A History of INDIAN Philosophy

THE SHANKARA SCHOOL OF VEDANTA | THE YOGA-VASISTHA
THE AYURVEDA AND ATHARVA-VEDA | THE BHAGAVAD GITA

VOLUME 2

SURENDRANATH DASGUPTA, M.A., Ph.D.,
Professor of Sanskrit, Government College, Chittagong, Bengal,
Lecturer in the University of Cambridge

FP
CLASSICS

निखिलमनुजचित्तं ज्ञानसूत्रैर्नवैर्यः
स्रजमिव कुसुमानां कालरन्ध्रैर्विधत्ते।
स लघुमपि ममैतं प्राच्यविज्ञानतन्तुं
उपहृतमतिभक्त्या मोदतां मे गृहीत्वा॥

May He, who links the minds of all people, through the apertures of time, with new threads of knowledge like a garland of flowers, be pleased to accept this my thread of Eastern thought, offered, though it be small, with the greatest devotion.

A History of INDIAN Philosophy

VOLUME 2

Published 2025

FINGERPRINT! CLASSICS
Prakash Books

Fingerprint Publishing
@FingerprintP
@fingerprintpublishingbooks
www.fingerprintpublishing.com

ISBN: 978 93 6214 911 4

PUBLISHER'S NOTE

We are pleased to present the highly anticipated Volume 2 of A History of Indian Philosophy by Professor S N Dasgupta.

In this benchmark five-volume study, originally published between 1922 and 1955, Professor Dasgupta examines the principal schools of thought that define Indian philosophy in great detail. A unifying force greater than art, literature, religion, or science, Professor Dasgupta describes philosophy as the most important achievement of Indian thought, arguing that an understanding of its history is necessary to appreciate the significance and potentialities of India's complex culture.

In the present volume of A History of Indian Philosophy Volume 2, which contains four chapters on Śaṅkara Vedānta, the Medical Speculation of the Ancient Hindus, the Philosophy of the Yoga-Vāsiṣṭha and the Bhagavad-Gītā, numerous unpublished and almost unknown manuscripts have been referred to by the author, making it the most valuable addition to the study of Indian philosophy.

The study presented here is strictly faithful to the original Sanskrit texts within the limits of the present writer's capacities. Often the ground covered has been wholly new and the materials have been obtained by a direct and first-hand study of all available texts and manuscripts. Thus, the present attempt is mainly intended to give an exposition of Indian thought strictly based on the original texts and commentaries.

The most important inclusion in this volume is the speculation of the Indian medical school (Ayurveda or the Medicine). Biology has always played a great part in liberating philosophy from its old-world ideas. In ancient India, Biology had not grown into a separate science; whatever biological ideas were present in India were mixed up with medical, osteological and physiological speculations, the only branch of study in ancient India which may be regarded as constituting an experimental science. It was, therefore, thought that a comprehensive work of the History of Indian Philosophy would be sadly defective without a chapter on these speculations, which introduce also some distinctly new ethical and eschatological concepts and a view of life which is wholly original. The biological notions of growth, development and heredity of these schools are no less interesting, and their relations to the logical categories of Nyāya are very instructive.

The chronological views regarding the antiquity of the Gītā may appear heretical, but it is hoped that they may be deemed excusable, for this is an age of toleration, and they are not more heretical than the views of many distinguished writers on Indian chronology. In the chapter on the Gītā, some repetition of the same views in different contexts were inevitable on account of the looseness of the structure of the Gītā, which is an ethico-religious treatise and not a system of philosophy. Neither the Yoga-Vāsiṣṭha nor the Gītā are systematic works on philosophy, and yet no treatment of Indian philosophy can legitimately ignore their claims. For in a country where philosophy and religion have been inseparably associated, the value of such writings as breath, the spirit of philosophy cannot be over-estimated, and no history of Indian philosophy worth the name can do without them.

It is hoped that this volume, like the previous one (volume-I) will be appreciated by the people who seek to know the Indian Philosophy in its totality.

NOTE ON THE TRANSLITERATION OF SANSKRIT AND PĀLĪ (IN DEVANAGARI SCRIPT)

When Sanskrit is written in another script, the corresponding letters in that script are transliterated according to this table.

Vowels and Diphthongs (see Note 1)

अ	a	ॠ	ṝ
आ	ā	ऌ	ḷ
इ	i	ए	e
ई	ī	ऐ	ai
उ	u	ओ	o
ऊ	ū	औ	au
ऋ ṛ			

Consonants (see Note 2)

Gutturals		Palatals		Cerebrals		Dentals	
क	ka	च	ca	ट	ṭa	त	ta
ख	kha	छ	cha	ठ	ṭha	थ	tha
ग	ga	ज	ja	ड	ḍa	द	da
घ	gha	झ	jha	ढ	ḍha	ध	dha
ङ	ṅa	ञ	ña	ण	ṇa	न	na
Labials		**Semivowels**		**Sibilants**		**Aspirate**	
प	pa	य	ya	श	śa	ह	ha
फ	pha	र	ra	ष	ṣa		
ब	ba	ल	la	स	sa		
भ	bha	ळ	ḻa				
म	ma	व	va				
Anusvāra		**Anunāsika**		**Visarga**		**Jihvāmūlīya**	
◌ं	ṃ	◌ँ	m̐	◌ः	ḥ	)(	ẖ

Upadhmānīya		Avagraha (see Note 4)	
ᳵ	ẖ	ऽ	’ (apostrophe)

Notes

1. Only the vowel forms that appear at the beginning of a syllable are listed; the forms used for vowels following a consonant can be found in grammars; no distinction between the two is made in transliteration.
2. The vowel a is implicit after all consonants and consonant clusters and is supplied in transliteration, with the following exceptions:

a) when another vowel is indicated by its appropriate sign; and
b) when the absence of any vowel is indicated by the subscript sign (्) called halanta or virāma.

3. Exception: Anusvāra is transliterated by:
   a) ṅ before gutturals,
   b) ñ before palatals,
   c) ṇ before cerebrals,
   d) n before dentals, and
   e) m before labials.
4. When doubled, avagraha is transliterated by two apostrophes (”).

NOTES ON THE PRONUNCIATION OF TRANSLITERATED SANSKRIT AND PĀLĪ WORDS

The vowels are pronounced almost in the same way as in Italian, except that the sound of *a* approaches that of *o* in *bond* or *u* in *but*, and *ā* that of *a* as in *army.* The consonants are as in English, except *c*, *ch* in church; *ṭ, ḍ*, *ṇ* are cerebrals, to which English *t, d*, *n* almost correspond; *t, d, n* are pure dentals; *kh, gh, ch, jh, ṭh*, *ḍh, th, dh, pit, bh* are the simple sounds plus an aspiration; *ñ* is the French *gn*; *ṛ* is usually pronounced as *ri,* and *ś, ṣ* as *sh.*

PREFACE

Nine years have passed away since the first volume of this work was published, and the present volume has been in the press for more than two years. During the last seven years bad health has been responsible for many interruptions. In the first volume manuscripts were sparingly used, but in the present work numerous unpublished and almost unknown manuscripts have been referred to. These could not be collected easily, and it took time to read them; many of them were old and moth-eaten and it was not often easy to decipher the handwriting. It has not always been possible, however, to give an elaborate account of the content of all these manuscripts, for in many cases they contained no new matter and had therefore only been mentioned by name, a fact which could be ascertained only after long and patient study, since records of them were previously unknown. A considerable delay was also caused in the writing of this volume by the fact that large portions of what will appear in the third volume had to be compiled before the manuscripts had left the author's hands. In any event, the author offers his sincere apologies for the delay.

The manuscript of the third volume has made good progress and, barring illness and other accidents, will soon be sent to press. This volume will contain a fairly elaborate account of the principal dualistic and pluralistic systems, such as the philosophy of the *Pañ-ca-rātra*, Bhāskara, Yāmuna, Rāmānuja and his followers, Mādhva and his followers, the *Bhāgavata-purāṇa* and the Gauḍīya school of Vaiṣṇavism. The fourth and the fifth volumes will deal with the philosophy of Vallabha and some other lesser known schools of Vaiṣṇavism, the philosophy of the Purāṇas, Tantras, the different schools of Śaivas, Śāktas, Indian Aesthetics, the philosophy of right and law and the religious systems that have found their expression in some of the leading vernaculars of India.

A new impression of the first volume is now in the press. The present volume contains four chapters on Śaṅkara Vedānta, the Medical Speculations of the Ancient Hindus, and the Philosophy of the *Yoga-vāsiṣṭha* and the *Bhagavadgītā.* A good deal of the Śaṅkara Vedānta, especially in regard to its controversy with Bhāskara, Rāmānuja, Mādhva and their followers, still remains to be treated in the third volume.

A word of explanation may be needed with regard to the inclusion in a work on Indian philosophy of the speculations of the Indian medical schools. Biology has recently played a great part in liberating philosophy from its old-world ideas. In ancient India, Biology had not grown into a separate science; whatever biological ideas were current in India were mixed up with medical, osteological and physiological speculations, the only branches of study in ancient India which may be regarded as constituting an experimental science. It was therefore thought that a comprehensive work on the history of Indian philosophy would be sadly defective without a chapter on these speculations, which introduce also some distinctly new ethical and eschatological concepts and a view of life which is wholly original. The biological notions of growth, development and heredity of these schools are no less interesting, and their relations to the logical categories of Nyāya are very instructive.

No attempt has been made to draw any comparisons or contrasts with Western philosophy, since in a work of this type it would most likely have been misleading and would have obscured the real philosophical issues. The study here presented is strictly faithful to the original Sanskrit texts within the limits of the present writer's capacities. Often the ground covered has been wholly new and the materials have been obtained by a direct and first-hand study of all available texts and manuscripts. Nevertheless some sources, containing, possibly, valuable materials, inevitably remain unconsulted, for many new manuscripts will be discovered in future, and our knowledge of Indian philosophy must advance but slowly. In spite of the greatest care, errors of interpretation, exposition and expression may have crept in and for these the author craves the indulgence of sympathetic readers.

Since the publication of the first volume of the present work, many treatises on Indian philosophy have appeared in India and elsewhere. But it has not been possible to refer to many of these. The present attempt is mainly intended to give an exposition of Indian thought strictly on the basis of the original texts and commentaries, and not to eradicate false views by indulging in controversy; and, since the author takes upon himself the responsibility of all the interpretations of the texts that he has used, and since he has drawn his materials mostly from them, it has seldom been possible to refer to the efforts of his fellow-workers in the field. Occasionally, however, he has had to discuss and sometimes to borrow the views of other writers in the assessment of chronological facts, and he also expresses his indebtedness to such other writers who have worked upon some of the special problems of Indian thought. It has been suggested to him that it would have been better if the views of other writers had been fully criticized, but however that may be, such criticism has been considered as beyond the scope of this work, which, as at present planned, will cover some 3000 pages when completed.

The chronological views regarding the antiquity of the *Gītā* may appear heretical, but it is hoped that they may be deemed excusable, for this is an age of toleration, and they are not more heretical than the views of many distinguished writers on Indian chronology. In the chapter on the *Gītā,* some repetition of the same views in different contexts was inevitable on account of the looseness of the structure of the *Gītā,* which is an ethico-religious treatise and not a system of philosophy. This, however, has been studiously avoided in the other chapters. Neither the *Yoga-vāsiṣṭha* nor the *Gītā* are systematic works on philosophy, and yet no treatment of Indian philosophy can legitimately ignore their claims. For in a country where philosophy and religion have been inseparably associated, the value of such writings as breathe the spirit of philosophy cannot be over-estimated, and no history of Indian philosophy worth the name can do without them.

I have no words sufficient to express my gratitude to my esteemed friend, Dr F. W. Thomas, Boden Professor of Sanskrit, Oxford, who went through the proofs in two of their stages and thus co-operated with me in the trouble of correcting them. I fear that in spite of our joint efforts many errors have escaped our eyes, but had it not been for his kind help the imperfections of the book would have been greater. I must similarly thank my friend, Mr Douglas Ainstie, for help with the proofs. My thanks are also due to my pupils, Dr M. Eleade (Bucharest), Mr Janakiballabh Bhattacharyya, MA., and my other friends, Messrs Satkari Mookerjee, M.A., Durgacharan Chatterjee, M.A., Srish Chandra Das Gupta, M.A., and my daughter, Miss Maitreyi Devi, for the assistance they rendered me in getting the manuscript ready for the press, inserting diacritical marks, comparing the references and the like, and also in arranging the index cards. But as none of them had the whole charge of any of these tasks, and as their help was only of an occasional nature, the responsibility for imperfections belongs to the author and not to them.

Calcutta, 1931 SURENDRANATH DASGUPTA

CONTENTS

CHAPTER XI *(continued)*

THE ŚAṄKARA SCHOOL OF VEDĀNTA 1-262

The World-Appearance; Thought and its Object in Buddhism and in Vedānta; Śaṅkara's Defence of Vedānta; Philosophy of Bādarāyaṇa and Bhartṛprapañca; Teachers and Pupils in Vedānta; Vedānta Doctrine of Soul and the Buddhist Doctrine of Soullessness; Vedāntic Cosmology; Śaṅkara and his School; Maṇḍana, Sureśvara and Viśvarūpa; Maṇḍana (AD 800); Sureśvara (AD 800); Padmapāda (AD 820); Vācaspati Miśra (AD 840); Sarvajñātma Muni (AD 900); Ānandabodha Yati; *Mahā-vidyā* and the Development of Logical Formalism; Vedānta Dialectic of Śrīharṣa (AD 1150); Application of the Dialectic to the Different Categories and Concepts; Citsukha's Interpretations of the Concepts of Śaṅkara Vedānta; The Dialectic of Nāgārjunā and the Vedānta Dialectic; Dialectical criticisms of Śāntarakṣita and Kamalaśīla (AD 760) as forerunners of Vedānta Dialectics (*a*) Criticisms of Sāṃkhya *Pariṇāma* Doctrine (*b*) Criticism od Īśvara (*c*) Refutation of the Soul Theory (*d*) Refutation of the Mīmāṃsā Theory of the Self (*e*) Refutation of the Sāṃkhya View of the Self (*f*) Refutation of the Upaniṣad View of the Self (*g*) Refutation of the Theory of the Persistence of Existing Entities (*h*) Refutation of Criticism of the Non-permanancy of Entities (*i*) Refutation of the Nyāya Vaiśeṣika Categories; Dialectic of Śaṅkara and Ānandajñāna; Philosophy of the *Prakaṭārtha-vivaraṇa* (AD 1200); Vimuktātman (AD 1200);–Rāmādvaya (AD 1300); Vidyāraṇya (AD 1350) Nṛsiṃhāśrama Muni (AD 1500); Appaya Dīkṣita (AD 1550); Prakāśānanda (AD 1550–1600); Madhusūdana Sarasvatī (AD 1500).

CHAPTER XII

THE PHILOSOPHY OF THE YOGA-VĀSIṢṬHA 263-316

Yoga-vāsiṣṭha; The Ultimate Entity; Origination; *Karma, Manas* and the Categories; The World-Appearance; Nature of Agency (*Kartṛtva*) and the Illusion of World Creation; The Stage of the Saint (*Jīvan-mukta*); Energy of Free-will (*Pauruṣa*); *Prāṇa* and its Control Stages of Progress; Methods of Right Conduct; *Yoga-vāsiṣṭha*, Śaṅkara Vedānta and Buddhist Vijñānavāda.

CHAPTER XIII

SPECULATIONS IN THE MEDICAL SCHOOLS 317-509

Āyurveda and the *Atharva-veda*; Bones in the Atharva-veda and Āyurveda; Organs in the *Atharva-veda* and Āyurveda; Practice of Medicine in the *Atharva-veda*; The Foetus and the Subtle Body; Foetal Development; Growth and Disease; *Vāyu, Pitta* and *Kapha*; Head and Heart; The Circulatory and the Nervous System; The Nervous System of the Tantras; The Theory of *Rasas* and their Chemistry; The Psychological Views and other Ontological Categories; Logical Speculations and Terms relating to Academic Dispute; Did Logic Originate in the Discussions of Āyurveda Physicians; Āyurveda Ethics; Springs of action in the *Caraka-samhitā*; Good Life in Caraka; Āyurveda Literature.

CHAPTER XIV

THE PHILOSOPHY OF THE BHAGAVAD-GĪTĀ 511-643

The *Gītā* Literature; *Gītā* and Yoga; Sāṃkhya and Yoga in the *Gītā*; Sāṃkhya Philosophy in the *Gītā*; Avyakta and Brahman; Conception of Sacrificial Duties in the *Gītā*; Sense-control in the *Gītā*; The Ethics of the *Gītā* and the Buddhist Ethics; Analysis of Action; Eschatology; God and Man; Viṣṇu, Vasudeva and Kṛṣṇa; Bhāgavata and the *Bhagavad-gītā*.

INDEX 645-714

CHAPTER XI

THE ŚAṄKARA SCHOOL OF VEDĀNTA (*Continued*)

The treatment of the school of Śaṅkara Vedānta in the preceding chapter may be considered fairly sufficient for all ordinary purposes. But the reputation of this school of thought stands so high, and so many people are interested in it, that it was pointed out to me that it would be desirable to go into a little more detailed study of it. An additional justification for such a suggestion is to bc found in the regrettable fact that, though numerous elementary and half-informed treatises have been published both in this country and in Europe, I do not know of any systematic study of the system in any of the modern languages of Europe or Asia which has been based on a first-hand study of the works of the great thinkers of this school who followed Śaṅkara and developed his system in a remarkably recondite manner. The comparatively small compass of this chapter in a History of Indian Philosophy cannot be expected to fulfil adequately such a demand; but still it may be expected that an attempt to bring out some of these materials by some amount of detailed study will be excusable, though it may seem slightly to disturb the general plan of this work.

THE WORLD-APPEARANCE

The Upaniṣads, called also the Vedānta, contain passages which indicate very different lines of thought, theistic, pantheistic, of self as the only ultimate reality, creationism, etc. The works of those commentators who wrote commentaries on the Upaniṣads before Śaṅkara and tried to interpret them on the supposition that there was one uniform, systematic, dogmatic philosophy in them are now practically all lost, and all that we can know of them is contained in the meager references that are found in Śaṅkara's commentaries or the works of other, later, commentators. As an example I may refer to Bhartṛprapañca, who tried to give a realistic interpretation of the *Bṛhadāraṇyaka Upaniṣad* by treating the world and souls as real emanations from God or Brahman.[1] Śaṅkara inherited from his predecessors the opinion that the Upaniṣads teach us one consistent systematic philosophy, but, being under the influence of Gauḍapāda, differed from them on the nature of this philosophy, which he propounded so elaborately in all his commentaries on the Upaniṣads and the *Brahma-sūtras.*

The main thesis of Śaṅkara, as has already been pointed out in the preceding chapter, consists of the view that Brahman alone is the ultimate reality, while everything else is false. He was interested in proving that this philosophy was preached in the Upaniṣads; but in the Upaniṣads there are many passages which are clearly of a theistic and dualistic purport, and no amount of linguistic trickery could convincingly show that these could yield a meaning which would support Śaṅkara's thesis. Śaṅkara therefore introduces the distinction of a common-sense view (*vyāvahārika*) and a philosophic view (*pāramārthika*), and explains the Upaniṣads on the supposition that, while there are some passages in them which describe things from a purely philosophic point of view, there are many others which speak of things only from a common-sense dualistic view of a real world, real souls and a real God as creator. Śaṅkara has applied this method of interpretation not only in his commentary on the Upaniṣads, but also in his commentary

1 Fragments of Bhartṛprapañca from the writings of Śaṅkara and his commentator Ānandajñāna and from Sureśvara's *Vārttika* have been collected by Prof. Hiriyanna, Mysore, in a short paper read at the *Third Oriental Conference in Madras* in 1924, published in Madras in 1925.

on the *Brahma-sūtra.* Judging by the *sūtras* alone, it does not seem to me that the *Brahma-sūtra* supports the philosophical doctrine of Śaṅkara, and there are some *sūtras* which Śaṅkara himself interpreted in a dualistic manner. He was never afraid of indulging in realistic interpretations; for he could easily get out of the difficulty by asserting that all the realistic conceptions found in the *sūtras* or in the Upaniṣad passages were merely an estimate of things from the common-sense point of view. Though on the basis of Śaṅkara's own statements, as well as those of his later commentators and other adherents of his school, there is hardly any room for doubt regarding the meaning and force of Śaṅkara's philosophy, yet at least one Indian scholar has sought to prove that Śaṅkara's philosophy was realistic.[1] That there was some amount of realism in Śaṅkara is proved by his own confession, when he criticizes the uncompromising Buddhistic idealists (*vijñāna-vādins*) or the so-called Buddhistic nihilists (*śūnya-vādins*). I have already discussed in a general way in what sense according to the Vedānta, from the point of view of the Śaṅkara school of Vedānta as interpreted by his later adherents, the world is an illusion. But in the present section I propose to discuss Śaṅkara's own statements, as well as the statements of some of his important followers, on the subject of the nature of world-illusion. This is one of the most important points of the Śaṅkara school of philosophy and needs a discussion in some detail.

But before I take it up, I am naturally reminded of the views of Buddhist idealism and the so-called Buddhistic nihilism, and it seems desirable that Śaṅkara's doctrine of illusion should be treated in connection with the doctrines of illusion in those systems of Buddhistic thought which preceded Śaṅkara. Taking the *Śūnyavāda* theory of Nāgārjuna and Candrakīrti, we see that they also introduced the distinction between limited truth and absolute truth. Thus, Nāgārjuna says in his *Mādhyamika-sūtras* that the Buddhas preach their philosophy on the basis of two kinds

1 *Advaita Philosophy* by K. Vidyāratna, published by the Calcutta University Press, 1924.

of truth, truth as veiled by ignorance and depending on common-sense presuppositions and judgments (*saṃvṛti-satya*) and truth as unqualified and ultimate (*paramārtha-satya*).[1] The word *saṃvṛti* literally means "closed." Candrakīrti explains *saṃvṛti* as meaning "closing on all sides" and says that it is ignorance (*ajñāna*) which is denoted by the term *saṃvṛti* here, because it covers the truth of all things.[2] In this sense the whole of the world of our experience of causes and effects, which we perceive and of which we speak, presents an appearance which is hidden by ignorance. This world is not contradicted in our world-experience; but, as each and every entity of this world is produced by other things or entities, and they again by others, and as we cannot specify the nature of each one of them without referring to others which produced them or from which they originated, and tracing those again to other causes and so on, it is not possible to assert anything as to the nature or characteristic (*svabhāva*) of anything as it is. Things are known to us only as being the result of the combination of many entities or as product complexes. Nothing is produced of itself, and so the products are never by themselves self-existent, but exist only through the coming together of different entities. That which has any nature of its own cannot owe its origination to other complexes, and so there is nothing in our world-experience which has a nature of its own. The apparent reality of the world has therefore the

---

1 द्वेसत्ये समुपाश्रितत्य बुद्धानां धर्मदेशना।
लोकसंवृतिसत्यं च सत्यं च परमार्थतः॥
dve satye samupāśritya buddhānāṃ dharma-deśanā
loka-saṃvṛti-satyaṃ ca satyaṃ ca paramārthataḥ
Mādhyamika-sūtra, XXIV.8, p. 492, B.B. edition.

2 *Ajñānaṃ hi samantāt sarva-padārtha-tattvāvacchādanāt saṃvṛtir ity ucyate. Ibid,* Candrakīrti however gives two other meanings of the word *saṃvṛti,* which do not seem to be so closely connected with the etymology. In the first of the two meanings *saṃvṛti* means interdependent origination or *pratītya-samutpāda,* and in the second it means the conventional world of common-sense, which can be expressed or indicated by speech and language and which we are supposed to know and refer to in all our experiences involving the knower and the known—*saṃvṛtiḥ saṃketo loka-vyavahāraḥ, sa ca abhidhānābhidheya-jñāna-jñeyādilakṣaṇaḥ.*

mysterious veil of ignorance over it, and it is this veil of ignorance which is referred to by the term *loka-saṃvṛta.* This is spoken of also as *tathya-saṃvṛti* (real ignorance), as distinguished from *mithyā-saṃvṛti* (false ignorance), properly used of the ordinary illusions and hallucinations of magic, mirage reflections, etc.[1] Those appearances which are due to sense-defects or other causes and are therefore contradicted in experience are called *mithyā-saṃvṛta*, because their falsehood is discovered in experience. The falsehood of the world-appearances, however, can be realized only when their real nature (*paramārtha-rūpa*) as a succession of essenceless products of causal complexes is properly understood. The world holds good and remains uncontradicted and has all the appearance of reality in all our practical experiences, and it is only when it is understood that these phenomena have no nature of their own that they are considered false. All teachings in philosophy take for granted the world-appearances, subjective and objective, and try to give a rational analysis and estimate of them; and it is only through an experience of these world-phenomena and a rational understanding of them that one realizes their truth as being a mere flow of causes and effects devoid of essence. The appearance of the world as reality is therefore true only in a limited manner during the period when the veil of ignorance is not removed from our eyes; and this is signified by designating the truth (*satya*) of the world as only *loka-saṃvṛta.* This world-appearance is however relatively true when compared with the ordinary illusions of perception (when, *e.g.*, a piece of rope is perceived as a snake, or when one sees a mirage in a desert).

But a question arises—if the world-appearance has no essence of its own, how is it that it appears to have one, or how is it that the world-phenomena appear at all? To such a question Nāgārjuna's answer is that the appearance of the world is like the appearance of mirages or dreams, which have no reality of their own, but still present an objective appearance of reality.[2] The world is not a mere

1 *Bodhi-caryāvatāra-pañjikā,* p. 353, Biblioteca Indica Series, 1902.

2 *Mādhyamika-sūtra,* XXIII.8.

nothing, like a lotus of the sky or the hare's horn, which are simply non-existent (*avidyamāna*). Thus there is not only the ultimate truth (*paramārtha*); there is also the relative truth of the phenomenal world (*loka-saṃvṛti-satya*); there are, further, the sense-illusions, hallucinations and the like which are. contradicted in ordinary experience (*aloka-saṃvṛta* or *mithyā-saṃvṛta*), and also that which is merely non-existent, like the hare's horn. The error (*viparyāsa*) of world-appearance is considered as being of four kinds, viz. the consideration of the momentary as eternal, the consideration of the painful as being pleasurable, the consideration of the unholy as holy, and of that which has no soul as having a soul.[1] And this error is due to ignorance (*avidyā*). Candrakīrti quotes a passage from the *Ārya-dṛḍhāśaya-paripṛcchā,* in which it is said that, just as a man may see in a dream that he is spending the night with the wife of the king, and, suddenly realizing that he is discovered, tries to fly for fear of his life (thus perceiving the presence of a woman, where there is none), so we are always falling into the error of asserting that we have perceived the manifold world-appearance where there is none.[2]

Such analogies of error naturally suggest the supposition that there must be some reality which is mistaken as some other thing; but, as has already been explained, the Buddhists emphasized the fact that, in dreams, the illusory appearances were no doubt objectively known as objective presentations of which we had previously become aware—experiences through which we pass, though there is no reality on which these appearances rest or are imposed. It was here that Śaṅkara differed. Thus, in his introduction to the commentary on the *Brahma-sūtra* he says that the essence of all

1 *Iha catvāro viparyāsā ucyante: tadyathā pratikṣaṇa-vināśini skandha-pañcake yo nityam iti grāhaḥ sa viparyāsaḥ… duḥkhātmake skandha-pañcake yaḥ sukham iti viparīto grāhaḥ so'paro viparyāsaḥ,… śarīram aśuci-svabhāvaṃ tatra yo śucitvena grāhaḥ sa viparyāsaḥ, … pañca-skandhaṃ nirātmakaṃ tasmin ya ātma-grāhaḥ anātmani ātmābhiniveśaḥ sa viparyāsaḥ.* Candrakīrti's commentary on *ibid.* XXIII.13. Compare it with the *Yoga-sūtra,* II.5, Ānandāśrama Series.

2 Candrakīrti's commentary on the *Mādhyamika-sūtra,* XXIII.13.

illusory perception is that one thing is mistaken for another, that the qualities, characteristics or attributes of one thing are taken for the qualities, characteristics or attributes of another. Illusion is defined as the false appearance in some object of something experienced before, resembling a memory image. It is explained by some as being the false affirmation of the characteristics of one thing in regard to another; others explain it as an error due to the non-apprehension of the difference between that which is wrongly apprehended and the misapprehended object which the former is wrongly supposed to be; others think that, when one thing is misapprehended as another, the illusion consists in the fancying of the former entity as being endowed with strange characteristics (*viparīta-dharmatva*); but in all these different ways of analysis illusion fundamentally is nothing but the false appearance of one thing with the characteristics of another. So also it may be that a conch-shell appears as silver or that one moon appears as two moons.[1] Śaṅkara then suggests that, since the universal self (*pratyag-ātman*) is felt through our feeling of "I" and since it is immediate in all experience (*aparokṣa*), it is not absolutely unrelated and unindicated (*aviṣaya*) in experience, and consequently it is quite possible that the non-self (*anātman*) and its characteristics may be illusorily imposed upon the universal self. This illusory imposition of the non-self and its characteristics on the universal self is called nescience (*avidyā*).

In his commentary on Gauḍapāda's *Kārikā*, I.17, Śaṅkara says that, when a piece of rope falsely appears as a snake, this is merely false imposition or appearance, not existence. The illusory appearance of the snake did not really bring into existence a snake, which later on became non-existent when right knowledge supervened. It was a mere illusion, and the rope-snake had no existence at all.[2] Śaṅkara in commenting on Gauḍapāda's *Kārikā*

---

1 Śaṅkara's *Adhyāsa-bhāṣya* on the *Brahma-sūtra,* Nirṇaya-Sāgara Press, Bombay, 1904.

2 *Rajjvāṃ sarpa iva kalpitatvāt na tu sa vidyate... na hi rajjvāṃ bhrānti-buddhyā kalpitaḥ sarpo vidyamānaḥ san vivekato nivṛttaḥ; tathedaṃ prapañcākhyaṃ māyā-mātram.*—Gauḍapāda's *Kārikā,* I.17, Ānandāśrama Series.

explains with approval Gauḍapāda's view that the world of common experience is as illusory as a dream. Dreams are false; for in a dream a man may have the experience of going to distant places, and yet, when he wakes up, he finds that he has been asleep for a few seconds only, and has not moved a foot from his bed. The dream experiences are therefore false, because they are contradicted by the waking experiences. But the waking experiences, being similar to dream experiences, are equally false. For both sets of experiences involve the duality of subject and object, and are therefore fundamentally more or less the same: so that, if one of them is false, the other also is false. The world-experience is like other well-known instances of illusion—the mirage, for example. Since it had no existence in the beginning, and will not have any existence in the end, neither can it have existence in the intervening period of appearance. The objection that our waking experiences fulfil practical purposes and have thus associated with them the pragmatic test of truth, which is absent in the case of dream experiences, is invalid; for the pragmatic tests of the waking experiences may well be contradicted by dream experiences; a man who goes to sleep after a sumptuous feast may well dream that he has been starving for days together. Both our inner world of mind and its experiences and the outer objective world are thus false creations.[1] But Gauḍapāda and Śaṅkara differ from the Śūnyavādin Buddhists in this—that they think that even false creations must have some basis in truth. If a rope appears as a snake, the false creation of the snake has some basis in the truth of the rope: there could not be false creations and false appearances without any firm basis of truth (*āspada*) underlying them.[2] Nāgārjuna, it will be remembered, tried to prove the falsity of all appearances on the ground of their being interdependent and not having anything which could be pointed out as their own nature. The dialectic being applicable to all appearances, there was nothing left which was not relative and interdependent, nothing which was self-evident by nature and which was intelligible by

1 Śaṅkara's commentary on Gauḍapāda's *Kārikā,* II.1-12.

2 *Na hi nirāspadā rajju-sarpa-mṛgatṛṣṇikādayaḥ kvacit upalabhyante. Ibid.* I.6.

itself without reference to anything else. It is this interdependence and relativity of all appearances that was called "nothingness" or *śūnyatā* by Nāgārjuna. There was nothing which could be affirmed of anything independently by itself without reference to something else; nothing therefore could be conceived as having any essence by itself. All appearances were therefore only interdependent phantom creations; and it was precisely this interdependence that proved the essencelessness of their natures. There was no basis of truth anywhere. There was nothing which had any essence. But neither Śaṅkara nor Gauḍapāda appears to have tried to show why the inner world of thoughts, ideas, emotions, volitions and the outer world of objects should be considered as being illusory appearances. Their main point seems to consist in a dogmatic statement that all appearances or experiences are false just as dream experiences are false. The imperfect analogy of waking experiences is made into an argument, and the entire manifold of appearances is declared to be false. But it is urged at the same time that these false creations must have some basis of truth; the changing appearances must have some unchanging basis on which they are imposed—and this basis is the self (*ātman*), or Brahman, which is the only thing that is permanent, unchanging and real. This self is the being of pure intelligence, which is one identical unit, negating all differences and duality (*viśuddha-vijñapti-mātra-sattā-dvaya-rūpeṇa*).[1] Just as the false creation of "snake" appears in the case of the "rope," so all such judgments as "I am happy," "I am unhappy," "I am ignorant," "I am born," "I am old," "I am with a body," "I perceive," etc., are all merely false predications associated with the self; they are all false, changing and illusory predications, and it is only the self which remains permanent through all such judgments. The self is entirely different from all such predications; it is self-luminous and self-manifesting, shining independently by itself.

By applying the dialectic of mutual interdependence, *pratītya-samutpāda,* Nāgārjuna tried to prove that there was nothing which could be pointed out as the essence of anything as it is; but he

1 Gauḍapāda's *Kārikā*, II.17.

did not explain how the appearances which were nothing more than phantom creations came to be what they were. How did the world-appearance of essenceless interdependent phenomena show itself? Śaṅkara did not try to prove with a keen logical dialectic that the world-appearance was false: he simply took it for granted, since the Upaniṣads proclaimed Brahman as the ultimate reality. But how did the world-appearance manifest itself? Śaṅkara does not seem to go deeply into this question and simply passes it over in asserting that this world-appearance is all due to ignorance *(avidyā*); it could not be spoken of as either existing or non-existing; it was merely illusory, like the conch-shell silver. But Padmapāda, who wrote the commentary known as *Pañca-pādikā* on the first four *sūtras* of Śaṅkara's commentary on the *Brahma-sūtras,* says that the precise meaning of the term "false conception" (*mithyā-jñāna*) in Śaṅkara's introduction to his commentary on the *Brahma-sūtras* is that there is a force or power or potency (*śakti*) of nescience which constitutes materiality (*jaḍātmikā avidyā-śaktiḥ*), and that it is this potency which transforms itself into the stuff *(upādāna*) of the world-appearance.[1] It is well to remember in this connection that, according to Śaṅkara's philosophy, it is not only the objective world that constitutes the world of appearance, but also the subjective world of all experiences and predicates that may be associated with the self. Thus, when one says "I," this ego-hood is analysed as involving two parts—the one, pure intelligence or pure consciousness; and the other, the concept of subjectivity, which is illuminated, expressed or manifested by the underlying pure intelligence with which it is falsely associated. The concept of subjectivity stands here as materiality, or objectivity, which is made to float up by the power of pure intelligence, thus causing the judgment "I am" or "I am a man."[2] This *avidyā-śakti,* or power of *avidyā*, subsists in the pure self and, on the one hand, arrests the

---

1 *Pañca-pādikā,* p. 4, the Vizianagram Sanskrit Series, 1891.

2 *asmat-pratyaye yo'nidam-aṃśaś cid-eka-rasaḥ tasmiṃs tad-bala-nirbhāsita-tayā lakṣaṇato yuṣmad-arthasya manuṣ yābhimānasya sambhedaivāvabhāsaḥ sa eva adhyāsaḥ.—Ibid.* p. 3.

revelation of its true nature as Brahman, and, on the other hand, transforms itself into the various concepts associated with the psychological self of our ordinary experience.[1] The illusion consists in the association of the psychological qualities of thinking, feeling, willing, etc. with the transcendent or universal self (*pratyak-citi*). These psychological determinations are all mutually connected with one another. Thus, to be able to enjoy pleasures, one must first act; one can only act when one has attachments, antipathies and desires, and one can have attachments and desires only when one has experienced joys and sorrows—so these psychological determinations in a beginningless cycle are always naturally associated with the transcendent self-luminous self.[2]

It should be clear from the foregoing discussion that, as Padmapāda or Prakāśātman explains, *ajñāna* or nescience is some kind of indefinable stuff out of the transformations of which subjective psychological experiences and the world of objects have come into being. This *ajñāna* is not the *ajñāna* of the Buddhists, i.e. a wrong notion or misconception, and this *adhyāsa,* or illusion, is not the *viparyaya* of Nāgārjuna; for here it is a positive power or stuff. Thus Prakāśātman argues that all effects have at their back some cause, which forms their stuff or material; the world-appearance, being also an effect, must have some stuff out of which it has evolved or was made up; and *ajñāna*, lying in the transcendent self as a separate power, is such a material cause.[3] This *avidyā-* potency in the transcendent self is positive in its nature. This positive *ajñāna* is directly perceived in such immediate perceptions as "I do not know myself or others," and can also be inferred or comprehended

1 *ataḥ sā pratyak-citi brahma-svarūpāvabhāsaṃ pratibadhnāti ahaṃkārādy-atad-rūpa-pratibhāsa-nimittaṃ ca bhavati. Ibid.* p. 5.

2 Prakāśātman's *Pañca-pādikā-vivaraṇa,* p. 10, the Vizianagram Sanskrit Series, 1892.

3 *sarvaṃ ca kāryam sopādānaṃ bhāva-kāryatvāt ghaṭādivad ity anumānāt... tasmān mithyārtha-taj-jñānātmakaṃ mithyā-bhūtam adhyāsam upādā-na-kāraṇa-sāpekṣam... mithyā-jñānam eva adhyāsopādānam.*
—*Pañca-pādikā-vivaraṇa,* pp. 11-12.

by implication.[1] The fact that *ajñāna* or *avidyā* is spoken of as a power inherent in the transcendent self shows that it is dependent thereon; *avidyā* is not, however, a power, but a substance or entity which has certain powers by which it transforms itself into the cosmic appearances, subjective and objective; yet it is called a power, or *śakti*, because of its dependence (*para-tantratā*) on the transcendent self, and it is in consideration of the entire dependence of *avidyā* and its transformations on the self that the self is regarded as the material cause of all effects—the cosmic appearances of the world and the mind.[2] The self thus not only holds the *ajñāna* within it as a dependent function, but in spite of its self-luminosity it can be reacted upon by the *ajñāna* with its manifold powers in such a way that it can be veiled by this *ajñāna* and made the underlying basis of all world-appearances of *ajñāna*-transformations.[3]

Appaya Dīkṣita, referring in his *Siddhānta-leśa* to the view of the writer of the *Padārtha-tattva*, summarizes the matter thus: Brahman and Māyā form together the material cause (*ubhayam upādānam*), and hence it is that in the world-appearance there are two distinct characteristics, "being" (*sattā*) from Brahman and materiality (*jāḍya*) from Māyā. Brahman is the cause, as the unchanging basis of the Māyā, which is the cause as being the stuff that actually undergoes transformation.[4] Vācaspati Miśra also conceives Brahman, jointly with its *avidyā*, to be the material cause of the world (*avidyā-sahita-brahmopādānam*).[5] In his adoration hymn at the beginning of his *Bhāmatī* he describes Brahman as being in association with its companion, the indefinable *avidyā*, the

1 *Ibid.* p. 13.

2 *Śaktir ity ātma-para-tantratayā ātmanaḥ sarva-kāryopādānasya nirvoḍhṛtvam. Ibid.* p. 13. *Ātma-kāraṇatva-nirvoḍhṛtvād ātma-para-tantratvā ca śakti-matyām api śakti-śabda upacāritaḥ.* Akhaṇḍānanda Muni's *Tattva-dīpana,* p. 65, Chowkhambā Sanskrit Book Depot, Benares, 1902.

3 *ataḥ svaprakāśe'pi ātmani vicitra-śakti-bhāva-rūpāvidyā-prayuktam āvaraṇaṃ durapahṇavam.* Rāmānanda Sarasvatī's *Vivaraṇopanyāsa,* p. 16, Chowkhambā Sanskrit Book Depot, Benares, 1901.

4 *Siddhānta-leśa,* p. 12, V.S. Series, 1890.

5 *Bhāmatī* on Śaṅkara's *Bhāṣya,* I.1.2, Nirṇaya-Sāgara Press, 1904.

unchanging cause of the entire objective universe.[1] Sarvajñātma Muni, however, does not wish to give *māyā* the same degree of co-operation in the production of the world-appearance as Brahman, and considers the latter to be the real material cause of the world through the instrumentality of Māyā; for Brahman, being absolutely changeless, cannot by itself be considered as cause, so that, when Brahman is spoken of as cause, this can only be in a remote and modified sense (*upalakṣaṇa*), through the instrumentality of *māyā*.[2] The author of the *Siddhānta-muktāvalī* is referred to by Appaya Dīkṣita as holding that it is the *māyā* and *māyā* alone that forms the stuff of the world-appearance; and that Brahman is not in any way the material cause of the universe, but that it is only the basis of the subsistence of *māyā* and is only from that point of view spoken of as being the material cause.[3]

It is clear that the above differences of view regarding the nature of the relation between *māyā* and the self or Brahman in the production of the world-appearance are mere scholastic disputes over words or modes of expression, and have but little philosophical significance. As has already been said, these questions do not seem to have arisen in Śaṅkara's mind. He did not think it worthwhile to explain anything definitely regarding the nature of *avidyā* and its relation with Brahman, and the part that it played in supplying the material stuff of the universe. The world was an illusion, and Brahman was the basis of truth on which these illusions appeared; for even illusions required something on which they could appear. He never faced squarely the difficulties that are naturally connected with the theory, and was not therefore concerned to explain the definite relation of *māyā* to Brahman in connection with the production of the phantom show of the universe. The natural objection against such views is that the term *avidyā* (formed by compounding the negative particle *a* and *vidyā*

1 *Anirvācyāvidyā-dvitaya-sacivasya prabhavato vivartā yasyaite viyad-anila-tejob-avanayaḥ. ibid.* p. 1.

2 *Saṃkṣepa-śārīraka*, I.333, 334, Bhāū Śāstri's edition.

3 *Siddhānta-leśa,* p. 13, V.S. Series, 1890.

"knowledge") may mean either absence of knowledge (*vidyā-bhāvaḥ*) or false knowledge (*mithyā-jñānam*); and in neither of these meanings can it be supposed to behave as the material cause or substance-stuff of anything; for a false knowledge cannot be a substance out of which other things are made.[1] The answer given by Ānandabodha Bhaṭṭāraka to such an objection is that this *avidyā* is not a psychological ignorance, but a special technical category, which is beginningless and indefinable (*anādy-anirvācyāvidyāśra-yaṇāt*). The acceptance of such a category is a hypothesis which one is justified in holding as valid, since it explains the facts. Effects must have some cause behind them, and a mere instrumental cause cannot explain the origination of the substratum of the effect; again, effects which are not true cannot have for their material cause (*upādāna-kāraṇa*) that which is true, nor can they have for their material cause that which is absolutely non-existent. So, since the material cause of the world can neither be true nor be anything which is absolutely non-existent, the hypothesis is naturally forced upon the Vedāntists that the material cause of this false world-appearance is an entity which is neither existent nor non-existent.[2] Ānandabodha in his *Pramāṇa-mālā* quotes approvingly from the *Brahma-tattva-samīkṣā* of Vācaspati to show that *avidyā* is called *avidyā* or nescience because it is a hypothetic category which is neither "is" nor "is not," and is therefore unintelligible; *avidyā* signifies particularly the unintelligibility of this category.[3] Ānandabodha points out that the acceptance of *avidyā* is merely the logical consequence of indicating some possible cause of the world-appearance—considering the nature of the world-appearance as it is, its cause can only be something which neither is nor is not; but what we understand by such a category, we cannot say; it is

1 *avidyā hi vidyābhavo mithyā-jñānaṃ vā na cobhayaṃ kasya cit sam-avāyi-kāraṇam adravyatvāt.* Ānandabodha's *Nyāya-makaranda,* p. 122, Chowkhambā Sanskrit Book Depot, Benares, 1901.

2 *Ibid.* pp. 122-124.

3 *sad-asad-ubhayānubhayādi-prakāraiḥ anirvacanīyatvam eva hy avidyānām avidyātvam. Brahma-tattva-samīkṣā* as quoted in *Pramāṇa-mālā,* p. 10, Chowkhambā Sanskrit Book Depot, Benares, 1907.

plainly unintelligible; the logical requirements of such a category merely indicate that that which is the material cause of this false world-appearance cannot be regarded either as existing or as non-existing; but this does not make this concept either intelligible or consistent.[1] The concept of *avidyā* is thus plainly unintelligible and inconsistent.

THOUGHT AND ITS OBJECT IN BUDDHISM AND IN VEDĀNTA

The Vedānta takes a twofold view of things; the first view refers to ultimate reality and the second to appearance. This ultimate reality is pure intelligence, as identical with pure bliss and pure being. This is called ultimately real in the sense that it is regarded as changeless. By pure intelligence the Vedānta does not mean the ordinary cognitional states; for these have a subjective and an objective content which are extraneous to them. This pure intelligence is pure immediacy, identical with the fact of revelation found in all our conscious states. Our apprehensions of objects are in some sense events involving both a subjective and an objective content; but their special feature in every case is a revelatory inwardness or immediacy which is non-temporal and changeless. The fact that we see, hear, feel, touch, think, remember is equivalent to saying that there are various kinds of cognizings. But what is the nature of this cognizing? Is it an act or a fact? When I see a blue colour, there is a blue object, there is a peculiar revelation of an appearance as blue and a revelation of the "I" as perceiver. The revelation is such that it is both a revelation of a certain character as blue and of a certain thing called the blue object. When a revelation occurs in perception, it is one and it reveals both the object and its appearance in a certain character as blue. The revelation is not the product of a certain relation which happens to subsist at any

1 *Vailakṣaṇya-vāco-yuktir hi pratiyogi-nirūpaṇād yauktikatva-prakaṭana-phalā na tv evaṃ-rūpatāyāḥ sāmañjasya-sampādanāya ity avocāma.*
—*Pramāṇa-mālā,* p. 10.

time between the character-appearance and the object; for both the character-appearance as blue and the object are given in revelation. The revelation is self-evident and stands unique by itself. Whether I see, or hear, or feel, or change, the fact remains that there is some sort of an awareness which does not change. Awareness is ever present by itself and does not undergo the changes that its contents undergo. I may remember that I had seen a blue object five minutes previously; but, when I do this, what I perceive is the image of a blue object, with certain temporal and spatial relations, which arises or becomes revealed; but the revelation itself cannot be revealed again. I may be conscious, but I cannot be conscious of consciousness. For consciousness as such, though ever present in its immediacy, cannot become an object of any other consciousness. There cannot be any such thing as the awareness of an awareness or the awareness of the awareness of an awareness, though we may multiply such phrases in language at our pleasure. When I remember that I have been to Trinity College this morning, that only means that I have an image of the way across the commons, through Church Street and Trinity Street; my movements through them are temporally pushed backward, but all this is a revelation as image at the present moment and not a revelation of a past revelation. I cannot say that this present image in any way reveals that particular image as the object of the present revelation. But the former revelation could not be held to be distinct from the present one; for distinction is always based on content and not on revelation. Revelation as such is identical and, since this is so, one revelation cannot be the object of another. It is incorrect to say that "*A* is *A*" means that one *A* becomes itself over again. It is owing to the limitations of grammatical terminology that identity is thus described. Identity thus understood is different from what we understand by identity as a relation. Identity understood as a relation presupposes some difference or otherness and thus is not self-contained. And it is because it is not self-contained that it can be called a relation. When it is said that *A* is identical with *A*, it means that on all the various occasions or contents in which *A* appeared it always signified the same thing, or that it had the same shape or that it was the same first letter of the English alphabet. Identity in this sense is a function of thought not existing by itself, but in relation to a sense of opponency or otherness. But revelation has no otherness in it; it is absolutely ubiquitous and homogeneous. But the identity of revelation of which we are speaking does not mean that the revelation signifies the same thing amidst a diversity of contents: it is simply the one essence identical in itself and devoid of any numerical or other kinds of difference. It is absolutely free from "now" and "then," "here" and "there," "such" or "not such" and "this" or "that." Consciousness of the self-shining self taken in this way cannot be regarded as the relation of an appearance to an object, but it is the fact of the revelation or the entity of the self. If we conceive of revelation in this way, it is an error to make any distinction in revelation as the revelation of the past or the revelation of the present moment. For moments are revealed as objects are revealed; they do not constitute revelation or form any part of it. This revelation is identical with the self-shining self to which everything else has to be related in order to be known.

"Is cognizing an act or a fact?" Before this can be answered the point to be made clear is what is meant by cognizing. If we ignore the aspect of revelation and speak of mental states which can be looked at from the point of view of temporal or qualitative change of character, we must speak of them as acts or events. If we look at any mental state as possessing certain characters and relations to its objects, we have to speak of these aspects. But, if we look at cognizing from the point of view of its ultimate truth and reality as revelation, we cannot call it either an act or a fact; for, as revelation, it is unique and unchangeable in itself. All relations and characters are revealed in it, it is self-evident and is at once in and beyond them all. Whether we dream or wake, whether we experience an illusion or a truth, revelation is always there. When we look at our mental states, we find that they are always changing, but this is so only with reference to the contents. Apart from this there is a continuity in our conscious life. By this continuity the Vedānta apprehends not any sort of coherence in our ideas, but the fact of the permanence of revelation. It may be asked what remains of revelation, if the mental states are taken away. This question is not admissible; for the mental states do not form part of revelation; they are rendered conscious by coming into relation with revelation. This category is the ultimate reality. It is not self or subject in the sense in which self or ego is ordinarily understood. For what is ordinarily understood as the ego or the "I" is as much a content of the perception of the moment as any other objective content. It is not impossible that any particular objective content may be revealed at any time without the corresponding "I perceive" being explicitly revealed at the same time. The notion of ego or "I" does not refer to an everlasting abiding independent self or person; for this notion is as changing as any other objective content. The "I" has no definite real content as referring to an existing entity, but is only a particular mode of mind which is often associated, as a relatively abiding content, with other changing contents of the mind. As such, it is as changeable as is any other object. "I know this" only means that there is a revelation which at one sweep reveals both the "this" and the "I." So far as the revelation appears as revealing the "this" and the "I," it is manifested in a subjective mental state having a particular conscious centre different from other similar centres. But, since revelation cannot in reality be individuated, all that we may say about "I" or "mine," "thou" or "thine," falls outside it. They are all contents, having some indefinite existence of their own and revealed by this principle of revelation under certain conditions. This principle of revelation thus has a reality in quite a different sense from that which is used to designate the existence of any other object. All other objects are dependent upon this principle of revelation for their manifestation, and their nature or essence, out of connection with it, cannot be defined or described. They are not self-evident, but are only expressed by coming into some sort of relation with this principle. We have already seen that this principle cannot be either subjective or objective. For all considerations of subject or object fall outside it and do not in any way qualify it, but are only revealed by it. There are thus two principles, the principle of revelation and all that which is revealed by it. The principle of revelation is one; for there is nothing else like it; it alone is real in the highest and truest sense. It is absolute in the sense that there is no growth, decay, evolution or change in it, and it is perfectly complete in itself. It is infinite in the sense that no finitude can form part of it, though through it all finitude is being constantly revealed. It is all-pervading in the sense that no spatial or temporal limits can be said to affect it in any way, though all these are being constantly revealed by it. It is neither in my head nor in my body nor in the space before me; but yet there is nowhere that it is not. It has sometimes been designated as the "Self" or *ātman*, but only in the sense of denoting its nature as the supreme essence and transcendent reality of all—the Brahman.

Apart from this principle of revelation, all else is constituted of a substanceless indefinable stuff called *māyā.* In some schools of Śaṅkara Vedānta it is said that all is pure and simple illusion, that things exist only when they are perceived and dissolve into nothingness as soon as we cease to perceive them; this school has been designated the *Dṛṣṭi-sṛṣṭi* school, a doctrine which has been briefly explained in the tenth chapter of the present work.[1] One of the most important texts of this school is the *Siddhānta-muktāvalī* by Prakāśānanda.[2] Prakāśānanda seems to have taken his

---

1 *A History of Indian Philosophy,* vol. I. pp. 477-478, by S. N. Dasgupta, published by the Cambridge University Press, 1922.

2 Prakāśānanda refers to the arguments of Prakāśātman's (AD 1200) *Pañca-pādikā-vivaraṇa* and Sarvajñātma Muni's (AD 900) *Saṃkṣepa-śārīraka* and refers approvingly to Sureśvara, the author of the *Naiṣkarmya-siddhi.* Appaya Dīkṣita (AD 1620) refers to Prakāśānanda in his *Siddhānta-leśa* (pp. 13, 72). Nānā Dīkṣita, a follower of the school of Prakāśānanda and author of the*Siddhānta-dīpikā,* in a commentary on the *Siddhānta-muktāvalī,* gives a list of Vedānta teachers. In this list he mentions the names of Prakāśānubhavānanda, Nṛsiṃha and RāghavendraYati. Venis thinks (see *The Pandit,* 1890, pp. 487-490) that Prakāśānubhava is the same as Prakāśātman and Nṛsiṃha the same as Nṛsiṃhāśrama Muni, who is said to have converted Appaya Dīkṣita to Śaṅkara Vedānta, and thinks that Prakāśānanda lived in the last quarter of the sixteenth century, being wedged in between Nṛsiṃha and Appaya. Though it would be difficult to settle his time so precisely and definitely, yet it would not be wrong

inspiration from the *Yoga-vāsiṣṭha*, and he denied the existence of things when they are not perceived (*ajñāta-sattvānabhyupagama*). He tried to show that there were no grounds for holding that external objects existed even when they were not perceived or that external objects had a reality independent of their perceptions. Examining the capacity of perception as a proof to establish this difference between perception and its object, he argued that, since the difference between the awareness and its object was a quality of the awareness, the awareness itself was not competent to grasp this quality in the object, as it was one of the constituents of the complex quality involving a difference of the awareness and its object; to assert the contrary would be a fallacy of self-dependence (*ātmāśrayatva*). If the apprehended difference is a complex, such as "difference-between-awareness-and-its-object," and if this complex is a quality which is apprehended as existing in the object, it has to be assumed that, in order that the nature of awareness may be realized, vindicated or established, it must depend upon itself involved as a constituent in the complex "difference-between-awareness-and-its-object" directly and immediately—which comes to the same thing as saying that awareness becomes aware of itself by being aware of itself; this is impossible and is called the logical fallacy of self dependence.[1] If it is held that the complex quality ("difference-of-awareness-from-the-object") is directly perceived in the object through the senses, then it has to be assumed that the said complex quality existed in the object even before the production of the awareness, and this would involve the impossible supposition that the complex quality of which the awareness was a constituent was already present even before such

---

to suppose that he lived some time towards the latter half of the sixteenth century. Prakāśānanda's doctrine of *Dṛṣṭi-sṛṣṭi* is apparently unknown to the earlier Vedantic works and even the *Vedānta-paribhāṣā,* a work of the early sixteenth century, does not seem to be aware of him, and it appears that the earliest mention of his name can be traced only to Appaya, who lived in the sixteenth and the seventeenth centuries. Prakāśānanda may thus be believed to have lived in the latter half of the sixteenth century.

1 *Siddhānta-muktāvalī,* as printed in the Pandit, 1889, pp. 247-249.

an awareness had already come into being. If perception or direct awareness cannot be said to prove the difference between the awareness and its object, there can be no inference which may be supposed to do it. For such an inference has to take form thus—"the object is different from its own awareness, because it is associated with entirely different kinds of qualities or characteristics."[1] But how could it be known that the object has qualities of an entirely different character from its awareness, since a difference between an awareness and its object was contested and could not be proved by perception or any other means? Prakāśānanda further says that the argument by implication (*arthāpatti*), that awareness involves the acceptance of something different from the awareness of which the awareness is affirmed, because there cannot be any knowledge without a corresponding object, is invalid. In proving the invalidity of the supposition that knowledge necessarily implies an object, Prakāśānanda raises the question whether such an implication of an object as conditioning knowledge refers to the production (*utpatti*) of knowledge, its persistence (*sthiti*) or its secondary cognition. As regards the first alternative Prakāśānanda says that according to the Vedānta consciousness is ever-existent and is never a product; and, even if it is regarded as a product, the process of cognition can itself be regarded as a sufficient cause for its production. It can by no means be urged that the presence of an external object is in all cases necessary for the production of knowledge; for, though it is arguable that in perception an object is necessary, no one will suggest that an external object is to be considered necessary in the production of inferential knowledge—a fact which shows that the presence of an external object is not indispensable for the production of knowledge as such. As regards the persistence of knowledge it is said that awareness has not the object that it knows for its locus or substance (*āśraya*), in such a way that the absence of the object, as apart from the awareness, would make it impossible for the awareness to persist; and, if knowledge is

1 *Vimato viṣayaḥ sva-viṣaya-jñānād bhidyate tad-viruddha-dharmāśrayatvāt. Ibid.* p. 252.

supposed to be persisting in anything, that something would not be a cognized object, but the cognizer itself—as in the Nyāya view, where knowledge is regarded as an attribute of the self and the self is then regarded as the substance or locus (*āśraya*) of knowledge. Since again cognition and its object do not exist in the same space or in the same time (this is proved by the possibility of our knowing a past or a future object), there cannot be any such concomitance between the two that it would be right for anyone to infer the external presence of an object because of there being a subjective cognition or awareness. So he argues that there is no proof that cognition and cognized objects are different.

In the above account of Prakāśānanda's views it is clear that he does not attempt to give any positive proof in support of his thesis that the world-appearance and all objects contained in it have no existence while they are not perceived or that the being of all objects cognized is their *percipi.* He only tries to show that it cannot be logically established that awareness of blue and blue are two different objects; or, in other words, that it cannot be proved that the cognized object is different from its cognition. It could not legitimately be held that awareness (*pratīti*) was different from its object (*pratyetavya*). The whole universe, as we perceive it, is nothing but cognition without there being any object corresponding to it. As dreams are nothing but mere awareness, without there being any real objects behind them which manifest themselves in different ways of awareness and their objects, so also is the world of awaking consciousness.[1] The world has thus no independent

---

1 प्रत्येतव्यप्रतीत्योश्च भेदः प्रामाणिकः कुतः
प्रतीतिमात्रमेवैतद्भाति विश्वं चराचरम्।
ज्ञानज्ञेयप्रभेदेन यथा स्वाप्नं प्रतीयते
विज्ञानमात्रमेवैतत्तथा जाग्रच्चराचरम्॥

pratyetavya-pratītyoś ca bhedaḥ prāmāṇikaḥ kutaḥ
pratīti-mātram evaitad bhāti viśvaṃ carācaram
jñāna-jñeya-prabhedena yathā svāpnaṃ pratīyate
vijñāna-mātram evaitat tathā jāgrac carācaram.

—*Siddhānta-muktāvalī,* p. 258.

substratum, but is mere cognition or mere awareness (*vijñāna-mātra* or *bhāva-mātra*).

This scheme of Vedānta philosophy is surprisingly similar to the idealism of Vasubandhu (AD 280-360), as taught in his *Viṃśatikā* with a short commentary of his own and in his *Triṃśikā* with a commentary by Sthiramati.[1] According to this idealism (*vijñāna-vāda*) of Vasubandhu all appearances are but transformations of the principle of consciousness by its inherent movement, and none of our cognitions are produced by any external objects which to us seem to be existing outside of us and generating our ideas. Just as in dreams one experiences different objects at different places and countries without there being any objective existence of them, or as in dreams many people may come together and perform various actions, so what seems to be a real world of facts and external objects may well be explained as a mere creation of the principle of intelligence without any objective basis at all. All that we know as subjective or objective is mere ideation (*vijñapti*) and there is no substantive reality, or entity corresponding to it; but that does not mean that pure non-conceptual (*anabhilapyenātmanā*) thought, which the saints realize, is also false.[2] It is possible that the awareness of anything may become the object of a further awareness, and that of another; but in all such cases where the awarenesses are significant (*arthavatī*) there is no entity or reality represented by them; this, however, should not be interpreted as a denial of the principle of intelligence or pure knowledge as such. Vasubandhu then undertakes to show that the perceptual evidence of the existence of the objective world cannot be trusted. He says that, taking visual perception as an example, we may ask ourselves if the objects of the visual perception are one as a whole or many

---

1 *Vijñapti-mātratā-siddhi,* containing two treatises, *Viṃśatikā and Triṃśikā,* Paris, 1925. It seems probable that Vasubandhu flourished in AD 280-360 rather than in AD 420-500 as held by me in the first volume of the present work. See B. Bhattacharya's foreword to the *Tattva-saṃgraha.*

2 *Yo bālair dhārmāṇāṃ svabhāvo grāhya-grāhakādiḥ parikalpitaḥ tena kalpitenātmanā teṣāṃ nairātmyaṃ na tv anabhilāpyenātmanā yo buddhānāṃ viṣaya iti.* Commentary on *Viṃśatikā,* p. 6.

as atoms. They cannot be mere wholes, since wholes would imply parts; they cannot be of the nature of atoms, since such atoms are not separately perceived; they cannot be of the nature of combinations of atoms, since the existence of atoms cannot be proved.[1] For, if six atoms combine from six sides, that implies that the atoms have parts; if however six atoms combine with one another at one identical point, that would mean that the combined group would not have a size larger than that of one atom and would therefore be invisible. Again, if the objects of awareness and perception were only wholes, then succession and sequence would be inexplicable, and our perception of separate and distinct things would remain unaccountable. So they have no real objective existence, though perception leads us to believe that they have. People are dreaming of the world of objects in the sleep of the sub-conscious habit of false imaginative construction (*vitatha-vikalpābhyāsa-vāsanā-nidrayā*), and in their dreams they construct the objective world; it is only when they become awake with the transcendent indeterminate knowledge (*lokottara-nirvikalpa-jñāna-lābhāt prabuddho bhavati*) that they find the world-construction to be as false as the dream-construction of diverse appearances. In such a view there is no objective material world, and our cognitions are not influenced by external objects; how then are our minds influenced by good instructions and associations? and, since none of us have any real physical bodies, how can one kill another? Vasubandhu explains this by the theory that the thought-currents of one person can sometimes determine the thought-currents of another. Thus the idea of killing of a certain type may produce such a disturbance of the vital powers of another as to produce a cessation of the continuity of the thought-processes, which is called death.[2] So also the good ideas of one may influence the ideas of another for good.

---

1 *Nāpi te saṃhatā viṣayī-bhavanti, yasmāt paramāṇur ekaṃ dravyaṃ na sidhyati. Ibid.* p. 7.

2 *para-vijñapti-viśeṣādhipatyāt pareṣāṃ jīvitendriya-virodhinī kācit vikriyā utpadyate yayā sabhāga-santati-vicchedākhyaṃ maraṇam bhavati.* Commentary on *Viṃśatikā,* p. 10.

In the *Triṃśikā* of Vasubandhu and its commentary by Sthiramati this idealism is more clearly explained. It is said that both the soul (or the knower) and all that it knows as subjective ideas or as external objects existing outside of us are but transformations of pure intelligence (*vijñāna-pariṇāma*). The transformation (*pariṇāma*) of pure intelligence means the production of an effect different from that of the causal moment simultaneously with the cessation of the causal moment.[1] There is neither externality nor subjectivity in pure intelligence, but these are imposed upon it (*vijñāna-svarūpe parikalpita eva ātmā dharmāśca*). All erroneous impositions imply that there must be some entity which is mistaken for something else; there cannot be erroneous impositions on mere vacuity; so it has to be admitted that these erroneous impositions of various kinds of external characteristics, self, etc. have been made upon the transformations of pure intelligence.[2] Both Vasubandhu and Sthiramati repudiate the suggestion of those extreme idealists who deny also the reality of pure intelligence on grounds of interdependence or relativity (*saṃvṛti*).[3] Vasubandhu holds that pure consciousness (*vijñapti-mātratā*) is the ultimate reality. This ultimate consciousness is a permanent entity, which by its inherent power (*śakti*) undergoes threefold transformations as the inherent indeterminate inner change (*vipāka*), which again produces the two other kinds of transformations as the inner psychoses of mental operations (*manana*) and as the perception of the so-called external sensibles (*viṣaya-vijñapti*). The apprehension of all appearances or characterized entities (*dharma*) as cognized objects and that of selves as cognizers, the duality of perceivers and the perceived, are due to the threefold transformations of *vipāka, manana* and *viṣaya-*

1 *kāraṇa-kṣaṇa-nirodha-sama-kālaḥ kāraṇa-kṣaṇa-vilakṣaṇa-kāryasya ātma-lābhaḥ pariṇāmaḥ.* Sthiramati's commentary on *Triṃśikā,* p. 16.

2 *upacārasya ca nirādhārasyāsambhavād avaśyaṃ vijñāna-pariṇāmo vastuto'sty upagantavyo yatra ātma-dharmopacāraḥ pravartate. Ibid.* Compare Śaṅkara's commentary on Gauḍapāda's *Kārikā,* "*na hi nirāspadā mṛgatṛṣṇikādayaḥ.*"

3 Thus *Laṅkāvatāra,* one of the most important works on Buddhistic idealism, denies the real transformation of the pure intelligence or *ālaya-vijñāna.* See *Laṅkāvatāra,* p. 46, published by the Otani University Press, Kyoto, 1923.

vijñapti. The ultimate consciousness (*vijñapti-mātra*) which suffers all these modifications is called *ālaya-vijñāna* in its modified transformations, because it is the repository of all experiences. The ultimate principle of consciousness is regarded as absolutely permanent in itself and is consequently also of the nature of pure happiness (*sukha*); for what is not eternal is painful, and this, being eternal, is happy.[1] When a saint's mind becomes fixed (*pratiṣṭhita*) in this pure consciousness (*vijñapti-mātra*), the tendency to dual thought of the subjective and the objective (*grāhya-grāhakānuśaya*) ceases and there dawns the pure indeterminate (*nirvikalpa*) and transcendent (*lokottara*) consciousness. It is a state in which the ultimate pure consciousness returns from its transformations and rests in itself. It is divested of all afflictions (*kleśa*) or touch of vicious tendencies and is therefore called *anāsrava.* It is unthinkable and undemonstrable, because it is, on the one hand, pure self-consciousness (*pratyātma-vedya*) and omniscience (*sarvajñatā*), as it is divested of all limitations (*āvaraṇa*), and, on the other hand, it is unique in itself.[2] This pure consciousness is called the container of the seed of all (*sarva-bīja*), and, when its first indeterminate and indefinable transformations rouse the psychosis-transformations and also the transformations as sense-perceptions, these mutually act and react against one another, and thus the different series rise again and again and mutually determine one another. These transformations are like waves and ripples on the ocean, where each is as much the product of others as well as the generator of others.[3]

---

1 *dhruvo nityatvād akṣayatayā; sukho nityatvād eva yad anityaṃ tad duḥkham ayaṃ ca nitya iti asmāt sukhaḥ.* Sthiramati's commentary on *Triṃśikā,* p. 44.

2 *Ālaya-vijñāna* in this ultimate state of pure consciousness (*vijñapti-mātratā*) is called the cause (*dhātu*) of all virtues, and, being the ultimate state in which the dharmas or characterized appearances have lost all their limitations it is called the *dharma-kāya* of the Buddha (*mahā-muniḥ bhūmi-pāramitādi-bhāva-nayā kleśa-jñeyāvaraṇa-prahāṇāt... sarva-dharma-vibhutva-lābhataś ca dharma-kāya ity ucyate). Ibid.*

3 *tac ca varttate srotasaughavat. Ibid.* p. 21.

In this view thought (*vijñāna*) is regarded as a real substance, and its transformations are also regarded as real; and it is these transformations that are manifested as the selves and the characterized appearances.[1] The first type of transformations, called *vipāka,* is in a way the ground of the other two transformations, which contain the indeterminate materials out of which the manifestations of the other two transformations appear. But, as has already been pointed out, these three different types of transformations again mutually determine one another. The *vipāka* transformations contain within them the seeds of the constructive instincts (*vikalpa-vāsanā*) of the selves as cognizers, the constructive instincts of colours, sounds, etc., the substantive basis (*āśraya*) of the attribution of these twofold constructive instincts, as well as the sense-faculties and the localization of space-determinations (*sthāna-vijñapti* or *bhājana-loka-sanniveśa-vijñapti*). They are also associated in another mode with sense-modifications involving the triune of the sense (*indriya*), sense-object (*viṣaya*) and cognition (and each of these triunes is again associated with a characteristic affective tone corresponding to the effective tones of the other two members of the triune in a one-to-one relation), attention (*manaskāra*), discrimination (*saṃjñā*), volition (*cetanā*) and feeling (*vedanā*).[2] The *vipāka* transformations have no determinate or limited forms (*aparicchinnālambanākāra*),

1 *avaśyaṃ vijñāna-pariṇāmo vastuto'sty upagantavy oyatrātmadharmopacāraḥ pravarttate. Ibid.* p. 16.

2 Feeling *(vedanā)* is distinguished here as painful, pleasurable and as the basic entity which is neither painful nor pleasurable, which is feeling *per se (vedanā anubhava-svabhāvā sā punar viṣayasya āhlādaka-paritāpaka-tadubhaya-kara-vivikta-svarūpa-sākṣātkaraṇa-bhedāt).* This feeling *per se* must be distinguished again from the non-pleasurable-painful feeling existing along with the two other varieties, the painful and the pleasurable. Here the *vipāka* transformations are regarded as evolving the basic entity of feeling, and it is therefore undifferentiated in it as pleasure or pain and is hence called "feeling as indifference (*upekṣā)"* and undifferentiated (*avyākṛta*). The differentiation of feeling as pleasurable or as painful takes place only as a further determination of the basic entity of feeling evolved in the *vipāka* transformations of good and bad deeds (*śubhāśubha-karma-vipāka).* Good and bad (*śubhāśubha*) are to be distinguished from moral and immoral as potential and actual determinations of virtuous and vicious actions.

and there are here no actualized emotional states of attachment, antipathy or the like, which are associated with the actual pleasurable or painful feelings. The *vipāka* transformations thus give us the basic concept of mind and its principal functions with all the potentialities of determinate subject-object consciousness and its processes. There are here the constructive tendencies of selves as perceivers, the objective constructive tendencies of colours, sounds, etc., the sense-faculties, etc., attention, feeling, discrimination, volition and sense-functioning. But none of these have any determinate and actualized forms. The second grade of transformations, called *manana,* represents the actual evolution of moral and immoral emotions; it is here that the mind is set in motion by the ignorant references to the mental elements as the self, and from this ignorance about the self is engendered self-love (*ātma-sneha*) and egoism (*ātma-māna*). These references are again associated with the fivefold universal categories of sense-functioning, feeling, attention, volition and discrimination. Then comes the third grade of transformations, which is associated with the fivefold universal categories together with the special manifestations of concrete sense-perceptions and the various kinds of intellectual states and moral and immoral mental states, such as desire (*chandaḥ*) for different kinds of sense-experiences, decisions (*adhimokṣa*) in conclusions firmly established by perceptions, reasoning, etc., memory, attentive reflection (*samādhi*), wisdom (*prajñā*), faith and firm will for the good (*śraddhā*), shamefulness (*hrī*) for the bad, etc. The term *ālaya-vijñāna* is given to all these three types of transformations, but there is underneath it, as the permanent passive ground, the eternal and unchangeable pure thought (*vijñapti-mātratā*).

It may be pointed out here that in this system of philosophy the eternal and unchangeable thought-substance undergoes by virtue of its inner dynamic three different orders of superficial changes, which are compared to constantly changing streams and waves. The first of these represents the basic change which later determines all subjective and objective possibilities; the second starts the process of the psychosis by the original ignorance and false attribution of self-hood to non-self elements, self-love and egoism; and in the third grade we have all the concrete mental and extra-mental facts. The fundamental categories which make the possibility of mind, mental processes and the extra-mental relations, are evolved in the first stage of transformations; and these abide through the other two stages of transformations and become more and more complex and concrete in course of their association with the categories of the other transformations. In analysing the knowledge situation Vasubandhu does not hold that our awareness of blue is only a modification of the "awareness," but he thinks that an awareness has always two relations, a relation with the subject or the knower (*grāhaka-graha*) and a relation with the object which is known (*grāhya-graha*). Blue as an object is essential for making an awareness of blue possible; for the awareness is not blue, but we have an awareness of the blue. But Vasubandhu argues that this psychological necessity is due to a projection of objectivity as a necessary function of determinate thought, and it does not at all follow that this implies that there are real external objects existing outside of it and generating the awareness as external agent. Psychological objectivity does not imply ontological objectivity. It is argued that, if the agency of objective entities in the production of sense-knowledge be admitted, there could not be any case where sense-knowledge could be admitted to be produced without the operation of the objective entities; but, since in dreams and illusions such sense-knowledge is universally regarded as being produced without the causal operation of such objective entities, no causal operation can be conceded to the objective entities for the production of sense-knowledge.

Śaṅkara, in attempting to refute the Buddhist idealism in his commentary on the *Brahma-sūtra,* II.11.28, seems to refer to a school of idealism which is the same as that described by Śāntarakṣita in his *Tattva-saṃgraha* (commented upon by Kamalaśīla), but largely different from that described in Vasubandhu's *Triṃśikā.* The positive arguments against the impossibility of an external world constituted by partless atoms are the same.[1] But it is further argued on behalf of the Buddhist idealists that the awareness of a pillar, the awareness of a wall or of a jug or of a piece of cloth, implies that these individual awarenesses are mutually different in nature among themselves; and that consequently the apparent differences among objects are but differences among the ideas; and that therefore the objects are of the same nature as the particular ideas by which we are supposed to know them; and, if that be so, the hypothesis of an external world of objects becomes unnecessary. Moreover the fact that both the idea of the object and the object are taken at one and the same moment proves that both the object and the idea are identical, just as the illusory second moon perceived simultaneously with the moon is identical with it.[2] When one of them is not perceived the other also is not perceived. If they were by nature separate and different, there would be no reason why there should be such a uniform and invariable relation between them. The reason for the diversity of our ideas is to be sought not in the diversity of external objects which are ordinarily supposed to

---

1 Vācaspati, however, in his *Bhāmatī* commentary, II.11.28, introduces some new points. He says that spatial extension, as perceived in visual perception, cannot be due to the perception of partless atoms. Nor can it be said that the colour particles produced in uninterrupted succession generate the notion of spatial extension, though there is no spatial extension in the individual atom; for it is not possible that the groups of colour particles are not interrupted by taste, smell and the tactual particles. So it has to be admitted that the colour particles are at some distance from one another and are interrupted by other particles, and that the continuous appearance of colour in spatial distribution is a false appearance, like the appearance of continuous trees from a distance constituting a forest *(gandha-rasa-sparśa-paramāṇvantaritā hi te rūpa-paramāṇavo na nirantarāḥ; tasmād ārāt sāntareṣu vṛkṣeṣu eka-ghana-pratyayavad eṣa sthūla-pratyayaḥ paramāṇuṣu sāntareṣu bhrānta eva)*.

2 This simile is adduced by Vācaspati probably from a quotation from Diṅnāga—*sahopalambha-niyamād abhedo nīla-tad-dhiyoḥ bhedaś ca bhrānti-vijñānair dṛsyetendāv ivādvaye.* Since both the blue and the idea of the blue are taken at the same moment, they are one and the same; for any two things which are taken simultaneously are identical. As one moon appears as two in an illusory manner, so the difference between the idea and the object is also perceived only illusorily. This argument of *sahopalambha-niyayma* is absent in Vasubandhu's *Viṃśatikā* and *Triṃśikā.*

produce them, but in the beginningless diversity of the instinctive sub-conscious roots (*vāsanā*) which produce all our ideas in the waking state, just as they produce dreams during sleep; as dreams are admitted by all to be produced without any external objects, so are all ideas produced without any external real objects; for as ideas the dream ideas are just the same as the waking ideas. But in both cases there are the instinctive sub-conscious roots (*vāsanā*), without which no ideas, whether in the dream state or in the waking state, can be produced; so these, being invariably present in all cases of production of ideas, are the cause of all ideas.[1]

Śaṅkara in refuting the above position says that such a view is untenable because it contradicts our experience, which always distinguishes the subject and the object from the awareness. We are directly aware of our sense-contact with external objects which we perceive, and the object of awareness and the awareness are not one and the same. Our awareness itself shows that it is different from its object. The awareness of a pillar is not the same as a pillar, but a pillar is only an object of the awareness of a pillar. Even in denying external objects, the Buddhist idealists have to say that what is knowable only within appears as if it was existing outside.[2] Śaṅkara argues thus: if externality is absolutely non-existent, how can any

1 Vācaspati summarizes in this connection the inference of the Sautrāntikas for the existence of an external world of objects as the causes of the corresponding ideas. The argument of the Sautrāntikas runs thus: When, the old causes remaining the same, there is a new effect, that new effect must be due to a new cause. Now, though it should be admitted that in the passing series of inner consciousness each particular moment generates the succeeding one, and that this power of productivity is called *vāsanā (tat-pravṛtti-vijñāna-janana-śaktir vāsanā),* and that its tendency to effectuate itself is called its power of fruition (*paripāka*), even then it would be difficult to understand how each particular moment should have a power altogether different from other moments; for, since there is nothing else to change the character of the moments, each moment is just as much a moment as any other. So it has to be admitted that there are other things which make one moment different in its power of effectuation from any other; and these are the external objects.

2 Śaṅkara says *yad antar-jñeya-rūpaṃ tad bahirvad avabhāsate.* This seems to be a quotation from Diṅnāga. Diṅnāga's verse, as quoted by Kamalaśīla in his commentary on the *Tattva-saṃgraha,* verses 2082-2084, runs as follows:

sense-cognition appear as external? Viṣṇumitra cannot appear as the son of a barren woman. Again, the fact that an idea has the same form as its object does not imply that there are no objects; on the other hand, if there were no objects, how could any idea have the same form as its corresponding object? Again, the maxim that any two things which are taken simultaneously are identical is false; for, if the object and its awareness are comprehended at the same moment, the very fact that one is taken along with the other shows that they cannot be identical. Moreover, we find that in all our awarenesses of blue or yellow, a jug or a wall, it is the qualifying or predicative factors of objects of knowledge that differ; awareness as such remains just the same. The objects of knowledge are like so many extraneous qualities attributed to knowledge, just as whiteness or blackness may be attributed to a cow; so whether one perceives blue or red or yellow, that signifies that the difference of perception involves a difference in objects and not in the awareness itself. So the awareness, being one, is naturally different from the objects, which are many; and, since the objects are many, they are different from the one, the awareness. The awareness is one and it is different from the objects, which are many.[1] Moreover, the argument that the appearance of world objects may be explained on the analogy of dreams is also invalid; for there is a great difference between our knowledge of dreams and of worldly objects—dreams are contradicted by the waking experience, but the waking experiences are never found contradicted.

It is curious to note here the contradictions in Śaṅkara's own statements. It has been already pointed out that he himself in his

---

यदन्तर्ज्ञेयरूपं तुबहिर्वदवभासते।
सोऽर्थो विज्ञानरूपत्वात्तत्प्रैययतयापि च॥
yad antar-jñeya-rūpaṃ tu bahirvad avabhāsate
so'rtho vijñāna-rūpatvāt tat-praiyayatayāpi ca.

This shows that Śaṅkara had Diṅnāga in his mind when he attempted to refute the Buddhist idealists.

1 *dvābhyāṃ ca bheda ekasya siddho bhavati ekasmāc ca dvayoḥ; tasmād artha-jñānayor bhedaḥ.* Śaṅkara's *Bhāṣya,* II.11.28, Nirṅaya-Sāgara Press, Bombay, 1904.

commentary on Gauḍapāda's *Kārikā* built a powerful argument for the non-existence of all objects of waking experience on the analogy of the non-existence of the objects of dream experience. Śāntarakṣita (AD 705) and Kamalaśīla (AD 728) in refuting a position similar to that of the view of Śaṅkara—that consciousness is one and unchangeable and that all objects are changing, but that the change of objects does not imply any change of the consciousness itself—argue that, had this been so, then that would imply that all sensibles of different kinds of colours, sounds, etc. were known at one and the same time, since the consciousness that would reveal those objects is constant and unchangeable.[1] Kamalaśīla therefore holds that consciousness is not unchangeable and one, but that there are only the changeable ideas of the sensibles and each idea is different from the other which follows it in time. Śaṅkara's view that consciousness is only one and that it is only the objects that are many seems to be based on a separation due to an arbitrary abstraction. If the commentary on Gauḍapāda's *Kārikā* be admitted to be a work of Śaṅkara, then it may be urged that Śaṅkara's views had undergone a change when he was writing the commentary on the *Brahma-sūtra*; for in the commentary on Gauḍapāda's *Kārikā* he seems again and again to emphasize the view that the objects perceived in waking experience are as false and as non-existent as objects of dream experience. His only realism there consisted in the assertion that the world was but the result of a false illusory imposition on the real Brahman, since illusions such as mirage, etc. must have some underlying basis upon which they are imposed. But in the commentary on the *Brahma-sūtra* the world of objects and sensibles is seen to have an existence of some sort outside individual thought. Vācaspati in his *Bhāmatī* commentary distinguishes the position of Śaṅkara from that of Buddhist idealism by saying that

1 *tad yadi nityaika-jñāna-pratibhāsātmakā amī śabdādayaḥ syus tadā vic-itrās-taraṇa-pratibhāsavat sakṛd eva pratibhāseran; tat-pratibhāsātmakasya jñānasya sarvadā vasthitatvāt.* Kamalaśīla's commentary on the *Tattva-saṃgra-ha,* sl. 331. Gaekwad's Oriental Series, 1926.

Neither Śāntarakṣita nor Kamalaśīla seems to be familiar with Śaṅkara.

the Vedānta holds that the "blue" is not an idea of the form of blue, but "the blue" is merely the inexplicable and indefinable object.[1]

In discussing the views of Vasubandhu in the *Viṃśatikā* and *Triṃśikā* it has been pointed out that Vasubandhu did not try to repudiate the objectivity of the objects of awareness, but he repudiated the idea that objects of awareness existed outside of thought and produced the different kinds of awareness. His idea seems to have been that the sensibles are made up of thought-stuff and, though they are the psychological objects of awareness, they do not exist outside of thought and determine the different ideas that we have of them. But both the sensibles and their ideas are determined by some inner law of thought, which determines the nature and methods of the whole process of the growth and development of the psychosis, and which determines not only its cognitional character, but also its moral and emotional character. All the arguments of Śaṅkara in which he emphasizes the psychological duality of awareness and its object would have no force against Vasubandhu, as Vasubandhu admits it himself and holds that "blue" (*nīla*) is different from the idea of blue; the blue is an object (*ālambana*) and the idea of the blue is an awareness. According to him thought splits itself into subject and object; the idea therefore expresses itself as a subject-object awareness. The subject and the object are as much products of thought as the idea itself; the fact that he considers the blue to be thought does not mean that he denies the objectivity of the blue or that the only existence of the blue is the blue-idea. The blue is objectively present before the idea of blue as a presentation, just as there is the subject to perceive it, but this objectivity does not imply that the blue is somewhere outside thought in the space outside; for even space-locations are thought-products, and so there is no sense in attributing the sensibles of presentation to the outside world. The sensibles are objects of awareness, but they are not the excitants of the corresponding awareness. It does not seem that Śaṅkara says anything to refute such a view. Śaṅkara's position in

1 *na hi brahma-vādino nīlādyākārāṃ vittim abhyupagacchanti, kintu anirvacanīyaṃ nīlādīti. Bhāmatī*, II.ii.28.

the commentary on Gauḍapāda's *Kārikā* seems to have been the same sort of view as that of Diṅnāga, which he takes so much pains to refute in the *Brahma-sūtra-bhāṣya*, and as such it was opposed to the view of Nāgārjuna that there must be some essence or reality on which the illusory impositions are made. But in the *Brahma-sūtra-bhāṣya* he maintains the view that the objective world, as it appears to our consciousness, is present before it objectively and independently—only its ultimate nature is inexplicable. The difference of the objects from the awareness and their independent existence and activity have been accepted by most of the later Vedānta teachers of the Śaṅkara school; and it is well known that in sense-perception the need of the mind-contact with the object of perception through the specific sense is considered indispensable.[1]

Prakāśātman (AD 1200) in his *Pañca-pādikā-vivaraṇa* raises this point and says that the great difference between the Mahāyānists and the Vedāntins consists in the fact that the former hold that the objects (*viṣaya*) have neither any separate existence nor any independent purpose or action to fulfil as distinguished from the momentary ideas, while the latter hold that, though the objects are in essence identical with the one pure consciousness, yet they can fulfil independent purposes or functions and have separate, abiding and uncontradicted existences.[2] Both Padmapāda and Prakāśātman argue that, since the awareness remains the same while there is a constant variation of its objects, and therefore that which remains constant (*anuvṛtta*) and that which changes (*vyāvṛtta*) cannot be considered identical, the object cannot be regarded as being only a modification of the idea.[3] It is suggested that the Buddhist idealist urges that, if the object (*e.g.*, blue) is different from the awareness,

1 See *Vedānta-paribhāṣā*, ch. 1, Śrīveṅkaṭeśvar Press, Bombay, 1911.

2 *tattva-darśinas tu advitīyāt saṃvedanāt abhede'pi viṣayasya bhedenāpi artha-kriyā-sāmarthya-sattvaṃ sthāyitvaṃ cābādhitam astīti vadanti. Pañca-pādikā-vivaraṇa*, p. 73. In addition to this work Prakāśātman also wrote two independent commentaries on *Brahma-sūtra* called *Śārīraka-ṃimāṃsā-nyāya-saṃgraha* and *Laukika-nyāya-muktāvalī*.

3 *anuvṛttasya vyāvṛttān na bhedo'nuvṛttatvād ākāśa-ghaṭādivat.*
—*Pañca-pādikā-vivaraṇa*, p. 73.

it cannot be revealed in it, and, if the blue can be revealed in the awareness, at that moment all the other things of the world might as well be revealed; for there is no such specific relation with the blue that the blue alone should appear in consciousness at that moment. If it is urged that the blue produces the awareness of the blue, then what would be the function of the visual organ? It is better, therefore, the Buddhist suggests, to admit a natural and unique relation of identity of the idea and the object.[1] The Vedāntist objects to this and says that such a supposition cannot be true, since we perceive that the subject, object and the idea are not one and the same. To such an objection the Buddhist is supposed to reply that these three do not form a complex unity, but arise at three successive moments of time, and then by virtue of their potency or root-impression a complex of the three appears; and this complex should not therefore be interpreted as being due to a relationing of three distinct entities.[2] Thus the fact that "I perceive blue" is not to be interpreted as a conscious relationing of "I," "the blue" and the awareness, but as an ideation arising at one particular point of

---

1 *Tasmāt svābhāvikāsādharaṇābhedasambandhād eva vijñāne nīlam avabhāsate. Pañca-pādikā-vivaraṇa,* p. 74. Arguing from a similar point of view, Śāntarakṣita and Kamalaśīla urge that, if the object was not identical with the awareness, there must be some immutable law why they should appear simultaneously. This law according to the Buddhists could only be either of identity *(tādātmya)* or of causality as invariability of production *(tad-utpatti).* The first alternative is what the Buddhists here are contending for as against the Vedāntists. There cannot be the law of causality here; for there cannot be any operation of the law of causality as production between two entities which are simultaneous. *Tattva-saṃgraha* and *Pañjikā,* 2030, 2031.

2 *tad vāsanā-sameta-samanantara-pratyaya-samutthaṃ saṅkalanātmakaṃ pratyayāntaram etan neha sambandhāgamaḥ.*
Padmapāda's (AD 820) *Pañca-pādikā,* p. 25. This work exerted the greatest influence on the development of Vedāntic thought for about six or seven centuries, and several commentaries were written on it. Most important of these are Prakāśātman's *Pañca-pādikā-vivaraṇa, Pañca-pādikādhyāsa-bhāṣya-vyākhyā, Pañca-pādikā-śāstra-darpaṇa* by Amṛtānanda, *Tattva-dīpana* by Amṛtānandanātha, and also a commentary by Ānandapūrṇa Yati. Prakāśātman's commentary on it, called *Pañcapādikā-vivaraṇa,* was commented upon by Akhaṇḍānanda Muni in his *Tattva-dīpana,* by Rāmānanda Sarasvatī in his *Vivaraṇopanyāsa,* and by Nṛsiṃhāśrama in his *Pañca-pādikā-vivaraṇa-bhāva-prakāśikā.*

time, involving all the three constituents in it. Such a supposition is necessary, because all appearances are momentary, and because the relationing of the three as three independent entities would necessarily be impossible without the lapse of some time for their operation of relationing. The theory of momentariness naturally leads us to the above supposition, that what appears as relationing is nothing but one momentary flash, which has the above three as its constituent elements; so the Buddhist is supposed to admit that, psychologically, the awareness and its object seem to be different, but such a psychological appearance can at best be considered as a mental illusion or fiction; for logically the Buddhist cannot admit that a momentary appearance could subsist long enough to have the possibility of being relationed to the self and the awareness, as in "I know the blue"; and, if the blue was not considered to be identical with awareness, there would remain no way to explain the possibility of the appearance of the blue in the awareness.[1]

Padmapāda points out that the main point with the Buddhists is the doctrine of causal efficiency (*artha-kriyā-kāritva*), or the maxim that that alone exists which can prove its existence by effecting some purpose or action. They hold further that this criterion of existence can be satisfied only if all existents are momentary and if all things are momentary; the only epistemological view that can consistently be accepted is the identity of the awareness and the object. The main reason why only momentary existents can satisfy the criterion of causal efficiency is that, if the existents were not assumed to be momentary, they could not affect any purpose or action.[2] Padmapāda urges in refutation of this that, if causal efficiency means the productivity of its own awareness (*sva-viṣaya-jñāna-jananam*), then an awareness or idea has no existence; for it does not produce any other knowledge of itself (*saṃvidāṃsva-*

---

1 *Nānubhavam āśritya saṃvedanād abhinnaṃ nīlaṃ brūmaḥ kintu vijñānena nīlasya pratibhāsānyathānupapattyā; kṣaṇikasya tv āgantuka-sambandhābhāve... pratibhāsa eva nasyāt.* —*Pañca-pādikā-vivaraṇa*, p. 74.

2 See the first volume of this work, pp. 163-164, where the reasons in justification of the doctrine are briefly stated.

viṣaya-jñānā-jananādasallakṣaṇatvam), and the awareness of one cannot be known by others except by inference, which again would not be direct cognition.[1] If causal efficiency means the production of another moment, then the last moment, having no other moment to produce, would itself be non-existent; and, if the last moment is proved to be non-existent, then by turns all the other moments would be non-existent. Existence is a nature of things; and even when a thing remains silent after an operation it does not on that account cease to exist.[2] On such a basis Prakāśātman points out that the supposed three notions of "I," "awareness" and the object are really not three distinct notions appearing as one on account of their similarity, but all the three are joined together in one identical subject-object-awareness which does not involve the three successive stages which the Buddhists suppose. This identity is proved by the fact that they are recognized (*pratyabhijñā*) to be so. We are, again, all conscious of our own identity, that we persist in all our changing states of consciousness, and that, though our ideas are continually changing with the changing objects, we remain unchanged all the same; and this shows that in knowing ourselves as pure awareness we are successively connected with the changing objects. But the question arises who is to be convinced of this identity, a notion of which can be produced only by a relationing of the previous existence (through sub-conscious impressions of memory) to the existence of the present moment; and this cannot be done by the Vedāntic self, which is pure self-revealing consciousness that cannot further be made an object of any other conscious state; for it is unchangeable, indestructible, and there cannot be in it a consciousness of relationing between a past

1 Padmapāda derives the possibility of one's being aware of an awareness, which however hardly appears to be convincing. He thinks that an awareness, being of the nature of light, does not stand in need of any other light to illuminate it. *na ca saṃvit saṃvido viṣayaḥ saṃvid-ātmanā bhedābhāvāt pradīpasyeva pradīpān-taram. Pañca-pādikā,* p. 27.

2 *nārtha-kriyā-kāritva-lakṣaṇam sattvaṃ kintu svābhāvikam iti sakṛt kāryyaṃ kṛt-vā tuṣṇīmbhūtasyāpi sthāyinaḥ sattvaṃ na virudhyate.*

—*Pañca-pādikā-vivaraṇa,* p. 80.

state and a present state through the sub-conscious impressions of memory.[1] The mere persistence of the same consciousness is not the recognition of identity; for the recognition of identity would be a relation uniting the past as past with the present as present; and, since there is no one to perceive the relation of identity, the appearance of identity is false. The Vedāntic answer to such an objection is that, though the pure consciousness cannot behave as an individual, yet the same consciousness associated with mind (*antaḥkaraṇa-viśiṣṭa*) may behave as an individual who can recognize his own identity as well as that of others. The mind is associated with the sub-conscious impressions of a felt ego (*ahaṃvṛtti-saṃskāra-sahitam*), due to the experience of the self as associated with a past time; being responsible for the experience of the self as associated with the present time, it produces the notion of the identity of the self as persisting both in the past and in the present. A natural objection against such an explanation is that, since the Vedānta does not admit that one awareness can be the object of another awareness, the revival of a past awareness is impossible, without which recognition of identity would be impossible. The answer of the Vedāntist is that, just as an idea is remembered through its sub-conscious impressions, so, though recognition of identity was absent in the preceding moment, yet it could arise through the operation of the sub-conscious impressions at a later moment.[2] According to the Vedānta the pure consciousness is the only unchanging substance underlying; it is this consciousness associated with mind (*antaḥkaraṇa*) that behaves as the knower or the subject, and it is the same consciousness associated with the previous and later time that appears as the objective self with which the identity is felt and which is known to be identical with the knower—the mind-associated consciousness. We all have

1 *pūrvānubhava-saṃskāra-sahitād idānīṃtana-vastu-pramiti-kāraṇāj jātam ekasya kāla-dvaya-saṃbandha-viṣayakaṃ pratyakṣa-jñānaṃ pratyabhijñā iti cet, na tarhi ātmani sā sambhavati... vijñāna-svabhāvasya hy ātmanaḥ... jñānānta-rāgamyatvāt...* —*Pañca-pādikā-vivaraṇa,* p. 75.

2 *Pañca-pādikā-vivaraṇa,* p. 76.

notions of self-identity and we feel it as "I am the same"; and the only way in which this can be explained is on the basis of the fact that consciousness, though one and universal, can yet be supposed to perform diverse functions by virtue of the diverse nature of its associations, by which it seems to transform itself as the knower and the thousand varieties of relations and objects which it knows. The main point which is to be noted in connection with this realization of the identity of the self is that the previous experience and its memory prove that the self existed in the past; but how are we to prove that what existed is also existing at the present moment? Knowledge of identity of the self is something different from the experience of self in the past and in the present. But the process consists in this, that the two experiences manifest the self as one identical entity which persisted through both the experiences, and this new experience makes the self known in the aforesaid relation of identity. Again, when I remember a past experience, it is the self as associated with that experience that is remembered; so it is the self as associated with the different time relations that is apprehended in an experience of the identity of self.

From all these discussions one thing that comes out clearly is that according to the Śaṅkara Vedānta, as explained by the *Vivaraṇa* school of Padmapāda and his followers, the sense-data and the objects have an existence independent of their being perceived; and there is also the mind called *antaḥkaraṇa,* which operates in its own way for the apprehension of this or that object. Are objects already there and presented to the pure consciousness through the mind? But what then are the objects? and the Śaṅkarite's answer is that they in themselves are unspeakable and indescribable. It is easy to notice the difference of such a view from that of the Buddhistic idealism of Diṅnāga or the *Laṅkāvatāra* on the one hand and that of Vasubandhu in his *Triṃśikā* on the other. For in the case of the former there were no objects independent of their being perceived, and in the case of the latter the objects are transformations of a thought-principle and are as such objective to the subject which apprehends them. Both the subject and the object are grounded in the higher and superior principle, the principle of thought. This grounding implies that this principle of thought and its transformations are responsible for both the subject and the object, as regards material and also as regards form. According to the Śaṅkara Vedānta, however, the stuff of world-objects, mind, the senses and all their activities, functionings and the like are but modifications of *māyā,* which is indescribable (*anirvācya*) in itself, but which is always related to pure consciousness as its underlying principle, and which in its forms as material objects hides from the view and is made self-conscious by the illuminating flash of the underlying principle of pure consciousness in its forms as intellectual states or ideas. As already described, the Śūnyavādins also admitted the objective existence of all things and appearances; but, as these did not stand the test of criticism, considered them as being essenceless (*nihsvabhāva*). The only difference that one can make out between this doctrine of essencelessness and the doctrine of indescribableness of the Śaṅkara school is that this "indescribable" is yet regarded as an indescribable something, as some stuff which undergoes changes and which has transformed itself into all the objects of the world. The idealism of the Śaṅkara Vedānta does not believe in the *sahopalam-bha-niyama* of the Buddhist idealists, that to exist is to be perceived. The world is there even if it be not perceived by the individual; it has an objective existence quite independent of my ideas and sensations; but, though independent of my sensations or ideas, it is not independent of consciousness, with which it is associated and on which it is dependent. This consciousness is not ordinary psychological thought, but it is the principle that underlies all conscious thought. This pure thought is independent and self-revealing, because in all conscious thought the consciousness shines by itself; all else is manifested by this consciousness and when considered apart from it, is inconceivable and unmeaning. This independent and uncontradicted self-shiningness constitutes being (*abādhita-svayaṃ-prakāśataiva asya sattā*).[1] All being is pure consciousness, and all appearance

1 Vācaspati Miśra's *Bhāmatī*, p. 13, Nirṇaya-Sāgara edition, 1904.

hangs on it as something which is expressed by a reference to it and apart from which it has no conceivable status or meaning. This is so not only epistemologically or logically, but also ontologically. The object-forms of the world are there as transformations of the indescribable stuff of *māyā*, which is not "being," but dependent on "being"; but they can only be expressed when they are reflected in mental states and presented as ideas. Analogies of world objects with dream objects or illusions can therefore be taken only as popular examples to make the conception of *māyā* popularly intelligible; and this gives the Vedāntic idealism its unique position.

ŚAṄKARA'S DEFENCE OF VEDĀNTA PHILOSOPHY OF BĀDARĀYAṆA AND BHARTṚPRAPAÑCA

Śaṅkara's defensive arguments consisted in the refutation of the objections that may be made against the Vedāntic conception of the world. The first objection anticipated is that from the followers of Sāṃkhya philosophy. Thus it is urged that the effect must be largely of the same nature as the cause. Brahman, which is believed to be intelligent (*cetana*) and pure (*śuddha*), could not be the cause of a world which is unintelligent (*jaḍa* and *acetana*) and impure (*aśuddha*). And it is only because the world is so different in nature from the intelligent spirits that it can be useful to them. Two things which are identical in their nature can hardly be of any use to each other—two lamps cannot be illuminating to each other. So it is only by being different from the intelligent spirits that the world can best serve them and exist for them. Śaṅkara's answer to this objection is that it is not true that the effect should in every way be similar to the cause—there are instances of inanimate hair and nails growing from living beings, and of living insects growing out of inanimate objects like cow-dung. Nor can it be denied that there is at least some similarity between Brahman and the world in this, that both have being. It cannot be urged that, because Brahman is intelligent, the world also should be intelligent; for there is no reason for such an expectation. The converse of it also has not been found to be true—it has not been found that what is unintelligent has been known to have been derived from a source other than Brahman.[1] The whole point of this argument seems to lie in the fact that, since the Upaniṣads assert that Brahman is the cause of the world, the apparent incompatibility of the production of an impure and unintelligent world from the intelligent and pure Brahman has to be explained away; for such ultimate truths can be discovered not by reason, but by the testimony of the Upaniṣads. Another objection supposed to be raised by Sāṃkhya against Vedānta is that at the time of dissolution (*pralaya*), when the world of effects will dissolve back into Brahman the cause, the impurities of the worldly state might also make the causal state of Brahmahood impure. Śaṅkara refutes it by pointing out two sets of instances in which the effects do not affect the causal state when they return to it. Of these, one set of instances is to be found in those cases where articles of gold, silver, etc. are melted back into their original material states as unformed gold and silver, and are not seen to affect them with their specific peculiarities as formed articles. The other instance is to be found in the manifestation of magic by a magician. The magical creations of a magician are controlled by him and, when they vanish in this way, they cannot in any way affect the magician himself; for the magical creations have no reality. So also a dreamer is not affected by his dreams when he is awake. So the reality is one which remains altogether untouched by the changing states. The appearance of this reality as all the changing states is mere false show (*māyā-mātram*), like the appearance of a rope as a snake. Again, as a man may in deep sleep pass into a state where there is no trace of his mundane experiences and may yet, when he becomes awake, resume his normal vocation in life, so after the dissolution of the world into its causal state there may again be the same kind of creation as there was before the dissolution. So there

1 *kiṃ hi yac caitanyenānanvitaṃ tad abrahma-prakṛtikaṃ dṛṣṭam iti brahma-vādinaṃ praty udāhriyeta samastasya vastujātasya brahma-prakṛtikatvābhyu-pagamāt.* —Śaṅkara's *Bhāṣya,* II.1.6.

can be no objection that the world of impure effects will affect the pure state of Brahman at the time of dissolution or that there could be no creation after dissolution.

These arguments of Śaṅkara in answer to a supposed objection that the world of effects, impure and unintelligent as it is, could not have been the product of pure and intelligent Brahman are not only weak but rather uncalled for. If the world of effects is mere *māyā* and magic and has no essence (*vastutva*), the best course for him was to rush straight to his own view of effects as having no substantiality or essence and not to adopt the *pariṇāma* view of real transformations of causes into effects to show that the effects could be largely dissimilar from their causes. Had he started with the reply that the effects had no real existence and that they were merely magical creations and a false show, the objection that the impure world could not come out of pure Brahman would have at once fallen to the ground; for such an objection would have validity only with those who believed in the real transformations of effects from causes, and not with a philosopher like Śaṅkara, who did not believe in the reality of effects at all. Instead of doing that he proceeded to give examples of the realistic return of golden articles into gold in order to show that the peculiar defects or other characteristics of the effect cannot affect the purity of the cause. Side by side with this he gives another instance, how magical creations may vanish without affecting the nature of the magician. This example, however, does not at all fit in with the context, and it is surprising how Śaṅkara failed to see that, if his examples of realistic transformations were to hold good, his example of the magic and the magician would be quite out of place. If the *pariṇāma* view of causation is to be adopted, the *vivarta* view is to be given up. It seems however that Śaṅkara here was obliged to take refuge in such a confusion of issues by introducing stealthily an example of the *vivarta* view of unreality of effects in the commentary on *sūtras* which could only yield a realistic interpretation. The *sūtras* here seem to be so convincingly realistic that the ultimate reply to the suggested incompatibility of the production of effects dissimilar from their causes is found in the fact that the Upaniṣads hold that this impure and unintelligent world had come out of Brahman; and that, since the Upaniṣads assert it, no objection can be raised against it on grounds of reason.

In the next section the theory of realistic transformation of causes is further supported by the *sūtra* which asserts that in spite of the identity of effects with their cause their plurality or diversity may also be explained on the analogy of many popular illustrations. Thus, though the waves are identical with the sea, yet they have an existence in their plurality and diversity as well. Here also Śaṅkara has to follow the implication of the *sūtra* in his interpretation. He, however, in concluding his commentary on this *sūtra*, says that the world is not a result of any real transformation of Brahman as effect; Brahman alone exists, but yet, when Brahman is under the conditioning phenomena of a world-creation, there is room for apparent diversity and plurality. It may be pointed out, however, that such a supplementary explanation is wholly incompatible with the general meaning of the rule, which is decidedly in favour of a realistic transformation. It is unfortunate that here also Śaṅkara does not give any reason for his supplementary remark, which is not in keeping with the general spirit of the *sūtra* and the interpretation which he himself gave of it.

In the next section the *sūtras* seem plainly to assert the identity of cause and effect, "because of the possibility of the effect, because the cause exists, because the effect exists in the cause and is due to an elaboration of the cause and also for other reasons and the testimony of the Upaniṣads." Such a meaning is quite in keeping with the general meaning of the previous sections. Śaṅkara, however, interprets the *sūtra* as meaning that it is Brahman, the cause, which alone is true. There cannot therefore be any real transformation of causes into effects. The omniscience of Brahman and His being the creator of the world have thus only a limited validity; for they depend upon the relative reality of the world. From the absolute point of view therefore there is no Īśvara who is the omniscient creator of the world.[1] Śaṅkara supports this generally on the ground of the testimony of some Upaniṣad texts (*e.g., mṛttiketyevasatyam,* etc.). He however introduces an argument in support of the *sat-kārya-vāda* theory, or the theory that the effect is already existent in the cause. This theory is indeed common both to the *pariṇāma* view of real transformation and the *vivarta* view, in two different ways. It is curious however that he should support the *sat-kārya-vāda* theory *on pariṇāma* lines, as against the generative view of *a-sat-kārya-vāda* of the Nyāya, but not on *vivarta* lines, where effects are treated as non-existent and false. Thus he says that the fact that curd is produced from milk and not from mud shows that there is some such intimate relation of curd with milk which it has not with anything else. This intimate relation consists in the special power or capacity (*śakti*) in the cause (*e.g.,* the milk), which can produce the special effect (*e.g.,* the curd). This power is the very essence of the cause, and the very essence of this power is the effect itself. If a power determines the nature of the effect, it must be already existent in the cause as the essence of the effect. Arguing against the Nyāya view that the cause is different from the effect, though they are mutually connected in an inseparable relation of inherence (*samavāya*), he says that, if such a *samavāya* is deemed necessary to connect the cause with the effect, then this also may require a further something to connect the *samavāya* with the cause or the effect and that another and that another *ad infinitum.* If it is urged that *samavāya*, being a relation, does not require any further relation to connect it with anything else, it may well be asked in reply how "conjunction" (*saṃyoga*), which is also regarded as a relation, should require the relation of inherence (*samavāya*) to connect it with the objects which are in conjunction (*saṃyogin*).

---

1 *kūṭa-stha-brohmātma-vādinaḥ ekatvaikāntyā tīśitrīśitavyabhāvaḥ īśvara-kāraṇa-pratijñā-virodha iti cet;na; avidyātmaka-nāma-rūpa-bīja-vyākaraṇā-pek-ṣarvāt sarvajñatvasya.* —Śaṅkara's *Bhāṣya* on *Brahma-sūtra.* II.i.14.

Na tāttvikam aiśvaryyaṃ sarvajñatvaṃ ca brahmaṇaḥ kintv avidyopādhikam iti tadāśrayam pratijñā-sūtram, tattvāśrayaṃ tu tad ananyatva-sūtram.

—*Bhāmatī* on the above *Bhāṣya.*

The conception of *samavāya* connecting substances with their qualities is unnecessary; for the latter always appear identified with the former (*tādātmya-pratīti*). If the effect, say a whole, is supposed to be existing in the cause, the parts, it must exist in them all taken together or in each of the separate parts. If the whole exist only in the totality of the parts, then, since all the parts cannot be assembled together, the whole as such would be invisible. If the whole exist in the parts in parts, then one has to conceive other parts of the whole different from its constituent parts; and, if the same questions be again repeated, these parts should have other parts and these others; and thus there would be a vicious infinite. If the whole exists wholly in each of the parts at the same time, then there would be many wholes. If it exists successively in each of the parts, then the whole would at one time be existent only in one part, and so at that time the functions of the whole would be absent in the other parts. If it is said that, just as a class-concept (*e.g.*, cow) exists wholly in each of the individuals and yet is not many, so a whole may also be wholly existent in each of the parts, it may well be replied that the experience of wholes is not like the experience of class-concepts. The class-concept of cow is realized in each and every cow; but a whole is not realized in each and every part. Again, if the effect is non-existent before its production, then, production being an action, such an action would have nothing as its agent, which is impossible—for, since the effect is non-existent before its production, it could not be the agent of its production; and, since being non-existent, it cannot be the agent of its production, such a production would be either itself non-existent or would be without any agent. If, however, production is not defined as an action, but as a relationing of an effect with its cause (*svakāraṇa-sattā-samavāya*), then also it may be objected that a relation is only possible when there are two terms which are related, and, since the effect is as yet non-existent, it cannot be related to its cause.

But, if the effect is already existent, what then is the necessity of the causal operation (*kāraka-vyāpāra*)? The answer to such a question is to be found in the view that the effect is but an elaboration of the cause into its effect. Just as a man may sit with his limbs collected together or stretched out and yet would be considered the same man, so an effect also is to be regarded as an expansion of the cause and as such identical with it. The effect is thus only a transformed state of the cause; and hence the causal operation is necessary for bringing about this transformation; but in spite of such a transformation the effect is not already existing in the cause as its potency or power.

There are seven other smaller sections. In the first of these the objection that, if the world is a direct product of the intelligent Brahman, there is no reason why such an intelligent being should create a world which is full of misery and is a prison-house to himself, is easily answered by pointing out that the transcendent creator is far above the mundane spirits that suffer misery in the prison-house of the world. Here also Śaṅkara adds as a supplementary note the remark that, since there is no real creation and the whole world is but a magical appearance, no such objection that the creator should not have created an undesirable world for its own suffering is valid. But the *sūtras* gave him no occasion for such a remark; so that indeed, as was the case with the previous sections, here also his *māyā* theory is not in keeping even with his general interpretation of the *sūtras*, and his remarks have to be appended as a note which hangs loosely and which does not appear to have any relevancy to the general meaning and purport of the *sūtras*.

In the next section an objection is raised that Brahman cannot without the help of any other accessory agents create the world; the reply to such an objection is found in the fact that Brahman has all powers in Himself and can as such create the world out of Himself without the help of anything else.

In the next section an objection is raised that, if the world is a transformation of Brahman, then, since Brahman is partless, the transformation must apply to the whole of Brahman; for a partial transformation is possible only when the substance which is undergoing the transformation has parts. A reply to such an objection is to be found in the analogy of the human self, which is in itself formless and, though transforming itself into various kinds of dream experiences, yet remains unchanged and unaffected as a whole by such transformations. Moreover, such objections may be levelled against the objectors themselves; for Sāṃkhya also admits the transformation of the formless *prakṛti.*

In another section it is urged that, since Brahman is complete in Himself, there is no reason why He should create this great world, when He has nothing to gain by it. The reply is based on the analogy of play, where one has nothing to gain and yet one is pleased to indulge in it. So Brahman also creates the world by His *līlā* or play. Śaṅkara, however, never forgets to sing his old song of the *māyā* theory, however irrelevant it may be, with regard to the purpose of the *sūtras*, which he himself could not avoid following. Thus in this section, after interpreting the *sūtra* as attributing the world-creation to God's playful activity, he remarks that it ought not to be forgotten that all the world-creation is but a fanciful appearance due to nescience and that the ultimate reality is the identity of the self and Brahman.

The above discussion seems to prove convincingly that Bādarāyaṇa's philosophy was some kind of *bhedābheda-vāda* or a theory of transcendence and immanence of God (Brahman)—even in the light of Śaṅkara's own commentary. He believed that the world was the product of a real transformation of Brahman, or rather of His powers and energies (*śakti*). God Himself was not exhausted by such a transformation and always remained as the master creator who by His play created the world and who could by His own powers create the world without any extraneous assistance. The world was thus a real transformation of God's powers, while He Himself, though remaining immanent in the world through His powers, transcended it at the same time, and remained as its controller, and punished or rewarded the created mundane souls in accordance with their bad and good deeds.

The doctrine of *bhedābheda-vāda* is certainly prior to Śaṅkara, as it is the dominant view of most of the *purāṇas.* It seems probable also that Bhartṛprapañca refers to Bodhāyana, who is referred to as *vṛttikāra* by Rāmānuja, and as *vṛttikāra* and *Upavarṣa* by Śaṅkara, and to Dramiḍācārya, referred to by Śaṅkara and Rāmānuja; all held some form of *bhedābheda* doctrine.[1] Bhartṛprapañca has been referred to by Śaṅkara in his commentary on the *Bṛhadāraṇyaka Upaniṣad*; and Ānandajñāna, in his commentary on Śaṅkara's commentary, gives a number of extracts from Bhartṛprapañca's *Bhāṣya* on the *Bṛhadāraṇyaka Upaniṣad.* Prof. M. Hiriyanna collected these fragments in a paper read before the Third Oriental Congress in Madras, 1924, and there he describes Bhartṛprapañca's philosophy as follows. The doctrine of Bhartṛprapañca is monism, and it is of the *bhedābheda* type. The relation between Brahman and the *jīva,* as that between Brahman and the world, is one of identity in difference. An implication of this view is that both *the jīva* and the physical world evolve out of Brahman, so that the doctrine may be described as *Brahma-pariṇāma-vāda.* On the spiritual side Brahman is transformed into the *antaryāmin* and the *jīva*; on the

1 Prof. S. Kuppusvāmī Śāstrī, in an article read before the Third Oriental Conference, quotes a passage from Veṅkaṭa's *Tattva-ṭīkā* on Rāmānuja's commentary on the *Brahma-sūtras,* in which he says that Upavarṣa is a name of Bodhāyana—*vṛttikārasya Bodhāyanasyaiva hi Upavarṣa iti syān nāma*—*Proceedings of the Third Oriental Conference,* Madras, 1924. The commentators on Śaṅkara's *Bhāṣya* say that, when he refers to Vṛttikāra in I.1.9, I.1.23, I.11.23 and III.111.53, he refers to Upavarṣa by name. From the views of Upavarṣa referred to in these *sūtras* it appears that Upavarṣa believed in the theory of *jñāna-karma-samuccaya,* held also by Bhāskara (an adherent of the *bhedābheda* theory), Rāmānuja and others, but vehemently opposed by Śaṅkara, who wanted to repudiate the idea of his opponents that the performance of sacrificial and Vedic duties could be conceived as a preliminary preparation for making oneself fit for Brahma-knowledge.

References to Dramiḍācārya's commentary on the *Chāndogya Upaniṣad* are made by Ānandagiri in his commentary on Śaṅkara's commentary on the *Chāndogya Upaniṣad.* In the commentary of Sarvajñātma Muni's *Saṃkṣepa-śārīraka,* III . 217-227, by Nṛsiṃhāśrama, the Vākyakāra referred to by Sarvajñātma Muni as Ātreya has been identified with Brahmanandin or Ṭaṅka and the bhāṣyakāra (a quotation from whose *Bhāṣya* appears in *Saṃkṣepa-śārīraka*, III.221, *"antar-guṇā bhagavatī paradevateti,"* is referred to as a quotation from Dramiḍācārya in Rāmānuja's *Vedārtha-saṃgraha,* p. 138, Pandit edition) is identified with Dramiḍācārya, who wrote a commentary on Brahmanandin's *Chāndogyopaniṣad-vārttika.*

physical side into *avyakta, sūtra, virāj* and *devatā,* which are all cosmic; and *jāti* and *piṇḍa,* which are not cosmic. These are the *avasthās* or modes of Brahman, and represent the eight classes into which the variety of the universe may be divided. They are again classified into three *rāśis, para-mātma-rāśi, jīva-rāśi* and *mūrttāmūrtta-rāśi,* which correspond to the triple subject-matter of Religion and Philosophy, viz. God, soul and matter. Bhartṛprapañca recognized what is known as *pramāṇa-samuccaya,* by which it follows that the testimony of common experience is quite as valid as that of the Veda. The former vouches for the reality of variety and the latter for that of unity (as taught in the Upaniṣads). Hence the ultimate truth is *dvaitādvaita. Mokṣa*, or life's end, is conceived as being achieved in two stages—the first leading to *apavarga*, where *saṃsāra* is overcome through the overcoming of *āsaṅga*; and the second leading to Brahmahood through the dispelling of *avidyā.* This means of reaching either stage is *jñāna-karma-samuccaya,* which is a corollary on the practical side to *pramāṇa-samuccaya* on the theoretical side.

It is indeed difficult to say what were the exact characteristics of Bādarāyaṇa's *bhedābheda* doctrine of Vedānta; but there is very little doubt that it was some special type of *bhedābheda* doctrine, and, as has already been repeatedly pointed out, even Śaṅkara's own commentary (if we exclude only his parenthetic remarks, which are often inconsistent with the general drift of his own commentary and the context of the *sūtras*, as well as with their purpose and meaning, so far as it can be made out from such a context) shows that it was so. If, however, it is contended that this view of real transformation is only from a relative point of view (*vyavahārika*), then there must at least be one *sūtra* where the absolute (*pāramārthika*) point of view is given; but no such *sūtra* has been discovered even by Śaṅkara himself. If experience always shows the causal transformation to be real, then how is one to know that in the ultimate point of view all effects are false and unreal? If, however, it is contended that there is a real transformation (*pariṇāma*) of the *māyā* stuff, whereas Brahman remains always unchanged, and if *māyā* is regarded as the power (*śakti*) of Brahman, how then can the *śakti* of Brahman as well as its transformations be regarded as unreal and false, while the possessor of the *śakti* (or the *śaktimat,* Brahman) is regarded as real and absolute? There is a great diversity of opinion on this point among the Vedāntic writers of the Śaṅkara school. Thus Appaya Dīkṣita in his *Siddhānta-leśa* refers to the author of *Padārtha-nirṇaya* as saying that Brahman and *māyā* are both material causes of the world-appearance—Brahman the *vivarta* cause, and *māyā* the *pariṇāma* cause. Others are said to find a definition of causation intermediate between *vivarta* and *pariṇāma* by defining material cause as that which can produce effects which are not different from itself (*svā-bhinna-kārya janakatvam upādānatvam*). The world is identical with Brahman inasmuch as it has being, and it is identical with nescience inasmuch as it has its characteristics of materiality and change. So from two different points of view both Brahman and *māyā* are the cause of the world. Vācaspati Miśra holds that *māyā* is only an accessory cause (*sahakāri*), whereas Brahman is the real *vivarta* cause.[1] The author of the *Siddhānta-muktāvalī*, Prakāśānanda, however, thinks that it is the *māyā* energy (*māyā-śakti*) which is the material cause of the world and not Brahman. Brahman is unchangeable and is the support of *māyā*; and is thus the cause of the world in a remote sense. Sarvajñātma Muni, however, believes Brahman alone to be the *vivarta* cause, and *māyā* to be only an instrument for the purpose.[2] The difficulty that many of the *sūtras* of Bādarāyaṇa give us a *pariṇāma* view of causation was realized by Sarvajñātma Muni, who tried to explain it away by suggesting that the *pariṇāma* theory was discussed approvingly

---

1 Vācaspati Miśra flourished in about AD 840. In addition to his *Bhāmatī* commentary on the *Brahma-sūtra* he wrote many other works and commentaries on other systems of philosophy. His important works are: *Tattva-bindu, Tattva-vaiśāradī* (yoga), *Tattva-samīkṣā Brahma-siddhi-ṭīkā, Nyāya-kaṇikā* on *Vidhi-viveka, Nyāya-tattvāloka, Nyāya-ratna-ṭīkā, Nyāya-vārttika-tātparya-ṭīkā, Brahma-tattva-saṃhitoddīpanī, Yukti-dīpikā* (*Sāṃkhya*), *Sāṃkhya-tattva-kaumudī, Vedānta-tattva-kaumudī.*

2 He lived about AD 900 during the reign of King Manukulāditya and was a pupil of Deveśvara.

in the *sūtras* only because this theory was nearest to the *vivarta*, and by initiating people to the *pariṇāma* theory it would be easier to lead them to the *vivarta* theory, as hinted in *sūtra* II.1.14.[1] This explanation could have some probability, if the arrangement of the *sūtras* was such as to support the view that the *pariṇāma* view was introduced only to prepare the reader's mind for the *vivarta* view, which was ultimately definitely approved as the true view; but it has been shown that the content of almost all the *sūtras* of II. i. consistently support the *pariṇāma* view, and that even the *sūtra* II.1.14 cannot be explained as holding the *vivarta* view of causation as the right one, since the other *sūtras* of the same section have been explained by Śaṅkara himself on the *pariṇāma* view; and, if the content be taken into consideration, this *sūtra* also has to be explained on the *pariṇāma* view of *bhedābheda* type.

TEACHERS AND PUPILS IN VEDĀNTA

The central emphasis of Śaṅkara's philosophy of the Upaniṣads and the *Brahma-sūtra* is on Brahman, the self-revealed identity of pure consciousness, bliss and being, which does not await the performance of any of the obligatory Vedic duties for its

---

1 विवर्तवादस्य हि पूर्वभूमिर्वेदान्तवादे परिणामवादः।
व्यवस्थितेऽस्मिन् परिणामवादे स्वयं समायाति विवर्तवादः॥
vivarta-vādasya hi pūrva-bhūmir
vedānta-vāde pariṇāma-vādaḥ
vyavasthite'smin pariṇāma-vāde
svayaṃ samāyāti vivarta-vādaḥ. —*Saṃkṣepa-śārīraka*, II.61.
उपायम् आतिष्ठति पूर्वम् उच्चैरुपायम् आप्तुं जनता यथैव।
श्रुतिर्मुनीन्द्रश्च विवर्त-सिद्ध्यै विकारवादं वदतस्तथैव॥
Upāyam ātiṣṭhati pūrvam uccair
Upāyam āptuṃ janatā yathaiva
Śrutir munīndraś ca vivarta-siddhyai
vikāra-vādaṃ vadata stathaiva. —*Ibid.* II.62.
विकारवादं कपिलादिपक्षम् उपेत्य वादेन तु सूत्रकारः।
श्रुतिश्च संजल्पति पूर्वभूमौस्थित्वा विवर्तप्रतिपादनय॥
vikāra-vādaṃ Kapilādi-pakṣam
upetya vādena tu sūtra-kāraḥ
śrutiś ca saṃjalpati pūrvabhūmau
sthitvā vivarta-pratipādanāya. —*Ibid.* II.64.

realization. A right realization of such Upaniṣad texts as "That art thou," instilled by the right teacher, is by itself sufficient to dispel all the false illusions of world-appearance. This, however, was directly against the Mīmāṃsā view of the obligatoriness of certain duties, and Śaṅkara and his followers had to fight hard on this point with the Mīmāṃsakas. Different Mīmāṃsā writers emphasized in different ways the necessity of the association of duties with Brahma-wisdom; and a brief reference to some of these has been made in the section on Sureśvara. Another question arose regarding the nature of the obligation of listening to the unity texts (*e.g.*, "that art thou") of the Vedānta; and later Vedānta writers have understood it differently. Thus the author of the *Prakaṭārtha,* who probably flourished in the twelfth century, holds that it is only by virtue of the mandate of the Upaniṣads (such as "thou shouldst listen to these texts, understand the meaning and meditate") that one learns for the first time that one ought to listen to the Vedānta texts—a view which is technically called *apūrva-vidhi.* Others, however, think that people might themselves engage in reading all kinds of texts in their attempts to attain salvation and that they might go on the wrong track; and it is just to draw them on to the right path, viz. that of listening to the unity texts of the Upaniṣads, that the Upaniṣads direct men to listen to the unity texts—this view is technically called *niyama-vidhi.* The followers of Sarvajñātma Muni, however, maintain that there can in no sense be a duty in regard to the attainment of wisdom of Brahma-knowledge, and the force of the duty lies in enjoining the holding of discussions for the clarification of one's understanding; and the meaning of the obligatory sentence "thou shouldst listen to" means that one should hold proper discussions for the clarification of his intellect. Other followers of Sureśvara, however, think that the force of the obligation lies in directing the student of Vedānta steadily to realize the truth of the Vedānta texts without any interruption; and this view is technically called *parisaṃkhyā-vidhi.* Vācaspati Miśra and his followers, however, think that no obligation of duties is implied in these commands; they are simply put in the form of commands in order to show the great importance of listening to Vedānta texts and holding discussions on them, as a means of advancement in the Vedāntic course of progress.

But the central philosophical problem of the Vedānta is the conception of Brahman—the nature of its causality, its relation with *māyā* and the phenomenal world of world-appearance, and with individual persons. Śaṅkara's own writings do not always manifest the same uniform and clear answer; and many passages in different parts of his work show tendencies which could be more or less diversely interpreted, though of course the general scheme was always more or less well-defined. Appaya Dīkṣita notes in the beginning of his *Siddhānta-leśa* that the ancients were more concerned with the fundamental problem of the identity of the self and the Brahman, and neglected to explain clearly the order of phenomenal appearance; and that therefore many divergent views have sprung up on the subject. Thus shortly after Śaṅkara's death we have four important teachers, Sureśvara and his pupil Sarvajñātma Muni, Padmapāda and Vācaspati Miśra, who represent three distinct tendencies in the monistic interpretation of the Vedānta. Sureśvara and his pupil Sarvajñātma Muni held that *māyā* was only an instrument (*dvāra*), through which the one Brahman appeared as many, and had its real nature hidden from the gaze of its individual appearances as individual persons. In this view *māyā* was hardly recognized as a substance, though it was regarded as positive; and it was held that *māyā* had, both for its object and its support, the Brahman. It is the pure Brahman that is the real cause underlying all appearances, and the *māyā* only hangs on it like a veil of illusion which makes this one thing appear as many unreal appearances. It is easy to see that this view ignores altogether the importance of giving philosophical explanations of phenomenal appearance, and is only concerned to emphasize the reality of Brahman as the only truth. Vācaspati's view gives a little more substantiality to *māyā* in the sense that he holds that *māyā* is coexistent with Brahman, as an accessory through the operation of which the creation of world-appearance is possible; *māyā* hides the

Brahman as its object, but it rests on individual persons, who are again dependent on *māyā*, and *māyā* on them, in a beginningless cycle. The world-appearance is not mere subjective ideas or sensations, but it has an objective existence, though the nature of its existence is inexplicable and indescribable; and at the time of dissolution of the world (or *pralaya*) its constitutive stuff, psychical and physical, will remain hidden in *avidyā*, to be revived again at the time of the next world-appearance, otherwise called creation. But the third view, namely that of Padmapāda, gives *māyā* a little more substantiality, regarding it as the stuff which contains the double activity or power of cognitive activity and vibratory activity, one determining the psychical process and the other the physical process, and regarding Brahman in association with *māyā*, with these two powers as Īśvara, as the root cause of the world. But the roots of a very thoroughgoing subjective idealism also may be traced even in the writings of Śaṅkara himself. Thus in the *Bṛhadāraṇyaka-bhāṣya* he says that, leaving aside theories of limitation (*avaccheda*) or reflection (*pratibimba*), it may be pointed out that, as the son of Kuntī is the same as Rādheya, so it is the Brahman that appears as individual persons through beginningless *avidyā*; the individual persons so formed again delusively create the world-appearance through their own *avidyā*. It will be pointed out in a later section that Maṇḍana also elaborated the same tendency shortly after Śaṅkara in the ninth century. Thus in the same century we have four distinct lines of Vedāntic development, which began to expand through the later centuries in the writers that followed one or the other of these schools; and some additional tendencies also developed. The tenth century seems to have been very barren in the field of the Vedānta, and, excepting probably Jñānottama Miśra, who wrote a commentary on Sureśvara's *Vārttika*, no writer of great reputation is known to us to have lived in this period. In other fields of philosophical development also this century was more or less barren, and, excepting Udayana and Śrīdhara in Nyāya-Vaiśeṣika, Utpala in Astronomy and Abhinavagupta in Śaivism, probably no other persons of great reputation can be mentioned. There were, however, a few Buddhistic writers of repute in this period, such as Candragomin (junior) of Rajshahi, the author of *Nyāya-loka-siddhi,* Prajñākara Gupta of Vikramaśilā, author of *Pramāṇa-vārtikālaṅkāra* and *Sahopalambha-niścaya*, Ācārya Jetāri of Rajshahi, the author of *Hetu-tattvopadeṣa, Dharma-dharmi-viniścaya* and *Bālāvatāra-tarka,* Jina, the author of *Pramāṇa-vārtikālaṅkāra-ṭīkā,* Ratnakīrti, the author of the *Apoha-siddhi, Kṣaṇa-bhaṅga-siddhi* and *Sthira-siddhi-dūṣaṇa,* and Ratna Vajra, the author of the *Yukti-prayoga.* The eleventh century also does not seem to have been very fruitful for Vedānta philosophy. The only author of great reputation seems to have been Ānandabodha Bhaṭṭārakācārya, who appears to have lived probably in the latter half of the eleventh century and the first half of the twelfth century. The *mahāvidyā* syllogisms of Kulārka Paṇḍita, however, probably began from some time in the eleventh century, and these were often referred to for refutation by Vedāntic writers till the fourteenth century, as will be pointed out in a later section. But it is certain that quite a large number of Vedāntic writers must have worked on the Vedānta before Ānandabodha, although we cannot properly trace them now. Ānandabodha says in his *Nyāya-makaranda* that his work was a compilation (*saṃgraha*) from a large number of Vedāntic monographs (*nibandha-puṣpāñjali*). Citsukha in his commentary on the *Nyāya-makaranda* points out (p. 346) that Ānandabodha was refuting a view of the author of the *Brahma-prakāśikā.* According to Govindānanda's statement in his *Ratna-prabhā*, p. 311, Amalānanda of the thirteenth century refuted a view of the author of the *Prakaṭārtha.* The author of the *Prakaṭārtha* may thus be believed to have lived either in the eleventh or in the twelfth century. It was a commentary on Śaṅkara's *Bhāṣya*, and its full name was *Śārīraka-bhāṣya-prakaṭārtha*; and Ānandajñāna (called also Janārdana) wrote his *Tattvāloka* on the lines of Vedāntic interpretation of this work. Mr Tripathi says in his introduction to the *Tarka-saṃgraha* that a copy of this work is available in Tekka Maṭha; but the present writer had the good fortune of going through it from a manuscript in the Adyar Library, and a short account of its philosophical views is given below in a separate section. In the *Siddhānta-leśa* of Appaya Dīkṣita we hear of a commentary on it called *Prakaṭārtha-vivaraṇa.* But, though Ānandajñāna wrote his *Tattvāloka* on the lines of the *Prakaṭārtha*, yet the general views of Ānandajñāna were not the same as those of the author thereof; Ānandajñāna's position was very much like that of Sarvajñātma Muni, and he did not admit many *ajñānas*, nor did he admit any difference between *māyā* and *avidyā.* But the author of the *Prakaṭārtha, so* far as can be judged from references to him in the *Siddhānta-leśa,* gave a separate place to the *antaḥkaraṇas* of individual persons and thought that, just as the *jīvas* could be cognizers through the reflection of pure intelligence in the *antaḥkaraṇa* states, so Īśvara is omniscient by knowing everything through *māyā* modifications. The views of the author of the *Prakaṭārtha* regarding the nature of *vidhi* have already been noted. But the way in which Ānandajñāna refers to the *Prakaṭārtha* in *Muṇḍaka*, p. 32, and *Kena*, p. 23, shows that he was either the author of the *Prakaṭārtha* or had written some commentary to it. But he could not have been the author of this work, since he refers to it as the model on which his *Tattvāloka* was written; so it seems very probable that he had written a commentary to it. But it is surprising that Ānandajñāna, who wrote commentaries on most of the important commentaries of Śaṅkara, should also trouble himself to write another commentary on the *Prakaṭārtha*, which is itself a commentary on Śaṅkara's commentary. It may be surmised, therefore, that he had some special reasons for respecting it, and it may have been the work of some eminent teacher of his or of someone in his parental line. However it may be, it is quite unlikely that the work should have been written later than the middle of the twelfth century.[1]

It is probable that Gaṅgāpurī Bhaṭṭāraka also lived earlier than Ānandabodha, as Citsukha points out. Gaṅgāpurī must then have lived either towards the latter part of the tenth century or the first half of the eleventh century. It is not improbable that he may have

1 See Tripathi's introduction to the *Tarka-saṃgraha.*

been a senior contemporary of Ānandabodha. His work, *Padārtha-tattva-nirṇaya,* was commented on by Ānandajñāna. According to him both *māyā* and Brahman are to be regarded as the cause of the world. All kinds of world-phenomena exist, and being may therefore be attributed to them; and being is the same whatever may be the nature of things that exist. Brahman is thus the changeless cause in the world or the *vivarta-kāraṇa*; but all the changing contents or individual existents must also be regarded as products of the transformation of some substance, and in this sense *māyā* is to be regarded as the *pariṇāmi-kāraṇa* of the world. Thus the world has Brahman as its *vivarta-kāraṇa* and *māyā* as its *pariṇāmi-kāraṇa.* The world manifests both aspects, the aspect of changeless being and that of changing materiality; so both *māyā* and Brahman form the material cause of the world in two different ways (*Brahma māyā ca ity ubhayopādānam;sattva-jāḍya-rūpobhaya-dharmānugaty-upapattiś ca*). *Tarka-viveka* and *Siddhānta-viveka* are the names of two chapters of this book, giving a summary of Vaiśeṣika and Vedānta philosophy respectively. The view' of Gaṅgāpurī in the *Padārtha-tattva-nirṇaya* just referred to seems to have been definitely rejected by Ānandabodha in his *Pramāṇa-mālā*, p. 16.

When Kulārka had started the *mahā-vidyā* syllogisms, and great Nyāya authors such as Jayanta and Udayana in the ninth and tenth centuries had been vigorously introducing logical methods in philosophy and were trying to define all that is knowable, the Vedāntic doctrine that all that is knowable is indefinable was probably losing its hold; and it is probable that works like Ānandabodha's *Pramāṇa-mālā* and *Nyāya-dīpāvalī* in the eleventh century or in the early part of the twelfth century were weakly attempting to hold fast to the Vedāntic position on logical grounds. It was Śrīharṣa who in the third quarter of the twelfth century for the first time attempted to refute the entire logical apparatus of the Naiyāyikas. Śrīharṣa's work was carried on in Citsukha's *Tattva-pradīpikā* in the early part of the thirteenth century, by Ānandajñāna in the latter part of the same century in his *Tarka-saṃgraha* and by Nṛsiṃhāśrama Muni in his *Bheda-dhikkāra* in the sixteenth century. On the last-named a pupil, Nārāyaṇāśrama, wrote his *Bheda-dhikkāra-satkriyā,* and this had a sub-commentary, called *Bheda-dhikkāra-satkriyojjvalā.* The beginnings of the dialectical arguments can be traced to Śaṅkara and further back to the great Buddhist writers, Nāgārjuna, Āryadeva, Candrakīrti, etc. Interest in these dialectical arguments was continuously kept up by commentaries written on these works all through the later centuries. The names of these commentators have been mentioned in the sections on Śrīharṣa, Citsukha and Ānandajñāna.

Moreover, the lines of Vedānta interpretation which started with Sureśvara, Padmapāda and Vācaspati were vigorously continued in commentaries and in independent works throughout the later centuries. Thus in the middle of the thirteenth century Vācaspati's *Bhāmatī* was commented on by Amalānanda in his *Kalpa-taru*; and this *Kalpa-taru* was again commented on by Appaya Dīkṣita in the latter part of the sixteenth century and the first quarter of the seventeenth century, and by Lakṣmīnṛsiṃha in his *Ābhoga* towards the end of the seventeenth century or the beginning of the eighteenth.[1]

Padmapāda's *Pañca-pādikā* was commented on by Prakāśātman in the thirteenth century in his *Pañca-pādikā-vivaraṇa,* by Akhaṇḍānanda in the fourteenth century in his *Tattva-dīpana,* by Vidyāraṇya in the same century in his *Vivaraṇa-prameya-saṃgraha,* by Ānandapūrṇa and Nṛsiṃha in the sixteenth century and by Rāma Tīrtha in the seventeenth century.[2] The line of Sureśvara

---

1 Allāla Sūri, son of Trivikramācārya, wrote a commentary on the *Bhāmatī,* called the *Bhāmatī-tilaka.*

2 Samyagbodhendra Saṃyamin, pupil of Gīrvāṇendra (AD 1450), wrote a summary of the main contents of the *Pañca-pādikā-vivaraṇa* in six chapters *(varṇaka),* and this work is called by two names, *Advaita-bhūṣaṇa* and *Vivaraṇa-prameya-saṃgraha.* There are again two other commentaries on Prakāśātman's *Pañca-pādikā-vivaraṇa:* the *Riju-vivaraṇa* by Viṣṇubhaṭṭa, son of Janārdana Sarvajña and pupil of Svāmīndrapūrṇa, and the *Ṭīkā-ratna* by Ānandapūrṇa. The *Riju-vivaraṇa* had again another commentary on it, called the *Trayyanta-bhāva-pradīpikā,* by Rāmānanda, pupil of Bhāratī Tīrtha. There are, however, two other commentaries on the *Pañca-pādikā* called *Pañca-pādikā-vyākhyā* (by an author whose name is not definitely known) and the *Prabandha-pariśodhinī*

also continued in the summary of his great *Vārttika* (called *Vārttika-sāra*) by Vidyāraṇya and its commentaries, and also in the commentaries on the *Saṃkṣepa-śārīraka* from the sixteenth century onwards. Many independent works were also written by persons holding more or less the same kinds of views as Sarvajñātma Muni.[1] The philosophy of *dṛṣṭi-sṛṣṭi-vāda* Vedānta, which was probably started by Maṇḍana, had doubtless some adherents too; but we do not meet with any notable writer on this line, except Prakāśānanda in the sixteenth century and his pupil Nānā Dīkṣita. The *Vedānta-kaumudī* is an important work which is referred to by Appaya Dīkṣita in his *Siddhānta-leśa.* In this work the omniscience of Brahman consists in the fact that the pure consciousness as Brahman manifests all that exists either as actually transformed or as potentially transformed, as future, or as latently transformed, as the past in the *māyā*; and it is the Parameśvara who manifests Himself as the underlying consciousness (*sākṣin*) in individual persons, manifesting the *ajñāna* transformations in them, and also their potential *ajñāna* in dreamless sleep. Many other important Vedānta views of an original character are expressed in this book. This work of Ramādvaya has been found by the present writer in the Govt. Oriental MSS. Library, Madras, and a separate section has been devoted to its philosophy. From references in it to followers of Madhva it may be assumed that the *Vedānta-kaumudī* was written probably in the fourteenth century.

From the fourteenth century, however, we have a large number of Vedānta writers in all the succeeding centuries; but with the notable exception of Prakāśānanda, Madhusūdana Sarasvatī in

by Ātmasvarūpa, pupil of Nṛsiṃhasvarūpa. Dharmarāyādhvarīndra also wrote a commentary on *Pañca-pādikā*, called the *Pañca-pādikā-ṭīkā.*

1 Apart from the two published commentaries on the *Saṃkṣepa-śārīraka,* there is another work called the *Saṃkṣepa-śārīraka-sambandhokti* by Vedānanda, pupil of Vedādhyakṣa-bhagavat-pūjyapāda, in which the author tries to show the mutual relation of the verses of it as yielding a consistent meaning. Nṛsiṃhāśrama also wrote a commentary on the *Saṃkṣepa-śārīraka,* called the *Tattva-bodhinī.* One Sarvajñātma Bhagavat wrote a small Vedāntic work, called *Pañca-prakriyā;* but it is not probable that he is the same as Sarvajñātma Muni.

his *Advaita-siddhi* (in which he tried to refute the objections of Vyāsa Tīrtha against the monistic Vedānta in the sixteenth century) and probably Vidyāraṇya's *Vivaraṇa-prameya-saṃgraha* and Dharmarājādhvarīndra *Paribhāṣā*, and its *Śikhāmaṇi* commentary by Rāmakṛṣṇa, there are few writers who can be said to reveal any great originality in Vedāntic interpretations. Most of the writers of this later period were good compilers, who revered all sorts of past Vedāntic ideas and collected them in well-arranged forms in their works. The influence of *the Pañca-pādikā-vivaraṇa,* however, is very strong in most of these writers, and the *Vivaraṇa* school of thought probably played the most important part in Vedāntic thought throughout all this period.

These Vedāntic writers grew up in particular circles inspired by particular teachers, whose works were carried on either in their own families or among their pupils; a few examples may make this clear. Thus Jagannāthāśrama was a great teacher of south India in the latter half of the fifteenth century; he had a pupil in Nṛsiṃhāśrama, one of the most reputed teachers of Vedānta in the early half of the sixteenth century. He was generally inspired on the one hand by the *Vivaraṇa* and on the other by Śrīharṣa and Citsukha and Sarvajñātma Muni: he wrote a number of Vedānta works, such as *Advaita-dīpikā* (his pupil, Nārāyaṇāśrama, wrote a commentary called *Advaita-dīpikā-vivaraṇa* on it), *Advaita-pañca-ratna*, *Advaita-bodha-dīpikā, Advaita-ratna-koṣa*, *Tattva-bodhinī,* a commentary on the *Saṃkṣepa-śārīraka*, *Tattva-viveka* (which had two commentaries, *Tattva-viveka-dīpana* of Nārāyaṇāśrama and *Tattva-vivecana* of Agnihotra, pupil of Jñānendra Sarasvatī), *Pañca-pādikā-vivaraṇa-prakāśikā*, *Bheda-dhikkāra*, *Advaita-ratna-vyākhyāna* (a commentary on Mallanārodīya's *Advaita-ratna*), and *Vedānta-tattva-viveka.* The fact that he could write commentaries both on Sarvajñātma Muni's work and also on the *Vivaraṇa*, and also write a *Bheda-dhikkāra* (a work on dialectic Vedānta on the lines of Śrīharṣa's dialectical work) shows the syncretistic tendencies of the age, in which the individual differences within the school were all accepted as different views of one Vedānta, and in which people were more interested in Vedānta as a whole and felt no hesitation in accepting all the Vedāntic ideas in their works. Nṛsiṃhāśrama had a pupil Dharmarājādhvarīndra, who wrote a *Vedānta-paribhāṣā,* a commentary called *Tarka-cūḍāmaṇi* on the *Tattva-cintāmaṇi* of Gaṅgeśa, and also on the *Nyaya-siddhānta-dīpa* of Śaśadhara Ācārya, and a commentary on the *Pañca-pādikā* of Padmapāda. His son and pupil Rāmakṛṣṇa Dīkṣita wrote a commentary on the first, called *Vedānta-śikhāmaṇi*; and Amaradāsa, the pupil of Brahmavijñāna, wrote another commentary on this *Śikhāmaṇi* of Rāmakṛṣṇa.[1] Rāmakṛṣṇa had also written a commentary on Rucidatta's *Tattva-cintāmaṇi-prakāśa,* called *Nyāya-śikhāmaṇi,* and a commentary on the *Vedānta-sāra.* Other authors, such as Kāśīnātha Śāstrin and Brahmendra Sarasvatī, had also written separate works bearing the name *Vedānta-paribhāṣā* after the *Vedānta-paribhāṣā* of Dharmarāja in the seventeenth century. Under the sphere of Nṛsiṃha's influence, but in the Śaiva and Mīmāṃsaka family of Raṅgarāja Adhvarin, was born Appaya Dīkṣita, who became one of the most reputed teachers of the sixteenth and the seventeenth centuries. His works have all been noted in the section devoted to him. He again was a teacher of Bhaṭṭojī Dīkṣita, who in addition to many works on grammar, law and ritual (*smṛti*) wrote two important works on Vedānta, called *Tattva-kaustubha* and *Vedānta-tattva-dīpana-vyākhyā,* the latter a commentary on the commentary, *Tattva-viveka-dīpana*, of Nārāyaṇāśrama (a pupil of Nṛsiṃhāśrama) on the latter's work, *Vedānta-tattva-viveka.* This Nārāyaṇāśrama had also written another commentary on Nṛsiṃhāśrama's *Bheda-dhikkāra*, called *Bheda-dhikkāra-satkriyā*; and later on in the eighteenth century another commentary was written on Nṛsiṃha's *Bheda-dhikkāra*, called *Advaita-candrikā*, by Narasiṃha Bhaṭṭa, pupil of Rāmabhadrāśrama and Nāgeśvara in the eighteenth century. Bhaṭṭojī Dīkṣita's son Bhānujī Dīkṣita was a commentator on the *Amara-koṣa* (*Vyākhyā-sudhā* or *Subodhinī*). Bhaṭṭojī was, however, a pupil not only of Appaya, but also of Nṛsiṃhāśrama Muni.

1 Pettā Dīkṣita, son of Nārāyaṇa Dīkṣita, also wrote a commentary on the *Vedānta-paribhāṣā,* called *Vedānta-paribhāṣā-prakāśikā.*

Bhaṭṭojī's younger brother and pupil, Raṅgojī Bhaṭṭa, wrote two works, the *Advaita-cintāmaṇi* and the *Advaita-śāstra-sāroddhāra*, more or less on the same lines, containing a refutation of Vaiśeṣika categories, a determination of the nature of the self, a determination of the nature of *ajñāna* and the nature of the doctrine of reflection, proofs of the falsity of world-appearance and an exposition of the nature of Brahman and how Brahmahood is to be attained. His son Koṇḍa Bhaṭṭa was mainly a grammarian, who wrote also on Vaiśeṣika. Again Madhusūdana Sarasvatī, who was a pupil of Viśveśvara Sarasvatī (pupil of Sarvajña Viśveśa and pupil's pupil of Govinda Sarasvatī), lived in the early half of the sixteenth century and was probably under the influence of Nṛsiṃhāśrama, who is reputed to have defeated Madhusūdana Sarasvatī's teacher, Mādhava Sarasvatī. Madhusūdana had at least three pupils, Puruṣottama, who wrote on Madhusūdana's commentary the *Siddhānta-tattva-bindu* a commentary called *Siddhānta-tattva-bindu-ṭīkā;*[1] the others were Bālabhadra and Śeṣagovinda (the latter of whom wrote a commentary on Śaṅkara's *Sarva-darśana-siddhānta-saṃgraha*, called *Sarva-siddhānta-rahasya-ṭīkā*). Again Sadānanda, the author of the *Vedānta-sāra,* one of the most popular and well-read syncretistic works on Vedānta, was a contemporary of Nṛsiṃhāśrama; Nṛsiṃha Sarasvatī wrote in 1588 a commentary thereon, called *Subodhinī.* Devendra, the author of the *Svānubhūti-prakāśa,* was also a contemporary of Nṛsiṃhāśrama. It has already been pointed out that Prakāśānanda was probably a contemporary of Nṛsiṃhāśrama, though he does not seem to have been under his influence. This shows how some of the foremost Vedānta writers of the sixteenth and seventeenth centuries grew up together in a Vedāntic circle, many of whom were directly or indirectly under the influence of Nṛsiṃhāśrama and Appaya Dīkṣita.

Passing to another circle of writers, we see that Bhāskara Dīkṣita, who lived in the latter half of the seventeenth century, wrote a commentary, *Ratna-tūlikā*, on the *Siddhānta-siddhāñjana* of his

1 Brahmānanda wrote on the *Siddhānta-bindu* another commentary, called *Siddhānta-bindu-ṭīkā.*

teacher Kṛṣṇānanda. The *Siddhānta-siddhāñjana* is an excellent syncretistic work on Vedānta, which contains most of the important Vedānta doctrines regarding the difference of *dharma-vicāra* and *brahma-vicāra*, the relation of Mīmāṃsā theories of commands, and the need of Brahma-knowledge; it introduces many Mīmāṃsā subjects and treats of their relations to many relevant Vedānta topics. It also introduces elaborate discussions on the nature of knowledge and ignorance. It seems, however, to be largely free from the influence of the *Vivaraṇa*, and it does not enter into theories of perception or the nature of the *antaḥkaraṇa* and its *vṛtti*. It is thus very different from most of the works produced in the sixteenth century in the circles of Nṛsiṃha or Appaya. Kṛṣṇānanda lived probably in the middle of the seventeenth century. He had for teacher Rāmabhadrānanda; and Rāmabhadrānanda was taught by Svayaṃprakāśānanda, the author of the *Vedānta-naya-bhūṣaṇa*, a commentary on the *Brahma-sūtra* on the lines of Vācaspati Miśra's *Bhāmatī*. This Svayaṃprakāśa must be distinguished from the other Svayaṃprakāśa, probably of the same century, who was a pupil of Kaivalyānanda Yogīndra and the author of the *Rasābhi-vyañjikā*, a commentary of *Advaita-makaranda* of Lakṣmīdhara Kavi. Rāmabhadrānanda had as his teacher Rāmānanda Sarasvatī, the author of the *Vedānta-siddhānta-candrikā*, on which a commentary was written by Gaṅgādharendra Sarasvatī (AD 1826), pupil of Rāmacandra Sarasvatī and pupil's pupil of Sarvajña Sarasvatī, and author of the *Sāṃrājya-siddhi* with its commentary, the *Kaivalya-kalpadruma*. Prakāśānanda was a pupil of Advaitānanda, author of the *Brahma-vidyābharaṇa*, a commentary on Śaṅkara's *Śārīraka-bhāṣya*—Advaitānanda was a disciple of Rāmatīrtha, author of the *Anvaya-prakāśikā* (a commentary on the *Saṃkṣepa-śārīraka* of Sarvajñātma Muni) and a disciple of Kṛṣṇatīrtha, a contemporary of Jagannāthāśrama, the teacher of Nṛsiṃhāśrama. Rāmatīrtha's *Anvaya-prakāśikā* shows an acquaintance with Madhusūdana's *Advaita-siddhi*; and he may thus be considered to have lived in the middle of the seventeenth century. Svayaṃprakāśānanda, again, had for pupil Mahādevānanda, or Vedāntin Mahādeva, the author of the *Advaita-cintā-kaustubha* or *Tattvānusandhāna.* It seems very clear that these writers of the seventeenth and the early eighteenth centuries flourished in a different circle of Vedāntic ideas, where the views of Vācaspati, Sureśvara and Sarvajñātma Muni had greater influence than the authors of the *Vivaraṇa* school of Vedānta. Another important syncretistic Vedānta writer is Sadānanda Kāśmīraka, author of the *Advaita-brahma-siddhi,* who lived in the early part of the eighteenth century. The *Advaita-brahma-siddhi* is an excellent summary of all the most important Vedānta doctrines, written in an easy style and explaining the chief features of the Vedāntic doctrines in the different schools of Advaita teachers. Narahari's *Bodha-sāra* may be mentioned as one of the important products of the late eighteenth century.[1]

---

1 A number of other important Vedānta works, written mostly during the seventeenth to nineteenth centuries, may also be mentioned. Thus Lokanātha, son of Sarvajñanārāyaṇa and grandson of Nṛsiṃhāśrama, wrote a metrical work in three chapters refuting the views of the dualists, called *Advaita-muktā-sāra* with a commentary on it called *Kānti*;Brahmānanda Sarasvatī wrote the *Advaita-siddhānta-vidyotana*; Gopālānanda Sarasvatī, pupil of Yogānanda, wrote the *Akhaṇḍātma-prakāśikā*;Harihara Paramahaṃsa, pupil of Śivarāma, pupil of Viśveśvarāśrama, wrote the *Anubhava-vilāsa,* and early in the nineteenth century Sāmin, a pupil of Brahmānanda, wrote a big work in twelve chapters, called *Brahmānanda-vilāsa.* In this connection it may not be out of place to mention the names of some important works of Vedānta dialectics in refutation of other systems of philosophical views more or less on the lines of those dialectical writings which have been noticed in the present volume. Thus Ānandapūrṇa (AD 1600), who commented on Śrīharṣa's *Khaṇḍana-khaṇḍa-khādya,* wrote the *Nyāya-candrikā* in four chapters, refuting the views of the Nyāya, Mīmāṃsā and Vaiśesika; Ānandānubhava, pupil of Nārāyaṇa Jyotisha, who lived probably in the same century, wrote a similar work, called *Padārtha-tattva-nirṇaya;*Jñānaghana, who probably lived in the thirteenth century, wrote an elaborate dialectical work in thirty-three chapters *(prakaraṇa),* called *Tattva-śuddhi;*ŚrīnivāsaYajvan, who probably lived in the sixteenth century, wrote the *Vādāvalī* in twenty-six chapters in refutation of Viśistādvaita and Dvaita views; Bhavānīśaṅkara also wrote a similar dialectical work, called *Siddhānta-dīpikā.* As examples of semi-popular Vedānta works of a syncretistic type, such works as the *Tattva-bodha* of Vāsudevendra, the *Guṇa-traya-viveka* of SvayaṃprakāśaYogīndra, the *Jaganmīthyātvadipikā* of Rāmendra Yogin, the *Ānanda-dīpa* of ŚivānandaYati (which had a commentary called *Ānanda-dīpa-ṭīkār* by Rāmanātha), the *Svātma-yoga-pradīpa*by Yogīśvara (which had a commentary by Amarānanda) and the

The sort of relationship of teachers and students in particular circles that has been pointed out holds good of the earlier authors also, though it is difficult to trace them as well as can be done in the later years, since many of the earlier books are now missing and the footprints of older traditions are becoming more and more faint. Thus it may be pointed out that Vidyāraṇya was a contemporary of Amalānanda in the fourteenth century, as both of them were pupils of Śaṅkarānanda and Anubhavānanda respectively; these in turn were both pupils of Ānandātman. Śaṅkarānanda was the author of the *Gītā-tātparya-bodhinī* and of a number of commentaries on the various Upaniṣads, and also of a summary of the Upaniṣads, called *Upaniṣad-ratna.* Amalānanda, however, had as teacher not only Anubhavānanda, but also Sukhaprakāśa Muni, who again was a disciple of Citsukha, himself a disciple of Gauḍeśvara Ācārya (called also Jñānottama).

VEDĀNTA DOCTRINE OF SOUL AND THE BUDDHIST DOCTRINE OF SOULLESSNESS

One of the most important points of Śaṅkara's criticism of Buddhism is directed against its denial of a permanent soul which could unite the different psychological constituents or could behave as the enjoyer of experiences and the controller of all thoughts and actions.

The Buddhists argue that for the production of sense-cognition, as the awareness of a colour or sound, what is required in addition to the sense-data of colours, etc. is the corresponding sense-faculties, while the existence of a soul cannot be deemed indispensable for the purpose.[1] Vasubandhu argues that what is experienced is the sense-

---

Vedānta-hṛdaya (on the lines of the *Yoga-vāsiṣṭha* and *Gauḍapāda*) by Varada Paṇḍita may be mentioned. This latter work was probably later than Prakāśānanda's *Vedānta-siddhānta-muktāvalī,* which followed the same line of thought.

1 The arguments here followed are those of Vasubandhu, as found in his *Abhidharma-kośa,* and are based on Prof. Stcherbatsky's translation of the appendix to ch. viii of that work, called the *Pudgala-viniścaya,* and Yaśomitra's commentary in manuscript from Nepal, borrowed from Viśvabhāratī, Śāntiniketan, Bengal.

data and the psychological elements in groups called *skandhas*. What one calls self (*ātman*) cannot be anything more than a mere apparent cognitional existence (*prajñapti-sat*) of what in reality is but a conglomeration of psychological elements. Had the apparent self been something as different from the psychological elements as colours are from sounds, it would then be regarded as an individual (*pudgala*); but, if its difference from these psychological elements be of the same nature as the difference of the constituents of milk from the appearance of milk, then the self could be admitted only to have a cognitional existence (*prajñapti-sat*).[1] The self has, in fact, only a cognitional appearance of separateness from the psychological elements; just as, though milk appears to have a separate existence from the proper combination of its constituent elements, yet it is in reality nothing more than a definite kind of combination of its constituent elements, so the self is nothing more than a certain conglomeration of the psychological elements (*skandha*), though it may appear to have a separate and independent existence. The Vātsīputrīyas, however, think that the individual is something different from the *skandhas* or psychological entities, as its nature is different from the nature of them. The Vātsīputrīyas deny the existence of a permanent soul, but believe in momentary individuals (*pudgala*) as a category separate and distinct from the *skandhas*. Just as fire is something different from the fuel that conditioned it, so the name "individual" (*pudgala*) is given to something conditioned by the *skandhas* at a given moment in a personal life.[2] Vasubandhu, however, argues against the acceptance of such an individual and says that there is no meaning in accepting such an individual. Rain and sun have no effects on mere vacuous space,

---

1 *Yadi yathā rūpādiḥ śabdāder bhāvāntaram abhipreyate pudgala itiabhyupagato bhavati bhinna-lakṣaṇaṃ hi rūpaṃ śabdād ityādi kṣīrādivat samudāyaś cet prajñaptitaḥ. —Abhidharma-kośa-vyākhyā,* Viśvabhāratī MS. p. 337.

2 Stcherbatsky's translation of the *Pudgala-viniścaya, Bulletin de l'Académie des Sciences de Russie,* p. 830.

The exact text of Vasubandhu, as translated from Tibetan in a note, runs thus: *gṛhīta-pratyutpannābhyantara-skandhaṃ upādāya pudgala-prajñaptiḥ. Ibid.* p. 953.

they are of use only to the skin; if the individual is, like the skin, a determiner of the value of experiences, then it must be accepted as external; if it is like vacuous space, then no purpose is fulfilled by accepting it.[1] The Vātsīputrīyas, however, thought that, just as the fuel conditioned the fire, so the personal elements conditioned the individual. By this conditioning the Vātsīputrīyas meant that the personal elements were some sort of a coexisting support.[2] What is meant by saying that the *pudgala* is conditioned by the personal elements is that, when the *skandhas* or psychological elements are present, the *pudgala* is also present there.[3] But Vasubandhu urges that a mere conditioning of this kind is not sufficient to establish the cognitional existence of an individual; for even colour is conditioned by the visual sense, light and attention in such a way that, these being present, there is the perception of light; but can anybody on that ground consider the existence of colour to be a cognitional one? And would cognitional entities deserve to be enumerated as separate categories? Again it may be asked, if such an individual exists, how is it experienced? For, if it be experienced by any of the senses, it must be a sense-datum: for the senses can grasp only their appropriate sense-data, and the individual is no sense-datum. Therefore, just as milk is nothing but the collected sense-data of colour, taste, etc., so also the so-called individual is nothing more than the conglomerated psychological elements.[4]

---

1 वात्सीपुत्रीयाणां तीर्थिकदृष्टिः प्रसज्यते निष्प्रयोजनत्वं च
वर्षातपाभ्यां किं व्योम्नश्चर्मण्यस्ति तयोः फलम्।
चर्मोपमश्चेत् स नित्यः खतुल्यश्चेदसत्फलः॥
Vātsīputrīyāṇāṃ tīrthika-dṛṣṭiḥ prasajyate niṣprayojanatvaṃ ca
varṣāta-pābhyāṃ kiṃ vyomnaś carmaṇy-asti tayoḥ phalam
carmopamaś cet sa nityaḥ khatulyaś ced asatphalaḥ.
—MS. of Yaśomitra's commentary, p. 338.

2 आश्रयभूतः सहभूतश्च।
āśraya-bhūtaḥ saha-bhūtaś ca. —*Ibid.*

3 रूपस्यापि प्रज्ञप्तिर्वक्तव्या चक्षुरादिषु सत्सु तस्योपलम्भात्, तानि चक्षुरादीन्युपादाय रूपम् प्रज्ञाप्यते।
Rūpasyāpi prajñaptir vaktavyā cakṣur-ādiṣu satsu tasyopalambhāt, tāni cakṣur-ādīny upādāya rūpam prajñāpyate. —*Ibid.*

4 *Yathā rūpādīny eva samastāni samuditāni kṣīram iti udakam iti vā prajñāpyate, tathā skandhāś ca samastā pudgala iti prajñāpyate, iti siddham.*
—MS. of Yaśomitra's commentary, p. 339 A.

The Vātsīputrīyas argue that, since the psychological elements, the sense-data, etc., are the causes of our experience of the individual, the individual cannot be regarded as being identical with these causal elements which are responsible for their experience; if it were so, then even light, eye, attention, etc., which are causes of the experience of the sense-data, would have to be regarded as being identical in nature with the individual.[1] But it is not so maintained; the sense-datum of sounds and colours is always regarded as being different from the individual, and one always distinguishes an individual from a sense-datum and says "this is sound," "this is colour" and "this is individual."[2] But the individual is not felt to be as distinct from the psychological elements as colour is from sound. The principle of difference or distinctness consists in nothing but a difference of moments; a colour is different from a sound because it is experienced at a different moment, while the psychological elements and the individual are not experienced at different moments.[3] But it is argued in reply that, as the sense-data and the individual are neither different nor identical (*ratio essendi*), so their cognition also is neither different nor identical in experience (*ratio cognoscendi*).[4] But Vasubandhu says that, if such a view is taken in this case, then it might as well be taken in all cases wherever there is any conglomeration.[5] Moreover, the separate senses are all limited to their special fields, and the mind which acts with them is also limited to the data supplied by them; there is, therefore, no way in which the so-called individual can be experienced. In the Ajita sermon Buddha is supposed to say: "A visual consciousness depends upon the organ of sight and a visible object. When these

1 *Yathā rūpam pudgalopalabdheḥ kāraṇaṃ bhavati sa ca tebhyo'nyo na vaktavyaḥ āloka-cakṣur-manaskārā api rūpopalabdheḥ kāraṇaṃ bhavati tad api tad-abhinna-svabhāvaḥ pudgalaḥ prāpnoti. Ibid.*

2 *Ibid.* p. 339 B.

3 *svalakṣaṇād api kṣaṇāntaram anyad ity udāhāryam. Ibid.*

4 *Yathā rūpa-pudgalayor anyānanyatvam avaktavyam evaṃ tadupalabdhyor api anyānanyatvam avaktavyam. Ibid.*

5 *yo'yaṃ siddhāntaḥ pudgala eva vaktavyaḥ so'yam bhidyate saṃskṛtam api avaktavyam iti kṛtvā. Ibid.*

three (object, sense organ and consciousness) combine, a sensation is produced. It is accompanied by a feeling, a representation and a volition. Only so much is meant, when we are speaking of a human being. To these (five sets of elements) different names are given, such as a sentient being, a man, Manu's progeny, a son of Manu, a child, an individual, a life, a soul. If with respect to them the expression is used 'he sees the object with his own eyes, ' it is false imputation (there being in reality nobody possessing eyes of his own). In common life such expressions with respect to them are current as 'that is the name of this venerable man, he belongs to such a caste and such a family, he eats such food, this pleases him, he has reached such an age, he has lived so many years, he has died at such an age.' These O brethren! accordingly are mere words, mere conventional designations.

"Expressions are they, (but not truth)!
Real elements have no duration:
Vitality makes them combine
In mutually dependent apparitions."[1]

The Vātsīputrīyas however refer to the *Bhāra-hāra-sūtra*, in which Buddha is supposed to say: "O brethren, I shall explain unto you the burden (of life), and moreover I shall explain the taking up of the burden, the laying aside of it and who the carrier is. . . . What is the burden? All the five aggregates of elements—the substrates of personal life. What is meant by the taking up of the burden? The force of craving for a continuous life, accompanied by passionate desires, the rejoicing at many an object. What is the laying aside of the burden? It is the wholesale rejection of this craving for a continuation of life, accompanied as it is by passionate desires and rejoicings at many an object, the getting rid of it in every circumstance, its extinction, its end, its suppression, an aversion to it, its restraint. its disappearance. Who is the carrier? We must answer: it is the individual, i.e. 'this venerable man having this name, of such a caste, of such a family, eating such food, finding pleasure or displeasure at such things, of such an age, who after a

1 Stcherbatsky's translation in *Bulletin de l'Académie des Sciences de Russie.*

life of such length will pass away having reached such an age.'"[1] But Vasubandhu points out that the carrier of the burden is not to be supposed to be some eternal soul or real individual. It is the momentary group of elements of the preceding moment that is designated as the burden, and the immediately succeeding one the carrier of the burden (*bhāra-hāra*).[2]

The Vātsīputrīyas again argue that activity implies an active agent, and, since knowing is an action, it also implies the knower who knows, just as the walking of Devadatta implies a Devadatta who walks. But Vasubandhu's reply to such a contention is that there is nowhere such a unity. There is no individual like Devadatta: what we call Devadatta is but a conglomeration of elements. "The light of a lamp is a common metaphorical designation for an uninterrupted production of a series of flashing flames. When this production changes its place, we say that the light has moved. Similarly consciousness is a conventional name for a chain of conscious moments. When it changes its place (i.e. appears in co-ordination with another objective element), we say that it apprehends that object. And in the same way we speak about the existence of material elements. We say matter 'is produced', 'it exists'; but there is no difference between existence and the element which does exist. The same applies to consciousness (there is nothing that cognizes, apart from the evanescent flashing of consciousness itself)."[3]

It is easy to see that the analysis of consciousness offered by the Vedānta philosophy of the Śaṅkara school is entirely different from this. The Vedānta holds that the fact of consciousness is entirely different from everything else. So long as the assemblage of the physical or physiological conditions antecedent to the rise of any cognition, as for instance, the presence of illumination, sense-

1 Stcherbatsky's translation.

2 Yaśomitra points out that there is no carrier of the burden different from the collection of the skandhas—*bhārādānavan na skandhebhyo'rthāntara-bhūtaḥ pudgala ity arthaḥ. —Abhidharma-kośa-vyākhyā,* Viśvabhāratī MS.

3 Stcherbatsky's translation in *Bulletin de l'Académie des Sciences de Russie,* pp. 938-939.

object contact, etc., is being prepared, there is no knowledge, and it is only at a particular moment that the cognition of an object arises. This cognition is in its nature so much different from each and all the elements constituting the so-called assemblage of conditions, that it cannot in any sense be regarded as the product of any collocation of conditions. Consciousness thus, not being a product of anything and not being further analysable into any constituents, cannot also be regarded as a momentary flashing. Uncaused and unproduced, it is eternal, infinite and unlimited. The main point in which consciousness differs from everything else is the fact of its self-revelation. There is no complexity in consciousness. It is extremely simple, and its only essence or characteristic is pure self-revelation. The so-called momentary flashing of consciousness is not due to the fact that it is momentary, that it rises into being and is then destroyed the next moment, but to the fact that the objects that are revealed by it are reflected through it from time to time. But the consciousness is always steady and unchangeable in itself. The immediacy (*aparokṣatva*) of this consciousness is proved by the fact that, though everything else is manifested by coming in touch with it, it itself is never expressed, indicated or manifested by inference or by any other process, but is always self-manifested and self-revealed. All objects become directly revealed to us as soon as they come in touch with it. Consciousness (*saṃvid*) is one. It is neither identical with its objects nor on the same plane with them as a constituent element in a collocation of them and consciousness. The objects of consciousness or all that is manifested in consciousness come in touch with consciousness and themselves appear as consciousness. This appearance is such that, when they come in touch with consciousness, they themselves flash forth as consciousness, though that operation is nothing but a false appearance of the non-conscious objects and mental states in the light of consciousness, as being identical with it. But the intrinsic difference between consciousness and its objects is that the former is universal (*pratyak*) and constant (*anuvṛtta*), while the latter are particular (*apratyak*) and alternating (*vyāvṛtta*). The awarenesses of a book, a table, etc. appear to be different not because these are different flashings of knowledge, but because of the changing association of consciousness with these objects. The objects do not come into being with the flashings of their awareness, but they have their separate existence and spheres of operation.[1] Consciousness is one and unchanging; it is only when the objects get associated with it that they appear in consciousness and as identical with it in such a way that the flashing of an object in consciousness appears as the flashing of the consciousness itself. It is through an illusion that the object of consciousness and consciousness appear to be welded together into such an integrated whole, that their mutual difference escapes our notice, and that the object of consciousness, which is only like an extraneous colour applied to consciousness, does not appear different or extraneous to it, but as a specific mode of the consciousness itself. Thus what appear as but different awarenesses, as book-cognition, table-cognition, are not in reality different awarenesses, but one unchangeable consciousness successively associated with ever-changing objects which falsely appear to be integrated with it and give rise to the appearance that qualitatively different kinds of consciousness are flashing forth from moment to moment. Consciousness cannot be regarded as momentary. For, had it been so, it would have appeared different at every different moment. If it is urged that, though different consciousnesses are arising at each different moment, yet on account of extreme similarity this is not noticed; then it may be replied that, if there is difference between the two consciousnesses of two successive moments, then such difference must be grasped either by a different consciousness or by the same consciousness. In the first alternative the third awareness, which grasps the first two awarenesses and their difference, must either be identical with them, and in that case the difference between the three awarenesses would vanish; or it may be different from them, and in that case, if

---

1 *tattva-darśī tu nityam advitīyaṃ vijñānaṃ viṣayāś ca tatrādhyastāḥ pṛthagartha-kriyā-samarthās teṣāṃ cābādhitaṃ sthāyitvam astīti vadati. Vivaraṇa-prameya-saṃgraha,* p. 74, the Vizianagram Sanskrit Series, Benares, 1893.

another awareness be required to comprehend their difference and that requires another and so on, there would be a vicious infinite. If the difference be itself said to be identical with the nature of the consciousness (*saṃvit-svarūpa-bhūtobhedaḥ*), and if there is nothing to apprehend this difference, then the nonappearance of the difference implies the non-appearance of the consciousness itself; for by hypothesis the difference has been held to be identical with the consciousness itself. The non-appearance of difference, implying the non-appearance of consciousness, would mean utter blindness. The difference between the awareness of one moment and another cannot thus either be logically proved, or realized in experience, which always testifies to the unity of awareness through all moments of its appearance. It may be held that the appearance of unity is erroneous, and that, as such, it presumes that the awarenesses are similar; for without such a similarity there could not have been the erroneous appearance of unity. But, unless the difference of the awarenesses and their similarity be previously proved, there is nothing which can even suggest that the appearance of unity is erroneous.[1] It cannot be urged that, if the existence of difference and similarity between the awarenesses of two different moments can be proved to be false, then only can the appearance of unity be proved to be true; for the appearance of unity is primary and directly proved by experience. Its evidence can be challenged only if the existence of difference between the awarenesses and their similarity be otherwise proved. The unity of awareness is a recognition of the identity of the awarenesses (*pratyabhijñā*), which is self-evident.

It has also been pointed out that the Buddhists give a different analysis of the fact of recognition. They hold that perception reveals the existence of things at the moment of perception, whereas recognition involves the supposition of their existence through a period of past time, and this cannot be apprehended by perception, which is limited to the present moment only. If it is suggested that recognition is due to present perception as associated with

1 *Vivaraṇa-prameya-saṃgraha*, p. 76.

the impressions (*saṃskāra*) of previous experience, then such a recognition of identity would not prove the identity of the self as "I am he"—for in the self-luminous self there cannot be any impressions. The mere consciousness as the flash cannot prove any identity; for that is limited to the present moment and cannot refer to past experience and unite it with the experience of the present moment. The Buddhists on their side deny the existence of recognition as the perception of identity, and think that it is in reality not one but two concepts—"I" and "that"—and not a separate experience of the identity of the self as persisting through time. To this the Vedāntic reply is that, though there cannot be any impressions in the self as pure consciousness, yet the self as associated with the mind (*antaḥkaraṇa*) can well have impressions (*saṃskāra*), and so recognition is possible.[1] But it may be objected that the complex of the self and mind would then be playing the double role of knower and the known; for it is the mind containing the impressions and the self that together play the part of the recognizer, and it is exactly those impressions together with the self that form the content of recognition also—and hence in this view the agent and the object have to be regarded as one. But in reply to this Vidyāraṇya Muni urges that all systems of philosophy infer the existence of soul as different from the body; and, as such an inference is made by the self, the self is thus both the agent and the object of such inferences. Vidyāraṇya says that it may further be urged that the recognizer is constituted of the self in association with the mind, whereas the recognized entity is constituted of the self as qualified by past and present time.[2] Thus the recognition of self-identity does not strictly involve the fact of the oneness of the agent and its object. If it is urged that, since recognition of identity of self involves two concepts, it also involves two moments, then the assertion that all knowledge is momentary also involves two

1 *Kevale cidātmani janya-jñāna-tat-saṃskārayor asambhave'py antaḥ-karaṇa-viśiṣṭe tat-sambhavād ukta-pratyabhijñā kiṃ na syāt. —Ibid.* p. 76.

2 *antaḥkaraṇa-viśiṣṭatayaivātmanaḥ pratyabhijñātṛtvaṃ pūrvāpara-kāla-viśiṣṭa-tayā ca pratyabhijñeyatvam. —Vivaraṇa-prameya-saṃgraha,* p. 77.

concepts, for momentariness cannot be regarded as being identical with knowledge. The complexity of a concept does not mean that it is not one but two different concepts occurring at two different moments. If such a maxim is accepted, then the theory that all knowledge is momentary cannot be admitted as one concept, but two concepts occurring at two moments; and hence momentariness cannot be ascribed to knowledge, as is done by the Buddhists. Nor can it be supposed, in accordance with the Prabhākara view, that the existence of the permanent "this self" is admitted merely on the strength of the recognizing notion of "self-identity"; for the self which abides through the past and exists in the present cannot be said to depend on a momentary concept of recognition of self-identity. The notion of self-identity is only a momentary notion, which lasts only at the present time; and hence the real and abiding self cannot owe its reality or existence merely to a psychological notion of the moment.

Again, if it is argued that memory, such as "I had an awareness of a book," shows that the self was existing at the past time when the book was perceived, it may be replied that such memory and previous experience may prove the past existence of the self, but it cannot prove that the self that was existing in the past is identical with the self that is now experiencing. The mere existence of self at two moments of time does not prove that the self had persisted through the intervening times. Two notions of two different times cannot serve to explain the idea of recognition, which presupposes the notion of persistence. If it were held that the two notions produce the notion of self-persistence through the notion of recognition, then that would mean that the Buddhist admits that one can recognize himself as "I am he." It cannot be said that, since the self itself cannot be perceived, there is no possibility of the perception of the identity of the self through recognition; for, when one remembers "I had an experience," that very remembrance proves that the self was perceived. Though at the time when one remembers it the self at the time of such memory is felt as the perceiver and not as the object of that self-perception, yet at the time of the previous experience which is now being remembered the self must have been itself the object of the perception. If it is argued that it is only the past awareness that is the object of memory and this awareness, when remembered, expresses the self as its cognizer, then to this it may be replied that since at the time of remembering there is no longer the past awareness, the cognizer on whom this awareness had to rest itself is also absent. It is only when an awareness reveals itself that it also reveals the cognizer on whom it rests; but, if an awareness is remembered, then the awareness which is remembered is only made an object of present awareness which is self-revealed. But the past awareness which is supposed to be remembered is past and lost and, as such, it neither requires a cognizer on which it has to rest nor actually reveals such a cognizer. It is only the self-revealed cognition that also immediately reveals the cognizer with its own revelation. But, when a cognition is mediated through memory, its cognizer is not manifested with its remembrance.[1] So the self which experienced an awareness in the past can be referred to only through the mediation of memory. So, when the Prabhākaras hold that the existence of the self is realized through such a complex notion as "I am he," it has to be admitted that it is only through the process of recognition (*pratyabhijñā*) that the persistence of the self is established. The main point that Vidyāraṇya Muni urges in his *Vivaraṇa-prameya-saṃgraha* is that the fact of recognition or the experience of self-identity cannot be explained by any assumption of two separate concepts, such as the memory of a past cognition or cognizer and the present awareness. We all feel that our selves are persisting through time and that I who experienced pleasure yesterday and I who am experiencing new pleasures to-day are identical; and the only theory by which this notion of self-persistence or self-identity can be explained is by supposing that the self exists and persists through time. The Buddhist attempts at explaining this notion of self-identity by the supposition of the operation of two separate concepts are wholly inadequate, as has

---

1 *svayaṃprakāśamānaṃ hi saṃvedanam āśrayaṃ sādhayati na tu smṛti-viṣaya-tayā para-prakāśyam.* —*Vivaraṇa-prameya-saṃgraha*, p. 78.

already been shown. The perception of self-identity can therefore be explained only on the basis of a permanently existing self.

Again, the existence of self is not to be argued merely through the inference that cognition, will and feeling presuppose some entity to which they belong and that it is this entity that is called self; for, if that were the case, then no one would be able to distinguish his own self from that of others. For, if the self is only an entity which has to be presupposed as the possessor of cognition, will, etc., then how does one recognize one's own cognition of things as differing from that of others? What is it that distinguishes my experience from that of others? My self must be immediately perceived by me in order that I may relate any experience to myself. So the self must be admitted as being self-manifested in all experience; without admitting the self to be self-luminous in all experience the difference between an experience as being my own and as belonging to others could not be explained. It may be objected by some that the self is not self-luminous by itself, but only because, in self-consciousness, the self is an object of the cognizing operation (*saṃvit-karma*). But this is hardly valid; for the self is not only cognized as an object of self-consciousness, but also in itself in all cognitional operations. The self cannot be also regarded as being manifested by ideas or percepts. It is not true that the cognition of the self occurs after the cognition of the book or at any different time from it. For it is true that the cognition of the self and that of the book take place at the same point of time; for the same awareness cannot comprehend two different kinds of objects at the same time. If this was done at different points of time, then that would not explain our experience—"I have known this." For such a notion implies a relation between the knower and the known; and, if the knower and the known were grasped in knowledge at two different points of time, there is nothing which could unite them together in the same act of knowledge. It is also wrong to maintain that the self is manifested only as the upholder of ideas; for the self is manifested in the knowing operation itself. So, since the self cannot be regarded as being either the upholder or cognizer of ideas or their object, there is but one way in which it can be considered as self-manifesting or self-revealing (*sva-prakāśa*). The immediacy of the self is thus its self-revealing and self-manifesting nature. The existence of self is thus proved by the self-luminous nature of the self. The self is the cognizer of the objects only in the sense that under certain conditions of the operation of the mind there is the mind-object contact through a particular sense, and, as the result thereof, these objects appear in consciousness by a strange illusion; so also ideas of the mind, concepts, volitions and emotions appear in consciousness and themselves appear as conscious states, as if consciousness was their natural and normal character, though in reality they are only illusorily imposed upon the consciousness—the self-luminous self.

Ānandabodha Bhaṭṭārakācārya, from whom Vidyāraṇya often borrows his arguments, says that the self-luminosity of the self has to be admitted, because it cannot be determined as being manifested by anything else. The self cannot be regarded as being perceived by a mental perception (*mānasa pratyakṣa*); for that would involve the supposition that the self is the object of its own operation; for cognition is at any rate a function of the self. The functions of cognition belonging to the self cannot affect the self itself.[1] The Vedānta has also to fight against the Prabhākara view which regards cognition as manifesting the object and the self along with itself, as against its own view that it is the self which is identical with knowledge and which is self-manifesting. Ānandabodha thus objects to the Prabhākara view, that it is the object-cognition which expresses both the self and the not-self, and holds that the self cannot be regarded as an object of awareness. Ānandabodha points out that it may be enunciated as a universal proposition that what is manifested by cognition must necessarily be an object of cognition, and that therefore, if the self is not an object of cognition, it is not manifested by cognition.[2] Therefore the self or the cognizer is not

1 *tathā sati svādhāra-vijñāna-vṛtti-vyāpyatvād ātmanaḥ karmatve svātmani vṛtti-virodhād iti brūmaḥ. —Nyāya-makaranda,* p. 131.

2 *Ibid.* pp. 134-135.

manifested by cognition; for, like cognition, it is self-manifested and immediate without being an object of cognition.[1]

The self-luminosity of cognition is argued by Ānandabodha. He says that, if it is held that cognition does not manifest itself, though it manifests its objects, it may be replied that, if it were so, then at the time when an object is cognized the cognizer would have doubted if he had any cognition at the time or not. If anyone is asked whether he has seen a certain person or not, he is sure about his own knowledge that he has seen him and never doubts it. It is therefore certain that, when an object is revealed by any cognition, the cognition is itself revealed as well. If it is argued that such a cognition is revealed by some other cognition, then it might require some other cognition and that another and so on *ad infinitum*; and thus there is a vicious infinite. Nor can it be held that there is some other mental cognition (occurring either simultaneously with the awareness of the object or at a later moment) by which the awareness of the awareness of the object is further cognized. For from the same mind-contact there cannot be two different awarenesses of the type discussed. If at a later moment, then, there is mind-activity, cessation of one mind-contact, and again another mind-activity and the rise of another mind-contact, that would imply many intervening moments, and thus the cognition which is supposed to cognize an awareness of an object would take place at a much later moment, when the awareness which it has to reveal is already passed. It has therefore to be admitted that cognition is itself self-luminous and that, while manifesting other objects, it manifests itself also. The objection raised is that the self or the cognition cannot affect itself by its own functioning (*vṛtti*); the reply is that cognition is like light and has no intervening operation by which it affects itself or its objects. Just as light removes darkness, helps the operation of the eye and illuminates the object and manifests itself all in one moment without any intervening operation of any other

1 *saṃveditā na saṃvid-adhīna-prakāśaḥ saṃvit-karmatām antareṇa aparokṣatvāt saṃvedanavat. Nyāya-makaranda*, p. 135. This argument is borrowed verbatim by Vidyāraṇya in his *Vivaraṇa-prameya-saṃgraha*, p. 85.

light, so cognition also in one flash manifests itself and its objects, and there is no functioning of it by which it has to affect itself. This cognition cannot be described as being mere momentary flashes, on the ground that, when there is the blue awareness, there is not the yellow awareness; for apart from the blue awareness, the yellow awareness or the white awareness there is also the natural basic awareness or consciousness, which cannot be denied. It would be wrong to say that there are only the particular awarenesses which appear and vanish from moment to moment; for, had there been only a series of particular awarenesses, then there would be nothing by which their differences could be realized. Each awareness in the series would be of a particular and definite character, and, as it passed away, would give place to another, and that again to another, so that there would be no way of distinguishing one awareness from another; for according to the theory under discussion there is no consciousness except the passing awarenesses, and thus there would be no way by which their differences could be noticed; for, even though the object of awareness, such as blue and yellow, differed amongst themselves, that would fail to explain how the difference of a blue awareness and a yellow awareness could be apprehended. So the best would be to admit the self to be of the nature of pure consciousness.

It will appear from the above discussion that the Vedānta had to refute three opponents in establishing its doctrine that the self is of the nature of pure consciousness and that it is permanent and not momentary. The first opponent was the Buddhist, who believed neither in the existence of the self nor in the nature of any pure permanent consciousness. The Buddhist objection that there was no permanent self could be well warded off by the Vedānta by appealing to the verdict of our notion of self-identity—which could not be explained on the Buddhist method by the supposition of two separate notions of a past "that self" and the present "I am." Nor can consciousness be regarded as being nothing more than a series of passing ideas or particular awarenesses; for on such a theory it would be impossible to explain how we can react upon our mental states and note their differences. Consciousness has thus to be admitted as permanent. Against the second opponent, the Naiyāyika, the Vedānta urges that the self is not the inferred object to which awarenesses, volitions or feelings belong, but is directly and immediately intuited. For, had it not been so, how could one distinguish his own experiences as his own and as different from those of others? The internalness of my own experiences shows that they are directly intuited as my own, and not merely supposed as belonging to some self who was the possessor of his experiences. For inference cannot reveal the internalness of any cognition or feeling. Against the third opponent, the Mīmāṃsaka, the Vedānta urges that the self-revealing character belongs to the self which is identical with thought—as against the Mīmāṃsā view, that thought as a self-revealing entity revealed the self and the objects as different from it. The identity of the self and thought and the self-revealing character of it are also urged; and it is shown by a variety of dialectical reasoning that such a supposition is the only reasonable alternative that is left to us.

This self as pure consciousness is absolutely impersonal, unlimited and infinite. In order to make it possible that this one self should appear as many individuals and as God, it is supposed that it manifests itself differently through the veil of *māyā.* Thus, according to the *Siddhānta-leśa*, it is said in the *Prakaṭārtha-vivaraṇa* that, when this pure consciousness is reflected through the beginningless, indescribable *māyā*, it is called Īśvara or God. But, when it is reflected through the limited parts of *māyā* containing powers of veiling and of diverse creation (called *avidyā*), there are the manifestations of individual souls or *jīvas.* It is again said in the *Tattva-viveka* of Nṛsiṃhāśrama that, when this pure consciousness is reflected through the pure *sattva* qualities, as dominating over other impure parts of *prakṛti,* there is the manifestation of God. Whereas, when the pure consciousness is reflected through the impure parts of *rajas* and *tamas,* as dominating over the *sattva* part of *prakṛti* (called also *avidyā*), there are the manifestations of the individual selves or *jīvas.* The same *prakṛti* in its two aspects, as predominating in *sattva* and as predominating in *rajas* and *tamas*, goes by the name of *māyā* and *avidyā* and forms the conditioning factors (*upādhi*) of the pure consciousness, which on account of the different characters of the conditioning factors of *māyā* and *avidyā* appear as the omniscient God and the ignorant individual souls. Sarvajñātma Muni thinks that, when the pure consciousness is reflected through *avidyā,* it is called Īśvara, and, when it is reflected through mind (*antaḥkaraṇa*), it is called *jīva.*

These various methods of accounting for the origin of individual selves and God have but little philosophical significance. But they go to show that the principal interest of the Vedānta lies in establishing the supreme reality of a transcendental principle of pure consciousness, which, though always untouched and unattached in its own nature, is yet the underlying principle which can explain all the facts of the enlivening and enlightening of all our conscious experiences. All that is limited, be it an individual self or an individual object of awareness, is in some sense or other an illusory imposition of the modification of a non-conscious principle on the principle of consciousness. The Vedānta is both unwilling and incapable of explaining the nature of the world-process in all its details, in which philosophy and science are equally interested. Its only interest is to prove that the world-process presupposes the existence of a principle of pure consciousness which is absolutely and ultimately real, as it is immediate and intuitive. Reality means what is not determined by anything else; and in this sense pure consciousness is the only reality—and all else is indescribable—neither real nor unreal; and the Vedānta is not interested to discover what may be its nature.

VEDĀNTIC COSMOLOGY

From what has been said above it is evident that *māyā* (also called *avidyā* or *ajñāna*) is in itself an indefinable mysterious stuff, which has not merely a psychological existence, but also an ontological existence as well. It is this *ajñāna* which on the one hand forms on the subjective plane the mind and the senses (the self alone being Brahman and ultimately real), and on the other hand, on the objective plane, the whole of the objective universe. This *ajñāna* has two powers, the power of veiling or covering (*āvaraṇa*) and the power of creation (*vikṣepa*). The power of veiling, though small, like a little cloud veiling the sun with a diameter of millions of miles, may, in spite of its limited nature, cover up the infinite, unchangeable self by veiling its self-luminosity as cognizer. The veiling of the self means veiling the shining unchangeable self-perception of the self, as infinite, eternal and limitless, pure consciousness, which as an effect of such veiling appears as limited, bound to sense-cognitions and sense-enjoyments and functioning as individual selves.[1] It is through this covering power of *ajñāna* that the self appears as an agent and an enjoyer of pleasures and pains and subject to ignorant fears of rebirth, like the illusory perception of a piece of rope in darkness as a snake. Just as through the creative power of ignorance a piece of rope, the real nature of which is hidden from view, appears as a snake, so does ignorance by its creative power create on the hidden self the manifold world-appearance. As the *ajñāna* is supposed to veil by its veiling power (*āvaraṇa-śakti*) only the self-cognizing and self-revealing aspect of the self, the other aspect of the self as pure being is left open as the basis on which the entire world-appearance is created by the creative power thereof. The pure consciousness, veiled as it is by *ajñāna* with its two powers, can be regarded as an important causal agent (*nimitta*), when its nature as pure consciousness forming the basis of the creation of the world-appearance is emphasized; it can be regarded as the material cause, when the emphasis is put on its covering part, the *ajñāna*. It is like a spider, which, so far as it weaves its web, can be regarded as a causal agent, and, so far as it supplies from its own body the materials of the web, can be regarded as the material cause of the web, when its body aspect

1 *vastuto 'jñānasyātmāchādakatvābhāve 'pi pramātṛ-buddhimātrāchādakatvena ajñānasyātmāchādakatvam upacārād ucyate. Subodhinī* on *Vedānta-sāra*, p. 13, Nirṇaya-Sāgara Press, Bombay, 1916.

is emphasized. The creative powers (*vikṣepa-śakti*) of *ajñāna* are characterized as being threefold, after the manner of Sāṃkhya *prakṛti*, as *sattva*, *rajas* and *tamas*. With the pure consciousness as the basis and with the associated creative power of *ajñāna* predominating in *tamas*, space (*ākāśa*) is first produced; from *ākāśa* comes air, from air fire, from fire water, from water earth. It is these elements in their fine and uncompounded state that in the Sāṃkhya and the Purāṇas are called *tan-mātras*. It is out of these that the grosser materials are evolved as also the subtle bodies.[1] The subtle bodies are made up of seventeen parts, excluding the subtle elements, and are called *sūkṣma-śarīra* or *liṅga-śarīra*. This subtle body is composed of the five cognitive senses, the five cognitive senses, the five *vāyus* or biomotor activities, *buddhi* (intellect) and *manas*, together with the five subtle elements in tanmātric forms. The five cognitive senses, the auditory, tactile, visual, gustatory and olfactory senses, are derived from the *sattva* parts of the five elements, *ākāśa*, *vāyu*, *agni*, *ap* and *pṛthivī* respectively. *Buddhi*, or intellect, means the mental state of determination or affirmation (*niścayātmikā antaḥkaraṇa-vṛtti*). *Manas* means the two mental

1 As to how the subtle elements are combined for the production of grosser elements there are two different theories, viz. the *trivṛt-karaṇa* and the *pañcī-karaṇa*. The *trivṛt-karaṇa* means that fire, water and earth (as subtle elements) are each divided into two halves, thus producing two equal parts of each; then the three half parts of the three subtle elements are again each divided into two halves, thus producing two quarter parts of each. Then the original first half of each element is combined with the two quarters of other two elements. Thus each element has half of itself with two quarter parts of other two elements. Vācaspati and Amalānanda prefer *trivṛt-karaṇa* to *pañcī-karaṇa*; for they think that there is no point in admitting that air and *ākāśa* have also parts of other elements integrated in them, and the Vedic texts speak of *trivṛt-karaṇa* and not of *pañcī-karaṇa*. The *pañcī-karaṇa* theory holds that the five subtle elements are divided firstly into two halves, and then one of the two halves of these five elements is divided again into four parts, and then the first half of each subtle element is combined with the one-fourth of each half of all the other elements excepting the element of which there is the full half as a constituent. Thus each element is made up of one-half of itself, and the other half of it is constituted of the one-fourth of each of the other elements (i.e. one-eighth of each of the other four elements), and thus each element has at least some part of other elements integrated into it. This view is supported by the *Vedānta-paribhāṣā* and its *Śikhāmaṇi* commentary, p. 363.

functions of *vikalpa* and *saṅkalpa* or of *saṅkalpa* alone resulting in doubt.[1] The function of mind (*citta*) and the function of egoism (*ahaṃkāra*) are included in *buddhi* and *manas.*[2] They are all produced from the *sattva* parts of the five elements and are therefore elemental. Though they are elemental, yet, since they are produced from the compounded *sattva* parts of all the elements, they have the revealing function displayed in their cognitive operations. *Buddhi* with the cognitive senses is called the sheath of knowledge (*vijñānamaya-koṣa*). *Manas* with the cognitive senses is called the sheath of *manas* (*manomaya-koṣa*). It is the self as associated with the *vijñānamaya-koṣa* that feels itself as the agent, enjoyer, happy or unhappy, the individual self (*jīva*) that passes through worldly experience and rebirth. The conative senses are produced from the *rajas* parts of the five elements. The five *vāyus* or biomotor activities are called *Prāṇa* or the breathing activity, *Udāna* or the upward activity and *Samāna* or the digestive activity. There are some who add another five *vāyus* such as the Nāga, the vomiting *Apāna troyānes* activity, Kūrma, the reflex activity of opening the eyelids, Kṛkala, the activity of coughing, Devadatta, the activity of yawning, and Dhanañjaya, the nourishing activity. These *prāṇas* together with the cognitive senses form the active sheath of *prāṇa* (*prāṇamaya-koṣa*). Of these three sheaths, the *vijñānamaya*, *manomaya* and *prāṇamaya,* the *vijñānamaya* sheath plays the part

1 The *Vedānta-sāra* speaks of *saṅkalpa* and *vikalpa,* and this is explained by the *Subodhinī* as meaning doubt. See *Vedānta-sāra* and *Subodhinī,* p. 17. The *Vedānta-paribhāṣā* and its commentators speak of *saṅkalpa* as being the only unction of *manas,* but it means "doubt." See pp. 88-89 and 358.

2 *smaraṇākāra-vṛttimad antaḥkaraṇaṃ cittam* (*Vedānta-paribhāṣā-Maṇi-prabhā,* p. 89). *anayor eva cittāhaṃkārayor antarbhāvaḥ* (*Vedānta-sāra,* p. 17). But the *Vedānta-paribhāṣā* says that *manas, buddhi, ahaṃkāra* and *citta,* all four, constitute the inner organ (*antaḥkaraṇa*). See *Vedānta-paribhāṣā,* p. 88. The *Vedānta-sāra* however does not count four functions *buddhi, manas, citta, ahaṃkāra*; *citta* and *ahaṃkāra* are regarded as the same as *buddhi* and *manas.* Thus according to the *Vedānta-sāra* there are only two categories. But since the *Vedānta-paribhāṣā* only mentions *buddhi* and *manas* as constituents of the subtle body, one need not think that there is ultimately any difference between it and the *Vedānta-sāra.*

of the active agent (*kartṛ-rūpaḥ*); the *manomaya* is the source of all desires and volition, and is therefore regarded as having an instrumental function; the *prāṇamaya* sheath represents the motor functions. These three sheaths make up together the subtle body or the *sūkṣma-śarīra.* Hiraṇyagarbha (also called *Sūtrātmā* or *prāṇa*) is the god who presides over the combined subtle bodies of all living beings. Individually each subtle body is supposed to belong to every being. These three sheaths, involving as they do all the subconscious impressions from which our conscious experience is derived, are therefore called a dream (*jāgrad-vāsanāmayatvāt svapna*).

The process of the formation of the gross elements from the subtle parts of the elements is technically called *pañcīkaraṇa.* It consists in a compounding of the elements in which one half of each rudimentary element is mixed with the eighth part of each other rudimentary element. It is through such a process of compounding that each element possesses some of the properties of the other elements. The entire universe consists of seven upper worlds (*Bhuḥ, Bhuvaḥ, Svar*, *Mahar, Janaḥ, Tapaḥ* and *Satyam*), seven lower worlds (*Atala*, *Vitala*, *Sutala, Rasātala, Talātala, Mahātala* and *Pātāla*) and all the gross bodies of all living beings. There is a cosmic deity who presides over the combined physical bodies of all beings, and this deity is called Virāṭ. There is also the person, the individual who presides over each one of the bodies, and, in this aspect, the individual is called Viśva.

The *ajñāna* as constituting *antaḥkaraṇa* or mind, involving the operative functions of *buddhi* and *manas*, is always associated with the self; it is by the difference of these *antaḥkaraṇas* that one self appears as many individual selves, and it is through the states of these *antaḥkaraṇas* that the veil over the self and the objects are removed, and as a result of this there is the cognition of objects. The *antaḥkaraṇa* is situated within the body, which it thoroughly pervades. It is made up of the *sattva* parts of the five rudimentary elements, and, being extremely transparent, comes into touch with the sense objects through the specific senses and assumes their forms.

It being a material stuff, there is one part inside the body, another part in touch with the sense-objects, and a third part between the two and connected with them both as one whole. The interior part of the *antaḥkaraṇa* is the ego or the agent. The intervening part has the action of knowledge, called also *vṛtti-jñāna*. The third part, which at the time of cognition is transformed into the form of the sense-objects, has the function of making them manifested in knowledge as its objects. The *antaḥkaraṇa* of three parts being transparent, pure consciousness can well be manifested in it. Though pure consciousness is one, yet it manifests the three different parts of the *antaḥkaraṇa* in three different ways, as the cognizer (*pramātṛ*), cognitive operation (*pramāṇa*) and the cognition, or the percept (*pramiti*). In each of the three cases the reality is the part of the pure consciousness, as it expresses itself through the three different modifications of the *antaḥkaraṇa*. The sense-objects in themselves are but the veiled pure consciousness, *brahman*, as forming their substance. The difference between the individual consciousness (*jīva-caitanya*) and the *brahman*- consciousness (*brahma-caitanya*) is that the former represents pure consciousness, as conditioned by or as reflected through the *antaḥkaraṇa*, while the latter is the unentangled infinite consciousness, on the basis of which all the cosmic creations of *māyā* are made. The covering of *avidyā*, for the breaking of which the operation of the *antaḥkaraṇa* is deemed necessary, is of two kinds, viz. subjective ignorance and objective ignorance. When I say that I do not know a book, that implies subjective ignorance as signified by "I do not know," and objective ignorance as referring to the book. The removal of the first is a precondition of all kinds of knowledge, perceptual or inferential, while the second is removed only in perceptual knowledge. It is diverse in kind according to the form and content of the sense-objects; and each perceptual cognition removes only one specific ignorance, through which the particular cognition arises.[1]

1 See Madhusūdana Sarasvatī's *Siddhānta-bindu*, pp. 132-150; and Brahmānanda Sarasvatī's *Nyāya-ratnāvalī*, pp. 132-150, Śrīvidyā Press, Kumbakoṇam, 1893.

ŚAṄKARA AND HIS SCHOOL

It is difficult to say exactly how many books were written by Śaṅkara himself. There is little doubt that quite a number of books attributed to Śaṅkara were not written by him. I give here, a list of those books that seem to me to be his genuine works, though it is extremely difficult to be absolutely certain. I have chosen only those works which have been commented on by other writers, since this shows that these have the strength of tradition behind them to support their authenticity. The most important works of Śaṅkara are his commentaries on the ten Upaniṣads, *Iśā, Kena, Kaṭha, Praśna, Muṇḍaka, Māṇḍūkya, Aitareya, Taittirīya, Chāndogya* and *Bṛhadāraṇyaka* and the *Śārīraka-mīmāṃsā-bhāṣya.* The main reasons why a number of works which probably were not written by him were attributed to him seem to be twofold; first, becausc there was another writer of the same name, i.e. Śaṅkarācārya, and second, the tendency of Indian writers to increase the dignity of later works by attributing them to great writers of the past. The attribution of all the Purāṇas to Vyāsa illustrates this very clearly. Śaṅkara's *Iśopaniṣad-bhāṣya* has one commentary by Ānandajñāna and another, *Dīpikā*, by the other Śaṅkara Ācārya. His *Kenopaniṣad-bhāṣya* has two commentaries, *Kenopaniṣad-bhāṣya-vivaraṇa* and a commentary by Ānandajñāna. The *Kāṭhakopaniṣad-bhāṣya* has two commentaries, by Ānandajñāna and by Bālagopāla Yogīndra. The *Praśnopaniṣad-bhāṣya* has two commentaries, by Ānandajñāna and Nārāyaṇendra Sarasvatī. The *Muṇḍakopaniṣad-bhāṣya* has two commentaries, by Ānandajñāna and Abhinavanārāyaṇendra Sarasvatī. The *Māṇḍūkyopaniṣad-bhāṣya* has two commentaries, by Ānandajñāna and Mathurānātha Śukla, and a summary, called *Māṇḍūkyopaniṣad-bhāṣyārtha-saṃgraha*, by Rāghavānanda. The *Aitareyopaniṣad-bhāṣya* has six commentaries, by Ānandajñāna, Abhinavanārāyaṇa, Nṛsiṃha Ācārya, Bālakṛṣṇadāsa, Jñānāmṛta Yati, and Viśveśvara Tīrtha. The *Taittirīyopaniṣad-bhāṣya* seems to have only one commentary on it, by Ānandajñāna. The *Chāndogyopaniṣad* has two commentaries, called *Bhāṣya-ṭippaṇa*, and a commentary by Ānandajñāna. The *Bṛhadāraṇyakopaniṣad-*

bhāṣya has a commentary by Ānandajñāna and a big independent work on it by Sureśvara, called *Bṛhadāraṇyakopaniṣad-bhāṣya-vārttika,* or simply *Vārttika,* which has also a number of commentaries; these have been noticed in the section on Sureśvara. His *Aparokṣānubhava* has four commentaries, by Śaṅkara Ācārya, by Bālagopāla, by Caṇḍeśvara Varman (*Anubhava-dīpikā*), and by Vidyāraṇya. His commentary on Gauḍapāda's *Māṇḍūkya-kārikā,* called *Gauḍapādiya-bhāṣya* or *Āgama-śāstra-vivaraṇa,* has two commentaries, one by Śuddhānanda and one by Ānandajñāna. His *Ātma-jñānopadeśa* has two commentaries, by Ānandajñāna and by Pūrṇānanda Tīrtha; the *Eka-śloka* has a commentary called *Tattva-dīpana,* by Svayaṃprakāśa Yati; no commentary however is attributed to the *Viveka-cūḍāmaṇi,* which seems to be genuinely attributed to Śaṅkara; the *Ātma-bodha* has at least five commentaries, by Advayānanda, Bhāsurānanda, Bodhendra (*Bhāva-prakāśika*), Madhusūdana Sarasvatī and Rāmānanda Tīrtha; The *Ātmānātma-viveka* has at least four commentaries, by Padmapāda, Pūrṇānanda Tīrtha, Sāyaṇa and Svayaṃprakāśa Yati. The *Ātmopadeśa-vidhi* is said to have a commentary by Ānanda-jñāna; the *Ānanda-laharī* has about twenty-four commentaries, by Appaya Dīkṣita, Kavirāja, Kṛṣṇa Ācārya (*Mañju-bhāṣiṇī*), Keśavabhaṭṭa, Kaivalyāśrama (*Saubhāgya-vardhinī*), Gaṅgāharī (*Tattva-dīpikā*), Gaṅgādhara, Gopīrāma, Gopīkānta Sārvabhauma (*Ānandalaharī-tarī*), Jagadīśa?, Jagannātha Pañcānana, Narasiṃha, Brahmānanda (*Bhāvārtha-dīpikā*), Malla Bhaṭṭa, Mahādeva Vidyāvagīśa, Mahādeva Vaidya, Rāmacandra, Rāmabhadra, Ramānanda Tīrtha, Lakṣmīdhara Deśika and Viśvambhara and Śrīkaṇṭha Bhaṭṭa and another called *Vidvan-manoramā.* The *Upadeśa-sāhasrī* has at least four commentaries, by Ānandajñāna, by Rāmā Tīrtha (*Padayojanikā*), *Bodha-vidhi* by a pupil of Vidyādhāman, and by Śaṅkarācārya. His *Cid-ānanda-stava-rāja,* called also *Cid-ānanda-daśaślokī* or simply *Daśa-ślokī,* has also a number of commentaries and sub commentaries, such as the *Siddhānta-tattva-bindu* by Madhusūdana Sarasvatī; Madhusūdana's commentary was commented on by a number of persons, such as Nārāyaṇa Yati

(*Laghu-ṭīkā*), Puruṣottama Sarasvatī (*Siddhānta-bindu-sandīpana*), Pūrṇānanda Sarasvatī (*Tattva-viveka*), Gauḍa Brahmānanda Sarasvatī (*Siddhānta-bindu-nyāya-ratnāvalī*), by Saccidānanda and Śivalāla Śarman. Gauḍa Brahmānanda's commentary, *Siddhānta-bindu-nyāya-ratnāvalī,* was further commented on by Kṛṣṇakānta (*Siddhānta-nyāya-ratna-pradīpikā*). Śaṅkara's *Dṛg-dṛśya-prakaraṇa* was commented on by Rāmacandra Tīrtha; his *Pañcīkaraṇa-prakriyā* has again a number of commentaries—that by Sureśvara is *Pañcī-karaṇa-vārttika,* and this has a further commentary, called *Pañcī-karaṇa-vārttikābharaṇa,* by Abhinava-nārāyaṇendra Sarasvatī, pupil of Jñānendra Sarasvatī. Other commentaries on the *Pañcīkaraṇa-prakriyā* are *Pañcīkaraṇa-bhāva-prakāśikā, Pañcīkaraṇa-ṭīkā-tattva-candrikā, Pañcīkaraṇa-tātparya-candrikā* and *Pañcīkaraṇa-vivaraṇa* by Ānandajñāna, *Pañcī-karaṇa-vivaraṇa* by Svayaṃprakāśa Yati and by Prajñānānanda, and a sub-commentary called *Tattva-candrikā.* Śaṅkara also commented on the *Bhagavad-gītā;* this commentary has been examined in the chapter on the *Bhagavad-gītā* in the present volume. His *Laghu-vākya-vṛtti* has a commentary called *Puṣpāñjali*, and another, called *Laghu-vākya-vṛtti-prakāśikā,* by Rāmānanda Sarasvatī; his *Vākya-vṛtti* has a commentary by Ānandajñāna, and another commentary, called *Vākya-vṛtti-prakāśikā,* by Viśveśvara Paṇḍita. He starts his *Vākya-vṛtti* in the same manner as Īśvarakṛṣṇa starts his *Sāṃkhya-kārikā,* namely by stating that, suffering from the threefold sorrows of life, the pupil approaches a good teacher for instruction regarding the ways in which he may be liberated from them. Sureśvara in his *Naiṣkarmya-siddhi* also starts in the same manner and thus gives a practical turn to the study of philosophy, a procedure which one does not find in his *Brahma-sūtra-bhāṣya.* The answer, of course, is the same as that given in so many other places, that one is liberated only by the proper realization of the Upaniṣad texts that declare the unity of the self with Brahman. He then goes on to show that all external things and all that is called mind or mental or psychical is extraneous to self, which is of the nature of pure consciousness; he also declares here that the effects of one's deeds are disposed by God (Īśvara), the superior illusory form of Brahman, and not by the mysterious power of *apūrva* admitted by the Mīmāṃsists. He concludes this short work of fifty-three verses by insisting on the fact that, though the unity texts (*advaita-śruti*) of the Upaniṣads, such as "that (Brahman) art thou," may have a verbal construction that implies some kind of duality, yet their main force is in the direct and immediate apperception of the pure self without any intellectual process as implied by relations of identity. The *Vākya-vṛtti* is thus conceived differently from the *Aparokṣānubhūti*, where *yoga* processes of posture and breath-regulations are described, as being helpful for the realization of the true nature of self. This may, of course, give rise to some doubts regarding the true authorship of the *Aparokṣānubhūti,* though it may be explained as being due to the different stages of the development of Śaṅkara's own mind; divergences of attitude are also noticeable in his thoroughgoing idealism in his commentary on Gauḍapāda's *Kārikā,* where the waking life is regarded as being exactly the same as dream life, and external objects are deemed to have no existence whatsoever, being absolutely like dream-perceptions—as contrasted with his *Śārīraka-mīmāṃsā-bhāṣya*, where external objects are considered to have an indescribable existence, very different from dream-creations. The *Upadeśa-sāhasrī*, which in its nineteen chapters contains only six hundred and seventy-five stanzas, is more in a line with the *Vākya-vṛtti*, and, though the well-known Vedānta topics are all slightly touched upon, greater emphasis is laid on the proper realization of the Vedāntic unity texts, such as "that art thou," as means to the attainment of Brahmahood. There are also a number of short poems and hymns attributed to Śaṅkarācārya, such as the *Advaitānubhūti, Ātma-bodha*, *Tattvopadeśa*, *Prauḍhānubhūti*, etc., some of which are undoubtedly his, while there are many others which may not be so; but in the absence of further evidence it is difficult to come to any decisive conclusion.[1] These hymns do not contain any additional

1 The *Ātma-bodha* was commented upon by Padmapāda in his commentary *Ātma-bodha-vyākhyāna,* called also *Vedānta-sāra.*

philosophical materials, but are intended to stir up a religious fervour and emotion in favour of the monistic faith. In some cases, however, the commentators have found an excuse for extracting from them Vedāntic doctrines which cannot be said to follow directly from them. As an illustration of this, it may be pointed out that out of the ten ślokas of Śaṅkara Madhusūdana made a big commentary, and Brahmānanda Sarasvatī wrote another big commentary on that of Madhusūdana and elaborated many of the complex doctrines of the Vedānta which have but little direct bearing upon the verses themselves. But Śaṅkara's most important work is the *Brahma-sūtra-bhāṣya,* which was commented on by Vācaspati Miśra in the ninth century, Ānandajñāna in the thirteenth, and Govindānanda in the fourteenth century. Commentaries on Vācaspati's commentary will be noticed in the section on Vācaspati Miśra. Subrahmaṇya wrote a verse summary of Śaṅkara's commentary which he calls *Bhāṣyārtha-nyāya-mālā*; and Bhāratī Tīrtha wrote also the *Vaiyāsika-nyāya-mālā*, in which he tried to deal with the general arguments of the *Brahma-sūtra* on the lines of Śaṅkara's commentary. Many other persons, such as Vaidyanātha Dīkṣita, Devarāma Bhaṭṭa, etc., also wrote topical summaries of the main lines of the general arguments of the *Brahma-sūtra* on the lines of Śaṅkara's commentary, called *Nyāya-mālā* or *Adhikaraṇa-mālā.* But many other persons were inspired by Śaṅkara's commentary (or by the commentaries of Vācaspati Miśra and other great writers of the Śaṅkara school) and under the name of independent commentaries on the *Brahma-sūtra* merely repeated what was contained in these. Thus Amalānanda wrote his *Śāstra-darpaṇa* imitating the main lines of Vācaspati's commentary on Śaṅkara's commentary; and Svayaṃprakāśa also wrote his *Vedānta-naya-bhūṣaṇa*, in which for the most part he summarized the views of Vācaspati's *Bhāmatī* commentary. Hari Dīkṣita wrote his *Brahma-sūtra-vṛtti,* Śaṅkarānanda his *Brahma-sūtra-dīpikā* and Brahmānanda his *Vedānta-sūtra-muktāvalī* as independent interpretations of the *Brahma-sūtra*, but these were all written mainly on the lines of Śaṅkara's own commentary, supplementing it with additional Vedāntic ideas that had been developed after Śaṅkara by the philosophers of his school of thought or explaining Śaṅkara's *Bhāṣya.*[1]

MAṆḌANA, SUREŚVARA AND VIŚVARŪPA

General tradition has always identified Maṇḍana with Sureśvara and Viśvarūpa; and Col. G.A. Jacob in his introduction to the second edition of the *Naiṣkarmya-siddhi* seems willing to believe this tradition. The tradition probably started from Vidyāraṇya's *Śaṅkara-dig-vijaya*, where Maṇḍana is spoken of as being named not only Umbeka, but also Viśvarūpa (VIII.63). He further says in x.4 of the same work that, when Maṇḍana became a follower of Śaṅkara, he received from him the name Sureśvara. But the *Śaṅkara-dig-vijaya* is a mythical biography, and it is certainly very risky to believe any of its statements, unless corroborated by other reliable evidences. There is little doubt that Sureśvara was the author of a *Vārttika*, or commentary in verse, on Śaṅkara's *Bṛhad-*

1 Some of these commentaries are: *Brahma-sūtra-bhāṣyārtha-saṃgraha* by Brahmānanda Yati, pupil of Viśveśvarānanda, *Brahma-sūtrārtha-dīpikā* by Veṅkaṭa, son of Gaurī and Śiva, *Brahma-sūtra-vṛtti* (called also *Mitākṣarā)* by Annam Bhaṭṭa, and *Brahma-sūtra-bhāṣya-vyākhyā* (called also *Vidyā-śrī)* by Jñānottama Bhaṭṭāraka, pupil of Jñānaghana. The peculiarity of this last work is that it is the only commentary on the *eka-jīva-vāda* line that the present writer could trace. In addition to these some more commentaries may be mentioned, such as *Brahma-sūtra-vṛtti* by Dharma Bhaṭṭa, pupil of Rāmacandrārya and pupil's pupil of Mukundāśrama, *Sūtra-bhāṣya-vyākhyāna* (called also *Brahma-vidyā-bharaṇa)* by Advaitānanda, pupil of Rāmānanda and pupil's pupil of Brahmānanda, *Brahma-sūtra-bhāṣya-vyākhyā* (called also *Nyāya-rakṣāmaṇi)* by Appaya Dīkṣita, *Brahma-tattva-prakāśikā* (which is different from an earlier treatise called *Brahma-prakāśikā*) by Sadāśivendra Sarasvatī, *Brahma-sūtropanyāsa* by Rāmeśvara Bhāratī, by a pupil of Rāmānanda, *Śārīraka-mīmāṃsā-sūtra-siddhānta-kaumudi* by Subrahmaṇya Agnicin Makhīndra, *Vedānta-kaustubha* by Sītārāma; none of which seem to be earlier than the sixteenth century. But Ananyānubhava, the teacher of Prakāśātman (AD 1200), seems to have written another commentary, called *Śārīraka-nyāya-maṇimālā*. Prakāśātman himself also wrote a metrical summary of the main contents of Śaṅkara's *Bhāṣya* called *Śāriraka-mīmāṃsā-nyāya-saṃgraha,* and Kṛṣṇānubhūti, in much later times, wrote a similar metrical summary, called *Śārīraka-mīmāṃsā-saṃgraha.*

āraṇyaka Upaniṣad (which was also summarized by Vidyāraṇya in a work called *Vārttika-sāra,* which latter was further commented on by Maheśvara Tīrtha in his commentary, called the *Laghu-saṃgraha*). The *Vārttika* of Sureśvara was commented on by at least two commentators, Ānandagiri in his *Śāstra-prakāśikā* and Ānandapūrṇa in his *Nyāya-kalpa-latikā.* In a commentary on the *Parāśara-smṛti* published in the Bib. Ind. series (p. 51) a quotation from this *Vārttika* is attributed to Viśvarūpa; but this commentary is a late work, and in all probability it relied on Vidyāraṇya's testimony that Viśvarūpa and Sureśvara were identically the same person. Vidyāraṇya also, in his *Vivaraṇa-prameya-saṃgraha* p. 92, quotes a passage from Sureśvara's *Vārttika* (IV.8), attributing it to Viśvarūpa. But in another passage of the *Vivaraṇa-prameya-saṃgraha* (p. 224) he refers to a Vedānta doctrine, attributing it to the author of the *Brahma-siddhi.* But the work has not yet been published, and its manuscripts are very scarce: the present writer had the good fortune to obtain one. A fairly detailed examination of the philosophy of this work will be given in a separate section. The *Brahma-siddhi* is an important work, and it was commented on by Vācaspati in his *Tattva-samīkṣā,* by Ānandapūrṇa in his *Brahma-siddhi-vyākhyā-ratna,* by Śaṅkhapāṇi in his *Brahma-siddhi-ṭīkā,* and by Citsukha in his *Abhiprāya-prakāśikā.* But only the latter two works are available in manuscripts. Many important works however refer to the *Brahma-siddhi* and its views generally as coming from the author of *Brahma-siddhi* (*Brahma-siddhi-kāra*). But in none of these references, so far as it is known to the present writer, has the author of *Brahma-siddhi* been referred to as Sureśvara. The *Brahma-siddhi* was written in verse and prose, since two quotations from it in Citsukha's *Tattva-pradīpikā* (p. 381, Nirṇaya-Sāgara Press) and *Nyāya-kaṇikā* (p. 80) are in verse, while there are other references, such as *Tattva-pradīpikā* (p. 140) and elsewhere, which are in prose. There is, however, little doubt that the *Brahma-siddhi* was written by Maṇḍana or Maṇḍana Miśra; for both Śrīdhara in his *Nyāyakandalī* (p. 218) and Citsukha in his *Tattva-pradīpikā* (p. 140) refer to Maṇḍana as the author of the *Brahma-siddhi.* Of these the evidence of Śrīdhara, who belonged to the middle of the tenth century, ought to be considered very reliable, as he lived within a hundred years of the death of Maṇḍana; whoever Maṇḍana may have been, since he lived after Śaṅkara (AD 820), he could not have flourished very much earlier than the middle of the ninth century. It is, therefore, definitely known that the *Naiṣkarmya-siddhi* and the *Vārttika* were written by Sureśvara, and the *Brahma-siddhi* by Maṇḍana. The question regarding the identity of these two persons may be settled, if the views or opinions of the *Brahma-siddhi* can be compared or contrasted with the views of the *Naiṣkarmya-siddhi* or the *Vārttika*. From the few quotations that can be traced in the writings of the various writers who refer to it is possible to come to some fairly decisive conclusions.[1]

Of all passages the most important is that quoted from the *Brahma-siddhi* in the *Vivaraṇa-prameya-saṃgraha* (p. 224). It is said there that according to the author of the *Brahma-siddhi* it is the individual persons (*jīvāḥ,* in the plural) who by their own individual ignorance (*svāvidyayā*) create for themselves on the changelcss Brahman the false world-appearance. Neither in itself, nor with the *māyā*, or as reflection in *māyā*, is Brahman the cause of the world (*Brahma na jagat-kāraṇam*). The appearances then are but creations of individual ignorance, and individual false experiences of the world have therefore no objective basis. The agreement of individual experiences is due to similarity of illusions in different persons who are suffering under the delusive effects of the same kinds of ignorance; this may thus be compared with the delusive experience of two moons by a number of persons. Not all persons experience the same world; their delusive experiences

1 A copy of the manuscript of the *Brahma-siddhi* and its commentary was consulted by me in the Adyar and the Govt. Sanskrit MSS. Libraries after the above section had been written, and a thorough examination of its contents, I am happy to say, corroborates the above surmises. The *Brahma-siddhi* is expected to be shortly published by Prof. Kuppusvāmi Śāstrī, and I consulted the tarka-pāda of it in proof by the kind courtesy of Prof. Śāstrī in Madras in December 1928. A separate section has been devoted to the philosophy of Maṇḍana's *Brahma-siddhi.*

are similar, but the objective basis of their experience is not the same (*saṃvādas tu bahu-puruṣāvagata-dvitīya-candravatsādṛśyād upapadyate*). If this account is correct, as may well be supposed, then Maṇḍana Miśra may be regarded as the originator of the Vedāntic doctrine of *dṛṣṭi-sṛṣṭi-vāda,* which was in later times so forcefully formulated by Prakāśānanda. Again, in Prakāśātman's *Pañca-pādikā-vivaraṇa* (p. 32), it is held that according to the author of the *Brahma-siddhi* both *māyā* and *avidyā* are nothing but false experiences (*avidyā māyā mithyā-pratyayaiti*). About the function of knowledge as removing doubts he is said to hold the view (as reported in the *Nyāya-kandalī,* p. 218) that doubt regarding the validity of what is known is removed by knowledge itself. In the *Nyāya-kaṇikā* (p. 80) it is said that Maṇḍana held that reality manifests itself in unlimited conceptions of unity or universality, whereas differences appear only as a result of limited experience. Again, in the *Laghu-candrikā* (p. 112, Kumbakoṇam edition) Maṇḍana is introduced in the course of a discussion regarding the nature of the dispersion of ignorance and its relation to Brahma-knowledge or Brahmahood. According to Śaṅkara, as interpreted by many of his followers, including Sureśvara, the dissolution of ignorance (*avidyā-nivṛtti*) is not a negation, since negation as a separate category has no existence. So dissolution of ignorance means only Brahman. But according to Maṇḍana there is no harm in admitting the existence of such a negation as the cessation of ignorance; for the monism of Brahman means that there is only one positive entity. It has no reference to negations, i.e. the negation of duality only means the negation of all positive entities other than Brahman (*bhāvādvaita*). The existence of such a negation as the cessation of ignorance does not hurt the monistic creed. Again, Sarvajñātma Muni in his *Saṃkṣepa-śārīraka* (II.174) says that ignorance (*avidyā*) is supported (*āśraya*) in pure consciousness (*cin-mātrāśrita-viṣayamajñānam*)*,* and that, even where from the context of Śaṅkara's *Bhāṣya* it may appear as if he was speaking of the individual person (*jīva*) as being the support of *ajñāna*, it has to be interpreted in this sense. Objections of Maṇḍana, therefore, to such a view, viz. that ignorance rests with the individuals, are not to be given any consideration; for Maṇḍana's views lead to quite different conclusions (*parihṛtya Maṇḍana-vācaḥ tad dhy anyathā prasthitam*).[1] The commentator of the *Saṃkṣepa-śārīraka*, Rāmatīrtha Svāmin, also, in commenting on the passage referred to, contrasts the above view of Maṇḍana with that of Sureśvara, who according to him is referred to by an adjective *bahu-śruta* in the *Saṃkṣepa-śārīraka* text, and who is reported to have been in agreement with the views of Sarvajñātma Muni, as against the views of Maṇḍana. Now many of these views which have been attributed to Maṇḍana are not shared by Sureśvara, as will appear from what will be said below concerning him. It does not therefore appear that Maṇḍana Miśra and Sureśvara were the same person. But, if Vidyāraṇya, who knows so much about the views of Maṇḍana, had identified them in the *Śaṅkara-dig-vijaya,* that might lead one to pause. Now Mr Hiriyanna seems to have removed this difficulty for us by his short note in *J.R.A.S.* 1924, where he points out that Vidyāraṇya in his *Vārttika-sāra* refers to the author of the *Brahma-siddhi* as a different authority from the author of the *Vārttika,* viz. Sureśvara. Now, if Vidyāraṇya, the author of the *Vārttika-sāra,* knew that Maṇḍana, the author of the *Brahma-siddhi,* was not the same person as Sureśvara, he could not have identified them in his *Śaṅkara-dig-vijaya.* This naturally leads one to suspect that the Vidyāraṇya who was the author of the *Vivaraṇa-prameya-saṃgraha* and the *Vārttika-sāra* was not the same Vidyāraṇya as the author of *Śaṅkara-dig-vijaya.* Another consideration also leads one to think that Vidyāraṇya (the author of the *Vivaraṇa-prameya-saṃgraha*) could not have written the *Śaṅkara-dig-vijaya.* Ānandātman had two disciples, Anubhavānanda and Śaṅkarānanda. Anubhavānanda had as his disciple Amalānanda, and Śaṅkarānanda had Vidyāraṇya as his disciple. So Amalānanda may be taken as a contemporary of Vidyāraṇya. Now Amalānanda had another teacher in Sukhaprakāśa, who had Citsukha as his teacher. Thus Citsukha may be taken to be

1 Mr Hiriyanna, in *J.R.A.S.* 1923, mentions this point as well as the point concerning *avidyā-nivṛtti* in Maṇḍana's view as admission of negation.

a contemporary of the grand teacher (*parama-guru*), Ānandātman, of Vidyāraṇya. If this was the case, he could not have written in his *Śaṅkara-dig-vijaya* (XIII.5) that Citsukha, who lived several centuries after Padmapāda, was a disciple of Padmapāda. It may therefore be safely asserted that the author of the *Śaṅkara-dig-vijaya* was not the author of the *Vivaraṇa-prameya-saṃgraha.* Now, if this is so, our reliance on the author of the *Vivaraṇa-prameya-saṃgraha* cannot be considered to be risky and unsafe. But on p. 92 of the *Vivaraṇa-prameya-saṃgraha* a passage from the *Vārttika* of Sureśvara (IV.8) is attributed to Viśvarūpa Ācārya. It may therefore be concluded that Maṇḍana, the author of the *Brahma-siddhi,* was not the same person as Sureśvara, unless we suppose that Maṇḍana was not only a Mīmāṃsā writer, but also a Vedānta writer of great repute and that his conversion by Śaṅkara meant only that he changed some of his Vedāntic views and accepted those of Śaṅkara, and it was at this stage that he was called Sureśvara. On this theory his *Brahma-siddhi* was probably written before his conversion to Śaṅkara's views. It seems likely that this theory may be correct, and that the author of the *Vidhi-viveka* was also the author of the *Brahma-siddhi*; for the passage of the *Brahma-siddhi* quoted by Vācaspati in his *Nyāya-kaṇikā* is quoted in a manner which suggests that in all probability the author of the *Vidhi-viveka* was also the author of the *Brahma-siddhi.* It may also be concluded that in all probability Viśvarūpa was the same person as Sureśvara, though on this subject no references of value are known to the present writer other than by the author of the *Vivaraṇa-prameya-saṃgraha.*

MAṆḌANA (AD 800)

Maṇḍana Miśra's *Brahma-siddhi* with the commentary of Śaṅkhapāṇi is available in manuscript, and Mahāmahopādhyāya Kuppusvāmi Śāstrī of Madras is expected soon to bring out a critical edition of this important work. Through the courtesy of Mahāmahopādhyāya Kuppusvāmi Śāstrī the present writer had an opportunity of going through the proofs of the *Brahma-siddhi* and through the courtesy of Mr C. Kunhan Raja, the Honorary Director of the Adyar Library, he was able also to utilize the manuscript of Śaṅkhapāṇi's commentary.[1] The *Brahma-siddhi* is in four chapters, *Brahma-kāṇḍa, Tarka-kāṇḍa, Niyoga-kāṇḍa,* and *Siddhi-kāṇḍa,* in the form of verses (*kārikā*) and long annotations (*vṛtti*). That Maṇḍana must have been a contemporary of Śaṅkara is evident from the fact that, though he quotes some writers who flourished before Śaṅkara, such as Śabara, Kumārila or Vyāsa, the author of the *Yoga-sūtra-bhāṣya,* and makes profuse references to the Upaniṣad texts, he never refers to any writer who flourished after Śaṅkara.[2] Vācaspati also wrote a commentary, called *Tattva-samīkṣā,* on Maṇḍana's *Brahma-siddhi*; but unfortunately this text, so far as is known to the present writer, has not yet been discovered. In the *Brahma-kāṇḍa* chapter Maṇḍana discusses the nature of Brahman; in the *Tarka-kāṇḍa* he tries to prove that we cannot perceive "difference" through perception and that therefore one should not think of interpreting the Upaniṣad texts on dualistic lines on the ground that perception reveals difference. In the third chapter, the *Niyoga-kāṇḍa,* he tries to refute the Mīmāṃsā view that the Upaniṣad texts are to be interpreted in accordance with the Mīmāṃsā principle of interpretation, that all Vedic texts command us to engage in some kind of action or to restrain ourselves from

1 Citsukha, the pupil of Jñānottama, also wrote a commentary on it, called *Abhiprāya-prakāśikā,* almost the whole of which, except some portions at the beginning, is available in the Government Oriental Manuscript Library, R. No. 3853. Ānandapūrṇa also wrote a commentary on the *Brahma-siddhi,* called *Bhāva-śuddhi.*

2 Maṇḍana's other works are *Bhāvanā-viveka, Vidhi-viveka, Vibhrama-viveka* and *Sphoṭa-siddhi.* Of these the *Vidhi-viveka* was commented upon by Vācaspati Miśra in his *Nyāya-kaṇikā,* and the *Sphoṭa-siddhi* was commented upon by the son of Bhavadāsa, who had also written a commentary, called *Tattva-vibhāvanā,* on Vācaspati Miśra's *Tattva-bindu.* The commentary on the *Sphoṭa-siddhi* is called *Gopālika.* Maṇḍana's *Vibhrama-viveka* is a small work devoted to the discussion of the four theories of illusion (*khyāti), ātma-khyāti, asat-khyāti, anyathā-khyāti* and *ākhyāti.* Up till now only his *Bhāvanā-viveka* and *Vidhi-viveka* have been published.

certain other kinds of action. This is by far the longest chapter of the book. The fourth chapter, the *Siddhi-kāṇḍa,* is the shortest: Maṇḍana says here that the Upaniṣad texts show that the manifold world of appearance does not exist at all and that its apparent existence is due to the *avidyā* of *jīva.*

In the *Brahma-kāṇḍa* the most important Vedāntic concepts are explained by Maṇḍana according to his own view. He first introduces the problem of the subject (*draṣṭṛ*) and the object (*dṛśya*) and says that it is only by abolishing the apparent duality of subject and object that the fact of experience can be explained. For, if there was any real duality of subject and object, that duality could not be bridged over and no relation between the two could be established; if, on the other hand, there is only the subject, then all things that are perceived can best be explained as being illusory creations imposed on self, the only reality.[1] Proceeding further with the same argument, he says that attempts have been made to bring about this subject-object relation through the theory of the operation of an intermediary mind (*antaḥkaraṇa*); but whatever may be the nature of this intermediary, the pure unchangeable intelligence, the self or the subject, could not change with its varying changes in accordance with its connection with different objects; if it is held that the self does not undergo any transformation or change, but there is only the appearance of a transformation through its reflection in the *antaḥkaraṇa*, then it is plainly admitted that objects are not in reality perceived and that there is only an appearance of perception. If objects are not perceived in reality, it is wrong to think that they have a separate and independent existence from the self.[2] Just as the very same man sees his own image in the mirror

---

1 *Ekatva evāyaṃ draṣṭṛ-dṛśya-bhāvo'vakalpate, draṣṭur eva cid-ātmanaḥ tathātathā vipariṇāmād vivartanād vā; nānātve tu vivikta-svabhāvayor asaṁsṛṣṭa-paraspara-svarūpayor asambaddhayoḥ kīdṛśo draṣṭṛ-dṛśya-bhāvaḥ.* Kuppusvāmi Śāstrī's edition of *Brahma-siddhi,* p. 7. (In the press.)

2 *ekāntaḥkaraṇa-saṃkrāntāvasty eva sambandha iti cet, na, citeḥ śuddhatvād apariṇāmād aprati-saṃkramāc ca; dṛśyā buddhiḥ citi-sannidheś chāyaya vivartata iti ced atha keyaṃ tac chāyatā?a-tad-ātmanaḥ tad-avabhāsaḥ; na tarhi paramārthato dṛśyaṃ dṛśyate, paramārthataś ca dṛśyamānaṃ draṣṭṛ-vyat-*

to be different from him and to exist outside of him as an object, so the same self appears as all the diverse objects outside of it. It is difficult to conceive how one could admit the existence of external objects outside the pure intelligence (*cit*); for in that case it would be impossible to relate the two.[1]

According to Maṇḍana *avidyā* is called *māyā*, or false appearance, because it is neither a characteristic (*sva-bhāva*) of Brahman nor different from it, neither existent nor non-existent. If it was the characteristic of anything, then, whether one with that or different from it, it would be real and could not therefore be called *avidyā;* if it was absolutely non-existent, it would be like the lotus of the sky and would have no practical bearing in experience (*navyavahāra-bījam*) such as *avidyā* has; it has thus to be admitted that *avidyā* is indescribable or unspeakable (*anirvacanīyā*).[2]

According to Maṇḍana *avidyā* belongs to the individual souls (*jīva*). He admits that there is an inconsistency in such a view; but

---

iriktam asti iti durbhaṇam. Ibid. Śaṅkhapāṇi in commenting on this discards the view that objects pass through the sense-channels and become superimposed on the *antaḥkaraṇa or durbhaṇam* and thereby become related to the pure intelligence of the self and objectified: *na tu sphaṭikopame cetasi indriya-praṇālī-saṃkrāntānām arthānāṃ tatraiva saṃkrāntena ātma-caitanyena sambaddhānāṃ tad-dṛśyatvaṃ ghaṭiṣyate.* Adyar MS. p. 75. It may not be out of place to point out in this connection that the theory of Padmapāda, Prakāśātman, as developed later on by Dharmarā jādhvarīndra, which held that the mind (*antaḥkaraṇa*) becomes superimposed on external objects in perception, was in all probability borrowed from the Sāṃkhya doctrine of *cic-chāyāpatti* in perception, which was somehow forced into Śaṅkara's loose epistemological doctrines and worked out as a systematic epistemological theory. The fact that Maṇḍana discards this epistemological doctrine shows, on the one hand, that he did not admit it to be a right interpretation of Śaṅkara and may, on the other hand, be regarded as a criticism of the contemporary interpretation of Padmapāda. But probably the reply of that school would be that, though they admitted extra-individual reality of objects, they did not admit the reality of objects outside of pure intelligence *(cit)*.

1 *Tathā hi darpaṇa-tala-stham ātmānaṃ vibhaktam ivātmanaḥ pratyeti; cites tu vibhaktam asaṃsṛṣṭaṃ tayā cetyata iti dur-avagamyam. Ibid.*

2 *Ibid.* p. 9. It may not be out of place here to point out that Ānandabodha's argument in his *Nyāya-makaranda* regarding the unspeakable nature of *avidyā,* which has been treated in a later section of this chapter, is based on this argument of Maṇḍana.

he thinks that, *avidyā* being itself an inconsistent category, there is no wonder that its relation with *jīva* should also be inconsistent and unexplainable. The inconsistency of the relationship of *avidyā* with the *jīvas* arises as follows: the *jīvas* are essentially identical with Brahman, and the diversity of *jīvas* is due to imagination (*kalpanā*); but this imagination cannot be of Brahman, since Brahman is devoid of all imagination (*tasyā vidyātmanaḥ kalpanā-śūnyatvāt*); it cannot be the imagination of *the jīvas,* since the *jīvas* themselves are regarded as being the product of imagination.[1] Two solutions may be proposed regarding this difficulty, firstly, that the word *māyā* implies what is inconsistent; had it been a consistent and explainable concept, it would be reality and not *māyā.*[2] Secondly, it may be said that from *avidyā* come the *jīvas* and from *the jīvas* comes the *avidyā*, and that this cycle is beginningless and therefore there is no ultimate beginning either of the *jīvas* or of the *avidyā.*[3] This view is held by those who think that *avidyā* is not the material cause of the world: these are technically called *avidyopādāna-bheda-vādins.* It is through this *avidyā* that the *jīvas* suffer the cycle of births and rebirths, and this *avidyā* is natural to *the jīvas,* since *the jīvas* themselves are the products of *avidyā.*[4] And it is through listening to the Vedāntic texts, right thinking, meditation, etc. that true knowledge dawns and the *avidyā* is destroyed; it was through this *avidyā* that the *jīvas* were separated from Brahman; with its destruction they attain Brahma-hood.[5]

---

1 इतरेतराश्रयप्रसङ्गात् कल्पनाधीनो हि।
जीव विभागः जीवाश्रया कल्पना।
Itaretarāśray aprasaṅgāt kalpanādhīno hi
Jīva vibhāgaḥ, jīvāśrayā kalpanā. —*Ibid. p.* 10.

2 *Anupapadyamānārthaiva hi māyā; upapadyamānārthatve vathārtha-bhāvān na māyā syāt. Ibid.*

3 *Anāditvān netaretarāśrayatva-doṣaḥ.* —*Ibid.*

4 *na hi jīveṣu nisarga-jā vidyāsti, avidyaiva hi naisargikī, āgantukyā vidyāyāh pravilayaḥ.* —*Ibid.* pp. 11-12.

5 *Avidyayaiva tu brahmaṇo jīvo vibhaktaḥ, tan-nivṛttau brahma-svarūpam eva bhavati, yathā ghaṭādi-bhede tad-ākāśam pariśuddham paramākāśam eva bhavati.*

—Ibid.

In defining the nature of Brahman as pure bliss Śaṅkhapāṇi the commentator raises some very interesting discussions. He starts by criticizing the negative definition of happiness as cessation of pain or as a positive mental state qualified by such a negative condition.[1] He says that there are indeed negative pleasures which are enjoyed as negation of pain (*e.g.*, a plunge into cold water is an escape from the painful heat); but he holds that there are cases where pleasures and pains are experienced simultaneously and not as negation of each other. A man may feel painful heat in the upper part of his body and yet feel the lower part of his body delightfully cool and thus experience pleasure and pain simultaneously (*sukha-duḥkhe yugapaj janyete*). Again, according to the scriptures there is unmixed pain in Hell, and this shows that pain need not necessarily be relative. Again, there are many cases (*e.g.*, in the smelling of a delightful odour of camphor) where it cannot be denied that we have an experience of positive pleasure.[2] Śaṅkhapāṇi then refutes the theory of pain as unsatisfied desire and happiness as satisfaction or annulment of desires (*viṣaya-prāptiṃ vinā kāma eva duḥkham ataḥ tan-nivṛttir eva sukham bhaviṣyati*) by holding that positive experiences of happiness are possible even when one has not desired them.[3] An objection to this is that experience of pleasures satisfies the natural, but temporarily inactive, desires in a sub-conscious or potential condition.[4] Again, certain experiences produce more pleasures in some than in others, and this is obviously due to the fact that one had more latent desires to be fulfilled than the other. In reply to these objections Śaṅkhapāṇi points out that, even if a thing is much desired, yet, if it is secured after much trouble, it does not satisfy one so much as a pleasure which comes easily. If pleasure is defined as removal of desires, then one should feel happy before

1 *duḥkha nivṛttir vā tad-viśiṣṭātmopalabdhir vā sukham astu, sarvathā sukham nāma na dharmāntaram asti.*
—Adyar MS. of the Śaṅkhapāṇi commentary, p. 18.

2 *Ibid.* pp. 20, 21.

3 *Ibid.* p. 22.

4 *sahajo hi rāgaḥ sarva-puṃsām asti sa tu viṣaya-viśeṣeṇa āvir-bhavati. Ibid.* p. 23

the pleasurable experience or after the pleasurable experience, when all traces of the desires are wiped out, but not at the time of enjoying the pleasurable experience; for the desires are not wholly extinct at that time. Even at the time of enjoying the satisfaction of most earnest desires one may feel pain. So it is to be admitted that pleasure is not a relative concept which owes its origin to the sublation of desires, but that it is a positive concept which has its existence even before the desires are sublated.[1] If negation of desires be defined as happiness, then even disinclination to food through bilious attacks is to be called happiness.[2] So it is to be admitted that positive pleasures are in the first instance experienced and then are desired. The theory that pains and pleasures are relative and that without pain there can be no experience of pleasure and that there can be no experience of pain without an experience of pleasure is false and consequently the Vedāntic view is that the state of emancipation as Brahmahood may well be described as an experience of positive pure bliss.[3]

Śaṅkara in his commentary on the *Brahma-sūtra* and in his commentaries on some of the Upaniṣads and the *Māṇḍūkya-kārikā* had employed some elements of dialectical criticism, the principles of which had long been introduced in well-developed forms by the Buddhists. The names of the three great dialecticians, Śrīharṣa, Ānandajñāna and Citsukha, of the Śaṅkara school, are well known, and proper notice has been taken of them in this chapter. But among the disciples of Śaṅkara the man who really started the dialectical forms of argument, who was second to none in his dialectical powers and who influenced all other dialecticians of the Śaṅkara school, Ānandabodha, Śrīharṣa, Ānandajñāna, Citsukha, Nṛsiṃhāśrama and others, was Maṇḍana. Maṇḍana's great dialectical achievement is found in his refutation of the perception of difference (*bheda*) in the *Tarka-kāṇḍa* chapter of his *Brahma-siddhi.*

1 *ataḥ kāma-nivṛtteḥ prāg-bhāvi sukha-vastu-bhūtam eṣṭavyam.* —*Ibid.* p. 27.

2 *Ibid.* p. 25.

3 *Yadi duḥkhā-bhāvaḥ sukhaṃ syāt tataḥ syād evaṃ bhāvāntare tu sukhe duḥkhābhāve ca tathā syād eva.* —*Ibid.* p. 161.

The argument arose as follows: the category of difference (*bheda*) is revealed in perception, and, if this is so, the reality of difference cannot be denied, and therefore the Upaniṣad texts should not be interpreted in such a way as to annul the reality of "difference." Against such a view-point Maṇḍana undertakes to prove that "difference," whether as a quality or characteristic of things or as an independent entity, is never experienced by perception (*pratyakṣa*).[1] He starts by saying that perception yields three possible alternatives, viz. (1) that it manifests a positive object, (2) that it presents differences from other objects, (3)that it both manifests a positive object and distinguishes it from other objects.[2] In the third alternative there may again be three other alternatives, viz. (i) simultaneous presentation of the positive object and its distinction from others, (ii) first the presentation of the positive object and then the presentation of the difference, (iii) first the presentation of the difference and then the presentation of the positive object.[3] If by perception differences from other objects are experienced, or if it manifests both the object and its differences, then it has to be admitted that "difference" is presented in perception; but, if it can be proved that only positive objects are presented in perception, unassociated with any presentation of difference, then it has to be admitted that the notion of difference is not conveyed to us by perception, and in that case the verdict of the Upaniṣads that reality is one and that no diversity can be real is not contradicted by perceptual experience. Now follows the argument.

Perception does not reveal merely the difference, nor does it first reveal the difference and then the positive object, nor both of them simultaneously; for the positive object must first be revealed, before any difference can be manifested. Difference must concern itself in a relation between two positive objects, *e.g.*, the cow is

1 This discussion runs from page 44 of the *Brahma-siddhi* (in the press) to the end of the second chapter.

2 *Tatra pratyakṣe trayaḥ kalpāḥ, vastu-svarūpa-siddhiḥ vastv-antarasya vyavac-ched ahubhayaṃ vā.* —*Brahma-siddhi*, II.

3 *Ubhayasminn api traividhyam, yaugapadyam, vyavaccheda-pūrvako vidhiḥ, vidhi-pūrvako vyavacchedaḥ.* —*Ibid.*

different from the horse, or there is no jug here. The negation involved in the notion of difference can have no bearing without that which is negated or that of which it is negated, and both these are positive in their notion. The negation of a chimerical entity (*e.g.,* the lotus of the sky) is to be interpreted as negation of a false relation of its constituents, which are positive in themselves (*e.g.,* both the lotus and the sky are existents, the incompatibility is due to their relationing, and it is such a relation between these two positive entities that is denied), or as denying the objective existence of such entities, which can be imagined only as a mental idea.[1] If the category of difference distinguishes two objects from one another, the objects between which the difference is manifested must first be known. Again, it cannot be held that perception, after revealing the positive object, reveals also its difference from other objects; for perception is one unique process of cognition, and there are no two moments in it such that it should first reveal the object with which there is present sense-contact and then reveal other objects which are not at that moment in contact with sense, as also the difference between the two.[2] In the case of the discovery of one's own illusion, such as "this is not silver, but conch-shell," only the latter knowledge is perceptual, and this knowledge refers to and negates after the previous knowledge of the object as silver has been negated. It was only when the presented object was perceived as "this before" that it was denied as being the silver for which it was taken, and when it was thus negated there was the perception of the conch-shell. There is no negative concept without there first being a positive concept; but it does not therefore follow that a

---

1 कुतश्चिन् निमित्तद्बुद्धौ लब्धरूपाणाम् बहिर्निषेधः क्रियते।
Kutaścin nimittād buddhau labdha-rūpāṇām bahir niṣedhaḥ kriyate.
—*Brahma-siddhi,* II.

2 क्रमः सम्गच्छते युक्त्या नैकविज्ञानकर्मणोः
न सन्निहितजं तच्च तदन्यामर्शि जायते॥
kramaḥ samgacchate yuktyā naika-vijñāna-karmaṇoḥ
Na sannihita-jaṃ tac ca tadanyāmarśi jāyate. —*Ibid.* ii. *Kārikā* 3.

positive concept cannot be preceded by a negative concept.[1] This is therefore not a case where there are two moments in one unique perception, but there are here different cognitive experiences.[2]

Again, there is a view (Buddhist) that it is by the power or potency of the indeterminate cognition of an object that both the positive determinate cognition and its difference from others are produced. Though the positive and the negative are two cognitions, yet, since they are both derived from the indeterminate cognition, it can well be said that by one positive experience we may also have its difference from others also manifested (*eka-vidhir eva anya-vyavacchedaḥ*).[3] Against such a view Maṇḍana urges that one positive experience cannot also reveal its differences from all other kinds of possible and impossible objects. A colour perceived at a particular time and particular place may negate another colour at that particular place and time, but it cannot negate the presence of taste properties at that particular place and time; but, if the very perception of a colour should negate everything else which is not that colour, then these taste properties would also be negated, and, since this is not possible, it has to be admitted that perception of a positive entity does not necessarily involve as a result of that very process the negation of all other entities.

There is again a view that things are by their very nature different from one another (*prakṛtyaiva bhinnā bhāvāḥ*), and thus, when by perception an object is experienced, its difference from other objects is also grasped by that very act. In reply to this objection Maṇḍana says that things cannot be of the nature of differences; firstly, in that case all objects would be of the nature

---

1 *pūrva-vijñāna-vihiterajatādau "idam" iti ca sannihitārtha-sāmānye niṣedho vidhi-pūrva eva, śuktikā-siddhis tu virodhi-niṣedha-pūrva ucyate;vidhi-pūrvatā ca niyamena niṣedhasyocyate, na vidher niṣedha-pūrvakatā niṣidhyate.*

—*Brahma-siddhi*, II. *Kārikā* 3.

2 *na ca tatra eka-jñānasya kramavad-vyāpāratā ubhaya-rūpasya utpatteḥ. Ibid.*

3 *Nīlasya nirvikalpaka-darśanasya yat sāmarthyaṃ niyataika-kāraṇatvaṃ tena anādi-vāsanā-vaśāt pratibhāsitaṃ janitam idam nedam iti vikalpo bhāvābhā-va-vyavahāram pravartayati... satyaṃ jñāna-dvayam idaṃ savikalpakaṃ tu nir-vikalpakaṃ tayor mūla-bhūtaṃ tat pratyakṣaṃ tatra ca eka-vidhir eva anya-vya-vaccheda iti brūma iti.* —Śaṅkhapāṇi's commentary, *ibid.*

of difference, and hence there would be no difference among them; secondly, as "difference" has no form, the objects themselves would be formless; thirdly, difference being essentially of the nature of negation, the objects themselves would be of the nature of negation; fourthly, since difference involves duality or plurality in its concept, no object could be regarded as one; a thing cannot be regarded as both one and many.[1] In reply to this the objector says that a thing is of the nature of difference only in relation to others (*parāpekṣaṃ vastuno bheda-svabhāvaḥ nātmāpekṣam*), but not in relation to itself. In reply to this objection Maṇḍana says that things which have been produced by their own causes cannot stand in need of a relation to other entities for their existence; all relationing is mental and as such depends on persons who conceive the things, and so relationing cannot be a constituent of objective things.[2] If relationing with other things constituted their essence, then each thing would depend on others—they would depend on one another for their existence (*itaretarāśraya-prasaṅgāt*). In reply to this it may be urged that differences are different, corresponding to each and every oppositional term, and that each object has a different specific nature in accordance with the different other objects with which it may be in a relation of opposition; but, if this is so, then objects are not produced solely by their own causes; for, if differences are regarded as their constituent essences, these essences should vary in accordance with every object with which a thing may be opposed. In reply to this it is urged by the objector that, though an object is produced by its own causes, yet its nature as differences appears in relation to other objects with which it is held in opposition. Maṇḍana rejoins that on such a view it would be difficult to understand the meaning and function of this oppositional

---

1 न भेदोवस्तुनो रूपं तदभावप्रसङ्गतः
अरूपेण च भिन्नत्वं वस्तुनो नावकल्पते ॥
Na bhedo vastuno rūpaṃ tad-abhāva-prasaṅgataḥ
arūpeṇa ca bhinnatvaṃ vastuno nāvakalpate. —*Brahma-siddhi*, n. 5.

2 *nāpekṣā nāma kaścid vastu-dharmo yena vastuni vyavasthāpyeran, na khalusva-hetu-prāpitodayeṣu sva-bhāva-vyavasthiteṣu vastuṣu sva-bhāva-sthitaye vastvantarāpekṣā yujyate. Ibid.* II.6, *vṛtti*.

relation (*apekṣā*); for it does not produce the object, which is produced by its own causes, and it has no causal efficiency and it is also not experienced, except as associated with the other objects (*nānāpekṣa-pratiyoginām bhedaḥ pratīyate*). Difference also cannot be regarded as being of the essence of oppositional relation; it is only when there is an oppositional relation between objects already experienced that difference manifests itself. Relations are internal and are experienced in the minds of those who perceive and conceive.[1] But it is further objected to this that concepts like father and son are both relational and obviously externally constitutive. To this Maṇḍana's reply is that these two concepts are not based on relation, but on the notion of production; that which produces is the father and that which is produced is the son. Similarly also the notions of long and short depend upon the one occupying greater or less space at the time of measurement and not on relations as constituting their essence.

In reply to this the objector says that, if relations are not regarded as ultimate, and if they are derived from different kinds of actions, then on the same ground the existence of differences may also be admitted. If there were no different kinds of things, it would not be possible to explain different kinds of actions. But Maṇḍana's reply is that the so-called differences may be but differences in name; the burning activity of the same fire is described sometimes as burning and sometimes as cooking. In the Vedānta view it is held that all the so-called varied kinds of actions appear in one object, the Brahman, and so the objection that varied kinds of actions necessarily imply the existence of difference in the agents which produce them is not valid. Again, the difficulty in the case of the Buddhist is in its own way none the less; for according to him all appearances are momentary, and, if this be so, how does he explain the similarities of effects that we notice? It can be according to them only on the basis of an illusory notion of the sameness of causes; so, if the Buddhist can explain our experience of similarity on the false appearance of sameness of causes, the Vedāntist may

1 *pauruṣeyīm apekṣām na vastv anuvartate, ato na vastu-svabhāvaḥ. —Ibid.*

also in his turn explain all appearances of diversity through illusory notions of difference, and there is thus no necessity of admitting the reality of differences in order to explain our notions of difference in experience.[1] Others again argue that the world must be a world of diversity, as the various objects of our experience serve our various purposes, and it is impossible that one and the same thing should serve different purposes. But this objection is not valid, because even the self-same thing can serve diverse purposes; the same fire can burn, illuminate and cook. There is no objection to there being a number of limited (*avacchinna*) qualities or characters in the self-same thing. It is sometimes urged that things are different from one another because of their divergent powers (*e.g.,* milk is different from sesamum because curd is produced from milk and not from sesamum); but divergence of powers is like divergence of qualities, and, just as the same fire may have two different kinds of powers or qualities, namely, that of burning and cooking, so the same entity may at different moments both possess and not possess a power, and this does not in the least imply a divergence or difference of entity. It is a great mystery that the one self-same thing should have such a special efficiency (*sāmarthyātiśaya*) that it can be the basis of innumerable divergent appearances. As one entity is supposed to possess many divergent powers, so one self-same entity may on the same principle be regarded as the cause of divergent appearances.

Again, it is held by some that "difference" consists in the negation of one entity in another. Such negations, it may be replied, cannot be indefinite in their nature; for then negations of all things in all places would make them empty. If, however, specific negations are implied with reference to determinate entities, then, since the character of these entities, as different from one another, depends on these implied negations, and since these implied negations can operate only when there are these different entities, they depend mutually upon one another (*itaretarāśraya*)

1 *Atha nir-anvaya-vināśānām api kalpanā-viṣayād abhedāt kāryasya tulyatā hanta tarhi bhedād eva kalpanā-viṣayāt kāryābheda-siddher mūḍhā kāraṇa-bheda-kalpanā. —Ibid.*

and cannot therefore hold their own. Again, it cannot be said that the notion of "difference" arises out of the operation of perceptual processes like determinate perception (occurring as the culmination of the perceptual process); for there is no proof whatsoever that "difference," as apart from- mutual negation, can be definitely experienced. Again, if unity of all things as "existents" (*sat*) was not realized in experience, it would be difficult to explain how one could recognize the sameness of things. This sameness or unity of things is by far the most fundamental of experiences, and it is first manifested as indeterminate experience, which later on transforms itself into various notions of difference.[1] In this connection Maṇḍana also takes great pains in refuting the view that things are twofold in their nature, both unity and difference, and also the Jaina view that unity and difference are both true in their own respective ways. But it is not necessary to enter into these details. The main point in his refutation of the category of difference consists in this, that he show's that it is inconceivable and dialectically monstrous to suppose that the category of difference can be experienced through perception and that it is philosophically more convenient to suppose that there is but one thing which through ignorance yields the various notions of difference than to suppose that there are in reality the infinite agreements of unity and difference just as they are experienced in perception.[2]

In the third chapter of the *Brahma-siddhi*, called the *Niyoga-kāṇḍa,* Maṇḍana refutes the Mīmāṃsā view that the Vedāntic texts are to be interpreted in accordance with the Mīmāṃsā canon of interpretation, viz. that Vedic texts imply either a command or a

---

1 प्रत्येकम् अनुबिद्धत्वादभेदेन मृषामतः
भेदो यथा तरङ्गाणाम् भेदाद्भेदः कलावतः ॥
Pratyekam anubiddhatvād abhedena mṛṣā mataḥ
Bhedo yathā taraṅgāṇām bhedād bhedaḥ kalāvataḥ.
—*Brahma-siddhi*, II. *Kārikā* 31.

2 एकस्यैवास्तु महिमा यन्नानेव प्रकाशते
लाघवान् न तु भिन्नानाम् यच्चकाशत्यभिन्नवत् ॥
Ekasyaivāstu mahimā yan nāneva prakāśate
Lāghavān na tu bhinnānām yac cakāśaty abhinnavat.
—*Brahma-siddhi*, II. *Kārikā* 32.

prohibition. But, as this discussion is not of much philosophical importance, it is not desirable to enter into it. In the fourth chapter, called the *Siddhi-kāṇḍa*, Maṇḍana reiterates the view that the chief import of the Upaniṣad texts consists in showing that the manifold world of appearance does not exist and that its manifestation is due to the ignorance (*avidyā*) of the individual souls *(jīva*). The sort of ultimate reality that is described in the Upaniṣad texts is entirely different from all that we see around us, and it is as propounding this great truth, which cannot be known by ordinary experience, that the Upaniṣads are regarded as the only source from which knowledge of Brahman can be obtained.

SUREŚVARA (AD 800)

Sureśvara's chief works are the *Naiṣkarmya-siddhi* and *Bṛhad-āraṇyakopaniṣad-bhāṣya-vārttika.* The *Naiṣkarmya-siddhi* has at least five commentaries, such as the *Bhāva-tattva-prakāśikā* by Citsukha, which is based on Jñānottama's *Candrikā.* This *Candrikā* is thus the earliest commentary on the *Naiṣkarmya-siddhi.* It is difficult to determine Jñānottama's date. In the concluding verses of this commentary the two names Satyabodha and Jñānottama occur; and Mr Hiriyanna points out in his introduction to *the Naiṣkarmya-siddhi that* these two names also occur in the Sarvajña-pīṭha of Conjeeveram, to which he claims to have belonged as teacher and pupil, and according to the list of teachers of that Maṭha Jñānottama was the fourth from Śaṅkara. This would place Jñānottama at a very early date; if, however, the concluding verses are not his, but inserted by someone else, then of course they give no clue to his date except the fact that he must have lived before Citsukha, since Citsukha's commentary was based on Jñānottama's commentary *Candrikā.* Another commentary is the *Vidyā-surabhi* of Jñānāmṛta, the pupil of Uttamāmṛta; another is the *Naiṣkarmya-siddhi-vivaraṇa* of Akhilātman, pupil of Daśarathapriya; and there is also another commentary, called *Sārārtha,* by Rāmadatta, which is of comparatively recent date.

Sureśvara's *Naiṣkarmya-siddhi* is divided into four chapters. The first chapter deals with discussions regarding the relation of Vedic duties to the attainment of Vedāntic wisdom. *Avidyā* is here defined as the non-perception in one's experience of the ultimate oneness of the self: through this rebirths take place, and it is the destruction of this ignorance which is emancipation (*tannāśo muktir ātmanaḥ*). The Mīmāṃsists think that, if one ceases to perform actions due to desire (*kāmya-karma*) and prohibited actions, then the actions which have already accumulated will naturally exhaust themselves in time by yielding fruits, and so, since the obligatory duties do not produce any new *karma,* and since no other new *karmas* accumulate, the person will naturally be emancipated from *karma.* There is, however, in the Vedas no injunction in favour of the attainment of right knowledge. So one should attain emancipation through the performance of the Vedic duties alone. As against this Mīmāṃsā view Sureśvara maintains that emancipation has nothing to do with the performance of actions. Performance of Vedic duties may have an indirect and remote bearing, in the way of purifying one's mind, but it has certainly no direct bearing on the attainment of salvation. Sureśvara states a view attributed to Brahmadatta in the *Vidyā-surabhi* commentary, that ignorance is not removed merely by the knowledge of the identity of oneself with Brahman, as propounded in Vedānta texts, but through long and continuous meditation on the same. So the right apprehension of the Upaniṣadic passages on the identity of the Brahman and the individual does not immediately produce salvation; one has to continue to meditate for a long time on such ideas of identity; and all the time one has to perform all one's obligatory duties, since, if one ceased to perform them, this would be a transgression of one's duties and would naturally produce sins, and hence one would not be able to obtain emancipation. So knowledge must be combined with the performance of duties (*jñāna-karma-samuccaya*), which is vehemently opposed by Śaṅkara. Another view which occurs also in the *Vārttika*, and is there referred to by the commentator Ānandajñāna as being that of Maṇḍana, is that, as the knowledge derived from the Vedāntic texts is verbal and conceptual, it cannot of itself lead to Brahma-knowledge, but, when these texts are continually repeated, they produce a knowledge of Brahman as a mysterious effect by just the same kind of process as gives rise to the mysterious effects of sacrificial or other Vedic duties. The *Vārttika* refers to various schools among the adherents of the joint operation of knowledge and of duties (*jñāna-karma-samuccaya*:), some regarding *jñāna* as being the more important, others regarding *karma* as more important, and still others regarding them both as being equally important, thus giving rise to three different schools of *jñāna-karma-samuccaya.* Sureśvara tries to refute all these views by saying that true knowledge and emancipation are one and the same thing, and that it does not in the least require the performance of any kind of Vedic duties. Sureśvara also refutes the doctrine of the joint necessity of *karma* and *jñāna* on the view of those modified dualists, like Bhartṛprapañca, who thought that reality was a unity in differences, so that the doctrine of differences was as true as that of unity, and that, therefore, duties have to be performed even in the emancipated state, because, the differences being also real, the necessity of duties cannot be ignored at any stage of progress, even in the emancipated state, though true knowledge is also necessary for the realization of truth as unity. Sureśvara's refutation of this view is based upon two considerations, viz. that the conception of reality as being both unity and difference is self-contradictory, and that, when the oneness is realized through true knowledge and the sense of otherness and differences is removed, it is not possible that any duties can be performed at that stage; for the performance of duties implies experience of duality and difference.[1]

The second chapter of the *Naiṣkarmya-siddhi* is devoted to the exposition of the nature of self-realization, as won through the proper interpretation of the unity texts of the Upaniṣads by a proper teacher. The experience of the ego and all its associated experiences of attachment, antipathy, etc., vanish with the dawn of true self-knowledge of unity. The notion of ego is a changeful and extraneous

1 See also Prof. Hiriyanna's introduction to his edition of the *Naiṣkarmya-siddhi.*

element, and hence outside the element of pure consciousness. All manifestations of duality are due to the distracting effects of the *antaḥkaraṇa.* When true knowledge dawns, the self together with all that is objectivity in knowledge vanishes. All the illusory appearances are due to the imposition of *ajñāna* on the pure self, which, however, cannot thereby disturb the unperturbed unity of this pure self. It is the *antaḥkaraṇa*, or the intellect, that suffers all modifications in the cognitive operations; the underlying pure consciousness remains undisturbed all the same. Yet this non-self which appears as mind, intellect, and its objects is not a substantive entity like the *prakṛti* of the Sāṃkhya; for its appearance is due merely to ignorance and delusion. This world-appearance is only a product of nescience (*ajñāna*) or false and indescribable illusion on the self, and is no real product of any real substance as the Sāṃkhya holds. Thus it is that the whole of the world-appearance vanishes like the illusory silver in the conch-shell as soon as truth is realized.

In the third chapter Sureśvara discusses the nature of *ajñāna,* its relation with the self, and the manner of its dissolution. There are two entities, the self and the non-self; now the non-self, being itself a product of *ajñāna* (nescience or ignorance), cannot be regarded as its support or object; so the *ajñāna* has for its support and object the pure self or Brahman; the ignorance of the self is also in regard to itself, since there is no other object regarding which ignorance is possible—the entire field of objective appearance being regarded as the product of ignorance itself. It is the ignorance of the real nature of the self that transforms itself into all that is subjective and objective, the intellect and its objects. It is thus clear that according to Sureśvara, unlike Vācaspati Miśra and Maṇḍana, the *avidyā* is based not upon individual persons (*jīva*), but upon the pure intelligence itself. It is this ignorance which, being connected and based upon the pure self, produces the appearances of individual persons and their subjective and objective experiences. This *ajñāna,* as mere ignorance, is experienced in deep dreamless sleep, when all its modifications and appearances shrink within it and it is experienced in itself as pure ignorance, which again in the waking state manifests itself in the whole series of experiences. It is easy to see that this view of the relation of *ajñāna* to pure intelligence is different from the idealism preached by Maṇḍana, as noticed in the previous section. An objection is raised that, if the ego were as much an extraneous product of *ajñāna* as the so-called external objects, then the ego should have appeared not as a subject, but as an object like other external or internal objects (*e.g.,* pleasure, pain, etc.). To this Sureśvara replies that, when the *antaḥkaraṇa* or mind is transformed into the form of the external objects, then, in order to give subjectivity to it, the category of the ego (*ahaṃkāra*) is produced to associate objective experiences with particular subjective centres, and then through the reflection of the pure intelligence by way of this category of the ego the objective experience, as associated with this category of the ego, appears as subjective experience. The category of the ego, being immediately and intimately related to the pure intelligence, itself appears as the knower, and the objectivity of the ego is not apparent, just as in burning wood the fire and that which it burns cannot be separated. It is only when the pure intelligence is reflected through the *ajñāna* product of the category of the ego that the notion of subjectivity applies to it, and all that is associated with it is experienced as the "this," the object, though in reality the ego is itself as much an object as the objects themselves. All this false experience, however, is destroyed in the realization of Brahman, when Vedāntic texts of unity are realized. In the third chapter of the *Naiṣkarmyasiddhi* the central ideas of the other three chapters are recapitulated. In the *Vārttika* Sureśvara discusses the very same problems in a much more elaborate manner, but it is not useful for our present purposes to enter into these details.

PADMAPĀDA (AD 820)

Padmapāda is universally reputed to be a direct disciple of Śaṅkarācārya, and, since the manner of his own salutation to Śaṅkarācārya confirms this tradition, and since no facts are known that can contradict such a view, it may safely be assumed that he was a younger contemporary of Śaṅkarācārya. There are many traditional stories about him and his relations with Śaṅkarācārya; but, since their truth cannot be attested by reliable evidence, it is not possible to pronounce any judgment on them. Only two works are attributed to him, viz. the *Pañca-pādikā*, which is a commentary on Śaṅkara's commentary on the first four *sūtras* of the *Brahma-sūtra* and Śaṅkara's introduction to his commentary known as the *adhyāsa* and the *sambhāvanā-bhāṣya*, and the *Ātma-bodha-vyākhyāna*, called also *Vedānta-sāra*. This *Pañca-pādikā* is one of the most important of the Vedānta works known to us. It was commented on by Prakāśātman (AD 1200) in his *Pañca-pādikā-vivaraṇa.*[1] The *Pañca-pādikā-vivaraṇa* was further commented on by Akhaṇḍānanda (AD 1350), a pupil of Ānandagiri, in his *Tattva-dīpana*. Ānandapūrṇa (AD 1600), who wrote his *Vidyā-sāgarī* commentary on Śrīharṣa's *Khaṇḍana-khaṇḍa-khādya* and also a commentary on the *Mahā-vidyā-viḍambana,* wrote a commentary on the *Pañca-pādikā.*[2] Nṛsiṃhāśrama also wrote a commentary on the *Pañca-pādikā-vivaraṇa,* called the *Pañca-pādikā-vivaraṇa-prakāśikā*, and Śrīkṛṣṇa also wrote one on the *Pañca-pādikā-vivaraṇa.* Aufrecht refers to another commentary by Amalānanda as *Pañca-pādikā-śāstra-darpaṇa*; but this is undoubtedly a mistake for his *Śāstra-darpaṇa,* which is noticed below. Amalānanda was a follower of the Vācaspati line and not of the line of Padmapāda and Prakāśātman. Rāmānanda Sarasvatī, a pupil of Govindānanda, the author of the *Ratna-prabhā* commentary on the *Śaṅkara-bhāṣya,* wrote his *Vivaraṇopanyāsa* (a summary of the main theses of the *Vivaraṇa*) as a commentary on Śaṅkara's *Bhāṣya*; but this was strictly on the lines of the *Pañca-pādikā-vivaraṇa,*

---

1 Prakāśātman also wrote a metrical summary of Śaṅkara's *Bhāṣya* and a work called *Śabda-nirṇaya,* in which he tried to prove the claims of scriptural testimony as valid cognition.

2 As Mr Telang points out in his introduction to the *Mahā-vidyā-viḍambana,* it seems that Ānandapūrṇa lived after Śaṛkara Miśra (AD 1529), as is seen from his criticism of his reading of a passage of the *Khaṇḍana-khaṇḍa-khādya,* p. 586 (Chowkhambā).

though it was not a direct commentary thereon. Vidyāraṇya also wrote a separate monograph, called *Vivaraṇa-prameya-saṃgraha,* in which he interpreted the Vedāntic doctrines on the lines of the *Pañca-pādikā-vivaraṇa.* Of all these the *Vivaraṇopanyāsa* of Rāmānanda Sarasvatī was probably the last important work on the *Vivaraṇa* line; for Rāmānanda's teacher Govindānanda, the pupil of Gopāla Sarasvatī and the pupil's pupil of Śivarāma, refers in his *Ratna-prabhā* commentary to Jagannāthāśrama's commentary on the *Śaṅkara-bhāṣya,* called the *Bhāṣya-dīpikā*, and also to Ānandagiri's commentary as "*vṛddhāḥ,"* p. 5 (Nirṇaya-Sāgara Press, 1904). Jagannātha was the teacher of Nṛsiṃhāśrama; Govindānanda must therefore have lived towards the end of the sixteenth century. Rāmānanda may therefore be placed in the early part of the seventeenth century. Govindānanda himself also in his *Ratna-prabhā* commentary followed the *Vivaraṇa* line of interpretation, and he refers to Prakāśātman with great respect as *Prakāśātma-śrī-caraṇaiḥ* (*Ratna-prabhā*, p. 3).

Padmapāda's method of treatment, as interpreted by Prakāśātman, has been taken in the first and the second volumes of the present work as the guide to the exposition of the Vedānta. It is not therefore necessary that much should be said in separate sections regarding the Vedāntic doctrines of these two great teachers. But still a few words on Padmapāda's philosophy may with advantage be read separately. Padmapāda says that *māyā, avyākṛta*, *prakṛti, agrahaṇa*, *avyakta*, *tamaḥ*, *kāraṇa*, *laya*, *śakti*, *mahāsupti*, *nidrā*, *kṣara* and *ākāśa* are the terms which are used in older literature as synonymous with *avidyā.* It is this entity that obstructs the pure and independently self-revealing nature of Brahman, and thus, standing as the painted canvas (*citra-bhitti*) of ignorance (*avidyā*), deeds (*karma*) and past impressions of knowledge (*pūrva-prajñā-saṃskāra*) produce the individual persons (*jīvatvāpādikā*). Undergoing its peculiar transformations with God as its support, it manifests itself as the two powers of knowledge and activity (*vijñāna-kriyā-śakti-dvayāśraya*) and functions as the doer of all actions and the enjoyer of all experiences (*kartṛtva-bhoktṛtvaikā-*

dhāraḥ). In association with the pure unchangeable light of Brahman it is the complex of these transformations which appears as the immediate ego (*ahaṃkāra*). It is through the association with this ego that the pure self is falsely regarded as the enjoyer of experiences. This transformation is called *antaḥkaraṇa*, *manas, buddhi* and the ego or the ego-feeler (*ahaṃ-pratyayin*) on the side of its cognitive activity, while on the vibratory side of its activity (*spanda-śaktyā*), it is called *prāṇa* or biomotor functions. The association of the ego with the pure *ātman*, like the association of the redness of a *japā* flower with a crystal, is a complex (*granthi*) which manifests the dual characteristics of activity of the *avidyā* stuff and the consciousness of the pure self (*saṃbhinnobhaya-rūpatvāt*).

On the question as to whether *avidyā* has for both support (*āśraya*) and object (*viṣaya*) Brahman Padmapāda's own attitude does not seem to be very clear. He only says that *avidyā* manifests itself in the individual person (*jīva*) by obstructing the real nature of the Brahman as pure self-luminosity and that the Brahman by its limitation (*avaccheda*) through beginningless *avidyā* is the cause of the appcarance of infinite individual persons. But Prakāśātman introduces a long discussion, trying to prove that Brahman is both the support and the object of *avidyā* as against the view of Vācaspati Miśra that *avidyā* has the Brahman as its object and the *jīva* as its support (*āśraya*). This is thus one of the fundamental points of difference between the *Vivaraṇa* line of interpretation and the interpretation of the Vācaspati line. In this Prakāśātman agrees with the view of Sureśvara and his pupil Sarvajñātman, though, as will be noticed, Sarvajñātman draws some nice distinctions which are not noticed by Sureśvara.

Padmapāda draws a distinction between two meanings of falsehood (*mithyā*), viz. falsehood as simple negation (*apahnava-vacana*) and falsehood as the unspeakable and indescribable (*anirvacanīyatā-vacana*). It is probably he who of all the interpreters first described *ajñāna* or *avidyā* as being of a material nature (*jaḍātmikā*) and of the nature of a power (*jaḍātmikā-avidyā-*

śakti), and interpreted Śaṅkara's phrase "*mithyā-jñāna-nimittaḥ*" as meaning that it is this material power of *ajñāna* that is the constitutive or the material cause of the world-appearance. Prakāśātman, however, elaborates the conception further in his attempts to give proofs in support of the view that *avidyā* is something positive (*bhāva-rūpa*). These proofs have been repeatedly given by many other later writers, and have already been dealt with in the first volume of the present work. Padmapāda is also probably the first to attempt an explanation of the process of Vedāntic perception which was later on elaborated by Prakāśātman and later writers, and his views were all collected and systematized in the exposition of the *Vedānta-paribhāṣā* of Dharmarāja Adhvarīndra in the sixteenth century. Describing this process, Padmapāda says that, as a result of the cognitive activity of the ego, the objects with which that is concerned become connected with it, and, as a result of that, certain changes are produced in it, and it is these changes that constitute the subject-object relation of knowledge (*jñātur jñeya-sambandhaḥ*). The *antaḥkaraṇa,* or psychical frame of mind, can lead to the limited expression of the pure consciousness only so far as it is associated with its object. The perceptual experience of immediacy (*aparokṣa*) of objects means nothing more than the expression of the pure consciousness through the changing states of the *antaḥkaraṇa.* The ego thus becomes a perceiver (*pramātṛ*) through its connection with the underlying consciousness. Prakāśātman, however, elaborates it by supposing that the *antaḥkaraṇa* goes out to the objective spatial positions, and assumes the spatial form of the objects perceived. Hence what Padmapāda conceived merely as the change of the *antaḥkaraṇa* states through the varying relation of the *antaḥkaraṇa* with its objects, is interpreted in the definite meaning of this relation as being nothing more than spatial superposition of the *antaḥkaraṇa* on its objects. In inference, however, there is no immediate knowledge, as this is mediated through relations with the reason (*liṅga*). Knowledge however would mean both mediate and immediate knowledge; for it is defined as being the manifestation of the object (*artha-prakāśa*).

On the subject of the causality of Brahman Padmapāda says that that on which the world-appearance is manifested, the Brahman, is the cause of the world. On this point Prakāśātman offers three alternative views, viz. (1) that, like two twisted threads in a rope, *māyā* and Brahman are together the joint cause of the world, (2) that that which has *māyā* as its power is the cause, and (3) that the Brahman which has *māyā* supported on it is the cause of the world, but in all these the ultimate causality rests with Brahman, since *māyā* is dependent thereon. Brahman is *sarvajña* (omniscient) in the sense that it manifests all that is associated with it, and it is the Brahman that through its *māyā* appears as the world of experience. The doctrines of *avaccheda-vāda* and *pratibimba-vāda* explained in the first volume of the present work are also at least as old as Padmapāda's *Pañca-pādikā*, and both Padmapāda and Prakāśātman seem to support the reflection theory (*pratibimba-vāda*), the theory that the *jīva* is but a reflected image of Brahman.[1]

VĀCASPATI MIŚRA (AD 840)

Vācaspati Miśra, the celebrated author of a commentary called *Bhāmatī* on Śaṅkara's commentary, is the author of a *Tattva-samīkṣā,* a commentary on Maṇḍana's *Brahma-siddhi*; he also commented on the *Sāṃkhya-kārikā, Vidhi-viveka*, *Nyāya-vārttika,* and he was the author of a number of other works. In his *Nyāya-sūcīni-bandha* he gives his date as 898 (*vasv-aṅka-vasu-vatsare*), which in all probability has to be understood as of the Vikrama-saṃvat, and consequently he can safely be placed in AD 842. In his commentary called *Bhāmatī* he offers salutation to Mārtaṇḍa-tilaka-svāmin, which has been understood to refer to his teacher. But Amalānanda in commenting thereon rightly points out that this word is a compound of the two names Mārtaṇḍa and Tilakasvāmin,

1 See volume I, pp. 475, 476. These two doctrines were probably present in germinal forms as early as the ninth century. But gradually more and more attention seems to have been paid to them. Appaya Dīkṣita gives a fairly good summary of these two doctrines in the *Parimala,* pp. 335-343, Śri Vāṇi Vilāsa Press, Srirangam, without committing either himself or Vācaspati to any one of these views.

belonging to gods adored with a view to the fruition of one's actions. Tilakasvāmin is referred to in *Yājñavalkya*, I.294 as a god, and the *Mitākṣarā* explains it as being the name of the god Kārttikeya or Skanda. Udayana, however, in his *Nyāya-vārttika-tātparya-pariśuddhi* (p. 9), a commentary on Vācaspati's *Tātparya-ṭīkā*, refers to one Trilocana as being the teacher of Vācaspati, and Vardhamāna in his commentary on it, called *Nyāya-nibandha-prakāśa*, confirms this: Vācaspati himself also refers to Trilocanaguru, whom he followed in interpreting the word *vyavasāya* (*Nyāya-sūtra,* I.1.4) as determinate knowledge (*savikalpa*).[1] It is however interesting to note that in the *Nyāya-kaṇikā* (verse 3) he refers to the author of the *Nyāya-mañjarī* (in all probability Jayanta) as his teacher (*vidyā-taru*).[2] Vācaspati says at the end of his *Bhāmatī* commentary that he wrote that work when the great king Nṛga was reigning. This king, so far as the present writer is aware, has not yet been historically traced. *Bhāmatī* was Vācaspati's last great work; for in the colophon at the end of the *Bhāmatī* he says that he had already written his *Nyāya-kaṇikā*, *Tattva-samīkṣā, Tattva-bindu* and other works on Nyāya, Sāṃkhya and Yoga.

Vācaspati's Vedāntic works are *Bhāmatī* and *Tattva-samīkṣā* (on *Brahma-siddhi*). The last work has not yet been published. Aufrecht, referring to his work, *Tattva-bindu,* says that it is a Vedānta work. This is however a mistake, as the work deals with the *sphoṭa* doctrines of sound, and has nothing to do with Vedānta. In the absence of Vācaspati's *Tattva-samīkṣā*, which has not been published, and manuscripts of which have become extremely scarce, it is difficult to give an entirely satisfactory

---

1 त्रिलोचनगुरून्नीतमार्गानुगमनोन्मुखैः
यथामानं यथावस्तु व्याख्यातम् इदम् ईदृशम्॥
trilocana-gur ūnnīta-mārg ānug amanonmukhaiḥ
yathāmānaṃ yathā-vastu vyākhyātam idam īdṛśam.
—*Nyāya-vārttika-tātparya-ṭīkā,* p. 87. Benares, 1898.

2 अज्ञानतिमिरशमनीं न्यायमञ्जरीं रुचिराम्
प्रसवित्रे प्रभवित्रे विद्यातरवे नमो गुरवे॥
ajñāna-timira-śamanīṃ nyāya-mañjarīṃ rucirām
Prasavitre prabhavitre vidyā-tarave namo gurave.
—*Nyāya-kaṇikā,* introductory verse.

account of the special features of Vācaspati's view of Vedānta. But his *Bhāmatī* commentary is a great work, and it is possible to collect from it some of the main features of his views. As to the method of Vācaspati's commentary, he always tries to explain the text as faithfully as he can, keeping himself in the background and directing his great knowledge of the subject to the elucidation of the problems which directly arise from the texts and to explaining the allusions and contexts of thoughts, objections and ideas of other schools of thought referred to in the text. The *Bhāmatī* commentary on Śaṅkara's *Bhāṣya* is a very important one, and it had a number of important sub-commentaries. The most important and earliest of these is the *Vedānta-kalpa-taru* of Amalānanda (AD 1247-1260), on which Appaya Dīkṣita (about AD 1600) wrote another commentary called *Vedānta-kalpataru-parimala.*[1] The *Vedānta-kalpa-taru* was also commented on by Lakṣmīnṛsiṃha, author of the *Tarka-dīpikā*, son of Koṇḍa Bhaṭṭa and grandson of Raṅgojī Bhaṭṭa, towards the end of the seventeenth century, and this commentary is called *Ābhoga.* The *Ābhoga* commentary is largely inspired by the *Vedānta-kalpa-taru-parimala,* though in many cases it differs from and criticizes it. In addition to these there are also other commentaries on the *Bhāmatī*, such as the *Bhāmatī-tilaka,* the *Bhāmati-vilāsa,* the *Bhāmatī-vyākhyā* by Śrīraṅganātha and another commentary on the *Vedānta-kalpa-taru,* by Vaidyanātha Payaguṇḍa, called the *Vedānta-kalpa- taru-mañjarī.*

Vācaspati defines truth and reality as immediate self-revelation *(sva-prakāśatā)* which is never contradicted *(abādhita)*. Only the pure self can be said to be in this sense ultimately real. He thus

1 Amalānanda also wrote another work, called *Śāstra-darpaṇa,* in which, taking the different topics (*adhikaraṇas*) of the *Brahma-sūtras,* he tried to give a plain and simple general explanation of the whole topic without entering into much discussion on the interpretations of the different *sūtras* on the topic. These general lectures on the *adhikaraṇas* of the *Brahma-sūtras* did not, however, reveal any originality of views on the part of Amalānanda, but were based on Vācaspati's interpretation, and were but reflections of his views, as Amalānanda himself admits in the second verse of the *Śāstra-darpaṇa (Vācaspati-mati-vimbitam ādarśam prārabhe vimalam)*—ŚriVāṇiVilāsa Press, 1913, Srirangam, Madras.

definitely rejects the definition of reality as the participation of the class-concept of being, as the Naiyāyikas hold, or capacity of doing work *(artha-kriyā-kāritva),* as the Buddhists hold. He admits two kinds of *ajñāna*, as psychological and as forming the material cause of the mind and the inner psychical nature of man or as the material world outside. Thus he says in his commentary on the *Śaṅkara-bhāṣya*, I.111.30, that at the time of the great dissolution (*mahā-pralaya*) all products of *avidyā*, such as the psychical frame *(antaḥkaraṇa),* cease to have any functions of their own, but are not on account of that destroyed; they are at that time merged in the indescribable *avidyā*, their root cause, and abide there as potential capacities *(sūkṣmeṇa śakti-rūpeṇa)* together with the wrong impressions and psychological tendencies of illusion. When the state of *mahā-pralaya* is at an end, moved by the will of God, they come out like the limbs of a tortoise or like the rejuvenation during rains of the bodies of frogs which have remained inert and lifeless all the year round, and then, being associated with their proper tendencies and impressions, they assume their particular names and forms as of old before the *mahā-pralaya.* Though all creation takes place through God's will, yet God's will is also determined by the conditions of *karma* and the impressions produced by it. This statement proves that he believed in *avidyā* as an objective entity of an indescribable nature *(anirvācyāavidyā),* into which all world-products disappear during the *mahā-pralaya* and out of which they reappear in the end and become associated with psychological ignorance and wrong impressions which had also disappeared into it at the time of the *mahā-pralaya. Avidyā* thus described resembles very much the *prakṛti* of Yoga, into which all the world-products disappear during a *mahā-pralaya* together with the fivefold *avidyā* and their impressions, which at the time of creation become associated with their own proper *buddhis.* In the very adoration hymn of the *Bhāmatī* Vācaspati speaks of *avidyā* being twofold (*avidyā-dvitaya),* and says that all appearances originate from Brahman in association with or with the accessory cause *(sahakāri-kāraṇa)* of the two *avidyās (avidyā-dvitaya-sacivasya)*. In explaining this passage Amalānanda points out that this refers to two *avidyās*, one as a beginningless positive entity and the other as the preceding series of beginningless false impressions *(anyāpūrvāpūrva-bhrama-saṃskārah)*. There is thus one aspect of *avidyā* which forms the material stuff of the appearances; but the appearances could not have been appearances if they were not illusorily identified with the immediate and pure self-revelation *(sva-prakāśācit)*. Each individual person *(jīva)* confuses and misapprehends his psychical frame and mental experiences as intelligent in themselves, and it is by such an illusory confusion that these psychical states attain any meaning as appearances; for otherwise these appearances could not have been expressed at all. But how does the person come in, since the concept of a person itself presupposes the very confusion which it is supposed to make? To this Vācaspati's reply is that the appearance of the personality is due to a previous false confusion, and that to another previous false confusion (cf. Maṇḍana). So each false confusion has for its cause a previous false confusion, and that another false confusion and so on in a beginningless series. It is only through such a beginningless series of confusions that all the later states of confusion are to be explained. Thus on the one hand the *avidyā* operates in the individual person, the *jīva*, as its locus or support *(āśraya)*, and on the other hand it has the Brahman or pure self-revealing intelligence as its object *(viṣaya)*, which it obscures and through which it makes its false appearances to be expressed, thereby giving them a false semblance of reality, whereby all the world-appearances seem to be manifestations of reality.[1] It is easy to see how this view differs from the view of the *Saṃkṣepa-śārīraka* of Sarvajñātma Muni; for in the opinion of the latter, the Brahman is both the support *(āśraya)* and the object *(viṣaya)* of *ajñāna*, which means that the illusion does not belong to the individual person, but is of a transcendental character. It is not the individual person as such *(jīva)*, but the pure intelligence

1 It is in the latter view that Vācaspati differs from Maṇḍana, on whose *Brahma-siddhi* he wrote his *Tattva-samīkṣā*.

that shines through each individual person *(pratyak-cit),* that is both obscured and diversified into a manifold of appearances in a transcendental manner. In Vācaspati's view, however, the illusion is a psychological one for which the individual person is responsible, and it is caused through a beginningless chain of illusions or confusions, where each succeeding illusory experience is explained by a previous illusory mode of experience, and that by another and so on. The content of the illusory experiences is also derived from the indescribable *avidyā,* which is made to appear as real by their association with Brahman, the ultimately real and self-revealing Being. The illusory appearances, as they are, cannot be described as being existent or non-existent; for, though they seem to have their individual existences, they are always negated by other existences, and none of them have that kind of reality which can be said to defy all negation and contradiction; and it is only such uncontradicted self-revelation that can be said to be ultimately real. The unreality of world-appearances consists in the fact that they are negated and contradicted; and yet they are not absolutely non-existent like a hare's horn, since, had they been so, they could not have been experienced at all. So in spite of the fact that the appearances are made out of *avidyā,* they have so far as any modified existence can be ascribed to them, the Brahman as their underlying ground, and it is for this reason that Brahman is to be regarded as the ultimate cause of the world. As soon as this Brahman is realized, the appearances vanish; for the root of all appearances is their illusory confusion with reality, the Brahman. In the *Bhāmatī* commentary on Śaṅkara's commentary, II.111.28, Vācaspati points out that according to the Śaṅkara Vedānta the objects of knowledge are themselves indescribable in their nature *(anirvacanīyaṃ nīlādi*) and not mere mental ideas *(na hi brahma-vādino nīlādy-ākārāṃ vittim abhyupagacchanti kintu anirvacanīyaṃ nīlādi).* The external objects therefore are already existent outside of the perceiver, only their nature and stuff are indescribable and irrational (*anirvācya*). Our perceptions therefore refer always to such objects as their excitants or producers, and they are not of the nature of pure sensations or ideas generated from within, without the aid of such external objects.

SARVAJÑĀTMA MUNI (AD 900)

Sarvajñātma Muni was a disciple of Sureśvarācārya, the direct disciple of Śaṅkara, to whom at the beginning of his work *Saṃkṣepa-śārīraka* he offers salutation by the name Deveśvara, the word being a synonym of the word *sura* in Sureśvara. The identification of Deveśvara with Sureśvara is made by Rāma Tīrtha, the commentator on the *Saṃkṣepa-śārīraka*, and this identification does not come into conflict with anything else that is known about Sarvajñātma Muni either from the text of his work or from other references to him in general. It is said that his other name was Nityabodhācārya. The exact date of neither Sureśvara nor Sarvajñātma can be definitely determined. Mr Pandit in his introduction to the *Gauḍavaho* expresses the view that, since Bhavabhūti was a pupil of Kumārila, Kumārila must have lived in the middle of the seventh century, and, since Śaṅkara was a contemporary of Kumārila (on the testimony of the *Śaṅkara-dig-vijaya*), he must have lived either in the seventh century or in the first half of the eighth century. In the first volume of the present work Śaṅkara was placed between AD 780-820. The arguments of Mr Pandit do not raise any new point for consideration. His theory that Bhavabhūti was a pupil of Kumārila is based on the evidence of two manuscripts, where, at the end of an act of the *Mālatī-Mādhava*, it is said that the work was written by a pupil of Kumārila. This evidence, as I have noticed elsewhere, is very slender. The tradition that Śaṅkara was a contemporary of Kumārila, based as it is only on the testimony of the *Śaṅkara-dig-vijaya*, cannot be seriously believed. All that can be said is that Kumārila probably lived not long before Śaṅkara, if one can infer this from the fact that Śaṅkara does not make any reference to Kumārila. Hence there seems to be no reason why the traditionally accepted view that Śaṅkara was born in

Saṃvat 844, or AD 788, or Kali age 3889, should be given up.[1] Taking the approximate date of Śaṅkara's death to be about AD 820 and taking into consideration that Sureśvara, the teacher of Sarvajñātman, occupied his high pontifical position for a long time, the supposition that Sarvajñātman lived in AD 900 may not be very far wrong. Moreover, this does not come into conflict with the fact that Vācaspati, who probably wrote his earlier work the *Nyāya-sūcī-nibandha* in AD 842, also wrote his commentary on Maṇḍana's *Brahma-siddhi* when Sureśvara was occupying the pontifical position.

Sarvajñātma Muni was thus probably a younger contemporary of Vācaspati Miśra. In his *Saṃkṣepa-śārīraka* he tries to describe the fundamental problems of the Vedānta philosophy, as explained by Śaṅkara. This work, which is probably the only work of his that is known to us, is divided into four chapters, written in verses of different metres. It contains, in the first chapter 563 verses, in the second 248, in the third 365 and in the fourth 63. In the first chapter of the work he maintains that pure Brahman is the ultimate cause of everything through the instrumentality (*dvāra*) of *ajñāna.* The *ajñāna*, which rests on (*āśraya*) the pure self and operates on it as its object (*viṣaya*), covers its real nature (*ācchādya*) and creates delusory appearances (*vikṣipati*), thereby producing the threefold appearances of God (Īśvara), soul (*jīva*) and the world. This *ajñāna* has no independent existence, and its effects are seen only through the pure self (*cid-ātman*) as its ground and object, and its creations are all false. The pure self is directly perceived in the state of dreamless sleep as being of the nature of pure bliss and happiness without the slightest touch of sorrow; and pure bliss can only be defined as that which is the ultimate end and not under any circumstances a means to anything else; such is also the pure self, which cannot be regarded as being a means to anything else; moreover, there is the fact that everyone always desires his self as the ultimate object of attainment which he loves above anything else. Such an infinite love and such an ultimate end cannot be

---

1 See *Ārya-vidyā-sudhā-kara,* pp. 226, 227.

this limited self, which is referred to as the agent of our ordinary actions and the sufferer in the daily concerns of life. The intuitive perception of the seers of the Upaniṣads also confirms the truth of the self as pure bliss and the infinite. The illusory impositions on the other hand are limited appearances of the subject and the object which merely contribute to the possibility of false attribution and cannot therefore be real (*navāstavaṃ tat*). When the Brahman is associated with *ajñāna* there are two false entities, viz. the *ajñāna* and the Brahman as associated with the *ajñāna*; but this does not imply that the pure Brahman, which underlies all these false associations, is itself also false, since this might lead to the criticism that, everything being false, there is no reality at all, as some of the Buddhists contend. A distinction is drawn here between *ādhāra* and *adhiṣṭhāna*. The pure Brahman that underlies all appearances is the true *adhiṣṭhāna* (ground), while the Brahman as modified by the false *ajñāna* is a false *ādhāra* or a false object to which the false appearances directly refer. All illusory appearances are similarly experienced. Thus in the experience "I perceive this piece of silver" (in the case of the false appearance of a piece of conch-shell as silver) the silvery character or the false appearance of the silver is associated with the "this" element before the perceiver, and the "this" element in its turn, as the false object, becomes associated with the false silver as the "this silver." But, though the objectivity of the false silver as the "this" before the perceiver is false, the "this" of the true object of the conch-shell is not false. It is the above kind of double imposition of the false appearance on the object and of the false object on the false appearance that is known as *parasparādhyāsa*. It is only the false object that appears in the illusory appearance and the real object lies untouched. The inner psychical frame (*antaḥkaraṇa*) to a certain extent on account of its translucent character resembles pure Brahman, and on account of this similarity it is often mistaken for the pure self and the pure self is mistaken for the *antaḥkaraṇa*. It may be contended that there could be no *antaḥkaraṇa* without the illusory imposition, and so it could not itself explain the nature of illusion. The reply given to such an objection is that the illusory imposition and its consequences are beginningless and there is no point of time to which one could assign its beginning. Hence, though the present illusion may be said to have taken its start with the *antaḥkaraṇa*, the *antaḥkaraṇa* is itself the product of a previous imposition, and that of a previous *antaḥkaraṇa,* and so on without a beginning. Just as in the illusion of the silver in the conch-shell, though there is the piece of conch-shell actually existing, yet it is not separately seen, and all that is seen to exist is the unreal silver, so the real Brahman exists as the ground, though the world during the time of its appearance is felt to be the only existing thing and the Brahman is not felt to be existent separately from it. Yet this *ajñāna* has no real existence and exists only for the ignorant. It can only be removed when the true knowledge of Brahman dawns, and it is only through the testimony of the Upaniṣads that this knowledge can dawn; for there is no other means of insight into the nature of Brahman. Truth again is defined not as that which is amenable to proof, but as that which can be independently and directly felt. The *ajñāna*, again, is defined as being positive in its nature (*bhāva-rūpam*) and, though it rests on the pure Brahman, yet, like butter in contact with fire, it also at its touch under certain circumstances melts away. The positive character of *ajñāna* is felt in the world in its materiality and in ourselves as our ignorance. The real ground cause, however, according to the testimony of the Upaniṣads, is the pure Brahman, and the *ajñāna* is only the instrument or the means by which it can become the cause of all appearances; but, *AJÑĀNA* not being itself in any way the material cause of the world, Sarvajñātman strongly holds that Brahman in association and jointly with *ajñāna* cannot be regarded as the material cause of the world. The *ajñāna* is only a secondary means, without which the transformation of appearances is indeed not possible, but which has no share in the ultimate cause that underlies them. He definitely denies that Brahman could be proved by any inference to the effect that that which is the cause of the production, existence and dissolution of the world is Brahman, since the nature of Brahman can be understood only by the testimony of the scriptures. He indulges in long discussions in order to show how the Upaniṣads can lead to a direct and immediate apprehension of reality as Brahman.

The second chapter of the book is devoted mainly to the further elucidation of these doctrines. In that chapter Sarvajñātma Muni tries to show the difference of the Vedānta view from the Buddhist, which difference lies mainly in the fact that, in spite of the doctrine of illusion, the Vedānta admits the ultimate reality to be Brahman, which is not admitted by the Buddhists. He also shows how the experiences of waking life may be compared with those of dreams. He then tries to show that neither perception nor other means of proof can prove the reality of the world-appearance and criticizes the philosophic views of the Sāṃkhya, Nyāya and other systems. He further clarifies his doctrine of the relation of Brahman to *ajñāna* and points out that the association of *ajñāna* is not with the one pure Brahman, nor with individual souls, but with the pure light of Brahman, which shines as the basis and ground of individual souls (*pratyaktva*); for it is only in connection with this that the *ajñāna* appears and is perceived. When with the dawn of right knowledge pure Brahman as one is realized, the *ajñāna* is not felt. It is only in the light of Brahman as underlying the individual souls that the *ajñāna* is perceived, as when one says, "I do not know what you say"; so it is neither the individual soul nor the pure one which is Brahman, but the pure light as it reveals itself through each and every individual soul.[1] The true light of Brahman is always there, and emancipation means nothing more than the destruction of the *ajñāna*. In the third chapter Sarvajñātman describes the ways (*sādhana*) by which one should try to destroy this *ajñāna* and prepare oneself for this result and for the final Brahma knowledge.

---

1 नाज्ञानम् अद्वयसम् आश्रयम् इष्टम् एवं नाद्वैतवस्तुविषयं निशितेक्षणानाम्।
नानन्दनित्यविषयाश्रयम् इष्टम् एतत् प्रत्यक्त्वमात्रविषयाश्रयतानुभूतेः॥
Nājñānam advayasam āśrayam iṣṭam evaṃ
nādvaita-vastu-viṣayaṃ niśitekṣaṇānām
nānanda-nitya-viṣayāśrayam iṣṭam etat
pratyaktva-mātra-viṣayāśrayatānubhūteḥ. —Saṃkṣepa-śārīraka, II.211.

In the last chapter he describes the nature of emancipation and the attainment of Brahmahood.

The *Saṃkṣepa-śārīraka* was commented upon by a number of distinguished writers, none of whom seem to be very old. Thus Nṛsiṃhāśrama wrote a commentary called *Tattva-bodhinī,* Puruṣottama Dīkṣita wrote another called *Subodhinī*, Rāghavānanda another called *Vidyāmṛta-varṣiṇī,* Viśvadeva another called *Siddhānta-dīpa,* on which Rāma Tīrtha, pupil of Kṛṣṇatīrtha, based his commentary *Anvayārtha-prakāśikā.* Madhusūdana Sarasvatī also wrote another commentary, called *Saṃkṣepa-śāriraka-sāra-saṃgraha.*

ĀNANDABODHA YATI

Ānandabodha is a great name in the school of Śaṅkara Vedānta. He lived probably in the eleventh or the twelfth century.[1] He refers to Vācaspati's *Tattva-samīkṣā* and criticizes, but without mentioning his name, Sarvajñātman's view of the interpretation of the nature of self as pure bliss. He wrote at least three works on Śaṅkara Vedānta, viz. *Nyāya-makaranda*, *Nyāya-dīpāvalī* and *Pramāṇa-mālā.* Of these the *Nyāya-makaranda* was commented upon by Citsukha and his pupil Sukhaprakāśa in works called *Nyāya-makaranda-ṭīkā* and *Nyāya-makaranda-vivecanī.* Sukhaprakāśa also wrote a commentary on the *Nyāya-dīpāvalī*, called *Nyāya-dīpāvalī-tātparya-ṭīkā.* Anubhūtisvarūpa Ācārya (late thirteenth century), the teacher of Ānandajñāna, also wrote commentaries on all the three works of Ānandabodha. Ānandabodha does not pretend to have made any original contribution and says that he collected his materials from other works which existed in his time.[2] He starts his *Nyāya-makaranda* with the thesis that the apparent difference of different selves is false, since not only do the Upaniṣads hold

---

1 Mr Tripathi in his introduction to Ānandajñāna's *Tarka-saṃgraha* gives Ānandabodha's date as AD 1200.

2 नानानिबन्धकुसुमप्रभवावदात न्यायापदेशमकरन्दकदम्ब एष
Nānā-nibandha-kusuma-prabhavāvadāta-
nyāyāpadeśa-makaranda-kadamba eṣa. —*Nyāya-makaranda,* p. 359.

this doctrine, but it is also intelligible on grounds of reason that the apparent multiplicity of selves can be explained on an imaginary supposition of diversity (*kālpanika-puruṣa-bheda*), even though in reality there is but one soul. Arguing on the fact that even the illusory supposition of an imaginary diversity may explain all appearances of diversity, Ānandabodha tries to refute the argument of the *Sāṃkhya-kārikā* that the diversity of souls is proved by the fact that with the birth and death of some there is not birth or death of others. Having refuted the plurality of subjects in his own way, he turns to the refutation of plurality of objects. He holds that difference (*bheda*) cannot be perceived by sense-perception, since difference cannot be perceived without perceiving both the object and all else from which it differs. It cannot be said that first the object is perceived and then the difference; for perception will naturally cease with awareness of its object, and there is no way in which it can operate for the comprehension of difference; neither can it be held that the comprehension of difference can in any way be regarded as simultaneous with the perception of the sensibles. Nor is it possible that, when two sensibles are perceived at two different points of time, there could be any way in which their difference could be perceived; for the two sensibles cannot be perceived at one and the same time. It cannot, again, be said that the perception of any sensible, say blue, involves with it the perception of all that is not blue, the yellow, the white, the red, etc. ; for in that case the perception of any sensible would involve the perception of all other objects of the world. The negation of the difference of an entity does not mean anything more than the actual position of it. It is not, however, right to hold that all positive entities are of the nature of differences; for this is directly against all experience. If differences are perceived as positive entities, then to comprehend their differences further differences would be required, and there would thus be a vicious infinite. Moreover, differences, being negative in their nature, cannot be regarded as capable of being perceived as positive sensibles. Whether difference is taken as a subject or a predicate in the form "the difference of the jug from the pillar," or "the jug is different from the pillar," in either case there is comprehension of an earlier and more primitive difference between the two objects, on the basis of which the category of difference is realized.

Ānandabodha then discusses the different theories of error held by the Nyāya, Mīmāṃsā, Buddhism, etc. and supports the *anirvacanīya* theory of error.[1] In this connection he records his view as to why nescience (*avidyā*) has to be admitted as the cause of world-appearance. He points out that the variety and multiplicity of world-appearance cannot be explained without the assumption of a cause which forms its substance. Since this world-appearance is unreal, it cannot come out of a substance that is real, nor can it come out of something absolutely non-existent and unreal, since such a thing evidently could not be the cause of anything; hence, since the cause of world-appearance cannot be either real or unreal, it must have for its cause something which is neither real nor unreal, and the neither-real-nor-unreal entity is *avidyā.*[2]

He next proceeds to prove the doctrine that the self is of the nature of pure consciousness (*ātmanaḥ saṃvid-rūpatva*). This he does, firstly, by stating the view that awareness in revealing itself reveals also immediately its objects, and secondly, by arguing that even though objects of awareness may be varying, there is still the unvarying consciousness which continues the same even when there is no object. If there were only the series of awarenesses arising and ceasing and if there were constant and persistent awarenesses abiding all the time, how could one note the difference between one awareness and another, between blue and yellow? Referring to *avidyā,* he justifies the view of its being supported on Brahman, because *avidyā,* being indefinable in its nature, i.e. being neither negative nor positive, there can be no objection to its being regarded as supported on Brahman. Moreover, Brahman can only be regarded as omniscient in its association with *avidyā,* since all relations are of the nature of *avidyā* and there cannot be any

1 See the first volume of the present work, ch. X, p. 485.

2 *Nyāya-makaranda,* pp. 122, 123.

omniscience without a knowledge of the relations. In his *Nyāya-dīpāvalī* he tries by inference to prove the falsity of the world-appearance on the analogy of the falsity of the illusory silver. His method of treatment is more or less the same as the treatment in the *Advaita-siddhi* of Madhusūdana Sarasvatī at a much later period. There is practically nothing new in his *Pramāṇa-mālā.* It is a small work of about twenty-five pages, and one can recognize here the arguments of the *Nyāya-makaranda* in a somewhat different form and with a different emphasis. Most of Ānandabodha's arguments were borrowed by the later writers of the Vedānta school. Vyāsatīrtha of the Mādhva school of Vedānta collected most of the standard Vedānta arguments from Ānandabodha and Prakāśātman for refutation in his *Nyāyāmṛta,* and these were again refuted by Madhusūdana's great work, the *Advaita-siddhi,* and these refuted in their turn in Rāma Tīrtha's *Nyāyāmṛta-taraṅgiṇī.* The history of this controversy will be dealt with in the third volume of the present work.

MAHĀ-VIDYĀ AND THE DEVELOPMENT OF LOGICAL FORMALISM

The Buddhists had taken to the use of the dialectic method of logical discussions even from the time of Nāgārjuna. But this was by no means limited to the Buddhists. The Naiyāyikas had also adopted these methods, as is well illustrated by the writings of Vātsyāyana, Uddyotakara, Vācaspati, Udayana and others. Śaṅkara himself had utilized this method in the refutation of Buddhistic, Jaina, Vaiśeṣika and other systems of Indian philosophy. But, though these writers largely adopted the dialectic methods of Nāgārjuna's arguments, there seems to be little attempt on their part to develop the purely formal side of Nāgārjuna's logical arguments, viz. the attempt to formulate definitions with the strictest formal rigour and to offer criticisms with that overemphasis of formalism and scholasticism which attained their culmination in the writings of later Nyāya writers such as Raghunātha Śiromaṇi, Jagadīśa Bhaṭṭācārya, Mathurānātha Bhaṭṭācārya and Gadādhara Bhaṭṭācārya. It is generally believed that such methods of overstrained logical formalism were first started by Gaṅgeśa Upādhyāya of Mithilā early in the thirteenth century. But the truth seems to be that this method of logical formalism was steadily growing among certain writers from as early as the tenth and eleventh centuries. One notable instance of it is the formulation of the *mahā-vidyā* modes of syllogism by Kulārka Paṇḍita in the eleventh century. There is practically no reference to this *mahā-vidyā* syllogism earlier than Śrīharṣa (AD 1187).[1] References to this syllogism are found in the writings of Citsukha Ācārya (AD 1220), Amalānanda, called also Vyāsāśrama (AD 1247), Ānandajñāna (AD 1260), Veṅkaṭa (AD 1369), Śeṣa Śārṅgadhara (AD 1450) and others.[2] The *mahā-vidyā* syllogisms were started probably sometime in the eleventh century, and they continued to be referred to or refuted by writers till the fifteenth century, though it is curious to notice that they were not mentioned by Gaṅgeśa or any of his followers, such as Raghunātha, Jagadīśa and others, in their discussions on the nature of *kevalānvayi* types of inference.

In all probability *mahā-vidyā* syllogisms were first started by Kulārka Paṇḍita in his *Daśa-ślokī-mahā-vidyā-sūtra* containing sixteen different types of definitions for sixteen different types of *mahā-vidyā* syllogisms. Assuming that Kulārka Paṇḍita, the founder of *mahā-vidyā* syllogisms, flourished in the 131eleventh century, it may well be suggested that many other writers had written on

---

1 *Gandhe gandhāntara-prasañjikā na ca yuktir asti; tadastitve vā kā no hāniḥ;tasyā apy asmābhiḥ khaṇḍanīyatvāt.*
—Śrīharṣa's *Khaṇḍana-khaṇḍa-khādya,* p. 1181, Chowkhambā edition.

2 *Athavā ayam ghaṭaḥ etadghaṭānyatve sati vedyatvānadhikaraṇānya-padār-hatvāt paṭavad ity-ādimahāvidyā-prayogair api vedyatva-siddhir apy ūhanīyā.*—Citsukha Ācārya's *Tattva-pradipikā,* p. 13, also p. 304. The commentator Pratyag-rūpa-bhagavān mentions Kulārka Paṇḍita by name, *evaṃ sarvā mahavidyās tacchāyā vānye prayogāḥ khaṇḍanīyā iti.*—Amalānanda's *Vedānta-kalpa-taru,* p. 304 (Benares, 1895). *Sarvāsv eva mahāvidyāsu,* etc.—Ānandajñāna's *Tarka-saṃgraha,* p. 22. Also Veṅkaṭa's *Nyāya-pariśuddhi,* pp. 125, 126, 273-276, etc., and *Tattva-muktā-kalāpa* with *Sarvārtha-siddhi,* pp. 478, 485, 486-491. Mr M. R. Telang has collected all the above references to *mahā-vidyā* in his introduction to the *Mahā-vidyā-viḍambana,* Gaekwad's Oriental Series, Baroda, 1920.

this subject before Vādīndra refuted them in the first quarter of the thirteenth century. Not only does Vādīndra refer to the arguments of previous writers in support of *mahā-vidyā* and in refutation of it in his *Mahā-vidyā-viḍambana,* but Bhuvanasundara Sūri also in his commentary on the *Mahā-vidyā-viḍambana* refers to other critics of *mahā-vidyā.* Recently two different commentaries have been discovered on *mahā-vidyā*, by Puruṣottamavana and Pūrṇaprajña. Veṅkaṭa in his *Nyāya-pariśuddhi* refers to the *Mahā-vidyā*, the *Māna-manohara* and the *Pramāṇa-mañjarī,* and Śrīnivāsa in his commentary *Nyāya-sāra* on the *Nyāya-pariśuddhi* describes them as works which deal with roundabout syllogisms (*vakrānumāna*).[1] This shows that for four or five centuries *mahā-vidyā* syllogisms were in certain quarters supported and refuted from the eleventh century to the sixteenth century.

It is well known that the great Mīmāṃsā writers, such as Kumārila Bhaṭṭa and his followers, believed in the doctrine of the eternity of sounds, while the followers of the Nyāya and Vaiśeṣika, called also Yaugācāryas, regarded sound as non-eternal (*anitya*). *Mahā-vidyā* modes were special modes of syllogism, invented probably by Kulārka Paṇḍita for refuting the Mīmāṃsā arguments of the eternity of sounds and proving the non-eternity of sounds. If these modes of syllogism could be regarded as valid, they would also have other kinds of application for the proving or disproving of other theories and doctrines. The special feature of the *mahā-vidyā* syllogisms consisted in their attempt to prove a thesis by the *kevalānvayi* method. Ordinarily concomitance (*vyāpti*) consists in the existence of the reason (*hetu*) in association with the probandum and its non-existence in all places where the probandum is absent (*sādhyābhāvavad-avṛttitvam*). But the *kevalānvayi* form of inference which is admitted by the Naiyāyikas applies to those cases where the probandum is so universal that there is no case where it is absent, and consequently it cannot have a reason (*hetu*) whose concomitance with it can be determined by its non-existence in all cases where the probandum is absent and its

1 See M. R. Telang's introduction to the *Mahā-vidyā-viḍambana.*

existence in all cases where the probandum is present. Thus in the proposition, "This is describable or nameable (*idam abhidheyam*) because it is knowable (*prameyatvāt*)," both the probandum and the reason are so universal that there is no case where their concomitance can be tested by negative instances. *Mahā-vidyā* syllogisms were forms of *kevalānvayi* inference of this type, and there were sixteen different varieties of it which had this advantage associated with them, that, they being *kevalānvayi* forms of syllogism, it was not easy to criticize them by pointing out defects or lapses of concomitance of the reason and the probandum, as no negative instances are available in their case. In order to make it possible that a *kevalānvayi* form of syllogism should be applicable for affirming the non-eternity of sound, Kulārka tried to formulate propositions in sixteen different ways so that on *kevalānvayi* lines such an affirmation might be made about a subject that by virtue of it the non-eternity of sound should follow necessarily as the only consequence, other possible alternatives being ruled out. It is this indirect approach of inference that has been by the critics of *mahā-vidyā* styled roundabout syllogism. Thus *mahā-vidyā* has been defined as that method of syllogism by which a specific probandum which it is desired to prove by the joint method of agreement and difference (3, *anvaya-vyatireki-sādhya-viśeṣaṃ vādy-abhimatam sādhayati*) is proved by the necessary implication of the existence of a particular probandum in a particular subject (2, *pakṣe vyāpaka-pratītya-paryavasāna-balāt*), affirmed by the existence of *hetu* in the subject on *kevalānvayi* lines (1, *kevalān-vayini vyāpake pravartamāno hetuḥ*). In other words, a reason which exists in a probandum inseparably abiding in a subject (*pakṣa*) without failure (proposition 1) proves (*sādhayati*), by virtue of the fact, that such an unfailing existence of that probandum in that subject in that way is only possible under one supposition (proposition 2), namely, the affirmation of another probandum in another subject (*e.g.*, the affirmation of the probandum "noneternity" to the subject "sound"), which is generally sought to be proved by the direct method of agreement and difference (proposition 3). This may be understood by following a typical *mahā-vidyā* syllogism. Thus it is said that by reason of knowability (*meyatva*) as such the self, dissociated from the relations of all eternal and non-eternal qualities of all other objects excepting sound, is related to a non-eternal entity (*ātmā śabdetarānitya-nitya-yavṛttitvānadhikaraṇānitya-vṛtti-dharmavān meyatvād ghaṭavat*). Now by the qualifying adjunct of "self" the self is dissociated from all qualities that it shares with all other eternal and non-eternal objects excepting sound, and the consequence is that it is left only with some kind of non-eternal quality in relation with sound, as this was left out of consideration in the qualifying adjunct, which did not take sound within its purview. Since many relations are also on the Nyāya view treated as qualities, such a non-eternal relation of the self to sound may be their mutual difference or their mutual negation (*anyonyābhāva*). Now, if the self, which is incontestably admitted to be eternal, has such a non-eternal quality or relation to sound, then this can only be under one supposition, viz. that sound is non-eternal. But, since all other non-eternal relations that the self may have to other non-eternal objects, and all other eternal relations that it may have to other eternal objects, and all other such relations that it may have to all eternal and non-eternal objects jointly, except sound, have already been taken out of consideration by the qualifying phrase, the inseparable and unfailing non-eternal quality that the self may have, in the absence of any negative instances, is in relation to sound; but, if it has a non-eternal quality in relation to sound, then this can be so only under one supposition, viz. that sound is itself non-eternal; for the self is incontestably known as eternal. This indirect and roundabout method of syllogism is known as *mahā-vidyā*. It is needless to multiply examples to illustrate all the sixteen types of propositions of *mahā-vidyā* syllogism, as they are all formed on the same principle with slight variations.

Vādīndra in his *Mahā-vidyā-viḍambana* refuted these types of syllogism as false, and it is not known that anyone else tried to revive them by refuting Vādīndra's criticisms. Vādīndra styles himself in the colophon at the end of the first chapter of his *Mahā-vidyā-viḍambana*

"*Hara-kiṅkara-nyāyācārya-parama-paṇḍita-bhaṭṭa-vādīndra,*" and in the concluding verse of his work refers to Yogīśvara as his preceptor. The above epithets of *Hara-kiṅkara*, *nyāyācārya*, etc. do not show however what his real name was. Mr. Telang points out in his introduction to the *Mahā-vidyā-viḍambana* that his pupil Bhaṭṭa Rāghava in his commentary on Bhāsarvajña's *Nyāya-sāra,* called *Nyāya-sāra-vicāra*, refers to him by the name Mahādeva. Vādīndra's real name, then, was Mahādeva, and the rest of the epithets were his titles. Bhaṭṭa Rāghava says that the name of Vādīndra's father was Sāraṅga. Bhaṭṭa Rāghava gives his own date in the Śaka era. The sentence however is liable to two different constructions, giving us two different dates, viz. AD 1252 and 1352. But, judging from the fact that Vādīndra was a religious counsellor of King Śrīsiṃha (also called Śiṅghana), who reigned in Devagiri AD 1210-1247, and that in all probability he lived before Veṅkaṭa (AD 1267-1369), who refers to his *Mahā-vidyā-viḍambana,* Mr. Telang suggests that we should take AD 1252 to be the date of Bhaṭṭa Rāghava; and, since he was a pupil of Vādīndra, one may deduct about 27 years from his date and fix Vādīndra's date as AD 1225. Mr Telang points out that such a date would agree with the view that he was a religious counsellor of King Śrīsiṃha. Vādīndra refers to Udayana (AD 984) and Śivāditya Miśra (AD 975-1025). Mr. Telang also refers to two other works of Vādīndra, viz. *Rasa-sāra* and *Kaṇāda-sūtra-nibandha,* and argues from allusions contained in Vādīndra's *Mahā-vidyā-viḍambana* that he must have written other works in refutation of *mahā-vidyā.* Vādīndra's *Mahā-vidyā-viḍambana* consists of three chapters. In the first chapter he gives an exposition of the *mahā-vidyā* syllogisms; the second and third chapters are devoted to the refutation of these syllogisms. Vādīndra's *Mahā-vidyā-viḍambana* has two commentaries, one called *Mahā-vidyā-viḍambana-vyākhyāna*, by Ānandapūrṇa (AD 1600), and the other, called *Vyākhyāna-dīpikā,* by Bhuvanasundara Sūri (AD 1400). In addition to these Bhuvanasundara Sūri also wrote a small work called the *Laghu-mahā-vidyā-viḍambana* and a commentary, *Mahā-vidyā-vivaraṇa-ṭippaṇa,* on a *Mahā-vidyā-daśaślokī-vivaraṇa* by an unknown author.

The main points of Vādīndra's criticisms may briefly be stated as follows: He says that it is not possible that there should be a proper reason (*hetu*) which has no negative instances (*kevalānvayi-hetor eva nirvaktum aśakyatvāt*). It is difficult to prove that any particular quality should exist everywhere and that there should not be any instance or case where it does not occur. In the third chapter he shows that not only is it not possible to have *kevalānvayi hetus*, but that even in arguments on the basis of such *kevalānvayi hetu* there would be great scope for fallacies of self-contradiction (*sva-vyāghāta*) and fallacies of illicit distribution of the middle term (*anaikāntikatva*) and the like. He also shows how all these fallacies apply to all the *mahā-vidyā* syllogisms invented by Kulārka Paṇḍita. It is needless for our present purposes to enter into any elaborate logical discussion of Vādīndra; for the present digression on *mahā-vidyā* syllogisms is introduced here only to show that scholastic logicisms were not first introduced by Śrīharṣa, but had already come into fashion a few centuries before him, though Śrīharṣa was undoubtedly the most prominent of those who sought to apply these scholastic methods in philosophy.

It will thus be seen that the fashion of emphasizing the employment of logical formalism as a method in philosophy was inherited by the Naiyāyikas and Vedāntists alike from Buddhists like Nāgārjuna, Āryadeva and others in the third and the fourth centuries and their later successors in the fifth, sixth and seventh centuries. But during the eighth, ninth and tenth centuries one notices a steady development on this side in the works of prominent Nyāya writers such as Vātsyāyana, Uddyotakara, Vācaspati Miśra and Udayana and Vedāntic authors such as the great master Śaṅkarācārya, Vācaspati Miśra and Ānandabodha Yati. But the school of abstract and dry formalism may be said to have properly begun with Kulārka Paṇḍita, or the authors of the *Māna-manohara* and *Pramāṇa-mañjarī* in the latter part of the eleventh century, and to have been carried on in the works of a number of other writers, until we come to Gaṅgeśa of the early thirteenth century, who enlivened it with the subtleties of his acute mind by the introduction of the new concepts of *avacchedakatā*, which may be regarded as a new turning point after *vyāpti*. This work was further carried on extremely elaborately by his later successors, the great writers of this new school of logic (*navya-nyāya*), Raghunātha Śiromaṇi, Jagadīśa Bhaṭṭācārya, Gadādhara Bhaṭṭācārya and others. On the Vedānta side this formalism was carried on by Śrīharṣa (AD 1187), Citsukha of about AD 1220 (of whom Vādīndra was a contemporary), Ānandajñāna or Ānandagiri of about AD 1260 and through a number of minor writers until we come to Nṛsiṃhāśrama and Madhusūdana Sarasvatī of the seventeenth century. It may be surmised that formal criticisms of Śrīharṣa were probably largely responsible for a new awakening in the Naiyāyikas, who began to direct their entire attention to a perfecting of their definitions and discussions on strict lines of formal accuracy and preciseness to the utter neglect of the collection of new data, new experiences or the investigation of new problems or new lines of enquiry, which is so essential for the development of true philosophy. But, when once they started perfecting the purely logical appliances and began to employ them successfully in debates, it became essential for all Vedāntists also to master the ways of this new formalism for the defence of their old views, with utter neglect of new creations in philosophy. Thus in the growth of the history of the dialectic of logical formalism in the Vedānta system of thought it is found that during the eighth, ninth, tenth and eleventh centuries the element of formalism was at its lowest and the controversies of the Vedānta with the Buddhists, Mīmāṃsists and Naiyāyikas were based largely on the analysis of experience from the Vedāntic standpoint and its general approach to philosophy. But in the twelfth and the thirteenth centuries the controversy was largely with the Nyāya and Vaiśeṣika and dominated by considerations of logical formalism above everything else. Criticisms became for the most part nothing more than criticisms of Nyāya and Vaiśeṣika definitions. Parallel to this a new force was gradually growing during these centuries in the writings of Rāmānuja and his followers, and in the succeeding centuries the followers of Mādhva, the great Vaiṣṇava writer, began to criticize the Vedāntists (of the Śaṅkara school) very strongly. It is found therefore that from the thirteenth or fourteenth century the Vedāntic attack was largely directed against the followers of Rāmānuja and Mādhva. A history of this controversy will be given in the third and fourth volumes of the present work. But the method of logical formalism had attained such an importance by this time that, though the Vaiṣṇavas brought in many new considerations and points of view in philosophy, the method of logical formalism never lost its high place in dialectic discussions.

VEDĀNTA DIALECTIC OF ŚRĪHARṢA (AD 1150)

Śrīharṣa flourished probably during the middle of the twelfth century AD Udayana, the great Nyāya writer, lived towards the end of the tenth century, as is evident from the colophon of his *Lakṣaṇāvalī*.[1] Śrīharṣa often refutes the definitions of Udayana, and therefore must have flourished after him. Again, the great logician Gaṅgeśa of Mithilā refers to Śrīharṣa and refutes his views, and, since Gaṅgeśa lived in AD 1200, Śrīharṣa must have lived before that date. Accordingly Śrīharṣa was after Udayana and before Gaṅgeśa, i.e. between the tenth and twelfth centuries AD. At the end of his book he refers to himself as honoured by the King of Kanauj (*Kānyakubjeśvara*). It is probable that this king may be Jayacandra of Kanauj, who was dethroned about AD 1195.[2] In his poetical work *Naiṣadha-carita* he mentions at the end of the several chapters many works of his, such as *Arṇava-varṇana, Gauḍorvīśa-kula-praśasti*, *Nava-sāhasāṅka-carita*, *Vijaya-praśasti*, *Śiva-śakti-siddhi*, *Sthairya-vicāraṇa*, *Chandaḥ-praśasti*, and also

1 तर्काम्बराङ्क (९०६) प्रमितेष्वतीतेषु शकान्ततः
वर्षेसूदयनश्चक्रे सुबोधां लक्षणावलीम्
tarkāmbarāṅka (906) pramiteṣv atīteṣu śakāntataḥ
varṣesūdayanaś cakre subodhāṃ lakṣaṇāvalīm.
—*Lakṣaṇāvalī*, p. 72, SurendralālGosvāmin's edition, Benares, 1900.

2 Ānandapūrna in his commentary on the *Khaṇḍana-khaṇḍa-khādya*, called *Khaṇḍana-phakkikā*, explains Kānyakubjeśvara as Kāśīrāja, i.e. King of Kāśī or Benares.

Īśvarābhisandhi and *Pañcanalīya kāvya.*[1] The fact that he wrote a work eulogizing the race of the kings of Gauḍa leads one to suspect that he may have been one of the five Brahmans invited by Ādiśūra of Bengal from Kanauj in the early part of the eleventh century, in which case Śrīharṣa would have to be placed at that time, and cannot be associated with Jayacandra, who was dethroned in AD 1195. Śrīharṣa's most important philosophical contribution was the *Khaṇḍana-khaṇḍa-khādya* (lit. "the sweets of refutation"), in which he attempts to refute all definitions of the Nyāya system intended to justify the reality of the categories of experience and tries to show that the world and all world-experiences are purely phenomenal and have no reality behind them. The only reality is the self-luminous Brahman of pure consciousness.[2] His polemic is against the Nyāya, which holds that whatever is known has a well-defined real existence, and Śrīharṣa's main point is to prove that all that is known is indefinable and unreal, being only of a phenomenal

---

1 None of these however are available.

2 Śrīharṣa at the end of this work speaks of having purposely made it extremely knotty here and there, so that no one could understand its difficulties easily except when explained by the teacher. Thus he says:

ग्रन्थग्रन्थिरिह क्वचित् क्वचिद् अपि न्यासि प्रयत्नान् मया
प्राज्ञम्मन्यमना हठेन पथितीमास्मिन् खलः खेलतु
श्रद्धाराद्धगुरुः श्लथीकृतदृढग्रन्थिः समासादयत्
त्व् एतत्तर्करसोर्म्मिमज्जन सुखेष्वासङ्गनं सज्जनः

grantha-granthir iha kvacit kvacid api nyāsi prayatnān mayā
prājñammanya-manā haṭhena pathitīmāsmin khalaḥ khelatu,
śraddhārāddha-guruḥ ślathīkṛta-dṛḍha-granthiḥ samāsādayat
tv etat-tarkarasormmi-majjana sukheṣv āsañjanaṃ sajjanaḥ.

—*Khaṇḍana-khaṇḍa-khādya,* p. 1341. Chowkhambā Sanskrit Book Depot, Benares, 1914. Several commentaries have been written on this celebrated work by various people, *e.g., Khaṇḍana-maṇḍana* by Paramānanda, *Khaṇḍana-maṇḍana* by Bhavanātha, *Dīdhiti* by Raghunātha Śiromani, *Prakāśa* by Vardhamāna, *Vidyā-bharaṇī* by Vidyābharapa, *Vidyāsāgarī* by Vidyāsāgara, *Khaṇḍana-ṭīkā* by Padmanābha Paṇḍita, *Ānanda-vardkana* by Śaṅkara Miśra, *Śrī-darpaṇa* by Śubhaṅkara, *Khaṇḍana-mahā-tarka* by Caritrasimha, *Khaṇḍana-khaṇḍana* by Pragalbha Miśra, *Śiṣya-hitaiṣiṇī* by Padmanābha, *Khaṇḍana-kuṭhāra* by GokulanāthaUpādhyāya. At least one refutation of it was attempted by the Naiyāyikas, as is evidenced by the work of a later Vācaspati (AD 1350) from Bengal, called *Khaṇḍanoddhāra.*

nature and having only a relative existence based on practical modes of acceptance, customs and conventions. But, though his chief polemic is against the Nyāya, yet, since his criticisms are almost wholly of a destructive nature like those of Nāgārjuna, they could be used, with modifications, no less effectively against any other system. Those who criticize with the object of establishing positive definitions would object only to certain definitions or views of other schools; but both Śrīharṣa and the nihilists are interested in the refutation of all definitions as such, and therefore his dialectic would be valid against all views and definitions of other systems.[1]

He starts with the proposition that none of our awarenesses ever stand in need of being further known or are capable of being the objects of any further act of knowledge. The difference of the Vedānta from the idealistic Buddhists consists in this, that the latter hold that everything is unreal and indefinable, not even excepting cognitions (*vijñāna*); while the Vedānta makes an exception of cognitions and holds that all the world, excepting knowledge or awareness, is indefinable either as existent or non-existent (*sad-asadbhyāṃ vilakṣaṇam*)and is unreal.[2] This indefinableness is in the nature of all things in the world and all experiences (*meya-svabhāvānugāminyām anirvacanīyatā*), and no amount of ingenuity or scholarship can succeed in defining the nature of that which has no definable nature or existence. Śrīharṣa undertakes to show that all definitions of things or categories put forward by the Nyāya writers are absolutely hollow and faulty even according to the canons of logical discussions and definitions accepted by

---

1 Śrīharsa himself admits the similarity of his criticisms to those of Nāgāijuna and says: "*tathā hi yadi darśaneṣu śūnya-vādānirvacanīya-pakṣayor āśrayaṇaṃ tada tāvad amūṣāṃ nir-bādhaiva sārva-pathīnatā,*" etc. *Khaṇḍana-khaṇḍa-khādya*, pp. 229-230, —Chowkhambā Sanskrit Book Depot, Benares, 1914.

2 By the idealistic Buddhists Śrīharṣa here means the idealism of the *Laṅkāvatāra,* from which he quotes the following verse:

बुद्ध्या विविच्यमानां स्वभावो नावधार्यते।
अतो निरभिलप्यास्ते निस्स्वभावाश्च देशिताः ॥

buddhyā vivicyamānānāṃ svabhāvo nāvadhāryate
Ato nirabhilapyās te nissvabhāvāś ca deśitāḥ.

—*Laṅkāvatāra-sūtra,* p. 287, Otani University Press, 1923.

the Naiyāyika; and, if no definition can stand or be supported, it necessarily follows that there can be no definitions, or, in other words, that no definitions of the phenomenal world are possible and that the world of phenomena and all our so-called experiences of it are indefinable. So the Vedāntist can say that the unreality of the world is proved. It is useless for anyone to attempt to find out what is true by resorting to arguments; for the arguments can be proved to be false even by the canons on which they are based. If anyone, however, says that the arguments of Śrīharṣa are open to the same objection and are not true, then that would only establish his own contention. For Śrīharṣa does not believe in the reality of his arguments and enters into them without any assumption of their reality or unreality. It can be contended that it is not possible to argue without first admitting the reality of the arguments. But such reality cannot be established without first employing the *pramāṇas* or valid means of proof; and the employment of the *pramāṇas* would require further arguments, and these further employment of the *pramāṇas* and so on until we have vicious infinite regress. If, however, the very arguments employed in accordance with the canons of the opponents to destroy their definitions be regarded as false, this would mean that the opponents reject their own canons, so that the Vedāntic arguments in refuting their position would be effective. The Vedānta is here interested only in destroying the definitions and positions of the opponents; and so, unless the opponents are successful in defending their own positions against the attacks of the Vedānta, the Vedānta point of view is not refuted. So the manifold world of our experience is indefinable, and the one Brahman is absolutely and ultimately real.

Regarding the proof that may be demanded of the ultimate oneness Śrīharṣa says that the very demand proves that the idea of ultimate oneness already exists, since, if the idea were not realized, no one could think of asking for a proof of it. Now, if it is admitted that the idea of absolute oneness is realized (*pratīta*), then the question arises whether such realization is right knowledge (*pramā*) or error (*apramā*). If it is a right idea, then, whatever may have produced it, this right idea is to be regarded as valid proof. If such an idea is false, one cannot legitimately ask the Vedāntist to adduce any proofs to demonstrate what is false. It may be urged that, though the Naiyāyika considers it false, it is regarded by the Vedāntist as true and hence the Vedāntist may be called upon to prove that the way in which or the means of proof through which he came to have his idea was true. This, however, the Vedāntist would readily deny; for, even though the idea of the absolute oneness may be right, yet the way in which one happened to come by this idea may be wrong. There may be a fire on a hill; but yet, if one infers the existence of such a fire from fog appearing as smoke, then such an inference is false, even though the idea of the fire may itself be right. Leaving aside the discussion of the propriety of such demands on the part of the opponents, the Vedāntist says that the Upaniṣadic texts demonstrate the truth of the ultimate oneness of reality.

The ultimate oneness of all things, taught in the Upaniṣad texts, cannot be said to be negatived by our perceptual experience of "many." For our perception deals with individual things of the moment and therefore cannot apply to all things of the past, present, and future and establish the fact of their all being different from one another. Perception applies to the experience of the immediate present and is therefore not competent to contradict the universal proposition of the oneness of all things, as taught by the Upaniṣads. Again, as Śrīharṣa says, in our perception of the things of experience we do not realize the differences of the perceptual objects from ourselves, but the differences among the objects themselves. The self-revelation of knowledge also fails to show its difference from all objects of the world. The difference, again, of the perceived objects from all other things is not revealed in the nature of the perceived objects themselves as *svarūpa-bheda*, or difference as being of the nature of the objects which are differenced—if that were the case, then the false and erroneous perception of silver would also at once manifest its difference from the object (the conch-shell) on which the false silver is imposed. In this way Śrīharṣa tried to prove that the purport of non-duality, as asserted in the Vedic texts, is not contradicted by any other, stronger, proof. Most of these arguments, being of a verbal nature, may better here be dropped. The main stress seems to rest on the idea that the immediate differences between the things perceived do not in the least suggest or imply that they, in their essence or in their totality, could not ultimately, as a result of our progressive and better knowledge of things, be considered as one identical reality (as is asserted in the Upaniṣads). If perception cannot prove anything, inferences by themselves cannot stand alone or contradict the non-duality taught in the Upaniṣads. In our world of phenomenal experience our minds are always impressed with the concept of difference; but Śrīharṣa says that the mere existence of an idea does not prove its reality. Words can give rise to ideas relating even to absolutely non-existing things.

Again, the concept of "difference" can hardly be defined. If it lies involved within the essential nature of all things that differ, then difference would be identical with the nature of the things that differ. If difference were different from the things that differ, then it would be necessary to find out some way of establishing a relation between "difference" and the things that differ, and this might require another connection, and that another, and so we should have a vicious endless series. He says that "difference" may be looked upon from a number of possible points of view. Firstly, "difference" is supposed to be of the nature of things. But a "difference" which is of the nature of the things which differ must involve them all in one; for there cannot be any difference without referring to the things from which there is difference. If by "book" we mean its difference from table, then the table has to enter into the nature of the book, and that would mean the identity of the table and the book. There is no meaning in speaking of "difference" as being the thing, when such differences can only be determined by a reference to other things. If "difference" be the nature of a thing, such a nature cannot be in need of being determined by other things. One thing, say a book, is realized as being different from a table—the nature of the difference may here be described as being "the quality of being distinguished from a table"; but "the quality of being distinguished" would have no meaning or *locus standi*, unless "the table" were also taken with it. If anyone says that a book is identical with "the quality of being distinguished from," then this will invariably include "the table" also within the essence of the book, as "the table" is a constituent of the complex quality "to be distinguished from," which necessarily means "to be distinguished from a table." So on this view also "the table" and all other things which could be distinguished from the book are involved in the very essence of all things—a conclusion which contradicts the very concept of difference. It may also be pointed out that the concept of difference is entirely extraneous to the concept of things as they are understood or perceived. The notion of "difference" is itself different from the notion of the book and the table, whether jointly or separately. The joint notion of the book and the table is different from the notion that "the book differs from the table." For understanding the nature of a book it is not necessary that one should understand previously its difference from a table. Moreover, even though the notion of difference may in some sense be said to lead to our apprehension of individual things, the apprehension of such individual things does not carry with it the idea that it is on account of such difference that the individual things are perceived. It is through similarity or resemblance between two things—say between a wild cow (*gavaya*) and the domestic cow (*go*)—that a man can recognize an animal as a wild cow; but yet, when he so considers an animal as a wild cow, he does not invariably because of such a resemblance to a cow think the animal to be a wild cow. The mental decision regarding an animal as a cow or a wild cow takes place immediately without any direct participation of the cause which produced it. So, even though the notion of difference may be admitted to be responsible for our apprehension of the different individual things, an apprehension of an individual thing does not involve as a constituent any notion of difference. It is therefore wrong to think that things are of the nature of difference.

In another view, wherein difference is interpreted as "mental negation" or "otherness" (*anyonyābhāva*), this "otherness" (say of the book from the table) is explained as being the negation of the identity of one with the other. When one says that the book is other than the table, what is meant is that identity of the book with the table is denied. Śrīharṣa here raises the objection that, if the identity of the book with the table was absolutely chimerical, like the hare's horn, such a denial of identity would be absolutely meaningless. It cannot, again, be suggested that this mental negation, or negation as otherness, means the denial of one class-concept in respect of another (*e.g.,* that of book on the table); for there is in these class-concepts no such special characteristic (*dharma*) by virtue of which one could be denied of the other or they could be distinguished from each other, since the Naiyāyika, against whom Śrīharṣa's arguments are directed, does not admit that class-concepts possess any distinguishing qualities. In the absence of such distinguishing qualities they may be regarded as identical: but in that case the denial of one class-concept (say of the table) would involve the denial of the class-concept of the thing itself (*e.g.,* the book), since the class-concepts of the book and the table, not having any distinguishing qualities, are identical; and, further, through mental denial both the book and the table would be devoid of the class-concepts of book and table, and so there would be no way of distinguishing one thing from another, book from table. It is easy to see therefore that there is no way of making a special case regarding negation as otherness (*anyonyabhāva*). Again, if difference is regarded as the possession of opposite characters (*vaidharmya*), then also it may be asked whether the opposite characters have further opposite characters to distinguish them from one another, and these again others, and so there is a vicious infinite; if these are supposed to stop anywhere, then the final characters at that stage, not having any further opposite characters to distinguish them, would be identical, and hence all opposite characters in the backward series would be meaningless and all things would be identical. If on the contrary it is admitted at the very first stage that opposite or differing characters have no differing characters to distinguish them from one another, then the characters will be identical. Again, it may be asked whether these distinguishing characters are themselves different from the objects which possess them or not. If they are different, one may again ask concerning the opposing characters which lead to this difference and then again about other opposing characters of these, and so on. If these infinite differences were to hold good, they could not arrive in less than infinite time, whereas the object is finite and limited in time. If, again, they came all at once, there would be such a disorderly medley of these infinite differences that there would be no way of determining their respective substrates and their orderly successive dependence on one another. And, since in the series the earlier terms of difference can only be established by the establishment of the later terms of difference, the forward movement in search of the later terms of difference, in support of the earlier terms of difference, makes these earlier terms of difference unnecessary.[1]

It cannot, therefore, be said that our perception of differences has any such intrinsic validity that it can contradict the ultimate unity taught in the Upaniṣad texts. Śrīharṣa does not deny that we perceive seeming differences in all things, but he denies their ultimate validity, since he considers them to be due to *avidyā* or nescience alone.[2]

The chief method of Śrīharṣa's dialectic depends upon the assumption that the reality of the things that one defines depends upon the unimpeachable character of the definitions; but all definitions are faulty, as they involve the fallacy of argument in a circle (*cakraka*), and hence there is no way in which the real

---

1 *prathama-bhedāsvīkāra-prayojanasya bheda-vyavahārāder dvitīya-bhedād eva siddheḥ prathama-bhedo vyarthaḥ syād eva, dvitīya-bhedādi-prayojanasya tṛtīya-bhedādinaiva siddheḥ so pi vyarthaḥ syāt.*
—*Vidyā-sāgarī* on *Khaṇḍana-khaṇḍa-khādya,* p. 206. Chowkhambā Sanskrit Book Depot, Benares, 1914.

2 *Na vayaṃ bhedasya sarvathaivāsattvam abhyupagacchāmaḥ, kiṃ nāma na pāramārthikaṃ sattvaṃ; avidyā-vidyamānatvaṃ tu tadīyam iṣyata eva.*
—*Khaṇḍana-khaṇḍa-khādya,* p. 214.

nature of things can be demonstrated or defined. Our world of experience consists of knower, known and knowledge; if a knower is defined as the possessor of knowledge, knowledge can only be understood by a reference to the knower; the known, again, can be understood only by a reference to knowledge and the knower, and so there is a circle of relativity which defies all attempts at giving an independent definition of any of these things. It is mainly this relativity that in specific forms baffles all attempts at definition of all categories.

APPLICATION OF THE DIALECTIC TO THE DIFFERENT CATEGORIES AND CONCEPTS

Śrīharṣa first takes for his criticism the definitions of right cognition. Assuming the definition of right cognition to be the direct apprehension of the real nature of things, he first urges that such a definition is faulty, since, if one accidentally guesses rightly certain things hidden under a cover and not perceived, or makes a right inference from faulty data or by fallacious methods, though the awareness may be right, it cannot be called right cognition.[1] It is urged that cognition, in order to be valid, must be produced through unerring instruments; here, however, is a case of chance guesses which may sometimes be right without being produced by unerring instruments of senses. Nor can correspondence of the cognition with its object (*yathārthānubhavaḥ pramā*) be regarded as a proper definition of right cognition. Such correspondence can be defined as meaning either that which represents the reality of the object itself or similarity to the object. The real nature of an object is indeterminable, and so correspondence of awareness with the object may rather be defined as similarity of the former to the latter. If this similarity means that the awareness must have such a character as is possessed by the object (*jñāna-viṣayīkṛtena rūpeṇa*

1 *E.g.*, when a man rightly guesses the number of shells closed in another man's hand, or when one makes a false inference of fire on a hill from a fog looking like smoke from a distance and there is fire on the hill by chance—his judgment may be right though his inference may be false.

sādṛśyam), then this is clearly impossible; for qualities that belong to the object cannot belong to the awareness—there may be an awareness of two white hard marbles, but the awareness is neither two, nor white, nor hard.[1] It may be urged that the correspondence consists in this, that the whiteness etc. belong to the object as qualities possessed by it, whereas they belong to awareness as being qualities which it reveals.[2] But that would not hold good in the case of illusory perception of silver in a conch-shell; the awareness of "before me" in the perception of "before me the silver" has to be admitted as being a right cognition. If this is admitted to be a right cognition, then it was meaningless to define right cognition as true correspondence; it might as well have been defined as mere cognition, since all cognition would have some object to which it referred and so far as that only was concerned all cognitions would be valid. If, however, entire correspondence of thought and object be urged, then partial correspondence like the above can hardly be considered satisfactory. But, if entire correspondence is considered indispensable, then the correctness of the partial correspondence has to be ignored, whereas it is admitted by the Naiyāyika that, so far as reference to an object is concerned, all cognitions are valid; only the nature of cognition may be disputed as to right or wrong, when we are considering the correspondence of the nature of the object and the nature characterized by the awareness of the object. If entire correspondence with the object is not assured, then cognition of an object with imperfect or partial correspondence, due to obstructive circumstances, has also to be rejected as false. Again, since the correspondence always refers to the character, form or appearance of the thing, all our affirmations regarding the objects to which the characters are supposed to belong would be false.

---

1 *Dvau ghaṭau śuklav ityatra rūpa-saṃkhyādi-samavāyitvaṃ na jñānasya guṇat-vād ataḥ prakāśamāna-rūpeṇa artha-sādṛśyaṃ jñānasya nāsti—asti ca tasya jñānasya tatra ghaṭayoḥ pramātvam. —Vidyā-sāgarī* on *Khaṇḍana,* p. 398.

2 *Arthasya hi yathā samavāyād rūpaṃ viśeṣaṇībhavati tathā viṣayabhāvāj jñānasyāpi tad-viśeṣaṇam bhavaty eva. —Khaṇḍana,* p. 399.

Referring to Udayana's definition of right cognition as *samyakparicchitti,* or proper discernment, Śrīharṣa says that the word "*samyak*" (proper) is meaningless; for, if *samyak* means "entire," then the definition is useless, since it is impossible to see all the visible and invisible constituent parts of a thing, and no one but an omniscient being could perceive a thing with all its characters, properties or qualities. If right discernment means the discernment of an object with its special distinguishing features, this again is unintelligible; for even in wrong cognition, say of conch-shell as silver, the perceiver seems to perceive the distinguishing marks of silver in the conch-shell. The whole point lies in the difficulty of judging whether the distinguishing marks observed are real or not, and there is no way of determining this. If, again, the distinguishing features be described as being those characteristics without the perception of which there can be no certain knowledge and the perception of which ensures right cognition, then it may well be pointed out that it is impossible to discover any feature of any cognition of which one can be positively certain that it is not wrong. A dreamer confuses all sorts of characters and appearances and conceives them all to be right. It may be urged that in the case of right perception the object is perceived with its special distinguishing features, as in the case of the true perception of silver, whereas in the case of the false perception of silver in the conch-shell no such distinguishing features are observed. But even in this case it would be difficult to define the essential nature of the distinguishing features; for, if any kind of distinguishing feature would do, then in the case of the false perception of silver in the conch-shell the distinguishing feature of being before the eyes is also possessed by the conch-shell. If all the particular distinguishing features are insisted on, then there will be endless distinguishing features, and it would be impossible to make any definition which would include them all. The certitude of a cognition which contradicts a previous wrong cognition would often be liable to the same objection as the wrong cognition itself, since the nature of the special distinguishing features which would establish its validity cannot be established by any definition of right knowledge.

Arguing against the definition of right cognition as "apprehension which is not incorrect or not defective" (*avyabhicārīanubhavaḥ*), Śrīharṣa says that "not incorrect" or "not defective" cannot mean that the cognition must exist only at the time when the object exists; for then inferential cognition, which often refers to past and future things, would be false. Neither can it mean that the cognition coexists in space with its objects; nor can it mean that the right cognition is similar to its object in all respects, since cognition is so different in nature from the object that it is not possible that there should be any case in which it would be similar thereto in all respects. And, if the view that an awareness and its object are one and the same be accepted, then this would apply even to those cases where one object is wrongly perceived as another; and hence the word "*avyabhicārī*" is not sufficient to distinguish right knowledge from wrong cognition.

Arguing against the Buddhist definition of right cognition as "an apprehension which is not incompatible (*avisaṃvādi*) with the object known," Śrīharṣa tries to refute the definition in all the possible senses of incompatibility of cognition with object which determines wrong knowledge. If the definition is supposed to restrict right cognition to cognition which is cognized by another cognition as being in agreement with its object, then a wrong cognition, repeated successively through a number of moments and found to be in agreement with its object through all the successive moments until it is contradicted, would also have to be admitted as right, because in this case the previous cognition is certified by the cognition of the succeeding moments. If, again, right cognition is defined as a cognition the incompatibility of which with its object is not realized by any other cognition, then also there are difficulties in the way. For even a wrong cognition may for some time be not contradicted by any other cognition. Moreover, the vision of the conch-shell by the normal eye as white may be contradicted by the later vision by the jaundiced eye as yellow. If it is urged that the contradiction must be by a faultless later cognition, then it may be pointed out that, if there had been any way of defining faultless cognition, the definition of right cognition would have been very easy. On the other hand, unless right cognition is properly defined, there is no meaning in speaking of faulty or wrong cognition. If right cognition is defined as a cognition which has causal efficiency, that in fact is not a proper definition; for even the wrong cognition of a snake might cause fear and even death. If it is urged that the causal efficiency must be exercised by the object in the same form in which it is perceived, then it is very difficult to ascertain this; and there may be a false cognition of causal efficiency also; hence it would be very difficult to ascertain the nature of right cognition on the basis of causal efficiency. Śrīharṣa points out again that in a similar way Dharmakīrti's definition of right cognition as enabling one to attain the object (*artha-prāpakatva*) is also unintelligible, since it is difficult to determine which object can be actually attained and which not, and the notion that the thing may be attained as it is perceived may be present even in the case of the wrong perception of silver in the conch-shell. If right cognition is defined as cognition which is not contradicted, then it may be asked whether the absence of contradiction is at the time of perception only, in which case even the wrong perception of silver in the conch-shell would be a right cognition, since it is uncontradicted at least at the time when the illusion is produced. If it is urged that a right cognition is that which is not contradicted at any time, then we are not in a position to assert the rightness of any cognition; for it is impossible to be certain that any particular cognition will never at any time be contradicted.

After showing that it is impossible to define right cognition (*pramā*) Śrīharṣa tries to show that it is impossible to define the idea of instruments (*karaṇa*) or their operative action (*vyāpāra*) as involved in the idea of instruments of cognition (*pramāṇa*). Śrīharṣa attempts to show that instrumentality as an agent cannot be separately conceived as having an independent existence, since it is difficult to determine its separate existence. It would be a long tale to go into all the details of this discussion as set forth by Śrīharṣa, and for our present purposes it is enough to know that Śrīharṣa refuted the concept of "instrumentality" as a separate agent, both as popularly conceived or as conceived in Sanskrit grammar. He also discusses a number of alternative meanings which could be attributed to the concept of *"karaṇa"* or instrument, and shows that none of these meanings can be satisfactorily justified.[1]

In refuting the definition of perception he introduces a long discussion showing the uselessness of defining perception as an instrument of right knowledge. Perception is defined in the Nyāya as cognition which arises through the contact of a particular sense with its object; but it is impossible to know whether any cognition has originated from sense-contact, since the fact of the production of knowledge from sense-contact cannot itself be directly perceived or known by any other means. Since in perception the senses are in contact on the one hand with the self and on the other hand with the external objects, Śrīharṣa urges by a series of arguments that, unless the specific object with which the sense is in contact is mentioned in each case, it would be difficult to formulate a definition of perception in such a way that it would imply only the revelation of the external object and not the self, which is as much in contact with the sense as is the object. Again, the specification of the object in the case of each perception would make it particular, and this would defeat the purposes of definition, which can only apply to universal concepts. Arguing against a possible definition of perception as immediateness, Śrīharṣa supposes that, if perception reveals some specific quality of the object as its permanent attribute, then, in order that this quality may be cognized, there ought to be another attribute, and this would presuppose another attribute, and so there would be an infinite regress; and, if at any stage of the infinite regress it is supposed that no further attribute is necessary, then this involves the omission of the preceding determining

1 Among many other definitions Śrīharsa also refutes the definition of *karaṇa* as given by Uddyotakara—*"yadvān eva karoti tat karaṇam."* *Khaṇḍana*, p. 506.

attributes, until the possibility of the perception is also negatived. If this immediateness be explained as a cognition produced by the instrumentality of the sense-organs, this again is unintelligible; for the instrumentality of sense-organs is incomprehensible. Śrīharṣa takes a number of alternative definitions of perceptions and tries to refute them all more or less in the same way, mostly by pointing out verbal faults in the formulation of the definitions.

Citsukha Ācārya, a commentator on Śrīharṣa's *Khaṇḍana-khaṇḍa-khādya*, offers a refutation of the definition of perception in a much more condensed form. He points out that the definition of perception by Akṣapāda as an uncontradicted cognition arising out of sense-contact with the object is unintelligible. How can we know that a cognition would not be contradicted? It cannot be known from a knowledge of the faultlessness of the collocating circumstances, since the faultlessness can be known only if there is no contradiction, and hence faultlessness cannot be known previously and independently, and the collocating circumstances would contain many elements which are unperceivable. It is also impossible to say whether any experience will forever remain uncontradicted. Nor can it again be urged that right cognition is that which can produce an effort on the part of the perceiver (*pravṛtti-sāmarthya*); for even an illusory knowledge can produce an effort on the part of the perceiver who is deceived by it. Mere achievement of the result is no test for the rightness of the cognition; for a man may see the lustre of a gem and think it to be a gem and really get the gem, yet it cannot be doubted that his apprehension of the ray of the gem as the gem was erroneous.[1] In the case of the perception of stars and planets there is no chance of any actual attainment of those objects, and yet there is no reason to deny the validity of the cognitions.

Passing over the more or less verbal arguments of Śrīharṣa in refutation of the definitions of inference (*anumāna*) as *liṅga-*

1 *dṛśyate hi maṇi-prabhāyāṃ maṇi-buddhyā pravartamānasya maṇi-prāpteḥ pravṛtti-sāmarthyaṃ na cāvyabhicāritvam.—Tattva-pradīpikā,* p. 218. Nirṇaya-Sāgara Press, Bombay, 1915.

parāmarśa or the realization of the presence in the minor term (*pakṣa, e.g.,* the mountain) of a reason or probans (*liṅga, e.g.,* smoke) which is always concomitant with the major term (*sādhya, e.g.,* fire), or as invariable concomitance of the probans with the probandum or the major term (*sādhya, e.g.,* fire), and its other slightly modified varieties, I pass on to his criticism of the nature of concomitance (*vyāpti*), which is at the root of the notion of inference. It is urged that the universal relationship of invariable concomitance required in *vyāpti* cannot be established unless the invariable concomitance of all the individuals involved in a class be known, which is impossible. The Naiyāyika holds that the mind by a sort of mental contact with class-concepts or universals, called *sāmānya-pratyāsatti,* may affirm of all individuals of a class without actually experiencing all the individuals. It is in this way that, perceiving the invariable concomitance of smoke and fire in a large number of cases, one understands the invariable concomitance of smoke with fire by experiencing a sort of mental contact with the class-concept "smoke" when perceiving smoke on a distant hill. Śrīharṣa argues in refutation of such an interpretation that, if all individual smoke may be known in such a way by a mental contact with class-concepts, then by a mental contact with the class-concept "knowable" we might know all individual knowables and thus be omniscient as well. A thing is knowable only as an individual with its specific qualities as such, and therefore to know a thing as a knowable would involve the knowledge of all such specific qualities; for the class-concept "knowable" would involve all individuals which have a specific knowable character. It may be urged that knowability is one single character, and that things may be otherwise completely different and may yet be one so far as knowability is concerned, and hence the things may remain wholly unknown in their diversity of characters and may yet be known so far as they are merely know-able. To this Śrīharṣa answers that the class-concept "knowable" would involve all knowables and so even the diversity of characters would be involved within the meaning of the term "knowable."

Again, assuming for the sake of argument that it is possible to have a mental contact with class-concepts through individuals, how can the invariable concomitance itself be observed? If our senses could by themselves observe such relations of concomitance, then there would be no possibility of mistakes in the observation of such concomitance. But such mistakes are committed and corrected by later experience, and there is no way in which one can account for the mistake in the sense-judgment. Again, if this invariable concomitance be defined as *avinābhāva,* which means that when one is absent the other is also absent, such a definition is faulty; for it may apply to those cases where there is no real invariable concomitance. Thus there is no real concomitance between "earth" and "possibility of being cut"; yet in *ākāśa* there is absence of earth and also the absence of "possibility of being cut." If it is urged that concomitance cannot be determined by a single instance of the absence of one tallying with the absence of the other, it must be proved that universally in all instances of the absence of the one, *e.g.,* the fire, there is also the absence of the other, *e.g.,* the smoke. But it is as difficult to ascertain such universal absence as it is to ascertain universal concomitance. Again, if this concomitance be defined as the impossibility of the presence of the middle term, the reason or the probans, where the major term or the probandum is also absent, then also it may be said that it is not possible to determine such an impossibility either by sense-knowledge or by any other means.

Now *tarka* or eliminatory consideration in judging of possibilities cannot be considered as establishing invariable concomitance; for all arguments are based on invariable concomitance, and such an assumption would lead to a vicious mutual interdependence. The great logician Udayana objects to this and says that, if invariable concomitance between smoke and fire be denied, then there are strong arguments (*tarka*) against such a denial (*bādhakastarkaḥ*), namely, that, if smoke is not regarded as concomitant with fire, then smoke would either exist without any cause or not exist at all, which is impossible. But Śrīharṣa says that there is room for an alternative proposition which Udayana misses, namely, that smoke is due to some cause other than fire. It may be that there are smokes which are not caused by fire. How can one be sure that all smokes are caused by fire? There may be differences in these two classes of fire which remain unnoticed by us, and so there is always room for the supposition that any particular smoke may not be caused by fire, and such doubts would make inference impossible. Udayana had however contended that, if you entertain the doubt, with regard to a future case, that it is possible that there may be a case in which the concomitance may be found wrong, then the possibility of such a doubt (*śaṅkā*) must be supported by inference, and the admission of this would involve the admission of inference. If such an exaggerated doubt be considered illegitimate, there is no obstruction in the way of inference. Doubts can be entertained only so long as such entertainment of doubts is compatible with practical life. Doubts which make our daily life impossible are illegitimate. Every day one finds that food appeases hunger, and, if in spite of that one begins to doubt whether on any particular day when he is hungry he should take food or not, then life would be impossible.[1] Śrīharṣa, however, replies to this contention by twisting the words of Udayana's own *kārikā,* in which he says that, so long as there is doubt, inference is invalid; if there is no doubt, this can only be when the invalidity of the inference has been made manifest, and until such invalidity is found there will always be doubts. Hence the argument of possibilities (*tarka*) can never remove doubts.[2]

---

1 शङ्का चेदनुमास्त्येव न चेच्छङ्का ततस्तराम्
व्याघातावधि राशङ्का तर्कः शङ्कावधिर्मतः
Śaṅkā ced anumāsty eva
Na ced śaṅkā tatastarām
Vyāghātāvadhi rāśaṅkā
tarkaḥ śaṅkāvadhir mataḥ.
—*Kusumāñjali,* III, 7. Chowkhambā Sanskrit Book Depot, Benares, 1912.

2 व्याघातो यदि शङ्कास्ति न चेच्छङ्का ततस्तराम्
व्याघातावधिराशङ्का तर्कः शङ्कावधिः कुतः
Vyāghāto yadi śaṅkāsti
Na cec chañkā tatastarām
Vyāghātāvadhir āśaṅkā
tarkaḥ śaṅkāvadhiḥ kutaḥ. —*Khaṇḍana-khaṇḍa-khādya,* p. 693

Śrīharṣa also objects to the definition of "invariable concomitance" as a natural relation (*svābhāvikaḥ sambandhaḥ*). He rejects the term "natural relation" and says that invariable concomitance would not be justifiable in any of its possible meanings, such as (i) depending on the nature of the related (*sambandhi-svabhāva-śrita*), (ii) produced by the nature of the related (*sambandhi-svabhāva-janya*), (iii) not different from the nature constituting the relatedness, since, as these would be too wide and would apply even to those things which are not invariable concomitants, *e.g.*, all that is earthen can be scratched with an iron needle. Though in some cases earthen objects may be scratched with an iron needle, not all earthen objects can be so scratched. He further refutes the definition of invariable concomitance as a relation not depending upon conditional circumstances (*upādhi*). Without entering into the details of Śrīharṣa's argument it may be pointed out that it rests very largely on his contention that conditionality of relations cannot be determined without knowledge of the nature of invariable concomitance and also that invariable concomitance cannot be determined without a previous determination of the conditionality of relations.

Śrīharṣa's brief refutation of analogy, implication and testimony, as also his refutation of the definitions of the different fallacies of inference, are not of much importance from a philosophical point of view, and need not be detailed here.

Turning now to Śrīharṣa's refutation of the Nyāya categories, we note that he begins with the refutation of "being" or positivity (*bhāvatva*). He says that being cannot be defined as being existent in itself, since non-being is also existent in itself; we can with as much right speak of being as existing as of non-being as existing; both non-being and being may stand as grammatical nominatives of the verb "exists." Again, each existing thing being unique in itself, there is no common quality, such as "existence" or "being," which is possessed by them all. Again, "being" is as much a negation of "non-being" as "non-being" of "being"; hence "being" cannot be defined as that which is not a negation of anything. Negation is a mere form of speech, and both being and non-being may be expressed in a negative form.

Turning to the category of non-being (*abhāva*), Śrīharṣa says that it cannot be defined as negation of anything; for being may as well be interpreted as a negation of non-being as non-being of being (*bhāvābhāvayor dvayor api paraspara-pratikṣepātmakatvāt*). Nor again can non-being be defined as that which opposes being; for not all non-being is opposed to all being (*e.g.*, in "there is no jug on the ground" the absence of jug does not oppose the ground in respect of which the jug is denied); if non-being opposes some existent things, then that does not differentiate negation; for there are many existent things which are opposed to one another (*e.g.*, the horse and the bull).

In refuting the Nyāya definition of substance (*dravya*) as that which is the support of qualities, Śrīharṣa says that even qualities appear to have numeral and other qualities (*e.g.*, we speak of two or three colours, of a colour being deep or light, mixed or primary—and colour is regarded as quality). If it is urged that this is a mistake, then the appearance of the so-called substances as being endowed with qualities may also be regarded as equally erroneous. Again, what is meant by defining substance as the support (*āśraya*) of qualities? Since qualities may subsist in the class-concept of quality (*guṇatva*), the class-concept of quality ought to be regarded as substance according to the definition. It may be urged that a substance is that in which the qualities inhere. But what would be the meaning here of the particle "in"? How would one distinguish the false appearance, to a jaundiced eye, of yellowness in a white conch-shell and the real appearance of whiteness in the conch-shell? Unless the falsity of the appearance of yellow in the conch-shell is realized, there can be no difference between the one case and the other. Again, substance cannot be defined as the inhering or the material cause (*samavāyi-kāraṇa*), since it is not possible to know which is the inhering cause and which is not; for number is counted as a quality, and colour also is counted as a quality, and yet one specifies colours by numbers, as one, two, or many colours.

Furthermore, the Nyāya definition of quality as that which has a genus and is devoid of qualities is unintelligible; for the definition involves the concept of quality, which is sought to be defined. Moreover, as pointed out above, even qualities, such as colours, have numeral qualities; for we speak of one, two or many colours. It is only by holding to this appearance of qualities endowed with numeral qualities that the definition of quality can be made to stand, and it is again on the strength of the definition of quality that such appearances are to be rejected as false. If colours are known as qualities in consideration of other reasons, then these, being endowed with numeral qualities, could not for that very reason be called qualities; for qualities belong according to definition only to substances. Even the numerals themselves are endowed with the quality of separateness. So there would not be a single instance that the Naiyāyika could point to as an example of quality.

Speaking of relations, Śrīharṣa points out that, if relation is to be conceived as something subsisting in a thing, then its meaning is unintelligible. The meaning of relation as "in" or "herein" is not at all clear; for the notion of something being a container (*ādhāra*) is dependent on the notion of the concept of "in" or "herein," and that concept again depends on the notion of a container, and there is no other notion which can explain either of the concepts independently. The container cannot be supposed to be an inhering cause; for in that case such examples as "there is a grape in this vessel" or "the absence of horns in a hare" would be unexplainable. He then takes a number of possible meanings which can be given to the notion of a container; but these, not being philosophically important, are omitted here. He also deals with the impossibility of defining the nature of the subject-object relation (*viṣaya-viṣayi-bhāva*) of knowledge.

In refuting the definition of cause Śrīharṣa says that cause cannot be defined as immediate antecedence; for immediate antecedence can be ascribed only to the causal operation, which is always an intervening factor between the cause and the effect. If, on the theory that what (*e.g.*, the causal operation) belongs to a thing (*e.g.*, the cause) cannot be considered as a factor which stands between it (cause) and that which follows it (effect), the causal operation be not regarded as a separate and independent factor, then even the cause of the cause would have to be regarded as one with the cause and therefore cause. But, if it is urged that, since the cause of the cause is not an operation, it cannot be regarded as being one with the cause, one may well ask the opponent to define the meaning of operation. If the opponent should define it as that factor without which the cause cannot produce the effect, then the accessory circumstances and common and abiding conditions, such as the natural laws, space, and so forth, without which an effect cannot be produced, are also to be regarded as operation, which is impossible. Further, "operation" cannot be qualified as being itself produced by the cause; for it is the meaning of the concept of cause that has still to be explained and defined. If, again, cause is defined as the antecedence of that which is other than the not-cause, then this again would be faulty; for one cannot understand the "not-cause" of the definition without understanding what is the nature of cause, and vice-versa. Moreover, space, being a permanent substance, is always present as a not-cause of anything, and is yet regarded as the cause of sound. If, again, cause is defined as that which is present when the effect is present and absent when the effect is absent, this would not explain the causality of space, which is never known to be absent. If, again, cause is defined as invariable antecedence, then permanent substances such as space are to be regarded as the sole causes of effects. If, however, invariable antecedence be understood to mean unconditional antecedence, then two coexistent entities such as the taste and the colour of an earthen pot which is being burnt must mutually be the cause of the colour and the taste of the burnt earthen pot; for neither does the colour condition taste, nor does the taste condition colour. Moreover, if mere invariable antecedents be regarded as cause, then the invariably preceding symptoms of a disease are to be regarded as the cause of the disease on account of their invariable antecedence. Again, causality cannot be regarded as a specific character or quality belonging to certain things, which quality can be directly perceived by us as existing in things. Thus we may perceive the stick of the potter's wheel to be the cause of the particular jugs produced by it, but it is not possible to perceive causality as a general quality of a stick or of any other thing. If causality existed only with reference to things in general, then it would be impossible to conceive of the production of individual things, and it would not be possible for anyone to know which particular cause would produce a particular effect. On the other hand, it is not possible to perceive by the senses that an individual thing is the cause of a number of individual effects; for until these individual effects are actually produced it is not possible to perceive them, since perception involves sense-contact as its necessary condition. It is not necessary for our present purposes to enter into all the different possible concepts of cause which Śrīharṣa seeks to refute: the above examination is expected to give a fairly comprehensive idea of the methods of Śrīharṣa's refutation of the category of cause.

Nor is it possible within the limited range of the present work to give a full account of all the different alternative defences of the various categories accepted in Nyāya philosophy, or of all the various ways in which Śrīharṣa sought to refute them in his *Khaṇḍana-khaṇḍa-khādya.* I have therefore attempted to give here only some specimens of the more important parts of his dialectical argument. The chief defect of Śrīharṣa's criticisms is that they often tend to grow into verbal sophisms, and lay greater stress on the faults of expression of the opponent's definitions and do not do him the justice of liberally dealing with his general ideas. It is easy to see how these refutations of the verbal definitions of the Nyāya roused the defensive spirit of the Naiyāyikas into re-stating their definitions with proper qualificatory phrases and adjuncts, by which they avoided the loopholes left in their former definitions for the attack of Śrīharṣa and other critics. In one sense, therefore, the criticisms of Śrīharṣa and some of his followers had done a great disservice to the development of later Nyāya thought; for, unlike the older Nyāya thinkers, later Nyāya writers, like Gaṅgeśa,

Raghunātha and others, were mainly occupied in inventing suitable qualificatory adjuncts and phrases by which they could define their categories in such a way that the undesirable applications and issues of their definitions, as pointed out by the criticisms of their opponents, could be avoided. If these criticisms had mainly been directed towards the defects of Nyāya thought, later writers would not have been forced to take the course of developing verbal expressions at the expense of philosophical profundity and acuteness. Śrīharṣa may therefore be said to be the first great writer who is responsible indirectly for the growth of verbalism in later Nyāya thought.

Another defect of Śrīharṣa's criticisms is that he mainly limits himself to criticizing the definitions of Nyāya categories and does not deal so fully with the general ideas involved in such categories of thought. It ought, however, in all fairness to Śrīharṣa to be said that, though he took the Nyāya definitions as the main objective of his criticisms, yet in dealing with the various alternative variations and points of view of such definitions he often gives an exhaustive treatment of the problems involved in the discussion. But in many cases his omissions become very glaring. Thus, for example, in his treatment of relations he only tries to refute the definitions of relation as container and contained, as inherence, and as subject-object relation of cognitions, and leaves out many other varieties of relation which might well have been dealt with. Another characteristic feature of his refutation is, as has already been pointed out, that he has only a destructive point of view and is not prepared to undertake the responsibility of defining any position from his own point of view. He delights in showing that none of the world-appearances can be defined in any way, and that thus, being indescribable, they are all false. But incapacity to define or describe anything in some particular way cannot mean that the thing is false. Śrīharṣa did not and could not show that the ways of definition which he attempted to refute were the only ways of defining the different categories. They could probably be defined in other and better ways, and even those definitions which he refuted could be bettered and improved by using suitable qualificatory phrases. He did not attempt to show that the concepts involved in the categories were fraught with such contradictions that, in whatever way one might try to define, one could not escape from those inner contradictions, which were inherent in the very nature of the concepts themselves. Instead of that he turned his attention to the actual formal definitions which had been put forward by the Nyāya and sometimes by Prabhākara and tried to show that these definitions were faulty. To show that particular definitions are wrong is not to show that the things defined are wrong. It is, no doubt, true that the refutation of certain definitions involves the refutation of the concepts involved in those definitions; but the refutation of the particular way of presentation of the concept does not mean that the concept itself is impossible. In order to show the latter, a particular concept has to be analysed on the basis of its own occurrences, and the inconsistencies involved in such an analysis have to be shown.

CITSUKHA'S INTERPRETATIONS OF THE CONCEPTS OF ŚAṄKARA VEDĀNTA

Citsukha (about AD 1220), a commentator on Śrīharṣa, had all Śrīharṣa's powers of acute dialectical thought, but he not only furnishes, like Śrīharṣa, a concise refutation of the Nyāya categories, but also, in his *Tattva-pradīpikā*, commented on by Pratyagbhagavān (AD 1400) in his *Nayana-prasādinī,*[1] gives

1 Citsukha, a pupil of Gauḍeśvara Ācārya, called also Jñānottama, wrote a commentary on Ānandabodha Bhattārakācārya's *Nyāya-makaranda* and also on Śrīharṣa's *Khaṇḍana-khaṇḍa-khādya* and an independent work called *Tattva-pradīpikā* or *Cit-sukki,* on which the study of the present section is based. In this work he quotes Udayana, Uddyotakara, Kumārila, Padmapāda, Vallabha *(Līlāvatī)*, Śālikanātha, Sureśvara, Sivāditya, Kulārka Paṇḍita and Śrīdhara *(Nyāya-kandatī).* In addition to these he also wrote a commentary on the *Brahma-sūtra-bhāṣya* of Śaṅkara, called *Bhāṣya-bhāva-prakāśikā, Vivaraṇa-tātparya-dīpikā,* a commentary on the *Pramāṇa-mālā* of Ānandabodha, a commentary on Maṇḍana's *Brahma-siddhi,* called *Abhiprāya-prakāśikā,* and an index to the *adhikaraṇas* of the *Brahma-sūtra,* called *Adhikaraṇa-mañjarī.* His teacher

us a very acute analysis and interpretation of some of the most important concepts of Śaṅkara Vedānta. He is not only a protector of the *Advaita* doctrine of the Vedānta, but also an interpreter of the Vedāntic concepts.[1] The work is written in four chapters. In the first chapter Citsukha deals with the interpretation of the Vedānta concepts of self-revelation (*sva-prakāśa*), the nature of self as consciousness (*ātmanaḥ saṃvid-rūpatva*), the nature of ignorance as darkness, the nature of falsity (*mithyātva*), the nature of nescience (*avidyā*), the nature of the truth of all ideas (*sarva-pratyayānām yathā-thatvam*), the nature of illusions, etc. In the second chapter he refutes the Nyāya categories of difference, separateness, quality, action, class-concepts, specific particulars (*viśeṣa*), the relation of inherence (*samavāya*), perception, doubt, illusion, memory, inference, invariable concomitance (*vyāpti*), induction (*vyāpti-graha*), existence of the reason in the minor term (*pakṣa-dharmatā*), reason (*hetu*), analogy (*upamāna*), implication, being, non-being, duality, measure, causality, time, space, etc. In the third chapter, the smallest of the book, he deals with the possibility of the realization of Brahman and the nature of release through knowledge. In the fourth chapter, which is much smaller than the first two, he deals with the nature of the ultimate state of emancipation.

Citsukha starts with a formal definition of the most fundamental concept of the Vedānta, namely the concept of self-revelation or

---

Jñānottama wrote two works on Vedānta, called *Nyāya-sudhā* and *Jñāna-siddhi;* but he seems to have been a different person from the Jñānottama who wrote a commentary on Sureśvara's *Naiṣkarmyasiddhi-,* for the latter was a householder (as he styles himself with a householder's title, *miśra),* and an inhabitant of the village of Mangala in the Cola country, while the former was an ascetic and a preceptor of the King of Gauḍa, as Citsukha describes him in his colophon to his *Tativa-pradīpikā.* He is also said to have written the *Brahma-stuti, Viṣṇu-purāṇa-ṭīkā, Ṣaḍ-darśaṇa-saṃgraha-vṛtti, Adhikaraṇa saṅgati* (awork explaining the inter-relation of the topics of the *Brahma-sūtra)* and a commentary on the *Naiṣkarmya- siddhi,* called the *Naiṣkarmya-siddhi-ṭīkā* or the *Bhāva-tattva-prakāśikā.* His pupil Sukhaprakāśa wrote a work on the topics of the *Brahma-sūtra,* called *Adhikaraṇa-ratna-mālā.*

1 Thus Paṇḍita Harinātha Śarmā in his Sanskrit introduction to the *Tattva-pradipikā* or *Cit-sukhī* speaks of this work as *advaita-siddhānta-rakṣako'pyadvaita-siddhānta-prakāśako vyutpādakaś ca.*

self-illumination (*sva-prakāśa*). Both Padmapāda and Prakāśātman in the *Pañca-pādikā* and *Pañca-pādikā-vivaraṇa* had distinguished the self from the ego as self-revelation or self-illumination (*svayaṃ-prakāśa*). Thus Prakāśātman says that consciousness (*saṃvid*) is self-revealing and that its self-revelation is not due to any other self-revealing cause.[1] It is on account of this natural self-revelation of consciousness that its objects also appear as self-revealing.[2] Padmapāda also says the same thing, when he states that the self is of the nature of pure self-revealing consciousness; when this consciousness appears in connection with other objects and manifests them, it is called experience (*anubhava*), and, when it is by itself, it is called the self or *ātman.*[3] But Citsukha was probably the first to give a formal definition of the nature of this self-revelation.

Citsukha defines it as that which is entitled to be called immediate (*aparokṣa-vyavahāra-yogya*), though it is not an object of any cognition or any cognizing activity (*avedyatve'pi*).[4] It may be objected that desires, feelings, etc. also are not objects of any cognition and yet are entitled to be regarded as immediate, and hence the definition might as well apply to them; for the object of cognition has a separate objective existence, and by a mind-object contact the mind is transformed into the form of the object, and thereby the one consciousness, which was apparently split up into two forms as the object-consciousness which appeared as material objects and the subject-consciousness which appeared as the cognizer, is again restored to its unity by the super-imposition of the subjective form on the objective form, and the object-form is revealed in consciousness as a jug or a book. But in the case of

---

1 *saṃvedanaṃ tu svayam-prakāśa eva na prakāśāntara-hetuḥ. —Pañca-pādikā-vivaraṇa,* p. 52.

2 *Tasmād anubhavaḥ sajātīya-prakāśāntara-nirapekṣaḥ prakāśamāna eva viṣayeprakāśādi-vyavahāra-nimittaṃ bhavitum arhati avyavadhānena viṣaye prakāśā-di-vyavahāra-nimittatvāt. —Ibid.*

3 *Tasmāt cit-svabhāva evātmā tena tena prameya-bhedena upadhīyamāno'nubha-vābhidhāriīyakaṃ labhate avivakṣitopādhir ātmādi-śabdaiḥ.*

—Pañca-pādikā, p. 19.

4 *Avedyatve saty aparokṣa-vyavahāra-yogyatvaṃ svayam-prakāśa-lakṣaṇam.*

—Cit-sukhī, p. 9

our experience of our will or our feelings these have no existence separate from our own mind and hence are not cognized in the same way as external objects are cognized. According to Vedānta epistemology these subjective experiences of will, emotions, etc. are different mental constituents, forms or states, which, being directly and illusorily imposed upon the self-revealing consciousness, become experienced. These subjective states are therefore not cognized in the same way as external objects. But, since the experience of these states is possible only through a process of illusory imposition, they are not entitled to be called immediate.[1] So, though they appear as immediate, they have no proper *yogyatā*, or, in other words, they are not entitled to be called immediate. But in the true sense even external objects are but illusory impositions on the self-revealing consciousness, and hence they also cannot be said to be entitled to be called immediate. There is therefore no meaning in trying to distinguish the self-revealing consciousness as one which is not an object of cognition; for on the Vedānta theory there is nothing which is entitled to be called immediate, and hence the phrase *avedyatve* (not being an object of cognition) is unnecessary as a special distinguishing feature of the self-revealing consciousness; the epithet "immediate" is therefore also unnecessary. To such an objection Citsukha's reply is that the experience of external objects is only in the last stage of world-dissolution and Brahmahood found non-immediate and illusory, and, since in all our ordinary stages of experience the experience of world-objects is immediate, the epithet *avedyatva* successfully distinguishes self-revealing consciousness from all cognitions of external objects which are entitled to be called immediate and are to be excluded from the range of self-revealing consciousness only by being objects of cognition. In the field of ordinary experience the perceived world-objects are found to be entitled to be called immediate no less than the self-revealing consciousness, and

1 *avedyatve'pi nāparokṣa-vyavahāra-yogyatā teṣāṃ, adhyastatayaiva teṣāṃ siddheḥ. —Cit-sukhī,* p. 10. *Nirṇaya* -Sāgara Press, Bombay, 1915.

it is only because they are objects of cognition that they can be distinguished from the self-revealing consciousness.

The main argument in favour of the admission of the category of independent self-revealing consciousness is that, unless an independent self-revealing consciousness is admitted, there would be a vicious series in the process preceding the rise of any cognition; for, if the pure experience of self-revealing consciousness has to be further subjected to another process before it can be understood, then that also might require another process, and that another, and so there would be an unending series. Moreover, that the pure experience is self-revealing is proved by the very fact of the experience itself; for no one doubts his own experience or stands in need of any further corroboration or confirmation as to whether he experienced or not. It may be objected that it is well known that we may be aware of our awareness of anything (*anu-vyavasāya*), and in such a case the self-revealing consciousness may become further cognized. Citsukha's reply to this is that, when one perceives a jug, there is the mental activity, then a cessation of that activity, then a further starting of new activity and then the knowledge that I know the jug, or rather I know that I know the jug—and hence such a cognition cannot be said to be directly and immediately cognizing the first awareness, which could not have stayed through so many moments.[1] Again, since neither the senses nor the external objects can of themselves produce the self-revelation of knowledge, if knowledge were not admitted as self-revealing, the whole world would be blind and there would be no self-revelation. When one knows that he knows a book or a jug, it is the cognized object that is known and not the awareness that is cognized; there can be no awareness of awareness, but only of the cognized object.[2] If the previous awareness could be made the object of subsequent awareness, then this would amount

1 *ghaṭa-jñānodaya-samaye manasi kriyā tato vibhāgas tataḥ pūrva-saṃyoga-vināśas tata uttara-saṃyogotpattis tato jñānāntaram iti aneka-kṣaṇa-vilambena utpadyamānasya jñānasya aparokṣatayā pūrva-jñuna-grāhakatvānupapatteḥ. —Cit-sukhī,* p. 17.

2 *Vidito ghaṭa ity atraanuvyavasāyena ghaṭasyaiva viditatvam avasīyate na tu vitteḥ. Ibid.* p. 18.

to an admission of the possibility of the self being known by the self (*svasyāpi svena vedyatvāpātāt*)—a theory which would accord not with the Vedānta idealism, but with the Buddhistic. It is true, no doubt, that the pure self-revealing consciousness shows itself only on the occasion of a mental state; but its difference from other cognitive states lies in the fact that it has no form or object, and hence, though it may be focussed by a mental state, yet it stands on a different footing from the objects illuminated by it.

The next point that Citsukha urges is that the self is of the nature of pure self-revealing consciousness (*ātmanaḥ saṃvid-rūpatva*). This is, of course, no new contribution by Citsukha, since this view had been maintained in the Upaniṣads and repeated by Śaṅkara, Padmapāda, Prakāśātman and others. Citsukha says that, like knowledge, the self also is immediately revealed or experienced without itself being the object of any cognizing activity or cognition, and therefore the self is also of the nature of knowledge. No one doubts about his own self; for the self always stands directly and immediately self-revealed. Self and knowledge being identical, there is no relation between the two save that of identity (*jñānātmanoḥ sambandhasyaiva abhāvāt*).

Citsukha defines falsity (*mithyātva*) as the non-existence of a thing in that which is considered to be its cause.[1] He shows this by pointing out that a whole, if it is to exist anywhere, must exist in the parts of which it is made, and, if it does not exist even there, it does not exist anywhere and is false. It is, however, evident that a whole cannot exist in the parts, since, being a whole, it cannot be in the parts.[2] Another argument adduced by Citsukha for the falsity of the world-

---

1 सर्वेषामपि भावानाम् आश्रयत्वेन संमते।
प्रतियोगित्वम् अत्यन्ताभावं प्रतिमृषात्मता॥
sarveṣām api bhāvānām āśrayatvena saṃmate
Pratiyogitvam atyantābhāvaṃ prati mṛṣātmatā.
Cit-sukhī, p. 39. Some of these definitions of falsity are collected in Madhusūdana's *Advaita-siddhi,* a work composed much later than the *Cit-sukhī.*

2 *aṃśinaḥ svāṃśa-gātyantābhāvasya pratiyoginaḥ aṃśitvād itarāṃśīva... vimataḥ paṭaḥ etat-tantu-niṣṭhātyantābhāva-pratiyogī avayavitvāt paṭāntaravat.*
—*Cit-sukhī,* pp. 40, 41. 163

appearance is that it is impossible that there should be any relation between the self-revealing consciousness, the knower (*dṛk*), and the objects which are cognized (*dṛśya*). Knowledge cannot be said to arise through sense-con tact; for in the illusory perception of silver there is the false perception of silver without any actual sense-contact with silver. A reference to subject-object relation (*viṣaya-viṣayi-bhāva*) cannot explain it, since the idea of subject-object relation is itself obscure and unexplainable. Arguing as to the impossibility of properly explaining the subject-object relation (*viṣaya-viṣayi-bhāva*) in knowledge, Citsukha says that it cannot be held that the subject-object relation means that knowledge produces some change in the object (*viṣaya*) and that the knower produces such a change. For what may be the nature of such a change? If it be described as *jñātatā*, or the character of being known, how can such a character be by my knowledge at the present moment generated as a positive quality in an object which has now ceased to exist? If such a quality can be produced even in past objects, then there would be no fixed law according to which such qualities should be produced. Nor can such a relationship be explained on a pragmatic basis by a reference to actual physical practical action with reference to objects that we know or the internal volitions or emotions associated with our knowledge of things. For in picking up a piece of silver that we see in front of us we may quite unknowingly be drawing with it the dross contained in the silver, and hence the fact of the physical drawing of the dross cannot on that ground alone make it an object of my knowledge, and hence the subject-object relation of knowledge cannot be defined as a mere physical action following cognition. The internal mental states of volition and the emotions associated with knowledge belong to the knower and have nothing to do with the object of knowledge. If, however, it is urged that objectivity consists in the fact that whatever is known appears in consciousness, the question arises, what does this appearing in consciousness mean? It cannot mean that consciousness is the container and the object is contained in it; for, consciousness being internal and the object external, the object cannot be contained in it. It cannot be a mere undefined relatedness; for in that case the object may as well be considered subject and the subject, object. If objectivity be defined as that which can induce knowledge, then even the senses, the light and other accessories which help the rise of knowledge may as well be regarded as objects. Object cannot be defined as that to which knowledge owes its particular form; for, knowledge being identical with its form, all that helps the rise of knowledge, the senses, light, etc., may as well be regarded as objects. So, in whatever way one may try to conceive the nature of the subject-object relation, he will be disappointed.

Citsukha follows the traditional view of nescience (*ajñāna*) as a positive entity without beginning which disappears with the rise of true knowledge.[1] Nescience is different from the conception of positivity as well as of negativity, yet it is called only positive because of the fact that it is not negative.[2] Ignorance or nescience is described as a positive state and not a mere negation of knowledge; and so it is said that the rise of right knowledge of any object in a person destroys the positive entity of ignorance with reference to that object and that this ignorance is something different from what one would understand by negation of right knowledge.[3] Citsukha says that the positive character of ignorance becomes apparent when we say that "We do not know whether what you say is true." Here there is the right knowledge of the fact that what is said is known, but it is not known whether what is said is valid.[4] Here also there is a positive knowledge of ignorance of fact, which is not the same as mere absence of knowledge. Such an ignorance, however, is not experienced through sense-contact or sense-processes, but directly by the self-revealing consciousness—the *sākṣin.* Just before the rise

1 *anādi-bhāva-rūpaṃ yad-vijñānena vilīyate tad ajñānam iti prājñā-lakṣaṇam saṃpracakṣate anāditve sati bhāva-rūpaṃ vijñāna-nirāsyam ajñānam iti lakṣaṇaṃ iha vivakṣitam. —Cit-sukhī,* p. 57.

2 *bhāvābhāva-vilakṣaṇasya ajñānasya abhāva-vilakṣaṇatva-mātreṇa bhāvat-vo-pacārāt. —Ibid.*

3 *vigītaṃ Deva-datta-niṣṭha-pramāṇa-jñānaṃ Devadatta-niṣṭha-pramā-bhāvā-tiriktānādernivarttakaṃ pramāṇatvād Yajñadattādigata-pramāṇa-jñānavad ity anumānam. —Ibid.* p. 58.

4 *tvadukte'rthe pramāṇa-jñānaṃ mama nāsti ity asya viśiṣṭa-viṣaya-jñānasya pramātvāt. —Cit-sukhī,* p. 59.

of right knowledge about an object there is ignorance (*ajñāna*), and the object, as qualified by such an ignorance, is experienced as being unknown. All things are the objects of the inner unmoved intuitive consciousness either as known or as unknown.[1] Our reference to deep dreamless sleep as a state in which we did not know anything (*na kiṃcid-avediṣam*) is also referred to as a positive experience of ignorance in the dreamless state.

One of the chief tenets of Vedānta epistemology lies in the supposition that a presentation of the false is a fact of experience. The opposite view is that of Prabhākara, that the false is never presented in experience and that falsehood consists in the wrong construction imposed upon experience by the mind, which fails to note the actual want of association between two things which are falsely associated as one. According to this theory all illusion consists of a false association or a false relationing of two things which are not presented in experience as related. This false association is not due to an active operation of the mind, but to a failure to note that no such association was actually presented in experience (*asaṃsargāgraha*). According to Prabhākara, the great Mīmāṃsā authority, the false is never presented in experience, nor is the false experience due to an arbitrary positive activity of wrong construction of the mind, but merely to a failure to note certain distinctions presented in experience. On account of such a failure things which are distinct are not observed as distinct, and hence things which are distinct and different are falsely associated as one, and the conch-shell is thus regarded as silver. But here there is no false presentation in experience. Whatever is known is true; falsehood is due to omissions of knowledge and failure in noting differences.

Citsukha objects to this view and urges that such an explanation can never explain all cases of false apprehension.

---

1 *asman-mate ajñānasya sākṣi-siddhatayā pramāṇābodhyatvāt, pramāṇa-jñānodayāt prāk-kāle ajñānaṃ tad-viśeṣito'rthaḥ sākṣi-siddhaḥ ajñāta ity anuvāda gocaraḥ... sarvaṃ vastu jñātatayā ajñātatayā vā sākṣi-caitanyasya viṣayaḥ. Ibid.* p. 60.

Take the proposition, "There are false apprehensions and false presentations"; if this proposition is admitted to be correct, then Prabhākara's contention is false; if it is admitted to be false, then here is a false proposition, the falsehood of which is not due to a failure to note differences. If the falsity of all propositions be said to be due to a failure to note differences, then it would be hard to find out any true proposition or true experience. On the analogy of our false experience of the everchanging flame of a lamp as the same identical one all cases of true recognition might no less be regarded as false, and therefore all inferences would be doubtful. All cases of real and true association could be explained as being due to a failure to note differences. There could be no case in which one could assure himself that he was dealing with a real association and not a failure to apprehend the absence of association (*asaṃsargāgraha*). Citsukha therefore contends that it is too much to expect that all cases of false knowledge can be explained as being due to a mere non-apprehension of difference, since it is quite reasonable to suppose that false knowledge is produced by defective senses which oppose the rise of true knowledge and positively induce false appearance.[1] Thus in the case of the illusory perception of conch-shell as silver it is the conch-shell that appears as a piece of silver. But what is the nature of the presentation that forms the object (*ālambana*) of false perception? It cannot be regarded as absolutely non-existent (*asat*), since that which is absolutely non-existent cannot be the object of even a false perception, and moreover it cannot through such a perception (*e.g.*, the tendency of a man to pick up the piece of silver, which is but a false perception of a piece of conch-shell) induce a practical movement on the part of the perceiver. Neither can it be regarded as existent; for the later experience contradicts the previous false perception, and one says that there is no silver at the present time and there was no silver in the past—it was only the conch-shell that appeared as silver. Therefore the false

1 *Tathā doṣāṇām api yathārtha-jñāna-pratibandhakatvam ayathārtha-jñāna-janakatvaṃ ca kiṃ na syāt. —Cit-sukhī*, p. 66.

presentation, though it serves all the purposes of a perceptual object, cannot be described either as existent or as non-existent, and it is precisely this character that constitutes the indefinable nature (*anirvacanīyata*) of all illusions.[1]

It is unnecessary to deal with the other doctrines of Vedānta which Citsukha describes, since there is nothing new in them and they have already been described in chapter X of volume I of this work. It is therefore desirable to pass on to his dialectic criticism of the Nyāya categories. It will suffice, however, to give only a few of these criticisms, as they mostly refer to the refutation of such kinds of categories as are discussed in Śrīharṣa's great work *Khaṇḍana-khaṇḍa-khādya,* and it would be tedious to follow the refutation of the same kinds of categories by two different writers, though the arguments of Citsukha are in many cases new and different from those given by Śrīharṣa. Citsukha's general approach to such refutations is also slightly different from that of Śrīharṣa. For, unlike Śrīharṣa, Citsukha dealt with the principal propositions of the Vedānta, and his refutations of the Nyāya categories were not intended so much to show that they were inexplicable or indefinable as to show that they were false appearances, and that the pure self-revealing Brahman was the only reality and truth.

Thus, in refuting time (*kāla*), Citsukha says that time cannot be perceived either by the visual sense or by the tactual sense, nor can it be apprehended by the mind (*manas*), as the mind only operates in association with the external senses. Moreover, since there are no perceptual data, it cannot be inferred. The notions of before and after, succession and simultaneity, quickness and duration, cannot by themselves indicate the nature of time as it is in itself. It may be urged that, since the solar vibrations can only be associated with human bodies and worldly things, making them appear as young or old only through some other agency such as days, months, etc., such an agency, which brings about the connection of solar

1 *pratyekaṃ sad asattvābhyāṃ vicāra-padavīṃ na yad gāhate tad anirvācyam āhur vedānta-vedinaḥ. Ibid.* p. 79.

vibrations with worldly things, is called time.[1] To this Citsukha replies that, since the self itself can be regarded as the cause of the manifestation of time in events and things in accordance with the varying conditions of their appearance, it is unnecessary to suppose the existence of a new category called time. Again, it cannot be said that the notions of before and after have time as their material cause; for the validity of these notions is challenged by the Vedāntist. They may be regarded as the impressions produced by a greater or lesser quantity of solar vibrations. There is therefore no necessity to admit time as a separate category, since its apprehension can be explained on the basis of our known data of experience. From considerations of some data relative space (*dik*) has to be discarded; for relative space cannot be perceived by the senses or inferred for want of data of experience. Both time and relative space originate from a sense of relativity (*apekṣā-buddhi*), and, given that sense of relativity, the mind can in association with our experience of bodily movements form the notion of relative space. It is therefore unnecessary to admit the existence of relative space as a separate category.

In refuting the atomic theory of the Vaiśeṣikas Citsukha says that there is no ground for admitting the Vaiśeṣika atoms. If these atoms are to be admitted on the ground that all things are to be conceived as being divisible into smaller and smaller parts, then the same may apply to the atoms as well. If it is urged that one must stop somewhere, that the atoms are therefore regarded as the last state, and are uniform in size and not further divisible, then the specks of dust that are seen in the windows when the sun is shining (called *trasareṇus*) may equally be regarded as the last stage of divisible size. If it is contended that, since these are visible, they have parts and cannot therefore be considered as indivisible, it may

---

1 *taraṇi-parispanda-viśeṣāṇāṃ yuva-sthavira-śarīrādi-piṇḍeṣu māsādi-vicitra-buddhi-janana-dvāreṇa tad-upahiteṣu paratvāparatvādi-buddhi-janakatvaṃ na ca tair asaṃbaddhānāṃ tatra buddhi-janakatvaṃ, na ca sākṣāt sambandho ravi-parispandānāṃ piṇḍair asti ataḥ tat-sambandhakatayā kaścid aṣṭadravya-vilakṣaṇo dravya-viśeṣaḥ svīkartavyaḥ, tasya ca kāla iti saṃjñā.* (This is Vallabha's view of time.)*Nayana-prasādinī* commentary on *Cit-sukhī,* p. 321, by Pratyak-svarupa-bhagavat, Nirṇaya-Sāgara Press, Bombay, 1915.

be said in reply that, since the Nyāya writers admit that the atoms can be perceived by the yogins, visibility of the *trasareṇus* could not be put forward as a reason why they could not be regarded as indivisible. Moreover, if the atoms were partless, how could they be admitted to combine to produce the grosser material forms? Again, it is not indispensable that atoms should combine to form bigger particles or make grosser appearances possible; for, like threads in a sheet, many particles may make gross appearances possible even without combining. Citsukha then repeats Śaṅkara's refutation of the concept of wholes and parts, saying that, if the wholes are different from the parts, then they must be in the parts or they would not be there; if they are not in the parts, it would be difficult to maintain that the wholes were made of parts; if they are in the parts, they must be either wholly or partly in them; if they are wholly in the parts, then there would be many such wholes, or in each part the whole would be found; and, if they are partly in the parts, then the same difficulty of wholes and parts would appear.

Again, the concept of contact (*saṃyoga*) is also inexplicable. It cannot be defined as the coming together of any two things which are not in contact (*aprāptayoḥ prāptiḥ saṃyogaḥ*); for, until one knows the meaning of the concept of contact, one cannot understand the meaning of the phrase "not in contact." If it is defined as the coming together of two things which are unrelated, then contact (*saṃyoga*) would include even the relation of inherence, such as that which exists between a piece of cloth and the threads. If it is defined as a relation which is produced in time and is transitory (*anityaḥ sambandhaḥ janyatva-viśeṣito vā*). then cases of beginningless contact would not be included, and even the possession of an article by purchase would have to be included as contact, since this relation of possession is also produced in time. It cannot be objected that "possession" is not a relation, since a relation to be such must be between two things; for, if the objection were valid, the relation between substance and quality would not be a relation, since quality and substance exist together, and there are no two separate things which can be related. If the objector means that the relation must be between two terms, then there are two terms here also, namely, the article possessed and the possessor. Moreover, if contact is defined as relation which does not connect two things in their entirety (*avyāpya-vṛttitva-viśeṣito*), then again it would be wrong, since in the case of partless entities the relation of contact cannot connect the parts, as they have no parts. Citsukha refutes the concept of separation (*vibhāga*) on the same lines and passes over to the refutation of number, as two, three and the like.

Citsukha urges that there is no necessity of admitting the existence of two, three, etc. as separate numbers, since what we perceive is but the one thing, and then by a sense of oscillation and mutual reference (*apekṣā-buddhi*) we associate them together and form the notions of two, three, etc. These numbers therefore do not exist separately and independently, but are imaginatively produced by mental oscillation and association from the experience of single objects. There is therefore no necessity of thinking that the numbers, two, three, etc., are actually produced. We simply deal with the notions of two, three, etc. on the strength of our powers of mental association.[1]

Citsukha then refutes the notion of class-concept (*jāti*) on the ground that it cannot be proved either by perception or by inference. The question is what exactly is meant by class-concept. If it is said that, when in perceiving one individual animal we have the notion of a cow, and in perceiving other individual animals also we have the same notion of cow, there *is jāti,* then it may be replied that this does not necessarily imply the admission of a separate class-concept of cow; for, just as one individual had certain peculiarities which entitled it to be called a cow, so the other individuals had their peculiarities which entitled them to be called cows. We see reflections of the moon in different places and call each of them the moon. What constitutes the essentials of the concept of cow? It is difficult to formulate one universal characteristic of cows; if

1 *āropita-dvitva-tritvādi-viśeṣitaikatva-samuccayālambanā buddhir dvitvādi-janiketi cet; na; tathābhūtāyā eva buddher dvitvādi-vyavahāra-janakatvopapattaudvitvādy-utpādakatva-kalpanā-vaiyarthyāt. —Nayana-prasādinī,* p. 300.

one such characteristic could be found, then there would be no necessity of admitting the class-concept of cow. For it would then be an individual characteristic, and one would recognize it as a cow everywhere, and there would be no necessity of admitting a separate class-concept. If one admits a class-concept, one has to point out some trait or quality as that which indicates the class-concept. Then again one could not get at this trait or quality independently of the class-concept or at the class-concept independently of it, and this mutual dependence would make the definition of either of them impossible. Even if one admits the class-concept, one has to show what constitutes the essentials of it in each case, and, if such essentials have to be found in each case, then those essentials would be a sufficient justification for knowing a cow as cow and a horse as horse: what then is the good of admitting a class-concept? Again, even if a class-concept be admitted, it is difficult to see how it can be conceived to be related to the individuals. It cannot be a relation of contact, identity, inherence or any other kind of relation existing anywhere. If all class-concepts existed everywhere, there would be a medley of all class-concepts together, and all things would be everywhere. Again, if it is held that the class-concept of cow exists only in the existing cows, then how does it jump to a new cow when it is born? Nor has the class-concept any parts, so as to be partly here and partly there. If each class-concept of cow were wholly existent in each of the individual cows, then there would be a number of class-concepts; and, if each class-concept of cow were spread out over all the individual cows, then, unless all the individual cows were brought together, one could not have the notion of any class-concept.

Speaking of the refutation of cause (*kāraṇa*), Citsukha says that cause cannot be defined as mere antecedence (*pūrva-kāla-bhāvitva*); for then the ass which is always found in the house of a washerman and on the back of which the washerman carries his clothes might be regarded as a thing antecedent to the smoky fire kindled in the washerman's house and thus as a cause of fire. If this antecedence be further qualified as that which is present in all cases of the presence of the effect and absent in all cases of the absence of the effect, then also the washerman's ass may be considered to satisfy the conditions of such an antecedence with reference to the fire in the washerman's house (when the washerman is away from the house with his ass, the fire in the washerman's house is also absent, and it is again kindled when he returns to his house with his ass). If "unconditionality" (*ananyathā-siddha*) is further added as a qualifying condition of antecedence, even then the ass and the common abiding elements such as space, ether and the like may be regarded as causes of the fire. If it be argued that the ass is present only because of the presence of other conditioning factors, the same may be said of seeds, earth, water, etc., which are all however regarded as being causes for the production of the shoots of plants. If objection be raised against the possibility of ether (*ākāśa*) being regarded as the cause of smoke on the ground of its being a common, abiding and all-pervasive element, then the same argument ought to stand as an objection against the soul (which is an all-pervasive entity) being regarded on the Nyāya view as the cause of the production of pleasure and pain. The cause cannot be defined as that which being there the effect follows; for then a seed cannot be regarded as the cause of the shoot of the plant, since the shoots cannot be produced from seeds without the help of other co-operating factors, such as earth, water, light, air, etc. Cause, again, cannot be defined as that which being present in the midst of the co-operating factors or even accessories (*sahakāri*), the effect follows; for an irrelevant thing, like an ass, may be present among a number of co-operating circumstances, but this would not justify anybody calling an irrelevant thing a cause. Moreover, such a definition would not apply to those cases where by the joint operation of many co-operating entities the effect is produced. Furthermore, unless the cause can be properly defined, there is no way of defining the co-operating conditions. Nor can a cause be defined as that which being there the effect follows, and which not being there, there is no effect (*sati bhāvo 'saty abhāva eva*); for such a maxim is invalidated by the plurality of causes (fire may be produced by rubbing two pieces of wood, by striking hard against a flint, or by a lens). It may be urged that there are differences in each kind of fire produced by the different agencies: to which it may be replied that, even if there were any such difference, it is impossible to know it by observation. Even when differences are noticeable, such differences do not necessarily imply that the different effects belong to different classes; for the differences might well be due to various attendant circumstances. Again, a cause cannot be defined as a collocation of things, since such a collocation may well be one of irrelevant things. A cause cannot be defined as a collocation of different causes, since it has not so far been possible to define what is meant by "cause." The phrase "collocation of causes" will therefore be meaningless. Moreover, it may be asked whether a collocation of causes (*sāmagrī*) be something different from the causes, or identical with them. If the former alternative be accepted, then effects would follow from individual causes as well, and the supposition of a collocation of causes as producing the effects would be uncalled-for. If the latter alternative be accepted, then, since the individuals are the causes of the collocation, the individuals being there, there is always the collocation and so always the effect, which is absurd. Again, what does this collocation of causes mean? It cannot mean occurrence in the same time or place; for, there being no sameness of time and place for time and place respectively, they themselves would be without any cause. Again, it cannot be said that, if the existence of cause be not admitted, then things, being causeless, would be non-existent; for the Nyāya holds that there are eternal substances such as atoms, souls, etc., which have no cause.

Since cause cannot be defined, neither can effect (*kārya*) be satisfactorily defined, as the conception of effect always depends upon the notion of cause.

In refuting the conception of substance (*dravya*)Citsukha says that a substance can be defined only as being that in which the qualities inhere. But, since even qualities are seen to have qualities and a substance is believed by the Naiyāyikas to be without any quality at the moment of its origination, such a definition cannot properly distinguish or define a substance. If a substance be defined in a roundabout way as that in which there is no presence of the absolute negation of possessing qualities (*guṇavattvātyantābhāvānadhikaraṇatā*), then also it may be objected that such a definition would make us regard even negation (*abhāva*) as a quality, since the absence of the negation of qualities, being itself a negation, cannot exist in a negation.[1] It may again be asked whether the absence of the negation of qualities refers to the negation of a number of qualities or the negation of all qualities; in either case it is wrong. For in the first case a substance, which contains only some qualities and does not possess others, would not be called a substance, and in the latter case it would be difficult to find anything that cannot be called a substance; for where is the substance which lacks all qualities? The fact also remains that even such a roundabout definition cannot distinguish a substance from a quality; for even qualities have the numerical qualities and the qualities of separateness.[2] If it is argued that, if qualities are admitted to have further qualities, there will be a vicious infinite, it may be said in reply that the charge of vicious infinite cannot be made, since the qualities of number and separateness cannot be said to have any further qualities. Substances, again, have nothing in common by virtue of which they could be regarded as coming under the class-concept of substances.[3] Gold and mud and trees are all regarded as substances, but there is nothing common in them by virtue of which one can think that gold is the same as mud or tree; therefore it cannot be admitted that in the substances one finds any characteristic which remains the same in them all.[4]

---

1 *Tatraiva atyantābhave'tivyāpteḥ; sopi hi guṇavattvātyantābhāvas tasyādhi-karaṇam svasyasvasminnavṛtteḥ.* —*Cit-sukhī,* p. 176.

2 *Asminnapi vakra-lakṣaṇe guṇādiṣu api saṃkhyā-pṛthaktva-guṇayoḥ pratīteḥ kathaṃ nātivyāptiḥ.* —*Ibid.* p. 177.

3 *Jātim abhyupagacchatā tajjāti-vyañjakaṃ kiṃcid-avaśyam abhyupeyam na ca tannirupaṇam suśakam.* —*Ibid.* p. 178.

4 *dravyaṃ dravyam iti anugata-pratyayaḥ pramāṇam iti cenna suvarṇam-upalabhya mṛttikām-upalabhyamānasya laukikasya tad evedaṃ dravyam iti pratyayā-bhāvāt parīkṣakāṇāṃ cānugata-pratyaye vipratipatteḥ.* —*Ibid.* p. 179.

Referring to qualities (*guṇa*), Citsukha deals with the definition of *guṇa* in the *Vaiśeṣika-bhāṣya* of Praśastapāda. There Praśastapāda defines *guṇa* as that which inheres in a substance, is associated with the class-concept of substance, is itself without any quality and which has no motion (*niṣkriya*).[1] But the definition of a quality cannot involve the phrase "without a quality"; for quality is still to be defined. Again, unless the *guṇa* is properly defined, its difference from motion is not known, and so the phrase "which has no motion" is meaningless. The class-concept of quality, again, can be determined only when the general character of qualities is known and the nature of class-concepts also is determined. Hence, from whatever point of view one may look at the question, it is impossible to define qualities...

It is needless now to multiply examples of such refutation by Citsukha. It will appear from what has been adduced that Citsukha enters into detail concerning most concepts of particular categories and tries to show their intrinsic impossibility. In some cases, however, he was not equal to the task and remained content with criticizing the definitions given by the Naiyāyikas. But it may be well to point out here that, though Śrīharṣa and Citsukha carried out an elaborate scheme of a critique of the different categories in order to show that the definitions of these categories, as given by the Nyāya, are impossible, yet neither of them can be regarded as the originator of the application of the dialectic method in the Vedānta. Śaṅkara himself had started it in his refutation of the Nyāya and other systems in his commentary on the *Vedānta-sūtras,* II. II.

THE DIALECTIC OF NĀGĀRJUNA AND THE VEDĀNTA DIALECTIC

The dialectic of Śrīharṣa was a protest against the realistic definitions of the Nyāya-Vaiśeṣika, which supposed that all that was knowable was

1 *rūpādtnāṃ guṇānāṃ sarveṣāṃ guṇatvābhisambandho dravyāśritatvaṃ nirguṇatvaṃ niṣkriyatvaṃ. —Praśastapāda-bhāṣya,* p. 94, The Vizianagram Sanskrit Series, Benares, 1895.

also definable. It aimed at refuting these definitions in order to prove that the natures of all things are indefinable, as their existence and nature are all involved in *māyā.* The only reality is Brahman. That it is easy to pick holes in all definitions was taught long ago by Nāgārjuna, and in that sense (except for a tendency to find faults of a purely verbal nature in Nyāya definitions) Śrīharṣa's method was a continuation of Nāgārjuna's, and an application of it to the actual definitions of the Nyāya-Vaiśeṣika. But the most important part of Nāgārjuna's method was deliberately ignored by Śrīharṣa and his followers, who made no attempt to refute Nāgārjuna's conclusions. Nāgārjuna's main thesis is that all things are relative and hence indefinable in themselves, and so there is no way of discovering their essences; and, since their essences are not only indefinable and indescribable, but incomprehensible as well, they cannot be said to possess any essences of their own. Nāgārjuna was followed by Āryadeva, a Ceylonese by birth, who wrote a separate work on the same subject in 400 verses. For about two centuries after this the doctrines of Nāgārjuna lay dormant, as is evidenced by the fact that Buddhaghoṣa of the fourth century AD does not refer to them. During the Gupta empire, in the fifth century AD, Asaṅga and Vasubandhu flourished. In the sixth century AD the relativist philosophy of Nāgārjuna again flourished in the hands of Buddhapālita, of Valabhī in Surat, and of Bhavya, or Bhāvaviveka, of Orissa. The school of Bhavya was called Mādhyamika-Sautrāntika on account of his supplementing Nāgārjuna's arguments with special arguments of his own. At this time the Yogācāra school of Mahāyāna monism developed in the north, and the aim of this school was to show that for the true knowledge of the one consciousness (*vijñāna*) all logical arguments were futile. All logical arguments showed only their own inconsistency.[1] It seems very probable that Śrīharṣa was inspired by these Yogācāra authors, and their relativist allies from Nāgārjuna to Bhavya, and Candrakīrti, the master commentator on Nāgārjuna's *Mādhyamika-kārikā.* Buddhapālita sought to prove that the apprehension and realization of the idealistic monism cannot be made by any logical argument, since all logic

1 *The Conception of Buddhist Nirvāṇa,* pp. 66—67. Published by the Academy of Sciences of the U. S. S. R. Leningrad, 1927.

is futile and inconsistent, while Bhāvaviveka sought to establish his idealistic monism by logical arguments. Candrakīrti finally supported Buddhapālita's scheme as against the scheme of Bhāvaviveka and tried to prove the futility of all logical arguments. It was this Mādhyamika scheme of Candrakīrti that finally was utilized in Tibet and Mongolia for the realization of idealistic monism.

In taking up his refutation of the various categories of being Nāgārjuna begins with the examination of causation. Causation in the non-Buddhistic systems of philosophy is regarded as being production from the inner changes of some permanent or abiding stuff or through the conglomeration (*sāmagrī*) of several factors or through some factors operating upon an unchangeable and abiding stuff. But Nāgārjuna denies not only that anything is ever produced, but also that it is ever produced in any one of the above ways. Buddhapālita holds that things cannot arise of themselves, since, if they are already existing, there is no meaning in their being produced; if things that are existing are regarded as capable of being produced again, then things would eternally continue to be produced. Bhāvaviveka, criticizing Buddhapālita, says that the refutation of Buddhapālita should have been supplemented with reasons and examples and that his refutation would imply the undesirable thesis that, if things are not produced of themselves, they must be produced by other factors. But Candrakīrti objects to this criticism of Bhāvaviveka and says that the burden of proof in establishing the identity of cause and effect lies with the opponents, the Sāṃkhyists, who hold that view. There is no meaning in the production of what already exists, and, if that which is existent has to be produced again, and that again, there will be an infinite regress. It is unnecessary to give any new argument to refute the Sāṃkhya *sat-kārya-vāda* view; it is enough to point out the inconsistency of the Sāṃkhya view. Thus Āryadeva says that the Mādhyamika view has no thesis of its own which it seeks to establish, since it does not believe in the reality or unreality of anything or in the combination of reality and unreality.[1] This was exactly the point of view that was taken by Śrīharṣa. Śrīharṣa says that the Vedāntists have no view of their own regarding the things of the world and the various categories involved in them. Therefore there was no way in which the Vedānta view could be attacked. The Vedānta, however, is free to find fault with other views, and, when once this is done and the inconsistencies of other positions are pointed out, its business is finished; for it has no view of its own to establish. Nāgārjuna writes in his *Vigraha-vyāvartanī* thus:

When I have these (of my own to prove),
I can commit mistakes just for the sake (of proving);
But I have none. I cannot be accused (of being inconsistent).
If I did (really) cognize some (separate) things,
I could then make an affirmation or a denial
Upon the basis of these things perceived or (inferred).
But these (separate) things do not exist for me.
Therefore I cannot be assailed on such a basis.[2]

Candrakīrti thus emphasizes the fact that it is not possible for the Mādhyamikas to offer new arguments or new examples in criticizing any view, since they have no view of their own to support. They cannot even prove their own affirmations, and, if their affirmations contain any thesis, they quarrel with it also themselves. So the Mādhyamika scheme of criticism consists only in finding fault with all theses, whatever they may be, and in replying to the counter-charges so far as inconsistencies can be found in the opponents' theses and methods, but not in adducing any new arguments or any new counter-theses, since the Mādhyamikas have no theses of

1 सद् असत् सदसच् चेति यस्य पक्षो न विद्यते
उपालम्भश्चिरेणापि तस्य वक्तुं न शक्यते॥
sad asat sad-asac ceti yasya pakṣo na vidyate
Upālambhaś cireṇāpi tasya vaktuṃ na śakyate. —Mādhyamika-vṛtti, p. 16.

2 अन्यत् प्रतीत्य यदि नाम परोऽभविष्यत् जायेत तर्हि बहुलः शिखिनोऽन्धकारः।
सर्वस्य जन्म च भवेत् खलु सर्वतश्च तुल्यम् परत्वम् अखिलेऽजनकेऽपि यस्मात्॥
Anyat pratītya yadi nāma paro'bhaviṣyat
Jāyeta tarhi bahulaḥ śikhino'ndhakāraḥ
Sarvasya janma ca bhavet khalu sarvataś ca
Tulyam paratvam akhile'janake'pi yasmāt. —Ibid. p. 36.

their own. In an argument one can only follow the principles that one admits; no one can be defeated by arguments carried on, on the basis of principles admitted only by his opponents.

Things are not produced by any conglomeration of foreign factors or causes; for, were it so, there would be no law of such production and anything might come from any other thing, *e.g.*, darkness from light.[1] And, if a thing cannot be produced out of itself or out of others, it cannot be produced by a combination of them both. Again, the world could not have sprung into being without any cause (*ahetutaḥ*).

The Buddhist logicians try to controvert this view by pointing out that, whatever a view may be, it must be established by proper proof. So, in order to prove the thesis that all existents are unproduced, the Mādhyamikas must give some proofs, and this would involve a further specification of the nature of such proofs and a specification of the number of valid proofs admitted by them. But, if the thesis that "all existents are unproved" is a mere assertion without any proof to support it, then any number of counter assertions may be made for which no proof need be show[n]; and, if proofs are not required in one case, they cannot be required in the other. So one could with equal validity assert that all existents are real and are produced from causes. The Mādhyamika answer to such an objection, as formulated by Candrakīrti, is that the Mādhyamika has no thesis of his own and so the question whether his thesis is supported by valid proof or not is as meaningless as the question regarding the smallness or the greatness of a mule's horn. Since there is no thesis, the Mādhyamika has nothing to say regarding the nature of valid proofs (*pramāṇa*) or their number. But it may well be asked why, if the Mādhyamika has no thesis of his own, should he hold the proposition that all existents are unproduced (*sarve bhāvā anutpannāḥ*)? To this the Mādhyamika replies that such propositions appear as definite views only to ordinary people,

1 *Mādhyamika-vṛtti,* p. 36. See also Stcherbatsky's *The Conception of Buddhist Nirvāṇa*, to which the author is indebted for the translation and some of the materials of the last two paragraphs.

not to the wise. The proper attitude for the wise is always to remain silent. They impart instruction only from a popular point of view to those who want to listen to them. Their arguments are not their own or those which they believe to be right, but only such as would appeal to their hearers.

It is not out of place here to mention that the Mādhyamika school wishes to keep the phenomenal and the real or the transcendental views wide apart. In the phenomenal view things are admitted to be as they are perceived, and their relations are also conceived as real. It is interesting to refer to the discussion of Candrakīrti with Diṅnāga regarding the nature of sense-perceptions. While Diṅnāga urges that a thing is what it is in itself (*sva-lakṣaṇa*), Candrakīrti holds that, since relations are also perceived to be true, things are relational as well. Phenomenally substances exist as well as their qualities. The "thing in itself" of Diṅnāga was as much a relative concept as the relational things that are popularly perceived as true; that being so, it is meaningless to define perception as being only the thing in itself. Candrakīrti thus does not think that any good can be done by criticizing the realistic logic of the Naiyāyikas, since, so far as popular perceptions or conceptions go, the Nyāya logic is quite competent to deal with them and give an account of them. There is a phenomenal reality and order which is true for the man in the street and on which all our linguistic and other usages are based. Diṅnāga, in defining perception, restricts it to the unique thing in itself (*sva-lakṣaṇa*) and thinks that all associations of quality and relations are extraneous to perceptions and should be included under imagination or inference. This however does violence to our ordinary experience and yet serves no better purpose; for the definition of perception as given by Diṅnāga is not from the transcendental point of view. If that is so, why not accept the realistic conceptions of the Nyāya school, which fit in with the popular experience? This reminds us of the attitude of the Vedāntists, who on the one hand accepted the view-point of popular experience and regarded all things as having a real objective existence, and on the other hand considered them as false and unreal from the transcendental point of view of ultimate reality. The attitude of the Vedāntists on this point seems to have been directly inspired by that of the Mādhyamikas. The attempts of Śrīharṣa to refute the realistic definitions of the Nyāya were intended to show that the definitions of the Nyāya could not be regarded as absolute and true, as the Naiyāyikas used to think. But, while the Mādhyamikas, who had no view-points of their own to support, could leave the field of experience absolutely undisturbed and allow the realistic definitions of the Nyāya to explain the popular experience in any way they liked, the Vedānta had a thesis of its own, namely, that the self-luminous Brahman was the only reality and that it was through it that everything else was manifested. The Vedānta therefore could not agree with Nyāya interpretations of experience and their definitions. But, as the Vedānta was unable to give the manifold world-appearance a footing in reality, it regarded it as somehow existing by itself and invented a theory of perception by which it could be considered as being manifested by coming in touch with Brahman and being illusorily imposed on it.

Continuing the discussion on the nature of causation, Nāgārjuna and Candrakīrti hold that collocations of causal conditions which are different from the effect cannot produce the effect, as is held by the Hīnayāna Buddhists; for, since the effect is not perceived in those causal conditions, it cannot be produced out of them, and, if it is already existent in them, its production becomes useless. Production of anything out of some foreign or extraneous causes implies that it is related to them, and this relation must mean that it was in some way existent in them. The main principle which Nāgārjuna employs in refuting the idea of causation or production in various ways is that, if a thing exists, it cannot be produced, and, if it does not exist, it cannot be produced at all. That which has no essence in itself cannot be caused by anything else, and, having no essence in itself, it cannot be the cause of anything else.[1]

Nāgārjuna similarly examines the concepts of going and coming and says that the action of going is not to be found in the space traversed, nor is it to be found in that which is not traversed;

1 *Mādhyamika-vṛtti,* p. 90, 1. 6.

and apart from the space traversed and not traversed there cannot be any action of going. If it is urged that going is neither in the space traversed nor in the space untraversed, but in the person who continues to go, since going is in him in whom there is the effort of going, then this again cannot be right. For, if the action of going is to be associated with the person who goes, it cannot be associated with the space traversed. One action cannot be connected with both; and, unless some space is gone over, there cannot be a goer. If going is in the goer alone, then even without going one could be called a goer, which is impossible. If both the goer and the space traversed have to be associated with going, then there must be two actions and not one; and, if there are two actions, that implies that there are also two agents. It may be urged that the movement of going is associated with the goer and that therefore going belongs to the goer; but, if there is no going without the goer and if there is no goer without going, how can going be associated with the goer at all? Again, in the proposition "the goer goes" (*gantā gacchati*) there is only one action of going, and that is satisfied by the verb "goes"; what separate "going" is there by virtue of association with which a "goer" can be so called? and, since there are no two actions of going, there cannot be a goer. Again, the movement of going cannot even be begun; for, when there is the motion of going, there is no beginning and when there is no motion of going, there cannot be any beginning. Again, it cannot be urged that "going" must exist, since its opposite, "remaining at rest" (*sthiti*), exists; for who is at rest? The goer cannot be at rest, since no one can be a goer unless he goes; he who is not a goer, being already at rest, cannot be the agent of another action of being at rest. If the goer and going be regarded as identical, then there would be neither verb nor agent. So there is no reality in going. "Going" stands here for any kind of passage or becoming, and the refutation of "going" implies the refutation of all kinds of passage (*niṣkarṣaṇa*) as well. If seeds passed into the state of shoots (*aṅkura*), then they would be seeds and not shoots; the shoots neither are seeds nor are different from them; yet, the seeds being there, there are the shoots. A pea is from another pea, yet no pea becomes another pea. A pea is neither in another pea nor different from it. It is as one may see in a mirror the beautiful face of a woman and feel attracted by it and run after her, though the face never passed into the mirror and there was no human face in the reflected image. Just as the essenceless reflected image of a woman's face may rouse attachment in fools, so are world-appearances the causes of our delusion and attachment.

It is needless to multiply examples and describe elaborately Nāgārjuna's method of applying his dialectic to the refutation of the various Buddhistic and other categories. But from what has been said it may be possible to compare or contrast Nāgārjuna's dialectic with that of Śrīharṣa. Neither Nāgārjuna nor Śrīharṣa is interested to give any rational explanation of the world-process, nor are they interested to give a scientific reconstruction of our world-experience. They are agreed in discarding the validity of world-experience as such. But, while Nāgārjuna had no thesis of his own to uphold, Śrīharṣa sought to establish the validity and ultimate reality of Brahman. But, it does not appear that he ever properly tried to apply his own dialectic to his thesis and attempted to show that the definition of Brahman could stand the test of the criticism of his own dialectic. Both Nāgārjuna and Śrīharṣa were, however, agreed in the view that there was no theory of the reconstruction of world-appearance which could be supported as valid. But, while Śrīharṣa attacked only the definitions of the Nyāya, Nāgārjuna mainly attacked the accepted Buddhistic categories and also some other relevant categories which were directly connected with them. But the entire efforts of Śrīharṣa were directed to showing that the definitions of the Nyāya were faulty and that there was no way in which the Nyāya could define its categories properly. From the fact that the Nyāya could not define its categories he rushed to the conclusion that they were intrinsically indefinable and that therefore the world-appearance which was measured and scanned in terms of those categories was also false. Nāgārjuna's methods differ considerably from those of Śrīharṣa in this, that the concepts which he criticized were shown by him to have been intrinsically based and constructed on notions which had no essential nature of their own, but were understood only in relation to others. No concept revealed any intrinsic nature of its own, and one could understand a concept only through another, and that again through the former or through another, and so on. The entire world-appearance would thus be based on relative conceptions and be false. Nāgārjuna's criticisms are, however, largely of an *a priori* nature, and do not treat the concepts in a concrete manner and are not based on the testimony of our psychological experience. The oppositions shown are therefore very often of an abstract nature and occasionally degenerate into verbalism. But as a rule they are based on the fundamentally relative nature of our experience. They are never half so elaborate as the criticisms of Śrīharṣa; but at the same time they are fundamentally more convincing and more direct than the elaborate roundabout logical subtleties of Śrīharṣa's dialectic. It cannot be denied that, based on the dialectical methods of Nāgārjuna, Buddhapālita and Candrakīrti, Śrīharṣa's criticisms, following an altogether different plan of approach, show wonderful powers of logical subtlety and finesse, though the total effect can hardly be regarded as an advance from the strictly philosophical point of view, while the frequent verbalism of many of his criticisms is a discredit to his whole venture.

DIALECTICAL CRITICISMS OF ŚĀNTARAKṢITA AND KAMALAŚĪLA (AD 760) (AS FORERUNNERS OF VEDĀNTA DIALECTICS)

(*a*) *Criticisms of the Sāṃkhya Pariṇāma Doctrine.*

In tracing the history of the dialectical ways of thinking in the Vedānta it has been pointed out in the previous sections that the influence of Nāgārjuna and Candrakīrti on Śaṅkara and some of his followers, such as Śrīharṣa, Citsukha and others, was very great. It has also been pointed out that not only Nāgārjuna and Candrakīrti, but many other Buddhist writers, had taken to critical and dialectical ways of discussion. The criticism of the different schools of Indian thought, as contained in Śāntarakṣita's *Tattva-saṃgraha* with Kamalaśīla's commentary *Pañjikā,* is a remarkable instance of this. Śāntarakṣita lived in the first half of the eighth century AD, and Kamalaśīla was probably his junior contemporary. They refuted the views of Kambalāśvatara, a follower of the Lokāyata school, the Buddhist Vasumitra (AD 100), Dharmatrāta (AD 100), Ghoṣaka (AD 150), Buddhadeva (AD 200), the Naiyāyika Vātsyāyana (AD 300), the Mīmāṃsist Śabarasvāmin (AD 300), the Sāṃkhyist Vindhyasvāmin (AD 300), the Buddhist Saṅghabhadra (AD 350), Vasubandhu (AD 350), the Sāṃkhyist Īśvarakṛṣṇa (AD 390), the Buddhist Diṅnāga (AD 400), the Jaina Ācāryasūri (AD 478), the Sāṃkhyist Māṭhara Ācārya (AD 500), the Naiyāyika Uddyotakara (AD 600), the rhetorician Bhāmaha (AD 640), the Buddhist Dharmakīrti (AD 650), the grammarian-philosopher Bhartṛhari (AD 650), the Mīmāṃsist Kumārila Bhaṭṭa (AD 680), the Jaina Śubhagupta (AD 700), the Buddhist Yugasena (AD 700), the Naiyāyika Āviddhakarṇa (AD 700), Śaṅkarasvāmin (AD 700), Praśastamati (AD 700), Bhāvivikta (AD 700), the Jaina Pātrasvāmin (AD 700), Āhrika (AD 700), Sumati (AD 700), and the Mīmāṃsist Uveyaka (AD 700).[1] It is not possible here, of course, to enter into a complete analysis of all the criticisms of the different philosophers by Śāntarakṣita and Kamalaśīla; yet some of the important points of these criticisms may be noted in order to show the nature and importance of this work, which also reveals the nature of the critical thinking that prevailed among the Buddhists before Śaṅkara and by which Śaṅkara and his followers, like Śrīharṣa, Citsukha or Ānandajñāna, were in all probability greatly influenced.

In criticizing the Sāṃkhya views they say that, if the effects, the evolutes, be identical with the cause, THE *pradhāna,* why should they be produced from the *pradhāna*? If they are identical, then the evolutes themselves might be regarded as cause or the *pradhāna*

---

1 These dates are collected from Dr B. Bhaṭṭacharya's foreword to the *Tattva-saṃgraha.* The present author, though he thinks that many of these dates are generally approximately correct, yet, since he cannot spare the room for proper discussions, does not take responsibility for them.

as effect. The ordinary way of determining causality is invariable antecedence, and that is avowedly not available here. The idea of *pariṇāma,* which means identity in diversity, the causal scheme of the Sāṃkhya, is also inadmissible; for, if it is urged that any entity changes into diverse forms, it may be asked whether the nature of the causal entity also changes or does not change. If it does not change, then the causal and the effect states should abide together in the later product, which is impossible; if it changes, then there is nothing that remains as a permanent cause; for this would only mean that a previous state is arrested and a new state is produced. If it is urged that causal transformation means the assumption of new qualities, it may be asked whether such qualities are different from the causal substance or not; if they are, then the occurrence of new qualities cannot entitle one to hold the view that the causal substance is undergoing transformations (*pariṇāma*). If the changing qualities and the causal substance are identical, then the first part of the argument would reappear. Again, the very arguments that are given in favour of the *sat-kārya-vāda* (existence of the effect in the cause) could be turned against it. Thus, if curds, etc. already exist in the nature of the milk, then what is the meaning of their being produced from it? If there is no idea of production, there is no idea of causality. If it is urged that the effects are potentially existent in the cause, and causal operations only actualize them, then it is admitted that the effects are actually non-existent in the cause, and we have to admit in the cause some specific characteristic, brought about by the causal operation, on account of the absence of which the effects remained in the potential state in the cause, and that the causal operations which actualize the effects produce some specific determinations in the cause, in consequence of which the effect, which was non-existent before, is actualized; this would mean that what was non-existent could be produced, which would be against the *sat-kārya-vāda* theory. In the light of the above criticisms, since according to the *sat-kārya-vāda* theory causal productions are impossible, the arguments of Sāṃkhya in favour of *sat-kārya-vāda*, that only particular kinds of effects are produced from particular kinds of causes, are also inadmissible.

Again, according to Sāṃkhya, nothing ought to be capable of being definitely asserted, since according to the *sat-kārya-vāda* theory doubts and errors are always existent as a modification of either *buddhi*, *manas* or *caitanya.* Again, the application of all Sāṃkhya arguments might be regarded as futile, since all arguments are intended to arrive at decisive conclusions; but decisive conclusions, being effects, are already existent. If, however, it is contended that decisive conclusions were not existent before, but were produced by the application of arguments, then there is production of what was non-existent, and thus the *sat-kārya-vāda* theory fails. If it is urged that, though the decisive conclusion (*niścaya*) is already existent before the application of the argumentative premises, yet it may be regarded as being manifested by the application of those premises, the Sāṃkhyist may be asked to define what he means by such manifestation (*abhivyakti*). This manifestation may mean either some new characteristic or some knowledge or the withdrawal of some obscuration to the comprehension. In the first alternative, it may again be asked whether this new character (*svabhāvātiśaya*) that is generated by the application of the premises is different from the decisive conclusion itself or identical with it. If it is identical, there is no meaning in its introduction; if it is different, no relation is admissible between these two, since any attempt to introduce a relation between two unrelated entities would launch us into a vicious infinite (*anavasthā*). It cannot mean the rise of the knowledge about that particular object for the manifestation of which the premises are applied; for, according to the *sat-kārya-vāda* theory, that knowledge is already there. Again, it cannot mean the removal of the obscuration of knowledge; for, if there is obscuration, that also must be ever-existent. As a matter of fact, the whole of the teachings of Sāṃkhya philosophy directed to the rise of true knowledge ought to be false, for true knowledge is ever-existent, and therefore there ought to be no bondage, and therefore all persons should always remain emancipated. Again, if there is any false knowledge, it could not be destroyed, and therefore there could be no emancipation.

Śāntarakṣita and Kamalaśīla then urge that, though the above refutation of the *sat-kārya-vāda* ought naturally to prove the *a-sat-kārya-vāda* (the production of that which did not exist before) doctrine, yet a few words maybe said in reply to the Sāṃkhya refutation of *a-sat-kārya-vāda.* Thus the argument that that which is nonexistent has no form (*nairūpya*) and therefore cannot be produced is false; for the operation of production represents itself the character of the thing that is being produced. As the Satkāryavādins think that out of the same three *guṇas* different kinds of effects may be produced according to causal collocations, so here also, according to the law of different kinds of causal forces (*karaṇa-śakti-pratiniyamāt*), different kinds of non-existing effects come into being. It is meaningless to hold that the limitation of causal forces is to be found in the pre-existence of effects; for, in reality, it is on account of the varying capacities of the causal forces that the various effects of the causes are produced. The production of various effects is thus solely due to the diverse nature of the causal forces that produce them. The law of causal forces is thus ultimately fundamental. The name *a-sat-kārya-vāda,* however, is a misnomer; for certainly there is no such non-existent entity which comes into being.[1] Production in reality means nothing more than the characteristic of the moment only, divested from all associations of a previous and a succeeding point of time.[2] The meaning of *a-sat-kārya-vāda* is that an entity called the effect is seen immediately after a particular causal operation; and it certainly did not exist before this second moment, since, if it did exist at the first moment of the causal operation, it would have been perceived; it is therefore said that the effect did not exist before; but this should not be interpreted to mean that the Buddhists believed

1 *Na hy asan-nāma kiñcid asti yad utpattim āviśet, kintu kālpaniko 'yaṃ vyavahāro yad asad utpadyata iti yāvat. —Tattva-saṃgraha-pañjikā,* p. 33.

2 *vastūnāṃ pūrvāpara-koṭi-śūnya-kṣaṇa-mātrāvasthāyī svabhāva eva utpādaḥ ity ucyate. —Ibid.*

in the non-existing existence of the effect, which suddenly came into being after the causal operation.

Refuting the other Sāṃkhya doctrines, Śāntarakṣita and Kamalaśīla point out that, if an effect (*e.g.,* curd) is said to exist in the cause (*e.g.,* milk), it cannot do so in the actual form of the effect, since then milk would have tasted as curd. If it is said to exist in the form of a special capacity or potency (*śakti*), then the existence of the effect in the cause is naturally denied; for it is the potency of the effect that exists in the cause and not the effect itself. Again, the Sāṃkhyists believe that all sensible things are of the nature of pleasure and pain; this, however, is obviously impossible, since only conscious states can be regarded as pleasurable or painful. There is no sense at all in describing material things as of the nature of pleasure or pain. Again, if objective material things were themselves pleasurable or painful, then the fact that the same objects may appear pleasurable to some and painful to others would be unexplainable. If, however, it is held that even pleasurable objects may appear painful to someone, on account of his particular state of mind or bad destiny, then the objects themselves cannot be pleasurable or painful. Again, if objects are regarded as being made up of three *guṇas*, there is no reason for admitting one eternal *prakṛti* as the source of them all. If causes are similar to effects, then from the fact that the world of objects is many and limited and non-eternal one ought to suppose that the cause of the objects also should be many, limited and noneternal. It is sometimes held that, as all earthen things are produced from one earth, so all objects are produced from one *prakṛti;* but this also is a fallacious argument, since all earthen things are produced not out of one lump of earth, but from different lumps. Thus, though it may be inferred that the world of effects must have its causes, this cannot lead us to infer that there is one such cause as the *prakṛti* of the Sāṃkhyists.

(*b*) *Criticism of Īśvara.*

One of the chief arguments of the Naiyāyika theists in favour of the existence of God is based on the fact that the specific forms and shapes of the different objects in the world cannot be explained except on the supposition of an intelligent organizer or shaper. To this Śāntarakṣita and Kamalaśīla reply that we perceive only the different kinds of visual and tactile sensibles and that there are no further shaped wholes or so-called objects, which men fancy themselves to be perceiving. It is meaningless to think that the visual sensibles and tactile sensibles go together to form one whole object. When people say that it is the same coloured object, seen in the day, that we touched in the night when we did not see it, they are wrong; for colour sensibles or sense-data are entirely different kinds of entities from tactile sense-data, and it is meaningless to say that it is the same object or whole which has both the colour and tactile characteristics. If two colour sensibles, say yellow and blue, are different, then still more different are the colour sensibles and the tactile ones. What exist therefore are not wholes having colour and tactile characters, but only discrete elements of colour and tactile sense-data; the combining of them into wholes is due only to false imagination. There are no objects which can be perceived by the two senses; there is no proof that it is one identical object that is perceived by the eye as well as touched. There exist therefore only loose and discrete sense-data. There being thus no shaped wholes, the supposition of the existence of God as shaper and organizer is inadmissible. The mere fact that there are the effects cannot lead to the inference that there is one intelligent creator and organizer, since a causal inference cannot be made from mere similarity of any description; there must be a law of unconditional and invariable connection (*pratibandha*). The argument that, since jugs, etc. are made by an intelligent potter, so trees, etc. must also have been made by an intelligent creator, is faulty; for trees, etc., are so different in nature from jugs, etc., that it is wrong to make any assertion from the former to the latter. The general Buddhist arguments against the existence of any eternal entity will also apply against the existence of any eternal God.

The argument that, since a state of arrest breaks up into a state of motion or production in all natural phenomena, there must be an intelligent creator, is wrong; for there is no state of arrest in nature; all things in the world are momentary. Again, if things are happening in succession, at intervals, through the operation of a causal agent, then God also must be operating at intervals and, by the arguments of the opponents themselves, He must have another being to guide His operations, and that another, and that another, and there would thus be a vicious infinite. If God had been the creator, then everything would have sprung into being all at once. He ought not to depend on accessory assistance; for, He being the creator of all such accessory circumstances, they could not render Him any assistance in His creation. Again, if it is urged that the above argument does not hold, because God only creates when He wishes, then it may be replied that, since God's will is regarded as eternal and one, the old objection of simultaneous production holds good. Moreover, since God is eternal and since His will depends only on Him and Him alone, His will cannot be transitory. Now, if He and His will be always present, and yet at the moment of the production of any particular phenomenon all other phenomena are not produced, then those phenomena cannot be regarded as being caused by God or by His will. Again, even if for argument's sake it may be granted that all natural objects, such as trees, hills, etc., presuppose intelligent creators, there is no argument for supposing that one intelligent creator is the cause of all diverse natural objects and phenomena. Therefore there is no argument in favour of the existence of one omniscient creator.

The arguments urged in refutation of *prakṛti* and Īśvara would also apply against the Pātañjala-Sāṃkhya, which admits the joint causality of Īśvara and *prakṛti*; for here also, *PRAKṚTI* and Īśvara being eternal causes, one would expect to have simultaneous production of all effects. If it is urged that the three *guṇas* behave as accessory causes with reference to God's operation, then also it may be asked whether at the time of productive activity (*sarga*) the activity of dissolution or of maintenance (*sthiti*) may also be expected to be operated, or whether at the time of dissolution, there might be productive operation as well. If it is urged that, though all kinds of forces are existent in *prakṛti*, yet it is only those that become operative that take effect, it may be objected that some other kind of cause has to be admitted for making some powers of *prakṛti* operative, while others are inoperative, and this would introduce a third factor; thus the joint causality of *puruṣa* and *prakṛti* is also easily refuted. Again, the view that God produces the world through kindness is also false; for, had it been so, the world would not have been so full of misery. Again, there being before creation no beings, God could not feel kindness to nonexistent beings. He would not have destroyed the world had He been so kind; if He created and destroyed the world in accordance with the good or bad deeds, then He would not be independent. Had He been independent, He would not have allowed Himself to be influenced by the consequences of bad deeds in producing misery in the world. If He created the world out of mere playful instincts, then these playful instincts would be superior to Him. If He derived much enjoyment from His productive and destructive play, then, if He were able, He would have created and destroyed the world simultaneously. If He is not capable of creating and destroying the world simultaneously, then there is no reason to suppose that He would be able to do it at intervals. If it is urged that the world was produced naturally by His own existence, then there would be simultaneous production. If it is objected that, just as spiders, though they naturally go on producing webs, yet do not produce them all at once, so God also may be producing the world gradually and not all at once, it may then be pointed out that the analogy of spider's webs is false, since the spider does not naturally produce webs, but only through greed for eating insects, and its activities are determined by such motives. God, however, is One who can have only one uniform motive. If it is urged that creation flows from God unconsciously, as it were, it may readily be objected that a being who creates such a great universe without any intelligent purpose would indeed be very unintelligent.

(c) *Refutation of the Soul Theory.*

The Nyāya view of the soul, that our thoughts must have a knower and that our desires and feelings must have some entity in which they may inhere and that this entity is soul and that it is the existence of this one soul that explains the fact of the unity of all our conscious states as the experience of one individual, is objected to by Śāntarakṣita and Kamalaśīla. They hold that no thought or knowledge requires any further knower for its illumination; if it had been so, there would be a vicious infinite. Again, desires, feelings, etc., are not like material objects, which would require a receptacle in which they might be placed. The so-called unity of consciousness is due to a false unifying imagination of the momentary ones as one. It is also well known that different entities may be regarded as combined on account of their fulfilling the same kinds of functions. It is knowledge in its aspect of ego that is often described as the self, though there is no objective entity corresponding to it. It is sometimes argued that the existence of the soul is proved by the fact that a man is living only so long as his vital currents are connected with the soul, and that he dies when they are disconnected from it; but this is false, since, unless the existence of soul be proved, the supposition of its connection with vital currents as determining life is untenable. Some, however, say that the self is directly perceived in experience; if it had not been, there would not have been such diversity of opinion about its existence. The sense of ego cannot be said to refer to the self; for the sense of ego is not eternal, as it is supposed to be. On the other hand, it refers sometimes to our body (as when I say, "I am white"), sometimes to the senses (as when I say, "I am deaf"), and sometimes to intellectual states. It cannot be said that its reference to body or to senses is only indirect; for no other permanent and direct realization of its nature is found in experience. Feelings, desires, etc., also often arise in succession and cannot therefore be regarded as inhering in a permanent self. The conclusion is that, as all material objects are soulless, so also are human beings. The supposed eternal soul is so different from the body that it cannot be conceived how one can help the other or even be related to it. Thus there is hardly any argument in favour of the soul theory of the Nyāya and Vaiśeṣika.

(*d*) *Refutation of the Mīmāṃsā Theory of the Self.*

Kumārila believed that, though the nature of the self as pure consciousness was eternal and unchangeable, yet it passed through various changing phases of other feeling and volitional states. That the self was of the nature of pure consciousness was proved by the fact that it perceives itself to be knower in the past and in the present. So the existence of the self is proved by the fact of self-consciousness. To this Śāntarakṣita and Kamalaśīla reply that, if the self is regarded as one eternal consciousness, then knowledge or the knowing faculty (*buddhi*) ought also to be regarded as similarly one and eternal; but seemingly Kumārila does not consider *buddhi* to be such. If the knowing faculty be regarded as eternal and one, how are the varying states of cognition, such as colour-cognition, taste-cognition, etc., to be explained? If it is urged that, though the knowing faculty is one, yet (just as a fire, though it has always a capacity of burning, yet bums only when combustible substances are put in it) it only passes through various kinds of perception according as various kinds of objects are presented to it; or, just as a mirror, though it has always the power of reflecting, yet only reflects when the objects are presented to it, so the selves are eternally conscious and yet operate only in connection with their specific bodies and grasp the various kinds of sense-data, and all cognitions are forged from them (selves). If the change of cognitions is due to the changing operations of the senses and the sense-objects, then such a cognizing faculty cannot be regarded as eternal and one. If the knowing faculty is to be regarded as eternal owing to an experience of continuity of consciousness, then how can one explain the variety of cognitions? If it is urged that the variety of cognitions is due to the assumption by the cognizing faculty of various forms of objects, then how can one explain the experience of the variety of cognitions in hallucinations, when there are no objects? Moreover the Mīmāṃsist does not think that the cognizing faculty assumes the forms of the objects cognized, but believes that cognition reveals the objects in the objective world and the cognizing faculty has itself no forms (*nirākārā buddhiḥ*). The fact that there may be cognitions without a corresponding real objective presentation proves that our cognitions are subjective and self-revealed and that they do not reveal objective entities. If it is urged that the knowing faculty has always the power of revealing all things, then sound-cognition would be the same as colour-cognition. The analogy of fire is also false, since there is not one fire that is constant; the analogy of the reflecting mirror is also false, since there is really no reflection in the mirror itself; one can see a reflection in a mirror at a particular angle, the mirror therefore is only an apparatus for producing an illusory cognition. Again, the *buddhi* cannot be compared to a mirror as an apparatus for producing illusory images; for then some other *buddhi* would be necessary for perceiving illusory images. Again, if the self is regarded as one and eternal, then it cannot pass through the varying feeling and volitional states. If these states are not entirely different from the self, then their changes would imply the change of the self; and again, if they are entirely different from the self, how should their change affect the self? Again, if these states all belong to the self and it is urged that it is when the pleasurable state is submerged in the nature of the common self, that the painful state may arise, it may be pointed out in objection that, if the pleasurable states could be submerged in the nature of the self in identity with itself, then they would be identical with the nature of the self. It is also wrong to suppose that the sense of self-consciousness refers to a really existing entity corresponding to it. It has in reality no specific object to refer to as the self. It may therefore be safely asserted that the existence of the self is not proved by the evidence of self-consciousness.

(*e*) *Refutation of the Sāṃkhya View of the Self.*

Against the Sāṃkhya view of the self it is pointed out that the Sāṃkhya regards the self as pure consciousness, one and eternal, and that, as such, it ought not to be able to enjoy diverse kinds of experiences. If it is held that enjoyment, etc., all belong to *buddhi* and the *puruṣa* only enjoys the reflections in the *buddhi*, it may well be objected that if the reflections in the *buddhi* are identical with *puruṣa*, then with their change the *puruṣa* also undergoes a change; and if they are different, the *puruṣa* cannot be considered to be their enjoyer. Again, if the *prakṛti* concentrates all its activities for the enjoyment of the *puruṣa*, how can it be regarded as unconscious? Again, if all actions and deeds belong to *buddhi*, and if *buddhi* be different from *puruṣa*, why should the *puruṣa* suffer for what is done by the *buddhi*?. If, again, the nature of *puruṣa* cannot be affected by the varying states of pleasure and pain, then it cannot be regarded as an enjoyer; and, if it could be affected, it would itself be changeable.

(*f*) *The Refutation of the Upaniṣad View of the Self.*

The Upaniṣadic thinkers hold that it is one eternal consciousness that illusorily appears as all objects, and that there is in reality no perceiver and perceived, but only one eternal consciousness. Against this view it is urged by Śāntarakṣita and Kamalaśīla that, apart from the individual cognitions of colour, taste, etc., no eternal, unchangeable consciousness is experienced. If one eternal consciousness is the one reality, then there cannot be a distinction of false knowledge and right knowledge, bondage and emancipation. There being only one reality, there is no right knowledge which need be attained.

(*g*) *Refutation of the Theory of the Persistence of Existing Entities.*

Śāntarakṣita and Kamalaśīla point out that the Naiyāyikas divide existing entities into two classes, as produced (*a-kṛtaka*) and unproduced (*a-kṛtaka*), and they hold that those which are produced are destructible. The Vātsīputrīyas also similarly divide existing entities into momentary (*e.g.*, ideas, sound, flame, etc.) and non-momentary (*e.g.*, earth, sky, etc.). On this point Śāntarakṣita and Kamalaśīla urge that whatever is produced is momentary, since the destructibility of momentary things does not depend on any cause excepting the fact that they are produced; for, had the destructibility of such entities depended on conditions or causes other than the fact of their being produced, then the premise that whatever is produced is necessarily destructible would be false. The Naiyāyika view, therefore, that produced entities depend for their destruction on other conditions, is false. If produced entities do not depend for their destruction on any other condition or cause than the fact of their being produced, then they must be destroyed the moment they are produced, or in other words they are momentary. Moreover, destruction, being negation, is not a positive entity and is absolutely contentless, and only positive entities depend on other conditions or causes for their production. Destruction, being negation, is not produced by any conditions or causes like a positive entity. Destruction therefore is not generated by any separate causal apparatus, but the very causes that lead to the production of an entity lead also to its destruction the next moment. Destructibility being a necessary characteristic of productibility, destruction cannot need the interference of any causes. It has also been stated above that destruction is pure negation and has therefore no characteristics which have to be generated by any positive set of causes or conditions.[1]

Kamalaśīla and Śāntarakṣita urge that existence (*sattva*) can be affirmed only of those entities which are capable of serving a purpose (*artha-kriyā-samarthā*). They urge that entities can only serve a purpose, if they are momentary. Entities that persist cannot

1 The word *kṣaṇika,* which is translated as "momentary," is, according to Śāntarakṣita, a technical term. The character in an entity of dying immediately after production, is technically called *kṣaṇa,* and whatever has this quality is called *kṣaṇika* (*utpādānāntara-vināśi-svabhāvo vastunaḥ kṣaṇa ucyate, sa yasyāsti sa kṣaṇika iti. Tattva-saṃgraha,* p. 142); *kṣaṇa* therefore does not mean time-moment. It means the character of dying immediately after being produced. The objection of Uddyotakara that what only stays for a moment of time *(kṣaṇa)* cannot be called *kṣaṇika*, because at the expiry of the moment nothing remains which can be characterized as momentary, is therefore inadmissible. There is, however, no entity separate from the momentary character, and the use of the term *kṣaṇika,* which grammatically distinguishes the possessor of the momentary character from the momentary character itself, is due only to verbal license.

serve any purpose and therefore cannot have any existence. In order to prove their thesis they enter into the following argument. If any purpose is to be served, then that can be either in succession or simultaneously, and no middle alternative is possible. If an existing entity persists in time, then all its effects ought to come about simultaneously; for, the complete cause being there, the effects must also be there, and there is no reason why the effects should happen in succession; but it is well known in experience that effects happen only in succession and not simultaneously. If, however, it is objected that even a persisting entity can perform actions in succession owing to its association with successive accessories (*kramiṇaḥ sahakāriṇaḥ*), then one may well enquire as to the nature of the assistance given by the successive accessories to the persisting entity in the production of the effect; is it by producing a special modification (*atiśayādhāna*) of the persisting cause or by independent working in consonance with the productive action of the persisting entity? In the first alternative, the special modification may be either identical with or different from the nature of the persisting entity, and both these alternatives are impossible; for, if it is identical, then, since the effect follows in consequence of the special modification of the accessories, it is the element of this special modification that is to be regarded as the cause of the effect, and not the persisting entity. If it is again urged that the effect is due to the association of the special modification with the persisting entity, then it would be impossible to define the nature of such association; for an association may be either of identity or of productivity (*tādātmya* and *tad-utpatti*), and neither of them is possible in the present case, since the special modification is recognized as being different from the persisting entity and is acknowledged by assumption to be produced by the accessories. Again, such association cannot be regarded as being of the nature of *samavāya*; for this special modification, being of the nature of an additional assistance (*upakāra*), cannot be regarded as being of the nature of inseparable inherence (*samavāya*). If this special modification be regarded as being neither of the nature of an additional assistance (*upakāra*) nor of the nature of an essence identical with the persisting entity, and if it is still regarded as being associated with the persisting entity in a relation of *samavāya*, then anything in the world could be regarded as being in the *samavāya* relation with anything else. In the other alternative, in which it is maintained that the persisting entity awaits only the independent working of the accessories, it may well be asked whether the causal nature of the persisting entity is the same together with the totality of the accessories as it is without them? In the former case, the accessories would also be persistent. In the latter case, the persisting entity can no longer be regarded as persisting.

Regarding the objection of Bhadanta Yogasena, that the same difficulties would arise in the assumption of entities as momentary, Śāntarakṣita and Kamalaśīla reply that in their view the accessories behave in two ways, firstly, as independent co-operation (*ekārtha-kriyā-kāritā*) and, secondly, as mutual help (*parasparopakāritā*). Thus in the first moment the different accessory-units are only independently co-operant, since, in one moment, their mutual actions cannot help one another; but in the second moment, the effects may be regarded as being of a joint nature, and therefore mutually determining one another, in the production of the effect of the third moment. In this view', though each entity operates independently, yet none of their operations are irrelevant. They are all being produced and determined by the respective causes and conditions in a beginningless series.

The objection against the momentariness of all things on the ground that things are perceived and recognized to be the same, and as persisting, is not a valid one. For the fact of persistence cannot be perceived by the senses and must be regarded as due to false imagination. All recognition is due to the operation of memory, which is almost universally recognized as invalid for purposes of right knowledge. On this point it may be argued that in recognition, if the entity now perceived be the same as the entity perceived at a previous time, then how can a cognition in the past comprehend an entity of the present time? If they are held to be different, then it is acknowledged that the entities perceived as the same in recognition are not really the same. The objector's argument that, since things pass by the same name, they must be persistent is invalid; for it is well known that even in ordinary perception, where a flame is known to be destroyed every moment, and produced anew, it is still said in common verbal usage to be the same flame. Thus all existing things must be regarded as momentary.

(*h*) *Refutation of Criticisms of the Non-permanency of Entities.*

It is objected by the Naiyāyikas and others that, if things are momentary, then the theory of *karma* would fail; for how can it be understood that the deeds be performed by one, and the fruits reaped by another? How, again, can it be understood that a momentary cause which does not abide till the rise of the effect should produce the same? Again, if objects are momentary, how can they be perceived by the eye? The phenomena of recognition would also be inexplicable, as there would be no permanent perceiver who would identify the present and the past as being one. How, again, would the phenomenon of bondage and of emancipation apply to a non-permanent being? In reply to this Śāntarakṣita and Kamalaśīla say that, just as a seed by means of its invariable power produces the shoots, without being superintended by any conscious agent, so the inner states of a man may generate other states, without being superintended by any permanent conscious agent; the formula (*dharma-saṃketa*) for all production is, "this happening, that happens"; "this being produced, that is produced." It is through ignorance that a man cannot discern that all subsequent states are determined by the natural forces of the preceding ones and thinks of himself as performing this or that action or as striving for emancipation. The true nature of things cannot be determined by the illusory experience of ignorant people. It is sometimes objected that the parts of a seed attain a due constitution by assimilating nutritive elements at the second stage, and then again at the third stage attain a new constitution by further accretion of new nutritive elements, and that therefore it cannot be held that the parts of the seed are entirely destroyed at the second stage. To this the reply of Śāntarakṣita is that in the second moment the effect is produced in dependence on the undestroyed causal efficiency of the first causal moment; so that the effect is produced by the causal efficiency of the first moment, when the cause is not destroyed. The cause however perishes in the second moment; for, once the cause has produced the effect, it cannot be producing it again and again; if it did, there would be a vicious infinite. It must therefore be admitted that the causal efficiency of the cause ceases immediately after production.[1] The view that the effect is produced simultaneously with the cause (*saha-bhūtaṃ kāryam*) is unreasonable, since the cause cannot produce the effect before it is itself produced; again, it cannot produce after it is itself produced; for then the effect also has to be acknowledged to be of the same nature as the cause; but at the same moment it can have no scope for its efficiency. Thus the cause and effect cannot be produced simultaneously. There is no necessity also for admitting a causal operation (*vyāpāra*), as separate and distinct from the cause. Invariable antecedence is the only qualification of cause.[2] If a causal operation has to be admitted for connecting the cause with the effect, then that would require another operation, and that another, and there would be a vicious infinite. If the causal operation is admitted to be able to generate the effect independently by itself, so can the cause be also admitted to be able to produce the effect. The objection that, if antecedence be admitted to be alone the determinant of causality, then the fact, that a thing is smelled after it is seen may also lead one to infer that colour is the cause of smell, is invalid, for the Buddhists have no objection to regarding colour as an accessory cause of smell. It must also be remembered that the Buddhists do not regard mere antecedence as the definition of cause, but invariable and necessary antecedence.[3] Again, no difficulty need be experienced in perception,

1 The Vaibhāṣikas are spoken of by Śāntarakṣita as holding the view that the effect is produced at the third moment. In this view the effect is produced by the destroyed cause.

2 *idam eva hi kāryasya kāraṇāpekṣā yat tad-anantara-bhāvitvam.—Tattva-saṃgraha,* p. 177.

3 *na hi vayam ānantarya-mātraṃ kārya-kāraṇa-bhāvādhigati-nibandhanaṃ... yasyaivānantaraṃ yad bhavati tat tasya kāraṇam iṣyate. Ibid.* p. 180.

if the objects are admitted to be momentary; for ideas may be considered to have forms akin to the objects, or to be formless, but revealing the objects. In either case the ideas are produced by their causes, and the momentariness or permanence of objects has nothing to do with their determination.[1] There are in reality no agent and no enjoyer, but only the series of passing mental phenomena. Causality consists in the determination of the succeeding states by the previous ones. The objection of Uddyotakara, that, if the mind is momentary, it cannot be modified (*vāsanā*) by deeds (*karma*), is invalid; for, in the Buddhist view, this modification (*vāsanā*) means nothing more than the production of a new mental state of a modified nature. There is again no permanent perceiver who remembers and recognizes; it is only when in a particular series of conscious states, on account of the strength of a particular perception, such particularly modified mental states are generated as may be said to contain seeds of memory, that memory is possible. The Buddhists also do not consider that there is one person who suffers bondage and is liberated; they think that bondage means nothing more than the production of painful states due to ignorance (*avidyā*) and other mental causes, and that liberation also means nothing more than purity of the mental states due to cessation of ignorance through right knowledge.

(*i*) *Refutation of the Nyāya Vaiśeṣika Categories.*

Śāntarakṣita and Kamalaśīla attempt to refute the categories of substance (*dravya*) with its subdivisions, quality (*guṇa*), action (*karma*), generality, or class concepts (*sāmānya*), specific peculiarities (*viśeṣa*), relation of inherence (*samavāya*), and the connotation and denotation of words (*śabdārtha*). This refutation may briefly be set out here.

Speaking against the eternity of atoms, they hold that, since no special excellence can be produced in eternal entities, no conditions or collocations of any kind can produce any change in the nature of the atoms; thus, the atoms being always the same in nature, all objects

1 Śāntarakṣita and Kamalaśīla are Buddhists who style themselves *nirākāra-vijñā-na-vādin*.

should be produced from them either at once, or not at all. The mere fact that no cause of atoms is known is no ground for thinking that they are causeless. Again, substance, as different from characters and qualities, is never perceived. The refutation of wholes (*avayavī*), which has already been effected, also goes against the acceptance of substantive wholes, and so the four substances earth, water, air and fire, which are ordinarily regarded as substantive—wholes made up of atoms also stand refuted. Again, it is not easy to prove the existence of separate and independent time and space entities; for spatial and temporal determinations may well be explained as mental modifications due, like other facts of experience, to their specific causes. The Buddhists of course accept the existence of *manas* as an instrument separate from the sense-organs, but they do not admit its existence as an eternal and single entity.

The refutation of substances implies the refutation of *guṇas,* which are supposed to be dependent on substances. If the substances do not exist, there can also be no relation of inherence, in which relation the *guṇas* are supposed to exist in substances. There is, again, no meaning in acknowledging colours, etc., as different from the atoms in which they are supposed to exist. The perception of numbers also ought to be regarded as due to mental modifications associated with particular cognitions. There is no reason for holding that numbers should stand as separate qualities. In a similar manner Śāntarakṣita and Kamalaśīla proceed with the refutation of the other Nyāya qualities.

Proceeding with the refutation of action (*karma*), they hold that, if all things are admitted to be momentary, then action cannot be attributed to them; for action, involving as it does successive separation of parts and association of contact-points, implies many moments for its execution. If things are admitted to be persistent or eternal, then also movement cannot be explained. If things are admitted to be always moving, then they will be in motion while they are perceived to be at rest, which is impossible. If things are at rest by nature, there cannot be any vibratory movement in them. The main principle involved in the refutation of *guṇas* and *karmas* consists in the fact that the *guṇas* and *karmas* are regarded by the Buddhists as being identical with the particular sense-data cognized. It is wrong, in their view, to analyse the sense-data as substances having qualities and motion as different categories inhering in them. Whatever may be the substance, that is also the quality which is supposed to be inhering in it, as also the motion which it is supposed to execute.

Regarding the refutation of class-concepts the main drift of Buddhist argument is that, though the perception of class-natures may be supposed to be due to some cause, yet it is wrong to assume the existence of eternal class-nature existing constantly in all the changing and diverse individual members of a class. For, howsoever we may try to explain it, it is difficult to see how one thing can remain constantly the same, though all the individual members in which it is supposed to exist are constantly changing. If class-natures are said to inhere owing to specific qualities, *e.g.*, cooking in the cook, then also it may be objected that, since the operation of cooking is different in each case, there is no one character "cooking" by virtue of which the class-nature of cook is admissible. Moreover, a cook is called a cook even when he is not cooking. Considerations like these should lead any thinking person to deny the existence of eternal class-natures.

Regarding the refutation of specific qualities (*viśeṣa*) it is held that, if *yogins* can perceive the ultimate specific qualities as different from one another, they might equally perceive the atoms to be different from one another; if the atoms cannot be perceived as different except through some other properties, then the same may be required of the specific properties themselves.

Regarding the refutation of *samavāya,* or relation of inherence, the Buddhist objects mainly to the admission of a permanent *samavāya* relation, though all the individuals in which this relation may be supposed to exist should be changing or perishing. It is a false supposition that the relation of inherence, such as that of the cloth in the thread, is ever felt to be, as if the one (*e.g.,* the cloth) was existing in the other (threads), as the Naiyāyikas suppose.

DIALECTIC OF ŚAṄKARA AND ĀNANDAJÑĀNA

It is well known that Śaṅkarācārya in his commentary on the *Brahma-sūtra,* II. ii 11-17, criticizes the atomic theory of the Vaiśeṣikas. His first thesis is that the production of an effect different in nature from the cause, as in the case of the production of the impure world from pure Brahman, can be justified on the analogy of even the critics of the Vedānta, the Vaiśeṣikas. The Vaiśeṣikas hold that in the production of the *dvy-aṇuka* (containing two atoms) from *the paramāṇu* (single atom) and of the *catur-aṇuka* (containing four atoms) from the *dvy-aṇuka,* all other qualities of the *paramāṇu* and the *dvy-aṇuka* are transferred to the *dvy-aṇuka* and *catur-aṇuka* respectively, excepting the specific measures of *pārimāṇḍalya* (specific atomic measure) and *aṇu-hrasva* (specific measure of the dyads), which are peculiar to *paramāṇu* and *dvy-aṇuka* respectively. Thus, though all other qualities of *paramāṇus* pass over to *dvy-aṇukas* produced by their combination, yet the specific *pārimāṇḍalya* measure of the *paramāṇus* does not pass to the *dvy-aṇukas,* which are of the *aṇu-hrasvaparimāṇa.* So also, though all the qualities of *dvy-aṇukas* would pass on to the *catur-aṇukas* made out of their combination, yet their own specific *aṇu-hrasvaparimāṇa* would not pass on to the *catur-aṇukas,* which are possessed of their own measure, viz. the *mahat parimāṇa,* uncaused by the *parimāṇa* of the *dvy-aṇukas.* This shows that the Vaiśeṣikas believe that the *pārimāṇḍalya* measure (*parimāṇa*) of the *paramāṇus* may produce an altogether different measure in their product, the *dvy-aṇukas*, and so the *aṇu-hrasva* measure of the *dvy-aṇukas* may produce an altogether different measure in their product, the *catur-aṇukas*, viz. the *mahat parimāṇa.* On this analogy it may be contended that the Vaiśeṣikas have nothing to object to in the production of an altogether different effect (viz. the impure world) from an altogether different cause, the pure Brahman. If it is urged that the measure of the *paramāṇu* cannot pass on to the *dvy-aṇuka* only because its passage is rendered impossible by the taking possession of it by an opposite quality (the *aṇu-hrasva parimāṇa*), then a similar reply may be given in the case of the difference between the world and Brahman. Moreover, since, according to the Vaiśeṣika theory, all products remain for a moment without qualities, there is no reason why, when the *dvy-aṇuka* was produced, the *pārimāṇḍalya* measure should not pass on to it. At that moment, since the *pārimāṇḍalya* measure did not pass on to it as did the other qualities, it follows, not that the passing of the *pārimāṇḍalya* measure is opposed by the other *parimāṇa,* but that it naturally did not pass on to it. Again, it cannot be objected that the analogy of dissimilarity of qualities (*guṇa*) cannot be cited in support of the dissimilarity of substances.

Śaṅkara's second thesis is that the Vaiśeṣika view that atoms combine is wrong, because, since the atoms are partless, and since combination implies contact and contact implies parts which come in contact, there cannot be any combination of atoms. Moreover, since before creation there is no one who can make an effort, and since the contact of atoms cannot be effected without effort, and since the selves, being unconscious at that time, cannot themselves make any effort, it is impossible to account for the activity without which the contact of the atoms would also be impossible. So the atoms cannot combine, for want of the effort needed for such a contact. Śaṅkara's third point is that the relation of *samavāya* upheld by the Vaiśeṣikas cannot be admitted; for, if to unite two different objects the relation of *samavāya* is needed, then *samavāya,* being itself different from them, would require another *samavāya* to connect itself with them, and that another, and that another, and so on *ad infinitum.* If the relation of contact requires a further relation of *samavāya* to connect it with the objects in contact, there is no reason why *samavāya* should not require some other relation in its turn. Again, if the atoms are regarded as always operative and combining, then there can be no dissolution (*pralaya*), and, if they are always disintegrating, then creation would be impossible. Again, since the atoms possess the qualities of colour, etc., they must be the product of some simpler causes, just as other objects having qualities are made up of simpler entities. Moreover, it is not right to suppose that, since we have the idea of non-eternality, this must imply eternality and that therefore the atoms must be eternal; for, even though it implies the existence of eternality, it does not imply that the atoms should be eternal, since there is such an eternal thing as Brahman. Again, the fact that the cause of the destruction of the atoms is not known does not imply that they are eternal; for mere ignorance of the ways of destruction does not imply eternality. Again, the Vaiśeṣikas are wrong in speaking of six different categories and yet hold that all the five other categories depend on substance for their existence or manifestation. A substance and its quality do not appear to be as different as two substances. A substance appears black or white, and this implies that the qualities are at bottom identical with the substance (*dravyātmakatā guṇasya*). It cannot, moreover, be urged that the dependence of other categories on substance consists in their inseparableness (*ayuta-siddhatva*) from it. This inseparableness cannot be inseparableness of space; for, when threads constitute as their product a piece of cloth, then the threads and the cloth cannot be regarded as having the same space, yet, being cause and effect, they are to be regarded as *ayuta-siddha*, or inseparable; and yet the whiteness of the cloth is not regarded as abiding in the threads. If inseparableness means inseparableness of time, then the two horns of a bull, which exist at the same time, should also be regarded as inseparable; and, if inseparableness means inseparableness of character or sameness of character, then quality cannot be regarded as being different from substance. Again, since the cause exists prior to the effect, it cannot be regarded as inseparable from the cause, and yet it is asserted by the Vaiśeṣikas that their relation is one of *samavāya*, since they are inseparable in their nature.

Śaṅkara, however, seldom indulges in logical dialectic like the above, and there are only a few rare instances in which he attacks his opponents from a purely logical point of view. But even here he does not so much criticize the definitions of the Vaiśeṣikas as point out the general logical and metaphysical confusions that result from some of the important Vaiśeṣika theories. It is easy to note the difference of a criticism like this from the criticism of Śrīharṣa in his *Khaṇḍana-khaṇḍa-khādya,* where he uses all the power of his dialectical subtleties to demolish the cherished principles of pure logic as formulated by the Nyāya logicians. It is not a criticism of certain doctrines in support of others, but it is a criticism which aims at destroying the possibility of logical or perceptual knowledge as a whole. It does not touch any specific metaphysical views, but it denies the power of perception and inference to give us right knowledge, and it supposes that it achieves its purpose by proving that the Nyāya modes of definition of perception and inference are faulty and self-contradictory. Citsukha's attempts are more positive; for he criticizes not only the Nyāya categories of logic, but also the categories of Vaiśeṣika metaphysics, and makes some positive and important statements, too, about the Vedānta doctrine itself. Ānandajñāna's *Tarka-saṃgraha* is another important work of negative criticism of the Vaiśeṣika categories and in that sense a continuation on a more elaborate scale of Citsukha's criticisms of the Vaiśeṣika categories. The importance of the Vaiśeṣika was gradually increasing, as it was gradually more and more adopted by Vaiṣṇava realistic writers, such as Mādhva and his followers, and it was supposed that a refutation of the Vaiśeṣika would also imply a refutation of the dualistic writers who draw their chief support from Vaiśeṣika physics and metaphysics.

Ānandajñāna, also called Ānandagiri, was probably a native of Gujarat and lived in the middle of the thirteenth century. Mr Tripathi points out in his introduction to Ānandajñāna's *Tarka-saṃgraha* that Ānandajñāna was a spiritual head of the Dvārakā monastery of Śaṅkara, of which Sureśvarācārya was the first teacher. He was a pupil of two teachers, Anubhūtisvarūpācārya and Śuddhānanda. Anubhūtisvarūpācārya wrote five works, viz. (1) a grammatical work called *Sārasvata-prakriyā,* (2) a commentary on Śaṅkara's commentary on Gauḍapāda's *Māṇḍūkya-kārikā,* (3) a commentary on Ānandabodha Yati's *Nyāya-makaranda,* called *Nyāya-makaranda-saṃgraha*, (4) a commentary, called *Candrikā,* on Ānandabodha's *Nyāya-dīpāvalī,* and (5) another commentary, called *Nibandha,* on Ānandabodha's *Pramāṇa-mālā.* Nothing is known about his other teacher, Śuddhānanda, who is different from the other Śuddhānanda, the teacher of Svayaṃprakāśa of the seventeenth century, author of the *Advaita-makaranda-ṭīkā.* One of the most distinguished of Ānandagiri's pupils was Akhaṇḍānanda, author of the *Tattva-dīpana,* a commentary on Prakāśātman's *Pañca-pādikā-vivaraṇa,* as he refers to him as *Śrīmad-ānanda-śailāhva-pañcāsyaṃ satataṃ bhaje* in the fourth verse of his *Tattva-dīpana.* Ānandagiri wrote a large number of works, which are mostly commentaries. Of these his *Īśāvāsya-bhāṣya-ṭippaṇa, Kenopaniṣad-bhāṣya-ṭippaṇa, Vākya-vivaraṇa-vyākhyā, Kaṭhopaniṣad-bhāṣya-ṭīkā, Muṇḍaka-bhāṣya-vyākhyāna, Māṇḍūkya-Gauḍapādiya-bhāṣya-vyākhyā, Taittirīya-bhāṣya-ṭippaṇa, Chāndogya-bhāṣya-ṭīkā, Taittirīya-bhāṣya-vārttika-ṭīkā, Śāstra-prakāśikā, Bṛhad-āraṇyaka-bhāṣya-vārttika-ṭīkā, Bṛhad-āraṇyaka-bhāṣya-ṭīkā, Śāriraka-bhāṣya-ṭīkā* (called also *Nyāya-nirṇaya*), *Gītā-bhāṣya-vivecana, Pañcīkaraṇa-vivaraṇa,* with a commentary called *Tattva-candrikā* by Rāma Tīrtha, a pupil of Jagannāthāśrama (latter part of the fifteenth century), and *Tarka-saṃgraha* have already been printed. But some of his other works, such as *Upadeśa-sāhasrī-vivṛti, Vākya-vṛtti-ṭīkā, Ātma-jñānopadeśa-ṭīkā, Svarūpa-nirṇaya-ṭīkā,* TRIPURĪ*-prakaraṇa-ṭīkā, Padārtha-tattva-nirṇaya-vivaraṇa* and *Tattvāloka,* still remain to be printed. It will thus be seen that almost all his works are but commentaries on Śaṅkara's commentaries and other works. The *Tarka-saṃgraha* and *Tattvāloka* (attributed to "Janārdana," which was probably the name of Ānandagiri when he was a householder) seem to be his only two independent works.[1] Of these the manuscript of the second work, in which he refutes the doctrines of many other philosophers, including Bhāskara's *pariṇāma* doctrines, has, unfortunately, not been available to the present writer. The *Tarka-saṃgraha* is devoted almost wholly to a detailed refutation of the Vaiśeṣika philosophy. The book is divided into three chapters. In

1 See Mr Tripathi's introduction to his edition of the *Tarka-saṃgraha,* Baroda, 1917.

the first chapter, dealing with the criticism of substances (*dravya*), he starts with a refutation of the concepts of duality, reality (*tattva*), existence (*sattva*), non-existence, positivity (*bhāva*) and negativity (*abhāva*). Ānandojñāna then passes on to a refutation of the definition of substance and its division into nine kinds (according to the Vaiśeṣika philosophy). He then criticizes the first substance, earth, and its diverse forms, as atoms (*paramāṇu*) and molecules (*dvyaṇuka*), and its grosser forms and their modified states, as bodies, senses and sense-objects, and continues to criticize the other substances such as water, fire, air, and the theory of creation and dissolution, *ākāśa*, time, space, self (*ātman*) and *manas*. In the second chapter he goes on to the criticism of qualities (*guṇa*), such as colour (*rūpa*), taste (*rasa*), smell (*gandha*), touch (*sparśa*), the effects of heat on the transformations of objects through molecular or atomic changes (*pīlu-pāka* and *piṭhara-pāka*), number (*saṅkhyā*), measure (*parimāṇa*), separateness (*pṛthaktva*), contact (*saṃyoga*), separation (*vibhāga*), the nature of knowledge, illusion and dreams, the nature of right knowledge and its means (*pramāṇa* and *pramā*), perception (*pratyakṣa*), inference (*anumāna*), concomitance (*vyāpti*), reason (*hetu*), fallacies (*hetv ābhāsa*), examples (*dṛṣṭānta*), discussions, disputations and wranglings, testimony of the scriptures (*āgama*), analogy (*upamāna*), memory, pleasure, pain, will, antipathy (*dveṣa*), effort (*prayatna*), heaviness, liquidity (*dravatva*), virtue, vice, etc. In the third chapter he refutes the notion of action, class-concept or universality (*jāti*), the relation of inherence (*samavāya*) and different kinds of negation. The thesis designed to be proved in all these refutations is the same as that of Śrīharṣa or Citsukha, viz. that in whatsoever manner the Vaiśeṣikas have attempted to divide, classify or define the world of appearances they have failed.

The conclusion at which he arrives after this long series of criticisms and refutations reminds us of Ānandabodha's conclusions in his *Nyāya-makaranda*, on which a commentary was written by his teacher Anubhūtisvarūpa Ācārya, to which reference has already been made when Ānandabodha's views were under discussion. Thus Ānandajñāna says that an illusory imposition cannot be regarded as existent (*sat*); for, since it is non-existent in the substratum (*adhiṣṭhāna*) of its appearance, it cannot be existent anywhere else. Neither can it be regarded as absolutely non-existent (*atyantāsat*); for, had it been so, it would not have appeared as immediately perceived (*aparokṣa-pratīti-virodhāt*); nor can it be regarded as existent and non-existent in the same object. The only alternative left is that the illusory imposition is indescribable in its nature.[1] This indescribability (*anirvācyatva*) means that, in whichever way one may try to describe it, it is found that none of those ways can be affirmed of it or, in other words, that it is indescribable in each and every one of those ways.[2] Now, since all appearances must have something for their cause and since that which is not a real thing cannot have a real thing as its material cause (*na ca avastuno vastu upādānam upapadyate*), and, since they are all indescribable in their nature, their cause must also be of that nature, the nescience of the substratum.[3]

He then asserts that this nescience (*ajñāna*), which is the material out of which all appearances take their form, is associated with Brahman; for Brahman could not be regarded as omniscient or the knower of all (*sarvajña*)without its association with *ajñāna*, which is the material stuff of the *all* (the knower, the means of knowledge, the objects and their relations).[4] Everything else that appears except the one reality, the self, the Brahman, is the product of this *ajñāna*. This one *ajñāna* then can explain the infinite kinds of appearances, and there is not the slightest necessity of admitting

---

1 *pāriśeṣyād anirvācyam āropyam upagamyatāṃ sattvādīnāṃ prakārāṇāṃ prāg-ukta-nyāya-bādhanāt. Tarka-saṃgraha,* p. 135.

2 येन येन प्रकारेण परो निर्वक्तुम् इच्छति।
तेन तेनात्मनाऽयोगस्तदनिर्वाच्यता मता॥
yena yena prakāreṇa paro nirvaktum icchati
Tena tenātmanā 'yogas tad-anirvācyatā matā. —Tarka- saṃgraha, p. 136.

3 *Tasmād rūpyādi-kāryasyānirvācyatvāt tad-upādānam api adhiṣṭhānājñānam upādeyam. —Ibid.* p. 137.

4 *pramāṇataḥ sarvajñatve'pi pramātṛtvasya pramāṇa-prameya-sambandhasya cājñāna-sambandham antareṇāsiddheḥ tasmin ajñānavattvam avaśyam āsray-ita-vyam anyathā sarvajñatvāyogāt. —Ibid. pp.* 137, 138.

a number of *ajñānas* in order to explain the diversity or the plurality of appearances. The many selves are thus but appearances produced by this one *ajñāna* in association with Brahman.[1] It is the one *ajñāna* that is responsible for appearances of the dream state as well as of the waking state. It is the one *ajñāna* which produces all kinds of diversity by its diversity of functions or modes of operation. If there is only one reality, which through one *ajñāna* appears in all diverse forms of appearances, how is the phenomenon of self-consciousness or self-recognition to be explained? To this difficulty Ānandajñāna's reply is that both the perceiving and the perceived self are but false appearances in the *antaḥkaraṇ* (an *ajñāna* product), and that it does not in any way infect the one true self with any kind of activity. Thus there is the one Brahman and there is one beginningless, indescribable *ajñāna* in connection with it, which is the cause of all the infinitely diverse appearances through which the former appears impure and suffers bondage, as it were, and again appears liberated, as it were, through the realization of the Vedāntic truth of the real nature of the self.[2] In fact there is neither bondage nor emancipation.

In view of the above it may be suggested that Ānandajñāna is following the same line of interpretation of the relation of *ajñāna* to Brahman which was upheld by Vācaspati and Ānandabodha. Ānandajñāna's position as an interpreter of Śaṅkara's philosophy is evident from the number of able commentaries which he wrote on the commentaries of Śaṅkara and also from the references made to him by later writers. Mr Tripathi collects the names of some of these writers, as Prajñānānanda, Śeṣa Śārṅgadhara, Vādivāgīśvara,

1 *Ekas tāvad ātmā dvayor api āvayoḥ sampratipanno'sti, tasya svājñānād eva avivāda-siddhād ekasmād atiriktaṃ sarvam pratibhāti;... samastasyaiva bheda-bhānasyā pāramārthikasyaikajñāna-sāmarthyād eva sambhavān nājñāna-bhede hetu rasti. —Ibid.* pp. 138, 139.

2 *Advitīyam ātma-tattvam, tatra ca anādy anirvācyam ekam ajñānam ananta-bheda-pratibhāna-nidānam, tataś cānekārtha-kaluṣitam ātma-tattvam baddham ivānubhūyamānam, vedānta-vākyottha-tattva-sākṣātkāra-parākṛta-sakāryājñānaṃ muktam iva bhāti; paramārthato na bandho na muktir iti sakaryājñāna-nivṛtty-upalakṣitam paripūrṇam ātma-tattvam eva parama-puruṣārtha-rūpaṃ sidhyati. —Tarka-saṃgraha,* p. 141.

Vādīndra, Rāmānanda Sarasvatī, Sadānanda Kāśmīraka (AD 1547), Kṛṣṇānanda (AD 1650), Maheśvara Tīrtha (AD 1650) and others.

PHILOSOPHY OF THE PRAKAṬĀRTHA-VIVARAṆA (AD 1200)

The *Prakaṭārtha-vivaraṇa* (as the writer himself calls it in the colophon of the work—*prārabhyate vivaraṇaṃ parkaṭārtham etat*) is an important commentary still in manuscript on Śaṅkara's commentary on the *Brahma-sūtra,* which the present writer had an opportunity of going through from a copy in the Adyar Library, Madras, through the kind courtesy of the Librarian, Mr T. R. Chintamani, who is intending to bring out an edition. The author, however, does not anywhere in the work reveal his own name and the references which can be found in other works are all to its name as *Prakaṭar* or to the author of the *Prakaṭārtha* (*parkaṭārtha-kāra*), and not to the author's personal name.[1] This work has been referred to by Ānandajñāna, of the thirteenth century (*Muṇḍaka,* p. 32; *Kena*, p. 23; Ānandāśrama editions AD 1918 and 1917), and it may well be supposed that the author of the work lived in the latter half of the twelfth century. He certainly preceded Rāmādvaya, the author of the *Vedānta-kaumudī,* who not only refers to the *Prakaṭārtha,* but has been largely influenced in many of his conceptions by the argument of this work.[2] The author of the latter holds that the indefinable *māyā* in association with pure consciousness (*cinmātra-sambandhinī*) is the mother of all existence (*bhūta-prakṛti*). Through the reflection of pure consciousness in *māyā* is produced Īśvara (God), and by a transformation of Him there arises the creator Brahmā, and it is

1 The colophon of the work runs as follows:

ज्ञात्वापि यस्य बहुकालम् अचिन्तनेन व्याख्यातुम् अक्षमतया परितापि चेतः
तस्योपतापहरणाय मयेह भाष्ये प्रारभ्यते विवरणम् प्रकटार्थम् एतत्॥

jñātvāpi yasya bahu-kālam acintanena
Vyākhyātum akṣamatayā paritāpi cetaḥ
tasyopatāpa-haraṇāya mayeha bhāṣye
prārabhyate vivaraṇam prakaṭārtham etat.

—MS. No. I, 38. 27, Govt. MSS. Library, Madras.

2 *Vedānta-kaumudī,* MS. transcript copy, p. 99.

by the reflection of the pure consciousness in the infinite parts of this Brahmā that there arise the infinite number of individual souls through the veiling and creating functions of the *māyā. Māyā* or *ajñāna* is not negation, but a positive material cause, just as the earth is of the jug (*ajñānaṃ nābhāva upādānatvān mṛdvat*). But, being of the nature of veiling (*āvaraṇatvāt*) and being destructible through right knowledge (*prakāśa-heyatvāt*), it cannot be known as it is: still it may well be regarded as the positive cause of all illusions.[1] The well-known Vedāntic term *svaprakāśa* is defined in the *Prakaṭārtha* as illumination without the cognition of its own idea (*sva-saṃvin-nairapekṣeṇa sphuraṇam*). The self is to be regarded as self-revealing; for without such a supposition the revelation of the self would be inexplicable.[2] The author of the *Prakaṭārtha* then criticizes the Kumārila view of cognition as being a subjective act, inferable from the fact of a particular awareness, as also the Nyāyā-Vaiśeṣika and Prabhākara views of knowledge as an illumination of the object inhering in the subject (*ātma-samavāyīviṣaya-prakāśojñānam*), and the Bhāskara view of knowledge as merely a particular kind of activity of the self; and he ultimately holds the view that the mind or *manas* is a substance with a preponderance of *sattva,* which has an illuminating nature, and that it is this *manas* which, being helped by the moral destiny (*adṛṣṭādi-sahakṛtam*), arrives at the place where the objects stand like a long ray of light and comes in contact with it, and then as a result thereof pure consciousness is reflected upon the object, and this leads to its cognition. Perceptual cognition, thus defined, would be a mental transformation which can excite the revelation of an object (*manaḥ-pariṇāmaḥ samvid-vyañjakojñānam*).[3] In the

---

1 *āvaraṇatvāt prakāśa-heyatvād vā tamovat-svarūpeṇa pramāṇa-yogyatve'pyabhāva-vyāvṛtti-bhrama-kāraṇatvādi-dharma-viśiṣṭasya prāmāṇikatvaṃ na viru-dhyate.* —MS. p. 12.

2 आत्मा स्वप्रकाशस् ततोऽन्यथाऽनुपपद्यमानत्वे सति
प्रकाशमानत्वान् न य एवं न स एवं यथा कुम्भः ॥
ātmā sva-prakāśas tato'nyathā'nupapadyamānatve sati
Prakāśamānatvān na ya evaṃ na sa evaṃ yathā kumbhaḥ. —*Prakaṭārtha* MS.

3 MS. p. 54.

case of inference, however, the transformation of *manas* takes place without any actual touch with the objects; and there is therefore no direct excitation revealing the object; for the *manas* there, being in direct touch with the reason or the *liṅga,* is prevented from being in contact with the object that is inferred. There is here not an operation by which the knowledge of the object can be directly revealed, but only such a transformation of the *manas* that a rise of the idea about the object may not be obstructed.[1] The author of the *Prakaṭārtha* accepted the distinction between *māyā* and *ajñāna* as conditioning *Īśvara* and *jīva.*

VIMUKTĀTMAN (AD 1200)

Vimuktātman, a disciple of Avyayātman Bhagavat Pūjyapāda, wrote his *Iṣṭa-siddhi* probably not later than the early years of the thirteenth century. He is quoted and referred to by Madhusūdana in his *Advaita-siddhi* and by Rāmādvaya in his *Vedānta-kaumudī* of the fourteenth century. It was commented upon by Jñānottama, the teacher of Citsukha, and this commentary is called *Īṣṭa-siddhi-vyākhyā* or *Īṣṭa-siddhi-vivaraṇa.* For reasons stated elsewhere Jñānottama could not have flourished later than the latter half of the thirteenth century. Vimuktātman wrote also another work, called *Pramāṇa-vṛtti-nirṇaya*, to which he refers in his *Īṣṭa-siddhi* (MS. p. 72). The work has not yet been published, and the manuscript from the Adyar Library, which is a transcript copy of a manuscript of the Nāḍuvil Maṭham, Cochin State, and which has been available to the present writer, is very fragmentary in many parts; so much so, that it is often extremely difficult to follow properly the meaning of the discussions. The work is divided into eight chapters, and is devoted in a very large part to discussions

1 *upalabdha-sambandhārtha kāreṇa pariṇatam mano*
'nāvabhāsa-vyāvṛtti-mātraphalam, na tu saṃvid-vyañjakam
liṅgādi-samvid-vyavadhāna-pratibandhāt. —MS. p. 54.

It is easy to see how Dharmarājādhvarīndra elaborated his vedāntic theory of perception and inference with these and other data worked out by his predecessors.

relating to the analysis of illusions in the Vedānta school and in the other schools of philosophy. This work is to be regarded as one of the four traditional *Siddhis,* such as the *Brahma-siddhi* by Maṇḍana, the *Naiṣkarmya-siddhi* by Sureśvara, the *Īṣṭa-siddhi* by Vimuktātman and the *Advaita-siddhi* by Madhusūdana. Hitherto only the *Naiṣkarmya-siddhi* and the *Advaita-siddhi* have been published. The *Brahma-siddhi* is expected to be published soon in Madras; but as yet the present writer is not aware of any venture regarding this important work.

The work begins with the interpretation of a salutation made by the author, in which he offers his adoration to that birthless, incognizable, infinite intuitive consciousness of the nature of self-joy which is the canvas on which the illusory world-appearance has been painted. Thus he starts the discussion regarding the nature of the ultimate reality as pure intuitive consciousness (*anubhūti*). Nothing can be beginningless and eternal, except pure consciousness. The atoms are often regarded as beginningless; but, since they have colours and other sense-properties, they are like other objects of nature, and they have parts also, as without them no combination of atoms would be possible. Only that can be indivisible which is partless and beginningless, and it is only the intuitive consciousness that can be said to be so. The difference between consciousness and other objects is this, that, while the latter can be described as the "this" or the object, the former is clearly not such. But, though this difference is generally accepted, dialectical reasoning shows that the two are not intrinsically different. There cannot logically be any difference between the perceiving principle (*dṛk*) and the perceived (*dṛśya*); for the former is unperceived (*adṛśyatvāt*). No difference can be realized between a perceived and an unperceived entity; for all difference relates two cognized entities. But it may be argued that, though the perceiver may not be cognized, yet he is self-luminous, and therefore the notion of difference ought to be manifested. A reply to this objection involves a consideration regarding the nature of difference. If difference were of the nature of the entities that differed, then difference should not be dependent on a reference to another (*nasvarūpa-dṛṣṭiḥ prati-yogy-apekṣā*). The difference has thus to be regarded as a characteristic (*dharma*) different from the nature of the differing entities and cognized by a distinct knowing process like colours, tastes, etc.[1] But this view also is not correct, since it is difficult to admit "difference" as an entity different from the differing entities; for such a difference would involve another difference by which it is known, and that another and that another, we should have an infinite regress; and the same objection applies to the admission of mutual negation as a separate entity. This being so, it is difficult to imagine how "difference" or mutual negation between the perceiver and the perceived can be cognized; for it is impossible that there should be any other cognition by which this "difference," or mutual negation which has the perceiver as one of its alternating poles, could be perceived.[2] Moreover, the self-luminous perceiving power is always present, and it is impossible that it could be negated—a condition without which neither difference nor negation could be possible. Moreover, if it is admitted that such a difference is cognized, then that very fact proves that it is not a characteristic of the perceiving self. If this difference is admitted to be self-luminous, then it would not await a reference to another, which is a condition for all notions of difference or mutual negation. Therefore, "difference" or "mutual negation" cannot be established, either as the essence of the perceiving self or as its characteristics; and as there is no other way in which this difference can be conceived, it is clear that there is no difference between the perceiving self and its characteristics.

Again, negation is defined as the non-perception of a perceivable thing; but the perceiving self is of the very nature of

1 *Tasmāt kathañcit bhinno jñānāntara-gamyo rūpa-rasādivad bhedo 'bhyupeyaḥ.*
—Adyar *Iṣṭa-siddhi* MS. p. 5.

2 एवं च सति न दृग्दृश्ययोर्भेदो द्रष्टुम् शक्यः नाप्यन्योन्याभावः न हि दृशः स्वयं दृष्टेः प्रतियोग्यपेक्षदृष्ट्यन्तरदृश्यं रूपान्तरं स्वं समस्ति स्वयं दृष्टित्वहानात्
evaṃ ca sati na dṛg-dṛśyayor bhedo draṣṭum śakyaḥ
Nāpy anyonyābhāvaḥ na hi dṛśaḥ svayaṃ dṛṣṭeḥ
prati-yogy-apekṣa-drṣṭy-antara-dṛśyaṃ rūpāntaraṃ svaṃ
samasti svayaṃ dṛṣṭitva-hānāt. —MS. p. 6.

perception, and its non-perception would be impossible. Admitting for the sake of argument that the perceiving self could be negated, how could there be any knowledge of such a negation? for without the self there could be no perception, as it is itself of the nature of perception. So the notion of the negation of the perceiving self cannot be anything but illusion. Thus the perceiving self and the perceived (*dṛk* and *dṛśya*) cannot be differentiated from each other. The difficulty, however, arises that, if the perceiving self and the perceived were identical, then the infinite limitations and differences that are characteristic of the perceived would also be characteristic of the perceiver; and there are the further objections to such a supposition that it is against all ordinary usage and experience. It may be argued that the two are identical, since they are both experienced simultaneously (*sahopalambha-niyamāt*); but the reply is that, as two are experienced and not one, they cannot be regarded as identical, for in the very experience of the two their difference is also manifested.[1] In spite of such obvious contradiction of experience one could not venture to affirm the identity of the perceiver and the perceived.[2] The maxim of identity of the perceiver and the perceived because of simultaneous perception cannot be regarded as true; for, firstly, the perceiver is never a cognized object, and the perceived is never self-luminous, secondly, the perceiver is always self-revealing, but not so the perceived, and, thirdly, though the "perceived" cannot be revealed without the perceiver, the latter is always self-revealed. There is thus plainly no simultaneity of the perceiver and the perceived. When a perceived object *A* is illuminated in consciousness, the other objects *B, C, D*, etc. are not illuminated, and, when the perceived object *B* is illuminated, *A* is not illuminated, but the consciousness (*samvid*) is always self-illuminated; so no consciousness can be regarded as being always qualified by a particular objective content; for, had

1 *abhede saha-bhānāyogād dvayor hi saha-bhānam na ekasyaiva na hi dṛśaiva dṛk saha bhātlti bhavatāpy ucyate, nāpi dṛśyenaiva dṛśyaṃ saha bhātīti kintu dṛg-dṛśyayoḥ saha bhānam ucyate atas tayor bhedo bhāty eva.* —MS. p. 25.

2 *Tasmāt sarva-vyavahāra-lopa-prasaṅgān na bhedo dṛg-dṛśyaoḥ. Ibid.*

it been so, that particular content would always have stood self-revealed.[1] Moreover, each particular cognition (*e.g.*, awareness of blue) is momentary and self-revealed and, as such, cannot be the object of any other cognition; and, if any particular awareness could be the object of any other awareness, then it would not be awareness, but a mere object, like a jug or a book. There is thus an intrinsic difference between awareness and the object, and so the perceiver, as pure awareness, cannot be identified with its object.[2] It has already been pointed out that the perceiver and the perceived cannot be regarded as different, and now it is shown that they cannot be regarded as identical. There is another alternative, viz. that they may be both identical and different (which is the *bhedābheda* view of Bhāskara and Rāmānuja and others), and Vimuktātman tries to show that this alternative is also impossible and that the perceiver and the perceived cannot be regarded as being both identical and different. The upholder of the *bhedābheda* view is supposed to say that, though the perceiver and the perceived cannot, as such, be regarded as identical, yet they may be regarded as one in their nature as Brahman. But in reply to this it may be urged that, if they are both one and identical with Brahman, there would be no difference between them. If it is argued that their identity with Brahman is in another form, then also the question arises whether their forms as perceiver and perceived are identical with the form in which they are identical with Brahman; and no one is aware of any form of the perceiver and the perceived other than their forms as such, and therefore it cannot be admitted that in spite of their difference they have any form in which they are one and identical. If again it is objected that it is quite possible that an identical entity should have two different forms, then also the question arises whether these forms are one, different or both identical with that entity and

1 *kiṃ vidyud-viśeṣitatā nāma saṃvidaḥ svarūpam uta saṃvedyasya, yadisamvidaḥ sāpi bhāty eva saṃvid-bhānāt saṃvedya-svarūpaṃ cet tadā bhānān na saṃvido bhānam. Ibid.* p. 27.

2 *asaṃvedyaiva saṃvit samvedyaṃ cāsaṃvid eva, ataḥ saṃvedyasya ghaṭa-sukhādeḥ saṃvidaś cābheda-gandho'pi na pramāṇavān. Ibid.* p. 31.

different. In the first alternative the forms would not be different; in the second they would not be one with the entity. Moreover, if any part of the entity be identical with any particular form, it cannot also be identical with other forms; for then these different forms would not be different from one another; and, if again the forms are identical with the entity, how can one distinguish the entity (*rūpin*) from the forms (*rūpa*)? In the third alternative the question arises whether the entity is identical with one particular form of it and different from other forms, or whether it is both identical with the same form and different. In the first case each form would have two forms, and these again other two forms in which they are identical and different, and these other two forms, and so on, and we should have infinite regress: and the same kind of infinite regress would appear in the relation between the entity and its forms. For these and similar reasons it is impossible to hold that the perceiver and the perceived are different as such and yet one and identical as Brahman.

If the manifold world is neither different nor identical nor both different and identical with the perceiver, what then is its status? The perceiver is indeed the same as pure perception and pure bliss, and, if it is neither identical nor different nor both identical with the manifold world and different, the manifold world must necessarily be unsubstantial (*avastu*); for, if it had any substantiality, it might have been related in one of the above three ways of relation. But, if it is unsubstantial, then none of the above objections would apply. But it may again be objected that, if the world were unsubstantial, then both our common experience and our practical dealing with this world would be contradicted. To this Vimuktātman's reply is that, since the world is admitted to be made up of *māyā* (*māyā-nirmitatvābhyupagamāt*), and since the effects of *māyā* cannot be regarded either as substantial or as unsubstantial, none of the above objections would be applicable to this view. Since the manifold world is not a substance, its admission cannot disturb the monistic view, and, since it is not unsubstantial, the facts of experience may also be justified.[1] As an instance of such an appearance which is neither *vastu* (substance) nor *avastu,* one may refer to dream-appearances, which are not regarded as unreal because of their nature as neither substance nor not-substance, but because they are contradicted in experience. Just as a canvas is neither the material of the picture painted on it nor a constituent of the picture, and just as the picture cannot be regarded as being a modification of the canvas in the same way as a jug is a modification of clay, or as a change of quality, like the redness in ripe mangoes, and just as the canvas was there before the painting, and just as it would remain even if the painting were washed away, whereas the painting would not be there without the canvas, so the pure consciousness also is related to this world-appearance, which is but a painting of *māyā* on it.[2]

Māyā is unspeakable and indescribable (*anirvacanīyā*), not as different from both being and non-being, but as involving the characters of both being and non-being. It is thus regarded as a power of ignorance (*avidyā-śakti*) which is the material cause of all objects of perception otherwise called matter (*sarva-jaḍopādāna-bhūtā*). But, just as fire springing from bamboos may burn up the same bamboos even to their very roots, so Brahma-knowledge, which is itself a product of ignorance and its processes, destroys the self-same ignorance from which it was produced and its processes and at last itself subsides and leaves the Brahman to shine in its own radiance.[3] The functions of the *pramāṇas,* which are all mere processes of ignorance, *ajñāna* or *avidyā,* consist only in the removal of obstructions veiling the illumination of the self-

1 *Prapañcasya vastutvābhāvātinādvaita-hōniḥ avastutvābhāvāc ca pratyakṣādy-aprāmāṇyam' apy-ukta-doṣābhāvāt.* MS. p. 64.

2 *Yatha citrasya bhittiḥ sākṣāt nopādānam nāpi sahajaṃ citraṃ tasyāh nāpy-avasthāntaraṃ mṛda iva ghaṭādiḥ nāpi guṇāntarāgamah āmrasyeva raktatādiḥ na cāsyāh janmādiś citrāt prāg ūrdhaṃ ca bhāvāt, yady api bhittiṃ vinā citraṃ na bhāti tathāpi na sā citraṃ vinā bhāti ity evam-ādy-anubhūtir bhitti-jagac-citrayoryojyam. Ibid.* p. 73.

3 MS. p. 137.

luminous consciousness, just as the digging of a well means the removal of all earth that was obstructing the omnipresent *ākāśa* or space; the *pramāṇas* have thus no function of manifesting the self-luminous consciousness, and only remove the veiling *ajñāna.*[1] So Brahma-knowledge also means the removal of the last remnants of *ajñāna,* after which Brahma-knowledge as conceptual knowledge, being the last vestige of *ajñāna,* also ceases of itself. This cessation of *ajñāna* is as unspeakable as *ajñāna* itself. Unlike Maṇḍana, Vimuktātman does not consider *avidyā* to be merely subjective, but regards it as being both subjective and objective, involving within it not only all phenomena, but all their mutual relations and also the relation with which it is supposed to be related to the pure consciousness, which is in reality beyond all relations. Vimuktātman devotes a large part of his work to the criticism of the different kinds of theories of illusion (*khyāti*), and more particularly to the criticism of *anyathākhyāti.* These contain many new and important points; but, as the essential features of these theories of illusion and their criticisms have already been dealt with in the tenth chapter of the first volume, it is not desirable to enter into these fresh criticisms of Vimuktātman, which do not involve any new point of view in Vedāntic interpretation. He also deals with some of the principal Vedāntic topics of discussion, such as the nature of bondage, emancipation, and the reconciliation of the pluralistic experience of practical life with the monistic doctrine of the Vedānta; but, as there are not here any strikingly new modes of approach, these may be left out in the present work.

RĀMĀDVAYA (AD 1300)

Rāmādvaya, a pupil of Advayāśrama, wrote an important work, called *Vedānta-kaumudī,* in four chapters, in which he discussed in a polemical way many Vedāntic problems while dealing with the subject matter of Śaṅkara's commentary on the first four topics of the *Brahma-sūtra.* The work has not yet been published; but at

1 MS. p. 143.

least one manuscript of it is available in the Government Oriental Manuscript Library, Madras: this through the kindness of the Curator the present author had the opportunity of utilizing. Rāmādvaya also wrote a commentary on his *Vedānta-kaumudī*, called *Vedānta-kaumudī-vyākhyāna*, a manuscript of the first chapter of which has been available to the present writer in the library of the Calcutta Asiatic Society. These are probably the only manuscripts of this work known till now. The date of the writing of the copy of the *Vedānta-kaumudī-vyākhyāna* is given by the copyist Śeṣanṛsiṃha as AD 1512. It is therefore certain that the work cannot have been written later than the fifteenth century. Rāmādvaya in the course of his discussions refers to many noted authors on Nyāya and Vedānta, none of whom are later than the thirteenth century. Vimuktātman, author of the *Īṣṭa-siddhi*, has been placed by the present author in the early half of the thirteenth century; but Rāmādvaya always refers to him approvingly, as if his views were largely guided by his; he also in his *Vedānta-kaumudī-vyākhyāna* (MS. p. 14) refers to Janārdana, which is Ānandajñāna's name as a householder; but Janārdana lived in the middle of the thirteenth century; it seems therefore probable that Rāmādvaya lived in the first half of the fourteenth century.

In the enunciation of the Vedāntic theory of perception and inference Rāmādvaya seems to have been very much under the influence of the views of the author of the *Prakaṭārtha*; for, though he does not refer to his name in this connection, he repeats his very phrases with a slight elaboration.[1] Just as the cloudless sky covers itself with clouds and assumes various forms, so the pure consciousness veils itself with the indefinable *avidyā* and appears in diverse limited forms. It is this consciousness that forms the real ground of all that is known. Just as a spark of fire cannot manifest itself as fire if there are no fuels as its condition, so the pure consciousness, which is the underlying reality of all objects, cannot illuminate them

1 See *Vedānta-kaumudī*, MS. transcript copy, pp. 36 and 47.

if there are not the proper conditions to help it in its work.[1] Such a conditioning factor is found in *manas*, which is of the stuff of pure *sattva:* on the occasion of sense-object contact this *manas*, being propelled by the moral destiny (*adṛṣṭādi-kṣubdhaṃ*), transforms itself into the form of a long ray reaching to the object itself.[2] The pure consciousness, as conditioned or limited by the *antaḥkaraṇa* (*antaḥkaraṇā vacchinnaṃcaitanyaṃ*), does by such a process remove its veil of *avidyā,* (though in its limited condition as individual soul this *avidyā* formed its own body), and the object also being in contact with it is manifested by the same process. The two manifestations of the subject and the object, having taken place in the same process (*vṛtti*) there, are joined together in the same cognition as "this object is known by me" (*vṛtter ubhayasaṃlagnatvāc ca tad-abhivyakta-caitanya-syāpi tathātvena mayedam viditam iti saṃśleṣa-pratyayaḥ*); and, as its other effect, the consciousness limited by the *antaḥkaraṇa,* transformed into the form of the process (*vṛtti*) of right knowledge (*pramā*), appears as the cognizer (*vṛtti-lakṣaṇa-pramāśrayāntaḥ-karaṇāvacchinnas tat-pramātetyapivyapadiśyate*).[3] The object also attains a new status in being manifested and is thus known as the object (*karma-kārakābhivyaktaṃ ca tat*

1 Rāmādvaya refers here to the *daharādhikaraṇa* of Śaṅkara's commentary on the *Brahma-sūtra,* presumably to I.3, 19, where Śaṅkara refers to the supposed distinction between the individual soul (*jiva*) and Brahman. Here Śaṅkara says that his commentary is directed towards the regulation of those views, both outside and inside the circle of *Upaniṣadic* interpreters, which regard individual souls as real (*apare tu vādinaḥ pāramārthikam eva jaivaṃ rūpam iti manyante asmadīyāś ca kecit).* Such a view militates against the correct understanding of the self as the only reality which through *avidyā* manifests itself as individual souls and with its removal reveals itself in its real nature in right knowledge as *parameśvara,* just as an illusory snake shows itself as a piece of rope. *Parameśvara,* the eternal unchangeable and upholding consciousness, is the one reality which, like a magician, appears as many through *avidyā.* There is no consciousness other than this *(eka eva parameśvaraḥ kūṭastha-nityo vijñāna-dhātur avidyayā-māyayā māyāvivad anekadhā vibhāvyate nānyo vijñāna-dhātur asti).*

2 This passage seems to be borrowed directly from the *Prakaṭārtha,* as may be inferred from their verbal agreement. But it may well be that both the *Vedānta-kaumudī* and the *Prakaṭārtha* borrowed it from the *Pañca-pādikā-vivaraṇa.*

3 *Vedānta-kaumudī,* MS. transcript copy, p. 36.

prakāśātmanā phala-vyapadeśa-bhāk). In reality it is the underlying consciousness that manifests the *vṛtti* transformation of the *antaḥkaraṇa*; but, as it is illusorily identified with the *antaḥkaraṇa* (*antaḥkaraṇa-caitanyayor aikyādhyāsāt*), like fire and iron in the heated iron, it is also identified with the *vṛtti* transformation of the *antaḥkaraṇa,* and, as the *vṛtti* becomes superimposed on the object, by manifesting the *vṛtti* it also manifests the object, and thus apart from the subjective illumination as awareness, there is also the objective fact of an illumination of the object (*evaṃ vṛtti-vyañjakam api taptā-yaḥ-piṇḍa-nyāyena tad-ekatām ivāptaṃ vṛttivad-viṣaya-prākaṭyāt-manā sampadyate*).[1] The moments in the cognitive process in perception according to Rāmādvaya may thus be described. The sense-object contact offers an occasion for the moral destiny (*adṛṣṭa*) to stir up the *antaḥkaraṇa*, and, as a result thereof, the *antaḥkaraṇa* or mind is transformed into a particular state called *vṛtti.* The pure consciousness underlying the *antaḥkaraṇa* was lying dormant and veiled, as it were, and, as soon as there is a transformation of the *antaḥkaraṇa* into a *vṛtti*, the consciousness brightens up and overcomes for the moment the veil that was covering it. The *vṛtti* thus no longer veils the underlying consciousness, but serves as a transparent transmitter of the light of consciousness to the object on which the *vṛtti* is superimposed, and, as a result thereof, the object has an objective manifestation, separate from the brightening up of consciousness at the first moment of the *vṛtti* transformation. Now, since the *vṛtti* joins up the subjective brightening up of consciousness and the objective illumination of the object, these two are joined up (*saṃśleṣa-pratyaya*) and this results in the cognition "this object is known by me"; and out of this cognition it is possible to differentiate the knower as the underlying consciousness, as limited by the *antaḥkaraṇa* as transformed into the *vṛtti*, and the known as that which has been objectively illuminated. In the *Vedānta-paribhāṣā* we hear of three consciousnesses (*caitanya*), the *pramātṛ-caitanya* (the consciousness conditioned by the *antaḥkaraṇa*), the *pramāṇa-caitanya* (the same consciousness condi-

1 MS, p. 37.

tioned by the *vṛtti* of the *antaḥkaraṇa*), and the *viṣaya-caitanya* (the same consciousness conditioned by the object). According to this perception (*pratyakṣa*) can be characterized either from the point of view of cognition (*jñāna-gata-pratyakṣatva*) or from the point of view of the object, both being regarded as two distinct phases, cognitional and objective, of the same perceptual revelation. From the point of view of cognition it is defined as the non-distinction (*abheda*) of the *pramāṇa-caitanya* from the *viṣaya-caitanya* through spatial superimposition of the *vṛtti* on the object. Perception from the point of view of the object (*viṣaya-gata-pratyakṣatva*) is defined as the non-distinction of the object from the *pramātṛ-caitanya* or the perceiver, which is consciousness conditioned by the *antaḥkaraṇa.* This latter view, viz. the definition of perception from the point of view of the object as the non-distinction of the object from the consciousness as limited by *antaḥkaraṇa* (*ghaṭāder antaḥkaraṇāva-cchinna-caitanyābhedaḥ*), is open to the serious objection that really the non-distinction of the object (or the consciousness conditioned by the *antaḥkaraṇa—antaḥkaraṇāvacchinna-caitanya*) but with the cognition *(pramāṇa-caitanya* or *vṛtti-caitanya*); for the cognition or the *vṛtti* intervencs between the object and the perceiver, and the object is in immediate contact with the *vṛtti* and not with the perceiver (*antaḥkaraṇāvacchinna-caitanya*). That this is so is also admitted by Dharmarāja Adhvarīndra, son of Rāmakṛṣṇa Adhvarin, in his *Śikhāmaṇi* commentary on the *Vedānta-paribhāṣā.*[1] But he tries to justify Dharmarāja Adhvarīndra by pointing out that he was forced to define *viṣaya-gata-pratyakṣatva* as non-distinction of the object from the subject, since this view was taken in Prakāśātman's *Vivaraṇa* and also in other traditional works on Vedānta.[2] This however seems to be an error. For the passage of the *Vivaraṇa* to which reference is made here expounds an entirely different

1 *yad vā yogyatve sati viṣaya-caitanyābhinna-pramāṇa-caitanya-viṣayatvaṃ ghaṭāder viṣayasya pratyakṣatvaṃ tathāpi viṣayasyāparokṣatvaṃ samvida-bhedāt iti vivarane tatra tatra ca sāṃpradāyikaiḥ pramātrabhedasyaiva viṣaya-pratyakṣa-lakṣaṇatvenābhidhānād evaṃ uktam. —Śikhā-maṇi on Vedānta-pari-bhāṣā,* p. 75, Bombay, 1911, Venkatesvara Press.

2 *Ibid.*

view.[1] It says there that the perceptibility of the object consists in its directly and immediately qualifying the cognitional state or sense-knowledge (*saṃvid*).[2] That other traditional Vedāntic interpreters entirely disagreed with the view of Dharmarāja Adhvarīndra is also evident from the account of the analysis of the perceptual process given by Rāmādvaya. Rāmādvaya says, as has just been pointed out, that it is the illuminated cognitive process, or the *vṛtti,* that has the subject and the object at its two poles and thus unites the subject and the object in the complex subject-predicate form "this is known by me." The object is thus illuminated by the *vṛtti*, and it is not directly with the subject, but with the *vṛtti,* that the object is united. Dharmarāja Adhvarīndra himself raises an objection against his interpretation, that it might be urged, if in perception there was non-distinction of the object from the subject, then in perceiving an object, *e.g.,* a book, one should feel "I am the book," and not "I perceive the book"; in reply to such an objection he says that in the perceptual process there is only a non-distinction between the consciousness underlying the object and the consciousness underlying the perceiver, and this non-distinction, being non-relational, does not imply the assertion of a relation of identity resulting in the notion "I am the book."[3] This is undoubtedly so, but it is hardly an answer to the objection that has been raised. It is true that the object and the subject are both but impositions of *avidyā* on one distinctionless pure consciousness; but that fact can hardly be taken as an explanation of the various modes of experiences of the complex world of subject-object experience. The difference of the Vedāntic view of perception, as expounded in the *Pañca-pādikā-vivaraṇa*, from the Buddhist idealism (*vijñāna-vāda*) consists in this, that,

1 *Tasmād avyavadhānena saṃvid-upādhitayāparokṣatā viṣayasya. Pañcapādikā-vivaraṇa*, p. 50, Benares, 1892.

2 It should be noted here that saṃvid means cognitional idea or sense-knowledge and not the perceiver (*antaḥkaraṇāvacchinna-caitanya*), as the author of the *Śikhāmaṇi* says. Thus Akhaṇḍānanda in his *Tattva-dīpana* commentary explains the word *saṃvid* as *saṃvic-chabdena indriyārtha-samprayoga-ja-jñānasya vivakṣitatvāt. Tattva-dīpana*, p. 194, Benares, 1902.

3 *Vedānta-paribhāṣā,* pp. 76, 77.

while the Buddhists did not accord any independent status to objects as outside the ideas or percepts, the Vedānta accepted the independent manifestation of the objects in perception in the external world.[1] There is thus a distinction between visional percept and the object; but there is also a direct and immediate connection between them, and it is this immediate relationship of the object to its awareness that constitutes the perceptivity of the object (*avyavadhānena-samvid-upādhitā aparokṣatā viṣayasya*—*Vivaraṇa*, p. 50). The object is revealed in perception only as an object of awareness, whereas the awareness and the subject reveal themselves directly and immediately and not as an object of any further intuition or inference (*prameyaṃ karmatvena aparokṣam pramātṛ-pramitī punar aparokṣe eva kevalaṃ na karmatayā*).[2]

The views of the *Vedānta-kaumudī,* however, cannot be regarded as original in any sense, since they are only a reflection of the exposition of the subject in Padmapāda's *Pañca-pādikā* and Prakāśātman's *Pañca-pādikā-vivaraṇa.* The development of the whole theory of perception may be attributed to the *Pañca-pādikā-vivaraṇa,* since all the essential points of the perceptual theory can be traced in that work. Thus it holds that all the world objects are veiled by *avidyā*; that, as the *antaḥkaraṇa* is transformed into states by superimposition on objects, it is illuminated by the underlying consciousness; and that through the spatial contact with the objects the veil of the objects is removed by these *antaḥkaraṇa* transformations; there are thus two illuminations, namely of the *antaḥkaraṇa* transformations (called *vṛtti* in the *Vedānta-kaumudī,* and *Vedānta-paribhāṣā* and pure consciousness); to the question that, if there were unity of the consciousness underlying the object and the consciousness underlying the *antaḥkaraṇa* (i.e. the subject) and the consciousness underlying the *antaḥkaraṇa* modification (or *vṛtti*), there would be nothing to explain the duality in perception (*e.g.*, "I perceive the book," and not "I am the book," and it is only

1 *na ca vijñānābhedād eva āparokṣyam avabhāsate bahiṣṭvasyāpi rajatāderāparokṣyāt.* —*Pañca-pādikā-vivaraṇa,* p. 50.

2 *Pañca-pādikā,* p. 17, Benares, 1891.

the latter form that could be expected from the unity of the three consciousnesses), Prakāśātman's reply is that, since the unity of the object-consciousness with the *antaḥkaraṇa*-consciousness (subject) is effected through the modification or the *vṛtti* of the *antaḥkaraṇa* and, since the *antaḥkaraṇa* is one with its *vṛtti,* the *vṛtti* operation is rightly attributed to the *antaḥkaraṇa* as its agent, and this is illuminated by the consciousness underlying the *antaḥkaraṇa* resulting in the perception of the knower as distinguished from the illumination of object to which the operation of the *vṛtti* is directed in spatial superimposition—the difference between the subject and the object in perception is thus due to the difference in the mode or the condition of the *vṛtti* with reference to the subject and the object.[1] This is exactly the interpretation of the *Vedānta-kaumudī*, and it has been pointed out above that the explanations of the *Vedānta-paribhāṣā* are largely different therefrom and are in all probability inexact. As this unity is effected between individual subjects (consciousness limited by specific *antaḥkaraṇas*) and individual objects (consciousness limited by specific *avidyā* materials constituting the objects) through the *vṛtti*, it can result only in revelation of a particular subject and a particular object and not in the revelation of all subjects and all objects.[2] This has been elaborated into the view that there is an infinite number of *ajñāna*-veils, and that each cognitive illumination removes only one *ajñāna* corresponding to the illumination of one object.[3] But this also is not an original contribution of Rāmādvaya, since it was also propounded by his predecessor Ānandajñāna in his *Tarka-saṃgraha* and by others.[4] The upshot of the whole discussion is that

1 See *Pañca-pādikā-vivaraṇa,* p. 70, and *Tattva-dīpana,* pp. 256-259, Benares, 1902.

2 *Etat prarnātṛ-caitanyābhinnatayaiva abhivyaktaṃ tad viṣaya-caitanyaṃ napramātr-antara-caitanyābhedena abhivyaktam ato na sarveṣām avabhāsyat-vam.* —*Pañca-pādikā-vivaraṇa,* p. 71.

3 *Yāvanti jñānāni tāvanti sva-tantrāṇi para-tantrāṇi vā ajñānāni tato na doṣaḥ. Vedānta-kaumudī*, MS. copy, p. 43.

4 The theory is that there is an infinite number of the *ajñāna-* veils; as soon as there is the *vṛtti*-object contact, the veil is removed and the object is illuminated; the next moment there is again an *ajñāna*-veil covering the object, and again there

on the occasion of a cognitive operation of the mind both the mind and the cognitive operation become enlivened and illuminated by the indwelling pure consciousness as subject-consciousness and awareness, and through contact with this cognitive operation the object also becomes revealed not as a mere content of awareness, but as an objective fact shining forth in the external world. Cognition of objects is thus not a mere quality of the self as knower, as the Nyāya holds, nor is there any immediate contact of the self with the object (the contact being only through the cognitive operation); the cognition is also not to be regarded as unperceived movement, modification or transformation of the self which may be inferred from the fact of the enlightenment of the object (*jñātatā*), as Kumārila held, nor is the illumination of the object to be regarded mere form of awareness without there being a corresponding as an objective entity (*viṣayābhivyaktir nāma vijñāne tad-ākārollekha-mātraṃ na bahir-aṅga-rūpasya vijñānābhivyāptiḥ*), as is held by the Buddhist subjective idealists. The cognitive operation before its contact with the object is a mere undifferentiated awareness, having only an objective reference and devoid of all specifications of sense characters, which later on assumes the sense characteristics in accordance with the object with which it comes in contact. It must be noted, however, that the cognitive operation is not an

---

is the vrtti-object contact, and again illumination of the object, and thus there is very quick succession of veils and their removals, as the perception of the object continues in time. On account of the rapidity of this succession it is not possible to notice it (*vṛtti-vijñānasya sāvayavatvāc ca hrāsa-daśāyāṃ dīpa-jvālāyā iva tamo'ntaraṃ mohāntaram āvaritum viṣayaṃ pravartate tato'pi kramamāṇaṃ kṣaṇāntare sāmagry-anusāreṇa vijñānāntaraṃ viṣay īvaraṇa-bhaṅgenaiva sva-kāryaṃ karoti, tathā sarvāṇy api atiśaighryāt tu jñāna-bhedavad āvaraṇān-taraṃ na lakṣyate.*

Vedānta-kaumudī, MS. copy, p. 46). This view of the *Vedānta-kaumudī* is different from the view of the *Vedānta-paribhāṣā,* which holds that in the case of continuous perception of the same object there are not different successive awarenesses, but there is *one* unchanged continuous *vṛtti* and not different *vṛt-tis* removing different *ajñānas (kiñ ca siddhānte dhārā-vāhika-buddhi-sthale na jñānā-bhedaḥ kintu yāvād ghaṭa-sphuraṇam tāvad ghaṭākār āntaḥkaraṇa-vrttir ekaiva na tu nānā vṛtteḥ sva-virodhi-vṛtty-utpatti-paryaṇtaṃ sthāyitvābhyupag-amāt. Vedānta-paribhāṣā,* pp. 26, 27, Bombay, 1911).

abstract idea, but an active transformation of a real *sattva* stuff, the mind (*antaḥkaraṇa*).[1] Since in the continuous perception of the same object we have only a rapid succession of cognitive acts, each dispelling an intellectual darkness enfolding the object before its illumination, there is no separate perception of time as an entity standing apart from the objects; perception of time is but the perception of the succession of cognitive acts, and what is regarded as the present time is that in which the successive time-moments have been fused together into one concrete duration: it is this concrete duration, which is in reality but a fusion of momentary cognitive acts and awarenesses, that is designated as the present time.[2] According to Rāmādvaya the definition of perception would not therefore include the present time as a separate element over and above the object as a separate datum of perception; for his view denies time as an objective entity and regards it only as a mode of cognitive process.

Rāmādvaya's definition of right knowledge is also different from that of Dharmarāja Adhvarīndra. Rāmādvaya defines right knowledge *(pramā)* as experience which does not wrongly represent its object (*yathārthānubhavaḥ pramā*), and he defines the instrument of right knowledge as that which leads to it.[3] Verbally this definition is entirely different from that of Dharmarāja Adhvarīndra, with whom the two conditions of *pramā* or right knowledge are that it should not be acquaintance with what was already known (*anadhigata*) and that it should be uncontradicted.[4] The latter condition, however, seems to point only to a verbal

---

1 *ataḥ sāvayava-sattvātm akamantaḥkaraṇam eva anudbhūta-rūpa-sparśam adṛśyam aspṛśyaṃ ca viṣayākāreṇa pariṇamate. —Vedānta-kaumudī,* MS. copy, p. 42.

2 *Na kālaḥ pratyakṣa-gocaraḥ... stambhādir eva prāg-abhāva-nivṛtti-pradh-vaṃ-sānutpatti-rūpo vartamānaḥ tad-avacchinaḥ kālo'pi vartamānaḥ sa ca tathā-vidho'neka-jñāna-sādhāraṇa eva, na caitāvatā jñāna-yaugapadyāpattiḥ sūksma-kālāpekṣayā kramạ-sambhavāt, na ca sūkṣma-kālopādhīnām apratītiḥ kārya-krameṇaiva unnīyamānatvāt. —Vedānta-kaumudī,* MS. copy, pp. 20-22.

3 *Ibid.* p. 16.

4 *Tatra smṛti-vyāvṛttam pramātvam anadhigatābādhitārtha-viṣaya-jñānatvam.*
—Vedānta-paribhāṣā, p. 20.

difference from Rāmādvaya's definition; but it may really mean very much more than a verbal difference. For, though want of contradiction (Dharmarāja Adhvarīndra's condition) and want of wrong representation (Rāmādvaya's condition) may mean the same thing, yet in the former case the definition of truth becomes more subjective than in the latter case; for want of wrong representation refers to an objective correspondence and objective certainty. An awareness may wrongly represent an object, but yet may not be found contradicted in the personal history of one or even many observers. Such a definition of truth becomes very relative, since its limits are not fixed by correspondence with its object. Considering the fact that the Vedānta speaks of a real spatial superimposition of the modification of the *antaḥkaraṇa* (which is its cognitive operation) on the object, a Vedānta definition of truth might well be expected to be realistic and not subjectivistic or relativistic. The idealism of the Vedānta rests content in the view that, however realistic these cognitive relations to objects may be, they are impositions and appearances which have as their ultimate ground one changeless consciousness. The definition of *pramā* by Rāmādvaya as an awareness which does not give a wrong representation (*yathārth ānubhava*) of objects could not be-found faulty because of the fact that according to the Vedānta all dual experience of the world was false; for, though it was ultimately so, for all practical purposes it had a real existence, and Rāmādvaya refers to the *Iṣṭa-siddhi* to justify his view on this point.

As to the other point, viz. that a *pramā* must always be that which acquaints us with what is unknown before (*anadhigata*), Rāmādvaya definitely repudiates such a suggestion.[1] He says that it often happens that we perceive things that we perceived before, and this makes recognition possible, and, if we deny that these are cases of right knowledge, we shall have to exclude much that is universally acknowledged as right knowledge. Also it cannot be conceived how in the case of the continuous perception of an object there can be new qualities accruing to

1 *ajñāta-jñāpanaṃ pramāṇam iti tad asāram. Vedānta-kaumudī,* MS. copy, p. 18.

the object, so as to justify the validity of the consciousness as right knowledge at every moment; nor can it be said that the sense-organs after producing the right knowledge of an object (which lasts for some time and is not momentary) may cease to operate until a new awareness is produced. There is therefore no justification for introducing *anadhigatatva* as a condition of perception. Turning to the difference between perception and inference, Rāmādvaya says that in inference the inferred object does not form a datum and there is no direct and immediate contact of the *antaḥkaraṇa* with the inferred object (*e.g.,* fire). In inference the *antaḥkaraṇa* is in touch only with the reason or the *liṅga* (*e.g.,* smoke), and through this there arises (*liṅgādi-bala-labdhākārollekha-mātreṇa*) an idea in the mind (*e.g.,* regarding the existence of fire) which is called inference.[1]

On the subject of the self-validity of knowledge (*svataḥ-prāmāṇya*) Rāmādvaya does not, like Dharmarājādhvarīndra, include the absence of defects (*doṣābhāva*) in the definition of *svataḥ-prāmāṇya.* It may well be remembered that Dharmarāja Adhvarīndra defines validity (*prāmāṇya*) of knowledge as an awareness that characterizes an object as it is (*tadvati tat-prakāraka-jñānatvam*), while self-validity (*svataḥ-prāmāṇya*) is defined as the acceptance by the underlying *sākṣi* consciousness of this validity in accordance with the exact modes of the awareness (of which the validity is affirmed), and in accordance with the exact objective conditions of the awareness, in absence of any defects.[2] Rāmādvaya, however, closely follows Kumārila's view of the self-validity of knowledge and defines it as that which, being produced by the actual data of that cognition, does not contain any

1 *Ibid.* p. 47. One of the earliest explanations of the Vedāntic view of inference occurs in the *Prakaṭārtha-vivaraṇa,* to which the *Vedānta-kaumudī* is in all probability indebted.

2 *doṣābhāve sati yāvat-svāśraya-grāhaka-sāmagrī-grāhyatvarn;svāśrayovṛt-ti-jñānam, tad-grāhakaṃ sākṣi-jñānam tenāpi vṛtti-jñāne gṛhyamāṇe tad-gata-prāmāṇyam api gṛhyate.* —*Vedānta-paribhāṣā,* pp. 336, 337.

element which is derived from other sources.[1] Later knowledge of the presence of any defects or distorting elements may invalidate any cognition; but, so long as such defects are not known, each cognition is valid of itself for reasons similar to those held by Kumārila and already discussed.[2] In this connection Rāmādvaya points out that our cognitions are entirely internal phenomena and are not in touch with objects, and that, though the objects are revealed outside, yet it is through our own internal conditions, merit and demerit, that they may be perceived by us.[3]

VIDYĀRAṆYA (AD 1350)

In addition to the *Sarva-darśana-saṃgraha* Mādhava wrote two works on the Śaṅkara Vedānta system, viz. *Vivaraṇa-prameya-saṃgraha* and *Pañcadaśī*; and also *Jīvan-mukti-viveka.* Of these the former is an independent study of Prakāśātman's *Pañca-pādikā-vivaraṇa*, in which Mādhava elaborates the latter's arguments in his own way. His other work, *PAÑCADAŚĪ,* is a popular compendium in verse. Both these works attained great celebrity on account of their clear and forcible style and diction. Vidyāraṇya is reputed to be the same as Mādhava, brother of Sāyaṇa, the great Vedic commentator. He was a pupil of Śaṅkarānanda, who had written some works of minor importance on the Upaniṣads.[4]

Vidyāraṇya in his *Pañcadaśī* repeats the *Vivaraṇa* view of the Vedānta, that, whether in our awakened state or in our dreams or in our dreamless condition, there is no moment when there is no consciousness; for even in dreamless sleep there must be some consciousness, as is evident from the later remembrance of the

---

1 *vijñāna-sāmagrī-janyatve sati yat tad-anya-janyatvaṃ tad-abhāvasyaivas-vatastvokty-angīkārāt. —Vedānta-kaumudī,* MS. copy, p. 52. *jñaptāvapi jñā-na-jñāpaka-sāmagrl-mātra-jñāpyatvaṃ svatastvam. Ibid.* p. 61.

2 *A History of Indian Philosophy,* vol. 1, Cambridge, 1922, pp. 372-375.

3 *prākaṭyena yuktasyāpi tasya na sarvair viditatvaṃ sva-prakāśam apiprākaṭyaṃ kasyacid evādṛṣṭa-yogāt sphurati na guṇatve jñānasya kathañcid artha-yo-gaḥ-samastīti. Vedānta-kaumudī,* MS. copy, pp. 67, 68.

4 Bhāratītīrtha and his teacher Vidyātīrtha also were teachers of Vidyāraṇya. Vidyāraṇya thus seems to have had three teachers, BhāratīTīrtha, VidyāTīrtha and Śaṅkarānanda.

experience of the dreamless state. The light of consciousness is thus itself ever present without any change or flickering of any kind. It should therefore be regarded as ultimately real. It is self-luminous and neither rises nor sets.[1] This self is pure bliss, because nothing is so much loved by us as our own selves. If the nature of self had been unobscured, we could not have found any enjoyment in sense-objects. It is only because the self is largely obscured to us that we do not rest content with self-realization and crave for other pleasures from sense-objects. *Māyā* is the cause of this obscuration, and it is described as that power by which can be produced the manifold world-appearance. This power (*śakti*), cannot be regarded either as absolutely real or as unreal. It is, however, associated only with a part of Brahman and not with the whole of it, and it is only in association with a part of Brahman that it transforms itself into the various elements and their modifications. All objects of the world are thus but a complex of Brahman and *māyā.* The existence or being of all things is the Brahman, and all that appears identified with being is the *māyā* part. *Māyā* as the power of Brahman regulates all relation and order of the universe. In association with the intelligence of Brahman this behaves as an intelligent power which is responsible for the orderliness of all qualities of things, their inter-relations and interactions.[2] He compares the world-appearance to a painting, where the white canvas stands for the pure Brahman, the white paste for the inner controller (*antaryāmin*), the dark colour for the dispenser of the crude elements (*sūtrātman*) and the coloration for the dispenser of the concrete elemental world (*virāṭ*), and all the figures that are manifested thereon are the living beings and other objects of the world. It is Brahman that, being reflected through the *māyā*, assumes the diverse forms and characters. The false appearance of individual selves is due to the false identification of subjectivity—a product of *māyā*—

1 *Nodeti nāstamety ekā saṃvid eṣā svayam-prabhā. Pañcadaśī*, I.7, Basumati edition, Calcutta, 1907.

2 *Śaktir asty aiśvarī kācit sarva-vastti-niyāmikā.* 38. *cic-chāyāveśataḥ śaktiś cetaneva vibhātisā.* 40. *Ibid.* III.

with the underlying pure consciousness—Brahman. Vidyāraṇya then goes on to describe the usual topics of the Vedānta, which have already been dealt with. The chief and important feature of Vidyāraṇya's *Pañcadaśī* is the continual repetition of the well-established Vedāntic principles in a clear, popular and attractive way, which is very helpful to those who wish to initiate their minds into the Vedāntic ways of self-realization.[1] His *Vivaraṇa-prameya-saṃgraha* is a more scholarly work; but, as it is of the nature of an elaboration of the ideas contained in *Pañca-pādikā-vivaraṇa,* which has generally been followed as the main guide in the account of Vedānta given in this and the preceding chapter, and there being but few ideas which can be considered as an original contribution of Vidyāraṇya to the development of Vedāntic thought, no separate account of its contents need be given here.[2] The *Jīvan-mukti-viveka,* the substance of which has already been utilized in section 17 of chapter x, volume 1 of the present work, is an ethical treatise, covering more or less the same ground as the *Naiṣkarmya-siddhi* of Sureśvara.

NṚSIṂHĀŚRAMA MUNI (AD 1500)

Nṛsiṃhāśrama Muni (AD 1500) was a pupil of Gīrvāṇendra Sarasvatī and Jagannāthāśrama and teacher of Nārāyaṇāśrama, who wrote a commentary on his *Bheda-dḥikkāra.* He wrote many works, such as *Advaita-dīpikā, Advaita-pañca-ratna, Advaita-bodha-*

---

1 There are four commentaries on the *Pañcadaśī:—Tattva-bodhinī, Vṛtti-prabhākara* by Niścaladāsa Svāmin, *Tātparya-bodhinī* by Rāmakṛṣṇa and another commentary by Sadānanda. It is traditionally believed that the *Pañcadaśī* was written jointly by Vidyāranya and BhāratīTīrtha. NiścaladāsaSvāmin points out in his *Vṛtti-prabhākara* that Vidyāranya was author of the first ten chapters of the *Pañcadaśī* and BhāratīTīrtha of the other five. Rāmakṛṣṇa, however, in the beginning of his commentary on the seventh chapter, attributes that chapter to BhāratīTīrtha, and this fits in with the other tradition that the first six chapters were written by Vidyāraṇya and the other nine by Bhāratītīrtha.

2 He also wrote another work on the *Vivaraṇa,* called *Vivaraṇopanyāsa,* which is referred to by Appaya Dīṣkita in his *Siddhānta-leśa,* p. 68—*Vivaraṇopanycse Bhāratītvriha-vacanam.*

dīpikā, Advaita-vāda, Bheda-dhikkāra, Vācārambhaṇa, Vedānta-tattva-viveka, and commentaries on the *Saṃkṣepa-śārīraka* and *Pañca-pādikā-vivaraṇa*, called *Tattva-bodhinī* and *Pañca-pādikā-vivaraṇa-prakāśikā.* Nṛsiṃhāśrama was very well reputed among his contemporaries, but it does not seem that he introduced any new ideas into the Vedānta. He is more interested in emphasizing the fact of the identity of Brahman with the self and the illusory character of the world-appearance than in investigating the nature and constitution of *māyā* and the way in which it can be regarded as the material stuff of world-appearance. He defines the falsehood of world-appearance as its non-existence in the locus in which it appears (*pratipannopādhāv abhāva-pratiyogitva*).[1] When a piece of conch-shell appears to be silver, the silver appears to be existent and real (*sat*), but silver cannot be the same as being or existence (*na tāvad rajata-svarūpaṃ sat*). So also, when we take the world-appearance as existent, the world-appearance cannot be identical with being or existence; its apparent identification with these is thus necessarily false.[2] So also the appearance of subjectivity or egoistic characters in the self-luminous self is false, because the two are entirely different and cannot be identified. Nṛsiṃhāśrama, however, cannot show by logical arguments or by a reference to experience that subjectivity or egoism (*ahaṃkāra,* which he also calls *antaḥkaraṇa* or mind) is different from self, and he relies on the texts of the Upaniṣads to prove this point, which is of fundamental importance for the Vedānta thesis. In explaining the nature of the perceptual process he gives us the same sort of account as is given by his pupil Dharmarāja Adhvarīndra in his *Vedānta-paribhāṣā*, as described in the tenth chapter in the first volume of this work.[3] He considers the self to be bliss itself (*sukha-rūpa*) and does not admit

1 *Vedānta-tattva-viveka,* p. 12. *The Pandit,* vol. xxv, May 1903. This work has two important commentaries, viz. *Tattva-viveka-dīpana,* and one called *Tattva-viveka-dīpana-vyākhyā* by Bhaṭṭojī.

2 *Vedānta-tattva-viveka,* p. 15.

3 *Yadā antaḥkaraṇa-vṛttyā ghaṭāvacchinnaṃ caitanyam upadhīyate tadāantaḥ-karaṇāvacchinna-ghaṭāvacchinna-caiṭanyayor vastuta ekatve 'py upādhi-bhedād bhinnayor abhedopādhi-sambandhena aikyād bhavaty abheda ity antaḥkara-ṇā-*

that there is any difference between the self and bliss (*sa cātmā sukhān na bhidyate*).[1] His definition of *ajñāna* is the same as that of Citsukha, viz. that it is a beginningless constitutive cause, which is removable by true knowledge.[2] There is thus practically no new line of argument in his presentation of the Vedānta. On the side of dialectical arguments, in his attempts to refute "difference" (*bheda*) in his *Bheda-dhikkāra* he was anticipated by his great predecessors Śrīharṣa and Citsukha.

APPAYA DĪKṢITA-I (AD 1550)[3]

Appaya Dīkṣita lived probably in the middle of the sixteenth century, as he refers to Nṛsiṃhāśrama Muni, who lived early in that century. He was a great scholar, well-read in many branches of Sanskrit learning, and wrote a large number of works on many subjects. His grandfather was Ācārya Dīkṣita, who is said to have been famous for his scholarship from the Himalayas to the south point of India: the name of his father was Raṅgarāja Makhīndra (or simply Rāja Makhīndra). There is, however, nothing very noteworthy in his Vedāntic doctrines. For, in spite of his scholarship, he was only a good compiler and not an original thinker, and on many occasions where he had opportunities of giving original views he contents himself with the views of others. It is sometimes said that he had two different religious views at two different periods of his life, Śaiva and the Vedānta. But of this one cannot be certain; for he was such an all-round scholar that the fact that he wrote a Śaiva commentary and a Vedāntic commentary need not lead to the supposition that he changed his faith. In the beginning of his commentary *Śivārka-*

---

vacchinna-caitanyasya viṣayābhinna-tad-adhiṣṭhāna-caitanyasyābheda-siddhy-artham vṛtter nirgamanaṃ vācyam. —*Ibid.* p. 22.

1 *Ibid.* p. 29.

2 *Anādy upādānatve sati jñāna-nivartyam ajñānam, nikhila-prapañcopādāna-brahma-gocaram eva ajñānam. Ibid.* p. 43.

3 He was also called Appayya Dīkṣita and AvadhāniYajvā, and he studied Logic *(tarka)* with Yajñeśvara Makhīndra. See colophon to Appaya Dīkṣita's commentary on the *Nyāya-siddhānta-mañjarī* of Jānakīnātha, called *Nyāya-siddhānta-mañjarī-vyākhyāna* (MS.).

maṇi-dīpikā on Śrīkaṇṭha's Śaiva commentary to the *Brahma-sūtra* he says that, though the right interpretation of the *Brahma-sūtra* is the monistic interpretation, as attempted by Śaṅkara and others, yet the desire for attaining this right wisdom of oneness (*advaita-vāsanā*) arises only through the grace of Śiva, and it is for this reason that Vyāsa in his *Brahma-sūtra* tried to establish the superiority of the qualified Brahman Śiva as interpreted by Śrīkaṇṭhācārya. This shows that even while writing his commentary on Śrīkaṇṭha's *Śaiva-bhāṣya* he had not lost respect for the monistic interpretations of Śaṅkara, and he was somehow able to reconcile in his mind the Śaiva doctrine of qualified Brahman (*saguṇa-brahma*) as Śiva with the Śaṅkara doctrine of unqualified pure Brahman. It is possible, however, that his sympathies with the monistic Vedānta, which at the beginning were only lukewarm, deepened with age. He says in his *Śivārka-maṇi-dīpikā* that he lived in the reign of King Cinnabomma (whose land-grant inscriptions date from Sadāśiva, mahārāja of Vijayanagara, AD 1566 to 1575; *vide* Hultzsch, *S.I. Inscriptions*, vol. 1), under whose orders he wrote the *Śivārka-maṇi-dīpikā* commentary on Śrīkaṇṭha's commentary. His grandson Nīlakaṇṭha Dīkṣita says in his *Śiva-līlārṇava* that Appaya Dīkṣita lived to the good old age of seventy-two. In the *Oriental Historical Manuscripts* catalogued by Taylor, vol. II, it is related that at the request of the Pāṇḍya king Tirumalai Nayaka he came to the Pāṇḍya country in AD 1626 to settle certain disputes between the Śaivas and the Vaiṣṇavas. Kālahasti-śaraṇa-Śivānanda Yogīndra, in his commentary on the *Ātmārpaṇa-stava*, gives the date of Appaya Dīkṣita's birth as Kali age 4654, or AD 1554, as pointed out by Mahāmahopādhyāya Kuppusvāmi Śāstri in his Sanskrit introduction to the *Śiva-līlārṇava.* Since he lived seventy-two years, he must have died some time in 1626, the very year when he came to the Pāṇḍya country. He had for his pupil Bhaṭṭojī Dīkṣita, as is indicated by his own statement in the *Tantra-siddhānta-dīpikā* by the latter author. Bhaṭṭoji Dīkṣita must therefore have been a junior contemporary of Appaya Dīkṣita, as is also evidenced by his other statement in his *Tattva-kaustubha* that he wrote this work at the request of King Keladī-Veṅkaṭendra, who reigned from 1604 to 1626 (*vide* Hultzsch's second volume of *Reports on Sanskrit Manuscripts*).[1]

It is said that Appaya Dīkṣita wrote about four hundred works. Some of them maybe mentioned here: *Advaita-nirṇaya, Catur-mata-sāra-saṃgraha* (containing in the first chapter, called *Nyāya-muktāvalī*, a brief summary of the doctrines of Mādhva, in the second chapter, called *Naya-mayūkha-mālikā,* the doctrines of Rāmānuja, in the third chapter the decisive conclusions from the point of view of Śrīkaṇṭha's commentary called *Naya-maṇi-mālā* and in the fourth chapter, called *Naya-mañjarī*, decisive conclusions in accordance with the views of Śaṅkarācārya); *Tattva-muktāvalī,* a work on Vedānta; *Vyākaraṇa-vāda-nakṣatra-mālā*, a work on grammar; *Pūrvottara-mīmāṃsā-vāda-nakṣatra-mālā* (containing various separate topics of discussion in Mīmāṃsā and Vedānta); *Nyāya-rakṣā-maṇi,* a commentary on the *Brahma-sūtra* following the monistic lines of Śaṅkara; *Vedānta-kalpa-taru-parimala,* a commentary on Amalānanda's *Vedānta-kalpa-taru,* a commentary on Vācaspati's *Bhāmatī* commentary; *Siddhānta-leśa-saṃgraha,* a collection of the views of different philosophers of the monistic school of Śaṅkara on some of the most important points of the Vedānta, without any attempt at harmonizing them or showing his own preference by reasoned arguments, and comprising a number of commentaries by Acyutakṛṣṇānanda Tīrtha (*Kṛṣṇālaṃkāra*), Gaṅgādharendra Sarasvatī (*Siddhānta-bindu-śīkara*), Rāmacandra Yajvan (*Gūḍhārtha-prakāśa*), Viśvanātha Tīrtha, Dharmaya Dīkṣita and others; *Śivārka-maṇi-dīpikā,* a commentary on Śrīkaṇṭha's *Śaiva-bhāṣya* on the *Brahma-sūtra*; *Śiva-karṇāmṛta*; *Śiva-tattva-viveka*; *Śiva-purāṇa-tāmasatva-khaṇḍana*; *Śivādvaita-nirṇaya; Śivānanda-laharī-candrikā,* a commentary on Śaṅkara's *Śivānanda-laharī*; *Śivārcana-candrikā*; *Śivotkarṣa-candrikā*; *Śivotkarṣa-mañjarī*; *Śaiva-kalpa-druma; Siddhānta-ratnākara; Mādhva-mukha-bhaṅga,* an attempt to show that Mādhva's

1 See Mahāmahopādhyāya Kuppusvami Sastri's introduction to the *Śiva-līlārṇava,* Srirangam, 1911

interpretation of the *Brahma-sūtra* is not in accordance with the meaning of the texts of the Upaniṣads; *Rāmānuja-mata-khaṇḍana*; *Rāmāyaṇa-tātparya-nirṇaya*; *Rāmāyaṇa-tātparya-saṃgraha; Rāmāyaṇa-bhārata-sāra-saṃgraha*; *Rāmāyaṇa-sāra*; *Rāmāyaṇa-sāra-saṃgraha; Rāmāyaṇa-sāra-stava*; *Mīmāṃsādhikaraṇamālā Upa-krama-parākrama,* a short Mīmāṃsā work; *Dharma-mīmāṃsā-paribhāṣā; Nāma-saṃgraha-mālikā*; *Vidhi-rasāyana*; *Vidhi-rasā-yanopajīvanī; Vṛtti-vārttika,* a short work on the threefold meanings of words; *Kuvalayānanda,* a work on rhetoric on which no less than ten commentaries have been written; *Citra-mīmāṃsā,* a work on rhetoric; *Jayollāsa-nidhi,* a commentary on the *Bhāgavata-purāṇa*; *Yādavābhyudaya-ṭīkā,* a commentary on Veṅkaṭa's *Yādavā-bhyudaya*; a commentary on the *Prabodha-candrodaya nāṭaka*, etc.

PRAKĀŚĀNANDA (AD 1550-1600)

It has been pointed out that the Vedānta doctrine of monism as preached by Śaṅkara could not shake off its apparent duality in association with *māyā*, which in the hands of the later followers of Śaṅkara gradually thickened into a positive stuff through the evolution or transformation of which all the phenomena of world-appearance could be explained. The Vedāntists held that this *māyā*, though it adhered to Brahman and spread its magical creations thereon, was unspeakable, indescribable, indefinable, changeable and unthinkable and was thus entirely different from the self-revealing, unchangeable Brahman. The charge of dualism against such a system of philosophy could be dodged by the teachers of Vedānta only by holding that, since Brahman was the ultimate reality, *MĀYĀ* was unreal and illusory, and hence the charge of duality would be false. But when one considers that *māyā* is regarded as positive and as the stuff of the transformations of world-appearance, it is hardly intelligible how it can be kept out of consideration as having no kind of existence at all. The positive character of *māyā* as being the stuff of all world-appearance has to be given up, if the strictly monistic doctrine is to be consistently kept. Almost all the followers of Śaṅkara had, however, been interpreting their master's views in such a way that the positive existence of an objective world with its infinite varieties as the ground of perceptual presentation was never denied. The whole course of the development of Vedānta doctrine in the hands of these Vedānta teachers began to crystallize compactly in the view that, since the variety and multiplicity of world-appearance cannot be explained by the pure changeless Brahman, an indefinable stuff, the *māyā*, has necessarily to be admitted as the ground of this world. Prakāśānanda was probably the first who tried to explain Vedānta from a purely sensationalistic view-point of idealism and denied the objective existence of any stuff. The existence of objects is nothing more than their perception (*dṛṣṭi*). The central doctrine of Prakāśānanda has already been briefly described in chapter x, section 15, of volume 1 of the present work, and his analysis of the nature of perceptual cognition has already been referred to in a preceding section of the present chapter.

Speaking on the subject of the causality of Brahman, he says that the attribution of causality to Brahman cannot be regarded as strictly correct; for ordinarily causality implies the dual relation of cause and effect; since there is nothing else but Brahman, it cannot, under the circumstances, be called a cause. Nescience (*avidyā*), again, cannot be called a cause of the world; for causality is based upon the false notion of duality, which is itself the outcome of nescience. The theory of cause and effect thus lies outside the scope of the Vedānta (*kārya-kāraṇa-vādasya vedānta-bahir-bhūtatvāt*). When in reply to the question, "what is the cause of the world?" it is said that nescience (*ajñāna*—literally, want of knowledge) is the cause, the respondent simply wants to obviate the awkward silence. The nature of this nescience cannot, however, be proved by any of the *pramāṇas*; for it is like darkness and the *pramāṇas* or the valid ways of cognition are like light, and it is impossible to perceive darkness by light. Nescience is that which cannot be known except through something else, by its relation to something else, and it is inexplicable in itself, yet beginningless and positive. It will be futile for anyone to try to understand it as it is in itself. Nescience is proved by one's own consciousness: so it is useless to ask how nescience is proved. Yet it is destroyed when the identity of the self with the immediately presented Brahman is realized. The destruction of nescience cannot mean its cessation together with its products, as Prakāśātman holds in the *Vivaraṇa'*, for such a definition would not apply, whether taken simply or jointly. Prakāśānanda, therefore, defines it as the conviction, following the realization of the underlying ground, that the appearance which was illusorily imposed on it did not exist. This view is different from the *anyathā-khyāti* view, that the surmised appearance was elsewhere and not on the ground on which it was imposed; for here, when the underlying ground is immediately intuited, the false appearance absolutely vanishes, and it is felt that it was not there, it is not anywhere, and it will not be anywhere; and it is this conviction that is technically called *bādha.* The indefinability of nescience is its negation on the ground on which it appears (*pratipannopādhau niṣedha-pratiyogitvam*). This negation of all else excepting Brahman has thus two forms; in one form it is negation and in another form this negation, being included within "all else except Brahman," is itself an illusory imposition, and this latter form thus is itself contradicted and negated by its former form. Thus it would be wrong to argue that, since this negation remains after the realization of Brahman, it would not itself be negated, and hence it would be a dual principle existing side by side with Brahman.[1]

---

1 *Brahmaṇy adhyasyamānaṃ sarvaṃ kālatraye nāstītiniścayasya asti rūpad-va-yam ekam bādhātmakam aparam adhyasyamānatvaṃ; tatra adhyasy amānatvena rūpeṇa sva-viṣayatvam; bādhatvena viṣayitvam iti nātmāśraya ity arthah tathā ca nādvaita-kṣatiḥ.* Compare also *Bhāmatī* on *Adhyāsa-bhāṣya.* Nānā Dīkṣita seems to have borrowed his whole argument from the *Bhāmatī.* See his commentary on the *Siddhānta-muktāvalī. The Pandit,* 1890, p. 108. This idea, however, is not by any means a new contribution of Prakāśānanda. Thus Citsukha writes the same thing in his *Tattva-dīpikā* (also called *Pratyak-tat-tva-pradīpika),* p. 39, as follows: "*sarveṣām api bhāvānām āsrayatvena sum-mate pratiyogitvam atyantābhāvam prat imṛṣātmatā,*" which is the same as *prati-pannopādhau niṣedha-pratiyogitvam.* Compare also *Vedānta-paribhāṣā,*

True knowledge is opposed to false knowledge in such a way that, when the former dawns, the latter is dispelled altogether. An objection is sometimes raised that, if this be so, then the person who has realized Brahma knowledge will cease to have a bodily existence; for bodily existence is based on illusion and all illusion must vanish when true knowledge dawns. And, if this is so, there will be no competent Vedānta teacher. To this Prakāśānanda replies that, even though the Vedānta teacher may be himself an illusory production, he may all the same lead any one to the true path, just as the Vedas, which are themselves but illusory products, may lead any one to the right path.[1]

On the subject of the nature of the self as pure bliss (*ānanda*) he differs from Sarvajñātma Muni's view that what is meant by the statement that the self is of the nature of pure bliss is that there is entire absence of all sorrows or negation of bliss in the self. Bliss, according to Sarvajñātma Muni, thus means the absence of the negation of bliss (*an-ānanda-vyavṛtti-mātramānandatvam*).[2] He differs also from the view of Prakāśātman that *ānanda*, or bliss, means the substance which appears as blissful, since it is the object that we really desire. Prakāśātman holds that it is the self on which the character of blissfulness is imposed. The self is called blissful, because it is the ground of the appearance of blissfulness. What people consider of value and desire is not the blissfulness, but that which is blissful. Prakāśānanda holds that this view is not correct, since the self appears not only as blissful, but also as painful, and it would therefore be as right to call the self blissful as to call it painful. Moreover, not the object of blissfulness, which in itself is dissociated from blissfulness, is called blissful, but that which

pp. 219 and 220, *mithyātvaṃ ca svāśrayatvenābhimata-yāvanniṣṭhātyantābhāva-prati-yogitvam.* In later times Madhusūdana freely used this definition in his *Advaita-siddhi.*

1 कल्पितोऽप्युपदेष्टा स्याद् यथाशास्त्रं समादिशेत्
न चाविनिगमो दोषोऽविद्यावत्त्वेन निर्णयात्
kalpito 'pyupadeṣṭā syād yathā-śāstraṃ samādiśet
Na cāvinigamo doṣo 'vidyāvattvena nirṇayāt. —*The Pandit,* 1890, p. 160.

2 *Saṃkṣepa-śārīraka,* I.1.174.

is endowed with bliss is called blissful (*viśiṣṭasyaiva ānanda-padārthatvāt*).[1] If blissfulness is not a natural character of the self, it cannot be called blissful because it happens to be the ground on which blissfulness is illusorily imposed. So Prakāśānanda holds that the self is naturally of a blissful character.

Prakāśānanda raises the question regarding the beholder of the experienced duality and says that it is Brahman who has this experience of duality; but, though Brahman alone exists, yet there is no actual modification or transformation *(pariṇāma)* of Brahman into all its experiences, since such a view would be open to the objections brought against the alternative assumptions of the whole of Brahman or a part of it, and both of them would land us in impossible consequences. The *vivarta* view holds that the effect has no reality apart from the underlying ground or substance. So *vivarta* really means oneness with the substance, and it virtually denies all else that may appear to be growing out of this one substance. The false perception of world-appearance thus consists in the appearance of all kinds of characters in Brahman, which is absolutely characterless (*niṣprakārikāyāḥ saprakārakatvena bhāvaḥ*). Since the self and its cognition are identical and since there is nothing else but this self, there is no meaning in saying that the Vedānta admits the *vivarta* view of causation; for, strictly speaking, there is no causation at all (*vivartasya bāla-vyutpatti-prayojana-tayā*).[2] If anything existed apart from self, then the Vedāntic monism would be disturbed. If one looks at *māyā* in accordance with the texts of the Vedas, *MĀYĀ* will appear to be an absolutely fictitious non-entity (*tuccha*), like the hare's horn; if an attempt is made to interpret it logically, it is indefinable (*anirvacanīya*), though common people would always

1 *Siddhānta-muktāvalī. The Pandit,* 1890, p. 215.

2 बालान् प्रति विवर्तोऽयं ब्रह्मनः सकलं जगत्
अविवर्त्तितम् आनन्दम् आस्थिताह् कृतिनः सदा ॥
Bālān prati vivarto'yaṃ brahmanaḥ sakalaṃ jagat
Avivarttitam ānandam āsthitāḥ kṛtinaḥ sadā. —The Pandit, 1890, p. 326.

think of it as being real (*vāstavī*).[1] Prakāśānanda thus preaches the extreme view of the Vedānta, that there is no kind of objectivity that can be attributed to the world, that *māyā* is absolutely non-existent, that our ideas have no objective substratum to which they correspond, that the self is the one and only ultimate reality, and that there is no causation or creation of the world. In this view he has often to fight with Sarvajñātma Muni, Prakāśātman, and with others who developed a more realistic conception of *māyā* transformation; but it was he who, developing probably on the lines of Maṇḍana, tried for the first time to give a consistent presentation of the Vedānta from the most thorough-going idealistic point of view. In the colophon of his work he says that the essence of the Vedānta as preached by him is unknown to his contemporaries and that it was he who first thoroughly expounded this doctrine of philosophy.[2] Prakāśānanda wrote many other works in addition to his *Siddhānta-muktāvalī*, such as *Tārā-bhakti-taraṅgiṇī*, *Manoramātantra-rāja-ṭīkā*, *Mahā-lakṣmī-paddhati* and *Śrī-vidyā-paddhati,* and this shows that, though a thoroughgoing Vedāntist, he was religiously attached to *tantra* forms of worship. Nānā Dīkṣita wrote a commentary on the *Muktāvalī,* called *Siddhānta-pradīpikā*, at a time when different countries of India had become pervaded by the disciples and disciples of the disciples of Prakāśānanda.[3]

---

1 तुच्छानिर्वचनीया च वास्तवी चेत्यसौ त्रिधा
ज्ञेया माया त्रिभिर्बोधैः श्रौतयौक्तिकलौकिकैः
tucchānirvacanīyā ca vāstavī cety asau tridhā
Jñeyā māyā tribhir bodhaiḥ śrauta-yauktika-laukikaiḥ. —*Ibid.* p. 420.

2 वेदान्तसारसर्वस्वम् अज्ञेयम् अधुनातनैः
अशेषेण मयोक्तं तत् पुरुषोत्तमयत्नतः
Vedānta-sāra-sarvasvam ajñeyam adhunātanaiḥ
aśeṣeṇa mayoktaṃ tat puruṣottama-yatnataḥ. —*The Pandit,* 1890, p. 428

3 यच्छिष्यशिष्यसन्दोहव्याप्ताभारतभूमयः
वन्दे तम् यतिभिर्वन्द्यं प्रकाशानन्दम्॥
yacchiṣya-siṣya-sandoha-vyāptābhārata-bhūmayaḥ
vande tam yatibhir vandyaṃ Prakāśānandam īśvaram. —*Ibid.* p. 488.

MADHUSŪDANA SARASVATĪ (AD 1500)[1]

Madhusūdana Sarasvatī, who was a pupil of Viśveśvara Sarasvatī and teacher of Puruṣottama Sarasvatī, in all probability flourished in the first half of the sixteenth century. His chief works are *Vedānta-kalpa-latikā, Advaita-siddhi, Advaita-mañjarī, Advaita-ratna-rakṣaṇa, Ātma-bodha-ṭīkā, Ānanda-mandākinī, Kṛṣṇa-kutūhalanāṭaka, Prasthāna-bheda, Bhakti-sāmānya-nirūpaṇa, Bhagavad-gītā-gūḍhārtha-dīpikā, Bhagavad-bhakti-rasāyana, Bhāgavata-purāṇa-prathama-śloka-vyākhyā, Veda-stuti-ṭīkā, Śāṇḍilyasūtra-ṭīkā, Śāstra-siddhānta-leśa-ṭīkā, Saṃ-kṣepa-śārīraka-sāra-saṃgraha, Siddhānta-tattva-bindu, Hari-līlā-vyākhyā.* His most important work, however, is his *Advaita-siddhi*, in which he tries to refute the objections raised in Vyāsatīrtha's *Nyāyāmṛta*[2] against the monistic Vedānta of Śaṅkara and his followers. Materials from this book have already been utilized in sections 6, 7, 8, 9 and 10 of the tenth chapter of the present work. More will be utilized in the third volume in connection with the controversy between Vyāsatīrtha and Madhusūdana, which is the subject-matter of *Advaita-siddhi.* Madhusūdana's *Siddhānta-bindu* does not contain anything of importance, excepting that he gives a connected account of the perceptual process, already dealt with in the tenth chapter and also in the section "Vedāntic Cosmology" of the present volume. His *Advaita-ratna-rakṣaṇa* deals with such subjects as the validity of the Upaniṣads: the Upaniṣads do not

---

1 Rāmājñā Pāṇḍeya in his edition of Madhusūdana's *Vedānta-kalpa-latikā* suggests that he was a Bengali by birth. His pupil Purusottama Sarasvatī in his commentary on the *Siddhānta-bindu-ṭīkā* refers to Balabhadra Bhaṭṭācārya as a favourite pupil of his, and Pāṇḍeya argues that, since Bhaṭṭācārya is a Bengali surname and since his favourite pupil was a Bengali, he also must have been a Bengali. It is also pointed out that in a family genealogy (*Kula-pañjikā*) of Kotalipara of Faridpur, Bengal, Madhusūdana's father is said to have been Pramodapurandara Ācārya, who had four sons—Śrinātha Cūḍāmani, Yāda-vānanda Nyāyācārya, Kamalajanayana and Vāgiśa Gosvāmin. Some of the important details of Madhusūdana's philosophical dialectics will be taken up in the treatment of the philosophy of Madhva and his followers in the third volume of the present work in connection with Madhusūdana's discussions with Vyāsatīrtha.

2 The *Advaita-siddhi* has three commentaries, *Advaita-siddhy-upanyāsa, Bṛhat-ṭīkā,* and *Laghu-candrikā,* by Brahmānanda Sarasvatī.

admit duality; perception does not prove the reality of duality; the duality involved in mutual negation is false; indeterminate knowledge does not admit duality; duality cannot be proved by any valid means of proof, and so forth. There is practically nothing new in the work, as it only repeats some of the important arguments of the bigger work *Advaita-siddhi* and tries to refute the view of dualists like the followers of Mādhva, with whom Madhusūdana was in constant controversy. It is unnecessary, therefore, for our present purposes to enter into any of the details of this work. It is, however, interesting to note that, though he was such a confirmed monist in his philosophy, he was a theist in his religion and followed the path of *bhakti,* or devotion, as is evidenced by his numerous works promulgating the *bhakti* creed. These works, however, have nothing to do with the philosophy of the Vedānta, with which we are concerned in the present chapter. Madhusūdana's *Vedānta-kalpa-latikā* was written earlier than his *Advaita-siddhi* and his commentary on the *Mahimnaḥ Stotra.*[1] Rāmājñā Pāṇḍeya points out in his introduction to the *Vedānta-kalpa-latikā* that the *Advaita-siddhi* contains a reference to his *Gītā-nibandhana*; the *Gītā-nibandhana* and the *Śrīmad-bhāgavata-ṭīkā* contain references to his *Bhakti-rasāyana,* and the *Bhakti-rasāyana* refers to the *Vedānta-kalpa-latikā*; and this show's that the *Vedānta-kalpa-latikā* was written prior to all these works. The *Advaita-ratna-rakṣaṇa* refers to the *Advaita-siddhi* and may therefore be regarded as a much later work. There is nothing particularly new in the *Vedānta-kalpa-latikā* that deserves special mention as a contribution to Vedāntic thought. The special feature of the work consists in the frequent brief summaries of doctrines of other systems of Indian philosophy and contrasts them with important Vedānta views. The first problem discussed is the nature of emancipation (*mokṣa*) and the ways of realizing it: Madhusūdana attempts to prove that it is only the Vedāntic concept of salvation that can appeal to men, all other views being unsatisfactory and invalid. But it does not

1 He refers to the *Vedānta-kalpa-latikā* and *Siddhānta-bindu* in his *Advaita-siddhi,* p. 537 (*Nirṇaya* -Sāgara edition). See also *Mahimnaḥ-stotra-ṭīkā,* p. 5.

seem that he does proper justice to other views. Thus, for example, in refuting the Sāṃkhya view of salvation he says that, since the Sāṃkhya thinks that what is existent cannot be destroyed, sorrow, being an existent entity, cannot be destroyed, so there cannot be any emancipation from sorrow. This is an evident misrepresentation of the Sāṃkhya; for with the Sāṃkhya the destruction of sorrow in emancipation means that the *buddhi*, a product of *prakṛti* which is the source of all sorrow, ceases in emancipation to have any contact with *puruṣa*, and hence, even though sorrow may not be destroyed, there is no inconsistency in having emancipation from sorrow. It is unnecessary for our present purposes, however, to multiply examples of misrepresentation by Madhusūdana of the views of other systems of thought in regard to the same problem. In the course of the discussions he describes negation (*abhāva*) also as being made up of the stuff of nescience, which, like other things, makes its appearance in connection with pure consciousness. He next introduces a discussion of the nature of self-knowledge, and then, since Brahma knowledge can be attained only through the Upaniṣadic propositions of identity, he passes over to the discussion of import of propositions and the doctrines of *abhihitān-vaya-vāda*, *Anavitābhidhāna-vāda* and the like. He then treats of the destruction of nescience. He concludes the work with a discussion of the substantial nature of the senses. Thus the mind-organ is said to be made up of five elements, whereas other senses are regarded as being constituted of one element only. *Manas* is said to pervade the whole of the body and not to be atomic, as the Naiyāyikas hold. Finally, Madhusūdana returns again to the problem of emancipation, and holds that it is the self freed from nescience that should be regarded as the real nature of emancipation.

CHAPTER XII

THE PHILOSOPHY OF THE YOGA-VĀSIṢṬHA

INTRODUCTION OF THE YOGAVĀSIṢṬHA THEME

The philosophical elements in the various Purāṇas will be taken in a later volume. The *Yoga-vāsiṣṭha-Rāmāyaṇa* may be included among the *purāṇas*, but it is devoid of the general characteristics of the *purāṇās* and is throughout occupied with discussions of Vedāntic problems of a radically monistic type, resembling the Vedāntic doctrines as interpreted by Śaṅkara. This extensive philosophical poem, which contains twenty-three thousand seven hundred and thirty-four verses (ignoring possible differences in different manuscripts or editions) and is thus very much larger than the *Śrīmad-bhagavad-gītā*, is a unique work. The philosophical view with which it is concerned, and which it is never tired of reiterating, is so much like the view of Śaṅkara and of Vijñānavāda Buddhism, that its claim to treatment immediately after Śaṅkara seems to me to be particularly strong. Moreover, the various interpretations of the *Vedānta-sūtra* which will follow are so much opposed to Śaṅkara's views as to make it hard to find a suitable place for a treatment like that of the *Yoga-vāsiṣṭha* unless it is taken up immediately after the chapter dealing with Śaṅkara.

The work begins with a story. A certain Brahmin went to the hermitage of the sage Agastya and asked him whether knowledge or work was the direct cause of salvation (*mokṣa-sādhana*). Agastya replied that, as a bird flies with its two wings, so a man can attain the highest (*paramaṃ padaṃ*) only through knowledge and work. To illustrate this idea he narrates a story in which Kāruṇya, the son of Agniveśya, having returned from the teacher's house after the completion of his studies, remained silent and did no work. When he was asked for the reason of this attitude of his, he said that he was perplexed over the question as to whether the action of a man in accordance with scriptural injunction was or was not more fitted for the attainment of his highest than following a course of self-abnegation and desirelessness (*tyāga-mātra*). On hearing this question of Kāruṇya, Agniveśya told him that he could answer his question only by narrating a story, after hearing which he might decide as he chose. A heavenly damsel (*apsarāḥ*), Suruci by name, sitting on one of the peaks of the Himālayas, once saw a messenger of Indra flying through the sky. She asked him where he was going. In reply he said that a certain king, Ariṣṭanemi by name, having given his kingdom to his son and having become free from all passions, was performing a course of asceticism (*tapas*), and that he had had to go to him on duty and was returning from him. The damsel wanted to know in detail what happened there between the messenger and the king. The messenger replied that he was asked by Indra to take a well-decorated chariot and bring the king in it to heaven, but while doing so he was asked by the king to describe the advantages and defects of heaven, on hearing which he would make up his mind whether he would like to go there or not. In heaven, he was answered, people enjoyed superior, medium and inferior pleasures according as their merits were superior, medium or inferior: when they had exhausted their merits by enjoyment, they were reborn again on earth, and during their stay there they were subject to mutual jealousy on account of the inequality of their enjoyments. On hearing this the king had refused to go to heaven, and, when this was reported to Indra, he was very much surprised and he asked the messenger to carry the king to Vālmīki's hermitage and make Vālmīki acquainted with the king's refusal to enjoy the fruits of heaven and request him to give him proper instructions for the attainment of right knowledge, leading to emancipation (*mokṣa*). When this was done, the king asked Vālmīki how he might attain *mokṣa*, and Vālmīki in reply wished to narrate the dialogue of Vaśiṣṭha and Rāma (*Vaśiṣṭha-rāma-saṃvāda*) on the subject.

Vālmīki said that, when he had finished the story of Rāma—the work properly known as *Rāmāyaṇa*—and taught it to Bharadvāja, Bharadvāja recited it once to Brahmā (the god), and he, being pleased, wished to confer a boon on him. Bharadvāja in reply said that he would like to receive such instructions as would enable people to escape from sorrow. Brahmā told him to apply to Vālmīki and went himself to him (Vālmīki), accompanied by Bharadvāja, and asked him not to cease working until he finished describing the entire character of Rāma, by listening to which people will be saved from the dangers of the world. When Brahmā disappeared from the hermitage after giving this instruction, Bharadvāja also asked Vālmīki to describe how Rāma and his wife, brother and followers behaved in this sorrowful and dangerous world and lived in sorrowless tranquillity.

In answer to the above question Vālmīki replied that Rāma, after finishing his studies, went out on his travels to see the various places of pilgrimage and hermitages. On his return, however, he looked very sad every day and would not tell anyone the cause of his sorrow. King Daśaratha, Rāma's father, became very much concerned about Rāma's sadness and asked Vaśiṣṭha if he knew what might be the cause of it. At this time the sage Viśvāmitra also visited the city of Ayodhyā to invite Rāma to kill the demons. Rāma's dejected mental state at this time created much anxiety, and Viśvāmitra asked him the cause of his dejection.

Rāma said in reply that a new enquiry had come into his mind and had made him averse from all enjoyments. There is no happiness in this world, people are born to die and they die to be born again. Everything is impermanent (*asthira*) in this world. All existent things are unconnected (*bhāvāḥ...parasparam asaṅginaḥ*). They are collected and associated together only by our mental imagination (*manaḥ-kalpanaya*). The world of enjoyment is created by the mind (*manaḥ*), and this mind itself appears to be nonexistent. Everything is like a mirage.

Vaśiṣṭha then explained the nature of the world-appearance, and it is this answer which forms the content of the book. When Vālmīki narrated this dialogue of Vaśiṣṭha and Rāma, king Ariṣṭanemi found himself enlightened, and the damsel was also pleased and dismissed the heavenly messenger. Kāruṇya, on hearing all this from his father Agniveśya, felt as if he realized the ultimate truth and thought that, since he realized the philosophical truth, and since work and passivity mean the same, it was his clear duty to follow the customary duties of life. When Agastya finished narrating the story, the Brahmin Sutīkṣṇa felt himself enlightened.

There is at least one point which may be considered as a very clear indication of later date, much later than would be implied by the claim that the work was written by the author of the *Rāmāyaṇa.* It contains a *śloka* which may be noted as almost identical with a verse of Kālidāsa's *Kumāra-saṃbhava.*[1] It may, in my opinion, be almost unhesitatingly assumed that the author borrowed it from Kālidāsa, and it is true, as is generally supposed, that Kālidāsa lived in the fifth century AD. The author of the *Yoga-vāsiṣṭha,* whoever he may have been, flourished at least some time after Kālidāsa. It may also be assumed that the interval between Kālidāsa's time and that of the author of the *Yoga-vāsiṣṭha* had been long enough to establish Kālidāsa's reputation as a poet. There is another fact which deserves consideration in this connection. In spite of the fact that the views of the *Yoga-vāsiṣṭha* and Śaṅkara's interpretation of Vedānta have important points of agreement neither of them

---

1 *Yoga-vāsiṣṭha,* III.16.50:

अथ तामतिमात्रविह्वलाम् सकृपाकाशभवा सरस्वती।
शफरीं ह्रदशोषविह्वलां प्रथमा वृष्टिरिवान्वकम्पत॥

atha tām atimātra-vihvalāṃ
sakṛpākāśabhavā Sarasvatī
śapharīṃ hrada-śoṣa-vihvalāṃ
prathamā vṛṣṭir ivānvakampata.

refers to the other. Again, the views of the *Yoga-vāsiṣṭha* so much resemble those of the idealistic school of Buddhists, that the whole work seems to be a Brahmanic modification of idealistic Buddhism. One other important instance can be given of such a tendency to assimilate Buddhistic idealism and modify it on Brahmanic lines, viz. the writings of Gauḍapāda and Śaṅkara. I am therefore inclined to think that the author of the *Yoga-vāsiṣṭha* was probably a contemporary of Gauḍapāda or Śaṅkara, about AD 800 or a century anterior to them.

The work contains six books, or *prakaraṇas,* namely, *Vairāgya, Mumukṣu-vyavahāra, Utpatti, Sthiti, Upaśama* and *Nirvāṇa.* It is known also by the names of *Ārṣa-Rāmāyaṇa, Jñāna-vāsiṣṭha, Mahā-Rāmāyaṇa, Vāsiṣṭha-Rāmāyaṇa* or *Vāsiṣṭha.* Several commentaries have been written on it. Of these commentaries I am particularly indebted to the *Tātparya-prakāśa* of Ānandabodhendra.

The *Yoga-vāsiṣṭha* is throughout a philosophical work, in the form of popular lectures, and the same idea is often repeated again and again in various kinds of expressions and poetical imagery. But the writer seems to have been endowed with extraordinary poetical gifts. Almost every verse is full of the finest poetical imagery; the choice of words is exceedingly pleasing to the ear, and they often produce the effect of interesting us more by their poetical value than by the extremely idealistic thought which they are intended to convey.

The *Yoga-vāsiṣṭha* had a number of commentaries, and it was also summarized in verse by some writers whose works also had commentaries written upon them. Thus Advayāraṇya, son of Narahari, wrote a commentary on it, called *Vāsiṣṭha-Rāmāyaṇa-candrikā.* Ānandabodhendra Sarasvatī, pupil of Gaṅgādharendra Sarasvatī of the nineteenth century, wrote the *Tātparya-prakāśa.* Gaṅgādharendra also is said to have written a commentary of the same name. Rāmadeva and Sadānanda also wrote two commentaries on the work, and in addition to these there is another commentary, called *Yoga-vāsiṣṭha-tātparya-saṃgraha,* and another commentary, the *Pada-candrikā*, was written by Mādhava Sarasvatī. The names of some of its summaries are *Bṛhad-yoga-vāsiṣṭha*, *Laghu-jñāna-vāsiṣṭha*, *Yoga-vāsiṣṭha-ślokāḥ* and *Yoga-vāsiṣṭha-saṃkṣepa* by Gauḍa Abhinanda of the ninth century, *Yoga-vāsiṣṭha-sāra* or *Jñāna-sāra*, *Yoga-vāsiṣṭha-sāra-saṃgraha* and *Vāsiṣṭha-sāra* or *Vāsiṣṭha-sāra-gūḍhārthā* by Ramānanda Tirthā, pupil of Advaitānanda. The *Yoga-vāsiṣṭha-saṃkṣepa* of Gauḍa Abhinanda had a commentary by Ātmasukha, called *Candrikā*, and another called *Saṃsāra-taraṇī*, by Mummaḍideva. The *Yoga-vāsiṣṭha-sāra* also had two commentaries by Pūrṇānanda and Mahīdhara. Mr. Śivaprasāda Bhaṭṭacārya in an article on the *Yoga-vāsiṣṭha-Rāmāyaṇa* in the *Proceedings of the Madras Oriental Conference* of 1924 says that the *Mokṣopāya-sāra*, which is another name for the *Yoga-vāsiṣṭha-sāra*, was written by an Abhinanda who is not to be confused with Gauḍa Abhinanda. But he misses the fact that Gauḍa Abhinanda had also written another summary of it, called *Yoga-vāsiṣṭha-saṃkṣepa*. Incidentally this also refutes his view that the *Yoga-vāsiṣṭha* is to be placed between the tenth and the twelfth centuries. For, if a summary of it was written by Gauḍa Abhinanda of the ninth century, the *Yoga-vāsiṣṭha* must have been written at least in the eighth century. The date of the *Yoga-vāsiṣṭha* may thus be regarded as being the seventh or the eighth century.

THE ULTIMATE ENTITY

The third book of the *Yoga-vāsiṣṭha* deals with origination (*utpatti*). All bondage (*bandha*) is due to the existence of the perceptible universe (*dṛśya*), and it is the main thesis of this work that it does not exist. At the time of each dissolution the entire universe of appearance is destroyed, like dreams in deep sleep (*suṣupti*). What is left is deep and static (*stimita-gambhīra*), neither light nor darkness, indescribable and unmanifested (*anākhyam anabhivyaktam*), but a somehow existent entity. This entity manifests itself as another (*svayaṃ anya ivollasan*); and through this dynamic aspect it appears as the ever-active mind (*manas*)—like moving ripples from the motionless ocean. But in reality whatever appears as the diversified universe is altogether non-existent; for, if it was existent, it could not cease under any circumstances.[1] It does not exist at all. The ultimate indefinite and indescribable entity, which is pure extinction (*Nirvāṇa-mātra*), or pure intelligence (*paro bodhaḥ*), remains always in itself and does not really suffer any transformations or modifications. Out of the first movement of this entity arises ego (*svatā*), which, in spite of its appearance, is in reality nothing but the ultimate entity. Gradually, by a series of movements (*spanda*) like waves in the air, there springs forth the entire world-appearance. The ultimate entity is a mere entity of pure conceiving or imagining (*saṃkalpa-puruṣa*).[2] The Muni held that what appears before us is due to the imagination of *manas*, like dreamland or fairyland (*yathā saṃkalpa-nagaraṃ yathā gandharva-pattanam*). There is nothing in essence except that ultimate entity, and whatever else appears does not exist at all—it is all mere mental creations, proceeding out of the substanceless, essenceless mental creations of the ultimate entity. It is only by the realization that this world-appearance has no possibility of existence that the false notion of ourselves as knowers ceases, and, though the false appearance may continue as such, there is emancipation (*mokṣa*).

This *manas*, however, by whose mental creations everything springs forth in appearance, has no proper form, it is merely a name, mere nothingness.[3] It does not exist outside or subjectively inside us; it is like the vacuity surrounding us everywhere. That anything has come out of it is merely like the production of a mirage stream. All characteristics of forms and existence are like momentary

---

1 *Yoga-vāsiṣṭha,* III.3.

2 सर्वेषां भूतजातानां संसारव्यवहारिणाम् प्रथमोऽसौ प्रतिस्पन्दश् चित्तदेकः स्वतोदयः।
अस्मात् पूर्वात् प्रोतिस्पन्दाद् अनन्यैतत्स्वरूपिणी इयं प्रविसृता सृष्टिःस्पन्दसृष्टिर् इवानिलात्॥
sarveṣāṃ bhūta-jātānāṃ saṃsāra-vyavahāriṇām
prathamo 'sau pratispandaś citta-dekaḥ svatodayaḥ
asmāt pūrvāt protispandād ananyaitat-svarūpiṇī
iyaṃ pravisṛtā sṛṣṭiḥ spanda-sṛṣṭir ivānilāt. —III.3.14, 15.

3 रामास्य मनसो रूपं न किंचिद् अपि दृश्यते।
नाममात्राद् ऋते व्योम्नो यथा शून्यजडाकृतेः॥
Rāmasya manaso rūpaṃ na kiṃcid api dṛśyate
nāma-mātrād ṛte vyomno yathā śūnya-jaḍākṛteḥ. —III.4.38.

imaginations. Whatever appears and seems to have existence is nothing but *manas*, though this *manas* itself is merely a hypothetical starting-point, having no actual reality. For the *manas* is not different from the dreams of appearance and cannot be separated from them, just as one cannot separate liquidity from water or movement from air. *Manas* is thus nothing but the hypothetical entity from which all the dreams of appearance proceed, though these dreams and *manas* are merely the same and it is impossible to distinguish between them.[1] *Avidyā, saṃsṛti, citta, manas, bandha, mala, tamas* are thus but synonyms for the same concept.[2] It is the perceiver that appears as the perceived, and it is but the perceptions that appear as the perceiver and the perceived. The state of emancipation is the cessation of this world-appearance. There is in reality no perceiver, perceived or perceptions, no vacuity (*śūnya*), no matter, no spirit or consciousness, but pure cessation or pure negation, and this is what we mean by Brahman.[3] Its nature is that of pure cessation (*śānta*), and it is this that the Sāṃkhyists call *puruṣa,* the Vedāntins call "Brahman," the idealistic Buddhists call "pure idea" (*vijñāna-mātra*) and the nihilists "pure essencelessness" (*śūnya*).[4] It is of the nature of pure annihilation and cessation, pervading the inner and the outer world.[5] It is described as that essencelessness (*śūnya*) which does not appear to be so, and in which lies the ground and being of the essenceless world-appearance (*yasmin śūnyaṃ jagat sthitam*), and which, in spite of all creations, is essenceless.[6] The illusory world-appearance has to be considered as absolutely non-existent, like the water of the mirage or the son of a barren

---

1 पूर्णे पूर्णं प्रसरति शान्ते शान्तं व्यवस्थितम् व्योमन्य् एवोदितं व्योम ब्रमणि ब्रह्म तिष्ठति
न दृश्यम् अस्ति सद्रूपं न द्रष्टा न च दर्शनं न शून्यं न जडं नौ चिच्छान्तम् एवेदम् आततम्॥
pūrṇe pūrṇaṃ prasarati śānte śāntaṃ vyavasthitam
vyomany evoditaṃ vyoma brahmaṇi brahma tiṣṭhati
na dṛśyam asti sad-rūpaṃ na draṣṭā na ca darśanaṃ
na śūnyaṃ na jaḍaṃ no cic chāntam evedam ātatam. —III.4.69, 70.

2 III.4.46.

3 III.5.6-7.

4 *nāśa-rūpo vināśātmā.* III.5.16.

5 III.7.22.

6 III.9.59.

woman. The ultimate entity is thus neither existent nor non-existent and is both statical and dynamical (*spandāspandātmaka*);[1] it is indescribable and un-nameable (*kimapy avyapadeśātmā*) and neither being nor nonbeing nor being-non-being, neither statical being nor becoming (*na bhāvo bhavanaṃ na ca*). The similarity of the philosophy of the *Yoga-vāsiṣṭha* to the idealistic philosophy of the *Laṅkāvatārasūtra* is so definite and deep that the subject does not require any elaborate discussion and the readers are referred to the philosophy of the *Laṅkāvatāra* in the first volume of the present work. On Vedānta lines it is very similar to Prakāśānanda's interpretation of the Vedānta in later times, called *dṛṣṭi-sṛṣṭi-vāda,* which can probably be traced at least as far back as Gauḍapāda or Maṇḍana. Prakāśātman refers to the *Yoga-vāsiṣṭha* as one of his main authorities.

ORIGINATION

The world as such never existed in the past, nor exists now, nor will exist hereafter; so it has no production or destruction in any real sense.[2] But yet there is the appearance, and its genesis has somehow to be accounted for. The ultimate entity is, of course, of the nature of pure cessation (*śānta*), as described above. The order of moments leading to the manifestation of the world-appearance can be described in this way: At first there is something like a self-reflecting thought in the ultimate entity, producing some indescribable objectivity which gives rise to an egohood. Thus, on a further movement, which is akin to thought, is produced a state which can be described as a self-thinking entity, which is clear pure intelligence, in which everything may be reflected. It is only this

1 III.9.49.

2 बन्ध्यापुत्रव्योमबने यथा न स्तः कदाचन जगदाद्यखिलं दृश्यं तथा नास्ति कदाचन।
न चोत्पन्नं न च ध्वंर्न्सि यत् किलादौ न विद्यते उत्पत्तिःकीदृशी तस्य नाशशब्दस्य का कथा॥
bandhyā-putra-vyoma-bane yathā na staḥ kadācana
jagad-ādy akhilaṃ dṛśyaṃ tathā nāsti kadācana
na cotpannaṃ na ca dhvarnsi yat kilādau na vidyate
utpattiḥ kīdṛśī tasya nāśa-śabdasya kā kathā. —III.11.4, 5.

entity that can be called conscious intelligence (*cit*). As the thought-activity becomes more and more concrete (*ghana-saṃvedana*), other conditions of soul (*jīva*) arise out of it. At this stage it forgets, as it were, its subject-objectless ultimate state, and desires to flow out of itself as a pure essence of creative movement (*bhāvanā-mātra-sāra*). The first objectivity is *ākāśa,* manifested as pure vacuity. At this moment arise the ego (*ahaṃta*) and time (*kāla*). This creation is, however, in no sense real, and is nothing but the seeming appearances of the self-conscious movement (*sva-saṃvedana-mātrakam*) of the ultimate being. All the network of being is non-existent, and has only an appearance of existing. Thought (*saṃvit*), which at this moment is like the *ākāśa* and the ego and which is the seed (*bīja*) of all the conceivings of thought (*bhāvanā*), formulates by its movement air.[1] Again, following the *ākāśa* moment and from it as a more concrete state (*ghanībhūya*), comes forth the sound-potential (*kha-tan-mātra*). This sound-potential is the root of the production of all the Vedas, with their words, sentences and valid means of proof. Gradually the conceivings of the other *tan-mātras* of *sparśa*, *tejas, rasa* and *gandha* follow, and from them the entire objective world, which has no other reality than the fact that they are conceptions of the self-conscious thought.[2] The stages then are, that in the state of equilibrium (*sama*) of the ultimate indescribable entity called the Brahman, which, though pure consciousness in

---

1 मनः सम्पद्यते लोलं कलनाकलनोन्मुखम्; कलयन्ती मनः शक्तिर् आदौ भावयति क्षणात्।
आकाशभावामच्छां शब्दबीजरसोत्मुखीम्; ततस् तां घनतां जातम् घनस्पदक्रमान् मनः ॥
manaḥ saṃpadyate lolaṃ kalanā-kalanonmukham;
kalayantī manaḥ śaktir ādau bhāvayati kṣaṇāt.
ākāśa-bhāvanāmacchāṃ śabda-bīja-rasortmukhīm;
tatas tāṃ ghanatāṃ jātam ghana-spanda-kramān manaḥ. —IV.44.16, 17.

A comparison of numerous passages like these shows that each mental creation is the result of a creative thought-movement called *bhāvanā,* and each successive movement in the chain of a succession of developing creative movements is said to be *ghana,* or concrete. *Ghana* has been paraphrased in the *Tātparya-prakāśa* as accretion (*upacaya*). *Bhāvāna* is the same as *spanda*; as the result of each thought-movement, there was thought-accretion (*ghana),* and corresponding to each *ghana* there was a semi-statical creation, and following each *ghana* there was a *spanda* (*ghana-spanda-kramāt*).

2 III.12.

essence, is in an unmanifested state, there first arises an objectivity (*cetyatva*) through its self-directed self-consciousness of the objectivity inherent in it (*sataś cetyāṃśa-cetanāt*); next arises the soul, where there is objective consciousness only through the touch or connection of objectivity (*cetya-saṃyoga-cetanāt*) instead of the self-directed consciousness of objectivity inherent in itself. Then comes the illusory notion of subjectivity, through which the soul thinks that it is only the conscious subject and as such is different from the object (*cetyaika-paratā-vaśāt*). This moment naturally leads to the state of the subjective ego, which conceives actively (*buddhitvākalanaṃ*), and it is this conceiving activity which leads to the objective conceptions of the different *tan-mātras* and the world-appearance. These are all, however, ideal creations, and as such have no reality apart from their being as mere appearance. Since their nature is purely conceptual (*vikalpa*), they cannot be real at any time. All that appears as existent does so only as a result of the conceptual activity of thought. Through its desire, "I shall see," there comes the appearance of the two hollows of the eye, and similarly in the case of touch, smell, hearing and taste. There is no single soul, far less an infinite number of them. It is by the all-powerful conceptual activity of Brahman that there arises the appearance of so many centres of subjective thought, as the souls (*jīvas*). In reality, however, the *jīvas* have no other existence than the conceptualizing activity which produces their appearance. There is no materiality or form: these are nothing but the self-flashings of thought (*citta-camatkāra*).

Manas, according to this theory, is nothing but that function of pure consciousness through which it posits out of itself an object of itself. Here the pure conscious part may be called the spiritual part and its objectivity aspect the material part.[1] In its objectivity also the *cit* perceives nothing but itself, though it appears to perceive

---

1 चितो यच् चेत्यकलनम् तन्मनस्त्वम् उदाहृतम्
चिद्भागोऽत्राजड भागो जाड्यम् अत्र हि चेत्यता॥
cito yac cetya-kalanaṃ tan-manastvam udāhṛtam
cid-bhāgo 'trājaḍo bhāgo jāḍyam atra hi cetyatā. —III.91.37.

something other than itself (*svam evānyatayā dṛstvā*), and this objectivity takes its first start with the rise of egohood (*ahaṃtā*).

But to the most important question, namely, how the original equilibrium is disturbed and how the present development of the conceptual creation has come about, the answer given in the *Yoga-vāsiṣṭha* is that it is by pure accident (*kākatālīya-yogena*) that such a course of events took place. It is indeed disappointing that such a wonderful creation of world-appearance should have ultimately to depend on accident for its origin.[1] It is considered irrelevant to enquire into the possibility of some other cause of the ultimate cause, the Brahman.[2]

KARMA, MANAS AND THE CATEGORIES

Karma in this view is nothing but the activity of the *manas*. The active states of *manas* are again determined by their preceding moments and may in their turn be considered as determining the succeeding moments. When any particular state determines any succeeding state, it may be considered as an agent, or *kartā*; but, as this state is determined by the activity of the previous state, otherwise called the *karma*, it may be said that the *karma* generates the *kartā*, the *kartā* by its activity again produces *karma*, so that *karma* and *kartā* are mutually determinative. As in the case of the seed coming from the tree and the tree coming from the seed, the cycle proceeds on from *kartā* to *karma* and from *karma* to *kartā*, and no ultimate priority can be affirmed of any one of them.[3] But,

---

1 III.96.15, IV.54.7.

2 ब्रह्मणः कात्रृअणं किं स्याद् इति वक्तुं न युज्योते
स्वभावो निर्विशेषत्वात् परो वक्तुं न युज्यते॥
Brahmaṇaḥ kāṛaṇaṃ kiṃ syād iti vaktuṃ na yujyote
svabhāvo nirviśeṣatvāt paro vaktuṃ na yujyate. —IV.18.22.

3 यथा कर्म च कर्ता च पर्यायेणेह संगतौ
कर्मणा क्रियते कर्ता कर्त्रा कर्म प्रणीयते
बीजाङ्कुरादिवन्न्यायो लोकवेदोक्त एव सः॥
yathā karma ca kartā ca paryāyeṇeha saṃgatau
karmaṇā kriyate kartā kartrā karma praṇīyate
bījāñkurādivan-nyāyo loka-vedokta eva saḥ. —III.95.19, 20.

if this is so, then the responsibility of *karma* ceases; the root desire (*vāsanā*) through which a man is born also makes him suffer or enjoy in accordance with it; but, if *kartā* and *karma* spring forth together, then a particular birth ought not to be determined by the *karma* of previous birth, and this would mean that man's enjoyment and sorrow did not depend on his *karma.* In answer to such a question, raised by Rāmacandra, Vaśiṣṭha says that *karma* is due not to *ātman*, but to *manas.* It is the mental movement which constitutes *karma.* When first the category of *manas* rises into being from Brahman, *karma* also begins from that moment, and, as a result thereof, the soul and the body associated with it are supposed to be manifested. *Karma* and *manas* are in one sense the same. In this world the movement generated by action (*kriyā-spanda*) is called *karma*, and, as it is by the movement of *manas* that all effects take place, and the bodies with all their associated sufferings or enjoyments are produced, so even the body, which is associated with physical, external *karma*, is in reality nothing but the *manas* and its activity. *Manas* is essentially of the nature of *karma*, or activity, and the cessation of activity means the destruction of *manas* (*karma-nāśe mano-nāśaḥ*).[1] As heat cannot be separated from fire or blackness from collyrium, so movement and activity cannot be separated from *manas.* If one ceases, the other also necessarily ceases. *Manas* means that activity which subsists between being and non-being and induces being through non-being: it is essentially dynamic in its nature and passes by the name of *manas.* It is by the activity of *manas* that the subject-objectless pure consciousness assumes the form of a self-conscious ego. *Manas* thus consists of this constantly positing activity (*ekānta-kalanaḥ*). The seed of *karma* is to be sought in the activity of *manas* (*karma-bījaṃ manaḥ-spanda*), and the actions (*kriyā*) which follow are indeed very diverse. It is the synthetic function (*tad-anusandhatte*) of *manas* that is called the functioning of the conative senses, by which all actions are performed, and it is for this reason that *karma* is nothing but *manas. Manas*, *buddhi*, *ahaṃkāra*, *citta*,

1 III.95.

karma, kalpanā, saṃsṛti, vāsanā, vidyā, prayatna, smṛti, indriya, prakṛti, māyā and *kriyā* are different only in name, and they create confusion by these varied names; in reality, however, they signify the same concept, namely, the active functioning of *manas* or *citta*. These different names are current only because they lay stress on the different aspects of the same active functioning. They do not mean different entities, but only different moments, stages or aspects. Thus the first moment of self-conscious activity leading in different directions is called *manas*. When, after such oscillating movement, there is the position of either of the alternatives, as "the thus," it is called *buddhi*. When by the false notions of associations of body and soul there is the feeling of a concrete individual as "I," it is called *ahaṃkāra*. When there is reflective thought associated with the memory of the past and the anticipations of the future, it is called *citta*. When the activity is taken in its actual form as motion or action towards any point, it is called *karma*. When, leaving its self-contained state, it desires anything, we have *kalpanā*. When the *citta* turns itself to anything previously seen or unseen, as being previously experienced, we have what is called memory (*smṛti*). When certain impressions are produced in a very subtle, subdued form, dominating all other inclinations, as if certain attractions or repulsions to certain things were really experienced, we have the root inclinations (*vāsanā*). In the realization that there is such a thing as self-knowledge, and that there is also such a thing as the false and illusory world-appearance, we have what is called right knowledge (*vidyā*). When the true knowledge is forgotten and the impressions of the false world-appearance gain ground, we have what are called the impure states (*mala*). The functions of the five kinds of cognition please us and are called the senses (*indriya*). As all world-appearance has its origin and ground in the highest self, it is called the origin (*prakṛti*). As the true state can neither be called existent nor non-existent, and as it gives rise to all kinds of appearance, it is called illusion (*māyā*).[1] Thus it is the same

---

1 III.96.17-31.

appearance which goes by the various names of *jīva, manas*, *citta* and *buddhi.*[1]

One of the peculiarities of this work is that it is not a philosophical treatise of the ordinary type, but its main purpose lies in the attempt to create a firm conviction on the part of its readers, by repeating the same idea in various ways by means of stories and elaborate descriptions often abounding in the richest poetical imagery of undeniably high aesthetic value, hardly inferior to that of the greatest Sanskrit poet, Kālidāsa.

THE WORLD-APPEARANCE

The *Yoga-vāsiṣṭha* is never tired of repeating that this world is like a hare's horn, a forest in the sky, or a lotus in the sky. The state of Brahman is higher than the state of *manas*. It is by becoming *manas* that Brahman transforms itself into thought-activity and thus produces the seeming changeful appearances. But Brahman in itself cannot have anything else (*brahma-tattve 'nyatā nāsti*). But, though there is this change into *manas*, and through it the production of the world-appearance, yet such a change is not real, but illusory; for during all the time when this change makes its appearance and seems to stay, Brahman remains shut up within itself, changeless and unchangeable. All objective appearance is thus nothing but identically the same as the Brahman, and all that appears has simply no existence. The seer never transforms himself into objectivity, but remains simply identical with himself in all appearances of objectivity. But the question arises, how, if the world-appearance is nothing but the illusory creative conception of *manas*, can the order of the world-appearance be explained? The natural answer to such a question in this system is that the seeming correspondence and agreement depend upon the similarity of the imaginary products in certain spheres, and also upon accident. It is by accident that

1 जीव इत्य् इच्यते लोके मन इत्य् अपि कथ्यते
चित्तम् इत्य् उच्यते सैव बुद्धिर् इत्य् उच्यते तथा ॥
Jīva ity ucyate loke mana ity api kathyate
cittam ity ucyate saiva buddhir ity ucyate tathā. —III.96.34.

certain dream series correspond with certain other dream series.[1] But in reality they are all empty dream constructions of one *manas*. It is by the dream desires that physical objects gradually come to be considered as persistent objects existing outside of us. But, though during the continuance of the dreams they appear to be real, they are all the while nothing but mere dream conceptions. The self-alienation by which the pure consciousness constructs the dream conception is such that, though it always remains identical with itself, yet it seems to posit itself as its other, and as diversified by space, time, action and substance (*deśa-kāla-kriyā-dravyaiḥ*).

The difference between the ordinary waking state and the dream state consists in this, that the former is considered by us as associated with permanent convictions (*sthira-pratyaya*), whereas the latter is generally thought to have no permanent basis. Any experience which persists, whether it be dream or not, comes to be regarded as permanent, whereas, if even our waking conceptions come to be regarded as changeful, they lose their validity as representing permanent objects, and our faith in them becomes shaken. If the dream experiences persisted in time and the waking experiences were momentary, then the waking state would be considered as a dream and the dream experiences would be considered as ordinary experiences in the dream state. It is only with the coming of the waking state that there is a break of the dream experiences, and it is then that the latter are contradicted and therefore regarded as false. But so long as the dream experiences lasted in the dream state, we did not consider them to be false; for during that time those dream experiences appeared somehow to be permanent and therefore real. There is thus no difference between dream states and waking states except this, that the latter are relatively persistent,

1 मेलनम् अपि स्वकियपरकियस्वप्नानां दैवात् क्वचित् संवादवत् स्वान्तः कल्पनाल्मकम् एव ॥
Melanam api svakiya-parakiya-svapnānāṃ daivāt kvacit saṃwādavat svān-taḥ-kalpanālmakam eva. —*Yoga-vāsiṣṭha-tātparya-prakāśa,* IV.18.46.

continuous and permanent (*sthira*), while the former are changeful and impermanent (*asthira*).[1]

There is within us a principle of pure consciousness, which is also the vital principle (*jīva-dhātu*), vitality (*vīrya*), and body heat (*tejas*). In the active condition, when the body is associated with manas, action and speech, the vital principle moves through the body, and on account of this all sorts of knowledge arise, and the illusion of world-appearance inherent in it is manifested as coming from outside through the various sense apertures. This being of a steady and fixed character is called the waking state (*jāgrat*). The *suṣupta,* or deep sleep state, is that in which the body is not disturbed by the movement of the *manas,* action or speech. The vital principle remains still in itself, in a potential state without any external manifestation, as the oil remains in the sesamum (*taila-saṃvid yathā tile*).[2] When the vital principle (*jīva-dhātu*) is very much disturbed, we have experiences of the dream state.

Whenever the *manas* strongly identifies itself with any of its concepts, it appears to itself as that concept, just as an iron ball in fire becomes itself like fire. It is the *manas* that is both the perceiver (*puruṣa*) and the perceived universe (*viśva-rūpatā*).[3]

The followers of the Sāṃkhya consider *manas* to be pure consciousness; they have also explained their doctrines in other details, and they think that emancipation cannot be attained by any way other than that which the Sāṃkhya suggests. The followers of the Vedānta also consider that emancipation is attained if one understands that all this world is Brahman and if there is self-control and cessation of desires together with this knowledge, and that this is the only way of salvation. The Vijñānavādins (Idealistic

---

1 जाग्रत्स्वप्नदशाभेदो न स्थिरास्किरते विना समः सदैव सर्वत्र समस्तोऽनुभवोऽनयोः
स्वप्नोऽपि स्वप्नसमये स्थैर्याजाग्रत्त्वम् ऋच्छतिअसैत्यात् जाग्रद् एवास्ते स्वनस् तादृशबोधतः ॥
jāgrat-svapna-daśā-bhedo na sthirāstkirate vinā
samaḥ sadaiva sarvatra samasto 'nubhavo 'nayoḥ
svapno 'pi svapna-samaye sthairyājjāgrattvam ṛcchati
asthairyāt jāgrad evāste svapnas tādṛśa-bodhataḥ. —IV.19.23.

2 IV.19.23.

3 IV.20.4.

Buddhists) think that, provided there is complete self-control and cessation of all sense desires, one may attain emancipation, if he understands that the world-appearance is nothing but his own illusion. Thus each system of thought thinks too much of its own false methods of salvation (*svair eva niyama-bhramaiḥ*), springing from the traditional wrong notions. But the truth underlying all these conceptions is that *manas* is the root of all creations. There is nothing intrinsically pleasurable or painful, sweet or bitter, cold or hot, and such appearances arise only through the habitual creations of the mind. When one believes and thinks with strong faith in any particular manner, he begins to perceive things in that particular manner during that particular time.[1]

NATURE OF AGENCY (KARTṚTVA) AND THE ILLUSION OF WORLD CREATION

Whenever we ascribe agency (*kartṛtva*) to any person in respect of deeds producing pleasure or pain, or deeds requiring strenuous exercise of will-power, as those of the Yoga discipline, we do it wrongly; for agency consists in the grasp of will and resolution, and so it is an internal determination of the mind, of the nature of dominant and instinctive desires and inclinations (*vāsanābhidhānaḥ*).[2] The inner movement of feeling in the person towards the enjoyment of experiences takes place in accordance with these fixed desires or inclinations leading him to specific forms of enjoyment. All enjoyment is thus a natural consequence of our nature and character as active agents. Since all active agency (*kartṛtva*) consists in the inner effort of will, the enjoyment

---

1 न ज्ञेनेह पदार्थेषु रूपम् एकम् उदीर्यते दृढभावनया वेतो यद् यथा भावयत्य् अलम्
तत् तत्पलम् तदाकारं तावत्कालम् प्रपश्यति न तद् अस्ति न यत् सत्यं न तद् अस्ति न यन् मृषा ॥
Na jñeneha padārtheṣu rūpam ekam udīryate
dṛḍha-bhāvanayā ceto yad yathā bhāvayaty alam
tat tat-phalam tad-ākāraṃ tāvat-kālam prapaśyati.
na tad asti na yat satyaṃ na tad asti na yan mṛṣā. —IV.21.56, 57.

2 योह्यन्तरस्थायाः मनोवृत्तेर् निश्चयः उपादेयताप्रत्ययो वासनाभ्त्धानतत्कृत्वशब्देनोच्यते ॥
yohyantara-sthāyāḥ manovṛtter niścayaḥ upād eyatā-pratyayo vāsanābhtdhā-natat-kartṛtva-śabdenocyate. —IV.38.2.

following such an inner exercise of will is nothing but the feeling modifications of the mind following the lead of the active exercise of the will. All action or active agency is thus associated with root inclinations (*vāsanā*), and is thus possible only for those who do not know the truth and have their minds full of the root inclinations. But those who have no *vāsanā* cannot be said to have the nature of active agents or of enjoying anything. Their minds are no doubt always active and they are active all the time; but, as they have no *vāsanā,* they are not attached to fruit, and there is the movement without any attachment. Whatever is done by *manas* is done, and what is not done by it is not done; so it is the *manas* that is the active agent, and not the body; the world has appeared from the mind (*citta* or *manas*), is of the essence of *manas,* and is upheld in *manas*. Everything is but a mental creation and has no other existence.

Ultimately, everything comes from Brahman; for that is the source of all powers, and therefore all powers (*śaktayaḥ*) are seen in Brahman—existence, non-existence, unity, duality and multiplicity all proceed from Brahman. The *citta,* or mind, has evolved out of pure consciousness (*cit*) or Brahman, as has already been mentioned, and it is through the latter that all power of action (*karma*), root desires (*vāsanā*), and all mental modifications appear. But, if everything has proceeded from Brahman, how is it that the world-appearance happens to be so different from its source, the Brahman? When anything comes out of any other thing, it is naturally expected to be similar thereto in substance. If, therefore, the world-appearance has sprung forth from Brahman, it ought to be similar in nature thereto; but Brahman is sorrowless, while the world-appearance is full of sorrow; how is this to be explained? To such a question the answer is, that to a person who has a perfect realization of the nature of the world-appearance, as being a mere conceptual creation from the Brahman and having no existence at all, there is no sorrow in this world-appearance nor any such quality which is different from Brahman. Only in the eyes of a person who has not the complete realization does this difference between the world-appearance and Brahman seem to be so great, and the mere notion of the identity of Brahman and the universe, without its complete realization, may lead to all sorts of mischief. On this account instruction in the identity of the Brahman and the world-appearance should never be given to anyone whose mind has not been properly purified by the essential virtues of self-control and disinclination to worldly pleasures.[1] As in magic (*indrajāla*), non-existent things are produced and existent things are destroyed, a jug becomes a cloth, and a cloth becomes a jug, and all sorts of wonderful sights are shown, though none of these appearances have the slightest essence of their own; so is the entire world-appearance produced out of the imagination of the mind. There is no active agent (*kartṛ*) and no one enjoyer (*bhoktṛ*) of the pleasures and sorrows of the world, and there is no destruction whatsoever.[2]

Though the ultimate state is the indescribable Brahman or *cit,* yet it is from *manas* that all creation and destruction from cycle to cycle take their start. At the beginning of each so-called creation the creative movement of *manas* energy is roused. At the very first the outflow of this *manas* energy in the direction of a conceptual creation means an accumulation of energy in *manas*, called *ghana*, which is a sort of statical aspect of the dynamical energy (*spanda*). At the next stage there is a combination of this statical state of energy with the next outflow of energy, and the result is the stabilized accretion of energy of the second order; this is again followed by another outflow of energy, and that leads to the formation of the stabilized energy of the third order, and so on. The course of thought-creation is thus through the interaction of the actualized energy of thought with the active forms of the energy of thought, which join together, at each successive outflow from the supreme fund of potential energy. Thus it is said that the

---

1 आदौ शम दमप्रायैर् गिमैः शिष्यं विशोधयेत्
पश्चात् सर्वम् इदं ब्रह्म शुद्धस् त्वम् इति बोधयेत्॥
Ādau śama dama-prāyair gimaiḥ śiṣyaṃ viśodhayet
paścāt sarvam idaṃ brahma śuddhas tvam iti bodhayet. —IV.39.23.

2 नात्र कश्चित् कर्ता न भोक्ता न विनाशम्क् एति॥
Nātra kaścit kartā na bhoktā na vināśam eti. —IV.39.41.

first creative movement of *manas* manifests itself as the *ākāśa* creation, and that, as a result of this creative outflow of energy, there is an accretion of energy in *manas*; at this moment there is another outflow (*spanda*) or movement on the part of *manas*, as modified by the accretion of energy of the previous state, and this outflow of *manas* thus modified is the creation of air. The outflow of this second order, again, modifies *manas* by its accretion, and there is a third outflow of energy of the *manas* as modified by the previous accretion, and so on. This process of the modification of energy by the outflow of the *manas* modified at each stage by the accretion of the outflow of energy at each of the preceding states is called *ghana-spanda-krama.*[1] The creation of all the so-called *tan-mātras* (subtle states) of *ākāśa*, *vāyu, tejas, ap* and *kṣiti* takes place in this order, and afterwards that of the *ahaṃkāra* and *buddhi*, and thus of the subtle body (*pury-aṣṭaka*); thereafter the cosmic body of Brahman is formed and developed in accordance with the root desire (*vāsanā*) inherent in *manas*. Thus here we have first the *ākāśa tan-mātra*, then the *vāyu tan-mātra* from the *ākāśa tan-mātra* plus the outflow of energy, then, from the *ākāśa tan-mātra* plus the *vāyu tan-mātra* plus the outflow of energy of the third order, *tejas tan-mātra*, and so on. Then, after the *tan-mātra,* the *ahaṃkāra* and the *buddhi,* we have the subtle body of eight constituents (five *tan-mātras, ahaṃkāra, buddhi* and the root *manas*), called the *pury-aṣṭaka* of Brahmā. From this develops the body of Brahmā, and from the creative imagination of Brahmā we have the grosser materials and all the rest of the world-appearance. But all this is pure mental creation, and hence unreal, and so also are all the scriptures, gods and goddesses and all else that passes as real.

THE STAGE OF THE SAINT (JĪVAN-MUKTA)

Emancipation (*mukti*) in this system can be attained in the lifetime of a person or after his death; in the former case it is called *sa-deha-muktatā,* or *jīvan-muktatā.* The *jīvan-mukta* state is that in which

1 IV.44.13-30.

the saint has ceased to have any desires (*apagatai-ṣaṇaḥ*), as if he were in a state of deep sleep (*suṣuptavat*). He is self-contained and thinks as if nothing existed. He has always an inward eye, even though he may be perceiving all things with his external eye and using his limbs in all directions. He does not wait for the future, nor remain in the present, nor remember the past. Though sleeping, he is awake and, though awake, he is asleep. He may be doing all kinds of actions externally, though he remains altogether unaffected by them internally. He internally renounces all actions, and does not desire anything for himself. He is full of bliss and happiness, and therefore appears to ordinary eyes to be an ordinary happy man; but in reality, though he may be doing all kinds of things, he has not the delusion of being himself an active agent (*tyakta-kartṛtva-vibhramaḥ*). He has no antipathy, grief, emotions, or outbursts of pleasure. He is quite neutral to all who do him ill or well; he shows sympathetic interest in each person in his own way; he plays with a child, is serious with an old man, an enjoyable companion to a young man, sympathetic with the sorrows of a suffering man. He is wise and pleasant and loving to all with whom he comes in contact. He is not interested in his own virtuous deeds, enjoyments, sins, in bondage or emancipation. He has a true philosophic knowledge of the essence and nature of all phenomena, and, being firm in his convictions, he remains neutral to all kinds of happenings, good, bad, or indifferent. But from the descriptions it appears that this indifference on the part of a saint does not make him an exclusive and unnatural man; for, though unaffected in every way within himself, he can take part in the enjoyment of others, he can play like a child and can sympathize with the sorrows of sufferers.[1]

Jīvan-mukti, or emancipation while living, is considered by Śaṅkara also as a possible state, though he does not seem to have used the term in his works. Thus, on the basis of *Chāndogya*, VI.14.2, he says that knowledge destroys only those actions which have not already begun to yield their fruits; those actions which have already begun to yield fruits cannot be destroyed by true

1 V.77.

knowledge, and so it is not possible for anyone to escape from their effects, good or bad; and it has to be admitted that even after the dawning of true knowledge the body remains until the effects of the actions which have already begun to yield fruits are exhausted by enjoyment or suffering. In explaining such a condition Śaṅkara gives two analogies: (1) as a potter's wheel goes on revolving when the vessel that it was forming is completed, so the body, which was necessary till the attainment of true knowledge, may continue to exist for some time even after the rise of knowledge; (2) as, when a man through some eye-disease sees two moons instead of one, he continues to do so even when he is convinced that there are not two moons but one, so, even when the saint is firmly convinced of the unreality of the world-appearance, he may still continue to have the illusion of world-appearance, though internally he may remain unaffected by it.[1] Of the Upaniṣads only the later *Muktika Upaniṣad*, which seems to have drawn its inspiration from the *Yoga-vāsiṣṭha*, mentions the word *jīvan-mukta*, meaning those saints who live till their fruit-yielding actions (*prārabdha-karma*) are exhausted.[2] But, though the word is not mentioned, the idea seems to be pretty old.

The conception of *sthita-prajña* in the *Śrīmad-bhagavad-gītā* reminds us of the state of a *jīvan-mukta* saint. A *sthita-prajña* (man of steady wisdom) has no desires, but is contented in himself, has no attachment, fear or anger, is not perturbed by sorrow nor longs for pleasure, and is absolutely devoid of all likes and dislikes. Like a tortoise within its shell, he draws himself away from the sense-objects.[3] This conception of the *Śrīmad-bhagavad-gītā* is referred to in the *Yoga-vāsiṣṭha*, which gives a summary of it in its own way.[4] But it seems as if the conception of the saint in the *Yoga-vāsiṣṭha* has this advantage over the other, that here the saint, though absolutely unaffected by all pleasures and sufferings, by virtue and vice, is yet not absolutely cut off from us; for, though

1 Śaṅkara's *Sarīraka-bhāṣya* or the *Brahma-sūtra,* IV.1.15, 19.

2 *Muktika Upaniṣad,* I.42, also II.33, 35, 76.

3 *Śrīmad-bhagavad-gītā,* II.55-58.

4 *Yoga-vāsiṣṭha,* VI.52-58.

he has no interest in his own good, he can show enjoyment in the enjoyment of others and sympathy with the sufferings of others; he can be as gay as a child when with children, and as serious as any philosopher when with philosophers or old men. The *Śrīmad-bhagavad-gītā*, though it does not deny such qualities to a saint, yet does not mention them either, and seems to lay stress on the aspect of the passivity and neutral character of the saint; whereas the *Yoga-vāsiṣṭha*, as we have already said, lays equal stress on both these special features of a saint. He is absolutely unattached to anything, but is not cut off from society and can seemingly take part in everything without losing his mental balance in any way. The *Gītā*, of course, always recommends even the unattached saint to join in all kinds of good actions; but what one misses there is the taking of a full and proper interest in life along with all others, though the saint is internally absolutely unaffected by all that he may do.

The saint in the *Yoga-vāsiṣṭha* not only performs his own actions in an unattached manner, but to all appearance mixes with the sorrows and joys of others.

The question whether a saint is above the tyranny of the effects of his own deeds was also raised in Buddhist quarters. Thus we find in the *Kathā-vatthu* that a discussion is raised as to whether a saint can be killed before his proper time of death, and it is said that no one can attain *Nirvāṇa* without enjoying the fruits of accumulated intentional deeds.[1] A story is told in the *Dhamma-pada* commentary (the date of which, according to E. W. Burlingame, is about AD 450), how the great saint Moggallāna was torn in pieces by thieves, and his bones were pounded until they were as small as grains of rice; such a miserable death of such a great saint naturally raised doubts among his disciples, and these were explained by Buddha, who said that this was due to the crime of parricide, which Moggallāna had committed in some previous birth; even though he had attained sainthood (*arhattva*) in that life, he could not escape suffering the effect of his misdeeds, which were on the point of

1 *Kathā-vatthu,* XVII.2.

bearing fruit.[1] This would naturally imply the view that sainthood does not necessarily mean destruction of the body, but that even after the attainment of sainthood the body may continue to exist for the suffering of the effects of such actions as are on the point of bearing fruit.

The different Indian systems are, however, not all agreed regarding the possibility of the *jīvan-mukta* state. Thus, according to the Nyāya, *apavarga*, or emancipation, occurs only when the soul is absolutely dissociated from all the nine kinds of qualities (will, antipathy, pleasure, pain, knowledge, effort, virtue, vice and rooted instincts). Unless such a dissociation actually occurs, there cannot be emancipation; and it is easy to see that this cannot happen except after death, and so emancipation during the period while the body remains is not possible.[2] The point is noticed by Vātsyāyana in a discussion on *Nyāya-sūtra,* IV.2.42-45, where he raises the question of the possibility of knowledge of external objects through the senses and denies it by declaring that in emancipation (*apavarga*) the soul is dissociated from the body and all the senses, and hence there is no possibility of knowledge; and that with the extinction of all knowledge there is also ultimate and absolute destruction of pain.[3] The Vaiśeṣika holds the same view on the subject. Thus Śrīharṣa says that, when through right knowledge (*paramārtha-darśana*) all merit ceases, then the soul, being devoid of the seeds of merit and demerit, which produce the body and

---

1 *Buddhist Legends* by E. W. Burlingame, vol. II. p. 304. The same legend is repeated in the introduction to *Jātaka* 522.

2 तद् एवम् नवानाम् आत्मगुणानां निर्मूलोच्छेदोऽपवर्गः
तद् एवेदम् उक्तं भवति तदत्यन्तवियोगोऽपवर्गः ॥
tad evam navānām ātma-guṇānāṃ nirmūlocchedo 'pavargaḥ
tad evedam uktaṃ bhavati tad-atyanta-viyogo 'pavargaḥ.—*Nyāya-mañjarī,* p. 508.

3 यस्मात् सर्वदुःखबीजं सर्वदुःखायतनं चापवर्गे
विछिद्यते तस्मात् सर्वेण दुःखेन विमुक्तिः
अपवर्गो नौ निर्बीजं निरायतनंच दुःखम् उत्पद्यते ॥
Yasmāt sarva-duḥkha-bījaṃ sarva-duḥkhāyatanaṃ cāpavarge
vichidyate tasmāt sarveṇa duḥkhena vimuktiḥ
apavargo no nirbījaṃ nirāyatanaṃ ca duḥkham utpadyate.
—Vātsyāyana on *Nyāya-sūtra*, IV.2.43.

the senses, etc., and the present body having been destroyed by the exhaustive enjoyment of the fruits of merit and demerit, and there being no further production of any new body by reason of the destruction of all the seeds of *karma*, there is absolute cessation of the production of body, like the extinction of fire by the burning up of all the fuel; and such an eternal nonproduction of body is called *mokṣa* (emancipation).[1]

Prabhākara seems to hold a similar view. Thus Śālikanātha, in explaining the Prabhākara view in his *Prakaraṇa-pañcikā,* says that emancipation means the absolute and ultimate destruction of the body, due to the total exhaustion of merit and demerit.[2] The difficulty is raised that it is not possible to exhaust by enjoyment or suffering the fruits of all the *karmas* accumulated since beginningless time; he who, being averse to worldly sorrows and all pleasures which are mixed with traces of sorrow, works for emancipation, desists from committing the actions prohibited by Vedic injunctions, which produce sins, exhausts by enjoyment and suffering the good and bad fruits of previous actions, attains true knowledge, and is equipped with the moral qualities of passionless tranquillity, self-restraint and absolute sex-control, exhausts in the end all the potencies of his *karmas* (*niḥśeṣa-karmāśaya*) and attains emancipation.[3] This view, however, no doubt has reference to a very advanced state in this life, when no further *karma* is accumulating; but it does not call this state *mokṣa* during life; for *mokṣa,* according to this view, is absolute and ultimate non-production of body.

---

1 यथा दग्धेन्धनस्यानलस्योपशमः पुनर् अनुत्पाद एवं पुनः शरीरानुत्पादो मोक्षः ॥
Yathā dagdhendhanasyānalasyopaśamaḥ punar anutpāda evaṃ punaḥ śarīrānutpādo mokṣaḥ. —*Nyāya-kandalī,* p. 283.
Praśastapāda also writes:
तदा श्रोधात् निर्बीजस्यात्मनः शरिरादिनिवृत्तिः पुनः इअफ़ीराद्यनुत्पत्तौ दग्धेनधनानलवद् उपशमो मोक्ष इति ॥
tadā nirodhāt nirbījasyātmanaḥ śarirādi-nivṛttiḥ punaḥ iafīrādy-anutpattau dagdhendhanānalavad upaśamo mokṣa iti. —*Praśastapāda-bhāṣyh,* p. 282.

2 आत्यन्तिकस् तु देहोच्छेदो निःशेषधर्माधर्मपरिक्षयनिबन्धनो मोक्ष इति ॥
Ātyantikas tu dehocchedo niḥśeṣa-dharmādharma-parikṣaya-nibandhano mokṣa iti. —*Prakaraṇa-pañcikā,* p. 156.

3 *Ibid.* p. 157.

The *Sāṃkhya-kārikā,* however, holds that, when true knowledge is attained (*samyagjñānādhigama*), and when in consequence none of the *karmas* of undetermined fruition (*aniyata-vipāka*), accumulated through beginningless time, are able to ripen for bearing fruit, the body may still continue to remain simply by the inertia, as it were, of the old *avidyā;* just as even after the potter has ceased to operate the potter's wheel may continue to move as a result of the momentum which it has acquired (*cakra-bhramivad dhṛta-śarīraḥ*).[1]

The word *jīvan-mukta* is not used either in the *Kārikā* or in the *Tattva-kaumudī* or in the *Tattva-vibhākara.* The *Sāṃkhya-sūtra,* however, uses the term and justifies it on the same grounds as does Vācaspati.[2] The *Sāṃkhya-sūtra,* more particularly the *Pravacana-bhāṣya,* raises the threefold conception of *manda-viveka* (feeble discrimination), *madhya-viveka* (middle discrimination), and *viveka-niṣpatti* (finished discrimination).[3] The stage of *manda-viveka* is that in which the enquirer has not attained the desired discrimination of the difference between *prakṛti and puruṣa,* but is endeavouring to attain it; the *madhya-viveka* stage is the state of the *jīvan-mukta.* But this is an *asamprajñāta* state, i.e. a state in which there is still subject-object knowledge and a full conscious discrimination. The last stage, *viveka-niṣpatti,* is an *asamprajñāta* state in which there is no subject-object knowledge, and therefore there cannot in this stage be any reflection of pleasure or sorrow (due to the fructifying *karma—prārabdha-karma*) on the *puruṣa.*

The Yoga also agrees with the general conclusion of the Sāṃkhya on the subject. A man who nears the state of emancipation ceases to have doubts about the nature of the self, and begins to re-

1 *Sāṃkhya-kārikā,* 67,68. The *Tattva-kaumudī* here essays to base its remarks on *Chāndogya,* VI.14.2, as Śaṅkara did in his *bhāṣya* on the *Brahma-sūtra.* The *Tattva-vibhākara* of Vaṃśīdhara Miśra, in commenting on Vācaspati's *Tattva-kaumudī,* quotes *Muṇḍaka Upaniṣad,* II.2.8, and also *Śrīmad-bhagavad-gītā,* IV.37, for its support. Compare *Yoga-vāsiṣṭha: ghanā na vāsanā yasya punar-janana-varjitā.*

2 *Sāṃkhya-sūtra,* III.77-83.

3 *Ibid.* III.77, 78.

live the nature of his own self and to discriminate himself as being entirely different from his psychosis (*sattva*)-, but, as a result of the persistence of some decayed roots of old impressions and instincts, there may, in the intervals of the flow of true discriminative knowledge, emerge other ordinary cognitive states, such as "I am," "mine," "I know," "I do not know"; yet, inasmuch as the roots of the old impressions have already been burnt, these occasional ordinary cognitive states cannot produce further new impressions. The general impressions of cognition (*jñāna-saṃskāra*), however, remain until the final destruction of *citta*. The point here is that, the roots in the world of subconscious impressions being destroyed, and the occasional appearance of ordinary cognitive states being but remnants produced by some of the old impressions, the roots of which have already been burnt, these occasional ordinary cognitive states are like passing shadows which have no basis anywhere; they cannot, therefore, produce any further impressions and thus cannot be a cause of bondage to the saint. With the advance of this state the sage ceases to have inclinations even towards his processes of concentration, and there is only discriminative knowledge; this state of *samādhi* is called *dharma-megha*. At this stage all the roots of ignorance and other afflictions become absolutely destroyed, and in such a state the sage, though living (*jīvann eva*), becomes emancipated (*vimukta*). The next stage is, of course, the state of absolute emancipation (*kaivalya*), when the *citta* returns back to *prakṛti*, never to find the *puruṣa* again.[1]

Among later writers Vidyāraṇya wrote on this subject a treatise which he called *Jīvan-mukti-viveka*.[2] It is divided into five chapters. In the first he deals with the authorities who support *jīvan-mukti*; in the second, with the nature of the destruction of instinctive root inclinations (*vāsanā*); in the third, with the

1 *Yoga-sūtra* and *Vyāsa-bhāṣya*, IV.29-32.

2 This Vidyāraṇya seems to be later than the Vidyāraṇya who wrote the *Pañcadaśī*, as quotations from the chapter *Brahmānanda* of the *Pañcadaśī* are found in it (chap. II, pp. 195, 196, Chowkhambā edition). So my identification of the Vidyāraṇya of the *Pañcadaśī* with the writer of *Jīvan-mukti-viveka* in the first volume (p. 419) of the present work seems to be erroneous.

destruction of *manas*(*mano-nāśa*); in the fourth, with the final object for which *jīvan-mukti* is sought; and in the fifth, with the nature and characteristics of those saints who have attained *jīvan-mukti* by wisdom and right knowledge (*vidvat-saṃnyāsa*), and have virtually renounced the world, though living. The work is more a textual compilation from various sources than an acute philosophical work examining the subject on its own merits. The writer seems to have derived his main inspiration from the *Yoga-vāsiṣṭha,* though he refers to relevant passages in several other works, such as *Bṛhadāraṇyaka Upaniṣad, Maitreyī-brāhmaṇa, Kahola-brāhmaṇa, Śārīra-brāhmaṇa, Jābāla-brāhmaṇa, Kaṭha-vallī, Gītā, Bhāgavata, Bṛhaspati-smṛti, Sūta-saṃhitā, Gauḍa-pāda-kārikā, Śaṅkara-bhāṣya, Brahma-sūtra, Pañca-pādikā, Viṣṇu-purāṇa, Taittirīya-brāhmaṇa, Yoga-sūtra, Naiṣkarmya-siddhi, Kauṣītaki, Pañcadaśī, Antaryāmi-brāhmaṇa, Vyāsa-bhāṣya, Brahma-upaniṣad,* the works of Yama, Parāśara, Bodhāyana, Medhātithi, Viśvarūpa Acārya, etc.

Disinclination to passions and desires (*virakti*) is, according to him, of two kinds, intense (*tīvra*) and very intense (*tīvratara*). Intense *virakti* is that in which the person does not desire anything in this life, whereas very intense *virakti* is that in which the person ceases to have any desires for all future lives.[1] Vidyāraṇya takes great pains to prove, by reference to various scriptural texts, that there are these two distinct classes of renunciation (*sannyāsin*), though one might develop into the other.[2] As regards the nature

1 If the ascetic has ordinary desires he is called *haṃsa*; if he desires emancipation, he is called *parama-haṃsa.* The course of their conduct is described in the *Parāśara-smṛti, Jīvan-mukti-viveka,* I.11. When a man renounces the world for the attainment of right knowledge, it is called *vividiṣā-saṃnyāsa* (renunciation for thirst of knowledge), as distinguished from *vidvat-saṃnyāsa* (renunciation of the wise) in the case of those who have already attained right knowledge. The latter kind of *samnyāsa* is with reference to those who are *jīvan-mukta.*

2 It is pointed out by Vidyāranya that the *Āruṇikopaniṣad* describes the conduct and character of *vividiṣā-saṃnyāsa,* in which one is asked to have a staff, one loin-cloth and to repeat the Āraṇyakas and the Upanishads only, and the *Parama-haṃsopaniṣat* describes the conduct and character of *vidvat-saṃnyāsa,* in which no such repetition of the Upaniṣads is held necessary, since such a person

of *jīvan-mukti,* Vidyāraṇya follows the view of the *Yoga-vāsiṣṭha*, though he supports it by other scriptural quotations. On the subject of bodiless emancipation (*videha-mukti*) also he refers to passages from the *Yoga-vāsiṣṭha. Jīvan-mukti* is the direct result of the cessation of all instinctive root desires (*vāsanā-kṣaya*), the dawning of right knowledge (*tattva-jñāna*), and the destruction of *manas* (*mano-nāśa*). Vidyāraṇya, however, holds that on account of steady right knowledge even the seeming appearance of passions and attachment cannot do any harm to a *jīvan-mukta,* just as the bite of a snake whose fangs have been drawn cannot do him any harm. Thus he gives the example of Yājñavalkya, who killed Śākalya by cursing and yet did not suffer on that account, because he was already a *jīvan-mukta,* firm in his knowledge of the unreality of the world. So his anger was not real anger, rooted in instinctive passions, but a mere appearance (*ābhāsa*) of it.[1]

ENERGY OF FREE-WILL (PAURUṢA)

One of the special features of the *Yoga-vāsiṣṭha* is the special emphasis that it lays upon free-will and its immense possibilities, and its power of overruling the limitations and bondage of past *karmas. Pauruṣa* is defined in the *Yoga-vāsiṣṭha* as mental and physical exertions made in properly advised ways (*sādhūpadiṣṭa-mārgeṇa*), since only such actions can succeed.[2] If a person desires anything and works accordingly in the proper way, he is certain to attain it, if he does not turn back in midway.[3] *Pauruṣa* is of two

---

is fixed and steady in his Brahma knowledge. This makes the difference between the final stages of the two kinds of renunciation (*Jīvan-mukti-viveka,* I.20-24).

1 *Jīvan-mukti-viveka,* pp. 183-186.

2 साधूपदिष्टमार्गेण यन् मनोऽङ्गविचेष्टितम्
तत् पौरुषं तत् सफलम् अन्य् अद् उन्मत्तचेष्टितम्॥
sādhūpadiṣṭa-mārgeṇa yan mano-'ṅga-viceṣṭitam
tat pauruṣaṃ tat saphalam anyad unmatta-ceṣṭitam.—Yoga-vāsiṣṭha, II.4.11.

3 यो यम् अर्थं प्रार्थय्ते तदर्थं चेहते क्रमात्
अवश्यंस तर्न् आप्नोति न चेद् अर्धान् निवर्तते
yo yam arthaṃ prārthayate tad-arthaṃ cehate kramāt
avaśyaṃ sa tarn āpnoti na ced ardhān nivartate. —*Ibid.* II.4.12.

kinds, of the past life (*prāktana*) and of this life (*aihika*), and the past *pauruṣa* can be overcome by the present *pauruṣa.*[1] The *karma* of past life and the *karma* of this life are thus always in conflict with each other, and one or the other gains ground according to their respective strength. Not only so, but the endeavours of any individual may be in conflict with the opposing endeavours of other persons, and of these two also that which is stronger wins.[2] By strong and firm resolution and effort of will the endeavours of this life can conquer the effect of past deeds. The idea that one is being led in a particular way by the influence of past *karmas* has to be shaken off from the mind; for the efforts of the past life are certainly not stronger than the visible efforts of the moment.

All efforts have indeed to be made in accordance with the direction of the scriptures (*śāstra*). There is, of course, always a limit beyond which human endeavours are not possible, and therefore it is necessary that proper economy of endeavours should be observed by following the directions of the scriptures, by cultivating the company of good friends, and by adhering to right conduct, since mere random endeavours or endeavours on a wrong line cannot be expected to produce good results.[3] If one exerts his will and directs his efforts in the proper way, he is bound to be successful. There is nothing like destiny (*daiva*), standing as a separate force: it has a continuity with the power of other actions performed in this life, so that it is possible by superior exertions to destroy the power of the actions of previous lives, which would have led to many evil results. Whenever a great effort is made or a great energy is exerted, there is victory. The whole question, whether the *daiva* of the past life or the *pauruṣa* of this life will win, depends upon the relative strength of the two, and any part of the *daiva* which becomes weaker than the efforts of the present life

---

1 *Yoga-vāsiṣṭha,* II.4.17.

2 *Ibid.* II.5.5, 7.

3 स च सच्छास्त्रसत्सङ्गसदाचारैर्निजं फलं
दददातीति स्वभावोऽयम् अन्यथा नार्थसिद्धये ॥
sa ca sac-chāstra-sat-saṅga-sad-ācārair nijaṃ phalaṃ
dadātīti svabhāvo'yam anyathā nārtha-siddhaye. —*Ibid.* II.5.25.

in a contrary direction is naturally annulled. It is only he who thinks that destiny must lead him on, and consequently does not strive properly to overcome the evil destiny, that becomes like an animal at the mercy of destiny or God, which may take him to heaven or to hell. The object of all endeavours and efforts in this life is to destroy the power of the so-called destiny, or *daiva*, and to exert oneself to his utmost to attain the supreme end of life.

The *Yoga-vāsiṣṭha* not only holds that *pauruṣa* can conquer and annul *daiva*, but it even goes to the extreme of denying *daiva* and calling it a mere fiction, that, properly speaking, does not exist at all. Thus it is said that endeavours and efforts manifest themselves as the movement of thought (*saṃvit-spanda*), the movement of *manas* (*manaḥ-spanda*), and the movement of the senses (*aindriya*). Thought movement is followed by movement of the psychosis or *cetas;* the body moves accordingly, and there is also a corresponding enjoyment or suffering. If this view is true, then *daiva* is never seen anywhere. Properly speaking, there is no *daiva*, and wherever any achievement is possible, it is always by continual strenuous effort of will, standing on its own account, or exercised in accordance with the *śāstra* or with the directions of a teacher.[1] It is for all of us to exert ourselves for good and to withdraw our minds from evil. By all the *pramāṇas* at our disposal it is found that nothing but the firm exercise of will and effort achieves its end, and that nothing is effected by pure *daiva*; it is only by the effort of eating that there is the satisfaction of hunger, it is only by the effort of the vocal organs that speech is effected, and it is only by the effort of the legs and corresponding muscles that one can walk. So everything is effected by personal efforts, when directed with the aid of the *śāstra* and proper advisers or teachers. What passes as *daiva* is a mere fiction; no one has ever experienced it, and it cannot be used by any of the senses; and the nature of efforts being essentially vibratory

1 शास्त्रतो गुरुतश् चैव स्वतश् चेति त्रिसिद्धयः
सर्वत्र पुरुषार्थस्य न दैवस्य कदाचन॥
Śāstrato gurutaś caiva svataś ceti tri-siddhayaḥ
sarvatra puruṣār thasya na daivasya kadācana. —*Yoga-vāsiṣṭha,* II.7.11.

(*spanda*), one can never expect such movement from the formless, insensible, so-called *daiva*, which is only imagined and can never be proved. Visible efforts are all tangible and open to immediate perception; and, even if it is admitted that *daiva* exists, how can this supposed formless (*amūrta*) entity come in contact with it? It is only fools who conceive the existence of *daiva*, and depend on it, and are ruined, whereas those who are heroes, who are learned and wise, always attain their highest by their free-will and endeavour.[1]

Rāma points out to Vaśiṣṭha in II.9 that *daiva* is fairly well accepted amongst all people, and asks how, if it did not exist, did it come to be accepted, and what does it mean after all? In answer to this Vaśiṣṭha says that, when any endeavour (*pauruṣa*) comes to fruition or is baffled, and a good or a bad result is gained, people speak of it as being *daiva*. There is no *daiva*, it is mere vacuity, and it can neither help nor obstruct anyone in any way. At the time of taking any step people have a particular idea, a particular resolution; there may be success or failure as the result of operation in a particular way, and the whole thing is referred to by ordinary people as being due to *daiva*, which is a mere name, a mere consolatory word. The instinctive root inclinations (*vāsanā*) of a prior state become transformed into *karma*. A man works in accordance with his *vāsanā* and by *vāsanā* gets what he wants. *Vāsanā* and *karma* are, therefore, more or less like the potential and actual states of the same entity. *Daiva* is but another name for the *karmas* performed with strong desire for fruit, *karma* thus being the same as *vāsanā*, and *vāsanā* being the same as *manas*, and *manas* being the same as the agent or the person (*puruṣa*); so *daiva* does not exist as an entity separate from the *puruṣa*, and they are all merely synonyms for the same indescribable entity (*durniścaya*). Whatever the *manas* strives to do is done by itself, which is the same as being done by *daiva*. There are always in *manas* two distinct groups of *vāsanās*,

1 मूढैः प्रकल्पितं दैवं तपरास् ते क्षयं गताः
प्राज्ञास् तु पौरुषार्थेन पदम् उत्तमतां गताः ॥
mūḍhaiḥ prakalpitaṃ daivaṃ tat-parās te kṣayaṃ gatāḥ
prājñās tu pauruṣārthena padam uttamatāṃ gatāḥ. —*Yoga-vāsiṣṭha,* II.8.16.

operating towards the good and towards the evil, and it is our clear duty to rouse the former against the latter, so that the latter may be overcome and dominated by the former. But, since man is by essence a free source of active energy, it is meaningless to say that he could be determined by anything but himself; if it is held that any other entity could determine him, the question arises, what other thing would determine that entity, and what else that entity, and there would thus be an endless vicious regression.[1] Man is thus a free source of activity, and that which appears to be limiting his activity is but one side of him, which he can overcome by rousing up his virtuous side. This view of *puruṣa-kāra* and *karma* seems to be rather unique in Indian literature.

PRĀṆA AND ITS CONTROL

The mind (*citta*), which naturally transforms itself into its states (*vṛtti*), does so for two reasons, which are said to be like its two seeds. One of these is the vibration (*parispanda*) of *prāṇa,* and the other, strong and deep-rooted desires and inclinations which construct (*dṛḍha-bhāvanā*).[2] When the *prāṇa* vibrates and is on the point of passing through the nerves (*nāḍī-saṃsparśanodyata*), then there appears the mind full of its thought processes (*saṃvedanamaya*). But when the *prāṇa* lies dormant in the hollow of the veins (*śirā-saraṇi-kotare*), then there is no manifestation of mind, and its processes and the cognitive functions do not operate.[3] It is the vibration of the *prāṇa* (*prāṇa-spanda*) that manifests itself through the *citta* and causes the world-appearance out of nothing. The cessation of the vibration of *prāṇa* means cessation of all cognitive functions. As a result of the vibration of *prāṇa,*

1 अन्यस् त्वां चेतयति चेत् तं चेतयति कोऽपरः
क इमम् च्तयेत् तस्माद् अनवस्था न वास्तवी ॥
Anyas tvāṃ cetayati cet taṃ cetayati ko 'parah
ka imam cctayet tasmād anavasthā na vāstavī. —*Yoga-vāsiṣṭha*, II.9.20.

2 *Ibid.* V.81.14.

3 I have translated *śirā* as veins, though I am not properly authorized to do it. For the difference between veins and arteries does not seem to have been known.

the cognitive function is set in motion like a top (*vīṭā*). As a top spins round in the yard when struck, so, roused by the vibration of *prāṇa,* knowledge is manifested; and in order to stop the course of knowledge, it is necessary that the cause of knowledge should be first attacked. When the *citta* remains awake to the inner sense, while shut to all extraneous cognitive activities, we have the highest state. For the cessation of *citta* the yogins control *prāṇa* through *prāṇāyāma* (breath-regulation) and meditation (*dhyāna*), in accordance with proper instructions.[1]

Again, there is a very intimate relation between *vāsanā* and *prāṇa-spanda,* such that *vāsanā* is created and stimulated into activity, *prāṇa-spanda,* and *prāṇa-spanda* is set in motion through *vāsanā.* When by strong ideation and without any proper deliberation of the past and the present, things are conceived to be one's own—the body, the senses, the ego and the like—we have what is called *vāsanā.* Those who have not the proper wisdom always believe in the representations of the ideations of *vāsanā* without any hesitation and consider them to be true; and, since both the *vāsanā* and the *prāṇa-spanda* are the ground and cause of the manifestations of *citta,* the cessation of one promptly leads to the cessation of the other. The two are connected with each other in the relation of seed and shoot (*bījāṅkuravat*); from *prāṇa-spanda* there is *vāsanā,* and from *vāsanā* there is *prāṇa-spanda.* The object of knowledge is inherent in the knowledge itself, and so with the cessation of knowledge the object of knowledge also ceases.[2]

As a description of *prāṇa* we find in the *Yoga-vāsiṣṭha* that it is said to be vibratory activity (*spanda-śakti*) situated in the upper part of the body, while *apāna* is the vibratory activity in the lower part of the body. There is a natural *prāṇāyāma* going on in the body in waking states as well as in sleep. The mental outgoing tendency of the *prāṇas* from the cavity of the heart is called *recaka,*

1 *Yoga-vāsiṣṭha,* V.91. 20-27.

2 समूलं नश्यतः क्षिप्रं मूलच्छेदाद् इव द्रुमः संविदं विद्धि संवेद्यं बीजं धीरतया विना न संभवति संवेद्यं तैलहीनस् तिलो यथा न बहिर् नान्तरे किंचित् संवेद्यं विद्यते पृथक् ॥

and the drawing in of the *prāṇas* (*dvādaśāṅguli*) by the *apāna* activity is called *pūraka.* The interval between the cessation of one effort of *apāna* and the rise of the effort of *prāṇa* is the stage of *kumbhaka.* Bhuśuṇḍa, the venerable old crow who was enjoying an exceptionally long life, is supposed to instruct Vaśiṣṭha in VI.24 on the subject of *prāṇa.* He compares the body to a house with the ego (*ahaṃkāra*) as the householder. It is supposed to be supported by pillars of three kinds,[1] provided with nine doors (seven apertures in the head and two below), tightly fitted with the tendons (*snāyu*) as fastening materials and cemented with blood, flesh and fat. On the two sides of it there are the two *nāḍīs, iḍā* and *piṅgalā,* lying passive and unmanifested (*nimīlite*). There is also a machine (*yantra*) of bone and flesh (*asthi-māṃsa-maya*) in the shape of three double lotuses (*padma-yugma-traya*) having pipes attached to them running both upwards and downwards and with their petals closing upon one another (*anyonya-milat-komala-saddala*). When it is slowly filled with air, the petals move, and by the movement of the petals the air increases. Thus increased, the air, passing upwards and downwards through different places, is differently named as *prāṇa, apāna, samāna*, etc. It is in the threefold machinery of the lotus of the heart (*hṛt-padma-yantra-tritaye*) that all the *prāṇa* forces operate and spread forth upwards and downwards like the rays from the moon's disc. They go out, return, repulse and draw and circulate. Located in the heart, the air is called *prāṇa*: it is through its power that there is the movement of the eyes, the operation of the tactual sense, breathing through the nose, digesting of food and the power

---

samūlaṃ naśyataḥ kṣipraṃ mūla-cchedād iva drumaḥ.
saṃvidaṃ viddhi saṃvedyaṃ bījaṃ dhīratayā vinā
na saṃbhavati saṃvedyaṃ taila-hīnas tilo yathā
na bahir nāntare kiṃcit saṃvedyaṃ vidyate pṛthak.—Yoga-vāsiṣṭha, V.91.66 and 67.

1 *tri-prakāra-mahā-sthūṇam,* VI.24.14. The commentator explains the three kinds of pillars as referring to the three primal entities of Indian medicine—*vāyu* (air), *pitta* (bile) and *kapha* (phlegm)—*vāta-pitta-kapha-lakṣaṇa-tri-prakārāmahān-tah sthūṇā viṣṭambha-kāṣṭhāni yasya.* I am myself inclined to take the three kinds of pillars as referring to the bony structure of three parts of the body—the skull, the trunk, and the legs.

of speech.[1] The *prāṇa* current of air stands for exhalation (*recaka*) and the *apāna* for inhalation (*pūraka*), and the moment of respite between the two operations is called *kumbhaka*; consequently, if the *prāṇa* and *apāna* can be made to cease there is an unbroken continuity of *kumbhaka.* But all the functions of the *prāṇa,* as well as the upholding of the body, are ultimately due to the movement of *citta.*[2] Though in its movement in the body the *prāṇa* is associated with air currents, still it is in reality nothing but the vibratory activity proceeding out of the thought-activity, and these two act and react upon each other, so that, if the vibratory activity of the body be made to cease, the thought-activity will automatically cease, and vice-versa. Thus through *spanda-nirodha* we have *prāṇa-nirodha* and through *prāṇa-nirodha* we have *spanda-nirodha.* In the *Yoga-vāsiṣṭha*, III.13.31, *vāyu* is said to be nothing but a vibratory entity (*spandate yat sa tad vāyuḥ*).

In V.78 it is said that *citta* and movement are in reality one and the same, and are therefore altogether inseparable, like the snow and its whiteness, and consequently with the destruction of one the other is also destroyed. There are two ways of destroying the *citta,* one by Yoga, consisting of the cessation of mental states, and the other by right knowledge. As water enters through the crevices of the earth, so air (*vāta*) moves in the body through the *nāḍīs* and is called *prāṇa.* It is this *prāṇa* air which, on account of its diverse functions and works, is differently named as *apāna,* etc. But it is identical with *citta.* From the movement of *prāṇa* there is the movement of *citta*, and from that there is knowledge (*samvid*). As regards the control of the movement of *prāṇa*, the *Yoga-vāsiṣṭha* advises several alternatives. Thus it holds that through

---

1 *Yoga-vāsiṣṭha,* VI.24. It is curious to note in this connection that in the whole literature of the Āyur-veda there is probably no passage where there is such a clear description of the respiratory process. *Pupphusa*, or lungs, are mentioned only by name in *Suśruta-saṃhitā,* but none of their functions and modes of operation are at all mentioned. It is probable that the discovery of the respiratory functions of the lungs was made by a school of thought different from that of the medical school.

2 *Ibid.* VI.25.61-74.

concentrating one's mind on one subject, or through fixed habits of long inhalation associated with meditation, or through exhaustive exhalation, or the practice of not taking breath and maintaining *kumbhaka*, or through stopping the inner respiratory passage by attaching the tip of the tongue to the uvula,[1] or, again, through concentration of the mind or thoughts on the point between the two brows, there dawns all of a sudden the right knowledge and the consequent cessation of *prāṇa* activities.[2]

Professor Macdonell, writing on *prāṇa* in the *Vedic Index*, vol. 11, says, "*prāṇa*, properly denoting 'breath,' is a term of wide and vague significance in Vedic literature." In the narrow sense *prāṇa* denotes one of the vital airs, of which five are usually enumerated, viz. *prāṇa*, *apāna*, *vyāna*, *udāna* and *samāna*. The exact sense of each of these breaths, when all are mentioned, cannot be determined. The word *prāṇa* has sometimes merely the general sense of breath, even when opposed to *apāna*. But its proper sense is beyond question "breathing forth," "expiration." But, though in a few cases the word may have been used for "breath" in its remote sense, the general meaning of the word in the Upaniṣads is not air current, but some sort of biomotor force, energy or vitality often causing these air currents.[3] It would be tedious to refer to

1 तालुमूलगतां यत्नाज् जिह्वयाक्रम्य घन्टिकाम्
ऊर्ध्वरन्ध्रगते प्राणे प्राणस्पन्दो निरुध्यते,
tālu-mūla-gatāṃ yatnāj jihvayākramya ghanṭikām
ūrdhva-randhra-gate prāṇe prāṇa-spando nirudhyate,—Yoga-vāsiṣṭha, V.78.25.

2 It is important to notice in this connection that most of the forms of *prāṇa-yāma* as herein described, except the *haṭha-yoga* process of arresting the inner air passage by the tongue, otherwise known as *khecarī-mūdrā*, are the same as described in the *sūtras* of Patañjali and the *bhāṣya* of Vyāsa; and this fact has also been pointed out by the commentator Ānandabodhendra Bhikṣu in his commentary on the above.

3 Difference between *prāṇa* and *vāyu, Aitareya,* II.4; the *nāsikya prāṇa,* I.4. Relation of *prāṇa* to other functions, *Kauṣītaki,* II.5; *prāṇa* as life, II.8; *prāṇa* connected with *vāyu,* II.12; *prāṇa* as the most important function of life, II.14; *prāṇa* as consciousness, III.2. Distinction of *nāsikya* and *mukhyaprāṇa, Chāndogya,* II.1-9; the function of the five *vāyus,* III.3-5; *prāṇa* as the result of food, I.8.4; of water, VI.5.2, VI.6.5, VI.7.6; *prāṇa* connected with *ātman,* as everything else connected with *prāṇa,* like spokes of a wheel, *Bṛhadāraṇyaka,* II.5.15; *prāṇa* as

the large number of relevant Upaniṣad texts and to try to ascertain after suitable discussion their exact significance in each case. The best way to proceed therefore is to refer to the earliest traditional meaning of the word, as accepted by the highest Hindu authorities. I refer to the *Vedānta-sūtra* of Bādarāyaṇa, which may be supposed to be the earliest research into the doctrines discussed in the Upaniṣads. Thus the *Vedānta-sūtra,* II.4.9 (*na vāyu-kriye pṛthag upadeśāt*), speaking of what may be the nature of *prāṇa,* says that it is neither air current (*vāyu*) nor action (*kriyā*), since *prāṇa* has been considered as different from air and action (in the Upaniṣads). Śaṅkara, commenting on this, says that from such passages as *yaḥ prāṇaḥ sa eṣa vāyuḥ pañca'vidhaḥ prāṇo pāno vyāna udānaḥ samānaḥ* (what is *prāṇa* is *vāyu* and it is fivefold, *prāṇa, apāna, vyāna, udāna, samāna*), it may be supposed that *vāyu* (air) is *prāṇa,* but it is not so, since in *Chāndogya,* III.18.4, it is stated that they are different. Again, it is not the action of the senses, as the Śāṃkhya supposes; for it is regarded as different from the senses in *Muṇḍaka,* II.1.3. The passage which identifies *vāyu* with *prāṇa* is intended to prove that it is the nature of *vāyu* that has transformed itself into the entity known as *prāṇa*(just as the human body itself may be regarded as a modification or transformation of *kṣiti,* earth). It is not *vāyu,* but, as Vācaspati says, "*vāyu-bheda,*" which Amalānanda explains in his *Vedānta-kalpa-taru* as *vāyoḥ pariṇāma-rūpa-kārya-viśeṣaḥ,* i.e. it is a particular evolutionary product of the category of *vāyu.* Śaṅkara's own statement is equally explicit on the point. He says, "*vāyur evāyam adhyātmam āpannaḥ pañca-vyūho viśeṣātmanāvatiṣṭhamānaḥ prāṇo nāma bhaṇyate na tattvāntaraṃ nāpi vāyu-mātram,*" i.e. it is *vāyu* which, having transformed itself into the body, differentiates itself into a group of five that is called *vāyu; prāṇa* is not altogether a different category, nor simply air. In explaining the nature of *prāṇa* in II.4.10-12, Śaṅkara says that *prāṇa* is not as independent *as jīva* (soul), but performs everything on its behalf, like a prime minister (*rāja-mantrivaj*

---

strength, *ibid.* V.14.4; *prāṇa* as force running through the *suṣumṇā* nerve, *Maitrī,* VI.21; etc.

jīvasya sarvārtha-karaṇatvena upakaraṇa-bhūto na svatantraḥ). *Prāṇa* is not an instrument like the senses, which operate only in relation to particular objects; for, as is said in *Chāndogya,* V.1.6, 7, *Bṛhadāraṇyaka,* IV.3.12 and *Bṛhadāraṇyaka*, I.3.19, when all the senses leave the body the *prāṇa* continues to operate. It is that by the functioning of which the existence of the soul in the body, or life (*jīva-sthiti*), and the passage of the *jīva* out of the body, or death (*jīvotkrānti*), are possible. The five *vāyus* are the five functionings of this vital principle, just as the fivefold mental states of right knowledge, illusion, imagination (*vikalpa*), sleep and memory are the different states of the mind. Vācaspati, in commenting on *Vedānta-sūtra*, II.4.11, says that it is the cause which upholds the body and the senses (*dehendriya-vidhāraṇa-kāraṇaṃ prāṇaḥ*), though it must be remembered that it has still other functions over and above the upholding of the body and the senses (*na kevalaṃ śarīrendriya-dhāraṇam asya kāryam,* Vācaspati, *ibid.*). In *Vedānta-sūtra,* II.4.13, it is described as being atomic (*aṇu*), which is explained by Śaṅkara as "subtle" (*sūkṣma*), on account of its pervading the whole body by its fivefold functioning's. Vācaspati in explaining it says that it is called "atomic" only in a derivative figurative sense (*upacaryate*) and only on account of its inaccessible or indefinable character (*duradhigamatā*), though pervading the whole body. Govindānanda, in commenting upon *Vedānta-sūtra,* II.4.9, says that *prāṇa* is a vibratory activity which upholds the process of life and it has no other direct operation than that (*parispanda-rupa-prāṇanānukūlatvād avāntara-vyāpārābhāvāt*). This seems to be something like biomotor or life force. With reference to the relation of *prāṇa* to the motor organs or faculties of speech, etc., Śaṅkara says that their vibratory activity is derived from *prāṇa* (*vāg-ādiṣu parispanda-lābhasya prāṇāyattatvam,* II.4.19). There are some passages in the *Vedānta-sūtra* which may lead us to think that the five *vāyus* may mean air currents, but that it is not so is evident from the fact that the substance of the *prāṇa* is not air (*etat prāṇādi-pañcakam ākāśādi-gata-rajo-'ṃśebhyo militebhya utpadyate*), and the *rajas* element is said to be produced from the five *bhūtas,* and the *prāṇas* are called *kriyātmaka,* or consisting of activity. Rāma Tīrtha, commenting on the above passage of the *Vedānta-sāra,* says that it is an evolutionary product of the essence of *vāyu* and the other *bhūtas,* but it is not in any sense the external air which performs certain physiological functions in the body (*tathāmukhya-prāṇo'pi vāyor bāhyasya sūtrātmakasya vikāro na śārīra-madhye nabhovad vṛtti-lābha-mātreṇa avasthito bāhya-vāyur eva*).[1] Having proved that in Vedānta *prāṇa* or any of the five *vāyus* means biomotor force and not air current, I propose now to turn to the Sāṃkhya-Yoga.

The Sāṃkhya-Yoga differs from the Vedānta in rejecting the view that the *prāṇa* is in any sense an evolutionary product of the nature of *vāyu.* Thus Vijñānabhikṣu in his *Vijñānāmṛta-bhāṣya* on *Vedānta-sūtra,* II.4.10, says that *prāṇa* is called *vāyu* because it is self-active like the latter (*svataḥ kriyāvattvena ubhayoḥ prāṇa-vāyvoḥ sājātyāt*). Again, in II.4.9, he says that *prāṇa* is neither air nor the upward or downward air current (*mukhya-prāṇo na vāyuḥ nāpi śārirasya ūrdhv-ādho-vgamana-lakṣaṇā vāyu-kriyā*).

What is *prāṇa*, then, according to Sāṃkhya-Yoga? It is *mahat-tattva,* which is evolved from *prakṛti,* which is called *buddhi* with reference to its intellective power and *prāṇa* with reference to its power as activity. The so-called five *vāyus* are the different functionings of the *mahat-tattva* (*sāmānya-kārya-sādhāraṇaṃ yat kāraṇaṃ mahat-tattvaṃ tasyaiva vṛtti-bhedāḥ prāṇāpānādayaḥ*; see *Vijñānāmṛta-bhāṣya,* II.4.11). Again, referring to *Sāṃkhya-kārikā,* 29, we find that the five *vāyus* are spoken of as the common functioning of *buddhi, ahaṃkāra* and *manas,* and Vācaspati says that the five *vāyus* are their life. This means that the three, *buddhi, ahaṃkāra* and *manas,* are each energizing, in their own way, and it is the joint operation of these energies that is called the fivefold *prāṇa* which upholds the body. Thus in this view also *prāṇa* is biomotor force and no air current. The special feature of this view is that this biomotor force is in essence a mental energy consisting

1 *Viḍvan-mano-rañjanī,* p. 105, Jacob's edition, Bombay, 1916.

of the specific functionings of *buddhi, ahaṃkāra* and *manas.*[1] It is due to the evolutionary activity of *antaḥkaraṇa.* In support of this view the *Sāṃkhya-pravacana-bhāṣya,* II.31, *Vyāsa-bhāṣya,* III.39, Vācaspati's *Tattva-vaiśāradī,* Bhikṣu's *Yoga-vārttika,* and Nāgeśa's *Chāyā-vyākhyā* thereon may be referred to. It is true, no doubt, that sometimes inspiration and expiration of external air are also called *prāṇa*; but that is because in inspiration and expiration the function of *prāṇa* is active or it vibrates. It is thus the entity which moves and not mere motion that is called *prāṇa.*[2] Rāmānuja agrees with Śaṅkara in holding that *prāṇa* is not air (*vāyu*), but a transformation of the nature of air. But it should be noted that this modification of air is such a modification as can only be known by Yoga methods.[3]

The Vaiśeṣika, however, holds that it is the external air which according to its place in the body performs various physiological functions.[4] The medical authorities also support the view that *vāyu* is a sort of driving and upholding power. Thus the *Bhāva-prakāśa* describes *vāyu* as follows: It takes quickly the *doṣas*, *dhātus* and the *malas* from one place to another, is subtle, composed of *rajo-guṇa*; is dry, cold, light and moving. By its movement it produces all energy, regulates inspiration and expiration and generates all movement and action, and by upholding the keenness of the senses and the *dhātus* holds together the heat, senses and the mind.[5] Vāhaṭa in his *Aṣṭāṅga-saṃgraha* also regards *vāyu* as the one cause of all body movements, and there is nothing to suggest that he meant air currents.[6] The long description of Caraka (I.12), as will be noticed in the next chapter, seems to suggest that he considered the *vāyu* as the constructive and destructive force of the universe, and as

1 Gauḍapāda's *bhāṣya* on the *Śaṃkhya-kārikā,* 29 compares the action of *prāṇa* to the movement of birds enclosed in a cage which moves the cage: compare Śaṅkara's reference to *Vedānta-sūtra,* II.4.9.

2 *Rāmānuja-bhāṣya* on *Vedānta-sūtra,* II.4.8.

3 See the *Tattva-muktā-kalāpa,* 53-55, and also *Rāmānuja-bhāṣya* and *Śruta-prakāśikā,* II.4.1-15.

4 *Nyāya-kandalī* of Śrīdhara, p. 48.

5 *Bhāva-prakāśa,* Sen's edition, Calcutta, p. 47.

6 Vāhata's *Aṣṭāṅga-saṃgraha* and the commentary by Indu, Trichur, 1914, pp. 138, 212.

fulfilling the same kinds of functions inside the body as well. It is not only a physical force regulating the physiological functions of the body, but is also the mover and controller of the mind in all its operations, as knowing, feeling and willing. Suśruta holds that it is in itself *avyakta* (unmanifested or unknowable), and that only its actions as operating in the body are manifested (*avyakto vyakta-karmā ca*).

In the *Yoga-vāsiṣṭha*, as we have already seen above, *prāṇa* or *vāyu* is defined as that entity which vibrates (*spandate yat sa tad vāyuḥ.* III.13) and it has no other reality than vibration. *Prāṇa* itself is, again, nothing but the movement of the intellect as *ahaṃkāra.*[1]

Prāṇa is essentially of the nature of vibration (*spanda*), and mind is but a form of *prāṇa* energy, and so by the control of the mind the five *vāyus* are controlled.[2] The Śaiva authorities also agree with the view that *prāṇa* is identical with cognitive activity, which passes through the *nāḍīs* (nerves) and maintains all the body movement and the movement of the senses. Thus Kṣemarāja says that it is the cognitive force which passes in the form of *prāṇa* through the *nāḍīs*, and he refers to Bhaṭṭa Kallaṭa as also holding the same view, and *prāṇa* is definitely spoken of by him as force (*kuṭila-vāhinī prāṇa-śaktiḥ*).[3] Śivopādhyaya in his *Vivṛti* on the *Vijñāna-bhairava* also describes *prāṇa* as force (*śakti*), and the *Vijñāna-bhairava* itself does the same.[4] Bhaṭṭa Ānanda in his *Vijñāna-kaumudī* describes *prāṇa* as a functioning of the mind (*citta-vṛtti*).[5]

STAGES OF PROGRESS

It has been already said that the study of philosophy and association with saintly characters are the principal means with which a

---

1 *Yoga-vāsiṣṭha,* III.14.

2 *Ibid.* V.13, 78.

3 *Śiva-sūtra-vimarśinī,* III.43, 44.

4 *Vijñāna-bhairava* and *Vivṛti,* verse 67.

5 See *the Nyāya-kandalī* of Śrīdhara, p. 48, and also *Dinakarī* and *Rāmarūdrī* on the *Siddhānta-muktāvalī* on *Bhāṣā-parichcheda,* p. 44.

beginner has to set out on his toil for the attainment of salvation. In the first stage (*prathamā bhūmikā*) the enquirer has to increase his wisdom by study and association with saintly persons. The second stage is the stage of critical thinking (*vicāraṇā*); the third is that of the mental practice of dissociation from all passions, etc. (*asaṅga-bhāvanā*); the fourth stage (*vilāpanī*) is that in which through a right understanding of the nature of truth the world-appearance shows itself to be false; the fifth stage is that in which the saint is in a state of pure knowledge and bliss (*śuddha-saṃvit-mayā-nanda-rūpa*). This stage is that of the *jīvan-mukta*, in which the saint may be said to be half-asleep and half-awake (*ardha-supta-prabuddha*). The sixth stage is that in which the saint is in a state of pure bliss; it is a state which is more like that of deep dreamless sleep (*suṣupta-sadṛśa-sthiti*). The seventh stage is the last transcendental state (*turyātīta*), which cannot be experienced by any saint while he is living. Of these the first three stages are called the waking state (*jāgrat*), the fourth stage is called the dream state (*svapna*), the fifth stage is called the dreamless (*suṣupta*) state, the sixth stage is an unconscious state called the *turya*, and the seventh stage is called the *turyātīta.*[1]

Desire (*icchā*) is at the root of all our troubles. It is like a mad elephant rushing through our system and trying to destroy it. The senses are like its young, and the instinctive root inclinations (*vāsanā*) are like its flow of ichor. It can only be conquered by the close application of patience (*dhairya*). Desire means the imaginations of the mind, such as "let this happen to me," and this is also called *saṅkalpa.* The proper way to stop this sort of imagining is to cease by sheer force of will from hoping or desiring in this manner, and for this one has to forget his memory; for so long as memory continues such hopes and desires cannot be stopped. The last stage, when all movement has ceased (*aspanda*) and all thoughts and imaginations have ceased, is a state of unconsciousness (*avedanam*).[2] *Yoga* is also defined as the

1 *Yoga-vāsiṣṭha,* VI.120.

2 *Yoga-vāsiṣṭha,* VI.126.

ultimate state of unconsciousness (*avedana*), the eternal state when everything else has ceased.[1] In this state *citta* is destroyed, and one is reduced to the ultimate entity of consciousness; and thus, being free of all relations and differentiations of subject and object, one has no knowledge in this state, though it is characterized as *bodhātmaka* (identical with consciousness). This last state is indeed absolutely indescribable (*avyapadeśya*), though it is variously described as the state of Brahman, Śiva, or the realization of the distinction of *prakṛti* and *puruṣa*.[2] The *Yoga-vāsiṣṭha,* however, describes this state not as being, essentially one of bliss, but as a state of unconsciousness unthinkable and indescribable. It is only the fifth state that manifests itself as being of the nature of *ānanda*; the sixth state is one of unconsciousness, which, it seems, can somehow be grasped; but the seventh is absolutely transcendental and indescribable.

The division of the progressive process into seven stages naturally reminds one of the seven stages of *prajñā* (wisdom) in Patañjali's *Yoga-sūtra* and *Vyāsa-bhāṣya.* The seven stages of *prajñā* are there divided into two parts, the first containing four and the second three. Of these the four are psychological and the three are ontological, showing the stages of the disintegration of *citta* before its final destruction or *citta-vimukti*.[3] Here also the first four stages, ending with *vilāpanī*, are psychological, whereas the last three stages represent the advance of the evolution of *citta* towards its final disruption. But, apart from this, it does not seem that there is any one to one correspondence of the *prajñā* states of the *Yoga-vāsiṣṭha* with those of Patañjali. The *Yoga-vāsiṣṭha* occasionally mentions the name *Yoga* as denoting the highest state and defines it as the ultimate state of unconsciousness (*avedanaṃ vidur yogam*) or as the cessation of the poisonous effects of desire.[4] In the first

1 *Ibid.* VI.126. 99.
2 *Ibid.* VI.126.71-72.
3 See my *A History of Indian Philosophy,* vol. 1, Cambridge, 1922, p. 273.
4 *Icchā-viṣa-vikārasya viyogaṃ yoga-nāmakam. Yoga-vāsiṣṭha,* VI.37.1; also *ibid.* VI.126.99.

half of the sixth book, chapter 125, the ultimate state is described as the state of universal negation (*sarvāpahnava*). Existence of *citta* is pain, and its destruction bliss; the destruction of *citta* by cessation of knowledge—a state of neither pain nor pleasure nor any intermediate state—a state as feelingless as that of the stone (*pāṣāṇavat-samam*), is the ultimate state aimed at.[1]

Karma, according to the *Yoga-vāsiṣṭha*, is nothing but thought-activity manifesting itself as subject-object knowledge. Abandonment of *karma* therefore means nothing short of abandonment of thought-activity or the process of knowledge.[2] Cessation of *karma* thus means the annihilation of knowledge. The stirring of *karma* or activity of thought is without any cause; but it is due to this activity that the ego and all other objects of thought come into being; the goal of all our endeavours should be the destruction of all knowledge, the unconscious, stone-like knowledgeless state.[3]

As there are seven progressive stages, so there are also seven kinds of beings according to the weakness or strength of their *vāsanās*. There are *svapna-jāgara*, *saṅkalpa-jāgara, kevala-jāgrat-sthita*, *cirāj-jāgrat-sthita*, *ghana-jāgrat-sthita*, *jāgrat-svapna* and *kṣīṇa-jāgaraka.* *Svapna-jāgara* (dream-awake) persons are those who in some past state of existence realized in dream experience all our present states of being and worked as dream persons (*svapnanara*). The commentator in trying to explain this says that it is not impossible; for everything is present everywhere in the spirit, so it is possible that we, as dream persons of their dream experience, should be present in their minds in their *vāsanā* forms (*tad-antaḥ-karaṇevāsanātmanā sthitāḥ*).[4] As both past and present have no existence except in thought, time is in

---

1 This *turīyātīta* stage should not be confused with the sixth stage of *suṣupti,* which is often described as a stage of pure bliss.

2 सर्वेषां कर्मणाम् एवं वेदनं बीजम् उत्तमम्
स्वरूपं चेतयित्वान्तस् ततः स्पण्डः प्रवर्तते
sarveṣāṃ karmaṇām evaṃ vedanaṃ bījam uttamam
svarūpaṃ cetayitvāntas tataḥ spaṇḍaḥ pravartate.—Yoga-vāsiṣṭha, VI.11.2.26.

3 *Ibid.* III.15.16.

4 *Ibid.* VI.2.50.9. *Tātparya-prakāśa.*

thought reversible, so that our existence at a time future to theirs does not necessarily prevent their having an experience of us in dreams. For the limitations of time and space do not hold for thought, and as elements in thought everything exists everywhere (*sarvaṃ sarvatra vidyate*).[1] By dreams these persons may experience changes of life and even attain to final emancipation. The second class, the *saṅkalpa-jāgar as* those who without sleeping can by mere imagination continue to conceive all sorts of activities and existences, and may ultimately attain emancipation. The third class, the *kevala-jāgaras*, are those who are born in this life for the first time. When such beings pass through more than one life, they are called *cira-jāgaras*. Such beings, on account of their sins, may be born as trees, etc., in which case they are called *ghana-jāgaras*. Those of such beings suffering rebirth who by study and good association attain right knowledge are called *jāgrat-svapna-sthita;* and finally, those that have reached the *turya* state of deliverance are called *kṣīṇa-jāgaraka.*

Bondage (*bandha*), according to the *Yoga-vāsiṣṭha*, remains so long as our knowledge has an object associated with it, and deliverance (*mokṣa*) is realized when knowledge is absolutely and ultimately dissociated from all objects and remains in its transcendent purity, having neither an object nor a subject.[2]

METHODS OF RIGHT CONDUCT

The *Yoga-vāsiṣṭha* does not enjoin severe asceticism or the ordinary kinds of religious gifts, ablutions or the like for the realization of our highest ends, which can only be achieved by the control of attachment (*rāga*), antipathy (*dveṣa*), ignorance (*tamaḥ*), anger (*krodha*), pride (*mada*), and jealousy (*mātsarya*), followed by the

---

1 *Yoga-vāsiṣṭha,* VI.2.50.9. *Tātparya-prakāśa.*

2 ज्ञानस्य ज्ञेयतापतीर् बन्ध इत्य् अभिदीयते
तस्यैव ज्ञेयताशान्तिर् मोक्ष इत्य् अभिधीयते
Jñānasya jñeyatāpattir bandha it yabhidīyate
tasyaiva jñeyatā-śāntir mokṣa ity abhidhīyate. —*Yoga-vāsiṣṭha,* VI.11.190.1.

right apprehension of the nature of reality.[1] So long as the mind is not chastened by the clearing out of all evil passions, the performance of religious observances leads only to pride and vanity and does not produce any good. The essential duty of an enquirer consists in energetic exertion for the achievement of the highest end, for which he must read the right sort of scriptures (*sac-chāstra*) and associate with good men.[2] He should somehow continue his living and abandon even the slightest desire of enjoyment (*bhoga-gandham parityajet*), and should continue critical thinking (*vicāra*). On the question whether knowledge or *work, jñāna* or *karma,* is to be accepted for the achievement of the highest end, the *Yoga-vāsiṣṭha* does not, like Śaṅkara, think that the two cannot jointly be taken up, but on the contrary emphatically says that, just as a bird flies with its two wings, so an enquirer can reach his goal through the joint operation of knowledge and work.[3]

The main object of the enquirer being the destruction of *citta,* all his endeavours should be directed towards the uprooting of instinctive root inclinations (*vāsanā*), which are the very substance and root of the *citta.* The realization of the truth (*tattva-jñāna*), the destruction of the *vāsanās* and the destruction of the *citta* all mean the same identical state and are interdependent on one another, so that none of them can be attained without the other. So, abandoning the desire for enjoyment, one has to try for these three together; and for this one has to control one's desires on one hand and practise breath-control (*prāṇa-nirodhena*) on the other; and these two would thus jointly co-operate steadily towards the final goal. Such an advancement is naturally slow, but this progress, provided it is

1 स्वपौरुषप्रयत्नेन विवेकेन विकाशिना
स देवोज्ञायते राम न तपःस्नानकर्मभिः
sva-pauruṣa-prayatnena vivekena vikāśinā
sa devo jñāyate rāma na tapaḥ-snāna-karmabhiḥ. —*Yoga-vāsiṣṭha,* III.6.9.

2 Good men are defined in the *Yoga-vāsiṣṭha* as follows:
देशे यं सुजनप्राया लोकाः साधुं प्रचक्षते
स विशिष्टः स साधुः स्यात् तं प्रयत्नेन संश्रयेत्॥
deśe yaṃ sujana-prāyā lokāḥ sādhuṃ pracakṣate
sa viśiṣṭaḥ sa sādhuḥ syāt taṃ prayatnena saṃśrayet.—*Ibid.* III.6.20.

3 *Ibid.* I.1.7, 8.

steady, is to be preferred to any violent efforts to hasten (*hatha*) the result.[1] Great stress is also laid on the necessity of self-criticism as a means of loosening the bonds of desire and the false illusions of world-appearance and realizing the dissociation from attachment (*asaṅga*).[2]

YOGA-VĀSIṢṬHA, ŚAṄKARA VEDĀNTA AND BUDDHIST VIJÑĀNAVĀDA

To a superficial reader the idealism of the *Yoga-vāsiṣṭha* may appear to be identical with the Vedānta as interpreted by Śaṅkara; and in some of the later Vedānta works of the Śaṅkara school, such as *the Jīvan-mukti-viveka,* etc., so large a number of questions dealt with in the *Yoga-vāsiṣṭha* occur that one does not readily imagine that there may be any difference between this idealism and that of Śaṅkara. This point therefore needs some discussion.

The main features of Śaṅkara's idealism consist in the doctrine that the self-manifested subject-objectless intelligence forms the ultimate and unchangeable substance of both the mind (*antaḥkaraṇa*) and the external world. Whatever there is of change and mutation is outside of this Intelligence, which is also the Reality. But, nevertheless, changes are found associated with this reality or Brahman, such as the external forms of objects and the diverse mental states. These are mutable and have therefore a different kind of indescribable existence from Brahman; but still they are somehow essentially of a positive nature.[3] Śaṅkara's idealism does not allow him to deny the existence of external objects as apart from perceiving minds, and he does not adhere to the doctrine of *esse est percipi.* Thus he severely criticizes the views of the Buddhist idealists, who refuse to believe in the existence of external objects as apart from the thoughts which seem to represent them. Some of these arguments are of great philosophical interest and remind

1 *Yoga-vāsiṣṭha,* V.92.

2 *Ibid.* V.93.

3 See the account of Śaṅkara Vedānta in my *A History of Indian Philosophy,* vol. 1, Cambridge, 1922, chapter x.

one of similar arguments put forth by a contemporary British Neo-realist in refutation of Idealism.

The Buddhists there are made to argue as follows: When two entities are invariably perceived simultaneously they are identical; now knowledge and its objects are perceived simultaneously; therefore the objects are identical with their percepts. Our ideas have nothing in the external world to which they correspond, and their existence during dreams, when the sense-organs are universally agreed to be inoperative, shows that for the appearance of ideas the operation of the sense-organs, indispensable for establishing connection with the so-called external world, is unnecessary. If it is asked how, if there are no external objects, can the diversity of percepts be explained, the answer is that such diversity may be due to the force of *vāsanās* or the special capacity of the particular moment associated with the cognition.[1] If the so-called external objects are said to possess different special capacities which would account for the diversity of percepts, the successive moments of the mental order may also be considered as possessing special distinctive capacities which would account for the diversity of percepts generated by those cognition moments. In dreams it is these diverse cognition moments which produce diversity of percepts.

Śaṅkara, in relating the above argument of the Buddhist idealist, says that external objects are directly perceived in all our perceptions, and how then can they be denied? In answer to this, if it is held that there is no object for the percepts excepting the sensations, or that the existence of anything consists in its being perceived, that can be refuted by pointing to the fact that the independent existence of the objects of perception, as apart from their being perceived, can be known from the perception itself, since the perceiving of an object is not the object itself; it is always felt that the perception of the blue is different from the blue which is perceived; the blue stands forth as the object of perception and the two can never be identical.

1 *Kasyacid eva jñāna-kṣaṇasya sa tādṛśaḥ sāmarthyātiśayo vāsanā-panṇāmaḥ. Bhāmatī,* II.11. 28.

This is universally felt and acknowledged, and the Buddhist idealist, even while trying to refute it, admits it in a way, since he says that what is inner perception appears as if it exists outside of us, externally. If externality as such never existed, how could there be an appearance of it in consciousness? When all experiences testify to this difference between knowledge and its object, the inner mental world of thoughts and ideas and the external world of objects, how can such a difference be denied? You may see a jug or remember it: the mental operation in these two cases varies, but the object remains the same.[1]

The above argument of Śaṅkara against Buddhist idealism conclusively proves that he admitted the independent existence of objects, which did not owe their existence to anybody's knowing them. External objects had an existence different from and independent of the existence of the diversity of our ideas or percepts.

But the idealism of the *Yoga-vāsiṣṭha* is more like the doctrine of the Buddhist idealists than the idealism of Śaṅkara. For according to the *Yoga-vāsiṣṭha* it is only ideas that have some sort of existence. Apart from ideas or percepts there is no physical or external world having a separate or independent existence. *Esse est percipi* is the doctrine of the *Yoga-vāsiṣṭha*, while Śaṅkara most emphatically refutes such a doctrine. A. later exposition of Vedānta by Prakāśānanda, known as *Vedānta-siddhānta-muktāvalī,* seems to derive its inspiration from the *Yoga-vāsiṣṭha* in its exposition of Vedānta on lines similar to the idealism of the *Yoga-vāsiṣṭha*, by denying the existence of objects not perceived (*ajñāta-sattvānahhyupagama*).[2] Prakāśānanda disputes the ordinarily accepted view that cognition of objects arises out of the contact of senses with objects; for objects for him exist only so long as they are perceived, i.e. there is no independent external existence of objects apart from their perception. All objects have only perceptual existence (*prātītika-sattva*). Both Prakāśānanda and

1 Śaṅkara's *bhāṣya* on the *Brahma-sūtra,* II.2.28.

2 *Siddhānta-muktāvalī.* See *The Pandit,* new series, vol. XI, pp. 129-139.

the *Yoga-vāsiṣṭha* deny the existence of objects when they are not perceived, while Śaṅkara not only admits their existence, but also holds that they exist in the same form in which they are known; and this amounts virtually to the admission that our knowing an object does not add anything to it or modify it to any extent, except that it becomes known to us through knowledge. Things are what they are, even though they may not be perceived. This is in a way realism. The idealism of Śaṅkara's Vedānta consists in this, that he held that the Brahman is the immanent self within us, which transcends all changeful experience and is also ultimate reality underlying all objects perceived outside of us in the external world. Whatever forms and characters there are in our experience, internal as well as external, have an indescribable and indefinite nature which passes by the name of *māyā.*[1] Śaṅkara Vedānta takes it for granted that that alone is real which is unchangeable; what is changeful, though it is positive, is therefore unreal. The world is only unreal in that special sense; *māyā* belongs to a category different from affirmation and negation, namely the category of the indefinite.

The relation of the real, the Brahman, to this *māyā* in Śaṅkara Vedānta is therefore as indefinite as the *māyā;* the real is the unchangeable, but how the changeful forms and characters become associated with it or what is their origin or what is their essence, Śaṅkara is not in a position to tell us. The *Yoga-vāsiṣṭha* however holds that formless and characterless entity is the ultimate truth; it is said to be the Brahman, *cit*, or void (*śūnya*)*;* but, whatever it may be, it is this characterless entity which is the ultimate truth. This ultimate entity is associated with an energy of movement, by virtue of which it can reveal all the diverse forms of appearances. The relation between the appearances and the reality is not external, indefinite and indescribable, as it is to Śaṅkara, but the appearances, which are but the unreal and illusory manifestations of the reality, are produced by the operation of this inner activity of the characterless spirit, which is in itself nothing but a subject-objectless pure consciousness. But this inner and immanent

1 See my *A History of Indian Philosophy*, vol. I, ch. X.

movement does not seem to have any dialectic of its own, and no definite formula of the method of its operation for its productions can be given; the imaginary shapes of ideas and objects, which have nothing but a mere perceptual existence, are due not to a definite order, but to accident or chance (*kākatālīya*). Such a conception is indeed very barren, and it is here that the system of the *Yoga-vāsiṣṭha* is particularly defective. Another important defect of the system is that it does not either criticize knowledge or admit its validity, and the characterless entity which forms its absolute is never revealed in experience. With Śaṅkara the case is different; for he holds that this absolute Brahman is also the self which is present in every experience and is immediate and self-revealed. But the absolute of the *Yoga-vāsiṣṭha* is characterless and beyond experience. The state of final emancipation, the seventh stage, is not a stage of bliss, like the Brahmahood of the Vedānta, but a state of characterlessness and vacuity almost. In several places in the work it is said that this ultimate state is differently described by various systems as Brahman, distinction of *prakṛti* and *puruṣa*, pure *vijñāna* and void (*śūnya*), while in truth it is nothing but a characterless entity. Its state of *mukti* (emancipation) is therefore described, as we have already seen above, as *pāṣāṇavat* or like a stone, which strongly reminds us of the Vaiśeṣika view of *mukti*. On the practical side it lays great stress on *pauruṣa*, or exertion of free-will and energy, it emphatically denies *daiva* as having the power of weakening *pauruṣa* or even exerting a superior dominating force, and it gives us a new view of *karma* as meaning only thought-activity. As against Śaṅkara, it holds that knowledge (*jñāna*) and *karma* maybe combined together, and that they are not for two different classes of people, but are both indispensable for each and every right-minded enquirer. The principal practical means for the achievement of the highest end of the *Yoga-vāsiṣṭha* are the study of philosophical scripture, association with good men and self-criticism. It denounces external religious observances without the right spiritual exertions as being worse than useless. Its doctrine of *esse est percipi* and that no experiences have any objective validity outside of themselves, that there are no external objects to which they correspond and that all are but forms of knowledge, reminds us very strongly of what this system owes to Vijñānavāda Buddhism. But, while an important Vijñānavāda work like the *Laṅkāvatāra-sūtra* tries to explain through its various categories the origin of the various appearances in knowledge, no such attempt is made in the *Yoga-vāsiṣṭha,* where it is left to chance. It is curious that in the Sanskrit account of Vijñānavāda by Hindu writers, such as Vācaspati and others, these important contributions of the system are never referred to either for the descriptive interpretation of the system or for its refutation. While there are thus unmistakable influences of Vijñānavāda and Gauḍapāda on the *Yoga-vāsiṣṭha,* it seems to have developed in close association with the Śaiva, as its doctrine of *spanda*, or immanent activity, so clearly shows. This point will, however, be more fully discussed in my treatment of Śaiva philosophy.

CHAPTER XIII

SPECULATIONS IN THE MEDICAL SCHOOLS

It may be urged that the speculations of the thinkers of the medical schools do not deserve to be recorded in a History of Indian Philosophy. But the force of such an objection will lose much in strength if it is remembered that medicine was the most important of all the physical sciences which were cultivated in ancient India, was directly and intimately connected with the Sāṃkhya and Vaiśeṣika physics and was probably the origin of the logical speculations subsequently codified in the *Nyāya-sūtras.*[1] The literature contains, moreover, many other interesting ethical instructions and reveals a view of life which differs considerably from that found in works on philosophy; further, it treats of many other interesting details which throw a flood of light on the scholastic methods of Indian thinkers. Those, again, who are aware of the great importance of Hatha Yoga or Tantra physiology or anatomy in relation to some of the Yoga practices of those schools will no doubt be interested to know for purposes of comparison or contrast the speculations of the medical schools on kindred points of interest. Their speculations regarding embryology, heredity and other such points of general enquiry are likely to prove interesting even to a student of pure philosophy.

1 The system of Sāṃkhya philosophy taught in *Caraka-saṃhitā,* IV.1, has already been described in the first volume of the present work, pp. 213-217.

ĀYUR-VEDA AND THE ATHARVA-VEDA

Suśruta says that Āyur-veda (the science of life) is an *upāṅga* of the *Atharva-Veda* and originally consisted of 100,000 verses in one thousand chapters and was composed by Brahmā before he created all beings (*Suśruta-saṃhitā,* I.1.5). What *upāṅga* exactly means in this connection cannot easily be satisfactorily explained. Ḍalhaṇa (AD 1100) in explaining the word in his *Nibandha-saṃgraha,* says that an *upāṅga* is a smaller *aṅga* (part)—"*aṅgam eva alpatvād upāṅgam.*" Thus, while hands and legs are regarded as *aṅgas*, the toes or the palms of the hands are called *upāṅga.* The *Atharva-Veda* contains six thousand verses and about one thousand prose lines. If the Āyur-veda originally contained 100,000 verses, it cannot be called an *upāṇga* of the *Atharva-Veda*, if *upāṇga* is to mean a small appendage, as Ḍalhaṇa explains it. For, far from being a small appendage, it was more than ten times as extensive as the *Atharva-Veda.* Caraka, in discussing the nature of Āyur-veda, says that there was never a time when life did not exist or when intelligent people did not exist, and so there were always plenty of people who knew about life, and there were always medicines which acted on the human body according to the principles which we find enumerated in the Āyur-veda. Āyur-veda was not produced at any time out of nothing, but there was always a continuity of the science of life; when we hear of its being produced, it can only be with reference to a beginning of the comprehension of its principles by some original thinker or the initiation of a new course of instruction at the hands of a gifted teacher. The science of life has always been in existence, and there have always been people who understood it in their own way; it is only with reference to its first systematized comprehension or instruction that it may be said to have a beginning.[1] Again, Caraka distinguishes Āyur-veda as a distinct Veda, which is superior to the other Vedas because it gives us life, which is the basis of

1 *Caraka,* I.30.24. This passage seems to be at variance with *Caraka,* I.1.6; for it supposes that diseases also existed always, while *Caraka,* I.1.6 supposes that diseases broke out at a certain point of time. Is it an addition by the reviser Dṛḍhabala?

all other enjoyments or benefits, whether they be of this world or of another.[1] Vāgbhaṭa, the elder, speaks of Āyur-veda not as an *upāṇga*, but as an *upaveda* of the *Atharva-Veda*.[2] The *Mahā-bhārata,* II.11.33, speaks of *upaveda*, and Nīlakaṇṭha, explaining this, says that there are four *upavedas*, *Āyur-veda, Dhanur-veda*, *Gāndharva* and *Artha-śāstra*. *Brahma-vaivarta,* a later *purāṇa,* says that after creating the Ṛk, Yajus, Sāma and Atharva Brahmā created the Āyur-veda as the fifth Veda.[3] Roth has a quotation in his *Wörterbuch* to the effect that Brahmā taught Āyur-veda, which was a *vedāṅga*, in all its eight parts.[4]

We thus find that Āyur-veda was regarded by some as a Veda superior to the other Vedas and respected by their followers as a fifth Veda, as an *upaveda* of the *Atharva-Veda*, as an independent *upaveda*, as an *upāṅga* of the *Atharva- Veda* and lastly as a *vedāṅga.* All that can be understood from these conflicting references is that it was traditionally believed that there was a Veda known as Āyur-veda which was almost co-existent with the other Vedas, was entitled to great respect, and was associated with the *Atharva-Veda* in a special way. It seems, however, that the nature of this association consisted in the fact that both of them dealt with the curing of diseases and the attainment of long life; the one principally by incantations and charms, and the other by medicines. What Suśruta understands by calling Āyur-vedaan *upāṅga* of the *Atharva- Veda* is probably nothing more than this. Both the *Atharva-Veda* and Āyur-veda dealt with the curing of diseases, and this generally linked them together in the popular mind, and, the for-

---

1 *Caraka,* I.1.42 and *Āyur-veda-dīpikā* of Cakrapāṇi on it.

2 *Aṣṭāṅga-saṃgraha,* I.1.8. *Gopatha-Brāhmaṇa,* I.10, however, mentions five vedas, viz. *Sarpa-veda, Piśāca-veda, Asura-veda, Itihāsa-veda* and *Purāṇa-veda,* probably in the sense of *upaveda,* but Āyur-veda is not mentioned in this connection.

3 *Brahma-vaivarta-purāṇa,* I.16.9, 10.

4 *Brahmā vedāṅgam aṣṭāṅgam āyur-vedam abhāṣata.* This quotation, which occurs in the *Wörterbuch* in connection with the word *āyur-veda,* could not be verified owing to some omission in the reference. It should be noted that *vedāṅga* is generally used to mean the six *aṅgas,* viz. *Śikṣā, Kalpa, Vyākaraṇa, Chandas, Jyotiṣ* and *Nirukta.*

mer being the holier of the two, on account of its religious value, the latter was associated with it as its literary accessory. Dārila bhaṭṭa, in commenting upon *Kauśika-sūtra*, 25.2, gives us a hint as to what may have been the points of contact and of difference between Āyur-veda and the *Atharva-Veda.* Thus he says that there are two kinds of diseases; those that are produced by unwholesome diet, and those produced by sins and transgressions. The Āyur-veda was made for curing the former, and the Atharvan practices for the latter.[1] Caraka himself counts penance (*prāyaś-citta*) as a name of medicine (*bheṣaja*) and Cakrapāṇi,in commenting on this, says that as *prāyaś-citta* removes the diseases produced by sins, so medicines *(bheṣaja)* also remove diseases, and thus *prāyaś-citta* is synonymous with *bheṣaja.*[2]

But what is this Āyur-veda? We now possess only the treatises of Caraka and Suśruta, as modified and supplemented by later revisers. But Suśruta tells us that Brahmā had originally produced the Āyur-veda, which contained 100,000 verses spread over one thousand chapters, and then, finding the people weak in intelligence and short-lived, later on divided it into eight subjects, viz. surgery (*śalya*), treatment of diseases of the head (*śālākya),* treatment of ordinary diseases (*kāya-cikitsā*), the processes of counteracting the influences of evil spirits (*bhūta-vidyā*), treatment of child diseases (*kaumāra-bhṛtya*), antidotes to poisons (*agada-tantra*), the science of rejuvenating the body (*rasāyana*) and the science of acquiring sex-strength *(vājīkaraṇa).*[3] The statement of Suśruta that Āyur-veda was originally a great work in which the later subdivisions of its eight different kinds of studies were not differentiated seems to be fairly trustworthy. The fact that Āyur-veda is called an *upāṅga*, an *upaveda*, or a *vedāṅga* also points to its existence in some state during the period when the Vedic literature was being composed.

---

1 *dvi-prakārā vyādhayaḥ āhāra-ninñttā aśubhanimittāś ceti; tatra āhāra-samutthānāṃ vaiṣamya Āyur-vedaṃ cakāra adharma-samutthānāṃ tu śāstramidam ucyate.* Dārila's comment on *Kauśika-sūtra,* 25.2.

2 *Caraka,* VI.1.3 and *Āyur-veda-dipikā, Ibid.*

3 *Suśruta-saṃhitā,* I.1.5-9.

We hear of compendiums of medicine as early as the *Prātiśākhyas.*[1] It is curious, however, that nowhere in the Upaniṣads or the Vedas does the name "Āyur-veda" occur, though different branches of study are mentioned in the former.[2] The Aṣṭāṅga Āyur-veda is, however, mentioned in the *Mahā-bhārata*, and the three constituents (*dhātu*), *vāyu* (wind), *pitta* (bile) and *śleṣman* (mucus), are also mentioned; there is reference to a theory that by these three the body is sustained and that by their decay the body decays *(etaiḥ kṣīṇaiś ca kṣīyate),* and Kṛṣṇātreya is alluded to as being the founder of medical science *(cikitsitam).*[3] One of the earliest systematic mentions of medicines unmixed with incantations and charms is to be found in the *Mahā-vagga* of the *Vinaya-Piṭaka*, where the Buddha is prescribing medicines for his disciples.[4] These medicines are of a simple nature, but they bear undeniable marks of methodical arrangement. We are also told there of a surgeon, named Akāśagotto, who made surgical operations *(sattha-kamma)* on fistula (*bhagandara*). In Rockhill's *Life of the Buddha* we hear of Jīvaka as having studied medicine in the Taxila University under Ātreya.[5] That even at the time of the *Atharva-Veda* there were hundreds of physicians and an elaborate pharmacopoeia, treating diseases with drugs, is indicated by a *mantra* therein which extols the virtues of amulets, and speaks of their powers as being equal to thousands of

---

1 R.V. *Prātiśākhya,* 16.54 (55), mentioned by Bloomfield in *The Atharva-Veda and Gopatha-Brāhmaṇa,* p. 10. The name of the medical work mentioned is *Subheṣaja.*

2 *Ṛg-Vedaṃ bhagavo 'dhyemi Yajur-vedaṃ sāma-vedam ātharvaṇaś caturtham itihāsa-purāṇaṃ pañcamaṃ vedānāṃ vedam pitryaṃ rāśiṃ daivaṃ nidhiṃ vāko-vākyam ekāyanaṃ deva vidyāṃ brahma-vidyāṃ bhūta-vidyāṃ kṣattra-vidyāṃ nakṣatra-vidyāṃ sarpa-deva-jana-vidyāṃ. Chāndogya,* VII.1.2. Of these *bhūta- vidyā* is counted as one of the eight *tantras* of Āyur-veda, as we find it in the *Suśruta-saṃhitā* or elsewhere.

3 *Mahā-bhārata*, II.11.25, XII.342.86, 87, XII.210.21. Kṛṣṇātreya is referred to in *Caraka-saṃhitā*, VI.15.129, and Cakrapāṇi, commenting on this, says that Kṛṣṇātreya and Ātreya are two authorities who are different from Ātreya Punarvasu, the great teacher of the *Caraka-saṃhitā.*

4 *Vinaya-Piṭaka, Mahā-vagga*, VI.1-14.

5 Rockhill's *Life of the Buddha,* p. 65.

medicines employed by thousands of medical practitioners.[1] Thus it can hardly be denied that the practice of medicine was in full swing even at the time of the *Atharva-Veda*; and, though we have no other proofs in support of the view that there existed a literature on the treatment of diseases, known by the name of Āyur-veda , in which the different branches, which developed in later times, were all in an undifferentiated condition, yet we have no evidence which can lead us to disbelieve Suśruta, when he alludes definitely to such a literature. The *Caraka-saṃhitā* also alludes to the existence of a beginningless traditional continuity of Āyur-ved, under which term he includes life, the constancy of the qualities of medical herbs, diet, etc., and their effects on the human body and the intelligent enquirer. The early works that are now available to us, viz. the *Caraka-saṃhitā* and *Suśruta-saṃhitā,* are both known as *tantras.*[2] Even Agniveśa's work *(Agniveśa-saṃhitā),* which Caraka revised and which was available at the time of Cakrapāṇi, was a *tantra*. What then was the Āyur-veda, which has been variously described as a fifth Veda or an *upaveda*, if not a literature distinctly separate from the *tantras* now available to us?[3] It seems probable, therefore, that such a literature existed, that the systematized works of Agniveśa and others superseded it and that, as a consequence, it came ultimately to be lost. Caraka, however, uses the word "Āyur-veda" in the general sense of "science of life." Life is divided by Caraka into four kinds, viz. *sukha* (happy), *duḥkha* (unhappy), *hita* (good) and *ahita* (bad). *Sukham āyuḥ* is a life which is not affected by bodily or mental diseases, is endowed with vigour, strength, energy, vitality, activity and is full of all sorts of enjoyments and successes. The opposite of this is the *asukham āyuḥ. Hitam āyuḥ* is the life of a person who is always willing to do good to all beings, never steals others' property, is truthful, self-controlled, self-restrained and works with careful consideration, does not

1 *Atharva-veda,* II.9.3, *śataṃ hy asya bhiṣajaḥ sahasram uta vīrudhaḥ.*

2 *Gurv-ājñā-lābhānantaraṃ etat-tantra-karaṇam.* Cakrapāṇi's *Āyur-veda-dīpikā,* I.1.1; also *Caraka-saṃhitā,* I.1.52.

3 Cakrapāṇi quotes the *Agniveśa-saṃhitā* in his *Āyur-veda -dīpikā,* VI.3.177 - 185.

transgress the moral injunctions, takes to virtue and to enjoyment with equal zeal, honours revered persons, is charitable and does what is beneficial to this world and to the other. The opposite of this is called *ahita.* The object of the science of life is to teach what is conducive to all these four kinds of life and also to determine the length of such a life.[1]

But, if Āyur-veda means "science of life," what is its connection with the *Atharva-Veda*? We find in the *Caraka-saṃhitā* that a physician should particularly be attached (*bhaktir ādeśyā*) to the *Atharva-Veda.* The *Atharva-Veda* deals with the treatment of diseases (*cikitsā*) by advising the propitiatory rites (*svastyayana*), offerings *(bali),* auspicious oblations (*maṅgala-homa),* penances *(niyama),* purificatory rites *(prāyaś-citta),* fasting *(upavāsa)* and incantations *(mantra).*[2] Cakrapāṇi, in commenting on this, says that, since it is advised that physicians should be attached *to the Atharva-Veda*, it comes to this, that the *Atharva-Veda* becomes Āyur-veda *(Atharva-vedasya āyurvedatvam uktaṃ bhavati).* The *Atharva-Veda,* no doubt, deals with different kinds of subjects, andI so Āyur-veda is to be considered as being only a part of the *Atharva-Veda (Atharva-vedaikadeśa eva āyur-vedaḥ).* Viewed in the light of Cakrapāṇi's interpretation, it seems that the school of medical teaching to which Caraka belonged was most intimately connected with the *Atharva-Veda.* This is further corroborated by a comparison of the system of bones found in the *Caraka-saṃhitā* with that of the *Atharva-Veda.* Suśruta himself remarks that, while he considers the number of bones in the human body to be three

1 *Caraka,* I.1.40 and I.30.20-23:
हिताहितं सुखं दुखं दुःखम् आयुस् तस्य हिताहितं
मानं च तच् च यत्रोक्तम् आयुर्वेदः स उच्यते ॥
hitāhitaṃ sukhaṃ duḥkham āyus tasya hitāhitaṃ
mānaṃ ca tac ca yatroktam āyur-vedah sa ucyate.

In I.30.20 the derivation of Āyur-veda is given as *āyur vedayati iti āyur-vedaḥ,* i.e. that which instructs us about life. Suśruta suggests two alternative derivations—*āyur asmin vidyate anena vā āyur vindatīty āyur-vedaḥ,* i.e. that by which life is known or examined, or that by which life is attained. *Suśruta-saṃhitā,* I.1.14.

2 *Caraka,* I.30.20.

hundred, the adherents of the Vedas hold them to be three hundred and sixty; and this is exactly the number counted by Caraka.[1] The *Atharva-Veda* does not count the bones; but there are with regard to the description of bones some very important points in which the school to which Caraka belonged was in agreement with the *Atharva-Veda*, and not with Suśruta. Dr Hoernle, who has carefully discussed the whole question, thus remarks: "A really important circumstance is that the Atharvic system shares with the Charakiyan one of the most striking points in which the latter differs from the system of Suśruta, namely, the assumption of a central facial bone in the structure of the skull. It may be added that the Atharvic term *pratiṣṭhā* for the base of the long bones obviously agrees with the Charakiyaen trm *adhiṣṭhāna* and widely differs from the Suśrutiyan *kūrca.*"[2] The *Śatapatha-brāhmaṇa*, which, as Dr Hoernle has pointed out, shows an acquaintance with both the schools to which Caraka and Suśruta respectively belonged, counts, however, 360 bones, as Caraka did.[3] The word *veda-vādino* in *Suśruta-saṃhitā,* III.5.18 does not mean the followers of Āyur-veda as distinguished from the Vedas, as Ḍalhaṇa interprets it, but is literally true in the sense that it gives us the view which is shared by Caraka with the *Atharva-Veda,* the *Śatapatha-brāhmaṇa*, the legal literature and the *purāṇas*, which according to all orthodox estimates derive their validity from the Vedas. If this agreement of the Vedic ideas with those of the Ātreya school of medicine, as represented by Caraka, be viewed together with the identification by the latter of Āyur-Ve-

---

1 *Trīṇi saṣaṣṭhāny asthi-śatāni veda-vādino bhāṣante; śalya-tantre tu trīṇy eva śatāni. Suśruta-saṃhitā,* III.5.18. *Trīṇi ṣaṣṭhāni śatāny asthnāṃ saha danta-nakhena. Caraka-saṃhitā,* IV.7.6.

2 A. F. Rudolf Hoernle's *Studies in the Medicine of Ancient India,* p. 113.

3 *Ibid.* pp. 105-106. See also *Śatapatha-brāhmaṇa,* X.5.4.12, also XII.3.2.3 and 4, XII.2.4.9-14, VIII.6.2.7 and 10. The *Yājñavalkya-Dharma-śāstra, Viṣṇu-smṛti, Viṣṇu-dharmottara* and *Agni-Purāṇa* also enumerate the bones of the human body in agreement with Caraka as 360. The source of the last three was probably the first (*Yājñavalkya-Dharma-śāstra*), as has been suggested by Dr Hoernle in his *Studies in the Medicine of Ancient India,* pp. 40-46. But none of these non-medical recensions are of an early date: probably they are not earlier than the third or the fourth century AD.

da with *Atharva-Veda*, it may be not unreasonable to suppose that the Ātreya school, as represented by Caraka, developed from the *Atharva- Veda*. This does not preclude the possibility of there being an Āyur-veda of another school, to which Suśruta refers and from which, through the teachings of a series of teachers, the *Suśruta-saṃhitā* developed. This literature probably tried to win the respect of the people by associating itself.with the *Atharva-Veda*, and by characterizing itself as an *upāṅga* of the *Atharva-Veda.*[1]

Jayanta argues that the validity of the Vedas depends on the fact that they have been composed by an absolutely trustworthy person *(āpta)*. As an analogy he refers to Āyur-veda, the validity of which is due to the fact that it has been composed by trustworthy persons *(āpta)*. That the medical instructions of the Āyur-veda are regarded as valid is due to the fact that they are the instructions of trustworthy persons *(yato yatrāptavādatraṃ tatra prāmāṇyam iti vyāptir gṛhyate)*. But it may be argued that the validity of Āyur-veda is not because it has for its author trustworthy persons, but because its instructions can be verified by experience *(nanvāyur-vedādau prāmāṇyaṃ pratyakṣādi-saṃvādāt pratipannaṃ nāpta-prāmāṇyāt)*. Jayanta in reply says that the validity of Āyur-veda is due to the fact of its being composed by trustworthy persons; and it can be also verified by experience. He argues also that the very large number of medicines, their combinations and applications, are of such an infinite variety that it would be absolutely impossible for any one man to know them by employing the experimental methods of agreement and difference. It is only because the medical authorities are almost omniscient in their knowledge of things that they can display such superhuman knowledge regarding diseases and their cures, which can be taken only on trust on their authority. His attempts at refuting the view that medical discoveries may have been carried on by the applications of the experimental methods of agreement and difference and then accumulated through long ages are very weak and need not be considered here.

---

1 The word *upāṅga* may have been used, however, in the sense that it was a supplementary work having the same scope as the *Atharva-Veda*.

The fourth Veda, known as the *Atharva-Veda* or the *Brahma-Veda,* deals mainly with curatives and charms.[1] There is no reason to suppose that the composition of this Veda was later than even the earliest Ṛg-Vedic hymns; for never, probably, in the history of India was there any time when people did not take to charms and incantations for curing diseases or repelling calamities and injuring enemies. The *Ṛg-Veda* itself may be regarded in a large measure as a special development of such magic rites. The hold of the Atharvaṇic charms on the mind of the people was probably very strong, since they had occasion to use them in all their daily concerns. Even now, when the Ṛg-Vedic sacrifices have become extremely rare, the use of Atharvaṇic charms and of their descendants, the Tantric charms of comparatively later times, is very common amongst all classes of Hindus. A very large part of the income of the priestly class is derived from the performance of auspicious rites (*svastyayana*), purificatory penances *(prāyaś-citta*), and oblations (*homa*) for curing chronic and serious illnesses, winning a law-suit, alleviating sufferings, securing a male issue to the family, cursing an enemy, and the like. Amulets are used almost as freely as they were three or four thousand years ago, and snake-charms and charms for dog-bite and others are still things which the medical people find it difficult to combat. Faith in the

1 Some of the sacred texts speak of four Vedas and some of three Vedas, e.g. "*asya mahato bhūtasya nihśvasitam etad ṛg-vedoyajur-vedaḥ sāma-vedo 'tharvāñ-girasaḥ,*" *Bṛh.* I I.4.10 speaks of four Vedas; again "*Yam ṛṣayas trayī-vido viduḥ ṛcahsātnāniyajūṃṣi,*" *Taittirīya-brāhmaṇa,* I.11.1.26 speaks of three Vedas. Sāyaṇa refers to the *Mīmāṃsā-sūtra,* II.1.37 "*śeṣe Yajuḥ-śabdaḥ*" and says that all the other Vedas which are neither Ṛk nor Sāma are Yajuṣ (Sāyaṇa's *Upodghāta* to the *Atharva- Veda,* p. 4, Bombay edition, 1895). According to this interpretation the *Atharva-Veda* is entitled to be included within Yajuṣ, and this explains the references to the three Vedas. The *Atharva-Veda* is referred to in *the Gopatha-Brāhmaṇa,* II.16 as Brahma-Veda, and two different reasons are adduced. Firstly, it is said that the *Atharva-Veda* was produced by the ascetic penances of Brahman; secondlyit is suggested in the *Gopatha-Brahmāṇa* that all Atharvaṇic hymns are curative *(bheṣaja),* and whatever is curative is immortal, and whatever is immortal is Brahman—"*Ye 'tharvāṇas tad bheṣajaṃ, yad bheṣajaṃ tad amṛtaṃ, yad amṛtaṃ tad Brahma.*" *Gopatha-brāhmaṇa,* I I I.4. See also *Nyāya-mañjarī,* pp. 250-261.

mysterious powers of occult rites and charms forms an essential feature of the popular Hindu mind and it oftentimes takes the place of religion in the ordinary Hindu household. It may therefore be presumed that a good number of Atharvaṇic hymns were current when most of the Ṛg-Vedic hymns were not yet composed. By the time, however, that the *Atharva-Veda* was compiled in its present form some new hymns were incorporated with it, the philosophic character of which does not tally with the outlook of the majority of the hymns. The *Atharva-Veda,* as Sāyaṇa points out in the introduction to his commentary, was indispensable to kings for warding off their enemies and securing many other advantages, and the royal priests had to be versed in the Atharvaṇic practices. These practices were mostly for the alleviation of the troubles of an ordinary householder, and accordingly the *Gṛhya-sūtras* draw largely from them. The oldest name of the *Atharva-Veda* is *Atharvāṅgirasaḥ,* and this generally suggested a twofold division of it into hymns attributed to Atharvan and others attributed to Aṅgiras; the former dealt with the holy *(śānta),* promoting of welfare *(pauṣṭika)* and the curatives *(bheṣajāni),* and the latter with offensive rites for molesting an enemy (*ābhi-cārika*), also called terrible *(ghora).* The purposes which the Atharvaṇic charms were supposed to fulfil were numerous. These may be briefly summed up in accordance with the *Kauśika-sūtra* as follows: quickening of intelligence, accomplishment of the virtues of a Brahmacārin (religious student); acquisition of villages, cities, fortresses and kingdoms, of cattle, riches, food grains, children, wives, elephants, horses, chariots, etc.; production of unanimity (*aikamatya*) and contentment among the people; frightening the elephants of enemies, winning a battle, warding off all kinds of weapons, stupefying, frightening and ruining the enemy army, encouraging and protecting one's own army, knowing the future result of a battle, winning the minds of generals and chief persons, throwing a charmed snare, sword, or string into the fields where the enemy army may be moving, ascending a chariot for winning a battle, charming all instruments of war music, killing enemies, winning back a lost city demolished by the enemy; performing the coronation ceremony, expiating sins, cursing, strengthening cows, procuring prosperity; amulets for promoting welfare, agriculture, the conditions of bulls, bringing about various household properties, making a new-built house auspicious, letting loose a bull (as a part of the general rites—*śrāddha*), performing the rites of the harvesting month of Agrahāyaṇa (the middle of November to the middle of December); securing curatives for various otherwise incurable diseases produced by the sins of past life; curing all diseases generally, Fever, Cholera, and Diabetes; stopping the flow of blood from wounds caused by injuries from weapons, preventing epileptic fits and possession by the different species of evil spirits, such as the *bhūta, piśāca, Brahma-rākṣasa,* etc.; curing *vāta*, *pitta* and *śleṣman*, heart diseases, Jaundice, white leprosy, different kinds of Fever, Pthisis, Dropsy; curing worms in cows and horses, providing antidotes against all kinds of poisons, supplying curatives for the diseases of the head, eyes, nose, ears, tongue, neck and inflammation of the neck; warding off the evil effects of a Brahmin's curse; arranging women's rites for securing sons, securing easy delivery and the welfare of the foetus; securing prosperity, appeasing a king's anger, knowledge of future success or failure; stopping too much rain and thunder, winning in debates and stopping brawls, making rivers flow according to one's wish, securing rain, winning in gambling, securing the welfare of cattle and horses, securing large gains in trade, stopping inauspicious marks in women, performing auspicious rites for a new house, removing the sins of prohibited acceptance of gifts and prohibited priestly services; preventing bad dreams, removing the evil effects of unlucky stars under whose influence an infant may have been born, paying off debts, removing the evils of bad omens, molesting an enemy; counteracting the molesting influence of the charms of an enemy, performing auspicious rites, securing long life, performing the ceremonies at birth, naming, tonsure, the wearing of holy thread, marriage, etc.; performing funeral rites, warding off calamities due to the disturbance of nature, such as rain of dust, blood, etc., the appearance of *yakṣas rākṣasas,* etc., earthquakes, the appearance of comets, and eclipses of the sun and moon.

The above long list of advantages which can be secured by the performance of Atharvaṇic rites gives us a picture of the time when these Atharvaṇic charms were used. Whether all these functions were discovered when first the Atharvaṇic verses were composed is more than can be definitely ascertained. At present the evidence we possess is limited to that supplied by the *Kauśika-sūtra.* According to the Indian tradition accepted by Sāyaṇa the compilation of the *Atharva-Veda* was current in nine different collections, the readings of which differed more or less from one another. These different recensions, or *śākhās*, were Paippalāda, Tāṇḍa, Maṇḍa, Śaunakīya, Jājala, Jalada, Brahmavāda, Devādarśa, and Cāraṇavaidya. Of these only the Paippalāda and Śaunakīya recensions are available. The Paippalāda recension exists only in a single unpublished Tübingen manuscript first discovered by Roth.[1] It has been edited in facsimile and partly also in print. The Śaunakīya recension is what is now available in print. The Śaunakīya school has the *Gopatha-brāhmaṇa* as its Brāhmaṇa and five *sūtra* works, viz. *Kauśika, Vaitāna, Nakṣatra-kalpa, Āṅgirasa-kalpa* and *Śānti-kalpa;*[2] these are also known as the five *kalpas* (*pañca-kalpa*). Of these the *Kauśika-sūtra* is probably the earliest and most important, since all the other four depend upon it.[3] The *Nakṣatra-kalpa* and *Śānti-kalpa* are more or less of an astrological character. No manuscript of the *Āṅgirasa-kalpa* seems to be available; but from the brief notice of Sāyaṇa it appears to have been a manual for molesting one's enemies (*abhicāra-karma*). The *Vaitāna-sūtra* dealt with some sacrificial and ritualistic details. The *Kauśika-sūtra* was commented on by Dārila, Keśava, Bhadra and Rudra. The existence of

1 *Der Atharvaveda in Kashmir* by Roth.

2 The *Kauśika-sūtra is* also known as *Saṃhitā-vidhi* and *Saṃhitā-kalpa.* The three *kalpas, Nakṣatra, Aṅgirasa* and *Śānti*, are actually *Pariśiṣṭas.*

3 *'tatra Śākalyena saṃhitā-mantrāṇāṃ śāntika-pauṣṭikādiṣu karmasu viniyoga-vidhānāt saṃhitā-vidhir nāma Kauśikaṃ śūtraṃ; tad eva itarair upajīvyatvāt. Upodhghāta* of Sāyaṇa to the *Atharva-Veda, p. 25.*

the Cāraṇa-vaidya (wandering medical practitioners) *śākhā* reveals to us the particular *śākhā* of the *Atharva-Veda,* which probably formed the old Āyur-veda of the Ātreya-Caraka school, who identified the *Atharva-Veda* with Āyur-veda. The suggestion, contained in the word *Cāraṇa-vaidya*, that the medical practitioners of those days went about from place to place, and that the sufferers on hearing of the arrival of such persons approached them, and sought their help, is interesting.[1]

BONES IN THE ATHARVA-VEDA AND ĀYUR-VEDA

The main interest of the present chapter is in that part of the *Atharva-Veda* which deals with curative instructions, and for this the *Kauśika-sūtra* has to be taken as the principal guide. Let us first start with the anatomical features of the *Atharva-Veda.*[2] The bones counted are as follows: 1. heels (*pārṣṇī*, in the dual number, in the two feet);[3] 2. ankle-bones (*gulphau* in the dual number);[4]

1 Is it likely that the word *Caraka* (literally, a wanderer) had anything to do with the itinerant character of Caraka's profession as a medical practitioner?

2 Hymns II.33 and X.2 are particularly important in this connection.

3 Caraka also counts one *pārṣṇi* for each foot. Hoernle (*Studies in the Medicine of Ancient India,* p. 128) remarks on the fact, that Caraka means the backward and downward projections of the os calcis, that is, that portion of it which can be superficially seen and felt, and is popularly known as the heel. The same may be the case with the *Atharva-Veda.* Suśruta probably knew the real nature of it as a cluster (*kūrca*); for in *Śārīra-sthāna* VI he speaks of the astragalus as *kūrca-śiras,* or head of the cluster, but he counts the *pārṣṇi* separately. Hoernle suggests that by *pārṣṇi* Suśruta meant the os calcis, and probably did not think that it was a member of the tarsal cluster *(kūrca).* It is curious that Vāgbhaṭa I makes a strange confusion by attributing one *pārṣṇi* to each hand *(Aṣṭāṅga-saṃgraha,* I I. 5; also Hoernle, pp. 91-96).

4 *Gulpha* means the distal processes of the two bones of the leg, known as the malleoli. As counted by Caraka and also by Suśruta, there are four *gulphas.* See Hoernle's comment on Suśruta's division, Hoernle, pp. 81, 82, 102-104. Suśruta, III.V.19, has "*tala-kūrca-gulpha-saṃśritāni daśa,*" which Ḍalhaṇa explains as *tala* (5 *śalākās* and the one bone to which they are attached)—6 bones, *kūrca*—2 bones, *gulpha*—2 bones. Hoernle misinterpreted Ḍalhaṇa, and, supposing that he spoke of two *kūrcas* and two *gulphas* in the same leg, pointed out a number of inconsistencies and suggested a different reading of the Suśruta text. His translation of *valaya* as "ornament" in this connection is also hardly correct; *valaya* probably means "circular." Following Ḍalhaṇa, it is possible that the in-

3. digits (*aṅgulayaḥ* in the plural number);[1] 4. metacarpal and metatarsal bones (*ucchlaṅkhau* in the dual number, i.e. of the hands and feet);[2] 5. base (*pratiṣṭhā*);[3] 6. the knee-caps (*aṣṭhwantau* in the dual);[4] 7. the knee-joints (*jānunoḥ sandhī*);[5] 8. the shanks (*jaṅghe* in the dual);[6] 9. the pelvic cavity (*śroṇī* in the dual);[7] 10. the

---

terpretation is that there are two bones in one cluster *(kūrca)* in each leg, and the two bones form one circular bone *(valayāsthi)* of one *gulpha* for each leg. If this is accepted, much of what Hoernle has said on the point loses its value and becomes hypercritical. There are two *gulphas,* or one in each leg, according as the constituent pieces, or the one whole *valayāsthi,* is referred to. On my interpretation Suśruta knew of only two bones as forming the *kūrca,* and there is no passage in Suśruta to show that he knew of more. The os calcis would be the *pārṣṇi,* the astragalus, the *kūrca-śiras,* the two malleoli bones and the two *gulpha* bones.

1 Both Caraka and Suśruta count sixty of these phalanges *(pāṇi-pādāṅguli),* whereas their actual number is fifty-six only.

2 Caraka counts these metacarpal and metatarsal bones *(pāṇi-pāda-śalākā)* as twenty, the actual number. Suśruta collects them under *tala,* a special term used by him. His combined *tala-kūrca-gulpha* includes all the bones of the hand and foot excluding the *aṅguli* bones (phalanges).

3 Caraka uses the term *pāṇi-pāda-śalākādhiṣṭhāna,* Yājñavalkya, *sthāna,* and Suśruta, *kūrca.* Caraka seems to count it as one bone. *Kūrca* means a network of (1) flesh *(*māṁsa*),* (2) *śirā,* (3) *snāyu,* (4) bones (māṁsa-*śirā-snāyv-asthi-jālāni*). All these four kinds of network exist in the two joints of the hands and feet.

4 Hoernle remarks that in the *Atharva-Veda aṣṭhīvat* and *jānu* are synonymous; but the text, X.2.2, seems clearly to enumerate them separately. The *aṣṭhīvat* is probably the patella bone. Caraka uses the terms *jānu* and *kapālikā,* probably for the knee-cap (patella) and the elbow pan *(kapālikā). Kapālikā* means a small shallow basin, and this analogy suits the construction of the elbow pan. Suśruta uses the term *kūrpara* (elbow pan), not in the ordinary list of bones in *Śārīra,* V.19, but at the time of counting the *marma* in *Ibid.* VI.25.

5 This seems to be different from *aṣṭhīvat* (patella).

6 The tibia and the fibula in the leg. Caraka, Bhela, Suśruta and Vāgbhaṭa I describe this organ rightly as consisting of two bones. The *Atharva-Veda* justly describes the figure made bv them as being a fourfold frame having its ends closely connected together *(catuṣṭayaṃ yujyate saṃhitāntam).* The corresponding two bones of the fore-arm *(aratm)*—radius and ulna—are correctly counted by Caraka. Curiously enough, Suśruta does not refer to them in the bone-list. The *bāhu* is not enumerated in this connection.

7 Caraka speaks of two bones in the pelvic cavity, viz. the os innominatum on both sides. Modern anatomists think that each os innominatum is composed of three different bones: ilium, the upper portion, ischium, the lower part, and the pubis, the portion joined to the other innominate bone. The ilium and ischium, however, though they are two bones in the body of an infant, become fused together

thigh bones *(ūrū* in the dual);[1] 11. the breast bones *(uras)*;[2] 12. the windpipe *(grīvāḥ* in the plural);[3] 13. the breast *(stanau* in the

---

as one bone in adult life, and from this point of view the counting of ilium and ischium as one bone is justifiable. In addition to these a separate *bhagāsthi* is counted by Caraka. He probably considered (as Hoernle suggests) the sacrum and coccyx to be one bone which formed a part of the vertebral column. By *bhagāsthi* he probably meant the pubic bone; for Cakrapāṇi, commenting upon *bhagāsthi,* describes it as"*abhimukhaṃ kaṭi-sandhāna-kārakaṃ tiryag-asthi*" (the cross bone which binds together the haunch bones in front). Suśruta, however, counts five bones: four in the *guda, bhaga, nitamba* and one in the *trika. Nitamba* corresponds to the two *śroṇi-phalaka* of Caraka, *bhaga* to the *bhagāsthi,* or pubic bone, *guda* to the coccyx and *trika* to the triangular bone sacrum. Suśruta's main difference from Caraka is this, that, while the latter counts the sacrum and coccyx as one bone forming part of the vertebral column, the former considers them as two bones and as separate from the vertebral column. Vāgbhaṭa takes *trika* and *guda* as one bone, but separates it from the vertebral column.

1 Caraka, Suśruta and Vāgbhaṭa I count it correctly as one bone in each leg. Caraka calls it *ūru-nalaka.*

2 Caraka counts fourteen bones in the breast. Indian anatomists counted cartilages as new bones *(taruṇa asthi).* There are altogether ten costal cartilages on either side of the sternum. But the eighth, ninth and tenth cartilages are attached to the seventh. So, if the seventh, eighth, ninth and tenth cartilages are considered as a single bone, there are altogether seven bones on either side of the sternum. This gives us the total number of fourteen which Caraka counts. The sternum was not counted by Caraka separately. With him this was the result of the continuation of the costal cartilages attached to one another without a break. Suśruta and Vāgbhaṭa I curiously count eight bones in the breast, and this can hardly be accounted for. Hoernle's fancied restoration of the ten of Suśruta does not appear to be proved. Yājñavalkya, however, counts seventeen, i.e. adds the sternum and the eighth costal cartilage on either side to Caraka's fourteen bones, which included these three. Hoernle supposes that Yājñavalkya's number was the real reading in Suśruta; but his argument is hardly convincing.

3 The windpipe is composed of four parts, viz. larynx, trachea, and two bronchi. It is again not a bone, but a cartilage; but it is yet counted as a bone by the Indian anatomists, e.g. Caraka calls it "*jatru*" and Suśruta "*kaṇṭha-nāḍī.*" Hoernle has successfully shown that the word *jatru* was used in medical books as synonymous with windpipe or neck generally. Hoernle says that originally the word denoted cartilaginous portions of the neck and breast (the windpipe and the costal cartilages), as we read in the *Śatapatha-brāhmaṇa:* "*tasmād imā ubhayatra parśavo baddhāḥ kīkasāsu ca jatruṣu*" (the ribs are fastened at either end, exteriorly to the thoracic vertebrae and interiorly to the costal cartilages—*jatru).* In medical works it means the cartilaginous portion of the neck, i.e. the windpipe (Caraka), and hence is applied either to the neck generally or to the sterno-cla-

dual);[1] 14. the shoulder-blade *(kaphoḍau* in the dual);[2] 15. the shoulder-bones *(skandhān* in the plural);[3] 16. the backbone *(pṛṣṭīḥ* in the plu-

---

vicular articulation at the base of the neck (Suśruta). It is only as late as the sixth or seventh century AD that, owing to a misinterpretation of the anatomical terms *sandhi* and *aṃsa,* it was made to mean clavicle. See Hoernle's *Studies in the Medicine of Ancient India,* p. 168.

1 "*Pārśvayoś catur-viṃśatiḥ pārśvayos tāvanti caiva sthālakāni tāvanti caiva sthālakārbudāni* i.e. there are twenty-four bones in the *pārśva* (ribs), twenty-four *sthālakas* (sockets), and twenty-four *sthālakārbudas* (tubercles). Suśruta speaks of there being thirty-six ribs on either side. A rib consists of a shaft and a head; " at the point of junction of these two parts there is a tubercle which articulates with the transverse process of corresponding vertebrae, and probably this tubercle is *arbuda*." There are, no doubt, twenty-four ribs. The *sthālakas* and *arbudas* cannot properly be counted as separate bones; but, even if they are counted, the total number ought to be 68 bones, as Hoernle points out, and not 72, since the two lowest have no tubercles.

2 *Kaphoda* probably means scapula or shoulder-blade. Caraka uses the word *aṃsa-phalaka.* Caraka uses two other terms, *akṣaka* (collar-bone) and *aṃsa.* This word *aṃsa* seems to be a wrong reading, as Hoernle points out; for in reality there are only two bones, the scapula and the collar-bone. But could it not mean the acromion process of the scapula? Though Suśruta omits the shoulder-blade in the counting of bones in *Śārīra,* v. (for this term is *akṣaka-saṃjñe),* yet he distinctly names *aṃsa-phalaka* in *Śārīra,* VI.27, and describes it as triangular (*trika-saṃbaddhe*); and this term has been erroneously interpreted as *grīvāyā aṃsa-dvayasya ca* yaḥ *saṃyogas sa trikaḥ* by Ḍalhaṇa The junction of the collar-bone with the neck cannot be called *trika.*

3 Caraka counts fifteen bones in the neck. According to modem anatomists there are, however, only seven. He probably counted the transverse processes and got the number fourteen, to which he added the vertebrae as constituting one single bone.

Suśruta counts nine bones. The seventh bone contains spinous and transverse processes and was probably therefore counted by him as three bones, which, together with the other six, made the total number nine.

4 Caraka counts forty-three bones in the vertebral column (*pṛṣṭha-gatāsthi*), while the actual number is only twenty-six. Each bone consists of four parts, viz. the body, the spinous process, and the two transverse processes, and Caraka counts them all as four bones. Suśruta considers the body and the spinous process as one and the two transverse processes as two; thus for the four bones of Caraka, Suśruta has three. In Caraka the body and the spinous process of the twelve thoracic vertebrae make the number twenty-four; the five lumbar vertebrae (body + spine + two transverses) make twenty. He adds to this the sacrum and the coccyx as one pelvic bone, thus making the number forty-five; with Suśruta we have twelve thoracic vertebrae, six lumbar vertebrae, twelve transverses, i.e. thirty bones. The word *kīkasa* (A.V. II.33.2) means the whole of the spinal column, *anūkya* (A.V. II.33.2) means the thoracic portion of the spine, and *udara* the abdominal portion.

ral)[4]; 17. the collar-bones *(aṃsau* in the dual);[1] 18. the brow (*lalāṭa*); 19. the central facial bone (*kakāṭikā*);[2] 20. the pile of the jaw *(hanu-citya);*[3] 21. the cranium with temples (*kapālam*).[4]

ORGANS IN THE ATHARVA-VEDA AND ĀYUR-VEDA

We have no proofs through which we could assert that the writer of the *Atharva-Veda* verse knew the number of the different bones

---

1 Both Caraka and Suśruta call this *akṣaka* and count it correctly as two bones. Cakrapāṇi describes it as "*ahṣa-vivakṣakau jatru-sandheḥ kīlakau"* (they are called *akṣaka* because they are like two beams—the fastening-pegs of the junction of the neck-bones).

Suśruta further speaks of *aṃsa-pītha* (the glenoid cavity into which the head of the humerus is inserted) as a *samudga* (casket) bone. The joint of each of the anal bones, the pubic bone and the hip bone (*nitamba*) is also described by him as a *samudga.* This is the "acetabulum, or cotyloid cavity, in which the head of the femur, is lodged" (*Suśruta, Śārīra,* v.27, *arnsa-pīṭha-guda-bhaga-nitambeṣu samudgāḥ).*

2 *Lalāṭa* is probably the two superciliary ridges at the eye-brow and *kakāṣikā* the lower portion, comprising the body of the superior maxillary together with the molar and nasal bones. Caraka counts the two molar *(gaṇḍa-kūṭa*), the two nasal, and the two superciliary ridges at the eye-brows as forming one continuous bone (*ekāsthi nāsikā-gaṇḍa-kūṭa-lalāṭam*).

3 According to Caraka, the lower jaw only is counted as a separate bone *(ekaṃ hanv-asthi*), and the two attachments are counted as two bones *(dve hanu-mūla-bandhane).* Suśruta, however, counts the upper and the lower jaws as two bones (*hanvor dve).* Though actually each of these bones consists of two bones, they are so fused together that they may be considered as one, as was done by Suśruta. Caraka did not count the upper jaw, so he counted the sockets of the teeth (*dantolūkhala*) and the hard palate (*tāluṣaka*). Suśruta's counting of the upper *hanu* did not include the palatine process; so he also counts the *tālu* (*ekaṃ tāluni).*

4 *Śaṅkha* is the term denoting the temples, of which both Caraka and Suśruta count two. Caraka counts four cranial bones (*catvāri śiraḥ-kapālāni*) and Suśruta six (*śirasi ṣaṭ).* The brain-case consists of eight bones. Of these two are inside and hence not open to view from outside. So there are only six bones which are externally visible. Of these the temporal bones have already been counted as *Śaṅkha,* thus leaving a remainder of four bones. Suśruta divides the frontal, parietal and occipital bones into two halves and considers them as separate bones, and he thus gets the number six. Both the frontal and occipital are really each composed of two bones, which become fused in later life.

Though the author has often differed from Dr Hoernle, yet he is highly indebted to his scholarly explanations and criticisms in writing out this particular section of this chapter.

to which he refers; but it does not seem possible that the references made to bones could have been possible without a careful study of the human skeleton. Whether this was done by some crude forms of dissection or by a study of the skeletons of dead bodies in a state of decay is more than can be decided. Many of the organs are also mentioned, such as the heart *(hṛdaya),* the lungs (*kloma*),[1] the gall-bladder (*halikṣṇa*),[2] the kidneys (*matsnābhyām),*[3] the liver

1 Caraka counts *kloma* as an organ near the heart, but he does not count *pupphusa.* In another place (*Cikitsā*, XVII.34) he speaks of *kloma* as one of the organs connected with hiccough (*hṛdayaṃ kloma kaṇṭhaṃ ca tālukaṃ ca samāśritā mṛdvī sā kṣudra-hikveti nṛṇāṃ sādhyā prakīrtitā).* Cakrapāṇi describes it as *pipāsā-sthāna* (seat of thirst). But, whatever that may be, since Caraka considers its importance in connection with hiccough, and, since he does not mention *pupphusa* (lungs—*Mahā-vyutpatti,* 100), *kloma* must mean with him the one organ of the two lungs. Suśruta speaks of *pupphusa* as being on the left side and *kloma* as being on the right. Since the two lungs vary in size, it is quite possible that Suśruta called the left lung *pupphusa* and the right one *kloma.* Vāgbhaṭa I follows Suśruta. The *Atharva-Veda,* Caraka, Suśruta, Vāgbhaṭa and other authorities use the word in the singular, but in *Bṛhad-āraṇyaka,* I. the word *kloma* is used in the plural number; and Śaṅkara, in commenting on this, says that, though it is one organ, it is always used in the plural (*nitya-bahu-vacanānta).* This, however, is evidently erroneous, as all the authorities use the word in the singular. His description of it as being located on the left of the heart *(yakṛc ca klomātiaś ca hṛdayasyādhastād dakṣiṇottarau māṃsa-khaṇḍau,* Br. I.1, commentary' of Śaṅkara) is against the verdict of Suśruta, who places it on the same side of the heart as the liver. The *Bhāva-prakāśa* describes it as the root of the veins, where water is borne or secreted. That *kloma* was an organ which formed a member of the system of respiratory organs is further proved by its being often associated with the other organs of the neighbourhood, such as the throat (*kaṇṭha*) and the root of the palate (*tālu-mūla*). Thus Caraka says,
"उदकवहानां स्त्रोतसां तालुमूलं क्लों च...जिह्वाताल्वोष्टकण्ठक्लोमशोषम्...दृष्ट्वा"
"*udaka-vahānāṃ srotasāṃ tālu-mūlaṃ kloma ca....Jihvā-tālv-oṣṭha-kaṇṭha-kloma-śoṣam...dṛṣṭvā*" (*Vimāna,* V.10). *Śārṅgadhara,* I.V.45, however, describes it as a gland of watery secretions near the liver
(जलवाहिशिरामूलं तृष्णात्छादनकं तिलम्)
(*jala-vāhi-śirā-mūlaṃ tṛṣṇā-tchādanakaṃ tilam).*

2 This word does not occur in the medical literature. Sāyaṇa describes it as "*etat-saṃjñakāt tat-saṃbandhāt māṃsa-piṇḍa-viśeṣāt."* This, however, is quite useless for identification. Weber thinks that it may mean "gall" (*Indische Studien,* 13, 206). Macdonell considers it to be "some particular intestine" (*Vedic Index,* vol. II, p. 500).

3. Sāyaṇa gives an alternative explanation:
"मस्त्स्न्नाभ्याम् उधयपार्श्वसंबन्धाभ्यां वृक्याभ्यां तत्संईपस्थपिताधारपात्राभ्याम्"

(*yakna*), the spleen (*plīhan*), the stomach and the smaller intestine (*antrebhyaḥ*), the rectum and the portion above it *(gudābhyaḥ)*, the larger intestine *(vaniṣṭhu,* explained by Sāyaṇa as *sthavirāntra),* the abdomen (*udara*), the colon (*plāśi*),[1] the umbilicus (*nābhi*), the marrow (*majjābhyaḥ*), the veins *(snāvabhyaḥ)* and the arteries *(dhamanibhyaḥ).*[2] Thus we see that almost all the important organs reported in the later Ātreya-Caraka school or the Suśruta school were known to the composers of the Atharvaṇic hymns.[3]

Bolling raises the point whether the *Atharva-Veda* people knew the difference between the *śirā* and the *dhamani*, and says, "The apparent distinction between veins and arteries in I.17.3 is offset by the occurrence of the same words in VII.35.2 with the more-general sense of 'internal canals' meaning entrails, vagina, etc.—showing how vague were the ideas held with regard to such subjects."[4] But this is not correct; for there is nothing in I.17.3 which suggests a knowledge of the distinction between veins and arteries in the

---

"*matsnābhyām ubhaya-pārśva-saṃbandhābhyāṃ vṛkyābhyāṃ tat-saṃīpa-stha-pittādhāra-pātrābhyām.*"

If this explanation is accepted, then *matsnā* would mean the two sacs of *pitta* (bile) near the kidneys. The two *matsnās* in this explanation would probably be the gall bladder and the pancreas, which latter, on account of its secretions, was probably considered as another *pittādhāra.*

1 *Plāśi* is paraphrased by Sāvana as "*bahu-cchidrān mala-pātrāt*" (the vessel of the excreta with many holes). These holes are probably the orifices of the glands inside the colon *(mnla-pātra).* The *Śatapatha-brāhmaṇa,* XII.9.1.3 enumerates all these organs as being sacred to certain gods and sacrificial instruments—*hṛdayam evāsyaindraḥ puroḍāśaḥ, yakṛt sāvitraḥ, klomā vāruṇaḥ, matsne evāsyāśvatthaṃ ca pātram audumbaraṃ ca pittaṃ naiyagrodham antrāṇi sthālyaḥ gudā upāśayāni śyena-pātre plīhāsandī nābhih kumbho vaniṣṭhuḥ plāśiḥ śātātṛṇṇā tad yat sā bahudhā vitṛṇṇā bhavati tasmāt plāśir bahudhā vikṛttaḥ. Vasti,* or bladder, is regarded as the place where the urine collects (A.V. I.3.6).

2 Sāyaṇa says that *snāva* means here the smaller *śirās* and *dhamanī* the thicker ones (the arteries)—*sūksmāḥ śirāḥ snāva-śabdena uryante dhamani-śabdena sthūlāḥ* (A.V. II.33).

3 A.V. X. 9 shows that probably dissection of animals was also practised. Most of the organs of a cow are mentioned. Along with the organs of human beings mentioned above two other organs are mentioned, viz. the pericardium (*purītat*) and the bronchial tubes (*saha-kaṇṭhikā).* A.V. X.9.15.

4 *Encyclopaedia of Religion and Ethics,* "Diseases and medicine: Vedic."

modern sense of the terms, such as is not found in VII.35.2. The *sūkta* I.17 is a charm for stopping the flow of blood from an injury or too much hemorrhage of women. A handful of street-dust was to be thrown on the injured part and the hymn was to be uttered. In I.17.1 it is said, "Those *hirās* (veins?) wearing red garment (or the receptacles of blood) of woman which are constantly flowing should remain dispirited, like daughters without a brother."[1] Sāyaṇa, in explaining the next verse, I.17.2, says that it is a prayer to *dhamanis*. This verse runs as follows: "Thou (Sāyaṇa says 'thou *śirā*') of the lower part, remain (i.e. 'cease from letting out blood,' as Sāyaṇa says), so thou of the upper part remain, so thou of the middle part, so thou small, so thou the big *dhamani*."[2] In the third verse both the *hirās* and *dhamanis* are mentioned. "These in the middle were formerly (letting out blood) among a hundred *dhamanis* and thousands of *hirās* (and after that) all the other *(nāḍīs)* were playing with (others which have ceased from letting out blood)."[3] Hymn VII.35 is for stopping the issue of a woman who is an enemy. The third verse says, "I close with a stone the apertures of a hundred *hirās* and a thousand *dhamanis*." Sāyaṇa, in explaining this verse, says that the *hirās* are fine *nāḍīs* inside the ovary *(garbha-dhāraṇārtham antar-avasthitāḥ sūkṣmāyā nāḍyaḥ)* and the *dhamanis* the thicker *nāḍīs* round the ovary for keeping it steady *(garbhā-śayasya avaṣṭaṃbkikā bāhyā sthūlā yā nāḍyaḥ)*.

1 Sāyaṇa paraphrases *hirā* as *śirā* and describes it as a canal (nāḍī) for carrying blood (*rajo-vahana-nāḍyaḥ*), and the epithet "*lohita-vāsasaḥ*" as either wearing red garment" or "red," or "the receptacle of blood" *(rudhirasya nivāsa-bhūtāḥ)*.

2 The previous verse referred to *śirās* as letting out blood, whereas this verse refers to *dhamanis* as performing the same function. Sāyaṇa also freely paraphrases *dhamani* as *śirā (mahī mahatī sthūlatarā dhamaniḥ śirā tiṣṭhād it tiṣṭhaty eva, anena prayogeṇa nivṛtta-rudhira-srāvā avatiṣṭhatām)*.

3 Here both the *dhamani* and the *hirā* are enumerated. Sāyaṇa here says that *dhamanis* are the important *nāḍīs* in the heart (*hṛdaya-gatānām pradhāna-nāḍīnām)*, and *hirās* or *śirās* are branch *nāḍīs (śirāṇāṃ śākhā-nāḍinām)*. The number of *dhamanis,* as here given, is a hundred and thus almost agrees with the number of *nāḍīs* in the heart given in the *Kaṭha Upaniṣad,* VI.16 (*śatam caikā ca hṛdayas*· *nāḍyaḥ)*. The *Praśna Upaniṣad,* III.6 also speaks of a hundred *nāḍīs,* of ·· there are thousands of branches.

The only point of difference between this verse and those of I. 17 is that here *śirās* are said to be a hundred and *dhamanis* a thousand, whereas in the latter, the *dhamanis* were said to be a hundred and the *śirās* a thousand. But, if Sāyaṇa's interpretation is accepted, the *dhamanis* still appear as the bigger channels and the *śirās* as the finer ones. *Nāḍī* seems to have been the general name of channels. But nowhere in the *Atharva-Veda* is there any passage which suggests that the distinction between veins and arteries in the modern sense of the terms was known at the time. In A.V. I.3.6 we hear of two *nāḍīs* called *gavīnyau* for carrying the urine from the kidneys to the bladder.[1] The gods of the eight quarters and other gods are said to have produced the foetus and, together with the god of delivery (Sūṣā), facilitated birth by loosening the bonds of the womb.[2] The term *jarāyu* is used in the sense of placenta, which is said to have no intimate connection with the flesh and marrow, so that when it falls down it is eaten by the dogs and the body is in no way hurt. A reference is found to a first aid to delivery in expanding the sides of the vagina and pressing the two *gavīnikā nāḍīs*.[3] The *snāvas* (tendons) are also mentioned along with *dhamanis*, and Sāyaṇa explains them as finer *śirās (śuksmāḥ śirāh snāva-śabdena ucyante),* The division of *dhamanis, śirās* and *snāvas* thus seems to have been based on their relative fineness: the thicker channels *(nāḍīs)* were called *dhamanis,* the finer ones were called *śirās* and the still finer ones *snāvas*. Their general functions were considered more or less the same, though these probably differed according to the place in the body where they were situated and the organs with which they were associated. It seems to have been recognized

1 *antrebhyo vinirgatasya mūtrasya mūtrāśaya-prāpti-sādhane pārśva-dvayas-* ...*āḍyau gavīnyau ity ucyete.* Sāyaṇa's *Bhāṣya.* In I.11.5 two *nāḍīs* called ... are referred to and are described by Sāyaṇa as being the two *nāḍīs* on ...s of the vagina controlling delivery (*gavīnikā yoneḥ pārśva-vartin-* ...*pratibandhike nāḍyau*—Sāyaṇa). In one passage (A.V. II.12.7) ...lled *manya* are mentioned, and Sāyaṇa says that they are near ... *sikatāvatī,* on which strangury depends, is mentioned in

...ry, Sūṣāni, is also invoked.

...*gavīnike.* A.V. I.11.5.

that there was a general flow of the liquid elements of the body. This probably corresponds to the notion of *srotas*, as we get it in the *Caraka-saṃhitā*, and which will be dealt with later on. Thus A.V.X.2.11 says, "who stored in him floods turned in all directions moving diverse and formed to flow in rivers, quick (*tīvrā*), rosy *(aruṇā)*, red *(lohinī)*, and copper dark *(tāmra-dhūmrā)*, running all ways in a man upward and downward?" This clearly refers to the diverse currents of various liquid elements in the body. The semen, again, is conceived as the thread of life which is being spun out.[1] The intimate relation between the heart and the brain seems to have been dimly apprehended. Thus it is said, "together with his needle hath Atharvan sewn his head and heart."[2] The theory of the *vāyus,* which we find in all later literature, is alluded to, and the *prāṇa, apāna, vyāna* and *samāna* are mentioned.[3] It is however difficult to guess what these *prāṇa, apāna,* etc. exactly meant. In another passage of the *Atharva-Veda* we hear of nine *prāṇas (nava prāṇān navabhiḥ saṃmimīte),* and in another seven *prāṇas* are mentioned.[4] In another passage we hear of a lotus with nine gates (*nava-dvāraṃ*) and covered with the three *guṇas.*[5] This is a very familiar word in

---

1 *Ko asmin reto nyadadhāt tantur ātayatām iti* (Who put the semen in him, saying, Let the thread of life be spun out? A.V. X.2.17).

2 *Mūrdhānam asya saṃsīvyātharvā hṛdayaṃ ca yat* (A.V. X.2.26). See also Griffith's translations.

3 *Ko asmin prāṇam avayat ko apānaṃ vyānam u samānam asmin ko deve 'dhi śiśrāya pūruṣe* (Who has woven *prāṇa, apāna, vyāna* and *samāna* into him and which deity is controlling him? A.V. X.2.13).

4 *Sapta prāṇām aṣṭau manyas (or majjñas) tāṃs te vṛścāmi brahmaṇā* (A.V. II.12.7). The Taittrirīya-brāhmaṇa, I.2.3.3 refers to seven *prāṇas*, *sapta vai śīrśaṇyāh prāṇāh.* Again a reference to the seven senses is found in A.V. X.2.6: *kaḥ sapta khāni vitatarda śīrṣaṇi.* In A.V. XV.15.16.17 seven kinds of *prāṇa, apāna* and *vyāna* are described. These seem to serve cosmic functions. The seven *prāṇas* are *agni*, *āditya*, *candramāḥ*, *pavamāna*, *āpaḥ*, *paśavaḥ* and *prajāḥ*. The seven *apānas* are *paurṇamāsī*, *aṣṭakā*, *amōvāsyā*, *śraddhā*, *dīkṣā*, *yajña* and *dakṣiṇā.* The seven kinds of *vyāna* are *bhūmi*, *antarikṣaṃ*, *dyauḥ*, *nakṣatrāṇi*, *ṛtavaḥ*, *ārtavāḥ* and *saṃvatsarāḥ.*

5 पुण्डरीकंनवद्वारं त्रिभिर् गुणेभिर् आवृतं
तस्मिन् यद् यक्षम् आत्मन्वत् तद् वै ब्रह्मविदो विदुः
puṇḍarīkaṃ nava-dvāraṃ tribhir guṇebhir āvṛtaṃ
tasmin yad yakṣam ātmanvat tad vai Brahma-vido viduḥ.

later Sanskrit literature, as referring to the nine doors of the senses, and the comparison of the heart with a lotus is also very common. But one of the most interesting points about the passage is that it seems to be a direct reference to the *guṇa* theory, which received its elaborate exposition at the hands of the later Sāṃkhya writers: it is probably the earliest reference to that theory. As we have stated above, the real functions of the *prāṇa*, etc. were not properly understood; *prāṇa* was considered as vital power or life and it was believed to be beyond injury and fear. It was as immortal as the earth and the sky, the day and the night, the sun and the moon, the Brāhmaṇas and the Kṣattriyas, truth and falsehood, the past and the future.[1] A prayer is made to *prāṇa* and *apāna* for protection from death (*prāṇāpānau mṛtyor mā pātaṃ svāhā*).[2] In A.V.III.6.8 *manas* and *citta* are separately mentioned and Sāyaṇa explains *manas* as meaning *antaḥkaraṇa*, or inner organ, and *citta* as a particular state of the *manas* (*mano-vṛtti-viśeṣeṇa),* as thought.[3] Here also the heart is the seat of consciousness. Thus in a prayer in III.26.6 it is said, "O Mitra and Varuṇa, take away the thinking power *(citta)* from the heart *(hṛt)* of this woman and, making her incapable of judgment, bring her under my control."[4] The *ojas* with which we are familiar in later medical works of Caraka and others is mentioned in A.V. II.18, where Agni is described as being *ojas* and is asked to give *ojas* to the worshipper.[5]

(Those who know Brahman know that being to be the self which resides in the lotus flower of nine gates covered by the three *guṇas.* A.V. X.8 43.) The *nāḍis iḍā, piñgalā* and *suṣumṇā,* which figure so much in the later Tāntric works, do not appear in the *Atharva-Veda.* No reference to *prāṇāyāma* appears in the *Atharva- Veda.*

1 A.V. II.15.

2 *Ibid.* II.16.1. *Prāṇa* and *apāna* are asked in another passage to enter a man as bulls enter a cow-shed. Sāyaṇa calls *prāṇa, apāna* " *śarīras-dhāraka* " (A.V. III.11.5). They are also asked not to leave the body, but to bear the limbs till old age (III.11.6).

3 *Manas* and *citta* are also separately counted in A.V. III.6.8.

4 The word *cittinaḥ* is sometimes used to mean men of the same ways of thinking (*cittinaḥ samāna-citta-yuktāḥ*—Sāyaṇa. A.V. III.13 5).

5 *Ojo' sy ojo me dāḥ svāhā* (A.V. II.XVIII.1). Sāyaṇa, in explaining *ojaḥ,* says, "*ojaḥ śarīra-sthiti-kāraṇam aṣṭamo dhātuḥ.*" He quotes a passage as being spoken by the teachers (*ācāryaiḥ*):

PRACTICE OF MEDICINE IN THE ATHARVA-VEDA

As we have said above, there is evidence to show that even at the time of the *Atharva-Veda* the practice of pure medicine by professional medical men had already been going on. Thus the verse II.9.3, as explained by Sāyaṇa, says that there were hundreds of medical practitioners *(śataṃ hy asya bhiṣajaḥ)* and thousands of herbs *(sahasram uta vīrudhaḥ),* but what can be done by these can be effected by binding an amulet with the particular charm of this verse.[1] Again (II.9.5), the Atharvan who binds the amulet is described as the best of all good doctors (*subhiṣaktama*). In VI.68.2 Prajāpati, who appears in the Ātreya-Caraka school as the original teacher of Āyur-veda and who learnt the science from Brahmā, is asked to treat (with medicine) a boy for the attainment of long life.[2] In the *Kauśika-sūtra* a disease is called *liṅgi,* i.e. that which has the symptoms (*liṅga*), and medicine (*bhaiṣajya*) as that which destroys it *(upatāpa).* Dārila remarks that this *upatāpa-karma* refers not only to the disease, but also to the symptoms, i.e. a *bhaiṣajya* is that which destroys the disease and its symptoms.[3] In the *Atharva-Veda* itself only a few medicines are mentioned, such as *jaṅgiḍa* (XIX.34 and 35), *gulgulu* (XIX.38), *kuṣṭha* (XIX.39) and *śata-vāra* (XIX.36), and these are all to be.used as amulets for protection not

---

"क्सेत्रज्ञस्य तद् ओजस् तु केवलाश्रय इष्यते यथा स्नेहः प्रदीपस्य यथाभ्रम् अशनित्विषः"
"*ksetrajñasya tad ojas tu kevalāśraya iṣyate yathā snehaḥ pradīpasya yathbhram aśani-tviṣaḥ*" (Just as the lamp depends on the oil and the lightning on the clouds so the ojaḥ depends on the *kṣhetra-jña* (self) alone).

1 शतं या भेषजानि ते सुहस्त्रं संगतानि च।
श्रेष्ठम् आस्त्रावभेषजं वसिष्ठं रोगनाशनम्॥
Śataṃ yā bheṣajāni te suhasraṃ saṃgatāni ca
śreṣṭham āsrāva-bheṣajaṃ vasiṣṭhaṃ roga-nāśanam.
(Oh sick person! you may have applied hundreds or thousands of medicinal herbs; but this charm is the best specific for stopping hemorrhage. A.V. VI.45.2.) Here also, as in II.9.3, the utterance of the charm is considered to be more efficacious than the application of other herbs and medicines. Water was often applied for washing the sores (VI.57.2).

2 *Cikitsatu Prajāpatir dīrghāyutvāya cakṣase* (VI.68.2).

3 Dārila's comment on the *Kauśika-sūtra,* 25.2.

only from certain diseases, but also from the witchcraft *(kṛtyā)* of enemies. The effect of these herbs was of the same miraculous nature as that of mere charms or incantations. They did not operate in the manner in which the medicines prescribed in the ordinary medical literature acted, but in a supernatural way. In most of the hymns which appear as pure charms the *Kauśika-sūtra* directs the application of various medicines either internally or as amulets. The praise of Atharvan as physician *par excellence* and of the charms as being superior to all other medicines prescribed by other physicians seems to indicate a period when most of these Atharvaṇic charms were used as a system of treatment which was competing with the practice of ordinary physicians with the medicinal herbs. The period of the *Kauśika-sūtra* was probably one when the value of the medicinal herbs was being more and more realized and they were being administered along with the usual Atharvaṇic charms. This was probably a stage of reconciliation between the drug system and the charm system. The special hymns dedicated to the praise of certain herbs, such as *jaṅgiḍa*, *kuṣṭha*, etc., show that the ordinary medical virtues of herbs were being interpreted on the miraculous lines in which the charms operated. On the other hand, the drug school also came under the influence of the *Atharva-Veda* and came to regard it as the source of their earliest authority. Even the later medical literature could not altogether free itself from a faith in the efficacy of charms and in the miraculous powers of medicine operating in a supernatural and non-medical manner. Thus Caraka, VI.1.39 directs that the herbs should be plucked according to the proper rites (*yathā-vidhi*), and Cakrapāṇi explains this by saying that the worship of gods and other auspicious rites have to be performed *(maṅgala-devatārcanādi-pūrvakaṃ)*; in VI.1.77 a compound of herbs is advised, which, along with many other virtues, had the power of making a person invisible to all beings *(adṛśyo bhūtānāṃ bhavati)*; miraculous powers are ascribed to the fruit *āmalaka* (Emblic Myrobalan), such as that, if a man lives among cows for a year, drinking nothing but milk, in perfect sense-control and continence and meditating the holy *gāyatrī* verse, and if at the end of the year on a proper lunar day in the month of Pauṣa (January), Māgha (February), or Phālguna (March), after fasting for three days, he should enter an *āmalaka* garden and, climbing upon a tree full of big fruits, should hold them and repeat *(japan)* the name of Brahman till the *āmalaka* attains immortalizing virtues, then, for that moment, immortality resides in the *āmalaka*; and, if he should eat those *āmalakas*, then the goddess Śrī, the incarnation of the Vedas, appears in person to him *(svayaṃ cāsyopatiṣṭhantī śrīr vedavākya-rūpiṇī,* VI.3.6). In VI.1.80 it is said that the *rasāyana* medicines not only procure long life, but, if they are taken in accordance with proper rites (*yathā-vidhi*), a man attains the immortal Brahman. Again in VI.1.3 the word *prāyaś-citta* (purificatory penance) is considered to have the same meaning as *auṣadha* or *bheṣaja.* The word *bheṣaja* in the *Atharva-Veda* meant a charm or an amulet which could remove diseases and their symptoms, and though in later medical literature the word is more commonly used to denote herbs and minerals, either simple or compounded, the older meaning was not abandoned.[1] The system of simple herbs or minerals, which existed independently of *the Atharva-Veda*, became thus intimately connected with the system of charm specifics of the *Atharva-Veda*; whatever antagonism may have before existed between the two systems vanished, and Āyur-veda came to

1 The A.V. terms are *bheṣajam* (remedy), *bheṣajī* (the herbs), and *bheṣajīḥ* (waters). The term *bhaiṣajya* appears only in the *Kauśika* and other *sūtras* and Brāhmaṇas. Bloomfield says that the existence of such charms and practices is guaranteed moreover at least as early as the Indo-Iranian (Aryan) period by the stems *baeṣaza* and *baeṣazya (mañthra baeṣaza* and *baeṣazya; haoma baeṣazya),* and by the pre-eminent position of water and plants in all prayers for health and long life. Adalbert Kuhn has pointed out some interesting and striking resemblances between Teutonic and Vedic medical charms, especially in connection with cures for worms and fractures. These may perhaps be mere anthropological coincidences, due to the similar mental endowment of the two peoples. But it is no less likely that some of these folk-notions had crystallized in prehistoric times, and that these parallels reflect the continuation of a crude Indo-European folklore that had survived among the Teutons and Hindus. See Bloomfield's *The Atharva-Veda and Gopatha-Brāhmaṇa,* P. 58, and Kuhn's *Zeitschrift für vergleichende Sprachforschung,* XIII. PP. 49-74 and 113-157.

be treated as a part of the *Atharva-Veda.*[1] Prajāpati and Indra, the mythical physicians of the *Atharva-Veda,* came to be regarded in the Ātreya-Caraka school as the earliest teachers of Āyur-veda.[2]

Bloomfield arranges the contents of the *Atharva-Veda* in fourteen classes: 1. Charms to cure diseases and possession by demons *(bhaiṣajyāni)*; 2. Prayers for long life and health *(āyuṣyāṇi)*; 3. Imprecations against demons, sorcerers and enemies *(ābhicārikāni* and *kṛtyā-pratiharaṇāni)*; 4. Charms pertaining to women (*strī-karmāṇi*); 5. Charms to secure harmony, influence in the assembly, and the like *(saumanasyāni)*; 6. Charms pertaining to royalty (*rāja-karmāṇi*); 7. Prayers and imprecations in the interest of Brahmins; 8. Charms to secure property and freedom from danger *(pauṣṭikāni);* 9. Charms in expiation of sin and defilement *(prūyaścittāni)*; 10. Cosmogonic and theosophic hymns; 11. Ritualistic and general hymns; 12. The books dealing with individual themes (books 13-18); 13. The twentieth book; 14. *The kuntāpa* hymns;[3] of these we have here to deal briefly with 1, 2, 3, 4 and 9, more or less in the order in which they appear in the *Atharva-Veda.* A.V. I.2 is a charm against fever (*jvara*), diarrhoea (*atīsāra*), diabetes (*atimūtra*), glandular sores (*nāḍī-maṇa*); a string made of *muñja* grass is to be tied, the mud from a field or ant-hill is to be drunk, clarified butter is to be applied and the holes of the anus and penis and the mouth of the sore are to be aerated with a leather bladder and the charm is to be chanted. The disease *āsrāva*, mentioned in this

---

1 The *Atharva-Veda* itself speaks (XIX.34.7) of herbs which were current in ancient times and medicines which were new, and praises the herb *jaṅgiḍa* as being better than them all—*na tvā pūrva oṣadhayo na tvā taranti yā navāḥ.*

2 A.V. VI.68.2—*Cikitsatu prajāpatir dīrghāyutvāya cakṣase*; *Ibid.* XIX.35.1—*Indrasya nāma gṛhṇanto ṛṣayaḥ jaṅgiḍaṃ dadan* (The *ṛṣis* gave *jaṅgiḍa,* uttering the name of Indra). This line probably suggested the story in the *Caraka-saṃhitā,* that Indra first instructed the *ṛṣis* in Āyur-veda. See *Ibid.* XI.VIII.23—*yan mātatī rathakrītam amṛtaṃ veda bheṣajaṃ tad irtdro apsu prāveśayat tad āpo datta bheṣajam.* The immortalizing medicine which Mātali (the charioteer of Indra) bought by selling the chariot was thrown into the waters by Indra, the master of the chariot. Rivers, give us back that medicine!

3 Mr Bloomfield's *The Atharva-Veda and Gopatha-Brāhmaṇa,* P. 57.

hymn, is explained by Sāyaṇa as meaning diabetes (*mūtrātisāra*).[1] I. 3 is a charm against stoppage of urine and stool *(mūtra-purīṣa-nirodha)*. Along with a chanting of the hymn the patient is to be made to drink either earth from a rat's hole (*mūṣika-mṛttikā*), a *pūtikā* plant, curd, or saw-dust from old wood, or he is to ride an elephant or a horse, or to throw an arrow; a fine iron needle was to be passed through the urinal canal. This is probably the earliest stage of what developed in later times as the *vasti-kriyā*.[2] I.7 and I.8 are charms for driving away evil spirits, *yātudhānas* and *kimīdins*, when a man is possessed by them. I.10 is a charm for dropsy (*jalodara*): a jugful of water containing grass, etc. is to be sprinkled over the body of the patient. I.11 is a charm for securing easy delivery. I.12 is a charm for all diseases arising from disturbance of *vāta, pitta* and *śleṣman*—fat, honey and clarified butter or oil have to be drunk. Head-disease (*śīrṣakti*) and cough *(kāsa)* are specially mentioned. I.17 is a charm for stopping blood from an injury of the veins or arteries or for stopping too much hemorrhage of women. In the case of injuries a handful of street-dust is to be thrown on the place of injury or a bandage is to be tied with sticky mud.[3] I.22 is a charm against heart-discase and jaundice—hairs of a red cow are to be drunk with water and a piece of a red cow's skin is to be tied as an amulet. It is prayed that the red colour of the sun and the red cow may come to the patient's body and the yellow colour due to jaundice may go to birds of yellow colour. I.23, which mentions *kilāsa* or *kuṣṭha* (white leprosy) of the bone, flesh and skin and the disease by which hairs are turned grey (*palita*), is a charm against these.[4]

1 Bloomfield says that *āsrāva* means *atīsāra* or diarrhoea *(Ibid.* p. 59). The same physical applications for the same diseases are directed in A.V. II.3. *Āsrāva* denotes any disease which is associated with any kind of diseased ejection. Thus in II.3.2 Sāyaṇa says that *āsrāva* means *atīsārātimūtra-nāḍī-vraṇādayaḥ.*

2 *Pra te bhinadmi mehanaṃ vartraṃ veśantyā iva evā te mūtraṃ mucyatām bahir bāl iti sarvakam* (I open your urinal path like a canal through which the waters rush. So may the urine come out with a whizzing sound—A.V. I.3.7). All the verses of the hymn ask the urine to come out with a whizzing sound.

3 IV.12 is also a charm for the same purpose.

4 VI.135-137 is also a charm for strengthening the roots of the hair. *Kākamāci with bhṛṅga-rāja* has to be drunk.

The white parts are to be rubbed with an ointment made of cow-dung, *bhṛṅga-rāja*, *haridrā indravanmī* and *nīlikā* until they appear red. The black medicines applied are asked to turn the white parts black. I.25 is a charm against *takman,* or fever—the patient has to be sprinkled with the water in which a red-hot iron axe has been immersed. The description shows that it was of the malarial type; it came with cold *(śīta)* and a burning sensation (*śoci*). Three types of this fever are described: that which came the next day (*anyedyuḥ*), the second day (*ubhayedyuḥ*), or the third day (*tṛtīyaka*).[1] It was also associated with yellow, probably because it produced jaundice. II.9 and 10 are charms against hereditary (*kṣetrīya*) diseases, leprosy, dyspepsia, etc.[2] Amulets of *arjuna* wood, barley, sesamum and its flower had also to be tied when the charm was uttered.[3] II.31 is a charm against various diseases due to worms. The priest, when uttering this charm, should hold street-dust in his left hand and press it with his right hand and throw it on the patient. There are visible and invisible worms; some of them are called *algaṇḍu* and others *śaluna* they are generated in the intestines, head and heels; they go about through the body by diverse ways and cannot be killed even with various kinds of herbs. They sometimes reside in the hills and forests and in herbs and animals, and they enter into our system through sores in the body and through various kinds of food and drink.[4] II.33 is a charm for removing *yakṣman* from

---

1 नमः शीतय तक्मने नमो रुराय शोचिषे कृणोमि।
यो अन्येद्युर् उभयेद्युर् अभ्येति तृतीयकाय नमो अस्तु तक्मने॥
Namaḥ śītaya takmane namo rūrāya śocișe kṛṇomi
Yo anyedyur ubhayedyur abhyeti tṛtīyakāya namo astu takmane.
See also A.V. VII.123.10, where the third-day fever, fourth-day fever and irregular fevers are referred to.

2 The word *kṣetrīya* has been irregularly derived in Pāṇini's rule, V.2.92 (*kṣetriyac parakṣetre cikitsyaḥ).* Commentaries like the *Kāśika* and the *Pada-mañjarī* suggest one of its meanings to be "curable in the body of another birth" *(janmāntara-śarīre cikitsyaḥ),* that is, incurable. I, however, prefer the meaning "hereditary," as given by Sāyaṇa in his commentary on A.V. II.10.1, as being more fitting and reasonable.

3 *Yakṣman* is also counted as a *kṣetrīya* disease (II.10.6).

4 II.31.5. I have adopted Sāyaṇa's interpretation.

all parts of the body. III.7.1 is a charm for removing all hereditary (*kṣetrīya*) diseases; the horn of a deer is to be used as an amulet. III.11 is a charm against phthisis *(rāja-yakṣman)*—particularly when it is generated by too much sex-indulgence; the patient is to eat rotten fish,[1] IV.4 is a charm for attaining virility—the roots of the *kapittha* tree boiled in milk are to be drunk when the charm is uttered, IV.6 and 7 are charms against vegetable poisoning—the essence of the *kṛmuka* tree is to be drunk, V.4 is a charm against fever (*takman*) and phthisis; the patient is to take the herb *kuṣṭha* with butter when the charm is uttered,[2] V.11 is a charm against fever,[3] V.23 is a charm against worms—the patient is given the juice of the twenty kinds of roots,[4] VI.15 is a charm for eye-diseases; the patient has to take various kinds of vegetable leaves fried in oil, particularly the mustard plant,[5] VI.20 is a charm against bilious fever *(śuṣmiṇo jvarasya)*; it is said to produce a great burning sensation, delirium and jaundice, VI.21 is a charm for increasing the hair—the hair is to be sprinkled with a decoction of various herbs, VI.23 is a charm against heart-disease, dropsy and jaundice, VI.25 is a charm for inflammation of the glands of the neck *(jgaṇḍa-māla)*.[6] VI.85 is a charm against consumption *(rājay-akṣman);* VI.90 for

1 VII.78 is also a charm for inflammation of the neck (*gaṇḍa-mālā*) and phthisis *(yakṣma)*.

2 *Kuṣṭha* was believed to be good for the head and the eyes (V.4.10).

3 Gāndhāra Mahāvrṣa, Muñjavān, and particularly Bālhīka (Balkh), were regarded as the home of fever; so also the country of Aṅga and Magadha. It was accompanied by cold (*śīta*) and shivering (*rūraḥ*). It was often attended with cough (*kāsa*) and consumption (*valāsa)*. It attacked sometimes on the third or fourth day, in summer or in autumn (*śārada*), or continued all through the year.

4 This is one of the few cases where a large number of roots were compounded together and used as medicine along with the charms.

5 Some of the other plants are *alasālā, silāñjālā, nīlāgalasālā.*

6 Also VII.78, where *apacit* appears as a name for the inflammation of the neck *(gala-gaṇḍa)*. Three different types of the disease are described. *Apacit* is at first harmless, but when it grows, it continues more to secrete its discharges, like boils on the joints. These boils grow on the neck, the back, the thigh-joint and the anus. See further VI.83, where conch-shell is to be rubbed and applied. VIII.83 is also a charm for it. Blood had to be sucked off the inflamed parts by a leech or an iguana *(gṛha-godhikā)*.

colic pain (*śūla*);[1] VI.105 for cough and other such diseases due to phlegm (*śleṣmā*); VI.109 for diseases of the rheumatic type (*vāta-vyādhi).*[2] VI.127 is a charm for abscess (*vidradha*), phlegmatic diseases *(valāsa)* and erysipelatous inflammation (*visarpa*). Various kinds of *visarpa* in different parts of the body are referred to. Heart-disease and phthisis are also mentioned.[3] There are said to be a hundred kinds of death (*mṛtyu*) (A.V. VIII.5.7), which are explained by Sāyaṇa as meaning diseases such as fever, head-disease, etc. Several diseases are mentioned in IX.18—first the diseases of the head, *śīrṣakti*, *śīrṣāmaya*, *karṇa-śūla* and *visalpaka,* by which secretions of bad smell come out from the ear and the mouth, then fever proceeding from head troubles with shivering and cracking sensations in the limbs. *Takman,* the dreaded autumnal fever, is so described. Then comes consumption; then come *valāsa, kāhābāha* of the abdomen, diseases of *kloma,* the abdomen, navel and heart, diseases of the spine, the ribs, the eyes, the intestines, the *visalpa, vidradha*, wind-diseases *(vāṭīkāra), alaji* and diseases of the leg, knee, pelvis, veins and head.

Bolling, in his article on diseases and medicine (Vedic) in the *Encyclopaedia of Religion and Ethics*, makes the following remark concerning the theory of the origin of diseases. "To be noted however is the fact that the Hindu theory of the constitution of the body of three elements, bile, phlegm and wind, does not appear in early Atharvan texts. *Vātī-kṛta-nāśanī* of VI.44.3 cannot be urged as proof to the contrary, as it means, not destructive of (diseases) produced by the wind in the body *vātī-kṛta-nāśanī*), but destructive of that which has been made into wind. Evidently, from its association with diarrhoea, it refers to wind in the intestines." This does not seem to me to be correct. The phrase which Bolling quotes is indeed of doubtful meaning; Sāyaṇa takes it as being composed

1 A piece of iron is to be tied as an amulet.

2 *Pippalī* is also to be taken along with the utterance of the charm. It is regarded as the medicine for all attacked by the diseases of the wind (*vātī - kṛtasya bheṣajīm).* It is also said to cure madness (*kṣiptasya bheṣajīm).*

3 *Cīpudru* is a medicine for *valāsa. Cīpudrur abhicakṣaṇam* (VI.127.2).

of two words, *vātī* (healer by aeration) and *kṛta-nāśanī* (destroyer of evil deeds which brought about the disease). But, however that may be, there are other passages on the subject, which Bolling seems to have missed. Thus in I.12.3 diseases are divided into three classes, viz. those produced by water, by wind, and those which are dry—*yo abhrajā vātajā yaś ca śuṣmaḥ.*[1] The phlegm of the later medical writers was also considered watery, and the word *abhraja* probably suggests the origin of the theory of phlegm, as being one of the upholders and destroyers of the body. The word *vātaja* means, very plainly, diseases produced by wind, and the *pitta,* or bile, which in later medical literature is regarded as a form of fire, is very well described here as *śuṣma*, or dry. Again in VI.109 we have *pippalī* as *vātī-kṛtasya bheṣajīm.* The context shows that the diseases which are referred to as being curable by *pippalī* are those which are considered as being produced by wind in later literature; for "madness" *(kṣipta)* is mentioned as a *vātī-kṛta* disease. The word *śuṣma* comes from the root "*śuṣ*" to dry up, and in slightly modified forms is used to mean a "drying up," "burning," "strength," and "fiery." In one place at least it is used to describe the extremely burning sensation of delirious bilious fever, which is said to be burning like fire.[2] My own conclusion therefore is that at least some Atharvaṇic people had thought of a threefold classification of all diseases, viz. those produced by wind, those by water, and those by fire, or those which are dry and burning. This corresponds to the later classification of all diseases as being due to the three *doṣas,* wind *(vāyu),* phlegm *(kapha* or *śleṣma)* and bile *(pitta).* Apart from the ordinary diseases, many were the cases of possession by demons and evil spirits, of which we have quite a large number. Some of the prominent ones are *Yātudhāna*, *Kimīdin, Piśāca*, *Piśācī, Amīvā, Dvayāvin, Rakṣaḥ, Magundī, Alimṃśa*, *Vatsapa, Palāla, Anupalāla*, *Śarku, Koka, Malimluca, Palijaka, Vavrivā-*

1 Compare also *vāṭīkārasya* (IX.13.20).

2 VI.20.4. For other references where the word *śuṣma* occurs in more or less modified forms see I.12.3, III.9.3, IV.4.3, IV.4.4, V.2.4, V.20.2, VI.65.1, VI.73.2, IX.1.10, 20, IX.4.22, etc.

sas, Āśreṣa, Rkṣagrīva, Pramīlin, Durṇāmā, Sunāmā, Kukṣila, Kusūla, Kakubha, Śrima, Arāya, Karuma, Khalaja, Śakadhūmaja, Uruṇḍa, Maṭmaṭa, Kumbhamuṣka, Sāyaka, Nagnaka, Taṅgalva, Pavīnasa, Gandharva, Brahmagraha, etc.[1] Some of the diseases with their troublous symptoms were (poetically) personified, and diseases which often went together were described as being related as brothers and sisters. Diseases due to worms were well known, in the case of both men and of cattle. There were also the diseases due to sorcery, which played a very important part as an offensive measure in Vedic India. Many of the diseases were also known to be hereditary *(kṣetrīya)*. From the names of the diseases mentioned above it will be found that most of the diseases noted by Caraka existed in the Vedic age.

The view-point from which the Vedic people looked at diseases seems to have always distinguished the different diseases from their symptoms. Thus the fever was that which produced shivering, cold, burning sensation, and the like, i.e. the diagnosis was mainly symptomatic. In addition to the charms and amulets, and the herbs which were to be internally taken, water was considered to possess great medical and life-giving properties. There are many hymns which praise these qualities of water.[2] The medicinal properties of herbs were often regarded as being due to water, which formed their essence. Charms for snake poisons and herbs which were considered to be their antidotes were in use. Scanty references to diseases and their cures are found sparsely scattered in other ṚgVedic texts and Brāhmaṇas. But nothing in these appears to indicate

1 See I.28.35, II.9, II.14, VIII.6. The last passage contains a good description of some of these beings. There were some good spirits which fought with evil ones and favoured men, such as Piṅga, who preserved the babe at birth and chased the amorous Gandharvas as wind chases cloud, VIII.6.19, 25 says that sometimes the higher gods are also found to bring diseases. Thus Takman was the son of Varuṇa (VI.96.2) and he produced dropsy (I.10.1-4, II.10.1, IV.16.7, etc.). Parjanya (rain-god) produced diarrhoea, and Agni produced fever, headache and cough.

2 *apsu antar amṛtam apsu bheṣajam* (There is immortality and medicine in water—I.4.4). See also I.5.6, 33, II.3, III.7.5, IV.33, VI.24.92, VI.24.2, etc.

any advance on the *Atharva-Veda*[1] in medical knowledge. Apart from these curatives there were also the already mentioned charms, amulets and medicines for securing long life and increasing virility, corresponding to the *Rasāyana* and the *Vājī-karaṇa* chapters of Caraka and other medical works. We cannot leave this section without pointing to the fact that, though most diseases and many remedies were known, nothing in the way of *nidāna*, or causes of diseases, is specified. The fact that there existed a threefold classification of diseases, viz. *abhraja, vātaja* and *śuṣma*, should not be interpreted to mean that the Vedic people had any knowledge of the disturbance of these elements operating as *nidānas* as they were understood in later medical literature. The three important causes of diseases were evil deeds, the sorcery of enemies, and possession by evil spirits or the anger of certain gods.

THE FOETUS AND THE SUBTLE BODY

A human body is regarded by Caraka as a modification of the five elements, ether, air, fire, water and earth, and it is also the seat of consciousness (*cetanā*).[2] The semen itself is made of the four elements, air, fire, water and earth; ether is not a constituent of it, but becomes connected with it as soon as it issues forth, since *ākāśa* or *antariksa* (ether) is all-pervading. The semen that is ejected and passes into the ovary is constituted of equal parts of air, fire, water and earth; the ether becomes mixed with it in the ovary; for *ākāśa* itself is omnipresent and has no movement of its own;[3] the semen

1 For a brief survey of these Ṛg-Vedic and other texts see Bolling's article "Disease and Medicine (Vedic)" in *Encyclopaedia of Religion and Ethics.*

2 *garbhas tu khalu antarikṣa vāyv-agni-toya-bhūmi-vikāraś cetanādhiṣṭhāna-bhūtaḥ.*—Caraka, IV.4.6.

3 *vāyu-agni-bhūmy-ab-guṇa-pādavat tat ṣaḍbhyo rasebhyaḥ prabhāvaś ca tasya.* Caraka, IV.2.4.
आकाशं तु यदुअपि शुक्रे पञ्चभौतिकेऽस्ति तथापि न पुरुषशरीरान् निर्गत्य गर्भाशयं गच्छति, किन्तु भूतचतुष्टयम् एव क्रियावड् याति आकाशं तु व्यापकम् एव तत्रागतेन शुक्रेण संबद्धं भवति॥
ākāśaṃ tu yady-api śukre pāñca-bhautike 'sti tathāpi na puruṣa-śarīrān nirgatya garbhāśayaṃ gacchati, kintu bhūta-catuṣṭayam eva kriyāvad yāti ākāśaṃ tu vyāpakam eva tatrāgatena śukreṇa saṃbaddhaṃ bhavati.

is the product of six kinds of fluids *(rasa)*. But the foetus cannot be produced simply by the union of the semen of the father and the blood (*śoṇita*) of the mother. Such a union can produce the foetus only when the *ātman* with its subtle body, constituted of air, fire, water and earth, and *manas* (mind—the organ involved in all perception and thought), becomes connected with it by means of its *karma*. The four elements constituting the subtle body of the *ātman*, being the general causes of all productions, do not contribute to the essential bodily features of the child.[1] The elements that contribute to the general features are, (1) the mother's part—the blood, (2) the father's part—the semen, (3) the *karma* of each individual; the part played by the assimilated food-juice of the mother need not be counted separately, as it is determined by the *karma* of the individual. The mental traits are determined by the state of mind of the individual in its previous birth. Thus, if the previous state of life was that of a god, the mind of the child will be pure and vigorous, whereas, if it was that of an animal, it will be impure and dull.[2]

Cakrapāṇi's *Āyur-veda -dipikā*, IV.2.4. Suśruta however considers *śukra* (semen) as possessing the qualities of *soma,* and *ārtava* (blood) as possessing the qualities of fire. He says, however, that particles of the other *bhūtas* (earth, air and ether, as Ḍalhaṇa enumerates them) are separately associated with them सौम्यं शुक्रं आर्तवम् आग्नेयम् इतरेषाम् अप्य् अत्र भूतानां सान्निध्यं अस्त्य् अणुना विशेषेण परस्परोपकारात् परानुग्रहात् परस्परानुप्रवेशाच् च
(*saumyaṃ śukram ārtavam āgneyam itareṣām apy atra bhūtānāṃ sānnidhyaṃ asty aṇunā viśeṣeṇa parasparo-pakārāt parānugrahāt parasparānupraveśāc ca* —Suśruta, III.3.1), and they mutually co-operate together for the production of the foetus.

1 यानि त्व् आत्मनि सूक्ष्माणि भूतानि आतिवाहिकरूपाणि तानि सर्वसाधारणत्वेन अविशेषसादृश्यकारणारूति नेह बोद्धव्यानि ॥
yāni tv ātmani sūkṣmāṇi bhūtāni ātivāhika-rūpāṇi tāni sarva-sādhāraṇatvena aviśeṣa-sādṛśya-kāraṇārūti neha boddhavyāni.
Cakrapāṇi's *Āyur-veda-dīpikā,* IV.2.23-27.

2 तेषां वीशेषाद् बलवन्ति यानि भवन्ति मातापितृकर्मजानि
तानि व्यवस्येत् सदृशत्वलिङ्गं सत्वं यथानूकम् अपि व्यवस्येत् ॥
Teṣāṃ viśeṣād balavanti yāni
bhavanti mātā-pitṛ-karma-jāni
tāni vyavasyet sadṛśatva-liṅgaṃ
satvaṃ yathānūkam api vyavasyet. —Caraka, IV.2.27.

When a man dies, his soul, together with his subtle body, composed of the four elements, air, fire, water and earth, in a subtle state and *manas*, passes invisibly into a particular womb on account of its *karma*, and then, when it comes into connection with the combined semen and blood of the father and mother, the foetus begins to develop.[1] The semen and blood can, however, operate as causes of the production of the body only when they come into connection with the subtle body transferred from the previous body of a dying being.[2] Suśruta (III.1.16) says that the very subtle eternal conscious principles are manifested *(abhivyajyate)* when the blood and semen are in union (*parama-sūkṣmāś cetanāvantaḥ śāśvatā lohita-retasaḥ sanni-pāteṣv abhivyajyante)*. But later on (III.3.4) this statement is modified in such a way as to agree with Caraka's account; for there it is said that the soul comes into contact with the combined semen and blood along with its subtle elemental body *(bhūtātmanā)*. In another passage a somewhat different statement is found (Suśruta, III.4.3). Here it is said that the materials of the developing foetus are *agni*, *soma*, *sattva*, *rajas*, *tamas*, the five senses, and the *bhūtātmā*—all these contribute to the life of the foetus and are also called

---

अनूकं प्राक्तनाव्यवहिता देहजातिस् तेन यथानूकर्न्
अति यो देवोशरीराद् अव्यवधानेनागत्य भवति स
देवसत्वो भवति
Anūkaṃ prāktanāvyavahitā deha-jātis tena yathānūkarṃ
iti yo deva-śarīrād avyavadhānenāgatya bhavati sa
deva-satvo bhavati, etc. —Cakrapāṇi, IV.2.23-27.

1 भूतैश् चतुर्भिः सहितः सुसूक्ष्मैर्
मनोजवो देहम् उपैति देहात्
कर्मात्मकत्वान् न तु तस्य दृश्यां
दिव्यं विना डर्शनम् अस्ति रूपं
bhūtaiś caturbhiḥ sahitaḥ su-sūkṣmair
mano-javo deham upaiti dehāt
karmāt-makatvān na tu tasya dṛśyāṃ
divyaṃ vinā ḍarśanam asti rūpaṃ.—Caraka, IV.2.3.

2 यद्य् अपि सुक्ररजशी कारणे, तथापि यदैवातिवहिकं सूक्ष्मभूतरूपशरीरं प्राप्नुतः, तदैव ते शरीरम् जनयतः नान्यदा ॥
yady api sukra-rajaśī kāraṇe, tathāpi yadaivātivahikaṃ sūkṣma-bhūta-rūpa-śarīraṃ prāpnutaḥ, tadaiva te śarīram janayataḥ, nānyadā.
—Cakrapāṇi, IV.2.36.

the *prāṇas* (life).[1] Ḍalhaṇa, in explaining this, says that the *agni* (fire) spoken of here is the heat-power which manifests itself in the fivefold functionings of digestion *(pācaka)*, viz. brightening of the skin (*bhrājaka*), the faculty of vision *(ālocaka),* coloration of the blood, the intellectual operations and the heat operations involved in the formation and work of the different constituent elements (*dhātu*), such as chyle, blood, etc.; the *soma* is the root-power of all watery elements, such as mucus, chyle, semen, etc., and of the sense of taste; *vāyu* represents that which operates as the fivefold life-functionings of *prāṇa*, *apāna*, *samāna*, *udāna*, and *vyāna.* Ḍalhaṇa says further that *sattva*, *rajas* and *tamas* refer to *manas*, the mind-organ, which is a product of their combined evolution. The five senses contribute to life by their cognitive functionings. The first passage seemed to indicate that life was manifested as a result of the union of semen and blood; the second passage considered the connection of the soul with its subtle body (*bhūtātmā*) necessary for evolving the semen-blood into life. The third passage introduces, in addition to these, the five senses, *sattva*, *rajas*, and *tamas*, and the place of semen-blood is taken up by the three root-powers of *agni*, and *vāyu.* These three powers are more or less of a hypothetical nature, absorbing within them a number of functionings and body-constituents. The reason for these three views in the three successive chapters cannot be satisfactorily explained, except on the supposition that Suśruta's work underwent three different revisions at three different times. Vāgbhaṭa the elder says that the moment the semen and the blood are united, the life principle *(jīva),*

1 This *bhūtātmā,* i.e. the subtle body together with the soul presiding over it, is called by Suśruta *karma-puruṣa.* Medical treatment is of this *karma-puruṣa* and his body *(śa eṣa karma-puruṣaḥ cikitsādhikṛtaḥ*—Suśruta, III.1.16). Suśruta (I.1.21) again says,

"पञ्चमहाभूतशरीरिसमवायः पुरुष इत्य् उच्यते; तस्मिन् क्रिया सोऽधिष्ठानम्"

"pañca-mahābhūta-śarīri-samavāyaḥ puruṣa ity ucyate; tasmin kriyā so 'dhiṣṭhānam."

(In this science, the term *puruṣa* is applied to the unity of five elements and the self *(śarīrī),* and this is the object of medical treatment.)

being moved by *manas* (*mano-javena*), tainted, as the latter is, with the afflictions *(kleśa)* of attachment, etc., comes in touch with it.[1]

The doctrine of a subtle body, as referred to in the medical works, may suitably be compared with the Sāṃkhya view. Cakrapāṇi himself, in explaining *Caraka-saṃhitā*, IV.2.36, says that this doctrine of a subtle body (*ātivāhika śarira*) is described in the *āgama*, and by *āgama* the Sāṃkhya *āgama* is to be understood *(tena āgamād eva Sāṃkhya-darśana-rūpād ātivāhika-śarīrāt)*. The *Sāṃkhya-kārikā* 39 speaks of a subtle body *(sūkṣma deha)* and the body inherited from the parents. The *sūkṣma* continues to exist till salvation is attained, and at each birth it receives a new body and at each death it leaves it. It is constituted of *mahat*, *ahaṃkāra,* the eleven senses and the five *tan-mātras.* On account of its association with the *buddhi,* which bears the impress of virtue, vice, and other intellectual defects and accomplishments, it becomes itself associated with these, just as a cloth obtains fragrance through its connection with campak flowers of sweet odour; and hence it suffers successive rebirths, till the *buddhi* becomes dissociated from it by the attainment of true discriminative knowledge. The necessity

---

1 गते पुराणे रजसि नवेऽवस्थिते शुद्धे गर्भस्याशये मार्गे च बीजात्मना शुक्लम् अविकृतम् अविकृतेन वायुना प्रेरितम् अन्यैश् च महाभूतैर् अनुगतम् आर्तवेन अभिमूर्छितम् अन्वक्षम् एव रागादिक्लेशवशानुवर्तिना स्वकर्मचोदितेन मनोजवेन जीवेनाभिसंसृष्टंगर्भाशयम् उपायाति॥
gate purāṇe rajasi nave 'vasthite śuddhe garbhasyāśaye mārge ca bījātmanā śuklam avikṛtam avikṛtena vāyunā preritam anyaiś ca mahā-bhūtair anugatam ārtavena abhimūrchitam anvakṣam eva rāgādi-kleśa-vaśānuvartinā sva-karma-coditena mano-javena jīvenābhisaṃsṛṣṭaṃgarbhāśayam upayāti.

—*Aṣṭāṅga-saṃgraha,* II.2.

Indu, in explaining this, says,
"बीजात्मना गर्भकारणमहाभूतस्वभावेन..सूक्ष्मस्वरूपैः मनस्सहचारिभिस् तन्मात्राख्यैर् महाभूतैर् अनुगतं स्त्रीक्षेत्रप्राप्त्या कर्मवशाद् आर्तवेन मिश्रीभूतम् अन्वक्षं मिश्रीभावहीनकालम् एव मनोजवेन जीवेनाभिसंसृष्तम् प्राप्तसंयोगम् गर्भाशयं शुक्लम् उपयाति"॥
"*bījātmanā garbha-kāraṇa-mahā-bhūta-svabhāvena...sūkṣma-svarūpaiḥ manas-sahacāribhis tanmātrākhyair mahā-bhūtair anugataṃ sirī-kṣetra-prāptyā karma-vaśād ārtavena miśrī-bhūtam anvakṣaṃ miśrī-bhāva-hīna-kālam eva... mano-javena jīvenābhisaṃsṛṣṭam prāpta-saṃyogaṃ garbhāśayaṃ śuklam upayāti.*" His further explanations of the nature of applications of the *jīva* show that he looked up Patañjali's *Yoga-sūtras* for the details of *avidyā,* etc., and the other *kleśas.*

of admitting a subtle body is said to lie in the fact that the *buddhi*, with the *ahaṃkāra* and the senses,cannot exist without a supporting body; so in the interval between one death and another birth the *buddhi*, etc. require a supporting body, and the subtle body is this support.[1] In the *Sāṃkhya-pravacana-bhāṣya*, V.103, it is said that this subtle body is like a little tapering thing no bigger than a thumb, and that yet it pervades the whole body, just as a little flame pervades a whole room by its rays.[2] The *Vyāsa-bhāṣya*, in refuting the Sāṃkhya view, says that according to it the *citta* (mind), like the rays of a lamp in a jug or in a palace, contracts and dilates according as the body that it occupies is bigger or smaller.[3] Vācaspati, in explaining the Yoga view as expounded by *Vyāsa*, says that in the Sāṃkhya view the *citta* is such that it cannot, simply by contraction and expansion, leave any body at death and occupy another body without intermediate relationship with a subtle body *(ātivāhika-śarīra)*. But, if the *citta* cannot itself leave a body and occupy another, how can it connect itself with a subtle body at the time of death? If this is to be done through another body, and that through another, then we are led to a vicious infinite. If it is argued that the *citta* is connected with such a subtle body from beginningless time, then the reply is that such a subtle body has never been perceived by anyone *(na khalu etad adhyakṣa-gocaraṃ)*; nor can it be regarded as indispensably necessary through inference, since the Yoga view can explain the situation without the hypothesis of any such body. The *citta* is all-pervading, and each soul is associated with a separate *citta*. Each *citta* connects itself with a particular body by virtue of the fact that its manifestations *(vṛtti)* are seen in that body.

1 *Sāṃkhya-tattva-kaumudi*, 39, 40, 41.

2 यथा दीपस्य सर्वगृहव्यापित्वेऽपि कलिकाकारत्वं...तथैव लिङ्गदेहस्य देहव्यापित्वेऽप्य् अन्गुष्ठपरिमाणत्वम् ॥

yathā dīpasya sarva-gṛha-vyāpitve 'pi kalikā-kāratvaṃ... tathaiva liṅga-dehasya deha-vyāpitve 'py anguṣṭha-parimāṇatvam.

—*Sāṃkhya-pravacana-bhāṣya,* V.103.

3 घटप्रासादप्रदीपकल्पं सङ्कोचविकाशि चित्तम् शरीरपरिमाणाकारमात्रम् इत्य् अपरे प्रतिपन्नाः ॥

ghaṭa-prāsāda-pradīpa-kalpaṃ saṅkoca-vikāśi cittam śarīra-parimāṇākāra-mātram ity apare pratipannāḥ.

—*Vyāsa-bhāṣya* on Patañjali's *Yoga-sūtras,* IV.10.

Thus the manifestations of the all-pervading *citta* of a soul cease to appear in its dying body and become operative in a new body that is born. Thus there is no necessity of admitting a subtle body (*ātivāhikatvaṃ tasya na mṛṣyāmahe*).[1]

The Vaiśeṣika also declines to believe in the existence of a subtle body, and assigns to it no place in the development of the foetus. The development of the foetus is thus described by Śrīdhara in his *Nyāya-kandalī*:[2] "After the union of the father's semen and the mother's blood there is set up in the atoms constituting them a change through the heat of the womb, such that their old colour, form, etc. become destroyed and new similar qualities are produced; and in this way, through the successive formation of dyads and triads, the body of the foetus develops; and, when such a body is formed, there enters into it the mind *(antaḥkaraṇa),* which could not have entered in the semen-blood stage, since the mind requires a body to support it *(na tu śukra-śoṇitāvasthāyāṃ śari-rāśrayatvān manasaḥ).* Small quantities of food-juice of the mother go to nourish it. Then, through the unseen power (*adṛṣṭa*), the foetus is disintegrated by the heat in the womb into the state of atoms, and atoms of new qualities, together with those of the food-juice, conglomerate together to form a new body." According to this view the subtle body and the mind have nothing to do with the formation and development of the foetus. Heat is the main agent responsible

---

1 Vācaspati's *Tattva-vaiśāradī,* IV.10. Reference is made to *Mahā-bhārata,* III.296.17, *aṅguṣṭha-mātram puruṣaṃ niścakarṣa yamo balāt.* Vācaspati says that *puruṣa* is not a physical thing and hence it cannot be drawn out of the body. It must therefore be interpreted in a remote sense as referring to the cessation of manifestation of *citta* in the dying body
न चास्य निष्कर्षः सम्भवति, इत्य् औपचारिको व्याख्येयस् तथा च चितेस् चित्तस्य च तत्र वृत्त्यभाव एव निष्कर्षाठः
(na cāsya niṣkarṣaḥ sambhavati, ity aupacāriko vyākhyeyas tathā ca citeś cittasya ca tatra tatra vṛtty-abhāva eva niṣkarṣārṭhaḥ).

The *Sāṃkhya-pravacana-bhāṣya,* V.103, says that the thumb-like *puruṣa* referred to in *Mahā-bhārata,* III.296.17, which Yama drew from the body of Satyavān, has the size of the subtle body (*liṅga-deha*).

2 *Nyāya-kandalī*, Vizianagram Sanskrit series, 1895, p. 33.

for all disintegration and re-combination involved in the process of the formation of the foetus.

The Nyāya does not seem to have considered this as an important question, and it also denies the existence of a subtle body. The soul, according to the Nyāya, is all-pervading, and *the Mahā bhārata* passage quoted above, in which Yama draws out the *puruṣa* of the size of a thumb, has, according to Nyāya, to be explained away.[1] In rebirth it is only the all-pervading soul which becomes connected with a particular body *(ya eva dehāntara-saṃgamo 'sya, tam eva taj-jñāḥ-para-hkam āhuḥ).*[2]

Candrakīrti gives us an account of the Buddhist view from the *Śāli-stamba-sūtra.*[3] The foetus is produced by the combination of the six constituents (*ṣaṇṇāṃ dhātūnāṃ samavāyāt).* That which consolidates *(saṃśleṣa)* the body is called earth *(pṛthivī-dhātu)*; that which digests the food and drink of the body is called fire *(tejo-dhātu)*; that which produces inhalation and exhalation is called air *(vāyu-dhātu)*; that which produces the pores of the body *(antaḥ-sauṣiryam)* is called ether *(ākāśa-dhātu)*; that by which knowledge is produced is called the *vijñāna-dhātu.* It is by the combination of them all that a body is produced *(sarveṣāṃ samavāyāt kāyasyotpattir bhavati).* The seed of *vijñāna* produces the germ of name and form (*nāma-rūpāṅkura*) by combination with many other diverse causes. The foetus is thus produced of itself, not by another, nor by both itself and another, nor by god, nor by time, nor by nature, nor by one cause, nor by no cause, but by the combination of the mother's and the father's parts at the proper season.[4] The combination of father's and mother's parts gives us the five *dhātus*,

---

1 तस्मान् न हृत्पुण्डरीके यावदयावदवस्थानम् आत्मनः अंत एव अङ्गुष्ठमात्रं पुरुषं निश्चकर्ष बलाद् यम इति व्यासवचनम् एवम्परम् अवगन्तव्यम्
tasmān na hṛt-puṇḍarīke yāvad-avasthānam ātmanaḥ ata eva aṅguṣṭha-mātraṃ puruṣaṃ niścakarṣa balād yama iti Vyāsa-vacanam evam-param avagantavyam
—(Jayanta's *Nyāya-mañjarī,* p. 469).

2 *Ibid.* p. 473.

3 *Mādhyamika-vṛtti* (Bibliotheca Buddhica), pp. 560-61.

4 *Ibid.* p. 567.

which operate together when they are in combination with the sixth *dhātu,* the *vijñāna.*

The view that the foetus is the result of the joint effect of the six *dhātus* reminds us of a similar expression in *Caraka*, IV.3. Caraka gives there a summary of the discussions amongst various sages on the subject of the causes of the formation and development of the foetus: where there is a union between a man with effective semen and a woman with no defect of organ, ovary and blood, if at the time of the union of the semen and blood the soul comes in touch with it through the mind, then the foetus begins to develop.[1] When it is taken care of by proper nourishment, etc., then at the right time the child is born, and the whole development is due to the combined effect of all the elements mentioned above *(samudayād eṣāṃ bhāvānām).* The foetus is born of elements from the mother and the father, the self, the proper hygienic care of the parents' bodies (*sātmya*) and the food-juice; and there is also operant with these the *sattva* or *manas*, which is an intermediate vehicle serving to connect the soul with a former body when it leaves one *(aupapāduka).*[2] Bharadvāja said that none of these causes can be considered as valid; for, in spite of the union of the parents, it often happens that they remain childless; the self cannot produce the self; for, if it did, did it produce itself after being born or without being born? In both cases it is impossible for it to produce itself. Moreover, if the self had the power of producing itself, it would not have cared to take birth in undesirable places and with defective powers, as sometimes happens. Again, proper hygienic habits cannot be regarded as the cause; for there are many who have these, but have no children, and there are many who have not these, but have children. If it was due to food-juice, then all people would have got children. Again, it is not true that the *sattva* issuing forth from one body connects itself

1 In the Vaiśeṣika also the all-pervading *ātman* comes into touch with the foetus through the *manas*; but the difference is this, that here the *manas* is an operative factor causing the development of the foetus, whereas there the *manas* goes to the foetus when through the influence of body-heat it has already developed into a body.

2 *Caraka-saṃhitā,* IV.3.3.

with another; for, if it were so, we should all have remembered the events of our past life. So none of the above causes can be regarded as valid. To this Ātreya replied that it is by the combined effect of all the above elements that a child is produced, and not by any one of them separately.[1] This idea is again repeated in IV.3.20, where it is said that just as a medical room (*kūṭāgāraṃ vartulākāraṃ gṛhaṃ jaintāka-sveda-pratipāditam*—Cakrapāṇi) is made up of various kinds of things, or just as a chariot is made up of a collection of its various parts, so is the foetus made up of the combination of various entities which contribute to the formation of the embryo and its development (*nānā-vidhānāṃ garbha-kārāṇāṃ bhāvānāṃ samudayād abhinirvartate*).[2] The idea of such a combined effect of causes as leading to the production of a perfect whole seems to have a peculiar Buddhistic ring about it.

Bharadvāja, in opposing the above statement of Ātreya, asks what, if the foetus is the product of a number of combined causes, is the definite order in which they co-operate together to produce the various parts (*katham ayaṃ sandhīyate*)? Again, how is it that a child born of a woman is a human child and not that of any other animal? If, again, man is born out of man, why is not the son of a stupid person stupid, of a blind man blind, and of a madman mad? Moreover, if it is argued that the self perceives by the eye colours, by the ear sounds, by the smell odours, by the organ of taste the different tastes, and feels by the skin the different sensations of touch, and for that reason the child does not inherit the qualities of the father, then it has to be admitted that the soul can have knowledge only when there are senses and is devoid of it when there are no senses; in that case the soul is not unchangeable,but is liable to change (*yatra caitad ubhayaṃ sambhavati jñatvam ajñatvaṃ ca sa-vikāraś cātmā).*[3] If the soul perceives the objects of sense through the activity of the senses, such as perceiving and the like,

1 *neti bhagavān Atreyaḥ sarvebhya ebhyo bhāvebhyaḥ samuditebhyo garbho 'bhinirvartate. Ibid.* IV.3.11.

2 *Ibid.* IV.3.20.

3 *Caraka-sahṃitā*, IV.3.21.

then it cannot know anything when it has no senses, and, when it is unconscious, it cannot be the cause of the body-movements or of any of its other activities and consequently cannot be called the soul, *ātman.* It is therefore simple nonsense to say that the soul perceives colours, etc. by its senses.

To this Ātreya replies that there are four kinds of beings, viz. those born from ovaries, eggs, sweat and vegetables. Beings in each class exist in an innumerable diversity of forms.[1] The forms that the foetus-producing elements (*garbha-karā bhāvāḥ*) assume depend upon the form of the body where they assemble. Just as gold, silver, copper, lead, etc. assume the form of any mould in which they are poured, so, when the foetus-producing elements assemble in a particular body, the foetus takes that particular form. But a man is not infected with the defect or disease of his father, unless it be so bad or chronic as to have affected his semen. Each of our limbs and organs had their germs in the semen of the father, and, when the disease or defect of the father is so deep-rooted as to have affected *(upatāpa)* the germ part of any particular organ in the seed, then the child produced out of the semen is born defective in that limb; but, if the defect or disease of the father is so superficial that his semen remains unaffected, then the disease or defect is not inherited by the son. The child does not owe sense-organs to his parents; he alone is responsible for the goodness or badness of his sense-organs; for these are born from his own self *(ātma-jānindriyāṇi).* The presence or absence of the sense-organs is due to his own destiny or the fruits of *karma (daiva).* So there is no definite law that the sons of idiots or men with defective senses should necessarily be born idiots or be otherwise defective.[2] The self *(ātman)* is conscious only when the sense-organs exist. The self is never without the *sattva* or the mind-organ, and through it there is always some kind of consciousness in the self.[3] The self,

1 *Ibid.* IV.3.22, 23.

2 *Caraka-saṃhitā,* IV.3.25.

3 *Ibid.* IV.3.26, *na hy-asattvaḥ kadācid ātmā sattva-viśeṣāc copalabhyate jñāna-viśeṣaḥ.* Cakrapāṇi, in commenting on this, says that our knowledge of the

as the agent, cannot without the sense-organs have any knowledge of the external world leading to practical work; no practical action for which several accessories are required can be performed unless these are present; a potter who knows how to make a jug cannot succeed in making it unless he has the organs with which to make it.[1] The fact that the self has consciousness even when the senses do not operate is well illustrated by our dream-knowledge when the senses lie inoperative.[2] Ātreya further says that, when the senses are completely restrained and the *manas*, or mind-organ, is also restrained and concentrated in the self, one can have knowledge of all things even without the activity of the senses.[3] The self is thus of itself the knower and the agent.

This view of Caraka, as interpreted by Cakrapāṇi, seems to be somewhat new. For the self is neither pure intelligence, like the *puruṣa* of the Sāṃkhya-yoga, nor the unity of being, intelligence and bliss, like that of the Vedānta. Here the soul is the knower by virtue of its constant association with *manas*. In this, however, we are nearer to the Nyāya-Vaiśeṣika view. But in the Nyāya-Vaiśeṣika view the soul is not always in contact with *manas* and is not always conscious. The *manas* in that view is atomic. The view that the soul has always a formless consciousness has undoubtedly a Vedāntic or Sāṃkhyaic tinge; but the other details evidently separate this view

---

external world is due to the operation of the sense-organs in association with the mind-organ. If these sense-organs do not exist, we cannot have any knowledge of the external world, but the internal organ of mind is always associated with the self: so the knowledge which is due to this mind-organ is ever present in the self *(yat tu kevala-mano-janyam ātma-jñānaṃ, tad bhavaty eva sarvadā*). It seems that both *sattva* and *manas* are used to denote the mind-organ.

1 The word *kārya-jñānam* in *Caraka-saṃhitā,* IV.3.27, has been explained by Cakrapāṇi as *kārya-pravṛtti-janaka-bāhya-viṣaya-jñānam.* The knowledge that the self has when it has no sense-organs operating in association with the mind has no object *(nirviṣaya)*; in other words, this knowledge which the self always has is formless.

2 *Ibid.* IV.3.31.

3 विनापीन्द्रियैः समाधिबलाद् एव यस्मात् सर्वज्ञो भवति; तस्माज् ज्ञस्वभाव एव निरिन्द्रियोऽप्य् आत्मा
vināpīndriyaiḥ samādhi-balād eva yasmāt sarvajño bhavati; tasmāj jña-sva-bhāva eva nirindriyo 'py ātmā
—(Cakrapāṇi's *Caraka-tātparya-ūkā,* IV.3.28-29).

from the accepted interpretations of these schools. The theory of the soul, however, as here indicated comes as a digression and will have to be discussed more adequately later on.

On the subject of the existence of subtle bodies we have already quoted the views of different Indian schools of philosophy for the purpose of suggesting comparisons or contrasts with the views of Caraka. Before concluding this section reference must be made to the Vedānta views with regard to the nature of subtle bodies.

According to the Vedānta, as interpreted by Śaṅkara, the subtle body is constituted of five particles of the elements of matter (*bhūta-sūkṣmaiḥ*), with which are also associated the five *vāyus*, *prāṇa*, *apāna*, etc.[1] Those who perform good deeds go to the region of the moon, and those who commit sins suffer in the kingdom of Yama and then are again born in this world.[2] Those who, as a reward of their good deeds, go to the kingdom of the moon and afterwards practically exhaust the whole of their fund of virtue and consequently cannot stay there any longer, begin their downward journey to this earth. They pass through *ākāśa*, air, smoke and cloud and then are showered on the ground with the rains and absorbed by the plants and again taken into the systems of persons who eat them, and again discharged as semen into the wombs of their wives and are reborn again. In the kingdom of the moon they had watery bodies (*candra-maṇḍale yad am-mayam śarīram upabhogārtham ārabdham*) for the enjoyment available in that kingdom; and, when they exhaust their good deeds through enjoyment and can no longer hold that body, they get a body which is like *ākāśa* and are thus driven by the air and come into association with smoke and cloud. At this stage, and even when they are absorbed into the body of plants, they neither enjoy pleasure nor suffer pain. A difference must be made between the condition of those who are endowed with plant-bodies as a punishment for their misdeeds and those who pass through the plant-bodies merely as stations on their way to rebirth. In the case of the former the plant life is a life of enjoyment and sorrow, whereas in the case of the latter there is nei-

1 The *Bhāṣya* of Śaṅkara on the *Brahma-sūtra,* III.1.1-7.

2 *Ibid.* III.1.13.

ther enjoyment nor sorrow. Even when the plant-bodies are chewed and powdered the souls residing in them as stations of passage do not suffer pain; for they are only in contact with these plant-bodies (*candra-maṇḍala-skhalitānāṃ vrīhy ādi-saṃśleṣa-mātraṃ tad-bhāvaḥ*).[1]

We thus see that it is only the Sāṃkhya and the Vedānta that agree to the existence of a subtle body and are thus in accord with the view of Caraka. But Caraka is more in agreement with the Vedānta in the sense that, while according to the Sāṃkhya it is the *tan-mātras* which constitute the subtle body, it is the fine particles of the gross elements of matter that constitute the subtle bodies in the case both of the Vedānta and of Caraka. The soul in one atomic moment becomes associated successively with *ākāśa*, air, light, heat, water, and earth (and not in any other order) at the time of its entrance into the womb.[2]

FOETAL DEVELOPMENT[3]

When the different elements of matter in conjunction with the subtle body are associated with the self, they have the appearance

1 *Bhāṣya* of Śaṅkara, III.1.25, also III.1.22-27.

2 *Caraka-saṃhitā,* IV.4.8. Cakrapāṇi, commenting on this, says that there is no special reason why the order of acceptance of gross elements should be from subtler to grosser; it has to be admitted only on the evidence of the scriptures—*ayaṃ ca bhūta-grahaṇa-krama āgama-siddha eva nātra yuktis tathā-vidhā hṛdayaṅgamāsti.*

3 In the *Garbha Upaniṣad,* the date of which is unknown, there is a description of foetal development. Its main points of interest may thus be summarized: the hard parts of the body are earth, the liquid parts are water, that which is hot (*uṣṇa*) is heat-light (*tejaḥ),* that which moves about is *vāyu,* that which is vacuous is *ākāśa.* The body is further said to depend on six tastes *(ṣaḍ-āśraya),* sweet (*madhura*), acid (*amla*), salt *(lavaṇa),* bitter (*tikta),* hot (kaṭu) and pungent (*kaṣāya),* and it is made up of seven *dhātus* of chyle *(rasa),* blood (*śoṇita*) and flesh (*māṃsa*). From the six kinds of *rasa* comes the *śoṇita,* from *śoṇita* comes *māṃsa,* from *māṃsa* comes fat (*medas*), from it the tendons *(snāyu),* from the *snāyu* bones *(asthi),* from the bones the marrow (*majjā*), from the marrow the semen (*śukra).* By the second night after the union of semen and blood the foetus is of the form of a round lump called *kalala,* at the eighth night it is of the form of a vesicle called *budbuda,* after a fortnight it assumes the form of a spheroid, *piṇḍa;* in two months the head appears, in three months the feet, in four months the abdomen, heels and the pelvic portions appear, in the fifth month the spine

of a little lump of mucus *(kheta-bhūtd)* with all its limbs undifferentiated and undeveloped to such an extent that they may as well be said not to exist as to exist. Suśruta remarks that the two main constituents of the body, semen and blood, are respectively made up of the watery element of the moon (*saumya*) and the fiery element *(āgneya)*; the other elements in atomic particles are also associated with them, and all these mutually help one another and co-operate together for the formation of the body.[1] Suśruta further goes on to say that at the union of female and male the heat (*tejaḥ*) generated rouses the *vāyu*, and through the coming together of heat and air the semen is discharged.[2] Caraka, however, thinks that the cause of discharge of semen is joy (*harṣa*).[3] The semen is not produced from the body, but remains in all parts of the body, and it is the joy which causes the discharge and the entrance of the semen into the uterus.[4] Thus he says that, being ejected by the self as joy (*harṣa-bhūtenāt-*

appears, in the sixth month the mouth, nose, eyes and ears develop; in the seventh month the foetus becomes endowed with life *(jīvena saṃyukto bhavati),* in the eighth month it becomes fully developed. By an excess of semen over blood a male child is produced, by the excess of blood a female child is produced, when the two are equal a hermaphrodite is produced. When air somehow enters and divides the semen into two, twins are produced. If the minds of the parents are disturbed (*vyākulita-mānasaḥ*), the issue becomes either blind or lame or dwarf. In the ninth month, when the foetus is well developed with all its organs, it remembers its previous birth and knows its good and bad deeds and repents that, on account of its previous *karma,* it is suffering the pains of the life of a foetus, and resolves that, if it can once come out, it will follow the Sāṃkhya-yoga discipline. But as soon as the child is born it comes into connection with *Vaiṣṇava vāyu* and forgets all its previous births and resolutions. A body is called *śarīra,* because three fires reside in it *(śrayante),* viz. the *koṣṭhāgni, darśanāgni* and *jñānāgni.* The *koṣṭhāgni* digests all kinds of food and drink, by the *darśanāgni* forms and colours are perceived, by the *jñānāgni* one performs good and bad deeds. This Upaniṣad counts the cranial bones as being four, the vital spots (*marman*) as being 107, the joints as 180, the tissues *(snāyu)* as 109, the *śirās,* or veins, as 700, the marrow places as 500, and the bones as 300.

1 *Suśruta-saṃhitā,* III.3.3.

2 *Ibid.* III.3.4, Nirṇaya-Sāgara edition, 1915. Ḍalhaṇa, commenting on this, says, "*sukha-lakṣaṇa-vyāyāmajoṣma-vitīnaṃ vidrutam anilāc cyutam*"

3 *Caraka-saṃhitā,* IV.4.7.

4 Cakrapāṇi, commenting on *Caraka-saṃhitā,* IV.4.7, says that "*nāṅgebhyaḥ śukram utpadyate kintu śukra-rūpatayaiva vyajyate,*" i.e. the semen is not pro-

manodīritaś cādkiṣṭhitaś ca), the semen constituent or the seed, having come out of the man's body, becomes combined with the menstrual product (*ārtava*) in the uterus *(garbhāśaya)* after it has entrance thereinto through the proper channel (*ucitena pathā).* According to Suśruta the ejected semen enters into the female organ (*yonim abhiprapadyate*) and comes into association there with the menstrual product.[1] At that very moment, the soul with its subtle body comes into association with it and thus becomes associated with the material characteristics of *sattva*, *rajas* and *tamas*, and godly *(deva),* demonic (*asura*), and other characteristics. Caraka, referring to the question of the association of the soul with the material elements, says that this is due to the operation of the soul acting through the mind-organ *(sattva-karaṇa).*[2] Cakrapāṇi, in commenting on the above passage, says that the self *(ātman)* is inactive; activity is however attributed to the soul on account of the operative mind-organ which is associated with it. This, however, seems to be a compromise on the part of Cakrapāṇi with the views of the traditional Sāṃkhya philosophy, which holds the soul to be absolutely inactive; but the text of the *Caraka-saṃhitā* does not here say anything on the inactivity of the soul; for Caraka describes the soul as active *(pravartate*) as agent *(kartṛ)* and as universal performer *(viśvakarman),* and the *sattva* is described here only as an organ of the soul *(sattva-karaṇa).*

---

duced from the different parts of the body, but it exists as it is and is only manifested in a visible form after a particular operation (Suśruta, III.3.4).

1 As Ḍalhaṇa interprets this, the female organ here means the uterus; thus Ḍalhaṇa says, " *yones tritīyāvartāvasthita-garbhaśayyām pratipadyate*" i.e. the semen enters into the third chamber of the female organ, the place of the foetus. The uterus is probably considered here as the third chamber, the preceding two being probably the vulva and the vagina.

2 *Sattva-karaṇo guṇa-grahaṇāya pravartate—Caraka-saṃhitā,* IV.4.8. Cakrapāṇi rightly points out that *guṇa* here means material elements which possess qualities—*guṇavanti bhūtāni.* The word *guṇa* is used in all these passages in the sense of material entity or *bhūta.* Though *guṇa* means a quality and *guṇin* a substance, yet the view adopted here ignores the difference between qualities and substances, and *guṇa,* the ordinary word for quality, stands here for substance (*guṇa-guṇinor abhedopacārāt*—Cakrapāṇi, *Ibid.).*

In the first month, the foetus has a jelly-like form *(kalala);*[1] in the second month, the material constituents of the body having undergone a chemical change (*abhiprapacyamāna*) due to the action of cold, heat and air (*śītoṣmānilaiḥ*), the foetus becomes hard *(ghana).* If it is the foetus of a male child, it is spherical (*piṇḍa*); if it is of a female child, it is elliptical (*peśī*); if it is of a hermaphrodite, it is like the half of a solid sphere *(arbuda).*[2] In the third month five special eminences are seen, as also the slight differentiation of limbs. In the fourth month the differentiation of the limbs is much more definite and well manifested; and owing to the manifestation of the heart of the foetus the entity of consciousness becomes also manifested, since the heart is the special seat of consciousness; so from the fourth month the foetus manifests a desire for the objects of the senses. In the fifth month the consciousness becomes more awakened; in the sixth intelligence begins to develop; in the seventh the division and differentiation of limbs become complete; in the eighth, the vital element *(ojas)* still remains unsettled, and so, if a child is born at this time, it becomes short-lived.[3]

Caraka, in describing the part played by different material elements in the formation of the body, says that from the element *ākāśa* are formed sound, the organ of hearing, lightness *(lāghava),* subtleness of structure *(saukṣmya)* and porosity *(vireka*); from *vāyu* (air) are formed the sensation of touch, the organ of touch, roughness, power of movement, the disposition of the constituent elements *(dhātu-vyūhana),* and bodily efforts; from fire, vision, the organ of vision,digestion,heat,etc.;from water, the sensation of taste and the taste-organ, cold, softness, smoothness and watery characteristics; from earth, smell, organ of smell, heaviness, steadiness and hardness. The parts of the body which are thus formed from different material elements grow and develop with the acces-

1 Ḍalhaṇa explains *kalala* as *siṅghāna-prakhyam.*

2 On the meanings of the words *peśī* and *arbuda* there is a difference of opinion between Ḍalhaṇa and Gayī. Thus Gayī says that *peśī* means quadrangular (*catur-aśra*) and *arbuda* means the form of the bud of a silk cotton tree (*śālmali-mukulākāram).*

3 *Suśruta-saṃhitā,* III.3.30.

sion of those elements from which they have grown.[1] As the whole world is made up of five elements *(bhūta),* so the human body is also made up of five elements.[2] Caraka maintains that the senses and all other limbs of the body which grow before birth make their appearance simultaneously in the third month.[3] When, in the third month, the sense-organs grow, there grow in the heart feelings and desires. In the fourth month the foetus becomes hard, in the fifth it gets more flesh and blood, in the sixth there is greater development of strength and colour, in the seventh it becomes complete with all its limbs, and in the eighth month there is a constant exchange of vital power *(ojas)* between the mother and the foetus. The foetus being not yet perfectly developed, the vital fluid passes from the mother to the foetus; but, since the latter cannot retain it, it returns to the mother.[4] Cakrapāṇi, commenting on this, says that such an exchange is only possible because the foetus is still undeveloped, and the foetus, being associated with the mother, serves also as the mother's vital power *(ojas)*; for otherwise, if the *ojas* went out altogether from the mother, she could not live.

There is a good deal of divergence of opinion as regards the order of the appearance of the different limbs of the foetus. Two different schools of quarrelling authorities are referred to by Caraka and Suśruta. Thus, according to Kumāraśiras and Śaunaka the head appears first, because it is the seat of the senses; according to

---

1 *Caraka-saṃhitā*, IV.4.12.

2 *evam ayaṃ loka-sammitaḥ puruṣaḥ—yāvanto hi loke bhāva-viśeṣās tāvantaḥ puruṣe, yāvantaḥ puruṣe tāvanto loke* (*Caraka-saṃhitā,* IV.4.13). In *Ibid.* IV.3, it is said that the foetus gets its skin, blood, flesh, fat, navel, heart, *kloma,* spleen, liver, kidneys, bladder, colon, stomach, the larger intestines, and the upper and the lower rectum from the mother, and its hair, beard, nails, teeth, bones, veins and semen from the father; but, however this may be, it is certain that the development of all these organs is really due to the assimilation of the five elements of matter. So the development of the human foetus is, like the development of all other things in the world, due to the accretion of material elements.

3 *Ibid.* IV.4.14.

4 मातुर् ओजो गर्भं गच्छतिति यद् उच्यते, तद्गर्भौज एव मातृसम्बद्धं सन् मात्रोज इति व्यपदिश्यते ॥
mātur ojo garbhaṃ gacchatiti yad ucyate, tad-garbhauja eva mātṛ-sambaddhaṃ san mātroja iti vyapadiśyate. —Cakrapāṇi, IV.4.24.

Kāṅkāyana, the physician of Bālhīka, and Kṛtavīrya the heart appears first, because according to Kṛtavīrya (as reported in Suśruta) this is the seat of consciousness *(cetanā)* and of *buddhi* and *manas*; according to Bhadrakāpya (as reported by Caraka) the navel comes first, since this is the place where food is stored, and according to Pārāśara (as reported in Suśruta), because the whole body grows from there. According to Bhadra Śaunaka (as reported by Caraka) the smaller intestine and the larger intestine (*pakvāśaya*) appear first, since this is the seat of air *(mārutādhi-ṣṭhānatvāt)*; according to Baḍiśa (as reported by Caraka) the hands and feet come out first, because these are the principal organs, and according to Mārkaṇḍeya (as reported by Suśruta), because they are the main roots of all efforts *(tan-mūlatvāc ceṣṭāyāḥ)*; according to Vaideha Janaka (as reported by Caraka) the senses appear first, for they are the seats of understanding *(buddhy-adhiṣṭhāna)*; according to Mārici (as reported by Caraka) it is not possible to say which part of the body develops first, because it cannot be seen by anyone (*parokṣatvād acintyam);* according to Subhūti Gautama (as reported by Suśruta) the middle part of the body *(madhya-śarīra)* appears first, since the development of other parts of thc body is dependent on it *(tan-nibaddhatvāt sarva-gātra-sambhavasya);* according to Dhanvantari (as reported by both Caraka and Suśruta) all the parts of the body begin to develop together *(yugapat sarvāṅgābhinirvṛtti),* though on account of their fineness and more or less undifferentiated character such development may not be properly noticed, as with the parts of a growing bamboo-shootor a mango fruit *(garbhasya sūkṣmatvān nopalabhyante vaṃśāṅkuravat cūta-phalavac ca).*[1] Just as the juicy parts and the stone, which are undifferentiated in a green mango at its early stages, are all found clearly developed and differentiated when it is ripe, so, when the human foetus is even in the early stages of development, all its undifferentiated parts are already developing there *pari passu*, though on account of their fineness of structure and growth they cannot then be distinguished.

---

1 *Suśruta-saṃhitā,* iii.3.32 and *Caraka-saṃhitā,* IV.6.21.

Referring to the early process of the growth of the foetus, Suśruta says that, as the semen and blood undergo chemical changes through heat, seven different layers of skin (*kalā*) are successively produced, like the creamy lay *-ers(santānikā)* formed in milk. The first layer, one-eighteenth of a paddy seed *(dhānya)* in thickness, is called *avabhāsinī*; the second, one-sixteenth of a paddy seed, *lohitā*; the third, one-twelfth of a paddy seed, *śvetā;* the fourth, one-eighth, is called *tāmrā;* the fifth, one-fifth, *vedinī;* the sixth, of the size of a paddy seed, *rohiṇī*; the seventh, of the size of two paddy seeds, *māṃsa-dharā.* All these seven layers of skin come to about six paddy seeds, or roughly one inch. This is said to hold good only in those places of the body which are fleshy. Apart from these seven *kalās* of skin there are also seven *kalās* between the different *dhātus. A dhātu* (from the root *dhā*, to hold) is that which supports or sustains the body, such as chyle *(rasa),* blood *(rakta),* flesh *(māṃsa),* fat (*medas*), bone *(asthi),* marrow *(majjā),* semen *(śukra)* and the last vital fluid *(ojas).* Lymph *(kapha),* bile *(pitta)* and excreta *(puriṣa*) have also to be counted as *dhātus.* These *kalās,* however, are not visible; their existence is inferred from the fact that the different *dhātus* must have separate places allotted to them, and the *kalās* are supposed to divide the layer of one *dhātu* from another and are covered with lymph and tissues (*snāyu*).[1] In the first *kalā*, known as the *māṃsa-dharā*, the veins, tissues, etc. of the flesh are found; in the second, the *rakta-dharā*, is found the blood inside the flesh; in the third, called the *medo-dharā,* there is the fat which is found in the abdomen and also between the smaller bones.[2] The fourth *kalā* is the *śleṣma-dharā,* which exists in the joints; the fifth is the *puriṣa-dharā,* which exists in the intestine (*pakvāśaya*) and

---

1 The *kalā* is defined by Vṛddha-Vāgbhaṭa as
यस् तु धात्व् आशयान्तरेषु क्लेदोऽवतिष्ठते यथास्वम् उष्मभिर् विपक्वह् स्नायुश्लेष्मजरायुच्छन्नः काष्ठ इव सारो धातुसारश्षोल्ऽपत्वात् कलासंज्ञः
yas tu dhātv āśayāntareṣu kledo 'vatiṣṭhate yathāsvam uṣmabhir vipakvah snāyu-śleṣma-jarāyu-cchannaḥ kāṣṭha iva sāro dhātu-sāra-śeṣol 'patvāt kalā-saṃjñaḥ
—(*Aṣṭāṅga-saṃgraha, Śārīra,* v).

2 The fat inside the smaller bones is called *medas,* whereas that inside the larger ones is called *majjā,* or marrow, and the fat of pure flesh only is called *vapā,* or fat.

separates the excreta; the sixth and the seventh are the *pitta-dharā* and the *śukra-dhorā.*

Suśruta thinks that the liver and spleen are produced from blood, *pupphusa* (lungs) from the froth of blood, and *uṇḍuka* (a gland in the colon?) from the dirt of blood (*śoṇita-kitta-prabhava*). The best parts (*prasāda*) of blood and lymph are acted upon by bile, and *vāyu* works in association therewith; by this process the entrails, rectum and bladder are produced; and, when the heating process goes on in the abdomen, the tongue is produced, as the essence of lymph, blood and flesh. The air, being associated with heat, enters the flesh and changes the currents, the muscles *(peśī)* are differentiated, and by the oily part of fat the *vāyu* produces the veins *(śirā)* and tissues *(snāyu).* From the essential part of blood and fat the kidneys *(vṛkka)* are produced, from the essential part of flesh, blood, lymph and fat the testicles, and from the essence of blood and lymph the heart, which is the centre of the *dhamanis* through which flows the current of life *(prāṇa-vahā).* Underneath the heart on the left side there are the spleen and the *pupphusa,* and on the right side the liver and the *klōma* (right lung?), and this is particularly the place of consciousness. At the time of sleep, when it is covered with *śleṣman* having a superabundance of *tamas*, the heart remains contracted.

The foetus grows through the chyle of the mother and also through the inflation of the body of the foetus by air.[1] The navel of the body is the heating centre *(jyotiḥ-sthāna),* and the air, starting from here, continues to inflate the body.

It must be borne in mind that a foetus is the product of several causes operating jointly. A defect of any particular limb at birth is due to some defect in that part of one or more of the operating causes through the influence of which that particular limb was produced. The cause of foetal development is not a question of organs or limbs which were absolutely non-existent: they already existed, in the potential form, in the causes operating jointly. The joint causes did not produce something absolutely new, but their joint

1 *Suśruta-saṃhitā,* III.4.57.

operation helped to actualize all that was already inherent in them. Of all the joint causes the self remains unchanged in all changes of the body. The changes of pleasure and pain or such other characteristics as are considered to be due to the soul are really due either to *sattva* or *manas,* or to the body.[1] Cakrapāṇi, commenting on this, says that the fact that a soul may take its birth as this or that animal does not imply that the soul is liable to change *(paramātma-vikārā na bhavanti)*; for such a change is due to the excessive preponderance of *sattva, rajas* or *tamas*, which are in reality due to virtue and vice, which in themselves are but the characteristics of mind *(sattva-rajas-tamaḥ-prabalatā-rūpa-vikāraja-manojanya-dharmādharma-janyāny eva*).[2]

There are three kinds of morbid elements *(doṣa)* of the body, viz. *vāta, pitta* and *śleṣman*, and two morbid elements which affect the mind *(sattva),* viz. *rajas* and *tamas*. By the disorder of the first three the body becomes diseased, and by that of the second two the mind becomes affected. These, however, will be dealt with more fully later on.

GROWTH AND DISEASE

The three elements, *vāyu, pitta* and *kapha*, are counted both as constituents *(dhātus)* and as *doṣas*, or morbid elements. *Dhātus* are those elements which uphold the body. The body is the conglomeration *(samudāya)* of the modification of five *bhūtas*, or elements, and it works properly so long as these elements are in proper proportions *(sama-yoga-vāhin)* in the body.[3] The modifications of the five elements which co-operate together to uphold the body are called *dhātus*. When one or more of the *dhātus* fall off or exceed

1 निर्विकारः परस् त्व् आत्मा सर्वभूतानां निर्विशेषसत्त्वशरीरयोस् तु विशेषाद् विशेषोपलब्धिः
nir-vikāraḥ paras tv ātmā sarva-bhūtānāṃ nirviśeṣa-sattva-śarīrayos tu viśeṣād viśeṣopalabdhiḥ.

—*Caraka-saṃhitā,* IV.4.34.

2 Cakrapāṇi's commentary, *Caraka,* IV.4.

3 *Caraka-saṃhitā,* IV.6.4. Cakrapāṇi, in commenting on the word *sama-yoga-vāhin,* explains *sama* as meaning *ucita-pramāṇa* (proper quantity).

the proper quantity *(dhātu-vaiṣamya),* one or more *dhātus* may be in excess or deficient either in partial tendencies or in entirety *(akārtsnyena prakṛtyā ca).* It has to be noted that, as Cakrapāṇi explains, not every kind of excess or deficiency of *dhātus* produces *dhātu-vaiṣamya,* or disturbance of the equilibrium of the *dhātus:* it is only when such deficiency or excess produces affections of the body that it is called *dhātu-vaiṣamya.* That amount of excess or deficiency which does not produce trouble or affection of the body is called the normal measure of the *dhātus (prākṛta-māna).*[1] It is indeed obvious that such a definition of *prākṛta-māna* and *dhātu-vaiṣamya* involves a vicious circle, since the normal measure or *prākṛta-māna* of *dhātus* is said to be that which exists when there is no trouble or affection, and *dhātu-vaiṣamya* is that which exists when there is trouble in the body; the trouble or affection of the body has thus to be defined in terms of *dhātu-vaiṣamya.* The only escape from this charge is that *dhātu-vaiṣamya* and disease are synonymous, and the *prākṛta-māna* of *dhātus* is the same as health. When the *dhātus* are in their normal measure, there cannot be any *vaiṣamya*, except of a local nature, as when, for example, *the pitta* existing in its own proper measure is somehow carried by *vāyu* to a part of the body and there is consequently a local excess. Whatever leads to the increase of any particular *dhātu* automatically leads also to the decrease of other *dhātus* which are opposed to it. Things having the same sort of composition as a particular bodily *dhātu* increase it, and things having a different composition decrease it *(sāmānyam ekatva-karaṃ viśeṣas tu pṛthaktva-kṛt).*[2] The normal health of a man is but another name for his *dhātu-sāmya*; a man is said to be unhealthy, or to be in a state of *dhātu-vaiṣamya*, when symptoms of disease (*vikāra*) are seen. Slight variations of the due proportion of *dhātu* do not entitle us to call them instances of *dhātu-vaiṣamya* unless there is *vikāra* or symptoms of it exter-

---

1 एतद् एव धातूनं प्राकृतमानं यद् अविकारकारि ॥
etad eva dhātūnāṃ prākṛta-mānaṃ yad avikāra-kāri.
—Cakrapāṇi's comment on *Caraka-saṃhitā,* IV.6.4.

2 *Caraka-saṃhitā,* I.1.44.

nally expressed. The daily course of a healthy man ought to be such that the equilibrium of *dhātus* may be properly maintained. The sole aim of Āyur-veda is to advise diet, medicines, and a course of behaviour, such that, if they are properly followed, a normally healthy person may maintain the balance of his *dhātus* and a man who has lost the equilibrium of his *dhātus* may regain it. The aim of Āyur-veda is thus to advise men how to secure *dhātu-sāmya (dhātu-sāmya-kriyā coktā tantrasyāsya prayojanam).*[1]

If a normally healthy man wishes to keep his health at its normal level, he has to take things of different tastes, so that there may not be an excess of any particular kind of substance in the body. Diseases are caused through the excessive, deficient, and wrongful administration of sense-objects, the climatic characteristics of heat and cold, and the misuse of intelligence.[2] Thus the sight of objects with powerful light, the hearing of loud sounds like the roaring of thunder, the smelling of very strong odours, too much eating, the touching of too much cold or heat or too much bathing or massage are examples of *atiyoga*, or excessive association with sense-objects. Not to see, hear, smell, taste or touch at all would be *ayoga*, or deficient association with sense-objects. To see objects very near the eye, at a very great distance, or to see frightful, hideous, unpleasant and disturbing sights, would be examples of the improper use *(mithyā-yoga)* of the visual sense. To hear grating and unpleasant sounds would be examples of the improper use of the ear; to smell bad and nauseating odours would be examples of *mithyā-yoga* of the nose; to eat together different kinds of things, which in their combination are so opposed as to be unhealthy, is an example of the improper use of the tongue; to be exposed to sudden heat and cold are examples of the improper use of touch.[3] Similarly, all activities of speech, mind and body, when they are performed

1 *Ibid.* I.1.52.

2 कालबुद्धीन्द्रियार्थानां योगो मिथ्या न चाति च।
द्वयाश्रयाणां व्याधीनां त्रिविधो हेतुसंग्रहः ॥
kāla-buddhīndriyārthānām yogo mithyā na cāti ca
dvayāśrayāṇāṃ vyādhīnāṃ tri-vidho hetu-saṃgrahaḥ. —*Ibid.* I.1.53.

3 *Caraka-saṃhitā,* I.1.37

to an excessive degree, or not performed at all, or performed in an undesirable or unhealthy manner, are to be considered respectively as examples of *atiyoga*, *ayoga* and *mithyā-yoga* of the effort of speech, mind and body *(vāṅ-manaḥ-śarira-pravṛtti)*.[1] But these are all due to the misuse of intelligence *(prajñāparādha)*. When a particular season manifests its special characteristics of heat, cold or rains to an excessive degree or to a very deficient degree or in a very irregular or unnatural manner, we have what are called *atiyoga*, *ayoga* and *mithyā-yoga* of time *(kāla)*.[2] But the misuse of intelligence, or *prajñāparādha*, is at the root of all excessive, deficient or wrongful association with sense-objects;[3] for, when proper things are not taken at the proper time or proper things are not done at the proper time, it is all misuse of intelligence and is therefore included under *prajñāparādha*. When certain sinful deeds are performed by *prajñāparādha*, and, by the sins *(adharma)* associated with those deeds, which become efficient only after a certain lapse of time, illness is produced, the real cause of the illness is primarily *adharma* or its root cause, *prajñāparādha*; *kāla,* or time, however, may still be regarded in some sense as the cause through which the *adharma* is matured and becomes productive.

The principle of growth and decay is involved in the maxim that the different constituents of the body grow when articles of food having similar constituents are taken, and that they decay when articles of food having opposite qualities are taken *(evam eva sarva-dhātu-guṇānāṃ sāmānya-yogād vṛddhir vipar-yayādd*

1 *Ibid.* I.1.39, 40. Cakrapāṇi says that this includes sinful deeds which produce illness and unhappiness,
शारीरमानसिकवाचनिककर्ममिथ्यायोगेनैवाधर्मोत्पादावान्तरव्यापारेणैवूधर्मजन्यानां विकाराणाम् क्रियमानत्वात्॥
śārīra-mānasika-vācanika-karma-mithyā-yo-genaivā-dharmotpādāvāntara-vyāpāreṇaivūdharma-janyānāṃ vikārāṇām kriya-mānatvāt.

2 Three seasons only are mentioned, *Śītoṣma-varṣa-lakṣaṇāḥ punar heman-ta-grīṣma-varṣāḥ. Ibid.* I.11.42.

3 Thus Cakrapāṇi, commenting on this, says,
"बुद्ध्यपराधस्यैव इन्द्रियार्थातियोगादिहेतुत्वात्"
"*buddhy-aparādhasyaiva indri-yārthātiyogādi-hetutvāt.*" —*Ibid.* I.1.53.

hrāsaḥ).[1] Thus, flesh increases by the intake of flesh, so does blood by taking blood, fat by fat, bones by cartilages, marrow by marrow, semen by semen and a foetus by eggs.[2] But the principle applies not only to the same kind of substances as taken in the above example, but also to substances having largely similar qualities, just as the seminal fluid may be increased by taking milk and butter *(samāna-guṇa-bhūyiṣṭhānām anyaprakṛtīnām apy-āhāra-vikārāṇām upayogaḥ*).[3] The ordinary conditions of growth always hold good, namely, proper age of growth, nature, proper diet and absence of those circumstances that retard growth. The assimilation of food is effected by heat which digests, air which collects together all things for the action of heat, water which softens, fat which makes the food smooth, and time which helps the process of digestion.[4] As any particular food is digested and changed, it becomes assimilated into the body. The hard parts of the food form the hard parts of the body and the liquid parts form the liquid parts such as blood and the like; and unhealthy food, i.e. food which has qualities opposed to the natural qualities of the body, has a disintegrating influence on the body.

As regards the growth of the body through the essence of the food-juice, there are two different views summed up by Cakrapāṇi (I.28.3). Some say that the chyle is transformed into blood, and the blood into flesh, and so forth. As regards the method of this transformation, some say that, just as the whole milk is changed into curd, so the whole chyle is transformed into blood, while others say that this transformation is somewhat like the circulation in irrigation (*kedarī-kulyā-nyāya*). The rasa (chyle) produced as a result of the digestive process, coming into association with *rasa* as the body-constituent (*dhātu-rūpa-rasa*), increases it to a certain extent; another part of the *rasa,* having the same colour and smell as blood, goes to blood and increases it, and another part similarly goes to flesh

1 *Caraka-saṃhitā,* I.1.43 and 44, also IV.6.9 and particularly IV.6.10.

2 *Ibid.* IV.6.10. Cakrapāṇi explains *āma-garbha* as *aṇḍa.*

3 *Ibid.* IV.6.11.

4 *Ibid.* IV.6.14 and 15.

and increases it; and the same process takes place with reference to its increasing fat, etc. Here the whole circulation begins by the entrance of the entire chyle into the constituent *rasa* (*rasa-dhātu*); in passing through some part remains in the *rasa* and increases it, the unabsorbed part passes into blood, and what is unabsorbed there passes into flesh and so on to the other higher constituents of bones, marrow and semen.[1] But others think that, just as in a farm-house pigeons of different descriptions sit together *(khale kapota-nyāya),* so not all the digested food-juice passes through the channel of the *rasa-dhātu*, but different parts of it pass through different channels from the very first stage. That part of it which nourishes *rasa* enters into the channel of its circulation, that part of it which nourishes the blood goes directly into that, and so on. But there is generally this time limitation, that the part which nourishes the blood enters into it only when the part which nourishes *rasa-dhātu* has been absorbed in it; so again the part which enters into flesh can only do so when the part which nourishes blood has been absorbed in it. Thus the circulatory system is different from the very beginning; and yet the nourishment of blood takes place later than that of *rasa*, the nourishment of flesh later than that of blood, and so on (*rasād raktaṃ tato māṃsam ityāder ayam arthaḥ yad rasa-puṣṭi-kālād uttara-kālaṃ raktaṃ jāyate,* etc.). The upholders of the last view maintain that the other theory cannot properly explain how a nourishing diet *(vṛṣya),* such as milk, can immediately increase the seminal fluid, and that, if it had to follow the lengthy process of passing through all the circulatory systems, it could not do its part so quickly; but on the second theory, milk through its special quality *(prabhāva)* can be immediately associated with the seminal fluid and thereby increase it.[2] But Cakrapāṇi remarks that the earlier theory *(kedārī-kulyā)* is

1 There are two kinds of *rasa,* called *dhātu-rasa* and *poṣaka-rasa.* See Cakrapāṇi's comment on *Caraka-saṃhitā,* VI.15.14 and 15.

2 परिणामपक्षे, वृष्यप्रयोगस्य रक्तादिरूपापत्तिक्रमेणातिच्चिरेण शुक्रं भवतीति; क्षीरादयश् च सद्य एव वृष्या दृस्यन्ते, खलेकक्षे तु वृष्योत्पन्नो रसः प्रब् हावाच् छीघ्रम् एव शुक्रेण संबद्धः सन् तत्पुष्टिम् करोतिति युक्तम्॥

pariṇāma-pakṣe, vṛṣya-prayogasya raktādi-rūpāpatti-krameṇāticireṇa śukraṃ bhavatīti; kṣīrādayaś ca sadya eva vṛṣyā dṛsyante, khale-kapota-pakṣe tu vṛṣyot-

as good as the later one. For on that view also it might be held that by milk its special quality *(prabhāva)* passed quickly through the various stages and became associated with the seminal fluid. Nor can it be said that according to the first theory every case of impurity of *rasa* (*rasa-duṣṭi*) is also a case of impurity of blood (*rakta-duṣṭi),* as is argued; for not the whole of *rasa* is transformed into blood, but only a part of it. So the *rasa* part may be impure, but still the part that goes to form blood may be pure; thus both theories are equally strong, and nothing can be said in favour of either. In *Caraka-saṃhitā*, VI.15.14 and 15, it is said that from *rasa* there is *rakta* (blood), from *rakta* flesh, from flesh fat, from fat bones, from bones marrow, from marrow semen. The two theories above referred to deal with the supposed ways in which such transformations occur.

In addition to the seven *dhātus,* or body-constituents, spoken of above there are ten *upa-dhātus*, which are counted by Bhoja as *śirā, snāyu,* ovarial blood and the seven layers of skin.[1] Caraka says in VI.15.15 that from *rasa* is also produced milk, and from milk ovarial blood; again, the thick tissues or ligaments (*kaṇḍarā*) and *śirās* are produced from blood, and from flesh are produced fat *(vasā)* and the six layers of skin, and from fat *(medas)* are produced the five tissues. The chyle, or *rasa,* becomes tinged with red by the heat of bile. The blood, again, being worked upon by *vāyu* and heat, becomes steady and white, and is called fat *(medas).* The bones are a conglomeration of earth, heat and air and therefore, though produced from flesh and fat, are hard. They are made porous by *vāyu*

---

panno rasaḥ prabhāvāc chīghram eva śukreṇa saṃbaddhaḥ san tat-puṣṭim karotiti yuktam —(Cakrapāṇi on *Caraka-saṃhitā,* I.28.3).

Elsewhere *(Ibid.* VI.15.32) it is said that those articles of food which stimulate semen *(vṛṣyā)* are, according to some authorities, changed into semen in six days and nights, whereas in the ordinary course, as is said in *Suśruta,* it takes a month for the transformation of ordinary articles of food into semen. But Caraka does not favour any time limitation and urges that, just as the movement of a wheel depends upon the energy spent on it, so the time that a particular food takes for getting itself transformed into semen or into any other *dhātu* depends upon the nature of the food and the powers of digestion.

1 Cakrapāṇi on *Caraka-saṃhitā,* VI.15.14 and 15, a quotation from Bhoja. *Ojas* is counted as an *upa-dhātu.*

running through them, and the pores are filled in by fat, which is called marrow. From the oily parts of marrow, again, semen is produced. Just as water percolates through the pores of a new earthen jug, the semen percolates through the pores of the bones, and there is also a flow of this seminal fluid through the body by way of its own ducts. By the rousing of desires and sex joy and by the heat of the sex act the semen oozes out and collects in the testes, from which it is ultimately liberated through its proper channel.[1]

VĀYU, PITTA AND KAPHA

The qualities of the body are briefly of two kinds, those which make the system foul, the *mala,* and those which sustain and purify the body, the *prasāda.* Thus in the pores of the body are formed many undesirable bodily growths which seek egress; some constituents of the body, such as blood, are often turned into pus; the *vāyu* (air), *pitta* (bile) and *kapha* (phlegm or lymph) may become less or more than their normal measure (*prakupita),* and there are other entities which, existing in the body, tend to weaken or destroy it; these are all called *malas.* Others which go towards the sustenance and the growth of the body are called *prasāda.*[2]

But *vāyu, pitta* and *kapha* are primarily responsible for all kinds of morbidities of the body, and they are therefore called *doṣa.* It must, however, be noted that the *vāyu, pitta* and *kapha* and all other *malas,* so long as they remain in their proper measure *(svamāna),* do not pollute or weaken the body or produce diseases. So even *malas* like *vāyu, pitta* and *kapha,* or sweat, urine, etc., are called *dhātus*, or body-constituents, so long as they do not exceed their proper measure, and thus instead of weakening the body they serve to sustain it. Both the *mala-dhātus* and the *prasāda-dhātus* in their proper measure co-operate together in sustaining the body.[3] When

1 *Caraka-saṃhitā,* VI.15.22-29.

2 *Caraka-saṃhitā,* IV.6.17.

3 एवं रसमलौ स्वप्रमाणावस्थितव् आश्रयस्य समधातोर् धातुसाम्यम् अनुवर्तयतः ॥
evaṃ rasa-malau sva-pramāṇāvasthitav āśrayasya sama-dhātor dhātu-sām-yam anuvartayataḥ (Ibid. I.28.3).

various kinds of healthy food and drink are exposed in the stomach to the internal fire of the digestive organs, they become digested by heat. The essential part of the digested food is the chyle *(rasa),* and the impurities which are left out and cannot be assimilated into the body as its constituents are called *kitta* or *mala.* From this *kitta* are produced sweat, urine, excreta, *vāyu, pitta, śleṣman* and the dirt of ear, eye, nose, mouth and of the holes of the hairs of the body, the hair, beard, hair of the body, nails, etc.[1] The impurity of food is excreta and urine, that of *rasa* is phlegm *(kapha),* that of flesh bile *(pitta)* and that of fat *(medas)* sweat.[2] This view of *vāyu, pitta* and *kapha* seems to indicate that these are secretions, waste-products *(kitta),* like the other waste-products of the body. But the theory of waste-products is that, when they are in their proper measure, they serve to sustain the body and perform important functions, but, when they exceed the proper limit or become less than their proper measure, they pollute the body and may ultimately break it. But of all waste-products *vāyu, pitta* and *kapha* are regarded as being fundamentally the most important entities, and they sustain the work of the body by their mutual co-operation in proper measure, and destroy it by the disturbance of balance due to the rise or fall of one, two or all three of them.

As has already been said, the body is composed of certain constituents, such as *rasa* and *rakta.* The food and drink which we take go to nourish the different *dhātus.* Not all the food and drink that we take, however, can be absorbed into the system, and consequently certain waste-products are left.[3] The question arises, what is it that sustains the system or breaks it? It has already been noticed that the

1 *Ibid.* I.28.3.

2 *Ibid.* VI.15.30.

3 Śārṅgadhara (IV.5) counts seven visible waste-products which are different from the three *malas* referred to here as *vāyu, pitta* and *kaph.*These are the watery secretions from tongue, eyes and cheeks, the colouring *pitta,* the dirt of ears, tongue, teeth, armpits and penis, the nails, the dirt of the eyes, the glossy appearance of the face, the eruptions which come out in youth, and beards. Rāḍhamalla, in commenting on this, refers to *Caraka-saṃhitā,* VI.15.29-30, in support of the above passage of Śārṅgadhara. Most of the *malas* are *chidra-malas,* or impurities of the openings.

due proportion of the *dhātus* is what constitutes the health of the body. This due proportion, however, must, as is easy to see, depend on the proper absorption of food and drink in such a way that each of the *dhātus* may have its due share and that only, neither less nor more. It is also necessary that there should be a due functioning of the causes of waste or accretion, working in a manner conducive to the preservation of the proper proportion of the constituents with reference to themselves and the entire system. Deficiency or excess of waste-products is therefore an invariable concomitant of all disturbances of the balance of *dhātus*, and hence the deficiency or excess of waste-products is regarded as the cause of all *dhātu-vaiṣamya.* So long as the waste-products are not in deficiency or excess, they are the agents which constitute the main working of the system and may themselves be therefore regarded as *dhātus.* It is when there is excess or deficiency of one or more of them that they oppose in various ways the general process of that working of the system and are to be regarded as *doṣas* or polluting agents. There are various waste-products of the body; but of all these *vāyu, pitta* and *kapha* are regarded as the three most important, being at the root of all growth and decay of the body, its health and disease. Thus Ātreya says in answer to Kāpyavaca's remarks in the learned discussions of the assembly of the sages, "In one sense you have all spoken correctly; but none of your judgments are absolutely true. Just as it is necessary that religious duties *(dharma),* wealth *(artha)* and desires *(kāma)* should all be equally attended to, or just as the three seasons of winter, summer and rains all go in a definite order, so all the three, *vāta, pitta* and *śleṣman* or *kapha,* when they are in their natural state of equilibrium, contribute to the efficiency of all the sense-organs, the strength, colour and health of the body, and endow a man with long life. But, when they are disturbed, they produce opposite results and ultimately break the whole balance of the system and destroy it."[1] There is one important point to which the notice of the reader should particularly be drawn. I have sometimes translated *mala* as "polluting agents or impurities" and sometimes

1 *Caraka-saṃhitā,* I.12.13.

as "waste-products," and naturally this may cause confusion. The term *mala* has reference to the production of diseases.[1] *Kitta* means waste-products or secretions, and these may be called *mala* when they are in such proportions as to cause diseases. When, however, a *mala* is in such proportions that it does not produce any disease, it is not a *mala* proper but a *mala-dhātu (nirbādha-karān malādīn prasāṃde samcakṣ-mahe)*.[2] In another passage of *Caraka* (I.28.3), which has been referred to above, it is said that out of the digested food and drink there are produced *rasa* and *kitta* (secretion) called *mala (tatrāhāra-prasādākhya-rasaḥ kiṭṭaṃ ca malākhyam abhinirvartate)*, and out of this *kitta* is produced sweat, urine, excreta, *vāyu,pitta* and *śleṣman*. These *malas* are also *dhātus*, inasmuch as they sustain the body as much as the other *dhātus*, *rasa* or *rakta*, etc. do, so long as they are in their proper proportions and balance *(te sarva eva dhātavo malākhyāḥ prasādākhyāś ca)*.[3] Vāgbhaṭa, however, takes a different view of this subject. He separates the *doṣa, dhātu* and *mala* and speaks of them as being the roots of the body. Thus he says that *vāyu* sustains the body, contributing energy *(utsāha)*, exhalation *(ucchvāsa)*, inspiration (*niḥśvāsa*), mental and bodily movement *(ceṣṭā)*, ejective forces *(vega-pravartana)*; *pitta* helps the body by digestive function, heat, the function of sight, imagination *(medhā)*, power of understanding *(dhī)*, courage (*śaurya)*, softness of the body; and *śleṣman*, by steadiness, smoothness, by serving to unite the joints, etc. The functions of the seven *dhātus*, beginning with *rasa*, are said to be the giving of satisfaction through the proper functioning of the senses (*prīṇana* or *rasa)*, the contribution of vitality (*jīvana)*, the production of oiliness (*sneha*), the supporting of the burden *(dhāraṇa)* of the bones (*asthi*), the filling up of bone cavities (*pūraṇa* or *majjā*) and productivity (*garbhotpāda* of *śukra*); of males it is said that the excreta has the

1 *tatra mala-bhūtās te ye śarīrasya bādhakarāḥ syuḥ. Caraka-saṃhitā*, IV.6.17.

2 Cakrapāṇi on *Caraka-saṃhitā*. Compare *Śārṅgadhara*, IV.8: *vāyuḥ pittaṃ kapho doṣā dhātavaś ca malā matāḥ*, i.e. *vāyu, pitta* and *kapha* are known as *doṣa, dhātu* and *mala*.

3 Also *evaṃ rasa-malau sva-pramāṇāvasthitav āśrayasya sama-dhātor dhātu-sāmyam anuvartayataḥ* (*Caraka-saṃhitā*, I.28.3).

power of holding the body, while urine ejects the surplus water and sweat holds it back.[1] The elder Vāgbhaṭa distinguishes the *dhātus* from *vāyu, pitta* and *kapha* by calling the latter *doṣa* (polluting agents) and the former *dūṣya* (the constituents which are polluted). He further definitely denies that the *malas* of *dhātus* could be the cause of disease. He thus tries to explain away this view (that of Caraka as referred to above) as being *aupacārika,* i.e. a metaphorical statement.[2] The body, according to him, is a joint product of *doṣa, dhātu* and *mala.*[3] Indu, the commentator on the *Aṣṭāṅga-saṃgraha,* however, emphasizes one important characteristic of the *doṣas* when he says that the dynamic which sets the *dhātus* in motion (*doṣebhya eva dhātūnāṃ pravṛttiḥ*) is derived from the *doṣas,* and the circulation chemical activities, oiliness, hardness, etc. of the chyle *(rasa)* are derived from them.[4] Owing to the predominance of one or other of the *doṣas* from the earliest period, when the foetus begins to develop, the child is said to possess the special features of one or other of the *doṣas* and is accordingly called *vāta-prakṛti, pitta-prakṛti* or *śleṣma-prakṛti.* Vāgbhaṭa further says that disease is not *dhātu-vaiṣamya,* but *doṣa-vaiṣamya,* and the equilibrium of *doṣas* or *doṣa-sāmya* is health. A disease, on this view, is the disturbance of *doṣas,* and, as *doṣas* are entities independent of the *dhātus*, the disturbance of *doṣas* may not necessarily mean the disturbance of *dhātus.*[5] In another passage the

1 *Aṣṭāṅga-hṛdaya,* I.11.1-5.

2 तज्जान् इत्युपचारेण तान् आहुर् घृतदाहवत्
रसादिस्थेषु दोषेषु व्याधयस् सम्भवन्ति ये॥
tajjān ity-upacāreṇa tān āhur ghṛta-dāhavat
rasādistheṣu doṣeṣu vyādhayas sambhavanti ye.—Aṣṭāṅga-saṃgraha, I.1.

3 Indu, the commentator on the *Aṣṭāṅga-saṃgraha,* puts it as *śarīraṃ ca doṣa-dhātu-mala-samudāyaḥ* (I.1).

4 *tathā ca dhātu-poṣāya rasasya vahana-pāka-sneha-kāṭhinyādi doṣa-prasāda-labhyam eva —(Ibid.).*

5 Āyur-veda is closely associated with the Sāṃkhya and Nyāya-Vaiśeṣika, which alone deal with some sort of physics in Indian philosophy. It is pointed out by Narasiṃha Kavirāja (a writer from the south) in his *Vivaraṇa-siddhānta-cititāmaṇi* (the only manuscript of which is in possession of the present writer) that according to Sāṃkhya it is the *doṣa* transforming itself from a state of equilibrium to a state of unbalanced preponderance of any of them that is to

elder Vāgbhaṭa says that, as the manifold universe is nothing but a modification of the *guṇas,* so all diseases are but modifications of the three *doṣas,* or, as in the ocean waves, billows and foam are seen which are in reality the same as the ocean, so all the different diseases are nothing but the three *doṣas.*[1] The elder Vāgbhaṭa uses also in another place the simile of the three *guṇas* with reference to the three *doṣas.* Thus he says, "As the three *guṇas* co-operate together for the production of the world in all its diversity, in spite of the mutual opposition that exists among themselves, so the three *doṣas* also co-operate together, in spite of natural opposition, for the production of the diverse diseases."[2] In the treatment of the bone system the present writer agrees with Dr Hoernle that Vāgbhaṭa always attempted to bring about a reconciliation between Caraka and Suśruta by explaining away the unadjustable views of one or the other. Here also the same tendency is seen. Thus, on the one hand, he explained away as being metaphorical (*aupacārikī*) the expressed views of Caraka that the *dhātu-malas* are the *doṣas.* On the other hand, he followed the statements of the *Uttara- tantra* that the three *doṣas,* the *dhātus,* excreta and urine sustain a man's body. He further follows the *Uttara-tantra* in holding that the three

---

be called a disease *(vaiṣamya-sāmyāvasthā-bhinnāvasthā-viśeṣavad doṣatvaṃ rogatvam).* The Naiyāyikas, however, hold that disease is a separate entity or substance, which is produced by *doṣa,* but which is not itself a *doṣa (dravyatve sati doṣa-bhinna-doṣa-janyatvaṃ rogatvam).* So a disease is different from its symptoms or effects. Narasiṃha further holds that, since Caraka speaks of diseases as being fiery (*āgneya*) and aerial *(vāyavya),* he tacitly accepts the diseases as separate substances. That Caraka sometimes describes a disease as being *dhātu-vaiṣamya* is to be explained as due to the fact that, since *dhātu-vaiṣamyas* produce diseases, they are themselves also called diseases in a remote sense *(yat tu Carakena dhātu-vaiṣamyasya rogatvam uktaṃ tat teṣāṃ tathā-vidha-duhkha-kartṛtvād aupacārikam. —Vivaraṇa-siddhānta-cintāmaṇi,* MS.p. 3).

1 *Aṣṭāṅga-saṃgraha,* I.22.

2 आरम्भकं विरोधेऽपि मिथो यद् यद् गुणत्रयम्
विश्वस्य दृष्टं युगपद् व्याधेर् दोषत्रयं तथा ॥
ārambhakaṃ virodhe 'pi mitho yad yad guṇa-trayam
viśvasya dṛṣṭaṃ yugapad vyādher doṣa-trayaṃ tathā (Ibid. I.21).

doṣas are the three *guṇas (bhinnā doṣās trayo guṇāḥ).* Ḍalhaṇa identifies *vāyu* with *rajas, pitta* with *sattva* and *kapha* with *tamas.*[1]

In the *Sūtra-sthāna* Suśruta mentions blood *(śoṇita)* as having the same status as *vāyu, pitta* and *kapha* and holds that the body depends on food and drink as well as on the various combinations of *vāyu,pitta, kapha* and *śoṇita* in health and disease. Ḍalhaṇa, in commenting on this, says that, Suśruta's work being principally a treatise on surgery, its author holds that blood with all its impurities plays an important part in producing disturbances in all wounds.[2] Suśruta further speaks of *vāta, pitta* and *śleṣman* as the causes of the formation of the body *(deha-sambhava-hetavaḥ).* The *vāta, pitta* and *kapha,* situated in the lower, middle and upper parts of the body, are like three pillars which support the body, and blood also co-operates with them in the same work. Ḍalhaṇa remarks that *vāta, pitta* and *kapha* are concomitant causes, working in cooperation with semen and blood.[3] Suśruta further derives *vāta* from the root *vā,* to move, *pitta* from *tap,* to heat, and *śleṣman* from *śliṣ,* to connect together. The *Sūtra-sthāna* of Suśruta compares *kapha, pitta* and *vāyu* with the moon *(soma),* the sun *(sūrya)* and air *(anila)* but not with the three *guṇas,* as is found in the supplementary book, called the *Uttara-tantra.* In discussing the nature of *pitta,* he says that *pitta* is the fire in the body and there is no other fire but *pitta* in the body. *Pitta* has all the qualities of fire, and so, when it diminishes, articles of food with fiery qualities serve to increase it, and, when it increases, articles of food with cooling properties serve to diminish it. *Pitta,* according to Suśruta, is situated between the stomach *(āmāśaya)* and the smaller intestines *(pakvāśaya),* and it cooks all food and drink

1 *rajo-bhuyiṣṭho mārutaḥ, rajo hi pravartakaṃ sarva-bhāvānāṃ pittaṃ sattv-ot-kaṭaṃ laghu-prakāśakatvāt,rajo-yuktaṃ vā ity eke kaphas tamo-bahulaḥ,gu-ru-prā-varaṇātmakatvād ity āhur bhiṣajaḥ. Yady evam tat kathaṃ kapha-prakṛ-tike puṃsi sattva-guṇopapannatā paṭhitā, ucyate, guṇa-dvitayam api kaphe jñātavyaṃ sattva-tamo-bahulā āpa* (Ḍalhaṇa on Suśruta, *Uttara-tantra,* 66.9).

2 *etad dhi śalya-tantram, śalya-tantre ca vraṇaḥ pradhāna-bhūtaḥ vraṇe ca dūṣyeṣu madhye raktasya prādhānyam iti śoṇitopādānam (Ibid.).* Suśruta also uses the word *doṣa* to mean pus *(pūya)* (I.5.12).

3 Suśruta, I.21.3 and 4. Ḍalhaṇa, commenting on this, writes: "*śukrārtavādi sahakāritayā deha-janakā abhipretāḥ*"

and separates the chyle on the one hand, and the excreta, urine, etc. on the other. Being situated in the above place, between the stomach and the smaller intestines *(tatra-stham eva),* by its own power *(ātma-śaktyā)* it works in other *pitta* centres of the body and by its heating work *(agni-karma)* sets up the proper activities at those places. In its function of cooking it is called *pācaka,* in its function in the liver and spleen, as supplying the colouring matter of blood, it is called "colouring" *(rañjaka),* in its function in the heart it serves intellectual purposes *(sādhaka),* in its function in the eyes it is called "perceiving," or *locaka,* in its function of giving a glossy appearance to the skin it is called *bhrājaka.* It is hot, liquid and blue or yellow, possesses bad smell, and after passing through unhealthy digestive actions tastes sour. Coming to *śleṣman,* Suśruta says that the stomach is its natural place; being watery, it flows downwards and neutralizes the bile-heat, which otherwise would have destroyed the whole body by its excessive heat. Being in *āmāśaya,* it works in the other centres of *śleṣman,* such as the heart, the tongue, the throat, the head and in all the joints of the body. The place of *vāyu* is the pelvic regions and the rectum *(śroṇi-guda-saṃśraya)*; the main place of the blood, which is counted as *doṣa* by Suśruta, is regarded as being the liver and the spleen.[1] I have noticed above, that in the *Atharva-Veda* mention is found of three kinds of diseases, the airy *(vātaja),* the dry *(śuṣma)* and the wet (*abhraja*).[2] In the *Caraka-saṃhitā vāta, pitta* and *kapha* are regarded as being produced from *kitta,* or secretions. They are thus regarded here as being of the nature of internal waste-products of unassimilated food-juice at the different stages of its assimilation, as chyle, flesh, etc., which have important physiological functions to perform for the preservation of the process of the growth of the body, when they are in due proportions, and they break up the body when they are in undue proportions. What exactly *kitta* means is difficult to determine. It may mean merely the part of the food-juice unassimilated as chyle, or the part of it unassimilated

1 *Suśruta-saṃhitā,* I.11.8-16.

2 *Ye abhrajā vātajā yaś ca śuṣmo* (*Atharva- Veda,* I.12.3); again, *agner ivāsya hata eti śuṣmiṇaḥ* (*Ibid.* VI.20.4).

as blood, and so forth; or it may mean such unassimilated products, together with the secretions from the respective *dhātus,* which absorb the substantial part of the food-juice and throw off some of its impurities into the unabsorbed material; this at least is what *kitta* ought to mean, if it is interpreted as *dhātu-mala,* or impurities of *dhātus*. These secretions and waste-products form the source of most of the constructive and destructive forces of the body. The watery character of *kapha* and the fiery character of *pitta* are not ignored; but their essence or substance is considered to be secretive, or of the nature of waste-product. Suśruta, however, does not seem to refer to this secretive aspect, but he seems to have grasped the essential physiological activity of the body as being of the nature of digestive operation and the distribution of the heat and the products of digestion; and the analogy of cooking, as requiring fire, water and air, seems to have been well before his mind. Suśruta also seems to have leant more towards the view of the physiological operations of the body as being due to elemental activities, the food-juice taking the place of earth and the other three principles being fire *(pitta),* water *(śleṣman)* and air *(vāta)*. The reason why the principles of the body are here regarded as being transformations of fire, water and air is not explained by Suśruta. The supplementary *Uttara-tantra*, however, thinks that they are the three *guṇas*. Vāgbhaṭa, always fond of taking a middle course in his endeavour to reconcile the different attempts to grasp the principles under discussion, holds that they are comparable to the three *guṇas*, because, though opposed to one another, they also co-operate together; and, because diseases are but modifications of the *doṣas*, he further thinks that *doṣas*, *dhātus* and *dhātu-malas* are quite different entities; but he is unable to give any definite idea as to what these *doṣas* are. The person who seems to have had the most definite conception of the *doṣas* was Caraka. In the *Uttara-tantra* and by Vāgbhaṭa the Sāṃkhya analogy of the *guṇas* seems to have had a very distracting influence, and, instead of trying to find out the true physiological position of the *doṣas*, these writers explain away the difficulty by a vague reference to the Sāṃkhya *guṇas*.

Let us now return to Caraka. By him *vāyu* is described as being dry *(rukṣa),* cold (*śīta*), light *(laghu),* subtle (*sūkṣma*), moving *(cala),* scattering everything else in different directions *(viśada)* and rough *(khara).*[1] It is neutralized in the body by those things which have opposite qualities. In the healthy constructive process the *vāyu* is said to perform physiological functions as follows: it sustains the machinery of the body *(tantra-yantra-dharaḥ),* it manifests itself as *prāna, udāna, samāna* and *apāna* and is the generator of diverse kinds of efforts; it is the force which controls (*niyantā*) the mind from all undesirables and directs *(praṇetā)* it to all that is desirable, is the cause of the employment of the sense-organs, is the carrier of the stimulation of sense-objects, collects together the *dhātus* of the body, harmonizes the functions of the body as one whole, is the mover of speech, is the cause of touch and sounds, as also of the corresponding sense-organs, the root of joy and mental energy, the air for the digestive fire, the healer of morbidities, the ejecter of extraneous dirts, the operating agent for all kinds of circulation, the framer of the shape of the foetus, and is, in short, identical with the continuity of life *(āyuṣo 'nuvṛtti-pratyaya-bhūta).* When it is in undue proportions, it brings about all sorts of troubles, weakens the strength, colour, happiness and life, makes the mind sad, weakens the functions of the sense-organs, causes malformations of the foetus, produces diseases and all emotions of fear, grief, delirium, etc., and arrests the functions of the *prāṇas.*

It is interesting to note how Vāyorvida describes the cosmic functions of air as the upholding of the earth, causing the burning of fire, the uniform motion of the planets and stars, the production

---

1 *Caraka-saṃhitā,* I.1.58. Cakrapāṇi, in commenting on this,says that, though *vāyu* is described as neither hot nor cold according to the Vaiśeṣika philosophy, yet, since it is found to increase by cold and decrease by heat, it is regarded as cold. Of course, when connected with *pitta* it is found to be hot, but that is on account of its association with the heat of *pitta (yoga-vāhitvāt*). In the Vāta-kalā-kalīya chapter (I.12.4), six qualities of *vāta* are mentioned; *sūkṣma* is not mentioned, however, and, in place of *cala, dāruṇa* is mentioned. Cakrapāṇi says that *dāruṇa* means the same as *cala.* In the same chapter (I.12.7) *vāyu* is qualified as *śuṣira-kara,* i.e. that which makes holes.

of clouds, the showering of rains, the flow of rivers, the shaping of flowers and fruits, the shooting out of plants, the formation of the seasons, the formation of the strata of minerals, the production of the power of seeds to produce shoots, the growing up of crops, etc.[1] In the same discussion Mārīci considers fire to be contained in the *pitta* and productive of all good and bad qualities, digestion and indigestion, vision and blindness, courage and fear, anger, joy, ignorance, etc., according as it is in equilibrium or is disturbed. Kāpya maintains that *soma,* contained in *śleṣman*, produces all good and bad qualities, such as firmness and looseness of the body, fatness, leanness, energy and idleness, virility and impotence, knowledge and ignorance, etc.[2]

These discussions seem to indicate that before Ātreya's treatise was written attempts were made to explain the physiological functions of the body in health and disease by referring them to the operation of one operative principle. The *Chāndogya Upaniṣad* speaks of earth, water and fire as being world-principles of construction: the different *vāyus* were known as early as the *Atharva-Veda*, and *vāyu* is regarded in many of the Upaniṣads as the principle of life. It seems fairly certain that the theory of *vāta, pitta* and *kapha* is a later development of the view which regarded air *(pavana),* fire (*dahana*) and water (*toya*) as the fundamental constitutive principles of the body. Thus Suśruta refers to this view in III. 4.80: "Some say that the constitution (*prakrti*) of the human body is elemental (*bhautikī*), the three constitutive elements being air, fire and water."[3] The advance of the medical schools of thought over these speculations and over others which consider the body to be a product of one *bhūta* or of many *bhūtas* is to be sought in this, that, besides allowing the material causes *(upādāna)* of the body to be the *dhātus*, they emphasized the necessity of admitting one or

1 *Caraka-saṃhitā*, I.12.8.

2 *Ibid.* I.12.11and 12.

3 प्रकृतिम् इह नराणाम् भौतिकीं केचिद् आहुः
पवनदहनतोयैः कीर्तितास् तास् तु तिस्रः ॥
prakṛtim iha narānām bhautikiṃ kecid āhuḥ
pavana-dahana-toyaiḥ kīrtitās tās tu tisrah. —Śuśruta, III.4.80.

more inherent dynamic principles for the development and decay of the body. This explains how *vāta*, *pitta* and *kapha* are regarded both as *dhātu* and as *doṣa*, as *prakṛti* and as *vikṛti*. Thus Caraka says, as has already been mentioned, that from the time of the formation of the foetus the *vāta*, *pitta* and *kapha* are working, but in more or less diverse ways and in diverse systems, with equal *vāyu, pitta*, *mala* and *kapha (sama-pittānila-kapha)* or different degrees of predominance of them as *vātala, pittala* and *śleṣmala*.[1] Men of the *śleṣmala* type are generally healthy, whereas *vātala and pittala* persons are always of indifferent health. Later on, when there is a disease with the predominance of that *doṣa* which is predominant in man's constitution from his birth, the newly collected *doṣa* produces morbidity on the lines on which the predominating *doṣa* of his constitution is working; but this newly collected *doṣa* does not augment the corresponding original *doṣa*. The original *doṣa* is never increased, and, whatever may be the predominance of a *doṣa* due to any disease, the constitutional condition of the *doṣas* remains the same. Thus a *vāta-prakṛti* person does not become *śleṣma-prakṛti* or *pitta-prakṛti*, and vice-versa. The *doṣas* which are constitutional always remain as the constant part engaged in their physiological operations. The later accretion of the *doṣas* or their deficiency has a separate course of action in producing diseases, and there is no interchange between these later collections of *doṣas* or their de-

1 Caraka refers to a view that there are none who may be regarded as *sama-vāta-pitta-śleṣman* (or having equal *vāta*, *pitta* and *śleṣman)*. Since all men take various kinds of diet (*viṣamāhāropayogitvāt*), they must be either *vāta-prakṛti, pitta-prakṛti,* or *śleṣma-prakṛti*. Against this Caraka says that *sama-vāta-pitta-śleṣman* is the same thing as health or freedom from disease (*aroga)*. All medicines are applied for attaining this end, and there cannot be any doubt that such a state exists. Again, the terms *vāta-prakṛti, pitta-prakṛti* and *śleṣma-prakṛti* are incorrect; for *prakṛti* means health. What they mean by *vāta-prakṛti* is that *vāta* is quantitatively predominant (*ādhikya-bhāvāt sā doṣa-prakṛtir ucyate*), and quantitative predominance is the same as *vikāra*; so the proper terms are *vātala, pittala,* etc. When a *vātala* person takes things which increase *vāta,* his *vāta* increases at once; but when he takes things which increase *pitta* or *śleṣman,* these do not increase in him as rapidly as *vāta* does. So in the case of a *pittala* person *pitta* increases rapidly when articles which increase *pitta* are taken, and so with regard to *śleṣman* (*Caraka-saṃhitā*, III.6.14-18).

ficiency and the constitutional constant parts of the *doṣas* known as *prakṛti.*[1] The only sense (as Cakrapāṇi says) in which a *doṣa* is related to a constitutional *(prakṛti) doṣa* is that a *doṣa* grows strong in a system in which a corresponding *doṣa* is constitutionally predominant, and it grows weaker when the opposite is the case.[2] It is not out of place in this connection to say that, though the *doṣas* are mutually opposed to one another, they do not always neutralize one another, and it is possible for them to grow simultaneously violent in a system. In the six seasons of rains *(varṣā),* autumn *(śarat),* late autumn (*hemanta*), winter *(śīta),* spring *(vasanta)* and summer *(grīṣma)* there is an alternate collection *(caya),* disturbance *(prakopa)* and lowering down *(praśama)* of the three *doṣas, pitta, śleṣman* and *vāyu* respectively. Thus, for example, in the rains *(varṣā)* there is collection of *pitta,* in the autumn *(śarat)* there is disturbance of *pitta,* in the harvesting season *(hemanta)* there is lowering of *pitta* and collection of *śleṣman,* in the summer there is collection of *vāta,* and so forth.[3] Contrasting the functions of the *doṣas* in the normal

1 *Ibid.* I.7.38-41. The passage *prakṛti-sthaṃ yadā pittaṃ mārutaḥ śleṣmaṇaḥ kṣaye* (I.17.45) is often referred to in support of the view that the new accretions of *doṣas* affect the *prakṛti-doṣas.* But Cakrapāṇi explains it differently. He says that a disease may be caused by a *doṣa* which is not in excess of the constant constitutional quantity (*prakṛti-māna*) by virtue of the fact that it may be carried from one part of the body to another and thereby may produce a local accretion or excess, though the total quantity of *doṣa* may not be in excess.

2 *samānāṃ hi prakṛtiṃ prāpya doṣaḥ pravṛddha-balo bhavati, asamānāṃ tu prāpya tathā balavān na syāt* (Cakrapāṇi on *Caraka-saṃhitā,* I.17.62).

3 *Ibid.* I.17.112. See also Cakrapāṇi's comments on these. Ḍalhaṇa, in commenting on *Suśruta-saṃhitā,* I.21.18, says that *sañcaya* of *doṣas* means aggregation or accumulation in general *(dehe 'tirupāvṛddhiś cayaḥ*); *prakopa* of *doṣas* means that the accumulated *doṣas* are spread through the system (*vilayana-rūpā vṛddhiḥ prakopaḥ).* The external signs of the *caya* of *vāta* are fullness of the stomach and want of motions; of *pitta* yellowish appearance and reduction of heat (*mandoṣṇatā*); of *kapha* heaviness of the limbs and feeling of laziness. In all cases of *caya* there is a feeling of aversion to causes which increase the particular *doṣa* of which there has been *caya* (*caya-kāraṇa-vidveṣaś ca).* The stage of *caya* is the first stage of operation in the growth and prevention of diseases. If the *doṣas* can be removed or neutralized at this stage, there is no further disease. The usual indication of the disturbance (*prakopa*) of *vāyu* is disorders of the stomach; of *pitta* acidity, thirst and burning; of *kapha,* aversion to food, palpitation

(prakṛti) and abnormal *(vikṛti)* states, Caraka says that in the normal state the heat of *pitta* occasions digestion; *śleṣman* is strength and vitality, and *vāyu* is the source of all activities and the life of all living beings; but in the abnormal state *pitta* produces many diseases; *śleṣman* is the dirt of the system and the cause of many troubles, and *vāta* also produces many diseases and ultimately death. The places *(sthānāni)* at which the affections of *vāta, pitta* and *kapha* are mostly found are thus described by Caraka: of *vāta* the bladder, rectum, waist and the bones of the leg, but the smaller intestine *(pakvāśaya)* is its particular place of affection; of *pitta* sweat, blood and the stomach, of which the last is the most important; of *śleṣman* the chest, head, neck, the joints, stomach and fat, of which the chest is the most important. There are eighty affections of *vāta,* forty of *pitta* and twenty of *śleṣman.*[1] But in each of these various affections of *vāta*, *pitta* and *śleṣman* the special features and characteristics of the corresponding *dośas* are found. Thus Caraka in I.20.12-23 describes certain symptoms as leading to a diagnosis of the disease as being due to the disturbance of *vāta*, *pitta* or *kapha.* But a question may arise as to what may consistently with this view be

---

(hṛdayotkleda), etc. The *prakopa* of blood (*śoṇita*) is always due to the *prakopa* of *vāta, pitta* or *kapha.* This is the second stage of the progress of diseases. The third stage is called *prasāra.* At this stage there is something like a fermentation of the *doṣas* (*paryuṣita-kiṇvodaka-piṣṭa-samavāya iva).* This is moved about by *vāyu,* which though inanimate, is the cause of all motor activities. When a large quantity of water accumulates at any place, it breaks the embankment and flows down and joins on its way with other streams and flows on all sides; so the *doṣas* also flow, sometimes alone, sometimes two conjointly, and sometimes all together. In the whole body, in the half of it, or in whatever part the fermented *doṣas* spread, there the symptoms of diseases are showered down, as it were, like water from the clouds *(doṣo vikāraṃ nabhasi meghavat tatra varṣati).* When one *doṣa,* e.g. *vāyu,* spreads itself in the natural place of another *doṣa,* e.g. *pitta,* the remedy of the latter will remove the former (*vāyoḥ pitta-sthāna-gatasya pitta-vat praṭīkāraḥ).* The difference between *prakopa* and *prasāra* is thus described by Ḍalhaṇa: just as when butter is first stirred up, it moves a little; this slight movement is like *prakopa*; but, when it is continuously and violently stirred to flow out, in froths and foams, it may then be called *prasāra* (*Suśruta-saṃhitā,* I.21.18-32). The fourth stage is when the *pūrva-rūpa* is seen, and the fifth stage is the stage of *rūpa* or *vyādhi* (disease) *(Ibid.* 38, 39).

1 *Caraka-saṃhitā,* I.20.11.

considered to be the nature of *vāyu,pitta* and *kapha.* Are they only hypothetical entities, standing as symbols of a number of symptoms without any real existence? In such an interpretation reality would belong to the symptoms, and the agents of morbidity, or the *doṣas,* would only be convenient symbols for collecting certain groups of these symptoms under one name. Wherever there is one particular set of symptoms, it is to be considered that there is disturbance of *vāyu*; wherever there is another set of symptoms, there is disturbance of *pitta*, and so forth. But there are serious objections against such an interpretation. For, as we have shown above, there are many passages where these *doṣas* are described as secretions and waste-products, which in their normal proportions sustain and build the body and in undue proportions produce diseases and may ultimately break up the system. These passages could not be satisfactorily explained upon the above interpretation. Moreover, there are many passages which describe *pitta* and *kapha* as entities having a particular colour and material consistency, and it is also said that there are particular places in the body where they collect, and this would be impossible upon the interpretation that they are not real entities, but hypothetical, having only a methodological value as being no more than convenient symbols for a collective grasp of different symptoms.[1]

---

1 The secretory character of these *doṣas* is amply indicated by such passages as those which regard *vāta, pitta* and *śleṣman* as requiring some space in the stomach for digesting the food materials, e.g. *ekaṃ punar vāta-pitta-śleṣmaṇām (Ibid.* III.2.3); *śleṣma hi snigdha-ślakṣṇa-mṛdu-madhura-sāra-sāndra-manda-stimita-guru-ślta-vijjalācchaḥ (śleṣman* is smooth, pleasing, soft, sweet, substantial, compact, inert, benumbed, heavy, cold, moist and transparent—*Ibid.* III.8.14.7.5); *pittam uṣṇaṃ tīkṣṇaṃ dravaṃ visram amlaṃ kaṭukaṃ ca (pitta* is hot, sharp and liquid, and possesses bad odour, and is acid and pungent and bitter—*Ibid.* III.8.14.7.6); *vātas tu rūkṣa-laghu-cala-bahu-śīghra-śita-paruṣa-viśadaḥ* (*vāta* is rough, light, moving, manifold, quick, cold, coarse and scattering—*Ibid.* III.8.14.7.7).

It must, however, be noted that the translation I have given of some of these words cannot be regarded as satisfactory; for in the translation I could only give one sense of a word, which in the original Sanskrit has been used in a variety of senses which the word has. Thus, for example, I have translated *rūkṣa* as "rough." But it also means "slim," "lean," "having insomnia," or (of a voice)

The attribution of a certain number of specific qualities to the *doṣas* is due to a belief that the qualities of effects are due to the qualities of causes. So, from the diverse qualities of our bodies considered as effects, the causes were also considered as having those qualities from which those of the effects were derived. Thus, in connection with the description of the qualities of *vāta,* Caraka says that on account of the qualities of *raukṣya* the bodies of those having congenital *vāta* tendency are rough, lean and small, and the voices of such people are rough, weak, grating, slow and broken, and they cannot sleep well (*jāgarūka*); again, on account of the quality of lightness of *vāyu,* the movements of a man with congenital *vāta* tendency would be light and quick, and so would be all his efforts, eating, speech, and so forth. It is easy to see that the resemblance of the qualities of *vāyu* to the qualities of the body is remote; yet, since the special features and characteristics of one's body were considered as being due to one or the other of the body-building agents, these characteristics of the body were through remote similarity referred to them.

There is another point to be noted in connection with the enumeration of the qualities of the *doṣas.* The disturbance of a *doṣa* does not necessarily mean that all its qualities have been exhibited in full strength; it is possible that one or more of the qualities of a *doṣa* may run to excess, leaving others intact. Thus *vāyu* is said to possess the qualities of *rūkṣa*, *laghu, cala, bahu*, *śīghra, śīta,* etc., and it is possible that in any particular case the *śīta* quality may run to excess, leaving others undisturbed, or so may *śīta* and *rūkṣa,* or *śīta, rūkṣa* and *laghu,* and so forth. Hence it is the business of the

---

"broken," and so forth. There is no English synonym which would have so many senses. Mahāmahopādhyāya Kaviraj Gaṇanātha Sen, of Calcutta, tries to divide the *doṣas* into two classes, invisible *(sūkṣma)* and visible *(sthūla)—Siddhānta-nidāna,* pp. 9-11. But though such a distinction can doubtless be made, it has not been so distinguished in the medical literature, as it is of little value from the medical point of view; it also does not help us to understand the real nature of the *doṣas*. The nature and the functions of the *doṣas* do not depend in the least on their visibility or invisibility, nor can the visible *doṣa* be regarded as always the product of the invisible one.

physician not only to discover which *doṣa* has run to excess, but also to examine which qualities of which *doṣa* have run to excess. The qualities of *doṣas* are variable, i.e. it is possible that a *doṣa* in its state of disturbance will remain a *doṣa,* and yet have some of its qualities increased and others decreased. The nature of the disturbance of a *doṣa* is determined by the nature of the disturbance of the qualities involved *(aṃśāṃśa-vikalpa).*[1] The natural inference from such a theory is that, since the entities having this or that quality are but component parts of a *doṣa,* a *doṣa* cannot be regarded as a whole homogeneous in all its parts. On this view a *doṣa* appears to be a particular kind of secretion which is a mixture of a number of different secretions having different qualities, but which operate together on the same lines. When a particular *doṣa* is in a healthy order, its component entities are in certain definite proportions both with regard to themselves and to the total *doṣa.* But, when it is disturbed, some of the component secretions may increase in undue proportions, while others may remain in the normal state; of course, the quantity of the whole *doṣa* may also increase or decrease. A *doṣa* such as *kapha* or *pitta* should therefore be regarded as a name for a collection of secretions rather than one secretion of a homogeneous character. It will be easily seen that, on taking into consideration the comparative strengths of the different components of a *doṣa* and the relative strengths of the other components of other *doṣas* and the relative strengths and proportions of each of the *doṣas* amongst themselves, the number of combinations is innumerable, and the diseases proceeding from such combinations are also innumerable. The whole system of Caraka's treatment depends upon the ascertainment of the nature of these affections; the

1 *Caraka-saṃhitā,* II.1.10.4. Cakrapāṇi, in commenting on this, says: "*tatra doṣāṇām aṃśāṃśa-vikalpo yathā—vāte prakūpite 'pi kadācid vātasya śītāṃśo balavān bhavati, kadācil laghv-aṃśaḥ, kadācid rūkṣāṃśaḥ kadācil laghu-rūkṣāṃśaḥ.*" The *doṣa* or *doṣas* which become prominently disturbed in a system are called *anubandhya,* and the *doṣa* or *doṣas* which at the time of diseases are not primarily disturbed are called *anubandha.* When three of the *doṣas* are jointly disturbed, it is called *sannipāta,* and when two are so disturbed it is called *saṃsarga (Ibid.* I I I.6.I I).

names of diseases are intended to be mere collective appellations of a number of affections of a particular type.[1]

One further point which ought to be noted with regard to the constructive and destructive operations of *vāyu, pitta* and *kapha* is that they are independent agents which work in unison with a man's *karma* and also in unison with a man's mind. The operations of the mind and the operations of the body, as performed by *vāyu, pitta* and *kapha* on the materials of the *dhātus, rasa, rakta,* etc., run parallel to each other; for both follow the order of human *karma,* but neither of them is determined by the other, though they correspond to each other closely. This psycho-physical parallelism is suggested throughout Caraka's system. Caraka, in trying to formulate it, says: " *śārīram api satvam anuvidhīyate satvaṃ ca śārīram*" (the mind corresponds to the body and the body to the mind). It may be remembered in this connection that the ultimate cause of all *dhātu-vaiṣamya* or *abhighāta* (bodily injuries through accidents, a fall and the like) is foolish action *(prajñāparādha).* Again *vāta, pitta* and *kapha* are found to perform not only physical operations, but also intellectual operations of various kinds. But all intellectual operations belong properly to mind. What is meant by attributing intellectual functions to *vāyu, pitta* and *kapha* seems to be a sort of psycho-physical parallelism, mind corresponding to body, body corresponding to mind, and both corresponding to *karma.*

HEAD AND HEART[2]

The most vital centres of the body are the head, the heart and the pelvis *(vasti).* The *prāṇas*, i.e. the vital currents, and all the senses are said to depend (*śritāḥ*) on the head.[3] The difference between

1 *yad vātārabdhatvādi-jñānam eva kāraṇam rogāṇāṃ cikitsāyām upakāri; nāma-jñānaṃ tu vyavahāra-mātra-prayojanārtham* (Cakrapāṇi on *Caraka-saṃhitā,* I.18.53).

2 The different names of the heart in *Caraka-saṃhitā* are *mahat, artha, hṛdaya* (I.30.3).

3 Cakrapāṇi, however, explains it as *śritā iva śritāḥ,* i.e. "as if they depended on" (I.17.12), because, when the head is hurt, all the senses are hurt. It is said in *Ibid.* VI.26.1 that there are one hundred and seven vital centres (*marma*), and of these

head *(śīrṣa)* and brain *(mastiṣka)* was known as early as the *Atharva-Veda.* Thus in A.V. X.2.6 the word *śīrṣa* is used in the sense of "head," and in verses 8 and 26 of the same hymn the word *mastiṣka* is used in the sense of "brain."[1] Head-disease is also mentioned in the *Atharva-Veda,* I.12.3, as *śīrṣakti.* The brain-matter is called *mastuluṅga* in *Caraka-saṃhitā,* VIII.9.101; the word *mastiṣka* is used in the same chapter in the sense of brain-matter (VIII.9.80), as has also been explained by Cakrapāṇi.[2] The passage from Caraka, VIII.9.4, quoted above shows that at least Dṛḍhabala considered the head to be the centre of the senses and all sense currents and life currents. Cakrapāṇi, in commenting upon this passage, says that, though the currents of sensation and life pass through other parts of the body as well, yet they are particularly connected with the head *(śirasi viśeṣeṇa prabaddhāni),* because, when there is an injury to the head, they are also injured. According to Caraka and Dṛḍhabala all the senses are particularly connected with the head, as well as the *prāṇas,* but the heart is regarded as the vital centre of the *prāṇas,* as well as of the *manas,* as I shall point out later on. Bhela, who is as old as Caraka, considers the brain to be the centre of the *manas,* a view which is, so far as I know, almost unique in the field of Sanskrit literature. He says that *manas,* which is the highest of all senses *(sarvendriya-param),* has its seat between the head and the palate *(śiras-tālv-antara-gatam).* Being situated

---

the three most important are the head, the heart and the pelvis. Also in VIII.9.16, *hṛdi mūrdhni ca vastau ca nṛṇāṃ prāṇāḥ pratiṣṭhitāḥ.* In VIII.9.4 it is distinctly said that all the senses and the currents of senses and *prāṇa* are dependent on the head as the rays of the sun are dependent on the sun—*śirasi indriyāṇi indriya-prāṇa-vahāni ca srotāmsi sūryam iva gabhastayaḥ saṃśritāni.*

1 "Which was that god who (produced) his brain, his forehead, his hindhead (*kakāṭika*), who first his skull, who, having gathered a gathering in man's jaw, ascended to heaven" (A.V.X.2.8). "Atharvan, having sewed together his head (*mūrdhānam*) and also his heart, aloft from the brain the purifying one sent (them) forth, out of the head" *(Ibid.* 26). (Whitney's translation, Harvard oriental series.)

2 *Mastiṣkaṃ śiro-majjā.* Cakrapāṇi, VIII.9.80 of *Caraka-saṃhitā.* The word *mastiṣka* is sometimes, though rarely, used in the sense of head, as in the passage quoted by Cakrapāṇi in VIII.9.80—*mastiṣke 'ṣṭāṅgulam paṭṭam.*

there, it knows all the sense-objects *(viṣayān indriyāṇām)* and the tastes which come near it (*rasādikān samīpa-sthān*). The original cause of *manas* and the energy of all the senses and the cause of all feelings and judgments *(buddhi),* the *citta,* is situated in the heart. The *citta* is also the cause of all motor functions and activities, such that those who are possessed of good *cittas* follow a good course and those who are possessed of bad *cittas* follow a bad course. The *manas* knows the *citta,* and thence proceeds the choice of action; then comes the understanding, deciding what is worth doing and what is not. *Buddhi,* or understanding, is the understanding of certain actions as good *(śubha)* and certain others as bad (*aśubha*).[1] It seems plain that Bhela distinguishes between *manas, citta* and *buddhi.* Of these *manas* is entirely different from *citta* and, so far as can be made out from Bhela's meagre statements, it is regarded as the cause of all cognitions and as having its seat in the brain. The *citta* was regarded as the cause of all activities, feelings and judgments, and the heart was regarded as its seat. *Buddhi* was probably the determinate understanding and judgment which was but a function of the *citta.* Bhela says that the *doṣas* in the brain affect the *manas,* and, as a result of this, the heart is affected, and from the affections of the heart the understanding *(buddhi)* is affected, and this leads to madness.[2] In another passage, while describing the different functions of *pitta,* Bhela says that there is a special kind of

---

1 *śiras-tālv-antara-gataṃ sarvendriya-paraṃ manaḥ tatra-sthaṃ tad dh viṣayān indriyāṇām rasādikān...kāraṇaṃ sarva-buddhīnāṃ cittaṃ hṛdaya-saṃśritaṃ kriyāṇām cetarāsāṃ ca cittaṃ sarvasya kāraṇam.* Bhela's chapter on "*Unmāda-cikitsitam.*" Calcutta University edition, p. 149.

2 ऊरधवं प्रकुपिता दोषांः शिरस्ताल्वन्तरे स्थितां।
मानसं दूषयन्त्य् आशु ततश् चित्तं विपद्यते
चित्ते व्यापदम् आपन्ने बुद्धिर् नाशं नियच्छति
तत्स् तु बुद्धिव्यापत्त कार्याकार्यं न भुध्यते
एवं प्रवर्तते व्याधिर् उन्मादो नाम दारुणः ॥
ūrdhvaṃ prakupitā doṣāḥ śiras-tālv-antare sthitāḥ,
mānasaṃ dūṣayanty āśu tataś cittaṃ vipadyate
citte vyāpadam āpanne buddhir nāśaṃ niyacchti
tatas tu buddhi-vyāpattau kāryākāryaṃ na budhyate
evaṃ pravartate vyādhir unmādo nāma dāruṇaḥ. —Ibid. p. 149.

ālocaka pitta called the *cakṣur-vaiśeṣika,* which, by bringing about the contact of *manas* with the soul, causes cognition and, transmitting it to the *citta,* produces the discriminative visual knowledge by which different objects are comprehended by the eye. The judgmental state, however, is different, and it is produced by a special kind of *ālocaka pitta* called the *buddhi-vaiśeṣika,* which is situated at the point between the eyebrows, and, being there, holds together the subtle forms emanating from the self *(susūkṣmān arthān ātma-kṛtān),* associates the data (*dhārayati*), integrates them with other similar known facts (*pratyudāharati*), remembers the past, and, after producing our knowledge in conceptual and judgmental forms, wills for future realization, generates instructive actions, and is the force which operates in meditation (*dhyāna*) and restraint of thoughts (*dhāraṇā*).[1]

Suśruta does not state anything of importance concerning the brain; but there seems to be little doubt that he knew that particular nerves in the head were connected with particular sense functions. Thus he says in III.6.28 that there are two nerves *(śirā)* lower down the ears on their back, called *vidhurā,* which, if cut, would produce deafness; on both sides of the nasal aperture inside the nasal organ there are two nerves called *phciṇa,* which, if cut, would destroy the sensation of smell; at the back of the eyebrows, below the eyes, there are the nerves called the *apāṅga,* which, if cut, would produce blindness. All these cognitive nerves meet in passing at the centre of the eyebrow *(śṛṅgātaka).*[2] He further says that the nerves are attached to the brain inside the skull on the upper part of it *(mastakābhyantaroparişṭhāt śirā-sandhi-sannipāta)* and this place, called the *romāvarta,* is the supreme superintendent (*adhipati*). Caraka says that the head is the place for the senses. It cannot be decided whether he took this in any deeper sense or whether he means simply that the sense-organs of ear, eyes, nose and taste are situated in the head.

1 Bhela's chapter on "*Puruṣa-niścaya*" p. 81.

2 *ghrāṇa-śrotrākṣi-jihvā-santarpaṇīnāṃ śirāṇāṃ madhye śirā-sannipātaḥ śṛṅgāṭakāni.—Suśruta-saṃhitā,* III.6.28.

Caraka considers the heart *(hṛdaya)* to be the only seat of consciousness.[1] The seats of *prāṇa* are said to be the head, throat, heart, navel, rectum, bladder, the vital fluid *ojas,* semen, blood and flesh.[2] In I.19.3 Caraka, however, excludes navel and flesh and includes the temples *(śaṅkha)* in their place. It is difficult to determine what is exactly meant by *prāṇa* here. But in all probability the word is used here in a general way to denote the vital parts. In I.30.4 and 5 Caraka says that the whole body with the four extremities, the trunk, and the head, collectively called *ṣaḍ-aṅga*, knowledge *(vijñāna),* the senses, the sense-objects, the self, *manas* and the objects of thought *(cintya),* are all supported *(saṃśrita)* by the heart, just as a house is supported by pillars and rafters.[3] It is plain, as Cakrapāṇi explains, that the body cannot subsist in the heart. What is meant is that, when all is well with the heart, it is w^rell with all the rest. Caraka holds that the *manas* and the soul reside in the heart and so also do cognition, pleasure and pain, not, however, in the sense that the heart is the place where these reside, but in the sense that they depend on the heart for their proper functioning; if the heart is wrong, they also go wrong, if the heart is well, they also work well. Just as rafters are supported by pillars, so are they all supported by the heart. But Cakrapāṇi does not seem to agree with this view of Caraka, and he holds that, since the heart is affected by strong thoughts, pleasure and pain, the mind and the soul actually reside in the heart and so do pleasure and pain. The self, which is the cause of all knowledge of sense-objects and the upholder (*dhārin*) of the system, resides in the heart. It is for this reason that, if a man is struck in the heart, he swoons away, and, if the heart bursts, he dies. It is also the place of the supreme vitality (*param ojas*).[4] The heart

1 *Caraka-samhitō,* IV.7.8, *hṛdayaṃ cetanādhiṣṭhānam ekam.*

2 *Ibid.* 9.

3 *Caraka-saṃhitā,* I.30.5.

4 Cakrapāṇi says that the mention of *param ojas* here proves that Caraka believed in another, *aparam ojas.* The total quantity of *aparam ojas* in the bodv is half a handful *arrdhāñjali-parimāṇā),* while that of *param ojas* is only eight drops of a white-red and slightly yellowish liquid in the heart. The *dhamanīs* of the heart contain half a handful of *aparam ojas,* and in the disease known as *prameha* (uri-

is also regarded as the place where all consciousness is concentrated (*tatra caitanya-saṃgrahaḥ*). Caraka says that the heart is the centre of the *prāṇa* currents (*prāṇa-vahānāṃ srotasāṃ hṛdayaṃ mūlam,* III.5.9) and also of the currents of mental activity (II.7.3). In the *Apasmāra-nidāna* (II.8.4) Caraka speaks of the heart as being the supreme place of the inner self *(antar-ātmanaḥ śreṣṭham āyatanam).*

It may not be out of place here to point out that the *Taittirīya-upaniṣad* (I.6.1) also speaks of the heart as being the space where *manomaya puruṣa,* i.e. the mind-person, resides. In many other Upaniṣads the heart is the centre of many *nāḍīs,* or channels.[1] Śaṅkara, in explaining *Bṛh.* II.I.19, says that the *nāḍīs* or *śirās,* called *hitā,* which are developed out of the food-juice and are 272,000 in number, emanate from the heart and spread over the whole body (*purītat*).[2] The *buddhi* resides in the heart and from there controls the external senses. Thus, for example, at the time of hearing in the awakened state the *buddhi* passes through these *nāḍīs* to the ear and from there expands the auditory organ and superintends it. When the *buddhi* thus expands, we have the state of awakening, when it contracts, the state of deep sleep *(suṣupti).*

THE CIRCULATORY AND THE NERVOUS SYSTEM

The names *śirā* (also *hirā)* and *dhamani*, of two different kinds of channels in the body, seem to have been distinguished at a peri-

nary disease) it is this *ojas* that is wasted; but even with waste of this *ojas* a man may live, whereas with the slightest waste of the *param ojas* a man cannot live. *Ojas* ought not to be regarded as the eighth *dhātu;* for it only supports *(dhārayati)* the body, but does not nourish it. *Ojas,* however, is sometimes used also in the sense of *rasa* (*Caraka-saṃhitā* I.30.6, Cakrapāṇi's commentary). See also *Ibid.* I.17.74 and 75 and Cakrapāṇi's comment on the same. *Ojas* is, however, regarded in the *Atharva-Veda,* II.17, as the eighth *dhātu.*

1 See *Bṛh.*I I. I.19, IV.2.2 and 3, IV.3.20, IV.4.8 and 9; *Chānd.*VIII.6.6; *Kaṭha,* VI.16; *Kauṣ.* IV.19; *Muṇḍ.* II.2.6; *Maitrī,* Bibliotheca Indica, 1870, VI.21, VII.11; *Praśna,* iii.6 and 7.

2 The word *purītat* means principally the covering of the heart. But Śaṅkara takes it here to mean the whole body.

od as early as the *Atharva-Veda.*[1] *The Bṛhad-āraṇyaka Upaniṣad* describes the *hitā nāḍīs* of the heart as being as fine as a thousandth part of a hair, and they are said to carry white, blue, yellow and green liquids; Śaṅkara, commenting on this, says that these various colours are due to the various combinations of *vāta, pitta* and *śleṣman* which the *nāḍls* carry.[2] He states that the seventeen elements (five *bhūtas,* ten senses, *prāṇa* and *antaḥkaraṇa*) of the subtle body, which is the support of all instinctive desires, abide in these *nāḍīs.* In *Bṛhad-āraṇyaka*, IV.2.3 it is said that there is the finest essence of food-juice inside the cavity of the heart; it is this essence which, by penetrating into the finest *nāḍīs*, serves to support the body. It is surrounded by a network of *nāḍīs.* From the heart it rushes upwards through the extremely fine *hitā nāḍīs*, which are rooted in the heart. *Chāndogya*, VIII.6.6 speaks of 101 *nāḍīs* proceeding from the heart, of which one goes towards the head.[3] In *Muṇḍ.* II.2.6 it is said that, like spokes in a wheel, the *nāḍīs* are connected with the heart. *Praśna*, III.6 and 7, however, says that in the heart there are one hundred *nāḍīs* and in each of

---

1 *śataṃ hirāḥ sahasraṃ dhamanīr uta.* —*Atharva- Veda,* VII.36.2.
Sāyaṇa explains *hirā* as *garbha-dhāraṇārthaṃ antar-avasthitāḥ sūkṣmā nāḍyaḥ* and *dhamanī* as *garbhāśayasya avaṣṭambhikā sthūlā nāḍyaḥ.—Atharva-Veda,* I.17.1, 2, also seems to distinguish *hirā* from *dhamanī.*

In I.17.1 the *hirās* are described as being of red garments (*lohita-vāsasaḥ*), which Sāyaṇa explains as *lohitasya rudhirasya nivāsa-bhūtā hi* (the abode of blood) and paraphrases as *rajo-vahana-nāḍyaḥ.* It seems, therefore, that the larger ducts were called *dhamanis.*In I.17.3 the *Atharva-Veda* speaks of hundreds of *dhamanīs* and thousands of *hirās.*

2 *Bṛh.* IV.3.20, with Śaṅkara's commentary. Anandagiri, in commenting on the same, quotes a passage from Suśruta which is substantially the same as *Suśruta-saṃhitā,* III.7.18, to show that those *śirās* which carry *vāta* are rosy (*aruṇa*), those which carry *pitta* are blue, those which carry blood are red, and those which carry *śleṣman* are white:

अरुणाः शिरा वातवहानीलां पित्तवहाः शिराः
असृग्वहास् तु रोहिण्यो गौर्यः श्लेष्मवहाह् शिराः ॥
aruṇāḥ śirā vāta-vahā nīlāḥ pitta-vahāḥ śirāḥ
asṛg-vahās tu rohiṇyo gauryaḥ śleṣma-vahāh śirāḥ.

3 This passage is sometimes referred to in later literature to show that the *suṣumṇā nāḍī,* which goes towards the head, was known as early as the *Chāndogya Upaniṣad.* See also *Kaṭha,* VI.16.

these are twenty-two hundred branches and the *vyāna vāyu* moves through these. The *Maitrī Upaniṣad* mentions the *suṣumṇā nāḍī* proceeding upwards to the head, through which there is a flow of *prāṇa.*[1] None of these passages tell us anything definite about the *nāḍīs.* All that can be understood from these passages is that they are some kind of ducts, through which blood and other secretions flow, and many of these are extremely fine, being about the thousandth part of a hair in breadth. The *naḍa,* or hollow reed, is described in the *Ṛg-Veda* (VIII.1.33) as growing in ponds and in the *Atharva-Veda* (IV.19.1) as being *vārṣika,* or "produced in the rains." This word may have some etymological relation with *nāḍī.*[2] In another place it is said that women break *naḍa* with stones and make mats out of them.[3] The word *nāḍī* is also used in the *Atharva-Veda* in the sense of "ducts."[4] In *Atharva-Veda,* V.18.8 the word *nāḍikā* is used to denote the speech organ (*vāk*). The word *dhamani* is used in *Ṛg-Veda,* II.11.8 and is paraphrased by Sāyaṇa as

---

1 *Urdhva-gā nāḍī suṣumṇākhyā prāṇa-saṃcāriṇī.—Maitrī,* VI.21. Sāyaṇa, in his commentary on A.V.I.17.3, quotes the following verse:

मध्यस्थायाः सुषुणायाः पर्वपङ्कसंभवाः
शाखोपशाखतां प्राप्ताः शिरा लक्षत्रयात् परं अर्धलक्षम् इति
प्राहुः शरीरार्थविचारकाः ॥

madhya-sthāyāḥ suṣumṇāyāḥ parva-pañcaka-saṃbhavāḥ
śākhopaśākhatāṃ prāptāḥ śirā lakṣa-trayāt paraṃ ardha-lakṣam iti
prāhuḥ śarīrārtha-vicārakāḥ.

2 Macdonell makes the following remarks in his *Vedic Index,* vol. I, p. 433: "*Naḍa* is found in several passages of the *Ṛg-Veda* (I.32, 8; 179, 4; II.34, 3; VIII.69, 2; X.I I, 2; 105, 4) but its sense is still obscure. It is identified by Pischel *(Zeitschrift der Deutschen Morgenländischen Gesellschaft,* 35, 717 *et seq.; Vedische Studien,* I.183 *et seq.)* with *Naḍa,* being explained by him in one passage (I.32.8). Here Caland and Henry, *L'Agniṣṭoma,* p. 313 would read *nalam.* See also Wackernagel, *Altindische Grammatik,* I.173, as a reed boat, which is split, and over which the waters go, etc."

3 *yathā naḍaṃ kaśipune striyo bhindanty aśmanā (Atharva- Veda,* VI.138.5).

4 In the *Atharva-Veda,* VI.138.4, the *nāḍīs* are described as ducts over the testes, through which the seminal fluid flows: *ye te nādyau deva-kṛte yayos tiṣṭhati vṛṣṇyaṃ te te bhinadmi* (I break with a stone upon a stone those two ducts of yours made by God over your two testes, through which your semen flows). In X.7.15 and 16, the hollows of the seas are described as *nāḍīs* (*samudro yasya nāḍyaḥ),* and so also the interspace of the quarters of the sky (*yasya catasraḥ pradiśo nāḍyaḥ).*

sound *(śabda)* and by Macdonell as "reed" or "pipe."[1] If Sāyaṇa's explanations are to be accepted, then in A.V. II.33.6 the word *snāva* means fine *śirās (sūkṣmāḥ-sirāḥ)* and *dhamanī* the larger ducts *(dhamani-śabdena sthūlāḥ).* In VI.90.5 one hundred *dhamanis* are said to surround the body of a person suffering from colic or gout *(śūla),* and Sāyaṇa paraphrases *dhamani* here as *nāḍī.* In *Chāndogya,* III.19.2, the rivers are said to be *dhamanis (yā dhamanayas tā nāḍyaḥ*), and Śaṅkara paraphrases *dhamanī* as *śirā.* I have already referred to the use of the word *hirā* in the *Atharva-Veda;* the word is also used in the *Ṛg-Veda.*[2]

The above references show that *nāḍīs, śirās* (or *hirās)* and *dhamanīs* were all ducts in the body, but sometimes the *nāḍīs* or *śirās* had also the special sense of finer channels, whereas the *dhamanīs* were the larger ducts. I shall now come to Caraka: it will be found that there was not much advance towards a proper understanding of the significance of their distinction and functions.

Caraka plainly regards *dhamanīs, śirās* and *srotas* (secretory currents) as ducts and thinks that different names are applied to them on account of their different functions. He says that the roots of the ten *dhamanīs* are in the heart. These carry throughout the body the *ojas,* by which all people live and without which they all die. It is the essence by which the foetus is formed, and which goes to the heart at a later stage, when the heart is formed; when it is lost, life also ceases to exist; it is the essence of the body and the seat of the *prāṇas.* These ducts are called *dhamanīs,* because they are filled with chyle from outside; they are called *srotas,* because the chyle, etc. which nourish the body are secreted *(sravaṇāt)* out of these; and they are called *śirā,* because they go *(saraṇāt śirāḥ*) to the

1 "*Dhamanī*, 'reed,' appears to denote 'pipe' in a passage of the *Ṛg-Veda* (II.11.8) and in a citation appearing in the *Nirukta* (VI.24)." *Vedic Index,* vol. I, p. 390. The word *śirā* is spelt with a palatal "ś" in *Caraka* and with a dental in the Vedas, and it has therefore been differently spelt in this chapter in different contexts.

2 *Tvaṃ vṛtram āśayānaṃ sirāsu moho vajreṇa siṣvapaḥ.* R.V.I.121.11.The word *dhamanī* is spelt with a long "ī" in *Caraka* and with a short "i" in the *Atharva-Veda.*

different parts of the body.[1] The ten *dhamanīs* spread out in manifold branches throughout the body. In the *Caraka-saṃhitā srotas* means properly the path through which the successive evolutionary products of the body-constituents *(dhātus)* or other kinds of secretion run and accumulate together with elements of their own types.[2] Cakrapāṇi explains it thus: The transformation into blood takes place in connection with chyle *(rasa)*. The coming together of *rasa* with blood at a different part of the body cannot take place without a path of transmission, called *srotas*. So the transformation of *dhātus* takes place through the function of this path of transmission. So for each kind of product there is a separate *srotas*. *Vāyu, pitta* and *kapha* may be said to go about through all the *srotas*, though there are, no doubt, special channels for each of the three.[3] Gaṅgādhara, however, takes the *srotas* as being the apertures through which the *dhātus* and other waste-products flow.[4] In whatever way it may be looked at, the *srotas* is, according to Caraka, nothing but the duct of the *dhamanīs*. Caraka opposes the view of those who think that the body is nothing but a collection of *srotas*, for the simple reason that the substances which pass through these *srotas* and the parts of the body where they are attached are certainly different from the *srotas* themselves. There are separate *srotas* for the flow of *prāṇa*, water, food-juice, blood, flesh, fat, bony materials, marrow, semen, urine, excreta and sweat; *vāta, pitta* and *śleṣman*, however, flow through the body and all the channels *(sarva-srotāṃsi ayana-bhūtāni)*. For the supply of materials for the suprasensual elements of the body, such as *manas*, etc., the whole of the living body serves as a channel.[5] The heart is the root of all *prāṇa* channels, i.e. the channels of

1 *dhmānāḍ dhamanyaḥ sravaṇāt srotāṃsi saraṇāt śirāḥ. Caraka-saṃhitā,* I.30.11.

2 *Ibid.* III.5.3.

3 *Doṣāṇāṃ tu sarva-śarīra-caratvena yathā-sthūla-sroto 'bhidhāne 'pi sarva-srotāṃsy eva gamanārthaṃ vakṣyante...vātādīnām api pradhāna bhūtādhamanyaḥ santy eva.* —Cakrapāṇi's comment on *Ibid.*

4 *āhāra-pariṇāma-raso hi srotasāṃ chidra-rūpaṃ panthānaṃ vinā gantuṃ na śaknoti, na ca srotaś chidra-pathena gamanaṃ vinā tad-uttarottara-dhātutvena pariṇamati,* etc. —Gaṅgādhara's *Jalpa-kalpa-taru* on *Ibid.*

5 Gaṅgādhara, in commenting on this passage (*Caraka-saṃhitā,* III.5.7), "*tadvad atīndriyāṇāṃ punaḥ sattvādīnāṃ kevalaṃ cetanāvac charīram ayana-bhūtam*

the *prāṇa vāyu*; for *vāyu* in general moves through all parts of the body. When these are affected, there is either too much or too little respiration; the respiration may be very slow or very quick, and it is attended with sound and pain. From these signs therefore one can infer that the *prāṇa* channels have been affected. The source of water channels is the palate, and the seat of thirst is in the heart *(kloma)*.[1] When these are affected, the tongue, palate, lips, throat and *kloma* become dried up, and there is great thirst. The stomach is the source of all currents carrying food, and, when these are affected, there is no desire for food, but indigestion, vomiting and the like. The heart is the source, and the ten *dhamanīs* are the paths, of the chyle *(rasa)* currents. The liver and spleen are the source of blood currents. The tendons and skin are the sources of flesh currents. The kidneys are the sources of fat channels; fat and pelvis, of bone channels; the bones and joints, of marrow channels; the testes and penis, of semen channels; the bladder, the pubic and the iliac regions, of urine channels; the intestines and the rectum, of the excreta channels, and the fat and pores of hairs, of perspiration channels.[2] It is curious, however, to note that, in spite of the fact that here the *śirās* and *dhamanīs* are regarded as synonymous, their number is differently counted in IV.7.13, where it is said that there are two hundred *dhamanīs* and seven hundred *śirās*, and the finer endings of these are counted as 29,956. It is reasonable to suppose, in accordance with the suggestions found in *theAtharva-Ve-*

---

adhiṣṭhāna-bhūtaṃ ca," says, "*mana ātmā śrotra-sparśana-nayana-rasana-ghrāṇa-huddhy-ahaṅkārādināṃ kevalam cetanāvat sajīvaṃ śarīra-sroto ' yana-bhūtam adhiṣṭhāna-bhūtaṃ ca*" There are several passages in Caraka where we hear of *mano-vaha* currents (currents carrying *manas*); if *manas, buddhi, ahaṅkāra*, etc. can all be carried in currents, they must be considered as having some material spatial existence. These *manas, buddhi* and *ahaṅkāra* may be *atīndriya,* but they are not on that account non-physical.

1 *Caraka-saṃhitā,* III.5.10. Cakrapāṇi explains it *(klomā)* as *hṛdaya-stham pipāsā-sthānam,* and Gaṅgādhara as the point of conjunction between the throat and the heart (*kaṇṭhorasoḥ sandhiḥ).*

2 The synonyms for *srotas* given by Caraka are *śirā, dhamanī, rasa-vāhinī, nāḍī, panthā, mārga, śarīra-chidra, saṃvṛtāsaṃvṛtāni* (open at the root, but closed at the end), *sthāna, āśaya* and *niketa.*

da, that, though the *dhamanīs* and *śirās* were regarded by Caraka as having the same functions, the former were larger than the latter.[1] Gaṅgādhara, in commenting on this passage, says that *śirās, dhamanīs* and *srotas* are different on account of their being different in number and of their having different functions and different appearances. It is well known that a distinction between *śirās* and *dhamanīs* is drawn by Suśruta, to which I shall presently refer, but Caraka positively denies any such distinction; and this is accepted by his commentator Cakrapāṇi also.[2] Gaṅgādhara is unable to point out any passage in *Caraka* to prove his opinion or to state more explicitly what is the difference of functions and appearances between the *dhamanīs* and *śirās*. In fact Gaṅgādhara's remarks are directly borrowed from *Suśruta*, III.9.3, without acknowledgment, and it is very surprising that he should not know the difference of views on this point between Caraka and Suśruta and should try to support Caraka by a quotation from Suśruta on the very point on which they materially differ.

Suśruta refers to Caraka's view that *śirās, srotas* and *dharmanīs* are the same and opposes it, saying that they are different in appearance, number and functions. Ḍalhaṇa, in explaining this, says that the *śirās* carry *vāta*, *pitta*, *śleṣman*, blood, etc., and are rosy, blue, white and red, whereas the *dhamanīs* that carry sense-im-pressions of sound, etc. have no distinctive colour, and the *srotas* have the same colour as the *dhātus* which flow through them. Again, the principal *śvrās* are forty in number, the principal *dhamanīs* twenty-four and the principal *srotas* twenty-two in number. The *śirās* permit us to contract or expand our limbs or perform other motor functions, and they allow the mind and senses to operate in their own ways and serve also to fulfil other functions of moving rapidly *(prasyandana)*, etc., when *vāyu* works in them. When *pitta*

---

1 There is one passage of Dṛḍhabala *(Caraka-saṃhitā,* VI.29.23) which seems to draw a distinction between *śirās* and *dhamanīs", * for there, as a symptom of a disease, it is said that the *śirās* have expanded *(āyāma)* and the *dhamanīs* have become contracted *(saṅkoca).*

2 *na ca Carake Suśruta iva dhamanī-śirā-srotasāṃ bhedo vivakṣitaḥ.*
—Cakrapāṇi's commentary on *Caraka,* III.5.3.

flows through the *śirās,* they appear shining, create desire for food, increase digestive fire and health. When *śleṣman* passes through them, they give an oily appearance to the body, firmness of joints and strength. When blood passes through them, they become coloured and filled also with the different *dhātus* and produce the sense-cognition of touch. *Vāyu*, *pitta, śleṣman* and blood—any one of these may flow through any and every *śirā.*[1] The *dhamanīs* are more like sensory nerves, since they carry sensations of sound, colour, taste and smell *(śabda-rūpa-rasa-gandha-vahatvādikaṃ dhamanīnāni).* The *srotas* carry *prāṇa,* food, water, chyle, blood, flesh and fat.[2] It is on account of their close proximity, similar functions, fineness (*saukṣmyāt),* and also because of the fact that they have been referred to in similar terms by older authorities, that they have sometimes been regarded as performing the same work, though their functions are really different.[3] Ḍalhaṇa, in explaining this, says that, as, when a bundle of grass is burning, the burning of each separate blade of grass cannot be perceived on account of their contiguity, so the *śirās, dhamanīs* and *srotas* are situated so close to one another that it is very difficult to observe their separate functions and work. *Śirā, srotas*, *mārga, kha* and *dhamanī* are the general names used to denote the canals or ducts of the body.[4] It is on account of the similarity of action of all these ducts that their functions are sometimes confused.

The *dhamanīs* start from the navel; ten proceed to the upper part of the body, ten to the lower part and four crosswise (*tir-yag-gāḥ).* Those ten which go to the upper part of the body, branch out, are divided into three classes, and are thirty in number. Of these there are altogether ten for carrying *vāta*, *pitta, kapha*, *śoṇita* and *rasa,* two

1 *Suśruta-saṃhitā,* I I I.7.8-17.

2 Ḍalhaṇa on *Ibid.* III.9.3.

3 *Ibid.*

4 Thus Ḍalhaṇa remarks:

आकाशीयावकाशानं देहे नामानि देहिनां
शिराः स्रोतांसि मार्गाः खं धमन्यः ॥
Ākāśīy āvakāśānāṃ dehe nāmāni dehināṃ
śirāḥ srotāṃsi mārgāḥ khaṃ dhamanyaḥ.

for each; there are eight for carrying *śabda, rūpa*, *rasa* and *gandha,* two for each; there are two for the organ of speech, two for making noise *(ghoṣa),* as distinguished from speech; two for going to sleep, two for being awake; two for bearing tears, two for carrying milk in women, and it is the same two *dhamanīs* that carry the semen in men. It is by these *dhamanīs* that the body on the upper side of the navel (e.g. sides, back, chest, shoulders, hands, etc.) is held fast to the lower part. The carrying of *vāta*, etc. is the common quality of all these *dhamanīs.* Those *dhamanīs* which branch out downwards are thirty in number. They eject *vāta,* urine, excreta, semen, menstrual blood, etc. downwards. They are connected with the place of *pitta (pittāśaya),* draw downwards the materials not fit for being absorbed, and nourish the body with the assimilable products of digestion. The *dhamanīs* connected with the *pittāśaya* carry the food-juice throughout the body, as soon as it is digested by the action of heat, by supplying it to the upper circulatory *dhamanīs* and through them to the heart, which is designated as the seat of *rasa (rasa-sthāna).*[1] Ten *dhamanīs* carry *vāta, pitta*, *śoṇita*, *kapha* and *rasa*; two, connected with the intestines, carry the food-juice; two carry water; two are connected with the bladder for ejecting urine; two are for the production of semen *(śukra-prādur-bhāva),* two for its ejection, and it is these which regulate the menstrual flow in the case of women; two, connected with the larger intestines, eject the excreta; there are eight others which carry perspiration. It is by these *dhamanīs* that the intestines, waist, urine, excreta, rectum, bladder and penis are held together.

Each of the other four *dhamanīs*, which go crosswise *(tiryag-gāḥ),* has hundreds and thousands of branches, which, innumerable

1 *Suśruta*, *Śārīra*, IX.7 and 8; see also Ḍalhaṇa's commentary on it. The apertures of some *dhamanīs* by which the food-juice is circulated through the body are as fine as lotus fibres, and some grosser than them, as the apertures of lotus stalks. Thus some *dhamanīs* have very fine apertures, and others grosser apertures.

यथा स्वभावतः खानि मृणालेषु बिसेषु च
धमनीनां तथा खानि रसो यैर् उपचीयते ॥

yathā svabhāvataḥ khāni mṛṇāleṣu biseṣu ca
dhamanīnāṃ tathā khāni raso yair upacīyate.—Ibid. IX.10.

as they are, are spread all over the body, like so many windows; their mouths are at the holes of the hairs, through which perspiration goes out and which nourish the body with *rasa,* and through these the effective principles (*vīrya*) of oil, watery sprinklings, ointments, etc. enter the body after being acted on by *bhrājaka* (heat of the skin).[1] It is again these which carry the pleasurable and painful sense-impressions of touch.[2] The *dhamanīs* direct the five senses to the five sense-objects for their cognition. There is the cognizer (*mantṛ*) and the *manas* organ; the *dhamanī* which is connected with *manas* on one side and the *dhamanīs* which *carry* the different sense-impressions on the other make the sense-data cognized by the self.[3] The various sensory and motor *dhamanīs* are further named in Suśruta, III.VI.28. Down below the back of the ear there are two *dhamanīs,* called *vidhura,* which, when injured, produce deafness; inside the two nostrils there are the two *dhamanīs* called *phaṇa* which, when hurt, arrest the sensation of smell. Below the eyebrows on the two sides of the eye there are the two *dhamanīs,* called *apāṅga,* which, when hurt, produce blindness: there are also two other *dhamanīs,* above the eyebrows and below them, called *āvarta,* which, when

1 *Suśruta, Śārīra,* IX.7 and 8; see also Ḍalhaṇa's commentary on it.

2 Ḍalhaṇa in commenting on this passage of Suśruta, III.IX.9, says: "*tair eva mano-nugataiḥ sukhāsukha-rūpaṃ sparśaṃ karmātmā gṛhṇīte*" (It is through these *dhamanīs,* as connected by *manas,* that the self, as associated with the subtle body, receives the pleasurable and painful impressions of touch.)

3 पञ्चाभिभूतास् त्व् अथ पञ्चकृत्वः
पञ्चेन्द्रियं पञ्चसु भावयन्ति
पञ्चेन्द्रियं पञ्चसु भावयित्वा
पञ्चत्वम् आयान्ति विनाशकाले ॥
pañcābhibhūtās tv atha pañca-kṛtvaḥ
pañcendriyaṃ pañcasu bhāvayanti
pañcendriyaṃ pañcasu bhāvayitvā
pañcatvam āyānti vināśa-kāle.—Suśruta, III.IX.11.

Ḍalhaṇa, in commenting on the above, says:
"मन्ता हि शरीरे एक एव, मनोऽप्य् एकम् एव, तेन मनसा यैव
धमनी शब्दादिवहासु धमनीस्व् अभिप्रपन्ना सैव धमनी स्वधर्मं ग्राहयति मन्तारं नान्येति" ॥
"*mantā hi śarīre eka eva, mano 'py ekam eva, tena manasā yaiva dhamanī śabdādi-vahāsu dhamanīṣv abhiprapannā saiva dhamanī sva-dharmaṃ grāhayati mantāraṃ nānyeti.*"

hurt, also produce blindness. Suśruta also speaks in this connection of a place inside the skull on the upper part of the brain, where all the *śirās* have met together, as the *adhipati* superintendent.

In describing the *śirās* (700 in number) Suśruta says that these are like so many canals by which the body is watered and by the contraction and expansion of which the movements of the body are rendered possible. They start from the navel and branch out like so many fibres of leaves. The principal *śirās* are forty in number; of these ten are for the circulation of *vāta, ten* for *pitta,* ten for *kapha* and ten for *rakta* (blood). The *śirās* of *vāta* circulation again branch out into 175 *śirās,* and the same is the case with those which circulate *pitta*, *kapha* and *rakta.* We have thus altogether 700 *śirās.* When *vāta* is properly circulated through the *śirās*, it becomes possible for us to move our limbs without obstruction and to exercise our intellectual functions. But it should be noted that, though some *śirās* are regarded as mainly circulating *vāyu* or *pitta* or *kapha*, yet they all, at least to some extent, circulate all three.[1]

There are 900 *snāyus*, and these have also holes within them *(suṣirāḥ),* and these, as well as the *kaṇḍarās,* which are also but special kinds of *snāyus,* serve to bind the joints of the body, just as the several pieces of planks are held together in a boat. Suśruta also mentions five hundred muscles. The *marmas* are vital spots in flesh, *śirā, snāyu* and bones which are particularly the seats of *prāṇa:* when persons are hurt in these places, they may either lose their lives or suffer various kinds of deformity. The *srotas* are again described by Suśruta as being ducts, other than *śirā* and *dhamanī,* which start from the cavity of the heart and spread out through the body.[2] These *srotas* carry the currents of *prāṇa*, food-juice, water, blood, flesh, fat, urine, excreta, semen and menstrual blood.

---

1 न हि वातं शिराः कास्चिन् न पित्तं केवलं तथा
श्लेष्मानम् वा वहन्त्य् एता अंतः सर्ववहाः स्मृताः ॥
na hi vātaṃ śirāḥ kāscin na pittaṃ kevalaṃ tathā
śleṣmānam vā vahanty etā ataḥ sarvavahāḥ smṛtāḥ.—Suśruta, III.vii.16.

2 मूलात् खाद् अन्तरं देहे प्रसृतं त्व् अभिवाहि यत्
स्त्रोतस् तद् इति विज्ञेयं शिराधमनीवर्जितम् ॥
mūlāt khād antaraṃ dehe prasṛtaṃ tv abhivāhi yat
srotas tad iti vijñeyaṃ śirā-dhamanī-varjitam.—Suśruta, Śārīra, IX.13:

THE NERVOUS SYSTEM OF THE TANTRAS.

The nerve system of the Tantras, however, is entirely different from that of the medical systems of Caraka and Suśruta. It starts with the conception of the spinal column *(meru-daṇḍa),* which is regarded as one bone from the bottom of the back to the root of the neck. In the passage inside this spinal column there is a nerve *(nāḍī),* called *suṣumṇā,* which is again in reality made up of three *nāḍīs, suṣumṇā, vajrā* and *citriṇī.*[1] All *nāḍīs* start from the root at the end of the vertebral column, called *kāṇḍa,* and they proceed upwards to the highest cerebral nerve-plexus, called *sahasrāra,* and are seventy-two thousand in number. The place of the root of these *nāḍīs (kāṇḍa)* is an inch above the anus and an inch below the root of the penis. If *suṣumṇā* is the central nerve of the spinal cord, then on its extreme right side is the *iḍā,* and then parallel to it towards the *suṣumṇā* are the *gāndhārī,* stretching from the corner of the left eye to the left leg, *hasti-jihvā,* stretching from the left eye to the left foot, *śaṅkhinī,* branching on the left, *kuhū* (the pubic nerve on the left) and also the *viśvodarā,* the lumbar nerves. On the extreme left of it is th e*piṅgalā,* and between it and the *suṣumṇā* are the *pūṣā,* stretching from below the corner of the right eye to the abdomen, *paśyantī,* the auricular branch or the cervical plexus, *sarasvatī* and

1 But according to the *Tanira-cūḍāmaṇi, suṣumṇā* is not inside the spinal column but outside it. Thus it says,"*tad-bāhye tu tayor madhye suṣumṇā vahni-saṃyuta.*" This, however, is against the view of the *Saṭ-cakra-nirūpaṇa,* which takes *suṣumṇā* to be inside the passage of the spine. According to the *Nigama-tattva-sāra-tantra, iḍā* and *piñgalā* are both inside the spine, but this is entirely against the accepted view. Dr Sir B. N. Seal thinks that *suṣumṇā* is the central passage or channel of the spinal cord and not a separate *nāḍī* (*The Positive Sciences of the Ancient Hindus,* pp. 219, 226, 227). Mr Rele in his *The Mysterious Kuṇḍalinī* (pp. 3 5,3 6) thinks that it is a *nāḍī* which is situated centrally and passes through the spinal column (*meru-daṇḍa*); but, judging from the fact that it is said to originate in the sacrum, from which it goes upwards to the base of the skull, where it joins with the plexus of a thousand nerves called *brahma-cakra* (cerebrum in the vault of the skull) and is divided at the level of the larynx (*kaṇṭha*) into anterior and posterior parts between the two eyebrows (*ājñā-cakra*) and the cavity in the brain (*brahma-randhra*) respectively, Rele thinks that this *suṣumṇā nāḍī* is nothing but the spinal cord.

vāraṇā (the sacral nerve). The *śaṅkhinī* (the auricular branch or the cervical plexus on the left) goes parallel to the *suṣumṇā,* but takes a turn in the region of the neck and passes on to the root of the left ear-holes; in another branch it passes through the inner side of the region of the forehead, where it gets joined with the *citriṇī nāḍī* and enters into the cerebral region. The *suṣumṇā nāḍī* is a sort of duct inside the spine, which encases within it the *vajrā nāḍī,* and that again encases within it the *citriṇī nāḍī,* which has within it a fine aperture running all through it, which is the fine aperture running through the spinal cord.[1] This inner passage within the *citriṇī nāḍī* is also called *brahma-nāḍī*; for there is no further duct or *nāḍī* within the *citriṇī.*[2] The *suṣumṇā* thus in all probability stands for our spinal cord. The *suṣumṇā*, however, is said to take a turn and get connected with the *śaṅkhinī* in the inside region of the forehead, whence it becomes connected with the aperture of the *śaṅkhinī (śaṅkkinī-nālam ālambya)* and passes to the cerebral region. All the *nāḍīs* are connected with the *suṣumṇā. Kuṇḍalinī* is a name for supreme bodily energy, and, because the channel of the *suṣumṇā,* the *brahma-nāḍī*, is the passage through which this energy flows from the lower part of the trunk to the regions of the nerve-plexus of the brain, *suṣumṇā* is sometimes called *kuṇḍalinī*; but *kuṇḍalinī* itself cannot be called a nerve, and it is distinctly wrong to call it the vagus nerve, as Mr Rele does.[3] The *iḍā nāḍī* on the left side of the *suṣumṇā* outside the spine goes upwards to the nasal region, and *piṅgalā* follows a corresponding course on the

---

1 *Nāḍī* is derived by Pūrṇānanda Yati, in his commentary on the *Ṣaṭ-cakra-nirūpaṇa,* from the root *naḍ,* to go, as a passage or duct *(naḍa gatau iti dhātor naḍyate gamyate 'nayā padavyā iti nāḍī).* Mahāmahopādhyāya Gaṇanātha Sen makes a very serious mistake in his *Pratyakṣa-śārīraka* when he thinks that the *nāḍīs* are to be regarded as being without apertures (*nīrandhra*). They are certainly not so regarded in the Āyur-veda or in the *Saṭ-cakra-nirūpaṇa* and its commentaries. In Yoga and Tantra literature the term *nāḍī* generally supersedes the term *śirā* of the medical literature.

2 *Śabda-brahma-rūpāyaḥ kuṇḍalinyāḥ parama-śiva-sannidhi-gamana-patharūpa-citriṇī-nāḍy-antargata-śūnya-bhāga iti.* Pūrṇānanda's commentary on *Saṭ-cakra-nirūpaṇa,* St.2.

3 *Suṣumṇāyai kuṇḍalinyai. Haṭha-yoga-pradīpikā,* IV.64.

right side. Other accounts of these *nāḍīs* hold that the *iḍā* proceeds from the right testicle and the *piṅgalā* from the left testicle and passes on to the left and the right of the *suṣumṇā* in a bent form (*dhanur-ākōre*). The three, however, meet at the root of the penis, which is thus regarded as the junction of the three rivers, as it were (*triveṇī*), viz. of *suṣumṇā* (compared to the river Gaṅgā), *iḍā* (compared to Yāmuna) and *piṅgalā* (compared to Sarasvatī). The two *nāḍīs*, *iḍā* and *piṅgalā*, are also described as being like the moon and the sun respectively, and *suṣumṇā* as fire.[1] In addition to these *nāḍīs* the *Yogi-yājñavalkya* mentions the name of another *nāḍī,* called *alambuṣā*, making the number of the important *nāḍīs* fourteen, including *suṣumṇā* and counting *suṣumṇā* as one *nāḍī* (i.e. including *vajrā* and *citriṇī),* though the total number of *nāḍīs* is regarded as being seventy-two thousand. Śrīkaṇāda in his *Nāḍī-vijñāna* counts the number of *nāḍīs* as thirty-five millions. But, while the Tantra school, as represented in the works *Sat-cakra-nirūpaṇa, Jñāna-saṃkalinī, Yogi-yājñavalkya,* etc., regards the *nāḍīs* as originating from the nerve-plexus lying between the root of the penis and the anus, and while Caraka regards them as originating from the heart, Śrīkaṇāda regards them as originating from the region of the navel *(nābhi-kanda)* and going upwards, downwards and sideways from there. Śrīkaṇāda, however, compromises with the Tantra school by holding that of these thirty-five millions there are seventy-two thousand *nāḍīs* which may be regarded as gross and are also called *dhamanīs*, and which carry the sense-qualities of colour, taste, odour, touch and sound (*pañcendriya-guṇāvahā*). There are again seven hundred *nāḍīs* with fine apertures, which carry food-juice by which the body is nourished. Of these again there are twenty-four which are more prominent.

The most important feature of the Tantra school of anatomy is its theory of nerve-plexuses (*cakra*). Of these the first is the *ādhāra-cakra*, generally translated as sacro-coccygeal plexus. This plexus is situated between the penis and the anus, and there are eight elevations on it. It is in touch with the mouth of the *suṣumṇā.* In the

1 *Ṣaṭ-cakra-nirūpaṇa,* St. I and *Yogi-yājñavalkya-saṃhitā,* p. 18.

centre of the plexus there is an elevation called *svayaṃbhū-liṅga*, like a fine bud with an aperture at its mouth. There is a fine thread-like fibre, spiral in its form, attached to the aperture of the *svayaṃbhū-liṅga* on one side and the mouth of the *suṣumṇā* on the other. This spiral and coiled fibre is called *kula-kuṇḍalinī*; for it is by the potential mother-energy, as manifested in its movement of a downward pressure of the *apāna vāyu* and an upward pressure of the *prāṇa vāyu*, that exhalation and inhalation are made possible and life functions operate. Next comes the *svādhiṣṭhāna-cakra*, the sacral plexus, near the root of the penis. Next comes the lumbar plexus (*maṇi-pura-cakra*), in the region of the navel. Next is the cardiac plexus (*anāhata-cakra* or *viśuddha-cakra),* in the heart, of twelve branches. Next is the laryngeal and pharyngeal plexus, at the junction of the spinal cord and the medulla oblongata, called the *bhāratī-sthāna.* Next comes the *lalanā-cakra*, opposite the uvula. Next to this is the *ājñā-cakra* between the eyebrows, within which is the *manaś-cakra*, the centre of all sense-knowledge and dream-knowledge, and the seat of *manas*, the mind-organ. Vijñānabhikṣu says in his *Yoga-vārttika* that one branch of the *suṣumṇā* goes upwards from here, which is the *nāḍī* for carrying the functions of *manas* and is called *mano-vahā nāḍī;* the *Jñāna-sarnkalinī tantra* calls it *jñāna-nāḍī.* It seems, therefore, that it is through this *nāḍī* that connection is established between the soul, residing in the brain, and the *manas*, residing in the *manaś-cakra.* Śaṅkara Miśra argues in his commentary on the *Vaiśeṣika-sūtras*, v.2.14 and 15, that the *nāḍīs* are themselves capable of producing tactile impressions; for, had it not been so, then eating and drinking, as associated with their corresponding feelings, would not have been possible, as these are effected by the automatic functions of *prāṇa.*[1] Above the *ājñā-cakra* comes the *soma-cakra,* in the middle of the cerebrum, and finally, in the upper cerebrum, there is the *sahasrāra-cakra*, the seat of the soul. The process of Yoga consists in rousing the potential energy located in the *ādhāra-cakra*, carrying it upwards through the aperture of the *citriṇī* or the *brah-*

1 See Dr Sir B.N. Seal's *Positive Sciences of the Ancient Hindus*, pp. 222-225.

ma-nāḍī, and bringing it to the *brahma-randhra* or the *sahasrāra.* This *kuṇḍalinī* is described as a fine fibre like a lightning flash (*taḍid iva vilasat tantu-rūpa-svarūpa*), which raises the question whether this is actually a physical nerve or merely a potential energy that is to be carried upwards to the upper cerebrum in the *sahasrāra-cakra*; and it cannot, I think, be yet satisfactorily explained. But, judging from a wide comparison of the texts, it seems pretty certain that it is the *kuṇḍalī śakti* or the *kuṇḍalī* energy which is carried upwards. If the *kuṇḍalī* energy is inexhaustible in its nature, the whole discussion as to whether the *ādhāra-cakra* is depleted or not or whether the *kuṇḍalinī* herself rises or her eject, as raised in Sir John's *Serpent Power*, pp. 301-320, loses its point. How far the *cakras* can themselves be called nerve-plexuses is very doubtful, since the nerve-plexuses are all outside the spinal aperture; but, if the *kuṇḍalinī* is to pass through the aperture of the *citriṇī nāḍī* and at the same time pass through the *cakras*, the *cakras* or the lotuses *(padma)* must be inside the spinal cord. But, supposing that these nerve-plexuses represent the corresponding places of the *cakras* inside the spinal cord, and also because it has become customary to refer to the *cakras* as plexuses, I have ventured to refer to the *cakras* as such. But it must be borne in mind that, as the *kuṇḍalinī* is a mysterious power, so also are the *cakras* the mysterious centres in the path of the ascent of the *kuṇḍalinī.* A nerve-physical interpretation of them as nerve-plexuses would be very unfaithful to the texts. A more detailed discussion on these subjects will be found in the treatment of Tantra philosophy in a later volume of this work. The chief interest of the present section is only to show that the Tantra anatomy is entirely different in its conception from the Āyur-veda anatomy, which has been the subject of our present enquiry. Another fact of importance also emerges from these considerations, namely, that, though in Dṛḍhabala's supplementary part of the *Siddhi-sthānathe* head is associated with sensory consciousness, Caraka's own part refers to the heart as the central seat of the soul. But the Tantra school points to the upper cerebrum as the seat of the soul and regards the spinal cord and its lower end as being of supreme importance for the vital functions of the body.

THE THEORY OF RASAS AND THEIR CHEMISTRY

The theory of *Rasas* or tastes plays an important part in Āyur-veda in the selection of medicines and diet and in diagnosing diseases and arranging their cures. In I.26 of Caraka we hear of a great meeting of sages in the Caitraratha Forest, attended by Ātreya, Bhadrakāpya, Śākunteya, Pūrṇākṣa Maudgalya, Hiraṇyākṣa Kauśika, Kumāraśiras Bharadvāja, Vāryovida, the Vaideha king Nimi, Baḍiśa and Kāṅkāyana, the physician of Balkh, for the purpose of discussing questions of food and tastes.

Bhadrakāpya held that taste, or *rasa*, was that which could be perceived by the organ of the tongue and it was one, viz. that of water. Śākunteya held that there were two *rasas*, nutritive *(upaśamanīya)* and denutritive (*chedanīya*). Pūrṇākṣa held that there were three *rasas, upaśamanīya, chedanīya* and neutral *(sādhāraṇa).* Hiraṇyākṣa held that there were four *rasas,* sweet and good, sweet and harmful, distasteful and good, distasteful and harmful. Kumāraśiras held that there were five *rasas,* earthy, watery, fiery, airy and ethereal (*āntarikṣa*). Vāryovida held that there were six *rasas,* heavy *(guru),* light *(laghu),* cold *(śīta),* hot *(uṣṇa),* smooth *(snigdha)* and dry *(rūkṣa).* Nimi held that there were seven *rasas,* sweet *(madhura),* sour *(amla),* salt *(lavaṇa),* hot *(kaṭu),* bitter *(tikta),* pungent *(kaṣāya)* and alkaline *(kṣāra).* Baḍiśa added one more to these, viz. unmanifested *(avyakta),* and held that there were eight *rasas.* Kāṅkāyana held that the *rasas* were of infinite variety and could not be counted, on account of the diversity of substances in which they are located *(āśraya),* their specific properties as light or heavy *(guṇa),* their action in developing or reducing the constituents of the body *(karma)* and their diversity as apparent to the organ of taste. Ātreya Punarvasu held that there are six *rasas* only, sweet (*madhura*), acid *(amid),* saline *(lavaṇa),* hot and pungent (*kaṭu*), bitter *(tikta)* and astringent *(kaṣāya).* The source *(yoni)* of all these *rasas* is water. Its actions are sedative (*upaśamana*) and denutritive (*chedana*), and a basis of equilibrium *(sādhāraṇatva)* of the *rasas* is reached when those having the above opposite actions are mixed together. Pleasantness (*svādu*) or unpleasantness *(asvādu)* of taste depends on liking or disliking. The seats of *rasas* are the essences of the five elements (*pañca-mahā-bhūta-vikārāḥ*) modified in accordance with five conditions, viz. specific nature of the substance *(prakṛti*); as acted upon by heat or other agents (*vikṛti*); association with other things (*vicāra*); the place in which the substance is grown (*deśa*); the time at which it is produced *(kāla)*.[1] The *guṇas* of heaviness, lightness, cold, warm, moisture and dryness belong to the things to which the *rasas* belong. The alkaline (*kṣāra*) should not be counted as a separate *rasa*, as it is made up of more than one *rasa* and affects more than one sense-organ; for it has at least two important *rasas* (of "hot and pungent" and "saline") and it affects not only the organ of taste, but also that of touch, and does not naturally belong to any substance, but has to be created by artificial processes. There is no such separate *rasa* which can be called unmanifested *(avyakta)*. Water is the origin of all *rasas*; so all *rasas* may be considered as existing in an unmanifested state in water, but that is no reason why we should say that water has a separate taste called "unmanifested"; moreover, when a substance has two *rasas*, one dominant and the other extremely feeble, the feeble *rasa* may be regarded as unmanifested; or, when in a compound of different *rasas*, say, of a syrup, a slight hot taste is added, this may be considered as unmanifested; but certainly there is no *rasa* to which the name "unmanifested" *(avyakta)* could be given. The view that there is an infinite number of *rasas* is untenable; for, though it may be urged that the same *rasa* may occur differently in different objects, that would only go to show that there are various grades of

1 Thus *mudga* (a sort of kidney-bean), which is a *bhūta-vikāra,* has the *rasas* of astringent and sweet and is yet light by nature, though one would expect it to be heavy on account of its *rasas* of astringent and sweet. *Vikṛti* is best exemplified in the case of fried paddy, which is lighter than rice. It is well known that by composition wholly new properties may be generated in the product. Medicinal herbs vary in their properties in accordance with the time of plucking.

forms of each particular *rasa* and not prove that with each variety of a particular *rasa* the *rasa* itself is wholly different. Again, if different *rasas* are mixed together, the mixed *rasa* itself is not entitled to be counted as a separate *rasa*; for its qualities are just as the sum total of the qualities of the different *rasas* which are its constituents, and no independent work can be attributed to this mixed *rasa* *(na saṃsṛṣṭānāṃ rasānāṃ karmopadiśanti buddhimantaḥ)*, as in the case of a compound of two or more substances, as mentioned above *(vicāra)*.

Though on account of the predominance of one or the other of them they are called earthy *(pārtkiva)*, watery *(āpya),* fiery *(āgneya),* airy *(vāyavya)* or ethereal *(ākāśātmaka),* yet all substances are compounded of the five elements. All substances, whether animate or inanimate, are to be considered as medicines *(auṣadha),* provided they are applied in the proper way (*yukti*) and for specific purposes *(artha)*. A substance can be a medicine only when it is applied in the proper way and for specific purposes; nothing can unconditionally be considered a medicine. The medicative influence is exerted both by virtue of the specific agency of a substance *(dravya-prabhāva)* and by the specific agency of its qualities, as also by their joint influence.[1] The action of medicines is called *karman*, its potency *vīrya*, the place where they operate *adhi-karaṇa*, the time of operation *kāla,* the mode of operation *upāya,* and the result achieved *phala.*

As regards the origin of *rasas*, it is suggested that water gets mixed with the five elements in the air and also after its fall on the

1 The medicinal effect of substances may be distinguished from the medicinal effect of qualities, as when by certain stones (*maṇi*) poison may be removed or by the use of certain amulets certain diseases may be cured. Again, there may be cases where simply by the application of heat a certain disease may be cured, irrespective of the substance which possesses heat as its property. It seems that only the sense-properties and mechanical properties are here counted as *guṇas*; other kinds of properties were considered as being due to the thing (*dravya*) itself. For, in addition to the sense-properties, the twenty qualities, *guru, laghu, śīta, uṣṇa, snigdha, rūkṣa, manda, tīkṣṇa, sthira, sāra, mṛdu, kaṭhina, viśada, picchila, ślakṣṇa, khara, sūkṣma, sthūla, sāndra* and *drava,* are counted as *guṇas* (*Caraka-saṃhitā*, I.1.48; I.25.35; I.26.11).

ground. These *rasas* nourish the bodies of all plants and animals. All the five elements are present in all *rasas*; but in some *rasas* some of the elements predominate, and in accordance with this there are differences among the various *rasas*. Thus, with the predominance of *soma* there is a sweet taste, with the predominance of earth and fire an acid taste, with water and fire a saline taste, with air and fire, hot and pungent, with air and *ākāśa*, bitter, with air and earth, astringent. The different elements which take part in the formation of *rasas* are said to be instrumental causes *(nimitta-kāraṇa)* of the *rasas*; this explains how, though fire has no *rasa*, yet it may help the generation of a particular *rasa.*[1] Destiny or unknown cause *(adṛṣṭa)* is, however, the general cause of such combinations of elements with water.

In the very first chapter of the *Caraka-saṃhitā*, substances *(dravya)* are counted as being the five elements, viz. *ākāśa*, air, light, heat, water and earth, together with soul, *manas*, time and space. Of these those substances which possess sense-organs are called animate and those which do not are called inanimate.[2] The *guṇas* are the sense-properties of hearing, touch, colour, taste and smell, the mechanical and other properties which all elements have in common, such as heaviness, lightness, cold, heat, and moisture, dryness, dullness, sharpness, steadiness, mobility, softness, hardness, motion, slipperiness, smoothness, roughness, grossness, fineness, thickness, liquidity, etc., and desire, hatred, pleasure, pain and effort, intelligence (including memory), consciousness, patience, egoism, etc., distance *(para),* nearness *(apara),* combination (*yukti),* number, contact, disjunction (*vibhāga*), separateness, measure, inertia *(saṃskāra)* and repetition *(abhyāsa).* The definition of substance *(dravya)* is, that which possesses quality *(guṇa)* and action

1 *Iha ca kāraṇatvaṃ bhūtānāṃ rasasya madhuratvādi-viśeṣa eva nimitta-kāraṇatvam ucyate.* —Cakrapāṇi on Caraka, I.26.38.

2 *Caraka-saṃhitā,* I.1.47. Even trees were regarded as being possessed of senses and therefore animated or *cetana.* Cakrapāṇi says that, since the sunflower continues to turn its face towards the sun, it may be regarded as being possessed of the sense of sight; again, since the *lavali* (*Averrhoa acida*) plant fructifies through hearing the sound of thunder, the plants have auditory organs, etc.

(karma) in the relation of inherence and is also the inseparable material cause *(samavāyi-kāraṇa)* of all effects. *Guṇas* are things which are themselves inactive and exist in *dravyas* in an inseparable relation of inherence. The *guṇas* themselves cannot contain any further *guṇas*.[1]

The above being the theory of *dravya* and *guṇa*, the question arises as to the way in which medicines operate in human bodies. The most general and obvious way in which the different medicines were classified was by their different tastes, which were considered primarily to be six in number, as has already been pointed out. Each of the tastes was considered as being capable of producing certain good or bad physiological effects. Thus the sweet taste is said to increase blood, flesh, fat, marrow, semen, life, to do good to the six senses, and to produce strength and colour of the body; to do good to the skin and throat, to destroy *pitta*, poison and *māruta* (morbidity of air), and to produce moistening, cold and heaviness, etc. The acid (*amla*) is said to rouse digestion, develop the body, and to remove *vāta*; it is light, warm, moist, etc. The saline taste is digestive; it removes *vāta,* secretes *kapha*; and it is moist, warm, etc. And so on with the other tastes. But, of course, all these qualities cannot belong to the tastes; as has already been pointed out, the *guṇas* cannot possess further *guṇas*, and the tastes *(rasa)* are themselves *guṇas*; so, when certain functions or properties are attributed to the *rasas*, they must be considered as belonging to the substances which possess those specific *rasas (rasa iti rasa-yuktāni dravyāṇi)*.[2]

From Suśruta's statements it appears that there was a great difference of opinion regarding the relative prominence of *dravya* and its properties.[3] There were some who held that *dravya* was the most important, since *dravya* remained permanent, whereas *rasa,* etc. are always changed; so *dravya* is relatively permanent. Again,

1 *Ibid.* I.1.47, 48 and 50, with Cakrapāṇi's commentary.

2 *Caraka-saṃhitā,* I.26.39, Cakrapāṇi's commentary.

3 *Suśruta, Sūtra-sthāna, 40.3. Dravya* is defined by Suśruta as *kriyā-guṇavat samavāyi-kāraṇam.*

dravya is grasped by the five senses, and not its *guṇas*. The *dravya* is also the support of the *rasas,* etc. All operations have to be done with the *dravya,* and the authoritative texts also speak of operations with the *dravyas*, and not with the *rasas*; the *rasas* depend largely on the nature of the *dravyas.* Others hold that *rasas* are the most important, since it is of them that we become directly aware when we take our food, and it is said that they remove the various morbidities of *vāta,* etc. Others hold that the potency *(vīrya)* of things is the most important, since it is by their potency that medicines act.[1] This potency is of two kinds, hot *(uṣṇa)* and cold *(śīta);* some think that it is of eight kinds, hot *(uṣṇa),* cold *(śīta),* moist *(snigdha),* dry *(rūkṣa),* moving *(viśada),* slippery *(picchila),* soft *(mṛdu)* and sharp (*tīkṣṇa*). Sometimes potency or *vīrya* overcomes *rasa* by its power and makes its own tendencies felt; thus, though sugar-cane ought to remove *vāta* on account of its sweetness, it really increases it on account of its being *śīta-vīrya* (of cold potency).[2] Others say that the *rasa,* as digested by the stomach (*pāka*), is most important, since things can produce good or bad effects only when they are digested. Some hold that each *rasa* remains unchanged by digestion, though according to others there are only three kinds of *rasa* resulting from digestion or *pāka*, viz. sweet, acid and hot (*kaṭu*); whereas Suśruta held that there were only two kinds of *rasa* resulting from digestion, viz. sweet and hot; for, in his view, acid was not the result of digestion (*amlo vipāko nāsti).* According to Suśruta it is the *pitta* which is turned into acid. Those objects which have more of earth and water in them are turned into sweet taste, whereas those

---

1 *ihauṣadha-karmāṇi ūrdhvādho-bhāgobhayabhāga-saṃśodhana-saṃśamana-saṃgrāhakāgni-dīpaina-prapiḍana-lekhana-vṛṃhaṇa-rasāyana-vājīkaraṇa-śvaya-thūkara-vilayana-dahana-dāraṇa-mādana-prāṇaghna-viṣa-praśamanāni vīrya-prādhanyād bhavanti.—Suśruta,* I.40.5.

2 *etāni khalu vīryāṇi sva-bala-guṇotkarṣāt rasam abhibhuyātma-karma kurvanti. Suśruta, Ibid.* The *vīrya* is said to remain both in the *dravya* and in the *rasa.* Thus in Suśruta, I.40.5-8, it is said that, if in those *rasas* which remove *vāta* there is dryness (*raukṣya*), lightness (*lāghava*) and cold (*śaitya*), then they will not remove *vāyu*; so, if in those which remove *pitta* there is sharpness (*taikṣṇya),* heat *(auṣṇya)* and lightness (*laghutā),* then they will not remove *pitta,* and so on.

which have *tejas,* air and *ākāśa* as their ingredients are turned into hot taste *(kaṭu).*

Speaking of the differences of view regarding the relative importance of *dravya, rasa*, *vīrya* and *vipāka*, Suśruta says that they are all important, since a medicine produces effects in all those four ways according to its own nature.[1] The view of Suśruta, as explained by Cakrapāṇi in the *Bhānumatī,* seems to be that food, drink and medicine are all products of the five *mahābhūtas,* and *rasa, vīrya* and *vipāka* are dependent on the *dravya* and are like its potency *(śakti),* through which it works.[2] Cakrapāṇi, commenting on this in the *Bhānumatī,* says that even in those cases where certain *rasas* are said to remove or increase certain morbidities *(doṣa)* it is only because of their importance that they are so described; the real agent in all such cases is the *dravya,* since the *rasa,* etc. are always dependent on the *dravya.* Apart from the *śakti* as manifested in *rasa,* etc., the *dravya* also operates by itself in an unthinkable way *(acintya),* which is also called *prabhāva* and which is comparable with the attractive force exerted by magnets on iron. The *dravya* by itself is thus differentiated from its *śakti,* and it is said to have a peculiar operative mode of its own, as distinguished from that of its *śakti* or potency, as manifested in *rasa, vīrya* or *vipāka*, and this mode of operation is considered to be quite unthinkable (*acintya*) as to the way in which it operates.[3] Thus some medicines operate by *rasa,* some by *vipāka,* or the *rasa* resulting from the digestive operation (e.g. *śuṇṭhī,* which, though hot in taste and hot in *vīrya,* is sweet after digestive operation), some by *vīrya* (e.g. *kulattha,* though pungent, yet removes *vāyu* on account of its hot *vīrya),* some by both *rasa* and *vipāka,* some by *dravya-pr abhāva, vīrya* and *rasa,* some by *dravya-prabhāva, vīrya*, *rasa* and *vipāka.*

1 *caturṇām api sāmagryam icchanty atra vipaścitaḥ.* Suśruta, I.40.13.

2 *dravya-śakti-rūpakā rasa-vīrya-vipākā yathā-yogaṃ nimitta*-kāraṇatātṃ *samavāyi-kāraṇatāṃ vā bhajanto na kartṛtayā vyapadiśyante dravya-parā-dhīnatvāt. —Bhānumatī,* I.40.13.

3 *dravyam ātmanā śaktyā prabhāvākhyayā doṣaṃ hanti...atra dravya-śakti-kāryodāharaṇam yathā karṣaka-maṇir loha-śalyam ākarṣati. —Bhānumatī,* I.40.13.

Caraka, however, differs from Suśruta in this view of *drayva* and *rasa, vīrya* and *vipāka*; for, according to him, *rasa, vīrya* and *vipāka,* themselves being *guṇas,* cannot possess further *guṇas.* He does not admit a *śakti* as different from the *dravya.* Thus in the case of *prabhāva,* while Suśruta holds that it is a specific *śakti,* or the thing operating in unaccountable ways, Caraka thinks that this *śakti* is identical with the thing itself. Thus Cakrapāṇi in explaining *Caraka-saṃhitā*, I.26.72, says, "*śaktir hi svarūpam eva bhāvānāṃ, nātiriktaṃ kincid dharmāntaraṃ bhāvānām*" (potency is the nature of things and is no separate property distinct from them). *Vīrya* in its general sense means "the potency or power of medicines to produce effects," and as such includes within it both *rasa* and *vipāka;* but, since these have special names, the term *vīrya* is not applied to them.[1] Apart from this there is special *vīrya* in a technical sense *(pāribhāṣika*). In the view which considers this *vīrya* to be of two kinds, *snigdha* and *rūkṣa,* these are to be taken as specific characteristics; but in the view which considers the *vīrya* to be of eight kinds, these are to be taken as a different set of characteristics of *dravya* or substance.[2] This *vīrya* is believed to be more powerful than *rasa*, so that, when the *vīrya* and *rasa* of a thing come into conflict, it is the *vīrya* which predominates and not the *rasa.*

Vāgbhaṭa junior makes some remarks in support of the name *vīrya*, as given to the characteristics which go by that name. He says that, since the *vīrya* characteristics of things remain unchanged even after digestion, and since the things are primarily in use for medical purposes and each of them would include many substances and *rasas,* this character justly deserves to be called *vīrya,* or the potency-in-chief for producing medical effects.[3] He further says that *rasa* is baffled by *vipāka,* that *rasa* and *vipāka* can baffle *vīrya,* if they work in the same direction, and that they may all be baffled

---

1 *tasya pākasya tad-rasasya vipākasya ca pṛthañ-nirdeśān na vīrya-vyavahāraḥ śāstre...Carake tu sāmānya-vīrya-śabdena te 'pi gṛhītāḥ.—Bhānumatī,* I.40.5.

2 *yadā dvividhaṃ vīryam tadā snigdha-rūkṣādīnāṃ...rasādi-dharmata-yaiva kārya-grahaṇaṃ vakṣyati hi madhuro rasaḥ snigdha ity ādi aṣṭavidha-vīrya-pakṣe tu...balavat-kārya-kartṛtva-vivakṣayā vīryatvam iti sthitiḥ.—Ibid.* I.40.4.

3 *Aṣṭāṅga-hṛdaya,* I.9.15.

by *prabhāva.* These remarks, however, are true only in those cases where *rasa, vīrya* and *vipāka* exist in the same proportion, and it must be borne in mind that some objects may have *rasa* of such a predominant type that it may overcome the *vipāka* or the *vīrya.*[1] As regards the relative priority of *vīrya* and *vipāka,* Śivadāsa in commenting on Cakrapāṇi's *Dravya-guṇa-saṃgraha* says that *vīrya* is prior to *vipāka;* and this would imply that, as *vīrya* can supersede *rasa,* so *vipāka* may supersede *vīrya.*

If we look back to the earliest history of the development of Indian medical ideas in the *Atharva-Veda,* we see that there were two important classes of medicines, viz. the amulets, *maṇis* and water. *Atharva-Veda*, I.4.4, I.5, I.6, I.33, VI.24, VI.92, etc. are all in praise of water as medicine, and water is regarded there as the source of all *rasa* or taste. Thus from the earliest times two different kinds of medicines were used. Of these the amulets were more or less of a miraculous effect. It was not possible to judge which kind of amulet or *maṇi* would behave in which way; their mode of operation was unthinkable (*acintya*). It is easy to see that this mode of operation of medicines was what was considered a *prabhāva* by Caraka and Suśruta. With them *prabhāva* means the mysterious operation of a medicine acting in an unaccountable way, so that, though two medicines might be exactly similar in *rasa*, *vīrya* and *vipāka*, they might behave differently with regard to their medicinal effects.[2] Such an effect was thus naturally considered as unthinkable. But the analogy of the old *maṇis* was fresh in the minds of these medical thinkers when conceiving this *prabhāva*, and it was in reality an extension of that idea to other unaccountable effects of medicines.[3]

---

1 *Aṣṭāṅga-hṛdaya,* I.28.

2 *rasa-vīrya-vipākārtaṃ sāmānyaṃ yatra lakṣyate viśeṣaḥ karmaṇāṃ caiva prabhāvas tasya ca smṛtaḥ.—Caraka-saṃhitā,* I.26.69.
Cakrapāṇi, in commenting on this, says, "*rasādi-kāryatvena yati nāvadhārayituṃ śakyate kāryaṃ tat pra-bhāva-kṛtam iti sūcayati; ata evoktaṃ' prabhāvo 'cintya ucyate' rasa-vīrya-vipāka-tayācintya ity arthah.*"

3 *maṇīnāṃ dhāraṇīyānāṃ karma yad vividhātmakaṃ, tat-prabhāva-kṛtaṃ teṣām prabhavo 'cintya ucyate.* (The various actions of amulets are to be considered as being due to a *prabhāva* which is unthinkable—*Ibid.* I.26.72.)

As none of the chemical effects (in the modem sense) of medicines on human organs were known, the most obvious way in which the medical effects of herbs, roots, etc. could be classified was on the basis of taste, and by Caraka and Suśruta we are told the effects of the different *rasas* on the different morbidities of the body, *vāyu, pitta* and *kapha.* As the main source of all diseases was unequal increase or decrease of *vāyu, pitta* and *kapha*, a classification which described the *rasas* in such a way that one could know which *rasa* increased or decreased which of the morbidities was particularly useful. But it is obvious that such a classification, though simple, could not be universally true; for, though the taste is some indication of the medicinal property of any substance, it is not an infallible one. But no other mode of classification was known; it was supposed that the taste *(rasa)* of some substances changed altogether after digestion and that in such cases the taste which changed after digestion *(pāka)* would be operative. Cakrapāṇi says that in those cases where the taste on the tongue *(rasa)* agrees with the taste as produced after the digestive process, the effect in that direction becomes very strong, but in the case where the latter differs from the former the operation of *rasa* becomes naturally weak, because the force of the taste produced by the final operation of the digestive process is naturally strong.[1] Caraka thought that there were only three *rasas* as the result of digestion, viz. *kaṭu, madhura* and *amla*; Suśruta rejected the last, as has already been described. But even this was not sufficient; for there were many other effects of medicine which could not be explained on the above suppositions. In explaining this, the theory of *vīrya* was introduced. In addition to taste substances were considered to possess other properties of heat and cold, as judged by inference, tactual properties of slipperiness, movement, moisture and dryness, etc., sharpness, etc. as

---

1 Cakrapāṇi on Caraka, i.26.65. Cakrapāṇi points out that the hot (*kaṭu*) taste is at first useful in cleaning the phlegm of the throat, but, since it becomes sweet after digestion, it acts as a nutrient (*vṛṣya*). But, except in the case of such local actions, it is difficult to understand why the *rasa* which was altered by digestion should have any such effect as Cakrapāṇi suggests *(viparyaye tu durbalam iti jñeyam).*

manifested by odour, and these were supposed to produce effects in supersession of *rasa* and *vipāka.* It was only in the cases where no sensible data of any kind could be found to indicate the medical properties of the thing that the idea of *prabhāva* was introduced. The chapters in Āyur-veda on *dravya* and *guṇa* deal with the enumeration of *prabhāva* and also of *rasa, vipāka* and *vīrya* wherever there is a divergence among them, as determined by empirical observation. This is very necessary not only for the selection of medicines and diet in the cure of diseases, but also for prevention of diseases. It is well to remember that many diseases were supposed to arise through eating together things which are opposed to each other in *rasa*, *vipāka* or *vīrya.*

THE PSYCHOLOGICAL VIEWS AND OTHER ONTOLOGICAL CATEGORIES

Caraka in the eighth chapter of the *Sūtra-sthāna* counts the senses as being five in number. Though both the Sāṃkhya and the Vaiśeṣika systems, to which Āyur-veda is largely indebted for its philosophical ideas, admit *manas,* or mind-organ, as a separate sense *(indriya)*, Āyur-veda here differs from them and, as Cakrapāṇi says, separates *manas* from the ordinary senses by reason of the fact that it has many functions which are not possessed by any of the other senses (*cakṣur-ādibhyo 'dhika-dharma-yogitayā*).[1] Caraka himself, however, in another place speaks incidentally of a sixth sense (*ṣaḍ-indriya*) in connection with the description of sweet taste.[2] *Manas* is, however, here described as transcending the senses (*atīndriya*). Cakrapāṇi, in explaining the *atīndriya* character of *manas*, says that it is called *atīndriya* because it is not a cause of the knowledge of external objects like the other senses. *Manas* is, indeed, the direct cause of pleasure and pain, but it is the superintendent of all the senses (*adhiṣṭhāyaka*). *Manas* is also called *sattva* and *cetas.* The self is, however, the permanent subject of all acts

1 Cakrapāṇi's commentary on *Caraka-saṃhitā,* I.8.3.

2 *Caraka-saṃhitā,* I.26.41, *tatra madhuro rasaḥ...ṣaḍ indriya-prasādanaḥ.*

of consciousness (*cetanā-pratisandhātā*). When the *manas* comes into contact with its objects, viz. pleasure or pain or the objects of thought, and the self makes an effort at grasping these objects, then there is a movement on the part of *manas*, by which it feels pleasure or pain, or thinks the objects of thought, or moves the sense-organs. Thus, when the self makes an effort and the objects of pleasure or pain or thought are present, then the *manas* turns to these as its objects and moves the senses, and the senses, guided by it, grasp their respective objects and produce their knowledge.

The one *manas* appears as diverse on account of the diversity of its objects of thought (e.g. the mind may sometimes take religious thoughts and appear religious and at other times take lustful thoughts and appear lustful), diversity of sense-objects with which it is associated (e.g. the mind may grasp colour, smell or sound, etc.), and diversity of ways of imagination (e.g. "This will do good to me" or "This will do me harm," etc.). In the same man the mind may sometimes appear as angry, ignorant or virtuous. But in reality the *manas* is one and the same for each person; all these differences do not appear at the same time with the same person, as might have been the case if there were many minds for one and the same person. Moreover, the *manas* is atomic; for otherwise many different objects or functions could be performed by one and the same *manas* at the same time.

It may be asked, if one and the same *manas* can show different kinds of moral propensities, *sattva*, *rajas* or *tamas*, how can any person be characterized as *sāttvika*, *rājasika* or *tāmasika* ? The answer is that a man is called *sāttvika*, *rājasika* or *tāmasika* according as predominance of one or other of these *guṇas* is observed in that man.

Manas is supposed to move the senses, which are constituted of *ākāśa*, air, light, heat, water and earth; and the seats of the senses are the physical sockets of the eye, the ear, the nostrils, the tongue and the skin. The five sense-cognitions are produced through the contiguity of the senses, the sense-objects, *manas* and soul. They are short-lived *(kṣaṇika),* but not exactly momentary, as the Buddhists would like to have them.[1] They also are of determinate nature (*niścayātmikāḥ*). As Cakrapāṇi says, it is quite possible for transitory sense-cognitions to give a determinate report of their objects. Though all the senses are made up of the five elements, yet those senses which contain any element in a preponderating degree were conceived as made up of that element. The sense that has a particular element in a preponderating degree is regarded as having by virtue of that a special capacity for grasping that particular element.[2]

The connection of the body, the senses, the *manas* and the self is called life (*jīvita*).[3] The self is everywhere regarded as the agent which unites the acts of consciousness (*jñāna-pratisandhātā*). Cakrapāṇi says that, since the body is momentary (*śarīrasya kṣaṇikatvena*), it may be argued that the union of the self with the body is also momentary. The answer that Cakrapāṇi gives to such an objection is that, though the body is momentary, yet, since the momentary bodies are repeated in a series, the series as a whole may be looked upon as one; and, though the union of the self with each term of the series is momentary, yet, since the series may be looked upon as one, its union with the self may also be regarded as one (*santāna-vyavasthito 'yam ekatayā ucyate).*[4] In another place Caraka says that the *manas*, the self and the body are connected together like a tripod, on which life rests; if any one of the components is missing, the unity is broken.[5]

It has already been pointed out that, according to Caraka, the self is active and that by its activity the mind moves; and it is by the operation of mind that the senses move. The self is also regard-

---

1 Cakrapāṇi's commentary on *Caraka-saṃhitā,* I.8.11. *Kṣanikā ity āśutara-vināśinyaḥ na tu bauddha-siddhāntavad eka-kṣaṇāvasthāyinyaḥ.*

2 *tatra yad-yad-ātmakam* indriyaṃ *viśeṣāt tat-tad-ātmakam evārtham anu-gṛhṇāti tat-svabhāvād vibhutvāc ca.* —(Caraka, I.8.14.)

3 Caraka, I.1.41. The other synonyms of life are *dhāri, nityaga* and *anubandha.*

4 *Ibid.* I.1.41.

5 सत्तवम् आत्मा शरीरं च त्रयमेतत् त्रिदण्डवत्
लोकस् तिष्ठति संयोगात् तत्र सर्वं प्रतिष्ठितम् ॥
sattvam ātmā śarīraṃ ca trayam etat tri-daṇḍavat
lokas tiṣṭhati saṃyogāt tatra sarvaṃ pratiṣṭhitam.—Ibid. I.1.45.

ed as being *cetana* (conscious). But this consciousness does not belong to the self in itself, it is attained only by its connection with the senses through *manas.*[1] It is, however, necessary to note that apart from this self there is, according to Caraka, another transcendent self (*paraḥ ātmā),* different from the self which participates in the union of the body and the senses (which is also technically called the *saṃyogi-puruṣa*).[2] The subtler, or transcendent, self is unchangeable (*nir-vikāra*). Knowledge implies a process and a change, and this self manifests consciousness only in those parts where it becomes associated with *manas* and the senses. Thus, though the self is eternal, yet the rise of consciousness in it is occasional. The unchangeableness of the self consists in its being able to unite with itself its past and future states.[3] If the self were not permanent, it could not unite with itself all its past experiences. The sufferings and enjoyment that affect us should not be attributed to the self, but to *manas (dṛśyamāna-rāgādi-vikāras tu manasi).*

The special feature of this view of self is that it is permanent and unchangeable; this self seems to hold within it all the individual egos which operate in association with their respective senses, *manas* and body. It becomes endowed with consciousness only when it is in association with the senses. Pleasure, pain and the movements involved in thought-processes are attributed to *manas*, though the *manas* is also considered to derive its activity from the self. The states of consciousness that are produced are all united in the self. The self, thus diverted in its subtler aspect from the senses and *manas*, is eternal and unchangeable, whereas in its aspect as associated with *manas* and the senses it is in the sphere of change and consciousness. This view is therefore different from those of the orthodox schools of Indian philosophy.

---

1 *idam eva cātmanaś cetanatvaṃ, yad indriya-saṃyoge sati jñāna-śālitvaṃ, na nikṛṣṭasyātmanas' cetanatvam.* Cakrapāṇi on Caraka, I.1.47.

2 *nirvikāraḥ paras tv ātmā satva-bhūta-guṇendriyaiḥ.* Caraka, I.1.55. *tena sattva-śarīrātma-melaka-rūpo ya ātma-śabdena ucyate taṃ vyāvartayati.* Cakrapāṇi on the above.

3 *nityatvaṃ cātmanaḥ pūrvāpar āvasthānubhūt ārtha-pratisandhānāt.* Cakrapāṇi on Caraka, I.1.55.

It is well to note in this connection that the *Caraka-saṃhitā* begins with an enumeration of the Vaiśeṣika categories, and, though it often differs from the Vaiśeṣika view, it seems to take its start from the Vaiśeṣika. It enumerates the five elements, *manas*, time, space and self as substances (*dravya*); it enumerates the *guṇas*, such as the sensible qualities, the mechanical or physical qualities given in the list beginning with heaviness *(gurv ādayaḥ*), intelligence *(buddhi),* and those beginning with remoteness *(para)* and ending with effort *(prayatna)*. But what is this *gurv ādi* list? There is no such list in the *Vaiśeṣika-sūtras*. Cakrapāṇi, however, refers to an enumeration given in a later chapter (I.25.35) by Caraka, where however these *guṇas* are not enumerated as belonging to all substances, but only to the food and drink that we take.[1] But the list referred to as *parādi* (beginning with *parādi) prayatnānta* (ending in *prayatna)* is not to be found anywhere in the *Caraka-saṃhitā*. This may be a reference to the *Vaiśeṣika-sūtra*, I.1.6.[2] But, if this is so, it leaves out a number of other *guṇas* enumerated in the *Vaiśeṣika-sūtra* which were counted there in the *parādi* list.[3] Caraka himself gives a list of *guṇas* beginning with *para* which includes some of those *guṇas* included in the *Vaiśeṣika-sūtra* already referred to and some more. *The guṇas* enumerated are *para, apara, yukti, saṃkhyā, saṃyoga, vibhāga, pṛthaktva, parimāṇa, saṃskāra,* and *abhyāsa.*[4] *Para* means "superiority" or "importance" (*pradhāna), apara* means "inferiority" or "unimportance" (*apra-dhāna)*. This importance or unimportance is with reference to country, time, age, measure, the *rasa* resulting from digestion *(pāka),* potency *(vīrya)* and taste

1 *āhāratvam āhārasyaikavidham arthābhedāt sa punaḥ...viṃśati-guṇo guru-laghu-śītoṣṇa-snigdha-rūkṣa-manda-tīkṣṇa-sthira-sara-mṛdu - kaṭhina - viśada -pic-chila-ślakṣṇa-khara-sūkṣma-sthūla-sāndra-dravānugamāt.*
—*Caraka-saṃhitā,* I.5.35.

2 *paratvāparatve buddhayaḥ sukha-duhkhe icchā-dveṣau prayatnaś ca guṇāḥ.*
—*Vaiśeṣika-sūtra,* I.1.6.

3 *rūpa-rasa-gandha-śparśāḥ saṃkhyā-parimāṇāni pṛthaktvaṃ saṃyoga-vibhāgau paratvāparatve. —Ibid.*

4 *Parāparatve yuktiś ca saṃkhyā saṃyoga eva ca, vibhāgaś ca prthaktvaṃ ca parimaṇam athāpi ca, saṃskārābhyāsa ity ete guṇāḥ jñeyāḥ par ādayaḥ.*
—*Caraka-saṃhitā,* I.26.27-29.

(rasa). Thus, a dry country is called *para* and a marshy one *apara*; the rains *(visarga)* of early and late autumn *(śarat* and *hemanta)* are called *para,* whereas the season of drought (winter, spring and summer) is called *apara*; with reference to *pāka, vīrya* and *rasa, para* and *apara* mean "suitability" and "unsuitability"—that which is suitable to one is *para* and that which is unsuitable to him is *apara. Yukti* means proper selection of medicines with reference to certain diseases *(doṣādy-apekṣayā bheṣajasya samīcīna-kalpanā); saṃkhyā* means "number"; *saṃyoga,* the mixing up or compounding of two or more substances; *vibhāga,* separation; *pṛthaktva,* difference. The mountains Himalaya and Meru are *pṛthak,* because they are situated in different places and cannot unite; again, even though a pig and a buffalo may meet together, they always remain different from each other; and again, in the same class, say in a collection of peas, each pea is different in identity from the other; in the last case difference in number constitutes a difference in identity; thus, wherever there is a numerical difference *(anekatā)*, there is difference in identity. *Pṛthaktva* thus stands for three kinds of difference, spatial difference, difference of characters and difference of identity due to numerical distinction. *Parimāṇa* means measurement by weight, *saṃskāra* means the production of new qualities and *abhyāsa* means habit due to constant practice *(satata-kriya)*. It is evident from the above that, though the terms used are the same as those used by Kaṇāda in the *Vaiśeṣika-sūtra,* yet they are mostly used in different senses in accordance, probably, with medical tradition. But this list does not end with *prayatna*; it seems therefore that *parādi* and *prayatnānta* stand for two different lists and should not be combined together. We have above the *parādi* list. The *prayatnānta* is a different list of *guṇas*. It includes, as Cakrapāṇi says, *icchā* (desire), *dveṣa* (hatred), *sukha* (pleasure), *duḥkha* (pain) and *prayatna* (effort). *Prayatna* means that particular quality by the rise of which in the soul the *manas* is moved to activity.

Karma (movement) is described as *prayatnādi-ceṣṭitam.* i.e. a movement of the nature of conscious effort; the word *ādi* in *prayatnādi* is explained by Cakrapāṇi as meaning "of the nature of."[1]

1 *ādi-śabdaḥ prakāravācī.* Cakrapāṇi's commentary on *Caraka-saṃhitā,* I.1.48.

Samavāya means the relation of inseparable inherence, as in the case of qualities and substances. Cakrapāṇi, in explaining the nature of *samavāya*, says that it is eternal, so that, even when in a particular case it may disappear, it continues to exist in other cases. It is never destroyed or created anew, but only its appearance is or is not manifested in particular cases.[1] In the case of *sāmānya* and *viśeṣa*, again, Caraka seems to add a new sense to the words. In the Vaiśeṣika systems the word *sāmānya* means a class concept; but here it means the concrete things which have similar constituents or characteristics; and *viśeṣa*, which means in Vaiśeṣika ultimate specific properties differentiating one atom from another, means in Caraka concrete things which have dissimilar and opposite constituents or characteristics. *Sāmānya* and *viśeṣa* thus have a significance quite different from what they have in the *Vaiśeṣika-sūtras*. The principle of *sāmānya* and *viśeṣa* is the main support of Āyur-veda; for it is the principle which underlies the application of medicines and the course of diets. Substances having similar constituents or characteristics will increase each other, and those having dissimilar constituents or characteristics will decrease each other. Thus a substance having the characteristics of *vāta* will increase *vāta* and decrease *śleṣman*, which is dissimilar to it, and so on. *Sāmānya* is thus defined as *tulyārthatā*, i.e. performing similar purposes. Instead of having only a conceptual value, *sāmānya* and *viśeṣa* are here seen to discharge a pragmatic work of supreme value for Āyur-veda. As regards the theory of substances (*dravya*) also, though Caraka borrowed the enumeration of categories, Cakrapāṇi says that the simpler *bhūtas* formed parts of the complex ones *(bhūtāntarānupraveśa)*, and in support of this idea he quotes a *sūtra* from the *Nyāya-sūtra,* which, however, there occurs as an opponent's view, since the theory of *bhūtānupraveśa* was not believed in by the Nyāya-Vaiśeṣika school; with that school none of the elements entered into any other, and their qualities were fixed in themselves. However, in spite of these modifications, the relation of Nyāya-Vaiśeṣika with Caraka seems to be close. But the detailed

1 *Caraka-saṃhitā,* I.1.49.

description of the school of Sāṃkhya, in IV.I , as has already been mentioned and explained in the first volume of the present work, in the chapter on Sāṃkhya, does not seem to have much bearing on the needs of Āyur-veda; and so the whole chapter does not appear to fit in with the rest of the work, and it is not referred to in other parts of the book. It is not improbable that this chapter was somehow added to the book from some other treatise.

Suśruta does not, like Caraka, enumerate the categoıies of the Vaiśeṣika, and his account of Sāṃkhya is very faithful to the traditional account given in Īśvarakṛṣṇa's *Kārikā* and in the *Sāṃkhya-sūtra.* Having described the Sāṃkhya theory, Suśruta says that according to medical science the causes of things are sixfold, viz. nature of things (*svabhāva*), God (*Īśvara*), time (*kāla*), accidental happenings (*yadṛcchā*), destiny (*niyati*) and evolution (*pariṇāma*).[1]As Ḍalhaṇa points out, Suśruta has in several places referred to the operation of all these causes. Thus the formation of the limbs of the body in the foetus-state is said to be due to nature *(svabhāva)*; God as fire is said to operate as the digestive fire in the stomach and to help digestion; time as seasons is said to be the cause of the increase and decrease of *doṣas;* destiny means virtue and vice, and diseases and recovery from them are sometimes attributed to these. Jejjaṭa, in commenting on Suśruta (as reported by Ḍalhaṇa), says that all the above six causes, with the exception of God, are but different names of *prakṛti.* Gayī, however, thinks that the above six causes represent the instrumental cause, though *prakṛti* may still be considered as being the material cause *(upādāna-kāraṇa).*

As Ḍalhaṇa and Gayī think, there is no reason to suppose that Suśruta described the Sāṃkhya doctrine; for, immediately after describing the sixfold causes, he speaks of the elements as being constituted of the three *guṇas, sattva*, *rajas* and *tamas.* Even the senses are regarded as being material. Souls are according to Āyur-veda eternal, though they are limited to their bodies and are not all-pervasive. They are manifested when the semen and the blood com-

1 *Suśruta-saṃhitā*, III.1.11.

bine, and it is this bodily self, suffering transmigration owing to virtue and vice (called *karma-puruṣa*), with which medical science is concerned. When the self is in association with *manas*, it has the following qualities: pleasure, pain, desire, hatred, effort, *prāṇa* and *apāna* (the upward current of breath and the downward force acting in the direction of the rectum), the opening and closing of the eyelids, the action of the intellect as decision or *buddhi (niś-caya),* imagination *(saṃkalpa),* thought (*vicāraṇā*), memory (*smṛ-ti*), scientific knowledge *(vijñāna),* energy (*adhya-vasāya*) and sense-cognitions *(viṣayopalabdhi)*. The qualities of *manas* are divided into three classes, viz. *sāttvika*, *rājasa* and *tāmasa*; of these the *sāttvika* ones are kind actions, the desire of enjoying gradually, mercy, truthfulness, virtue, faith, self-knowledge, retentive power *(medhā),* intelligence *(buddhi),* self-control (*dhṛti*), and sense of duty for the sake of duty *(anabhiṣaṅga)*; the *rājasa* qualities are suffering, impatience, pride, untruthfulness, cruelty, boastfulness, conceit (*māna*), joy, passion and anger; the *tāmasa* qualities are dullness, viciousness, want of retentive power, idleness and sleepiness.

LOGICAL SPECULATIONS AND TERMS RELATING TO ACADEMIC DISPUTE

Things are either existent *(sat)* or non-existent *(asat),* and they can be investigated by the four *pramāṇas*, viz. the testimony of trusty persons (*āptopadeśa*), perception *(pratyakṣa*), inference *(anumāna)* and the coming to a conclusion by a series of syllogisms of probability *(yukti)*.[1]

Those whose minds are free from the impurities of *rajas* and *tamas* through the force of their ascetic endeavours, who possess unlimited knowledge extending through the past, present and future, are to be considered as trustworthy *(āpta)*. Such persons neither have any deficiency of knowledge nor would they willingly

1 *Caraka-saṃhitā*, I.11.17.

say anything untrue. They must be considered as absolutely trusty *(āpta),* and their testimony may be regarded as true.[1]

The valid and certain knowledge that arises as the result of the relation of self, senses, *manas* and sense-objects is called "perception." This contact of the sense with the object is regarded by Cakrapāṇi as being of five kinds, viz.(1) contact with the *dravya* (substance), called *saṃyoga*; (2)contact with the *guṇas* (qualities) through the thing (*saṃyukta-samavāya*) in which they inhere by *samavāya* (inseparable) relation; (3)contact with the *guṇas* (such as colour, etc.) in the generic character as universals of those qualities, e.g. colouredness (*rūpatva*), which exist in the *guṇas* in the *samavāya* relation; this is called *saṃyukta-samaveta-samavāya* since the eye is in contact with the thing and the colour is in the thing by *samavāya* relation, and in the specific colour there is the universal colour or the generic character of colour by *samavāya* relation; (4) the contact called *samavāya* by which sounds are said to be perceived by the ear: the auditory sense is *ākāśa*, and the sound exists in *ākāśa* by the *samavāya* relation, and thus the auditory sense can perceive sound by a peculiar kind of contact called *samaveta-samavāya*; (5)the generic character of sound as the sound universal *(śabdatva)* is perceived by the kind of contact known as *samaveta-samavāya.* It is only immediately resulting (*tadātve*) cognition of such a contact that is called perception *(pratyakṣa);* for inference, memory, etc. also may come in as a result of such a cognition at later stages through other successive processes (*pāraṃparya*). Cakrapāṇi further notes that the four kinds of contact spoken of here are the real causes of the phenomenon of perception; in reality, however, "knowledge that results as the effect of sense-contact" would be a sufficient definition of *pratyakṣa*; so in the perception of pleasure, though none of these contacts are necessary, it is regarded as a valid case of direct perception. Contact with the self is, of course, necessary for all kinds of cognition.[2] It is easy to see that the above theory of perception is of the same type as that found in

1 *Caraka-saṃhitā,* I.11.18, 19.

2 Cakrapāṇi on *Caraka-saṃhitā,* I.11.20.

the Nyāya system. The *nir-vikalpa* perception is not taken into consideration; for there is nothing corresponding to the term *avyapadeśya* in the *Nyāya-sūtra.*[1] Inference must be based on perception, by which the concomitance of the *hetu* can first be observed. Inference is of three kinds, viz. from *kārya* (effect) to *kāraṇa* (cause), as the inference of cohabitation from pregnancy; from cause to effect, as the inference of the future production of fruit from a seed with the other attendant causes, sprinkling with water and the like; and inference by associations other than that of cause and effect, as the inference of fire from smoke.[2]

Yukti is not counted as a separate *pramāṇa* by any other system of Indian thought. When our intelligence judges a fact by a complex weighing in mind of a number of reasons, causes or considerations, through which one practically attains all that is desirable in life, as virtue, wealth or fruition of desires, we have what may be called

---

1 The definition of *pratyakṣa* given in *Caraka-saṃhitā,* I.11.20, is:
आत्मेन्द्रियमनोऽर्थानां सन्निकर्शात् प्रवर्तते
व्यक्ता तडात्वे या बुद्धिः प्रत्यक्षं सा निरुच्यते॥
ātmendriya-mano-'rthānāṃ sannikarśāt pravartate
vyaktā tadātve yā buddhiḥ pratyakṣaṃ sā nirucyate.
The definition of *pratyakṣa* in the *Nyāya-sūtra* is as follows:
इन्द्रियार्थसत्मिकर्षोत्पन्नं ज्ञानम् अव्यपदेश्यम्
अव्यभिचारि व्यवसायात्मकं प्रत्यक्षम्॥
indriyārtha-satmikarṣotpannaṃ jñānam avyapadeśyam
avyabhicāri vyavasāyātmakaṃ pratyakṣam.
For a discussion thereon see vol. I, pp. 333-343.

2 प्रत्यक्षपूर्वं त्रिविधं त्रिकालं चानुमीयते
वह्निर् निगूढो धूमेन मैथुनं गर्भदर्शनात्॥
एवं व्यवस्यन्त्य् अतीतं बीजात् फलं अनागतं
दृष्ट्वा बीजात् फलं जातम् इहैव सदृशम् बुधाः
pratyakṣa-pūrvaṃ tri-vidhaṃ
tri-kālaṃ cānumīyate
vahnir nigūḍho dhūmena
maithunaṃ garbha-darśanāt.
Evaṃ vyavasyanty atītaṃ
dṛṣṭvā bījāt phalam anāgataṃ
dṛṣṭvā bījāt phalaṃ jātam
ihaiva sadṛśam budhāḥ.—Caraka-saṃhitā, III.21, 22.

yukti.[1] As Cakrapāṇi points out, this is not in reality of the nature of a separate *pramāṇa*; but, since it helps *pramāṇas,* it is counted as a *pramāṇa*. As an example of *yukti*, Caraka mentions the forecasting of a good or bad harvest from the condition of the ground, the estimated amount of rains, climatic conditions and the like. Cakrapāṇi rightly says that a case like this, where a conclusion is reached as the combined application of a number of reasonings, is properly called *ūha* and is current among the people by this name. It is here counted as a separate *pramāṇa.* It is in reality an inference of an effect from causes and, as such, cannot be used at the present time, and hence it cannot be called *tri-kāla*, valid in all the three times, past, present and future, as Caraka says.

The Buddhist, writes Śāntarakṣita in discussing Caraka's doctrine of *yukti* as a separate *pramāṇa,* holds that *yukti* consists in the observation that, since, when this happens, that happens, and, since, when this does not happen, that does not happen, this is the cause of that. It may be argued that this is not a case of inference, since there is no proposition equivalent to the proposition with a *dṛṣṭānta*, or example, in Nyāya inference (e.g. whatever is smoky is fiery, as the kitchen). It is held, as Kamalaśīla interprets, that the cause-effect idea is derived from the idea of "this happening, that happens," and there is no other idea in the notion of causality; if in any case any particular example is given, then another example might be asked for, and after that another, and we should have *regressus ad infinitum.*[2] These arguments in support of *yukti* as the concluding of

---

1 *buddhiḥ paśyati yā bhāvān bahu-kāraṇa-yogajān*
yuktis tri-kāla sā jñeyā tri-vargaḥ sādhyate yayā.—Ibid. I.11.25.

2 *dṛṣṭānte 'py ata eva tad-bhāva-bhāvitvāt kāryatā-pratipattiḥ, tatrāpi dṛṣṭānto 'nyo 'nveṣaṇīyaḥ, tatrāpy apara ity anavasthā.* Kamalaśīla as quoted by Cakrapāṇi on *Caraka-saṃhitā,* I.11.25. Śāntarakṣita misrepresents Caraka's view of *yukti* in a very strange manner. He says that, when from the fact that in all cases when *A* is present *B* is present and in all cases when *A* is absent *B* is also absent one thinks *A* to be the cause of *B,* this is regarded by Caraka as the new *pramāṇa* of *yukti.*
Śāntarakṣita's exact words are:

अस्मिन् सति भवत्य् एव न भवत्य् असतीति च
तस्माद् अतो भवत्य् एव युक्तिर् एषाऽभिध्ल्यते

the cause-effect relation from "this happening, that happens" relation are refuted by Śāntarakṣita and Kamalaśīla, who point out that there are no separate cognitive processes which link up the relation of "this happening, that happens" with the cause-effect relation, because both these convey the same concept. The cause-effect relation is the same as "this happening, that happens." It may be argued that, whenever anything invariably and unconditionally happens on the happening of any other thing, then the two are considered to be related as cause and effect, just as a jug, etc. are invariably seen to appear after the proper operations of the potter and his wheels. If this is *yukti,* then it is not a different source of knowledge.

Cakrapāṇi, however, points out that these criticisms are all beside the point, since *yukti*, according to Caraka, is not *kārya-kāraṇatā* from *tad-bhāva-bhāvitā*; it is the arriving at a conclusion as a result of a series of reasonings. But it is important to note that in III.4.6 and 7 Caraka speaks of three kinds of *pramāṇas,* viz. *pratyakṣa, anumāna* and *śabda,* and describes *anumāna* as being *tarka* depending on *yukti. Tarka* is explained by Cakrapāṇi as being the knowledge of things which cannot be perceived (*tarko 'pratyakṣa-jñānam*), *and yukti* is here paraphrased by Cakrapāṇi as the relation of *a-vinū-bhāva.* It is said in this connection that a disease is to be determined by *pratyakṣa,* the medical texts (*āpto - padeśa*) and inference. But in III.8.6.33 and 34 Caraka counts *aitihya* as *āptopadeśa,* though ordi-

---

प्रमाणान्तरम् एवेयम् इत्य् आह चरको मुनिः
नानुमानम् इयं यस्मास् दृष्टान्तोऽत्र न लभ्यते॥

asmin sati bhavaty eva na bhavaty asatīti ca
tasmād ato bhavaty eva yuktir eṣā 'bhidhlyate
pramāṇāntaram eveyam ity āha carako muniḥ
nānumānam iyaṃ yasmād dṛṣṭānto'tra na labhyate.

—*Tattva-saṃgraha,* p. 482.

This, however, is entirely different from what Caraka says, as is pointed out by Cakrapāṇi in his commentary on *Caraka-saṃhitā.* Caraka's idea of *yukti* is the logic of probability, i.e. when from a number of events, circumstances, or observations one comes to regard a particular judgment as probable, it is called *yukti,* and, as it is different from inference or any of the other accepted *pramāṇas,* it is to be counted as a separate *pramāṇa.* So far as I know, this is the only example of the introduction of the logic of probability in Indian thought.

narily *aitihya* is considered in Indian philosophy as being "tradition" or long-standing popular belief, different from *āptopadeśa*; *upamāna*, under the name of *aupamya,* is also referred to.

It may not be out of place here to note that the obstacles to perception referred to in the *Sāṃkhya-kārikā* are all mentioned here. Thus it is said that even those things which have colour *(rūpa)* cannot be perceived if they are covered by a veil, or if the senses are weak, or if the mind is unsettled, or if they are mixed up in any homogeneous medium indistinguishable from them, or when in the case of smaller lights they are overcome by stronger luminaries, or when they are too fine or too subtle.[1]

Logic was of use with Indian medical men not only in diagnosing a disease, but also in the debates which they had with one another. The rival practitioners often had to show their skill and learning in debates on occasions of the treatment of illness of rich patients. The art of carrying on a dispute successfully was considered an important acquisition among medical practitioners. Thus we have a whole set of technical terms relating to disputes, such as are never found in any other literature, excepting the *Nyāya-sūtra.* In the *Caraka-saṃhitā* almost the whole of the chapter called the "*Roga-bhiṣag-jitīya-vimāna*" (I I I.8) is devoted to this purpose. It is well to remember that different kinds of disputes and fallacies are mentioned in the *Nyāya-sūtra,* and it will be useful to refer to these when dealing with similar topics from either the *Caraka-saṃhitā* or the *Suśruta-saṃhitā.*

The four terms referred to in connection with disputes in the *Nyāya-sūtra* are *tarka, vāda, jalpa* and *vitaṇḍā. Tarka* is said to be the same as *ūha,* and this is explained as a process of reasoning carried on in one's mind before one can come to any right conclusion. It is a name for the subjective weighing of different alternatives on the occasion of a doubt before a conclusive affirmation or denial *(nirṇaya)* is made. Disputes are said to be of three kinds, *vāda, jalpa* and *vitaṇḍā. Vāda* means a discussion for the ascertainment of *truth, jalpa* a dispute in which the main object is the overthrow of the opponent rightly or wrongly, and *vitaṇḍā* a dispute in which

1 *Caraka-saṃhitā,* I.11.8.

attempts are made to discover the faults of the opponent's thesis without any attempt to offer any alternative thesis. *Vāda* is thus essentially different in its purpose from *jalpa* and *vitaṇḍā*; for *vāda* is an academical discussion with pupils, teachers, fellow-stūdents and persons seeking truth solely for the purpose of arriving at right conclusions, and not for fame or gain.[1] *Jalpa*, on the other hand, is that dispute which a man carries on while knowing himself to be in the wrong or unable to defend himself properly from his opponents except by trickery and other unfair methods of argument.

Caraka, in III.8, says that a medical man should hold discussions (*sambhāṣā*) with other medical men. Discussion increases zeal for knowledge (*saṃharṣa*), clarifies knowledge, increases the power of speech and of achieving fame, removes doubts in the learning acquired before and strengthens convictions. In the course of these discussions many new things may be learnt, and often out of zeal an opponent will disclose the most cherished secret teachings of his teachers. These discussions are of two classes, friendly *(sandhāya saṃbhāṣā)* and hostile *(vigṛhya saṃbhāṣā*). A friendly discussion is held among wise and learned persons who frankly and sincerely discuss questions and give their views without any fear of being defeated or of the fallacies of their arguments being exposed. For in such discussions, even though there may be the fallacies described, no one would try to take advantage of the other, no one is jubilant over the other's defeat and no attempt is made to misinterpret or misstate the other's views.

Caraka then proceeds to give instructions as to how one should behave in an assembly where one has to meet with hostile disputes. Before engaging oneself in a hostile discussion with an opponent a man ought carefully to consider whether his opponent is inferior *(para)* to him and also the nature of the assembly *(pariṣat)* in which the discussion is undertaken. A *pariṣat* may be learned *(jñānavatī)* or ignorant *(mūḍhā),* and these again may be friendly (*suhṛt*), neu-

1 *vādaṃ ca nirṇaya-phalārtkibhir eva śiṣya-sabrahmacāri-gurubhiḥ saha vlta-rāgaiḥ, na khyāti-lābha-rabhasa-prativardhamāna-spardhānubandha-vidhur ātma-bhir ārabheta.—Nyāya-mañjarī,* p. 594.

tral (*udāsīnā*), or hostile *(pratiniviṣṭā)*. When an opponent is to be judged, he is to be judged from two points of view, intellectual and moral. Thus, on the one hand, it has to be considered whether he is learned and wise, whether he remembers the texts and can reproduce them quickly and has powers of speech, and on the other hand, whether he is of an irritable temperament, or of a fearful nature, etc. A man must carefully consider whether his opponent is superior to him in these qualifications or not.

No disputes should be undertaken in a hostile assembly; for even the best arguments might be misinterpreted. In an ignorant, friendly or neutral assembly it is possible to win a debate by proceeding tactfully against an opponent who is looked down upon by famous or otherwise great persons. In beginning conversations with such persons attempts may be made to puzzle them by reciting long *sūtras* and to demoralize or stun them, as it were, by jokes, banter and gestures and by using satirical language.

When a man has to enter into a dispute with his equal, he should find out the special point in which his opponent is weak and attack him there and should try to corner him in such positions as are generally unacceptable to people in general. Caraka then proceeds to explain a number of technical terms in connection with such disputes. Like the Nyāya, Caraka divides such hostile disputes *(vāda)* into two classes, *jalpa* and *vitaṇḍā. Pratijñā* is the enunciation of a thesis which is sought to be proved, e.g. "The *puruṣa* is eternal." *Sthāpanā* is the establishing of a thesis by syllogistic reasonings involving propositions with *hetu, dṛṣṭānta, upanaya* and *nigamana.* Thus the above thesis *(pratijñā*), "The *puruṣa* is eternal," is to be supported by a reason *(hetu),* "because it is uncreated"; by an example *(dṛṣṭānta),* "The sky is uncreated and it is eternal"; by a proposition showing the similarity between the subject of the example and the subject of the thesis *(upanaya),* viz. "Just as the *ākāśa* is uncreated, so *the puruṣa* is also uncreated"; and finally by establishing the thesis *(nigamana),* "Therefore the *puruṣa* is eternal."[1]

1 It is easy to see that Caraka admitted in a syllogism all the five propositions that are admitted in the *Nyāya-sūtra.*

Pratiṣṭhāpanā is the attempt to establish a proposition contrary to the proposition or the thesis put forth by the opponent. Thus, when the thesis of the *sthāpanā* is "*Puruṣa* is eternal," the *pratisthāpanā* proposition would be "*Puruṣa* is non-eternal," because "it is perceivable by the senses," and "The jug which is perceptible to the senses is non-eternal," and "*Puruṣa* is like the jug," so "*Puruṣa* is non-eternal."

Caraka defines *hetu* as "the cause of knowledge" *(hetur nāma upalabdhi-kāraṇam),* and the cause of knowledge is the pramāṇas of *pratyakṣa, anumāna, aitihya* and *aupamya.* The definition of *hetu* in the *Nyāya-sūtra* refers only to the perceived *hetu* in the case of inference, through a similarity or dissimilarity to which a relation is established by inference.[1] Here Caraka points out that a *hetu* may be either perceived, inferred or found by analogy or from the scriptures, but, in whichever way it may be found, when it leads to knowledge, it is called a *hetu.* Thus, when I say, "The hill is fiery, because it smokes" (*parvato vahnimān dhūmavattvāt*), the smoke is the *hetu,* and it is directly perceived by the eye. But when I say, "He is ill, because he is of low digestion," the *hetu* is not directly perceived, but is only inferred; for the fact of one's being in low digestion cannot be directly perceived. Again, when it is said, "*Puruṣa* is eternal, because it is uncreated" (*nityaḥ puruṣaḥ a-kṛtakatvāt*), the uncreatedness *(a-kṛtakatva)* is the *hetu,* but it is neither perceived, nor inferred, but accepted from the testimony of the scriptures. Again, in the proposition, "His face is most beautiful, because it has been compared with the moon" (*asya mukhaṃ kāntatamaṃ candropamatvāt*), the fact of being compared with the moon is the *hetu* and it is known by *upamā.*[2] Thus Caraka's definition of *hetu* does not really come into conflict with that of Gautama: he only says that a *hetu* may be discovered by any of the *pramāṇas*, and, by whichever *pramāṇa* it may be discovered, it may be called

---

1 *udāharaṇa-sādharmyāt sādhya-sādhanaṃ hetuḥ tathā vaidharmyāt. —Nyāya-sūtra,* I.1.34, 35.

2 See Gaṅgādhara's *Jalpa-kalpa-taru,* III.8.122.

a *hetu*, if it is invariably and unconditionally (*a-vinā-bhāva*) associated with the major term (*sādhya*).[1]

Caraka then proceeds to describe *uttara*, which is in purport the same as the *jāti* of the *Nyāya-sūtras.* When an opponent wants to prove a thesis on the basis of a similarity of the subject of the thesis with the *hetu,* attempts have to be made to upset the thesis by showing its dissimilarity to the *hetu.* Thus one may say that the feeling of cold in a man must be due to his being affected by snow, dews, or chilly air, because effects arise from causes similar to them; in reply it may be said that effects are dissimilar from their causes, since a burning fever may often be an effect of cold.[2]

---

1 *hetuś cāvinābhāva-liṅga-vacanaṃ yady api, tathāpīha liṅga-pragrāhakāṇi pratyakṣādi-pramāṇāny eva yathokta-hetu-mūlatvena hetu-śabdenāha.*

—Cakrapāṇi on Caraka, I I I.8.6.25.

2 *sādharmya-vaidharmyābhyāṃ pratyavasthānaṃ jātiḥ. Nyāya-sūtra,* I.2.18. There are twenty-four kinds of this *jāti,* e.g. (1-2) *sādharmya-vaidharmya-sama,* (3-8) *utkarṣāpakarṣa-varṇyāvarṇya-vikalpa-sādhya-sama,* (9-10) *prāpty-aprāpti-sama,* (11-12) *prasaṅga-pratidṛṣṭānta-sama,* (13) *anutpatti-sama,* (14) *saṃśaya-sama,* (15) *prakaraṇa-sama,* (16) *ahetu-sama,* (17) *arthāpatti-sama,* (18) *aviśeṣa-sama,* (19) *upapatti-sama,* (20) *upalabdhi-sama,* (21) *anupalabdhi-sama,* (22) *nitya-sama,* (23) *anitya-sama,* (24) *kārya-sama.*

Sādharmya-vaidharmya-sama is that in which, when an argument is given on the basis of the similarity or dissimilarity to a certain *hetu,* it is pointed out that quite the opposite conclusions may be drawn from other points of similarity or dissimilarity with other *hetus.* Thus, when it is said, "*Śabda* is non-eternal, because it is produced by an effort, and whatever is produced by an effort is non-eternal, as a jug," it may be answered, "*Śabda* is eternal, because it is partless: a partless entity like the *ākāśa* is found to be eternal; there is no special reason why on account of its similarity to a jug sound should be non-eternal, and not eternal owing to its similarity to *ākāśa.*" An escape from the dilemma is possible by enquiring as to what may constitute an unconditional and invariable *(avyabhicārī)* similarity.

Utkarṣāpakarṣa-varṇyāvarṇya-vikalpa-sādhya-sama is that in which similarity is pressed too far. Thus it is urged that, because sound is non-eternal like a jug, it must also be visible like a jug, and, if it is not so, it cannot be non-eternal like a jug. Moreover, it may be said that the reason why sound is expected to be non-eternal like a jug is that the former is produced by an effort *(prayatnāntarīyaka).* But things which are produced by efforts differ in many of their qualities; thus a cloth is soft, and a jug is hard, though both of them are produced by effort; so it may be argued that, though *śabda* is as much a product of effort as a jug, it may not agree with the jug in being non-eternal. Moreover, instead of

The long list of *jātis* given in the *Nyāya-sūtra* and explained in the commentaries and in the *Nyāya-mañjarī* is not referred to by

---

arguing that sound is like a jug, it may as well be argued that a jug is like sound; so that the status of the jug is as uncertain as sound itself *(yadi yathā ghaṭas tathā śabdaḥ prāptaṃ tarhi yathā śabdaḥ tathā ghaṭa iti śabdaś cānityatayā sādhya iti ghato 'pi sādhya eva syād anyathā hi na tena tulyo bhavet—Nyāya-mañjarī*, p. 624). In answer to these kinds of fault-finding the proper argument is that no similarity should be extended beyond its limits, and an example (*dṛṣṭānta*) should not be considered to have the same status as a probandum *(sādhya);* for an example is that which is already agreed upon among the disputants and the common people (*laukika-parīkṣakāṇāṃ yasminn arthe buddhi sāmyaṃ sa dṛṣṭāntaḥ).*

Prāpty-aprāpti-sama is that in which it is urged that, if the *hetu* and the probandum are together, they cannot be distinguished from each other; if they are separate, *hetu* cannot lead us to the *sādhya.* The answer to this is that a *hetu* can produce an effect either by direct contact (e.g. the rope and the stick in contact with clay produce a jug) or from a distance (e.g. the *śyena* sacrifice can destroy an enemy from a distance).

Prasaṅga-sama is that in which a reason for the *hetu* is asked. Thus, if the character of immediately following an effort (*prayatnāntarīyakatva*) is the cause of non-eternality, what can establish the *prayatnāntarīyakatva* of a jug, etc.? The answer to this is that a reason is necessary only for that which is not directly experienced as being evident in itself. That a jug immediately follows the efforts that produce it is directly experienced ānd does not require any argument or reason to establish it, as no light is required to see a burning lamp.

Dṛṣṭānta-sama is that in which from the same *hetu* two different conclusions are seen to result. Thus it may be said that both the jug and *ākāśa* have the character of immediately following an effort (e.g. as by digging new space is produced in underground wells which before the effort of digging were solid earth without space—*kūpa-khanana-prayatnānantaraṃ tad-upalambhāt*—and this character is therefore to be regarded as *prayatnāntariyaka)*; yet, as a jug is non-eternal and *ākāśa* eternal, so *śabda,* though it immediately follows an effort, is eternal. The answer is that, if such an opposite conclusion is drawn, a separate *hetu* has to be given, which is not done in the present case.

If sound is non-eternal, it must possess the character of coming into existence immediately after an effort that produces it; but how can it possess that character before being produced or coming into existence? If it cannot at that stage possess that character, it must be eternal, since the cause of its non-eternality is absent. This objection is called *anutpatti-sama.* The reply is that, unless the sound is in existence, its eternality or non-eternality cannot be discussed. If it is non-existent, of what is the eternality to be affirmed by the opponent?

Again, it may be argued that *śabda* has *prayatnāntarīyakatva,* and therefore it may be expected to be non-eternal; it is perceived by the senses, and therefore it may be expected to be eternal, like so many other sensible objects. This doubt

Caraka; nor does the technical name of *jāti* find any place in Caraka's description of it. If these elaborate descriptions of *jāti* were

---

is called *saṃśaya-sama.* A doubt remains a doubt only so long as the special features which remove a doubt are not discovered. Though a man may have many qualities in common with a post, the doubt cannot remain when the special features of a man (e.g. his having a head and hands and feet) are known.

Prakaraṇa-sama is that in which an entity is equally related to *hetus,* so that no one conclusion can properly be drawn. Thus, sound has both *prayatnāntarīyakatva* and *niravayavatva* (partlessness). Though, according to the first, it may be said to be non-eternal, according to the second it may be said to be eternal; so it is eternal. The answer is that the second *hetu* cannot be pressed as leading to a conclusion, because the first also is admitted to exist.

Ahetu-sama is the objection that there can be no argument from a *hetu*; for, if there is no *sādhya* (probandum), what is it that the *hetu* produces? and again, if there is no *hetu* before the *sādhya,* how can the *sādhya* be produced? So, as *hetu* is only a concomitant of *sādhya,* no inference is possible from it. The answer is that it is quite possible that from the previously existing *hetu* the non-existing *sādhya* should be produced. *Arthāpatti-sama* is where, for example, owing to the fact that sound is partless, it appears to be similar to *ākāśa* and hence by implication to be eternal. This is against the previous thesis that it is non-eternal owing to its being *prayatnāntarīyaka. Aviśeṣa-sama* is the objection, that if on account of having the same characteristic of *prayatnāntarīyakatva, śabda* and *ghaṭa* are said to be equally non-eternal, then, owing to all things having the same quality of existence *(sattā),* they are all the same. The answer to this is that equality in one respect does not mean equality in all respects.

Upapatti-sama is where a jug may be expected to be non-eternal owing to its *prayatnāntarīyakatva* and eternal owing to its being partless like *ākāśa. Upalabdhi-sama* is where it is urged that, when by a terrible storm a tree is broken, there is sound which is not the result of any human effort (*prayatnāntarīyakatva*) I, and yet it is non-eternal; again, lightning is not the result of human effort, still it is non-eternal. The answer is that the concomitance is between *prayatnāntarīyakatva* and non-eternality and not between non-eternality and *prayatnāntarīyakatva*; so that all that is produced by human effort is noneternal, but not vice-versa. It should also be noted that by *prayatnāntarīyakatva* emphasis is laid on the fact that all things that possess this character are produced. *Anitya-sama* is an objection where it is urged, for example, that, if on account of the similarity of sound to a jug, the former is non-eternal, then, since in some way or other all things in the world must have some similarity to a jug, all things must be non-eternal. The *nitya-sama* objection runs as follows: Is non-eternality in sound non-eternal or eternal? If the latter, then in order that an eternal quality may abide in it, sound itself must be eternal. If the former, then on some occasions at least sound must be eternal.

known to Caraka, it is unlikely that he should have passed them over without referring to them.

An example *(dṛṣṭānta)* is that on which the common folk and the learned are of the same opinion, since examples involve facts which are perceived by all and known to all, e.g. the fire is hot, water is liquid, the earth is firm. A *siddhānta*, or conclusion, is that to which one could arrive after a searching enquiry and demonstration by proper reasons. This *siddhānta* is of four kinds, viz. (1)*sarva-tantra-siddhānta,* or conclusions accepted by all, e.g. "There are causes of diseases; there are diseases; curable ones can be cured";(2) *prati-tantra-siddhānta,* or conclusions which are not accepted by all, but are limited to particular books or persons: e.g. some say that there are eight *rasas,* others say that there are six; some say that there are five senses, others, that there are six; (3) *adhikaraṇa-siddhānta*, or conclusions which being accepted or proved, other conclusions also become proved or accepted: e.g. if it is proved that emancipated souls do not reap the fruits of *karma*, as they are without any desire, then the doctrine of the suffering of the fruits of *karma*, emancipation, the existence of soul and existence after death will have to be considered as refuted; (4)*abhyupagama-siddhānta*, or conclusions which are accepted only for the sake of an argument, and which are neither examined critically nor considered as proved.[1]

Śabda is a collection of letters which may be of four kinds, viz. (1) *dṛṣṭārtha*—of experienced purport (e.g. "The *doṣas* lose their equilibrium through three causes"); (2)*adṛṣṭārtha*—of unperceivable purport (e.g. "There is after-life; there is emancipation"); (3) *satya*, or truth, that which tallies With facts (e.g. "There is Āyur-veda; there are means for curing curable diseases");(4) *anṛta*, the op-

---

The *kārya-sama* objection suggests that *prayatnāntarīyakatva* leads to production in two ways, either by bringing into existence that which was non-existent, or by removing the veil from something which was in a veiled condition; and it remains undecided what sort of *prayatnāntarīyakatva* applies to *śabda*.

The above interpretations are all based on Jayanta's *Nyāya-mañjarī*

1 All these *siddhāntas* occur under the same names in the *Nyāya-sūtra,* I.1.28, 29, 30, 31.

posite of truth, untruth.[1] *Saṃśaya*, or doubt, occurs with reference to things about which no certainty is attained. Thus those who are unhealthy and inactive die soon, whereas those who are healthy and active live a long life. So there is a doubt whether in this world death happens timely or untimely. *Prayojana*, or the object of action, is that for which anything is begun. Thus one may think that, if there is untimely death, I shall form healthy habits and leave off unhealthy habits, so that untimely death may not touch me.[2] *Sa-vyabhicāra* means variability, e.g. "This may or may not be a medicine for this disease."[3] *Jijñāsā* means experimenting; a medicine is to be advised after proper experiments *(jijñāsā). Vyavasāya* means decision *(niścaya),* e.g. "This is a disease due to predominance of *vāyu*; this is the medicine for this disease." *Artha-prāpti* is the same as the well-known *arthāpatti*, or implication, when on making a statement, some other thing which was not said becomes also stated; it is a case of implication, e.g. the statement, "This disease cannot be cured by allowing the patient to take his normal food and drink," implies that it can be cured by fasting, or, if it is said, "He should not eat during the day," this means that "He should eat during the night."[4] *Saṃbhava* is the source from which anything springs, e.g. the six *dhātus* may be considered as the *saṃbhava* of the foetus; wrong diet, of disease; and right course of treatment, of health.

---

1 The first two divisions, *dṛṣṭārtha* and *adṛṣṭārtha,* occur in the *Nyāya-sūtra*, I.1.8, *sa dvividho dṛṣṭādṛṣṭārthatvāt.*

2 *Prayojana,* which means pleasure and pain, is referred to in the *Nyāya-sūtra,* I.1.1, though it is nowhere critically examined. It is explained by Vātsyāyana as that which goads men to action *(yena prayuktaḥ pravartate).* Uddyotakara explains it as the realization of pleasure and the fear of pain *(sukha-prāpti-duḥkha-hāni).*

3 *anaikāntikaḥ sa-vyabhicāraḥ. Nyāya-sūtra,* I.2.5. E.g. "sound is eternal" because it is untouchable; but untouchability does not lead to eternality, since the touchable atoms are eternal, whereas untouchable thoughts are shortlived.

4 Cakrapāṇi says that Caraka does not think that *artha-prāpti* is a separate *pramāṇa*; according to him it is a case of inference, and hence is not included in the list of *pramāṇas.*

Anuyojya means a faulty answer which omits such details as should have been given in the answer, e.g. "This disease can be cured by purificatory action"; such an answer is faulty, as it does not state whether the purification should be made by vomiting or purging. *Ananuyojya* is what is different from *anuyojya. Anuyoga* is a question put by a learned man in a discussion as an enquiry about the reason for a thesis put forward by a learned colleague: e.g. a learned man says, "*Puruṣa* is eternal," and another learned man asks, "What is the reason?" Such a question is called *anuyoga.* A counter-question, such as "What is the reason for your asking such a question?" is called *praty-anuyoga.*

Vākya-doṣa, or faulty statement, is of five kinds, viz. *nyūna, adhika*, *anarthaka*, *apārthaka* and *viruddha.* 1) *Nyūna*, or the fault of omission, is that in which any of the five propositions necessary for a syllogism is omitted. It may also be applied to those cases in which, when a statement has to be supported by a number of reasons, only one is offered and others are omitted, materially affecting the strength of the support of the original statement. Thus several reasons are given in support of the eternality of *puruṣa*, viz. beginninglessness, not being the product of any effort, unchangeableness, etc. Proposing to give all these reasons, and giving only one, is an instance of *nyūna. Adhika* is where, when Āyur-veda is being discussed, the opponent makes irrelevant references to learned works on politics or the art of government. It may also mean cases where words or statements are needlessly repeated. Such a repetition is of two kinds, verbal repetition and sense repetition. Verbal repetition is the repetition of the same word, while the other is the repetition of the sense only, though different words may be used.*Anarthaka* and *apārthaka* mean the use of meaningless and unconnected words or expressions. *Viruddha*, or contrary statement, means the making of a statement contrary to the example (*dṛṣṭānta-viruddha*) or the accepted conclusion *(siddhānta),* e.g. cold water is hot, for so is fever; or when a medical man *(vaidya)* says that medicine does not cure diseases.

Samaya-viruddha is the making of any statement against the accepted conclusions of any particular *śāstra.* Thus, for example, if a Mīmāṃsaka says that animals should not be sacrificed, it will be against his accepted doctrine that animals should be sacrificed. Or, if in any system of philosophy treating of emancipation (*mokṣa - śāstra*) it be said that injury to living beings is good, then this is against the accepted tenet of that *śāstra. Vākya-praśaṃsā* is that kind of statement in which the faults mentioned above in *vākya-doṣa* do not occur.

Chala means a rejoinder in which the statement of the opponent is wilfully misinterpreted. It is of two kinds, *vāk-chala* and *sāmānya-chala.* The word *nava* means "nine" as well as "new," and if, when one says about one's opponent, "This physician is *nava-tantra*" (has newly learnt his texts), and the opponent replies, "I have not nine text-books, I have one text," the other person objects, "I do not say you have nine texts, I say that you are *navābhyasta-tantra*" (have newly learnt the texts), *navābhyasta-tantra* might also mean "read nine times"; and then the opponent might well say, "I have several times read the texts, and not nine times, as you say." This is an example of *vāk-chala.*

Again, when a physician says "Medicine cures diseases," the opponent may take the most general characteristics of the terms and say that the above statement comes to this, that an existent entity cures another existent entity; and, if this is so, then, since bronchitis exists (*san kāsaḥ*) and consumption exists (*san kṣayaḥ),* bronchitis, being an existent entity, must cure another existent entity, consumption. This is called *sāmānya-chala.*[1]

1 *Chala* is treated in the *Nyāya-sūtra* exactly on the same lines as here. Thus the definition of *chala* there (*Nyāya-sūtra,* I.2.10) is *vacana-vighāto 'rtha-vikalpopapattyā chalam* (to attack one's speech by a wilful misinterpretation of it is *chala).* This is divided into three classes, *vāk-chala, sāmānya-chala* and *upacāra-chala*; of these *vāk-chala* is exactly the same as in *Caraka-saṃhitā,* and so also the *sāmānya-chala* (because a Brahman is well-read in scriptures, a *vrātya* (outcast Brahman) is also well-read, because he also is a Brahman in some sense). *Upacāra-chala,* which, however, resembles *vāk-chala,* is not mentioned in the *Caraka-saṃhitā.* Its definition in the *Nyāya-sūtra,* I.2.14, is *dharma-vikalpa-nirdeśe 'rtha-sad-bhāva-pratiṣedha upacāra-chalam* (to make

Fallacies (*a-hetu*) are of three kinds, *prakaraṇa-sama, saṃśaya-sama* and *varṇya-sama.*[1] *Prakaraṇa-sama* is where that

---

one's statement impossible by taking it in one sense, say the primary, when the secondary one was intended). Thus, if it is said, "This porter is an ass," it may be objected that the porter, being a man, cannot at the same time be an ass. Gautama, however, tentatively raises the objection that *chalas* should be regarded as three in number and not tw'o, taking *upacāra-chala* within *sāmānya-chala.* This means a criticism in view of Caraka's division of *chala* into two classes. For Gautama argues that, if on account of some similarity *upacāra-chala* should be included within *sāmānya-chala,* and *chalas* should be counted as being of two kinds instead of three, then for the very same reason of similarity *chalas* may as well be regarded as being of one kind instead of two. So, in view of the specific differences that exist between the *chalas,* they should be regarded as being of three kinds.

1 *Nyāya-sūtra,* I.2.4, describes the fallacies (*hetv-ābhāsa*) as of five kinds, *sa-vyabhicāra, viruddha, prakaraṇa-sama, sādhya-sama* and *kālātīta.*

Sa-vyabhicāra hetu is that which has no invariable concomitance with the probandum, e.g. sound is eternal because it is untouchable, and that which is touchable is non-eternal, like a jug. But untouchability has no invariable concomitance with eternality; for an atom is touchable and at the same time eternal, and thoughts (*buddhi*) are untouchable and at the same time non-eternal.

Viruddha hetu is where the reason *(hetu)* demolishes the very theory on which its security depends, e.g. this changeable world *(vikāro)* disappears *(vyakter apaiti),* because it is non-eternal *(nityatva-pratiṣedhāt);* but, though it disappears *(apeto 'pi),* yet it exists *(asti),* because it is not destructible *(vināśa-pratiṣedhāt).* Now a thing which is non-eternal cannot but be destructible. Destructibility and eternality cannot abide together.

Prakaraṇa-sama is where two opposite *hetus* exist in a thing, so that nothing can be affirmed by either of them. Thus it may be argued with as much force that "sound is eternal, because it has in it the qualities of eternal things," as that "sound is non-eternal, because it has in it the qualities of non-eternal things"; so no conclusion can be drawn from either of these *hetus.*

Sādhya-sama is where the *hetu* itself remains to be proved. Thus in the argument, "shadow is a substance because it moves," the movability of shadows is a doubtful point and is itself in need of proof. Does a shadow move like a man, or is it that because the covering entity moves that at different places the light is veiled and this gives rise to the formation of shadows at different places ?

Kālātīta is where the *hetus* in the case of the accepted example and the case to be proved vary, because in the latter case the *hetu* is not properly a *hetu;* for the *hetu* and *sādhya* exist in two successive moments and are therefore not concomitant; but in the former case they are concomitant and simultaneous, e.g. sound is eternal, because it is manifested, like colour, owing to a particular contact, like light, being manifested by the contact of a stick and a drum, just as which is given as the *hetu* remains to be proved. Thus, when it is said that, since the self is different from the body, it is eternal, and because the body is unconscious it is non-eternal, it may be urged (as by the Cārvāka school of philosophers) that both the points, viz. that the self is different from the body and that the body is not endowed with consciousness, which are offered as the *hetu*, are themselves to be proved; for according to the Cārvākas the body is endowed with consciousness and is non-eternal. A reference to the footnote below shows that this *prakaraṇa-sama* is different from the *prakaraṇa-sama* of the *Nyāya-sūtra*. *Saṃśaya-sama* is that in which that which is the cause of doubt is offered as the *hetu* for a particular conclusion, e.g. This person quotes a passage from Āyur-veda—is he or is he not a physician? Even a man who is not a physician might have heard a passage somewhere and quoted it. Now, therefore, quoting a passage from Āyur-veda leaves us in doubt as to the man's being a physician or not. If this itself is offered as the *hetu* for a particular conclusion and if it is said, "He is a physician because he has quoted a passage from Āyur-veda," it becomes a case of *saṃśaya-sama*. Gautama speaks of *saṃśaya-sama* as an instance of *jāti*; but the former is a case where a doubt is not removed because of the fact that the thing about which anything is affirmed possesses two opposite qualities, so that no affirmation can be made on the strength of any of these characteristics. Here, however, *saṃśaya-sama* is used in the sense that what is itself doubtful is adduced as the reason for a particular conclusion.

Varṇya-sama is where an affirmation is made about a thing on the strength of another affirmation which itself remains to be proved and is hence in the same condition as the previous affirmation, e.g. "Buddhi is non-eternal, like sound, as it is untouchable, like the latter." But the non-eternality of sound stands as much in need of proof as that of *buddhi*, and the former affirmation cannot

---

colour is manifested by the contact of light with a thing. But the similarity fails; for, while colour is manifested simultaneously with the contact of light and the things, sound is heard at a moment different from that at which actual contact of the stick and the drum takes place.

be made on the basis of the latter. This fallacy is similar to the *jāti* called *sādhya-sama* and the fallacy *sādhya-sama* of Gautama already described in the footnotes to page 451.

Atīta-kāla is that in which that which should be said first is said later, e.g. the thesis, or *pratijñā,* should be stated first and the conclusion, or *nigamana*, last; if instead the *nigamana* is stated first and the *pratijñā* after, then we have the fault of *kālātīta.*

Upālambha (criticism) is the finding fault with the *hetus*, also called *a-hetu,* as described above, or *hetv-ābhāsas. Parihāra* (reply) means the reply given to the objections pointed out by an opponent; e.g. the self is eternal, since so long as it remains in the body it shows signs of life, and, when it is away, though the body still remains the same, yet there is no sign of life; therefore the self is different from the body and is eternal. *Pratijñā-hāni* (to give up one's thesis) is where, being cornered by the opponent, one is forced to give up one's original thesis. Thus one may start with the thesis that *puruṣa* is eternal, but, being cornered, one may give it up and say that *puruṣa* is not eternal. *Abhyanujñā* (to bring a countercharge) is that in which a disputant, instead of refuting the charge brought against him by his opponent, charges his opponent with the same defects.[1] *Hetv-antara* (dodging with a wrong reason) is where, when the cause of some root fact *(prakṛti)* is asked, the reply refers to the cause of the modifications or manifestations *(vikṛti)* of that root fact.[2] *Arthāntara* (wrong answer) is where, when the definition of one thing (e.g. fever) is asked, a definition of another thing (e.g. diabetes) is given.[3] *Nigraha-sthāna* is where, in a learned

1 This corresponds to *matāmujñā* of the *Nyāya-sūtra,* V.1.42.

2 In *Nyāya-sūtrc,* V.2.6, we hear of a *hetv-antara,* but that seems to be different from this. The significance of *hetv-antara,* as it stands there, may be illustrated as follows. An adherent of Sāṃkhya says that all this world of things is derived from one root cause, because all these are limited and whatever is limited is derived from one root cause. This may be refuted by pointing out that there are many limited things which are derived from more than one root cause. To this the Sāṃkhya adherent replies that only those which are associated with pleasure and pain and ignorance are to be regarded as proceeding from one root cause; but this is an addition which was not contained in the original thesis.

3 This is also mentioned in the *Nyāya-sūtra,* V.2.7.

assembly, a statement, though thrice repeated, is not understood by the opponent. Caraka counts among the *nigraha-sthānas* many of the cases which have already been enumerated and described. Thus he counts *pratijñā-hāni, abhyanujñā, kālātīta, a-hetu, nyūna, atirikta, vyartha, apārthaka, punar-ukta, viruddha, hetv-antara, arthāntara.*[1]

After this Caraka further describes the ten categories, a knowledge of which he thinks is very necessary for a mastery of the subject-matter of Āyur-veda. These are *kāraṇa* (the agent or the mover), *karaṇa* (the instrument necessary for an agent to bring about an effort), *kārya-yoni* (the material cause by the modification of which effects are produced), *kārya* (that for the production of which the mover makes his effort), *kārya-phala* (that for which a particular effect is intended by the agent), *anubandha* (the good or bad result which attaches itself to the doer after the production of the effect), *deśa* (place), *kāla* (the seasons, days, etc.), *pravṛtti* (the effort and the action needed for the production of the effect) and *upāya* (the passivity and special aptitude of the agent, the instrument and the material cause which can make the effect possible). (same list, explained:) The physician is the cause *(kāraṇa),* the medicines the instruments *(karaṇa)*; the want of equilibrium of the *dhātus* the *kārya-yoni;* the restoration of the equilibrium of the *dhātus* the *kārya*; the happy state of body and mind the *kārya-phala*; length of life, *anubandha*; the place and the diseased person, *deśa*; the year and the condition of the diseased person, *kāla*; the efforts of the physician, *pravṛtti*; the qualifications of the physician, the qualities of the medicine, etc., *upāya.*

It may be pointed out in this connection that the *Uttara-tantra* of Suśruta also mentions thirty-two technical terms helpful to physicians in refuting the statements of hostile critics and in estab-

1 The *nigraha-sthānos* mentioned in the *Nyīya-sūtra,* V.2.1, are the following: *pratijñā-hāni, pratijñāntara, pratijñā-virodha, pratijñā-sannyāsa, hetv-antara, arthāntara, nirarthaka, avijñātārtha, apārthaka, aprāpta-kāla, nyūna, adhika, punar-ukta, ananubhāṣana, ajñāna, apratibhā, vikṣepa, matānujñā, paryanuyojyo-pekṣeṇa, niranuyojyānuyoga, apa-siddhānta, hetv-ābhāsa.* Many of these, however, are not mentioned by Caraka.

lishing their own points, which are called *tantra-yukti.*[1] These are said to be *adhikaraṇa, yoga, padārtha, hetv-artha, uddeśa, nirdeśa, upadeśa, apadeśa, pradeśa, atideśa, apavarja, vākya-śeṣa, arthāpatti, viparyaya, prasaṅga, ekānta, anekānta, pūrva-pakṣa, nirṇaya, anu-mata, vidhāna, anāgatāvekṣaṇa, atikrāntāvekṣaṇa, saṃśaya, vyā-khyāna, sva-saṃjñā, nirvacana, nidarśana, niyoga, samuccaya, vikalpa* and *ūhya.* But these technical terms are maxims for the interpretation of textual topics, like the maxims of Mīmāṃsā, and are not points of dispute or logical categories. It is said that these maxims are like the sun to a group of lotuses, or like a lamp to a house, for the illumination or the expression of the subject of discourse.[2] This remark very much resembles the remark of Vātsyāyana that *ānvīkṣikī* (logic) is like a light to all sciences *(pradīpaḥ sarva-vidyānām).* But the difference between *tantra-yukti* and *anvīkṣikī* is this, that, while the former refers to the laws of thought, the latter refers to technical modes of expression in medical science in general and in the *Suśruta-saṃhitā* in particular. They therefore refer to the ways of deducing the inner meaning or intention of the medical texts from their abbreviated forms of expression. Thus, when one reads in the text, "about *rasa* or *doṣa*" and nothing else is said, one understands that this style of expression signifies thst it is an *adhikaraṇa* (topic of discourse) and that something is going to be related about *rasa* or *doṣa,* though it is not explicitly so stated. Now the maxim *(tantra-yukti)* of *yoga* means that the verb at a distant part of the sentence may be joined with its relevant case in another part of the sentence.[3] The maxim

---

1 *asad-vādi-prayuktānāṃ vākyānāṃ pratiṣedhānaṃ sva-vākya-siddhir api ca kriyate tantra-yuktitaḥ. —Suśruta-saṃhitā, Uttara-tantra, 65.5.*

2 यथाम्बुजवनस्यार्कः प्रदिपो वेश्मनो यथा।
प्रबोध्यस्य प्रकाशार्थस् तथा तन्त्रस्य युक्तः॥
yathāmbuja-vanasyārkaḥ pradīpo veśmano yathā
prabodhyasya prakāśārthas tathā tantrasya yuktayaḥ.
—Suśruta-saṃhitā, Uttara-tantra, 65.7.

3 तैलम् पिवेच् चामृतवल्लि निम्बहिंस्राभयावृक्षकपिप्पलीन्हिः
सिद्धं बलाभ्यां च सदेवदारु हिताय मित्यं गलगण्डरोगे॥
tailam pivec cāmṛta-vallī-nimba-hiṃsrābhayā-vṛkṣaka-pippalībhiḥ
siddhaṃ balābhyāṃ ca sa-devadāru hitāya nityaṃ gala-gaṇḍa-roge. Ibid. 9, 10.

of *padārtha* means that, when a word having two or more senses is used, then that meaning alone has to be accepted which suits the previous and the later contexts. Thus, when it is said in a medical text that we shall now describe the origin of the Veda, then only Āyur-veda is to be meant and not Ṛg, Yajuṣ or Atharva. The maxim of *hetv-artha* illustrates the condition of invisible things by visible and known examples. Thus it is said that, just as a muddy ball becomes dissolved and sticky through water, so do milk and other drugs dissolve a boil by their application. The maxim of *uddeśa* is the method of briefly touching a subject without going into details. Thus, when one says "disease" (*śalya*), it means both internal and external diseases without any kind of specification. The maxim of *nirdeśa* is the method of describing a thing in detail. The maxim of *upadeśa* is the method of giving a general instruction. Thus it is said that one should not sit up at night nor sleep during the day. This is, however, only a general instruction which has its exceptions. The maxim of *apadeśa* is the method of showing the reasons of things. Thus it is said that phlegm *(śleṣman)* increases through the taking of sweet things *(madhureṇa śleṣmā 'bhivardhate)*. The maxim of *pradeśa* is the analogy by which a present difficulty is solved in the way in which a past difficulty was solved *(prakṛtasya atikrāntena sādhanam pradeśaḥ)*. Thus it may be said that, since this has cured Devadatta in this way in the past, it would also cure Yajñadatta in a similar way now. The maxim of *atideśa* is that of anticipating a future event from a present indication or prognostication. Thus from the fact of the increase of uprising wind in a man's system it may be predicted that he will have a specific bowel-disease (*udāvarta*). The maxim of *apavarja* consists in allowing exceptions to general directions (e.g. cases of poisoning should not be fomented, except in the case of poisoning through the bites of insects). The maxim of

---

In the above verse it is enjoined that a particular medical decoction is to be made with a number of drugs which are to be boiled (*siddham),* and this boiled decoction has to be drunk (*pivet).* But the word *pivet* is in the first line and the word *siddham* is in the third line, and it is allowed that these two distant words may be combined *(yoga).*

vākya-śeṣa consists in supplying an idea suggested by the context, but not expressly mentioned. Thus when it is said "of the head, hands, feet, sides, back, belly, heart," it is the whole man that is to be understood though it is not expressly stated in the context. That which is understood, by implication, though not directly mentioned, is called the maxim of *arthāpatti.* Thus, when a man says "I shall eat rice," it is understood that he is not thirsty, but hungry. The maxim of *viparyaya* is that by virtue of which from a positive or a negative assertion its contrary is asserted also, e.g. when it is said that those who are lean, weak and of fearful temperament are difficult to be cured. The maxim of *prasaṅga* is that by virtue of which allusion is made to things repeatedly described in another chapter. The maxim of *ekānta* allows of affirming a specific action of things unexception-ably (e.g. *madana* fruit induces vomiting, i.e. under all circumstances). The maxim of *anekānta* is that by virtue of which one understands that different opinions prevail on a particular subject. Thus some teachers think that substances are the most important, while others think that *rasa* is so; others, again, think that the inner essence *(vīrya)* is the most important, while still others think that chemical action through digestion *(vipāka)* is so. The maxims of *pūrva-pakṣa* and *uttara-pakṣa* allow of discussing a matter in the form of question and answer. The maxim of *anumata* is that by virtue of which it is to be understood that, when the opinion of other authorities is referred to and not contradicted, it is signified that it is approved. The maxim of *vidhāna* is that by virtue of which one understands that, when certain descriptions follow certain enumerations, the former are to be taken in the order in which the latter are related. The maxim of *anāgatāvekṣaṇa* allows of leaving certain things for future description and elaboration, and *atikrāntāvekṣaṇa* permits alluding to things described before (e.g. it is said in the *Śloka-sthāna* that this matter will be described in the *Cikitsā* chapter, and about another matter it may be said in the *Cikitsā* chapter that it has been described in the *Śloka-sthāna).* The maxim of *saṃśaya* allows a way of statement which may create doubt and confusion in the mind of the reader. The method of elaborate description is called *vyākhyāna.* The method of using words in a sense different from what they have in other literatures is called *sva-saṃjñā*, i.e. technical use (e.g. *mithuna* in Āyur-veda means honey and clarified butter). A definition is called *nirvacana.* The maxim of *nidarśana* allows of describing anything after the analogy of other things. Thus it may be said that, just as fire in a room grows bigger and bigger with wind, so does a boil grow with *vāta*, *pitta* and *kapha. Niyoga* means a direction (e.g. "only what is good to the system is to be taken"). *Samuccaya* means the taking of two or more things together as having equal value. *Vikalpa* is the method of giving alternative or optional directions. *Ūhya* is the maxim by which things which are apparent from the context can be understood.

It is easy to see that of these thirty-two maxims some are ways of interpreting ideas, others are ways of interpreting the arrangement and manner of textual words and their connections, while there are others which are but descriptions of specific peculiarities of style. The redactor (Nāgārjuna) says that he has collected all these maxims as general principles of textual understanding, and he calls them *śabda-nyāyārtha*, i.e. the meaning of the maxims of verbal interpretation.

DID LOGIC ORIGINATE IN THE DISCUSSIONS OF ĀYUR-VEDA PHYSICIANS?

Dr Mahāmahopādhyāya Satish Chandra Vidyabhusan in his *History of Indian Logic* supposes without adducing any reason that the *Caraka-saṃhitā* gives a summary of the principal doctrines of Ānvīkṣikī, possibly as propounded by Medhātithi Gautama. He further says that the doctrines of Ānvīkṣikī evidently did not constitute a part of the original Āyur-veda of Punarvasu Ātreya, and that these doctrines seem to have been incorporated into the *Caraka-saṃhitā* by the redactor Caraka, in whose time they were widely known and studied. Dr Vidyabhusan's theory is that both Caraka and Akṣapāda borrowed the Nyāya doctrines from Medhātithi Gautama, but, while Caraka accepted them in their crude forms, Akṣapāda pruned them thoroughly before they were assimilated in the *Nyāya-sūtra.*[1]

But Dr Vidyabhusan's Medhātithi Gautama is more or less a mythical person, and there is no proof that he ever wrote anything, or that Caraka borrowed anything from a Medhātithi Gautama, or that the Nyāya doctrines found in the *Caraka-saṃhitā* were not contained in the original treatise of Agniveśa, now lost. Dr Vidya-bhusan refers to the evidence of a number of works, such as the *Kusumāñjali, Naiṣadha-carita* and *Nyāya-sūtra-vṛtti*, which refer to Gautama as being the founder of Anvīkṣikī. But none of these authorities are earlier than the tenth century. He refers also to the authority of the *Padma-purāṇa*, *Skanda-purāṇa* and *Gandharva-tantra*, none of which can be regarded as a work of any considerable antiquity. Vātsyāyana himself refers to Akṣapāda as the person to whom Nyāya (the science of Logic) revealed itself.[2] Uddyotakara also refers to Akṣapāda as the utterer of the *Nyāya-śāstra,* and so also does Vācaspati.[3] There is therefore absolutely no reason why the original authorship of Nyāya should be attributed to a Gautama, as against Akṣapāda, on evidence which cannot be traced to any period earlier than the tenth century and which is collected from Purāṇa sources directly

---

1 *History of Indian Logic,* pp. *25* and *26,* by Mahāmahopādhyāya Satish Chandra Vidyabhusan. Calcutta University, 1921.

2 योऽक्षपादम् ऋषिं न्यायः प्रत्यभाद् वदतां वरं
तस्य वात्स्यायन इदं भाष्याजातम् अवर्तयत्॥
Yo 'kṣapādam ṛṣiṃ nyāyaḥ pratyabhād vadatāṃ varaṃ
tasya Vātsyāyana idaṃ bhāṣya-jātam avartayat.
—*Vātsyāyana-bhāṣya*, 2.24, AD 400.

Dr Vidyabhusan's translation of it as "The Nyāya philosophy manifested itself (in a regular form) before Akṣapāda" is inexact.

3 यद् अक्षपादः प्रवरो मुनीनां
शमाय शास्त्तं जगतो जगाद॥
yad Akṣapādaḥ pravaro munīnāṃ
śamāya śāstraṃ jagato jagāda.—Nyāya-vārttika of Uddyotakara (AD 600).

Opening lines, *atha bhagavatā Akṣapādena niḥśreyasa-hetau śāstre praṇīte. Nyāya-vārttika-tāt-parya-pkā* of Vācaspati. Dr Vidyabhusan's translation of the *Nyāya-vārttika* word *śāstra* as "Nyāyaśāstra in a systematic way" is again inexact.

contradicted by the earliest Nyāya authorities. The *Nyāya-śāstra,* therefore, cannot be traced on the evidence of the earliest Nyāya authorities to any earlier Gautama; for, had this been so, it would certainly have been mentioned by either Vātsyāyana, Uddyotakara or Vācaspati. Jayanta also attributes the elaborate Nyāya work to Akṣapāda and does not seem to know that this elaborate treatise, the *Nyāya-sūtra,* was based on the teachings of an earlier authority.[1] If any such authorities were known, they would certainly have been mentioned for the dignity and the prestige of the *Śāstra.* Gautama is an old name, and we find it attached to one of the Ṛṣis of the *Ṛg-Veda* (I.62.78.85; IV.4); he is mentioned in the *Śatapatha-brāhmaṇa* (I.4.1.10; III.3.4.19, etc.); in the *Taittirīya-prātiśākhya* (I.5), in the *Āśvalāyana-śrauta-sūtra* (I.3; II.6, etc.) and in other similar older works; but nowhere is he spoken of as being the author of the *Nyāya-śāstra.* Gautama is also mentioned in the *Mahā-bhārata* several times, but nowhere is he referred to as the author of the *Nyāya-śāstra.* The passage of the *Mahā-bhārata* on which Dr Vidyabhusan bases his theory of a Medhātithi Gautama does not say that Medhātithi was the author of Anvīkṣikī or Nyāya, nor does it say that Medhātithi and Gautama were identical persons.[2] The name Gautama is a patronymic, and the passage of the *Mahā-bhārata* referred to by Dr Vidyabhusan clearly means that the highly wise Medhātithi of the Gautama race was engaged in asceticism. This is corroborated by the fact that the passage of Bhāsa referred to by Dr Vidyabhusan mentions Medhātithi as a teacher of *Nyāya-śāstra* and does not call him Gautama, nor does it say that Medhātithi was the originator of Nyāya.[3] Dr Vidyabhusan's theory, therefore, of Medhātithi Gauta-

---

1 *Akṣapāda-praṇīto hi vitato Nyāya-pādapaḥ.*
Opening lines of the *Nyāya-mañjañ* of Jayantabhaṭṭa (AD 880).

2 मेधातिथिर् महाप्राज्ञो गौतमस् तपसि स्थितः विमृश्य तेन कालेन पत्न्याः संस्थ्याव्यतिक्रमम् ॥
Medhātithir mahā-prājño Gautamas tapasi sthitaḥ vimṛśya tena kālena patnyāḥ saṃsthyā-vyatikramam.
—*Mahā-bhārata, Śānti-parva,* 265.45, Vangavasi edition.

3 *Medhātither Nyāya-śāstram* (having learnt *Nyāya-śāstra* from Medhātithi). Bhāsa's *Pratimā-nāṭaka,* Act V, p. 79..M.M. Ganapati Sastri's edition.

ma being the originator of the *Nyāya-śāstra* falls down like a house of cards. His identification of Medhātithi Gautama's birthplace as Mithilā, his ascertainment of his date, his identification of Persian references to Medhātithi Gautama and his so-styled references to Medhātithi Gautama in the *Aṅguttara-nikāya* and the *Brahma-jāla-sutta* are no less fictitious.[1] The Gautama tradition of Nyāya need not be followed; but it may incidentally be mentioned that an Ātreya Gautama, who is described as being Sāṃkhya (probably in the sense of wise, philosopher, or learned), is counted in the list of the sages who assembled together to discover the causes and remedies of diseases; side by side with this Ātreya, another Ātreya is also mentioned as *bhikṣu Ātreya.*[2] A number of sages are mentioned in the *Caraka-saṃhitā* as persons who discussed the problem of the rise of diseases and how they could be removed. Among these Bharadvāja volunteered to proceed to Indra to learn from him the science of healing. Indra instructed him in the subject, being learned in the three subjects of the *(hetu)* causes (of diseases), knowledge of the *(liṅga)* signs (of diseases) and the knowledge of medicines. Bharadvāja, having learnt this elaborate science in three divisions, repeated it to the sages in exactly the same manner in which he learnt it. After this it is said that Punarvasu taught Āyur-veda to his six disciples, Agniveśa, Bhela and others. Cakrapāṇi, the commentator, says that Punarvasu was the disciple of Bharadvāja, and quotes as his authority a statement of Hārīta. But on this point Caraka himself is silent.

But one thing emerges from this half-mythical account of the origin of Āyur-veda, viz. that the Āyur-veda was occupied from the beginning with the investigation of the nature of causes *(hetu)* and reasons *(liṅga)* for legitimate inferences in connection with the enquiry into the causes of diseases and the apprehension of signs or indications of the same. In the *Nidāna-sthāna* of Caraka eight synonyms for reason *(hetu)* are given, viz. *hetu, nimitta, āyata-*

1 *History of Indian Logic,* by Dr Satish Chandra Vidyabhusan, pp. 17-21.

2 *Ātreyo Gautamaḥ sāṃkhyaḥ.* In this passage Ātreya may, however, be taken as a man separate from the wise Gautama.

na, kartṛ, kāraṇa, pratyaya, samutthāna and *nidāna.* It is curious enough that the words *pratyaya* and *āyatana* are used, which are presumably Buddhistic. The word *pratyaya,* in the sense of cause, is hardly found in Indian philosophy, except in Buddhism. The use of so many terms to denote cause evidently suggests that before Caraka's redaction there must have been an extensive literature which had used these words to denote cause. As a matter of fact, the word *pratyaya* is hardly ever used in the *Caraka-saṃhitā* to signify cause, though it is counted here as one of the synonyms of *hetu,* or cause. The natural implication of this is that the word *pratyaya* was used for *hetu* in some earlier literature, from which Caraka collected it; so with other words, such as *samutthāna, āyatana,* which are counted in the list as synonyms for *hetu,* but are not actually used in the body of the text. This may lead us to think that the discussion of *hetu* under various names is an old subject in Āyur-veda literature existing before Caraka, from which Caraka collected them.

We know that Āyur-veda was primarily concerned with three questions, viz. how diseases originated, how they were known, and what were their cures. It was in this connection that the principle of causality was first from a practical necessity applied in Āyur-veda. Thus, if it is known that a person has been exposed to sudden cold or has enjoyed a heavy feast, then, since it is known that cold leads to fever and over-feeding to indigestion, with the very first symptoms of uneasiness one may at once infer that the patient is likely to get fever or to have diarrhoea or acute indigestion. Or, if it is known that the patient has a strong diarrhoea, then it can similarly be inferred that he has eaten indigestible articles. Thus the two principal kinds of inference which were of practical use to the Āyur-veda physicians were inference of the occurrence of a disease from a knowledge of the presence of the causes of that disease, i.e. from cause to effect, and inference of the specific kinds of unhygienic irregularity from the specific kind of disease of the patient, i.e. from the effect to the cause. The other and third kind of inference is that of inference of disease from its early prognostications (*pūrva-rūpa*). Cakrapāṇi, in commenting on the possibility of inference of specific diseases from their early specific prognostications, compares it with inference of rain from an assemblage of dark clouds or of the future rise of the Kṛttika constellation from the rise of the constellation Rohiṇī, which immediately precedes it. Both these are cases of inference of future occurrences of causation or coexistence. The prognostication may, however, be of the nature of an immediately and invariably associated antecedent which may drop altogether when the disease shows itself. Thus before a high fever the hair of the patient may stand erect; this standing erect of the hair in a specific manner is neither the cause nor is it coexistent with fever, since it may vanish when the fever has actually come. It is, however, so invariably associated with a specific kind of fever that the fever can be inferred from it.[1] Again, when there is any doubt among a number of causes as to which may be the real cause of the disease, the physician has to employ the method of difference or the method of concomitant variation for its proper ascertainment. That similar things produce the same kind of effects and opposite things produce opposite results are two of the accepted postulates of the law of *sāmānya* and *viśeṣa* in the *Caraka-saṃhitā.*[2] Now, applying these two principles, it is held that in a case of doubt as to any kind of irregularity being the cause of any particular disease it has to be found out by experiment whether the application of the suspected cause (e.g. cold) increases the disease (e.g. fever); if it does, and if the application of its opposite (e.g. heat) decreases the disease, then cold is to be regarded as the cause of the disease. If the application of any particular kind of element increases an effect (a particular kind of disease) and the application of its opposite decreases it, then that particular element may be regarded as the cause of that effect. Caraka holds that the three

1 These two kinds of *pūrva-rūpa* are thus described by Cakrapāṇi in his commentary on *Caraka-saṃhitā,* II.1.7: *tac ca pūrva-rūpaṃ dvi-vidham ekarn bhāvi-vyādhy-avyakta-liṅgam...dvitlyaṃ tu doṣa-dūṣya - santmūrchanā-janyam avyakta-liṅgād anyad eva yathā jvare bāla-pradveṣa-roma-harṣādi.*

2 *Caraka-saṃhitā,* I.1.44.

methods, viz. the cause and effect relation (*nidāna*), the method of invariable prognostication *(pūrva-rūpa)* and the method of concomitant variation *(upaśaya,* which includes *anupaśaya* also) are to be employed either jointly or separately for the ascertainment of the nature of diseases which have already occurred or which are going to happen in the near future.[1] Caraka thus urges that the physician should examine carefully the causes of diseases by the application of all these methods, so that they may be ascertained from their visible effects. Caraka then goes on to give examples of a number of diseases and the causes or prognostications by which their nature can be ascertained. He then says that a disease which is at first only an effect of some other causes may act as a cause of other diseases and may thus be regarded both as an effect and as a cause. There is therefore no absolute difference between a cause and an effect, and that which is a cause may be an effect and that which is an effect may also in its turn be a cause. Sometimes a disease may behave as cause of another disease and then cease to exist itself, whereas again, one disease may exist side by side with another disease which it has produced and aggravate its effects. Then, again, a disease (cause) may produce a disease (effect), and that effect another effect. Thus one cause may produce one effect as well as many effects, and one effect may be due to one or too many causes, and again many causes may jointly produce many effects. Thus, though fever, delirium, etc. may all be produced by dryness (*rūkṣa*), yet under certain circumstances fever alone may be produced by it. Again, fever may also be produced by the combination of a number of causes which under other circumstances may produce jointly a number of diseases. So one entity may be an invariable concomitant *(liṅga)* of one event or of many events, and there may also be a number of invariable concomitants of one event. Thus fever is the invariable concomitant of hygienic irregularities in general, and all fevers have heat as their invariable concomitant. From certain kinds of hygienic irregularities fever

1 The other two methods of *saṃprāpti* and *rūpa* need not be discussed in this connection.

can be inferred; but these can also be associated with a number of other diseases.[1]

Hence it is evident that the determination of the nature of causes and effects and the inference of facts or events of invariable concomitance were an indispensable necessity for the Āyur-veda physicians in connection with the diagnosis of diseases and the ascertainment of their causes and cures. It was for this reason that Caraka divided inference into three classes, from causes to effects, from effects to causes and from the association of other kinds of invariable concomitants. The *Nyāya-sūtra* of Akṣapāda contains expressions which seem to have been borrowed from Nāgārjuna's *Mādhyamika-kārikā* and from the *Laṅkāvatāra-sūtra* and the regulations of Buddhistic idealism, and hence it is generally believed to have been composed in the second or the third century AD.[2] In this fundamental and earliest work of Nyāya philosophy inference *(anumāna)* is described as being of three kinds, viz. from cause to effect *(pūrvavat),* from effect to cause *(śeṣavat),* and inference from similarities *(sāmānyato-dṛṣṭa)* not comprehended under the cause-effect relation. Now it is exactly these three forms of inference that are described in the *Caraka-saṃhitā,* and, so far as is known to the present writer, this is the earliest work which describes inference in such a systematic manner, and so it may naturally be regarded as the source from which Akṣapāda drew his ideas. Now Caraka's work may be regarded as a revision of Agniveśa's work, based on Atri's teachings, based on Bharadvāja's instructions. Agniveśa's work is now lost, and it is not known what exactly were the contributions of Caraka in his revision of Agniveśa's work; but,

1 See *Caraka-saṃhitā,* II.8.22-27.

2 H. Ui's *The Vaiśeṣika Philosophy,* p. 16. L.Suali's *Filosofia Indiana,* p. 14.Jacobi, article in *J.A.O. Society,* vol. XXXI, p. 29, 1911.

A commentary on Nāgārjuna's *Pramāṇa-vidhvaṃsana* called *Pramāṇa-vidhvaṃsana-sambhāṣita-vṛtti* reproduces Nāgārjuna's definition of the categories, which are the same as the categories enumerated in the first *sūtra* of Aksapāda's *Nyāya-sūtra.* But, as Walleser points out in his *Life of Nāgārjuna from Tibetan and Chinese Sources,* it is impossible to fix Nāgārjuna's date exactly. He may have lived at any time between the second and the fourth centuries AD. So no fruitful result can be attained by considerations of this kind.

since we find no work of an earlier date, Hindu, Buddhist or Jaina, which treats of the logical subjects found in the *Caraka-saṃhitā*, and since these logical discussions seem to be inextricably connected with medical discussions of diagnosis of diseases and the ascertainment of their causes, it seems very natural to suppose that Caraka got his materials from Agniveśa, who probably got them from still earlier sources. Incidentally it may be mentioned that Jayanta, in his *Nyāyamañjarī*, discussing the question of the probable sources from which Akṣapāda drew his materials, suggests that he probably elaborated his work from what he may have gathered from some other science (*śāstrāntarābhyāsāt*); but it is difficult to say whether by *śāstrāntara* Jayanta meant Āyur-veda. The *Nyāya-sūtra*, however, expressly justifies the validity of the Vedas on the analogy of the validity of Āyur-veda, which is a part of the Vedas.[1]

The similarity of the *Nyāya-sūtra* definition of inference to Caraka's definition is also very evident; for while the former begins *tat-pūrvakaṃ tri-vidham* (where *tat-pūrvakaṃ* means *pratyakṣa-pūrvakaṃ),* the latter begins *pratyakṣa-pūrvakaṃ tri-mdham tri-kālaṃ.* But, while Caraka knows only the three forms of inference, he has no names for these three types such as are supplied by Akṣapāda, viz. *pūrvavat* (related to *pūrva,* the prior, or the cause), *śeṣavat* (related to *śeṣa,* the later, or the effect) and *sāmānyato-dṛṣṭa* (from observed similarity in the past, present and future, which is also emphasized by Caraka in the same manner).[2]

1 मन्त्रायुर्वेदप्रामाण्यवच् च तत्प्रामाण्यम् आप्तप्रामाण्यात् ॥
Mantrāyur-veda-prāmāṇyavac ca tat-prāmāṇyam āpta-prāmāṇyāt.
—*Nyāya-sūtra,* II.1.68.

Jayanta enters into a long discussion in his *Nyāya-mañjarī,* trying to prove that it was through his omniscience that Caraka could write his work and that he neither discovered the science by inductive methods nor derived it from previous traditional sources.

2 एवं व्यवस्यन्त्य् अतीतं बीजात् फलम् अनागतं
दृष्ट्वा बीजात् फलं जातम् इहैव सदृशं बुधाः ॥
Evaṃ vyavasyanty atītaṃ bījāt phalam anāgataṃ
dṛṣṭvā bījāt phalaṃ jātam ihaiva sadṛśaṃ budhāḥ.
—*Caraka-saṃhitā,* I.11.22.

From the considerations detailed in the preceding footnote it may well be assumed that Akṣapāda's contribution to the definition

---

Vātsyāyana, in his commentary on the *Nyāya-sūtra,* illustrates *pūrvavat* (from cause to effect) as the inference of rain from the rise of clouds, *śeṣavat* (from effect to cause) as the inference of rain in the uplands from the flooding of the river in the lower regions and *sāmānyato-dṛṣṭa* (from similar behaviour) as the inference of the motion of heavenly bodies from their changes of position in the sky at different times. But he also gives another meaning of these three terms *pūrvavat, śeṣavat* and *sāmānyato-dṛṣṭa.* He interprets *pūrvavat* here as the inference of fire from smoke "on the analogy of past behaviour of co-presence," *śeṣavat* as the inference of the fact that sound is quality because it is neither substance nor action, by the method of residues *(śeṣa),* and *sāmānyato-dṛṣṭa* as the inference of the existence of soul from the existence of desire, which is a quality and as such requires a substance in which it would inhere. This is not an inference from similarity of behaviour, but from the similarity of one thing to another (e.g. that of desire to other qualities), to extend the associations of the latter (inherence in a substance) to the former (desire), i.e. the inference that desire must also inhere in a substance.

In the case of the terms *pūrvavat* and *śeṣavat,* as these two terms could be grammatically interpreted in two different ways (with *matup* suffix in the sense of possession and *vati* suffix in the sense of similarity of behaviour), and as the words *pūrva* and *śeṣa* may also be used in two different ways, Vātsyāyana interprets them in two different ways and tries to show that in both these senses they can be justified as modes of inference. It seems obvious that the names *pūrvavat, śeṣavat* and *sāmānyato-dṛṣṭa* were given for the first time to the threefold inference described by Caraka, as this explains the difficulty felt by Vātsyāyana in giving a definite meaning to these terms, as they had no currency either in traditional or in the contemporaneous literature of Vātsyāyana. Uddyotakara, in his commentary on Vātsyāyana, contributes entirely original views on the subject. He takes Aksapāda's sūtra, b*atha tat-pūrvakaṃ tri-vidham anumānam pūrvavac cheṣavat sāmānyato-dṛṣṭaṃ ca,* and splits it up into *atha tat-pūrvakaṃ tri-vidham anumānaṃ* and *pūrvavac cheṣavat sāmānyato-dṛṣṭaṃ ca*; by the first *tri-vidha* he means inference from positive instances (*anvayi*), from negative instances (*vyatireki*) and from both together (*anvaya-vyatireki*). He gives two possible interpretations of the terms *pūrvavat, śeṣavat* and *sāmānyato-dṛṣṭa,* one of which is *that pūrvavat* means argument from cause to effect, *śeṣavat* that from effect to cause and *sāmānyato-dṛṣṭa* is the inference on the basis of relations other than causal. The *Sāṃkhya-kārikā* also mentions these kinds of inference.The *Māṭhara-vṛtti* again interprets the threefold character of inferences (*tri-vidha anumāna*) in two ways; it says, firstly, that *tri-vidha* means that an inference has three propositions, and, secondly, that it is of three kinds, viz. *pūrvavat* (from the effect, e.g. flooding of the river, to the inference of the cause, e.g. showers in the upper region), *śeṣavat* (from part to whole, e.g. tasting a drop of sea-water of inference consists in his giving names to the types of floating inference described in *Caraka-saṃhitā.* It is not improbable that the *Nyāya-sūtra* derived its theory of five propositions, and in fact most of the other logical doctrines, from Caraka, as there are no earlier works to which these can be traced.[1] Caraka's definition of perception as the knowledge that arises through the contact of the self, the senses, the mind and the objects seems very much like an earlier model for Akṣapāda's definition of perception, which adds three more qualifications to make the meaning more complex and precise.[2] The idea that in the first instance perception is indeterminate *(nir-vikalpa* or *a-vyapadeśya)* is a later development and can hardly be traced in Hindu philosophy earlier than the *Nyāya-sūtra.*[3] The similarity of the various categories of *vāda, jalpa, vitaṇḍā, chala, jāti, nigrahasthāna,* etc., as enumerated in Caraka, to those of the *Nyāya-sūtra* has been duly pointed out in a preceding section. The only difference between the two sets of enumeration and

---

to be saline, one infers that the whole sea is saline), and *sāmānyato-dṛṣṭa* (inference from general association, e.g. by seeing flowering mangoes in one place one infers that mangoes may have flourished in other places as well).Curiously enough, the *Māṭhara-vṛtti* gives another example of *sāmānyato-dṛṣṭa* which is very different from the examples of *sāmānyato-dṛṣṭa* hitherto considered. Thus it says that, when one says, "It is illuminated outside," another replies, "The moon must have risen."

1 For more or less fanciful reasons Mr Dhruva suggests that the terms *pūrvavat* and *śeṣavat* were borrowed in the *Nyāya-sūtra* from the *Mīmāṃsā-sūtra* and that this *sūtra* must therefore be very old (*Proceedings and Transactions of the First Oriental Conference,* Poona, 1922). This argument is invalid for more than one reason. Firstly, granting that the *Mīmāṃsā-sūtra* is very old (which is doubtful), the fact that these two logical terms were borrowed from it does not show that it must be a very old work; for even a modern work may borrow its terminology from an older treatise. Secondly, the fact that these three terms were borrowed from early sources does not show that the theory of *tri-vidha anumāna* in the *Nyāya-sūtra* is either its own contribution or very old. Mr Dhruva's arguments as to the *Māṭhara-vṛtti* being subsequent to Vātsyāyana's commentary are also very weak and do not stand criticism.

2 *indriyārtha-sannikarṣotparmam jñānam avyapadeśyam avyabhicāri vyavasā-yātmakāṃ pratyakṣam.—Nyāya-sūtra,* I.1.4.

3 Caraka uses the word *vikalpa* in II.1.10.4 in the sense of distinction *(bheda)* of superiority and inferiority *(utkarṣa-prakarṣa-rūpa).*

their elaboration is that Caraka's treatment, being the earlier one, is less full and less complex than that of Akṣapāda.

The fact that physicians in counsel earnestly discussed together, in order to arrive at right conclusions regarding both the theoretical causes of diseases and their cures and their actual practical discernment in individual cases, is abundantly clear from even a very superficial study of the *Caraka-saṃhitā.* The entire work seems to be a collection of discussions of learned physicians with Atri as their chairman. Where differences of opinion are great, they are all noted, and Atri's own opinion on them is given, and, where there was more or less unanimity, or where Atri himself lectured on specific problems, his own opinion alone is given. It is also related how a good and clever physician is to defeat his opponents in dispute, not only in a legitimate and scientific way, but also by sophistic wrangling and unfair logical tricks. It was a practical necessity for these physicians to earn their bread in the face of strong competition, and it is easy to see how the logical tricks of *chala, jāti* and *nigraha-sthōna* developed into a regular art of debate, not always for the discovery of truth, but also for gaining the victory over opponents. We hear of debates, discussions or logical disputes in literature much earlier than the '*Caraka-saṃhitā',* but nowhere was the acquirement of this art deemed so much a practical necessity for earning a living as among the medical men. And, since there is no mention of the development of this in any other earlier literature, it is reasonable to suppose that the art of debate and its other accessories developed from early times in the traditional medical schools, whence they are found collected in Caraka's work. The origin of the logical art of debate in the schools of Āyur-veda is so natural, and the illustrations of the modes of dispute and the categories of the art of debate are so often taken from the medical field, that one has little reason to suspect that the logical portions of the *Caraka-saṃhitā* were collected by Caraka from non-medical literature and grafted into his work.

ĀYUR-VEDA ETHICS

The length of the period of a man's lifetime in this iron age (*kali-yuga*) of ours is normally fixed at one hundred years. But sinful actions of great enormity may definitely reduce the normal length to any extent. Ordinary vicious actions, however, can reduce the length of life only if the proper physical causes of death, such as poisoning, diseases and the like, are present. If these physical causes can be warded off, then a man may continue to live until the normal length of his life, one hundred years, is reached, when the body-machine, being worn out by long work, gradually breaks down. Medicines may, however, in the case of those who are not cursed by the commission of sins of great enormity, prolong the normal length of life. It is here that Caraka and his followers differ from all other theories of *karma* that flourished on the soil of India. The theory is not accepted in any Indian system of thought except that of Caraka. In spite of the many differences that prevail amongst these theories, they may still be roughly divided into four classes. Thus there are, first, the *pauruṣa-vādins,* such as those who follow the *Yoga-vāsiṣṭha* school of thought and are idealists of the extreme type, thinking that all our experiences can be controlled by a determined effort of the will and that there is no bond of previous *karma,* destiny, or fatality which cannot be controlled or overcome by it. Human will is all-powerful, and by it we can produce any change of any kind in the development of our future well-being. There is, again, the view that God alone is responsible for all our actions, and that He makes those whom He wants to raise perform good actions and those whom He wants to take the downward path commit sinful deeds. There is also the view that God rewards or praises us in accordance with our good or bad deeds, and that we alone are responsible for our actions and free to act as we choose. There is a further view, elaborately dealt with in Patañjali's *Yoga-sūtra*, that our deeds determine the particular nature of our birth, the period of our lifetime and the nature of our enjoyments or sufferings. Ordinarily the fruits of the actions of a previous birth are reaped in the present birth, and the ripened fruits of the actions of the present birth determine the nature of the future birth, period of life and pleasurable or painful experiences, while the fruits of extremely good or bad actions are reaped in this life. In none of these theories do we find the sort of common-sense eclecticism that we find in Caraka. For here it is only the fruits of extremely bad actions that cannot be arrested by the normal efforts of good conduct. The fruits of all ordinary actions can be arrested by normal physical ways of well-balanced conduct, the administration of proper medicines and the like. This implies that our ordinary non-moral actions in the proper care of health, taking proper tonics, medicines and the like, can modify or arrest the ordinary course of the fruition of our *karma.* Thus, according to the effects of my ordinary *karma* I may have fallen ill; but, if I take due care, I may avoid such effects and may still be in good health. According to other theories the laws of *karma* are immutable. Only the fruits of unripe *karma* can be destroyed by true knowledge. The fruits of ripe *karma* have to be experienced in any case, even if true knowledge is attained. The peculiar features of Caraka's theory consist in this, that he does not introduce this immutability of ripe *karmas.* The effects of all *karmas*, excepting those which are extremely strong, can be modified by an apparently non-moral course of conduct, involving the observance of the ordinary daily duties of life. Ordinarily the law of *karma* implies the theory of a moral government of the universe in accordance with the good or bad fruits of one's own *karma.* We may be free to act as we choose; but our actions in this life, excepting those of great enormity, determine the experiences of our future lives, and so an action in this life cannot ordinarily be expected to ward off any of the evils of this life which one is predestined to undergo in accordance with the *karma* of a previous birth. Moreover, it is the moral or immoral aspects of an action that determine the actual nature of their good or bad effects, success or failure. This implies a disbelief in our power of directly controlling our fortunes by our efforts. The theory of *karma* thus involves a belief in the mysterious existence and ripening of the sinful and virtuous elements of our actions, which alone in their course of maturity produce effects. If the theory that sins bring their punishment, and virtues produce their beneficial effects, of themselves, is accepted, its logical consequences would lead us to deny the possibility of mere physical actions modifying the fruition of these *karmas*. So the acceptance of the moral properties of actions leads to the denial of their direct physical consequences. If through my honest efforts I succeed in attaining a happy state, it is contended that my success is not due to my present efforts, but it was predestined, as a consequence of the good deeds of my previous birth, that I should be happy. For, if the fruition was due to my ordinary' efforts, then the theory that all happy or unhappy experiences are due to the ripening of the *karmas* of the previous births falls to the ground. If, on the other hand, all success or failure is due to our proper or improper efforts, then the capacity of sins or virtues to produce misery or happiness may naturally be doubted, and the cases where even our best efforts are attended with failure are not explained. But, if our ordinary efforts cannot effect anything, and if the modes of our experiences, pleasures and sufferings, and the term of our life are already predestined, then none of our efforts are of any use in warding off the calamities of this life, and the purpose of the science of medicine is baffled. In common-sense ways of belief one refers to "fate" or "destiny" only when the best efforts fail, and one thinks that, unless there is an absolute fatality, properly directed efforts are bound to succeed. Caraka's theory seems to embody such a common-sense view. But the question arises how, if this is so, can the immutability of the law of *karma* be preserved? Caraka thinks that it is only the extremely good or bad deeds that have this immutable character. All other effects of ordinary actions can be modified or combated by our efforts. Virtue and vice are not vague and mysterious principles in Caraka, and the separation that appears elsewhere between the moral and the physical sides of an action is not found in his teaching.[1]

1 *Caraka-samkitā*, I I I.3.28-38.

He seems to regard the "good," or the all-round manifold utility *(hitā)* of an action, as its ultimate test. What a man has to do before acting is carefully to judge and anticipate the utility of his action, i.e. to judge whether it will be good for him or not; if the effects are beneficial for him, he ought to do it, and, if they are harmful, he ought not to do it.[1] Our ultimate standard of good actions lies in seeking our own good, and to this end the proper direction and guidance of our mind and senses are absolutely necessary. Caraka applies here also his old principle of the golden mean, and says that the proper means of keeping the mind in the right path consists in avoiding too much thinking, in not thinking of revolting subjects, and in keeping the mind active. Thoughts and ideas are the objects of the mind, and one has to avoid the *atiyoga*, *mithyā-yoga* and *a-yoga* of all thoughts, as just described. "Self-good," or *ātma-hita*, which is the end of all our actions, is described as not only that which gives us pleasure and supplies the material for our comfort, ease of mind and long life, but also that which will be beneficial to us in our future life. Right conduct *(sad-vṛtta)* leads to the health and well-being of body and mind and secures sense -control (*indriya-vijaya)*.

The three springs of action are our desire for self-preservation *(prāṇaiṣaṇā),* our desire for the materials of comfort (*dhanaiṣaṇā*), and our desire for a happy state of existence in the future life *(paralokaiṣaṇā).* We seek our good not only in this life, but also in the after-life, and these two kinds of self-good are summed up in our threefold desire—for self-preservation, for the objects that lead to happiness, and for a blessed after-life. Right conduct is not conduct in accordance with the injunctions of the Vedas, or conduct which leads ultimately to the cessation of all sorrows through cessation of all desires or through right knowledge and the extinction of false knowledge, but is that which leads to the fulfilment of the three ultimate desires. The cause of sins is not transgression of the in-

1 *buddhyā samyag idaṃ mama hitam idam mamāhitam ity avekṣyāvekṣya karmaṇāṃ pravṛttīnāṃ samyak pratipādanena ity ahita-karma-parityāgena hita-karmācaraṇena ca.*—Cakrapāṇi on Caraka, I.8.17.

junctions of the scriptures, but errors of right judgment or of right thinking *(prajñāparādha)*. First and foremost is our desire for life, i.e. for health and prolongation of life; for life is the precondition of all other good things. Next to our desire for life is our desire for wealth and the pursuit of such vocations of life as lead to it. The third is the desire for a blessed after-life. In this connection Caraka introduces a discussion to prove the existence of a future state of existence. He says that a wise man should not entertain doubts regarding the existence of a future life, since such doubts might hinder the performance of right conduct. The mere fact that we cannot experience its existence with our senses is not a sufficient negative proof. For there are few things which can be directly experienced by the senses, and there are many which exist, but are never experienced by the senses. The very senses with which we experience other things cannot themselves be subject to sense-experience.[1] Even sensible things cannot be perceived if they are too near or too distant, if they are covered, if the senses are weak or diseased, if the mind is otherwise engaged, if they are mixed up with similar things, if their light is overcome by stronger light, or if they are too small.[2] It is therefore wrong to say that what is not perceived by the senses does not exist. If, again, it is argued that the foetus must derive its soul from the parents, then it may be pointed out that, if the soul of the foetus migrated from either of the parents, then, since the soul is without parts, it could not have migrated in parts, and such a total migration would mean that the parents would be left without any soul and would die. As the soul could not migrate from the parents to the child, so neither can the mind nor the intellect be said to have so migrated. Moreover, if all life must be derived from the migration of other souls, then how can insects come into

1 *yair eva tāvad indriyaiḥ pratyakṣam upalabhyate tāny eva santi cāpratyak-ṣāṇi.* —Caraka, I.11.7.

2 *satāṃ ca rūpāṇām ati-sannikarṣād ati-viprakarṣād āvaraṇāt karaṇa-daur-ba-lyān mano 'navasthānāt samānābhihārāt abhibhavād ati-saukṣmyāc ca pratyakṣānu-palabdhiḥ.—Ibid.* II.8.

being, as many do, without parent insects?[1] Consciousness exists as a separate and beginningless entity, and it is not created by anyone else. If, however, the supreme soul be regarded as its cause, then in that sense it may be conceived as having been produced therefrom.[2] The theory of the after-life consists according to Caraka principally in the view that the soul is existent and uncreated, and that it is associated with the foetus at a certain stage of its development in the womb. He also refers to the evidence of rebirth which we have in the difference of the child from the parents; in the fact that, though other causes are more or less the same, two children differ in colour, voice, appearance, intelligence and luck; in the fact that some are servants, whereas others are their rich masters; in the fact that some are naturally in good health, while others are in bad, or are different in the length of life; from the fact that infants know how to cry, suck, smile or fear without any previous instruction or experience; that with the same kind of efforts two persons reap two different kinds of results; that some are naturally adepts in certain subjects and dull in others; and that there are at least some who remember their past lives; for from these facts the only hypothesis that can be made is that these differences are due to the *karma* of one's past life, otherwise called *daiva*, and that the fruits of the good and bad deeds of this life will be reaped in another. It has also been pointed out in a previous section that a child does not owe his or her intellectual parts to the father or to the mother. These gifts belong to the soul of the child, and there is therefore no reason to suppose that the son of an intellectually deficient person will on that account be necessarily dull.

Caraka further urges that the truth of rebirth can be demonstrated by all possible proofs. He first refers to the verdict of the Vedas and of the opinions of philosophers, which are written for the good of the people and are in conformity with the views of the wise

1 *saṃsveda-jānāṃ maśakādīnāṃ tathodbhij-jānāṃ gaṇḍūpadādināṃ cetanānām mātā-pitarau na vidyete tatas teṣām acaitanyaṃ syān mātā-pitroś cetana-kāraṇayorabhāvāt.*—Cakrapāṇi on Caraka, II.11.

2 On this point Cakrapāṇi gives a different interpretation in I.11.13.

and the virtuous and not in opposition to the opinions of the Vedas. Such writings always recommend gifts, penances, sacrifices, truthfulness, non-injury to all living beings and sex-continence as leading to heavenly happiness and to liberation *(mokṣa).* The sages say that liberation, or the cessation of rebirth, is only for those who have completely purged off all mental and bodily defects. This implies that these sages accepted the theory of rebirth as true; and there have been other sages who also have distinctly announced the truth of rebirth. Apart from the testimony of the Vedas and of the sages, even perception *(pratyakṣa)* also proves the truth of rebirth. Thus it is seen that children are often very different from their parents, and even from the same parents the children born are often very different in colour, voice, frame of body, mental disposition, intelligence and luck, as described above. The natural inference to be based on these data directly experienced is that no one can avoid the effects of the deeds he has performed, and that therefore what was performed in a past birth is indestructible and always follows a man in his present birth as his *daiva*, or *karma*, the fruits of which show in his present life. The deeds of the present birth will again accumulate fruits, which will be reaped in the next birth. From the present fruits of pleasurable or painful experiences their past seeds as past *karma* are inferred, and from the present deeds as seeds their future effects as pleasurable or painful experiences in another birth are also inferred. Apart from this inference other reasons also lead to the same condition. Thus the living foetus is produced by the combination of the six elements, to which connection with the self from the other world is indispensable; so also fruits can only be reaped when the actions have been performed and not if they are not performed—there cannot be shoots without seeds. It may be noted in this connection that in no other system of Indian thought has any attempt been made to prove the theory of rebirth as has here been done. A slight attempt was made in the Nyāya system to prove the theory on the ground that the crying, sucking and the natural fear of infants implies previous experience. But Caraka in a systematic manner takes up many more points and appeals to the different logical proofs that may be adduced. Again, we find the nature of the fruits of action *(karma)* discussed in the *Vyāsa-bhāṣya* on the *Yoga-sūtra* of Patañjali. It is said in the *Yoga-sūtra*, II.13, that the *karmas* of past life determine the particular birth of the individual in a good or bad or poor or rich family and the length of life and pleasurable or painful experiences. But that physical differences of body, colour, voice, temperament, mental disposition and special intellectual features are also due to the deeds of the past life seems to be a wholly new idea. It is, however, interesting to note that, though Caraka attributes the divergence of intelligence to deeds of the past life, yet he does not attribute thereto the weakness or the strength of the moral will.

Caraka further refers to the collective evil effects of the misdeeds of people living in a particular locality, which may often lead to the outbreak of epidemics. Speaking of the outbreak of epidemic diseases, he says that they are due to the pollution of air and water, and to country and climatic revolutions. The pollution of air consists in its being unnatural for the season, dull and motionless, too violent, too dry, too cold, too warm, stormy, of the nature of whirlwind, too humid, dusty, smoky, impure or of bad smell. The pollution of water consists in its being of unnatural colour, bad smell, bad taste, containing impurities (when devoid of its natural qualities), which are often avoided by water birds, and being unpleasant, and having its sources largely dried up. The pollution of a particular locality occurs when it is infested with lizards, wild animals, mosquitoes, flies, insects, mice, owls, predatory birds or jackals, or when it is full of wild creepers, grass, etc., or when there is a failure of crops, the air smoky, etc. The pollution of time consists in the happening of unnatural climatic conditions. The cause of these epidemic conditions is said to be the demerit (*adharma*) due to the evil deeds of past life, the commission of which is again due to bad deeds of previous life. When the chief persons of a country, city or locality transgress the righteous course and lead the people in an unrighteous manner, the people also in their conduct continue to grow vicious and sinful. And, as a result of the misdeeds of the people of the locality, the gods forsake that place, there is no proper rain, the air, water and the country as a whole become polluted and epidemics break out. Thus the misdeeds of a people can, according to Caraka, pollute the whole region and ultimately ruin it. When a country is ruined by civil war, then that also is due to the sins of the people, who are inflated with too much greed, anger, pride and ignorance. Thus epidemics are caused by the conjoint sins of the people of a particular region. But even at the time of the outbreak of such epidemics those who have not committed such bad actions as to deserve punishment may save themselves by taking proper medicines and by leading a virtuous life. Continuing to establish his theory that all climatic and other natural evils are due to the commission of sins or *adharma*, Caraka says that in ancient times people were virtuous, of strong and stout physique and extremely long-lived, and on account of their virtuous ways of living there were no climatic disturbances, no famines, no failure of crops, no drought and no pollutions leading to epidemics and diseases. But at the close of the *satya-yuga,* through over-eating some rich men became too fat, and hence they became easily tired, and hence became lazy, and on account of laziness they acquired the storing habit (*sañcaya*), and, through that, the tendency to receive things from others (*parigraha*), and, through that, greed *(lobha).* In the next, Tretā, age, from greed there arose malice, from malice lying, from lying desire, anger, conceit, antipathy, cruelty, violence (*abhighāta*), fear, sorrow and anxiety. Thus in the Tretā age *dharma* diminished by a quarter, and so the earthly production of harvest, etc. also diminished by a quarter, and the bodies of living beings lost their vitality accordingly; their length of life diminished, and diseases began to grow. So in the Dvāpara age there was a further diminution of the quantities of earthly productions and a further weakening of human constitution and shortening of the length of life.

It may be remembered that in Suśruta, III.I, it is said that many persons of the medical school of thought had conceived this world to have come into being either through time *(kāla)*, in the natural process by a blind destiny (*niyati*), or through a mere nature (*svabhāva*), accidental concourse of things (*yadṛcchā*), or through evolution *(pariṇāma)* by the will of God; and they called each of these alternatives the *prakṛti*, or the origin of the world.[1] But the notion of the Sāṃkhya *prakṛti* holds within it all these concepts, and it is therefore more appropriate to admit one *prakṛti* as the evolving cause of the world. Gayī, in interpreting this, holds that *prakṛti* is to be regarded as the evolving material cause, whereas time, natural process, etc. are to be regarded as instrumental causes for the world-manifestation. According to Suśruta the selves (*kṣetra-jña*) are not in the medical school regarded as all-pervasive (*a-sarva-gata*), as they are in the Sāṃkhya system of thought. These selves, on account of their virtues or vices, transmigrate from one life to another as men or as different animals; for, though not all-pervasive, they are eternal and are not destroyed by death. The selves are not to be regarded as self-revealing, as in Sāṃkhya or the Vedānta; but they can be inferred, as the substance or entity to which the feelings of pleasure and pain belong, and they are always endowed with consciousness, though they may not themselves be regarded as of the nature of pure consciousness. They are *cetanāvantaḥ* (endowed with consciousness) and not *cit-svarūpāḥ* (of the nature of consciousness). They are extremely subtle or fine (*parama-sūkṣma*), and this epithet is explained by Ḍalhaṇa as meaning that the selves are as small as atoms. But, being always endowed with consciousness, they can also through self-perception (*pratyakṣa*) be perceived as existing. The transmigration of

---

1 The primary use of *prakṛti* may have been due to the idea of an enquiry regarding the source and origin of the world. *Prakṛti* literally means "source" or "origin." So the term was probably used in reference to other speculations regarding the origin of the world before it was technically applied as a Sāṃkhya term. The ideas of *svabhāva, kāla,* etc. seem to have been combined to form the technical Sāṃkhya concept of *prakṛti,* and two schools of Sāṃkhya, the Kapila and the Patañjali schools, arose in connection with the dispute as to the starting of the evolution of *prakṛti* accidentally (*yadṛcchā*) or by the will of God. The idea of *prakṛti* was reached by combining all the alternative sources of world-manifestation that were current before, and so they are all conserved in the notion of *prakṛti.*

these selves is regulated by the merit and demerit of their deeds. Ḍalhaṇa says that through excessive sins they are born as animals, through an admixture of virtues and sins they are born as men, and through a preponderance of virtues they are born as gods. But according to Caraka not only is the nature of transmigration controlled by the good or bad deeds of a man, but even the productivity of nature, its purity or pollution; and the thousand and one things in which nature is helpful or harmful to men are determined by good and bad deeds (*dharma* and *adharma*). *Dharma* and *adharma* are therefore regarded as the most important factors in determining most of the human conditions of life and world-conditions of environment. Such a view is not opposed to the Sāṃkhya theory of world-creation; for there also it is held that the evolution of *prakṛti* is determined by the good or bad deeds of the selves; but, though implied, yet in no Sāṃkhya work is such a clear and specific determination of world-conditions and world-evolution through the merit and demerit of human beings to be found. Freedom of human will is almost wholly admitted by Caraka, and, where the fruits of previous actions are not of a confirmed character, they can be averted or improved.by our efforts. Our efforts thus have on the one hand a cosmical or universal effect, as determining the conditions of the development of the material world, and on the other hand they determine the fate of the individual. The fruits of our actions determine our birth, our experiences and many intellectual gifts; but they do not determine the nature of our will or affect its strength of application in particular directions.

SPRINGS OF ACTION IN THE CARAKA-SAṂHITĀ

The chief feature of Caraka's springs of action consists in the fact that he considers three primary desires as the motive causes of all our actions. These are, as has already been said, the desire for life, the desire for riches and the desire for future life. In this Caraka seems to have a view uniquely different from that of most of the systems of philosophy, which refer to a number of emotions as the root causes prompting us to action. Thus the Vaiśeṣika regards attraction to pleasure and aversion to pain as the cause of all our actions. Pleasure is defined as being a sort of feeling which is approved and welcomed and towards which an attraction is naturally felt. Pleasures, therefore, when they arise, must always be felt, and there cannot be anything like unfelt pleasures. Apart from sensory pleasures, Śrīdhara in his *Nyāya-kandalī* discusses the existence of other kinds of pleasure, due to the remembering of past things, or to calmness and contentedness of mind or self-knowledge. Pleasures are, however, regarded as the fruits of meritorious deeds *(dharma)* performed before. Pain, the reverse of pleasure, may be defined as an experience from which we are repelled and which is the result of past misdeeds. Desire, as the wish to have what is unattained (*aprāpta-prārthanā*), may be either for the self (*svārtha*) or for others *(parārtha)*. Such desires may be prompted by any of the following: longing for happiness in heaven or on earth *(kāma),* appetites (*abhilāṣa*), longing for the continuation and recurrence of the enjoyment of pleasurable objects, compassion for others (*karuṇā*), disinclination to worldly enjoyment *(vairāgya),* intention of deceiving others *(upadhā),* subconscious motives *(bhāva)*. Praśastapāda, however, distinguishes between desires for enjoyment and desires for work. But he does not include the positive Buddhist virtues of friendship *(maitrī)* and a feeling of happiness in the happiness of others *(muditā),* and he is content with only the negative virtue of compassion *(karuṇā)*. He also counts anger, malice, suppressed revengefulness *(manyu),* jealousy of the good qualities of others *(akṣamā),* and envy arising from a sense of one's inferiority *(amarṣa)*. But, in spite of this elaborate classification, Praśastapāda makes in reality two broad divisions, namely, desires arising from attachment to pleasures, and those from aversion to pain. Pain is as much a positive feeling as pleasure and cannot be regarded as mere negation of pleasure. Though Praśastapāda knows that there is such a thing as desire for work, yet he does not give it any prominent consideration, and the net result of his classification of the springs of action is that he thinks that all desires are prompted by attachment to feelings of pleasure and antipathy to pain. Feelings, therefore, are to be regarded here as fundamentally determining all desires and through them all actions.

The Naiyāyikas think that attachment and antipathy can be traced to a more fundamental root, viz. ignorance or delusion *(moha).* Thus Vātsyāyana, by tracing attachment or antipathy to ignorance, tends to intellectualize the psychological basis of Praśastapāda. For *moha* would mean want of knowledge, and, if attachment and antipathy be due to want of knowledge, then one can no longer say that feelings ultimately determine our actions, as it is the absence of right knowledge that is found to be ultimately the determinant of the rise of all feelings and emotions. Jayanta, however, in his *Nyāya-mañjarī,* counts ignorance *(moha),* attachment *(rāga)* and antipathy *(dveṣa)* as being three parallel defects *(doṣa)* which prompt our efforts.[1] Under attachment he counts sex-inclination *(kāma),* disinclination to part with that which would not diminish by sharing with others (*matsara*), jealousy *(spṛhā),* inclination towards birth again and again *(tṛṣṇā)* and inclination towards taking forbidden things *(lobha).* Under *dveṣa* he counts emotional outbursts of anger with burning bodily conditions, envy *(īrṣyā),* jealousy at the good qualities of others *(asūyā),* injuring others *(droha)* and concealed malice *(manyu).* Under ignorance he counts false knowledge *(mithyā-jñāna),* perplexity due to indecision *(vicikitsā),* sense of false superiority (*mada*) and mistakes of judgment *(pramāda).* But he adds that of the three defects, *rāga, dveṣa* and *moha, moha* is the worst, since the other two arise through it. For it is only the ignorant who are under the sway of attachment and antipathy. To the objection that in that case *moha* ought not to be counted as a defect in itself, but as the source of the other two defects, Jayanta replies that, though it is a source of the other two defects, it of itself also leads people to action and should therefore be counted as a defect in itself. It is no doubt true that all defects are due to false knowledge and are removed by right knowledge; yet it would

---

1 *Teṣāṃ doṣōṇāṃ trayo rāśayo bhavanti rāgo dveṣo moha iti.*

—*Nyāya-mañjarī*, p. 500

be wrong to count the defects as being of only one kind of false knowledge *(mithyā-jñāna)*; for the three defects are psychologically felt to have three distinctive characteristics. Jayanta, while admitting that the feelings of attachment or antipathy are due to ignorance, considers them to be psychologically so important as to be regarded as independent springs of action. Thus, while he was in nominal agreement with Vātsyāyana in regarding attachment and antipathy as being due to *moha*, he felt their independent psychological importance and counted them as parallel defects prompting our efforts.

Patañjali divides all our actions into two classes, vicious (*kliṣṭa*) and virtuous (*akliṣṭa*). The virtuous actions are prompted by our natural propensity towards emancipation, while the vicious ones are prompted by ignorance *(avidyā)*, egoism *(asmitā)*, attachment *(rāga)*, antipathy *(dveṣa)* and the will to live *(abhiniveśa)*. The latter four, though of the nature of feeling, are yet regarded as being only manifestations of the growth and development of ignorance *(avidyā)*. It is a characteristic peculiarity of the Sāṃkhya philosophy that thoughts and feelings are not regarded there as being intrinsically different; for the *guṇas* form the materials of both thoughts and feelings. What is thought in one aspect is feeling in another. It was on this account that false knowledge could be considered to have developed into the feelings of egoism, attachment and antipathy, and could be regarded as being of the same stuff as false knowledge. In the Nyāya psychology, thought and feelings being considered intrinsically different, a difficulty was felt in reconciling the fact that, while ignorance could be regarded as being the cause of the feelings of attachment and antipathy, the latter could not be regarded as being identical with ignorance *(moha)*. Jayanta, therefore, while he traced *rāga* and *dveṣa* to *moha*, ontologically considered them as parallel factors determining our actions psychologically. In the Sāṃkhya-Yoga metaphysics this difficulty could be obviated; for that school did not consider feelings to be different from thoughts, since the thoughts are themselves made up of feeling-stuff; hence even false knowledge *(avidyā)* need not be regarded as being wholly an intellectual element, since it is itself the product of the feeling-stuff—the *guṇas*.

It is needless to refer in detail to the theories of the springs of action in other systems of Indian thought. From what has already been said it would appear that most systems of Indian Philosophy consider false knowledge to be at the root of all our worldly activities through the mediation of feelings of attachment, antipathy and self-love. There is an inherent pessimism in most systems of Indian thought, which consider that normally we are all under the evil influence of false knowledge and are all gliding on the downward path of sins and afflictions. They also consider that all attachments lead to bondage and slavery to passions, and thereby lead us away from the path of liberation. Actions are judged as good or bad according as they lead to liberation or bondage; their efficacy is in securing the transcendental realization of the highest truth and the cessation of rebirth, or obscuration of the nature of reality and exposure to the miseries of rebirth.

But Caraka gives us a scheme of life in which he traces the springs of all our actions to the three fundamental motives or biological instincts of life-preservation, worldly desire of acquiring riches for enjoyment, and other worldly aspirations of self-realization. According to him these three fundamental desires sum up all springs of action. On this view will appears to be more fundamental than feeling or knowledge. Caraka does not seem to begin from the old and stereotyped idea that false knowledge is the starting-point of the world. His is a scheme of a well-balanced life which is guided by the harmonious play of these three fundamental desires and directed by perfect wisdom and unerring judgment. Evil and mischief creep in through errors of judgment, by which the harmony of these desires is broken. All kinds of misdeeds are traced, not to feelings of attachment or antipathy, but to errors of judgment or foolishness (*prajñāparādha*). *This prajñāparādha* may be compared to the *moha* or *avidyā* of the Nyāya and Yoga. But, while the Nyāya and Yoga seem to refer to this *moha* or *avidyā* as a fundamental defect inherent in our mental constitution and determining its activities as a formative element, Caraka's *prajñāparādha* is not made to occupy any metaphysical status, but expresses itself only in the individual lapses of judgment.

Caraka, however, did not dare to come into conflict with the prevailing ethical and philosophical opinions of his time, and we find that in *Śārīra*, 1 he largely accepts the traditional views. He says there that it is the phenomenal self (*bhūtātman* or *saṃyoga-puruṣa*) that feels pleasure and pain, and in connection with the duty of a physician to remove all physical sufferings produced by diseases he says that the ultimate healing of all pain consists in the permanent *naiṣṭhikī* (removal) of pain by the removal of grasping *(upadhā)*.[1] He says there that grasping (*upadhā*) is itself sorrowful and the cause of all sorrows. All sorrows can be removed by the removal of all grasping tendencies. Just as a silkworm draws out its cocoon thread to its own destruction, so does the miserable man of ignorance draw desires and longings from the objects of sense. He is wise indeed who considers all objects as fire and withdraws himself from them. With the cessation of all actions (*anārambha*) and dissociation from sense-objects there is no more fear of being afflicted with sorrows. Sorrows, again, are said to proceed from four causes, namely, the wrong notion of noneternal things (e.g. sense-objects) as eternal (*buddhi-vibhraṃśa*), the want of the power of controlling the mind from undesirable courses (*dhṛti-vibhraṃśa*), forgetfulness of the nature of right knowledge *(smṛti-vibhraṃśa)* and the adoption of unhygienic courses (*asātmya-arthāgamd). Prajñāparādha* is defined here as a wrong action that is done through the confusion of intelligence and want of selfcontrol and right knowledge (*dhi-dhṛti-smṛti-vibhraṣṭa*), and this is supposed to rouse up all maladies and defects (*sarva-doṣa-prakopaṇa*). Some of the offences that may be counted under *prajñāparādha* are as follows: to set things in motion, to try to stop moving objects, to let the proper time for doing things

1 Cakrapāṇi interprets *upadhā* as desire *(tṛṣṇā);* hut it seems to me that it would have been more correct to interpret it as the Buddhist *upādāna,* or grasping. Cakrapāṇi on Caraka, IV. I.3.

pass by, to begin an action in the wrong manner, not to behave in the accustomed manner, not to behave modestly and politely, to insult respected persons, to go about in wrong places or at wrong times, to take objects which are known to be harmful, not to abide by the proper course of conduct described in the *Caraka-saṃhitā*, I.1.6; the passions of jealousy, vanity, fear, anger, greed, ignorance, egoism, errors, all actions prompted by these and whatever else that is prompted by ignorance *(moha)* and self-ostentation *(rajas)*. *Prajñāparādha* is further defined as error of judgment *(viṣama-vijñāna)* and as wrong enterprise (*viṣama-pravartanā*), proceeding out of wrong knowledge or erroneous judgment. It will thus appear that it is wise to take *prajñāparādha* in the wider sense of error of judgment or misapplied intelligence, regarding it as the cause of all kinds of moral depravity, unhealthy and unhygienic habits and accidental injuries of all kinds. As Caraka admitted the existence of the self and of rebirth and regarded moral merit *(dharma)* and demerit *(adharma)* as the causes of all human enjoyment and sufferings, and of the productivity or unproductivity of the ground, and the hygienic or unhygienic conditions of water, air and the seasons, he had to include within *prajñāparādha* the causes that led to vices and sins. The causes of all sorrows are, firstly, wrong consideration of the non-eternal as eternal and of the injurious as good; secondly, want of self-control; and, thirdly, the defect of memory (*smṛti-bhraṃśa*), through which the right knowledge and right experience of the past cannot be brought into effect. Thus, though in a sense Caraka compromises with the traditional schools of philosophy in including philosophical ignorance or misconception within *prajñāparādha*, and though he thinks that philosophical ignorance produces sins, yet he takes *prajñāparādha* in the very wide sense of error of judgment, leading to all kinds of transgression of laws of health and laws of society and custom, risky adventures, and all other indiscreet and improper actions. *Prajñāparādha,* therefore, though it includes the philosophical *moha* of the traditional school of philosophy, is yet something very much more, and is to be taken in the wider sense of error of judgment. Caraka, no doubt, admits jealousy, vanity, anger, greed, ignorance *(moha),* etc., as producing improper action, but he admits many other causes as well. But the one supreme cause of all these subsidiary causes is *prajñāparādha,* or error of judgment, taken in its wide sense. It will not, therefore, be wrong to suppose that, according to Caraka, all proper actions are undertaken through the prompting of three fundamental desires, the desire for life, the desire for wealth and enjoyment, and the desire for spiritual good. And all improper actions are due to improper understanding, confusion of thought, and misdirected intelligence *(prajñāparādha).* The three fundamental desires, unassociated with any error of judgment or lack of understanding, may thus be regarded as the root cause of all proper actions. There is, therefore, nothing wrong in giving full play to the functioning of the three fundamental desires, so long as there is no misdirected understanding and confusion to turn them into the wrong path. Caraka does not seem to agree with other systems of philosophy in holding the feelings of attachment and antipathy to be the springs of all actions. Actions are prompted by the normal active tendencies of the three fundamental desires, and they become sinful when our energies are wrongly directed through lack of understanding. Though Caraka had to compromise with the acknowledged view of the systems of Indian Philosophy that the cessation of all sorrows can be only through the cessation of all actions, yet it seems clear that the course of conduct that he approves consists in the normal exercise of the three fundamental desires, free from the commission of any errors of judgment (*prajñāparādha*). Thus Caraka does not preach the ideal of leaving off desires, attachments, feelings and actions of all kinds, nor does he advocate the *Gītā* ideal of the performance of duties without attachment. His is the ideal of living one's life in a manner that is most conducive to health, long life, and proper enjoyment. Our only care should be that we do not commit any mistake in eating, drinking and other actions of life which may directly or indirectly (through the production of sins) produce diseases and sufferings or jeopardize our life and enjoyment in any way. This unique character of Caraka's ethical position is very clearly proved by the code of conduct, virtues and methods of leading a good life elaborated by Caraka. He no doubt shows a lip-sympathy with the ideal of giving up all actions *(sannyāsa)*; but his real sympathies seem to be with the normal scheme of life, involving normal enjoyments and fruition of desires. A normal life, according to Caraka, ought also to be a virtuous life, as vices and sins are the sources of all sorrows, sufferings and diseases in this life and the next.

GOOD LIFE IN CARAKA

It is well worth pointing out at the outset that "good life" in Caraka means not only an ethically virtuous life, but a life which is free from diseases, and which is so led that it attains its normal length. Moral life thus means a life that is free from the defect of *prajñāparādha.* It means wise and prudent life; for it is only the want of wisdom and prudence that is the cause of all physical, social, physiological, moral and spiritual mischiefs. To be a good man, it is not enough that one should practise the ethical virtues: a man should practise the physical, physiological and social virtues as well. He must try to live a healthy and long life, free from diseases and sufferings and free from reproaches of any kind. It is important to note that Caraka does not believe in the forced separation of the physical life from the mental and the moral. Physical diseases are to be cured by medicines, while mental diseases are to be cured by right and proper knowledge of things, self-control and self-concentration. The close interconnection between body and mind was well known from early times, and even the *Mahā-bhārata* (XII.16) says that out of the body arise the mental diseases and out of the mind arise the bodily diseases. Caraka also thinks that a physician should try to cure not only the bodily diseases but also the mental diseases. The *Mahā-bhārata* further says in the same chapter that there are three elements in the body, viz. heat, cold and air; when they are in a state of equipoise, the body is healthy, and when any one of them predominates, there is disease. The mind is constituted of *sattva, rajas* and *tamas*; when these are in a state of equipoise, the mind is in proper order, and when any one of them predominates, it becomes diseased. Caraka, however, thinks that it is only when *rajas* and *tamas* predominate that the mind gets diseased. But, whatever these differences may be, it is evident that, when Caraka speaks of life, he includes both mind and body, and it is the welfare of both that is the chief concern of the physician. Caraka's prohibitions and injunctions are therefore based on this twofold good of body and mind that ought to be aimed at.

After speaking of the harmfulness of attempting to control some of the bodily excretory movements, he recommends the necessity of attempting to control certain other mental and bodily tendencies. Thus he forbids all persons to indulge rashly in their unthinking tendencies to eommit mistakes of mind, speech and action. A man should also control his passion of greed, and his feelings of grief, fear, anger, vanity, shamelessness, envy, attachment and solicitude. He should not speak harshly or talk too much or use stinging words or lie or speak irrelevantly or untimely. He should not injure others by his body, indulge in unrestricted sex-gratifications, or steal. Injury to living beings (*hiṃsā*) is supposed to produce sins and thereby affects one's longevity. Non-injury is thus described as being the best way of increasing life (*ahiṃsā prāṇa-vardhanānām).* The man who follows the above right course of life is called virtuous, and he enjoys wealth, satisfies his desires, abides by the laws (*dharma*) of a good life, and is happy. Along with the proper and well-controlled exercise of the moral functions Caraka advises people to take to well-controlled bodily exercises (*vyāyāma*). When moderately performed, they give lightness, power of doing work, steadiness *(sthairya)* and fortitude (*duḥkha-sahiṣṇutā*). Avoidance of unwise courses and non-commission of errors of judgment (*tyāgaḥ prajñāparādhānām),* sense-control, remembrance of past experiences (*smṛti*), due knowledge of one's own powers, due regard to proper time and place and good conduct prevent the inrush of mental and bodily diseases; for it is these which are the essentials of a good life, and a wise man always does what is good for himself. Caraka further advises that one should not keep company with those who are sinful in character, speech and mind, or with those who are quarrelsome, greedy, jealous, crooked, light-minded or fond of speaking ill of others or cruel or vicious, or with those who associate with one's enemies. But one should always associate with those who are wise, learned, aged, with men of character, firmness, self-concentration, ready experience, with those who know the nature of things and are full of equanimity, and those who direct us in the right path, are good to all beings, possess a settled character and are peaceful and self-contented. In these ways a man should try, on the one hand, to secure himself against the inrush of mental troubles which upset one's moral life and, on the other hand, properly to attend to his bodily welfare by taking the proper kind of food at the proper time and attending to other details of physical well-being.[1] The rules of good conduct *(sad-vṛtta)* are described in detail by Caraka as follows:[2]

A man should respect gods, cows, Brāhmaṇas, preceptors *(guru),* elderly persons, saints and teachers (*acārya*), hold auspicious amulets, bathe twice and clean all the pores of the body and feet and cut his hair, beard and nails three times in a fortnight. He should be well-dressed, should always oil his head, ears, nose and feet, comb his hair, scent himself and smoke *(dhūma-pā).* He should recognize others with a pleasant face, help others in difficulties, perform sacrifices, make gifts, talk delightfully, nicely and for the good of others, be self-controlled (*vaśyātman*) and of a virtuous temperament. He should envy the cause of another's prosperity in the form of his good character and other causes of his personal efficiency *(hetāv īrṣyu),* but should not be jealous of the fruits of these in the form of a man's prosperity or wealth *(phale nerṣyu).* He should be of firm decision, fearless, susceptible to the feeling of shame, intelligent, energetic, skillful, of a forgiving nature, virtuous and a believer *(āstika).* He should use umbrellas, sticks, turbans and shoes, and should at the time of walking look four cubits of ground in front of him; he should avoid going to im-

1 See *Caraka-saṃhitā,* I.7.

2 *Ibid.* I.8.

pure, unclean and dirty places; he should try to appease those who are angry, soothe the fears of those who have become afraid, help the poor, keep his promises, bear harsh words, be self-controlled, remove the causes of attachments and antipathy *(rāga-dveṣa)* and behave as the friend of all living beings. Again, one should not tell lies, or take that which belongs to others, should not commit adultery, or be jealous at other people's wealth, should not be given to creating enemies, should not commit sins, or do wrong even to a sinner, or speak about the defects or secrets of others; should not keep company with the sinful or with those who are the king's enemies or with madmen, the mean, wicked, outcast, or those who make abortions. One should not climb into bad vehicles, lie on hard beds, or beds without sheets or pillows, should not climb steep mountain sides or trees or bathe in fast flowing rivers with strong currents; one should not go about places where there are great fires raging, or laugh loudly or yawn or laugh without covering the face, or pick one's teeth. Again, one should not break the laws ordained by a large number of persons, or other laws in general; should not go about at night in improper places, or make friends with youngsters, old or greedy people, fools, sinners or eunuchs; one should not be fond of wines, gambling, prostitutes, divulge secrets, insult others, be proud or boastful or speak ill of old people, teachers, kings or assemblages of persons, or talk too much; one should not turn out relations, friends or those who know one's secrets. One should attend at the proper time to every action, should not undertake to do anything without properly examining it, or be too procrastinating, or be under the influence of anger and pleasure; one should not be very down-hearted in afflictions, or too elated in success, or too disappointed in failures; should practice sex-continence, try to be wise, make gifts, be friendly and compassionate to all and always contented. It is needless to continue to enumerate all the qualities, which would commonly be included within the requisites of a good life. In this Caraka seems to cut an absolutely new way, and in no other branch of Indian thought can we note such an assemblage of good qualities of all the different kinds necessary not only for a virtuous life, but for the healthy and successful life of a good citizen.

It has already been pointed out that error of judgment or delusion, in whichever sphere it may be exercised, is the root of all mischiefs and all troubles. And Caraka demonstrates this by enumerating in his schedule of good conduct proper behaviour in all the different concerns and spheres of life. To Caraka the conception of life is not as moral or immoral, but as good *(hitā)* and bad *(ahita)*. It is true, no doubt, that here and there stray statements are found in the *Caraka-saṃhitā* which regard the cessation of all sorrow's as the ultimate end of life; but it is obvious that Caraka's main approach to the subject shows very clearly that, though moral virtues are always very highly appreciated, yet the non-moral virtues, such as the proper taking care of the well-being of one's own body and the observance of social rules and forms of etiquette or normal prudent behaviour, are regarded as being equally necessary for the maintenance of a good life. Transgressions and sins are the causes of mental worries, troubles and also of many mental and physical diseases, and one ought therefore to take proper care that they may not enter into one's life; and it is said that the diseases produced by strong sinful acts cannot be cured by the ordinary means of the application of medicines and the like, until with the proper period of their sufferings they subside of themselves. But sins and transgressions are not the only causes of our desires, accidents and other domestic, social and political troubles. It is through our imprudent behaviour and conduct, which are due to error of judgment (*prajñāparādha*), as our other sins and immoral acts are, that all our bodily and mental troubles happen to us. A good life, which is the ideal of every person, is a life of peace, contentment and happiness, free from desires and troubles of all kinds. It is a life of prudence and well-balanced judgment, where every action is done with due consideration to its future consequences and where all that may lead to troubles and difficulties is carefully avoided. It is only such a life that can claim to be good and can be regarded as ideal. A merely moral or virtuous life is not our ideal, which must be good in every respect. Any transgression, be it of the rules of hygiene, rules of polite society, rules of good citizenship, or any deviation from the path which prudence or good judgment would recommend to be wise, may disturb the peace of life. A scheme of good life thus means a wise life, and observance of morality is but one of the many ways in which wisdom can be shown.

Āyur-veda, or the Science of Life, deals primarily with the ways in which a life may be good *(hita),* bad (*ahita*), happy *(sukha)* or unhappy *(asukha).* A happy life is described as a life undisturbed by bodily and mental diseases, full of youth and proper strength, vitality, energy, power of launching new efforts, endowed with wisdom, knowledge and efficient sense-organs—a life which is full of all kinds of desirable enjoyments and in which the ventures that are undertaken are all successful. The opposite of this is what may be called an unhappy life. The happy life thus represents a life so far as it is happy and enjoyable and so far as it satisfies us. The good life is the life as it is moulded and developed by our right conduct. In a way it is the good life that makes a happy life. They who seek a good life should desist from the sins of taking other people's possessions and be truthful and self-controlled. They should perform every action with proper observation, care and judgment, and should not be hasty or make mistakes by their carelessness; they should attend to the attainment of virtue, wealth and the enjoyments of life without giving undue emphasis to any of them; they should respect those who are revered, should be learned, wise and of a peaceful mind and control their tendencies to attachment, anger, jealousy and false pride; they should always make gifts; they should lead a life of rigour (*tapas*) and attain wisdom, self-knowledge or philosophy (*adhyātma-vidaḥ*), and behave in such a way that the interests of both the present life on earth and the life hereafter may be attended to with care and judgment, always remembering the lessons of past experience.[1] It is now clear that the ideal of good life in Caraka is not the same as that of the different systems of philosophy which are technically called the Science of

1 *Caraka-saṃhitā,* I.30.22.

Liberation (*mokṣa-śāstra*). The fundamental idea of a good life is that a life should be so regulated that the body and mind may be free from diseases, that it should not run into unnecessary risks of danger through carelessness, that it should be virtuous, pure and moral; that it should be a prudent and wise life which abides by the laws of polite society and of good and loyal citizens, manifesting keen alertness in thought and execution and tending constantly to its own good—good for all interests of life, body, mind and spirit.

ĀYUR-VEDA LITERATURE

The systematic development of Indian' medicine proceeded primarily on two principal lines, viz. one that of Suśruta and the other that of Caraka. It is said in Suśruta's great work, *Suśruta-saṃhitā,* that Brahmā originally composed the Āyur-veda in one hundred verses, divided into one thousand chapters, even before he had created human beings, and that later on, having regard to the shortness of human life and the poverty of the human intellect, he divided it into the eight parts, *Śalya, Śālākya,* etc., alluded to in a previous section. But this seems to be largely mythical. It is further said in the same connection in the *Suśruta-saṃhitā*, I.1 that the sages Aupadhenava, Vaitaraṇa, Aurabhra, Pauṣkalāvata, Karavīrya, Gopurarakṣita, Suśruta and others approached Dhanvantari or Divodāsa, king of Kāśī, for medical instruction. Suśruta's work is therefore called a work of the Dhanvantari school. Though it was revised at a later date by Nāgārjuna, yet Suśruta himself is an old writer. A study of the Jātakas shows that the great physician Ātreya, a teacher of Jīvaka, lived in Taxila shortly before Buddha.[1] It has been said in a preceding section that in the enumeration of bones Suśruta shows a knowledge of Ātreya's system of osteology. Hoernle has further shown in sections 42, 56, 60 and 61 of his "Osteology," that the *Śatapatha-Brāhmaṇa,* which is at least as old as the sixth century BC, shows an acquaintance with Suśruta's views concerning the counting of bones. But, since Ātreya could not

1 Rockhill's *Life of Buddha,* pp. 65 and 96.

have lived earlier than the sixth century BC, and since the *Śatapatha-Brāhmaṇa* of about the sixth century BC shows an acquaintance with Suśruta's views, Hoernle conjectures that Suśruta must have been contemporary with Ātreya's pupil, Agniveśa.[1] But, admitting Hoernle's main contentions to be true, it may be pointed out that by the term *veda-vādinaḥ* in *Suśruta-saṃhitā*, III.5.18 Suśruta may have referred to authorities earlier than Ātreya, from whom Ātreya also may have drawn his materials. On this view, then, the lower limit of Suśruta's death is fixed as the sixth or seventh century BC, this being the date of the *Śatapatha-Brāhmaṇa,* while practically nothing can be said about the upper limit.

But it is almost certain that the work which now passes by the name of *Suśruta-saṃhitā* is not identically the same work that was composed by this elder Suśruta (*vṛddha Suśruta).* Ḍalhaṇa, who lived probably in the eleventh or the twelfth century, says in his *Nibandha-saṃgraha* that Nāgārjuna was the reviser of the *Suśruta-saṃhitā;*[2] and the *Suśruta-saṃhitā* itself contains a supplementary part after the *Kalpa-sthāna,* called the *Uttara-tantra* (later work). In the edition of Suśruta by P. Muralidhar, of Pharuknagar, there is a verse at the beginning, which says that that which was so well taught for the good of the people by the great sage Dhanvantari to the good pupil Suśruta became famous all over the world as *Suśruta-saṃhitā*, and is regarded as the best and the chief of the threefold Āyur-veda literature, and that it was strung together in the form of a book by no other person than Nāgārjuna.[3] Cakrapāṇi

1 Hoernle's *Medicine of Ancient India,* Part I, "Osteology," pp. 7 and 8.

2 *Pratisaṃskartāpīha Nāgārjuna eva.* Ḍalhaṇa's *Nibandha-saṃgraha,* I. I. I.

3 उपदिष्टा तु या सम्यग् धन्वन्तरिमहर्षिणा
सुश्रुताय सुशिष्याय लोकानां हितवान्छया
सर्वत्र भुवि विख्याता नाम्ना सुश्रुतसंहिता
आयुर्वेदत्रयीमध्ये स्रेष्ठा मान्या तथोत्तमा
सा च नागार्जुनेनैव ग्रथिता ग्रन्थरूपतः ॥
Upadiṣṭā tu yā samyag Dhanvantari-maharṣiṇā
Suśrutāya suśiṣyāya lokānāṃ hita-vānchayā
sarvatra bhuvi vikhyātā nāmnā Suśruta-saṃhitā
Āyur-vedat-rayīmadhye sreṣṭhā mānyā tathottamā
sā ca Nāgārjunenaiva grathitā grantha-rūpataḥ.

also in his *Bhānumatī* refers to a reviser (*pratisaṃskartṛ*); but he does not mention his name. Gayadāsa's *pañjikā* on Suśruta, *Suśruta-candrikā* or *Nyāya-candrikā,* has an observation on the eighth verse of the third chapter of the *Nidāna-sthāna*, in which he gives a different reading by Nāgārjuna, which is the same as the present reading of Suśruta in the corresponding passage.[1] Again, Bhaṭṭa Narahari in his *Ṭippaṇī* on the *Astāṅga-hṛdaya-saṃhitā,* called *Vāgbhaṭa-khaṇḍana-maṇḍana*, in discussing *mūḍha-garbha-nidāna,* annotates on the reading *vasti-dvāre vipannāyāh*, which Vāgbhaṭa changes in borrowing from Suśruta's *vastimāra-vipannā-yāḥ* (II.8.14), andsavsthat *vasti-dvāre* is the reading of Nāgārjuna.[2] That Nāgārjuna had the habit of making supplements to his revisions of works is further testified by the fact that a work called *Yoga-śataka,* attributed to Nāgārjuna, had also a supplementary chapter, called *Uttara-tantra*, in addition to its other chapters, *Kāya-cikitsā, Śālākya-tantra*, *Śalya-tantra, Viṣa-tantra, Bhūtavidyā*, *Kaumāra-tantra, Rasāyana-tantra* and *Vājīkaraṇa-tantra.* This makes it abundantly clear that what passes as the *Suśruta-saṃhitā* was either entirely strung together from the traditional teachings of Suśruta or entirely revised and enlarged by Nāgārjuna on the basis of a nuclear work of Suśruta which was available to Nāgārjuna. But was Nāgārjuna the only person who revised the *Suśruta-saṃhitā*? Ḍalhaṇa's statement that it was Nāgārjuna who was the reviser of the work *(pratisoṃskartāpīha Nāgārjuna eva*) is attested by the verse of the Muralidhar edition (*Nāgārjunenaiva grathitā*); but the use of the emphatic word *eva* in both suggests that there may have been other editions or revisions of Suśruta by other writers as well. The hopelessly muddled condition of the readings, chapter-divisions and textual arrangements in the chapters in different editions of the *Suśruta-saṃhitā* is such that there can be no doubt that from time

---

1 *Nāgārjunas tu paṭhati; śarkarā sikatā meho bhasmākhyo'śmari-vaikrtam iti.* In the Nirṇaya-Sāgara edition of 1915 this is II.3.13, whereas in Jīvānanda's edition it is I I.3.8. See also Dr Cordier's *Récentes Découvertes de MSS. Médicaux Sanserits dans l'Inde,* p. 13.

2 *ata eva Nāgārjunair vasti-dvāra iti paṭhyate.*

to time many hands were in operation on this great work. Nor it is proper to think that the work of revising Suśruta was limited to a pre-Cakrapāṇi period. It is possible to point out at least one case in which it can be almost definitely proved that a new addition was made to the *Suśruta-saṃhitā* after Cakrapāṇi, or the text of Suśruta known to Ḍalhaṇa was not known to Cakrapāṇi. Thus, in dealing with the use of catheters and the processes of introducing medicine through the anus *(vasti-kriyā)* in IV.38, the texts of the *Suśruta-saṃhitā* commented on by Ḍalhaṇa reveal many interesting details which are untouched in the chapter on *Vasti* in the *Caraka-saṃhitā* (*Uttara-vasti, Siddhi-sthāna,* XII). This chapter of the *Caraka-saṃhitā was* an addition by Dṛḍhabala, who flourished in Kāśmīra or the Punjab, probably in the eighth or the ninth century. When Cakrapāṇi wrote his commentary in the eleventh century, he did not make any reference to the materials found in the *Suśruta-saṃhitā*, nor did he introduce them into his own medical compendium, which passes by the name of *Cakradatta.* Cakrapāṇi knew his *Suśruta-saṃhitā* well, as he had commented on it himself, and it is extremely unlikely that, if he had found any interesting particulars concerning *vasti-kriyā* in his text, he should not have utilized them in his commentary or in his own medical work. The inference, therefore, is almost irresistible that many interesting particulars regarding *vasti-kriyā,* absent in the texts of the *Suśruta-saṃhitā* in the ninth and eleventh centuries, were introduced into it in the twelfth century. It is difficult, however, to guess which Nāgārjuna was the reviser or editor of the *Suśruta-saṃhitā*; it is very unlikely that he was the famous Nāgārjuna of the *Mādhyamika-kārikā,* the great teacher of Śūnyavāda; for the accounts of the life of this Nāgārjuna, as known from Chinese and Tibetan sources, nowhere suggest that he revised or edited the *Suśruta-saṃhitā.* Alberuni speaks of a Nāgārjuna who was born in Dihaka, near Somanātha (Gujarat), about one hundred years before himself, i.e. about the middle of the ninth century, and who had written an excellent work on alchemy, containing the substance of the whole literature of the subject, which by Alberuni's time had become very rare. It is not improbable that this Nāgārjuna was the author of the *Kakṣaputa-tantra,* which is avowedly written with materials collected from the alchemical works of various religious communities and which deals with the eightfold miraculous acquirements (*aṣṭa-siddhi*). But Vṛnda in his *Siddha-yoga* refers to a formula by Nāgārjuna which was said to have been written on a pillar in Pātaliputra.[1] This formula is reproduced by Cakrapāṇi Datta, Vaṅgasena and by Nityanātha Siddha in his *Rasa-ratnākara.* But since Vṛnda, the earliest of these writers, flourished about the eighth or the ninth century, and since his formula was taken from an inscription, it is not improbable that this Nāgārjuna flourished a few centuries before him.

Of the commentaries on the *Suśruta-saṃhitā* the most important now current is Ḍalhaṇa's *Nibandha-saṃgraha.* Ḍalhaṇa quotes Cakrapāṇi, of AD 1060, and is himself quoted by Hemādri, of AD 1260. He therefore flourished between the eleventh and the thirteenth centuries. It has been pointed out that sufficient textual changes in the *Suśruta-saṃhitā* had occurred between Cakrapāṇi and Ḍalhaṇa's time to have taken at least about one hundred years. I am therefore inclined to think that Ḍalhaṇa lived late in the twelfth, or early in the thirteenth, century at the court of King Sahapāla Deva. Cakrapāṇi had also written a commentary on the *Suśruta-saṃhitā,* called *Bhānumatī,* the first book of which has been published by Kaviraj Gangaprasad Sen. Dr Cordier notes that there is a complete manuscript of this at Benares. Niścala Kara and Śrīkaṇtha Datta sometimes quote from Cakrapāṇi's commentary on the *Suśruta-saṃhitā.* Ḍalhaṇa's commentary is called *Nibandha-saṃgraha,* which means that the book is collected from a number of commentaries, and he himself says in a colophon at the end of the *Uttara-tantra* that the physician Ḍalhaṇa, son of Bharata, had written the work after consulting many other commentaries.[2]

1 *Nāgārjunena likhitā stambhe Pāṭaliputrake,* V.149.

2 निबन्धान् बहुशो वीक्ष्य वैद्यः श्रीभारतात्मजः
उत्तरस्थानम् अकरोत् सुस्पष्टं डल्हणो भिषक् ॥
Nibandhān bahuśo vīkṣya vaidyaḥ Śrībhāratātmajaḥ
uttara-sthānam akarot suspaṣṭaṃ Ḍalhaṇo bhiṣak.

At the beginning of his *Nibandha-saṃgraha* he refers to Jaiyyata, Gayadāsa, Bhāskara's *pañjikā,* Śrimādhava and Brahmadeva. In his work he further mentions Caraka, Hārīta, Jatukarṇa, Kāśyapa, Kṛṣṇātreya, Bhadraśaunaka, Nāgārjuna, the two Vāgbhaṭas, Videha, Hariścandra, Bhoja, kārttika Kuṇḍa and others. Hari-ścandra was a commentator on the *Caraka-saṃhitā.* It is curious, however, that, though Ḍalhaṇa refers to Bhāskara and Śrimādhava Concluding verse of Ḍalhaṇa's commentary on Suśruta's *Uttara-tantra,* chap. 66. at the beginning of his commentary, he does not refer to them in the body of it. Hoernle, however, is disposed to identify Bhāskara and Kārttika Kuṇḍa as one person. Vijayarakṣita and Śrīkaṇtha Datta, commentators on Mādhava's *Nidāna*, refer to Kārttika Kuṇḍa in connection with their allusions to the *Suśruta-saṃhitā,* but not to Bhāskara. A Patna inscription (E.I.1.340, 345) says that King Bhoja had given the title of Vidyāpati to Bhāskara bhaṭṭa. Hoernle thinks that this Bhāskara was the same as Bhāskara bhaṭṭa. Hoernle also suggests that Vṛnda Mādhava was the same as Śrimādhava referred to by Ḍalhaṇa. Mādhava in his *Siddha-yoga* often modifies Suśruta's statements. It may be that these modifications passed as Mādhava's *Ṭippaṇa.* Since Gayadāsa and Cakrapāṇi both refer to Bhoja and do not refer to one another, it may be that Gayadāsa was a contemporary of Cakrapāṇi. Hoernle thinks that the Brahmadeva referred to by Ḍalhaṇa was Śrībrahma, the father of Maheśvara, who wrote his *Sāhasāñka-carita* in AD 1111. Maheśvara refers to Hariścandra as an early ancestor of his. It is not improbable that this Hariścandra was a commentator on Caraka. The poet Maheśvara was himself also a Kavirāja, and Heramba Sena's *Gūḍha-bodhaka-saṃgraha* was largely based on Maheśvara's work. Jejjaṭa's commentary passed by the name of *Bṛhal-laghu-pañjikā*; Gayadāsa's commentary was called the *Suśruta-candrikā* or *Nyāya-candrikā* and Śrīmādhava or Mādhava-Kara's *Ṭippaṇa* was called *Śloka-vārttika.* Gayadāsa mentions the names of Bhoja, Suranandī and Svāmidāsa. Gayadāsa's *pañjikā* has been discovered only up to the *Nidāna-sthāna,* containing 3000 *granthas.* Among other commentators of Suśruta we hear the names of Gomin, Āṣādhavarman, Jinadāsa, Naradanta, Gadādhara, Bāṣpacandra, Soma, Govardhana and Praśnanidhāna.

It may not be out of place here to mention the fact that the Sāṃkhya philosophy summed up in the *Śārīra-sthāna* of Suśruta is decidedly the Sāṃkhya philosophy of Īśvarakṛṣṇa, which, as I have elsewhere pointed out, is later than the Sāṃkhya philosophy so elaborately treated in the *Caraka-saṃhitā.*[1] This fact also suggests that the revision of Suśruta was executed after the composition of Īśvarakṛṣṇa's work (about AD 200), which agrees with the view expressed above that the revision of Suśruta was the work of Nāgārjuna, who flourished about the fourth or the fifth century AD. But it is extremely improbable that the elaborate medical doctrines of an author who lived at so early a date as the sixth century BC could have remained in a dispersed condition until seven, eight or nine hundred years later. It is therefore very probable that the main basis of Suśruta's work existed in a codified and well-arranged form from very early times. The work of the editor or reviser seems to have consisted in introducing supplements, such as the *Uttara-tantra*, and other chapters on relevant occasions. It does not seem impossible that close critical and comparative study of a number of published texts of the *Suśruta-saṃhitā* and of unpublished manuscripts may enable a future student to separate the original from the supplementary parts. The task, however, is rendered difficult by the fact that additions to the *Suśruta-saṃhitā* were probably not limited to one period, as has already been pointed out above.

It is well known that Atri's medical teachings, as collected by Agniveśa in his *Agniveśa-tantra*, which existed at least as late as Cakrapāṇi, form the basis of a revised work by Caraka, who is said to have flourished during the time of Kaṇiṣka, passing by the name of *Caraka-saṃhitā.*[2] It is now also well known that Caraka did not complete his task, but left it half-finished at a point in the *Cikitsā-sthāna,* seventeen chapters of which, together with the

1 *History of Indian Philosophy*, vol. I, pp. 313-322.

2 On Caraka's being the court-physician of Kaniṣka see S. Levi, *Notes sur les Indo-Scythes,* in *Journal Asiatique,* pp. 444 sqq.

books called *Siddhi-sthāna* and *Kalpa-sthāna*, were added by Kapilabala's son, Dṛḍhabala, of the city of Pañcanada, about the ninth century AD. The statement that Dṛḍhabala supplemented the work in the above way is found in the current texts of the *Caraka-saṃhitā*.[1] Niścala Kara in his *Ratna-prabhā* describes him as author of the *Caraka-pariśiṣṭa*, and Cakrapāṇi, Vijayarakṣita and Aruṇa-datta (AD 1240), whenever they have occasion to quote passages from his supplementary parts, all refer to Dṛḍhabala as the author. The city of Pañcanada was identified as the Punjab by Dr U. C. Dutt in his *Materia Medica,* which identification was accepted by Dr Cordier and referred to a supposed modem Panjpur,north of Attock in the Punjab. There are several Pañcanadas in different parts of India, and one of them is mentioned in the fifty-ninth chapter of the *Kāśī-khaṇḍa*; Gaṅgādhara in his commentary identifies this with Benares, assigning no reason for such identification. Hoernle, however, thinks that this Pañcanada is the modern village of Pantzinor ("five channels" in Kashmir) and holds that Dṛḍhabala was an inhabitant of this place. There are many passages in Caraka which the commentators believe to be additions of the Kāśmīra recension (*Kāśmīra-pāṭha*). Mādhava quotes a number of verses from the third chapter of the sixth section, on fevers, which verses are given with the omission of about twenty-four lines. Vijaya-rakṣita, in his commentary on Mādhava's *Nidāna,* says that these lines belong to the Kāśmīra recension. Existing manuscripts vary very much with regard to these lines; for, while some have the lines, in others they are not found. In the same chapter there are other passages which are expressly noted by Cakrapāṇidatta as belonging to Kāśmīra recensions, and are not commented upon by him. There are also other examples. Hoernle points out that Jīvānanda's edition of 1877 gives the Kāśmīra version, while his edition of 1896, as well as the editions of Gaṅgādhara, the two Sens and Abinas, have Caraka's original version. Mādhava never quotes readings belonging to the Kāśmīra recension. Hoernle puts together four points, viz. that Caraka's work was revised and completed by Dṛḍhabala, that there

1 *Caraka-saṃhitā,* VI.30 and *Siddhi-sthāna*, VII.8.

existed a Kāśmīra recension of the *Caraka-saṃhitā,*, that Dṛḍhabala calls himself a native of Pañcanada city, and that there existed a holy place of that name in Kāśmīra; and he argues that the so-called Kāśmīra recension represents the revision of the *Caraka-saṃhitā* by Dṛḍhabala. Judging from the fact that Mādhava takes no notice of the readings of the Kāśmīra recension, he argues that the latter did not exist in Mādhava's time and that therefore Mādhava's date must be anterior to that of Dṛḍhabala.

But which portions were added to the *Caraka-saṃhitā* by Dṛḍhabala? The obvious assumption is that he added the last seventeen chapters of the sixth book (*Cikitsā*) and the seventh and eighth books.[1] But such an assumption cannot hold good, since there is a great divergence in the counting of the number of the chapters in different manuscripts. Thus, while Jīvānanda's text marks Arśas, Atīsāra, Visarpa, Madātyaya and Dvivraṇīya as the ninth, tenth, eleventh, twelfth and thirteenth chapters of *Cikitsā* and therefore belonging to the original Caraka, Gaṅgādhara's text calls the ninth, tenth, eleventh, twelfth and thirteenth chapters Unmāda, Apasmāra, Kṣatakṣīṇa, Śvayathu and Udara. The seventeen chapters attributed to Dṛḍhabala have consequently different titles in the Gaṅgādhara and Jīvānanda editions. Hoernle has discussed very critically these textual problems and achieved notable results in attributing chapters to Caraka or Dṛḍhabala.[2] But it is needless for us to enter into these discussions.

Mahāmahopādhyāya Kaviraj Gaṇanātha Sen, merely on the strength of the fact that the *Rāja-taraṅgiṇī* is silent on the matter,[3] disputes the traditional Chinese statement that Caraka was the

---

1 अस्मिन् सप्तादशाध्या कल्पाःसिद्धय एव च
नासाद्यन्तेऽग्निवेशस्य तन्त्रे चरकसंस्कृते
तान् एतान् कापिलबलःशेषान् दृढबलोऽकरोत्
तन्त्रस्यास्य महार्थस्य पूरणार्थं यथायथम्॥
asmin saptādaśādhyā kalpāḥ siddhaya eva ca
nāsādyante 'gniveśasya tantre Carakasaṃskṛte
tān etān Kāpilabalaḥ śeṣān Dṛḍhabalo 'karot
tantrasyāsya mahārthasya pūraṇārthaṃ yathāyatham.—VI.30.274.

2 *J.R.A.S.*, 1908 and 1909.

3 *Pratyakṣa-śārīram,* introduction.

court-physician of Kaṇiṣka. There is no ground to believe as gospel truth a tradition, which cannot be traced to any earlier authority than Bhoja (eleventh century), that Patañjali was the author of a medical work, and that therefore Patañjali and Caraka could be identified. His comparisons of some passages from Caraka (IV.1) with some *sūtras* of Patañjali are hardly relevant and he finally has to rest for support of this identification on the evidence of Rāmabhadra Dīkṣita, a man of the seventeenth or the eighteenth century, who holds that Patañjali had written a work on medicine. He should have known that there were more Patañjalis than one, and that the alchemist and medical Patañjali was an entirely different person from Patañjali, the grammarian.

The most important commentary now completely available to us is the *Āyur-veda-dīpikā*, or *Caraka-tātparya-ṭīkā,* of Cakrapāṇi-datta. Another important commentary is the *Caraka-pañjikā* by Svāmikumāra. He was a Buddhist in faith, and he refers to the commentator Hariścandra. The *Caraka-tattva-pradīpikā* was written in later times by Śivadāsasena, who also wrote the *Tattva-candrikā*, a commentary on Cakradatta. We hear also of other commentaries on Caraka by Bāṣpacandra or Vāpyacandra, Īśāna-deva, Īśvarasena, Vakulakara, Jinadāsa, Munidāsa, Govardhana, Sandhyākara, Jaya nandī and the *Caraka-candrikā* of Gayadāsa.

Among other ancient treatises we may mention the *Kāśyapa-saṃhitā*, discovered in Kaṭhmāṇḍū, a medical dialogue between Kāśyapa, the teacher and Bhārgava, the student. It is interesting to note that it has some verses (MS., pp. 105-110) which are identical with part of the fifth chapter of the first book of Caraka. There is another important manuscript, called *Bhāradvāja-saṃhitā,* which contains within it a small work called *Bhesaja-kalpa*, a commentary by Veṅkaṭeśa.[1] Agniveśa's original work, the *Agniveśa-saṃhitā*, which was the basis of Caraka's revision, was available at least up to the time of Cakrapāṇi; Vijayarakṣita and Śrīkaṇṭhadatta also

1 See Dr Cordier's missing part- PDF 443*Récentes Découvertes de MSS. Médicaux Sanscrits dans l'Inde* (1898-1902).

quote from it.[1] Jatūkarṇa's work also existed till the time of the same writers, as they occasionally quote from *Jatūkarṇa-saṃhitā.*[2] The *Parāśara-saṃhitā* and *Kṣārapāṇi-saṃhitā* were also available down to Śrikaṇthadatta's, or even down to Śivadāsa's, time. The *Hārīta-saṃhitā* (different from the printed and more modem text) was also available from the time of Cakrapāṇi and Vijayarakṣita, as is evident from the quotations from it in their works. Bhela's work, called *Bhela-saṃhitā,* has already been published by the University of Calcutta. It may be remembered that Agniveśa, Bhela, Jatūkarṇa, Parāśara, Hārīta and Kṣārapāṇi were all fellow-students in medicine, reading with the same teacher, Ātreya-Punarvasu; Agniveśa, being the most intelligent of them all, wrote his work first, but Bhela and his other fellow-students also wrote independent treatises, which were read before the assembly of medical scholars and approved by them. Another work of the same school, called *Kharaṇada-saṃhitā*, and also a *Viśvāmitra-saṃhitā,* both of which are not now available, are utilized by Cakrapāṇi and other writers in their commentaries. The name *saṃhitā*, however, is no guarantee of the antiquity of these texts, for the junior Vāgbhaṭa's work is also called *Aṣṭāṅga-hṛ daya-saṃhitā.* We have further a manuscript called *Vararuci-saṃhitā,* by Vararuci, and a *Siddha-sara-saṃhitā* by Ravigupta, son of Durgāgupta, which are of comparatively recent date. The *Brahma-vaivarta-purāṇa* refers to a number of early medical works, such as the *Cikitsā-tattva-vijñāna* of Dhanvantari, *Cikitsā-darśana* of Divodāsa, *Cikitsā-kaumudī* of Kāśīrāja, *Cikitsā-sāra-tantra* and *Bhrama-ghna* of Āśvinī, *Vaidyaka-sarvasva* of Nakula, *Vyādhi-sindhu-vimardana* of Sahadeva, *Jñānārṇava* of Yama, *Jīvādana* of Cyavana, *Vaidya-sandeha-bhañjana* of Janaka, *Sarva-sāra* of Candrasuta, *Tantra-sāra* of Jābāla, *Vedāṅga-sāra* of Jājali, *Nidāna* of Paila, *Sarva-dhara* of Karatha and *Dvaidha-*

1 See Cakrapāṇi's commentary on *Caraka-saṃhitā,* I I.2, also Śrīkaṇṭha on the *Siddha-yoga, Jvarādhikāra.*

2 Cakrapāṇi's commentary, II.2 and II.5, also Śrīkaṇṭha on the *Nidāna* (*Kṣudra-roga*).

nirṇaya-tantra of Agastya.[1] But nothing is known of these works, and it is difficult to say if they actually existed.

It is well known that there were two Vāgbhaṭas (sometimes spelt Vāhaṭa). The earlier Vāgbhaṭa knew Caraka and Suśruta. It is conjectured by Hoernle and others that the statement of I-tsing (AD 675-685), that the eight arts formerly existed in eight books, and that a man had lately epitomized them and made them into one bundle, and that all physicians in the five parts of India practised according to that book, alludes to the *Aṣṭāṅga-saṃgraha* of Vāgbhaṭa the elder. In that case Vāgbhaṭa I must have flourished either late in the sixth century or early in the seventh century; for I-tsing speaks of him as having epitomized the work "lately," and on the other hand time must be allowed for the circulation of such a work in the five parts of India. A comparison of Suśruta and Vāgbhaṭa I shows that the study of anatomy had almost ceased to exist in the latter's time. It is very probable that Vāgbhaṭa was a Buddhist. The *Aṣṭāṅga-saṃgraha* has a commentary by Indu; but before Indu there had been other commentators, whose bad expositions were refuted by him.[2]

Mādhava, Dṛḍhabala and Vāgbhaṭa II all knew Vāgbhaṭa I. Mādhava mentions him by name and occasionally quotes from him both in the *Siddha-yoga* and in the *Nidāna*, and so also does Dṛḍhabala.[3] Hoernle has shown that Dṛḍhabala's 96 diseases of the eye are based on Vāgbhaṭa's 94. Vāgbhaṭa II towards the end of the *Uttara-sthāna* of his *Aṣṭāṅga-hṛdaya-saṃhitā* definitely expresses his debt to Vāgbhaṭa I. But they must all have flourished before Cakrapāṇi, who often refers to Dṛḍhabala and Vāgbhaṭa II. If, as Hoernle has shown, Mādhava was anterior to Dṛḍhabala, he

1 It is curious to notice that the *Brahma-vaivarta-purāṇa* makes Dhanvantari, Kāśīrāja and Divodāsa different persons, which is contrary to Suśruta's statement noted above.

2 *Durvyākhyā-viṣa-suptasya Vāhaṭasyāsmad-uktayaḥ santu saṃvitti-dāyinyas sad-āgama-pariṣkṛtā.* Indu's commentary, I.1.

3 *Siddha-yoga,* I.27, *Aṣṭāṅga-saṃgraha,* II.1, *Nidāna,* II.22 and 23, *Saṃ-graha,* I.266, *Caraka-saṃhitā* (Jivānanda, 1896), *Cikitsita-sthāna,* XVI.31, *Saṃgraha,* II.26.Again, *Cikitsita-sthāna,* XVI.53, etc., *Saṃgraha,* II.27, etc.

also must necessarily have flourished before Cakrapāṇi. Hoernle's argument that Mādhava flourished before Dṛḍhabala rests upon the fact that Suśruta counts 76 kinds of eye-diseases, while Vāgbhaṭa I has 94. Dṛḍhabala accepts Vāgbhaṭa I's 94 eye-diseases with the addition of two more, added by Mādhava, making his list come to 96. Mādhava had accepted Suśruta's 76 eye-diseases and added two of his own.[1] The second point in Hoernle's argument is that Mādhava in his quotations from Caraka always omits the passages marked by Vijayarakṣita as Kāśmīra readings, which Hoernle identifies with the revision work of Dṛḍhabala. These arguments of Hoernle appear very inconclusive; for, if the so-called Kāśmīra recension can be identified with Dṛḍhabala's revision, both Dṛḍhabala's Kāśmīra nativity and his posteriority to Mādhava can be proved; but this proposition has not been proved. On the other hand, Cakrapāṇi alludes to a Dṛḍhabala *saṃskāra* side by side with a Kāśmīra reading, and this seems to indicate that the two are not the same.[2] The suggestion of Mādhava's anteriority on the ground that he counts 78 eye-diseases is rather far-fetched. Mādhava's date, therefore, cannot be definitely settled. Hoernle is probably correct in holding that Dṛḍhabala is anterior to Vāgbhaṭa.[3] However, the relative anteriority or posteriority of these three writers does not actually matter very much; for they lived at more or less short intervals from one another and their dates may roughly be assigned to a period between the eighth and tenth centuries AD.

Vāgbhaṭa IIs *Aṣṭāṅga-hṛdaya-saṃhitā* has at least five commentaries, viz. by *Aruṇadatta* (*Sarvāṅga-sundarī*), Aśādhara, Candracandana (*Padārtha-candrikā*), Rāmanātha and Hemādri *(Āyur-veda-rasāyand)*. Of these *Aruṇadatta* probably lived in AD 1220. Mādhava's *Rug-viniścaya*, a compendium of patholo-

1 Hoernle thinks that the total number of 76 eye-diseases ordinarily found in the printed editions of Mādhava's *Nidāna* is not correct, as they do not actually tally with the descriptions of the different eye-diseases given by Mādhava and do not include *pakṣma-kopa* and *pakṣma-śātā* varieties. Hoernle's "Osteology," p. 13.

2 Cakra's commentary, I.7.46-50.

3 See Hoernle's "Osteology," pp. 14-16.

gy, is one of the most popular works of Indian Medicine. It has at least seven commentaries, viz. by Vijayarakṣita (*Madhu-kośa*), Vaidya-vācaspati (*Ātaṅka-dīpana*), Rāmanātha Vaidya, Bhavānī-sahāya, Nāganātha (*Nidāna-pradīpa*), *Gaṇeśa* Bhisaj and the commentary known as *Siddhānta-candrikā* or *Vivaraṇa-siddhōn-ta-candrikāy* by *Narasiṃha* Kavirāja.[1] Vijayarakṣita's commentary, however, closes with the 33rd chapter, and the rest of the work was accomplished by Śrīkaṇṭhadatta, a pupil of Vijayarakṣita. Vṛnda (who may be the same as Mādhava) wrote a *Siddha-yoga,* a book of medical formulas, well known among medical writers.

In connection with this brief account of Indian medical works the *Nava-nītaka*, and the other mutilated medical treatises which have been discovered in Central Asia and which go by the name of "Bower manuscript," cannot be omitted. This manuscript is written on birch leaves in Gupta characters and is probably as old as the fifth century AD. It is a Buddhist work, containing many medical formulas taken from Caraka, Suśruta and other unknown writers. It will, however, be understood that an elaborate discussion of chronology or an exhaustive account of Indian medical works would be out of place in a work like the present.'The Āyur-veda literature, and particularly that part which deals with medical formulas and recipes, medical lexicons and the like, is vast. Aufrecht's catalogue contains the names of about 1500 manuscript texts, most of which have not yet been published, and there are many other manuscripts not mentioned in Aufrecht's catalogue. Among the books now much in use may be mentioned the works of Śārṅgadhara, of the fourteenth century, Śivadāsa's commentary on Cakrapāṇi, of the fifteenth century, and the *Bhāva-prakāśa* of Bhāvamiśra, of the sixteenth. Vaṅ-

1 Narasiṃha Kavirāja was the son of Nīlakaṇṭha bhaṭṭa and the pupil of Rāmakṛṣṇa Bhaṭṭa. He seems to have written another medical work, called *Madhu-matī.* His *Vivaraṇa-siddhānta-candrikā,* though based on Vijaya's *Madhu-koṣa,* is an excellent commentary and contains much that is both instructive and new. The only manuscript available is probably the one that belongs to the family library of the author of the present work, who is preparing an edition of it for publication.

gasena's work is also fairly common. Among anatomical texts Bhoja's work and Bhāskara bhaṭṭa's *Śārīra-padminī* deserve mention. The *Aupadhenava-tantra, Pauṣkalāvata-tantra, Vaitaraṇa-tantra* and *Bhoja-tantra* are alluded to by Ḍalhaṇa. The *Bhāluki-tantra* and *Kapila-tantra* are mentioned by Cakrapāṇi in his *Bhānumatī* commentary. So much for the anatomical treatises. *Videha-tantra, Nimi-tantra, Kāṅkāyana-tantra, Sātyaki-tantra, Karāla-tantra* and *Kṛṣṇātreya-tantra* on eye-diseases are alluded to in Śrīkaṇṭha's commentary on Mādhava's *Nidāna.* The *Śaunaka-tantra* on eye-diseases is named in the commentaries of Cakrapāṇi and Ḍalhaṇa. The *Jivaka-tantra, Parvataka-tantra* and *Bandhaka-tantra* are alluded to by Ḍalhaṇa as works on midwifery. The *Hiraṇyākṣya-tantra* on the same subject is named by Śrīkaṇṭha, whereas the *Kāśyapa-saṃhitā* and *Ālambāyana-saṃhitā* are cited by Śrīkaṇṭha on toxicology. The *Uśanas-saṃhitā, Sanaka-saṃhitā, Lāṭyāyana-saṃhitā* are also mentioned as works on toxicology.

Among some of the other important Tantras may be mentioned Nāgārjuna's *Yoga-śataka,* containing the eight regular divisions of Indian Medicine, and Nāgārjuna's *Jīva-sūtra* and *Bheṣaja-kalpa,* all of which were translated into Tibetan. Three works on the *Aṣṭāṅga-hṛdaya,* called *Aṣṭāṅga-hṛdaya-nāma-vaidūryaka-bhāṣya, Padār-tha-candrikā-prabhāsa-nāma, Aṣṭāṅga-hṛdaya-vṛtti* and *Vaidyakā-ṣṭāṅga-hṛdaya-vṛtter bheṣaja-nāma-sūcī,* were also translated into Tibetan.

The *Āyur-veda-sūtra* is a work by Yogānandanātha, published with a commentary by the same author in the Mysore University Sanskrit series in 1922, with an introduction by Dr Shama Sastry. It is rightly pointed out in the introduction that this is a very modern work, written after the *Bhāva-prakāśa,* probably in the sixteenth century. It contains sixteen chapters and is an attempt to connect Āyur-veda with Patañjali's Yoga system. It endeavours to show how different kinds of food increase the *sattva, rajas* and *tamas* qualities and how *yoga* practices, fasting and the like, influence the conditions of the body. Its contribution, whether as a work of Āyur-veda or as a work of philosophy, is rather slight. It shows a tendency to connect *Yoga* with Āyur-veda, while the *Vīra-siṃhāvalokita* is a work which tries to connect astrology with the same.

CHAPTER XIV

THE PHILOSOPHY OF THE BHAGAVAD-GĪTĀ

THE GĪTĀ LITERATURE

The *Gītā* is regarded by almost all sections of the Hindus as one of the most sacred religious works, and a large number of commentaries have been written on it by the adherents of different schools of thought, each of which explained the *Gītā* in its own favour. Śaṅkara's *bhāṣya* is probably the earliest commentary now available; but from references and discussions found therein there seems to be little doubt that there were previous commentaries which he wished to refute.

Śaṅkara in his interpretation of the *Gītā* seeks principally to emphasize the dogma that right knowledge can never be combined with Vedic duties or the duties recommended by the legal scriptures. If through ignorance, or through attachment, a man continues to perform the Vedic duties, and if, as a result of sacrifices, gifts and *tapas* (religious austerities), his mind becomes pure and he acquires the right knowledge regarding the nature of the ultimate reality—that the passive Brahman is the all—and then, when all reasons for the performance of actions have ceased for him, still continues to perform the prescribed duties just like common men and to encourage others to behave in a similar manner, then such actions are inconsistent with right knowledge. When a man performs actions without desire or motive, they cannot be considered as *karma* at all. He alone may be said to be performing *karma*, or duties, who has any interest in them. But the wise man, who has no interest in his *karma*, cannot be said to be performing *karma* in the proper sense of the term, though to all outward appearances he may be acting exactly like an ordinary man. Therefore the main thesis of the *Gītā,* according to Śaṅkara, is that liberation can come only through right knowledge and not through knowledge combined with the performance of duties. Śaṅkara maintains that all duties hold good for us only in the stage of ignorance and not in the stage of wisdom. When once the right knowledge of identity with Brahman dawns and ignorance ceases, all notions of duality, which are presupposed by the performance of actions and responsibility for them, cease.[1] In interpreting *Gītā,* III.1, Śaṅkara criticizes the opinions of some previous commentators, who held that obligatory duties cannot be given up even when true wisdom is attained. In reply he alludes to legal scriptures *(smṛti-śāstrd),* and asserts that the mere non-performance of any duties, however obligatory, cannot lead to evil results, since non-performance is a mere negation and of mere negation no positive results can come out. The evil effects of the non-performance of obligatory duties can happen only to those who have not given up all their actions (*a-saṃnyāsi-viṣayatvāt pratyavāya-prāpteḥ).* But those who have attained true wisdom and have consequently given up all their actions transcend the sphere of duties and of the obligatory injunctions of the Vedas, and the legal scriptures cannot affect them at all. The performance of duties cannot by itself lead to liberation; but it leads gradually to the attainment of purity of mind (*sattva-śuddhi*) and through this helps the dawning of the right knowledge, with which all duties cease.[2] In a very lengthy discussion on the interpretation of *Gītā*, XVIII.67, Śaṅkara tries to prove that all duties presuppose the multiplicity of the world of appearance, which is due to ignorance

1 Śaṅkara's interpretation of the *Gītā,* II.69. Yogāśrama edition, Benares,1919.
2 *Ibid.* III.4.

or nescience, and therefore the sage who has attained the right knowledge of Brahman, the only reality, has no duties to perform. Final liberation is thus produced, not by true knowledge along with the performance of duties, but by true knowledge alone. The wise man has no duties of any kind. Śaṅkara's interpretation of the *Gītā* presupposes that the *Gītā* holds the same philosophical doctrine that he does. His method of interpretation is based not so much on a comparison of textual passages, as simply on the strength of the reasonableness of the exposition of a view which can be consistently held according to his Vedānta philosophy, and which he ascribes to the *Gītā.* The view taken in the present exposition of the *Gītā* philosophy is diametrically opposite to that of Śaṅkara. It has been repeatedly pointed out that the *Gītā* asserts that even the wise man should perform his allotted duties, though he may have nothing to gain by the performance of such duties. Even God Himself as Kṛṣṇa, though He had no unsatisfied cravings, passions or desires of any kind, performed His self-imposed duties in order to set an example to all and to illustrate the fact that even the wise man should perform his prescribed duties.[1]

Ānandajñāna wrote a commentary on Śaṅkara's *Bhagavad-Gītā-bhāsya,* called *Bhagavad-Gītā-bhāṣya-vivaraṇa,* and Rāmānanda wrote another commentary on that of Śaṅkara, called *Bhagavad-Gītā-bhāṣya-vyākhyā.* He is also said to have written another work on the *Gītā,* called *Gītāśaya.* After Śaṅkara, there seems to have been some pause. We have two commentaries, one in prose and one in verse, by two persons of the same name, Yāmunācārya. The Yāmunācārva who was the author of a prose commentary is certainly, though a *viśiṣṭādvaita-vādin,* not the celebrated Yāmuna, the teacher of Rāmānuja. His commentary, which has been published by the Sudarśana Press, Conjeeveram, is very simple, consisting mainly of a mere paraphrase of the *Gītā* verses. He thinks that the first six chapters of the *Gītā* deal with the nature of true knowledge of God as a means to devotion, the second six with the nature of God as attainable by devotion and adoration,

1 *Gītā*, III.22

and the third six repeat the same subjects for a further clearing up of the problems involved.

Yāmuna, the great teacher of Rāmānuja, who is said to have been born in AD 906, summarized the subject-matter of the *Gītā* in a few verses called *Gītārtha-saṃgraha,* on which Nigamānta Mahā-deśika wrote a commentary known as *Gītārtha-saṃgraha-rakṣā.* This also was commented on by Varavara Muni, of the fourteenth century, in a commentary called *Gītārtha-saṃgraha-dīpikā,* published by the Sudarśana Press, Conjeeveram. Another commentary, called *Bhagavad-Gītārtha-saṃgraha-ṭīkā,* by Pratyakṣa-devayathācārya, is mentioned by Aufrecht. Yāmuna says that the object of the *Gītā* is to establish the fact that Nārāyaṇa is the highest Brahman, attained only by devotion *(bhakti),* which is achieved through caste duties *(sva-dharma),* right knowledge and disinclination to worldly pleasures *(vairāgya).* It is said that the first six chapters of the *Gītā* describe the process of attaining self-knowledge by self-concentration *(yoga)* through knowledge and action along with self-subordination to God, the performance of all actions for God and detachment from all other things. Nigamānta Mahādeśika notes that *karma* may lead to self-realization either indirectly, through the production of knowledge, or directly by itself. From the seventh to the twelfth chapters the processes of the attainment of devotion (*bhakti-yoga*) by knowledge and by actions are described, and it is held that the true nature of God can be realized only by such devotion. From the thirteenth to the eighteenth chapters, the nature of *pradhāna*, of *puruṣa*, of the manifested world and of the supreme lord are described and distinguished along with the nature of action, of knowledge and of devotion. Yāmuna then goes on to describe the contents of the chapters of the *Gītā* one by one. Thus he says that in the second chapter the nature of the saint of imperturbable wisdom *(sthita-dhī)* is described. Such right knowledge can be achieved only by a knowledge of the self as immortal and the habit of performing one's duties in an unattached manner. In the third chapter it is said that a man should perform his duties for the preservation of the social order (*loka-rakṣā*) without attachment, leaving the fruits of all his actions to God, and considering at the same time that the *guṇas* are the real agents of actions and that it is wrong to pride oneself upon their performance. The fourth chapter describes the nature of God, how one should learn to look upon actions as implying no action (on account of unattachment), the different kinds of duties and the glory of knowledge. The fifth describes the advantages and the diverse modes of the path of duties and also the nature of the state of realization of Brahman. The sixth describes the nature of *yoga* practice, four kinds of *yogins,* the methods of *yoga*, the nature of *yoga* realization and the ultimate superiority of *yoga* as communion with God. The seventh describes the reality of God, how His nature is often veiled from us by *prakṛti* or the *guṇas*, how one should seek protection from God, the nature of the different kinds of devotees, and the superiority of the truly enlightened person. The eighth describes the lordly power of God and the reality of His nature as the unchanged and the unchangeable; it also describes the duties of those who seek protection in God and the nature of the true wisdom. The ninth describes the glory of God and His superiority even when He incarnates Himself as man, and the nature of devotional communion. The tenth describes the infinite number of God's noble qualities and the dependence of all things on Him, for initiating and increasing devotion. The eleventh describes how the true nature of God can be perceived, and demonstrates that it is only through devotion that God can be known or attained. The twelfth describes the superiority of devotion, methods of attaining devotion, and different kinds of devotion; it is also held that God is highly pleased by the devotion of His devotees. The thirteenth describes the nature of the body, the purification of the self for self-realization, the cause of bondage and right discrimination. The fourteenth describes how the nature of an action is determined by the ties of *guṇa,* how the *guṇas* may be made to cease from influencing us, and how God alone is the root of all the ways of the self's future destiny. The fifteenth describes how the supreme lord is different from the pure selves, as well as from selves in association with non-selves, on account of his all-pervasiveness and his nature as upholder and lord. The sixteenth describes the division of beings into godly and demoniac and also the privileged position of the scriptures as the authority for laying the solid foundation of knowledge of the true nature of our duties. The seventeenth distinguishes unscriptural things from scriptural. The eighteenth describes how God alone should be regarded as the ultimate agent of all actions, and states the necessity of purity and the nature of the effects of one's deeds. According to Yāmuna *karma-yoga,* or the path of duties, consists of religious austerities, pilgrimage, gifts and sacrifices; *jñāna-yoga*, or the path of knowledge, consists of self-control and purity of mind; *bhakti-yoga,or* the path of devotion, consists in the meditation of God, inspired by an excess of joy in the communion with the divine. All these three paths mutually lead to one another. All three are essentially of the nature of the worship of God, and, whether regarded as obligatory or occasional, are helpful for discovering the true nature of one's self. When by self-realization ignorance is wholly removed, and when a man attains superior devotion to God, he is received into God.

Rāmānuja, the celebrated Vaiṣṇava teacher and interpreter of the *Brahma-sūtra,* who is said to have been born in AD 1017, wrote a commentary on the *Gītā* on *viśiṣṭādvaita* lines, viz. monism qualified as theism. Veṇkaṭanātha, called also Vedāntācārya, wrote a sub-commentary thereon, called *Tātparya-candrikā.* Rāmānuja generally followed the lines of interpretation suggested in the brief summary by his teacher Yāmuna. On the question of the imperativeness of caste duties Rāmānuja says that the *Gītā* holds that the duties allotted to each caste must be performed, since the scriptures are the commands of God and no one can transgress His orders; so the duties prescribed by the scriptures as obligatory are compulsory for all. The duties have, therefore, to be performed without desire for their fruits and purely because they are the injunctions of the scriptures (*eka-śāstrārthatayā anuṣṭheyam).* It is only when duties performed simply to please God, and as adoration of Him, have destroyed all impurities of the mind, and when the senses have become controlled, that a man becomes fit for the path of wisdom. A man can never at any stage of his progress forsake the duty of worshipping God, and it is only through such adoration of God that the sins accumulating in him from beginningless time are gradually washed away and he can become pure and fit for the path of knowledge.[1] In interpreting III.8 Rāmānuja says that the path of duties (*karma-yoga*) is superior to the path of knowledge (*jñāna-yoga*). The path of duties naturally leads to self-knowledge; so self-knowledge is also included within its scope. The path of knowledge alone cannot lead us anywhere; for without work even the body cannot be made to live. Even those who adhere to the path of knowledge must perform the obligatory and occasional (*nitya-naimittika*) duties, and it is through the development of this course that one can attain self-realization by duty alone. The path of duties is to be followed until self-realization (*ātmāvalokana*) and, through it, emancipation are obtained. But the chief duty of a man is to be attached to God with supreme devotion.

Madhvācārya, or Ānandatīrtha, who lived in the first three-quarters of the thirteenth century, wrote a commentary on the *Bhagavad-Gītā,* called *Gītā-bhāṣya,* commented on by Jayatīrtha in his *Prameya-dīpikā,* and also a separate monograph interpreting the main purport of the *Gītā,* called *Bhagavad-Gītā-tātparya-nirṇaya,* commented on by Jayatīrtha in his *Nyāya-dīpikā.* His main emphasis was on the fact that God is different from everything else, and that the only way of attaining our highest goal is through devotion *(bhakti)* as love and attachment *(sneha).* In the course of his interpretation he also introduced long discussions in refutation of the monistic theory of Śaṅkara. Since everything is dominated by the will of Hari the Lord, no one ought to feel any attachment to mundane things. Duties are to be performed by all. Kṛṣṇabhaṭṭa Vidyādhirāja, the sixth disciple from Madhva, who lived in the first quarter of the fourteenth century, wrote a

1 *Anabhisaṃhita-phalena kevala-parama-puruṣārādhana-rūpenānuṣṭhitena karmaṇā vidhvasta-mano-malo 'vyākulendriyo jñāna-niṣṭkāyām adhikaroti.* Rāmānuja's commentary on the *Gītā,* III.3. See also *Ibid.* III.4. Gujarati Press, Bombay, 1908.

commentary on the *Gītā,* called *Gītā-ṭīkā.* Rāghavendra Svāmin, who lived in the seventeenth century and was a pupil of Sudhīndra Yati, wrote three works on the *Gītā*, called *Gītā-vivṛti, Gītārtha-saṃgraha* and *Gītārtha-vivaraṇa.* Commentaries were also written by Vallabhācārya, Vijñānabhikṣu, Keśava Bhaṭṭa of the Nimbārka school (called *Gītā-tattva-prakāśikā),* Āñjaneya (called *Hanumad-bhāṣya),* Kalyāṇa Bhaṭṭa (called *Rasika-rañjinī*), Jagaddhara (called *Bhagavad-Gītā-pradīpa), Jayarāma.* (called *Gītā-sārārtha-saṃgrahd),* Baladeva Vidyābhūṣaṇa (called *Gītā-bhūṣaṇa-bhāṣya),* Madhusūdana (called *Gūḍhārtha-dīpikā),* Brahmānanda Giri, Mathurānātha (called *Bhagavad-Gītā-prakāśa)*, Dattātreya (called *Prabodha-candrikā*), RāmaKṛṣṇa, Mukundadāsa, Rāma-Nārāyaṇa, Viśveśvara, Śaṅkarānanda, Śivadayālu Śrīdharasvāmin (called *Subodhinī*), Sadānanda Vyāsa (called *Bhāva-prakāśa),* Sūryapandita *(Paramārtha-prapā)*, Nīlakaṇtha (called *Bhāva-dīpikā),* and also from the Śaiva point of view by Rājānaka and Rāmakaṇtha (called *Sarvato-bhadra).* Many other works were also written on the general purport of the *Gītā*, such as *Bhagavad-Gītārtha-saṃgraha* by Abhinavagupta and Nṛsiṃha Thakkura, *Bhagavad-Gītārtha-sāra* by Gokulacandra, *Bhagavad-Gītā-lak-ṣābharaṇa* by Vādirāja, *Bhagavad-Gītā-sāra* by Kaivalyānanda Sarasvatī, *Bhagavad-Gītā-sāra-saṃgraha* by Narahari and *Bhagavad-Gītā-hetu-nirṇaya* by Vitthala Dīkṣita. Most of these commentaries are written either from the point of view of Śaṅkara's *bhāṣya*, repeating the same ideas in other language, or from the Vaiṣṇava point of view, approving of the hold of normal duties of men in all stages of life and sometimes differing only in the conception of God and His relation with men. These can claim but little originality either of argument or of opinions, and so may well be left out of detailed consideration for our present purposes.

GĪTĀ AND YOGA

Whoever may have written the *Gītā*, it seems very probable that he was not acquainted with the technical sense of *yoga* as the cessation of mental states (*citta-vṛtti-nirodha*), as used by Patañjali in his *Yoga-sūtra*, I.1.1 have elsewhere shown that there are three roots, *yujir yoge* and *yuj samādhau,* i.e. the root *yujir,* to join, and the root *yuj* in the sense of cessation of mental states or one-pointedness, and *yuj saṃyamane, i.e. yuj* in the sense of controlling. In the *Gītā* the word *yoga* appears to have been used in many senses, which may seem to be unconnected with one another; yet it may not be quite impossible to discover relations among them. The primary sense of the word *yoga* in the *Gītā* is derived from the root *yujir yoge* or *yuj,* to join, with which is connected in a negative way the root *yuj* in the sense of controlling or restricting anything to that to which it is joined. Joining, as it means contact with something, also implies disjunction from some other thing. When a particular type of mental outlook or scheme of action is recommended, we find the word *buddhi-yoga* used, which simply means that one has intimately to associate oneself with a particular type of wisdom or mental outlook. Similarly, when the word *karma-yoga* is used, it simply means that one has to associate oneself with the obligatoriness of the performance of duties. Again, the word *yoga* is used in the sense of fixing one's mind either on the self *(ātman)* or on God. It is clear that in all these varying senses the dominant sense is that of "joining." But such a joining implies also a disjunction, and the fundamental and indispensable disjunction implied is dissociation from all desires for pleasures and fruits of action *(phala-tyāga).* For this reason cases are not rare where *yoga* is used to mean cessation of desires for the fruits of action. Thus, in the *Gītā*, VI.2, it is said, "What is called cessation (of desires for the fruits of action) is what you should know, O Pāṇḍava, as Yoga: without renouncing one's desires *(na hy asaṃnyasta-saṅkalpa)* one cannot be a yogin."[1] The reason why this negative concept of cessation of desires should be regarded as *yoga* is that without

1 *Asaṃnyasto 'parityaktaḥ phala-viṣayaḥ saṅkalpo 'bhisandhir yena so 'saṃnyasta-saṅkalpaḥ.* Śaṅkara's commentary, VI.2. *Na saṃnyastaḥ phala-saṅkalpo yena.* Śrīdhara's commentary on the above. Yogāśrama edition, Benares, 1919.

such a renunciation of desires no higher kind of union is possible. But even such a dissociation from the fruits of desires (which in a way also means *saṃyamana*, or selfcontrol) is to be supplemented by the performance of duties at the preliminary stages; and it is only in the higher stages, when one is fixed in *yoga* (*yogārūḍha*), that meditative peace *(śama)* can be recommended. Unless and until one succeeds in conquering all attachments to sense-objects and actions and in giving up all desires for fruits of actions, one cannot be fixed in *yoga*. It is by our attempts at the performance of our duties, trying all the time to keep the mind clear from motives of pleasure and enjoyment, that we gradually succeed in elevating it to a plane at which it would be natural to it to desist from all motives of self-interest, pleasure and enjoyment. It is at this stage that a man can be called fixed in *yoga* or *yogārūḍha*. This naturally involves a conflict between the higher self and the lower, or rather between the real self and the false; for, while the lower self always inclines to pathological and prudential motives, to motives of self-interest and pleasure, it has yet within it the higher ideal, which is to raise it up. Man is both a friend and a foe to himself; if he follows the path of his natural inclinations and the temptations of sense-enjoyment, he takes the downward path of evil, and is an enemy to his own higher interests; whereas it is his clear duty to raise himself up, to strive that he may not sink down but may elevate himself to a plane of detachment from all sense-pleasures. The duality involved in this conception of a friend and a foe, of conqueror and conquered, of an uplifting power and a gravitating spirit, naturally involves a distinction between a higher self (*paramātman*) and a lower self *(ātman)*. It is only when this higher self conquers the lower that a self is a friend to itself. In a man who has failed to conquer his own passions and self-attachments the self is its own enemy. The implication, however, is that the lower self, though it gravitates towards evil, has yet inherent in it the power of self-elevation. This power of self-elevation is not something extraneous, but abides in the self, and the *Gītā* is emphatic in its command, "Thou shouldst raise thyself and not allow thyself to sink down; for the self is its own friend and its foe as well[1]."

It is only when the self thus conquers its lower tendencies and rises to a higher plane that it comes into touch with the higher self *(paramātman).* The higher self always remains as an ideal of elevation. The *yoga* activity of the self thus consists, on the one hand, in the efforts by which the *yogin* dissociates himself from the sense-attachments towards which he was naturally gravitating, and on the other hand, in the efforts by which he tries to elevate himself and to come into touch with the higher self. At the first stage a man performs his duties in accordance with the injunctions of the *śāstras*; then he performs his duties and tries to dissociate himself from all motives of self-interest and enjoyment, and at the next stage he succeeds in conquering these lower motives and is in touch with the higher self. Even at this stage he may still continue to perform his duties, merely for the sake of duty, or he may devote himself to meditative concentration and union with the higher self or with God. Thus the *Gītā* says that the person who has conquered himself and is at peace with himself is in touch with *paramātman.* Such a person is a true philosopher; for he not only knows the truths, but is happy in the inner realization and direct intuitive apperception of such truths; he is unshakable in himself; having conquered his senses, he attaches the same value to gold and to stones; he is the same to friends and to enemies, to the virtuous as to the sinful; he is in union (with *paramātman)* and is called a *yogin.*[2] The fact that the word *yogin* is derived here from the root

1 Śaṅkara's commentary, VI.5.

2 *Yukta ity ucyate yogī sama-loṣṭāśma-kāñcanaḥ,* VI.8. Śaṅkara, however, splits it up into two independent sentences, as follows: *Ya īdṛśo yuktaḥ samāhita iti sa ucyate kathyate; sa yogī sama-loṣṭāśma-kāñcanaḥ.* Śrīdhara, again, takes a quite different view and thinks it to be a definition of the *yogārūḍha* state and believes *yukta* to mean *yogārūḍha,* which in my opinion is unjustifiable. My interpretation is simpler and more direct than either of these and can be justified by a reference to the context in VI.7 and VI.10.

yuj, to join, is evident from a number of passages where the verb *yuj* is used in this connection.[1]

The *Gīṭā* advises a *yogin* who thus wants to unite himself with *paramātman*, or God, in a meditative union, to lead a lonely life, controlling his mind and body, desiring nothing and accepting nothing.[2] The *yogin* should seat himself on level ground, in a clean place, and, being firm on his threefold seat composed of *kuśa* grass, a leopard skin and soft linen, he should control his thoughts, senses and movements, make his mind one-pointed in God *(tatra),* gather himself up in union, and thus purify himself.[3] The *yogin* should eat neither too much nor too little, should neither sleep too much, nor dispense with sleep. He should thus lead the middle course of life and avoid extremes. This avoidance of extremes is very unlike the process of *yoga* advised by Patañjali. Patañ jali's course of *yoga* formulates a method by which *the yogin* can gradually habituate himself to a condition of life in which he can ultimately dispense with food and drink altogether and desist from all movements of body and mind. The object of a *yogin* in making his mind one-pointed is ultimately to destroy the mind. According to Patañjali the advancement of a *yogin* has but one object before it, viz. the cessation of all movements of mind *(citta-vṛtti-nirodha).* Since this absolute cessation cannot be effected without stopping all movements of the body, desires and passions are to be uprooted, not only because they would make the mind fly to different objects, but also because they would necessitate movements of the body, which would again disturb the mind. The *yogin* therefore has to practise a twofold control of movements of body and mind. He has

1 *Yogī yuñjīta satatatn ātmārtaṃ rahasi sthitaḥ.* Śaṅkara's commentary, VI.10.
Upaviśyāsane yuñjyād yogam ātma-viśuddhaye. VI.12.
Yukta āsīta mat-paraḥ. VI.14.
Yuñjann evaṃ sadātmānaṃ yogī niyata-mānasaḥ. VI.15, etc.

2 *Ekākī yata-cittātmā nirāśīr aparigrahaḥ.* VI.10. The word *ātmā* in *yata-cittātmā* is used in the sense of body *(deha),* according to Śaṅkara, Śrīdhara and others.

3 Both Śaṅkara and Śrīdhara make *tatra* an adjective to *āsane.* Such an adjective to *āsane* would not only be superfluous, but would also leave *ekāgram* without an object. The verb *yuñjyāt,* literally meaning "should link up," is interpreted by Śrīdhara as "should practise," apparently without any justification (VI.12).

to habituate himself to dispensing with the necessity of food and drink, to make himself used to all kinds of privations and climatic inconveniences of heat and cold and ultimately to prepare himself for the stoppage of all kinds of bodily movements. But, since this cannot be successfully done so long as one inhales and exhales, he has to practise *prāṇāyāma* for absolute breath-control, and not for hours or days, but for months and years. Moral elevation is regarded as indispensable in *yoga* only because without absolute and perfect cessation of all desires and passions the movements of the body and mind could not be absolutely stopped. The *yogin*, however, has not only to cut off all new' causes of disturbance leading to movements of body and mind, but also to practise one-pointedness of mind on subtler and subtler objects, so that as a result thereof the sub-conscious forces of the mind can also be destroyed. Thus, on the one hand, the mind should be made to starve by taking care that no new sense-data and no new percepts, concepts, thoughts, ideas or emotions be presented to it, and, on the other hand, steps are to be taken to make the mind one-pointed, by which all that it had apprehended before, which formed the great storehouse of the sub-conscious, is destroyed. The mind, thus pumped out on both sides, becomes absolutely empty and is destroyed. The ideal of Patañjali's Yoga is absolute extremism, consisting in absolute stoppage of all functions of body and mind.

The *Gītā,* on the other hand, prescribes the golden middle course of moderate food, drink, sleep, movements of the body and activity in general. The object of the *yogin* in the *Gītā* is not the absolute destruction of mind, but to bring the mind or the ordinary self into communion with the higher self or God. To the *yogin* who practises meditation the *Gītā* advises steadiness of posture; thus it says that the *yogin* should hold his body, head and shoulders straight, and, being unmoved and fixed in his posture, should avoid looking to either side and fix his eyes on the tip of his nose. The *Gītā* is, of course, aware of the process of breath-control and *prāṇāyāma*; but, curiously enough, it does not speak of it in its sixth chapter on *dhyāna-yoga*, where almost the whole chapter is devoted to *yoga* practice and the conduct of *yogins.* In the fifth chapter, V.27, it is said that all sense-movements and control of life-movements (*prāṇa-karmāṇi*) are like oblations to the fire of self-control. In the two obscure verses of the same chapter, V.29 and 30, it is said that there are some who offer an oblation of *prāṇa* to *apāna* and of *apāna* to *prāṇa* and thus, stopping the movement of inhalation and exhalation *(prāṇāpāna-gatī ruddhvā),* perform the *prāṇāyāma,* while there are others who, taking a low diet, offer an oblation of *prāṇa* to *prāṇa.* Such actions on the part of these people are described as being different kinds of sacrifices, or *yajña,* and the people who perform them are called *yajña-vidaḥ* (those who know the science of sacrifice), and not *yogin.* It is difficult to understand the exact meaning of offering an oblation of *prāṇa* to *prāṇa* or of *prāṇa* to *apāna* and of calling this sacrifice. The interpretations of Śaṅkara, Śrīdhara and others give us but little help in this matter. They do not tell us why it should be called a *yajña* or how an oblation of *prāṇa* to *prāṇa* can be made, and they do not even try to give a synonym for *juhvati* (offer oblation) used in this connection. It seems to me, however, that there is probably a reference to the mystical substitution-medita-tions *(pratīkopāsanā)* which were used as substitutes for sacrifices and are referred to in the Upaniṣads. Thus in the *Maitrī Upaniṣad*, VI.9, we find that Brahman is to be meditated upon as the ego, and in this connection, oblations of the five *vāyus* to fire with such *mantras* as *prāṇāya svāhā, apānāya svāhā*, etc. are recommended. It is easy to imagine that, in a later process of development, for the actual offering of oblations to fire was substituted a certain process of breath-control, which still retained the old phraseology of the offering of oblations in a sacrifice. If this interpretation is accepted, it will indicate how processes of breath-control became in many cases associated with substitution-meditations of the Vedic type.[1] The development of processes of breath-control in connection with substitution-meditations does not seem to be unnatural at all, and, as a matter of fact, the practice of *prāṇāyāma* in connection with such substitution-

1 See *Hindu Mysticism,* by S. N. Dasgupta, Chicago, 1927, pp. 18-20.

meditations is definitely indicated in *the Maitrī Upaniṣad,* VI.18. The movement of inhalation and exhalation was known to be the cause of all body-heat, including the heat of digestive processes, and Kṛṣṇa is supposed to say in the *Gītā,* XV.14, "As fire I remain in the body of living beings and in association with *prāṇa* and *apāna* I digest four kinds of food and drink." The author of the *Gītā,* however, seems to have been well aware that the *prāṇa* and *apāna* breaths passing through the nose could be properly balanced (*samau*), or that the *prāṇa vāyu* could be concentrated between the two eyebrows or in the head (*mūrdhni*).[1] It is difficult to say what is exactly meant by taking the *prāṇa* in the head or between the eyebrows. There seems to have been a belief in the *Atharva-śiras Upaniṣad* and also in the *Atharva-śikhā Upaniṣad* that the *prāṇa* could be driven upwards, or that such *prāṇa,* being in the head, could protect it.[2] Manu also speaks of the *prāṇas* of young men rushing upwards when old men approached them. But, whatever may be meant, it is certain that neither the balancing of *prāṇa* and *apāna* nor the concentrating of *prāṇa* in the head or between the eyebrows is a phrase of Patañjali, the Yoga writer.

In describing the course of a *yogin* in the sixth chapter the *Gītā* advises that the *yogin* should lead the austere life of a Brahmacārin, withdraw his mind from all mundane interests and think only of God, dedicate all his actions to Him and try to live in communion with Him (*yukta āsīta).* This gives to his soul peace, through which he loses his individuality in God and abides in Him

1 *prāṇāpānau samau hṛtvā nāsābhyantara-cāriṇau,* V.27. The phrase *samau kṛtvā* is left unexplained here by Śaṅkara. Śrīdhara explains it as "having suspended the movement of *prāṇa* and *apāna"—prāṇāpānāv ūrddhvādho-gati-fiirodhena samau kṛtvā kumbhakaṃ kṛtvā.* It is difficult, however, to say what is exactly meant by concentrating the *prāṇa vāyu* between the two eyebrows, *bhruvor madhye prāṇam āveśya samyak* (VIII.10). Neither Śaṅkara nor Śrīdhara gives us any assistance here. In *mūrdhny ādhāyātmanaḥ prāṇam āsthito yoga-dhāraṇām* (VIII.12) *mūrdhni* is paraphrased by Śrīdhara as *bhruvor madhye,* or "between the eyebrows."

2 *Atharva-śiras,* 4 and 6 and *Atharva-śikhā, 1.*

in the bliss of self-effacement.[1] *A yogin* can be said to be in union (with God) when he concentrates his mind on his own higher self and is absolutely unattached to all desires. By his efforts towards such a union *(yoga-sevayā)* he restrains his mind from all other objects and, perceiving his self in himself, remains in peace and contentment. At this higher state the *yogin* enjoys absolute bliss *(sukham ātyantikam)*, transcending all sense-pleasures by his pure reason, and, being thus fixed in God, he is never shaken away from Him. Such a *yogin* forsakes all his desires and controls all his senses by his mind, and, whenever the mind itself seeks to fly away to different objects, he tries to control it and fix it on his own self. Patiently holding his mind fixed in his self, he tries to desist from all kinds of thought and gradually habituates himself to shaking off attachments to sense-attractions. At this stage of union the *yogin* feels that he has attained his highest, and thus even the greatest mundane sorrows cannot affect him in the least. *Yoga* is thus sometimes defined as the negation of the possibility of all association with sorrows.[2] One can attain such a state only by

---

1 *śāntiṃ Nirvāṇa-paramāṃ mat-saṃsthām adhigacchati,* VI.15. The *Gītā* uses the words *śānti* and *Nirvāṇa* to indicate the bliss of the person who abides in God. Both these words, and particularly the word *Nirvāṇa,* have a definite significance in Buddhism. But the *Gītā* seems to be quite unacquainted with the Buddhistic sense of the word. I have therefore ventured to translate the word *Nirvāṇa* as "bliss of self-effacement." The word is primarily used in the sense of "extinguishing a light," and this directly leads to the Buddhistic sense of the absolute destruction of the *skandhas.* But the word *Nirvāṇa* is also used from very early times in the sense of "relief from sufferings" and "satisfaction." Thus the *Mahā-bhārata,* with which the *Gītā* is traditionally associated, uses it in this sense in III.10438:

स पीत्व शीतलं तोयम् पिपासार्त्तो महि पतिः।
निर्वाणम् अगमद् धीमान् सुसुखी चाभवत् तदा॥

sa pītvā śītalaṃ toyaṃ pipāsārtto mahī-patiḥ;
Nirvāṇam agamad dhīmān susukhī cābhavat tadā.

Again, in the *Mahā-bhārata,* XII.7150 and 13014, *Nirvāṇa* is described as being highest bliss *(paramaṃ sukham),* and it is also associated with *śānti,* or peace, as it is in the above passage—*śāntiṃ Nirvāṇa-paramāṃ.* In *Mahā-bhārata,* VI.1079, and in another place it is called a "state of the highest Brahman" *(paramaṃ brahma—Ibid.* XII.13239).

2 *taṃ vidyād duḥkha-saṃyoga-viyogaṃ yoga-saṃjñitam,* VI.23.

persistent and self-confident efforts and without being depressed by preliminary failures. When a *yogin* attains this union with himself or with God, he is like the motionless flame of a lamp in a still place, undisturbed by all attractions and unruffled by all passions.[1] The *yogin* who attains this highest state of union with himself or with God is said to be in touch with Brahman or to attain Brahmahood, and it is emphatically asserted that he is filled with ecstatic joy. Being in union with God, he perceives himself in all things, and all things in himself; for, being in union with God, he in one way identifies himself with God, and perceives God in all things and all things in God. Yet it is no mere abstract pantheism that is indicated here; for such a view is directly in opposition to the main tenets of the *Gītā*, so often repeated in diverse contexts. It is a mystical state, in which, on the one hand, *the yogin* finds himself identified with God and in communion with Him, and, on the other hand, does not cease to have relations with the beings of the world, to whom he gives the same consideration as to himself. He does not prefer his own happiness to the happiness of others, nor does he consider his own misery and suffering as greater or more important or more worthy of prevention than those of others. Being in communion with God, he still regards Him as the master whom he adores, as the supreme Lord who pervades all things and holds them in Himself. By his communion with God the *yogin* transcends his lower and smaller self and discovers his greater self in God, not only as the supreme ideal of his highest efforts, but also as the highest of all realities. As soon as the *yogin* can detach himself from his lower self of passions and desires, he uplifts himself to a higher universe, where the distinction of *meum* and *teum,* mine and thine, ceases and the interest of the individual loses its personal limitations and becomes enlarged and universalized and identified with the interests of all living beings. Looked at from this point of view, *yoga* is sometimes defined in the *Gītā* as the outlook of equality *(samatva).*[2]

1 *Yathā dīpo nivāta-stho neṅgate sopamā smṛtā,* VI.19.

2 *samatvaṃ yoga ucyate*, II.48.

In the *Gītā* the word *yoga* has not attained any definite technical sense, as it did in Patañjali's *Yoga-sūtra*, and, in consequence, there is not one definition of *yoga,* but many. Thus *yoga* is used in the sense of *karma-yoga,* or the duty of performance of actions, in V.I, and it is distinguished from the *sāṃkhya* path, or the path of knowledge, in II.39. The word *karma-yoga* is mentioned in III.3 as the path of the *yogins,* and it is referred to in III.7, V.2 and XIII.24. The word *buddhi-yoga* is also used at least three times, in II.49, X.10 and XVIII.57, and the *bhakti-yoga* also is used at least once, in XIV.26. The one meaning of *yoga* that suits all these different contexts seems to be "association." It has already been said that this primary meaning of the word is the central idea of *yoga* in the *Gītā.* One of the main teachings of the *Gītā* is that duties should be performed, and it is this obligatoriness of the performance of duties that in the *Gītā* is understood by *karma-yoga.* But, if such duties are performed from motives of self-interest or gain or pleasure, the performance could not lead to any higher end. It is advised, therefore, that they should be performed without any motive of gain or pleasure. So the proper way in which a man should perform his duties, and at the same time keep himself clean and untarnished by the good and bad results, the pleasures and sorrows, the praise and blame proceeding out of his own deeds, is to make himself detached from all desires for the fruits of actions. To keep oneself detached from the desires for the fruits of actions is therefore the real art (*kauśala*) of performing one's duties; for it is only in this way that a man can make himself fit for the higher union with God or his own higher self. Here, then, we have a definition of *yoga* as the art of performing one's duties (*yogaḥ karmasu kauśalam*— II.50). The art of performing one's duties, e.g. the art of keeping oneself unattached, cannot however be called *yoga* on its own account; it is probably so-called only because it is the indispensable step towards the attainment of the real *yoga*, or union with God. It is clear, therefore, that the word *yoga* has a gradual evolution to a higher and higher meaning, based no doubt on the primary root-meaning of "association."

It is important to note in this connection that the process of *prāṇāyāma*, regarded as indispensable in Patañjali's *Yoga*, is not considered so necessary either for *karma-yoga*, *buddhi-yoga*, or for the higher kind of *yoga*, e.g. communion with God. It has already been mentioned that the reference to *prāṇāyāma* is found only in connection with some kinds of substitution-meditations which have nothing to do with the main concept of *yoga* in the *Gītā*. The expression *samādhi* is used thrice in the noun form in the *Gītā*, in II.44, 53 and 54, and three times in the verb form, in VI.7, XII.9 and XVII.11; but the verb forms are not used in the technical sense of Patañjali, but in the simple root-meaning of *sam* + *ā* + √*dhā*, "to give" or "to place" (*arpaṇa* or *sthāpana)*. In two cases (II.44 and 53) where the word *samādhi* is used as a noun it has been interpreted by both Śaṅkara and Śrīdhara as meaning the object in which the mind is placed or to which it is directed for communion, viz. God.[1] The author of the *Gītā* is well aware of the moral conflict in man and thinks that it is only by our efforts to come into touch with our higher self that the littleness of passions and desires for fruits of actions and the preference of our smaller self-interests can be transcended. For, once man is in touch with his highest, he is in touch with God. He has then a broader and higher vision of man and his place in nature, and so he identifies himself with God and finds that he has no special interest of his own to serve. The low and the high, the sinful and the virtuous, are the same in his eyes; he perceives God in all things and all things in God, and it is this state of communion that is the real *yoga* of the *Gītā*; and it is because in this state all inequalities of race, creed, position, virtue and vice, high and low vanish, that this superior realization of universal equality is also called *yoga*. Not only is this union with God called *yoga*, but God Himself is called *Yogeśvara,* or the Lord of communion. As a result of this union, the *yogin* enjoys supreme

---

1 In II.44, however, Śaṅkara considers this object of mind to be *antahkaraṇa* or *buddhi.* But Śrīdhara considers this object to be God, and in II.53 Śaṅkara and Śrīdhara are unanimous that the object, or the support of the union or communion of the mind, is God.

bliss and ecstatic joy, and is free from the least touch of sorrow or pain; and this absolute freedom from pain or the state of bliss, being itself a result of *yoga*, is also called *yoga.* From the above survey it is clear that the *yoga* of the *Gītā* is quite different from the *yoga* of Patañjali, and it does not seem at all probable that the *Gītā* was aware of Patañjali's *yoga* or the technical terms used by him.[1]

The treatment of *yoga* in the *Gītā* is also entirely different from its treatment in almost all the Upaniṣads. The *Katha Upaniṣad* speaks of sense-control as being *yoga*; but sense-control in the *Gītā* is only a preliminary to *yoga* and not itself *yoga.* Most of the *yoga* processes described in the other Upaniṣads either speak of *yoga* with six accessories *(ṣaḍ-aṅga yoga)* or of *yoga* with eight accessories (*aṣṭāṅga-yoga*), more or less after the manner of Patañjali. They introduce elaborate details not only of breath-control or *prāṇāyāma*, but also of the nervous system of the body, *iḍā*, *piṅgalā* and *suṣumṇā*, the nerve plexus, *mūlādhāra* and other similar objects, after the manner of the later works on the *Ṣaṭ-cakra* system. Thus the *Amṛta-nāda* enumerates after the manner of Patañjali the six accessories of *yoga* as restraint (*pratyāhāra*), concentration *(dhyāna),* breath-control (*prāṇāyāma*), fixation *(dhā-raṇā*), reasoning *(tarka)* and meditative absorption *(samādhi),* and describes the final object of *yoga* as ultimate loneliness of the self *(kaivalya).* The *Amṛta-birtdu* believes in an all-pervading Brahman as the only reality, and thinks that, since mind is the cause of all bondage and liberation, the best course for a *yogin* to adopt is to deprive the mind of all its objects and thus to stop the activity of the mind, and thereby to destroy it, and bring about Brahma-hood. Brahman is described here as being absolutely indeterminate, uninferable, infinite and beginningless. The *Kṣurika* merely describes *prāṇāyāma, dhyāna, dhāraṇā* and *samādhi* in association with the nerves, *suṣumṇā, piṅgalā*, etc.

---

1 *paśya me yogam aiśvaram,* IX.5, *etārn vibhūtiṃ yogaṃ ca,* X.7. In the above two passages the word *yoga* seems to have a different meaning, as it is used there in the sense of miraculous powers; but even there the commentators Śaṅkara and Śrīdhara take it to mean "association" *(yukti)* and interpret *aiśvaraṃ yogaṃ* as "association of miraculous powers."

and the nerve plexuses. The *Tejo-bindu* is a Vedāntic Upaniṣad of the ultra-monistic type, and what it calls *yoga* is only the way of realizing the nature of Brahman as one and as pure consciousness and the falsity of everything else. It speaks of this *yoga* as being of fifteen accessories *(pañca-daśāṅga yoga)*. These are *yama* (sense-control through the knowledge that all is Brahman), *niyama* (repetition of the same kinds of thoughts and the avoidance of dissimilar ones), *tyāga* (giving up of the world-appearance through the realization of Brahman), silence, a solitary place, the proper posture, steadiness of mind, making the body straight and erect, perceiving the world as Brahman (*dṛk-sthiti*), cessation of all states and breath-control *(prāṇa-saṃyamana)*, perceiving all objects of the mind as Brahman *(pratyāhāra)*, fixing the mind always on Brahman *(dhāraṇā)*, self-meditation and the realization of oneself as Brahman. This is, however, a scheme of *yoga* quite different from that of Patañjali, as well as from that of the *Gītā*. The *Triśikha-brāhmaṇa* speaks of a *yoga* with eight accessories (*aṣṭāṅga-yoga*), where the eight accessories, though the same in name as the eight accessories of Patañjali, are in reality different therefrom. Thus *yama* here means want of attachment *(vairāgya)*, *niyama* means attachment to the ultimate reality *(anuraktiḥ pare tattve)*, *āsana* means indifference to all things, *prāṇa-saṃyamana* means the realization of the falsity of the world, *pratyāhāra* means the inwardness of the mind, *dhāraṇā* means the motionlessness of the mind, *dhyāna* means thinking of oneself as pure consciousness, and *samādhi* means forgetfulness of *dhyānas*. Yet it again includes within its *yama* and *niyama* almost all the virtues referred to by Patañjali. It also speaks of a number of postures after the *haṭha-yoga* fashion, and of the movement of *prāṇa* in the nerve plexuses, the ways of purifying the nerves and the processes of breath-control. The object of *yoga* is here also the destruction of mind and the attainment of *kaivalya*. The *Darśana* gives an *aṣṭāṅga-yoga* with *yama, niyama, āsana, prāṇāyāma, pratyāhāra, dhāraṇā, dhyāna* and *samādhi* more or less after the fashion of Patañjali, with a supplementary treatment of nerves *(nāḍī)* and the movement of the *prāṇa* and other *vāyus* in them. The final object of *yoga* here is the attainment of Brahmahood and the comprehension of the world as *māyā* and unreal. The *Dhyāna-bindu* describes the self as the essential link of all things, like the fragrance in flowers or the thread in a garland or the oil in sesamum. It describes a *ṣaḍ-aṅga yoga* with *āsana, prāṇa-saṃrodha, pratyāhāra, dhāraṇā, dhyāna* and *samādhi.* It also describes the four *cakras* or nerve plexuses, and speaks of the awakening of the serpent power *(kuṇḍalinī)* and the practice of the *mudrās.* It speaks further of the balancing or unifying of *prāṇa* and *apāna* as leading to *yoga.*[1] The object of this *yoga* is the attainment of the transcendent state of liberation or the realization of the *paramātman.* It is useless to refer to other Upaniṣads; for what has already been said will be enough to show clearly that the idea of *Yoga* in the *Gītā* is entirely different from that in the Yoga Upaniṣads, most of which are of comparatively late date and are presumably linked up with traditions different from that of the *Gītā.*

SĀṂKHYA AND YOGA IN THE GĪTĀ

In the *Gītā* Sāṃkhya and Yoga are sometimes distinguished from each other as two different paths, and sometimes they are identified. But though the *Gītā* is generally based on the doctrines of the *guṇas, prakṛti* and its derivatives, yet the word *sāṃkhya* is used here in the sense of the path of knowledge or of philosophic wisdom. Thus in the *Gītā,* II.39, the path of knowledge is distinguished from that of performance of duties. Lord Kṛṣṇa says there that he has just described the wisdom of Sāṃkhya and he is going to describe the wisdom of Yoga. This seems to give us a clue to what is meant by Sāṃkhya wisdom. This wisdom, however, seems to be nothing more than elaboration of the doctrine of the immortality of soul and the associated doctrine of rebirth, and also the doctrine that, howsoever the body might be affected and suffer

1 *Tadā prāṇāpānayor aikyaṃ kṛtvā*; see *Dhyāna-bindu,* 93-5 (Adyar Library edition, 1920). This seems to be similar to *prāṇāpānau samau kṛtvā* of the *Gītā.*

changes of birth, growth and destruction, the self is absolutely unaffected by all these changes; the self cannot be cut or burned; it is eternal, all-pervasive, unchangeable, indescribable and unthinkable. In another passage of the *Gītā*, XIII.25, it is said that there are others who perceive the self in accordance with *sāṃkhya-yoga*; and Śaṅkara explains this passage to mean that *sāṃkhya-yoga* means the realization of the self as being absolutely different from the three *guṇas*, *sattva*, *rajas* and *tamas*. If this is Sāṃkhya, the meaning of the word *yoga* in this passage (*anye sāṃkhyena yogena*) is not explained. Śaṅkara does not expound the meaning of the word *yoga*, but explains the word *sāṃkhya* and says that this *sāṃkhya* is *yoga*, which seems to be an evasion. Śrīdhara follows Śaṅkara's interpretation of *sāṃkhya*, but finds it difficult to swallow his identification of *sāṃkhya* with *yoga*, and he interprets *yoga* here as the *yoga* (of Patañjali) with eight accessories, but does not explain how this *aṣṭāṅga-yoga* can be identified with *sāṃkhya*. It is, no doubt, true that in the immediately preceding verse it is said that, howsoever a man may behave, if he knows the proper nature of *puruṣa* and of the *prakṛti* and the *guṇas*, he is never born again; but there is no reason to suppose that the phrase *sāṃkhyena yogena* refers to the wisdom recommended in the preceding verse; for this verse summarizes different paths of self-realization and says that there are some who perceive the self in the self through the self, by meditation, others by *sāṃkhya-yoga* and others by *karma-yoga*. In another passage it is said that the *Sāṃkhyas* follow the path of knowledge (*jñāna-yoga*), while the *Yogins* follow the path of duties (*Gītā*, III.3). If the word *yoga* means "association," as it does in various contexts, then *sāṃkhya* and *sāṃkhya-yoga* would mean more or less the same thing; for *sāṃkhya-yoga* would only mean association with *sāṃkhya*, and the phrase *sāṃkhyena yogena* might mean either association with *sāṃkhya* or the union of *sāṃkhya*. It has already been said that, following the indications of the *Gītā*, II.39, *sāṃkhya* should mean the realization of the true nature of the self as immortal, all-pervasive, unchangeable and infinite. It has also been pointed out that it is such a true realization of the self, with its corresponding moral elevation, that leads to the true communion of the self with the higher self or God. Thus this meaning of *sāṃkhya* on the one hand distinguishes the path of *sāṃkhya* from the path of *yoga* as a path of performance of duties, and at the same time identifies the path of *sāṃkhya* with the path of *yoga* as communion with God. Thus we find that the *Gītā*, V.4, 5, says that "fools only think Sāṃkhya and Yoga to be different, not so wise men," since, accepting either of them, one attains the fruit of them both. The goal reached by the followers of Sāṃkhya is also reached by the *Yogins*; he who perceives *Sāṃkhya* and *Yoga* to be the same perceives them in the right perspective. In these passages *sāṃkhya* and *yoga* seem from the context to refer respectively to *karma-sannyāsa* and *karma-yoga. Sāṃkhya* here can only in a secondary way mean the renunciation of the fruits of one's actions *(karma-sannyāsa).* The person who realizes the true nature of his self, and knows that the self is unchangeable and infinite, cannot feel himself attached to the fruits of his actions and cannot be affected by ordinary mundane desires and cravings. As in the case of the different uses of the word *yoga,* so here also the word *sāṃkhya,* which primarily means "true knowledge," is also used to mean "renunciation"; and since *karma-yoga* means the performance of one's duties in a spirit of renunciation, *sāṃkhya* and *yoga* mean practically the same thing and are therefore identified here; and they are both regarded as leading to the same results. This would be so, even if *yoga* were used to denote "communion"; for the idea of performance of one's duties has almost always communion with God as its indispensable correlate. Thus in the two passages immediately following the identification of *sāṃkhya* and *yoga* we find the *Gītā* (V.6, 7) saying that without *karma-yoga* it is hard to renounce *karma*; and the person who takes the path of *karma-yoga* speedily attains Brahman. The person who thus through *karma-yoga* comes into union (with Brahman) is pure in spirit and self-controlled, and, having identified himself with the universal spirit in all beings, he is not affected by his deeds.

One thing that emerges from the above discussion is that there is no proof that the word *sāṃkhya* in the *Gītā* means the discernment of the difference of *prakrti* and the *guṇas* from *puruṣa*, as Śaṅkara in one place suggests *(Gītā,* XIII.25), or that it refers to the cosmology and ontology of *prakṛti*, the *guṇas* and their evolutes of the traditional Kapila-Sāṃkhya. The philosophy of the *guṇas* and the doctrine of *puruṣa* were, no doubt, known to the *Gītā*; but nowhere is this philosophy called *sāṃkhya. Sāṃkhya* in the *Gītā* means true knowledge (*tattva-jñāna*) or self-knowledge *(ātma-bodha).* Śaṅkara, commenting on the *Gītā*, XVIII.13, interprets *sāṃkhya* to mean *vedānta*, though in verse XIII.25 he interprets the word as meaning the discernment of the difference between the *guṇas* and the *puruṣa,* which would decidedly identify the *sāṃkhya* of the *Gītā* with the Kapila-Sāṃkhya.

The *Mahā-bhārata* also refers to *sāṃkhya* and *yoga* in several places. But in almost all places *sāṃkhya* means either the traditional school of Kapila-Sāṃkhya or some other school of Sāṃkhya, more or less similar to it: *yoga* also most often refers either to the *yoga* of Patañjali or some earlier forms of it. In one place are found passages identifying *sāṃkhya* and *yoga*, which agree almost word for word with similar passages of the *Gītā.*[1] But it does not seem that the *sāṃkhya* or the *yoga* referred to in the *Mahā-bhārata* has anything to do with the idea of *Sāṃkhya* or *yoga* in the *Gītā.* As has already been pointed out, the *yoga* in the *Gītā* means the dedication to God and renunciation of the fruits of one's *karma* and being in communion with Him as the supreme Lord pervading the universe. The chapter of the *Mahābhārata* just referred to speaks of turning back the senses into the *manas* and of turning the *manas* into *ahaṃkāra* and *ahaṃkāra* into *buddhi* and *buddhi* into *prakṛti*, thus finishing with *prakṛti* and its evolutes and meditating upon pure *puruṣa.* It is clear that this system of *yoga* is definitely associated with the Kapila school of Sāṃkhya. In the *Mahā-bhārata*, xII. 306, the predominant feature of *yoga* is said to be *dhyāna*, and the latter

1 *yad eva yogāḥ paśyanti tat sāṃkhyair api dṛśyate ekaṃ sāṃkhyañ ca yogañ ca yah paśyati sa tattva-vit. Mahā-bhārata,* VII.316.4. Compare the *Gītā,* V.5.

is said to consist of concentration of mind *(ekāgratā ca manasaḥ)* and breath-control (*prāṇāyāma*). It is said that the *yogin* should stop the functions of his senses by his mind, and the movement of his mind by his reason *(buddhi),* and in this stage he is said to be linked up *(yukta)* and is like a motionless flame in a still place.[1] This passage naturally reminds one of the description of *dhyāna-yoga* in the *Gītā,* VI.11-13, 16-19 and 25,26; but the fundamental idea of *yoga,* as the dedication of the fruits of actions to God and communion with Him, is absent here.

It is needless to point out here that the *yoga* of the *Gītā* is in no way connected with the *yoga* of Buddhism. In Buddhism the sage first practises *śīla*, or sense-control and mind-control, and thus prepares himself for a course of stabilization or fixation of the mind (*samādhāna*, *upadhāraṇa, patitthā)*. This *samādhi* means the concentration of the mind on right endeavours and of its states upon one particular object (*ekārammana*), so that they may completely cease to shift and change *(sammā ca avikkhippamānā).* The sage has first to train his mind to view with disgust the appetitive desires for food and drink and their ultimate loathsome transformations as various nauseating bodily elements. When a man habituates himself to emphasizing the disgusting associations of food and drink, he ceases to have any attachment to them and simply takes them as an unavoidable evil, only awaiting the day when the final dissolution of all sorrows will come. Secondly, the sage has to habituate his mind to the idea that all his members are made up of the four elements, earth, water, fire and wind, like the carcass of a cow at the butcher's shop. Thirdly, he has to habituate his mind to thinking again and again (*anussati*) about the virtues or greatness of the Buddha, the Saṅgha, the gods and the law of the Buddha, about the good effects of *śīla* and the making of gifts (*cāgānussati*), about the nature of death (*maraṇānussati*) and about the deep nature and qualities of the final extinction of all phenomena (*upasamānussati*). He has also to pass through various purificatory processes. He has to go to the cremation grounds and notice the diverse horrifying changes of

1 Cf. the *Gītā,* VI.19, *yathā dīpo nivāta-sthaḥ,* etc.

human carcasses and think how nauseating, loathsome, unsightly and impure they are; from this he will turn his mind to living human bodies and convince himself that they, being in essence the same as dead carcasses, are as loathsome as the latter. He should think of the anatomical parts and constituents of the body as well as of their processes, and this will help him to enter into the first *jhāna*, or meditation, by leading his mind away from his body. As an aid to concentration the sage should sit in a quiet place and fix his mind on the inhaling (*passāsa*) and the exhaling *(assāsa)* of his breath, so that, instead of breathing in a more or less unconscious manner, he may be aware whether he is breathing quickly or slowly; he ought to mark this definitely by counting numbers, so that by fixing his mind on the numbers counted he may realize the whole process of inhalation and exhalation in all stages of its course. Next to this we come to *brahma-vihāra,* the fourfold meditation of *mettā* (universal friendship), *karuṇā* (universal pity), *muditā* (happiness in the prosperity and happiness of all) and *upekkhā* (indifference to any kind of preferment of oneself, one's friend, enemy or a third party). In order to habituate himself to meditation on universal friendship, a man should start with thinking how he would himself like to root out all misery and become happy, how he would himself like to avoid death and live cheerfully, and then pass over to the idea that other beings would also have the same desires. He should thus habituate himself to thinking that his friends, his enemies and all those with whom he is not connected might all live and become happy. He should fix himself to such an extent in this meditation that he should not find any difference between the happiness or safety of himself and that of others. Coming to *jhānas*, we find that the objects of concentration may be earth, water, fire, wind, colours, etc. In the first stage of concentration on an object there is comprehension of the name and form of the object; at the next stage the relational movement ceases, and the mind penetrates into the object without any quivering. In the next two stages there is a buoyant exaltation and a steady inward bliss, and, as a result of the one-pointedness which is the culminating effect of the progressive meditation, there is the final release of the mind *(ceto-vimutti)*—the *Nibbāna.*

It is easy to see that, though Patañjali's *yoga* is under a deep debt of obligation to this Buddhist *yoga*, the *yoga* of the *Gītā* is unacquainted therewith. The pessimism which fills the Buddhist *yoga* is seen to affect not only the outlook of Patañjali's *yoga*, but also most of the later Hindu modes of thought, in the form of the advisability of reflecting on the repulsive sides of things (*pratipakṣa-bhāvanā*) which are seemingly attractive.[1] The ideas of universal friendship, etc. were also taken over by Patañjali and later on passed into Hindu works. The methods of concentration on various ordinary objects also seem to be quite unlike what we find in the *Gītā.* The *Gītā* is devoid of any tinge of pessimism such as we find in the Buddhist *yoga.* It does not anywhere recommend the habit of brooding over the repulsive aspects of all things, so as to fill our minds with a feeling of disgust for all worldly things. It does not rise to the ideal of regarding all beings as friends or to that of universal compassion. Its sole aim is to teach the way of reaching the state of equanimity, in which the saint has no preferences, likes and dislikes—where the difference between the sinner and the virtuous, the self and the not-self has vanished. The idea of *yoga* as self-surrendering union with God and self-surrendering performance of one's duties is the special feature which is absent in Buddhism. This self-surrender in God, however, occurs in Patañjali's *yoga*, but it is hardly in keeping with the technical meaning of the word *yoga*, as the suspension of all mental states. The idea appears only once in Patañjali's *sūtras*, and the entire method of *yoga* practices, as described in the later chapters, seems to take no notice of it. It seems highly probable, therefore, that in Patañjali's *sūtras* the idea was borrowed from the *Gītā*, where this self-surrender to God and union with Him is defined as *yoga* and is the central idea which the *Gītā* is not tired of repeating again and again.

We have thus completely failed to trace the idea of the *Gītā* to any of the different sources where the subject of *yoga* is dealt with,

---

1 See *Nyāya-mañjarī*, *Vairāgya-śataka*, *Śānti-śataka.*

such as the Yoga Upaniṣads, Patañjali's *Yoga-sūtras*, Buddhist Yoga, or the *Mahā-bhārata.* It is only in the *Pañca-rātra* works that the *Gītā* meaning of *yoga* as self-surrender to God is found. Thus *Ahirbudhnya-saṃhitā* describes *yoga* as the worship of the heart (*hṛdayārādhana*), the offering of an oblation (*haviḥ*) of oneself to God or self-surrender to God *(bhagavate ātma-samarpaṇam),* and *yoga* is defined as the linking up *(saṃyoga)* of the lower self *(jīvātmari)* with the higher self *(paramātman).*[1] It seems, therefore, safe to suggest that the idea of *yoga* in the *Gītā* has the same traditional source as in the *Pañca-rātra* works.

SĀṂKHYA PHILOSOPHY IN THE GĪTĀ

It has been said before that there is no proof that the word *sāṃkhya* in the *Gītā* means the traditional Sāṃkhya philosophy; yet the old philosophy of *prakṛti* and *puruṣa* forms the basis of the philosophy of the *Gītā.* This philosophy may be summarized as follows:

Prakṛti is called *mahad brahma* (the great Brahma or the great multiplier as procreatress) in the *Gītā*, XIV.3.[2] It is said there that this *prakṛti* is described as being like the female part, which God changes with His energy for the creation of the universe. Wherever any living beings may be born, the great Brahman or *prakṛti* is to be considered as the female part and God as the father and fertilizer. Three types of qualities are supposed to be produced from *prakṛti* (*guṇāḥ prakṛti-sambhavāḥ*).[3] These are *sattva*, *rajas* and *tamas*, which bind the immortal self in its corporeal body. Of these, *sattva*, on account of its purity, is illuminating and untroubling (*anāmayam*, which Śrīdhara explains as *nirupadravam* or *śāntam),* and consequently, on account of these two qualities,

1 The *Ahirbudhnya-saṃhitā,* of course, introduces many observations about the nerves *(nāḍī)* and the *vāyus,* which probably became associated with the *Pañca-rātra* tradition in later times.

2 *mama yonir mahad brahma tasmin garbhaṃ dadhāmy aham.* XIV.3. I have interpreted *mahad brahma* as *prakṛti,* following Śrīdhara and other commentators. Śaṅkara surreptitiously introduces the w'ord *māyā* between *mama* and *yoni* and changes the whole meaning.

3 *Gītā*, XIV.5.

binds the self with the attachment for knowledge *(jñāna-saṅgena)* and the attachment for pleasure (*sukha-saṅgena*). It is said that there are no living beings on earth, or gods in the heavens, who are not pervaded by the three *guṇas* produced from the *prakṛti.*[1] Since the *guṇas* are produced from *the prakṛti* through the fertilization of God's energy in *prakṛti*, they may be said to be produced by God, though God always transcends them. The quality of *sattva*, as has been said above, associates the self with the attachments for pleasure and knowledge. The quality of *rajas* moves to action and arises from desire and attachment (*tṛṣṇā-saṅga-samudbhavam),* through which it binds the self with egoistic attachments for action. The quality of *tamas* overcomes the illumination of knowledge and leads to many errors. *Tamas,* being a product of ignorance, blinds all living beings and binds them down with carelessness, idleness and sleep. These three qualities predominate differently at different times. Thus, sometimes the quality of *sattva* predominates over *rajas* and *tamas*, and such a time is characterized by the rise of knowledge in the mind through all the different sense-gates; when *rajas* dominates *sattva* and *tamas*, the mind is characterized by greed, efforts and endeavours for different kinds of action and the rise of passions, emotions and desires; when *tamas* predominates over *sattva* and *rajas*, there is ignorance, lethargy, errors, delusions and false beliefs.

The different categories are *avyakta*, or the undifferentiated *prakṛti, buddhi* (intellect*), ahaṃkāra* (egohood), *manas* (mind-organ) and the ten senses, cognitive and conative. *Manas* is higher and subtler than the senses, and *buddhi* is higher than the *manas,* and there is that (probably self) which transcends *buddhi. Manas* is regarded as the superintendent of the different senses; it dominates them and through them enjoys the sense-objects. The relation between the *buddhi* and *ahaṃkāra* is nowhere definitely stated. In addition to these, there is the category of the five elements *(mahābhūta).*[2] It is difficult to say whether these categories

1 *Gītā,* XVIII.40.
2 *Ibid.* III.42, XIII.6 and 7, XV. 9.

were regarded in the *Gītā* as being the products of *prakṛti* or as separately existing categories. It is curious that they are nowhere mentioned in the *Gītā* as being products of *prakṛti*, which they are in Sāṃkhya, but on the other hand, the five elements, *manas, ahaṃkāra* and *buddhi* are regarded as being the eightfold nature *(prakṛti)* of God.[1] It is also said that God has two different kinds of nature, a lower and a higher; the eightfold nature just referred to represents the lower nature of God, whereas His higher nature consists of the collective universe of life and spirit.[2] The *guṇas* are noticed in relation to *prakṛti* in III.5, 27, 29, XII.21, XIV.5, xvIII.40, and in all these places the *guṇas* are described as being produced from *prakṛti,* though the categories are never said to be produced from *prakṛti.* In the *Gītā,* IX.10, however, it is said that *prakṛti* produces all that is moving and all that is static through the superintendence of God. The word *prakṛti* is used in at least two different senses, as a primary and ultimate category and as a nature of God's being. It is quite possible that the primary meaning of *prakṛti* in the *Gītā* is God's nature; the other meaning of *prakṛti,* as an ultimate principle from which the *guṇas* are produced, is simply the hypostatization of God's nature. The whole group consisting of pleasure, pain, aversion, volition, consciousness, the eleven senses, the mind-organ, the five elements, egohood, intellect *(buddhi),* the undifferentiated *(avyakta,* meaning *prakṛti* existing, probably, as the sub-conscious mind) power of holding the senses and the power of holding together the diverse mental functions *(saṃghāta)* with their modifications and changes, is called *kṣetra.* In another place the body alone is called *kṣetra.*[3] It seems, therefore, that the word *kṣetra* signifies in its broader sense not only the body, but also the entire mental plane, involving the diverse mental functions, powers, capabilities, and also the undifferentiated sub-conscious element. In this connection it may be pointed out that *kṣetra* is a term which is specially reserved to denote the complex of body and

1 *Gītā*, VII.4.
2 *Ibid.* VII.5.
3 *Ibid.* XIII.2.

mind, exclusive of the living principle of the self, which is called *kṣetra-jña,* or the knower of the *kṣetra,* or *kṣetrin,* the possessor of the *kṣetra* or the body-mind complex. It is said that, just as the sun illuminates this whole world, so does the *kṣetrin* illuminate the whole *kṣetra.*[1]

It will be remembered that it is said in the *Gītā* that God has two different natures, one the complex whole of the five elements, *ahaṃkāra, buddhi*, etc., and the other the collective whole of life and spirit (*jlva-bhūta*). It will also be remembered that, by the fertilization of God's power in *prakṛti,* the *guṇas*, or the characteristic qualities, which pervade all that is living, come into being. The *guṇas,* therefore, as diverse dynamic tendencies or characteristic qualities, pervade the entire psychosis-complex of *ahaṃkāra, buddhi,* the senses, consciousness, etc., which represents the mental side of the *kṣetra. Kṣetra-jña,* or the *kṣetrin,* is in all probability the same as *puruṣa,* an all-pervading principle as subtle as *ākāśa* (space), which, though it is omnipresent, remains untouched by any of the qualities of the body, in which it manifests itself. It is difficult to say what, according to the *Gītā, prakṛti* is in itself, before the fertilization of God's energy. It does not seem that *prakṛti* can be regarded as being identical with God. It appears more to be like an ultimate principle coexistent with God and intimately connected with Him. There is, however, no passage in the *Gītā* by which the lower *prakṛti* of God, consisting of the categories, etc., can be identified with *prakṛti*; for *prakṛti* is always associated with the *guṇas* and their production. Again, it is nowhere said in the *Gītā* that the categories *ahaṃkāra,* senses, etc., are in any way the products of the *guṇas;* the word *guṇa* seems to imply only the enjoyable, emotional and moral or immoral qualities. It is these *guṇas* which move us to all kinds of action, produce attachments and desires, make us enjoy or suffer, and associate us with virtues and vices. *Prakrti* is regarded as the mother-source from which all the knowable, enjoyable, and dynamic qualities of experience, referred to as being generated by the successive preponderance of

1 *Gītā.* XIII.34.

the *guṇas,* are produced. The categories of the psychosis and the five elements, which form the mental ground, do not, therefore, seem to be products of the *guṇas* or the *prakṛti*. They seem to constitute a group by themselves, which is referred to as being a lower nature of God, side by side with His higher nature as life and spirit. *Kṣetra* is a complex of both the *guṇa* elements of experience and the complex categories of body and mind. There seem, therefore, to be three different principles, the *aparā prakṛti* (the lower nature), *parā prakṛti* or *puruṣa*, and *prakṛti. Prakṛti* produces the *guṇas,* which constitute experience-stuff; the *aparā prakṛti* holds within itself the material world of the five elements and their modifications as our bodies, the senses and the mind-categories. It seems very probable, therefore, that a later development of Sāṃkhya combined these two *prakṛtis* as one, and held that the *guṇas* produced not only the stuff of our experience, but also all the mind-categories, the senses, etc., and the five gross elements and their modifications. The *guṇas,* therefore, are not the products of *prakṛti,* but they themselves constitute *prakṛti,* when in a state of equilibrium. In the *Gītā prakṛti* can only produce the *guṇas* through the fertilizing energy of God; they do not constitute the *prakṛti,* when in a state of equilibrium. It is hard to realize the connection between the *aparā prakṛti* and *the prakṛti and* the *guṇas*. The connection, however, can be imagined to take place through the medium of God, who is the fertilizer and upholder of them both. There seems to be but one *puruṣa,* as the all-pervading fundamental life-principle which animates all bodies and enjoys and suffers by its association with its experiences, remaining at the same time unaffected and untouched by the effects of the *guṇas*. This naturally presumes that there is also a higher and a lower *puruṣa,* of which the former is always unattached to and unaffected by the *guṇas,* whereas the lower *puruṣa,* which is different in different bodies, is always associated with the *prakṛti* and its *guṇas* and is continually affected by their operations. Thus it is said that the *puruṣa,* being in *prakṛti,* enjoys the *guṇas* of *prakṛti* and this is the cause of its rebirth in good or bad bodies.[1] There is

1 *Gītā*, XIII.21.

also in this body the higher *puruṣa (puruṣaḥ parah),* which is also called *paramātman,* being the passive perceiver, thinker, upholder, enjoyer and the great lord.[1] The word *puruṣa* is used in the *Gītā* in four distinct senses, firstly, in the sense of *puruṣottama,* or God;[2] secondly, in the sense of a person;[3] and the *Gītā* distinctly speaks of the two other *puruṣas* as *kṣara* (changeable) and *akṣara* (unchangeable). The *kṣara* is all living beings, whereas the *akṣara* is changeless. It is this higher self *(uttamaḥ puruṣaḥ*), different from the other *puruṣa* and called also *paramātman*, that pervades the three worlds and upholds them as their deathless God.[4] God, however, transcends both the *kṣara puruṣa* and the *akṣara puruṣa* and is therefore called *puruṣottama.*[5] Both *prakṛti* and the *paramātman puruṣa* are beginningless. The *paramātman puruṣa,* being changeless and beyond the sphere of the *guṇas*, is neither the agent of anything nor affected by the *guṇas,* though it resides in the body. *Prakṛti* is regarded as the ground through which all causes, effects, and their agents are determined. It is the fundamental principle of all dynamic operations, motivations and actions, whereas *puruṣa* is regarded as the principle which makes all experiences of joys and sorrows possible.[6] The *paramātman puruṣa,* therefore, though all-pervasive, yet exists in each individual, being untouched by its experiences of joy, sorrow and attachment, as its higher self. It is only the lower self that goes through the experiences and is always under the influence of the *guṇas*. Any attempts that may be made to rise above the sphere of the *guṇas,* above attachments and desires, above pleasures and pains, mean the subordination of the lower self

---

1 उपद्रष्टानुमन्ता च भर्ता भोक्ता महेश्वरः
परमात्मेति चाप्युक्ता देहेऽस्मिन् पुरुषः परः ॥
upadraṣṭānumantā ca bhartā bhoktā maheśvaraḥ
paramātmeti cāpy ukto dehe 'smin puruṣaḥ paraḥ.—Ibid. XIII.:43.

2 *sanātanas tvam puruṣo mato me. Gītā* xI.18.
tvam ādi-devaḥ puruṣaḥ purāṇaḥ. Ibid xI.38.
For puruṣottama see *Ibid.* VIII.1, X.15, XI.3, XV.18 and XV.19.

3 *Ibid.* II.15, II.21, II.60, III.4, etc

4 *Ibid.* xv.16 and 17.

5 *Ibid.* xv.15 and 18

6 *Ibid.* XIII.20.

to the pure and deathless higher self. Every attempt in this direction implies a temporary communion *(yoga)* with the higher self. It has already been pointed out that the *Gītā* recognizes a conflict between the higher and the lower selves and advises us to raise the lower self by the higher self. In all our moral efforts there is always an upward and a downward pull by the higher *puruṣa* on the one side, and the *guṇas* on the other; yet the higher *puruṣa* does not itself make the pulls. The energy of the downward pull is derived from the *guṇas* and exerted by the lower self. In all these efforts the higher self stands as the unperturbed ideal of equanimity, steadiness, unchangeableness in good or evil, joys or sorrows. The presence of this superior self is sometimes intuited by self-meditation, sometimes through philosophic knowledge, and sometimes by our moral efforts to perform our duties without attachment and without desires.[1] Each moral effort to perform our allotted duties without attachment means also a temporary communion (*yoga)* with the higher self or with God. A true philosophic knowledge, by which all actions are known to be due to the operations of the *prakṛti* and its *guṇas* and which realizes the unattached nature of the true self, the philosophic analysis of action and the relation between God, the higher self, the lower self, and the *prakṛti,* and any devotional realization of the nature of God and dedication of all action to Him, and the experience of the supreme bliss of living in communion with Him, mean a communion with the higher self or God, and are therefore *yoga.*

It is easy to notice here the beginnings of a system of thought which in the hands of other thinkers might well be developed into the traditional school of Sāṃkhya philosophy. It has already been pointed out that the two *prakṛtis* naturally suggested the idea of unifying them into the one *prakṛti* of the Sāṃkhya. The higher and the lower *puruṣas,* where the latter enjoys and suffers, while

---

1 ध्यानेनात्मनि ओअश्यन्ति केचिद् आत्मानम् आत्मनक़
अन्ये सांख्येन योगेन कर्मयोगेन चापरे
dhyānenātmani paśyanti kecid ātmānam ātmanā
anye sāṃkhyena yogena karma-yogena cāpare.—Gitā, XIII.25.

the former remains unchanged and unperturbed amidst all the experiences of joy and sorrow on the part of the latter, naturally remind one of the Upaniṣadic simile of the two birds in the same tree, of whom the one eats tasteful fruits while the other remains contented without them.[1] The *Gītā* does not seem to explain clearly the nature of the exact relation between the higher *puruṣa* and the lower *puruṣa.* It does not definitely state whether the lower *puruṣa* is one or many, or describe its exact ontological states. It is easy to see how any attempt that would aim at harmonizing these two apparently loosely-connected *puruṣas* into one self-consistent and intelligible concept might naturally end in the theory of infinite, pure, all-pervasive *puruṣas* and make the lower *puruṣa* the product of a false and illusory mutual reflection of *prakṛti* and *puruṣa.* The *Gītā* uses the word *māyā* in three passages (VII.14 and 15, XVII.61); but it seems to be used there in the sense of an inscrutable power or ignorance, and not in that of illusory or magical creation. The idea that the world or any of the mental or spiritual categories could be merely an illusory appearance seems never to have been contemplated in the *Gītā.* It is not, therefore, conceivable that the lower, or the *kṣara, puruṣa* might be mere illusory creation, accepted as a necessary postulate to explain the facts of our undeniable daily experience. But it is difficult to say how this *kṣetra-jña puruṣa* can have a separate existence from the *para puruṣa* (which is absolutely free from the *guṇas),* as enjoying the *guṇas* of *prakṛti*, unless the former be somehow regarded as the result of the functioning of the latter. Such a view would naturally support a theory that would regard the lower *puruṣa* as being only the *para puruṣa* as imaged or reflected in the *guṇas.* The *para puruṣa*, existing by itself, free from the influence of the *guṇas*, is in its purity. But even without losing its unattached character and its lonely purity it may somehow be imaged in the *guṇas* and play the part of the phenomenal self, the *jīva* or the lower *puruṣa*, enjoying the *guṇas* of *prakṛti* and having the superior *puruṣa* as its ultimate ground. It cannot be denied that the *Gītā* theory of *puruṣa* is much

1 *Muṇḍaka,*III.1.1 and *Śvetāśvatara,* 4.6.

looser than the later Sāṃkhya theory; but it has the advantage of being more elastic, as it serves better to explain the contact of the lower *puruṣa* with the higher and thereby charges the former with the spirit of a higher ideal.

The qualities of *sattva*, *rajas* and *tamas* were regarded as the universal characteristics of all kinds of mental tendencies, and all actions were held to be prompted by specific kinds of *sattva*, *rajas* or *tamas*. Mental tendencies were also designated accordingly as *sāttvika*, *rājasa* or *tāmasa*. Thus religious inclinations *(śraddhā)* are also described as being of a threefold nature. Those who are of *sāttvika* nature worship the gods, those who are of *rājasa* nature worship the *yakṣas* and the *rakṣas* and those who are of *tāmasa* nature worship ghosts and demons. Those who, prompted by vanity, desires and attachments, perform violent ascetic penances unauthorized by the scriptures and thereby starve and trouble their body and spirit, are really demoniac in their temperament. Again, *sāttvika* sacrifices are those performed solely out of reverence for the scriptural injunctions and from a pure sense of duty, without any desire or motive for any other kind of worldly or heavenly good. Again, *rājasa* sacrifices are those which are performed for the realization of some benefits or good results or for the satisfaction of some vanity or pride. *Tāmasa* sacrifices are those which are performed without proper faith, with improper ceremonials, transgressing Vedic injunctions. Again, *tapas* also is described as being threefold, as of body *(śārīra)*, of speech *(vāñmaya)* and of mind (*mānasa*). Adoration of gods, Brahmins, teachers and wise men, sincerity and purity, sex-continence and non-injury are known as physical or bodily *tapas*. To speak in a manner that would be truthful, attractive, and conducive to good and would not be harmful in any way, and to study in the regular and proper way are regarded as the *tapas* of speech *(vāñ-maya tapas)*. Mental *(mānasa) tapas* consists of sincerity of mind, friendliness of spirit, thoughtfulness and mental control, self-control and purity of mind. The above threefold *tapas* performed without any attachment for a reward is called *sāttvika tapas*. But *tapas* performed out of vanity, or for the sake of higher position, respectability in society, or appreciation from people, is called *rājasa*—such a *tapas* can lead only to unsteady and transient results. Again, the *tapas* which is performed for the destruction of others by ignorant self-mortification is called *tāmasa tapas*. Gifts, again, are called *sāttvika* when they are made to proper persons (holy Brahmins) on auspicious occasions, and in holy places, merely out of sense of duty. Gifts are called *rājasa* when they are made as a return for the good done to the performer, for gaining future rewards, or made unwillingly. Again, gifts are called *tāmasa* when they are made slightingly, to improper persons, in unholy places, and in ordinary places. Those who desire liberation perform sacrifices and *tapas* and make gifts without aiming at the attainment of any mundane or heavenly benefits. Knowledge also is regarded as *sāttvika*, *rājasa* and *tāmasa*. *Sāttvika* wisdom consists in looking for unity and diversity and in realizing one unchangeable reality in the apparent diversity of living beings. *Rājasa* knowledge consists in the scientific apprehension of things or living beings as diverse in kind, character and number. *Tāmasa* knowledge consists in narrow and untrue beliefs which are satisfied to consider a little thing as the whole and entire truth through sheer dogmatism, and unreasonable delusion or attachment. An action is called *sāttvika* when it is performed without any desire for a reward, without attachment and without aversion. It is called *rājasa* when it is performed with elaborate endeavours and efforts, out of pride and vanity, for the satisfaction of one's desires. It is called *tāmasa* when it is undertaken out of ignorance and without proper judgment of one's own capacities, and when it leads to waste of energy, harm and injury. An agent *(kartṛ)* is called *sāttvika* when he is free from attachment and vanity and absolutely unruffled in success and failure, persevering and energetic. Again, an agent is called *rājasa* if he acts out of motives of self-interest, is impure, is filled with sorrow or joy in failure or success, and injures others. An agent is called *tāmasa* if he is careless, haughty, thoughtless, deceptive, arrogant, idle, procrastinating and melancholic. Understanding *(buddhi)* is said to be *sāttvika* when it grasps how a man has to set himself in the path of virtue, how to refrain from vice, what ought and what ought not to be done, of what one has to be afraid and how to be fearless, what is bondage, and what is liberation. *Rājasa* understanding is that by which one wrongly grasps the nature of virtue and vice, and of right and wrong conduct. *Tāmasa* understanding is that which takes vice as virtue and out of ignorance perceives all things wrongly. That mental hold *(dhṛti)* is called *sāttvika* which by unfailing communion holds together the sense-functions and biomotor and mind activities. That happiness which in the beginning appears to be painful, but which is in the end as sweet as nectar, and which is the direct result of gaiety of mind, is called *sāttvika sukha*. The happiness arising out of sense-object contact, which in the beginning is as attractive as nectar, but in the end is as painful as poison, is *rājasa*. That happiness which arises out of sleep, idleness and errors, and blinds one in the beginning and in the end, is called *tāmasa*. So also the food which increases life, facilitates mind-function, increases powers of enjoyment, makes one healthy and strong, and is sweet, resistible and delightful is liked by the *sāttvika* people. That food is liked by *rājasa* people which is hot, sour, salt, dry and causes pain and brings on diseases. The food which is impure, tasteless, old and rotten is liked by *tāmasa* people. All this goes to show that the *guṇas*, *sattva*, *rajas* and *tamas*, are determinants of the tendencies of, or rather the stuff of, the moral and immoral, pleasurable and painful planes or characteristics of our experience. *Sattva* represents the moral and supermoral planes, *rajas* the ordinary mixed and normal plane, and *tamas* the inferior and immoral characteristics of our experience.

AVYAKTA AND BRAHMAN

The word *avyakta* is primarily used in the *Gītā* in the sense of "the unmanifested." Etymologically the word consists of two parts, the negative particle *a* meaning "negation," and *vyakta* meaning "manifested," "differentiated" or "revealed." In this sense the word is used as an adjective. There is another use of the word in the neuter gender (*avyaktam*), in the sense of a category. As an illustration of the first sense, one may refer to the *Gītā,* II.25 or VIII.21. Thus in II.25 the self is described as the unmanifested; unthinkable and unchangeable. In the Upaniṣads, however, it is very unusual to characterize the self as *avyakta* or unmanifested; for the self there is pure consciousness and self-manifested. In all later Vedāntic works the self is described as *anubhūti-svabhāva,* or as being always immediately intuited. But in the *Gītā* the most prominent characteristic of the self is that it is changeless and deathless; next to this, it is unmanifested and unthinkable. But it does not seem that the *Gītā* describes the self as pure consciousness. Not only does it characterize the self as *avyakta* or unmanifested, but it does not seem anywhere to refer to it as a self-conscious principle. The word *cetanā*, which probably means consciousness, is described in the *Gītā* as being a part of the changeable *kṣetra*, and not the *kṣetra-jña.*[1] It may naturally be asked how, if the self was not a conscious principle, could it be described as *kṣetra-jña* (that which knows the *kṣetra*)? But it may well be replied that the self here is called *kṣetra-jña* only in relation to its *kṣetra*, and the implication would be that the self becomes a conscious principle not by virtue of its own inherent principle of consciousness, but by virtue of the principle of consciousness reflected or offered to it by the complex entity of the *kṣetra.* The *kṣetra* contains within it the conscious principle known as *cetanā*, and it is by virtue of its association with the self that the self appears as *kṣetra-jña* or the knower.

It may not be out of place here to mention that the term *kṣetra* is never found in the Upaniṣads in the technical sense in which it is used in the *Gītā.* The term *kṣetra-jña*, however, appears in *Śvetāśvatara,* VI.16 and *Maitrāyaṇa,* II.5 in the sense of *puruṣa,* as in the *Gītā.* The term *kṣetra,* however, as used in the *Gītā,* has more or less the same sense that it has in Caraka's account of Sāṃkhya in the *Caraka-saṃhitā,* III.1.61-63. In Caraka, however, *avyakta* is excluded from the complex constituent *kṣetra,* though in the *Gītā* it is included within the constituents of *kṣetra.* Caraka again considers

1 *Gītā*, XIII.7.

avyakta (by which term he means both the Sāṃkhya *prakṛti* and the *puruṣa*) as *kṣetra-jña,* whereas the *Gītā* takes only the *puruṣa* as *kṣetra-jña.* The *puruṣa* of the *Gītā* is further characterized as the life-principle (*jīva-bhūta,* VII.5 and XV.7) by which the whole world is upheld. The *Gītā* does not, however, describe in what particular way the life-principle upholds the world. In Caraka's account also the *ātman* is referred to as the life-principle, and it is held there that it is the principle which holds together the *buddhi*, the senses, the mind and the objects—it is also the principle for which good, bad, pleasure, pain, bondage, liberation, and in fact the whole world-process happens. In the *Caraka-saṃhitā puruṣa* is regarded as *cetanā-dhātu*, or the upholder of consciousness; yet it is not regarded as conscious by itself. Consciousness only comes to it as a result of the joint operation of *manas*, the senses, the objects, etc. In the *Gītā puruṣa* is not regarded as the *cetanā-dhātu*, but *cetanā* or consciousness is regarded as being a constituent of the *kṣetra* over which the *puruṣa* presides. Thus knowledge can accrue to *puruṣa* as *kṣetra-jña*, only in association with its *ksetra.* It may well be supposed that *puruṣa* as *kṣetra-jña* and as a life-principle upholds the constituents of the *kṣetra*, and it is probable that the *puruṣa's* position as a cognizer or knower depends upon this intimate association between itself and the *kṣetra.*

Another relevant point is suggested along with the considerations of the nature of the *puruṣa* as the cognizer, namely, the consideration of the nature of *puruṣa* as an agent (*kartṛ*). It will be pointed out in another section that the fruition of actions is rendered possible by the combined operations of *adhiṣṭhāna*, *kartṛ*, *kāraṇa*, *ceṣṭā* and *daiva*, and this doctrine has been regarded as being a Sāṃkhya doctrine, though it has been interpreted by Śaṅkara as being a Vedāntic view. But both Sāṃkhya and the Vedānta theories are explicitly of the *sat-kārya-vāda* type. According to the *sat-kārya-vāda* of the traditional Sāṃkhya philosophy the fruition of actions is the natural result of a course of unfolding evolution, consisting in the actualization of what was already potentially present. On the Vedāntic *sat-kārya-vāda* view all operations are but mere appearances, and the cause alone is true. Neither of these doctrines would seem to approve of a theory of causation which would imply that anything could be the result of the joint operation of a number of factors. That which is not cannot be produced by the joint operation of a collocation of causes. It may be remembered, however, that the *Gītā* explicitly formulates the basic principle of *sat-kārya-vāda*, that what exists cannot be destroyed and that what does not exist cannot ctime into being. This principle was applied for proving the deathless character of the self. It is bound to strike anyone as very surprising that the *Gītā* should accept the *sat-kārya-vāda* doctrine in establishing the immortality of the self and should assume the *a-sat-kārya-vāda* doctrine regarding the production of action. It is curious, however, to note that a similar view regarding the production of action is to be found in Caraka's account of Sāṃkhya, where it is said that all actions are produced as a result of a collocation of causes—that actions are the results of the collocation of other entities w'ith the agent *(kartṛ)*.[1]

The word *avyakta* is also used in the sense of "unknowability" or "disappearance" in the *Gītā*, II.28, where it is said that the beginnings of all beings are invisible and unknown; it is only in the middle that they are known, and in death also they disappear and become unknown. But the word *avyakta* in the neuter gender means a category which is a part of God Himself and from which all the manifested manifold world has come into being. This *avyakta* is also referred to as a *prakṛti* or nature of God, which, under His superintendence, produces the moving and the unmoved—the entire universe.[2] But God Himself is sometimes referred to as being *avyakta* (probably because He cannot be grasped by any of our senses), as an existence superior to the *avyakta*, which is described as a part of His nature, and as a category from which all things have come into being.[3] This *avyakta* which is identical with God is also

1 *Caraka-saṃhitā,* IV.I.54.

2 *Gītā,* IV.10, *mayādhyakṣeṇa prakṛtiḥ sūyate sacarācaram.*

3 *Ibid.* VIII.20 and VIII.21; also IX.4, where it is said, "All the world is pervaded over by me in my form as *avyakta;* all things and all living beings are in me, but I am not exhausted in them."

called *akṣara*, or the immortal, and is regarded as the last resort of all beings who attain their highest and most perfect realization. Thus there is a superior *avyakta*, which represents the highest essence of God, and an inferior *avyakta,* from which the world is produced. Side by side with these two *avyaktas* there is also the *prakṛti,* which is sometimes described as a coexistent principle and as the *māyā* or the blinding power of God, from which *the guṇas* are produced.

The word "Brahman" is used in at least two or three different senses. Thus in one sense it means *prakṛti,* from which the *guṇas* are produced. In another sense it is used as an essential nature of God. In another sense it means the Vedas. Thus in the *Gītā*, III.15, it is said that the sacrificial duties are derived from Brahman (Vedas). Brahman is derived from the eternal; therefore the omnipresent Brahman is always established in the sacrifices.[1] The idea here is that, since the Vedas have sprung from the eternal Brahman, its eternal and omnipresent character is transmitted to the sacrifices also. The word "omnipresent" (*sarva-gata*) is probably used in reference to the sacrifices on account of the diverse and manifold ways in which the sacrifices are supposed to benefit those who perform them. In the *Gītā,* IV.32, also the word "Brahman" in *Brahmaṇo rnukhe* is used to denote the Vedas. But in IV.24 and 25, where it is said that all sacrifices are to be made with the Brahman as the object and that the sacrificial materials, sacrificial fire, etc. are to be looked upon as being Brahman, the word "Brahman" is in all probability used in the sense of God.[2] In v.6, 10, 19 also the word "Brahman" is used in the sense of God or Īśvara; and in most of the other cases the word is used in the sense of God. But according to the *Gītā* the personal God as Īśvara is the supreme principle, and Brahman, in the sense of a qualityless, undifferentiated ultimate principle as taught in the Upaniṣads, is a principle which, though

1 *Gītā,* III.15.

2 Śrīdhara, in interpreting this verse (IV.24), explains it by saying, *tad evam parameśvarārādhana-lakṣaṇaṃ kar,na jñāna-hetutvena bandhakatvābhāvād akar-maiva.*

great in itself and representing the ultimate essence of God, is nevertheless upheld by the personal God or Īśvara. Thus, though in VIII.3 and X.12 Brahman is referred to as the differenceless ultimate principle, yet in XIV.27 it is said that God is the support of even this ultimate principle, Brahman. In many places we also hear of the attainment of Brahmahood (*brahma-bhūta*, V.24, VI.27, XVIII.54, or *brahma-bhūya,* XIV. 26), and also of the attainment of the ultimate bliss of Brahman *(Brahma-Nirvāṇa,* II.72, V.24, 25, 26). The word *brahma-bhūta* does not in the *Gītā* mean the differenceless merging into oneness, as in the Vedānta of Śaṅkara. It is wrong to think that the term "Brahman" is always used in the same sense in which Śaṅkara used it. The word "Brahman" is used in the sense of an ultimate differenceless principle in the Upaniṣads, and the Upaniṣads were apprized by all systems of Hindu thought as the repository of all sacred knowledge. Most systems regarded the attainment of a changeless eternal state as the final goal of realization. As an illustration, I may refer to the account of Sāṃkhya given by Caraka, in which it is said that, when a man gives up all attachment and mental and physical actions, all feelings and knowledge ultimately and absolutely cease. At this stage he is reduced to Brahmahood *(brahma-bhūta),* and the self is no longer manifested. It is a stage which is beyond all existence and which has no connotation, characteristic or mark.[1] This state is almost like a state of annihilation, and yet it is described as a state of Brahmahood. The word "Brahman" was appropriated from the Upaniṣads and was used to denote an ultimate superior state of realization, the exact nature of which differed with the different systems. In the *Gītā* also we find the word "Brahman" signifying a high state of self-realization in which, through a complete detachment from all passions, a man is self-contented within himself and his mind is in a perfect state of equilibrium. In the *Gītā,* V.19, Brahman is defined as the faultless state of equilibrium

1 निःसृतः सर्वभवेभ्यश् चिह्नं यस्य न विद्यते॥
nihsṛtaḥ sarva-bhavebhyaś cihnaṃ yasya na vidyate.—Caraka-saṃhitā, IV.1.153.

(nirdoṣaṃ hi samaṃ brahma), and in all the verses of that context the sage who is in a state of equanimity and equilibrium through detachment and passionlessness is said to be by virtue thereof in Brahman; for Brahman means a state of equanimity. In the *Gītā,* XIII.13, Brahman is described as the ultimate object of knowledge, which is beginningless, and cannot be said to be either existent or non-existent *(na sat tan nāsad ucyate).* It is said that this Brahman has His hands and feet, eyes, head, mouth and ears everywhere in the world, and that He envelopes all. He is without senses, but He illuminates all sense-qualities; Himself unattached and the upholder of all, beyond the *guṇas,* He is also the enjoyer of the *guṇas.* He is both inside and outside of all living beings, of all that is moving and that is unmoved. He is both near and far, but unknowable on account of His subtle nature. Being one in many, yet appearing as many, the upholder of all living beings, the devourer and overpowerer of all, He is the light of all light, beyond all darkness, He is both knowledge and the object of knowledge, residing in the heart of all. It is easy to see that the whole concept of Brahman, as herein stated, is directly borrowed from the Upaniṣads. Towards the end of this chapter it is said that he who perceives the many living beings as being in one, and realizes everything as an emanation or elaboration from that, becomes Brahman. But in the next chapter Kṛṣṇa as God says, "I am the upholder of the immortal and imperishable Brahman of absolute bliss and of the eternal *dharma.*" In the *Gītā,* XIV.26, it is said that "he who worships me unflinchingly through devotion, transcends all *guṇas* and becomes Brahman." It has just been remarked that the *Gītā* recognizes two different kinds of *avyaktas.* It is the lower *avyakta* nature of God which has manifested itself as the universe; but there is a higher *avyakta,* which is beyond it as the eternal and unchangeable basis of all. It seems very probable, therefore, that Brahman is identical with this higher *avyakta.* But, though this higher *avyakta* is regarded as the highest essence of God, yet, together with the lower *avyakta* and the selves, it is upheld in the super-personality of God.

The question whether the *Gītā* is a Sāṃkhya or a Vedānta work, or originally a Sāṃkhya work which was later on revised, changed, or enlarged from a Vedānta point of view, need not be elaborately discussed here. For, if the interpretation of the *Gītā*, as given herein, be accepted, then it will be evident that the *Gītā* is neither a Sāṃkhya work nor a Vedānta work. It has been pointed out that the word *Sāṃkhya*, in the *Gītā*, does not mean the traditional Sāṃkhya philosophy, as found in Īśvarakṛṣṇa's *Kārikā.* But there are, no doubt, here the scattered elements of an older philosophy, from which not only the Sāṃkhya of Īśvarakṛṣṇa or the *Saṣṭi-tantra* (of which Īśvarakṛṣṇa's work was a summary) developed, but even its earlier version, as found in Caraka's account, could be considered to have developed. There is no doubt that the *Gītā's* account of Sāṃkhya differs materially from the Sāṃkhya of the *Saṣṭi-tantra* or of Īśvarakṛṣṇa, from the Sāṃkhya of Caraka, from the Sāṃkhya of Pañcaśikha in the *Mahā-bhārata* and from the Sāṃkhya of Patañjali and the *Vyāsa-bhāṣya.* Ordinarily the Sāṃkhya of Patañjali is described as a theistic Sāṃkhya *(seśvara-sāṃkhya)*; but the īśvara of Patañjali is but loosely attached to the system of Sāṃkhya thought as expounded in Yoga. The īśvara there appears only as a supernormal, perfect being, who by his permanent will removes the barriers in the path of the evolution of *prakṛti* in accordance with the law of *karma.* He thus merely helps the fulfilment of the teleology of the blind *prakṛti.* But in the *Gītā* both the *puruṣas* and the root of the cosmic nature are but parts of God, the super-person *(puruṣottama*). The *prakṛti,* from which *the guṇas* which have only subjectivistic characteristics are derived, is described as the *māyā* power of God, or like a consort to Him, who, being fertilized by His energies, produces the *guṇas.* The difference of the philosophy of the *Gītā* from the various schools of Sāṃkhya is very evident. Instead of the one *prakṛti* of Sāṃkhya we have here the three *prakṛtis* of God. The *guṇas* here are subjectivistic or psychical, and not cosmical. It is because the *Gītā* admits a *prakṛti* which produces the subjectivistic *guṇas* by which the *puruṣas* are bound with ties of attachment to their experiences, that such a *prakṛti* could fitly be described as *guṇamayī māyā (māyā* consisting of *guṇas).* The *puruṣas*, again, though they are many, are on the whole but emanations from a specific *prakṛti* (divine nature) of God. The *puruṣas* are not stated in the *Gītā* to be of the nature of pure intelligence, as in the Sāṃkhya; but the cognizing element of consciousness *(cetanā)* is derived from another *prakṛti* of God, which is associated with *the puruṣa.* It has also been pointed out that the *Gītā* admits the *sat-kārya-vāda* doctrine with reference to immortality of the self, but not with reference to the fruition of actions or the rise of consciousness. The Sāṃkhya category of *tan-mātra* is missing in the *Gītā*, and the general teleology of the *prakṛti* of the Sāṃkhya is replaced by the super-person of God, who by his will gives a unity and a purpose to all the different elements that are upheld within Him. Both the Sāṃkhya of Kapila and that of Patañjali aim at securing, either through knowledge or through Yoga practices, the final loneliness of the translucent *puruṣas.* The *Gītā*, however, is anxious to secure the saintly equanimity and a perfect, unperturbed nature by the practice of detachment of the mind from passions and desires. When such a saintly equanimity and self-contentedness is achieved, the sage is said to be in a state of liberation from the bondage of guṇa-attachments, or to be in a state of Brahmahood in God. The philosophy of the *Gītā* thus differs materially from the traditional Sāṃkhya philosophy on almost every point. On some minor points (e.g. the absence of *tan-mātras*, the nature of the production of knowledge and action, etc.) the *Gītā* philosophy has some similarities with the account of the Sāṃkhya given in the *Caraka-saṃhitā,* IV.I, as already described in the first volume of this work.[1]

The question whether the *Gītā* was written under a Vedāntic influence cannot be answered, unless one understands what is exactly meant by this Vedāntic influence; if by Vedāntic influence one means the influence of the Upaniṣads, then the *Gītā* must plainly be admitted to have borrowed very freely from the Upaniṣads, which from the earliest times had been revered for their wisdom.

1 *A History of Indian Philosophy*, vol. 1, 1922, pp. 213-222.

If, however, by Vedāntic influence one means the philosophy of Vedānta as taught by Śaṅkara and his followers, then it must be said that the *Gītā* philosophy is largely different therefrom. It has already been pointed out that, though Brahman is often described in Upaniṣadic language as the highest essence of God, it is in reality a part of the super-personality of God. The *Gītā*, moreover, does not assert anywhere that Brahman is the only reality and all else that appears is false and unreal. The word *māyā* is, no doubt, used in the *Gītā* in three passages; but its meaning is not what Śaṅkara ascribes to it in his famous interpretation of Vedāntic thought. Thus in the *Gītā*, VII.14, *māyā* is described as being of the nature of *guṇas*, and it is said that he who clings to God escapes the grip of the *māyā* or of the *guṇas*. In the *Gītā*, VII.15, the word *māyā* is also probably used in the same sense, since it is said that it is ignorant and sinful men who, through demoniac ideas, lose their right wisdom under the influence of *māyā* and do not cling to God. In all probability, here also *māyā* means the influence of *rajas* and *tamas*; for it has been repeatedly said in the *Gītā* that demoniac tendencies are generated under the preponderating influence of *rajas* and *tamas*. In the *Gītā*, XVIII.61, it is said that God resides in the heart of all living beings and moves them by *māyā*, like dolls on a machine. It has been pointfed out that the psychical tendencies and moral or immoral propensities which move all men to action are produced under the influence of the *guṇas*, and that God is the ultimate generator of the *guṇas* from the *prakṛti*. The *māyā*, therefore, may well be taken here to mean *guṇas*, as in the *Gītā*, VII.14. Śrīdhara takes it to mean the power of God. The *guṇas* are, no doubt, in a remote sense, powers of God. But Śaṅkara's paraphrasing of it as deception (*chadmanā*) is quite inappropriate. Thus it is evident that the *Gītā* does not know the view that the world may be regarded as a manifestation of *māyā* or illusion. It has also been pointed out that the word "Brahman" is used in the *Gītā* in the sense of the Vedas, of faultless equanimity, of supreme essence and of *prakrti*, which shows that it had no such crystallized technical sense as in the philosophy of Śaṅkara. The word had in the *Gītā* all the looseness of Upaniṣadic usage. In the *Gītā* the word *avidyā,* so famous in Śaṅkara's philosophy of the Vedānta, is nowhere used. The word *ajñāna* is used several times (V.15, 16; X.11; XIII.11; XIV.8, 16, 17; XVI.4); but it has no special technical sense in any of these passages. It has the sense of "ignorance" or "misconception," which is produced by *tamas (ajñānam tamasaḥ phalam,* XIV.16) and which in its turn produces *tamas (tamas tv ajñāna-jaṃ viddhi*, XIV.8).

CONCEPTION OF SACRIFICIAL DUTIES IN THE GĪTĀ

The Vedic view of the obligatoriness of certain kinds of sacrifices or substitution-meditations permeated almost all forms of Hindu thought, excepting the Vedānta philosophy as interpreted by Śaṅkara. The conception of the obligatoriness of duties finds its best expression in the analysis of *vidhi* in the Mīmāṃsā philosophy. *Vidhi* means the injunctions of the Vedas, such as, "Thou should'st perform such and such sacrifices"; sometimes these are conditional, such as, "Those who wish to attain Heaven should perform such and such sacrifices"; sometimes they are unconditional, such as, "Thou should'st say the three prayers." The force of this *vidhi,* or injunction, is differently interpreted in the different schools of Mīmāṃsā. Kumārila, the celebrated commentator, in interpreting Jaimini's definition of *dharma,* or virtue, as a desirable end *{artha)* or good which is enjoined by the Vedic commands *(codanā-lakṣaṇo' rtho dharmaḥ, Mīmāṃsā-sūtra,* I.1), says that it is the performance of the Vedic injunctions, sacrifices, etc. *(yāgādiḥ)* that should be called our duty. The definition of virtue, then, involves the notion that only such a desired end (on account of the pain associated with it not exceeding the associated pleasure) as is enjoined by Vedic commands is called *dhartna.* The sacrifices enjoined by the Vedas are called *dharma,* because these would in future produce pleasurable experiences. So one's abstention from actions prohibited by Vedic commands is also called *dharma,* as by this means one can avoid the undesirable effects and sufferings of punishments as a result of transgressing those commands. Such sacrifices, however, are ultimately regarded as *artha,* or desired ends, because they produce pleasurable experiences. The imperative of Vedic commands is supposed to operate in a twofold manner, firstly, as initiating a volitional tendency in obedience to the verbal command *(śābdī bhāvanā),* and, secondly, in releasing the will to the actual performance of the act enjoined by the command *(ōrthī bhāvanā).* The propulsion of verbal commands is not like any physical propulsion; such a propulsion only arises as a result of one's comprehension of the fact that the performance of the acts enjoined will lead to beneficial results, and it naturally moves one to perform those acts out of self-interest.[1] So of the twofold propulsion *(bhāvanā)* implied in a Vedic imperative the propulsion to act, as communicated by the verbal command, is called *śābdī bhāvanā*; and this is followed by the actual efforts of the person for the performance of the act.[2] The prescriptive of the command *(vidhi)* is comprehended directly from the imperative suffix *(lin)* of the verb, even before the meaning of the verb is realized. If this is so, it is contended that the imperative, as it is communicated by the command, is a pure contentless form of command. This contention is admitted by the Bhaṭṭa School, which thinks that, though in the first stage we have communication of the contentless pure form of the imperative, yet at the successive stages the contentless form of duty is naturally supplemented by a more direct reference to the concrete context, as denoted by the verb with which the suffix is associated. So the process of the propulsion of *bhāvanā*, though it starts at the first instance with the communication of a pure contentless

1 *adṛṣṭe tu viṣaye śreyaḥ-sādhanādhigamaḥ śabdaika-nibandhana iti tad-adhi-gamopāyaḥ śabda eva pravartakah; ata eva śabdo 'pi na svarūpa-mātreṇa pra-vartako vāyv-ādi-tulyatva-prasaṅgāt;...arthapratītim upajanayataḥ śab-dasya pra-vartakatvam. Nyāya-mañjarī,* p. 342. The Vizianagram Śanskrit Series, Benares, 1895.

2 *Liṅ-ādeḥ śabdasya na pratīti-janana-mātre vyāparaḥ kintu puruṣa-pravṛttav api; sa cāyam liṅ-ādi-vyāpāraḥ śabda-bhāvanā-nāmadheyo vidhir ity ucyate sa eva ca pravartakah...yo bhavana-kriyā-kartṛ-viṣayaḥ prayojaka-vyāpāraḥ pu-ruṣa-stho yatra bhavana-kriyāyāḥ kartā svargādikarmatāṃ āpadyate so 'rtha-bhāvanā-śab-dena ucyate.—Ibid.* p. 343.

form, passes, by reason of its own necessity and the incapacity of a contentless form of duty to stand by itself, gradually through more and more concrete stages to the actual comprehension of the duty implied by the concrete meaning of the associated verb.[1] So the communication of the contentless duty and its association with the concrete verbal meaning are not two different meanings, but are rather the prolongation of one process of communication, just as cooking includes all the different associated acts of putting the pan on the fire, lighting the fire, and the like.[2] These two *bhāvanās*, therefore, mean nothing more than the reasoning of the will and its translation into definite channels of activity, as the performance of the sacrifice, etc., and *vidhi* here means simply the prompting or the propulsion (*vyāpāraḥ preraṇā-rūpaḥ*); and it is such prompting that initiates in the performer the will, which is later on translated into concrete action.

Another Mīmāṃsā view objects to this theory of dual *bhāvanā* and asserts that the suffix *liṅ* involves the notion of an order to work *(preraṇa)*, as if the relation of the Vedas to us were one of master and servant, and that the Vedic *vidhi* as expressed in the *liṅ* suffix conveys thc command *(praiṣya-praiṣayoḥ sambandhaḥ)*. The *vidhi* goads us to work, and, being goaded by it, we turn to work. It does not physically compel us to act; but the feeling we have from it

---

1 यद्य् अप्य् अंशैर् असंपृष्तां विधिः स्पृशति भावनाम्
तथाप्य् अशक्तितो नासौ तन्मात्रे पर्यवस्यति
अनुष्ठेये हि विष्ये विधिः पुंसां प्रवर्तकः
अंशत्रयेन चापूर्णां नानुतिष्ठति भावनाम्
तस्मात् प्रक्रान्तरूपोऽपि विधिस् तावत् प्रतीक्षते
यावद् योज्ञत्वम् आपन्ना भावनाऽन्यानपेक्षिणी ॥
Yady apy aṃśair asaṃspṛṣṭāṃ vidhiḥ spṛśati bhāvanām
tathāpy aśaktito nāsau tan-mātre paryavasyati
anuṣṭheye hi viṣaye vidhiḥ puṃsāṃ pravartakah
aṃśa-trayena cāpūrṇāṃ nānutiṣṭhati bhāvanām
tasmāt prakrānta-rūpo 'pi vidhis tāvat praṅkṣate
yāvad yogyatvam āpannā bhāvanā 'nyānapekṣiṇī.—Ibid. p. 344.

2 *Yathā hi sthāly-adhiśrayaṇāt prabhṛtyā nirākāṅkṣaudana-niṣpatter ekaiveyaṃ pāka-kriyā salilāvaseka-taṇḍulāvapana-darvī-vighaṭṭanāsrāvaṇādy-aneka-kṣaṇa-samudāya-svabhāvā tathā prathama-pada-jñānāt prabhṛti ānirākāñṣa-vākyārtha-paricchedād ekaiveyaṃ śābdī pramitiḥ.—Nyāya-mañjarī*, p. 345.

that we have been ordered to act constitutes the driving power. The knowledge of *vidhi* thus drives us to our Vedic duties. When a man hears the command, he feels that he has been commanded and then he sets to work. This setting to work is quite a different operation from the relation of the command and the commanded, and comes after it. The essence of a Vedic sentence is this command or *niyoga.* A man who has formerly tasted the benefits of certain things or the pleasures they produced naturally intends to have them again; here also there is a peculiar mental experience of eagerness, desire or intention *(ākūta),* which goads him on to obey the Vedic commands. This *akūta* is a purely subjective experience and cannot, therefore, be experienced by others, though one can always infer its existence from the very fact that, unless it were felt in the mind, no one would feel himself goaded to work.[1] *Niyoga,* or a prompting to work *(preraṇa),* is the sense of all *vidhis,* and this rouses in us the intention of working in accordance with the command. The actual performance of an action is a mere counterpart of the intention *(ākūta),* that is subjectively felt as roused by the *niyoga* or the driving power of the *vidhi.* This view differs from the view of Kumārila in this, that it does not suppose that the propulsion of the Vedic command takes effect in a twofold *bhāvanā*, through the whole process of the conception and the materialization of the action in accordance with the Vedic commands. The force of the command is exhausted in prompting us to action and arousing in us the inward resolution *(ākūta)* to obey the command. The actual performance of the action comes as a natural consequence *(artha).* The force of the *vidhi* has a field of application only when our ordinary inclinations do not naturally lead us to the performance of action. *Vidhi*, therefore, operates merely as a law of command which has to be obeyed for the sake of the law alone, and it is this psychological factor of inward resolution to obey the law that leads to the performance of action.

---

1 *Ayam api bhautika-vyāpāra-hetur ātmākūta-viśeṣo na pramāṇāntara-vedyo bhavati na ca na vedyate tat-saṃvedane sati ceṣṭā yadvantaṃ dṛṣṭvā tasyāpi tādṛk-preraṇā'vagamo 'numīyate.—Nyāya-mañjarī.* p. 348.

Maṇḍana, in his *Vidhi-viveka,* discusses the diverse views on the significance of *vidhi.* He interprets *vidhi* as a specific kind of prompting *(pravartanā*). He distinguishes the inner volitional intention of attaining an end and its translation into active effort leading to muscular movements of the body. *Pravartanā* here means the inner volitional direction of the mind towards the performance of the action, as well as actual nervous changes which are associated with it.[1] The command of the Vedas naturally brings with it a sense of duty or of "oughtness" (*kartavyatā*), and it is this sense of *kartavyatā* that impels people to action without any reference to the advantages and benefits that may be reaped by such actions. The psychological state associated with such a feeling of "oughtness" is said to be of the nature of instincts *(pratibhā).* It is through an instinctive stimulus to work, proceeding from the sense of "oughtness," that the action is performed.

The Nyāya doctrine differs from the above view of *vidhi* as a categorically imperative order and holds that the prompting of the Vedic commands derives its force from our desire for the attainment of the benefits that we might reap if we acted in accordance with them. So the ultimate motive of the action is the attainment of pleasure or the avoidance of pain, and it is only with a view to attaining the desired ends that one is prompted to follow the Vedic commands and perform the sacrifices. In this view, therefore, the prompting, or *preraṇā,* has not in it that self-evident call of the pure imperative or the rousing of the volitional tendency through the influence of the imperative; the prompting felt is due only to the rise of desires for the end.

Most of the above interpretations of *vidhi* are of much later date than the *Gītā.* No systematic discussion of the nature of *vidhi* which can be regarded as contemporaneous with or prior to the date

---

1 *Bhāva-dharma eva kaścit samīhita-sādhanānuguṇo vyāpāra-padōrthaḥ; tad yathā ātmano buddhy-ādi-janana-pravṛttasya manaḥ-saṃyoga evā'yaṃ bhāva-dharmaḥ tadvad atrāpi spandas tad-itaro vā bhāva-dharmaḥ pravṛtti-jananā'-nukiīlatayā vyāpāra-viśeṣaḥ pravartanā.* Vācaspati's *Nyāya-kaṇikā* on *Vidhi-viveka,* pp. 243, 244.

of the *Gītā* is now available. But even these latter-day explanations are useful in understanding the significance of the force of the notion of the imperative in the *Gītā*. It is clear from the above discussion that the notion of the imperative of *vidhi* cannot be called moral in our sense of the term, as has been done in a recent work on Hindu Ethics.[1] For the imperative of *vidhi* is limited to the injunctions of the Vedas, which are by no means coextensive with our general notion of morality. According to the Mīmāṃsā schools just described virtue (*dharma*) consists in obedience to Vedic injunctions. Whatever may be enjoined by the Vedas is to be considered as virtue, whatever is prohibited by the Vedas is evil and sin, and all other things which are neither enjoined by the Vedas nor prohibited by them are neutral, i.e. neither virtuous nor vicious.[2] The term *dharma* is therefore limited to actions enjoined by the Vedas, even though such actions may in some cases be associated with evil consequences leading to punishments due to the transgression of some other Vedic commands. The categorical imperative here implied is scriptural and therefore wholly external. The virtuous character of actions does not depend on their intrinsic nature, but on the external qualification of being enjoined by the Vedas. Whatever is not enjoined in the Vedas or not prohibited in them is simply neutral. It is clear, therefore, that the term *dharma* can be translated as "virtue" only in a technical sense, and the

---

1 S.K. Maitra's *Hindu Ethics,* written under Dr Seal's close personal supervision and guidance.

2 Kumārila holds that even those sacrifices which are performed for the killing of one's enemies are right, because they are also enjoined by the Vedas. Prabhākara, however, contends that, since these are performed only out of the natural evil propensities of men, their performance cannot be regarded as being due to a sense of duty associated with obedience to the injunctions of the Vedas. Kumārila thus contends that, though the Śyena sacrifice is attended with evil consequences, yet, since the performer is only concerned with his duty in connection with the Vedic commands, he is not concerned with the evil consequences; and it is on account of one's obedience to the Vedic injunctions that it is called right, though the injury to living beings that it may involve will bring about its punishment all the same. Sāṃkhya and some Nyāya writers, however, would condemn the Śyena sacrifice on account of the injury to living beings that it involves.

words "moral" and "immoral" in our sense have nothing to do with the concept of *dharma* or *adharma.*

The *Gītā* distinguishes between two kinds of motives for the performance of sacrifices. The first motive is that of greed and self-interest, and the second is a sense of duty. The *Gītā* is aware of that kind of motive for the performance which corresponds to the Nyāya interpretation of Vedic *vidhis* and also to the general Mīmāṃsā interpretation of *vidhi* as engendering a sense of duty. Thus it denounces those fools who follow the Vedic doctrines and do not believe in anything else; they are full of desires and eager to attain Heaven, they take to those actions which lead to rebirth and the enjoyment of mundane pleasures. People who are thus filled with greed and desires, and perform sacrifices for the attainment of earthly goods, move in an inferior plane and are not qualified for the higher scheme of life of devotion to God with right resolution.[1] The Vedas are said to be under the influence of mundane hankerings and desires, and it is through passions and antipathies, through desires and aversions, that people perform the Vedic sacrifices and think that there is nothing greater than these. One should therefore transcend the sphere of Vedic sacrifices performed out of motives of self-interest. But the *Gītā* is not against the performance of Vedic sacrifices, if inspired by a sheer regard for the duty of performing sacrifices. Anyone who looks to his own personal gain and advantages in performing the sacrifices, and is only eager to attain his pleasurable ends, is an inferior type of man; the sacrifices should therefore be performed without any personal attachment, out of regard for the sacred duty of the performance.

1 *Vyavasāyātmikā buddhiḥ samādhau na vidhīyate. Gītā,* II.44. The word *samādhau* is explained by Śrīdhara as follows:*samādhiś cittaikāgryaṃ, para-meivarābhx-mukhatvam iti yāvat;tasmin niścayātmikā buddhis tu na vidhīyate. Samādhi* is thus used here to mean one-pointedness of mind to God. But Śaṅkara gives a very curious interpretation of the word *samādhi,* as meaning mind (*antaḥkaraṇa* or *buddhi*), which is hardly justifiable. Thus he says,*samā-dhīyate 'smin puruṣ-opabhogāya sarvam iti samādhir antaḥkaraṇaṃ buddhiḥ.* The word *vyavasāyāt-mikā* is interpreted by commentators on II.41and II.44 as meaning *niścayātmikā* (involving correct decision through proper *pramāṇas* or proof). I prefer, however, to take the word to mean "right resolution."

Prajāpati created sacrifices along with the creation of men and said, "The sacrifices will be for your good—you should help the gods by your sacrifices, and the gods will in their turn help you to grow and prosper. He who lives for himself without offering oblations to the gods and supporting them thereby is misappropriating the share that belongs to the gods."

This view of the *Gītā* is different from that of the later Mīmāṃsā, which probably had a much earlier tradition. Thus Kumārila held that the final justification of Vedic sacrifices or of *dharma* was that it satisfied our needs and produced happiness—it was *artha*. The sacrifices were, no doubt, performed out of regard for the law of Vedic commands; but that represented only the psychological side of the question. The external ground for the performance of Vedic sacrifices was that it produced happiness for the performer and satisfied his desires by securing for him the objects of desire. It was in dependence on such a view that the Nyāya sought to settle the motive of all Vedic sacrifices. The Naiyāyikas believed that the Vedic observances not only secured for us all desired objects, but that this was also the motive for which the sacrifices were performed. The *Gītā* was well aware of this view, which it denounces. The *Gītā* admitted that the sacrifices produced the good of the world, but its whole outlook was different; for the *Gītā* looked upon the sacrifices as being bonds of union between gods and men. The sacrifices improved the mutual good-will, and it was by the sacrifices that the gods were helped, and they in their turn helped men, and so both men and the gods prospered. Through sacrifices there was rain, and by rain the food-grains grew' and men lived on the food-grains. So the sacrifices were looked upon as being sources not so much of individual good as of public good. He who looks to the sacrifices as leading to the satisfaction of his selfish interests is surely an inferior person. But those who do not perform the sacrifices are equally wicked. The Vedas have sprung forth from the deathless eternal, and sacrifices spring from the Vedas, and it is thus that the deathless, all-pervading

Brahman is established in the sacrifices.[1] The implied belief of the *Gītā* was that the prosperity of the people depended on the fertility of the soil, and that this again depended upon the falling of rains, and that the rains depended on the grace of gods, and that the gods could live prosperously only if the sacrifices were performed; the sacrifices were derived from the Vedas, the Vedas from the all-pervading Brahman, and the Brahman again forms the main content of the Vedas. Thus there was a complete cycle from Brahman to sacrifices, from sacrifices to the good of the gods and from the good of the gods to the good and prosperity of the people. Everyone is bound to continue the process of this cycle, and he who breaks it is a sinful and selfish man, who is not worth the life he leads.[2] Thus the ideal of the *Gītā* is to be distinguished from the ideal of the Mīmāṃsā in this, that, while the latter aimed at individual good, the former aimed at common good, and, while the latter conceived the Vedic commands to be the motives of their action, the former valued the ideal of performing the sacrifices in obedience to the law of continuing the process of the cycle of sacrifices, by which the world of gods and of men was maintained in its proper state of prosperity. When a man works for the sacrifices, such works cannot bind him to their fruits; it is only when works are performed from motives of self-interest that they can bind people to their good and bad fruits.[3]

The word *dharma* in the *Gītā* does not mean what Jaimini understood by the term, viz. a desirable end or good enjoined by the sacrifices (*codanā-lokṣano 'rtho dharmaḥ).* The word seems to be used in the *Gītā* primarily in the sense of an unalterable customary order of class-duties or caste-duties and the general approved course of conduct for the people, and also in the sense of prescribed schemes of conduct. This meaning of *dharma* as "old customary order" is probably the oldest meaning of the word, as it is also found

1 *Gītā*, III.15.
2 *Ibid*, III.16.
3 *Ibid*. III.9.

in the *Atharva-Veda*, 18.3.1 (*dharmaṃ purā-ṇam anupālayanti).*[1] Macdonell, in referring to *Maitrāyaṇa,* IV.1 9, *Kāthaka,* XXXI.7 and *Taittirīya,* III.2.8.11, points out that bodily defects (bad nails and discoloured teeth) and marrying a younger daughter while her elder sister is unmarried are coupled with murder, though not treated as equal to it, and that there is no distinction in principle between real crimes and what are now regarded as fanciful bodily defects or infringements of merely conventional practices. In the *Śatapatha-brāhmaṇa*, XIV.4.2.26, also we find *dharma* for a Kṣattriya[2] is illustrated as being the characteristic duties of a Kṣattriya. The central meaning of the word *dharma* in the *Gītā* is therefore the oldest Vedic meaning of the word, which is a much earlier meaning than the latter-day technical meaning of the word as it is found in Mīmāṃsā. *Dharma* does not in the *Gītā* mean sacrifices *(yajña)* or external advantages, as it does in Mīmāṃsā, but the order of conventional practices involving specific caste-divisions and caste-duties. Accordingly, the performance of sacrifices is *dharma* for those whose allotted duties are sacrifices. Adultery is in the Vedas a vice, as being transgression of *dharma*, and this is also referred to as such *(dharme naṣṭe,* I.39) in the *Gītā.* In the *Gītā*, II.7, Arjuna is said to be puzzled and confused regarding his duty as a Kṣattriya and the sinful course of injuring the lives of his relations *(dharma-saṃmūḍha-cetāḥ).* The confusion of *dharma* and *adharma* is also referred to in XVIII.31 and 32. In the *Gītā*, IV.7 and 8, the word *dharma* is used in the sense of the established order of things and conventionally accepted customs and practices. In II.40 the way of performing one's duties without regard to pleasures or sorrows is described as a particular and specific kind of *dharma (asya dharmasya),* distinguished from *dharma* in general.

The *yajña* (sacrifice) is said to be of various kinds, e.g. that in which oblations are offered to the gods is called *daiva-yajña*; this is

---

1 *dharma, dharman* are the regular words, the latter in the *Ṛg-Veda* and both later, for "law" or "custom." See Macdonell's *Vedic Index,* p. 390.

2 *tad etat kṣattrasya ksattraṃ yad dharmaḥ tasmād dharmāt paraṃ nāsti.* Dr Albrecht Weber's edition, Leipzig, 1924.

distinguished from *brahma-yajña,* in which one dedicates oneself to Brahman, where Brahman is the offerer, offering and the fire of oblations, and in which, by dedicating oneself to Brahman, one is lost in Brahman.[1] Then sense-control, again, is described as a kind of *yajña*, and it is said that in the fire of the senses the sense-objects are offered as libations and the senses themselves are offered as libations in the fire of sense-control; all the sense-functions and vital functions are also offered as libations in the fire of sense-control lighted up by reason. Five kinds of sacrifices *(yajña)* are distinguished, viz. the *yajña* with actual materials of libation, called *dravya-yajña*, the *yajña* of asceticism or self-control, called *tapo-yajña,* the *yajña* of union or communion, called *yoga-yajña,* the *yajña* of scriptural studies, called *svādhyāya-yajña,* and *the yajña* of knowledge or wisdom, called *jñāna-yajña.*[2] It is easy to see that the extension of the application of the term *yajña* from the actual material sacrifice to other widely divergent methods of self-advancement is a natural result of the extension of the concept of sacrifice to whatever tended towards self-advancement. The term *yajña* had high and holy associations, and the newly discovered systems of religious endeavours and endeavours for self-advancement came to be regarded as but a new kind of *yajña*, just as the substitution-meditations *(pratikopāsanā*) were also regarded as being but new forms of *yajña.* Thus, while thought advanced and newer modes of self-realization began to develop, the older term of *yajña* came to be extended to these new types of religious discipline on account of the high veneration in which the older institution was held.

But, whatever may be the different senses in which the term *yajña* is used in the *Gītā,* the word *dharma* has not here the technical sense of the Mīmāṃsā. The *Gītā* recommends the performance of sacrifices to the Brahmins and fighting to the Kṣattriyas, and thus aims at continuity of conventional practices which it regards as *dharma.* But at the same time it denounces the performance of

1 *Gītā,* IV.24 and 25.

2 *Ibid.* IV.26-28; see also 29 and 30.

actions from desire, or passions or any kind of selfish interest. A man should regard his customary duties as his *dharma* and should perform them without any idea of the fulfilment of any of his own desires. When a man performs *karma* from a sense of disinterested duty, his *karma* is no longer a bondage to him. The *Gītā* does not, on the one hand, follow the old *korma-* ideal, that one should perform sacrifices in order to secure earthly and heavenly advantages, nor does it follow, on the other hand, the ideal of the Vedānta or of other systems of philosophy that require us to abandon our desires and control our passions with a view to cleansing the mind entirely of impurities, so as to transcend the sphere of duties and realize the wisdom of the oneness of the spirit. The *Gītā* holds that a man should attain the true wisdom, purge his mind of all its desires, but at the same time perform his customary duties and be faithful to his own *dharma.* There should be no impelling force other than regard and reverence for his own inner law of duty with reference to his own *dharma* of conventional and customary practices or the duties prescribed by the *śāstra.*

SENSE-CONTROL IN THE GĪTĀ

The uncontrollability of the senses was realized in the *Kafha Upaniṣad*, where the senses are compared with horses. The *Gītā* says that, when the mind is led on by fleeting sense-attractions, the man loses all his wisdom, just as a boat swings to and fro in deep waters in a strong gale. Even in the case of the wise man, in spite of his efforts to keep himself steady, the troubled senses might lead the mind astray. By continually brooding over sense-objects one becomes attached to them; out of such attachments there arise desires, out of desires there arises anger, out of anger blindness of passions, through such blindness there is lapse of memory, by such lapse of memory a man's intelligence is destroyed, and as a result of that he himself is destroyed.[1] Man is naturally inclined towards the path of evil, and in spite of his efforts to restrain himself he

1 *Gītā,* II.60, 62, 63.

tends towards the downward path. Each particular sense has its own specific attachments and antipathies, and attachment *(rāga)* and antipathy are the two enemies. The *Gītā* again and again proclaims the evil effects of desires and attachments *(kāma),* anger *(krodha)* and greed *(lobha)* as the three gates of Hell, being that which veils wisdom as smoke veils fire, as impurities sully a mirror or as the foetus is covered by the womb.[1] Arjuna is made to refer to Kṛṣṇa the difficulty of controlling the senses. Thus he says, "My mind, O Kṛṣṇa, is violent, troubled and changeful; it is as difficult to control it as it is to control the winds."[2] True *yoga* can never be attained unless and until the senses are controlled.

The Pāli work *Dhamma-pada* is also filled with similar ideas regarding the control of attachments and anger. Thus it says, "He has abused me, beaten me, worsted me, robbed me—those who dwell not upon such thoughts are freed from hate. Never does hatred cease by hating, but hatred ceases by love; this is the ancient law.... As the wind brings down a weak tree, so Māra overwhelms him who lives looking for pleasures, has his senses uncontrolled, or is immoderate in his food, slothful and effeminate....As rain breaks through an ill-thatched house, so passion will break through an undisciplined mind."[3] Again, speaking of mind, it says, "As an arrow-maker levels his arrow, so a wise man levels his trembling, unsteady mind, which it is difficult to guard and hold back....Let the wise man guard his mind, incomprehensible, subtle, and capricious though it is. Blessed is the guarded mind."[4] Again, "Not nakedness, nor matted hair, not dirt, nor fastings, not lying on earth, nor ashes, nor ascetic postures, none of these things purify a man who is not free from desires."[5] Again, "From attachment *(piyato)* comes grief, from attachment comes fear; he who is free from attachment knows neither grief nor fear. From affection *(pemato)* come grief and fear.

---

1 *Gītā.* III.34, 37-39; XVI.21.
2 VI.34.
3 *Dhamma-pada* (Poona, 1923), I.4, 5, 7, 13.
4 *Ibid.* III.36, 38.
5 *Ibid.* X.141.

He who is free from affection knows neither grief nor fear. From lust *(rati)* come grief and fear. He who is free from affection knows neither grief nor fear. From lust *(kāma)* come grief and fear. He who is free from lust knows neither grief nor fear. From desire *(taṇhā)* come grief and fear. He who is free from desire knows neither grief nor fear."[1]

It is clear from the above that both the *Gītā* and the *Dhamma-pada* praise sense-control and consider desires, attachments, anger and grief as great enemies. But the treatment of the *Gītā* differs from that of the *Dhamma-pada* in this, that, while in the *Dhamma-pada* there is a course of separate lessons or moral instructions on diverse subjects, the *Gītā* deals with sense-control as a means to the attainment of peace, contentment and desirelessness, which enables a man to dedicate all his actions to God and follow the conventional courses of duties without looking for anything in them for himself. The *Gītā* knows that the senses, mind and intellect are the seats of all attachments and antipathies, and that it is through the senses and the mind that these can stupefy a man and make his knowledge blind.[2] All the sense-affections of cold and heat, pleasure and sorrow, are mere changes of our sensibility, are mere touches of feeling which are transitory and should therefore be quietly borne.[3] It is only by controlling the senses that the demon of desire, which distorts all ordinary and philosophic knowledge, can be destroyed. But it is very hard to stifle this demon of desire, which always appears in new forms. It is only when a man can realize within himself the great being which transcends our intellect that he can control his lower self with his higher self and uproot his desires. The self is its own friend as well as its own foe, and one should always try to uplift oneself and not allow oneself to sink down. The chief aim of all sense-control is to make a man's thoughts steady, so that he can link himself up in communion with God.[4]

---

1 *Dhatnma-pada,* XVI.212-216.

2 *Gita,* III.40.

3 *Ibid.* II.14.

4 *Ibid.* II.61; III.41, 43; VI.5, 6.

The senses in the *Gītā* are regarded as drawing the mind along with them. The senses are continually changing and fleeting, and they make the mind also changeful and fleeting; and, as a result of that, the mind, like a boat at sea before a strong wind, is driven to and fro, and steadiness of thought and wisdom *(prajñā)* are destroyed. The word *prajñā* is used in the *Gītā* in the sense of thought or wisdom or mental inclinations in general. It is used in a more or less similar sense in the *Bṛhad-āraṇyaka Upaniṣad,* IV.4.21, and in a somewhat different sense in the *Māṇḍūkya Upaniṣad*, 7. But the sense in which Patañjali uses the word is entirely different from that in which it is used in the *Gītā* or the Upaniṣads. Patañjali uses the word in the technical sense of a specific type of mystical cognition arising out of the steady fixing of the mind on an object, and speaks of seven stages of such *prajñā* corresponding to the stages of *yoga* ascension. *Prajñā* in the *Gītā* means, as has just been said, thought or mental inclination. It does not mean *jñāna,* or ordinary cognition, or *vijñāna* as higher wisdom; it means knowledge in its volitional aspect. It is not the *kriyākhya-jñāna,* as moral discipline of *yama, niyama,* etc., of the *Pañca-rātra* work *Jayākhya-saṃhitā.* It means an intellectual outlook, as integrally connected with, and determining, the mental bent or inclination. When the mind follows the mad dance of the senses after their objects, the intellectual background of the mind determining its direction, the *prajñā* is also upset. Unless the *prajñā* is fixed, the mind cannot proceed undisturbed in its prescribed fixed course. So the central object of controlling the senses is the securing of the steadiness of this *prajñā* *(vaśe hi yasyendriyāṇi tasya prajñā pratiṣṭhitā*—II.57). *Prajñā* and *dhī* are two words which seem to be in the *Gītā* synonymous, and they both mean mental inclination. This mental inclination probably involves both an intellectual outlook, and a corresponding volitional tendency. Sense-control makes this *prajñā* steady, and the *Gītā* abounds in praise of the *sthita-prājña* and *sthita-dhī,* i.e. of one who has mental inclination or thoughts fixed and steady.[1] Sense-attachments are formed by continual association with sense-

1 *Gita,* II.54-56.

objects, and attachment begets desire, desire begets anger, and so on. Thus all the vices spring from sense-attachments. And the person who indulges in sense-gratifications is rushed along by the passions. So, just as a tortoise collects within itself all its limbs, so the person who restrains his senses from the sense-objects has his mind steady and fixed. The direct result of sense-control is thus steadiness of will, and of mental inclinations or mind *(prajñā)*. The person who has *his prajñā* fixed is not troubled in sorrows and is not eager to gain pleasures, he has no attachment, no fear and no anger.[1] He is indifferent in prosperity and in adversity and neither desires anything nor shuns anything.[2] He alone can obtain peace who, like the sea receiving all the rivers in it, absorbs all his desires within himself; not so the man who is always busy in satisfying his desires. The man who has given up all his desires and is unattached to anything is not bound to anything, has no vanity and attains true peace. When a man can purge his mind of attachments and antipathies and can take to sense-objects after purifying his senses and keeping them in full control, he attains contentment *(prasāda)*. When such contentment is attained, all sorrows vanish and his mind becomes fixed *(buddhiḥ paryavati-ṣṭhate)*.[3] Thus sense-control, on the one hand, makes the mind unruffled, fixed, at peace with itself and filled with contentment, and on the other hand, by making the mind steady and fixed, it makes communion with God possible. Sense-control is the indispensable precondition of communion with God; when once this has been attained, it is possible to link oneself with God by continued efforts.[4] Thus sense-control, by producing steadiness of the will and thought, results in contentment and peace on the one hand, and on the other makes the mind fit for entering into communion with God.

One thing that strikes us in reading the *Gītā* is that the object of sense-control in the *Gītā* is not the attainment of a state of

---

1 *Gītā,* II.56.
2 *Ibid.* II.57.
3 *Ibid.* II.65; see also II.58, 64, 68, 70, 71.
4 *Ibid.* VI.36.

emancipated oneness or the absolute cessation of all mental processes, but the more intelligible and common-sense ideal of the attainment of steadiness of mind, contentment and the power of entering into touch with God. This view of the object of selfcontrol is therefore entirely different from that praised in the philosophic systems of Patañjali and others. The *Gītā* wants us to control our senses and mind and to approach sense-objects with such a controlled mind and senses, because it is by this means alone that we can perform our duties with a peaceful and contented mind and turn to God with a clean and unruffled heart.[1] The main emphasis of this sense-control is not on the mere external control of volitional activities and the control of motor propensities in accordance with the direction of passions and appetites, but on the inner control of the mind behind these active senses. When a person controls only his physical activities, and yet continues to brood over the attractions of sense, he is in reality false in his conduct (*mithyācāra*). Real self-control does not mean only the cessation of the external operations of the senses, but also the control of the mind. Not only should a man cease from committing actions out of greed and desire for sense-gratification, but his mind should be absolutely clean, absolutely clear of all impurities of sense-desires. Mere suspension of physical action without a corresponding control of mind and cessation from harbouring passions and desires is a vicious course.[2]

THE ETHICS OF THE GĪTĀ AND THE BUDDHIST ETHICS

The subject of sense-control naturally reminds one of Buddhism. In the Vedic religion performance of sacrifices was considered

1 रागद्वेषविमुक्तैस् तु विषयान् इन्द्रियैस् चरन्।
आत्मवश्यैर् विधेयात्मा प्रसादम् अधिगच्छती
rāga-dveṣa-vimuktais tu viṣayān indriyaiś caran
ātma-vaśyair vidheyātmā prasādam adhigacchati.—Ibid. II.64.

2 Cf. *Dhamma-pada,* I.2. All phenomena have mind as their precursor, are dependent upon mind and are made up of mind. If a man speaks or acts with a pure mind, happiness accompanies him, just as a shadow follows a man incessantly.

as the primary duty. Virtue and vice consisted in obedience or disobedience to Vedic injunctions. It has been pointed out that these injunctions implied a sort of categorical imperative and communicated a sense of *vidhi* as law, a command which must be obeyed. But this law was no inner law of the spirit within, but a mere external law, which ought not to be confused with morality in the modern sense of the term. Its sphere was almost wholly ritualistic, and, though it occasionally included such commands as "One should not injure anyone" (*mā hiṃsyāt*), yet in certain sacrifices which were aimed at injuring one's enemies operations which would lead to such results would have the imperative of a Vedic command, though the injury to human beings would be attended with its necessary punishment. Again, though in later Sāṃkhya commentaries and compendiums it is said that all kinds of injuries to living beings bring their punishment, yet it is doubtful if the Vedic injunction "Thou shouldst not injure" really applied to all living beings, as there would be but few sacrifices where animals were not killed. The Upaniṣads, however, start an absolutely new line by the substitution of meditations and self-knowledge for sacrificial actions. In the primary stage of Upaniṣadic thoughts a conviction was growing that instead of the sacrificial performances one could go through a set form of meditations, identifying in thought certain objects with certain other objects (e.g. the dawn as the horse of horse-sacrifice) or even with symbolic syllables, OM and the like. In the more developed stage of Upaniṣadic culture a new conviction arose in the search after the highest and the ultimate truth, and the knowledge of Brahman as the highest essence in man and nature is put forward as the greatest wisdom and the final realization of truth and reality, than which nothing higher could be conceived. There are but few moral precepts in the Upaniṣads, and the whole subject of moral conflict and moral efforts is almost silently dropped or passes unemphasized. In the Taittirlya *Upaniṣad*, I.II, the teacher is supposed to give a course of moral instruction to his pupil after teaching him the Vedas—Tell the truth, be virtuous, do not give up the study of the Vedas; after presenting the teacher with the stipulated honorarium (at the conclusion of his studies) the pupil should (marry and) continue the line of his family. He should not deviate from truth or from virtue (*dharma*) or from good. He should not cease doing good to others, from study and teaching. He should be respectful to his parents and teachers and perform such actions as are unimpeachable. He should follow only good conduct and not bad. He should make gifts with faith (*śraddhā*), not with indifference, with dignity, from a sense of shame, through fear and through knowledge. If there should be any doubt regarding his course of duty or conduct, then he should proceed to act in the way in which the wisest Brahmins behaved. But few Upaniṣads give such moral precepts, and there is very little in the Upaniṣads in the way of describing a course of moral behaviour or of emphasizing the fact that man can attain his best only by trying to become great through moral efforts. The Upaniṣads occupy themselves almost wholly with mystic meditations and with the philosophic wisdom of self knowledge. Yet the ideas of self-control, peace and cessation of desires, endurance and concentration are referred to in Bṛhadāraṇyaka, IV.4.23, as a necessary condition for the realization of the self within us.[1] In *Katha*, VI.11, the control of the senses (*indriya-dhāraṇa*) is referred to as *yoga*, and in *Muṇḍaka*, III.2.2, it is said that he who consciously desires the objects of desire is again and again born through desires; but even in this world all desires vanish for him who is self-realized in himself and is self-satisfied.[2] The idea that the path of wisdom is different from the path of desires was also known, and it was felt that he who sought wisdom (vidyābhīpsita) was not drawn by many desires.[3]

---

1 *śānto dānta uparatas titikṣuḥ samāhito bhūtvātmany eva ātmānam paśyati. Bṛḥ.* IV.4.23.

2 *kāmān yah kāmayate marryamānaḥ sa kāmabhir jāyate tatra tatra paryāpta-kāmasya kṛtātmanas tu ihaiva sarve pravilīyanti kāmāḥ.—Muṇḍaka,* III.2.2.

3 *Kaṭha,* II.4.

The point to be discussed in this connection is whether the central idea of the *Gītā*, namely, sense-control and more particularly the control of desires and attachments, is derived from the Upaniṣads or from Buddhism. It has been pointed out that the Upaniṣads do not emphasize the subject of moral conflict and moral endeavours so much as the nature of truth and reality as Brahman, the ultimate essence of man and the manifold appearance of the world. Yet the idea of the necessity of sense-control and the control of desires, the settling of the mind in peace and contentment, is the necessary precondition for fitness for Vedic knowledge. Thus Śaṅkara, the celebrated commentator on the Upaniṣads, in commenting on *Brahma-sūtra*, I.1.1, says that a man is fit for an enquiry after Brahman only when he knows how to distinguish what is permanent from what is transitory (nityānitya-*vastu*-viveka), and when he has no attachment to the enjoyment of the fruits of his actions either as mundane pleasures or as heavenly joys (ihāmutra-*phala*-bhoga-*virāga*). The necessary qualifications which entitle a man to make such an enquiry are disinclination of the mind for worldly joys (*śama*), possession of proper control and command over the mind, by which it may be turned to philosophy (*dama*), power of endurance (*viṣaya-titikṣā*), cessation of all kinds of duties (uparati), and faith in the philosophical conception of truth and reality (*tattva*-śraddhā). It may be supposed, therefore, that the Upaniṣads presuppose a high degree of moral development in the way of self-control and disinclination to worldly and heavenly joys. Detachment from sense-affections is one of the most dominant ideas of the *Gītā*, and the idea of Muṇḍaka, III.2.2, referred to above, is re-echoed in the *Gītā*, II.70, where it is said that, just as the waters are absorbed in the calm sea (though poured in continually by the rivers), so the person in whom all desires are absorbed attains peace, and not the man who indulges in desires. The *Gītā*, of course, again and again emphasizes the necessity of uprooting attachments to pleasures and antipathy to pains and of controlling desires (*kāma*); but, though the Upaniṣads do not emphasize this idea so frequently, yet the idea is there, and it seems very probable that the *Gītā* drew it from the Upaniṣads. Hindu tradition also refers to the Upaniṣads as the source of the *Gītā*. Thus the *Gītā*-māhātmya describes the Upaniṣads as the cows from which Kiṣṇa, the cowherd boy, drew the *Gītā* as milk.[1]

But the similarity of Buddhist ethical ideas to those of the *Gītā* is also immense, and, had it not been for the fact that ideas which may be regarded as peculiarly Buddhistic are almost entirely absent from the *Gītā*, it might well have been contended that the *Gītā* derived its ideas of controlling desires and uprooting attachment from Buddhism. Tachibana collects a long list of Buddhist vices as follows:[2]

aṇganaṃ, impurity, lust, *Sn*. 517.
ahankāro, selfishness, egoism, *A*. I.132; *M*. III.18, 32.
mamaṅkaro, desire, *A*. I.132; *M*. III.18, 32.
mamāyitaṃ, selfishness, *S.N*. 466.
mamattaṃ, grasping, egoism, *S.N*. 872, 951.
apekhā, desire, longing, affection, *S.N*. 38; *Dh*. 345.
icchā, wish, desire, covetousness.
ejā, desire, lust, greed, craving, *S.N*. 751; *It*. 92.
āsā, desire, longing, *S.N*. 634, 794, 864; *Dh*. 397.
pipāsā, thirst.
esā, *esanā*, wish, desire, thirst, *Dh*. 335.
ākāñkhā, desire, longing, *Tha*. 20.
kiñcanaṃ, attachment, *S.N*. 949; *Dh*. 200.
gantho, bond, tie, *S.N*. 798; *Dh*. 211.
ādāna-gantho, the tied knot of attachment, *S.N*. 794.
giddhi, greed, desire, *Sn*. 328; *M*. I.360, 362.
gedho, greed, desire, *Sn*. 65, 152.
gahanaṃ, entanglement, *Dh*. 394.
gāho, seizing, attachment.
jālinī, snare, desire, lust, *Dh*.180; *A*. II.211.
pariggaho, attachment, *Mahānid*. 57.
chando, wish, desire, intention, *S.N*. 171, 203, etc.

1 *Sarvopaniṣado gāvo dogdhā gopāla-nandanaḥ*.
2 *The Ethics of Buddhism*, by S. Tachibana, p. 73.

jatā, desire, lust, *S.N.* I.13; *V.M.* I.
jigiṃsanatā, covetousness, desire for, *Vibhaṅga*, 353.
nijigiṃsanatā, covetousness, *V.M.* I.23.
toṇhā, *tasinā*, lust, unsatisfied desire, passion.
upādānam, clinging, attachment, *Dh.* II.58, III.230.
paṇidhi, wish, aspiration, *Sn.* 801.
pihā, desire, envy, *Tha.* 1218.
pemaṃ, affection, love, *A.* III.249.
bandho, thong, bondage, attachment, *Sn.* 623; *Dh.* 344.
bandhanaṃ, bond, fetter, attachment, *Sn.* 522, 532; *Dh.*345.
nibandho, binding, attachment, *S.* II.17.
vinibandhanam, bondage, desire, *Sn.* 16.
anubandho, bondage, affection, desire, *M.* III. 170; *Jt.* 91.
upanibandho, fastening, attachment, *V.M.* I.235.
paribandho, Com. on *Thi.* p. 242.
rāgo, human passion, evil, desire, lust, *passim.*
sārāgo, sārajjanā, sārajjitattam, affection, passion, *Mahānid.* 242.
rati, lust, attachment, *Dh.* 27.
manoratho, desire, wish (?).
ruci, desire, inclination, *Sn.* 781.
abhilāso, desire, longing, wish, Com. on *Peta-vattu*, 154.
lālasā, ardent desire (?).
ālayo, longing, desire, lust, *Sn.* 535, 635; *Dh.* 411.
lobho, covetousness, desire, cupidity, *Sn.* 367; *Dh.* 248.
lobhanam, greed, *Tha.* 343.
lubhanā, *lobhitattam*, do. (?).
vanaṃ, desire, lust, *Sn.* 1131; *Dh.* 284, 344.
vanatho, love, lust, *Dh.* 283, 284.
nivesanam, clinging to, attachment, *Sn.* 470, 801.
Saṅgo, fetter, bond, attachment, *Sn.* 473, 791; *Dh.* 397.
āsatti, attachment, hanging on, clinging, *Sn.* 777; *Vin.* II.156 *S.* I.212.
visattikā, poison, desire, *Sn.* 333; *Dh.* 180.
Santhavaṃ, friendship, attachment, *Sn.* 207, 245; *Dh.* 27.
ussado, desire (?), *Sn.* 515, 783, 785.
sneho, *sineho*, affection, lust, desire, *Sn.* 209, 943; *Dh.* 285.

āsayo, abode, intention, inclination, *V.H.* I.140.
anusayo, inclination, desire, *A.* I.132; *Sn.* 14, 369, 545.
sibbanī, desire (?), *Sn.* 1040.
kodho, anger, wrath, *Sn.* I.245, 362, 868, 928; *Dh.* 221-3; *It.* 4, 12, 109.
kopo, anger, ill-will, ill-temper, *Sn.* 6.
āghāto, anger, ill-will, hatred, malice, *D.* I.3, 31; *S.* I.179.
patigho, wrath, hatred, *Sum.* 116.
doso, anger, hatred, passim.
viddeso, enmity, hatred (?).
dhūmo, anger (?), *Sn.* 460.
upanāho, enmity, *Sn.* 116.
vyāpādo, wish to injure, hatred, fury, *Sum.* 211; *It.* 111.
anabhiraddhi, anger, wrath, rage, *D.* I.3.
Veraṃ, wrath, anger, hatred, sin, *Sn.* 150; *Dh.* 3-5, 201.
virodho, opposition, enmity (?).
roso, anger (?).
rosanam, anger (?).
vyāroṣaṇam, anger, *Sn.* 148.
aññāṇam, ignorance, *It.* 62.
moho, fainting, ignorance, folly, *passim*.
mohanam, ignorance, *S.N.* 399, 772.
avijjā, ignorance, error, passion.

It is interesting to note that three vices, covetousness, hatred and ignorance, and covetousness particularly, appear under different names and their extirpation is again and again emphasized in diverse ways. These three, ignorance, covetousness and hatred or antipathy, are the roots of all evils. There are, of course, simpler commandments, such as not to take life, not to steal, not to commit adultery, not to tell a lie, and not to take intoxicating drinks, and of these stealing gold, drinking liquors, dishonouring one's teacher's bed, and killing a Brahmin are also prohibited in the *Chāndogya Upaniṣad*, v.10.9-10.[1] But, while the *Chāndogya*

1 There is another list of eightfold prohibitions called *aṭṭhaṅgāsīla;* these are not to take life, not to take what is not given, to abstain from sex-relations, to ab-

only prohibits killing Brahmins, the Buddha prohibited taking the life of any living being. But all these vices, and others opposed to the *atthaṅga-sīla* and *dasa-kusala*-kamma, are included within covetousness, ignorance and hatred. The *Gītā* bases its ethics mainly on the necessity of getting rid of attachment and desires from which proceeds greed and frustration of which produces anger. But, while in Buddhism ignorance (*avidyā*) is considered as the source of all evil, the *Gītā* does not even mention the word. In the twelvefold chain of causality in Buddhism it is held that out of ignorance (avijjā) come the conformations (*saṅkhāra*), out of the conformations consciousness (*viññāna*), out of consciousness mind and body (*nāma-rūpa*), out of mind and body come the six fields of contact (*āyatana*), out of the six fields of contact comes sense-contact, out of sense-contact comes feeling, out of feeling come desires (*taṅhā*), out of desires comes the holding fast to things (*upādāna*), out of the holding fast to things comes existence (*bhava*), out of existence comes birth (*jāti*), and from birth come old age, decay and death. If ignorance, or avijjā, is stopped, then the whole cycle stops. But, though in this causal cycle ignorance and desires are far apart, yet psychologically desires proceed immediately from ignorance, and a frustration of desires produces anger, hatred, etc. In the *Gītā* the start is taken directly from attachment and desires (kāma). The Buddhist word *tṛṣnā* (*taṇhā*) is seldom mentioned in the *Gītā*; whereas the *Upaniṣadic* word kāma takes its place as signifying desires. The *Gītā* is not a philosophical work which endeavours to search deeply into the causes of attachments, nor does it seek to give any practical course of advice as to how one should get rid of attachment. The Vedānta system of thought, as interpreted by Śaṅkara, traces the origin of the world with all its evils to ignorance or nescience (*avidyā*), as an indefinable

---

stain from falsehood, from drinking liquors, from eating at forbidden times, from dancing and music and from beautifying one's 'body by perfumes, garlands, etc. There is also another list called *dasa-kusala-kamma,* such as not to take life, not to take what is not given, not to commit adultery, not to tell a lie, not to slander, not to abuse or talk foolishly, not to be covetous, malicious and sceptical.

principle; the Yoga traces all our phenomenal experience to five afflictions, ignorance, attachment, antipathy, egoism and self-love, and the last four to the first, which is the fountain-head of all evil afflictions. In the *Gītā* there is no such attempt to trace attachment, etc. to some other higher principle. The word *ajñāna* (ignorance) is used in the *Gītā* about six or eight times in the sense of ignorance; but this "ignorance" does not mean any metaphysical principle or the ultimate starting-point of a causal chain, and is used simply in the sense of false knowledge or ignorance, as opposed to true knowledge of things as they are. Thus in one place it is said that true knowledge of things is obscured by ignorance, and that this is the cause of all delusion.[1] Again, it is said that to those who by true knowledge (of God) destroy their own ignorance (*ajñāna*) true knowledge reveals the highest reality (*tat param*), like the sun.[2] In another place *jñāna* and *ajñāna* are both defined. *Jñāna* is defined as unvacillating and abiding self-knowledge and true knowledge by which truth and reality are apprehended, and all that is different from this is called ajñāna.[3] *Ajñāna* is stated elsewhere to be the result of *tamas*, and in two other places tamas is said to be the product of *ajñāna*.[4] In another place it is said that people are blinded by ignorance (*ajñāna*), thinking, "I am rich, I am an aristocrat, who else is there like me? I shall perform sacrifices make gifts and enjoy."[5] In another place ignorance is said to produce doubts (*saṃśaya*), and the *Gītā* lecture of Kṛṣṇa is supposed to dispel the delusion of Arjuna, produced by ignorance.[6] This shows that, though the word ajñāna is used in a variety of contexts, either as ordinary ignorance or ignorance of true and absolute philosophic knowledge, it is never referred to as being the source of attachment or desires. This need not be interpreted to mean that the *Gītā* was

1 *ajñānenāvṛtaṃ jñānaṃ tena muhyanti jantavaḥ*. V.15.

2 *jñānena tu tad-ajñānaṃ yeṣām nāśitaṃ ātmanaḥ*. V.16.

3 *adhyātma-jñāna-nityatvaṃ tattva-jñānārīha-darśanam etaj-jñānam iti prok-tam ajñānam yad ato 'nyathā.—Gītā,* XIII.12.

4 *Ibid.* XIV.16, 17; x.11; XIV.8.

5 *Ibid.* V.16.

6 *Ibid,* IV.42; XVIII.72.

opposed to the view that attachments and desires were produced from ignorance; but it seems at least to imply that the *Gītā* was not interested to trace the origin of attachments and desires and was satisfied to take their existence for granted and urged the necessity of their extirpation for peace and equanimity of mind. Buddhist Hīnayāna ethics and practical discipline are constituted of moral discipline (*śīla*), concentration (*samādhi*) and wisdom (*paññā*). The śīla consisted in the performance of good conduct (caritta) and desisting (vāritta) from certain other kinds of prohibited action. Śīla means those particular volitions and mental states, etc. by which a man who desists from committing sinful actions maintains himself on the right path. Śīla thus means (1) right volition (*cetanā*), (2) the associated mental states (*cetasika*), (3) mental control (*saṃvara*), and (4)the actual non-transgression (in body and speech) of the course of conduct already in the mind by way of the preceding three *sīlas*, called *avitikkama*. *Saṃvara* is spoken of as being of five kinds, viz. (1) *pātimokkha-saṃvara* (the control which saves him who abides by it), (2)*sati-saṃvara* (the control of mindfulness),(3) *ñāna-saṃvara* (the control of knowledge), (4) khanti-saṃvara (the control of patience) and (5) *viriya-saṃvara* (the control of active restraint). *Pātimokkha-saṃvara* means all self-control in general. *Sati-saṃvara* means the mindfulness by which one can bring in the right and good associations, when using one's cognitive senses. Even when looking at any tempting object, a man will, by virtue of his mindfulness (sati), control himself from being tempted by not thinking of its tempting side and by thinking on such aspects of it as may lead in the right direction. *Khanti-saṃvara* is that by which one can remain unperturbed in heat and cold. By the proper adherence to *śila* all our bodily, mental and vocal activities (*kamma*) are duly systematized, organized and stabilized (*samādhānam, upadhāraṇam, patitthā*). The practice of *śīla* is for the practice of *jhāna* (meditation). As a preparatory measure thereto, a man must train himself continually to view with disgust the appetitive desires for eating and drinking (*āhāre patikūla-saṇñā*) by emphasizing in the mind the various troubles that are associated with seeking food and drink and their ultimate loathsome transformations as various nauseating bodily elements. He must habituate his mind to the idea that all the parts of our body are made up of the four elements, viz. *kṣiti* (earth), ap (water), etc. He should also think of the good effects of *śīla*, the making of gifts, of the nature of death and of the deep nature and qualities of the final extinction of all phenomena, and should practise *brahma-vihāra*, as the fourfold meditation of universal friendship, universal pity, happiness in the prosperity and happiness of all, and indifference to any kind of preferment for himself, his friend, his enemy or a third party.[1]

The *Gītā* does not enter into any of these disciplinary measures. It does not make a programme of universal altruism or hold that one should live only for others, as is done in Mahāyāna ethics, or of the virtues of patience, energy for all that is good (*vīrya* as *kuśalotsāha*), meditation and true knowledge of the essencelessness of all things. The person who takes the vow of saintly life takes the vow of living for the good of others, for which he should be prepared to sacrifice all that is good for him. His vow does not limit him to doing good to his co-religionists or to any particular sects, but applies to all human beings, irrespective of caste, creed or race, and not only to human beings, but to all living beings. Mahāyāna ethical works like the *Bodhi-caryāvatāra-pañjikā* or *Śikṣā-samuccaya* do not deal merely with doctrines or theories, but largely with practical instructions for becoming a Buddhist saint. They treat of the practical difficulties in the path of a saint's career and give practical advice regarding the way in which he may avoid temptations, keep himself in the straight path of duty, and gradually elevate himself to higher and higher states.

The *Gītā* is neither a practical guide-book of moral efforts nor a philosophical treatise discussing the origin of immoral tendencies and tracing them to certain metaphysical principles as their sources; but, starting from the ordinary frailties of attachment and desires, it tries to show how one can lead a normal life of duties and responsibilities and yet be in peace and contentment in a state of

1 See *A History of Indian Philosophy*, by S.N. Dasgupta, vol. I, p. 103.

equanimity and in communion with God. The *Gītā* has its setting in the great battle of the *Mahā-bhārata*. Kṛṣṇa is represented as being an incarnation of God, and he is also the charioteer of his friend and relation, Arjuna, the great Pāṇḍava hero. The Pāṇḍava hero was a Kṣattriya by birth, and he had come to the great battle-field of Kurukṣetra to fight his cousin and opponent King Duryodhana, who had assembled great warriors, all of whom were relations of Arjuna, leading mighty armies. In the first chapter of the *Gītā* a description is given of the two armies which faced each other in the holy field (*dharma-kṣetra*) of Kurukṣetra. In the second chapter Arjuna is represented as feeling dejected at the idea of having to fight with his relations and of eventually killing them. He says that it was better to beg from door to door than to kill his respected relations. Kṛṣṇa strongly objects to this attitude of Arjuna and says that the soul is immortal and it is impossible to kill anyone. But, apart from this metaphysical point of view, even from the ordinary point of view a Kṣattriya ought to fight, because it is his duty to do so, and there is nothing nobler for a Kṣattriya than to fight. The fundamental idea of the *Gītā* is that a man should always follow his own caste-duties, which are his own proper duties, or sva-dharma. Even if his own proper duties are of an inferior type, it is much better for him to cleave to them than to turn to other people's duties which he could well perform. It is even better to die cleaving to one's caste-duties, than to turn to the duties fixed for other people, which only do him harm.[1] The caste-duties of Brahmins, Kṣattriyas, Vaiśyas and Śūdras are fixed in accordance with their natural qualities. Thus sense-control, control over mind, power of endurance, purity, patience, sincerity, knowledge of worldly things and philosophic wisdom are the natural qualities of a Brahmin. Heroism, bravery, patience, skill, not to fly from battle, making of gifts and lordliness are the natural duties of a Kṣattriya. Agriculture, tending of cattle and trade are the natural duties of a Śūdra. A man can attain his highest only by performing the specific duties of his own caste. God pervades this world, and it is He who moves all beings to

1 *Gītā*, III.35.

work. A man can best realize himself by adoring God and by the performance of his own specific caste-duties. No sin can come to a man who performs his own caste-duties. Even if one's caste-duties were sinful or wrong, it would not be wrong for a man to perform them; for, as there is smoke in every fire, so there is some wrong thing or other in all our actions.[1] Arjuna is thus urged to follow his caste-duty as a Kṣattriya and to fight his enemies in the battle-field. If he killed his enemies, then he would be the master of the kingdom; if he himself was killed, then since he had performed the duties of a Kṣattriya, he would go to Heaven. If he did not engage himself in that fight, which was his duty, he would not only lose his reputation, but would also transgress his own *dharma*.

Such an instruction naturally evokes the objection that war necessarily implies injury to living beings; but in reply to such an objection Kṛṣṇa says that the proper way of performing actions is to dissociate one's mind from attachment; when one can perform an action with a mind free from attachment, greed and selfishness, from a pure sense of duty, the evil effects of such action cannot affect the performer. The evil effects of any action can affect the performer when in performing an action he has a motive of his own to fulfil. But, if he does not seek anything for himself, if he is not overjoyed in pleasures, or miserable in pains, his works cannot affect him. A man should therefore surrender all his desires for selfish ends and dedicate all his actions to God and be in communion with Him, and yet continue to perform the normal duties of his caste and situation of life. So long as we have our bodies, the necessity of our own nature will drive us to work. So it is impossible for us to give up all work. To give up work can be significant only if it means the giving up of all desires for the fruits of such actions. If the fruits of actions are given up, then the actions can no longer bind us to them. That brings us in return peace and contentment, and the saint who has thus attained a perfect equanimity of mind is firm and unshaken in his true wisdom, and nothing can sway him to and fro. One may seek to attain this state either by philosophic wisdom or

1 *Gītā*, XVIII.44-48.

by devotion to God, and it is the latter path which is easier. God, by His grace, helps the devotee to purge his mind of all impurities, and so by His grace a man can dissociate his mind from all motives of greed and selfishness and be in communion with Him; he can thus perform his duties, as fixed for him by his caste or his custom, without looking forward to any reward or gain.

The *Gītā* ideal of conduct differs from the sacrificial ideal of conduct in this, that sacrifices are not to be performed for any ulterior end of heavenly bliss or any other mundane benefits, but merely from a sense of duty, because sacrifices are enjoined in the scriptures to be performed by Brahmins; and they must therefore be performed from a pure sense of duty. The *Gītā* ideal of ethics differs from that preached in the systems of philosophy like the Vedānta or the Yoga of Patañjali in this, that, while the aim of these systems was to transcend the sphere of actions and duties, to rise to a stage in which one could give up all one's activities, mental or physical, the ideal of the *Gītā* was decidedly an ideal of work. The *Gītā*, as has already been pointed out, does not advocate a course of extremism in anything. However elevated a man may be, he must perform his normal caste-duties and duties of customary morality.[1] The *Gītā* is absolutely devoid of the note of pessimism which is associated with early Buddhism. The *śīla, samādhi* and *paññā* of Buddhism have, no doubt, in the *Gītā* their counterparts in the training of a man to disinclination for joys and attachments, to concentration on God and the firm and steady fixation of will and intelligence; but the significance of these in the *Gītā* is entirely different from that which they have in Buddhism. The *Gītā* does not expound a course of approved conduct and prohibitions, since, so far as these are concerned, one's actions are to be guided by the code of caste-duties or duties of customary morality. What is required of a man is that he should cleanse his mind from the impurities of attachment, desires and cravings. The samādhi of the *Gītā* is not a mere concentration of the mind on some object, but

1 Śaṅkara, of course, is in entire disagreement with this interpretation of the *Gītā*, as will be discussed in a later section.

communion with God, and the wisdom, or *prajñā*, of the *Gītā* is no realization of any philosophic truth, but a fixed and unperturbed state of the mind, where the will and intellect remain unshaken in one's course of duty, clear of all consequences and free from all attachments, and in a state of equanimity which cannot be shaken or disturbed by pleasures or sorrows.

It may naturally be asked in this connection, what is the general standpoint of Hindu Ethics? The Hindu social system is based on a system of fourfold division of castes. The *Gītā* says that God Himself created the fourfold division of castes into Brahmins, Kṣattriyas, Vaiśyas and Śūdras, a division based on characteristic qualities and specific duties. Over and above this caste division and its corresponding privileges, duties and responsibilities, there is also a division of the stages of life into that of *Brahma-cārin*—student, *gṛha-stha*—householder, *vāna-prastha*—retired in a forest, and *bhikṣu*—mendicant, and each of these had its own prescribed duties. The duties of Hindu ethical life consisted primarily of the prescribed caste-duties and the specific duties of the different stages of life, and this is known as *varṇāśrama-dharma*. Over and above this there were also certain duties which were common to all, called the *sādhāraṇa-dharmas*. Thus Manu mentions steadiness (*dhairya*), forgiveness (*kṣamā*), self-control (*dama*), non-stealing (*cauryābhāva*), purity (*śauca*), sense-control (indriya-*nigraha*), wisdom (*dhī*), learning (*vidyā*), truthfulness (*satya*) and control of anger (*akrodha*) as examples of *sādhāraṇa-dharma. Praśastapāda* mentions faith in religious duties (dharma-śraddhā), non-injury (*ahiṃsā*), doing good to living beings (*bhūta-hitatva*), truthfulness (*satya-vacana*), non-stealing (*asteya*), sex-continence (*brahma-carya*), sincerity of mind (*anupadhā*), control of anger (*krodha-varjana*), cleanliness and ablutions (*abhiṣecana*), taking of pure food (*śuci-dravya-sevana*), devotion to Vedic gods (*viśiṣṭa-devatā-bhakti*), and watchfulness in avoiding transgressions (*apramāda*). The caste-duties must be distinguished from these common duties. Thus sacrifices, study and gifts are common to all the three higher castes, Brahmins, Kṣattriyas and Vaiśyas. The specific duties of a

Brahmin are acceptance of gifts, teaching, sacrifices and so forth; the specific duties of a Kṣattriya are protection of the people, punishing the wicked, not to retreat from battles and other specific tasks; the duties of a Vaiśya are buying, selling, agriculture, breeding and rearing of cattle, and the specific duties of a Vaiśya. The duties of a Śūdra are to serve the three higher castes.[1]

Regarding the relation between *varṇa*-dharma and sādhāraṇa-dharma, a modern writer says that "the sādhāraṇa-dharmas constitute the foundation of the *varṇāśrama-dharmas*, the limits within which the latter are to be observed and obeyed. For example, the Brahmin in performing religious sacrifice must not appropriate another's property, non-appropriation being one of the common and universal duties. In this way he serves his own community as well as subserves (though in a negative way) the common good of the community—and so, in an indirect way, serves the common good of humanity. Thus the individual of a specific community who observes the duties of his class does not serve his own community merely, but also and in the same process all other communities according to their deserts and needs, and in this way the whole of humanity itself. This, it will be seen, is also the view of Plato, whose virtue of justice is the common good which is to be realized by each class through its specific duties; but this is to be distinguished from the common good which constitutes the object of the *sādhāraṇa-dharmas* of the Hindu classification. The end in these common and universal duties is not the common well-being, which is being correctly realized in specific communities, but the common good as the precondition and foundation of the latter; it is not the good which is common-in-the-individual, but common-as-the-prius-of-the-individual. Hence the *sādhāraṇa* duties are

---

1 The *Gītā,* however, counts self-control (*śama*), control over the mind *(dama),* purity *(śauca),* forgiving nature *(kṣānti),* sincerity *(ārjova),* knowledge *(jñāna),* wisdom *(vijñāna)* and faith *(āstikya)* as the natural qualities of Brahmins. The duties of Kṣattriyas are heroism *(śaurya),* smartness *(tejas),* power of endurance *(dhṛti),* skill *(dākṣya),* not to fly in battle *(yuddhe cāpy apalāyana),* making of gifts *(dāna)* and power of controlling others *(īśvara-bhāva).* The natural duties of Vaiśyas are agriculture, rearing of cows and trade. *Gītā,* XVIII.42-44.

obligatory equally for all individuals, irrespective of their social position or individual capacity."[1] The statement that the common good (*sādhāraṇa-dharma*) could be regarded as the precondition of the specific caste-duties implies that, if the latter came into conflict with the former, then the former should prevail. This is, however, inexact; for there is hardly any instance where, in case of a conflict, the *sādhāraṇa-dharma*, or the common duties, had a greater force. Thus, for example, non-injury to living beings was a common duty; but sacrifices implied the killing of animals, and it was the clear duty of the Brahmins to perform sacrifices. War implied the taking of an immense number of human lives; but it was the duty of a Kṣattriya not to turn away from a battle-field, and in pursuance of his obligatory duty as a Kṣattriya he had to fight. Turning to traditional accounts, we find in the *Rāmāyaṇa* that Śambūka was a Śūdra saint (*muni*) who was performing ascetic penances in a forest. This was a transgression of caste-duties; for a Śūdra could not perform *tapas*, which only the higher caste people were allowed to undertake, and hence the performance of tapas by the Śūdra saint Śambūka was regarded as *adharma* (vice); and, as a result of this adharma, there was a calamity in the kingdom of Rāma in the form of the death of an infant son of a Brahmin. King Rāma went out in his chariot and beheaded Śambūka for transgressing his caste-duties. Instances could be multiplied to show that, when there was a conflict between the caste-duties and the common duties, it was the former that had the greater force. The common duties had their force only when they were not in conflict with the caste-duties. The *Gītā* is itself an example of how the caste-duties had preference over common duties. In spite of the fact that Arjuna was extremely unwilling to take the lives of his near and dear kinsmen in the battle of Kurukṣetra Kṛṣṇa tried his best to dissuade him from his disinclination to fight and pointed out to him that it was his clear duty, as a Kṣattriya, to fight. It seems therefore very proper to hold that the common duties had only a general application, and that the

1 *Ethics of the Hindus,* by S.K. Maitra under Dr Seal's close personal supervision and guidance, pp. 3-4.

specific caste-duties superseded them, whenever the two were in conflict.

The *Gītā* does not raise the problem of common duties, as its synthesis of *nivṛtti* (cessation from work) and *pravṛtti* (tending to work) makes it unnecessary to introduce the advocacy of the common duties; for its instruction to take to work with a mind completely detached from all feelings and motives of self-seeking, pleasure-seeking and self-interest elevates its scheme of work to a higher sphere, which would not be in need of the practice of any select scheme of virtues.

The theory of the *Gītā* that, if actions are performed with an unattached mind, then their defects cannot touch the performer, distinctly implies that the goodness or badness of an action does not depend upon the external effects of the action, but upon the inner motive of action. If there is no motive of pleasure or self-gain, then the action performed cannot bind the performer; for it is only the bond of desires and self-love that really makes an action one's own and makes one reap its good or bad fruits. Morality from this point of view becomes wholly subjective, and the special feature of the *Gītā* is that it tends to make all actions non-moral by cutting away the bonds that connect an action with its performer. In such circumstances the more logical course would be that of Śaṅkara, who would hold a man who is free from desires and attachment to be above morality, above duties and above responsibilities. The *Gītā*, however, would not advocate the objective nivṛtti, or cessation of work; its whole aim is to effect subjective nivṛtti, or detachment from desires. It would not allow anyone to desist from his prescribed objective duties; but, whatever might be the nature of these duties, since they were performed without any motive of gain, pleasure or self-interest, they would be absolutely without fruit for the performer, who, in his perfect equanimity of mind, would transcend all his actions and their effects. If Arjuna fought and killed hundreds of his kinsmen out of a sense of his caste-duty, then, howsoever harmful his actions might be, they would not affect him. Yudhiṣṭhira, however, contemplated an expiation of the sin of killing his kinsmen by repentance, gifts, asceticism, pilgrimage, etc., which shows the other view, which was prevalent in the Mahā-*bhārata* period, that, when the performance of caste-duties led to such an injury to human lives, the sinful effects of such actions could be expiated by such means.[1] Yudhiṣṭhira maintained that of asceticism (*tapas*), the giving up of all duties (*tyāga*), and the final knowledge of the ultimate truth (*avadhi*), the second is better than the first and the third is better than the second. He therefore thought that the best course was to take to an ascetic life and give up all duties and responsibilities, whereas Arjuna held that the best course for a king would be to take upon himself the normal responsibilities of a kingly life and at the same time remain unattached to the pleasures of such a life.[2] Regarding also the practice of the virtues of non-injury, etc., Arjuna maintains that it is wrong to carry these virtues to extremes. Howsoever a man may live, whether as an ascetic or as a forester, it is impossible for him to practise non-injury to all living beings in any extreme degree. Even in the water that one drinks and the fruits that one eats, even in breathing and winking many fine and invisible insects are killed. So the virtue of non-injury, or, for the matter of that, all kinds of virtue, can be practised only in moderation, and their injunctions always imply that they can be practised only within the bounds of a commonsense view of things. Non-injury may be good; but there are cases where non-injury would mean doing injury. If a tiger enters into a cattle-shed, not to kill the tiger would amount

---

1 *Mahā-bhārata,* XII.7. 36 and 37.

2 Thus Arjuna says:

अशक्तः शक्तवद् गच्छन् निह्सङ्गो मुक्तबन्धनः
समः शत्रौ च मित्रे च स वै मुक्तो महीपते॥
aśaktaḥ śaktavad gacchan nihsaṅgo mukta-bandhanaḥ
samaḥ śatrau ca mitre ca sa vai mukto mahīpate;

to which Yudhiṣṭhira replies:

तपस् त्यागोऽवधिर् इति निश्चयस् त्व् एष धीमताम्
परस्परं ज्याय एषां येषां नैःश्रेयसी मतिः॥
tapas tyāgo 'vadhir iti niścayas tv eṣa dhīmatām
parasparaṃ jyāya eṣāṃ yeṣāṃ naihśreyasl matiḥ.

Ibid. XII.18.31 and XII.19.9.

to killing the cows. So all religious injunctions are made from the point of view of a practical and well-ordered maintenance of society and must therefore be obeyed with an eye to the results that may follow in their practical application. Our principal object is to maintain properly the process of the social order and the well-being of the people.[1] It seems clear, then, that, when the *Gītā* urges again and again that there is no meaning in giving up our normal duties, vocation and place in life and its responsibilities, and that what is expected of us is that we should make our minds unattached, it refers to the view which Yudhiṣṭhira expresses, that we must give up all our works. The *Gītā* therefore repeatedly urges that tyāga does not mean the giving up of all works, but the mental giving up of the fruits of all actions.

Though the practice of detachment of mind from all desires and motives of pleasure and enjoyment would necessarily involve the removal of all vices and a natural elevation of the mind to all that is high and noble, yet the *Gītā* sometimes denounces certain types of conduct in very strong terms. Thus, in the sixteenth chapter, it is said that people who hold a false philosophy and think that the world is false and, without any basis, deny the existence of God and hold that there is no other deeper cause of the origin of life than mere sex-attraction and sex-union, destroy themselves by their foolishness and indulgence in all kinds of cruel deeds, and would by their mischievous actions turn the world to the path of ruin. In their insatiable desires, filled with pride, vanity and ignorance, they take to wrong and impure courses of action. They argue too much and think that there is nothing greater than this world that

---

1 लोकयात्रार्थम् एवेदं धर्मप्रवचनं कृतम्
अहिंसा साधु हिंसेति श्रेयान् धर्मपरिग्रहः
नात्यन्तं गुणवत् किंचिन् न चाप्य् अत्यन्त निर्गुणम्
उभयं सर्वकार्येषु दृश्यते साध्व् असाधु वा ॥
Loka-yātrārtham evedaṃ dharma-pravacanaṃ kṛtam
ahiṃsā sādhu hiṃseti śreyōn dharma-parigrahaḥ
nātyantaṃ guṇavat kiṃcin na cāpy atyanta-nirguṇam
ubhayaṃ sarva-kāryeṣu dṛśyate sādhv asādhu vā.
Mahā-bhārati, XII.15.49 and 50.

we live in, and, thinking so, they indulge in all kinds of pleasures and enjoyments. Tied with bonds of desire, urged by passions and anger, they accumulate money in a wrongful manner for the gratification of their sense-desires. "I have got this to-day," they think, "and enjoy myself; I have so much hoarded money and I shall have more later on"; "that enemy has been killed by me, I shall kill other enemies also, I am a lord, I enjoy myself, I am successful, powerful and happy, I am rich, I have a noble lineage, there is no one like me, I perform sacrifices, make gifts and enjoy." They get distracted by various kinds of ideas and desires and, surrounded by nets of ignorance and delusion and full of attachment for sense-gratifications, they naturally fall into hell. Proud, arrogant and filled with the vanity of wealth, they perform improperly the so-called sacrifices, as a demonstration of their pomp and pride. In their egoism, power, pride, desires and anger they always ignore God, both in themselves and in others.[1] The main vices that one should try to get rid of are thus egoism, too many desires, greed, anger, pride and vanity, and of these desire and anger are again and again mentioned as being like the gates of hell.[2]

Among the principal virtues called the divine equipment (*daivī sampat*) the *Gītā* counts fearlessness (*abhaya*), purity of heart *(sattva-saṃśuddhi),* knowledge of things and proper action in accordance with it, giving, control of mind, sacrifice, study, *tapas*, sincerity (*ārjava*), non-injury *(ahimsā),* truthfulness *(satya),* control of anger *(akrodha),* renunciation *(tyāga),* peacefulness of mind *(śānti),* not to backbite *(apaiśuna)*, kindness to the suffering *(bhūteṣu dayā),* not to be greedy *(alolupatva),* tenderness (*mārdava),* a feeling of shame before people in general when a wrong action is done *(hrī),* steadiness *(acapala),* energy *(tejas),* a forgiving spirit (*kṣānti*), patience *(dhṛti),* purity *(śauca),* not to think ill of others (*adroha*), and not to be vain. It is these virtues which liberate our spirits, whereas vanity, pride, conceit, anger, cruelty and ignorance are

1 *Gītā*, XVI.8-18.
2 *Ibid.* XVI.21.

vices which bind and enslave us.[1] The man who loves God should not hurt any living beings, should be friendly and sympathetic towards them, and should yet be unattached to all things, should have no egoism, be the same in sorrows and pleasures and full of forgivingness for all. He should be firm, self-controlled and always contented. He should be pure, unattached, the same to all, should not take to actions from any personal motives, and he has nothing to fear. He is the same to friends and enemies, in appreciation and denunciation; he is the same in heat and cold, pleasure;and pain; he is the same in praise and blame, homeless and always satisfied with anything and everything; he is always unperturbed and absolutely unattached to all things.[2] If one carefully goes through the above list of virtues, it appears that the virtues are pre-eminently of a negative character—one should not be angry, hurtful to others, egoistic, proud or vain, should not do anything with selfish motives, should not be ruffled by pleasure and pain, heat and cold and should be absolutely unattached. Of the few positive virtues, sincerity and purity of heart, a forgiving spirit, tenderness, friendliness, kindness, alertness and sympathy seem to be most prominent. The terms *maitra* (friendliness) and *karuṇā* (compassion) might naturally suggest the Buddhist virtues so named, since they do not occur in the Upaniṣads.[3] But in the *Gītā* also they are mentioned only once, and the general context of the passage shows that no special emphasis is put on these two virtues. They do not imply any special kind of meditation of universal friendship or universal piety or the active performance of friendly and sympathetic deeds for the good of humanity or for the good of living beings in general. They seem to imply simply the positive friendly state of the mind that must accompany all successful practice of non-injury to fellow-beings. The *Gītā* does not advocate the active performance of friendliness, but encourages a friendly spirit as a means of discouraging the

1 *Gītā.* XVI.1-5.

2 *Ibid.* XVI.13-19; see also *Ibid.* XIII.8-11.

3 The term *maitra* occurs only once in the *Muktikopaniṣat,* I I.34, and the *Muktika* is in all probability one of the later Upaniṣads.

tendency to do harm to others. The life that is most admired in the *Gītā* is a life of unattachedness, a life of peace, contentment and perfect equanimity and unperturbedness in joys and sorrows. The vices that are denounced are generally those that proceed from attachment and desires, such as egoism, pride, vanity, anger, greediness, etc. There is another class of virtues which are often praised, namely those which imply purity, sincerity and alertness of mind and straightness of conduct. The negative virtue of sense-control, with its positive counterpart, the acquirement of the power of directing one's mind in a right direction, forms the bed-rock of the entire superstructure of the *Gītā* code of moral and virtuous conduct.

The virtue of sameness *(samatva),* however, seems to be the great ideal which the *Gītā* is never tired of emphasizing again and again. This sameness can be attained in three different stages: subjective sameness, or equanimity of mind, or the sameness in joys and sorrows, praise and blame and in all situations of life; objective sameness, as regarding all people, good, bad or indifferent, a friend or an enemy, with equal eyes and in the same impartial spirit; and the final stage of the achievement of this equanimity is the self-realized state when one is absolutely unperturbed by all worldly things—a state of transcendence called *guṇātīta.* Thus in the *Gītā,* II.15, it is said that he whom sense-affections and physical troubles cannot affect in any way, who is unperturbable and the same in joys and sorrows, attains immortality. In II.38 Kṛṣṇa asks Arjuna to think of joys and sorrows, gain and loss, victory and defeat as being the same, and to engage himself in the fight with such a mind; for, if he did so, no sin would touch him. In II.47 Kṛṣṇa says to Arjuna that his business is only to perform his duties and not to look for the effects of his deeds; it is wrong to look for the fruits of deeds or to desist from performing one's duties. In II.48 this sameness in joys and sorrows is described as *yoga,* and it is again urged that one should be unperturbed whether m success or in failure. The same idea is repeated in II.55, 56 and 57, where it is said that a true saint should not be damped in sorrow or elated in joy, and that he should not be attached to anything and should take happiness or misery indifferently, without particularly welcoming the former or regretting the latter. Such a man is absolutely limited to his own self and is self-satisfied. He is not interested in achieving anything or in not achieving anything; there is no personal object for him to attain in the world.[1] To such a man gold and stones, desirables and undesirables, praise and blame, appreciation and denunciation, friends and foes are all alike.[2] Such a man makes no distinction whether between a friend and foe, or between a sinner and a virtuous man.[3] Such a man knows that pleasures and pains are welcomed and hated by all and, thinking so, he desires the good of all and looks upon all as he would upon himself—on a learned Brahmin of an elevated character, on a cow, an elephant, a dog or a *caṇḍāla*; and the wise behave in the same way.[4] He sees God in all beings and knows the indestructible and the immortal in all that is destructible. He, who knows that all beings are pervaded by all, and thus regards them all with an equal eye, does not hurt his own spiritual nature and thus attains his highest.[5] As the culmination of this development, there is the state in which a man transcends all the corporeal and mundane characteristics of the threefold *guṇas*, and, being freed from birth, death, old age and sorrow, attains immortality. He knows that the worldly qualities of things, the *guṇas*, are extraneous to his own spiritual nature, and by such thoughts he transcends the sphere of all worldly qualities and attains Brahmahood.[6]

Apart from the caste-duties and other deeds that are to be performed without any attachment, the *Gītā* speaks again and again of sacrifices, *tapas* and gifts, as duties which cannot be ignored at any stage of our spiritual development. It is well worth pointing out that the *Gītā* blames the performance of sacrifices either for the

1 *Gītā*, III.17, 18.
2 *Ibid.* XIV.24, 25.
3 *Ibid.* VI.9.
4 *Ibid.* VI.31; also v.18.
5 *Ibid.* XIII.28.
6 *Ibid,* XIV.20, 23, 26.

attainment of selfish ends or for making a display of pomp or pride. The sacrifices are to be performed from a sense of duty and of public good, since it is only by the help of the sacrifices that the gods may be expected to bring down heavy showers, through which crops may grow in plenty. Physical *tapas* is described as the adoration of gods, Brahmins, teachers and wise men, as purity, sincerity, sex-continence and non-injury; *tapas* in speech is described as truthful and unoffending speech, which is both sweet to hear and for the good of all, and also study; mental *tapas* is described as serenity of mind (*manaḥ-prasāda*), happy temper (*saumyatva*), thoughtfulness (*mauna*), self-control (*ātma-vini-graha*) and sincerity of mind; and the higher kind of *tapas* is to be performed without any idea of gain or the fulfilment of any ulterior end.[1] Gifts are to be made to good Brahmins in a holy place and at an auspicious time, merely from a sense of duty. This idea that gifts are properly made only when they are made to good Brahmins at a holy time or place is very much more limited and restricted than the Mahāyāna idea of making gifts for the good of all, without the slightest restriction of any kind. Thus it is said in the *Śikṣā-samuccaya* that a Bodhisattva need not be afraid among tigers and other wild animals in a wild forest, since the Bodhisattva has given his all for the good of all beings. He has therefore to think that, if the wild animals should eat him, this would only mean the giving his body to them, which would be the fulfilment of his virtue of universal charity. The Bodhisattvas take the vow of giving away their all in universal charity.[2]

Thus the fundamental teaching of the *Gītā* is to follow caste-duties without any motive of self-interest or the gratification of sense-desires. The other general duties of sacrifices, *tapas* and gifts are also to be practised by all and may hence be regarded in some sense as being equivalent to the *sādhāraṇa-dharmas* of the Vaiśeṣika and Smrti literature. But, if caste-duties or customary duties come into conflict with the special duties of non-injury (*ahiṃsā*), then the caste-duties are to be followed in preference.

1 *Gītā*. XVI.11-17.

2 *Śikṣā-samuccaya*, ch. XIX, p. 349.

It does not seem that any of the other special duties or virtues which are enjoined can come into conflict with the general caste-duties; for most of these are for the inner moral development, with which probably no caste-duties can come into conflict. But, though there is no express mandate of the *Gītā* on the point, yet it may be presumed that, should a Śūdra think of performing sacrifices, *tapas* or gifts or the study of the Vedas, this would most certainly be opposed by the *Gītā*, as it would be against the prescribed caste-duties. So, though non-injury is one of the special virtues enjoined by the *Gītā*, yet, when a Kṣattriya kills his enemies in open and free fight, that fight is itself to be regarded as virtuous (*dharmya*) and there is for the Kṣattriya no sin in the killing of his enemies. If a person dedicates all his actions to Brahman and performs his duties without attachment, then sinfulness in his actions cannot cleave to him, just as water cannot cleave to the leaves of a lotus plant.[1] On the one hand the *Gītā* keeps clear of the ethics of the absolutist and metaphysical systems by urging the necessity of the performance of caste and customary duties, and yet enjoins the cultivation of the great virtues of renunciation, purity, sincerity, non-injury, selfcontrol, sense-control and want of attachment as much as the absolutist systems would desire to do; on the other hand, it does not adopt any of the extreme and rigorous forms of selfdiscipline, as the Yoga does, or the practice of the virtues on an unlimited and universalist scale, as the Buddhists did. It follows the middle course, strongly emphasizing the necessity of selfcontrol, sense-control and detachment from all selfish ends and desires along with the performance of the normal duties. This detachment from sense-pleasures is to be attained either through wisdom or, preferably, through devotion to God.

ANALYSIS OF ACTION

The consideration of the *Gītā* ethics naturally brings in the problem of the analysis of the nature of action, volition and agent.

---

1 *Gītā*, V.10.

The principal analysis of volition in Hindu Philosophy is to be found in the Nyāya-Vaiśeṣika works. Praśastapāda divides animal activities into two classes, firstly, those that are of a reflex nature and originate automatically from life-functions (*jīvana-pūrvaka*) and subserve useful ends (*kārn api artha-kriyām*) for the organism, and, secondly, those conscious and voluntary actions that proceed out of desire or aversion, for the attainment of desirable ends and the avoidance of undesirable ones. Prabhākara holds that volitional actions depend on several factors, firstly, a general notion that something has to be done *(kāryatā-jñāna),* which Gaṅgabhaṭṭa in his *Bhātta-cintāmaṇi* explains as meaning not merely a general notion that a particular work can be done by the agent, but also the specific notion that an action must be done by him—a sense which can proceed only from a belief that the action would be useful to him and would not be sufficiently harmful to him to dissuade him from it. Secondly, there must be the belief that the agent has the power or capacity of performing the action (*kṛti-sādhyatā-jñāna).* This belief of *kṛti-sādhyatā-jñāna* leads to desire (*cikīrṣā*). The Prabhākaras do not introduce here the important factor that an action can be desired only if it is conducive to the good of the agent. Instead of this element they suppose that actions are desired when the agent identifies himself with the action as one to be accomplished by him—an action is desired only as a kind of selfrealization. The Nyāya, however, thinks that the fact that an action is conducive to good and not productive of serious mischief is an essential condition of its performance.

The *Gītā* seems to hold that everywhere actions are always being performed by the *guṇas* or characteristic qualities of *prakṛti*, the primal matter. It is through ignorance and false pride that one thinks himself to be the agent.[1] In another place it is said that for the occurrence of an action there are five causes, viz. the body, the agent, the various sense-organs, the various life-functions and biomotor activities, and the unknown objective causal elements or

1 *Gītā,* III.27; XIII.29.

the all-controlling power of God *(daiva).*[1] All actions being due to the combined operation of these five elements, it would be wrong to think the self or the agent to be the only performer of actions. Thus it is said that, this being so, he who thinks the self alone to be the agent of actions, this wicked-minded person through his misapplied intelligence does not see things properly.[2] Whatever actions are performed, right or wrong, whether in body, speech or mind, have these five factors as their causes.[3] The philosophy that underlies the ethical position of the *Gītā* consists in the fact that, in reality, actions are made to happen primarily through the movement of the characteristic qualities of *prakṛti*, and secondarily, through the collocation of the five factors mentioned, among which the self is but one factor only. It is, therefore, sheer egoism to think that one can, at his own sweet will, undertake a work or cease from doing works. For the *prakṛti*, or primal matter, through its later evolutes, the collocation of causes, would of itself move us to act, and even in spite of the opposition of our will we are led to perform the very action which we did not want to perform. So Kṛṣṇa says to Arjuna that the egoism through which you would say that you would not fight is mere false vanity, since the *prakṛti* is bound to lead you to action.[4] A man is bound by the active tendencies or actions which necessarily follow directly from his own nature, and there is no escape. He has to work in spite of the opposition of his will. *Prakṛti*, or the collocation of the five factors, moves us to work. That being so, no one can renounce all actions. If renouncing actions is an impossibility, and if one is bound to act, it is but proper that one should perform one's normal duties. There are no duties and no actions which are absolutely faultless, absolutely above all criticism; so the proper way in which a man should purify his

---

1 अधिष्ठानं तथा कर्ता कर्ता करणं च पृथग्विधम्
विविधाश् च पृथक् चेष्टा दैवं चैवात्र पञ्चमन्त्॥
adhiṣṭhānaṃ tathā kartā karaṇaṃ ca pṛthag-vidham
vividhāś ca pṛthak ceṣṭā daivaṃ caivātra pañcamant. Gītā. XVIII.14.

2 *Ibid*, XVIII.16.

3 *Ibid.* XVIII.15.

4 *Ibid.* XVIII.59.

actions is by purging his mind of all imperfections and impurities of desires and attachment. But a question may arise how, if all actions follow necessarily as the product of the five-fold collocation, a person can determine his actions? The general implication of the *Gītā* seems to be that, though the action follows necessarily as the product of the fivefold collocation, yet the self can give a direction to these actions; if a man wishes to dissociate himself from all attachments and desires by dedicating the fruits of all his actions to God and clings to God with such a purpose, God helps him to attain his noble aim.

ESCHATOLOGY

The *Gītā* is probably the earliest document where a definite statement is made regarding the imperishable nature of existent things and the impossibility of that which is non-existent coming into being. It says that what is non-existent cannot come into being, and that what exists cannot cease to be. In modern times we hear of the principle of the conservation of energy and also of the principle of the conservation of mass. The principle of the conservation of energy is distinctly referred to in the *Vyāsa-bhāṣya* on *Patañjali-sūtra,* IV.3, but the idea of the conservation of mass does not seem to have been mentioned definitely anywhere. Both the Vedāntist and the Sāṃkhyist seem to base their philosophies on an ontological principle known as *sat-kārya-vāda*, which holds that the effect is already existent in the cause. The Vedānta holds that the effect as such is a mere appearance and has no true existence; the cause alone is truly existent. The Sāṃkhya, on the other hand, holds that the effect is but a modification of the causal substance, and, as such, is not non-existent, but has no existence separate from the cause; the effect may therefore be said to exist in the cause before the starting of the causal operation (*kāraṇa-vyāpāra*). Both these systems strongly object to the Buddhist and Nyāya view that the effect came into being out of non-existence, a doctrine known as *a-sat-kārya-vāda.* Both the Sāṃkhya and the Vedānta tried to prove their theses, but neither of them seems to have realized that their doctrines are based upon an *a priori* proposition which is the basic principle underlying the principle of the conservation of energy and the conservation of mass, but which is difficult to be proved by reference to *a posteriori* illustration. Thus, the Sāṃkhya says that the effect exists in the cause, since, had it not been so, there would be no reason why certain kinds of effects, e.g. oil, can be produced only from certain kinds of causes, e.g. sesamum. That certain kinds of effects are produced only from certain kinds of causes does not really prove the doctrine of *sat-kārya-vāda*, but only implies it; for the doctrine of *sat-kārya-vāda* rests on an *a priori* principle such as that formulated in the *Gītā*—that what exists cannot perish, and that what does not exist cannot come into being.[1] The *Gītā* does not try to prove this proposition, but takes it as a self-evident principle which no one could challenge. It does not, however, think of applying this principle, which underlies the ontological position of the Sāṃkhya and the Vedānta, in a general way. It seems to apply the principle only to the nature of self *(ātman)*. Thus it says, "O Arjuna, that principle by which everything is pervaded is to be regarded as deathless; no one can destroy this imperishable one. The bodies that perish belong to the deathless eternal and unknowable self; therefore thou shouldst fight. He who thinks the self to be destructible, and he who thinks it to be the destroyer, do not know that it can neither destroy nor be destroyed. It is neither born nor does it die, nor, being once what it is, would it ever be again...Weapons cannot cut it, fire cannot burn it, water cannot dissolve it and air cannot dry it." The immortality of self preached in the *Gītā* seems to have been directly borrowed from the Upaniṣads, and the passages that describe it seem to breathe the spirit of the Upaniṣads not only in idea, but also in the modes and expressions. The ontological principle that what exists cannot die and that what is not cannot come into being does not seem to have been formulated in the Upaniṣads. Its formulation in the *Gītā*

1 *nāsato vidyate bhāvo nābhavo vidyate sataḥ.—Gītā*, II.16.

in support of the principle of immortality seems, therefore, to be a distinct advance on the Upaniṣadic philosophy in this direction.

The first argument urged by Kṛṣṇa to persuade Arjuna to fight was that the self was immortal and that it was the body only that could be injured or killed, and that therefore Arjuna need not feel troubled because he was going to kill his kinsmen in the battle of Kurukṣetra. Upon the death of one body the self only changed to another, in which it was reborn, just as a man changed his old clothes for new ones. The body is always changing, and even in youth, middle age and old age, does not remain the same. The change at death is also a change of body, and so there is no intrinsic difference between the changes of the body at different stages of life and the ultimate change that is affected at death, when the old body is forsaken by the spirit and a new body is accepted. Our bodies are always changing, and, though the different stages in this growth in childhood, youth and old age represent comparatively small degrees of change, yet these thought to prepare our minds to realize the fact that death is also a similar change of body only and cannot, therefore, affect the unperturbed nature of the self, which, in spite of all changes of body at successive births and rebirths, remains unchanged in itself. When one is born one must die, and when one dies one must be reborn. Birth necessarily implies death, and death necessarily implies rebirth. There is no escape from this continually revolving cycle of birth and death. From Brahmā down to all living creatures there is a continuous rotation of birth, death and rebirth. In reply to Arjuna's questions as to what becomes of the man who, after proceeding a long way on the path of *yoga,* is somehow through his failings dislodged from it and dies, Kṛṣṇa replies that no good work can be lost and a man who has been once on the path of right cannot suffer; so, when a man who was proceeding on the path of *yoga* is snatched away by the hand of death, he is born again in a family of pure and prosperous people or in a family of wise *yogins;* and in this new birth he is associated with his achievements in his last birth and begins anew his onward course of advancement, and the old practice of the previous birth carries him onward, without any effort on his part, in his new line of progress. By his continual efforts through many lives and the cumulative effects of the right endeavours of each life the *yogin* attains his final realization. Ordinarily the life of a man in each new birth depends upon the desires and ideas that he fixes upon at the time of his death. But those that think of God, the oldest instructor, the seer, the smallest of the small, the upholder of all, shining like the sun beyond all darkness, and fix their life-forces between their eyebrows, and control all the gates of their senses and their mind in their hearts, ultimately attain their highest realization in God. From the great Lord, the great unmanifested and incomprehensible Lord, proceeds the unmanifested *(avyakta),* from which come out all manifested things *(vyaktayah sarvāḥ),* and in time again return to it and again evolve out of it. Thus there are two forms of the unmanifested *(avyakta),* the unmanifested out of which all the manifested things come, and the unmanifested which is the nature of the eternal Lord from whom the former come.[1] The ideas of *deva-yāna* and *pitṛ-yāna, dakṣiṇāyana* and *uttarāyaṇa,* the black and the white courses as mentioned in the Upaniṣads, are also referred to in the *Gītā.* Those who go through smoke in the new-moon fortnight and the later six months (when the sun is on the south of the equator), and thus take the black course, return again; but those who take the white course of fire in the full-moon fortnight and the former six months (when the sun is on the north of the equator) do not return again.[2] No very significant meaning can be made out of these doctrines. They seem to be but the perpetuation of the traditional faiths regarding the future courses of the dead, as referred to in the *Chāndogya Upaniṣad.* The *Gītā*, again, speaking of others, says that those who follow the sacrificial duties of the Vedas enjoy heavenly pleasures in heaven, and, when their merits are exhausted by the enjoyments of the good fruits of their actions, they come back to earth. Those who follow the path of desires and take to religious duties for the attainment of pleasures must always

---

1 *Gītā*, VIII.16-23.
2 *Ibid*, VIII.24-26.

go to heaven and come back again—they cannot escape this cycle of going and coming. Again, in the *Gītā*, XVI.19, Kṛṣṇa says, "I make cruel vicious persons again and again take birth as ferocious animals."

The above summary of the eschatological views of the *Gītā* shows that it collects together the various traditionally accepted views regarding life after death without trying to harmonize them properly. Firstly, it may be noted that the *Gītā* believes in the doctrine of *karma.* Thus in XV.2 and in IV.9 it is said that the world has grown on the basis of *karma*, and the *Gītā* believes that it is the bondage of *karma* that binds us to this world. The bondage of *karma* is due to the existence of attachment, passions and desires. But what does the bondage of *karma* lead to? The reply to such a question, as given by the *Gītā*, is that it leads to rebirth. When one performs actions in accordance with the Vedic injunctions for the attainment of beneficial fruits, desire for such fruits and attachment to these desirable fruits is the bondage of *karma*, which naturally leads to rebirth. The proposition definitely pronounced in the *Gītā*, that birth necessarily means death and death necessarily means birth, reminds us of the first part of the twelvefold causal chain of the Buddha—"What being, is there death? Birth being, there is death." It has already been noticed that the attitude of the *Gītā* towards Vedic performances is merely one of toleration and not one of encouragement. These are actions which are prompted by desires and, like all other actions similarly prompted, they entail with them the bonds of *karma*; and, as soon as the happy effects produced by the merits of these actions are enjoyed and lived through, the performers of these actions come down from heaven to the earth and are reborn and have to pass through the old ordeal of life. The idea that, there being birth, there is death, and that, if there is death there is also rebirth, is the same in the *Gītā* as in Buddhism; but the *Gītā* form seems to be very much earlier than the Buddhistic form; for the Buddhistic form relates birth and death through a number of other causal links intimately connected together in an interdependent cycle, of which the *Gītā* seems to be entirely ignorant. The *Gītā* does not speak of any causal chain, such as could be conceived to be borrowed from Buddhism. It, of course, knows that attachment is the root of all vice; but it is only by implication that we can know that attachment leads to the bondage of *karma* and the bondage of *karma* to rebirth. The main purpose of the *Gītā* is not to find out how one can tear asunder the bonds of *karma* and stop rebirth, but to prescribe the true rule of the performance of one's duties. It speaks sometimes, no doubt, about cutting asunder the bonds of *karma* and attaining one's highest; but instruction as regards the attainment of liberation or a description of the evils of this worldly life does not form any part of the content of the *Gītā.* The *Gītā* has no pessimistic tendency. It speaks of the necessary connection of birth and death not in order to show that life is sorrowful and not worth living, but to show that there is no cause of regret in such universal happenings as birth and death. The principal ideas are, no doubt, those of attachment, *karma*, birth, death and rebirth; but the idea of Buddhism is more complex and more systematized, and is therefore probably a later development at a time when the *Gītā* discussions on the subject were known. The Buddhist doctrine that there is no self and no individual anywhere is just the opposite of the *Gītā* doctrine of the immortality of the self.

But the *Gītā* speaks not only of rebirth, but also of the two courses, the path of smoke and the path of light, which are referred to in the *Chāndogya Upaniṣad.*[1] The only difference between the Upaniṣad account and that of the *Gītā* is that there are more details in the Upaniṣad than in the *Gītā.* But the ideas of *deva-yāna* and *pitṛ-yāna* do not seem to fit in quite consistently with the idea of rebirth on earth. The *Gītā*, however, combines the idea of rebirth on earth with the *deva-yāna-pitṛ-yāna* idea and also with the idea of ascent to heaven as an effect of the merits accruing from sacrificial performances. Thus the *Gītā* combines the different trains of ideas just as it finds them traditionally accepted, without trying to harmonize them properly. It does not attempt to discuss the point

1 *Chāndogya Upaniṣad,* V.10.

regarding the power of *karma* in determining the nature of rebirths, enjoyments and sufferings. From some passages (IV.9 or VI.40-45) it might appear that the bonds of *karma* produced their effects independently by their own powers, and that the arrangement of the world is due to the effect of *karma.* But there are other passages (XVI.19) which indicate that *karma* does not produce its effects by itself, but that God rewards or punishes good and bad deeds by arranging good and bad births associated with joys and sorrows. In the *Gītā*, V.15, it is said that the idea of sins and virtues is due to ignorance, whereas, if we judge rightly, God does not take cognizance either of vices or of virtues. Here again there are two contradictory views of *karma:* one view in which *karma* is regarded as the cause which brings about all inequalities in life, and another view which does not attribute any value to good or bad actions. The only way in which the two views can be reconciled in accordance with the spirit of the *Gītā* is by holding that the *Gītā* does not believe in the objective truth of virtue or vice *(puṇya* or *pāpa).* There is nothing good or bad in the actions themselves. It is only ignorance and foolishness that regards them as good or bad; it is only our desires and attachments which make the actions produce their bad effects with reference to us, and which render them sinful for us. Since the actions themselves are neither good nor bad, the performance of even apparently sinful actions, such as the killing of one's kinsmen on the battle-field, cannot be regarded as sinful, if they are done from a sense of duty; but the same actions would be regarded as sinful, if they were performed through attachments or desires. Looked at from this point of view, the idea of morality in the *Gītā* is essentially of a subjective character. But though morality, virtue and vice, can be regarded from this point of view as subjective, it is not wholly subjective. For morality does not depend upon mere subjective conscience or the subjective notions of good and bad. The caste-duties and other duties of customary morality are definitely fixed, and no one should transgress them. The subjectivity of virtue and vice consists in the fact that they depend entirely on our good or bad actions. If actions are performed from a sense of obedience to scriptural commands, caste-duties or duties of customary morality, then such actions, in spite of their bad consequences, would not be regarded as bad.

Apart from these courses of rebirth and ascent to heaven, the last and best and ultimate course is described as being liberation, which transcends all that can be achieved by all kinds of merits attained by sacrifices, gifts or *tapas*. He who attains this highest achievement lives in God and is never born again.[1] The highest realization thus consists in being one with God, by which one escapes all sorrows. In the *Gītā* liberation *(mokṣa)* means liberation from old age and death. This liberation can be attained by true philosophic knowledge of the nature of *kṣetra*, or the mind-body whole, and the *kṣetra-jña*, the perceiving selves, or the nature of what is truly spiritual and what is non-spiritual, and by clinging to God as one's nearest and dearest.[2] This liberation from old age and death also means liberation from the ties of *karma* associated with us through the bonds of attachment, desires, etc. It does not come of itself, as the natural result of philosophic knowledge or of devotion to God; but God, as the liberator, grants it to the wise and to those who cling to Him through devotion.[3] But whether it be achieved as the result of philosophic knowledge or as the result of devotion to God, the moral elevation, consisting of dissociation from attachment and the right performance of duties in an unattached manner, is indispensable.

GOD AND MAN

The earliest and most recondite treatment regarding the nature and existence of God and His relation to man is to be found in the *Gītā*. The starting-point of the *Gītā* theism may be traced as far back as the *Puruṣa-sūkta*, where it is said that the one quarter of the *puruṣa* has spread out as the cosmic universe and its living beings, while

1 *Gītā*, VIII.28; IX.4.
2 *Ibid.* VII.29; XIII.34
3 *Ibid.* XVIII.66.

its other three-quarters are in the immortal heavens.[1] This passage is repeated in *Chāndogya*, III.12.6 and in *Maitrāyaṇī*, VI.4, where it is said that the three-quarter Brahman sits root upward above *(ūrdhva-mūlaṃ tripād Brahma).* This idea, in a slightly modified form, appears in the *Katha Upaniṣad*, VI.1, where it is said that this universe is the eternal Aśvattha tree which has its root high up and its branches downwards *(ūrdhva-mūlo 'vāk-śākhaḥ).* The *Gītā* borrows this idea and says, "This is called the eternal Aśvattha (*pipul* tree) with its roots high up and branches downwards, the leaves of which are the Vedas; and he who knows this, he knows the Vedas" (XV.I). Again it is said, "Its branches spread high and low, its leaves of sense-objects are nourished by the *guṇas*, its roots are spread downwards, tied with the knots of *karma*, the human world" (XV.2); and in the next verse, it is said, "In this world its true nature is not perceived; its beginning, its end, and the nature of its subsistence, remain unknown; it is only by cutting this firmly rooted Aśvattha tree with the strong axe of unattachment (*asaṅga-śastreṇa*) that one has to seek that state from which, when once achieved, no one returns." It is clear from the above three passages that the *Gītā* has elaborated here the simile of the Aśvattha tree of the *Katha Upaniṣad.* The *Gītā* accepts this simile of God, but elaborates it by supposing that these branches have further leaves and other roots, which take their sap from the ground of human beings, to which they are attached by the knots of *karma.* This means a duplication of the Aśvattha tree, the main and the subsidiary. The subsidiary one is an overgrowth, which has proceeded out of the main one and has to be cut into pieces before one can reach that. The principal idea underlying this simile throws a flood of light on the *Gītā* conception of God, which is an elaboration of the idea of the *Puruṣa-sūkta* passage already referred to. God is not only immanent, but transcendent as well. The immanent part, which

1 पादोऽस्य वुश्वा भूतानि
त्रिपाद् अस्यामृतं दिवि॥
pādo 'sya viśvā bhūtāni
tripād asyāmṛtaṃ divi.—Puruṣa-sūkta.

forms the cosmic universe, is no illusion or *māyā:* it is an emanation, a development, from God. The good and the evil, the moral and the immoral of this world, are all from Him and in Him. The stuff of this world and its manifestations have their basis, an essence, in Him, and are upheld by Him. The transcendent part, which may be said to be the root high up, and the basis of all that has grown in this lower world, is itself the differenceless reality—the Brahman. But, though the Brahman is again and again referred to as the highest abode and the ultimate realization, the absolute essence, yet God in His super-personality transcends even Brahman, in the sense that Brahman, however great it may be, is only a constitutive essence in the complex personality of God. The cosmic universe, the *guṇas*, the *puruṣas*, the mind-structure composed of *buddhi, ahaṃkāra,* etc., and the Brahman, are all constituents of God, having their separate functions and mental relations; but God in His super-personality transcends them all and upholds them all. There is, however, one important point in which the *Gītā* differs from the Upaniṣads—this is,its introduction of the idea that God takes birth on earth as man. Thus in the *Gītā*, IV.6 and IV.7, it is said that "whenever there is a disturbance of *dharma* and the rise of *adharma,* I create myself; though I am unborn, of immortal self and the lord of all beings, yet by virtue of my own nature *{prakṛti*) I take birth through my own *māyā* (blinding power of the *guṇas)*" This doctrine of the incarnation of God, though not dealt with in any of the purely speculative systems, yet forms the corner-stone of most systems of religious philosophy and religion, and the *Gītā* is probably the earliest work available to us in which this doctrine is found. The effect of its introduction and of the dialogue form of the *Gītā,* in which the man-god Kṛṣṇa instructs Arjuna in the philosophy of life and conduct, is that the instruction regarding the personality of God becomes concrete and living. As will be evident in the course of this section, the *Gītā* is not a treatise of systematic philosophy, but a practical course of introduction to life and conduct, conveyed by God Himself in the form of Kṛṣṇa to His devotee, Arjuna. In the *Gītā* abstract philosophy melts down to an insight into the nature of practical life and conduct, as discussed with all the intimacy of the personal relation between Kṛṣṇa and Arjuna,which suggests a similar personal relation between God and man. For the God in the *Gītā* is not a God of abstract philosophy or theology, but a God who could be a man and be capable of all personal relations.

The all-pervasive nature of God and the fact that He is the essence and upholder of all things in the world is again and again in various ways emphasized in the *Gītā.* Thus Kṛṣṇa says, "There is nothing greater than I, all things are held in me, like pearls in the thread of a pearl garland; I am the liquidity in water, the light of the sun and the moon, manhood *(pauruṣa)* in man; good smell in earth, the heat of the sun, intelligence in the intelligent, heroism in the heroes, strength in the strong, and I am also the desires which do not transgress the path of virtue."[1] Again, it is said that "in my unmanifested (*avyakta*) form I pervade the whole world; all beings exist completely in me, but I am not exhausted in them; yet so do I transcend them that none of the beings exist in me—I am the upholder of all beings, I do not exist in them and yet I am their procreator."[2] In both these passages the riddle of God's relation with man, by which He exists in us and yet does not exist in us and is not limited by us, is explained by the fact of the threefold nature of God; there is a part of Him which has been manifested as inanimate nature and also as the animate world of living beings. It is with reference to this all-pervasive nature of God that it is said that "as the air in the sky pervades the whole world, so are all beings in 'me' (God). At the end of each cycle *(kalpa)* all beings enter into my nature *(prakṛtiṃ yānti māmikām),* and again at the beginning of a cycle I create them. I create again and again through my nature *(prakrti)*; the totality of all living beings is helplessly dependent on *prakṛti.*"[3] The three *prakṛtis* have already been referred to in the previous sections—*prakṛti* of God as cosmic matter, *prakṛti* as the nature of God from which all life and spirit

1 *Gītā*, VII.7-11.

2 *Ibid*, IX.3-5.

3 *Ibid.* IX.6-8.

have emanated, and *prakṛti* as *māyā*, or the power of God from which the three *guṇas* have emanated. It is with reference to the operation of these *prakṛtis* that the cosmic world and the world of life and spirit may be said to be existent in God. But there is the other form of God, as the transcendent Brahman, and, so far as this form is concerned, God transcends the sphere of the universe of matter and life. But in another aspect of God, in His totality and superpersonality, He remains unexhausted in all, and the creator and upholder of all, though it is out of a part of Him that the world has come into being. The aspect of God's identity with, and the aspect of His transcendence and nature as the father, mother and supporter of the universe, are not separated in the *Gītā*, and both the aspects are described often in one and the same passage. Thus it is said, "I am the father, mother, upholder and grandfather of this world, and I am the sacred syllable OM, the three Vedas, Rk, Sāman and Yajus; I am the sacrifice, the oblations and the fire, and yet I am the master and the enjoyer of all sacrifices. I am the final destiny, upholder, matter, the passive illuminator, the rest, support, friend, the origin, the final dissolution, the place, the receptacle and the immortal seed. I produce heat and shower, I destroy and create, I am both death and the deathless, the good and the bad."[1] With reference to His transcendent part it is said, "The sun, the moon and fire do not illuminate it—it is my final abode, from which, when once achieved, no one returns."[2] And again, immediately after, it is said, "It is my part that forms the eternal soul-principle (*jīva-bhūta*) in the living, which attracts the five senses and the *manas* which lie buried in *prakṛti*, and which takes the body and goes out of it with the six senses, just as air takes out fragrance from the flowers."[3] And then God is said to be the controlling agent of all operations in this world. Thus it is said, "By my energy I uphold the world and all living beings

1 *Gītā*. IX.16-19, 24.

2 *Ibid*, XV.6.

3 *Ibid.* , XV.7 and 8. It is curious that here the word Īśvara is used as an epithet of *jīva*.

and fill all crops with their specific juices; as fire in the bodies of living beings, and aided by the bio motor *prāṇa* functions, I digest the four kinds of food; I am the light in the sun, the moon and fire." Again it is said, "I reside in the hearts of all; knowledge, forgetfulness and memory all come from me; I alone am to be known by the Vedas; I alone know the Vedas, and I alone am the author of the Vedānta."[1] From these examples it is evident that the *Gītā* does not know that pantheism and deism and theism cannot well be jumbled up into one as a consistent philosophic creed. And it does not attempt to answer any objections that may be made against the combination of such opposite views. The *Gītā* not only asserts that all is God, but it also again and again repeats that God transcends all and is simultaneously transcendent and immanent in the world. The answer apparently implied in the *Gītā* to all objections to the apparently different views of the nature of God is that transcendentalism, immanentism and pantheism lose their distinctive and opposite characters in the melting whole of the super-personality of God. Sometimes in the same passage, and sometimes in passages of the same context, the *Gītā* talks in a pantheistic, a transcendental or a theistic vein, and this seems to imply that there is no contradiction in the different aspects of God as preserver and controller of the world, as the substance of the world, life and soul, and as the transcendent substratum underlying them all. In order to emphasize the fact that all that exists and all that is worthy of existence or all that has a superlative existence in good or bad are God's manifestation, the *Gītā* is never tired of repeating that whatever is highest, best or even worst in things is God or God's manifestation. Thus it is said, "I am the gambling of dice in all deceptive operations, I am victory in all endeavours, heroism of the heroes and the moral qualities *(sattva)* of all moral men *(sattvavatām)*"; and after enumerating a number of such instances Kṛṣṇa says that, wherever there are special gifts or powers or excellence of any kind, they are to be regarded as

1 *Gītā*, XV.8, 12, 13, 14, 15.

the special manifestation of God.[1] The idea that God holds within Himself the entire manifold universe is graphically emphasized in a fabulous form, when Kṛṣṇa gives Arjuna the divine eye of wisdom and Arjuna sees Kṛṣṇa in his resplendent divine form, shining as thousands of suns burning together, with thousands of eyes, faces and ornaments, pervading the heavens and the earth, with neither beginning nor end, as the great cosmic person into whose mouths all the great heroes of Kurukṣetra field had entered, like rivers into the ocean. Kṛṣṇa, after showing Arjuna his universal form, says, "I am time *(kāla),* the great destroyer of the world, and I am engaged in collecting the harvest of human lives, and all that will die in this great battle of Kurukṣetra have already been killed by me; you will be merely an instrument in this great destruction of the mighty battle of Kurukṣetra. So you can fight, destroy your enemies, attain fame and enjoy the sovereignty without any compunction that you have destroyed the lives of your kinsmen."

The main purport of the *Gītā* view of God seems to be that ultimately there is no responsibility for good or evil and that good and evil, high and low, great and small have all emerged from God and are upheld in Him. When a man understands the nature and reality of his own self and its agency, and his relation with God, both in his transcendent and cosmic nature, and the universe around him and the *guṇas* of attachment, etc., which bind him to his worldly desires, he is said to have the true knowledge. There is no opposition between the path of this true knowledge *(jñāna-yoga)* and the path of duties; for true knowledge supports and is supported by right performance of duties. The path of knowledge is praised in the *Gītā* in several passages. Thus it is said, that just as fire bums up the wood, so does knowledge reduce all actions to ashes. There is nothing so pure as knowledge. He who has true faith is attached to God, and he who has controlled his senses, attains knowledge, and having attained it, secures peace. He who is foolish, an unbeliever, and full of doubts, is destroyed. He who

1 *Gītā*, x.36-41.

always doubting has neither this world, nor the other, nor does he enjoy any happiness. Even the worst sinner can hope to cross the sea of sins in the boat of knowledge.[1] In the *Gītā*, IV.42, Kṛṣṇa says to Arjuna, "Therefore, having destroyed the ignorance of your heart by the sword of knowledge, and having cut asunder all doubts, raise yourself up." But what is this knowledge? In the *Gītā,* IV.36, in the same context, this knowledge is defined to be that view of things by which all beings are perceived in this self or God. The true knowledge of God destroys all *karma* in the sense that he who has perceived and realized the true nature of all things in God cannot be attached to his passions and desires as an ignorant man would be. In another passage, already referred to, it is said that the roots of the worldly Aśvattha tree are to be cut by the sword of unattachment. The confusion into which Arjuna falls in the *Gītā,* III.1 and 2, regarding the relative excellence of the path of *karma* and the path of knowledge is wholly unfounded. Kṛṣṇa points out in the *Gītā,* III.3, that there are two paths, the path of knowledge and the path of duties (*jñāna-yoga* and *karma-yoga).* The confusion had arisen from the fact that Kṛṣṇa had described the immortality of soul and the undesirability of Vedic actions done with a motive, and had also asked Arjuna to fight and yet remain unattached and perform his duty for the sake of duty. The purpose of the *Gītā* was to bring about reconciliation between these two paths, and to show that the path of knowledge leads to the path of duties by liberating it from the bonds of attachment; for all attachment is due to ignorance, and ignorance is removed by true knowledge. But the true knowledge of God may be of a twofold nature. One may attain a knowledge of God in His transcendence as Brahman, and attain the philosophic wisdom of the foundation of all things in Brahman as the ultimate substance and source of all manifestation and appearance. There is another way of clinging to God as a super-person, in a personal relation of intimacy, friendship and dependence. The *Gītā* admits that both these ways may lead us to the attainment of our highest realization. But it is the latter which the *Gītā* prefers and considers easier.

1 *Gītā*, IV.37-41.

Thus the *Gītā* says (XII.3-5) that those who adore the indefinable, unchangeable, omnipresent, unthinkable, and the unmanifested, controlling all their senses, with equal eyes for all and engaged in the good of all, by this course attain Him. Those who fix their mind on the unmanifested *(avyakta)* find this course very hard. But those who dedicate all their actions to God and, clinging to Him as their only support, are devoted to Him in constant communion, them He saves soon from the sea of death and rebirth.[1]

The most important point in which the *Gītā* differs from the Upaniṣads is that the *Gītā* very strongly emphasizes the fact that the best course for attaining our highest realization is to dedicate all our actions to God, to cling to Him as our nearest and dearest, and always to be in communion with Him. The *Gītā* draws many of its ideas from the Upaniṣads and looks to them with respect. It accepts the idea of Brahman as a part of the essence of God, and agrees that those who fix their mind on Brahman as their ideal also attain the high ideal of realizing God. But this is only a compromise; for the *Gītā* emphasizes the necessity of a personal relation with God, whom we can love and adore. The beginning of our association with God must be made by dedicating the fruits of all our actions to God, by being a friend of all and sympathetic to all, by being self-controlled, the same in sorrow or happiness, self-contented, and in a state of perfect equanimity and equilibrium. It is through such a moral elevation that a man becomes apt in steadying his mind on God and ultimately in fixing his mind on God. In the *Gītā* Kṛṣṇa as God asks Arjuna to give up all ceremonials or religious courses and to cling to God as the only protector, and He promises that because of that God will liberate him.[2] Again, it is said that it is by devotion that a man knows what God is in reality and, thus knowing Him truly as He is, enters into Him. It is by seeking entire protection in God that one can attain his eternal state.[3]

1 *Gītā*, XII.6, 7.

2 *Ibid.* XVIII.66.

3 *Ibid.* XVIII.55, 62.

But, though in order to attain the height at which it is possible to fix one's mind on God, one should first acquire the preliminary qualification of detaching oneself from the bonds of passions and desires, yet it is sometimes possible to reverse the situation. The *Gītā* thus holds that those whose minds and souls are full of God's love, who delight in constantly talking and thinking of God and always adore God with love, are dear to Him, and God, through His great mercy and kindness, grants them the proper wisdom and destroys the darkness of their ignorance by the light of knowledge.[1] In the *Gītā*, XVIII.57-58, Kṛṣṇa as God asks Arjuna to leave all fruits of actions to God and to fill his mind with God, and He assures him that He will then, by His divine grace, save him from all sorrows, troubles or difficulties. Again, in IX.30-32 it is said that, even if a man is extremely wicked, if he adores God devotedly, he becomes a saint; for he has adopted the right course, and he soon becomes religious and attains eternal peace of mind. Even sinner's, women, Vaiśyas and Śūdras who cling to God for support, are emancipated. Kṛṣṇa as God assures Arjuna that a devotee *(bhakta)* of God can never be lost.[2] If a man clings to God, no matter whether he has understood Him rightly or not, no matter whether he has taken the right course of approaching Him or not, God accepts him in whichever way he clings to Him. No one can be lost. In whichever way one may be seeking God, one is always in God's path.[3] If a man, prompted by diverse desires, takes to wrong gods, then even unto those gods God grants him true devotion, with which he follows his worship of those gods, and, even through such worship, grants him his desires.[4] God is the Lord of all and the friend of all beings. It is only great-souled men who with complete constancy of mind worship God, and with firm devotion repeat the name of God, and, being always in communion with Him, adore Him with devotion. God is easily accessible to those who always think of God with

1 *Gītā,* X.9-11.
2 *Ibid.* IX.30-32.
3 *Ibid.* IV.11.
4 *Ibid.* VII.20-22.

inalienable attachment.[1] In another passage (VII.16, 17) it is said that there are four classes of people who adore God: those who are enquiring, those who are in trouble, those who wish to attain some desired things, and those who are wise. Of these the wise (*jñānin*), who are always in communion with Him and who are devoted to Him alone, are superior; the wise are dear to Him and He is dear to them. In this passage it has been suggested that true wisdom consists in the habit of living in communion with God and in being in constant devotion to God. The path of *bhakti*, or devotion, is thus praised in the *Gītā* as being the best. For the *Gītā* holds that, even if a man cannot proceed in the normal path of self-elevation and detach himself from passions and desires and establish himself in equanimity, he may still, simply by clinging to God and by firm devotion to Him, bring himself within the sphere of His grace, and by grace alone acquire true wisdom and achieve that moral elevation, with little or no struggle, which is attained with so much difficulty by others. The path of *bhakti* is thus introduced in the *Gītā*, for the first time, as an independent path side by side with the path of wisdom and knowledge of the Upaniṣads and with the path of austere self-discipline. Moral elevation, self-control, etc. are indeed regarded as an indispensable preliminary to any kind of true self-realization. But the advantage of the path of devotion (*bhakti*) consists in this, that, while some seekers have to work hard on the path of self-control and austere self-discipline, either by constant practice or by the aid of philosophic wisdom, the devotee makes an easy ascent to a high elevation—not because he is more energetic and better equipped than his fellow-workers in other paths, but because he has resigned himself completely to God; and God, being pleased with his devotees who cling fast to Him and know nothing else, grants them wisdom and raises them up through higher and higher stages of self-elevation, self-realization and bliss. Arjuna treated Kṛṣṇa, the incarnation of God on earth, as his friend, and Kṛṣṇa in the role of God exhorted him to depend entirely on Him and assured him that He would liberate him—He was asking him

1 *Gītā,* IV.13-15; V.29; VII.14.

to give up everything else and cling to Him as his only support. The *Gītā* lays down for the first time the corner-stone of the teachings of the *Bhāgavata-purāṇa* and of the later systems of Vaiṣṇava thought, which elaborated the theory of *bhakti* and described it as the principal method of self-elevation and self-realization.

Another important feature of the *Gītā* doctrine of devotion consists in the fact that, as, on the one hand, God is contemplated by His devotees in the intimate personal relation of a father, teacher, master and friend, with a full consciousness of His divinity and His nature as the substratum and the upholder of the entire animate and inanimate cosmic universe, so, on the other hand, the transcendent personality of God is realized not only as the culmination of spiritual greatness and the ultimate reconciliation of all relative differences, of high and low, good and bad, but as the great deity, with a physical, adorable form, whom the devotee can worship not only mentally and spiritually, but also externally, with holy offerings of flowers and leaves. The transcendent God is not only immanent in the universe, but also present before the devotee in the form of a great deity resplendent with brightness, or in the personal form of the man-god Kṛṣṇa, in whom God incarnated Himself. The *Gītā* combines together different conceptions of God without feeling the necessity of reconciling the oppositions or contradictions involved in them. It does not seem to be aware of the philosophical difficulty of combining the concept of God as the unmanifested, differenceless entity with the notion of Him as the super-person Who incarnates Himself on earth in the human form and behaves in the human manner. It is not aware of the difficulty that, if all good and evil should have emanated from God, and if there be ultimately no moral responsibility, and if everything in the world should have the same place in God, there is no reason why God should trouble to incarnate Himself as man, when there is a disturbance of the Vedic *dharma*. If God is impartial to all, and if He is absolutely unperturbed, why should He favour the man who clings to Him, and why, for his sake, overrule the world-order of events and in his favour suspend the law of *karma*? It is only by constant endeavours and practice that one can cut asunder the bonds of *karma.* Why should it be made so easy for even a wicked man who clings to God to release himself from the bonds of attachment and *karma,* without any effort on his part? Again, the *Gītā* does not attempt to reconcile the disparate parts which constitute the complex super-personality of God. How are the unmanifested or *avyakta* part as Brahman, the *avyakta* part as the cosmic substratum of the universe, the *prakṛti* part as the producer of the *guṇas*, and the *prakṛti* part as the *jīvas* or individual selves, to be combined and melted together to form a complex personality? If the unmanifested nature is the ultimate abode *(paraṃdhāma)* of God, how can God as a person, who cannot be regarded as a manifestation of this ultimate reality, be considered to be transcendent? How can there be a relation between God as a person and His diverse nature as the cosmic universe, *jīva* and the *guṇas*? In a system like that of Śaṅkara Brahman and Īśvara, one and the many could be combined together in one scheme, by holding Brahman as real and Īśvara and the many as unreal and illusory, produced by reflection of Brahman in the *māyā,* the principle of illusoriness. But, howsoever Śaṅkara might interpret the *Gītā*, it does not seem that it considered Īśvara or the world as in the least degree illusory. In the Upaniṣads also the notion of Īśvara and the notion of Brahman are sometimes found side by side. As regards God as Īśvara, the *Gītā* not only does not think him to be illusory, but considers him the highest truth and reality. Thus there is no way of escaping from any of the categories of reality—the two *avyaktas, prakṛti, jīva* and the super-personality of Īśvara comprehending and transcending them all. The concepts of Brahman, *jīva*, the unmanifested category from which the world proceeds, and the *guṇas* are all found in the Upaniṣads in passages which are probably mostly unrelated. But the *Gītā* seems to take them all together, and to consider them as constituents of Īśvara, which are also upheld by Him in His superior form, in which He transcends and controls them all. In the Upaniṣads the doctrine of *bhakti* can hardly be found, though here and there faint traces of it may be perceived. If the Upaniṣads ever speak of Īśvara, it is only to show His great majesty, power and glory, as the controller and upholder of all. But the *Gītā* is steeped in the mystic consciousness of an intimate personal relation with God, not only as the majestic super-person, but as a friend who incarnates Himself for the good of man and shares his joys and sorrows with him, and to whom a man could cling for support in troubles and difficulties and even appeal for earthly goods. He is the great teacher, with whom one can associate oneself for acquisition of wisdom and the light of knowledge. But He could be more than all this. He could be the dearest of the dear and the nearest of the near, and could be felt as being so intimate, that a man could live simply for the joy of his love for Him; he could cling to Him as the one dear friend, his highest goal, and leave everything else for Him; he could consider, in his deep love for Him, all his other religious duties and works of life as being relatively unimportant; he could thus constantly talk of Him, think of Him, and live in Him. This is the path of *bhakti* or devotion, and the *Gītā* assures us that, whatever may be the hindrances and whatever may be the difficulties, the *bhakta* (devotee) of God cannot be lost. It is from the point of view of this mystic consciousness that the *Gītā* seems to reconcile the apparently philosophically irreconcilable elements. The *Gītā* was probably written at a time when philosophical views had not definitely crystallized into hard-and-fast systems of thought, and when the distinguishing philosophical niceties, scholarly disputations, the dictates of argument, had not come into fashion. The *Gītā*, therefore, is not to be looked upon as a properly schemed system of philosophy, but as a manual of right conduct and right perspective of things in the light of a mystical approach to God in self-resignation, devotion, friendship and humility.

VIṢṆU, VASUDEVA AND KṚṢṆA

Viṣṇu, Bhagavat, Nārāyaṇa, Hari and Kṛṣṇa are often used in a large section of Indian religious literature as synonymous names of the supreme lord. Of these Viṣṇu is an important god of the *Ṛg-Veda*, who is one of the *ādityas* and who makes three strides in the sky, probably as he manifests himself in the eastern horizon, as he rises to the zenith and as he sets in the west. He is also represented in the *Ṛg-Veda* as a great fighter and an ally of Indra. It is further said that he has two earthly steps and another higher step which is known only to himself. But in the *Ṛg-Veda* Viṣṇu is certainly inferior to Indra, with whom he was often associated, as is evident from such names as *Indrā-viṣṇu* (RV.IV.55.4; VII.99.5; VIII.10.2, etc.). According to later tradition Viṣṇu was the youngest, the twelfth of the *ādityas*, though he was superior to them all in good qualities.[1] His three steps in the *Ṛg* -Vedic allusion have been explained in the *Nirukta* as referring to the three stages of the sun's progress in the morning, at midday and at evening. One of the names of Viṣṇu in the *Ṛg-Veda* is Śipiviṣṭa, which Durgācārya explains as "surrounded with the early rays" *(śipi-saṃjñair bāla-raśmibhir āviṣṭa).*[2] Again, the sage praises Viṣṇu in the *Ṛg-Veda* in the following terms: "I, a master of hymns and knowing the sacred customs, to-day praise that name of thine, Śipiviṣṭa. I, who am weak, glorify thee, who art mighty and dwellest beyond this world."[3] All this shows that Viṣṇu was regarded as the sun, or endowed with the qualities of the sun. The fact that Viṣṇu was regarded as dwelling beyond this world is probably one of the earliest signs of his gradually increasing superiority. For the next stage one must turn to the *Śatapatha-brāhmaṇa.* In I.2.4 of that work it is said that the demons *(asura)* and the gods were vying with one another; the gods were falling behind, and the demons were trying to distribute the world among themselves; the gods followed them, making Viṣṇu the sacrifice as their leader *(te yajñam eva Viṣṇuṃ puraskṛtyeyuḥ*), and desired their own shares; the demons felt jealous and said that they could

1 एकादशस् तथा त्वष्टा द्वादशो विष्णुर् उच्यते
जघन्यजस् तु सर्वेषाम् आदित्यानां गुणाधिकः ॥
Ekādaśas tathā Tvaṣṭā dvādaśo Viṣṇur ucyate
jaghanyajas tu sarveṣām ādityānāṃ guṇādhikaḥ.—Mahā-bhārata, I.65.16. Calcutta, Bangavasi Press, second edition, 1908.

2 *Nirukta,* v.9. Bombay edition, 1918.

3 *Ṛg-Veda,* VII.100.5, translated by Dr L. Sarup, quoted in *Nirukta, v.*8.

give only so much ground as would be occupied by Viṣṇu when he lay down, Viṣṇu being a dwarf (*vāmano ha Viṣṇur āsa*). The gods felt dissatisfied at this, and they approached him with various *mantras* and in consequence attained the whole world. Again, in XIV.1 of the same work, Kurukṣetra is referred to as being the place of the sacrificial performances of the gods, and it is said there that in industry, rigorism *(tapas),* faith, etc. Viṣṇu was the best of all gods and was regarded as being superior to them all *(tasmād āhur Viṣṇur devānāṃ śreṣṭhaḥ),* and was himself the sacrifice. Again, in *Taittirīya-saṃhitā*, I.7.5.4, in *Vājasaneyi-saṃhitā,* I.30; II.6.8; V.21, in *Atharva-Veda,* V.26.7; VIII.5.10, etc., Viṣṇu is referred to as the chief of the gods *(Viṣṇu-mukhā devā).* Again, Viṣṇu as sacrifice attained unlimited fame. Once he was resting his head on the end of his bow; and, when some ants, perceiving that, said, "How should we be rewarded, if we could gnaw the strings of the bow," the gods said that they would then be rewarded with food; and so the ants gnawed away the strings, and, as the two ends of the bow sprang apart, Viṣṇu's head was tom from his body and became the sun.[1] This story not only shows the connection of Viṣṇu with the sun, but also suggests that thc later story of Kṛṣṇa's being shot with an arrow by an archer originated from the legend of Viṣṇu's being killed by the flying ends of his bow. The place of Viṣṇu *(Viṣṇu-pada)* means the zenith, as the highest place of the sun, and it is probable that the idea of the zenith being the place of Viṣṇu led also to the idea that Viṣṇu had a superior place transcending everything, which was, however, clearly perceived by the wise. Thus, at the beginning of the daily prayer-hymns of the Brahmans, known as *sandhyā*, it is said that the wise see always that superior place of Viṣṇu, like an open eye in the sky.[2] The word *vaiṣṇava* is used in the literal sense of "belonging to Viṣṇu" in the *Vājasaneyi-saṃhitā,* V.21, 23, 25, *Taittirīya-saṃhitā,* V.6.9.2.3, *Aitareya-brāhmaṇa,* III.38, *Śatapatha-brāhmaṇa,* I.1.4.9; III.5.3.2, etc.; but the use

1 *Śatapatha-brāhmaṇa,* XIV.1.

2 *tad Viṣṇoḥ paramaṃ padaṃ sadā paśyanti sūrayah divīva cakṣur ātatam. Ācamana-mantra* of the daily *sandhyā* prayer-hymn.

of the word in the sense of a sect of religion is not to be found anywhere in the earlier literature. Even the *Gītā* does not use the word, and it is not found in any of the earlier Upaniṣads; it can be traced only in the later parts of the *Mahā-bhārata.*

Again, it is well known that the supreme man, *or puruṣa,* is praised in very high terms in the man-hymn (*Puruṣa-sūkta*) of the *Ṛg-Veda*, X.90, where it is said that *puruṣa* is all that we see, what is past and what is future, and that everythıng has come out of him; the gods performed sacrifice with him with the oblations of the seasons, and out of this sacrifice *puruṣa* was first born, and then the gods and all living beings; the various castes were born out of him; the sky, the heavens and the earth have all come out of him; he is the creator and upholder of all; it is by knowing him that one attains immortality; there is no other way of salvation. It is curious that there should be a word *nārāyana,* similar in meaning (etymologically *nara + phak,* born in the race or lineage of man) *to puruṣa,* which was also used to mean the supreme being and identified with *puruṣa* and Viṣṇu. In *Śatapatha-brāhmaṇa,* XIV.3.4, *puruṣa* is identified with *nārāyaṇa (purusaṃ ha nārāyaṇaṃ Prajāpatir uvāca).* Again,in *Śatapatha-brāhmaṇa*, XIII.6.1, the idea of the *puruṣa-sūkta* is further extended, and the *puruṣa nārāyaṇa* is said to have performed the *pañca-rātra* sacrifice (*pañcarātraṃ ya-jña-kratum*) and thereby transcended everything and become everything. This *pañca-rātra* sacrifice involves the (spiritual) sacrifice of *puruṣa (puruṣa-medho yajña-kratur bhavati,* XIII.6.7). The five kinds of sacrifice, five kinds of animals, the year with the five kinds of seasons, the five kinds of indwelling entities *(pañca-vidham adhyātmam)* can all be attained by the *pañca-rātra* sacrifices. The sacrifice was continued for five days, and the Vedic habit of figurative thinking associated each of the days of the sacrifice with various kinds of desirable things, so that the five-day sacrifice was considered to lead to many things which are fivefold in their nature. The reference to the five kinds of indwelling entities soon produced *the pañca-rātra* doctrine of the manifestation of God in various modes as the external deity of worship *(arcā),* inner controller *(antar-yāmin),* as various manifestations of His lordly power (*vibhava*), as successive deity-forms in intimate association as *vyūha* and as the highest God *(para).* This idea is also found in the later *Pānca-rātra* scriptures, such as *Ahirbudhnya-saṃhitā* (I.1) and the like, where God is described as having his highest form along with the *vyūha* forms. *Puruṣa* is thus identified with *nārāyaṇa,* who, by sacrifice of *puruṣa (puruṣa-medha),* became all this world. The etymological definition of *nārāyaṇa* as "one who has descended from man *(nara),*" as herein suggested in accordance with Pāṇini, IV.1.99, is not, however, accepted everywhere. Thus Manu, I.10, derives *nārāyaṇa* from *nāra,* meaning "water," and *ayana,* meaning "abode," and *nāra* (water), again, is explained as "that which has descended from *nara,*" or supreme man.[1] The *Mahā-bhārata*, III.12,952 and 15,819 and XII.13,168, accepts Manu's derivation; but in V.2568 it says that the supreme God is called *nārāyaṇa* because he is also the refuge of men.[2] The *Taittirīya-Āraṇyaka*, X.1.6, identifies *nārāyaṇa* with Vāsudeva and Viṣṇu.[3] It may be suggested in this connection that even the Upaniṣad doctrine of the self as the supreme reality is probably a development of this type of ideas which regarded man as supreme God. The word *puruṣa* is very frequently used in the Upaniṣads in the sense of man, as well as in that of the highest being or supreme reality. In the *Mahā-bhārata nara* and *nārāyaṇa* are referred to as being the forms of the supreme lord. Thus it is said, "The four-faced Brahmā, capable of being understood only with the aid of the *niruktas,* joined his hands and, addressing Rudra, said, "Let good happen to the three worlds. Throw down thy weapons, O lord of

1 आपो नारा इति प्रोक्ता आपो वै नरसूनवः ।
ता यद् अस्यायनं पूर्वं तेन नारायणः स्मृतः ॥
āpo nārā iti proktā āpo vai nara-sūnavaḥ
tā yad asyāyanaṃ pūrvaṃ tena nārāyaṇaḥ smṛtaḥ.—Manu, I.10.
Water is called *nāra*; water is produced from man, and, since he rested in water in the beginning, he is called *nārāyaṇa.* Kullūka, in explaining this, says that *nara,* or man, here means the supreme self, or Brahman.

2 *Narāṇām ayanāc cāpi tato nārāyaṇah smṛtaḥ.—Mahā-bhārata,* V.2568.

3 *Nārāyaṇāya vidmahe vāsudevāya dhīmahi tan no Viṣṇuḥ pracodayāt. Taittirlya Āranyaka,* p. 700. Ānandāśrama Press, Poona, 1898.

the universe, from desire of benefiting the universe. That which is indestructible, immutable, supreme, the origin of the universe, uniform and the supreme actor, that which transcends all pairs of opposites and is inactive, has, choosing to be displayed, been pleased to assume this one blessed form (for, though double, the two represent but one and the same form). This *nara* and *nārāyaṇa* (the displayed forms of supreme Brahman) have taken birth in the race of *dharma.* The foremost of all deities, these two are observers of the highest vows and endued with the severest penances. Through some reason best known to Him I myself have sprung from the attribute of His Grace Eternal, as thou hast; for, though thou hast ever existed since all the pure creations, thou too hast sprung from His Wrath. With myself then, these deities and all the great Rṣis, do thou adore this displayed form of Brahman and let there be peace unto all the worlds without any delay."[1] In the succeeding chapter (i.e. *Mahā-bhārata, Śānti-parva,* 343) *nara* and *nārāyaṇa* are described as being two foremost of sages *(ṛṣi)* and two ancient deities engaged in the practice of penances, observing high vows and depending upon their own selves and transcending the very sun in energy.

The word *bhagavat* in the sense of blissful and happy is a very old one and is used in the *Ṛg-Veda,* I.164.40; VII.41.4; X.60.12 and in the *Atharva-Veda*, II.10.2; V.31.11, etc. But in the *Mahā-bhārata* and other such early literature it came to denote Viṣṇu or Vāsudeva, and the word *bhāgavata* denoted the religious sect which regarded Viṣṇu as Nārāyaṇa or Vāsudeva as their supreme god. The Pali canonical work *Niddesa* refers to various superstitious religious sects, among which it mentions the followers of Vāsudeva, Baladeva, Puṇṇabhadda, Maṇibhadda, Aggi, Nāga, Suparṇa, Yakkha, Asura, Gandhabba, Mahārāja, Canda, Suriya, Inda, Brahmā, dog, crow, cow, etc. It is easy to understand why a Buddhist work should regard the worship of Vāsudeva as being of a very low type; but at any rate it proves that the worship of Vāsudeva was prevalent during

1 *Mahā-bhārata, Śānti-parva,* 342.124-129. P. C. Roy's translation, *Mokṣa-dharma-parva,* p. 817. Calcutta.

the period when the *Niddesa* was codified. Again, in commenting upon Pāṇini, IV.3.98 (*Vāsudevār-junābhyāṃ vuñ),* Patañjali points out that the word Vāsudeva here does not denote the Vāsudeva who was the son of Vasudeva of the Kṣattriya race of Vṛṣṇis, since, had it been so, the suffix *vuñ,* which is absolutely equivalent to *vuñ,* could well be by Pāṇini, IV.3.99 *(gotra-kṣattriyākhyebhyo bdhulaṃ vuñ),* by which *vuñ* is suffixed to names of Kṣattriya race. Patañjali thus holds that the word *Vāsudeva* is in this rule not used to refer to any Kṣattriya race, but is a name of the Lord *(saṃjñaiṣā tatra bhāgavataḥ).* If Patañjali's interpretation is to be trusted, for which there is every reason, Vāsudeva as God is to be distinguished from the Kṣattriya Vāsudeva, the son of Vasudeva of the race of Vṛṣṇis. It was well established in Pāṇini's time that Vāsudeva was God, and that His followers were called *Vāsudevaka,* for the formation of which word by the *vuñ* suffix Pāṇini had to make the rule (IV.3.98). Again, the Ghosuṇḍī inscription in Rajputana, which is written in Brāhmī, an early form of about 200-150 BC, contains a reference to the building of a wall round the temple of Vāsudeva and saṃkarṣaṇa. In the Besnagar inscription of about 100 BC Heliodorus, son of Diya, describes himself as a great devotee of Bhagavat (*parama-bhāgavata*), who had erected a pillar bearing an image of Garuda. In the Nānāghāt inscription of 100 BC Vāsudeva and saṃkarṣaṇa appear together as deities to whom adorations are addressed along with other gods. If the testimony of Patañjali is accepted, the religious sect of Vāsudevas existed before Pāṇini. It is generally believed that Patañjali lived in 150 BC, since in course of interpreting a grammatical rule which allowed the use of the past tense in reference to famous contemporary events not witnessed by the speaker he illustrates it by using a past tense in referring to the Greek invasion of the city of Sāketa (*aruṇad Yavanaḥ Sāketam);* as this event took place in 150 BC, it is regarded as a famous contemporary event not witnessed by Patañjali. Patañjali was the second commentator of Pāṇini, the first being Kātyāyana. Sir R. G. Bhandarkar points out that Patañjali notices variant readings in Kātyāyana's *Vārttikas,* as found in the texts used by the schools of Bhāradvājīyas, Saunāgas and others, some of which might be considered as emendations of the *Vārttikas*, though Patañjali's introduction of them by the verb *pathanti,* "they read," is an indication that he regarded them as different readings.[1] From this Sir R. G. Bhandarkar argues that between Kātyāyana and Patañjali a considerable time must have elapsed, which alone can explain the existence of the variant readings of Kātyāyana's text in Patañjali's time. He therefore agrees with the popular tradition in regarding Pāṇini as a contemporary of the Nandas, who preceded the Mauryas. Kātyāyana thus flourished in the first half of the 5th century BC But, as both Goldsṭūckerand Sir R.G. Bhandarkar have pointed out, the *Vārttika* of Kātyāyana notices many grammatical forms which are not noticed by Pāṇini, and this, considering the great accuracy of Pāṇini as a grammarian, naturally leads to the supposition that those forms did not exist in his time. Goldsṭūckerand gives a list of words admitted into Pāṇini's *sūtras* which had gone out of use by Kātyāyana's time, and he also shows that some words which probably did not exist in Pāṇini's time had come to be used later and are referred to by Kātyāyana. All this implies that Pāṇini must have flourished at least two or three hundred years before Kātyāyana. The reference to the Vāsudeva sect in Pāṇini's *sūtras* naturally suggests its existence before his time. The allusions to Vāsudeva in the inscriptions referred to above can be regarded as corroborative evidence pointing to the early existence of the Vāsudeva sect, who worshipped Vāsudeva or Bhagavat as the supreme Lord.

Turning to literary references to Vāsudeva and Kṛṣṇa, we find the story of Vāsudeva, who is also called-by his family name Kanha and Keśava (probably on account of his bunch of hair), in the *Ghaṭa-jātaka.* The story agrees in some important details with the usual accounts of Kṛṣṇa, though there are some new deviations. A reference to the Vṛṣṇi race of Kṣattriyas is found in Pāṇini, IV.1.114 *(ṛṣy-andhaka-vṛṣṇi-kurubhyaś ca).* The word is formed by an *uṇādi* suffix, and it literally means "powerful" or "a great leader."[2] It also

1 Sir R.G. Bhandarkar's *Early History of the Deccan*, p. 7.

2 *Yūthema vṛṣṇir ejati*, *Ṛg-Veda*, I.10.2.

means "heretic" *(pāṣaṇḍa)* and one who is passionately angry *(caṇḍa)*. It is further used to denote the Yādava race, and Kṛṣṇa is often addressed as Vārṣṇeya, and in the *Gītā*, X.37, Kṛṣṇa says, "Of the Vṛṣṇis I am Vāsudeva." The Vṛṣṇis are referred to in Kauṭilya's *Artha-śāstra,* where the group of Vṛṣṇis (*vṛṣṇi-saṅgha*) is said to have attacked Dvaipāyana. The *Ghaṭa-jātaka* also has the story of the curse of Kanha Dvaipāyana as the cause of the destruction of the Vṛṣṇis. But the *Mahā-bhārata* (XVI.1) holds that the curse was pronounced by Viśvāmitra, Kaṇva and Nārada upon Śāmba, the son of Kṛṣṇa. Two Vāsudevas are mentioned in the *Mahā-bhārata*: Vāsudeva, the king of the Pauṇḍras, and Vāsudeva or Kṛṣṇa, the brother of Samkar-ṣaṇa, and both of them are mentioned as being present in the great assemblage of kings at the house of King Drupada for the marriage of Draupadī; it is the latter Vāsudeva who is regarded as God. It is very probable that Vāsudeva originally was a name of the sun and thus became associated with Viṣṇu, who with his three steps traversed the heavens; and a similarity of Kṛṣṇa or Vāsudeva to the sun is actually suggested in the *Mahā-bhārata,* XII.341.41, where Nārāyaṇa says, "Being like the sun, I cover the whole world with my rays, and I am also the sustainer of all beings and am hence called Vāsudeva."

Again, the word *Sātvata* also is used as a synonym of Vāsudeva or Bhāgavata. The word *Sātvata* in the plural form is a name of a tribe of the Yādavas, and in the *Mahā-bhārata,* VII.7662, the phrase *Satvatāṃ varaḥ* is used to denote Sātyaki, a member of the Yādava race, though this appellation is applied to Kṛṣṇa in a large number of places in the *Mahā-bhārata.*[1] In the later *Bhāga-vata-purāṇa* (IX.9.50) it is said that the Sātvatas worship Brahman as Bhagavān and as Vāsudeva. In the *Mahā-bhārata*, VI.66.41, Saṃkarṣaṇa is said to have introduced the *sātvata* rites in worshipping Vāsudeva. If Sātvata was the name of a race, it is easy to imagine that the persons may have had special rites in worshipping Vāsudeva. Yāmunācārya, the great teacher of Rāmānuja in the tenth century AD, says that

1 *Mahā-bhārata,* V.2581, 3041, 3334, 3360, 4370; IX.2532, 3502; X.726; XII.1502, 1614, 7533.

those who adore God (*bhagavat*), the supreme person, with purity *(sattva),* are called *bhāgavata* and *sātvata.*[1] Yāmuna strongly urges that Sātvatas are Brāhmaṇas by caste, but are attached to Bhagavat as the supreme lord. Yāmuna, however, seems to urge this in strong opposition to the current view that Sātvatas were a low-caste people, who had not the initiation with the holy thread and were an outcast people originated from the Vaiśyas.[2] The Sātvatas are said to be the fifth low-caste people, who worship in the temples of Viṣṇu by the orders of the king, and are also called Bhāgavatas.[3] The Sātvatas and Bhāgavatas are those who make their living by worshipping images and are hence low and disreputable. Yāmuna urges that this popular view about the Bhāgavatas and the Sātvatas is all incorrect; for, though there are many Sātvatas who make a living by worshipping images, not all Sātvatas and Bhāgavatas do so; and there are many among them who worship Bhagavat, as the supreme person, solely by personal devotion and attachment.

From Patañjali's remarks in commenting on Pāṇini, IV.3.98, it is seen that he believed in the existence of two Vāsudevas, one a leader of the Vṛṣṇi race and the other God. as Bhagavat. It has already been pointed out that the name Vāsudeva occurs also in the *Ghaṭa-jātaka.* It may therefore be argued that the name Vāsudeva was an old name, and the evidence of the passage of the *Niddesa*, as well as that of Patañjali, shows that it was a name of

---

1 ततश् च सत्त्वाद् भगवान् भज्यते यैह् परः पुमान्
ते सात्वता भागवता इत्य् उच्यन्ते द्विजोत्तमैः ॥
tataś ca sattvād bhagavān bhajyate yaih paraḥ pumān
te sātvatā bhāgavatā ity ucyante dvijottamaiḥ.
Yāmuna's *Āgama-prāmāṇya,* p. 7.6.

2 Thus Manu (X.23) says:
वैश्यात् तु जायते व्रात्यात् सुधन्वाचार्य एव च।
कारूषश् च विजन्मा च मैत्रस् सात्वत एव च॥
vaiśyāt tu jāyate vrātyāt sudhanvācārya eva ca
kārūṣaś ca vijanmā ca maitras sātvata eva ca.

3 पञ्चमः सात्वतो नाम विष्णोर् आयतनं हि सः।
पूजयेद् आज्ञया राज्ञां स तु भागवतः स्मृतः॥
pañcamaḥ sātvato nāma Viṣṇor āyatanaṃ hi saḥ
pūjayed ājñayā rājñāṃ sa tu bhāgavataḥ smṛtaḥ.—Ibid. p. 8.

God or Bhagavat. The later explanation of Vāsudeva as "the son of Vasudeva" may therefore be regarded as an unauthorized surmise. It is very probable that Vāsudeva was worshipped by the race of Yādavas as a tribal hero according to their own tribal rites and that he was believed to be an incarnation of Viṣṇu, who was in his turn associated with the sun. Megasthenes, in his account of India as he saw' it, speaks of the Sourasenoi—an Indian nation in whose land are two great cities, Methora and Kleisobora, through which flows the navigable river Jobares—as worshipping Heracles. "Methora" in all probability means Mathura and "Jobares" Jumna. It is probable that Heracles is Hari, which again is a name of Vāsudeva. Again in the *Mahābhārata*, VI.65, Bhīṣma says that he was told by the ancient sages that formerly the great supreme person appeared before the assembly of gods and sages, and Brahmā began to adore Him with folded hands. This great Being, who is there adored as Vāsudeva, had first created out of Himself saṃkarṣaṇa, and then Pradyumna, and from Pradyumna Aniruddha, and it was from Aniruddha that Brahmā was created. This great Being, Vāsudeva, incarnated Himself as the two sages, Nara and Nārāyaṇa. He Himself says in the *Mahā-bhārata*, VI.66, that "as Vāsudeva I should be adored by all and no one should ignore me in my human body"; in both these chapters Kṛṣṇa and Vāsudeva are identical, and in the *Gītā* Kṛṣṇa says that "of the Vṛṣṇis I am Vāsudeva." It has also been pointed out that Vāsudeva belonged to the Kanhāyana *gotra.* As Sir R. G. Bhandarkar says, "It is very probable that the identification of Kṛṣṇa with Vāsudeva was due to the similarity of the *gotra* name with the name of Kṛṣṇa."[1] From the frequent allusions to Vāsudeva in Patañjali's commentary and in the *Mahābhārata,* where he is referred to as the supreme person, it is very reasonable to suppose that the word is a proper noun, as the name of a person worshipped as God, and not a mere patronymic name indicating an origin from a father Vasudeva. Kṛṣṇa, Janārdana, Keśava, Hari, etc. are not Vṛṣṇi names, but were used as personal appellations of Vāsudeva. Patañjali in his commentary on Pāṇini,

1 Sir R.G. Bhandarkar 's *Vaiṣṇavism and Śaivism*, pp. 11-12.

IV.3.98, notes that Vāsudeva, as the name of a Kṣattriya king of the race of Vṛṣṇis, is to be distinguished from Vāsudeva as the name of God. This God, worshipped by the Sātvatas according to their family rites, probably came to be identified with a Vṛṣṇi king Vāsudeva, and some of the personal characteristics of this king became also personal characteristics of the god Vāsudeva. The word Kṛṣṇa occurs several times in the older literature. Thus Kṛṣṇa appears as a Vedic *ṛṣi,* as the composer of *Ṛg-Veda,* VIII.74. In the *Mahā-bhārata Anukramaṇī* Kṛṣṇa is said to have descended from Aṅgiras. Kṛṣṇa appears in the *Chāndogya Upaniṣad* (III.17) as the son of DevakI, as in the *Ghaṭa-jātaka.* It is therefore probable that Vāsudeva came to be identified with Kṛṣṇa, the son of Devakī. The older conception of Kṛṣṇa's being a *ṛtvij* is found in the *Mahā-bhārata,* and Bhīṣma in the *Sabhā-parva* speaks of him as being a *ṛtvij* and well-versed in the accessory literature of the Vedas (*vedāṅga*). It is very probable, as Dr Ray Chaudhury points out, that Kṛṣṇa, the son of Devakī, was the same as Vāsudeva, the founder of the Bhāgavata system; for he is referred to in the *Ghaṭa-jātaka* as being Kanhāyana, or Kanha, which is the same as Kṛṣṇa, and as Devakī-putra, and in the *Chāndogya Upaniṣad,* III.17.6, also he is referred to as being Devakī-putra. In the *Ghaṭa-jātaka* Kṛṣṇa is spoken of as being a warrior, whereas in the *Chāndogya Upaniṣad* he is a pupil of Ghora Aṅgirasa, who taught him a symbolic sacrifice, in which penances *(tapas),* gifts *(dāna),* sincerity *(ārjava),* non-injury *(ahiṃsā)* and truthfulness *(satya-vacana)* may be regarded as sacrificial fees *(dakṣiṇā).* The *Mahā-bhārata,* II.317, describes Kṛṣṇa both as a sage who performed long courses of asceticism in Gandhamādana, Puṣkara and Badarī, and as a great warrior. He is also described in the *Mahā-bhārata* as Vāsudeva, Devakī-putra and as the chief of the Sātvatas, and his divinity is everywhere acknowledged there. But it is not possible to assert definitely that Vāsudeva, Kṛṣṇa the warrior and Kṛṣṇa the sage were not three different persons, who in the *Mahā-bhārata* were unified and identified, though it is quite probable that all the different strands of legends refer to one identical person.

If the three Kṛṣṇas refer to one individual Kṛṣṇa, he must have lived long before Buddha, as he is alluded to in the *Chāndogya,* and his *guru* Ghora Aṅgirasa is also alluded to in the *Kauṣītaki-brāhmaṇa,* XXX.6 and the *Kāṭhaka-saṃhitā*, I.1, which are pre-Buddhistic works. Jaina tradition refers to Kṛṣṇa as being anterior to Pārśvanātha (817 BC), and on this evidence Dr Ray Chaudhury thinks that he must have lived long before the closing years of the ninth century BC[1]

BHĀGAVATA AND THE BHAGAVAD-GITA

The *Mahā-bhārata* (XII.348) associates the *Bhagavad-Gītā* with the doctrines of the Ekānti-Vaiṣṇavas. It is said there that the God Hari (*bhagavān Hari*) always blesses those that are devoted to God without any idea of gain (*ekāntin*) and accepts their adorations, offered in accordance with proper rites *(vidhi-prayukta).*[2] This *ekānta* religion *(ekānta-dharma)* is dear to Nārāyaṇa, and those who adhere to it attain to Hari, as Nīlakaṇṭha, the commentator on the *Mahā-bhārata*, points out, without passing through the three stages of Aniruddha, Pradyumna and saṃkarṣaṇa. The *ekāntin* faith leads to much higher goals than the paths of those that know the Vedas and lead the lives of ascetics. The principles of this *ekāntin* faith were enunciated by the Bhagavat himself in the battle of the Pāṇḍavas and the Kurus, when Arjuna felt disinclined to fight. This faith can be traced originally to the *Sāma-veda.* It is said that, when Nārāyaṇa created Brahmā, he gave him this *sātvata* faith, and from that time forth, as the *Mahā-bhārata* states, there has been a host of persons who were instructed in this faith and followed it. It was at a much later stage briefly described in the *Hari-Gītā.*[3]

1 *Early History of the Vaiṣṇava Sect,* p. 39.

2 *Ekāntino niṣkāma-bhaktāḥ,* Nīlakaṇṭha's commentary on the *Mahā-bhārata,* XII.348.3.

3 *kaihito hari-Gītāsu samāsa-vidhi-kalpitaḥ, Hari-Gītā.* 53. The traditional teaching of the *Gītā* doctrines is represented as ancient in the *Gītā* itself (IV.1-3), where it is said that Bhagavān declared it to Vivasvān, and he related it to Manu, and Manu to Ikṣvāku, and so on, until after a long time it was lost; it was again revived by Kṛṣṇa in the form of the *Bhagavad-Gītā.* In the *Mahā-bhārata,* XII.348,

This faith is very obscure and very difficult to be practised, and its chief feature is cessation from all kinds of injury. In some places it is said to recognize one *vyūha:* in other places two, and in others three, *vyūhas* are mentioned. Hari, however, is the final and absolute reality; he is both the agent, the action and the cause, as well as the absolute beyond action (*akartā*). There are, how ever, but few *ekāntins* in the world: had the world been filled with *ekāntins*, who never injured anyone, were always engaged in doing good to others and attained self-knowledge, then the golden age, *kṛta yuga*, would have come again. This *ekānta* religion is a faith parallel to that of the Sāṃkhya-yoga, and the devotee who follows it attains Nārāyaṇa as his ultimate state of liberation. From this description in the *Mahābhārata* it seems that the doctrine of the *Gītā* was believed to be the *ekāntin* doctrine originally taught by Nārāyaṇa to Brahmā, Nārada and others long before the recital of the *Gītā* by Kṛṣṇa in the *Mahā-bhārata* battle. It is further known that it had at least four or five different schools or variant forms, viz. *eka-vyūha*, *dvi-vyūha, tri-vyūha, catur-vyūha* and *ekānta*, and that it was known as the Sātvata religion.

Yāmunācārya in his *Āgama-prāmāṇya* tries to combat a number of views in which the Bhāgavatas were regarded as being inferior to Brahmins, not being allowed to sit and dine with them. The Sātvatas, again, are counted by Manu as a low-caste people, born from outcast Vaiśyas and not entitled to the holy thread.[1] The Sātvatas were, of course, regarded as the same as Bhāgavatas, and their chief duties consisted in worshipping for their living in Viṣṇu

---

it is said that Sanatkumāra learned this doctrine from Nārāyaṇa, from him Prajāpati, from him Raibhya and from him Kukṣi. It was then lost. Then again Brahmā learned it from Nārāyaṇa, and from him the Barhiṣada sages learned it, and from them Jyeṣṭha. Then again it was lost; then again Brahmā learned it from Nārāyaṇa, and from him Dakṣa learned it, and from him Vivasvān, and from Vivasvān Manu, and from Manu Ikṣvāku. Thus the tradition of the *BhagavadGītā,* as given in the poem itself, tallies with the *Mahā-bhārata* account.

1 वैश्यात् तु जायते व्रात्यात् सुधन्वाचार्य एव च।
कारूषश् च विजन्मा च मैत्रस् सात्वत एव च॥
vaiśyāt tu jāyate vrātyāt sudhanvācārya eva ca
kārūṣaś ca vijanmā ca maitraḥ saśvata eva ca.—Agama-prāmāṇya, p. 8.

temples by the order of the king.[1] They also repaired or constructed temples and images for their living, and were therefore regarded as outcasts. That the Bhāgavatas did in later times worship images and build images and temples is also evident from the fact that most of the available *Pañca-rātra* works are full of details about image-building and image-worship. The *Gītā* (IX.26) also speaks of adoration with water, flowers and leaves, which undoubtedly refers to image-worship. saṃkarṣaṇa, as the brother or companion of Kṛṣṇa, is mentioned in Patañjali's *Mahā-bhāṣya* (II.2.24) in a verse quoted by him, and in II.2.34 he seems to quote another passage, in which it is related that different kinds of musical instruments were played in the temple of Dhana-pati, Rāma and Keśava, meaning Balarāma, Saṃkarṣaṇa and Kṛṣṇa.[2]

As Yāmuna points out, the opponents of the Bhāgavata school urge that, since the ordinary Brahminic initiation is not deemed a sufficient qualification for undertaking the worship of Viṣṇu, and since special and peculiar forms of initiation and ceremonial performances are necessary, it is clear that the Bhāgavata forms of worship are not Vedic in their origin. The fourteen Hindu sciences, viz. the six *vedāṅgas* on Vedic pronunciation (*śikṣā*), ritual *(kalpa)*, grammar *(vyākaraṇa),* metre *(chandas),* astronomy (*jyotiṣa*), lexicography *(nirukta),* the four Vedas, Mīmāṃsā, argumentative works or philosophy *(nyāya-vistara),* the mythologies *(purāṇa)* and rules of conduct *(dharma-śāstra),* do not refer to the *Pañca-rātra* scriptures as being counted in their number. So the Bhāgavata or the *Pañca-rātra* scriptures are of non-Vedic origin. But Yāmuna contends that, since Nārāyaṇa is the supreme god, the Bhāgavata

1 पञ्चमः सात्वतो नाम विष्णोर् आयतनं हि सः।
पूजयेद् आज्ञया राज्ञां स तु भागवतः स्मृतः॥
pañcamaḥ sātvato nāma Viṣṇor āyatanāṃ hi sa
pūjayed ājñayā rājñāṃ sa tu bhāgavataḥ smṛtaḥ.—Ibid.

2 *Saṅkarṣaṇa-dvitīyasya balaṃ Kṛṣṇasya ardḥitam.—Mahā-bhāṣya,* II.2.27.
मृदङ्गशङ्खपणवाः पृथङ्नदन्ति संसदि
प्रासादे धनपतिरामकेशवानाम्॥
mṛdaṅga-śaṅkha-paṇavāḥ pṛthañ nadanti saṃsadi
prāsāde dhana-pati-rāma-keśavānām.—Ibid. II.2.34.

literature, which deals with his worship, must be regarded as having the same sources as the Vedas; the Bhāgavatas also have the same kind of outer dress as the Brahmins and the same kinds of lineage. He further contends that, though *sātvata* means an outcast, yet *sātvata* is a different word from *sātvata*, which means a devotee of Viṣṇu. Moreover, not all Bhāgavatas take to professional priestly duties and the worshipping of images for their livelihood; for there are many who worship the images through pure devotion. It is very easy to see that the above defence of the Bhāgavatas, as put forward by one of their best advocates, Yāmunācārya, is very tame and tends to suggest very strongly that the Bhāgavata sect was non-Vedic in its origin and that image-worship, image-making, image-repairng and temple-building had their origin in that particular sect. Yet throughout the entire scriptures of the *Pañca-rātra* school there is the universal and uncontested tradition that it is based on the Vedas. But its difference from the Vedic path is well known. Yāmuna himself refers to a passage *(Āgama-prāmāṇya*, p. 51) where it is said that Śāṇḍilya, not being able to find his desired end *(puruṣārtha)* in all the four Vedas, produced this scripture. The *Gītā* itself often describes the selfish aims of sacrifices, and Kṛṣṇa urges Arjuna to rise above the level of the Vedas. It seems, therefore, that the real connection of the *Pañca-rātra* literature is to be found in the fact that it originated from Vāsudeva or Viṣṇu, who is the supreme God from whom the Vedas themselves were produced. Thus the *Īśvara-saṃhitā* (I.24-26) explains the matter, and states that the Bhāgavata literature is the great root of the Veda tree, and the Vedas themselves are but trunks of it, and the followers of Yoga are but its branches. Its main purpose is to propound the superiority of Vāsudeva, who is the root of the universe and identical with the Vedas.[1]

---

1 महतो वेदवृक्षस्य मुलभूतो महान् अयं स्कन्धभूता ऋगाद्यास् ते शाखाभूताश् च योगिनः
जगन्मूलस्य वेदस्य वासुदेवस्य मुख्यतः प्रतिपादकता सिद्धा मूलवेदाख्यता द्विजाः ॥
mahato veda-vṛkṣasya mulā-bhuto mahān ayaṃ
skandha-bhūtā ṛg-ādyās te śākhā-bhūtāś ca yoginaḥ
jagan-mūlasya vedasya Vāsudevasya mukhyataḥ
pratipādakatā siddhā mūla-vedākhyatā dvijāḥ.—Īśvara-saṃhitā, I.24-26.

The affinity of this school of thought to the Upaniṣad school becomes apparent when it is considered that Vāsudeva was regarded in this system as the highest Brahman.[1] The three other *vyūhas* were but subordinate manifestations of him, after the analogy of *prajñā, virāt, viśva* and *taijasa* in monistic Vedānta. Patañjali's *Mahā-bhāṣya* does not seem to know of the four *vyūhas,* as it mentions only Vāsudeva and saṃkarṣaṇa; and the *Gītā* knows only Vāsudeva. It seems, therefore, that the *vyūha* doctrine did not exist at the time of the *Gītā* and that it evolved gradually in later times. It is seen from a passage of the *Mahābhārata*, already referred to, that there were different variations of the doctrine and that some accepted one *vyūha*, others two, others three and others four. It is very improbable that, if the *vyūha* doctrine was known at the time of the *Gītā*, it should not have been mentioned therein. For the *Gītā* was in all probability the earliest work of the *ekāntin* school of the Bhāgavatas.[2] It is also interesting in this connection

---

1 यस्मात् सम्यक् परं ब्रह्म वासुदेवाख्यम् अव्ययम्
अस्माद् अवाप्यते शास्त्राज् ज्ञानपूर्वेण कर्मणा ॥
yasmāt samyak paraṃ brahma Vāsudevākhyam avyayam
asmād avāpyate śāstrāj jñāna-pūrveṇa karmaṇā.
Pauṣkarāgama, as quoted in *Rāmānuja-bhāṣya,* II.2.42.
The *Chāndogya Upaniṣad* (VII.1.2) refers also to the study of *ekāyana,* as in the passage *vāko-vākyam ekāyanaṃ*; *ekāyana* is also described as being itself a Veda in *Śrīpraśna-saṃhitā,* II.38, 39:
वेदम् एकायनं नाम वेदानाम् शिरसि स्थितम्
तदर्थकम् पञ्चरात्रम् मोक्षदं तत्क्रियावताम्
यस्मिन्न् एको मोक्षमार्गो वेदे प्रोक्तः सनातनः
मदाराधनरूपेण तस्माद् एकायनम् भवेत् ॥
vedam ekāyanaṃ nāma vedānām śirasi sthitam
tad-arthakam pañca-rātram mokṣa-daṃ tat-kriyāvatām
yasminn eko mokṣa-mārgo vede proktaḥ sanātanaḥ
mad-ārādhana-rūpeṇa tasmād ekāyanam bhavet.
See also the article "The Pañca-rātras or Bhāgavata-śāstra," by Govindācarya Svāmin, *J.R.A.S.* 1911.

2 That the *ekāntin* faith is the same as the Sātvata or the *Pañca-rātra* faith is evident from the following quotation from the *Pādma-tantra,* IV.2.88:
सूरिस् सुहृद् भागवतस् सात्वतः पञ्चकालवित्
एकान्तिकस् तन्मयश् च पञ्चरात्रिक इत्य् अपि ॥
sūris suhṛd bhāgavatas sātvataḥ pañca-kāla-vit
ekāntikas tan-mayaś ca pañca-rātrika ity api.

to note that the name Nārāyaṇa is never mentioned in the *Gītā*, and Vāsudeva is only identified with Viṣṇu, the chief of the *ādityas*. Thus Sir R.G. Bhandarkar says, "It will be seen that the date of the *Bhagavad-Gītā,* which contains no mention of the *vyūhas* or personified forms, is much earlier than those of the inscriptions, the *Niddesa* and Patañjali, i.e. it was composed not later than the beginning of the fourth century before the Christian era; how much earlier it is difficult to say. At the time when the *Gītā* was conceived and composed the identification of Vāsudeva with Nārāyaṇa had not yet taken place, nor had the fact of his being an incarnation of Viṣṇu come to be acknowledged, as appears from the work itself.... Viṣṇu is alluded to as the chief of the Ādityas and not as the supreme being, and Vāsudeva was Viṣṇu in this sense, as mentioned in chapter X, because the best thing of a group or class is represented to be his *vibhūti* or special manifestation."[1]

The date of the *Gītā* has been the subject of long discussions among scholars, and it is inconvenient for our present purposes to enter into an elaborate controversy. One of the most extreme views on the subject is that of Dr Lorinser, who holds that it was composed after Buddha, and several centuries after the commencement of the Christian era, under the influence of the *New Testament.* Mr Telang in the introduction to his translation of the *Bhagavad-Gītā* points out—as has been shown above—that the *Bhagavad-Gītā* does not know anything that is peculiarly Buddhistic. Attempt has also been made to prove that the *Gītā* not only does not know anything Buddhistic, but that it also knows neither the accepted Sāṃkhya philosophy nor the Yoga of Patañjali's *Yoga-sūtra.* This, together with some other secondary considerations noted above, such as the non-identification of Vāsudeva with Nārāyaṇa and the non-

---

This faith is also called *ekāvana,* or the path of the One, as is seen from the following passage from the *Īśvara-saṃhitā,* I.18:

मोक्षायनाय वै पन्था एतदन्यो न विद्यते
तस्माद् एकायनं नाम प्रवदन्ति मनीषिणः ॥

mokṣāyanāya vai panthā etad-anyo na vidyate
tasmād ekāyanaṃ nāma pravadanti manīṣiṇaḥ.

1 *Vaiṣṇavism and Śaivism*, p. 13.

appearance of *the vyūha* doctrine, seems to be a very strong reason for holding the *Gītā* to be in its general structure pre-Buddhistic. The looseness of its composition, however, always made it easy to interpolate occasional verses. Since there is no other consideration which might lead us to think that the *Gītā* was written after the *Brahma-sūtras*, the verse *Brahma-sūtra-padaiś caiva hetumadbhir viniścitaiḥ* has to be either treated as an interpolation or interpreted differently. Śaṅkara also thought that the *Brahma-sūtra* referred to the *Gītā* as an old sacred writing (*smṛti*), and this tallies with our other considerations regarding the antiquity of the *Gītā.* The view of Dr Lorinser, that the *Bhagavad-Gītā* must have borrowed at least some of its materials from Christianity, has been pretty successfully refuted by Mr Telang in the introduction to his translation, and it therefore need not be here again combated. Dr Ray Chaudhury also has discussed the problem of the relation of Bhāgavatism to Christianity, and in the discussion nothing has come out which can definitely make it seem probable that the Bhāgavata cult was indebted to Christianity at any stage of its development; the possibility of the *Gītā* being indebted to Christianity may be held to be a mere fancy. It is not necessary here to enter into any long discussion in refuting Garbe's view that the *Gītā* was originally a work on Sāṃkhya lines (written in the first half of the second century BC), which was revised on Vedāntic lines and brought to its present form in the second century AD; for I suppose it has been amply proved that, in the light of the uncontradicted tradition of the *Mahā-bhārata* and the *Pañca-rātra* literature, the *Gītā* is to be regarded as a work of the Bhāgavata school, and an internal analysis of the work also shows that the *Gītā* is neither an ordinary Sāṃkhya nor a Vedānta work, but represents some older system wherein the views of an earlier school of Sāṃkhya are mixed up with Vedāntic ideas different from the Vedānta as interpreted by Śaṅkara. The arbitrary and dogmatic assertion of Garbe, that he could clearly separate the original part of the *Gītā* from the later additions, need not, to my mind, be taken seriously. The antiquity of the Bhāgavata religion is. as pointed out by Tilak, acknowledged by Senart (*The Indian Interpreter*, October 1909 and January 1910) and 561Bühler *(Indian Antiquary*, 1894), and the latter says, "The ancient Bhāgavata, Sātvata or *Pañca-rātra* sect, devoted to the worship of Nārāyaṇa and his deified teacher Kṛṣṇa Devakī-putra, dates from a period long anterior to the rise of the Jainas in the eighth century BC" And assuredly the *Gītā* is the earliest available literature of this school. As regards external evidence, it may be pointed out that the *Gītā* is alluded to not only by Kālidāsa and Bāṇa, but also by Bhāsa in his play *Karṇa-bhāra.*[1] Tilak also refers to an article by T. G. Kale in the *Vedic Magazine*, VII. pp. 528-532, where he points out that the *Bodhāyana-Gṛhya-śeṣa-sūtra,* II.22.9, quotes the *Gītā,* IX.26, and the *Bodhāyana-Pitṛ-medha-sūtra,* at the beginning of the third *praśna,* quotes another passage of the *Gītā.*[2] Incidentally it may also be mentioned that the style of the *Gītā* is very archaic; it is itself called an Upaniṣad, and there are many passages in it which are found in the *Īśa (Īśa,* 5, cf. the *Bhagavad-Gītā,* XIII.15 and VI.29), *Muṇḍaka (Muṇḍ.*II.1.2, cf. the *Gītā*,

---

1 Tilak quotes this passage on page 574 of his *Bhagavad-Gītā-rahasya* (Bengali translation of his Marathi work) as follows:

हतोऽपि लभतेस्वर्गं जित्वा तु लभते यशः
उभे बहुमते लोके नास्ति निष्फलता रणे,
hato'pi labhate svargaṃ jitvā tu labhate yaśaḥ
ubhe bahumate loke nāsti niṣphalatā raṇe,

which repeats the first two lines of the *Gītā,* II.37.

2 *Bodhāyana-Gṛhya-śeṣa-sūtra:*

तद् आह भगवान्,
पत्रम् पुष्पम् फलं तोयं यो में भक्त्या प्रयच्छति
तद् अहम् भक्त्युपहृतम् अश्नार्नि प्ययतात्मनः ॥
tad āha bhagavān,
patram puṣpam phalaṃ toyaṃ yo me bhaktyā prayacchati
tad aham bhakty-upahṛtam aśnārni prayatātmanaḥ.

Also *Bodhāyana-Pitṛ-medha-sūtra:*

यतस्य वै मनुष्यस्य ध्रुवम् मरणम्
इति विजानीयात् तस्माज् जाते न प्रहृष्येन् मृते च न विषीदेत
yatasya vai manuṣyasya dhruvam maraṇam
iti vijānīyāt tasmāj jāte na prahṛṣyen mṛte ca na viṣīdeta.

Compare the *Gītā, jātasya hi dhruvo mṛtyuḥ,* etc.

N.B. These references are all taken from Tilak's *Bhagavad-Gītā-rahasya* pp. 574, etc.

XIII.15), *Kāthaka* (II.15, II.18 and 19 and II.7, cf. the *Gītā,* VIII.11; II.20 and 29) and other Upaniṣads. We are thus led to assign to the *Gītā* a very early date, and, since there is no definite evidence to show that it was post-Buddhistic, and since also the *Gītā* does not contain the slightest reference to anything Buddhistic, I venture to suggest that it is pre-Buddhistic, however unfashionable such a view may appear. An examination of the *Gītā* from the point of view of language also shows that it is archaic and largely un-Pāṇinean. Thus from the root *yudh* we have *yudhya* (VIII.7) for *yudhyasva; yat,* which is *ātmane-pada* in Pāṇinean Sanskrit, is used in *parasmai-pada* also, as in VI.36, VII.3, IX.14 and XV.11; *ram* is also used *in parasmai-pada* in X.9. The roots *kāṅkṣ, vraj, viś* and *iṅg* are used in Pāṇinean Sanskrit in *parasmai-pada,* but in the *Gītā* they are all used in *ātmane-pada* as well—*kāṅkṣ* in I.31, *vraj* in II.54, *viś* in XXIII.55 and *iṅg* in VI.19 and XIV.23. Again, the verb *ud-vij,* which is generally used in *ātmane-pada,* is used in *parasmai-pada* in V.20; *nivasiṣyasi* is used in XII.8 for *nivatsyasi, mā śucaḥ* for *mā śocīḥ* in XVI.5; and the usage of *prasaviṣyadhvam* in III.10 is quite ungrammatical. So *yamaḥ saṃyamatām* in X.29 should be *yamaḥ saṃyacchatām, he sakheti* in XI.41 is an instance of wrong *sandhi, priyāyārhasi* in XI.44 is used for *priyāyāḥ arhasi, senānīnām* in X.24 is used for *senānyām.*[1] These linguistic irregularities, though they may not themselves be regarded as determining anything definitely, may yet be regarded as contributory evidence in favour of the high antiquity of the *Gītā.* The *Gītā* may have been a work of the Bhāgavata school written long before the composition of the *Mahā-bhārata*, and may have been written on the basis of the Bhārata legend, on which the *Mahā-bhārata* was based. It is not improbable that the *Gītā*, which summarized the older teachings of the Bhāgavata School, was incorporated into the *Mahā-bhārata*, during one of its revisions, by reason of the sacredness that it had attained at the time.

1 For enumeration of more errors of this character see Mr. V.K. Rajwade's article in the Bhandarkar commemoration volume, from which these have been collected.

INDEX[1]

abādhita, 125
abādhita-svayaṃ-prakdāśataiva asya sattā, 41
Abdomen, 336, 412
abhaya, 595
abhāva, 165, 186, 223, 262
abheda, 239
abhedo nīla-tad-dhiyoḥ, 30n.
abhicāra-karma, 329
Abhidharma-kośa, 67n.
Abhidharma-kośa-vyākhyā, 68n.
abhidhānābhidheya-jñāna-jñeyādilak-ṣaṇaḥ, 4n.
abhighāta, 396, 478
abhihitānvaya-vāda, 262
abhilāso, 580
abhilāṣa, 481
Abhinanda, 267
Abhinavagupta, 56, 517
Abhinavanārayaṇa, 90
Abhinavanārāyaṇendra Sarasvatī, 90, 92
abhiniveśa, 483
abhiprapacyamāna, 367
Abhiprāya-prakāśikā, 96, 101n., 170n.
abhiṣecana, 589
abhivyajyate, 353
abhivyakti, 200
abhraja, 349, 351, 386n.
abhyanujñā, 453
abhyāsa, 420, 431
abhyupagama-siddhānta, 447
Ablutions, 309, 589
Abnormal states, 392
Abode, 581
Abscess, 348
Absence, 21
Absolute destruction, 287
Absolute oneness, 148
Absolute truth, 3
Absolutist, 600
Abstract idea, 244
Abstraction, 33
Abuse, 582n.
Academic dispute, 435
Academy of Sciences, 189n.
acapala, 595
Acceptance of gift, 590
Accessories, 185, 211, 212
Accessory cause, 126, 214
Accidental happenings, 434
Accretion, 272n 382; of energy, 283
Acetabulum, 334n.
acetana, 42
Acid, 393n., 417,419, 421,422
Acidity, 390 n.
acintya, 423, 425
Action, 171, 215, 223, 278, 420, 470-472, 480, 490, 514, 515, 545, 569, 591, 592, 600, 602
Active agent, 282
Active functioning, 276
Active operation, 178
Active restraint, 584
Activity, 266, 287, 401, 429, 430, 561, 588, 600; of the self, 226
Act of knowledge, 79
Acts, 17
Actual, 27n; data, 246

1 The words are arranged in the order of the English alphabet. Sanskrit and Pāli technical terms and words are in small italics; names of books are in italics with a capital. English words and other names are in Roman with a capital. Letters with diacritical marks come after ordinary ones.

Acyutakṛṣṇānanda Tīrtha, 253
Additional assistance, 211
adharma, 375, 477, 480, 486, 565, 568, 591, 612
adhika, 447, 449, 454 n.
adhikaraṇa, 125 n., 455
Adhikaraṇa-mañjari, 171 n.
Adhikaraṇa-mālā, 93
Adhikaraṇa-ratna-mālā, 170n.
Adhiknraṇa-saṅgati, 171n.
adhikaraṇa-siddhānta, 447
adhimokṣa, 28
adhipati, 399, 411
adhiṣṭhāna, 131, 222. 324, 551
adhiṣṭhāyaka, 427
adhya-vasāya, 435
adhyāsa, 11, 119
Adhyasa-bhāṣya, 7n., 256
adhyātma-vidaḥ,493
ad infinitum, 46, 81, 438
Adoration, 513
adroha, 595
adṛṣṭa, 238, 357, 420
adṛṣṭādi-kṣubdhaṃ, 237
adṛṣṭādi-sahakṛtam, 227
adṛṣṭārtha, 447
Adultery, 582n.
Advaita-bhūṣaṇa, 60n.
Advaita-bodha-dīpikā, 62
Advaita-brahma-siddhi, 66
Advaita-candrikā, 63
Advaita-cintā-kaustubha, 66
Advaita-cintāmaṇi, 64
Advaita-dīpikā, 61, 249
Advaita-dīpikā-vivaraṇa, 62
Advaita-makaranda, 65
Advaita-makaranda-ṭīkā, 222
Advaita-mañjarī, 260
Advaita-muktā-sāra, 66n.
Advaita-nirṇaya, 253
Advaita-pañca-ratna, 62, 249
Advaita Philosophy, 3n.
Advaita-ratna, 62
Advaita-ratna-koṣa, 62
Advaita-ratna-rakṣaṇa, 260, 261
Advaita-ratna-vyākhyāna, 62
Advaita-siddhānta-vidyotana, 66n.
Advaita-siddhi, 62, 65, 137, 228, 229, 257n., 260, 261
Advaita-siddhy-upanyāsa, 260n.
Advaita-śāstra-sāroddhāra, 64
advaita-śruti, 93
Advaita-vāda, 250
advaita-vāsanā, 252
Advaitānanda, 65, 95n., 268
Advaitānubhūti, 93
Advancement, 605
Advayānanda, 91
Advayāraṇya, 267
Advayāśrama, 235
Adyar, 57, 97n., 101
Affection, 571, 580
Affections of *vata*, 392
Affective tone, 27
Affirmations, 86, 191, 314, 452
Afflictions, 26, 355, 484, 583
agada-tantra, 320
Agasti, 263, 265
Agastya, 505
Age, 431
Agent, 89, 195, 361, 366, 417, 429, 515, 547, 548, 600, 602
Aggi, 628
Agni, 86, 339n., 350n, 2, 353, 354
Agnihotra, 62
agni-karma, 386
Agni-Purāṇa, 324n.
Agniṣṭoma, L', 403 n.
Agniveśa, 459, 461,465 495, 500, 503
Agniveśa-saṃhitā, 322, 503
Agniveśa-tantra, 500
Agniveśya, 264, 266
agrahaṇa, 120
Agrahāyaṇa, 328
Agriculture, 586, 590
ahaṃkāra, 87, 118, 121, 250, 275, 276, 283, 298, 304, 356, 404, 535, 540, 542, 612
ahaṃtā, 272, 274
a-hetu, 451
ahetu-sama, 444n. 4, 446n.
ahetutaḥ, 192
ahiṃsā, 589, 595, 599, 634
Ahirbudhnya-saṃhitā, 539, 627
ahita, 322, 323, 492, 493
aihika, 293
aikamatya, 327
aindriya, 294
Air, 86, 216, 223, 272, 352, 378, 385-389. 419. 420, 423, 488
Airy, 417. 419
Aitareya, 90, 300n. 3
Aitareya-brāhmaṇa, 625
Aitareyopaniṣad-bhāṣya, 90
aitihya, 439, 443
Ajita, 70

Index

ajñāna, 4, 10, 11. 58, 63, 84. 85. 87. 115, 118, 125, no, 129, 130, 133. 176. 177. 224. 225, 234, 250, 255, 454, 559, 582, 583; its nature, dependence on self and transformation into world-appearance, 11; its notion in Padmapāda or Prakāśātman different from that of Nāgārjuna,10; its transformations, 11, 61; Vacaspati's view of its causality, 12
ajñānaṃ nābhāva upādānatvān mṛdvat, 227
ajñāta-sattvānabhyupagama, 20, 313
akartā, 636
Akhaṇḍānanda, 60, 119, 222
Akhaṇḍānanda Muni, 12n, 36n.
Akhaṇḍātma-prakāśika, 66n.
Akhilātman, 114
akhyāti, 101n,
akliṣṭa, 483
akrodha, 589, 595
a-kṛtaka, 209
akṣaka-saṃjñe, 333 n. 2
Akṣapāda, 458, 460, 465-469
alaji, 348
alambuṣā, 414
alasālā, 347n. 6
Alberuni, 497
Alchemy, 497
Alertness, 511; of mind, 596
algaṇḍu, 346
Alīṃsa, 349
Alkaline, 417, 418
All, 224
Allāla Sūri, 60n.
All-pervading, 18, 359n., 530, 566,
All-pervasive, 185
aloka-saṃvṛta, 6
alolupatva, 595
Alternating, 73
Alternative, 21, 440
Altindische Grammatik, 403n.
Amalānanda, 60, 67, 86n. 99, 119, 123, 125, 127, 138, 301
Amaradāsa, 63
Amara-koṣa, 63
amarṣa, 481
amāvasyā, 339n.
Amīvā, 349
amla, 364n. 3. 417, 421
Amṛtānanda, 36, 530
Amulets, 321, 326, 328, 341, 346, 351, 490
amūrta, 295
aṃsa, 333n. 2
aṃsa-phalaka, 333n. 2
aṃsa-pītha, 334 n.1
aṃśāṃśa-vikalpa, 395
anabhilapyenātmanā, 23
anabhiraddhi, 581
anabhiṣaṅga, 435
anadhigata, 244, 245
anadhigatatva, 246
anaikāntikatva, 143
Analogy, 33, 171, 179, 208, 218, 456; of dreams, 32; of play, 48
Analysis, 75; of consciousness, 72
ananubhāṣaṇa, 454n.
ananuyojya, 449
ananyathā-siddha, 185
Ananyānubhava, 95n.
anarthaka, 448, 449
Anatomical texts, 508
Anatomical treatises, 508
Anatomy, 414, 505
anavasthā, 200
anādy-anirvācyāvidyāśrayaṇāt, 14
anāgatāvekṣaṇa, 455, 457
anāhata-cakra, 415
anākhyam anabhivyaktam, 268
anāmayam, 539
anārambha, 485
anāsrava, 26
anātman, 7
anekatā, 432
anekānta, 455
anekāntha, 457
Anger, 309, 388, 435, 478, 574, 581. 589, 595
Angry, 428
anila, 385
Animal, 372, 601
Animate, 419, 420
Aniruddha, 633, 635
anirvacanīyaṃ nīlādi, 128
anirvacanīyatā, 179
anirvacanīyatā-vacana, 121
anirvacanīyā, 103, 136, 234, 258
anirvācya, 41, 128
anirvācyatva, 223
anirvācyā avidyā, 126
anitya, 25, 138
anitya-sama, 444n. 2
aniyata-vipāka, 287
Ankle-bones, 329
Annam Bhaṭṭa, 95n.
Annihilation, 308
Annotations, 100
anṛta, 446
antaḥkaraṇa-caitanyayor aikyādhyāsāt, 237

antaḥkaraṇas, 39, 58, 64, 75, 83, 86n., 87, 89, 101, 103n., 116, 120-122, 126, 130, 131, 237-241, 250, 310, 339, 343, 356, 401, 528, 565n. 1
antahkarana-viśiṣṭa, 38
antaḥkaraṇa-viśiṣṭa, 38
antaḥkaraṇāvacchinnaṃ caitanyaṃ, 237
antaḥ-sauṣiryam, 358
antarikṣaṃ, 339n,
Antaryāmi-brāhmaṇa, 290
antaryāmin, 247, 626
Antecedence, 184, 198
Antipathy, 28, 115, 283, 286, 309, 477, 480-482, 571, 581, 582
antrebhyaḥ, 334
anubandha, 395n., 429n., 454, 580
anubandhya, 395n.
anubhava, 172
Anubhava-dīpikā, 90
Anubhava-vilāsa, 66n.
Anubhavānanda, 67, 99
anubhūti, 229
anubhūti-svabhāva, 549
Anubhūtisvarūpācārya, 134, 220, 223
anumata, 454, 456
anumāna, 160, 223, 435, 438, 441. 464, 468n,
anupadhā, 589
anupalabdhi-sama, 444n. 2
anupaśaya, 463
Anupatāla, 349
anus, 344, 496
anusayo, 580
anutpatti-sama, 444n.
anuvṛtta, 73
anu-vyavasāya, 174
anuyoga, 448
anuyojya, 448
anūkya, 333
Anvaya-prakaśikā, 64
anvaya-vyatireki, 467
anvaya-vyatireki-sādhya-viśeṣaṃ vādy-abhimatam sādhayati, 140
Anvayārtha-prakāśsikā, 134
anvayi, 467 n.
anvitābhidhāna-vāda, 261
anyathā-khyāti, 101 n., 234, 255
anyā pūrvāpurva-bhrama-saṃskāraḥ, 126
anyedyuḥ, 345
anyonya-milat-komala-saddala, 297
anyonynābhāva, 141, 151, 152
aṅgam eva alpatvād upāṅgam, 317
aṅganaṃ, 578
Aṅgiras, 326, 634
Aṅgirasa-kalpa, 328
aṅgulayaḥ, 331
Aṅguttara-nikāya, 460
aṅkura, 195
aññāṇam, 581
aṇu, 302
aṇu-hrasva, 217
aṇu-hrasva measure, 218
aṇuharsva parimāṇa, 217
aṇḍa, 376n.
ap, 86. 584
apacit, 347n. 7
apadeśa, 454, 456
apagataiṣaṇaḥ, 283
apahnava-vacana, 121
apaiśuna, 595
apara, 420, 431
aparam ojas, 400n.
aparā prakṛti, 543
aparicchinnālambanākāra, 26
aparokṣa, 7, 73, 121
aparokṣa-pratīti-virodhāt, 223
aparokṣa-vyavahāra-yogya, 172
Aparokṣānubhava, 90
Aparokṣānuhhūti, 92
apa-siddhānta, 454n.
Apasmāra, 502
apavarga, 51, 286
apavarja, 454, 456
apāna, 298 301, 338, 362, 387, 435, 523. 514, 531
apāna vāyu, 414
apānāya svāhā, 523
apāṅga, 399, 409
apārthaka, 448, 449, 453, 454n.
apekhā, 578
apekṣā, 110
apekṣā-buddhi, 181, 182
Aperture, 177 414, 415
Apoha-siddhi, 56
a posteriori, 603
Apparatus, 207
Apparent reality, 4
Appaya Dīkṣita, 11, 12, 19, 51, 54. 56. 60-64, 91, 95n., 123n., 125, 248 251, 252; his date, lineage and works, 251 ff.
Appearance, 4, 5, 9, 15, 23-25, 32, 36, 43, 116, 121, 126, 223, 224, 267, 271, 272, 276, 291, 432, 512, 603;
of unity, 75
Appetites, 575
Appetitive desire, 584
Appreciation, 597

Apprehension, 25
apradhāna, 431
apramā, 148
apramāda, 589
apratibhā, 454 n.
apratyak, 73
aprapta-kāla, 454 n.
aprāpta-prārthanā, 480
aprāptayoḥ prāptiḥ saṃyogaḥ, 182
a priori, 603
apsarāḥ, 263
apūrva, 92
apūrva-vidhi, 53
Arāya, 349
arbuda, 332 n. 3, 366
arcā, 626
Ardent desire, 580
ardha-supta-prabuddha, 305
ardhāñjali-parimāṇa, 400 ft.
Argument, 20, 30n., 33, 322, 438
arhatattva, 286
Ariṣṭanemi, 264
Arjuna, 568, 570, 583, 586, 591, 592. 597. 602, 604, 612, 616-620, 635
Armpits, 380 n.
Arṇava-varṇana, 145
aroga, 390n.
arpaṇa, 529
Arrogant, 595
Arśas, 501
Arteries, 296n., 336, 337
artha, 381, 396, 419, 559, 562, 566
artha-kriyā-kāritva, 37, 125
artha-kriya-sāmarthya, 210
artha-kriya-sāmarthya-sattvam, 35n.
artha-prāpakatva, 158
artha-prāpti, 448
Artha-śāstra, 318, 630
arthavalī, 23
arthāntara, 453, 454n.
arthāpatti, 20, 454, 456
arthāpatti-sama, 444n. 2, 446 n.
Artificial process, 417
Aruṇadatta, 500, 505
aruṇā, 338, 402 n.
asamprajñāta, 289
asaṃsargāgraha, 177, 179
Asaṅga, 189
asaṅga, 310
asaṅga-bhāvanā, 305
asaṅga-śāstreṇa, 611
a-sarva-gata, 478
asat, 179, 435
a-sat-kārya-vāda, 45, 206, 552, 603
asat-khyāti, 101 n.
asātmya-arthāgama, 485
Ascetic, 435; life, 592; postures, 570
Asceticism, 264, 309, 592
Asiatic Society of Bengal, 236
asmitā, 483
aspanda, 306
Aspects, 275
Aspiration, 580
Ass, 184, 450 82.
Assembly, 441
Assimilation, 386
Associated, 584
Association, 17, 24, 29, 39, 180, 210. 216. 224, 276, 374, 417, 430, 437, 217, 528. 531, 583
asteya, 589
asthi, 370, 382
asthi-māṃsa-maya, 297
asthira, 265, 278
asti, 451n.
Astragalus, 330 n. 3
Astringent, 417, 419
Astrology, 508
Astronomy, 56
asukha, 492
asukham āyuḥ, 321
asura, 366, 623, 628
Asura-veda, 319n., 2
asūyā, 481
asvādu, 417
asubha, 397
aśuddha, 41
Aśvattha. 611
Aśvattha tree, 610, 611
aṣṭakā, 339
aṣṭa-siddhi, 497
Aṣṭāṅga Āyur-veda, 320
Aṣṭāṅga-hṛdaya, 424 7t., 508
Aṣṭāṅga-hṛdaya-nāma-vaidūryaka- bhāṣya, 508
Aṣṭāṅga-hṛdaya-saṃhitā, 495, 503- 505
Aṣṭāṅga-hṛdaya-vṛtti, 508
Aṣṭāṅga-saṃgraha, 304, 319n. 3, 330n. 3, 355n. 1, 370n. 1, 382, 384n., 504
aṣṭānga-yoga, 530-531
aṣṭhīvantau, 331
aṣṭhīvat, 331n. 4
Atala, 87
Atharva, 318, 455
Atharvan texts, 348
Atharvaṇic charms, 326

Atharvaṇic hymns, 336
Atharvaṇic rites, 328, 342
Atharva-śikhā Upaniṣad, 524
Atharva-śiras *Upaniṣad*, 524
Alharva-Veda, 317-319, 321-325, 328, 329, 334, 337, 338, 340-343, 350, 386, 396, 400 401- 403, 424. 567, 625, 628; as Atharva and Aṅgiras, 326; Ayur-veda an *upāṅga* of it, 317; Āyur-veda its *upaveda*, 318; diseases and their symptoms in, 350 ff.; diseases mentioned in, 344 ff.; distinguishes *śirā* and *dhamanī*, 401 n .; head and brain in, 396; its bone system critically compared and contrasted with that of Caraka, Suśruta, Vāgbhaṭa, 329 ff.; its contents as arranged by Bloomfield, 343 ff; its principal contents, 326 ff.; its probable priority to *Ṛg-veda*, 325, 326; its relation with Ayur-veda, 319; its *śākhās*, 328 ff.; its theory of *vāyus*, 338, 339; on *śirā* and *dhamanī*, 336 ff.; rivalry between drugs and charms in, 340 ff.; theory of the origin of diseases in, 348 ff.; *vāyu, pitta* and *kapha* in, 386; what *nāḍī* means in, 402
Atharva-Veda and Gopatha-Brāhmaṇa, 343n. 1, 344n. 1
Atharvaveda in Kashmir, 329n.
Atharvāṅgirasaḥ, 326
atideśa, 454, 456
atikrāntāvekṣaṇa, 454, 457
atimūtra, 344
atirikta, 453
atiśayādhāna, 210
atiyoga, 373, 374, 472
atīndriya, 404, 427
atīsāra, 344, 501
Atīta-kāla, 452
Atomic, 428; changes, 223; measure, 217; theory, 174, 217
Atoms, 23, 29, 181, 215- 218, 222, 229, 356, 432
Atri, 465. 468. 500
Attachment, 28, 116, 280, 354, 480- 482, 570, 571, 580-582 584 587, 588, 591, 595, 596, 598, 599, 602, 607-610
Attention, 26, 28
Attentive reflection, 28
Attock, 500
Attractions, 276
atyantāsat, 223
aṭṭhaṅga-sīla, 581
Auditory organ, 401
Auditory sense, 436
Aufrecht, Th., 507, 513
aupacārika, 382, 384
Aupadhenava, 494
Aupadhenava-tantra, 507
aupamya, 440, 441
aupapāduka, 359
Aurabhra, 494
Auricular. 412
Auspicious rites, 326
Austerities, 515
auṣadha, 343
auṣadhi, 419
auṣṇya, 422n.
Authenticity, 90
Autumn, 390, 431
Autumnal fever, 348
avabhāsinī, 370
avaccheda, 121
avacchedakatā, 143
avaccheda-vāda, 122
avacchinna, 111
Avadhāni Yajvā, 251n.
avadhi, 592
avasthā, 51
avastu, 232, 233
avayavī, 215
avedanaṃ, 306
avedyatva, 172, 173
avedyatve saty aparokṣa-vyavahāra- yogyatvaṃ, 172n.
Averrhoa acida, 420 n.
Aversion, 390, 600
Aviddhakarṇa, 198
avidyamāna, 6
avidyā, 6, 7, 9, 10, 13, 15, 51, 55, 58, 83, 84. 97, 98, 101-104, 113, 114. 120, 121, log-iii, 135, 136, 171, 215, 234-237, 240, 254, 270, 287, 354, 482, 484, 559, 581, 582; described as *śakti* by Gauḍapāda, 9; in neither of its senses can be material cause, 13; its meanings. 13; nature of its causality according to Ānandabodha, also according to Vācaspati's *Brahma-tattva-samīkṣā*, 13; not psychological ignorance, but special technical category, 13; Padmapāda's interpretation regarding the creative power of, 10; so called because of its unintelligibility, 13
avidyā-dvitaya,126
avidyā-dvitaya-sacivasya, 126
avidyā māyā mithyā-pratyaya iti, 97
avidyā-nivṛtti, 98
avidyā-potency, 11

avidyā-sahita-brahmopādānam, ii
avidyā stuff, 120
avidyā-śakti, 10, 233
avidyopādāna-bheda-vādins, 104
avijjā, 581
avijñātārtha, 454 n.
avinābhāva, 161, 438, 443
avisaṃvādi, 157
aviśeṣa-sama, 444n. 2, 446 n.
aviṣaya, 7
avitikkama, 583
avyabhicārī, 157, 444n.
avyabhicārī anubhavaḥ, 156 *avyakta*, 49, 120, 304, 416, 417, 539, 540, 548, 549, 552, 555. 605, 612, 618. 621
avyakto vyakta-karmā, 304
avyapadeśātmā, 270
avyapadeśyay, 306, 436, 468
Avyayātman Bhagavat Pūjyapāda, 227
avyākṛta, 27n., 120
avyāpya-vṛttitva-viśeṣito, 183
Awaking consciousness, 21
Awareness, 15, 16, 19-23, 29-34, 36n., 37, 73-75, 77, 78, 81, 82, 84, 135, 136, 154, 174, 226, 231, 237. 242. 244, 246; of blue, 31
Ayodhyā, 265
ayoga, 374, 472
ayuta-siddha, 219
ayuta-siddhatva, 219
ābhāsa, 291
ābhicārika, 326
Ābhoga, 60, 125
ācārya, 489
Ācārya Dīkṣita, 251
Ācārya Jetāri, 56
Ācāryasūri, 197
ācchādya, 129
ādāna-gantho,578
ādhāra, 130, 166
ādhāra-cakra, 414, 415
Ādiśūra, 145
ādityas, 339 n., 623. 639
āgama, 354
Āgama-prāmāṇya, 633 ft. 2. 636, 637
Āgama-śāttra-vivaraṇa, 90
āghāto, 580
āgneya, 365. 384 n., 419
āhāre paṭikūla-saññā, 584
Āhrika, 198
ājñā-cakra, 412 414, 415
ākāṅkṣā, 578
ākāśa, 85, 86, 120, 184, 223, 234, 271, 282, 351, 364, 367, 420, 422, 428, 432, 436. 441
ākāśa-dhātu, 358
Ākāśagotto, 320
Ākāśa tan-mātra, 283
ākāśātmaka, 419
ākūta, 561, 562
ālambana, 33, 179
Ālamvāyana-saṃhitā, 507
ālaya-vijñāna, 25, 28
ālayo, 580
ālocaka, 354, 397
ālocaka-pitta, 399
āma-garbha, 376n,
āmalaka, 342
Amalānanda, 94
āmāśaya, 385, 386
ānanda, 257
Ānandabodha, 58, 59, 81, 103n., 106, 134, 135, 143, 170n,, 223, 225; his doctrine of *avidyā* probably borrowed from Maṇḍana, 104; as inspirer of many later works of Vedānta, 136; his date and works, 134; his interpretation of the nature of the self, 136; his refutation of "difference", 134, 135; his view of the nature of *avidyā*, 135
Ānandabodha Bhaṭṭārakācārya, 13, 56, 79, 170 n,
Ānandabodhendra, 266
Ānandabodhendra Bhikṣu, 300n 2
Ānandabodhendra Sarasvatī, 266
Ānanda-dīpa, 66 n.
Ānanda-dīpa-ṭīkā, 66 n.
Ānandagiri, 50n,, 95, 119, 143, 220, 222, 401
Ānandajñāna, i n., 49, 56-59, 90-93, 106. 115, 134, 137, 143, 198. 217, 220, 223, 225, 236, 241, 513; contents of his work *Tarka-saṃgraha*, 222, 223; his criticism of Nyāya-Vaiśeṣika categories, 222, 223; his interpretation of the indescribableness of world-appearance and *ajñāna*, 223, 224; his teachers, 220; his works, 222
Ānanda-laharī, 91
Ānanda-laharī-tarī, 91
Ānanda-mandākini, 259
Ānandapūrṇa, 60, 66, 95, 101n., 119, 142, 145n.
Ānandatīrtha, 516
Ānanda-vardhana, 146n.
Ānandānubhuva, 66 n.
Ānandāśrama, 225
Ānandātman, 67, 99
āntarikṣa, 416
Ānvīkṣikī, 455, 457

Index

Āñjaneya, 517
āpaḥ, 339n.
āpta, 325, 435
āptopadeśa, 435, 438 440
āpya, 419
ārambhakaṃ, 384n.
ārjava, 590n., 595, 634
Ārṣa-Rāmāyaṇa, 266
ārtava, 365
ārtavāḥ, 339 n.
ārthī bhāvanā, 560
Āruṇikopaniṣad, 291n .
Āryadeva, 59, 143, 189, 190
Ārya-dṛḍhāśaya-paripṛcchā, 6
Ārya-vidyā-sudhā-kara, 130n.
āsana, 530, 531
āsanga, 51
āsatti, 580
āsayo, 580
āsā, 578
āspada, 8
āsrāva, 344
āssāsa, 536
āstika, 489
āstikya, 590n.
Āśādhara, 505
āśraya, 21, 26, 98, 416
āśraya-bhūtaḥ, 69n.
Āśreṣa, 349
Āśvalāyana-śrauta-sūtra, 460
Āśvinī, 503
Āṣāḍhavarman, 499
Ātaṅka-dīpana, 505
ātivāhika śarīra, 355
Ātma-bodha, 91, 93
Ātma-bodha-vyākhyāna, 93n ., 119
ātma-dharmopacāraḥ, 25n.
ātma-jānīndriyāṇi, 361
Ātma-jñānopadeśa, 90
Ātma-jñānopadeśa-ṭīkā, 222
ātma-khyāti, 101n .
ātma-māna, 28
ātman, 9, 24, 67, 172,223, 275, 351, 359n. 1, 360 361, 472, 519, 520, 551. 604
ātmanaḥ samvid-rupatva, 136, 171,
ātma-samavāyī viṣaya-prakāśo jñānam, 226
ātma-sneha, 28
Ātmasukha, 267
Ātmasvarūpa, 61n.
ātma-śaktyā, 385
ātma-vinigraha, 598
Ātmānātma-viveka, 91
Ātmārpaṇa-stava, 252
ātmāśrayatva, 19
ātmāvalokana, 516
Ātmopadeśa-vidhi, 91
Ātreya, 321, 359. 361, 381, 388, 461, 494
Ātreya bhikṣu, 461
Ātreya-Caraka, 329, 340, 343
Ātreya-Caraka school, 336
Ātreya Gautama, 460
Ātreya Punarvasu, 321 n., 416, 503
āvaraṇa, 25, 84
āvaraṇa-śakti, 85
āvaraṇatvāt, 226
āvartta, 409
āyatana, 461, 581
āyāma, 405 If.
Āyur-veda, 299n., 317-320, 322, 325, 334, 340, 343, 373, 383 n., 413 n.. 416. 426. 427, 432. 433, 446, 449. 452, 454. 455. 457, 458. 461. 462, 464. 465. 469, 491, 493, 508; an *upaveda* of *Atharva-Veda*, 318; a part of *Atharva-Veda*, 322; apertures of the *dhamanīs* in, 408; application of inductive methods for the discovery of cause in Caraka, 462 ff.; are *vāyu, pitta* and *kapha* only hypothetical entities? 392 ff.; as a science of life, 321; a separate Veda superior to the other Vedas, 318, 319; a *vedāṅga*, 318; brain the centre of *manas* in, according to Bhela, 396; brain the seat of sensations, 403; Caraka school closely associated with *Atharva-Veda*, 322, 324; Caraka's view of *nāḍī, śirā, dhamanī* and *srotas* as ducts, 403 ff.; categories of Caraka and Vaiśeṣika, 430-433; causes of things according to Suśruta, 433; circulation of *dhātu* in growth, 375, 377; cognitive currents in, 404; constructive and destructive operations of *vāyu, pitta* and *kapha*, 395; control of body and mind, 488, 489; Dṛḍhabala's distinction of *śirās* and *dhamanīs*, 405n.; *dhamanīs* in relation to cognition according to Suśruta, 409 ff.; *dhātu-mala* in, 386; different functions of *vāyu, pitta* and *kapha*, 393, 394; different kinds of ducts in, 404; dispute, methods of, 440 ff.; disputes, terms of, 441 ff,; disturbance of *doṣas* according to seasons, 390; divergent views on the development of the foetus referred to in *Caraka-saṃhitā*, 358, 359; divergent views regarding vāyu as narrated in Caraka, 387 ff.; *doṣa* as *prakṛti*, 389; *dravya, rasa, vīrya, vipāka, prabhāva*, 422-427; early references to, 320, 321; epidemics caused by

collective evil effects, 476 ff.; equilibrium of *dhātus*, 381; ethical position of Caraka, 487; fallacies, 443 ff.; foetal development in Suśruta and Caraka, its different stages, 365 ff.; formation of foetus in Caraka, Suśruta and Vāgbhaṭa, 351-354; freedom of will in, 479; Āyur-veda, function of *dhamanīs* in, according to Suśruta, 408 ff.; function of the different ducts, 404 ff.; future life, belief in, 473; good, conception of, 471, 472; good life and happy life, 491, 493; good life in Caraka, 487 ff.; good of the body and of the mind, 487, 488; heart in the Upaniṣads contrasted with, 401; heart the vital centre of the *prāṇas* in, 396; *hetu-vidyā* in Caraka, 461; inference in, compared with Nyāya and Sāṃkhya, 465, 467; is beginningless, 318; its relation with *Atharva-Veda*, 319; Its theory of *dhātu-sāmya* and *dhātu-vaiṣamya*, 372 ff.; its unbroken tradition, 318; *jāti* fallacy, conception of, compared with Nyāya, 443-446; *yukti*, misrepresentation by Sāntarakṣita, 438; *yukti pramāṇa* of, 437; *yukti pramāṇa* refuted by Sāntarakṣita, 437 » 438; life, its definition, 428; literature, 492 ff., 507; *manas* and the senses, 428; *manas*, its theory, 427. 428; meaning of *ojas* in, 400 II.; medical discussions in, 441; *nāḍī, śirā* and *dhamanī* as ducts in, 402, 403; natural place of *vāyu, pitta* and *kapha*, 386, 392; nature of *pitta*, 385, 386; necessity of logical tricks in, 468, 469; number of *śirā, srotas* and *dhamanī* according to Suśruta, 407; number of *śirās* in, according to Suśruta, 411; number of *snāyus* in, according to Suśruta, 411; origin in the knowledge of *hetu* and *liṅga*, 461; (origin of the world, Suśruta on, 478; *param* and *aparam* ojas in, 400; perception, obstruction of. 440; perception theory of. 435, 436; period of life in, 469; possible existence of a pre-Caraka literature of it, 321; *prajñāparādha,* according to Caraka, 485, 486; *pramāṇas* in, 435; *prāṇa* in, 304; principles of growth, 374, 375; psychological theories of perception of Bhela in, 397; psycho-physical parallelism in, according to Caraka, 395; *rasas*, their number, 416-419; *rasas*, their origin, 419, 420; rebirth, nature of, determined by past life, 474, 475; rebirth, proofs of, 475, 476; relation of head and heart in, 400; right conduct, rules of, according to Caraka, 489ff.; *saṃyogi-puruṣa*, its conception, 429; *sañcaya* and *prakopa* of *doṣas*, 390; scheme of life in Caraka, 484; seat of *prāṇa* according to Caraka, 399; secretory character of *vāyu*, *pitta* and *kapha*, 394, self and the body, 429; self and knowledge, 429; self and *manas*, 430; self and the transcendent self (*parah ātmā*), 429; self, in association with *manas*, 435; self, nature of, according to Suśruta, 478; sorrows, cause of, according to Caraka, 484, 485; soul, conception of, 433; special categories in Caraka, 454; special categories in Suśruta, 454 ff.; springs of action and right conduct in, 473; springs of action in Caraka compared with those of other systems, 479 ff.; substance and qualities, 420-421; subtle body and self in Caraka, 361; Suśruta and Sāṃkhya, 433; Suśruta's distinction of *sirās* and *dhamanīs*, 405. ff.; Suśruta's views regarding brain as the seat of cognitive and conative nerves, 399; synonyms for *srotas*, 405n.; the combination of the *doṣas* in different relations, 394; the organs in relation to the ducts, 405; theory of *dhātus* and *upa-dhātus*, 375–378; theory of *doṣa* according to Suśruta, 384, 385; theory of the formation of the body, 389; theory of *karma* in, compared with other theories of *karma*, 469-471; theory of *mala-dhātus*, 379 ff.; theory of *prabhāva*, 377; three classes of inference in Caraka, 464, 465; transgressions (*prajñāparādha*) the obstacle to good life, in Caraka, 491, 492; transmigration determined by *dharma* and *adharma*, 479; ultimate healing in, 484; *upāṅga* of *Atharva-Veda*, 317; validity of the Vedas established through it, 324, 325; views of the different Upaniṣads regarding the *nāḍīs* contrasted with, 402; *vāyu, pitta* and *kapha* and their operations in the building of the body, 389 ff.; what is its nature? 320

Āyur-veda-dīpikā, 319n. 2, 320n., 351, 502
Āyur-veda-rasāyana, 506
Āyur-veda-sūtra, 508
āyuṣo 'nuvṛtti-pratyaya-bhūta, 388
āyuṣyāṇi, 343

Backbite, 595
Backbone, 332
Bad, 284; deeds, 479
Badness, 591
Baḍiśa, 368, 416

baeṣaza, 343*n*. 1
baeṣazya, 343n. 1
bahu-śruta, 98
Balabhadra Bhaṭṭācārya, 2601n.
Baladeva, 628
Baladeva Vidyābhūṣaṇa, 517
Balance, 380
bali, 322
Balkh, 416
bandha, 267, 270, 309
Bandhaku-tantra, 507
bandhanaṃ, 580
bandho, 580
Barren woman, 270
Basic concept of mind, 28
Basic entity, 27*n*.
Basis, 12, 33; of truth, 12
Battle, 589
Battle-field, 608
Bādarāyaṇa, 52, 301; his philosophy, 48; his philosophy is some kind of *bhedābheda-vāda* or immanence in transcendence, 48
bādha, 255
bādhakas tarkaḥ, 162
bāhu, 331n. 6, 394
Bālabhadra, 63
Bālagopāla, 90
Bālagopāla Yogīndra, 90
Bālakṛṣṇadāsa, 90
Bālāvatāra-tarka, 56
Bālhīka, 347n. 4, 368
Bāṇa, 641
Bāṣpacandra, 499, 502
Beard, 379
Beginningless, 13, 224, 249, 530; *avidyā*, 55; contact, 182; series, 211; time, 287
Being, 11, 41, 53, 171, 233, 270, 275, 584
Being-non-being, 270
Benares, 500
Bengal, 145, 260n.
Besnagar, 628
Bhadanta Yogasena, 211
Bhadra, 329
Bhadrakāpya, 368, 416
Bhadraśaunaka, 498
bhaga, 332n. 8
bhagandara, 320
Bhagavad-bhakti-rasāyana, 259
Bhagavad-gītā, 91, 516
Bhagavad-gītā-bhāṣya, 513
Bhagavad-gītā-bhāṣya-vivaraṇa, 513
Bhagavad-gītā-bhāṣya-vyākhyā, 513
Bhagavad-gītā-gūḍhārtha-dīpikā, 259
Bhagavad-gītā-hetu-nirṇaya, 517
Bhagavad-gītā-lakṣābharaṇa, 517
Bhagavad-gītā-pradīpa, 517
Bhagavad-gītā-prakāśa, 517
Bhagavad-gītā-rahasya, 641, 642n. 1
Bhagavad-gītārtha-saṃgraha, 517
Bhagavad-gītārtha-saṃgraha-ṭīkā, 513
Bhagavad-gītārtha-sāra, 517
Bhagavad-gītā-sāra, 517
Bhagavad-gītā-sāra-saṃgraha, 517
Bhagavad-gītā-tātparya-nirṇaya, 516
Bhagavat, 628–631; and Viṣṇu, 628, 629
bhagāsthi, 332n. 8
bhaiṣajya, 340, 343
bhakti, 260, 516, 513, 619, 620, 622
Bhakti-rasāyana, 260
bhaktir ādeśyā, 322
Bhakti-sāmānya-nirūpaṇa, 259
bhakti-yoga, 514, 515, 527
Bhandarkar, R.G., 629, 633, 638
Bharadvāja, 264, 359, 461, 465
Bharata, 498
Bhartṛhari, 197
Bhartṛprapañca, 2, 41, 49, 51, 115; his philosophy of *bhedābheda*, 49
Bhaṭṭacarya Sivaprasad, 267
Bhaṭṭacharya, B., 23n., 198n.
Bhaṭṭa Ānanda, 305
Bhaṭṭa Kallaṭa, 304
Bhaṭṭa Narahari, 495
Bhaṭṭa Rāghava, 141, 142
Bhaṭṭoji Dīkṣita, 62, 63, 249, 251
bhautikī, 389
bhava, 581
Bhavabhūti, 128, 129
Bhavadāsa, 101n.
Bhavanātha, 146n.
Bhavanīsahāya, 506
Bhavya, 189
Bhāgavata, 290, 634-637, 643; and the *ekāntins*, 635; sect, 635 ff.
Bhāgavata-purāṇa, 252, 620, 631
Bhāgavata-purāṇa-prathama-śloka-vyākhyā, 259
Bhāgavatism, 641
bhājana-loka-sanniveśa-vijñapti, 26
Bhāluki-tantra, 507
Bhāmatī, 12, 30n., 33, 41, 60, 64, 94, 122-126, 128, 197, 252, 256n., 312n. 2, 498
Bhāmatī-tilaka, 60n., 125
Bhāmatī-vilāsa, 125
Bhāmatī-vyākhyā, 125

Bhānujī Dīkṣita, 63
Bhānumatī, 421, 423n., 495, 507
Bhāradvāja-saṃhitā, 502
Bhāradvājīyas, 629
bhāra-hāra, 72
Bhāra-hāra-sūtra, 70
Bhārata legend, 643
bhārati sthāna, 414
Bhārati Tīrtha, 60n., 93, 248n.
Bhārgava, 502
Bhāsa, 460, 641
Bhāsarvajña, 141
Bhāskara, 50n., 222, 231, 498, 499
Bhāskara Bhaṭṭa, 507
Bhāskara Dīkṣita, 64
Bhāsurānanda, 91
Bhāṣā-pariccheda, 305n.
Bhāṣya-bhāva-prakāśikā, 170n.
Bhāṣya-dīpikā, 119
Bhāṣya-ṭippana, 90
Bhāṣyārtha-nyāya-mālā, 93
Bhāṭṭa-cintāmaṇi, 600
Bhāū Śāstri, 13n.
bhāva, 222, 480
Bhāva-dīpikā, 517
bhāva-mātra, 21
Bhāvamiśra, 507
bhāvanā, 271, 560-562
bhāvanā-mātra-sāra, 271
Bhāvanā-viveka, 101n.
Bhāva-prakāśa, 304, 335n. 1, 505, 507, 508
Bhāva-prakāśikā, 91
bhāva-rūpa, 121, 131
Bhāva-śuddhi, 101n.
Bhāva-tattva-prakāśikā, 113, 171
bhāvatva, 164
Bhāvaviveka, 189, 190
bhāvābhāvayor dvayor api paraspara-pratikṣepātmakatvāt, 164
bhāvādvaita, 98
Bhāvārtha-dīpikā, 91
Bhāvivikta, 198
bheda, 106, 134, 250, 468n.
Bheda-dhikkāra, 59, 62, 63, 248, 250
Bheda-dhikkāra-satkriyā, 59, 63
Bheda-dhikkāra-satkriyojjvalā, 59
bhedābheda, 51, 53, 231, 232; earliest references to, 49; philosophy of Bhartṛprapañca, 49
bhedābheda-vāda, 48, 49
Bhela, 331n. 6, 396, 397, 461, 503; his psycho-physiological theories, 396 ff.
Bhela-saṃhitā, 503
bheṣaja, 319, 343, 431
Bheṣaja-kalpa, 503, 508
bheṣajāni, 326
bhikṣu, 589
Bhīṣma, 633
bhoga-gandham parityajet, 309
Bhoja, 378n., 498, 499, 507
Bhoja-tantra, 507
bhoktṛ, 282
Bhrama-ghna, 503
bhrājaka, 352, 385, 409
bhruvor madhye, 525n. 2
bhṛnga-rāja, 345
Bhuśuṇḍa, 297
Bhuvaḥ, 87
Bhuvanasundara Sūri, 139, 142
Bhūḥ, 87
bhūmi, 339n.
bhūta, 302, 327, 351n. 2, 366n., 367, 372, 389, 432
bhūta-hitatva, 589
bhūta-prakṛti, 226
bhūta-sūkṣmaiḥ, 362
bhūta-vidyā, 320, 495
bhūta-vikāra, 418n.
bhūtātman, 352, 354, 484
bhūteṣu daya, 595
Bibliotheca Indica, 401n.
Bile, 320, 369, 379
Bilious fever, 346
Billows, 384
Binding, 580
Biomotor, 302, 600; forces, 86, 299, 303; functions, 120
Birth, 581, 597, 605
Bitter, 279, 393n., 416, 419
bīja, 271
bījāṅkuravat, 297
Blackness, 275
Bladder, 336, 337, 392, 405, 409
Blame, 597
Blind, 360
Blindness, 388, 399
Bliss, 53, 526, 588; of mind, 598
Blissfulness, 257
Blood, 327, 346, 354, 358, 365, 369, 371, 375-378, 384-386, 390, 404, 407, 411, 421, 433; currents, 405
Bloomfield, 321n., 343
Blue, 15, 21, 30, 31, 33, 34-37, 82, 135, 203, 385, 401; 407; awareness, 81, 82
Boastfulness, 435
Bodha-sāra, 66

Bodha-vidhi, 91
bodhātmaka, 306
Bodhāyana, 49, 290
Bodhāyana-Gṛhya-śeṣa-sūtra, 641
Bodhāyana-Pitṛ-medha-sūtra, 641
Bodhendra, 91
Bodhi-caryāvatāra-pañjikā, 5n., 584
Bodhisattva, 598
Bodiless emancipation, 291
Bodily, 583; exercises, 488
Body, 286, 302, 373, 379, 381, 386, 396, 411, 426, 452, 522, 547, 581, 584
Body-building, 394
Bolling, 336, 348, 351n. 2
Bond, 580
Bondage, 200, 208, 215, 234, 267, 284, 291, 309, 484, 548, 569, 580, 606
Bone, 322, 324, 369, 378, 405, 411; channels, 405
Bony materials, 404
"Bower Manuscripts" 507
brahma-bhūta, 553, 554
brahma-bhūya, 553
brahma-caitanya, 89
brahma-cakra, 412n.
brahma-carya, 589
Brahmacārin, 327, 524, 589
Brahmadatta, 114
Brahmadeva, 498, 499
Brahmagraha, 349
Brahmahood, 43, 63, 93, 106, 526, 554, 556, 598
Brahma-jāla-sutta, 460
Brahma-knowledge, 49, 54, 64, 98, 100, 115, 133, 233, 234, 257, 261, 291
Brahman, 2, 9, 11, 12, 18, 32, 41–45, 47, 48, 52-55, 59, 84, 92, 97, 101, 104, 111, 114–117, 120–122, 127, 129-133, 136, 145, 148, 180, 188, 194, 196, 218, 219, 224, 225, 232, 233, 236, 247, 249, 253, 255, 270, 272-275, 277, 280-283, 306, 314, 319, 396, 450, 511, 513, 514, 523, 526, 530, 552-555, 566, 567, 576, 577, 599, 610, 611, 618, 621, 622, 627, 638; nature of causality, 11, 12
Brahmana jagat-kāraṇam, 97
Brahmanandin, 50n.
brahma-nāḍī, 413, 415
brahman-consciousness, 89
Brahma-nirvāṇa, 553
Brahmaṇo mukhe, 553
Brahma-pariṇāma-vāda, 49
Brahma-prakāśikā, 56, 95n.
brahma-randhra, 412n., 415
Brahma-rākṣasa, 327
Brahma-siddhi, 95, 97, 99-101, 106, 107, 110, 113, 122, 135, 127n., 129, 205, 227, 229
Brahma-siddhi-ṭīkā, 52, 95
Brahma-siddhi-vyākhyā-ratna, 95
Brahma-stuti, 171n.
Brahma-sūtra, 3, 6, 9, 29, 32, 33, 50n., 53, 64, 94, 106, 119, 125n., 171n., 217, 225, 234, 236, 250, 252, 285n., 289n., 290, 456, 577, 640; discussion as to whether it professes pure monism or *bhedābheda*, 51 ff.; does not support Śaṅkara's philosophy, 2
Brahma-sūtra-bhāṣya, 34, 92, 93, 170n.
Brahma-sūtra-bhāṣya-vyākhyā, 95n.
Brahma-sūtra-bhāṣyārtha-saṃgraha, 95n.
Brahma-sūtra-dīpikā, 94
Brahma-sūtra-vṛtti, 94
Brahma-sutro-panyāsa, 95n.
Brahma-tattva-prakāśikā, 95n.
Brahma-tattva-samīkṣā, 13
Brahma-tattva-saṃhitoddīpanī, 52n.
Brahma-vaivarta, 318, 503, 505n.
Brahmavāda, 328
Brahma-Veda, 326n.
brahma-vicāra, 64
Brahma-vidyā-bharaṇa, 64, 95n.
brahma-vihāra, 537, 584
Brahmavijñāna, 62
brahma-yajña, 568
Brahmā, 226, 264, 283, 318, 493, 605, 628, 636
Brahmānanda Giri, 517
Brahmānanda Sarasvatī, 62, 66n., 89., 91, 93, 94, 290n.
Brahmānanda-vilāsa, 66n.
Brahmānanda Yati, 94
Brahmin Sutīkṣṇa, 265
Brahmopaniṣat, 290
Brain, 396, 412n., 415
Bravery, 586
Brāhmaṇas, 339, 343n. 1, 350, 489
Brāhmins, 263, 547, 569, 581, 586, 588, 589-591, 597, 598, 628
Breast, 332
Breath, 299
Breath-control, 310, 519, 522, 523, 531
Breathing activity, 86
Breathing forth, 299
Breath-regulation, 296
Breeding, 589
Broken, 393, 394
Bronchi, 332n. 2
Bronchial tubes, 336n. 3

Bronchitis, 450
Brow, 333
Bṛhad-āraṇyaka-bhāṣya-ṭīkā, 222
Bṛhad-āraṇyaka-bhāṣya-vārttika-ṭīkā, 222
Bṛhad-āraṇyaka Upaniṣad, 2, 84, 90, 95, 290, 300n. 3, 301, 335n. 1, 401, 402, 456, 460
Bṛhad-āraṇyukopaniṣad-bhāṣya, 55, 90
Bṛhad-āraṇyakopaniṣad-bhāṣya- vārttika, 90, 113
Bṛhad-yoga-vāsiṣṭha, 267
Bṛhad-laghu-pañjikā, 499
Bṛhaspati-smṛti, 290
budbuda, 364n. 3
Buddha, 25n., 70, 320, 494, 536, 581, 606
Buddhadeva, 197
Buddhaghoṣa, 189
Buddhapālita, 189, 190
Buddhas,
Buddhi, 86, 87, 120, 126, 206–208, 275, 276, 283, 303, 355, 397, 401, 406n., 430, 435, 450, 452, 535, 540, 541, 565n. 1, 611
Buddhism, 67, 135, 263, 526n. 1, 536, 538, 577, 581, 588, 607; analysis of recognition, 75; and Vedānta on the notion of self-consciousness and recognition of identity, 38 ff.; *avidyā* in, and in *Gītā*, 581-583; criticisms of the concept of God of Nyāya and Yoga, 203-205; criticism of the Sāṃkhya *pariṇāmu* doctrine, 197 ff.; development of the foetus in the *Śali-stamba-sūtra*, 358; ideal life of Mahāyāna, 584; its arguments against the self as individual entity, 67 f.; its attempt to interpret self-identity by the assumption of two separate concepts, 78; its criticism of Nyāya-Vaiśeṣika categories, 215 ff.; its criticism of the Vedāntic identity of self as shown in memory, 76; its doctrine of momentariness and *artha-kriyā-kāritā,* 209 ff.; its idealism compared with that of Śaṅkara and *Yoga-vāsiṣṭha*, 310 ff.; its refutation of criticism of the non-permanency of entities by heretical thinkers, 213 ff.; refutation of the soul theory of various systems of Indian thought in, 205-208; *sīla* in, 583, 584; status of the object in, 40; the Vātsīputrīyas doctrine of soul, 68 ff.; Vasubandhu's refutation of the soul theory of the Vātsīputrīyas in, 67 ff.; views, list of, in, 578 ff.
Buddhist arguments, 203, 216
Buddhistic, 138, 174, 196, 461, 607, 642
Buddhistic idealism, 3, 25n., 29–31, 33, 34, 40, 236, 312, 464; its explanation of the apparent duality of object and awareness, and the diversity of objects, 30; its theory that things simultaneous are identical, 30n.; that all ideas are due to *vāsanās*, 30
Buddhistic nihilism, 3
Buddhist Legends, 287n.
Buddhist logicians, 191, 196
Buddhists, 6, 10, 36, 37, 38, 75, 77, 78, 82, 111, 125, 130, 133, 136, 143, 144, 157, 197, 198, 214-217, 311, 428, 437, 465, 480, 484, 505, 507, 578, 582-584, 596, 599, 603, 607; deny any being as the ground of world-appearance which is like dreams, 5; their quarrel with the Vedāntins regarding the nature of existence as causal efficiency, 37
Buddhist subjective idealists, 242
Buddhist writers, 59, 197
buddhitvākalanaṃ, 272
buddhi-vaiśeṣika, 399
buddhi-vibhraṃśa, 485
buddhi-yoga, 519, 527, 528
buddhy-adhiṣṭhāna, 368
Bulletin de l'Académie des Sciences de Russie, 68n., 71n., 72n.
Burlingame, E.W., 286
Burning, 112, 391n.
Bühler, G., 641

caitanya, 238
Caitraratha Forest, 416
cakra, 414, 531
cakra-bhramivad-dhṛta-śarīraḥ, 289
Cakradatta, 496, 502
Cakrapāṇidatta, 319, 322n., 321, 352n., 354, 359, 361, 365n., 366, 367, 371, 372n., 375n., 377, 378n., 381n., 387n., 390, 394n., 395n., 396, 400, 404, 405n., 407, 420n., 421n., 421–432, 435-438, 443n., 448n., 461, 462, 473n., 474n., 484n., 495–499, 501-507
Cakra system, 530
cakṣur-vaiśeṣika, 397
cala, 387, 394
Caland, W., 403n.
Calcutta University, 3n.
Camphor, 105
Canals, 411
Canda, 628
Candracandana, 506
Candragomin, 56
Candrakīrti, 4, 59, 189–194, 197, 358; and Diṅnāga, 192

candramāḥ, 339n.
Candrikā, 113, 114, 220, 267
Canvas, 229
caṇḍāla, 597
Caṇḍeśvara Varman, 90
Capacity, 46
Caraka, 304, 318, 319, 324, 331n., 332n., 339, 350, 351, 354, 358, 364, 366-368, 375n., 381, 384, 387, 389-392, 395, 396, 399, 400, 403, 405, 407, 411, 414-416, 419n., 420n., 422-427, 429, 430, 432, 433, 437, 438, 441-443, 446, 446, 448n., 450n., 453, 454, 458, 461-463, 465, 467, 468-477, 479, 484, 486-493, 498-500, 502-507, 549-552, 554
Caraka-candrikā, 502
Caraka-pañjikā, 502
Caraka-pariśiṣṭa, 500
Caraka-saṃhitā, 317n., 321, 322, 338, 351n., 359n., 361n., 365n., 366, 367n., 371n., 372n., 377n., 378, 380n., 381n., 386, 387n., 389n., 390n., 392n., 395n., 396, 399n., 404, 405n., 420, 421n., 422, 427n., 428n., 430, 431n., 432, 435n., 436n., 437n., 438n., 440, 450n., 457, 458, 461, 462n., 463-469, 479, 485, 492, 496, 498, 500, 549, 551, 552n., 556
Caraka-tattva-pradīpikā, 502
Caraka-tātparya-ṭīkā, 362n., 502
Cardiac plexus, 414
Caritrasiṃha, 146n.
caritta, 583
Cartilages, 332n., 375
Caste, 584, 587, 589
Caste-duty, 567, 568, 586-589, 591, 592, 598, 599
Categorical imperative, 575
Category, 13, 17, 28, 168, 169, 181, 188, 196, 215, 219, 273, 427, 430, 433, 454
Cattle, 350
Cattle-shed, 593
catur-aṇuka, 217, 218
Catur-mata-sāra-saṃgraha, 251
cauryābhāva, 589
Causal, 203, 607; agent, 85. 204; apparatus, 209; complexes, 4; efficiency, 37, 110, 157, 158, 213; forces, 200; moment, 213; nature, 211; operation, 29, 47, 166, 199, 201, 214, 603; state, 43; substance, 198; transformation, 51, 198
Causality, 36n., 171, 198, 214, 253, 462; of Brahman, 122; of the world due jointly to Brahman and Māyā according to *Padārtha-tattva*, 11
Causation, 189, 194
Cause, 3, 12, 25n., 44-46, 110, 166, 167, 175, 184, 185, 191, 210, 214, 216, 218, 219, 224, 233, 247, 393, 427, 433, 436, 437, 454, 462-464, 602, 603; and effect, 219; of atoms, 215; of the world, 43; unknown, 420
Cause-effect, 437, 438
Causeless, 185, 215
Cavity, 411
caya, 390
caya-kāraṇa-vidveṣa, 391n.
cāgānussati, 536
Cāraṇa-vaidya, 328, 329
Cārvāka, 452, 469
Central Asia, 507
Central seat, 416
Centres, 18
Cerebral region, 412, 413
Cerebrum, 412n., 415, 416
Ceremonies, 546
Cervical plexus, 412
Cessation, 24, 270, 279; from work, 591; of desires, 519; of work, 592
ceṣṭā, 381, 551
ceṣṭitam, 432
cetanā, 26, 41, 351, 368, 420n., 429, 549, 556, 583
cetanā-dhātu, 551
cetanā-pratisandhātā, 427
cetanāvantaḥ, 478
cetas, 294, 427
cetasika, 583
ceto-vimutti, 537
cetya-saṃyoga-cetanāt, 272
cetyatva, 272
Ceylonese, 189
chadmanā, 557
chala, 449, 450n., 468
Chandaḥ-praśasti, 145
Chandas, 28, 319n., 578, 637
Change, 52
Changeable, 18, 253
Changeful, 278
Changeless, 12, 15, 277; being, 59
Changing, 217; association, 73; contents, 17; materiality, 59; objects, 38; states, 38
Channel, 338, 378, 401, 404
Character, 17, 20, 31n., 152, 215, 216
Character-appearance, 15
Characteristic, 4, 7, 20, 44, 187, 203, 209, 229, 230, 263, 269, 290, 432, 597

Characterized appearances, 26n., 26; entities, 25
Characterless entity, 314
Chariot, 264
Charm, 325, 326, 340-348, 350; system, 342
Chāndogya, 90, 284, 289n., 300n., 301, 321n., 402, 403, 606
Chāndogya-bhāṣya-ṭīkā, 222
Chāndogya Upaniṣad, 49n., 388, 402n., 581, 607, 634, 639n.
Chāndogya-Upaniṣad-vārttika, 50n.
Chāyā-vyākhyā, 303
chedana, 417
chedanīya, 416
Cheeks, 380n.
Chemical changes, 369
Chemistry, 416
Chest, 392
chidra-malas, 380n.
Chimerical, 151
Chintamani, T.R., 225
Cholera, 327
Christianity, 641
Church Street, 16
Chyle, 369, 375-378, 382, 385, 386, 405, 407
cic-chāyāpatti, 103n.
Cid-ānanda-daśaśloki, 91
Cid-ānanda-stava-rāja, 91
cid-ātman, 129
cikitsā, 322, 335n., 457, 501
Cikitsā-darśana, 503
Cikitsā-kaumudī, 503
Cikitsā-sāra-tantra, 503
Cikitsā-sthāna, 500
Cikitsā-tattva-vijñāna, 503
cikitsitam, 320
cikīrṣā, 600
cin-mātra-sambandhinī, 226
cin-mātrāśrita-viṣayam ajñānam, 98
Cinnabomma, 251
cintya, 400
cira-jāgara, 309
cirāj-jāgrat-sthita, 308
Circular bone, 330n. 4
Circulation, 377
Circulatory system, 377
Circumstance, 269
cit, 102, 103n., 271, 280, 282, 314
citra-bhitti, 120
Citra-mīmāṃsā, 252
citriṇī, 412, 415
citriṇī nāḍī, 413, 415
Citsukha, 56-59, 61, 67, 95, 99, 101n., 106, 134, 138, 143, 159, 169, 171, 171n., 175, 177, 180, 181, 184-188, 197, 198, 220, 223, 227, 249, 250, 255n.; awareness of awareness impossible, 173, 174; his analysis of illusion, 179; his criticism of the atomic theory, 181, 182; his criticism of "cause" *(kāraṇa)*, 184 ff.; his criticism of Nyāya categories, 180; his date and works, 171; his definition of self-revealing consciousness, 171-173; his quarrel with Prabhākara on the subject of illusion, 177 ff.; his refutation of the category of time, 180, 181; his refutation of class-concepts *(jāti)*, 184; his refutation of *dravya*, 185, 187; his refutation of numbers, 182; his refutation of qualities (*guṇa)*, 187, 188; his refutation of space, 181; his treatment of the falsehood of the world-appearance, 175, 176; his treatment of nescience (*ajñāna),* 176; main content of his *Tattva-pradīpikā*, 171*n*.; nature of self, 174, 175
Citsukha Ācārya, his refutation of the Nyāya definition of perception, 159
cit-svarūpāḥ, 479
citta, 86, 270, 275, 276, 280, 289, 296, 298, 306, 339, 355, 356, 397
citta-camatkāra, 272
citta-vimukti, 306
citta-vṛtti, 305
cittinaḥ, 340n. 4
Cīpudru, 348n. 2
Class-concept, 46, 125, 151, 152, 160, 171, 183, 187, 188, 215, 216, 223, 432
Class-duties, 567
Class-nature, 216, 217
Clavicle, 333n. 2
Cleanliness, 589
Clinging, 580
"Closed," 4
Cloth, 217
Clouds, 236
Coarse, 393n.
Coccyx, 332n., 333n.
Cognition, 20-24, 26, 81, 157, 172, 176, 207, 216, 246, 276, 280, 318
Cognitional character, 33
Cognitional existence, 67
Cognitive activities, 296
Cognitive functions, 296
Cognitive nerves, 399
Cognitive operation, 242
Cognitive process, 237

Cognitive relation, 245
Cognitive senses, 87, 583
Cognitive states, 174, 289, 290
Cognized object, 21, 25
Cognizer, 21, 25, 26, 409
Cognizing, 17; activity, 120, 172; faculty, 207
Coherence, 17
Cola country, 171n.
Cold, 279, 350, 373, 374, 387, 393n., 416, 417, 420, 421, 422n., 426, 476, 488, 583, 595, 596
Colic, 403; pain, 346
Collar bone, 333n., 333
Collocating, 159, 184; conditions, 185
Collocation, 194, 200, 215, 602; of causes, 185, 551, 552; of things, 185
Collyrium, 275
Colour, 28, 69, 208, 214, 216, 219, 223, 229, 336, 381, 385, 414, 420, 428, 440; cognition, 207; particles, 29n.
Colouredness, 436
Colouring *pitta,* 380n.
Combination, 217, 420
Combinations of atoms, 23
Command, 55
Commentary, 31n., 33, 44, 49, 60, 62, 114, 117, 119, 123, 125, 225, 251, 267, 413n.
Commentator, 59, 189
Common duty, 589-591
Common good, 590
Common self, 208
Commonsense, 4; view, 2, 592
Common well-being, 590
Communion, 527, 534-536, 544, 545, 548, 571, 574, 584, 587, 588, 618
Community, 590
Compact, 393n.
Compassion, 596
Compendium, 246
Compilation, 56
Compilers, 61
Complex, 4, 29, 75, 247; quality, 19, 20
Compounding, 431
Conative senses, 86
Conceit, 435, 477, 595
Conceive, 294
Concentration, 537, 583, 588
Concept, 270; of contact, 182
Conception, 272, 285, 611
Conception of Buddhist Nirvāṇa, The, 189n., 192n.
Concepts of duality, 222
Conceptual, 272; activity, 272; creation, 273, 280, 282
Conch-shell, 7, 116, 131, 154-158, 179
Conclusion, 188, 199, 435, 438-441, 446, 452
Concomitance, 21, 140, 161, 162, 223, 436, 451n., 463
Concrete, 29, 271n.; duration, 244; individual, 276; state, 272
Conditional, 164
Conditionality of relations, 164
Conditioning knowledge, 20
Conditions, 18, 209, 211
Conduct, 583, 587
Conformations, 581
Congenital *vāta*, 393
Conglomeration, 189, 191
Conjeeveram, 113
Conjunction, 46
Connection, 414
Connotation, 554
Conscious, 17, 432; centre, 18; moments, 72; states, 15, 215
Consciousness, 16, 20, 32, 34, 38, 40, 72-75, 79, 82, 83, 171, 172, 176, 189, 229, 231, 236-238, 240, 241, 245, 247, 255, 270, 314, 361, 366, 371, 420, 427, 429, 430, 452, 474, 549, 556, 581, 620; of relationing, 38; pure, 25
Consequence, 210
Conservation of energy, 603
Constant, 73
Constituent, 19, 20, 85, 375, 432, 612; elements, 68, 354
Constitution, 389
Constitutional, 390
Constitutive stuff, 55
Constructive, 386; instincts, 26; principles, 388; tendencies, 28
Consumption, 346, 450
Contact, 218, 223, 420, 435, 436, 445*n.*; of atoms, 218
Contact-points, 216
Container, 25, 166
Contemporary, 58
Contentless, 209
Contentment, 571, 574, 584, 587
Content of recognition, 76
Contiguity, 428
Continuity, 17, 24; of consciousness, 207
Continuous, 278; appearance, 30n.; perception, 245
Contradiction, 127, 158, 169
Contrary, 19

Control, 296, 488; of anger, 589, 595; of mind, 589, 595
Controller, 247
Controversy, 144
Cooking, 112, 216, 386
Co-operant, 211
Co-operation, 12, 380
Cordier, Dr P., 496n., 498, 500
Co-religionists, 584
Coronation ceremony, 327
Corporeal, 597
Correspondence, 154
Cosmic universe, 611
Cosmic world, 613
Costal cartilages, 332n. 1
Cotyloid cavity, 335n.
Cough, 344, 346, 347n.
Country, 431
Courage, 382, 388
Course, 605
Covetous, 581, 582n.
Covetousness, 580, 581
Cow, 183, 489, 593, 597
Cranial bones, 334n.
Cranium, 333
Craving, 588
Creation, 83, 205, 270, 271, 279
Creationism, 2
Creative power, 85
Creative thought movement, 271n.
Creator, 2, 45, 47, 203, 204
Creed, 584
Critical thinking, 305
Criticism, 40, 168, 180, 190, 191, 197, 220, 234, 453; of qualities, 223
Cruelty, 435, 477, 595
Cupidity, 580
Curatives, 325
Curator, 236
Curd, 46
Cures, 325
Currents of sensation, 396
Cursing, 327
Customary morality, 588, 610
Customs, 146, 570, 587
Cyavana, 503
Cycle, 613

dahana, 388
daharādhikaraṇa, 237n.
daiva, 292-295, 361, 475, 476, 551, 600
daiva yajña, 568
daivī sampat, 595
dakṣiṇā, 339, 634
dakṣiṇāyana, 605
dama, 577, 589
Damsel, 264
Dancing, 582n.
dantolūkhala, 334n. 3
darśana, 531
dasa-kusala-kamma, 581
Dasgupta, S.N., 19, 524n. 1, 585n.
Daśarathapriya, 114
Daśa-śloki-mahā-vidyā-sūtra, 139
Daśa-ślokī, 91
Data of experience, 181
Dattātreya, 517
Datum of perception, 244
Days, 180
dākṣya, 590n.
dāna, 590n., 634
Dārila, 329, 340
Dārila Bhaṭṭa, 319
dāruṇa, 388n.
Death, 286, 348, 392, 581, 584, 597, 610, 613
Deathless, 604, 613
Debate, 440
Decay, 581
Deccan, Early History of the, 630n. 1
Decisions, 28, 435, 448
Decoction, 456n.
Deeds, 279, 286
Deep sleep, 267
Defeat, 597
Defects, 44, 246
Deficiency, 372, 380, 390
Definition, 146, 157, 165, 167, 183-185, 220; of cause, 214; of perception, 158
deha, 522n. 3
deha-sambhava-hetavaḥ, 385
Dejection, 265
Delirium, 346, 388
Deliverance, 309
Delivery, 338n. 3
Delusion, 196, 283, 582, 583, 595
Demerit, 287, 477, 485
Demons, 265, 343, 349, 546, 557, 623
Denotation of words, 215
Denunciation, 597
Denutritive, 416, 417
Dependence, 11, 616
Dependent on being, 41
Desirable, 597
Desire, 28, 105, 205, 206, 291, 305, 378, 420, 431, 435, 437, 477, 479, 480, 492, 516, 526, 527, 529, 556. 564, 569, 577, 581,

584, 587, 588, 591-596, 602, 605, 606, 608, 616; bonds of, 310; for life, 473
Desirelessness, 263, 571
Desisting, 583
Destiny, 292, 413, 420, 431, 471, 613
Destroyed cause, 214n.
Destructibility, 451n.
Destructible, 226, 597
Destruction, 209, 271, 275; of the atoms, 219; of *citta*, 310; of mind, 523
Destructive, 386; play, 205
deśa, 417, 454
deśa-kāla-kriyā-dravyaiḥ, 277
Detached, 528
Detachment, 554
Determinant of causality, 214
Determinate, 26; perception, 112; thought, 29
Determination, 26n., 63, 86, 214
Determine, 26
deva, 366
Devadatta, 72, 86
Devagiri, 142
Devakī, 634
Devakī-putra, 634
Devarāma Bhaṭṭa, 93
devatā, 49
deva-yāna, 605, 607
Devādarśa, 328
Devendra, 63
Deveśvara, 128
Devotee, 620
Devotion, 513-515, 587, 610, 619, 622, 637; to Vedic gods, 589
dhairya, 305, 589
dhamanī, 336, 337, 400, 402n., 403– 408, 409n., 411, 414; its pre-Carakian senses discussed, 402, 403
Dhamma-pada, 286, 570, 571, 575
dhanaiṣaṇā, 473
Dhanañjaya, 86
dhanur-ākāre, 413
Dhanur-veda, 318
Dhanvantari, 368, 494, 495, 503, 505
dharma, 24, 26n., 151, 229, 381, 478-480, 485, 488, 559, 563, 564, 567-569, 576, 587, 612, 627
Dharma-dharms-viniścaya, 56
dharma-kāya, 26n.
Dharmakīrti, 158, 197
dharma-kṣetra, 586
dharma-megha, 290
Dharma-mīmāṃsā-paribhāṣā, 252
Dharmarāja Ādhvarīndra, 61n., 61, 62, 103n., 121, 227n., 239, 244, 246, 249
dharma-saṃketa, 213
dharma-śāstra, 637
dharma-śraddhā, 589
Dharmatrāta, 197
dharma-vicāra, 64
Dharmaya Dīkṣita, 252
dharmya, 599
dhānya, 369
dhāraṇa, 382, 399, 530, 531
dhārin, 400,
dhātu, 26n., 320, 354, 358, 369, 372, 373, 378-384, 386-388, 400, 404, 407, 454
dhātu-mala, 386, 387
dhātu-rasa, 377n.
dhātu-rūpa-rasa, 375
dhātu-sāmyam, 382n.
dhātu-vaiṣamya, 372, 373, 380, 382, 384, 395
dhātu-vyūhana, 367
dhī, 382, 589
dhī-dhṛti-smṛti-vibhraṣṭa, 485
Dhruva, Mr, 468n.
dhruvo, 26n.
dhṛti, 435, 548, 590n., 595
dhṛti-vibhraṃśa, 485
dhūma-pā, 489
dhūmo, 580
dhyāna, 296, 399, 530, 531
Dhyāna-bindu, 531
dhyāna-yoga, 523, 535
Diabetes, 327, 344
Diagnosis, 350
Dialectic, 136, 146, 196, 197, 259n.; criticism, 180; methods, 138; Nāgārjuna and Vedānta, 188; of Śaṅkara, 217; Śrīharṣa and Nāgārjuna, 188 ff.
Dialectical, 59, 83, 168; arguments, 250; criticism, 106; subtleties, 220; thought, 169
Diarrhoea, 237, 348, 350n. 2
Diet, 448
Difference, 16, 19, 20, 31n., 31, 34, 73, 75, 87, 101, 106, 110-112, 134, 135, 146, 150-152, 171, 185, 229, 230, 232, 240, 241, 431; numerical, 16; of characters, 431; of identity, 431
Difference between awareness and object, 19
Difference-of-awareness-from-the-object, 20
Different, 32, 74, 417, 419; classes, 185; effects, 185; measure, 218
Differentiate, 165
Differentiation, 27n.

Digestion, 352, 375, 378n., 392, 421– 422, 426n., 431
Digestive fire, 388
Digestive function, 382
Digits, 331
Dihaka, 496
dik, 181
Dinakarī, 305n.
Diṅnāga, 30n., 31n., 34, 40, 192, 197; and Candrakīrti, 192
Direct cognition, 37
Direct perception, 436
Disciplinary measure, 584
Discipline, 599
Discoveries, 325
Discrimination, 26, 28, 289
Discriminative knowledge, 289, 290, 355
Discussion, 114, 149, 440, 441, 457
Disease, 325, 350, 373, 381-387, 391n., 392n., 393, 419, 427, 431, 433, 438, 440, 448, 449, 455, 458, 463; as modifications of *doṣas*, 384; its causes, 373 ff.; its theory according to Sāṃkhya and Nyāya, 382, 384n.
Diseases of the legs, 348
Disgust, 584
Disinclination, 282, 290, 588
Disintegrating, 219, 306, 356
Disjunction, 420
Disliking, 417
Dispute, 440, 442
Dissection, 334
Dissociation, 286, 310, 610
Dissolution, 43, 126, 204, 219, 223, 613; of ignorance, 98
Distance, 420
Distasteful, 416
Distinct entities, 36
Distinction, 16, 17, 468n.
Disturbance, 390
Diverse, 428
Diversity, 30, 44, 45, 224, 416, 428; of contents, 16
Divine equipment, 595
Divodāsa, 494, 503, 505n. 1
Dīdhiti, 146n.
dīkṣā, 339n.
Dīpikā, 90
Doctrine, 261, 437, 584, 603, 606, 607, 612
Dogs, 338, 597
Doing good to living beings, 589
Dominant, 417
Dormant, 189
doṣa, 349, 372, 379, 381, 382, 387, 389-393, 395, 397, 421, 427, 433, 446, 455, 482, 580; according to Suśruta, 384, 385
doṣa-prakṛtiḥ, 390n.
doṣābhāva, 246
Doubt, 162, 171, 440, 446, 583
Dramiḍācārya, 49
draṣṭṛ, 101
drava, 419n.
dravya, 215, 222, 419–422, 426, 430, 432, 435
Dravya-guṇa-saṃgraha, 424
dravya-prabhāva, 419, 422
dravya-yajña, 568
dravyātmakatā guṇasya, 219
Dream appearances, 233
Dream conceptions, 277
Dream construction, 24, 277
Dream experience, 7, 9, 32, 278, 308
Dream ideas, 30
Dream knowledge, 361, 414
Dreamless sleep, 61, 116, 177, 247
Dream life, 92
Dream objects, 41
Dream perceptions, 92
Dream persons, 308
Dream state, 224, 277
Dreams, 5, 21–24, 29, 30, 223, 311, 312, 328
Drink, 385, 584
droha, 482
Dropsy, 327
Drought, 431
Drugs, 321
Drug system, 342
Drupada, 630
Dry, 387, 416, 421, 476; country, 431
Dryness, 417, 420, 422n., 426
Dṛḍhabala, 407n., 419, 496, 500-502, 505, 506
Dṛḍhabala saṃskāra, 506
dṛḍha-bhāvanā, 296
Dṛg-dṛśya-prakaraṇa, 91
dṛk, 175, 229
dṛk and *dṛśya*, 230
dṛk-sthiti, 530
dṛśaḥ adṛśyatvāt, 229
dṛśya, 101, 175, 229, 267
dṛśyamāna, 430
dṛṣṭānta, 223, 437, 441, 445n., 446
dṛṣṭānta-sama, 445n.
dṛṣṭānta-viruddha, 449
dṛṣṭārtha, 446
dṛṣṭi, 253

Dṛṣṭi-ṣṛṣṭi, 20n.
Dṛṣṭi-sṛṣṭi school, 18
dṛṣṭi-sṛṣṭi-vāda, 60, 97, 424
Dual experience, 245
Dualistic, 2; writers, 220
Duality, 110, 116, 171, 253, 258, 260, 280; of subject and object, 101
Ducts, 402n., 402, 403
duḥkha, 321, 432
duḥkha-sahiṣṇutā, 488
duḥkham, 26n.
duḥkhābhāve, 106n.
Dullness, 352, 420, 435, 476
duradhigamatā, 302
Duration, 180
Durgācārya, 623
Durgāgupta, 503
durniścaya, 295
Durṇāmā, 349
Duryodhana, King, 586
Dusty, 476
Dutt, Dr U.C., 500
Duty, 435, 512, 513, 516, 519, 520, 534, 560, 564, 584, 589-592, 606-610
dūṣya, 382
Dvaidha-nirṇaya-tantra, 503
Dvaita, 66n.
dvaitādvaita, 51
Dvayāvin, 349
dvādaśāṅguli, 297
Dvāpara age, 478
dvāra, 54, 129
Dvārakā monastery, 220
dveṣa, 309, 431, 482, 483
Dvivrañīya, 501
dvy-aṇuka, 217, 218, 222
Dyads, 217, 356
dyauḥ, 339n.
Dying, 210n.
Dynamical, 270, 275
Dynamic principle, 389
Ḍalhana, 317, 321, 324, 333n. 4, 352n. 2, 352, 365n. 2., 366n. 2, 384, 385, 392n., 407, 408, 409n., 433, 479, 494–499, 507

Ear, 379, 380n.
Earth, 85, 215, 351, 419, 420, 421, 428, 584
Earthquake, 328
Earthy, 416, 419
Eating, 394, 584
Eclipses, 328
Ecstatic joy, 526, 529
Effect, 4, 13, 44, 45, 47, 167, 185, 200– 203, 210, 211, 214, 218, 384n., 419n., 420, 436, 462-464, 592, 603
Effective tones, 26
Effectuation, 31n.
Efficiency, 214, 381
Effort, 286, 292, 294, 420, 430, 432, 435
Egg (born from), 360, 375
Ego, 17, 89, 116, 117, 120, 206, 269, 271, 308, 430
Ego-feeler, 120
Egoism, 28, 86, 420, 483, 595, 596
Egoistic, 249, 596
ejā, 578
Ejective forces, 381
eka-jīva-vāda, 95n.
Eka-śloka, 90
eka-vidhir eva anyavyavacchedaḥ, 108
ekānta, 454, 456, 636
ekānta-dharma, 635
ekānta-kalanaḥ, 275
ekāntin, 635
Ekānti-Vaiṣṇavas, 635
ekārammana, 536
ekārtha-kriyā-kārītā, 211
ekāyana, 639n. 3
Element, 261, 351, 401, 417–420, 430, 433, 476, 584, 600, 602
Elemental, 389; body, 352; world, 247
Elephant, 597
Elevation, 620
Eliminatory, 161
Emanations, 2, 611
Emancipation, 106, 114, 115, 133, 171, 208, 213, 234, 261, 264, 270, 279, 283, 284, 286, 287, 290, 308, 446, 449
Emblic Myrobalan, 342
Embryology, 317
Emotional, 541
Emotions, 172, 175, 176, 283, 479
Empirical, 427
Encyclopaedia of Religion and Ethics, 336n. 4, 348, 351n. 2
Endeavour, 295
Endurance, 577, 586, 590n.
Enemy, 343, 584, 593-596, 599
Energy, 282, 381, 388, 435, 595
Enjoyable, 541
Enjoyer, 208, 214, 613
Enjoyment, 208, 264, 275, 284, 429, 521, 548, 593, 608
Enmity, 580
Entity, 13, 17, 23, 24, 27n., 78, 215, 269, 272

Entrails, 336
Envy, 580
Epidemics, 476
Epistemological, 37, 103n.
Epistemologically, 41
Equanimity, 554, 556, 583, 584, 588, 592, 596, 597, 618, 619; of mind, 596
Equilibrium, 272, 273, 381, 383n., 388, 417, 618
Erroneous, 74; appearance, 75; impositions, 24
Error, 6, 486; of judgment, 485
Eruptions, 380n.
Erysipelatous inflammation, 348
esanā, esā, 578
Eschatological, 606
Eschatology, 603
esse est percipi, 310, 315
Essence, 44, 46, 149, 189, 194, 272, 280, 417
Essenceless, 9, 40, 195, 269; products, 5
Essencelessness, 8, 40, 270
Essentials, 183
Established, 21
Eternal, 28, 73, *84*, 140, 206, 207, 216, 430, 433, 442, 443; consciousness, 208; entities, 215; soul, 206; substances, 185; thing, 219
Eternality, 219, 451n.
Eternity of atoms, 215
Ether, 351
Ethereal, 416, 419
Ethical ideas, 578
Ethics, 583, 584, 599
Ethics of Buddhism, The, 579n. 2
Ethics of the Hindus, 591n.
Ever-existent, 20
Evil, 520, 580, 581; effects, 476
Evolutes, 198
Evolution, 18, 28, 433, 479n.
Excitants, 33
Excitation, 227
Excitement, 477, 478
Excreta, 369, 379, 381-385, 404, 408-411; channels, 405
Exhalation, 298, 524, 536, 537
Existence, 31n, 37, 210, 222, 280, 581. 603; of the soul, 446
Existent, 13, 179, 223, 270, 276, 435; entity, 267
Existing entity, 208–210
Experience, 23, 25, 31, 38, 39, 51, 67, 76, 78, 83, 86, 97, 108, 116, 128, 149 159, 172, 173, 192, 206, 215, 233, 308, 312, 314, 325, 429, 471, 543, 546, 582
Experimenting, 448
Expiating sins, 327
Expiation, 592
Expiration, 299, 303
External, 314; characteristics, 24; *karma*, 275; object, 19, 20, 23, 24, 30, 31, 174, 311, 312, 315, 327, 427; senses, 180, 401; sensibles, 25; world, 29, 30, 30n., 240, 242, 312
Extinction, 287, 584
Extra-individual reality, 103n.
Extra-mental, 28
Extreme, 592; idealists, 24
Extremism, 588
Eye, 380, 380n.
Eyebrows, 399, 412n., 525
Eye-diseases, 284, 346

Fact, 272
Factor, 602
Fainting, 581
Faith, 28, 435, 576, 589, 597
Fallacies, 19, 142, 223, 440, 441, 450, 452
Fallacious argument, 201
False, 23, 31, 75, 149, 175, 179, 205, 209, 245, 249; appearance, 7, 29n., 111,130, 180, 269; association, 177; cognition, 157; creations, 8, 9; experience, 117, 177, 179; ignorance, 5; knowledge, 9, 13, 179, 269, 483; object, 130; perception, 179, 258; predications, 9; presentations, 179; relationing, 177; show, 43, 44
Falsehood, 177, 249, 582n.; two meanings of, 121
Falsity, 175; of the world, 530
Faridpur, 260n.
Fasting, 322, 580
Fat, 369, 371, 375, 378, 379, 392, 404-407, 411, 421; channel, 405
Fatality, 471
Fate, 471
Fatness, 388
Faults of expression, 168
Faulty answer, 448
Faulty statement, 448
Fear, 388, 574, 595
Feeble discrimination, 289
Feeling, 27n., 28, 82, 205, 206. 304, 397, 480, 483, 581; as indifference, 26n.; of disgust, 538
Feeling-stuff, 483
Fellow-being, 596
Fermentation, 392n.
Fetter, 580

Fever, 327, 349, 462, 464
Fibula, 331n. 7
Fiery, 416, 419; character, 386
Filosofia Indiana, 465n.
Fineness, 420
Finished discrimination, 289
Finitude, 18
Fire, 85, 161, 162, 184, 215, 223, 275, 351, 386-389, 419, 613
Firm will, 28
Fistula, 320
Five *vāyus*, 86
Fixation of will, 588
Flame, 209, 211
Flashing, 74
Flesh, 338, 369, 375, 378, 386, 399, 404, 407, 411, 421; currents, 405
Flies, 477
Flowers, 388
Fluids, 351
Foam, 384
Foe, 597
Foetal development, 371; according to Ātreya, 360, 361; divergences of view referred to, 368; in the *Garbha Upaniṣad*, 364n.; its processes in Caraka and Suśruta, 369 ff.
Foetus, 337, 351, 352, 356–359, 366-369, 375, 388, 403, 448, 474, 476
Folklore, 343n. 1
Folk-notions, 343n. 1
Folly, 581
Food, 385, 405, 407, 508, 584
Food-juice, 359, 386, 402, 404, 408-411, 414
Foolishness, 484, 593, 608
Force, 292
Forehead, 413
Forgiveness, 589, 595
Forgiving nature, 590n.
Forgiving spirit, 595, 596
Formalism, 138, 143, 144
Formative, 484
Formless, 294
Foundation, 590
Free-will, 291, 295
Friend, 595-597
Friendly, 441, 596
Friendship, 537, 580, 616, 622
Frogs, 126
Fruition, 295; of actions, 551
Fruits, 388
Fruit-yielding actions, 284, 285
Fuel, 287
Full-moon, 606
Function, 36, 206, 276, 427, 428, 612; of thought, 16
Fury, 580

Gadādhara, 499
Gadādhara Bhaṭṭācārya, 138, 143
gahanaṃ, 578
Gain, 587, 592, 597
gala-guṇḍa, 347n.
Gall-bladder, 334
gandha, 223, 272, 408
Gandhabba, 628
Gandhamādana, 634
Gandharva, 349
gandharva-pattanam, 269
Gandharva-tantra, 458
gantā gacchati, 195
gantho, 578
Gaṅgabhaṭṭa, 600
Gaṅgā, 413
Gaṅgādhara, 91, 404-407, 443n. 2., 500-502
Gaṅgādharendra Sarasvatī, 64, 252, 266
Gaṅgāharī, 91
Ganṅgāpurī Bhaṭṭāraka, 58, 59
Gaṅgeśa, 62, 144, 145, 168
Gaṅgeśa Upādhyāya, 138
Gaṇanātha Sen, Mahāmahopādhyāya, 393n., 413n.
gaṇḍa-mālā, 346
Gaṇeśa Bhisaj, 506
Garbe, R., 641
garbha-karā bhāvāḥ, 360
Garbha Upaniṣad, 364n. 3
garbhāśaya, 365
garbhotpāda, 382
Garland, 582n., 612
Garuḍa, 629
Gauḍa, 145
Gauḍa Abhinanda, 267
Gauḍa Brahmānanda Sarasvatī, 91
Gauḍapāda, 2, 8, 25n., 32, 34, 67n., 90, 92, 266, 270, 304n. 1, 315
Gauḍa-pāda-kārikā, 7, 290
Gauḍapādīya-bhāṣya, 90
Gauḍavaho, 128
Gauḍeśvara Ācārya, 67
Gauḍorvīśa-kula-praśasti, 145
Gaurī, 95n.
Gautama, 443, 451n., 452, 460
gavaya, 151
gavīnikā, 338n. 3
gavīnyau, 337
Gayadāsa, 495, 498, 499, 502

Gayī, 433, 478
gāho, 578
Gāndhāra, 318, 347n. 4
gāndhārī, 412
gāyatrī, 342
gedho, 578
Generality, 215
Generator, 26
Generic, 436
Genesis, 271
ghana, 272n., 282, 366
ghana-jāgaras, 309
ghana-jāgrat-sthita, 308
ghana-saṃvedana, 271
ghana-spanda-kramāt, 272n., 283
ghanībhūya, 272
Ghaṭa-jātaka, 630, 631, 634
ghora, 326
Ghosuṇḍī, 628
ghoṣa, 408
Ghoṣaka, 197
giddhi, 578
Gifts, 309, 511, 515, 584, 598, 599
Gīrvāṇendra Sarasvatī, 60n., 249
Gītā, 290, 487, 511-513, 517-523, 526n. 1, 528-531, 534-536, 539-546, 548-552, 554-559, 563-569, 571, 574, 577, 578, 581-589, 591-603, 605-613, 616, 619-622, 625, 630, 635, 636, 638, 640, 642, 643; analysis of how actions are performed, 600, 602; *avidyā* in and in Buddhism, 581-583; Aśvattha simile of the Upaniṣads, how applied in, 610, 611; *avyakta*, its meanings in, 548 ff.; Brahman, its meanings in, 552 ff.; clinging to God, necessity of, 616, 618; conception of *sādhāraṇa-dharma* and *varṇa-dharma*, 589 ff.; conflict between caste-duties and other duties, 598, 599; conservation of energy principle applied to the problem of immortality, 604; conservation of energy principle in, compared with that of Yoga, Vedānta and Nyāya, 603; crude beginnings of Sāṃkhya in, 545 ff.; ethical ideas compared with those of the Upaniṣads and Buddhism, 575 ff.; ethics, basis of, 581; God and his doctrine in, 618 ff.; God, his nature in, 541 ff., 611 ff; idea of God in, and in the Upaniṣads, 618; ideal as performance of *sva-dharma* in, 584, 586; ideal in, compared with the sacrificial and other ideals, 587, 588; ideal of self-surrender, 587; ideal of *tapas*, 598; immortality in, 604, 605; important commentaries on, 517; interpretation by Madhva, 516; interpretation by Rāmānuja, 515, 516; interpretation by Śaṅkara, 511, 512; interpretation by Yāmuna, 513; its conception of *dharma* and sacrifices, 567 ff.; its date, 640 ff.; its difference from Mīmāṃsā, 563 ff.; its relation to Sāṃkhya, 555, 556; its relation to Vedānta, 556 ff.; *karma*, rebirth, and liberation, 606 ff.; *kṣetra* and *kṣetra-jña* theory of, 540, 541; meaning of *Yoga* in, 517 ff.; path of knowledge and of duty, 615, 616; performance of duties with unattached mind in, 591 ff.; *prakṛti, puruṣa* and God in, 541–544; *prakṛti-puruṣa* philosophy in, 538 ff.; principal virtues in, 595 ff.; *puruṣa-sūkta* conception of God and the conception of God in, 611; rebirth and life after death, 605, 606; *sattva, rajas* and *tamas* in, 546 ff.; Sāṃkhya, its meaning different from that of classical Sāṃkhya in, 534, 535; *sāṃkhya-yoga*, discussion on the meaning of, in. 531-534; sense-control in, 569 ff.; sense-control in, different from that of Buddhism, 571; sense-control in, different from that of Patañjali, 573, 574; some vicious tendencies denounced in, 593, 595; standpoint of ethics in, compared with the general stand-point of Hindu ethics, 588 ff.; virtue of sameness, 596, 597; *yoga* in, akin to that of *Pañca-rātrayoga*, 538; *yoga* in Patañjali, indebted to *yoga* in, 537, 538; *yoga* of, different from that of Patañjali, 527 ff.; *yoga* of, different from the Upaniṣad *yoga,* 529 ff.; *yoga* instructions in, 521 ff.; *yoga,* its meaning different from that of Buddhism in, 536, 537; *yogin*, his characteristics, 524, 526; *yogin*, his relation with God, 526, 527
Gītā-bhāṣya, 516
Gītā-bhāṣya-vivecana, 222
Gītā-bhūṣaṇa-bhāṣya, 517
Gītā-nibandhana, 260
Gītārtha-saṃgraha, 513, 517
Gītārtha-saṃgraha-dīpikā, 513
Gītārtha-vivaraṇa, 517
Gītā-sārārtha-saṃgraha, 517
Gītāśaya, 513
Gītā-tattva-prakāśikā, 517
Gītā-tātparya-bodhini, 67
Gītā-ṭikā, 517
Gītā-vivṛti, 517
Glandular sores, 344
Glenoid cavity, 334n. 2

go, 151
God, 2, 51, 83, 92, 129, 203–205, 226, 264, 294, 433, 469, 470, 478n., 512-519, 521, 522, 526-529, 534, 536, 538-545, 552, 553, 555, 556, 564, 571, 574, 582, 584-588, 593, 595, 597, 599-602, 605, 608-613, 616, 621, 626, 631, 635, 637
Goddesses, 283
God's powers, 48
God's will, 126
Gods, 283, 489, 568
Going, 195
Gokulacandra, 517
Gokulanātha Upādhyāya, 146n.
Gold, 43, 597
Goldstücker, Th., 629
Gomin, 499
Good, 24, 284,314, 473; and bad, 26n.; deeds, 479; life, 492
Goodness, 591
Gopatha-Brāhmaṇa, 319n. 3, 321n., 326n., 328
Gopāla Sarasvatī, 119
Gopālānanda Sarasvatī, 66n.
Gopālika, 101n.
Gopikānta Sārvabhauma, 91
Gopirāma, 91
Gopurarakṣita, 494
Govardhana, 499, 502
Government, 234
Govinda Sarasvatī, 63
Govindānanda, 56, 93, 119, 120, 302
Grace, 587
Grammarian-philosopher, 197
Grammatical, 164
granthī, 120
Grass, 408
Grating, 394
grāhaka-graha, 29
grāhya-grāhakānuśaya, 25
Greed, 477, 580, 581, 595
Greediness, 596
Greedy, 595
Grief, 285, 388
Griffith, 339n.
grīṣma, 390
grīvāh, 332
Gross, 414
Grossness, 420
Grounds, 19
Growing, 41
Growth, 33; of the body, 375
gṛha-godhikā, 348n. 7
gṛha-stha, 589
Gṛhya-sūtras, 326
guda, 332n. 8
gudābhyaḥ, 334
Gujarat, 220
gulgulu, 458
gulpha, 330n. 4
gulphau, 329
guṇa, 187, 200, 201, 215, 216, 218, 223, 339, 366n., 384, 385, 387, 416, 417, 419n., 420, 421, 422, 427, 428, 430, 431, 433-436, 483, 514, 515, 531-535, 539, 543-545, 555-557, 597, 600, 611, 612
guṇa-attachments, 556
guṇamayī māyā, 556
Guṇa-traya-viveka, 66n.
guṇatva, 165
guṇavattvātyantābhāvānadhikara ṇatā, 187
guṇatīta, 597
guṇin, 366n. 1
Gupta empire, 189, 507
guru, 416, 419n., 489
gurv-ādayaḥ, 430
gurv-ādi, 430
Gūḍha-bodhaka-saṃgraha, 499
Gūḍhārtha-dīpikā, 517
Guḍhārtha-prakāśa, 252

Hair, 379
halikṣṇa, 334
Hallucinations, 5, 207
haṃsa, 291n.
Handful, 400n.
hanu-citya, 333
Hanumad-bhāṣya, 517
hanvor dve, 334n. 4
Happiness, 130, 584, 597, 618
Happy, 321; temper, 598
Hara-kiṅkara, 141
Hara-kiṅkara-nyāyācārya-parama-paṇḍi-ta-bhaṭṭa-vādīndra, 141
Hardness, 382, 420
Hare's horn, 5, 128, 277
Hari, 516, 623, 633
Hari Dīkṣita, 94
haridra indravaruṇī, 345
Hari-gītā, 635
Harihara Paramahaṃsa, 66n.
Hari-līlā-vyākhyā, 259
Harinātha Śarmā, 171n.
Hariścandra, 498, 502
Harmful, 416
harṣa, 365
hasti-jihvā, 412
Hate, 570

Hatred, 420, 431, 435, 580-582
haṭha, 310
Haṭha-Yoga, 435, 531
Haṭha-yoga-pradīpikā, 413n.
haviḥ, 538
Hārīta, 463, 498
Hārīta-saṃhitā, 503
Head, 345, 392, 396, 400
Headache, 350n. 2
Head disease, 344, 396
Health, 385, 448
Hearing, 272, 420
Heart, 334, 337n. 2, 368, 396, 401n., 402, 404, 411, 414
Heart diseases, 348
Heat, 223, 275, 278, 373, 374, 379, 382, 386, 417, 420, 422n., 426, 488, 583, 595, 596
Heaven, 264, 587, 606, 610
Heaviness, 391n., 417, 420, 421, 430
Heavy, 393n., 416
Heels, 329
Heliodorus, 629
Hell, 105, 570, 595
hemanta, 390, 431
hemanta-griṣma-varṣāḥ, 375n.
Hemādri, 498, 506
Hemorrhage, 336; of women, 345
Heracles, 633
Heramba Sena, 499
Herb, 346, 417n., 426
Heredity, 317
Hermaphrodite, 365n. 3
Hermitage, 264
Heroism, 586, 590n., 612
hetāv īrṣyu, 489
hetu, 139-142, 171, 223, 436, 442, 443, 445n., 451n., 452, 453, 461
Hetu-tattvopadeśa, 56
hetv-antara, 453
hetv-artha, 454, 455
hetv-ābhāsa, 223, 451n., 453, 454n.
Higher self, 529, 544
Himālayas, 264, 431
hiṃsā, 488
Hindu Ethics, 563, 588; standpoint of, 58 ff.
Hindu Mysticism, 524n. 1
Hindu philosophy, 600
Hiraṇyagarbha, 87
Hiraṇyākṣa Kauśika, 416
Hiraṇyākṣya-tantra, 507
hirā, 336, 337, 401, 403
Hiriyanna, 2n., 49, 99n., 99, 113, 116n.
History of Indian Logic, 457
History of Indian Philosophy, 1, 19, 307n. 4, 311n. 1, 314n. 1, 557n. 1,
History of the Vaiṣṇava Sect, Early, 635n.
hitā, 321, 401, 473, 489, 492
hitā nāḍīs, 402
Hīnayāna, 583
Hīnayāna Buddhists, 194
Hoernle, R., 324, 330n. 3, 331n. 4, 332n. 1,n. 2,n. 3,n. 4, 5, 384, 494, 499-502, 505, 506
Holes, 388n.
homa, 326
Homogeneous, 16, 440
Horns, 219
Hostile, 441
Hot, 279, 364n., 416-419, 421-422, 426n.
Householder, 589
hrāsaḥ, 375
hrī, 28, 595
hṛdaya, 334, 396n.
hṛdaya-stham pipāsā-sthānam, 406n.
hṛdayotkleda, 392n.
hṛt, 339
hṛt-padma-yantra-tritaye, 298
Hultzsch, E., 251
Human body, 322, 351
Humanity, 590
Human passion, 580
Human self, 48
Humid, 476
Humility, 622
Hunger, 294
Hygienic habits, 359
Hypothesis, 13, 30, 74
Hypothetical, 393; entities, 269, 392

icchā, 305, 431, 578
Idea, 30, 34, 36, 209, 214, 437, 584, 595, 612
Ideal, 587, 588; creations, 272
Idealism, 21, 24, 29, 40, 117, 245, 253, 296, 310, 312; refutation of, 311
Idealistic, 266; Buddhism, 266, 270, 279; monism, 189; philosophy, 270
Idealists, 469
Ideation, 23, 36
Identical, 17, 30, 31, 34, 36n., 37, 38, 41, 44, 74, 78, 104, 175, 176, 195, 198, 199, 210, 211, 232, 258; entity, 39, 232; object, 203; point, 23
Identity, 16, 36, 38, 39, 75, 83, 151, 175, 261, 431, 613; as a relation, 16; function of thought, 16; in diversity, 198; of the awareness, 37, 190; of cause and effect, 190; of the self, 39, 54, 75, 77

Idleness, 388, 435
iḍā, 297, 339n., 412, 529
iḍā nāḍī, 413
Ignorance, 4, 5, 6, 9, 28, 84, 85, 113, 116, 120, 171, 176, 177, 213, 215, 233, 234, 290, 309, 388, 477, 482, 483, 485, 539, 559, 581-583, 593, 595, 608, 616, 618
Ignorant, 428, 441
ihāmutra-phala-bhoga-virāga, 577
Iliac, 405
Ilium, 331n. 8
Ill-temper, 580
Illumination, 72, 205, 234, 241, 242n., 244
Illuminator, 613
Illusion, 3, 7, 10, 12, 18, 29, 33, 37, 41, 54, 74, 79, 116, 127, 131, 171, 223, 226, 227, 230, 234, 257, 276, 278, 302, 611; difference in the_theory of, between Nāgārjuna and Śaṅkara and Gauḍāpada, 8
Illusoriness, 621
Illusory, 30, 32, 84, 116, 126, 208, 253, 270, 277; appearances, 116, 130; character, 249; cognition, 207; creation, 546; experience, 213; images, 207; impositions, 34, 130, 131, 173, 223; knowledge, 160; perception, 84, 154, 175; products, 257; silver, 136; snake, 237n.
Ill-will, 580
Image, 16, 636
Imaginary, 314
Imagination, 104, 269, 302, 308, 382, 428, 435
Imaginative construction, 24
Immanent, 48, 611; self, 314
Immediacy, 15, 16, 73, 79, 121
Immediate, 172, 173; antecedence, 166; contact, 242
Immediateness, 159
Immoral, 26n., 541, 557, 564, 584
Immortal, 552, 555, 586, 597, 612, 613
Immortality, 342, 532, 597, 598, 604, 607, 626
Immutable law, 36n.
Impatience, 435
Imperative, 563
Imperishable, 555, 603, 604
Impermanent, 265, 278
Implication, 20, 171, 448, 607
Importance, 431
Impossible, 183, 195, 216
Impotency, 388
Imprecations, 343
Impressions, 75, 276, 289
Improper use, 374
Impure, 41, 43, 44, 352, 476; states, 276
Impurities, 381, 587, 588
Inactive, 420
Inanimate, 41, 419, 420
Incantations, 322, 326
Incarnation, 586, 612
Inclinations, 276, 279, 290, 580
Incomprehensible, 189
Inconsistencies, 191
Inda, 628
Indefinability of nescience, 255
Indefinable, 13, 18, 25, 33, 59, 136, 146, 148, 180, 188, 189, 236, 253, 258, 582, 616; nature, 179; stuff, 253
Indefinite existence, 18
Independent co-operation, 211
Independent existence, 68
Indescribable, 40, 41, 55, 169, 189, 223, 224, 233, 253, 267-270, 272, 306, 314; nature, 126
Indescribableness, 40
Indestructible, 38, 597, 627
Indeterminable, 154
Indeterminate, 25, 468, 530; cognition, 108; experience, 112; knowledge, 24; materials, 26
Index, 170n.
India, 469
Indian anatomists, 332n. 2
Indian Antiquary, 641
Indian Interpreter, The, 641
Indian literature, 296
Indian medical men, 440
Indian Medicine, 493, 508
Indian philosophy, 138, 261, 317, 430, 440, 461, 483, 486; pessimism in, 483
Indian thought, 437, 439n., 476, 491
Indifference, 284, 584
Indigestion, 405
Indignation, 388, 580
Indische Studien, 335n. 2
Indispensable, 20, 610
Indistinguishable, 440
Individual, 38, 67-69, 133, 151, 160, 183, 217, 430; consciousness, 89; good, 566; ignorance, 97; members, 216; persons, 97, 126; self, 86; soul, 83, 236n.
Individuality, 524
Indivisible, 181, 229
Indo-Iranian, 343n. 1
Indra, 264, 344n. 3, 354, 382, 505
indrajāla, 282
Indrā-viṣṇu, 623

indriya, 26, 275, 276, 427
indriya-dhāraṇa, 576
indriya-nigraha, 589
indriya-vijaya, 473
Indu, 354, 382, 505
Induction, 171
Indulgence, 593
Inequality, 264
Inert, 393n.
Inertia, 420
Inexhaustible, 415
Inexplicable, 23, 33, 55, 180, 182, 213
Inference, 20, 31n., 37, 73, 76, 78, 83, 122, 136, 139, 149, 160, 162, 171, 183, 192, 203, 220, 223, 227, 245, 351, 426, 435-438, 443, 462, 464, 476
Inferential, 89; cognition, 156; knowledge, 20
Inferior, 441
Inferiority, 431, 468n.
Infinite, 18, 73, 84, 130, 530; consciousness, 89; differences, 152; number, 417; regressus, 232; time, 152
Inflammation, 327
Inhalation, 298, 299, 524, 536, 537
Inherence, 420
Inherent, 25; movement, 23
Inhering cause, 166
Initiation, 637
Injunction, 593, 606
Inner change, 25
Inner consciousness, 31n.
Inner dynamic, 28
Inner law of thought, 33
Inner psychoses, 25
Inner states, 213
Inoperative, 204, 311
Inscriptions, S.I., 251
Insects, 477
Insensible, 294
Inseparable, 219, 436; inherence, 210, 432
Inseparableness, 219; of character, 219; of space, 219; relation, 420; relation of inherence, 46
Insomnia, 393n.
Inspiration, 303
Instinctive passions, 291
Instinctive subconscious roots, 30
Instincts, 484
Instructions, 24, 264, 584
Instrument, 52
Instrumental cause, 13, 420, 433, 478
Instrumentality, 12, 129
Instruments of cognition, 158
Intellect, 86, 435, 474
Intellectual, 441; states, 206
Intelligence, 102, 310, 373, 374, 420, 430, 435, 437, 588, 602
Intelligent, 41, 44
Intelligible, 41
Intense, 290
Intention, 580
Interdependence, 8, 9, 25
Interdependent origination, 4n.
Internal canals, 336
Internal organ, 362n. 2
Interpretation, 2, 415
Intervening, 166
Intestine, 334, 345, 405, 409
Intimate relation, 46
Intoxicating drinks, 581
Intrinsically, 279
Intrinsic difference, 231
Introduction, 56
Intuitive, 84; consciousness, 177, 229; perception, 130
Invalid, 20, 162, 211, 214
Invariability, 36n.
Invariable, 198, 214; antecedence, 167, 214, 380, 450, 464; concomitance, 160-164, 171; connection, 203; power, 213; prognostication, 463
Invariably and unconditionally associated, 443
Invariably associated, 462
Invisible, 394n.
Inward resolution, 562
Iron age, 469
Irrelevant, 184
Ischium, 331n. 8
itaretarāśraya, 112
itaretarāśraya-prasaṅgāt, 110
Itihāsa-veda, 317n. 3
I-tsing, 505
īrṣyā, 482
Īśa Upaniṣad, 642
Īśā, 90
Iśāvāsya-bhāṣya-tippaṇa, 222
Īsopaniṣad-bhāṣya, 90
Īśvara, 45, 55, 58, 83, 92, 129, 203, 204, 226, 433, 553, 621; its criticisms by Kamalaśīla, 203 ff.
īśvara-bhāva, 590n.
Īśvarakṛṣna, 92, 197, 433, 499, 555
Īśvara-saṃhitā, 637, 638n. 1
Īśvarasena, 502
Īśvarābhisandhi, 145

Īṣṭa-siddhi, 227, 229, 236, 245
Īṣṭa-siddhi-vivaraṇa, 227
Īṣṭa-siddhi-vyākhyā, 227

Jackals, 477
Jacob, G.A., 94
Jacobi, H., 465n.
jaḍa, 41
jaḍātmikā, 121
jaḍātmikā avidyā-śakti, 121
Jagaddhara, 517
Jagadīśa, 91
Jagadīśa Bhaṭṭācārya, 138, 143
jagan-mithyātva-dīpikā, 66n.
Jagannātha Pañcānana, 91
Jagannāthāśrama, 61, 64, 119, 222, 248
Jaimini, 559, 567
Jaina, 113, 138, 197, 198, 465, 634, 641
Jaiyyaṭa, 498
Jalada, 328
jalpa, 440-442, 468
Jalpa-kalpa-taru, 405n., 443n. 2
Janaḥ, 87
Janārdana, 56, 236, 633
Janārdana Sarvajña, 60n.
jaṅghe, 331
jaṅgiḍa, 340, 342, 344n.
Japan, 342
jarāyu, 338
jatru, 332n.
Jatūkarṇa, 498, 503
Jatūkarṇa-saṃhita, 503
jaṭā, 578
Jaundice, 327, 345, 346
Jaundiced eye, 165
Jayacandra, 145
Jayanandi, 502
Jayanta, 59, 123, 324, 325, 358n. 1, 460, 465, 482, 483
Jayarāma, 517
Jayatīrtha, 516
Jayākhya-saṃhitā, 573
Jayollāsa-nidhi, 252
Jābāla-brāhmaṇa, 290
jāḍya, 11
jāgarūka, 394
jāgrad-vāsanāmayatvāt svapna, 87
jāgrat, 278, 305
jāgrat-svapna, 308
jāgrat-svapna sthita, 309
Jājala, 328, 503
jālinī, 578
Jānakīnātha, 251n.
jānu, 331n. 4
jānunoḥ sandhī, 331
Jātaka, 287n., 494
jāti, 49, 183, 223, 443–446, 452, 468, 581
Jealousy, 309
Jejjata, 433, 499
jhāna, 536, 537, 583
jigiṃsanatā, 578
jijñāsā, 448
Jina, 56, 58, 83, 86, 97, 98, 101-104, 271, 272, 276, 354
Jinadāsa, 499, 502
jīva, 120, 121, 126, 127, 129
jīva-bhūta, 541, 551
jīva-caitanya, 89
jīva-dhātu, 278
Jīvaka, 320, 494
Jīvaka-tantra, 507
jīvana, 382
jīvana-pūrvaka, 600
jīvan-mukta, 283-285, 289
jīvan-mukta state, 286
jīvan-muktatā, 283
Jīvan-mukti, 284, 290, 291
Jīvan-mukti-viveka, 246, 248, 290, 291n., 310
jīvann eva, 290
jīva-rāśi, 51
jīva-sthiti, 301
Jīva-sūtra, 508
jīvatvāpādikā, 120
Jīvādana, 503
Jīvānanda, 501, 502
jīvātman, 538
jīvita, 429
jīvitendriya-virodhinī, 24n.
jīvotkrānti, 301
jñāna, 115, 315, 573, 582, 590n.
jñāna-gata-pratyakṣatva, 238
Jñānaghana, 95n.
jñāna-karma-samuccaya, 51, 115
jñāna-nāḍī, 414
jñāna-pratisandhātā, 429
Jñāna-saṃkalinī, 413, 414
jñāna-saṃskāra, 289
Jñāna-sāra, 267
Jñāna-siddhi, 171n.
jñānavatī, 441
Jñāna-vāsiṣṭha, 266
jñāna-viṣayīkṛtena rūpeṇa sādṛśyam, 154
jñāna-yoga, 515, 516, 532, 568, 616
Jñānāmṛta, 114
Jñānāmṛta Yati, 90
Jñānārṇava, 503

Jñanendra Sarasvatī, 62, 91
jñānin, 619
Jñānottama, 67, 101n., 113, 114, 171n., 227
Jñānottama Bhaṭṭāraka, 95n.
Jñānottama Miśra, 55
jñātatā, 175, 242
jñātur jñeya-sambandhaḥ, 121
Jobares, 633
Joint causality, 204
Joint nature, 211
Joint operation, 551
Joints, 386, 392, 405
Joy, 388, 435, 545, 577, 588, 596, 597
Judgments, 397
Jug, 165, 174
juhvati, 523
jvara, 344
jyotiḥ-sthāna, 371
Jyotiṣ, 319n.
jyotiṣa, 637

Kahola-brāhmaṇa, 290
kaivalya, 290, 530
Kaivalya-kalpadruma, 64
Kaivalyānanda Sarasvatī, 517
Kaivalyananda Yogīndra, 64
Kaivalyāśrama, 91
kakāṭīkā, 333
Kakṣapuṭa-tantra, 496
Kakubha, 349
kalpa, 319n., 613, 637
kalpanā, 104, 275, 276, 366, 431
Kalpa-sthāna, 494, 500
Kalpa-taru, 60
Kalyāṇa Bhaṭṭa, 517
Kamalajanayana, 260n.
Kamalaśīla, 29, 31n., 32, 36n., 197, 198, 201, 203, 205, 206, 208-213, 215n., 215, 216, 437, 438; criticisms against the non-permanency of entities answered by, 213 ff.; Yogasena's criticisms against the doctrine of momentariness answered by, 211; his criticism of the concept of God, 203 ff.; his criticism of the concept of Īśvara or God, 203 ff.; his treat-ment of the different views of the nature of momentariness, 214; his criticism of the doctrine of soul (Nyāya), 205, 206; his criticism of the soul theory of Kumārila, 206 ff.; his criticism of the Yoga concept of God, 204 ff.; his doctrine of momentariness, 209 ff.; his refutation of Nyāya-Vaiśeṣika categories, 215 ff.; his refutation of the Sāṃkhya theory of soul, 208; his refutation of the theory of the persistence of entities, 209 ff.; his refutation of the Upaniṣad theory of self, 208; his theory of causal efficiency (*artha-kriyā-samarthā*), 210 ff.
Kamalśīla and Śāntarakṣita, their criticisms of the Sāṃkhya doctrine of *pariṇāma*, 198 ff.; writers mentioned in their work *Tattva-saṃgraha* and its *Pañjikā*, 197
Kambalāśvatara, 197
kamma, 583
Kanauj, 145
Kanha, 630, 634
Kanhāyana, 634
Kaṇāda, 431
Kaṇāda-sūtra-nibandha, 142
kaṇḍarā, 378, 411
Kaniṣka, 500n. 1, 502
kaṇṭha, 412n.
kaṇṭha-nāḍī, 332n. 3
kaṇṭhorasoḥ sandhiḥ, 406n.
kapālam, 333
kapālikā, 331n. 4
kapha, 298n. 2, 349, 369, 379-386, 388, 389, 391n., 392, 393, 395, 408-411, 421, 426, 457
kaphoḍa, 333n. 2
kaphoḍau, 332
Kapila, 479n., 556
Kapilabala, 500
Kapila-Sāṃkhya, 535
Kapila-tantra, 507
karaṇa, 454
karaṇa-śakti-pratiniyamāt, 200
Karaṭha, 503
Karavīrya, 494
Karāla-tantra, 507
karma, 116, 120, 213-216, 273-276, 280, 287, 292, 295, 296, 351, 361, 395, 416, 419, 420, 432, 446, 469-471, 476, 511, 513, 569, 606-608, 611, 621
karma-bījaṃ manaḥ-spanda, 275
karma-nāśe mano-nāśaḥ, 275
karma-puruṣa, 352n., 435
karma-sannyāsa, 534
karma-yoga, 515, 516, 519, 527, 528, 534, 616
Karṇa-bhāra, 641
karṇa-śūla, 348
kartavyatā, 562
kartā, 273, 366
kartṛ, 282, 461, 547, 551, 552
kartṛtva, 279

kartṛtva-bhoktṛtvaikā-dhāraḥ, 120
Karuma, 349
karuṇā, 480, 537, 596
kaṣāya, 364n., 416, 417
Kathā-vatthu, 285, 286n.
Kaṭha Upaniṣad, 90, 337n. 2, 401n., 402, 529, 569, 576, 610, 611
Kaṭha-vallī, 290
kaṭhina, 419n.
Kaṭhopaniṣad-bhāṣya-ṭīkā, 222
kaṭu, 364n. 3, 416, 417, 421, 426n.
kaumāra-bhṛtya, 320
Kaumāra-tantra, 495
kauśala, 528
Kauśika-sūtra, 319, 327-329, 340
Kauṣītaki, 290, 300n. 3, 328
Kauṣītaki-brāhmaṇa, 634
Kauṣītaki-Upaniṣad, 300n.
Kauṭilya, 630
Kaviraj Gangaprasad Sen, 498
Kaviraj Gaṇanātha Sen, 502
Kavirāja, 91
kāhābāha, 348
kākatālīya, 314
kāla, 180, 271, 369, 374, 417, 419, 433, 454, 478
Kālahasti-śaraṇa-Śivānanda Yogīndra, 251
kālātīta, 451n., 452
Kālidāsa, 265, 266, 276, 469, 641
kālpanika-puruṣa-bheda, 134
kāma, 381, 480, 482, 570, 571, 578, 582
kām api-artha kriyām, 600
kāmya-karma, 114
kānti, 66n.
Kānyakubjeśvara, 145
Kāṅkāyana, 368, 416
Kāṅkāyana-tantra, 507
kāṇḍa, 412
Kāpya, 388
Kāpyavaca, 381
kāraka-vyāpāra, 47
kāraṇa, 120, 158, 184, 436, 454, 461, 551
kāraṇa-kṣaṇa-nirodha-sama-kālaḥ, 25n.
kāraṇa-kṣaṇa-vilakṣaṇa-kāryasya, 25n.
kāraṇa-vyāpāra, 603
Kārikā, 25n., 32, 34, 100, 289, 431
Kārttika Kuṇḍa, 498, 499
Kārttikeya, 123
Kāruṇya, 263, 265
kārya, 185, 436, 454
kārya-jñānam, 362n.
kārya-kāraṇatā, 438
kārya-kāraṇa-vādasya vedānta-bahir-bhūtat-vāt, 253
kārya-phala, 454
kārya-sama, 444n. 4, 447n.
kāryatā-jñāna, 600
kārya-yoni, 454
kāsa, 344, 347n. 4
Kāśika, 346n. 4
Kāśī, 494
Kāśī-khaṇḍa, 500
Kāśinātha Śāstrin, 62
Kāśirāja, 503, 505n. 1
Kāśmīra, 506
Kāśmīra-pāṭha, 501
Kaśyapa, 498
Kaśyapa-saṃhitā, 502, 507
Kāṭhaka, 567, 642
Kāṭhaka-saṃhitā, 634
Kaṭhakopaniṣad-bhāṣya, 90
Kāṭhmāṇḍu, 502
Kātyāyana, 629
Kāya-cikitsā, 320, 495
kedārī-kulyā, 377
Kenopaniṣad, 90, 225
Kenopaniṣad-bhāṣya, 90
Kenopaniṣad-bhāṣya-ṭippana, 222
Kenopaniṣad-bhāṣya-vivaraṇa, 90
Keśava-bhaṭṭa, 91, 329, 517, 630, 633
kevala-jāgarat, 308
kevala-jāgrat-sthita, 308
kevalānvayi, 139, 140, 142
kevalānvayi-hetor eva nirvaktum aśakyatvāt, 142
kevalānvayini vyāpake pravartamāno hetuḥ, 140
Khalaja, 349
khale-kapota-nyāya, 377
khanti-saṃvara, 583
Khaṇḍana-khaṇḍa-khādya, 66n., 119, 138n., 145, 146, 152, 153n., 154, 162, 168, 180, 220
Khaṇḍana-khaṇḍanam, 146n.
Khaṇḍana-kuṭhāra, 146n.
Khaṇḍana-mahā-tarka, 146n.
Khaṇḍana-maṇḍanam, 146n.
Khaṇḍana-phakkikā, 146n.
Khaṇḍana-ṭīkā, 146n.
Khaṇḍanoddhāra, 146n.
khara, 387, 419n.
Kharaṇada-saṃhitā, 503
kha-tan-mātra, 272
khyāti, 101n., 234
Kidney, 334, 405

Kidney-bean, 418n.
kilāsa, 345
Kimīdin, 344, 349
Kindness, 596; to the suffering, 595
King Ariṣṭanemi, 265
King Daśaratha, 265
King Keḷadi-Veṅkaṭendra, 251
King of Gauḍa, 171n.
King of Kanauj, 145
kiñcanaṃ, 578
kiṭṭa, 379, 381, 386
kīkasāsu, 332n. 2
Kleisobora, 633
kleśa, 354
kleśa-jñeyāvaraṇa, 26n.
kliṣta, 483
kloma, 334, 371, 405
Knowability, 161
Knowable, 161
Knower, 39, 175
Knowing, 304; faculty, 206, 207
Knowledge, 20, 21, 76, 146, 171, 174-176, 263, 284, 286, 296, 308, 315, 388, 429, 435, 436, 438, 441, 470, 511, 514, 539, 547, 554, 582, 583-586, 589n., 592, 595, 610, 616, 622
Knowledge situation, 29
kodho, 580
Koka, 349
Koṇḍa Bhaṭṭa, 63, 125
kopo, 580
Kotalipara, 260n.
kramiṇaḥ sahakāriṇaḥ, 210
kriyā, 275, 301
kriyākhya-jñāna, 573
kriyā-spanda, 275
kriyātmaka, 302
krodha, 309, 570
krodha-varjana, 589
Kṛkala, 86
kṛmuka, 346
Kṛṣṇa, 512, 524, 531, 570, 583, 586, 587, 591, 597, 602, 604-606, 612, 616-620, 623, 630, 633, 634, 636, 637; and Vasudeva, 630 ff.
Kṛṣṇa Ācārya, 91
Kṛṣṇabhaṭṭa Vidyādhirāja, 516
Kṛṣṇa Devakī-putra, 641
Kṛṣṇakānta, 91
Kṛṣṇa-kutūhala nāṭaka, 259
Kṛṣṇatīrtha, 64, 133
Kṛṣṇālaṃkāra, 252
Kṛṣṇānanda, 225
Kṛṣṇānubhūti, 95n.
Kṛṣṇātreya, 320, 498
Kṛṣṇātreya-tantra, 507
kṛtaka, 209
kṛta-nāśanī, 348
Kṛtavīrya, 368
kṛta yuga, 636
kṛti-sādhyatā-jñāna, 600
Kṛttika, 462
kṛtyā, 340
kṣamā, 589
kṣaṇa, 210n.
Kṣaṇa-bhaṅga-siddhi, 56
kṣaṇika, 210n., 428
kṣaṇikasya, 37n.
kṣaṇikatva, 429
kṣara, 120
kṣara puruṣa, 546
Kṣatakṣīna, 502
Kṣatriya, 339, 567, 568, 586-591, 599
kṣānti, 590n., 595
kṣāra, 416, 417, 544
Kṣārapāṇi-saṃhitā, 503
Kṣemarāja, 304
kṣetra, 540-543, 549, 551, 610
kṣetra-jña, 340, 478, 541, 546, 610
kṣetrin, 541
kṣetrīya, 345, 346, 350
kṣipta, 349
kṣiti, 283, 584
kṣīṇa-jāgaraka, 308, 309
Kṣurika, 530
kuhū, 412
Kukṣila, 349
kula-kuṇḍalinī, 414
Kula-pañjikā, 260n.
kulattha, 422
Kulārka Paṇḍita, 56, 59, 138-140, 142, 143, 170n.; introduction of his *Mahā-vidyā* syllogisms, 139-141
Kullūka, 627n. 1
Kumāra-saṃbhava, 265
Kumāraśira Bharadvāja, 416
Kumāraśiras, 368
Kumārila, 100, 128, 129, 139, 169, 197, 206, 226, 246, 559, 562, 563, 566
kumbhaka, 297, 298
Kunhan Raja, Dr, 100
kuntāpa, 344
Kuntī, 55
kuṇḍalinī, 413, 415, 531
kuṇḍalī energy, 415
kuṇḍalī śakti, 415
Kuppusvami Śāstri, 50n., 97n., 100, 102n.

Kurukṣetra, 586, 591, 604, 625
Kurus, 635
Kusumāñjali, 162, 458
Kusūla, 349
kuśa grass, 521
kuśalotsāha, 584
kuṣṭha, 340, 342, 345, 346
Kuvalayānanda, 252
kūrca, 324, 330n.
kūrca-śiras, 330n. 3
Kūrma, 86
kūrpara, 331

laghu, 387, 394, 416, 419n.
Laghu-candrikā, 98, 260n.
Laghu-jñāna-vāsiṣṭha, 267
Laghu-mahā-vidyā-viḍambana, 142
Laghu-saṃgraha, 95
laghutā, 422n.
Laghu-ṭīkā, 91
Laghu-vākya-vṛtti, 92
Laghu-vākya-vṛtti-prakāśikā, 92
Lakṣaṇāvalī, 144
Lakṣmīdhara Deśika, 91
Lakṣmīdhara Kavi, 64
Lakṣmīnṛsiṃha, 60, 125
lalaṇā-cakra, 414
lalāṭa, 333
Laṅkāvatāra-sūtra, 25n., 40, 146, 270, 315, 464
Larger intestine, 336
Laryngeal plexus, 414
Larynx, 332n. 2, 414n.
Laukika-nyāya-muktāvalī, 35n.
lavalī, 420n.
lavaṇa, 364n. 3, 416, 417
Law, 575; of causality, 36n.
laya, 120
Laziness, 390
lāghava, 367, 422n.
lālasā, 580
Lāṭyāyana-saṃhitā, 507
Lean, 393n.
Leanness, 388
Learned, 441
Learning, 589
Legal literature, 324
Leprosy, 345
Lévi, S., 500n. 1
Liberation, 215, 483, 484, 511, 512, 531, 547, 548, 610, 636
Lie, 582n.
Life, 420, 429, 473, 582n.
Life-functions, 600
Life of Nāgārjuna from Tibetan and Chinese Sources, 465n.
Life of the Buddha, 320, 494n. 1
Life-principle, 551
Ligaments, 378
Light, 81, 176, 387, 416, 420; of consciousness, 238
Lightness, 417, 420, 422n.
Liking, 417
Limitations, 16, 25, 230, 291
Limited forms, 26
Limited self, 130
Limited truth, 3
Limitless, 84
Linguistic, 192
liṅ, 560
liṅga, 122, 160, 227, 340, 461, 464
liṅga-deha, 356*n.*, 1
liṅga-parāmarśa, 160
liṅga-śarīra, 86
liṅgādibala-labdhākārollekha- mātreṇa, 245
liṅgī, 340
Lips, 405
Liquid, 394n.
Liquidity, 420
Liquors, 581
Literature, 440
Liver, 334, 371, 405
Living beings, 41
Lizards, 477
līlā, 48
Līlāvatī, 170n.
lobha, 477, 482, 570, 580
lobhanaṃ, 580
lobhitattaṃ, 580
locaka, 385
Localization, 26
Locus, 21, 127
Locus standi, 150
Logic, 440, 455, 457; of probability, 439n.
Logical, 219, 435; apparatus, 59; argument, 189; categories, 454; consequence, 13; dialectic, 219; discussions, 146; disputes, 468; fallacy, 19; formation, 136, 138, 144, 149; methods, 59; tricks, 468
Logically, 21
lohinī, 338
lohita-vāsasaḥ, 402n.
lohitā, 369
Lokanātha, 66n.
loka-rakṣā, 514

loka-saṃvṛta, 4
loka-saṃvṛti-satya, 5
loka-vyavahāraḥ, 4n.
Lokāyata, 197
lokottara, 25
lokottara-nirvikalpa-jñāna-lābhāt, 24
Longing, 580
Looseness, 388
Lord, 516; of communion, 529
Lorinser, Dr, 640
Loss, 597
Lotus, 415; in the sky, 6, 277; stalks, 409n.
Love, 580
Lower *prakṛti*, 541
Lower *puruṣa*, 543, 545, 546
lubhanā, 580
Lumbar nerve, 412
Lumbar plexus, 414
Lumbar vertebrae, 333n. 1
Lungs, 334, 371
Lust, 571, 580
Lustful, 428
Lymph, 369, 371, 379

Macdonell, A.A., 299, 335n., 402, 403, 567
mada, 309, 482
madana, 456
Madātyaya, 501
Madhu-kośa, 506
Madhu-matī, 507n. 4
madhura, 364n. 3, 416, 417
Madhusūdana Sarasvatī, 61, 63, 64, 89n., 91, 93, 134, 136, 143, 227, 229, 257n., 260, 261, 517; his lineage, date and works, 259, 260; his philosophy in his *Vedānta-kalpa-latikā*, 261
Madhva, 144, 220, 516, 517
Madhva-mukha-bhaṅga, 252
Madhva school, 136
madhya-śarīra, 368
madhya-viveka, 289
Madras, 97n., 100
Magic, 43, 44, 282; rites, 326
Magical creations, 43, 44, 545
Magician, 43, 44, 237n.
Magundī, 349
mahad brahma, 539
mahat, 355, 396n.
mahat parimāṇa, 217
Mahā-bhārata, 318, 320, 356, 460, 487, 488, 526n., 535, 538, 555, 586, 593n., 624n., 625, 627, 628, 630-636, 638, 641, 643
Mahā-bhārata Anukramaṇī, 634
Mahābhārata period, 592
Mahā-bhāṣya, 636, 638
mahābhūta, 421, 540
Mahādeva, 141
Mahādeva Vaidya, 91
Mahādeva Vidyāvagīśa, 91
Mahā-lakṣmī-paddhati, 259
Mahāmahopādhyāya Kuppusvāmi, 251
mahā-muniḥ, 26n.
mahā-pralaya, 126
Mahārāja, 628
Mahā-Rāmāyaṇa, 266
mahāsupti, 120
Mahātala, 87
Mahā-vagga, 320
Mahā-vidyā, 56, 59, 133, 138-143; nature of its syllogisms, 139-141; referred to, defended and criticized by Nyāya and Vedānta writers, 136– 139; syllogisms refuted by Vādīndra, 141-143
Mahā-vidyā-daśaśloki-vivaraṇa, 142
Mahā-vidyā-viḍambana, 119, 138n., 139, 141
Mahā-vidyā-viḍambana-vyākhyāna, 142
Mahā-vidyā-vivaraṇa-ṭippana, 142
Mahāvṛṣa, 347n. 4
Mahā-vyutpatti, 335n. 1
Mahāyāna, 584, 598
Mahāyāna monism, 189
Mahāyānists, 34
Maheśvara, 499
Maheśvara Tīrtha, 95, 225
Mahimnaḥ Stotra, 260
Mahīdhara, 267
maitra, 596
Maitra, S.K., 564n. 1, 591n.
Maitrāyana, 549
Maitrāyaṇī, 567, 610
Maitreyī-brāhmaṇa, 290
Maitri Upaniṣad, 301n., 401n., 402, 480, 523, 524
majjā, 369, 382
majjābhyaḥ, 336
Major term, 160
mala, 270, 276, 379, 381, 382, 389
mala-dhātu, 379, 381
mala-pātra, 336n. 1
Malformations, 388
Malice, 580
Malicious, 582n.
Malimluca, 349
Malla Bhaṭṭa, 91
Malleoli, 330n. 4
mamaṅkaro, 578

mamattaṃ, 578
mamāyitaṃ, 578
Man, 520
Manaḥ, 265
manaḥ-kalpanayā, 265
manaḥ-pariṇāmaḥ saṃvid-vyañjako jñānam, 227
manaḥ-prasāda, 598
manaḥ-spanda, 294
manana, 25, 28
manas, 26, 86, 87, 120, 180, 215, 223, 225, 237, 261, 267-270, 272-276, 278, 280, 282, 284, 295, 303, 339, 352, 354, 359n. 5, 359, 397, 400, 406n., 414, 415, 417, 420, 427, 428-430, 432, 435, 535, 540
manasi, 430
manaś-cakra, 414
manda, 419n.
manda-viveka, 289
Man-god, 612, 620
Manhood, 612
Man-hymn, 626
Manifestation, 26, 200, 271; of mind, 296
Manifests, 59
Manifold world, 233
mano-javena, 354
manomaya, 87
manomaya-koṣa, 86
manomaya puruṣa, 401
mano-nāśa, 290, 291
Manoramā tantra-rāja-ṭīkā, 259
manoratho, 580
mano-vahā, 406n.
mano-vahā-nāḍī, 414
mantra, 321, 322, 625
mantṛ, 409
Manu, 70, 524, 589, 632n. 3, 636
Manukulāditya, 52n.
Manuscript, 56, 129, 234, 236
manya, 338n. 3
manyu, 480, 482
maṅgala-homa, 322
Mañju-bhāṣiṇi, 91
Maṇḍana, 60, 94-100, 111-117, 127, 129, 170n., 227, 234, 258, 328, 390n., 562; all relations are mental in, 110, 111; *Brahma-kāṇḍa* of *Brahma-siddhi* holds that perception does not apprehend diversity of objects, 101, 102; his divergence of view from Sarvajñātma Muni, 98; his identity with Sureśvara the author of the *Naiṣkarmya-siddhi* disproved, 99; his refutation of the category of difference, 106 ff.; his refutation of "difference as negation," 112; his view of *avidyā* and *māyā*, 102; his view of Brahman as pure bliss, as elaborated by Śaṅkhapāṇi, 104; references to his doctrine by other Vedāntic writers, 97, 98; the author of *Brahma-siddhi*, 95; the content of the *Niyoga-kāṇḍa* and *Siddhi-kāṇḍa* chapters of the *Brahma-siddhi* of, 113; the general content of the fourth chapter of his *Brahma-siddhi*, 100, 101
maṇi, 419n., 424
Maṇibhadda, 628
maṇi-pūra-cakra, 414
maraṇānussati, 536
Marbles, 154
marma, 396n.
marman, 365n.
Marrow, 336, 338, 369, 375, 378, 404, 405, 421
Marshy, 431
mastakābhyantaroparişṭhāt śirāsan- dhi-sannipāta, 399
Master, 613
mastiṣka, 396
mastiṣkam śiro-majjā, 397n.
mastuluṅga, 396
matānujñā, 454n.
Material, 11; cause, 11-13, 52, 59, 85, 131, 165, 224, 226, 389, 420, 433, 454, 478; objects, 205; power, 121; staff, 12, 87, 224, 249; stuff, 126; things, 201; world, 24, 125
Materiality, 11, 52, 131, 272
Materia Medica, 500
Mathuranatha, 517
Maṭhurānātha Bhaṭṭācārya, 138
Mathurānātha Śukla, 90
matsara, 482
matsnā, 336n. 3
matsnābhyām, 334
Matter, 51, 364, 613
matup, 467n.
maṭha, 114
Maṭmaṭa, 349
mauna, 598
Mauryas, 629
Maxim, 31, 37, 76, 185, 454, 456, 457; of identity, 231
Mādhava, 246, 247, 499, 505-507
Mādhava Sarasvatī, 267
Mādhva-Kara, 499
Mādhyamika, 190–192
Mādhyamika-kārikā, 189, 464, 496
Mādhyamika-Sautrāntika, 189

Mādhyamika-sūtra, 3, 6n.
Mādhyamika-vṛtti, 191n., 192n., 194n., 358n. 3
māgha, 342
mā hiṃsyāt, 575
Mālatī-Mādhava, 129
māṃsa, 331, 364n. 3, 369
māṃsa-dharā, 369
māna, 435
Māna-manohara, 139, 143
mānasa, 547
mānasa pratyakṣa, 79
Māṇḍūkya, 90
Māṇḍūkya-Gauḍapādīya-bhāṣya-vyākhyā, 222
Māṇḍūkya-kārikā, 90, 106, 220
Māṇḍūkya-Upaniṣad-bhāṣya, 90
Māṇḍūkya-Upaniṣad-bhāṣyārtha- saṃgraha, 90
Māra, 570
mārdava, 595
mārga, 406n., 408
Mārīci, 368, 388
Mārkaṇḍeya, 368
Mārtaṇḍa-tilaka-svāmin, 123
māruta, 421
mārutādhiṣṭhānatvāt, 368
mātsarya, 309
Māṭhara Ācārya, 197
Māṭhara-vṛtti, 467n., 468n.
māyā, 11, 12, 18, 41, 47, 51, 52, 54, 55, 58, 59, 83, 84, 89, 97, 102, 120, 122, 188, 226, 247, 249, 253, 258, 275, 276, 314, 552, 556, 611, 612, 621; alone the cause of the world, 12; as an instrumental cause (Brahman being the material cause) according to Sarvajñātma Muni, 12; differences of view regarding its relation with Brahman, 12; scholastic disputes as to the nature of its causality, 12
māyā-mātram, 43
māyā-nirmitatvābhyupagamāt, 233
māyā power, 555
māyā theory, 48
Measure, 171, 223, 420, 431
Mechanical, 420, 430
medas, 364n. 3, 369, 378, 379
medhā, 382, 435
Medhātithi, 290, 460
Medhātithi Gautama, 458
Medical, 413n., 433, 435, 438, 441; formulas, 507; herbs, 321, 342; literature, 343, 349, 350, 413n.; practitioners, 321; science, 320; system, 411; treatment, 352n. 4; writers (later), 348
Medicinal, 419n.
Medicine, 319, 324, 325, 373, 416, 419, 420, 422-426, 431, 432, 454, 470
Medicine of Ancient India, 495n. 2
Meditation, 104, 296, 299, 522, 537, 575, 576. 583, 584, 596
Meditative union, 521
Medium, 264
medo-dharā, 369
Medulla oblongata, 414
Megasthenes, 633
Memory, 28, 171, 302, 305, 435, 436
Mendicant, 589
Menstrual blood, 408, 411
Menstrual flow, 409
Menstrual product, 365
Mental, 28, 583, 588; causes, 215; contact, 160; control, 583; creation, 269, 271, 280, 283; diseases, 487; functions, 541; inclinations, 573; modifications, 280; movement, 275; operations, 25; phenomena, 214; state, 17, 176, 215, 298, 583; tendencies, 546
Mercy, 435
Merit, 286, 287, 485
Meru, 431
meru daṇḍa, 411, 412n.
Messenger, 265
Metacarpal, 331
Metaphorical, 384
Metaphysical, 219, 220, 582, 584, 586, 599
Metatarsal, 331
Method of interpretation, 2
Methodological, 393
Methods, 33, 191
Methora, 633
mettā, 537
meya-svabhāvānugāminyām anirvacanīyatā, 146
meyatva, 140
Mice, 477
Middle discrimination, 161, 289
Migration, 474
Milk, 68, 69, 112, 201, 375-378, 408
Mind, 40, 87, 177, 180, 249, 267, 280, 296, 386, 395, 414, 428, 429, 440, 474, 488, 522, 547, 581, 583-586, 592, 597, 618
Mind activities, 548
Mind-associated consciousness, 39
Mind-body, 610
Mind-contact, 81
Mindfulness, 583

Mind-object contact, 79
Mind-organ, 261, 361, 366, 427
Mind-person, 401
Mind-structure, 611
Mineral, 388
Minor term, 160
Miraculous, 342; effect, 424
Mirage, 5, 33, 265, 270; stream, 269
Mirror, 207
Misconception, 559
Misdeeds, 476
Misery, 47, 205
Mitākṣarā, 94n., 123
Mithilā, 138, 144, 460
mithuna, 457
mithyā, 121
mithyācāra, 575
mithyā-jñānam, 9, 13, 482
mithyā-jñāna-nimittaḥ, 121
mithyā-saṃvṛta, 6
mithyātva, 171, 175
mithyā-yoga, 374, 473
Mitra, 339
Mixed *rasa*, 419
Mixing up, 431
Mīmāṃsaka, 53, 62, 83, 449
Mīmāṃsā, 53, 64, 66n., 99, 101, 113, 135, 139, 177, 251, 454, 515, 559, 563-569; *vidhi* conception, 559 ff.; *vidhi* conception, diverse views on, 561, 562
Mīmāṃsādhikaraṇa-mālā, 252
Mīmāṃsā-sūtra, 326n., 468n., 559
Mīmāṃsā view, 114
Mīmāṃsists, 92, 114, 144, 197, 198, 207
Mode of mind, 17
Modes of Brahman, 51
Modification, 25, 29, 34, 116, 210, 214, 241, 247, 269, 280, 433
Modifications of *māyā,* 40
Moggallāna, 286
moha, 482-486, 581
mohanam, 581
Moist, 393n., 421
Moistening, 421
Moisture, 417, 420, 426
mokṣa, 51, 261, 264, 287, 309, 475, 610
mokṣa-sādhana, 263
mokṣa-śāstra, 449, 493
Mokṣopāya-sāra, 267
Molecular, 223
Momentariness, 76, 211, 214
Momentary, 6, 37, 73, 81, 82, 111, 204, 209, 211-214, 231, 428, 429; appearance, 37; cause, 213; character, 209n.; existents, 37; flashing, 36, 73; ideas, 34; imaginations, 269; individuals, 68
Moments, 17, 31n., 69, 75, 174, 209, 211, 237, 272, 275
Mongolia, 189
Monism, 49
Monistic, 234; interpretation, 250; type, 263; Vedānta, 251; view, 233
Moon, 7, 30, 385, 612
Moral, 26n., 28, 441, 471, 541, 564, 596, 610; conflict, 529, 577; destiny, 237, 238; discipline, 583; efforts, 544, 545; elevation, 522, 534; injunctions, 322; life, 487; precepts, 576
Morality, 608
Morbid elements, 372
Morbidities, 379
Morbidity, 392, 420, 421, 426
Mosquitoes, 477
Mother-energy, 414
Motion, 188, 420
Motionless, 476
Motor *dhamanī*, 409
Motor organs, 302
Mouth, 180, 379
Movement, 216, 271, 411, 426, 432; of thought, 294
Moving, 387, 421
mṛdu, 419n., 421
mṛgatṛṣṇikādayaḥ, 25n.
mṛtyu, 348
Mucus, 320
Mudga, 418n.
muditā, 480, 537
mudrās, 531
mukhya, 300n. 3
Muktāvalī, 259
mukti, 283, 315
Muktika, 596*n.*
Muktika-Upaniṣad, 284, 285n., 596n.
Mukundadāsa, 517
Mukundāśrama, 95n.
Multiplicity, 280
Mummaḍideva, 267
Mumukṣu-vyavahāra, 266
Mundane, 597
muni, 269, 590
Munidasa, 502
Muñja grass, 344
Muñjavān, 344n. 4
Muṇḍaka, 402, 642
Muṇḍaka-bhāṣya-vyākhyāna, 222

Muṇḍaka-Upaniṣad, 58, 90, 289n., 301, 402, 576, 577, 642
Muṇḍaka-Upaniṣad-bhāṣya, 90
Muralidhar, P., 494
Muscles, 294
Music, 582n.
Mutual dependence, 183
Mutual help, 211
Mutual interdependence, 161
Mutual negation, 141, 230, 260
Mutual reference, 182
Mutual relations, 234
mūḍhā, 441
mūlādhāra, 529
mūrdhni, 524
mūrttāmūrtta-rāśi, 51
mūtrātisāra, 344
Mysterious centre, 415
Mysterious Kuṇḍalinī, The, 412n.
Mysterious operation, 424
Mysterious power, 415
Mystic, 622
Mystical cognition, 573
Mystical state, 527

naḍa, 402
Nagnaka, 349
Nails, 379, 380n.
nairūpya, 200
Naiṣadha-carita, 145, 458
Naiṣkarmya-siddhi, 19, 92, 94, 97, 114, 115, 117, 171n., 227, 229, 248, 290.
Naiṣkarmya-siddhi-ṭīkā, 171n.
Naiṣkarmya-siddhi-vivaraṇa, 114
naiṣṭhikī, 484
Naiyāyika, 59, 82, 125, 136, 139, 143, 146, 148, 151, 154, 160, 166, 168, 188, 192, 197, 198, 203, 209, 213, 217, 261, 384, 480
na kiṃcid avediṣam, 177
Nakṣatra-kalpa, 328
Nakula, 503
Naḷam, 403n.
Nara, 626, 633
Naradanta, 499
Narahari, 66, 266, 517
Narasiṃha, 91
Narasiṃha Bhaṭṭa, 63
Narasiṃha Kavirāja, 383n., 506
na svarūpa-dṛṣṭiḥ prati-yogy- apekṣā, 229
Natural forces, 213
Natural quality, 586
Nature, 418n., 584, 612; of consciousness, 74; of knowledge, 223; of things, 433
Nauseating, 584
nava, 449
nava-dvāraṃ, 339
Nava-nītaka, 507
Nava-sāhasāṅka-carita, 145
nava-tantra, 449
navābhyasta-tantra, 449
Navel, 371, 399, 408, 411, 414
navya-nyāya, 143
na vyavahāra-bījam, 102
Naya-maṇi-māla, 251
Naya-mayūkha-mālikā, 251
Nayana-prasādinī, 169, 181n.
nābhi, 336
nābhi-kanda, 414
nāḍī, 297, 304, 338n., 337, 338, 401-403, 405, 412–415; its meaning, 402; its number, 402n., 405; its pre-Carakian senses, 402, 403
nāḍīkā, 402
nāḍī-saṃsparśanodyata, 296
Nāḍī-vijñāna, 413
nāḍī-vraṇa, 344
Nāḍuvil Maṭham, 227
Nāga, 86, 628
Nāganātha, 506
Nāgārjuna, 3, 5, 8, 9, 11, 34, 59, 138, 143, 146, 188–190, 194, 196, 197, `433, 464, 494-499, 508; his criticism of causation as interpreted by Bhavya and Candrakīrti, 189, 191; his criticism of causation contrasted with that of the Hīnayānists, 194; his criticism of the concept of "going," 194 ff.; his distinction of limited truth (*saṃvṛta*) and absolute truth (*paramārtha*), 3; his view regarding production and nature of things, 47; his main thesis of "no thesis," 188, 189, 191, 192
Nāgeśa, 303
Nāgeśvara, 63
nākṣatrāṇi, 339n.
nāma-rūpa, 581
nāma-rūpāṅkura, 358
Nāma-saṃgraha-mālikā, 252
Nānā Dīkṣıta, 19, 60, 256n., 259
nānāpekṣa-pratiyogināṃ bhedaḥ pratīyate, 110
nāra, 627
nārāyaṇa, 513, 623, 626, 628, 630, 633, 635, 636, 638, 640; conception of, 626, 627
Nārāyaṇa Dīkṣita, 63n.
Nārāyaṇa Jyotisha, 66n.
Nārāyaṇa Yati, 91

Nārāyaṇāśrama, 61, 62, 248
Nārāyaṇendra Sarasvatī, 90
nāsikya, 300n. 3
ñāna-samvara, 583
Nearness, 420
Necessary antecedence, 214
Neck, 392
Negation, 98, 105, 110, 112, 127, 135, 151, 152, 165, 187, 209, 223, 255, 257, 314, 512
Negative, 135, 140, 176; criticism, 220; instances, 140; pleasures, 104
Negativity, 222
Neither-real-nor-unreal, 135
Neo-realist, 311
Nepal, 67n.
Nerve-physical, 415
Nerve-plexus, 412-415, 529, 531
Nerves, 296, 399, 415
Nervous system, 401, 411, 529
Nescience, 7, 10, 52, 116, 135, 171, 176, 224, 253, 255, 261, 524
Neutral, 416, 441
New bones, 332n. 1
New moon, 605
New Testament, 640
Nibandha, 220, 580
nibandha-puṣpāñjali, 56
Nibandha-saṃgraha, 317, 494, 498
Nibbāṇa, 537
nidarśana, 454, 457
Nidāna, 350, 461, 463, 499, 501, 503, 505
Nidana-pradīpa, 506
Nidāna-sthāna, 461, 495, 499
Niddesa, 628, 631, 640
nidrā, 120
nigamana, 442, 452
Nigama-tattva-sāra-tantra, 412n.
Nigamānta Mahādeśika, 513
nigraha-sthāna, 453, 468
Nihilists, 146, 270
niḥsvabhāva, 40
niḥśeṣa-karmāśaya, 287
niḥśvāsa, 381
nijigiṃsanatā, 578
Nimbārka school, 517
Nimi, 416
Nimi-tantra, 507
nimitta, 85, 461
nimitta-kāraṇa, 420
nimīlite, 297
niranuyojyānuyoga, 454n.
nirarthaka, 454n.
nirākārā buddhiḥ, 207
nirāspadā, 25n.
nirdeśa, 454, 455
nirṇaya, 454
Nirukta, 319n., 404n., 623, 637
nirvacana, 454, 457
nirvāṇa, 266, 285, 526n. 1
nirvāṇa-mātra, 269
nir-vikalpa, 25, 436, 468
nir-vikāra, 429
Niścaladāsa Svāmin, 249n.
Niścala Kara, 498, 500
niścaya, 199, 435, 448
niścayātmikā, 565n. 1
niścayātmikā antaḥkaraṇa-vṛtti, 86
niścayātmikāḥ, 428
niṣkarṣaṇa, 195
niṣkriya, 188
niṣprakārīkāyāḥ saprakārakatvena bhāvaḥ, 258
nitamba, 331n. 8, 334n. 2
Nityabodha Ācārya, 128
nityaga, 429n.
nitya-naimittika, 516
Nityanātha Siddha, 498
nitya-sama, 444n. 4, 446n.
nityatva-pratiṣedhāt, 451n.
nityatvād, 26n.
nityānitya-vastu-viveka, 577
nivasiṣyasi, 642
nivesanam, 580
nivṛtti, 591, 592
niyama, 322, 530, 531, 573
niyama-viddhi, 53
niyantā, 387
niyati, 433, 478
niyoga, 457, 561
Niyoga-kāṇḍa, 100, 101, 113
nīla, 33
Nīlakaṇṭha, 318, 517, 635
Nīlakaṇṭha Bhaṭṭa, 507n.
Nīlakaṇṭha Dīkṣita, 251
nīlāgalaṣālā, 346n. 7
nilikā, 345
nīrandhra, 413n.
Non-appropriation, 590
Non-being, 165, 171, 233, 275
Non-Buddhistic, 189
Non-distinction, 238-240
Non-eternal, 139-141, 451n., 452
Non-eternality, 219
Non-existence, 32, 222, 249, 280, 603

Non-existent, 13, 32, 37, 47, 128, 139, 140, 175, 179, 185, 199, 223, 258, 270, 271, 282, 299, 603
Non-existing effects, 200
Non-injury, 547, 589, 590, 592-596, 599
Non-momentary, 209
Non-moral, 470
Non-perception, 230
Non-permanency of entities, 213
Non-pleasurable-painful, 27n.
Non-production, 287
Non-self, 7, 116; elements, 28
Non-stealing, 589
Non-transgression, 583
Normal, 390; duty, 593, 599, 602; measure, 372; state, 395
Nose, 379
Nostrils, 428
Nothingness, 18
Nourishment, 358
Nṛga, 123
Nṛsiṃhasvarūpa, 61n.
Nṛsiṃha Ṭhakkura, 517
Nṛsiṃhāśrama Muni, 19, 36, 50n., 59-64, 66n., 83, 90, 106, 119, 143, 248-250; his date and works, 248; nature of his Vedāntic interpretations, 249
Number, 182, 187, 216, 420, 431
Numerical, 16; difference, 431; qualities, 187
Nutrient, 426n.
Nutritive, 416, 417; elements, 213
Nyāya, 21, 46, 59, 66n., 123, 133, 135. 139, 141, 144-146, 158, 165, 168,
Nyāya (*cont*). 169, 184, 185, 194, 196, 206, 220, 236, 242, 286, 356, 358, 437, 442, 458, 460, 484, 562, 563n. 2, 564, 566, 600, 603; its arguments in favour of the existence of God criticized by Kamalaśīla, 203 ff.; its idea of emancipation, 286; its theory of the subtle body, 356; origin of, 457 ff.; springs of action in, 480, 482
Nyāya, categories, 169, 171, 180, 220; definitions, 188; logic, 192; logicians, 220; perceptions, 194; philosophy, 167, 464; psychology, 483; school, 192; system, 436, 476; view, 205; writers, 143, 146, 168, 181
Nyāya-candrikā, 66n., 495, 499
Nyāya-dīpāvalī, 59, 134, 136, 220
Nyāya-dīpāvalī-tātparya-ṭīkā, 134
Nyāya-dīpikā, 516
Nyāya-kalpa-latikā, 95
Nyāya-kandalī, 95, 98, 288n., 304n. 1, 356, 480
Nyāya-kaṇikā, 52n., 95, 98, 100, 123, 563n. 1
Nyāya-loka-siddhi, 56
Nyāya-makaranda, 13, 56, 80n., 81n., 103n., 134-136, 170n., 220, 223
Nyāya-makaranda-saṃgraha, 220
Nyāya-makaranda-ṭīkā, 134
Nyāya-makaranda-vivecanī, 134
Nyāya-mañjarī, 123, 287n., 326n., 358n. 1, 445, 447n., 466n., 465, 482, 538n. 1, 560n. 1
Nyāya-mālā, 93
Nyāya-muktāvalī, 251
Nyāya-nibandha-prakāśa, 123
Nyāya-nirṇaya, 222
Nyāya-pariśuddhi, 138, 139
Nyāya-rakṣā-maṇi, 95n., 252
Nyāya-ratna-ṭīkā, 52n.
Nyāya-ratnāvalī, 89n.
Nyāya-sāra, 139, 141
Nyāya-sāra-vicāra, 141
Nyāya-siddhānta-dīpa, 62
Nyāya-siddhānta-mañjarī, 251n.
Nyāya-siddhānta-mañjari-vyākhyāna, 251n.
Nyāya-sudhā, 171n.
Nyāya-sūcī-nibandha, 123, 129
Nyāya-sūtra, 123, 286, 317, 432, 436, 440, 442-445, 446n. 1, 450n., 452, 453n., 458, 460, 464-468
Nyāya-sūtra-vṛtti, 458
Nyāya-śāstra, 458, 460
Nyāya-śikhāmaṇi, 62
Nyāya-tattvāloka, 52n.
Nyāya-Vaiśeṣika, 56, 188, 226, 361, 382, 432, 433, 600; analysis of volition, 600; criticism of its categories by Śriharṣa, 146 ff.; its categories criticized by Ānandajñāna, 222, 223; its categories refuted by Citsukha, 181 ff.; its categories refuted by Kamalaśīla, 215 ff.; its categories refuted by Śaṅkara, 217 ff.
Nyāya-vārttika, 122
Nyāya-vārttika-tātparya-pariśuddhi, 123
Nyāya-vārttika-tātparya-ṭīkā, 52n.
nyāya-vistara, 637
nyāyācārya, 141
Nyāyāmṛta, 136, 259
Nyāyāmṛta-taraṅgiṇī, 136
nyūna, 448, 449, 453, 454

Object, 19, 21, 29, 31, 33–36, 40, 101, 417, 428, 468; of awareness, 23, 33, 240; of consciousness, 74; of knowledge, 31
Object-consciousness, 172

Objection, 36, 116, 176
Objective, 24, 25, 28, 592; consciousness, 272; content, 17; entities, 29; existence, 24, 172; experience, 117; ignorance, 89; plane, 84; self, 39; world, 23, 272
Objectively, 272
Objectivity, 33, 116, 176
Oblations, 523, 613
Obligatoriness, 53
Obligatory duty, 114, 590
Observation, 200, 427, 437
Obstacle, 440
Occasion, 440
Occasional, 429
Occipital, 334n. 5
Ocean waves, 384
Odour, 373, 414, 426
Oiliness, 382
ojas, 340, 367-369, 378n., 400, 403
Old age, 597, 610
Older literature, 120
OM, 576, 613
Omnipresent, 234, 616
Omniscience, 25, 45, 61
Omniscient, 58, 136, 204; being, 156; God, 83
Oneness, 258; of reality, 149
Ontological, 41, 306, 427, 603, 604; existence, 84; objectivity, 29
Operation, 166, 204, 227
Operative, 204; action, 158; functions, 87; principle, 388
Opposite quality, 218
Opposition, 580
Oppositional relation, 110
Oppositional term, 110
Organ, 416, 417, 426
Organism, 600
Organized, 583
Organizer, 203
Oriental Historical Manuscripts, 251
Oriental Manuscript Library, 236
Origin, 276, 479n., 613
Origination, 4, 185, 271; of the sub-stratum, 13
Orissa, 189
Orthodox school, 430
Os calcis, 330n. 3
Oscillating movement, 275
Oscillation, 182
Os innominatum, 331n. 8
"Osteology," 494, 506
Otherness, 151, 152
Oughtness, 562
Outbursts of pleasure, 283
Ovary, 337, 351, 358, 360
Owls, 477

Pada-candrikā, 267, 506
Pada-mañjarī, 346n. 4
Pada-yojanikā, 91
padārtha, 454, 455
Padārtha candrikā-prabhāsa-nāma, 508
Padārtha-nirṇaya, 51
Padārtha-tattva, 11
Padārtha-tattva-nirṇaya, 58, 59, 66n.
Padārtha-tattva-nirṇaya-vivaraṇa, 222
Paddy, 418n.
padma, 415
Padmanābha Paṇḍita, 146n.
Padmapāda, 9, 10, 34, 36n., 37, 39, 54, 55, 59, 62, 91, 99, 102n., 117, 122, 169-172, 174, 240; causality of Brahman, 122; his followers, 117, 119; his view of perception, etc., 121, 122; meaning of *ajñāna*, 120, 121; quarrel with Buddhists re-garding the nature of existence, 37; regarding the nature of self-consciousness, 38 ff.
Padma-purāṇa, 458
padma-yugma-traya, 297
Paila, 503
Pain, 201, 208, 233, 279, 286, 400, 420, 427, 430, 432, 435, 480, 540, 548, 595-597
Painful, 27n., 279
Painting, 233
Paippalāda, 328
pakṣa, 140, 160
pakṣa-dharmatā, 171
pakṣe vyāpaka-pratītya-paryavasāna-balāt, 140
pakvāśaya, 368, 369, 385, 392
Palate, 405
Palatine process, 334n. 4
palita, 345
Palījaka, 349
Pancreas, 336n. 3
Pandit, 19n., 249, 256n., 257n., 258n., 259n., 313n.
Pandit, Mr, 128, 129
Panjpur, 500
panthā, 406n.
Pantheism, 527
Pantheistic, 1
Pantzinor village, 500, 501
pañca-daśāṅga yoga, 530
Pañcadasī, 246, 247, 248n., 290n.
pañca-mahā-bhūta-vikārāḥ, 417

Pañcanada, 500
Pañcanalīya kāvya, 145
Pañca-pādikā, 9, 36n., 60, 62, 117, 119, 122, 171, 240, 290
Pañca-pādikā-dhyāsa-bhāṣya-vyā-khyā, 36n.
Pañca-pādikā-śāstra-darpaṇa, 36n., 119
Pañca-pādikā-vivaraṇa, 19, 34, 36n., 37, 38n., 39n., 60, 61, 91, 97, 119, 171, 172, 222, 237n., 239-241, 246, 248
Pañca-pādīkā-vivaraṇa-bhāva- prakāśikā, 36n.
Pañca-pādikā-vivaraṇa-prakāśikā, 62, 119, 249
Pañca-*pādikā-vyākhyā*, 60n.
Pañca-prakriyā, 61n.
Pañca-rātra, 538, 573, 636, 637. 639n.
Pancaśikha, 555
pañca-vidham adhyātman, 626
pañcendriya-guṇāvahā, 414
pañcīkaraṇa, 86n., 87
pañcīkaraṇa-bhāva-prakāśikā, 91
pañcīkaraṇa-prakriyā, 91
Pañcīkaraṇa-tātparya-candrikā, 91
Pañcīkaraṇa-ṭīkā-tattva-candrikā, 91
Pañcīkaraṇa-vārttika, 91
Pañcīkaraṇa-vārṭṭikābharaṇa, 91
Pañcīkaraṇa-vivaraṇa, 91, 222
Pañjikā, 36n., 197
paññā, 583, 588
paṇidhi, 580
para, 420, 430, 431, 441
paraḥ ātmā, 429
paralokaiṣaṇā, 473
parama-guru, 99
parama-haṃsa, 291n.
Parama-haṃsa-Upaniṣad, 291n.
Paramaṃ padaṃ, 263
parama-sūkṣma, 479
Paramānanda, 146n.
paramāṇu, 217, 222
paramārtha, 5
paramārtha-darśana, 286
paramārtha-prapā, 517
paramārtha-rūpa, 5
paramārtha-satya, 4
paramātman, 520, 521, 531, 538, 543, 544
paramātma-rāśi, 51
Parameśvara, 61, 237
param ojas, 400
paraṃ dhāma, 621
para puruṣa, 546
parasparādhyāsa, 130
parasparopakāritā, 211
para-tantratā, 11
para-vijñapti-viśeṣādhipatyāt, 24n.
parādi, 430
parā prakṛti, 543
parārtha, 480
Parāśara, 290
Parāśara-saṃhitā, 503
Parāśara-smṛti, 95, 291n.
paribandho, 580
Paribhāṣā, 61
Parietal, 334n. 5
pariggaho, 578
parigraha, 477
parihāra, 453
Parimala, 123n.
pariṇāma, 24, 44, 45, 51, 53, 198, 218, 222, 223, 258, 431, 433, 478; cause, 52; doctrine, 197; view of causation, 52
pariṇāmi-kāraṇa, 59
paripāka, 31n.
parisaṃkhyā-vidhi, 54
parispanda, 296
pariṣat, 441
Parjanya, 350n. 2
parokṣatvād acintyam, 368
Particles, 181
Particular, 73
Partless, 181, 182, 218, 229
Parts, 46
Parvataka-tantra, 507
Paryanuyojyo-pekṣaṇa, 454n.
Passion, 264, 435, 483, 488, 527, 529, 536, 556, 570, 575, 580, 581, 616, 619
Passionlessness, 554
Passive, 28
paśavaḥ, 339n.
paśyanti, 412
Patañjali, 300n., 306, 355n., 470, 476, 479n., 483, 502, 508, 517, 522, 527-531, 535, 537, 538, 555, 556, 573, 574, 588, 628, 629, 631, 633, 636, 638, 640
Patañjali-sūtra, 603
Patella bone, 331n. 4
Path of wisdom, 577
Pathology, 506
Patience, 420, 583-586, 595
Patient, 344
patiṭṭhā, 536, 583
paṭigho, 580
paurṇamāsī, 339n.
pauruṣa, 291-294, 315, 612
pauruṣa-vādins, 469
Pauṣa, 342

Pauṣkalāvata, 494
Pauṣkalāvata-tantra, 507
pauṣṭika, 326, 344
pavamāna, 339n.
pavana, 388
Pavīnasa demon, 349
pācaka, 352, 385
Pādma-tantra, 639n. 3
pāka, 421 426, 431
Pāṇḍava, 586, 635
Paṇḍya, 251
Pāṇini, 346n., 627-629, 631, 633
pāṇi-pāda-salākādhiṣṭhāna, 331n. 3
pāṇi-pādāṅguli, 331n. 1
pāpa, 608
pāramārthika, 2, 51
pāraṃparya, 436
Pārāśarya, 368
pārıbhāṣika, 422
pārimāṇḍalya, 217; measure, 218
Pārśvanātha, 634
pārṣṇī, 329
pārthiva, 419
pāṣaṇḍa, 630
pāṣāṇavat-samam, 308
Pātañjala-Sāṃkhya, 204
pātāla, 87, 349
Pātrasvāmin, 198
Pāṭaliputra, 498
pāṭimokkha-saṃvara, 583
Pea, 195
Peace, 519, 526, 571, 583, 584, 587, 596
Peacefulness of mind, 595
Pearl, 612
Peculiarities, 183
Pelvic bone, 333n.
Pelvic cavity, 331
Pelvis, 396, 405
pemaṃ, 580
Penancos, 628
Penis, 344, 380n.
People, 593
Perceived universe, 278
Perceiver, 25, 77, 156, 160, 179, 230-232, 240, 270, 397
Perceiving, 385; power, 230; principle, 229
Perceiving-self, 230
Perception, 19, 20, 23, 24, 75, 101, 106, 134, 135, 156, 167, 171, 183, 192, 207, 215, 220, 223, 230, 232, 236, 238, 239, 244, 245, 260, 270, 294, 311, 312, 351, 435, 436, 440, 468, 475; of identity, 75
Percepts, 312
Perceptual, 89; data, 180; experience, 121; knowledge, 89, 220; process, 239, 249
Percipi, 21
Performance, 586
Perfumes, 582n.
Pericardium, 336n. 3
Permanence, 214
Permanent, 25, 206, 278, 429, 430; consciousness, 82; convictions, 277; entity, 25; perceiver, 215; self, 82, 206; subject, 427; substance, 167
Persistence, 20, 77; of knowledge, 20
Persistent, 216, 278
Persisting cause, 210
Persisting entity, 210, 211
Person, 291, 295, 428
Personality, 127, 611
Perspiration, 409; channels, 405
Pessimism, 483, 588
Pessimistic tendency, 607
pesī, 366, 371
Pettā Dīkṣita, 63n.
phala, 419
phala-tyāga, 519
phale nerṣyu, 489
Phantom show, 12
phaṇa, 399, 409
Pharmacopœia, 321
Pharyngeal plexus, 414
Phālguna, 342
Phenomena, 204, 584
Phenomenal, 145, 146, 192, 582; appearance, 55; reality, 192; self, 484
Phenomenon, 436
Philosopher, 44, 521
Philosophic, 586; analysis, 545; knowledge, 284, 610; truth, 588; view, 2; wisdom, 576
Philosophical, 263, 584; development, 55; idea, 427; ignorance, 486; truth, 265
Philosophy, 51, 59, 76, 84, 263, 588, 593, 603, 612; of Bādarāyaṇa, 41
Phlegm, 348, 349, 379, 426, 456
Phlegmatic diseases, 348
Physical, 275, 430, 471, 588; diseases, 487; process, 55; propulsion, 560; sciences, 317; trouble, 597; world, 312
Physician, 321, 322, 394, 416, 452, 454, 457, 484
Physiological activity, 386
Physiological effects, 420
Physiological functions, 302, 304, 386, 388
Physiological operations, 387, 390
Physiological position, 387

picchila, 419n., 421
pihā, 580
Pilgrimage, 265, 515, 592
Pillar, 30
Piṅgalā, 297, 339, 412n., 413, 529, 530
piṇḍa, 49, 364n., 366
pipāsā, 578
pipāsā-sthāna, 335n. 1
Pipe, 403
pippalī, 348n. 1
Pischel, R., 403n.
Piśāca, 327, 349
Piśāca-veda, 319n. 3
Pitṛ-yāna, 605, 607
pitta, 297, 320, 327, 344, 349, 369, 372, 373, 379-393, 395, 397, 401, 404, 407, 408, 421, 421, 426, 457, 611; nature of, 385, 386
pitta-dharā, 369
pittala, 390n.
pitta-prakṛti, 382, 389
pittāśaya, 408
piṭhara-pāka, 223
pivato, 571
pīlu-pāka, 223
Placenta, 338
Planet, 388
Plant, 388, 419
Plato, 590
Playful activity, 48
Playful instincts, 205
plāśī, 336
Pleasantness, 417
Pleasing, 393n.
Pleasurable, 27n., 279; experience, 105; state, 208
Pleasure, 78, 201, 285, 286, 400, 420, 427, 430, 432, 435, 436, 471, 480, 528, 540, 568, 588, 592-597, 606
Pleasure-seeking, 591
Plexus, 412n., 415
plīhan, 334
Pluralistic experience, 234
Plurality, 44, 45, 110, 185, 224; of causes, 185
Points of dispute, 454
Poison, 419n., 421, 580
Polemic, 145, 146
Polemical, 234
Poles, 239
Politics, 449
Polluting agents, 380–382
Pollution, 476, 477
Popular belief, 440
Positive, 54; cause, 226; entity, 209; experience, 177; knowledge, 177; quality, 175; unity, 176
Positive Sciences of the Ancient Hindus, 412n., 415n.
Positivity, 222
Possession, 182
Postures, 531
poṣaka-rasa, 377n.
Potency, 9, 36, 201, 419, 421-422, 431
Potency-in-chief, 424
Potential, 26n.; *ajñāna*, 61; energy, 415
Potentialities, 28
Potter, 287
Potter's wheel, 284
Power, 9, 25, 247, 280, 595; of controlling others, 590n.; of productivity, 31n.
Prabandha-pariśodhinī, 60n.
Prabhākara, 76, 77, 79, 169, 177, 179, 226, 287, 563, 600; his analysis of illusion, 177; his idea of emanci-pation, 287
prabhāva, 377, 421, 424–427
Prabodha-candrikā, 517
Prabodha-candrodaya nāṭaka, 252
Practical action, 175
Practical discipline, 583
Practical movement, 179
Practice, 568, 583, 599
pradeśa, 454, 456
pradhāna, 198, 431, 514
Pradyumna, 633, 635
Pragalbha Miśra, 146n.
Pragmatic, 432; basis, 175
Praise, 597
Praiṣya-praiṣayoḥ sambandhaḥ, 561
prajāḥ, 339n.
Prajāpati, 564
prajñapti-sat, 67
prajñā, 28, 306, 573, 588, 638
Prjñākara Gupta, 56
Prajñānānanda, 91, 225
prajñāparādha, 374, 395, 473, 484-487, 492
prakaraṇa, 66n., 266
Prakaraṇa-pañcikā, 287
prakaraṇa-sama, 444n., 446n., 450, 452
Prakaṭārtha-vivaraṇa, 53, 56, 58, 83, 225-227, 236, 237, 245; its philosophy, dates, etc., 225–227
prakāśa-heyatvāt, 226
Prakāśānanda, 19-21, 60, 63, 63, 64, 97, 253, 257-259, 312; Brahma and the world in, 258; discussions regarding awareness in,

19-21; discussions regarding subjective idealism in, 19; *māyā* in, 258; nature of *ajñāna* in, 255; nature of *ānanda* in, 257; negative dialectics of, 20, 21; quarrel with Vasubandhu of, 21; theory of causality in, 253-257; view-point of his work, 252, 253; works of, 259
Prakāśānubhavānanda, 19n.
Prakāśātman, 10, 11, 19, 34, 38, 94, 97, 102, 119-122, 136, 171, 172, 174, 222, 239-241, 246, 255-258, 270; his quarrel with the Buddhists regarding nature of objects, 34, 36
Prakāśātma-śrī-caraṇaiḥ, 120
prakopa, 391n.
prakṛti, 48, 83, 116, 120, 126, 201, 204, 208, 275, 276, 289, 298, 306, 315, 389, 390, 433, 453, 478, 514, 531. 534, 538-543, 545, 552, 556, 557, 562, 600, 602, 612, 613, 621, 622
prakṛti-doṣas, 391n.
prakṛti-māna, 391n.
prakṛtıṃ yānti māmikām, 613
pralaya, 43, 55, 219
pramā, 148, 158, 223, 237, 244, 245
pramāda, 482
pramāṇa, 89, 148, 158, 192, 223, 234, 255, 294, 435. 437, 438, 442, 443, 448n.
pramāṇa-caitanya, 238, 239
Pramāṇa-mañjarī, 139, 143
Pramāṇa-mālā, 13, 15, 59, 134, 136, 171, 220
Pramāṇa-samuccaya, 51
Pramāṇa-vārttikālaṅkāra, 56
Pramāṇa-vārttikālaṅkāra-ṭīkā, 56
Pramāṇa-vidhvaṃsana, 465n.
Pramāṇa-vidhvaṃsana-sambhāṣita-vṛtti, 465n.
Pramāṇa-vṛtti-nirṇaya, 227
pramātṛ, 89, 121
prameha, 400n.
Prameya-dīpikā, 516
prameyatvāt, 140
pramiti, 89
Pramodapurandara Ācārya, 260n.
praṇetā, 387
prasaṅga, 454, 456
prasaṅga-pratidṛṣṭānta-sama, 444n. 4
prasaṅga-sama, 445n.
prasāda, 371, 379, 574
prasāda-dhātu, 379
prasāra, 392n.
Prasthāna-bheda, 259
prasyandana, 407
praśama, 390
Praśastamati, 198
Praśastapāda, 187, 287, 480, 482, 589, 600
Praśastapāda-bhāṣya, 188n.
Praśnanidhāna, 499
Praśna-Upaniṣad, 90, 337n., 401n., 402
Praśna-Upaniṣad-bhāṣya, 90
prathamā-bhūmikā, 305
pratibandha, 203
pratibimba, 55
pratibimba-vāda, 122
pratijñā, 442, 452
pratijñā-hāni, 453
pratijñāntara, 454n.
pratijñā-sannyāsa, 454n.
Pratimā-nāṭaka, 460n.
pratiniviṣṭā, 441
pratipakṣa-bhāvanā, 537
pratipannopādhau niṣedha-pratiyogitvam, 255
pratipannopādhāva-pratiyogitva, 249
pratisaṃskartṛ, 495
pratiṣṭhā, 324, 331
pratıṣṭhāpanā, 442
prati-tantra-siddhānta, 446
pratikopāsanā, 523, 569
pratīta, 21, 148
pratītya-samutpāda, 4n., 9
pratyabhijñā, 38, 75, 77
pratyag ātman, 7
Pratyagbhagavān, 169
Pratyag-rūpa-bhagavān, 138n.
pratyak, 73
pratyak-cit, 127
pratyak-citi, 10
Pratyak-svarūpa-bhagavat, 181n.
Pratyakṣa, 106, 223, 238, 435, 436, 438, 442, 475, 479
Pratyakṣadevayathācārya, 513
Pratyakṣa-śārīram, 413n.
Pratyak-tattva-pradīpikā, 256n.,
pratyaktva, 133
praty-anuyoga, 448
pratyaya, 461
pratyāhāra, 530, 531
pratyātma-vedya, 25
pratyetavya, 21
pratyudāharati, 399
Prauḍhānubhūti, 93
Pravacana-bhāṣya, 289
pravartanā, 562
pravartate, 366
pravṛtti, 454, 591

pravṛtti-sāmarthya, 150
prayatna, 275, 430-432
prayatnādi, 432
prayatnānta, 430, 431
prayatnāntarīyaka, 445n.
prayatnāntarīyakatva, 446n.
prayojana, 446, 448n. 1
prākṛta-māna, 372, 373
prāktana, 292
prāmāṇya, 246
prāṇa, 86, 87, 120, 298-301, 303, 338, 339, 352, 362, 387, 388, 396, 399, 401, 403, 404, 407, 411, 415, 435, 523, 524; as depending on the head, 396; as vibration, 304; as vital parts, 399; channels of, 404, 405; heart the centre of, 396; history of the meaning of, 299 ff.; seat of, according to Caraka, 399
prāṇaiṣaṇā, 473
prāṇa-karmāṇi, 523
prāṇamaya-koṣa, 87
prāna-nirodha, 298, 310
prāṇa-saṃyamana, 530
prāṇa-spanda, 296, 297
prāṇa-vahā, 371
prāṇa-vahānāṃ srotasāṃ hṛdayaṃ mūlam, 400
prāṇa vāyu, 405, 414
prāṇāpāna-gatī ruddhvā, 523
prāṇāya svāhā, 523
prāṇāyāma, 296, 297, 522-524, 528-531, 535
prāpty-aprāpti-sama, 444n. 4, 445n.
prārabdha-karma, 285, 289
Prātiśākhyas, 320
prātītika-sattva, 312
prāyaś-citta, 319, 322, 326, 343, 344
Pre-condition, 473, 590
Predatory birds, 477
Predominance, 428
Preferment, 584
Preparatory measure, 583
preraṇa, 561
Presentation of the false, 177
Pride, 309, 435, 477, 593-596
Principle of consciousness, 23, 25
Principle of difference, 69
Principle of intelligence, 23
Principle of thought, 40
Privilege, 589
prīṇana, 382
Probability, 435
Probandum, 139, 140, 160, 161
Probans, 160
Proceedings and Transactions of the First Oriental Conference, Poona, 468n.
Proceedings of the Madras Oriental Conference, 268
Process, 296, 440
Procreator, 612
Product, 15, 20, 26, 386; complexes, 4
Production, 12, 20, 29, 37, 43, 44, 47, 72, 191, 194, 199, 200, 204, 209, 211, 214, 215, 218, 271, 272; of action, 552; of knowledge, 20
Prognostication, 462, 463
Prohibitions, 588
Projection of objectivity, 29
Proof, 148
Proper discernment, 154
Proper measure, 379
Proper proportion, 381
Property, 416-420, 426, 590
Propulsion, 561, 562
Prosperity, 584
Protection, 589
Proud, 595, 596
pṛṣṭha-gatāsthi, 333n. 1
pṛṣṭih, 332
pṛthak, 431
pṛthaktva, 223, 431
pṛthivī, 86
Psychical frame, 121
Psychical process, 55
Psychological, 125, 306, 427; appearance, 37; constituents, 67; duality of awareness, 33; elements, 67-69; entities, 68; existence, 84; experience, 196; ignorance, 13, 126; necessity, 29; objectivity, 29; objects of awareness, 33; self, 10; thought, 40
Psychologically, 36
Psycho-physical parallelism, 395
Psychosis, 28, 33, 289, 294, 541
Psychosis-transformations, 25
Pthisis, 334, 348
Pubic, 405; bone, 334n. 8; nerve, 412
Pubis, 334n. 8
Public good, 566
pudgala, 67, 68
Pudgala-viniścaya, 67n., 68n.
punar-ukta, 453, 454n.
Punarvasu, 461
Punarvasu Ātreya, 458
Pungent, 393n., 416–419, 422
Puṇṇabhadda, 628
Puṇya, 608
pupphusa, 299n., 371
Purāṇa, 49, 85, 90, 263, 324, 382, 637

Purāṇa-veda, 319n. 3
Pure, 41, 352; annihilation, 270; awareness, 38; being, 15; bliss, 15, 104, 130, 247, 257; blissfulness, 106, cessation, 270; consciousness, 25, 34, 38-40, 53, 75, 82–85, 89, 116, 121, 136, 206, 208, 226, 233-238, 240, 242, 261, 271, 272, 275, 278-280; essencelessness, 270; extinction, 269; happiness, 25; idea, 270; intelligence, 9, 15, 24, 25, 58, 102n., 117, 138, 269, 556; negation, 270; thought, 28; vacuity, 271
Purificatory rites, 322
Purity, 547, 586, 589, 595, 596, 598, 599, 631; of heart, 595; of mind, 512, 515
purīṣa, 369
purīṣa-dharā, 369
purītat, 401
puruṣa, 208, 270, 278, 289, 290, 295, 306, 315, 442, 443, 449, 453, 514, 534, 535, 538, 543-545, 551, 556, 611, 626
puruṣaḥ paraḥ, 543
puruṣa-kāra, 296
puruṣa-nārāyaṇa, 626
Puruṣa-niścaya, 399n.
Puruṣa-sūkta, 610, 611, 626
puruṣārtha, 637
puruṣottama, 63, 485, 544
Puruṣottama Dīkṣita, 133
Puruṣottama Sarasvatī, 91, 259
Puruṣottamavana, 139
pury-aṣṭaka, 283
Pus, 379, 385
Puṣpāñjali, 92
pūraka, 297, 298
Pūrṇaprajña, 139
Pūrṇākṣa Maudgalya, 416
Pūrṇānanda, 267, 413n.
Pūrṇānanda Sarasvatī, 91
Pūrṇānanda Tīrtha, 90, 91
Pūrṇānanda Yati, 413n.
pūrva, 467n.
pūrva-kāla-bhāvitva, 184
pūrva-pakṣa, 454, 456
pūrva-prajñā-saṃskāra, 120
pūrva-rūpa, 392n., 462, 463
pūrvavat, 464-467
Pūrvottara-mīmāṃsā-vāda-nakṣatra-mālā, 251
pūṣā, 412
pūtikā, 344
pūya, 385n.

Qualification, 214
Qualitative change, 17
Qualities, 7, 165, 171, 175, 182, 185, 187, 215, 218, 419, 420, 430-436, 441, 539, 584, 590n., 600
Quick, 393n.
Quickness, 180

Race, 584
Radius, 331n. 7
Rage, 580
Raghunātha, 168
Raghunātha Śiromaṇi, 138, 146n.
Rains, 68, 374, 381, 390, 431
143,
rajas, 83, 85, 86, 352, 366, 372 384, 428, 433, 488, 508, 532, 546
rajas element, 302
rajo-vahana-nāḍyaḥ, 402n.
Rajputana, 628
Rajshahi, 56
Rajwade, V.K., 643n.
Rakṣaḥ, 349
rakta, 369, 378, 380, 381, 395, 411
rakta-dharā, 369
rakta-duṣṭi, 378
ram, 642
Raṅgarāja Adhvarin, 62
Raṅgarāja Makhīndra, 250
Raṅgojī Bhaṭṭa, 63, 125
rañjaka, 385
rasa, 223, 272, 351, 364n. 3, 369, 375-379, 381, 382, 395, 401n., 404, 405, 408, 416-427, 455, 456
rasa-dhātu, 377
rasa-duṣṭi, 378
Rasa-ratnākara, 498
Rasa-sāra, 142
rasa-sthāna, 408
rasa-vāhinī, 406n.
Rasābhivyañjikā, 64
Rasātala, 87
rasāyana, 320, 350
Rasāyana-tantra, 495
Rasika-rañjinī, 517
rati, 571, 580
Ratnakīrti, 56
Ratna-prabhā, 119, 120, 500
Ratna-tūlikā, 64
Ratna Vajra, 56
raukṣya, 393, 422n.
Ravigupta, 503
Ray Chaudhury, Dr, 634, 641
Rādheya, 55

Rāḍhamalla, 380n.
rāga, 309, 482, 483, 570, 580
rāga-dveṣa, 489
rāgādi, 430
Rāghavānanda, 90, 133
Rāghavendra Svāmin, 517
Rāghavendra Yati, 19n.
rāja-karmāṇi, 344
Rāja Makhīndra, 250
rājasa, 428, 435, 546-548
Rāja-taraṅgiṇī, 502
Rājānaka, 517
rākṣasas, 328
Rāma, 264, 265, 295, 591, 636
Rāmabhadra, 91
Rāmabhadra Dīkṣita, 502
Rāmabhadrānanda, 64
Rāmabhadrāśrama, 63
Rāmacandra, 91, 275
Rāmacandra Tīrtha, 91
Rāmacandra Yajvan, 252
Rāmacandrārya, 95n.
Rāmadatta, 114
Ramadeva, 266
Rāmakaṇṭha, 517
Rāmakṛṣṇa, 61, 249n., 517
Rāmakṛṣṇa Adhvarin, 239
Rāmakṛṣṇa Bhaṭṭa, 504n.
Rāmakṛṣṇa Dīkṣita, 62
Rāmanārāyaṇa, 517
Rāmanātha, 66n., 506
Rāmanātha Vaidya, 506
Rāmarūdrī, 305n.
Rāmatīrtha, 60, 64, 91, 98, 128, 133, 136, 222
Rāmādvaya, 226, 227, 234, 236, 239, 244-246; *ajñānas* as many, 241, 242; continuity of perception through a rapid succession *ajñāna* covering and its removal in, 242; his date and work, 234, 236; his definition of right knowledge different from that of *Vedānta-paribhāṣā*, 244; his reation with *Pañca-pādikā*, 240, 241; his theory of Vedāntic perception in contrast to that of *Vedānta-paribhāṣā* and *Śikhāmaṇi*, 259 ff.; his view different from that of the *Vedānta-paribhāṣā* on the subject of the continuity of perception, 242; his view of time, 242, 244; movement of *vṛtti* and perception, 239-241; place of *antaḥkaraṇa* in perception, 239-244; pure consciousness and perception, 242
Rāmājña Pāṇḍeya, 260n., 260
Rāmānanda, 60n., 95n., 513
Rāmānanda Sarasvatī, 11, 36n., 64, 92, 119, 225
Rāmānandatīrtha, 91, 267
Rāmānuja, 49, 144, 231, 251, 303, 513, 515, 516, 631
Rāmānuja-bhāṣya, 304n. 2
Rāmānuja-mata-khaṇḍana, 252
Rāmāyaṇa, 264, 265, 590
Rāmāyaṇa-bhārata-sāra-saṃgraha, 252
Rāmāyaṇa-sāra, 252
Rāmāyaṇa-sāra-saṃgraha, 252
Rāmāyaṇa-sāra-stava, 252
Rāmāyaṇa-tātparya-nirṇaya, 252
Rāmāyaṇa-tātparya-saṃgraha, 252
Rāmendra Yogin, 66n.
Rāmeśvara Bhāratī, 95n.
rāśi, 51
React, 26
Real, 135, 192, 314; God, 2; ignorance, 5; objects, 30; souls, 2; substance, 26; transformation, 44, 45, 51; world, 2, 23
Realism, 314
Realistic, 2, 3, 245; definitions, 188, 194; interpretation, 44; logic, 192; transformation, 44, 45, 51
Reality, 5, 17, 23, 84, 133, 190, 208, 214, 222, 224, 238n., 272, 283, 310, 582
Realization, 269, 276, 611
Rearing, 589; of cows, 590n.
Reason, 139, 140, 142, 160, 171, 223, 437
Reasoning, 28, 438, 440
Rebirths, 86, 104, 355, 475, 543, 606-610, 618
recaka, 297, 298
Récentes Découvertes de MSS. Médicaux Sanscrits dans l'Inde, 503n.
Receptacle, 206, 613
Recognition, 75, 77, 211
Recognition of identity, 38, 39, 76; in Buddhism and Vedānta, 38 ff.
Rectum, 334, 371, 386, 392, 405, 409
Red, 31, 402n., 407
Reed, 403
Reflection, 58, 63
Refutation, 146, 168, 169, 184, 216, 217, 220; of action, 216
Relation, 17, 25, 28, 29, 39, 51, 111, 122, 140, 166, 168, 175, 182, 183, 192, 199, 219, 233, 234, 433, 436, 463; of identity, 39; of inherence, 171, 182, 215-217; of inseparability, 223
Relationing, 36
Relationship, 175
Relative concept, 105

Relative space, 181
Relativistic, 189, 245; philosophy, 189
Relativity, 181
Rele, 412n., 413
Religion, 612
Religious, 428, 593, 612; discipline, 569; duty, 589; endeavours, 569
Remoteness, 430
Renunciation, 291, 519, 534, 535, 595, 599
Repentance, 592
Repetition, 420
Reply, 453
Reports on Sanskrit Manuscripts, 251
Repository, 25
Repulsions, 276
Resemblance, 151
Resolution, 292
Respiratory process, 299n. 1
Responsibility, 584, 589, 591, 592
Result, 438
Retentive power, 435
Revelation, 15-18, 226
Reward, 587
Rhetoric, 252
Rhetorician, 197
Ribs, 332n.
Rice, 418n.
Right cognition, 154, 157, 158
Right conduct, 473, 474, 493
Right knowledge, 114, 176, 208, 215, 223, 237, 244, 245, 264, 276, 286, 290, 302
Right perception, 156
Right thinking, 104
Right volition, 583
Ritual, 637
Ritualistic, 329
Rockhill, W., 320, 321, 494n. 1
roga-bhiṣag-jitīya-vimāna, 440
rohiṇī, 369, 462
romāvarta, 399
Root, 404, 426; desires, 280; inclinations, 280, 295
Rooted instincts, 286
Root-impression, 36
Rope, 7, 43, 84, 122
Rosy, 407
Roth, 318, 328
Rough, 387, 394
Roughness, 420
ruci, 580
Rudimentary element, 87
Rudra, 627
Rug-viniścaya, 506
rūkṣa, 387, 394, 416, 419. 421, 422, 464
rūpa, 440
rūpatva, 436
rūpin, 232
rūraḥ, 347n. 4
Ṛg-Veda, 326, 402, 403, 460, 567, 623, 626
Ṛg-Vedic, 350; hymns, 325; sacrifices, 326
Ṛju-vivaraṇa, 60n.
Ṛk, 318, 455, 613
Ṛkṣagrīva, 349
ṛṣi, 344n. 2, 460, 628
ṛtavaḥ, 339n.

sabhāga-santati-vicchedākhyaṃ, 24n.
Sabhā-parva, 634
sac-chāstra, 309
Saccidānanda, 91
Sacral nerve, 412
Sacral plexus, 414
Sacrifice, 445n., 511, 515, 523, 552, 559, 563, 566, 568, 584, 588-590, 595, 598, 599, 610, 613, 623, 626
Sacrificial, 50n., 576; actions, 575; duties, 553, 559; performance, 608 sacro-coccygeal plexus, 414
Sacrum, 332n., 333n.
sad-asadbhyāṃ vilakṣaṇam, 146
Sadānanda, 63, 266
Sadānanda Kāśmiraka, 66, 225
Sadānanda Vyāsa, 517
Sadāśiva, 251
Sadāśivendra Sarasvatī, 95n.
sa-deha-muktatā, 283
sad-vṛtta, 473, 489
Sages, 461, 628
Saguṇa-brahma, 250
sahabhūtam kāryam, 214
Sahadeva, 503
saha-kaṇṭhikā, 336n.
sahakāri, 184
sahakāri-kāraṇa, 126
Sahapāla Deva, 498
sahasrāra, 412, 415
sahasrāra-cakra, 415
sahopalambha-niścaya, 56
sahopalambha-niyama, 30n., 40
sahopalambha-niyamād, 30n.
Saint, 285, 489, 584, 590
Saintly persons, 305
Saline, 417, 419
Salt, 416
Salvation, 263, 355
sama, 272

sama-dhātoḥ, 382n.
sama-pittānila-kapha, 389
samatva, 527, 596
sama-vāta-pitta-śleṣman, 390n.
samavāya, 46, 171, 210, 211, 215, 217-219, 223, 432, 436; relation, 436
samavāyi-kāraṇa, 165, 420
samaveta-samavāya, 436
samaya-viruddha, 449
sama-yoga-vāhin, 372
samādhāna, 536, 583
samādhi, 28, 290, 528, 530, 531, 565n., 583, 588
samāna, 86, 298, 301, 338, 387
sambandhi-svabhāva-janya, 164
sambandhi-svabhāva-śrita, 164
sambhāvanā-bhāṣya, 119
Sameness, 596; in all situations of life, 596; in blame, 596; in joy, 596; in praise, 596; in sorrow, 596
samīcīna, 431
samuccaya, 454, 457
samudga, 333
samutthāna, 461
Samyagbodhendra Saṃyamin, 60n.
samyagjñānādhigama, 287
samyak, 156
samyak-paricchitti, 154
saṃbhava, 448
saṃbhāṣā, 441
saṃbhinnobhaya-rūpatvāt, 120
saṃghāta, 540
saṃgraha, 56
saṃmharṣa, 441
Saṃhitā-kalpa, 329n.
Saṃhitā-vidhi, 329n.
Saṃjñā, 26
Saṃkalpa, 435
Saṃkalpa-nagaraṃ, 269
Saṃkalpa-puruṣa, 269
Saṃkarṣaṇa, 628, 631, 633, 635, 636, 638
Saṃkhyā, 431
Saṃkṣepa-śārīraka, 13n., 19, 50n., 53n., 60, 62, 64, 98, 127-129, 133, 248, 257n.
Saṃkṣepa-śārīraka-sambandhokti, 61n.
Saṃkṣepa-śārīraka-sāra-saṃgraha,134, 259
Saṃprāpti, 464n.
Saṃsarga, 395n.
Saṃsāra, 51
Saṃsāra-taraṇī, 267
Saṃskāra, 75, 420, 431
Saṃsṛti, 270, 275
Saṃśaya, 446, 454, 457, 583
Saṃśaya-sama, 444n., 446n., 450, 452
Saṃślesa, 358
Saṃśleṣa-pratyaya, 238
Saṃvara, 583
Saṃvatsarāḥ, 339n.
Saṃvedanamaya, 296
Saṃvid, 73, 172, 231, 239, 271, 299
Saṃvit-karma, 78
Saṃvit-spanda, 294
Saṃvit-svarūpa-bhūto bhedaḥ, 74
Saṃvṛta, 5
Saṃvṛtāsaṃvṛtām, 406n.
Saṃvṛti, 4, 25; as *mithyā-saṃvṛti* and *loka-saṃvṛti*, 4; its meanings, 3
Saṃvṛti-satya, 4
Saṃyamana, 519
Saṃyoga, 46, 182, 223, 435
Saṃyoga-puruṣa, 484
Saṃyoga-vibhāga, 431
Saṃyogin, 46
Saṃyogi-puruṣa, 429
Saṃyukta-samavāya, 436
Saṃyukta-samaveta-samavāya, 436
Sanaka-saṃhitā, 507
sandhāya saṃbhāṣā, 441
sandhi, 333n. 2
Sandhyākara, 502
san kāsaḥ, 450
san kṣayaḥ, 450
sannipāta, 395n.
sannyāsa, 487
sannyāsin, 291
santānikā, 369
santhavaṃ, 580
Saṅgha, 536
Saṅghabhadra, 197
Saṅgo, 580
Saṅkalpa, 86, 305
Saṅkalpa-jāgara, 308
Saṅkhāra, 581
Saṅkhyā, 223
Saṅkoca, 407n.
sañcaya, 477
saraṇāt śirāḥ, 404
Sarasvatī, 413
sarasvalī, 412
sarga, 204
Sarpa-veda, 319n.
sarva-bīja, 25
Sarva-darśana-saṃgraha, 246
Sarva-darśana-siddhānta-saṃgraha, 63
Sarva-dhara, 503
sarva-doṣa-prakopaṇa, 485

sarva-gala, 553
sarva-jaḍopādāna-bhūtā, 233
sarva-jña, 122, 224
Sarvajñanārāyaṇa, 66n.
Sarvajña-pītha, 113
Sarvajña Sarasvatī, 64
sarvajñatā, 25
Sarvajña Viśveśa, 63
Sarvajñātma Bhagavat, 61n.
Sarvajñātma Muni, 12, 19, 50n., 54, 58, 60-62, 66. 83, 98, 121, 127-129, 133, 134, 257, 258; *ajñāna* and truth, 131; *ajñāna* in relation with Brahman, 129 ff.; association of *ajñāna* in, 133; commentaries on his *Saṃkṣepa-śārīraka*, 133, 134; difference of his view with that of Maṇḍana, 98; his date, 129; his view of the causality of *māyā*, 12; nature of *ajñāna*, 129; nature of Brahman, 131; Vedānta and Buddhism in, 133
sarva-pratyayāṇāṃ yathārthatvam, 171
Sarva-siddhānta-rahasya-ṭīkā, 63
sarva-srotāṃsi ayana-bhūtāni, 404
sarva-tantra-siddhānta, 446
Sarvato-bhadra, 517
Sarvāṅga-sundarī, 506
sarvāpahnava, 306
Sarvārtha-siddhi, 138n.
sarve bhāvā amutpannāḥ, 192
sarvendriya-param, 397
sat, 223, 435
sataś cetyāṃśa-cetanāt, 272
satata-kriyā, 431
sati, 583
sati-saṃvara, 583
sat-kārya-vāda, 45, 190, 198-200, 551, 552, 556, 603; its criticisms by Kamalśīla and Santarakṣita, 198 ff.
sattā, 11
satthakamma, 320
sattva, 83, 85, 210, 222, 226, 237, 289, 352, 359, 365, 372, 384, 427, 428, 433, 488, 508, 532, 539, 546, 631
sattva-saṃśuddhi, 595
sattva stuff, 242
sattva-śuddhi, 512
satya, 4, 87, 446, 589, 595
Satyabodha, 113
satya-vacana, 589, 634
Satyavān, 357n. 1
satya-yuga, 477
Saubhāgya-vardhinī, 91
Saukṣmya, 367
Sauksṃyāt, 407
saumanasyani 344
saumya, 365
saumyatva, 598
Saunāgas (grammarians), 629
Sautrāntikas, 31n.
sa-vikalpa, 123
sa-vyubhicāra, 448, 451n.
sa-vyabhicāru hetu, 451n.
sādhaka, 385
sadhana, 133
sādharmya-vaidharmya-sama, 444n. 4
sādhāraṇa, 416, 590
sādhāraṇa-dharma, 589, 590, 599
sādhāraṇatva, 182
sādhūpadiṣṭa-mārgeṇa, 291, 292
sādhya, 160, 443, 446n.
sadhya-sama, 451n., 452
sādhyābhāvavad-avṛttitvam, 139
Sāhasāṅka-carita, 499
Sāketa (city), 629
sākṣi consciousness, 246
sākṣin, 61, 177
Sāma, 318
sāmagrī, 185, 189
Sāman, 613
Sāmarthyātiśaya, 112
sāmānya, 432, 463
sāmānya-chala, 449, 450
sāmānya-pratyāsatti, 160
sāmānyato-dṛṣṭa, 464, 465, 467n.
Sāmin, 66n.
Sāṃkhya, 41, 43, 48, 85, 103n., 116, 123, 133, 190, 198-201, 208, 261, 279, 289, 301, 339, 349, 354, 364, 366, 382n., 385n., 387, 433, 453n., 460, 478, 479, 483, 527, 531-535, 538, 540, 543, 545, 546, 551, 552, 554-556, 575, 603. 604, 640, 641; arguments, 199: its general criticisms by Kamalaśila, 201; philosophy, 317n., 499; physics, 317; *prakṛti*, 85; refutation of its soul theory by Kamalaśila, 208; system, 427
Sāṃkhya and Nyāya, on the theory of doṣas, 382, 384n.
Sāṃkhya-kārikā, 92, 122, 134, 287, 289n., 303, 354, 440, 467n.
Sāṃkhya pariṇāma, criticisms of, by Sāntarakṣita and Kamalaśila, 197 ff.
Sāṃkhya-purvacana-bhāṣya, 303, 355, 357n. 1
Sāṃkhya-sūtra, 289, 433
Sāṃkhya-tattva-kaumudī, 52n., 356n.
Sāṃkhya-Yoga, 302, 303, 361, 365n., 483, 636; its doctrine of subtle body, 354, 355;

its idea of emancipation, 287, 289; *prāṇa* in, 302, 303
Sāṃkhyic, 362
Sāṃkhyist, 190, 197, 199, 270, 603
Sāṃrājya-siddhi, 64
sāndra, 419n.
sāra, 419n.
sārajjanā, 580
sārajjitattam, 580
Sāraṅga, 142
Sārasvata-prakriyā, 220
sārāgo, 580
Sārārtha, 114
sātmya, 359
sāttvika, 428, 435,546
Sātvata, 630-633, 636, 637
Sātyaki, 630
Sātyaki-tantra, 507
Sāyaṇa, 91, 215, 247, 326n., 326, 328, 335n., 336, 337, 339, 340, 346n., 348, 402n., 403n., 403
Scapula, 333n.
Scattering, 393n.
Sceptical, 582n.
Scheme of life, 484
Scholastic, 12, 143; logicism, 143
Scholasticism, 138
Science, 84; of life, 322
Scriptural command, 608
Scriptural injunction, 263
Scriptural text, 291
Scriptures, 131, 292, 309
Seal, Dr Sir B. N., 415n., 564n., 591n.
Seasons, 454
Seat of consciousness, 351
Second moon, 30
Secretions, 334n., 379, 381, 386, 393-395. 402
Secretive aspect, 386
Secretory character, 393n.
Secretory currents, 403
Seed, 184, 213, 271
Seeds of memory, 215
Seeming appearances, 271
Self, 1, 9, 18, 24, 26, 28, 38, 39, 48, 75, 78, 82, 84, 87, 116, 129, 171, 175, 180, 207, 208, 223, 226, 237n., 242, 247, 249, 257, 359-361, 400, 409, 428-430, 435, 452, 453, 468, 519-521, 539, 549, 552, 597, 602, 604, 612
Self-abnegation, 263
Self-alienation, 277
Self-cognizing, 85
Self-conscious, 271; ego, 275
Self-consciousness, 25, 78, 208, 224, 272
Self-contained, 16; state, 276
Self-contentedness, 556
Self-contradiction, 142
Self-control, 279, 282, 321, 435, 515, 523, 575. 583, 589, 598, 599
Self-controlled, 489
Self-criticism, 315
Self-dependence, 19
Self-directed, 272; consciousness, 272
Self-dissociated, 140
Self-evident, 15, 18, 563
Self-flashing, 272
Self-gain, 591
Self-good, 473
Self-hood, 28
Self-identity, 39, 76-78, 82
Self-illumination, 171
Self-interest, 548, 567, 591, 592, 598
Selfish interest, 566
Selfishness, 587
Self-knowledge, 261, 276, 435, 511, 516, 575, 582
Self-love, 28, 483, 591
Self-luminosity, 81, 84, 120
Self-luminous, 9, 75, 78, 81, 145, 194, 229-231, 249; consciousness, 234
Self-manifesting, 9, 79
Self-meditation, 544
Self-mortifications, 547
Self-ostentation, 485
Self-perception, 77, 84
Self-persistence, 77, 78
Self-realization, 532, 600, 620
Self-realized state, 597
Self-recognition, 224
Self-reflecting, 271
Self-restrained, 321
Self-revealed, 175, 207, 231
Self-revealing, 79, 83, 85, 120, 127, 180, 226, 231, 253; consciousness, 38, 173, 175, 177
Self-revelation, 73, 126, 127, 149, 171, 172, 174
Self-same, 112
Self-satisfied, 597
Self-seeking, 591
Self-shining, 17
Self-shiningness, 41
Self-surrendering, 538
Self-thinking, 271
Self-validity, 246; of knowledge, 246
Selling, 589

Semen, 351, 354, 358, 365, 369, 375, 377n., 385, 404, 411, 421, 433; channels, 405
Seminal fluid, 375-378
Semi-statical creation, 272n.
Senart, E., 641
Sensation, 55, 311; of smell, 399
Sense, 26, 40, 174, 176, 223, 276, 294, 302, 339, 401, 420, 427, 429, 430, 468, 474, 570, 575
Sense-affections, 597
Sense-attraction, 526, 569
Sense-channels, 102n.
Sense-cognition, 67, 84, 407, 428, 435
Sense-contact, 159, 167, 175, 177, 436, 581
Sense-control, 529, 536, 568, 571, 573, 586, 589, 596, 599
Sense-data, 39, 67, 69, 203, 207, 216, 409
Sense-desire, 598
Sense-enjoyments, 84
Sense-experiences, 28
Sense-faculties, 26, 28, 67
Sense-functioning, 28
Sense-gates, 539
Sense-gratification, 595
Sense-illusions, 6
Sense-impressions, 407, 409
Sense-knowledge, 29, 239, 414
Sense-modifications, 26
Sense-object, 26, 72, 87, 89, 207, 223, 237, 238, 247, 373, 374, 387, 400, 409, 428, 435, 540
Sense-organ, 159, 215, 245, 311, 360. 361, 367, 381, 387, 388, 417, 420, 427, 600
Sense-perception, 26, 28, 34, 134, 192
Sense-pleasure, 599
Sense-property, 229, 419n., 420
Sense-quality, 414
Sense-uncontrollability, 569
Sensible, 32, 33, 430
Sensory consciousness, 416
Sensory *dhamani*, 409
Sensory nerves, 407
Sentence, 272
Separateness, 171, 187, 223, 420
Separation, 223, 431
Sequence, 23
Series, 26, 30n.
Serpent Power, 415
Sesamum, 112
seśvara-Sāṃkhya, 555
Sex-attraction, 593
Sex-continence, 491, 547, 589, 598
Sex Joy, 378
Sex-relation, 581n.
Sex-strength, 320
Sex-union, 593
Shama Sastry, Dr, 508
Shamefulness, 28
Sharp, 421
Sharpness, 420, 422n., 426
Sheath of knowledge, 86
Shivering, 347n., 350
Shoots, 184, 195
Shoulder-blade, 332
sibbanī, 580
siddham, 455
Siddha-sāra-saṃhitā, 503
Siddha-yoga, 498, 499, 505, 507
siddhānta, 446, 449
Siddhanta-bindu, 89n., 260
Siddhānta-bindu-nyāya-ratnāvalī, 91
Siddhānta-bindu-sandīpana, 91
Siddhānta-bindu-śīkara, 252
Siddhānta-bindu-ṭīkā, 260n.
Siddhānta-candrikā, 506
Siddhānta-dīpa, 133
Siddhānta-dīpikā, 19, 66n.
Siddhānta-leśa, 11, 12, 19, 51, 54, 56, 58, 61, 83, 249n.
Siddhānta-leśa-saṃgraha, 252
Siddhānta-muktāvalī, 12, 19, 20n., 2565n., 258n., 259, 305n.; its view that *māyā* alone is the cause of world-appearance; and Brahman the basis of *māyā,* 12
Siddhānta-nidāna, 394n.
Siddhānta-nyāya-ratna-pradīpikā, 91
Siddhānta-ratnākara, 252
Siddhānta-siddhāñjana, 64
Siddhānta-tattva-bindu, 63, 91, 259
Siddhānta-tattva-bindu-ṛtkā, 63
Siddhānta-viveka, 59
Siddhi-kāṇḍa, 100, 101, 113
Siddhi-sthāna, 416, 496, 500
Significance, 588
sikatāvatī, 338n. 3
silāñjālā, 347n.
Silver, 43, 130, 156
Similarity, 151, 154
Simile, 30n., 384
Simultaneity, 180
Simultaneous, 36n., 452n.; production, 205
Simultaneously, 30, 31, 36n., 205
Sin, 284, 471, 477, 483, 492, 516, 592, 608
Sincerity, 547, 586, 590n., 595, 596, 598, 599; of mind, 589
sineho, 580

Sinful, 477
Sinner, 597
Sītārāma, 95n.
Skanda, 123
Skanda-purāṇa, 458
skandha, 67, 68, 332, 526n.
Skeleton, 334
Skill, 586, 590n.
Skin, 369, 378, 385, 405, 421, 428
Skull, 324, 411, 412n.
Slander, 582n.
Sleep, 297, 302
Sleepiness, 435
Slim, 393
Slipperiness, 420, 426
Slippery, 421
Slow, 394
Smaller intestine, 392
Smaller self, 527
Smartness, 590n.
Smell, 223, 272, 385, 420, 428
Smoky, 184, 476
Smooth, 393n., 416
Smoothness, 382, 420
Smṛti, 62, 275, 276, 435. 599, 640
smṛti-bhraṃśa, 486
smṛti-śāstra, 512
smṛti-vibhraṃśa, 485
Snake, 8, 43, 85
Snake-charms, 326
snāva, 336, 403
snāyu, 297, 331n., 364n., 365n., 371, 411
sneha, 382, 516, 580
snigdha, 416, 419n., 421, 422
Social order, 593
Society, 593
Sockets, 333n.
Soft, 393n., 421
Softness, 420
Solar, 167, 171; vibrations, 180, 181
soma, 352, 385, 388, 419, 499
soma-cakra, 415
Sorcery, 350
Sorrow, 287, 343, 362, 485, 545, 588, 596-598, 618
Soul, 51, 205, 272, 286, 352, 356, 360, 362, 366, 400, 415, 416, 420, 428, 432, 433, 474, 618
Soul theory (Kumārila), criticized by Kamalaśīla, 206 ff.
Soul theory (Nyāya), criticized by Kamalaśīla, 205, 206
Sound, 28, 69, 209, 414, 428, 446n., 451n., 452
Sound-cognition, 207
Sound-potential, 272
Sour, 386, 416
Sourasenoi, 633
Source, 417, 479n.
South India, 61
Space, 194, 223, 420, 430, 445n.
Space-determinations, 26
Space-locations, 33
spanda, 272n., 282, 294, 304
spanda-sakti, 120, 297
spandāspandātmaka, 270
sparśa, 223, 272
Spatial, 18; difference, 431; extension, 29n.
Special capacity, 201
Special efficiency, 112
Special power, 46
Specific, 416, 436; agency, 419; caste-duty, 590, 591; duty, 589, 590, 599; ignorance, 89; nature, 417; par-ticulars, 171; peculiarities, 215; purpose, 419; qualities, 160, 217; relation, 36
Speculation, 435, 479n.
Speech, 278, 294, 388, 394, 547; organ, 403
Sphoṭa-siddhi, 101n.
Spider, 85, 205
Spider's webs, 205
Spinal column, 333n., 411, 412
Spinal cord, 412, 414-416
Spine, 412n.
Spiral, 414
Spirit, 270, 327
Spiritual categories, 545
Spleen, 334, 405
Spring, 390, 431
Springs of action, 479, 482
spṛhā, 482
srutas, 338, 403-408, 411
Stabilized, 583
Stage, 272, 275
stana, 332
Star, 388
State, 272, 289; of deep sleep, 283
Statical, 270
Stcherbatsky, 67n., 68n., 71n., 192n.
Steadiness, 382, 420, 488, 589, 595; of mind, 574
Steady, 573
Sternum, 332n.
sthairya, 488
Sthairya-vicāraṇa, 145

sthavırāntra, 336
sthālakas, 332n. 3
sthālakārbudas, 333n. 3
sthāna-vijñapti, 26
sthānāni, 392
sthāpanā, 528
sthāpanā, 442
sthira, 278, 419n.
Sthiramati, 21, 24, 25n.
sthira-pratyaya, 277
Sthira-siddhi-dūṣaṇa, 56
sthita-dhī, 514, 573
sthita-prājña, 285. 573
sthiti, 20, 195, 204, 266
sthūla, 393n., 419n.
stimita-gambhīra, 267
Stomach, 385, 386, 392, 421
Stone, 597
Stormy, 476
Straightness of conduct, 596
Strength, 381, 392
strī-karmāni, 344
Student, 589
Studies in the Medicine of Ancient India, 324n., 329n., 332n.
Study, 589, 595, 599
Stuff, to; of world-objects, 40
Suali, L., 464n.
Sub-conscious, 24, 38, 39; impressions, 38. 289
Subheṣaja, 320n.
subhiṣuktama, 340
Subhūti Gautama, 368
Subject, 31, 33, 36, 40, 101
Subject-consciousness, 172, 242
Subjective, 25, 28, 207, 215, 234, 440, 592, 608; act, 226; character, 608; cognition, 21; conscience, 608; ego, 272; experiences, 117, 172; ideas, 24, 55; idealism, 55; ignorance, 89; illumination, 237; mental, 18; same-ness, 596; states, 172; thought, 272
Subjectively, 249, 269
Subjectivistic, 245
Subjectivity, 10
Subject-object awareness, 33, 38
Subject-object consciousness, 28
Subject-object knowledge, 289, 308
Subject-objectless, 271, 275, 314
Subject-object relation, 101, 121, 166, 168, 175, 176
Subodhinī, 63, 84. 86n., 133, 517
Subrahmanya, 93
Subrahmanya Agnıcın Makhindra, 831n.
Substance, 21, 54, 59, 135, 165, 182, 185, 187, 192, 198, 215, 216, 219, 222, 223, 233, 302, 417-420, 422, 430-432, 435
Substanceless, 18, 269
Substance-stuff, 13
Substantial, 393n.
Substantiality, 44, 55
Substantive, 215; basis, 26; reality, 23
Substitution-meditation, 524, 528, 559, 569
Substraturn, 21, 223, 224
Subtle, 198, 440; states, 283
Subtle body, 86, 283, 351, 356. 409n.; in Sāṃkhya-yoga, Vaiśeṣıka and Nyāya, 354-356; agreement of the Vedānta and Caraka, 364
Subtler, 429
Success, 597
Succession, 23, 180, 206
Successive processes, 436
Sudhīndra Yatī, 517
Suffering, 275, 285, 429, 435, 471, 559, 608
Sufficient cause, 20
Sugar-cane, 421
Suhṛt, 441
Suitability, 431
Suitable, 431
sukha, 25, 321, 431, 492
sukha-duḥkhe yugapaj janyete, 105
sukham āyuḥ, 321
Sukhaprakāśa Muni, 67, 99, 134, 171n.
sukha-rúpa, 249
sukha-saṅga, 539
Sumati, 198
Summer, 381, 390, 431
Sun, 385, 582, 612
Sunāmā (demon), 349
Suparṇa, 628
Superficial changes, 28
Super-imposed, 237
Super-imposition, 172, 240, 245
Superior, 205
Superiority, 431, 468n.
Super-person, 555, 616, 621
Super-personality, 557, 611, 612
Support, 165; of *māyā*, 52
Supposition, 20, 36
Supreme bliss, 529
Supreme essence, 18
sura, 128
Suranandī, 499
Surat, 189
Sureśvarācārya, 2n., 19, 53, 55, 59, 60, 66, 90-92, 94-100, 113-117, 121, 128, 129, 169n.,

171 n, 220, 227, 248; *karma* and emancipation in, 114; *karma* and *jñāna*, 115; nature of *ajñāna*, 116, 117; nature of self and self-realization, 115, 116
Surgery, 320, 385
Suriya, 628
susūkṣmān, 399
Suśruta, 304, 317, 554-324, 329n., 331n., 332n., 339n., 351n., 352n., 354,368,369, 384n., 385-388, 389n., 399, 401n., 405, 407, 408n., 409, 411, 185n., 421–426, 433, 454, 478, 493-496, 500, 505, 507; his de-scription of the apertures of the *dhamants,* 408; his description of the function of the *dhamanis,* 408ff.; on *dhātu-mala,* 386; his view re-garding the relation of *dhamanis* to cognition, 409 ff.; his view re-gard-ing strás and *dhamants*, 407; his view that the cognitive and conative nerves are attached to the brain, 399; his view that foṇita is a doṣa, 384
Suśruta-candrikā, 495, 499
Suśruta-saṃhitā, 298n., 317, 320n., 321,324,365n., 367n., 371n., 386n., 390n., 392., 399n., 401n., 407n., 433n., 440n., 454n., 455, 493-500
Suśruta school, 336
Suśruta-Sotra-sthāna, 421n.
suṣirāḥ, 411
suṣumṇā, 339, 412-414. 529, 530
suṣumṇā nāḍī, 402
suṣupta, 278, 305
suṣupta-sudṛśa-sthiti, 305
suṣuptavat, 283
suṣupti, 267, 401
Sutala, 87
sūkṣma, 355, 387, 393, 419
sūkṣma-deha, 354
sūkṣma-śarīra, 86, 87
sūkṣmāḥ-śirāḥ, 403
Sūryapaṇḍita, 517
Sūṣā, 337
Sūṣāṇi, 337n. 4
Sūta-saṃhitā, 290
Sūtra-bhāṣya-vyākhyāna, 94n.
Sitras, 44, 45, 47, 51
Sūtra-sthāna, 384, 385, 427
sūtrātman, 87, 247
svabhāva, 4, 102, 433, 478
svabhāvātiśaya, 199
sva-dharma, 513, 586
svakāraṇa-sattā-samavāya, 47
sva-lakṣaṇa, 192
sva-māna, 379
svapna, 305
svapna-jāgara, 308
svapna-nara, 308
sva-prakāśa, 79, 171, 226
sva-prakāśatā, 125
sva-prakāśā cit, 126
Svar (world), 87
svarūpa-bheda, 149
Svarūpa-nirṇaya-ṭīkā, 222
sva-samjñā, 454
sva-samvedana-mātrakam, 271
sva-samvin-nairapekṣeṇa sphuraṇam, 226
svastyayana, 322, 326
svasyāpi svena vedyaṭvāpātāt, 174
svataḥ-prāmāṇya, 246
sva-viṣaya-jñāna-jananam, 37
sva-vyāghāta, 142
svayaṃbhū-liṅga, 414
svayaṃ-prakāśa, 172
Svayaṃprakāśa, 64, 94, 220
Svayaṃprakāśa Yati, 91
Svayaṃprakāśa Yogindra, 66n.
Svayamprakāśānanda, 64
svābhāvikaḥ sambandhaḥ, 162
stābhanna-kārya-janakatvam upādā-natuam, 52
svādhıṣṭhāna-cakra, 414
svādu, 417
Svāmidāsa, 499
Svāmikumāra, 502
Svāmīndrapūrna, 60n.
Svānubhūti-prakāśa, 63
svārtha, 480
Svāima-yoga-pradīpa, 66n.
svāvidyayā, 97
Sweet, 279, 360, 379, 381, 393n., 404, 416-419. 421, 426n., 427
Sweetness, 421
Syllogism, 138–141, 435
Symbolic sacrifice, 634
Symbolic syllables, 582
Symbols, 393
Sympathy, 285, 596
Symptoms, 340, 343, 373, 384n., 392, 393, 405n.
Syncretistic, 62; works, 63
Synonymous, 405
Syrup, 417
System, 437, 612
Systematic study, 1
Systematized, 583
Śabara, 100, 197

śabda, 403, 438, 445n., 446
śabda-brahma, 413n.
Śubda-nirṇaya, 119n.
śabda-nyāyārtha, 457
sabdatva, 436
śabdartha, 215
śaitya, 422n.
Śaiva, 62, 250, 251, 517; authorities, 304; commentary, 250; philosophy, 315
Śaiva-bhāṣya, 250, 252
śaiva-kalpa-druma, 252
Śaivism, 56
śakadhumaje (demon), 349
śaktayuh, 280
śakti, 9, 11, 25, 46, 51, 120, 201, 247, 250, 421, 422
śaktimat, 51
śaluna, 345
śalya, 320, 455, 494
Śalya-tantram, 385n., 495
śuma, 519, 577, 589n.
Śambūka, 590, 591
Śaṅkara, 2, 5-10, 12, 24, 29, 31-34, 40, 43-45, 47-51, 53, 55, 59, 89-91, 93, 98-100, 102, 106, 114, 115, 117, 121, 125, III, 129, 138, 143, 174, 197, 198, 217, 219, 225, 250-253, 263, 266, 284, 289, 301-303, 309, 310, 312, 315, 334n., 362, 401, 403, 511, 512, 516, 517, 521, 523, 524, 528, 529. 532-535, 553, 557, 577, 582, 588, 591, 621, 640; and some Buddhists differ regarding the ontology of illusion, 5; attempts to prove that his philosophy was realistic, 2; *bhedāhhedu* interpretation prior to, 49; contradicts his own view on idealism, 32 did not elaborate the exact nature of the causality of avidyd or of Brahman, 12; emphasizes that waking experience is as faise as dream experience in Gauḍapada's commentary, 32, 33; his assertion that the world-appearance is mere illusion is dogmatic, as also the doctrine that the self is the only ground on which all illusions are imposed, 9; his commentary cannot satisfactorily convince that the *sūtras* professed unqualified monism, 48; his criticism of the atomic theory, 217 ff.; his criticism of the theory of *samavāya*, 218; his definition of il-lusion, 5, 7; his dialectic arguments, 217 ff.; his explanation as to the illusory creation by ignorance: in-terpretation of his explanation by his other followers, 9; his explanation of the causal theory on realistic lines. as against Nyāya, 45-47; his four important followers and the divergence of their views, 54, 55; his idealism compared with that of *Yoga-vāsiṣtha* and Buddhist idealism, 310 ff.; his interpretation of the *Brahma-sūtra* and the Upaniṣads as reconciliation of the pantheistic and dua-listic tendencies, 2; his interpretation of illusion in Gauḍapāda's *Kāri*-kā, 7, his realistic interpretation of the Brahma-*sūtras* with parenthetic reservation, how far justifiable, 45; his refutation of Buddhist idealism, 301, 312; his refutation of Buddhistic idealism, 31; his refutation of the charge of the incompatibility of the production of the impure world from the pure Brahman, 43; his refutation of the Sāṃkhya criticism of Vedānta, 41, 43; his two different analogies regarding the production of the world from Brahman, 43; his view of the *naḍīs* and the heart, 401; his views regarding sird and *dhumuni,* 401; his works and followers, 89-94: how far he is justified in sometimes taking *pariṇāma* analogies and sometimes the view of magical creation, 44; originator of Vedānta dialectics, 188; special nature of his dialectic as distinguished from that of Śrtharsa and Citsukha, 219, 220
Śaṅkara-bhāṣya, 12, 119, 125, 290
Śaṅkara-dig-vijaya, 94, 99, 129
Śaṅkara Miśra, 119n., 145n., 415
Śaṅkara school, 3, 34, 51, 72
Śaṅkarasvāmin, 198
Śaṅkara Vedānta, 12, 18, 19, 39, 40, 128, 171, 246
Śaṅkara-vnjaya, 128
Śaṅkarānanda, 94, 99, 247, 517
Śaṅkā, 162
Śaṅkha, 339n., 399
Śaṅkhapāṇi, 95, 100, 102n., 104, 105, 108, 412, 413
śarat, 390
śarīra-chidra, 405n.
śariri, 352n. 4
śarku (demon), 349
Śaśadhara Ācārya, 62
Satapatha-brahmana, 324, 332, 336, 429, 460, 494, 567, 623-626
śauca, 589, 595
Śaunaka, 368
Śaunaka-tantra, 507
Śaunakīya, 328
śaurya, 382, 431, 589n.

śābdi *bhāvanā*, 559, 560
Śākalya, 291
śākhā, 328
śākhā-nāḍīnām, 230n. 2
Śākunteya, 416
śālākya, 320, 494
Sālākya-tantra, 495
Śālikanātha, 169n., 287
Sali-stamba-sūtra, 358
śānta, 270, 271, 326
Santarakṣita, 29, 32, 36n., 67n., 197, 198, 201, 203, 205, 206, 208-216, 437, 438; his argument against the Upanıṣadic view similar to that of Śaṅkara, 32
śānti, 526n., 595
Sānti-kalpa, 328
Śānti-śataka, 537n. 1
Śāṇḍilya-sūtra-ṭīkā, 259
śārada, 346n.
Śārira, 408n., 409n., 411n., 484, 547
Śartra-brāhmaṇa, 290
Śārīraka-bhāṣya, 64, 284n.
Śārīraka-bhāṣya-prakaṭārtha, 56
Śārīraka-bhāṣya-ṭikā, 222
Śārtraka-mīṃāmsā-bhāṣya, 64, 90, 92
Śārīraka-mīmāmsā-nyāya-saṃgraha, 30n., 94
Śārīraka-mīmāmsā-saṃgraha, 94n.
Sūrīraka-mīmāṃsā – sūtra – siddhānta-kaumudī, 94n.
Śārīraka-nyāya-maṇimālā, 94n.
Śarīra-padminī, 507
Śārīra-sthāna, 329n.
Śārṅgadhara, 334n., 380n., 381n., 507; *his view of mala*, 380
śāstra, 292, 294, 449, 520
Śāstra-darpaṇa, 94, 119, 125n.
Śāstra-prakāśikā, 95, 222
Śāstra-siddhānta-leśa-ṭīkā, 259
śāstrāntara, 465
śesa, 467n.
Śeṣagovinda, 63
Śeṣanrsiṃha, 236
Śeṣa Śārṅgadhara, 138, 225
śeṣavat, 464, 465, 467n.
Śikhāmaṇi, 61, 62, 85n., 239
śikṣā, 637
Śikṣā, 319n.
Śikṣā-samuccaya, 584, 598
Śiṅghana, 142
Śipiviṣṭa, 623
śırası ṣaṭ, 339n.
śiras-tālv-antara-gatam, 397
śirā, 296, 336, 338, 371, 399, 401, 403, 405-408, 411, 413
śirā-saraṇı-koṭare, 296
Śıṣya-hitaiṣinī, 145n.
Śiva, 94n., 250, 306
Śivadayālu Śrīdharasvāmin, 517
Śivadāsa, 424, 502, 503, 507
Śiva-karnāmṛta, 252
Śivalāla Śarman, 91
Śiva-līlārṇava, 251
Śiva-purāṇa-tāmasatva-khaṇḍana, 252
Śivarāma, 66n., 119
śiva-sūtra-vimarśinī, 304n.
Śiva-śakti-siddhi, 145
Śiva-tattva-viveka, 252
Śivāditya, 169n.
Śivāditya Miśra, 142
Śivādvaita-mrnaya, 252
śivānanda-laharī, 252
Śıvānanda-laharī-candrikā, 252
Śivānanda Yati, 66n.
Śivārcana-candrikā, 252
Śivārka-maṇi-dīpikā, 251, 252
Śivopādhyaya, 304
Śıvotkarṣa-candrikā, 252
Śivotkarṣa-mañjarī, 252
śīghra, 394
śīla, 536, 583, 584, 588
śīrsa, 396
śīrṣaktı, 344, 348, 396
śirṣāmaya, 348
śīta, 387, 390, 394, 416, 419, 421
śīta-vīrya, 421
śtoṣma-varṣa-lakṣaṇāḥ, 374n.
śītoṣmānilaiḥ, 366
ślakṣṇa, 419n.
śleṣma, 348
śleṣma-dharā, 369
śteṣmala, 389
śleṣman, 320, 327, 344, 372, 379, 381, 382, 385-388. 390, 392, 393n., 401, 404. 407, 432, 456
śleṣma-prakṛti, 382, 389
śleṣmā, 348
ślıṣ. 385
śloka, 265
Śloka-sthāna, 457
Śloka-vārttika, 499
śoci, 345
śoṇita, 351, 364n., 384, 385, 390n., 408
śrāddha, 339, 546, 576
śrāddha, 327
Śrima (demon), 349
śritāḥ, 396
Śrī, 342
Śrībrahma, 499

Śrī-darpaṇa, 145n.
Śrīdhara, 56, 169n., 305n., 356, 480, 519, 521, 524n., 528, 529n., 532, 539, 553, 557, 564
Śrīharṣa, 28, 59, 61, 62, 64, 66, 95, 106, 119, 138, 143-149, 151-153, 156, 158-160, 162, 165-169, 188, 189, 194, 196-198, 220, 223, 250, 286; awareness and its object cannot be similar, 154; Buddhist precursors of pre-Śaṅkara Vedānta dialectic, Kamalasīla and Śāntarakṣita, 197 ff.; compared and contrasted with Nāgārjuna, 196, 197; his assertion of indefinability of all appearances is a direct challenge to Nyāya-Vaiśeṣıka, which thinks that all that is knowable is definable, 146; his criticism of "being," 164; his criticism of the Buddhist definition of right cognition, 157; his criticism of the definition of "invariable concomitance," 162, 164; his criticism of the nature of concomitance (*vyāpti*), 160, 161; his criticism of non-being, 164; his criticisms often refer to Nyāya definitions rather than to Nyāya thought, 168, his criticism of the Nyāya definition of "cause," 166; his criticism of the Nyāya definition of right cognition, 153 ff.; his criticism of the Nyāya theory of relation, 166; his criticism of the possibility of knowing the class-concepts, 160, 161; his criticism of substance and quality, 165; his criticism of *tarka,* 161, 162; his criticism of Udayana, 162; his date, works and followers, 144, 145; his dialectic compared with that of Nāgārjuna, 188; his dialectic distinguished from that of Śaṅkara, 219, 220; his difference with the Mādhyamika position, 194; his difference with Vācaspati and Maṇḍana, 116; his ontologic argument for the existence of Brahman, 148; his refutation of analogy, 164; his refutation of "difference," 149; his refutation of the category of "difference," 149 ff.; his refutation of the definition of cause, 165-167; his refutation of the definition of perception, 158, 159; his refutation of the notion of instruments of knowledge in, 158; his view that all definitions may be proved false, 148 ff.; his view that world-appearances are false because all definitions of any of their categories are self-contradictory, 169; method of his dialectic, 153; perception cannot challenge the instruction of the Upaniṣads, 149; precursors of his dialectic, Kamalśīla and Śāntarakṣita, 197 ff.; responsible for the growth of verbalism in the new school of Nyāya, 168; similarity of his dialectic to that of Nāgārjuna, 146
Śrīkaṇāda, 413, 414
Śrīkaṇṭha, 250, 251
Śrīkaṇṭha Bhaṭṭa, 91, 498, 503
Śrīkaṇṭha Datta, 499, 507
śrīmad-ānanda-śailāhva-pañcāsyam satatam bhaje, 222
Śrīmad-bhagavad-gītā, 263, 285, 289
śrīmad-bhāgavata-ṭīkā, 260
Śrīmādhava, 498, 499
Śrīnatha Cūḍāmani, 259n.
Śrīnivāsa, 139
Śrīnivāsa Yajvan, 66n.
Śrīraṅganātha, 125
Śrīsiṃha, 142
Śrī-vidyā-paddhati, 259
Śroṇī-guda-saṃśrayu, 386
śroṇī, 331
śroṇī-phalaka, 331n. 8
Śruta-prakāśikā, 303n.
śṛṅgāṭaka, 399
śubha, 397
Śubhagupta, 198
Śubhankara, 145n.
Śubhāśubha, 26n.
śubhāśubha-karma-vipāka, 26n.
śuci-dravya-sevana, 589
śuddha, 41
śuddha-suṃvit-mayā-nanda-rūpa, 305
Śuddhānanda, 220
śukra, 364n., 369, 382
śukra-dharā, 369
śukra-prādur-bhāva, 409
śuṇṭhī, 422
śuṣira-kara, 387n.
śuṣma, 349, 350, 386
śuṣmiṇo jvarasya, 346
Śūdra, 586, 588, 590, 599, 619

śūla, 346, 403
śūnya, 270, 314, 385
śūnyatā, 8
Śūnya-vāda, 496
Śūnya-vāda theory, 3
śūnya-vādin, 3, 40
Śūnya-vādin Buddhists, 8
Śvayathu, 502
śvetā, 369
Śvetāśvatara, 549
śyena sacrifice, 445n., 563n.

śaḍ-aṅga, 400
ṣaḍ-aṅga yoga, 529, 531
ṣaḍ-āśraya, 364n.
Ṣaḍ-darśuṇa-saṃgraha-vṛtti, 171n.
ṣaḍ-indriya, 427
Ṣaṣti-tantra, 555
Ṣaṭ-cakra-*nirūpaṇa,* 414n., 413

Tachibana, 578
Tactile, 203
Tactual particles, 29n.
Tactual sense, 180
tad anusandhatte, 275
tadātve, 436
tad-bhāva-bhāvitā, 438
tad-utpatti, 210
tadvati tat-prakāraka-jñānatvam, 246
taijasa, 638
taikṣnva, 422n.
Taittirīya, 90, 567
Taittirīya-Āraṇyaka, 627
Taittirīya-bhāṣya-ṭippaṇa, 222
Taittirīya-bhāṣya-vārṭṭika-tīkā, 222
Taittirīya-brāhmana, 290, 325n., 338n.
Taittirīya-prātiśākhya, 460
Taittirīya-saṃhatā, 625
Taittirīya Upaniṣad, 576
Tattırıiyopariṣad-bhāṣya, 90
Taking of pure food, 589
takman, 346, 348, 349n. 2
tala-kūrca-gulpha, 331n.
Talātalu, 87
tamas, 83, 85, 120, 270, 309, 352, 354, 366, 371, 372, 384, 428, 433, 488. 508, 532, 539, 546, 582
tan-mātras, 85, 272, 283, 355, 556
tannāśomuktır ātmanaḥ, 114
tantra, 320n., 411
Tantra anatomy, 415, 416
Tuntra-cūdāmaṇi, 414n.
Tantra literature, 413n.
Tantra philosophy, 415
Tantra physiology, 317
Tantras, *nāḍi-cakras* in, 413-415; *su-ṣuniṇā,* its position in, 412, 414n., 413; system of nāḍts in, 411-413
Tantra-sāra, 503
Tantra school, 413, 414, 416
Tantra-siddhānta-dīpikā, 251
tantra-yantra-dharaḥ, 387
tantra-yukti, 454, 455
Taṅgalva, 349
Taṅka, 49n.
taṇhā, 571, 578, 582
tapaḥ, 87, 264, 493, 511, 547, 590, 592, 595, 598, 599, 610, 625, 634
tapo-yajña, 568
tarka, 161, 162, 438, 530
Tarka-cudamani, 62
Tarka-dīpikā, 125
Tarka-kāṇda, 100, 101, 106
Tarka-pāda, 97n.
Tarka-saṃgraha, 56, 58n., 59, 134n., 137n., 220, 222, 223n., 241, 242, 440
Tarka-viveka, 59, 91
tarko '*pratyaksa-jñānam,* 438
taruṇa asthi, 332n.
Taste, 208, 223, 229, 272, 414, 416-420, 421-427, 431
Taste cognition, 207
tathya-saṃvṛti, 5
tat param, 582
tattva, 222
Tattva-bindu, 52n., 100n., 123
Tattva-bodha, 66n.
Tattva-bodhinī, 60n., 62, 133, 248n., 249
Tattva-candrikā, 91, 222, 502
Tattva-cintāmaṇi, 62
Tattva-cintāmaṇi-prakāśa, 62
Tattva-dīpana, 11, 60, 91, 119, 222, 239n., 241
Tattva-dīpikā, 91, 255n.
tattva-jñāna, 291
Tattva-kaumudī, 289
Tattva-kaustubha, 62, 251
Tattva-muktā-kalāpa, 137n., 303n. 3
Tattva-muktāvalī, 251
Tattva-pradīpikā, 59, 95, 137n., 160, 169, 171n.
Tattva-samīkṣā, 52n., 95, 100, 122, 123, 127n., 127
Tattva-saṁgraha, 23n., 29, 31n., 32n., 36n., 197, 198n., 209n., 214n.
Tattva-saṃgraha-pañjikā, 201n.
tattva-śraddhā, 577
Tattva-suddhi, 66n.
tattva-ṭikā, 49n.
Tattva-vaiśāradī, 52n., 303, 356n.
Tattva-vibhākara, 289
Tuttva-vibhāvanā, 100n.
Tattva-vivecana, 62
Tattva-viveka, 62, 83
Tattva-riveka-dīpanu, 62, 250n.
Tattvāloka, 56, 58, 222
Tattvānusandhāna, 64
Tattvopadeśa, 93

Taxila, 320, 494
Taylor, 251
tādātmya, 36n., 210
tādātmya-pratīti, 46
tālu, 339n. 4
tālu-mūla, 334n. 1
tāluṣaka, 339n. 4
tāmasa, 435, 546
tāmasika, 428
tāmrā, 369
Tāntric charms, 326
Tāṇḍa, 328
Tārā-bhakti-taranginī, 259
Tātparyu-bodhinī, 248n.
Tātparya-candrika, 515
Tātparya-prakāśa, 266, 271n., 308
Tātparya-ṭīkā, 123
Teacher, 294, 441, 489, 598, 622
Teaching, 441, 589
Technical term, 440
Teeth, 380n.
tejas, 272, 278, 283, 364, 365, 421, 589n., 595
Tejo-bindu, 530
tejo-dhātu, 358
Tekka Maṭha, 56
Telang, K. T., 141, 142, 640, 641
Temperament, 441
Temples, 333
Temporal, 17, 18, 399; bones, 339n. 5; determinations, 215
Temptation, 584
Tendons, 405, 584, 595, 596, 602
Term, 435
Terminology, 16
Testicles, 371
Testimony, 45, 131, 196, 435
Texts, 19
Theist, 260
Theistic, 2
Theology, 612
Theory, 416, 584; of creation, 223; of momentariness, 36; of pain, 105; of perception, 194; of substances, 432
Thesis, 21, 24, 33, 188, 190, 191, 196, 210, 217, 223, 267, 452
Thickness, 420
Thing, 419n., 581, 595
Third Oriental Conference, 2n.
Thirst, 390n., 405
Thoracic vertebrae, 332n., 339n.
Thought, 26, 217, 219, 272, 308, 351, 428, 435, 473, 483
Thought-activity, 271, 277, 315
Thought-creation, 271n., 282
Thoughtfulness, 598
Thought-movement, 271n., 294
Thought-principle, 40
Thought-processes, 24, 296, 430
Thought-stuff, 33
Thought-substance, 28
Throat, 386, 405, 421, 426
Tibet, 189
Tibetan, 68n., 189
Tibia, 331n. 7
Tiger, 593, 598
tikta, 364n. 3, 408, 416, 417
Tilak, 641, 642n.
Tilakasvāmin, 123
Time, 78, 171, 180, 181, 215, 223, 374, 417, 420, 430, 431, 433; and space, 308
Tirumalai Nayaka, 251
tiryag-ga, 409
tīkṣṇa, 419, 421
tīvratara, 290
tīvrā, 338
Tongue, 380n., 386, 405, 428
Topic. 440
Tortoise, 126
Touch, 223, 272, 414, 417, 420
Toxicology, 507
toya, 388
Trachea, 332n. 2
Trade, 589n.
Tradition, 90, 117, 440
Tranquillity, 264
Transcendence, 597
Transcendent, 24, 25, 611, 613; reality, 18; self, 11, 429; state, 531
Transcendental, 194; principle, 83
Transformation of Brahman, 48
Transformations, 23-26, 29, 40, 41, 44, 59, 101, 120, 131, 197, 204, 227, 237, 238, 241, 242, 253, 258, 267, 269, 387, 404, 584
Transgression, 115, 319, 473, 492, 589
Transitory, 571
Transmigration, 433, 479
Transparent, 393n.
Trasareṇu, 181
Trayyanta-bhāva-pradīpikā, 60n.
Tretā age, 477, 478
Triads, 356
Trickery, 441
trika, 331n. 8
trika-saṃbaddhe, 332n. 4
tri-kāla, 437
Trilocana, 123

Trilocanaguru, 123
Triṃśikā, 24, 25n., 29, 30n., 33, 40
Trinity College, 16
Trinity Street, 16
Tripathi, 56, 58n., 134, 220, 222n., 225
tri-prakāra-mahā-sthūṇam, 297n. 2
Tripurī-prakaraṇa-ṭīkā, 222
Triśikha-brāhmaṇa, 530
Triune, 26
Triveṇī, 413
tri-vidha, 468n.
Trivikramācārya, 60n.
trivṛt-karaṇa, 85n.
Troubles, 584
True associations, 179
True experience, 179
True knowledge, 189, 200, 284, 534
True proposition, 179
True recognition, 179
Trunk, 400
Truth, 4, 131, 136, 441, 576, 577, 622
Truthful, 598
Truthfulness, 435, 589, 595
Tṛṣṇā, 482, 484n., 582
tṛtīyaka, 345
Tubercles, 332n. 3
tuccha, 258
tulyārthatā, 432
turya, 305, 309
turyātīta, 305, 308n.
Tübingen, 328
tyakta-kartṛtva-vibhiamaḥ, 283
tyāga, 589, 592, 595
tyāga-mātra, 263
Ṭippaṇa, 495, 499
Ṭīkā-ratna, 60n.

ubhayedyuḥ, 345
Ubiquitous, 16
Ucchlaṅkhau, 331
ucchvāsa, 381
ucitena pathā, 365
Udara, 502
udara, 339n. 1, 336
Udayana, 56, 59, 123, 138, 142–145, 154, 161, 162, 169n.; criticized by Śrīharṣa on the subject of *tarka,* 162
udāna, 86, 299, 301, 387
udāsīnā, 441
udāvarta, 456
uddeśa, 454, 455
Uddyotakara, 138, 143, 158n., 169n., 197, 209n., 214, 448n., 458, 460, 467n.
Ui, H., 464n.
Ulna, 331n. 7
Ultimate, 269, 272; being, 271; causality, 122; cause, 128, 131, 273; consciousness, 25; entity, 267-270; principle, 553; reality, 9, 15, 25, 48, 113, 194, 229, 253, 314, 530; specific properties, 432; truth, 17, 576, 592
Umbilicus, 336
Unaffected, 48
Unattached, 595, 596
Unattachedness, 596
Unattachment, 611
Uncaused, 73
Unchangeable, 28, 38, 48, 52, 73, 84, 189, 206, 237n., 253, 277, 314, 429, 430, 555; consciousness, 208
Uncompounded, 85
Unconditional, 203
Unconditionality, 184
Unconnected, 265
Unconscious, 208
Unconsciousness, 306
Uncontradicted existence, 34
Undemonstrable, 25
Underlying consciousness, 61, 237, 238, 240
Undesirable, 597
Undetermined fruition, 287
Undifferentiated, 26n., 553; awareness, 242
Unhappy, 321
Unhealthy, 373
Uniform motive, 205
Unimportance, 431
Uninferable, 530
Unintelligent, 41-44
Unintelligible, 13, 159, 165
Uninterrupted succession, 29n.
Unique, 15, 263; relation, 36
Unity, 98, 280; of consciousness, 206; texts, 53, 93
Universal, 73, 160, 436; altruism, 584; characteristic, 183; compassion, 538; concomitance, 161; duty, 590; friendship, 584, 596; piety, 596; pity, 584; self, 7, 10; spirit, 534
Universality, 98, 223
Universe, 12
Unknowable, 304
Unlimited, 73
Unmanifested, 267, 304, 416, 417, 549, 605, 612, 618; state, 272
Unmāda, 502
Unmada-cikitsitam, 397n.
Unnameable, 270
Unperceivable, 159

Unperceived, 229
Unperturbed, 583, 595, 597
Unperturbedness, 596
Unproduced, 73, 209
Unreal, 146, 314; appearances, 55
Unreality, 148, 190, 284, 291
Unreasonable, 214
Unrighteous, 477
Unspeakable, 40, 102n., 233, 234, 253
Unsubstantial, 232, 233
Unsuitable, 431
Unsuitability, 431
Untenable, 417
Unthinkable, 25, 253, 421–424, 616
Untruthfulness, 435
uṇādi, 630
uṇḍuka, 371
upacaryate, 302
upacaya, 271n.
upacāra-chala, 450n.
upadeśa, 454, 455
Upadeśa-sāhasrī, 91, 93
Upadeśa-sāhasrī-vivṛti, 222
upadhā, 480, 484
upadhāraṇa, 536, 583
upa-dhātu, 378
upakāra, 210
Upakrama-parākrama, 252
upalabdhi-sama, 443n., 446n.
upalakṣaṇa, 12
upumā, 443
upamāna, 171, 440
upanaya, 442
upanāho, 580
upanibandho, 580
Upaniṣadic, 236n., 576, 582; simile, 545
Upaniṣad-ratna, 67
Upaniṣads, 1, 2, 9, 43-34, 53, 67, 90, 106, 113, 115, 130, 131, 134, 149, 174, 247, 260, 299, 301, 320, 388, 401. 523, 529, 531, 549, 554, 557, 575, 577, 578, 596n., 604, 606, 612, 618, 620, 625, 638, 642; as one consistent philosophy borrowed by Śaṅkara from his predecessors, 2; commentators before Śaṅkara, 1; ethical ideas in, 576. 577; heart in, 401; nature of its philosophy under Gauḍapāda's influence, 2; their view of self criticized by Kamalaśīla, 208; their views regarding the *nāḍīs*, 401 ff.
Upaniṣad texts, 92, 100, 101, 113, 152
upapatti-sama, 443n. 4, 446n.
uparati, 577
upasamānussati, 536
Upaśama, 266
Upaśamana, 417
upaśamanīya, 416
upaśaya, 463
upatāpa, 340, 360
Upavarṣa, 49
upavāsa, 322
upaveda, 318, 320
upādāna, 10, 389, 580, 581
upādāna-kāraṇa, 13, 433
upādhi, 83, 164
upālambha, 453
upāṅga, 317, 318, 320, 324
upāya, 419, 454
upekkhā, 537
upekṣā, 26n.
Upholder, 613
Upodghāta, 325n., 328n.
Upper worlds, 87
uras, 332
Urinal canal, 344
Urinary disease, 400
Urine, 379, 381-385, 404, 408-411
Uruṇḍa, 349
ussado, 580
Uśanas-saṃhitā, 507
uṣṇa, 364n., 416, 419n., 421
Uterus, 365
Utkarṣa-prakarṣa-rūpa, 468 n
utkarṣāpakarṣa-varṇyāvarṇya-vikalpa-sādhya-sama, 443n., 445n.
Utpala, 56
Utpatti, 266
utpatti, 267
utsāha, 381
uttamaḥ puruṣah, 544
Uttamāmṛta, 114
uttara, 443, 456
Uttara-sthāna, 505
Uttara-tantra, 384, 385, 387, 454, 494, 495, 498, 500
Uttara-vasti, 496
Uttarāyaṇa, 605
Uveyaka, 198
Uvula, 299. 414
ūha, 437, 440
ūhya, 454, 457
ūrdhra-gā nāḍi, 402n.
ūrdhva-mūlam tripād Brahma, 610
ūru-nalaka, 331n. 9
ūrū, 331

Vacuity, 24, 270

Vacuous space, 68
Vagina, 32, 337n., 338, 365n.
vahana-pāka-sneha, 382n.
Vaibhāṣikas, 214n.
Vaideha Janaka, 368
Vaideha king, 416
vaidharmya, 152
vaidya, 449
Vaidyaka-sarvasva, 503
Vaidyakāṣṭāṅga-hṛdaya-vṛtter bheṣaja-nāma-sūcī, 508
Vaidyanātha Dīkṣita, 93
Vaidyavācaspati, 506
Vain, 596
vairāgya, 266, 480, 513, 530
Vairāgya-śataka, 537n.
Vaiśeṣika, 59, 63, 138, 139, 144, 181, 206, 217-220, 223, 286, 303, 315, 351, 358n., 430, 480, 599; cate-gories, 63, 220; its theory of the subtle body, 356; philosophy, 222, 387n., 464n.; physics, 220, 317; springs of action in, 480; system, 427, 432; theory, 218
Vaiśeṣika-bhāṣya, 187
Vaiśeṣika-sūtras, 415, 430–432
Vaiśya, 586, 588, 589, 619, 631, 636
vaiṣamya, 373
Vaiṣṇava, 144, 220, 251, 515, 517. 620
Vaiṣṇavism and Śaivism, 633n., 640n.
Vaitaraṇa, 494
Vaitārana-tantra, 507
vaitāna, 328
Vaitāna-sūtra, 329
Vaiyāsika-nyāya-mālā, 93
Vajrā, 412, 413
vakrānumāna, 139
Vakulakara, 502
Valabhī, 189
valaya, 329n. 4
valayāsthi, 329n. 4
valása, 346n., 348
Valid, 13, 182, 191, 211; means of proof, 272; proofs, 192
Validity, 191, 196
Vallabhācārya, 169n., 180n., 517
Vaṃśīdhara Miśra, 289n.
Vanaṃ, 580
vanatho, 580
vaniṣthu, 336
Vanity, 593-596
Vaṅgasena, 498, 507
Varada Paṇḍita, 66n.
Vararuci, 503
Vararuci-saṃhitā, 503
Vardhamāna, 123, 145n.
Variability, 448
Varṇa-dharma, 589
vorṇaka, 60n.
varṇāśrama-dharma, 589
varṇya-sama, 450, 452
varsā, 390
Varuṇa, 339, 349n. 2
Varying states, 207
vasanta, 390
Vasiṣṭha, 264, 297
vasti, 336n. 1, 396, 496
vasti-kriyā, 344, 496
vastu, 233
vasturva, 44
Vasubandhu, 21-24, 29, 30n., 33. 40, 67-69, 72, 189, 197; admits pure knowledge, 23; arguments of Śaṅkara for psychological duality of awareness do not apply to Va-su-bandhu, 33; central features of his philosophy, 28, 29; did not deny objectivity of objects of awareness, but regarded objects as awarenesses, 33; experiences like dreams, 23; his date, 23n.; his denial of the doctrine of pure vacuity, 24; his idealistic conceptional space, 29; his idealistic explanation of physical events, 24; his refutation of the atomic theory, 23; his theory of *ālaya-vijñāna*, 25; his theory of pure consciousness and its power, 25; his theory of thought transformations, 24; his view of thought as real substance and its threefold transformations, 26 ff; his view that illusory impositions must have an object, 24; perceptual know-ledge of the material world not trust-worthy, 23; *sahopalambha-niyama* absent in, 30n. 1; world-construction as false as dream-construction, 24
Vasumitra, 197
vasu-aṅka-vasu-vatsare, 123
Vaśiṣtha-rāma-samvāda, 264
vaśyātman, 489
vati, 467n.
Vatsapa, 349
Vavṛvāsas, 349
vā, 385
Vācaspati Miśra, 12, 13, 29 n,, 33, 36n., 52, 54, 55, 59, 60, 64, 66, 85n., 93-95, 100, 116, 119, 121, 122, 126, 128, 129, 134, 138, 143, 145n., 225, 252, 289, 301, 303, 315, 355, 356n., 458, 460; admuts *jīva* as the locus of *avidyā* and Brahman as its ob-

ject, 127; admits two kinds of *ajñāna*, 125; discussions regarding his date and teachers, 123; his account of the Sautrāntika view of the existence of the external world, 30n. 2; his de-finition of truth, 125, 126; his difference with Sarvajñātma Muni, 127; his explanation regarding the nature of object, 33; his followers, 125; his reference to other Buddhistic arguments regarding the falsity of space, 32n.; his view of illusion, 127; his view of the status of the object of knowledge, 128; method of his commentary, 125; on the Sāṃkhya-Yoga theory of the subtle body, 355
Vācārambhaṇa, 248
vāda, 440, 442, 468
Vādāvalī, 66n.
Vādirāja, 517
Vādivāgīśvara, 225
Vādīndra, 139, 141–143, 225; his date and works, 141, 142
Vāgbhaṭa, 318, 329n. 3, 331n. 7, 332n. 1, 334n. 1, 354, 381, 384, 387, 495, 498, 503-506; diseases as modifications of doṣas, 384; his view of *doṣa*, *dhātu* and *dhātu-mala*, 387; his view of *doṣa*, *dhātu* and *mala*, 381 ff.
Vāgbhaṭa junior, 422
Vāgbhaṭa-khaṇḍana-maṇḍana, 495
Vāgīśa Gosvāmin, 259n.
Vāhaṭa, 304, 505
Vājasaneyi-saṃhitā, 625
vājīkaraṇa, 320, 350
Vājīkaraṇa-tantra, 495
vāk, 403
vāk-chala, 449, 450n.
vākya-doṣa, 448, 449
Vākyakāra, 49n.
vākya-praśaṃsā, 449
vākya-śeṣa, 454. 456
Vākya-vivaraṇa-vyākhyā, 222
Vākya-vṛtti, 92, 93
Vākya-vṛtti-prakāśikā, do
Vākya-vṛtti-ṭīkā, 222
Vālmīki, 264, 265
vāna-prastha, 589
vān-manaḥ-śarīra-pravṛtti, 374
vāṅmaya, 547
Vāpyacandra, 502
vāraṇā, 412
vāritta, 583
vārṣika, 402
Vārttika, 1n., 55, 60, 90, 95, 97, 115, 117
Vāryovida, 416
vāsanā, 30, 31n., 214, 215, 273-276, 280, 283, 290, 295-297, 305, 308, 310, 311
vāsanābhidhānaḥ, 279
vāsanā-kṣaya, 291
Vāsiṣṭha, 265, 266, 275, 295
Vāsiṣṭha-Rāmāyaṇa, 266
Vāsiṣṭha-Rāmāyaṇa-candrikā, 266
Vāsiṣṭha-sára, 267
Vāsiṣṭha-sāra-gūḍhārthā, 267
vāstavī, 258
Vāsudeva, 623, 627-634. 638, 640; and Kṛṣṇa, 630 ff.
Vāsudevaka, 628
Vāsudevendra, 66n.
vála, 298, 327, 344, 372, 381, 385-389, 390n., 392, 393n., 395, 401, 407, 408, 411, 421, 422n., 432, 457
vātaja, 349, 350, 386
Vāta-kalā-kalīya, 387n.
vātala, 389
vāta-prakṛti, 382, 389
vāti, 348
vātīkāra, 348
vātī-kṛta-nāśanī, 348
vātī-kṛtasya-bheṣajīm, 349
Vātsīputrīyas, 68, 69, 72, 209
Vātsyāyana, 138, 143, 197, 286, 448n. 1., 455, 458, 465n., 467 n., 468n., 482
Vāyorvida, 388
vāyu, 86, 283, 297n., 299n., 301, 303, 304, 320, 338, 349, 354, 362, 365, 367. 371, 379-386, 387n., 388-392, 394, 395, 402. 405. 407, 422n., 422, 426, 448; according to Caraka, 387ff.
vedanā, 26
Vedas, 51, 258, 272, 318, 319, 321, 324. 325, 342, 388, 455, 473, 475, 512, 557, 561, 564, 568, 575. 576, 599, 606, 611, 606, 635, 637, 638
Veda-stuti-ṭīkā, 259
vedavādinah, 494
Vedādhyakṣa bhagavat pūjyapāda, 60n.
Vedānanda, 60n.
Vedānta, 1, 3, 15, 17, 20, 21, 33, 38, 39, 43, 51, 54, 61, 62, 64, 66, 79, 82-84, 99, 111, 123, 133, 136, 143, 144, 146, 148, 180, 194, 220, 227, 236, 239, 248, 249, 252, 257, 258, 261, 266, 270, 279, 302, 314, 361, 362, 478, 512, 551, 553, 555, 557, 559, 569, 582, 588, 597, 604, 638, 641; *ajñāna* and *prakṛti* in, 85; all subjective notions are only contents, and therefore outside the

revelation in, 18; analysis of consciousness in, 73 ff.; apprehension of objects involving objective characters, objects and the pure immediacy of revelation in, 15; Ānandabodha's arguments in favour of the self-luminosity of the self and its criticism of the Prabhākara in, 79, 81; beginnings of the dialectical arguments in, 59; Buddhist criticism of the identity of the self and its reply in, 76, 77, cognitional revelation not a product in, 15; con-tinuation of the school of Vācaspati up to the seventeenth century in, 59, 60; continuation of the schools of Sureśvara, Padmapāda and Maṇḍana up to the fourteenth century in, 60, 61; continuity of conscious life in, 17; criticism of Buddhistic analysis of recognition in, 75; difference between pure intelligence and cognitional states in, 15; does not admit any relation between the character and the object, but both are manifested in one simple revelation, 15; eleventh century writers in, 56; everything else which is not a principle of revelation is *māyā* in, 18; existence of self cannot be proved by inference in, 78; existence of self is only proved through its immediacy and self-revelation in, 78, 79; general writers after the fourteenth century greatly under the influence of the *Vivaraṇa* school in, 61; idea of *jıvan-mukti* in, 290; in what sense cognizing is an act, in what sense it is a fact in, 17; "I" only a particular mode of mind in, 17; its account of the *antuḥkaraṇa,* 86; its account of the *koṣas*, 86, 87; its account of the possibility of recognition, 75, 76; its account of the universe, 87; its account of the *vāvus*, 86; its central philosophical problem, 54; its chief emphasis is on the unity of the self, 83, 84; its conception of identity differentiated from the ordinary logical concept of identity, 16; its cosmology, 84-*89*; its difference with the Mahāyānists regarding nature of objects in the *vivaraṇa* school, 34; its theory of the subtle body, 362; its three opponents, Buddhist, Naiyāyika and Mīmāṃsaka, 82, 83; its twofold view, 15, logical explanation as regards the nature of identity in, 16: meaning of cognizing in, 17; meaning of *prāṇa* in, 301, 302; memory does not indicate awareness of awareness in, 77; mental states and revelation in, 17; nature of *ajñāna* and its powers in, 84, 85: nature of the *antaḥkaraṇa* in, 87, 89*;* nature of the obligatoriness of its study in, 53; no cognition cannot be cognized again in, 16; notion of "I" as content in, 17; possible borrowing of its theory of perception from Śāṃkhya by Padmapāda in, 102n.; principle of revelation designated as self or *ātman* in, 18; principle of revelation is self-content, infinite and non-temporal in, 18; principle of revelation neither subjective nor objective in, 18; quarrel with the Prabhākaras on the subject of revelation in, 77; reasons adduced as to why cognition cannot be cognized in, 16; refutation of the arguments against the self-luminosity of the self in, 78, 79; revelation cannot be individuated, 18; revelation identical with self in, 17; self-identity proved through memory in, 77; seventeenth and eighteenth century writers more under the influence of Vācaspati, Sureśvara and Sarvajñātma than of the *Vivaraṇa* in, 64, Śrīharṣa, Citsukha and the *mahā-vidyā* syllogism of Kulārka in, 59; status of the object in, 40; tenth century writers in and Buddhism in, 55, 56; the evolution of the microcosmos and macrocosmos from *ajñāna,* 85, 86; the self limited by *māyā* behaves as individuals and as God in, 83; the theory of trivrt-karaṇa and *pañcī-karaṇa* in, 85; Vidyāraṇya's analysis of the recognizer in, 76, Vidyāraṇya's contention that the self-identity cannot be explained by the assumption of two separate concepts in, 77, 78; writers from the seventeenth to the nine-teenth century in, 66n. 1; writers inspired by Jagannāthāśrama Nṛsiṃha and Appaya in, 63; writers in-spired by Kṛṣṇānanda of the seventeenth century in, 64; writers of the Sixteenth and seventeenth centuries in, 63

Vedānta arguments, 136, 148

Vedānta dialectic, 144; history of its rise and growth, 143, 144; *mahā-tudyā syllogisms* of Kulārka as its direct precursor in, 143, 144

Vedānta dialectics. 66n., 188, 197; forerunners of, 197 ff.

Vedānta epistemology, 172, 177

Vedānta-hṛdaya, 66n.

Vedānta idealism, 174

Vedānta-kalpa-latikā, 259, 260

Vedānta-kalpa-taru, 125, 137n., 301

Vedānta-kalpa-taru-mañjarī, 125

Vedānta-kalpa-taru-parimala, 125, 260
Vedānta-kaumudī, 60, 61, 226, 227, 234-237, 240, 241, 242n.
Vedānta-kaumudī-vyākhyāna, 236
Vedānta-kaustubha, 94n.
Vedānta-naya-bhūṣaṇa, 64, 94
Vedānta-paribhāṣā, 19n., 34, 62, 85n., 86n., 121, 238, 239, 240n., 242n., 249, 257n.
Vedānta-paribhāṣā-prakāśikā, 62n.
Vedānta philosophy, 21, 59, 72, 129
Vedānta-sāra, 62, 63, 85n., 86., 93n., 119, 302
Vedānta-siddhānta-candrikā, 64
Vedānta-siddhānta-muktāvalī, 66n., 312
Vedānta-sūtra, 263, 301-303
Vedānta-sūtra-muktāvalī, 94
Vedānta-sikhāmaṇi, 62
Vedānta-tattva-dīpana-vyākhyā, 62
Vedānta-tattva-kaumudī, 52n.
Vedānta-tattva-viveka, 62, 248, 250n.
Vedānta teachers, 19, 34
Vedānta texts, 54
Vedānt topics, 93
Vedānta writers, 63
Vedāntācārva, 515
Vedāntic, 36n., 60n., 106, 362; attack, 144; Circle, 63; concept of salvation, 261; concepts, 171; cosinology, 84. 260; development, 55; doctrines, 263, idealism, 41; influence, 556, 557; interpretation, 56; interpretation by Bhartrprapañca, 1; interpreters, 239; monism, 258; problems, 263; self, 15; texts, 104, 113. 114, 117, writers, 51, 61
Vedāntin, 34, 270
Vedāntist, 13, 36, 111, 143, 144, 148, 181, 192, 194, 259, 603
Vedāṅga, 318, 320
Vedānga-sāra, 503
Vedārtha-saṃgraha, 49n.
Vedic commands, 559. 561-567
Vedic commentator, 247
Vedic dharma, 621
Vedic duties, 49n., 53, 114, 115.511
Vedic index, 402n., 403n., 567n. 3
Vedic India, 350
Vedic injunctions, 546
Vedic knowledge, 577
Vedic religion, 575
Vedic texts, 85n., 113, 149
Vedische Studien, 402n.
rega-pravartana, 381
Vegetables (born from), 349
Veins, 296, 336, 337, 371
Venis, 19n.
Veṅkaṭa, 49n., 94n, 138, 139, 142, 230
Veṅkaṭanātha, 515
Veṅkaṭeśa, 503
Veraṃ, 580
Verbal command, 559
Verbal definitions, 168
Verbalism, 197
Verbal nature, 188
Verbal repetition, 449
Verbal sophisms, 168
Verbal usage, 211
Vertebrae, 339n. 1
Vertebral column, 331n. 1, 339n. 1, 412
vibhava, 626
vibhāga, 182, 223, 420
Vibhrama-viveka, 100n.
vibhūti, 640
Vibration, 296; of the *prāṇa*, 296
Vibratory, 294; activity, 297, 298, 302; movement, 216
vicāra, 417, 419
vicāraṇā, 305, 435
Vice, 223, 286, 355, 435, 568, 575, 581, 591, 595, 596, 608
vicikitsā, 482
Vicious, 25, 26.477, 483, endless series, 150, infinite, 46, 81, 135, 152, 187, 200, 205, 213; infinite regress, 148, 295
Viciousness, 435
Victory, 597
viddeso, 581
Videha, 499
videha-mukti, 292
Videha-tantra, 508
vidhāna, 455, 457
vidhi, 58. 559 561
Vidh-rasāvana, 254
Vidhi-rasā-yanopajīvanī, 254
Vidhi-viveka, 52n., 99, 100, 122, 562
vidhura, 409
vidhurā, 399
vidradha, 348
Vidran-manoramā, 91
Vidvan-mano-rañjanī, 302n.
vidvat-saṁnyāsa, 290, 291n
Vidyabhusan. Dr, 219, 460
vidvā, 13, 275, 251. 589
Vidyābharaṇa, 145n.
vidyābhāva, 13
vidyābhīpsita, 577
Vidyādhāman, 91
Vidyāmṛta-varṣinī, 133

Vidyāraṇya, 60. 61. 66, 79, 81n., 90, 94, 95, 99, 119, 246, 248, 290, 291; a follower of the Vivaraṇa view, 247; his date and works, 246, 248; his idea of *Jīran-mukti*, 290; his view that *māyā* and Brahman are the joint cause of the world-appearance, 247; the writer of *Pañcadaśī* and of the *Jīvan-mukti-viveka*, 290n.
Vidyāraṇya Muni, 76, 77
Vidyāratna, K., 3n.
Vidyā sāgarī, 119, 145n., 152, 154n.
Vidyā-surabhi, 114
Vidyā-śrī, 94n.
vidyā-taru, 123
Vidyātīrtha, 247n.
View, 427, 430, 441; of things, 15
Vigorous, 352
Vigraha-vyāvartanī, 190
vigrhya-saṃbhāṣā, 441
Vijayanagara, 251
Vijaya-praśasti, 145
Vijayarakṣita, 499-501, 503, 506, 507
vijñapti, 23
vijñapti-mātratā, 25, 28
Vyñapti-mātratā-siddhi, 21n.
vrjñāna, 26, 146, 189, 358, 400, 435, 573, 589n.
Vijñāna-bhairava, 305
Vijñānabhiksu, 303, 517
vijñāna-dhātu, 358
Vijñāna-kaumudī, 305
vijñāna-krtvā-śakti-dvayāśraya, 120
vijñānamaya, 87
vijñānamaya-koṣa, 86
vijñāna-mātra, 21, 25, 270
vipiāna-parināma, 24
vyjñána-vāda, 23, 240, 263, 315
vijñāna-vādins, 3, 279
Vijñānāmrta-bhāṣya, 303
vikalpa, 86 n, 272, 302, 443, 457, 468n.
vikalpa-vāsanā, 26
vikāra, 373, 430
Vikrama-saṃvat, 123
Vikramaśilā, 56
vikrti, 389, 390, 417, 450n., 453
vikṣepa, 84. 454n
viksepa-śakti, 85
vikṣipati, 129
vilayana-rūpā vrddhiḥ prakopah, 390n.
vilāpanī, 305, 236
vumukta, 290
Viruktātman, 227, 229, 231, 233-236: criticism of the *bhedābheda* view by, 231, 232; criticism of the *sahopa-lambha-myamāt* by, 231; his date and works, 227; his refutation of "ditference," 229, 230; nature of pure consciousness in, 229; tries to prove an intrinsic difference between awareness and its object, 231; world-appearance like a painting on canvas in. 233
Viṃśatīkā, 21, 23n., 24n., 30n., 33
Vinaya-Piṭaka, 320
vināśa-pratiṣedhāt, 450n.
Vindhyasvāmin, 197
vinibandhanam, 580
viññāna, 581
Violent, 476
viparīta-dharmatva, 7
viparyaya, 11, 445, 456
viparyāsa, 6; (error), four kinds of, 5
vipāka, 25–28, 421–424, 427, 456
virakti, 290, 291
virāj, 49
virāt, 247, 638
vireka, 367
Virility, 350, 388
viriya-saṃvara, 583
virodho, 580
Virtue, 223, 286, 355, 435, 471, 575, 592, 595, 596, 599, 608
Virtuous, 26, 428, 483, 596, 597, 599; deeds, 284
viruddha, 448, 449, 450n., 453
viruddha hetu, 450n.
visalpa, 348
visalpaka, 348
visarga, 431
visarpa, 240, 501
visattikā, 580
Visible, 181, 393n.; *doṣa*, 393n.
Vision, 388
Visual, 203, consciousness, 70; organ, 36; perception, 23, 29n.; sense, 180
Viśada, 387, 419 n., 421
viśesa, 171, 215, 217, 432, 463
viśiṣṭa-devatā-bhakti, 589
viśiṣṭasyaiva ānanda-padārthatvāt, 257
Viśiṣṭādvaita, 66n., 515
Viśiṣṭādvaita-vādin, 513
viśuddha-cakra, 414
viśva, 87, 638
Viśvabhāratī, 67n.
Viśvadeva, 133
Viśvambhara, 91
Viśvanātha Tīrtha, 252
Viśvarūpa Ācārya, 94, 95, 99, 100, 290

viśva-rūpatā, 278
Viśvāmitra, 265, 630
Viśvāmītra-suṃhitā, 503
Viśveśvara, 517
Viśveśvara Paṇḍita, 92
Viśveśvara Sarasvatī, 63
Viśveśvara Tīrtha, 90
Viśveśvarānanda, 94n.
Viśveśvarāśrama, 66n.
Viśvodārā, 412
viṣama-pravartanā, 485
viṣama-vijñāna, 485
visamāhāropayogitvāt. 389n.
Viṣa-tantra, 495
Viṣaya, 26, 34, 120, 127, 130, 175
viṣaya-caitanya, 238
viṣaya-gata-pratyakṣatva, 239
viṣaya-titikṣā, 577
viṣaya-vijñapti, 25
viṣaya-viṣayi-bhāva, 166, 175
viṣayān indriyāṇām, 397
viṣayopalabdhi, 435
Viṣṇu, 623, 625, 627, 636-640; and *bhagavat*, 628, 629; conception of, 623, 625; conception of, and of *nārāyaṇa,* 626, 627
Viṣṇubhaṭṭa, 60n.
Viṣṇu-dharmottara, 324n.
Viṣṇu-mukhā, 625
Viṣṇu-pada, 625
Viṣṇu-purāṇa, 290
Viṣṇu-purāṇa-ṭīkā, 171n.
Viṣṇu-smṛti, 324n.
Vital centres, 396
Vital currents, 206
Vital element, 367, 368
Vital functions, 416, 568
Vitality, 278, 382, 392
Vital parts, 399
Vital powers, 24
Vital principle, 278
vitaṇḍā, 440, 442, 468
Viṭṭhala Dīkṣita, 517
Vivaraṇa, 61, 62, 64, 119, 239, 231, 248n., 255; line, 120; school, 39, 61, 66
Vivaraṇa-prameya-saṃgraha, 60, 61, 60n., 74n., 75n., 77, 81 n, 95, 97, 99, 100, 119, 246, 248
Vivaraṇa-siddhānta-candrikā, 506
Vivaraṇa-siddhānta-cintāmaṇi, 384n.
Vivaraṇa-tātparya-dīpikā, 171n.
Vivaraṇopanyāsa, 11, 36n., 119, 248n.
Vivaraṇopanyāse Bhāratītīrtha-vaca-nam, 248n.
vivarta, 44, 45, 258; cause, 52; view, 53, 247; view of causation, 258
vivarta-kāraṇa, 58, 59
Viveka-cūdāmaṇi, 91
viveka-mṣpatti, 289
vividiṣā-saṃnyāsa, 291n.
Vīrasiṃhāvalokita, 508
vīrya, 278, 409, 419, 421-427, 431, 456, 584
vīṭā, 296
Vocal activities, 583
Vocal organs, 294
Void, 315
Volition, 26, 28, 82, 175, 176, 540, 600
Volitional states, 206, 207
Volitional tendency, 559
Voluntary, 600
Vomiting, 405
vraṇah, 385n.
Vṛddha-Vāgbhaṭa, 369n. 1
vṛddhāḥ, 119
vṛddhi, 375
vṛkka, 371
Vṛnda, 498, 507
Vṛṣṇis, 628, 630, 633
vṛsya, 377, 426n.
vṛtti, 64, 81, 100, 237, 238, 241, 296, 356
vṛtti-caitanya, 239
vṛtti-jñāna, 89
vṛitikāra, 49
vṛtti-prabhākara, 248n.
vṛtti transformation, 237
Vṛtti-vārttika, 252
vyakta, 548
vyakter *apaiti*, 450n.
vyartha, 453
vyatireki, 467n.
vyavasāya, 123, 448
vyavasāyātmikā, 564n. 1
vyādhi, 392n.
Vyādhi-sindhu-vimarduna, 503
Vyākaraṇa, 319n., 637
Vyākaraṇa-vāda-nakṣatra-mālā, 251
vyākhyāna, 454, 457
Vyākhyāna-dīpikā, 142
Vyākhyā-sudhā, 63
vyākulita-mānasaḥ, 364n. 3
vyāna, 299, 301, 338
vyāpādo, 580
vyāpāra, 158, 214
vyāpāraḥ preraṇā-rūpaḥ, 561
vyāpti, 139, 160, 171, 223
vyāpti-graha, 171
vyāroṣanam, 581

Vyāsa, 90, 100, 299n. 2
Vyāsa-bhāṣya, 290, 303, 306, 355, 476, 555, 603
Vyāsatīrtha, 136, 259, 260
Vyāsāśrama, 138
vyāvahārika, 2, 51
vyāvṛtta, 73
vyāyāma, 488
vyūha, 635, 636, 638

Wackernagel, 402n.
Waking experiences, 7, 9, 32
Waking ideas, 30
Waking life, 92, 133
Waking state, 30, 277, 278, 297
Walleser, 464n.
Warm, 417, 421, 476
Washerman, 184
Waste-products, 379, 381, 386, 393
Watchfulness, 589
Water, 85, 215, 223, 351, 386-389, 404, 407, 411, 416-420, 421, 424, 428, 584; channels, 405
Watery, 386, 416, 419; character, 386
Way, 133, 428
Weak, 394
Wealth, 595
Weber, Dr Albrecht, 334n., 567n.
Well-being, 593
Whirlwind, 476
White, 407; leprosy, 327
Whitney, W. D., 396n.
Whole, 23, 46, 175, 181, 215
Will, 172, 286, 469, 484; force of, 305; to live, 483
Willing, 304
Will-power, 279
Windpipe, 332
Winter, 381, 390, 431
Wisdom, 28, 297, 516, 519, 573, 576, 583, 586, 588, 589, 599, 618, 620 Wise, 441, 619
Wish, 580
World, 2, 4, 12, 59, 131, 265, 272
World-appearance, 1, 5, 10-13, 21, 52, 53, 55, 63, 85, 113, 116, 121, 122, 127, 128, 135, 136, 169, 175, 194, 196, 247, 249, 253, 258, 265, 269-272, 276-283, 296, 310
World-construction, 24
World-creation, 45, 48, 279
World-experience, 4, 196
Worldly life, 607
World-manifestation, 478n.
World-objects, 24, 32, 41
World-order, 621
World-phenomena, 58
World-process, 84, 196
Worms, 345, 346, 349
Worship, 626
Wounds, 385
Wrath, 580
Wrong construction, 177
Wrong notion, 10
Wrong perception, 158

yad antar-jñeya-rūpaṃ, 31n.
yadṛcchā, 433, 478
yajña, 339n., 523, 568, 569
yajña-vidaḥ, 523
Yajñeśvara Makhīndra, 251n.
Yajus, 318, 455, 613
Yakkha, 628
Yakna, 334
Yakṣas, 328, 546
Yakṣman, 345n. 5, 346
Yama, 290, 362, 503, 530. 531, 573
yantra, 297
yasmin śūnyam jagat sthitam, 270
Yaśomitra, 67n., 72
yathārthānubhava, 245
yathārthānubhavaḥ pramā, 153, 244
yathā-vidhi, 342, 343
Yaugācāryas, 139
Yādava, 630, 633
Yādavābhyudaya, 252
Yādavābhyudaya-ṭīkā, 252
Yadavānanda Nyāyācārya, 259n.
Yājñavalkya, 123, 291, 332n. 1
Yājñavalkya-Dharma-śāstra, 324n.
Yāmunācārya, 513-515, 630, 636, 637
yātudhānas, 344, 349
Yellow, 31, 203, 385; awareness, 81, 82
Yellowness, 165
Yoga, 123, 126, 289, 298, 306, 415, 454, 455, 484, 513, 514, 517-520, 522, 527-529, 532, 534, 537, 538, 544, 545, 570, 582, 588, 597, 599, 605, 637; concept of God criticized, 204; springs of action in, 483
yoga-dhāraṇā, 524n. 2
Yoga discipline, 279
Yoga literature, 413n.
Yoga practices, 317, 508, 514, 523, 556
Yoga processes, 529
yoga-sevā, 526
Yoga-sūtra, 6n., 290, 306, 354n., 470, 476, 517, 527, 538, 640

Yoga-sūtra-bhāṣya, 100
Yoga system, 508
yoga-śataka, 495, 508
Yoga Upaniṣads, 531,538
yoga-vāhitvāt, 387n.
Yoga-vārttika, 303, 414
Yoga-vāsiṣṭha, 19, 66n., 263, 265n., 266-270. 273, 277, 284, 285, 289n., 290-294, 294, 304, 305n., 306-310, 312-315, 469; cītta and movement, 298; conception of *jīvan-mukti*, 283 ff.; denial of *daiva* in, 295; energy and its evolution, 400 ff; energy and world-appearance, 280 ff; estimate of its philosophy, 314, 315; free-will and destiny, 292; its doctrine of *prārabdha-karma,* 284, 285. its idealism compared with that of Prakāśānanda, 312, 314; its idealism compared with that of Śaṅkara and Buddhist idealism, 310ff; *jīvan-mukti* and Nyāya emancipation, 286; *jīvan-mukti* and the Prabhākara idea of emanicpation, 287; *jīvan-mukti* and the Śāṃkhya idea of emancipation, 287, 289; *jivan-mukti* and the Sāṃkhya-yoga idea of emancipation, 287–290; *jīvan-mukti* and Vidyāraṇya's doctrine of *jīvan-mukti*, 290; *jīvan-mukti* compared with Buddhist sainthood, 285, 286; *jīvan-mukti* compared with *sthita-prājña*, 285; *karma, manas* and the categories, 273-276; nature of *kartṛtva*, 279 ff.; nature of the work, other works on it and its date, 263-267; origination of the world through thought-movement, 271-273; place of free-will in, 294; *prāṇa* and *prāṇāyāma* in, 297 ff.; *prāṇa* vibration and knowledge in, 296; right conduct and final attainment in, 309, 310; stages of progress to-wards saintliness in, 305 ff.; theory of *spanda,* 271-273; ultimate reality is pure intelligence, 267, 269; *vāsanā* and *prāṇa* vibration in, 296, 297; world-appearance is entirely mental creation and absolutely false, 269,270
Yoga-vāsiṣṭha-Rāmāyaṇa, 263, 267
Yoga-vāsıṣṭha-saṃkṣepa, 267
Yoga-vāsiṣṭha-sāra, 267
Yoga-vāsiṣṭha-sāra-saṃgraha, 267
Yoga-vāsiṣṭha-ślokāḥ, 267
Yoga-vāsiṣṭha-tātparya-prakāśa, 277n.
Yoga-vāsiṣṭha-tātparya-saṃgraha, 267
Yogācāra, 189
Yogānanda, 66n.
Yogānandanātha, 508
yogārūḍha, 519, 520, 521n.
Yogeśvara, 529
Yogins, 217, 296, 514, 519, 521-527, 530
Yogi-yājñavalkya-saṃhitā, 413
Yogīśvara, 66n., 141
yogyatā, 173
yoni, 417
yuddhe cāpy apalāyana, 589n.
yudh, 642
Yudhiṣṭhira, 592, 593
Yugasena, 198
yuj, 517, 519, 521
yujir, 517, 519
yujir yoge, 517, 519
yuj samādhau, 517
yukta, 521n. 1, 535
yukta āsīta, 524
yukti, 419, 420, 431, 435, 437, 438
Yukti-dīpikā, 52n.
Yukti-prayoga, 56
yuñjyāt, 521n. 4

Zeitsahrift der Deutschen Morgenländi-schen Gesellschaft, 402n.

* * *